Lecture Notes in Computer Science 3586

Commenced Publication in 1973
Founding and Former Series Editors:
Gerhard Goos, Juris Hartmanis, and Jan van Leeuwen

T0181029

Andrew P. Black (Ed.)

ECOOP 2005 – Object-Oriented Programming

19th European Conference
Glasgow, UK, July 25-29, 2005
Proceedings

 Springer

Volume Editor

Andrew P. Black
Portland State University
Maseeh College of Engineering and Computer Science
Department of Computer Science
Portland OR 97207, USA
E-mail: black@cs.pdx.edu

Library of Congress Control Number: 2005929057

CR Subject Classification (1998): D.1, D.2, D.3, F.3, C.2, K.4, J.1

ISSN   0302-9743
ISBN-10   3-540-27992-X Springer Berlin Heidelberg New York
ISBN-13   978-3-540-27992-1 Springer Berlin Heidelberg New York

Springer is a part of Springer Science+Business Media

springeronline.com

© Springer-Verlag Berlin Heidelberg 2005
Printed in Germany

Typesetting: Camera-ready by author, data conversion by Scientific Publishing Services, Chennai, India
Printed on acid-free paper   SPIN: 11531142   06/3142   5 4 3 2 1 0

Preface

The 19th Annual Meeting of the European Conference on Object-Oriented Programming—ECOOP 2005—took place during the last week of July in Glasgow, Scotland, UK. This volume includes the refereed technical papers presented at the conference, and two invited papers. It is traditional to preface a volume of proceedings such as this with a note that emphasizes the importance of the conference in its respective field. Although such self-evaluations should always be taken with a large grain of salt, ECOOP is undisputedly the preeminent conference on object-orientation outside of the United States. In its turn, object-orientation is today's principal technology not only for programming, but also for design, analysis and specification of software systems. As a consequence, ECOOP has expanded far beyond its roots in programming to encompass all of these areas of research—which is why ECOOP has remained such an interesting conference.

But ECOOP is *more* than an interesting conference. It is the nucleus of a technical and academic *community*, a community whose goals are the creation and dissemination of new knowledge. Chance meetings at ECOOP have helped to spawn collaborations that span the boundaries of our many subdisciplines, bring together researchers and practitioners, cross cultures, and reach from one side of the world to the other. The ubiquity of fast electronic communication has made maintaining these collaborations easier than we would have believed possible only a dozen years ago. But the role of conferences like ECOOP in *establishing* collaborations has not diminished. Indeed, as governments make it harder to travel and emphasize the divisions between nations, it becomes ever more important that we strengthen our personal and professional networks and build bonds between individuals, institutions, and countries.

As we have moved into the electronic age, we have realized that it is not so much a shared locality or a shared language that defines a community, but a shared set of values. As a scientific community, we value evidence-based inquiry. We value truth, and demand a high standard of evidence in ourselves and in our colleagues as we search for it. We value integrity, because without integrity we cannot build upon the results of our colleagues, and the scientific process will grind to a halt. We value technology, because technology gives us new tools in the search for truth. We value clear communication, because without communication new knowledge cannot be evaluated by our colleagues, or influence the way that others think. We value the slow social process by which one individual's discoveries become accepted knowledge, because we recognize that this process is the best way yet found to minimize subjectivity.

ECOOP's refereed technical program consisted of 24 papers that were selected by the Program Committee from 172 submissions. Every paper was read by at least three members of the Program Committee; some papers, which appeared controversial, were read by four or five PC members. In addition, the committee sought the opinions of 147 co-reviewers, selected because of their expertise on particular topics. As is usual, the selection took place at a two-day meeting. However, because of the difficulty that many of the European PC members would have experienced in traveling to my home institution in the United States, the meeting was held in Bern, Switzerland. I am very grateful to Prof. Oscar Nierstrasz, a founding member of AITO and Programme Chair for ECOOP '93, for offering the use of his facilities at the SCG in Bern, and to Oscar, Therese Schmid and the students of the SCG who went to extraordinary lengths to help me with the local arrangements.

For many of us, the invited talks, tutorials and workshops at ECOOP are at least as important as the talks based on refereed papers. This year, we featured two invited technical talks, described more fully on page VII, in addition to the banquet address, which was given by Dr. Gilad Bracha. The schedule for the week included 19 workshops and 16 tutorials, selected for their topicality, interest and diversity. Many of the tutorials were offered more than once, to reduce scheduling conflicts for attendees who wished to attend multiple events. It also gave me great pleasure to host Prof. Emeritus Peter Wegner as guest of honor at the conference banquet. Peter has the distinction of having defined the term "object-oriented language" in his 1987 OOPSLA paper, and has been involved with ECOOP as a workshop participant and panelist at least since 1988. While traveling to Lisbon to give the banquet address at ECOOP '99, Peter was struck down by a bus in London, and suffered life-threatening injuries. He has made a most remarkable recovery, and I was absolutely delighted to be able to welcome him back into the ECOOP community.

The continued success of ECOOP depends on the dedication and hard work of a large number of people; not only is most of this work performed voluntarily, but we compete with each other to volunteer! In addition to me, 24 distinguished researchers served on the Program Committee, writing sometimes lengthy reviews of many papers, working very long hours to meet the conference deadlines, and behaving (almost always!) in a most professional manner. The conference could not have taken place at all without the efforts of the 373 authors who submitted papers, the board of AITO, which sponsored the conference, the conference Organizing Committee, the Tutorials and Workshops Committees, and the local organizers and student volunteers. Richard van de Stadt also deserves a special mention for the excellence of his technical support through CyberChairPRO.

June 2005   Andrew P. Black
                                                    ECOOP 2005 Program Chair

The AITO Dahl-Nygaard Prize

It was a great loss to our community when both Ole-Johan Dahl and Kristen Nygaard passed away in 2002, not long after ECOOP in Málaga. Pioneers in the areas of programming and simulation, their foundational work on object-oriented programming, made concrete in the Simula language, can now be seen as one of the most significant inventions in software engineering. Their key ideas took shape around 1965, but more than 20 years were to pass before these ideas were fully absorbed into and appreciated by the broader software community. Since then, object-orientation has profoundly transformed the landscape of software design and the process of software development.

In remembrance of Dahl and Nygaard's scholarship and their enthusiastic encouragement of young researchers, AITO has established a pair of annual prizes. The senior prize is awarded to a researcher with outstanding career contributions, and the junior prize is awarded to a younger researcher who has demonstrated great potential for following in the footsteps of these pioneers.

This year, the first time that the prizes have been awarded, the Prize Committee selected Bertrand Meyer to receive the Dahl-Nygaard Senior Prize, and Gail Murphy to receive the Dahl-Nygaard Junior Prize.

Bertrand Meyer was one of the most influential researchers in the 1980s, in the initial period of wide adoption of object-oriented programming. He designed the Eiffel language, which pioneered the concept of *design by contract*. He provided strong arguments for object-oriented software architecture in his book "Object-Oriented Software Construction", which remains to this day a highly influential work. Many of his contributions have proven to be of lasting value.

Like Nygaard, Meyer has not backed away from controversy and has consistently followed his own vision of object orientation. Design by contract established an essential bridge between axiomatic specification and object-oriented programming. Bertrand Meyer is currently Professor of Software Engineering at ETH Zürich in Switzerland. His research on trusted components continues to explore challenging problems in software engineering.

Gail Murphy has shown promising potential as a young researcher by proposing innovative ideas and by proving that these are conceptually sound and realistically implementable. She focuses her research and teaching on software engineering, and she has made contributions to understanding and reducing the problems associated with the evolution of large software systems.

Gail Murphy is currently an Associate Professor at the University of British Columbia in Canada. Like Dahl and Nygaard, Murphy challenges students to examine new proposals with a disciplined and questioning eye. She is preparing a new generation of researchers by encouraging the development of sound theories backed by solid prototype implementations.

Both Meyer and Murphy agreed to present lectures at ECOOP 2005. Invited papers corresponding to these lectures are included in this volume. Meyer's paper is entitled "Attached Types and Their Application to Three Open Problems of Object-Oriented Programming" and begins on page 1. Murphy's paper is entitled "The Emergent Structure of Development Tasks" and begins on page 33.

June 2005

Jean Bézivin
Markku Sakkinen
Dave Thomas
AITO Dahl-Nygaard Prize Committee

Organization

ECOOP 2005 was organized by the Universities of Glasgow and Strathclyde, under the auspices of AITO (Association Internationale pour les Technologies Objets), and in cooperation with ACM SIGPLAN.

Executive Committee

General Co-chairs
    Peter Dickman (University of Glasgow)
    Paddy Nixon (University of Strathclyde)
Program Chair
    Andrew P. Black (Portland State University)
Organizing Chair
    Peter Dickman (University of Glasgow)

Organizing Committee

Workshops
    Marc Roper (University of Strathclyde)
    Wolfgang De Meuter (Vrije Universiteit Brussels)
Tutorials
    Karen Renaud (University of Glasgow)
    Elisa Baniassad (The Chinese University of Hong Kong)
Demos and Posters
    Rob Pooley (Heriott-Watt University)
PhD Workshop/Doctoral Symposium
    Alex Potanin (Victoria University of Wellington)
    David Lievens (University of Strathclyde)
Treasurer
    David Watt (University of Glasgow)
Catering Liaison/Coordination
    Simon Gay (University of Glasgow)
Venue Liaison/Coordination
    Sotirios Terzis (University of Strathclyde)
IT Facilities Liaison
    Tony Printezis (Sun Microsystems Laboratories)

Registration
    Murray Wood (University of Strathclyde)
Sponsorship
    Steve Neely (University of Strathclyde)
Publicity and Web
    Ian Ferguson (University of Strathclyde)
    Richard Cooper (University of Glasgow)
    Karen Renaud (University of Glasgow)
Workshops Review Committee
    Marc Roper (University of Strathclyde)
    Wolfgang De Meuter (Vrije Universiteit Brussels)
    Martine Devos (Avaya Labs Research)
    Michel Tilman (Real Software)
    Maximo Prieto (Universidad de la Plata)
    Stéphane Ducasse (University of Bern)
    Ralf Lämmel (CWI Amsterdam)
Doctoral Symposium Committee
    Alex Potanin (Victoria University of Wellington)
    David Lievens (University of Strathclyde)
    István Zólyomi (Eötvös Loránd University)
    Gregory de Fombelle (Thales Research and UPMC (Paris 6))
    Jérôme Darbon (Ecole Nationale Supérieure des Télécommunications)

As Organizing Chair I would like to thank the support staff and event planners at the Glasgow Convention Bureau, the Scottish Exhibition and Conference Centre, the Moat House Hotel Glasgow, the Glasgow Science Centre and the Arches. Administrative and support staff at the Universities of Glasgow and Strathclyde also contributed to the organization of ECOOP 2005 and their efforts are much appreciated. Most importantly, thanks are due to the many student volunteers who kept things running smoothly during the meeting and who were critical to the success of the conference.

Peter Dickman

Program Committee

Mehmet Akşit	University of Twente, Netherlands
Luca Cardelli	Microsoft, UK
Shigeru Chiba	Tokyo Institute of Technology, Japan
Yvonne Coady	University of Victoria, Canada
William Cook	University of Texas, Austin, USA
Theo D'Hondt	Vrije Universiteit Brussel, Belgium
Christophe Dony	Montpellier-II University, France
Stphane Ducasse	University of Bern, Switzerland
Erik Ernst	University of Aarhus, Denmark
Richard P. Gabriel	Sun Microsystems, USA
Tony Hosking	Purdue University, USA
Jean-Marc Jzquel	Irisa/Univ. Rennes 1, France
Eric Jul	University of Copenhagen, Denmark
Luigi Liquori	INRIA, France
James Noble	Victoria University of Wellington, New Zealand
Martin Odersky	EPFL, Switzerland
Christian Queinnec	Universit Pierre et Marie Curie, France
Martin Robillard	McGill University, Canada
Jrg Striegnitz	Research Centre Jlich, Germany
Peri Tarr	IBM Research, USA
Dave Thomas	Bedarra, Canada
Mads Torgersen	University of Aarhus, Denmark
Todd Veldhuizen	Chalmers University, Sweden
Allen Wirfs-Brock	Microsoft, USA

Referees

Jonathan Aldrich	Gavin Bierman
Davide Ancona	Stephen Blackburn
Francoise André	Mireille Blay-Fornarino
Gabriela Arévalo	Bard Bloom
Uwe Assmann	Guillaume Bonfante
Thomas Baar	Chandrasekhar Boyapati
Arnaud Bailly	Gilad Bracha
Jennifer Baldwin	Jean-Pierre Briot
Daniel Bardou	Pim van den Broek
Mike Barnett	Dennis Brylow
Don Batory	Michele Bugliesi
Benoit Baudry	Cristiano Calcagno
Klaas van den Berg	Michelle Cart
Alexandre Bergel	Emmanuel Chailloux
Lodewijk Bergmans	Stephen Chong

Mark C. Chu-Carroll
Dave Clarke
Thomas Cleenewerck
Pierre Cointe
Pascal Costanza
Vincent Cremet
Tom Van Cutsem
Ferruccio Damiani
Jessie Dedecker
Robert DeLine
Marcus Denker
Iulian Dragos
Sophia Drossopoulou
Roland Ducournau
Pascal Durr
Peter Ebraert
Tatjana Eitrich
Burak Emir
Jean Ferrié
John Field
Franck Fleurey
Remi Forax
Robert Fuhrer
Markus Gälli
Vladimir Gapeyev
Jacques Garrigue
Sofie Goderis
Paul Grace
Orla Greevy
Wolfgang Grieskamp
Dan Grossmann
Gurcan Gulesir
Mads Haahr
Richard Hamlet
William Harrison
Tom Hirschovitz
Marianne Huchard
Atsushi Igarashi
Radha Jagadeesan
Suresh Jagannathan
Nadeem Jamali
Harmen Kastenberg
Andy Kellens
Pertti Kellomäki
Andrew Kennedy

Joseph Kiniry
Shriram Krishnamurthi
Neel Krishnaswami
Doug Lea
Christopher League
Gary T. Leavens
Thérèse Libourel
Henry Lieberman
Hanbing Liu
Cristina Videira Lopes
Roberto Lopez-Herrejon
Jacques Malenfant
Jean-Yves Marion
Michel Mauny
Wolfgang De Meuter
Isabel Michiels
Nikolay Mihaylov
Todd Millstein
Stijn Mostinckx
Peter Müller
Gail Murphy
Istvan Nagy
Srinivas Nedunuri
Philippe Nguyen
Joost Noppen
Johan Nordlander
Nathaniel Nystrom
Harold Ossher
Ellen Van Paesschen
Amit Paradkar
Didier Parigot
Renaud Pawlak
Frédéric Peschanski
Filip Pizlo
Noël Plouzeau
Erik Poll
Laura Ponisio
Anne Pons
Isabelle Puaut
Philip Quintslund
Vadakkedathu T. Rajan
Arend Rensink
Coen De Roover
Guido van Rossum
Claudio Russo

Table of Contents

Language Design

Program Analysis

Types

Testing

Concurrency

Attached Types and Their Application to Three Open Problems of Object-Oriented Programming

Bertrand Meyer

ETH Zurich and Eiffel Software
http://se.inf.ethz.ch — http://www.eiffel.com

Abstract. The three problems of the title — the first two widely discussed in the literature, the third less well known but just as important for further development of object technology — are:

- Eradicating the risk of **void calls**: $x \cdot f$ with, at run time, the target x not denoting any object, leading to an exception and usually a crash.
- Eradicating the risk of "**catcalls**": erroneous run-time situations, almost inevitably leading to crashes, resulting from the use of covariant argument typing.
- Providing a simple way, in concurrent object-oriented programming, to **lock** an object handled by a remote processor or thread of control, or to access it *without* locking it, as needed by the context and in a safe way.

A language mechanism provides a combined solution to all three issues.

This mechanism also allows new solutions to two known problems: how to check that a certain object has a certain type, and then use it accordingly ("Run-Time Type Identification" or "downcasting"), for which it may provide a small improvement over previously proposed techniques; and how to provide a "once per object" facility, permitting just-in-time evaluation of certain object properties.

The solution relies on a small extension to the type system involving a single symbol, the question mark. The idea is to declare certain types as "attached" (not permitting void values), enforce some new validity rules that rule out void calls, and validate a number of common programming schemes as "Certified Attachment Patterns" guaranteed to rule out void calls. (In addition, the design replaced an existing type-querying construct by a simpler one.)

The mechanism is completely static: all checks can be performed by compilers as part of normal type system enforcement. It places no undue burden on these compilers — in particular, does not require dataflow analysis — and can be fairly quickly explained to programmers. Existing code, if reasonably well-written, will usually continue to work without change; for exceptions to this rule, often reflecting real risks of run-time crashes, backward-compatible options and a clear transition path are available.

The result is part of the draft ECMA (future ISO) standard for Eiffel.

There is one and only one kind of acceptable language extension: the one that dawns on you with the sudden self-evidence of morning mist. It must provide a complete solution to a real problem, but usually that is not enough: almost all good extensions solve several potential prob-

A.P. Black (Ed.): ECOOP 2005, LNCS 3586, pp. 1–32, 2005.

lems at once, through a simple addition. It must be simple, elegant, explainable to any competent user of the language in a minute or two. (If it takes three, forget it.) It must fit perfectly within the spirit and letter of the rest of the language. It must not have any dark sides or raise any unanswerable questions. And because software engineering is engineering, and unimplemented ideas are worth little more than the whiteboard marker with serves to sketch them, you must see the implementation technique. The implementors' group in the corner of the room is grumbling, of course — how good would a nongrumbling implementor be? — but you and they see that they can do it.

When this happens, then there is only one thing to do: go home and forget about it all until the next morning. For in most cases it will be a false alarm. If it still looks good after a whole night, then the current month may not altogether have been lost.

From "Notes on Language Design and Evolution" in [6]

1   Overview

The design of a programming language is largely, if the designer cares at all about reliability of the resulting programs, the design of a type system. Object-oriented programming as a whole rests on a certain view of typing, the theory of abstract data types; this makes it natural, when searching for solutions to remaining open problems, to turn for help to typing mechanisms.

One such problem is **void-safety**: how to guarantee that in the fundamental object-oriented operation, a feature call $x.f(args)$, the target x will always, at execution time, denote an object. If it does not — because x is "void" — an exception will occur, often leading to a crash.

This article shows that by fine-tuning the type system we may remove this last significant source of run-time errors in object-oriented programs. The basic language extension is just one symbol (the question mark).

As language extensions should, the mechanism yields other benefits beyond its initial purpose. It provides a solution to the "catcall" issue arising from covariant argument redefinition; a better technique of run-time object type identification; a flexible approach to object locking in concurrent programming; and a simple way to perform lazy computation of attributes ("once per object").

1.1   Mechanism Summary

Here is a capsule description of the mechanism:

- A call $x.f(args)$ is only valid (as enforced statically) if its target x is **attached**.
- The simplest way for a variable to be attached is to be declared of an "attached type", guaranteeing that no value can be void. Types are indeed attached by default. To get the "detachable" version of a type T (permitting void values) use $?\ T$.

- For variables of a detachable type, some simple and common program schemes guarantee a non-void value. For example, immediately after **create** *x*... or the test **if** *x* /= *Void* **then** ... , *x* is not void. The mechanism uses a small catalog of such *"Certified Attachment Patterns"* or CAPs, easy for programmers to understand and for compilers to implement. A variable used in such a CAP is attached (again, statically), even if its type is not. CAPs are particularly important in ensuring that reasonably-written existing software will run unmodified. Initial evaluation suggests that this will be the case with the vast majority of current code.

- Outside of these patterns, a call of target *x* requires *x* to be of an attached type. The remaining problem is to guarantee that such a variable will never be void. The basic rule concerns assignment and argument passing: if the target is attached, the source must be attached too. This leaves only the question of initialization: how to ensure that any attached variable is, on first access, not void.

- Some types guarantee non-void initialization by providing a default initialization procedure that will produce an object. We call them "self-initializing types".

- A variable that is not of such a type may provide its own specific initialization mechanism. We call it a "self-initializing variable".

- Generic classes can use a question mark to specify a self-initializing type parameter.

- This leaves only the case of a variable that could be accessed while void (because no CAP applies, the type is not self-initializing, and neither is the variable itself). The "Object Test" construct makes it possible to find out if the variable is attached to an object of a specific type, and then to use it safely.

1.2   The Void Safety Issue

The basic idea of typed object-oriented languages is to ensure, thanks to validity rules on program texts enforced statically (at compile-time), that the typical object-oriented operation, *x*. *f* (*args*), known as a "qualified call", will never find *x* attached to an object not equipped to execute the operation *f*. The validity rules essentially require the programmer to declare every variable, routine argument, routine result and other entity with an explicit type (based on a class, which must include the appropriate *f* with the appropriate arguments), and to restrict polymorphic assignments *x* := *y*, as well as actual-to-formal argument associations, to those in which the type of *y* **conforms** to the type of *x*; conformance is governed by inheritance between classes, so that if *f* is available for the type of *y* it will also be available, with a compatible signature, for the type of *x*.

This technique, pioneered by Eiffel and Trellis-Owl and since implemented in various ways in typed O-O languages, eliminates many potential run-time errors, and has succeeded in establishing static typing firmly. But — notice the double negation in the above phrasing of the "basic idea" — it only works if the target entity, *x*, is **attached** to an object at the time of execution. Rather than directly denoting an object, *x* is often a *reference* to a potential object; to support the description of flexible data structures, programming languages generally permit a reference to be *void*, or "null", that is to say attached to no object. If *x* is void at the time of the call, an exception will result, often leading to a crash.

The initial goal for the work reported here was once and for all to remove this sword of Damocles hanging over the execution of even a fully type-checked program.

1.3   General Description

The basis of the solution is to extend the type system by defining every type as "*at-tached*" or "*detachable*", where an attached type guarantees that the corresponding values are never void. Attached is the default. A qualified call, $x.f(args)$, is now valid **only** if the type of x is attached. Another new validity rule now allows us to assign (or perform argument passing) from the attached version of a type to the detachable version, but not the other way around without a check of non-voidness. Such a check, applied to an expression exp of a detachable type, is a new kind of boolean expression: an "Object Test" of the form $\{x: T\}\ exp$, where T is the desired attached type and x is a fresh variable. In the Conditional instruction

```
if {x: T} exp then                                              /1/
    ... Instructions, in particular calls of the form x.f (args)...
end
```

if the Object Test evaluates to true, meaning that exp is indeed attached to an object of type T, x is bound to that value of exp over the "scope" of the Object Test, here the whole **then** clause. Calls of target x are then guaranteed to apply to a non-void target over that scope. It is necessary to use such a locally bound variable, rather than directly working on exp, because if exp is a complex expression or even just an attribute of the class many kinds of operation occurring within the **then** clause, such as calls to other routines of the class, could perform assignments that make exp void a gain and hence hang the sword of Damocles back up again. The variable x is a "read-only", like a formal routine argument in Eiffel: it cannot figure as the target of an assignment, and hence will keep, over the scope of the Object Test, the original value of exp, guaranteed to be non-void.

The Object Test resembles mechanisms found in typed object-oriented languages under names such as "Run-Time Type Identification", "type narrowing", "downcasting", and the "with" instruction of Oberon; it addresses their common goal in a compact and general form and is intended to subsume them all. In particular, it replaces Eiffel's original "Assignment Attempt" instruction, one of the first such mechanisms, written $x\ ?=\ exp$ with (in the absence of a specific provision for attached types) the semantics of assigning exp to x if exp happens to be attached to an object of the same type as x or conforming, and making x void otherwise. An assignment attempt is typically followed by an instruction that tests x against *Void*. The Object Test, thanks to its bound variable and its notion of scope, merges the assignment and the test.

Relying on the Object Test instruction alone would yield a complete solution of the Void Call Eradication problem, but would cause considerable changes to existing code. Sometimes it is indeed necessary to add an Object Test for safety, but in a huge number of practical cases it would do nothing but obscure the program text, as the context guarantees a non-void value. For example, immediately after a creation instruction **create Result...**, we know that **Result**, even if declared of a detachable type, has an attached value and hence can be used as the result of a function itself declared attached. We certainly do not want in such a case to be forced to protect **Result** through an Object Test, which would be just noise. An important part of the mechanism is the notion of *Certified Attachment Patterns*: a catalog of program schemes officially guaranteeing that a certain variable, even if declared of an attached type, will in certain contexts always have a certifiably attached value. The catalog is limited to cases that can be safely and universally guaranteed correct, both easily explainable to programmers and easily implementable by compilers; these cases cover a vast number of practical situations, ensuring that the Object Test, however fundamental to the soundness of the approach as a whole, remains — as it should be — a specialized technique to be used only rarely.

An immediate consequence of these techniques will be to remove preconditions, occurring widely in libraries of reusable classes as well as in production applications, of the form **require** *x* / = *Void* for a routine argument *x* (sometimes for an attribute as well). Informal surveys shows that in well-written Eiffel code up to 80% of routines contain such a precondition. With the new type system, it is no longer necessary if we declare *x* of an attached type. Going from preconditions to a static declaration, and hence a compile-time check, is a great boost to reliability and a significant simplification of the program text.

To go from these basic ideas to a full-fledged language mechanism that delivers on the promise of total, statically-enforced Void Call Eradication, the solution must address some delicate issues:

- In a language framework guaranteeing for reliability and security that all variables, in particular object fields, local variables of routines and results of functions, are automatically initialized (an idea also pioneered by Eiffel and widely adopted by recent languages), how to ensure that variables declared of an attached type are indeed initialized to attached values.

- How to handle attached type in the context of genericity. For example, the Eiffel library class *ARRAY* [*G*] is generic, describing arrays of an arbitrary type *G*. Sometimes the corresponding actual parameter will be attached, requiring — or not! — automatic initialization of array entries; sometimes it will be detachable, requiring automatic initialization of all entries to *Void*. It would be really unpleasant, for this and all other container classes, to have to provide two versions, one for detachable types and one for attached types, or even three depending on initialization requirements for attached types. The solution to this issue is remarkably simple (much shorter to explain than the details of the issue itself): if a generic class needs to rely on automatic initialization of variables of the formal generic type (here *G*), make this part of the declaration for the parameter, requiring clients to provide an initialization mechanism for actual parameters that are attached types.

- How to make the whole mechanism as invisible as possible to programmers using the language. We must not force them to use any complicated scheme to attain ordinary results; and we must guarantee an "effect of least surprise". In other words they should be able to write their application classes in a simple and intuitive way, the way they have always done, even if they do not understand all the subtleties of attachment, and it is then our responsibility to ensure that they get safely operating programs and the semantics corresponding to their intuition.

- How to ensure that the resulting type system achieves its goal of total Void Call Eradication. The authors of Spec#, a previous design which influenced this work, write that they expect *"fewer unexpected non-null reference exceptions"* [3]. We are more ambitious and expect to remove such exceptions entirely and forever. Here it must be mentioned that although we believe that the design described here reaches this goal we have not provided a mathematical proof or, for that matter, do not yet have a formal framework in which to present such a proof.

- In the case of Eiffel, a well-established language with millions of lines of production code, how to provide a smooth transition to the new framework. The designers of Spec# have the advantage of working on a new research language; Eiffel has commercial implementations with heavy customer investment in business-critical applications, and we must guarantee either backward compatibility or a clear migration path. This alone is a make-or-break requirement for any proposed Eiffel solution.

Our solutions to these issues will be described below.

In finalizing the mechanism we realized that it appears to help with two other pending issues, one widely discussed and the other more esoteric at first sight but important for the future of object technology:

- A *covariant* type system (where both arguments and results of functions can be redefined in descendant classes to types conforming to their originals) raises, in a framework supporting polymorphism and dynamic binding, the specter of run-time type mismatches, or "catcalls", another source of crashes. We suggest the following solution to remove this other threat to the reliability of our software: permit covariant redefinition of an argument (covariant result types are not a problem) *only* if the new type is detachable. Then the new version must perform an Object Test, and no catcall will result. This is a way of allowing the programmer to perform covariant redefinition but forcing him to recognize that polymorphism may yield at run time an actual argument of the old type, and to deal with that situation explicitly. The rule also applies to the case of "anchored types", which is a form of implicit covariance, and appears to resolve the issue.

- An analysis of what it takes to bring *concurrent programming* to the level of quality and trust achieved by sequential programming, and bring it up to a comparable level of abstraction, has led to the development of the SCOOP mechanism [11] based on the transposition to a concurrent context of the basic ideas of Design by Contract. One of the conclusions is to allow a call $x.f(args)$ to use a target x representing a "separate" object — an object handled by a different processor — and hence to support asynchronous handling, one of the principal benefits of concurrency, *only* if x is one of the formal arguments of the enclosing routine. Then a call to that routine, using as actual argument for x a reference to such a separate object, will block until the object becomes available, and then will place an exclusive hold on it for the duration of the routine's execution. But it turns out that, conversely, a call using a separate actual argument should not always reserve the object; for example we might only want to pass to another routine a reference to that object, without performing any call on it. It would not be appropriate to decide on the basis of the routine's code whether object reservation is needed or not, as a kind of compiler optimization: clients should not have to know that code, and in any case the body of a routine may be redefined along the inheritance hierarchy, so that the language would not guarantee a specific semantics for a routine under polymorphism. Instead, the rules will now specify that passing a separate object as actual argument causes the call to place a reservation on the object *if and only if* the corresponding formal argument is declared of an *attached* type. If not, the routine can assign the argument to another variable, or pass it on to another routine; the target of the assignment, or the corresponding formal argument, must themselves be of an unattached type in accordance with the basic rule stated above. To perform a *call* using such an argument as target, one must check its attachment status, relying as usual on an Object Test; the final new semantic rule is that an Object Test on a separate expression will (like its use as actual argument to a routine with a corresponding attached formal) cause reservation of the object. So a simple convention to define the effect of combining two type annotations, "separate" and "attached", appears to provide the flexible and general solution sought.

In passing, we will see that the mechanism additionally addresses two problems for which solutions were available before, but perhaps addresses them better. One of the problem is Run-Time Type Identification: the Object Test construct provides a simple and general approach to this issue. The other, for which Eiffel already provided a specific mechanism, is "once per object": how to equip a class with a feature that will be computed only once for a given object, and only if needed at execution time. For example a field in objects representing the stock of a company might denote the price history of the share over several years. If needed, this field, pointing to a large list of values, will have to be initialized from a database. If only because of the time and space cost, we want to retrieve these values only if needed, and then the first time it is needed.

The following sections detail the mechanism and these applications.

2   Previous Work, Context and Acknowledgments

The "non-null types" of Spec# are the obvious inspiration for the design presented here. It is a pleasure to acknowledge the influence of that work. Our goal has been to try for a simpler and more general mechanism. The reader who would like to compare the two designs should note that references to Spec# in this article are based on 2003-2004 publications [3] [1] and check more recent work since Spec# has been progressing rapidly.

Other work addressing some of the same issues has included the Self language's attempt to eliminate Void values altogether [2] and my own earlier (too complicated) attempt to provide void-avoidance analysis [10]. I also benefited from early exposure to the type system work of Erik Meijer and Wolfram Schulte [5].

The design reported here resulted from the work of the ECMA standardization effort for Eiffel (ECMA TC39-TG4), intended to yield an ISO standard [4]. The basic ideas are due to Éric Bezault, Mark Howard, Emmanuel Stapf (TG4 convener and secretary) and Kim Waldén. Mark Howard first proposed, I believe, the idea of replacing Eiffel's Assignment Attempt by a construct also addressing void call eradication. The actual design of that construct, the Object Test, is due to Karine Arnout and Éric Bezault. This article largely reports on the ideas developed by this group of people. As the editor of the standard I bear responsibility for any remaining mistakes in the mechanism and of course in this article.

Numerous discussions with Peter Müller from ETH have been particularly fruitful in shaping the ideas. The application of the mechanism to SCOOP (the last problem) is part of joint work with Piotr Nienaltowski of ETH. Also helpful have been comments on the Eiffel draft standard from David Hollenberg and Paul-Georges Crismer.

In addition I am grateful to Andrew Black and Richard van de Stadt for their toler-ance and kind assistance (extending beyond the normal duties of editors) in getting this article to press.

3   Syntax Extension

In Eiffel's spirit of simplicity the advances reported here essentially rely on one single-letter symbol: it is now permitted to prefix a type by a question mark, as in

> *x*: **?** *T*

instead of the usual *x*: *T*. (The other syntactical novelty, Object Test, is not an addition but a replacement for the previous Assignment Attempt mechanism.) The question mark turns the type from attached to detachable. It is also possible to prefix a formal generic parameter with a question mark, as in

> **class** *ARRAY* [**?** *G*] ...

with semantics explained in section 7.

The standards committee decided that in the absence of a question mark **types are attached by default** and hence do not support *Void* as a possible value. This is based on the analysis that void values are of interest to authors of fundamental data structure libraries such as EiffelBase [7], which include classes representing linked data struc-tures such as void-terminated linked lists, but much less to authors of application pro-grams; classes *COMPANY_STOCK* in a financial application or *LANDING_ROUTE* in an aeronautic application are unlikely to require support for void values. So we ask professional library developers working on the basic "plumbing" to specify the possi-bility of void values when they need it, by using detachable types for example in the declaration of the neighboring item in class *LINKABLE* [*G*] describing linked list items:

> *right*: **?** *LINKABLE* [*G*]   (*LINKABLE*) ▮▮▶
>   *item   right*

but leave application programmers in peace when, as should usually be the case, they don't care about void values and, more importantly, don't want to worry about the re-sulting possibility of void calls.

This choice of default semantics raises a backward compatibility problem in the context, mentioned above, of preserving the huge commercial investment of Eiffel users; in the previous versions of the language, reference types support void by default, and some programs take advantage of that convention. To address this issue, we provide the symbol **!** as a transition facility. **!** *T* means the attached version of type *T*. In standard Eiffel this will mean the same as *T*, so the exclamation mark symbol is redundant. But offering an explicit symbol enables compilers to provide a migration option whereby the default semantics is reversed (*T* means **?** *T*), compatible with the previous convention. Programmers can then continue to use their existing classes with their original semantics, while starting to take advantage of void-call avoidance guarantees by declaring attached types with the explicit **!**. In the final state, the need for **!** will go away. In the rest of this article we stick with the Standard option: we don't need to use **!** at all, with the understanding that *T* means **!** *T*.

The **?** and **!** symbols are inspired by the conventions of Spec#. There has been criticism on the part of some Eiffel users that these are cryptic symbols ("*it looks like C++ !*") not in the Eiffel style; the symbol **!** in particular has bad karma since it was part of a short-lived syntax variant for the creation instruction now written in the normal Eiffel style as **create** *x*. Although the symbols have the benefit of brevity, they might similarly go away in favor of keywords, not affecting the validity rules, semantics and discussion of the present article.

To understand the rest of that discussion, note that Eiffel has two kinds of type: *reference* types, the default, whose values are reference to objects (or void in the case of detachable types); and *expanded* types, equipped with copy semantics. (The "value" types of C# are a slightly more restricted form of expanded types.) A type is expanded if it is based on a class declared as **expanded class** *C* ... rather than just **class** *C* ... Expanded types serve in particular to represent subobject fields of objects, as well as to model the basic types such as *INTEGER* and *REAL*, enabling Eiffel to have a consistent type system entirely based on the notion of class. Obviously expanded types do not support *Void* as one of their possible values. In the rest of this discussion the term "attached type" covers both non-detachable reference types (the most common case) and expanded types; that is to say, every type except a (reference) detachable type declared explicitly as **?** *T*.

4   Constraints on Calls and Attachment

The fundamental new constraint ensuring avoidance of void calls restricts the target of a qualified call:

> ## Target Validity rule
> A qualified call *a.f* or *a.f* (*args*) is valid only if the target expression *a* is attached.

An expression *a* is said to be attached, in the usual case, if its type is attached. This notion will be slightly generalized below.

A general note on the style of language description: "validity rules" in the specification of Eiffel **[6]** **[4]** **[12]** stand between syntax and semantics; they supplement the syntax by placing constraints (sometimes known as "static semantics") on acceptable language elements. Unlike in many other language descriptions, Eiffel's validity rules are always phrased in "if and only if" style: they don't just list individual permitted and prohibited cases, but give an exhaustive list of the necessary *and sufficient* conditions for a construct specimen to be valid, thus reinforcing programmer's confidence in the language. This property obviously does not apply to the rules as given in this article, since it is not a complete language description. The Target Validity rule, for example, appears above in "only if" style since it supplements other clauses on valid calls (such as *a* being of a type that has a feature *f* with the appropriate arguments, exported to the given client). The rules respect the spirit of the language definition, however, by essentially specifying all the supplementary clauses added to the existing rules.

The Target Validity rule will clearly ensure eradication of void calls if attached types live up to their name by not permitting void values at run time; the discussion will now focus on how to meet this requirement.

The other principal new constraint on an existing construct governs attachment. The term "attachment", for source *y* and target *x*, covers two operations: the assignment *x* := *y*, and argument passing *f* (..., *y*, ...) or *a*. *f* (..., *y*, ...) where the corresponding formal argument in *f* is *x*. The basic existing rule on attachment is *conformance* or *convertibility* of the source to the target; conformance, as mentioned, is based on inheritance (with provision for generic parameters), and convertibility is based on the Eiffel mechanism, generalizing ordinary conversions between basic types such as *INTEGER* and *REAL*, and allowing programmers to specify conversions as part of a class definition. Now we add a condition:

Attachment Consistency rule

An attachment of source *y* and target *x*, where the type of *x* is attached, is permitted only if the type of *y* is also attached.

This rule is trivially satisfied for expanded types (the only type that conforms to an expanded type *ET* is *ET* itself) but new for attached reference types.

A companion rule lets us, in the redefinition of a feature in a descendant of the original class, change a result type from detachable to attached, and an argument type from attached to detachable. The rationale is the same, understood in the context of polymorphism and dynamic binding.

This rule narrows down the risk of void call by guaranteeing that if a void value arises somewhere it will not be transmitted, through assignment or argument passing, to variables of attached types. There remains to guarantee that the values *initially* set for targets of attached type can never be void. This sometimes delicate initialization issue will indeed occupy most of the remaining discussion.

5   Initialization

5.1   Variables and Entities

Initialization affects not just variables but the more general notion of "entity". An entity is any name in the program that represents possible values at run time. This covers:

- *Variables*: local variables of routines, attributes of classes (each representing a field in the corresponding instances).
- "*Read-only*" entities: manifest constants, as in the declaration *Pi*: *REAL* = 3.141592, formal arguments of routines, **Current** representing the current objects (similar to this or self).

A variable *x* can be the target of an assignment, as in *x* := *y*. Read-only entities can't, as they are set once and for all. More precisely: a constant has a fixed value for the duration of the program; **Current** is set by the execution (for the duration of a call *x*. *f*, the new current object will be the object attached to *x*, as evaluated relative to the previous current object); formal arguments are attached to the value of the corresponding actuals at the time of each call, and cannot be changed during the execution of that call.

Local variables include a special case, the predefined local **Result** denoting the result to be returned by a function, as in the following scheme:

```
clicked_window (address: URL) : WINDOW                            /2/
                -- Window showing URL for address: depending on user
                -- request, either same as current display window or
                -- newly created one.
        do
                if must_open_in_new_window then
                        create Result. make (address)
                else      -- Keep current window, but display address
                        Result := display_window. displaying (address)
                end
        end
```

This example also illustrates the creation instruction, here using the creation procedure *make*. Unlike the constructors of C++, Java or C#, creation procedures in Eiffel are normal procedures of the class, which happen to be marked as available for creation (the class lists them in a clause labeled **create**).

The example also shows a typical context in which the initialization issue arises: *WINDOW* being an attached type, we must make sure that **Result** is attached (non-void) on exit. Clearly a creation instruction (first branch) produces an attached result. The second branch will work too if the function *displaying*, returning a *WINDOW* and hence required to produce an attached result, satisfies this requirement.

5.2   Self-initializing Types

In earlier versions of Eiffel, initialization has always been guaranteed for all variables, to avoid the kind of run-time situation, possible in some other languages, where the program suddenly finds a variable with an unpredictable value as left in memory by the execution of a previous program if any. This would be a reliability and security risk. Any solution to the initialization issue must continue to avoid that risk.

Since read-only entities are taken care of, it remains to ensure that every variable has a well-defined value before its *first use*, meaning more precisely:

- For local variables of a routine *r*, including **Result** for a function: the first use in any particular call to *r*.
- For attributes: the first use for any particular object. This doesn't just mean the first use in a routine call *x*. *r* (...) where *r* is a routine of the class: it can also be during a creation operation **create** *x*. *make* (...) at the time the object is being created, where *make* may try to access the attribute; or, if contract monitoring is on, in the evaluation of the class invariant, before or after the execution of a routine call.

Eiffel's earlier initialization rules were simple:

1 A variable of a reference type was initialized to *Void*. This policy will be retained for detachable types, but we need a different one for attached types; this is the crux of our problem.

2 The basic types *BOOLEAN, CHARACTER, INTEGER, REAL*, all of them expanded types, specify default initialization values, respectively **False**, null character, 0, 0.0.

3 Programmer-defined expanded types were required to include *default_create* among their creation procedures. *default_create* is a procedure defined in class *ANY* (the top-level class of which all other classes are descendants, similar to Object in other frameworks but in the context of multiple inheritance) where it does nothing; any class can redefine it to implement a specific initialization scheme. Although implicitly present in every class, *default_create* is not necessarily available as a creation procedure; this happens only if the class lists it explicitly in its **create** clause.

Case 2 is in fact an application of case 3, assuming proper versions of *default_create* in the basic types. Note that *default_create* only needs to create a new object in the case of reference types; for variables of expanded types, it can simply apply its algorithm to an existing object.

It is tempting to keep this *default_create* requirement for expanded types, extend it to attached types, and declare victory. This was, however, found too restrictive. First, it would break most existing code: as noted above, we would like to assume that most application classes do not need void values, and so can effortlessly be reinterpreted, under the new scheme, as attached; but we cannot assume that all or even a majority already support *default_create* as creation procedure. In fact this is not such a common case since most non-trivial class invariants require creation procedures with arguments. Even for new classes, the *default_create* requirement is not one we can easily impose on all application programmers.

Even if we can't use impose it universally, this requirement does address the initialization problem for variables of the corresponding types, so we may rely on it when applicable. We give such types a name:

Definition: Self-initializing type

A type is **self-initializing** if it is one of:

* A detachable type.
* A type (including the basic types) based on a class that makes *default_create* from *ANY* available for creation.

For variables of self-initializing types we adopt a policy of **lazy initialization**. The previous policy was systematically to initialize object fields (corresponding to attributes) on object creation, prior to the execution of any creation procedure such as *make* above, and local variables on routine entry, using in both cases the default value, language-set or provided by *default_create*. Instead, we can now afford a more flexible policy: no sweeping general initialization, but, on first access to a variable of a self-initializing type, check whether it has already been set; if not, call *default_create*. This actually implies a slight change of semantics for expanded types:

* Under the previous rules, the semantics for expanded types was that a variable directly denoted an object of that type, rather than a reference. For an attribute, this means a **subobject** of the current object; for a local variable, the compiler-generated code may allocate the object directly on the **stack** rather than on the heap. One of the disadvantages of this approach, apart from its too greedy approach to initialization with *default_create*, is that it requires a special rule prohibiting cycles in the client relation between expanded types: if both *A* and *B* are expanded classes, you can't have *A* declare an attribute of type *B* and conversely, since this would mean that every object of type *A* has a subobject of type *B* and conversely.

* The new semantics is simply that expanded types simply represent objects with **copy semantics** rather than the default *reference semantics*. Using such an object as source of an assignment will imply copying, rather than assign a reference.

* As a result, the clumsy prohibition of no client cycles between expanded classes goes away.

* We also removed the requirement that expanded types provide *default_create* for creation; in other words, they do not have to be self-initializing. When they are not, the same alternative initialization techniques as for attached reference types, discussed below, are available to them, and the same lazy initialization semantics.

* Compilers can now implement expanded types through references; this is purely a matter of implementation, as the only requirement is copy semantics.

* In the vast majority of cases, there are indeed no cycles in the client relation; compilers can then optimize the representation by using subobjects and stack-based allocation as before. In the general spirit of the language's evolution, the idea is to make things simpler and more easy to learn for programmers (just talk about copy semantics, don't worry about implementation), remove hard-to-justify restrictions, and expect a little more of the compiler writer.

- Previously, a creation instruction **create** *x.make* (...), where *make* can be *default_create*, would not (as noted) create an object for expanded *x*, but simply apply *make* to an existing stack object or subobject. Now it may have to create an object, in particular if the relation does have cycles. This is an implementation matter not affecting the semantics.

- Whether or not it actually creates an object, the creation instruction will be triggered the first time the execution needs a particular expanded variable. This change from a greedy policy (initialize everything on object creation or routine entry) to a lazy one can break some existing code if *make* or *default_create* performs some significant operations on the current object and others: this initialization can occur later, or not at all. The new policy seems better, but maintainers of existing software must be warned of the change and given a backward-compatibility option to keep the old semantics.

Except for copy semantics, the rest of this discussion applies to self-initializing reference types as well as to expanded types.

To summarize the results so far, we have narrowed down the initialization problem by taking care of one important case: self-initializing types, for which the policy will be to create the object (or possibly reinitialize an existing object in the expand case) if its first attempted use finds it uninitialized.

This leaves — apart from generic parameters — the case of non-self-initializing types.

5.3   Self-initializing Attributes

If the type is not self-initializing, we can make an individual *attribute* (instance variable) self-initializing. (The technique will not be available for local variables.)

Here, especially for readers steeped in C++ or its successors such as Java and C#, a little digression is necessary about what I believe to be a misunderstanding of object-oriented principles in a specific aspect of the design of these languages. They consider an attribute (also called *instance variable*, *member variable* or *field*) as fundamentally different from a function (or *method*); this is illustrated by the difference in call syntax, as in

$$y := x.\text{my\_attribute} \qquad\qquad\qquad\qquad /3/$$

versus

$$y := x.\text{your\_function ()} \qquad\qquad \text{-- Note the parentheses} \qquad /4/$$

which makes it impossible to change your mind — go from a storage-based implementation to a computation-based one for a certain query returning information on objects of a certain type — without affecting *every single client* using the query in the above styles. The Principle of Uniform Access [8] requires instead that such a choice of implementation should not be relevant to clients. In Eiffel (as already in Simula 67) the syntax in both cases is simply

$$x.\text{her\_query}$$

which could call either an attribute or a function; the term "query" covers both cases.

The problem goes further. Because a class in C++ etc., when it exports an attribute, exports the information that it is an attribute (rather than just a query), it exports it for both reading and writing, permitting remote assignments to object fields, such as x.my_attribute = new_value   /5/

This scheme is widely considered bad practice since it violates the principles of information hiding and data abstraction, which would require a procedure call

x.set_my_attribute (new_value)   /6/

with a proper set_my_attribute procedure. As a result, textbooks warn against exporting attributes — always a bad sign, since if a language design permits a construct officially considered bad the better solution would be to remove it from the language itself — and suggest writing instead an exported function that will return the value of the attribute, itself declared secret (private), so that instead of the plain attribute access /3/ one will call, in style /4/, a function whose sole purpose is to access and return the secret attribute's value. But this leads to lots of noise in the program text, with secret attributes shadowed by little functions all of the same trivial form (one line to return the value). "Properties", as introduced by Delphi and also present in C#, handle such cases by letting the programmer associate with such a secret attribute a "getter" function and a "setter" procedure, which will respectively return the value and set it. The advantage is to permit the assignment syntax /5/ with the semantics of a procedure call /6/ (as also now possible in Eiffel, with examples below). But the price is even more noise: in C#, altogether three keywords (value, set, get) in the language, and still two separate features in the class — the attribute and the property — for a single query.

The Eiffel policy is different. The Uniform Access Principle suggests that we should make as little difference as possible between attributes and functions. Each is just a query; if exported, it is exported as a query, for access only. The interface of a class (as produced by automatic documentation tools) doesn't show the difference between an attribute and a function; nor, as we have seen above, does the call syntax (no useless empty parentheses).

Standard Eiffel goes further in the application of the principle. In particular, it was previously not possible, largely for fear of performance overhead, to redefine an attribute into a function in a descendant class (while the reverse was permitted). Partly as a result, attributes could not have contracts — preconditions and postconditions — as functions do; postcondition properties can be taken care of in the class invariant, but there is no substitute for preconditions. These restrictions are now all gone, in part because of the availability of better implementation techniques that avoid penalizing programs that don't need the extended facilities. With a new keyword **attribute**, one can equip an attribute with a contract:

```
bounding_rectangle: RECTANGLE                                                    /7/
            -- Smallest rectangle including whole of current figure
      require
            bounded
      attribute
      ensure
            Result.height = height
            Result.width = width
            Result.lower_left = lower_left
            Result.contains (Current)
      end
```

With this convention the attribute can freely be redefined into a function and converse-ly. Note that **Result**, previously meaningful for functions only, is now available for at-tributes too; the example uses it for its postcondition. This further enhances the symme-try between the two concepts. The previous syntax for declaring an attribute, *x*: *SOME_TYPE*, remains available as an abbreviation for

```
x: SOME_TYPE
    attribute
```

End of digression. This new generality of the concept of attribute suggests another sim-ple mechanism taking care of explicit attribute initialization, and making attributes even more similar to functions: give them an optional algorithm by allowing instructions af-ter **attribute**, the same way a function has instructions after **do** (see e.g. /2/). So we can for example provide *shadow* with an explicit initialization:

```
bounding_rectangle: FIGURE                                        /8/
            -- Smallest rectangle including whole of current figure
            -- (Computed only if needed)
    require
            bounded
    attribute
            create Result. set (lower_left, width, height)
    ensure
            -- As above
    end
```

The semantics is to call this code if — and only if — execution finds, for a particular object, the attribute uninitialized on first use of that object.

An interesting benefit of this technique is to provide a **"once per object"** mecha-nism, letting us performing a certain operation at most one time on any object, and only when needed, in a lazy style. That's what the algorithm for *bounding_rectangle* does. Here is another example, from a class *COMPANY_STOCK*:

```
stock_history: LIST [VALUATION]                                   /9/
            -- Previous valuations over remembered period
    attribute
            if {l: LIST [VALUATION]}
                      database. retrieved (ticker_symbol) then
                Result := l   -- Yields list retrieved from database
            else
                create Result      -- Produces empty list
            end
    ensure
            -- ...
    end
```

The stock history list might be huge, so we only want to retrieve it into memory from the database for a particular company if, and when, we need it. This could be done manually by keeping a boolean attribute that says whether the list has been retrieved, but the technique is tedious is there are many such "lazy" queries. Self-initializing attributes solve the problem in a simpler way. Note the use of an Object Test to check whether the object structure retrieved from the database is of the expected type.

The presence of self-initialization for a particular attribute will, in the semantics, take precedence over self-initialization at the class level if also present.

This concept of self-initializing attribute further narrows down the initialization issue. But it does not yet solve it completely:

- It does not apply to local variables. In fact we could devise a similar notion of "self-initializing local", where the declaration includes an initialization algorithm. But this seems overkill for such a narrowly-scoped notion.

- For both attributes and local variables the requirement of self-initialization cannot be the only possibility. In some cases a human reader sees immediately that for every use of a variable at run time an assignment or creation will have happened before, giving it a well-defined attached value. Then the lazy initialization-on-demand of either self-initializing types or self-initializing attributes is not necessary, and would in fact be deceptive in the program text since the initialization code will be never be executed. We should simply let things go as originally written, after checking that there is no risk of undefined or void value.

5.4   Certified Attachment Patterns

The last observation leads to the third and last initialization technique: rely on compilers (or other static checking tools) to verify that explicit assignment or creation will have occurred before every use. The authors of Spec# have reached a similar conclusion, taking advantage of modern compiler technology; they write [1]:

Spec# stipulates the inference of non-nullity for local variables. This inference is performed as a dataflow analysis by the Spec# compiler.

We differ from this assessment in only one respect: it is not possible in Eiffel to refer to "the compiler". There are a number of Eiffel compilers, and one of the principal purposes of the ECMA standard is precisely to keep maintaining their specific personalities while guaranteeing full syntactical, validity and semantic interoperability for the benefit of users. Even if there were only one compiler as currently with Spec#, we do not wish to let programmers depend on the smartness of the particular implementation to find out — by trying a compilation and waiting for possible rejection — if a particular scheme will work or not. There should be precise rules stating what is permissible and what is not. These rules should be available in a descriptive style, like the rest of a good language specification, not in an operational style dependent on the functioning of a compiler. They should be valid for any implementation; after all, much of the progress in modern programming language description has followed from the decision to abstract from the properties of a particular compiler and provide high-level semantic specifications instead.

Apart from this difference of view, the Eiffel rules result from the same decision of relying — for cases not covered by self-initializing types or attributes — on statically enforceable rules of good conduct. We call them Certified Attachment Patterns:

Definition: Certified Attachment Pattern (CAP)

A Certified Attachment Pattern for a non-self-initializing variable *x* is a general program context in which *x* is guaranteed to be non-void.

Here is a typical Certified Attachment Pattern, for an arbitrary attribute or local variable *x*. If the body of the routine starts with a creation instruction or assignment of target *x*, then the immediately following instruction position is a CAP for *x*. This is a very important pattern; in fact (as the reader may have noted) neither of the last two examples /8/ /9/ would be valid without it, because they rely on a **create Result** ... instruction to ensure that **Result** is non-void on return from the attribute evaluation. This property is trivial — since the **create** instruction is the last in the routine — but without the CAP there would be no way to rely on it.

The stock history example /9/ also relies on another CAP: if *cap1* and *cap2* are two Certified Assignment Patterns for *x*, then so is **if** *c* **then** *cap1* **else** *cap2* **end** for any condition *c*.

Here is a third CAP, assuming that *x* is a local variable or formal routine argument:

```
if x /= Void then                                              /10/
    ... Any Instructions here, except for assignments of target x.
end
```

The **then** branch is a CAP for *x*. It would **not** be a valid CAP if *x* were an attribute, as the "Instructions" could include procedure calls that perform an assignment (of a possible void value) to *x*. But for a local variable we can ascertain just by looking locally at the **then** branch that there is no such assignment.

Certified Attachment Patterns, from the above definition, apply to "non-self-initializing variables". This includes variables of attached types that are not self-initializing, but also variables of **detachable** types, which we had not considered for a while. In fact, as the reader may have noted, /10/ is meaningful only for a detachable type; if the type of *x* is attached, and not self-initializing, then the attempt to evaluate it in the test *x* /= *Void* of /10/ would not work; and the test is meaningless anyway for *x* of an attached type. But for detachable *x* the CAP is useful, as it allows us to perform a call of target *x* as part of the Instructions.

Such calls are indeed valid. The Target Validity Rule, the basic constraint of the void-safe type system, stated that "A qualified call *a.f* is only valid if *a* is attached". As noted, this usually means that the type of *a* is attached, but we can generalize the definition to take advantage of CAPs:

Definition: Attached expression

An expression *a* is attached if and only if either:
- Its type is an attached type.
- It occurs as part of a Certified Attachment Pattern for *a*.

Without this CAP, we would have, for every use of a local variable *x* of a detachable types, to write an Object Test (with the need to shadow *x* with an explicitly declared Object-Test-Local *y*, as in **if** {*y*: *TYPE_OF_X*} *x* **then** ...) every time we want to use *x* as target of a call. Occasion ally this cannot be avoided, but often the routine's algorithm naturally includes **if** *x* /= *Void* **then** ..., which the CAP allows us to use as it stands, in the way we would normally do.

An associated CAP is for *x* in the else part of **if** *x* = *Void* **then** ... **else** ... end. Another one for *x*, particularly important for class invariants, is in *other_condition* in

> *x* /= *Void* **and then** *other_condition*

where **and then** is the nonstrict conjunction operator, guaranteeing that the second operand will not be evaluated if the first evaluates to false. This also works if we replace **and then** by **implies** (implication, nonstrict in Eiffel, i.e. *a* **implies** *b* is defined with value true if *a* has value false, even if *b* is not defined); it works for **or else** if we change the test to *x* = *Void*.

Another Certified Attachment Pattern, similar to the first, is particularly important for loops iterating on linked data structure. It is of the form

```
from
    ...
until
    x = Void
loop
    ... Any Instructions not assigning to x ...
end
```

If *x* is a local variable (again, not an attribute), it remains attached throughout the Instructions. This makes possible, without further ado — in particular, without any Object Test — a whole range of common traversal algorithms, such as this one for searching in a linked list:

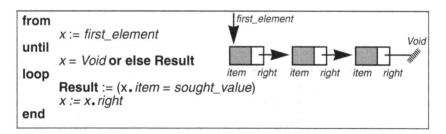

(**Result** starts out false; the loop will set it to true if and only if the item in one of the list cells has an *item* field equal to *sought_value*. *x* is as before a local variable) The CAP enables us to write the loop exactly as we would write it anyway, with the guarantee that it will not produce any void call. A look the previous version of the EiffelBase library suggests that many existing loops will similarly compile and run "as is"; occasionally, application of the Target Validity rule will require a slight rewrite, at worst inclusion of some instructions in an Object Test. This is extremely encouraging (especially given the complexity of some of the intermediate suggestions, some involving changes to the loop construct, that were experimented before we arrived at the general solution reported here). More generally, we see as particularly attractive the prospect of replacing, in such a library, hundreds of occurrences of

```
some_routine (x: SOME_TYPE)
      require
            x /= Void
            x.some_property
```

by just

```
some_routine (x: SOME_TYPE)
      require
            x.some_property
```

with the non-void test turned into a compile-time guarantee (*SOME_TYPE* being an attached type) that *x* indeed represents an object, so that we can concentrate on the more meaningful contractual properties such as *x.some_property*.

A CAP, very useful in practice, applies to the instructions that immediately follow a series of creation instructions **create** *a* ..., for one or more *a*: these instructions are a CAP for such *a*. Beyond local variables, this also applies to attributes, somewhat neglected by the previous CAPs, and enables us to handle many simple cases such as guaranteeing that a just created **Result** of a function, as in /8/ and /9/, is attached as expected.

Finally, as a concession to programmers who prefer to run the risk of an exception in the case of a variable that shouldn't be void but is, we include as CAP the position immediately following

```
check
      x /= Void
end
```

taking advantage of Eiffel's **check** instruction. This instruction will raise an exception if *x* is void. This CAP is an escape valve, as we do not feel like preventing programmers from using an exception-based style if that's their choice (which we may disapprove).

Using CAPs to guarantee attachment is a pessimistic policy, erring, if at all, on the side of safety: if we cannot absolutely guarantee the impossibility of a void value, the Target Validity rule will (except, as noted, under backward-compatibility compiler options, to avoid breaking existing code) reject the code. The design rule for CAPs is not that they *support all correct cases*, but that they *reject any incorrect case*. We can afford to miss some correct cases if they do not occur too frequently; the only drawback will be that programmers may have, in some extreme and (we hope) rare situations, an Object Test that appears unnecessary. (Remember that one of the reasons those cases are so rare is that CAPs are only a technique of next-to-last resort, and Object Tests of the last one: in many practical cases the Eiffel programmer can rely on self-initializing types or variables.) As a result we can afford not to care too much about cases that worry the Spec# designers [3] [1], such as a creation procedure that needs to access an attribute that one is not sure has already been initialized. In Eiffel, the attribute will often be of a self-initializing type, or itself be declared **attribute** ... so that it is self-initializing; if not, there might be a matching CAP; if not, the programmer can always get away with an Object Test or, if that's the preferred style, force a CAP with a **check** instruction as above. We don't have to turn our compilers into prodigies of dataflow analysis.

We do not, in fact, want CAPs to be too sophisticated. They should cover situations where it is immediately obvious to a human reader (and, besides, true!) that an expression cannot take on a void value even though it is neither of an attached type nor self-initializing. The argument should be simple and understandable. If it is convoluted, it may be just as well to force a slight rewrite of the immediate context to make the safety argument compelling. In other works, when it comes to establishing guaranteed attachment status, *we do not want Eiffel compilers to be too smart* about possible voidness. The argument should always remain clearly understandable to the reader of the program, in the Eiffel spirit of clarity and quality-focused software engineering. (There is still a great need for sophisticated dataflow analysis and more generally for very smart compiler writers: generate the fastest and most compact code possible.)

This approach rests under the assumption that a small number of simple CAPs capture the vast majority of practical situations. This seems to be the case with the set of CAPs sketched above, covering most of what has been included in the Eiffel standard, where they are of course specified much more precisely. On the organizational side, the existence of an international standards committee provides a good framework: even if the CAP catalog remains separate from the Eiffel standard proper, permitting more frequent additions, it should remain subject to strict quality control and approval by a group of experts after careful evaluation. Technically (beyond "proof by committee"), the goal should be, with the development of a proper mathematical framework, to *prove* — through machine-validated proofs — the validity of proposed CAPs. The three criteria that must remain in force throughout that process are:

- A guarantee of correctness beyond any doubt.
- Simple enforceability by any reasonable compiler, *without* dataflow analysis.
- Understandability of all CAPs by any reasonably qualified programmer.

6   Object Tests and Their Scopes

The Object Test form of boolean expression, {*x: T*} *exp*, was presented in the Overview, which gave the essentials. *T* is an attached type; *exp* is an expression; *x* is a fresh name not used for any entity in the enclosing context, and is known as the **Object-Test-Local** of the expression. Evaluation of the expression:

- Yields true if and only if the value of *exp* is attached to an object of type *T* (and so, as a particular consequence, not void).
- Has the extra effect of binding *x* to that value for the subsequent execution of the program extract making up the scope of the Object Test. *x* is a Read-Only entity and hence its value can never be changed over that scope.

The scope depends on where the Object Test appears. We saw that in **if** *ot* **then** ... **else** ... **end**, with *ot* an Object Test, the scope is the **then** part. Also, if a condition is of the form *ot* **and then** *boolexp* or *ot* **implies** *boolexp*, the scope includes *boolexp* as well. With a negated Object Test, **not** {*x*: *T*} *exp*, the scope, in a conditional instruction, is the **else** part; such negated variants are particularly important for loops, since in

> **from** ... **until not** {*x*: *T*} *exp* **loop** ... **end**

the whole loop clause — the loop body — is part of the scope.

The notion of scope has been criticized by some experienced Eiffel programmers who in line with the Eiffel method's emphasis on command-query separation **[8]** do not like the idea of an expression evaluation causing initialization of an entity as a side effect. But apart from some unease with the style there seems to be nothing fundamentally wrong there, and the construct does provide a useful and general scheme.

In particular, it is easier to use than Eiffel's earlier Assignment Attempt mechanism *x* ?= *y*. Although an effective and widely used method of run-time type ascertainment, the Assignment Attempt treats the non-matching case by reintroducing a void value (for *x*), which in light of this entire discussion doesn't seem the smartest idea. An Assignment Attempt almost always requires declaring the target *x* specially as a local variable; with Object Test we integrate the declaration in the construct. It should almost always be followed by a test *x* /= *Void*, yet it is possible for programmers to omit that test if they think the object will always match; this is a source of potential unreliability. Here we essentially force such a test through the notion of scope.

In general, the Object Test seems an attractive alternative to the various run-time type identification and ascertainment (including downcasting) in various languages; it seems to subsume them all.

7   Generic Classes

Perhaps the most delicate part of the attachment problem is the connection with genericity. There turns out to be a remarkably simple solution. (This needs to be pointed out from the start, because the detailed analysis leading to that solution is somewhat longish. But the end result is a four-line rule that can be taught in a couple of minutes.)

Consider a container class such as *ARRAY* [*G*] (a Kernel Library class) or *LIST* [*G*]. *G* is the "**formal generic parameter**", representing an arbitrary type. To turn the class into a type, we need to provide an "**actual generic parameter**", itself a type, as in *ARRAY* [*INTEGER*], *LIST* [*EMPLOYEE*]. This process is called a "**generic derivation**". The actual generic parameter may itself be generically derived, as in *ARRAY* [*LIST* [*EMPLOYEE*]].

Genericity can be constrained, as in *HASH_TABLE* [*ELEMENT*, *KEY* –> *HASHABLE*] which will accept a generic derivation *HASH_TABLE* [*T*, *STRING*] only if *STRING* conforms to (inherits from) the library class *HASHABLE* (in the Eiffel Kernel Library it does). Unconstrained genericity, as in *ARRAY* [*G*], is formally an abbreviation for *ARRAY* [*G* –> *ANY*].

None of these class declarations places any requirement on the attachment status of a type. You can use — subject to restrictions discussed now — *ARRAY* [*T*] as well as *ARRAY* [*? T*]. The same holds even for constrained genericity: attachment status does not affect conformance of types. (So if *U* inherits from *T*, *? U* still conforms to *T*. It's only for entities and expressions that the rules are stricter: With *x: T* and *y: ? U*, *y* does not conform to *x*, prohibiting the assignment *x := y*.) Without such rules, we would have to provide two versions of *ARRAY* and any other container class: once for attached types, one for detachable types. Not an attractive prospect.

Now consider a variable of type *G* in a generic class *C* [*G*]. What about its initialization *?* *G* stands for an arbitrary type: detachable or attached; if attached, self-initializing or not. Within the class we don't know. But a client class using a particular generic derivation needs to know! Perhaps the most vivid example is array access. Consider the declarations and instruction

```
x, y: T
i, j: INTEGER
arr: ARRAY [T]
...
arr. put (x, i)      -- Sets entry of index i to x; Can also be        /11/
                     -- written more conventionally as arr [i] := x
```

This sets a certain entry to a certain value. Now the client may want to access an array entry, the same or another:

```
y := arr. item (j)     -- Can also be written as y := arr [j]           /12/
```

T is an attached type. Instruction /11/ will indeed store an attached value into the *i*-th entry, assuming the array implementation does its job properly. Since the class *ARRAY* [*G*] will, as one may expect, give for function *item* the signature

```
item (i: INTEGER): G
```

and the actual generic parameter for *arr* is *T*, instruction /12/ correspondingly expects the call *arr. item* (*j*) to return a *T* result, for assignment to *y*. This should be the case for *j = i*, but what about other values of *j*, for which the entry hasn't been explicitly set by a *put* yet?

We expect default initialization for such items of container data structures, as for any other entities. But how is class *ARRAY* [*G*], or any other container class, to perform this initialization in a way that will work for all possible actual generic parameters:

detachable, as in *ARRAY* [? *T*], expanded, or attached as with *ARRAY* [*T*] but with *T* either self-initializing or not?

The tempting solution is to provide several versions of the class for these different cases, but, as already noted, we'd like to avoid that if at all possible. We must find a way to support actual generic parameters that are detachable, easy enough since we can always initialize a *G* variable to Void, or attached, the harder case since then we must be faithful to our clients and always return an attached result for queries such as *item* that yield a *G*.

The result of such a query will be set by normal instructions of the language, for example creations or assignments. For example the final instruction of a query such as *item* may be **Result** := *x* for some *x*. Then **Result** will be attached if an only if *x* is attached. Although *x* could be a general expression, the properties of expressions are deducible from those of their constituents, so in the end the problem reduces to guaranteeing that a certain entity *x* of the class, of type *G*, is attached whenever the corresponding actual parameter *T* is. Let's consider the possible kinds of occurrence of *x*:

G1   x may be a formal argument of a routine of C. From the conformance rules, which state that only *G* itself conforms to *G*, *x* will be of type *T* (the actual generic parameter of our example), detachable or attached exactly as we want it to be. Perfect! Other cases of read-only entities are just as straightforward. From then on we consider only variables.

G2   We may be using *x* as a target of a creation instruction **create x.** *make* (...) or just **create** *x*. That's the easiest case: by construction, *x* will always be attached, regardless of the status of *T*. (To make such creation instructions possible the formal generic parameter must satisfy some rules, part of the general Eiffel constraints: it must specify the creation procedures in the generic constraint, as in *C* [*G* –> *C* **create** *make* **end**], where *make* is a procedure of *C*, or similarly *C* [*G* –> *ANY* **create** *default_create* **end**]. Then the actual generic parameter *T* must provide the specified procedures available as creation procedures.)

G3   We may be using *x* as the target of an assignment *x* := *y*. Then the problem is just pushed recursively to an assessment of the attachment status of *y*.

G4   The last two cases generalize to that of an occurrence in a Certified Assignment Pattern resulting from the presence of such a creation instruction or assignment instruction guaranteed to yield an attached target, for example at the beginning of a routine.

G5   So the only case that remains in doubt is the use of *x* — for example in the source of an assignment — without any clear guarantee that it has been initialized. If *x*'s type were not a formal generic, we would then require *x* to be self-initializing: either by itself, through an **attribute** clause, or by being of a self-initializing type. But here — except if we get a self-initializing attribute *x* of type *G*, a possible but rare case — we expect the guarantee that *G* represents a self-initializing type.

We don't have that guarantee in the general case; *T*, as noted, may be of any kind. And yet if *T* is not self-initializing we won't be able to give the client what it expects. So what we need, to make the mechanism complete, is language support for specifying that a generic parameter must be self-initializing (that is to say, as defined earlier, either detachable or providing *default_create* as a creation procedure). The syntax to specify this is simply to declare the class, instead of just *C* [*G*], as

---
class *C* [**?** *G*] ...

This syntax is subject to criticism as it reuses a convention, the **?** of detachable types, with a slightly different meaning. But it seemed preferable to the invention of a new keyword; it might change if too many people find it repulsive, but what matters here is the semantic aspect, captured by the validity rule:

Generic Initialization rule

Consider a formal generic parameter *G* of a class C.
1. If any instruction or expression of C uses an entity of type *G* in a state in which it has not been provably initialized, the class declaration must specify **?** *G* rather than just *G*.
2. If the class declaration specifies **?** *G*, then any actual generic parameter for *G* must be self-initializing.

A formal generic parameter of the form is known as a **self-initializing formal**; clearly we must add this case to the list of possibilities in the definition of self-initializing types.

In the Standard these are two separate validity rules. There are both very easy to state and apply. The first is for the authors of generic classes — typically a relatively small group of programmers, mostly those who build libraries — and the second for authors of clients of such classes; they're a much larger crowd, typically including all application programmers, since it's hard to think of an application that doesn't rely on generic classes for arrays, lists and the like.

Class *ARRAY* will fall under clause 1, declared as *ARRAY* [**?** *G*]; this makes it possible to have arrays of *T* elements for an attached type *T*. The rule is very easy to explain to ordinary application programmers (the second group): *ARRAY* gives you a guarantee of initialization — you'll never get back a void entry from an *ARRAY* [*T*], through *arr. item* (*i*), or arr [*i*] which means the same thing —, so you must provide that default initialization yourself by equipping *T* with a *default_create*. Now if you can't, for example if *T* is really someone else's type, then don't worry, that's OK too: instead of an *ARRAY* [*T*] use an *ARRAY* [**?** *T*]; simply don't expect arr [*i*] to give you back a *T*, it will give you a **?** *T*, possibly void, which you'll have to run through an Object Test if you want to use it as attached, for example as the target of a call. Fair enough, don't you agree?

This **?** *G* declaration leading to a requirement of self-initializing actual generic parameters applies to class *ARRAY* because of the specific nature of arrays, where initialization has to sweep through all entries at once. It doesn't have to be carried through to data structures subject to finer programmer control. For example, in class *LIST* [*G*] and all its EiffelBase descendants representing various implementations of sequential lists, such as *LINKED_LIST[G]*, *TWO_WAY_LIST[G]*, *ARRAYED_LIST[G]* etc., the basic operation for inserting an item is *your_list. extend (x)*, adding *x* at the end, with implementations such as

```
extend (x: G)
            -- Add x at end.
    local
            new_cell: LINKABLE [G]
    do
            create new_cell.make (x)
    end
```

Then, to get the items of a list, we access fields of list cells, of type *LINKABLE[G]* for the same *G*, through queries that return a *G*. This is case <u>G1</u>, the easiest one, in the above list, guaranteeing everything we need to serve our attached and detachable clients alike.

Most generic classes will be like this and will require no modification whatsoever, taking just a *G* rather than a *? G. ARRAY* and variants (two-dimensional arrays etc.) are an exception, very important in practice, and of course there will be a few other cases.

8   Getting Rid of Catcalls

Having completed Void Call Eradication, we come to the second major problem, whose discussion (to reassure the reader) will be significantly shorter; not that the problem is easier or less important, but simply because the solution will almost trivially follow from the buildup so far.

Typed object-oriented programming languages are almost all *novariant*: if you redefine a routine in a descendant of the class containing its original declaration, you cannot change its signature — the type of its arguments and results.

And yet... modeling the systems of the world seems to require such variance. As a typical example, consider (see the figure on the opposing page) a class *VEHICLE* with a query and command

```
driver: DRIVER
register (d: DRIVER) do driver := d end                              /13/
```

A vehicle has a driver, of type *DRIVER* (a companion class) and a procedure *register* that assigns a driver. No we introduce descendant classes *TRUCK* and *BICYCLE* of *VEHICLE*, and *TRUCKER* and *BIKER* of *DRIVER*. Shouldn't *driver* change type, correspondingly, in *TRUCK* and *BICYCLE*, to *TRUCKER* and *BIKER* respectively? All signs are that it should. But novariance prevents this.

The policy that would allow such type redefinitions is called covariance (from terminology introduced by Luca Cardelli); "co" because the redefinition follows the direction of inheritance.

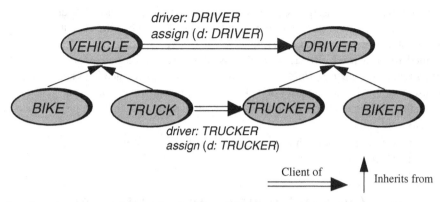

driver: DRIVER
assign (d: DRIVER)

driver: TRUCKER
assign (d: TRUCKER)

Client of ⟶   Inherits from ↑

In fact there is no type risk associated with redefining **query results**, such as *driver*, co-variantly. Still, most languages don't permit this, probably because then programmers wouldn't understand why they can also redefine **routine arguments** covariantly. If you redefine *driver*, you will also want to redefine register so that its signature reads

register (d: TRUCKER) **do** *driver := d* **end**	-- in *TRUCK* **/14/**
register (d: BIKER) **do** *driver := d* **end**	-- in *BIKE* **/15/**

and so on. Eiffel allows you to do this and in fact provides an important abbreviation; if you know ahead of time (that is to say, in the ancestor class) that an entity will be co-variant, you can avoid redefinitions altogether by declaring the entity from the start as "anchored" to another through the **like** keyword: here in *TRUCK* you can replace /13/ by

register (d: **like** *driver) ... Rest as before ...*   -- in *VEHICLE* **/16/**

where the **like** type declaration anchors *d* to driver, so that the redefinitions of /14/ and /15/ are no longer needed explicitly (but the effect is the same). **like**, avoiding explicit "redefinition avalanche", is the covariant mechanism par excellence.

With covariant arguments we have a problem **[9]** because of polymorphism and dynamic binding. The declarations and call

v: VEHICLE
d: DRIVER
...
v. register (d)

look reasonable enough; but what the call is preceded by the assignments

v := some_truck
d := some_biker

with the types of the assignment sources as implied by their names? We end up assigning to a truck a driver qualified only to ride a bike. Then when the execution attempts, on an object of type *TRUCKER*, to access a feature of the driver — legitimately assumed to be a truck driver, on the basis of the redefinition —, for example *driver. license_expiration_date*, we get a crash, known as a catcall (assuming truck licenses expire, but bike licenses don't). This is the reason novariance is the general rule: even though catcalls happen rarely in well-written programs, they are just as much of a risk as void calls.

The solution proposed here is simple: force the programmer who makes a covariant argument redeclaration to recognize the risk through the following rule:

Covariant argument redeclaration rule

The type of a covariant argument redeclaration, or of an anchored (like) argument declaration, must be detachable.

In our example an explicit redeclaration will have to be written, instead of /14/

```
register (d: ? TRUCKER) ...                -- in TRUCK          /17/
```

and an anchored one, instead of /16/:

```
register (d: ? like driver) ...            -- in VEHICLE        /18/
```

This requires the body of the routine (in the redefined version for the first case, already in the original version for the second case) to perform an explicit Object Test if it wants to apply a call to the argument, ascertaining it to be of the covariantly redefined type. Catcalls clearly go away.

The semantics of **?** U in the covariant redefinition of an argument *x* originally of type *T* is slightly different from the usual one involving possible void values. It really means "from *T* down to *U*". It also requires a particular convention rule for the semantics of a new precondition clause of the form require else *x. some_U_property* (we interpret it as {*y: U*} *x* **and then** *y. some_U_property*). So there is a certain amount of kludginess on the theoretical side. But in practice the technique seems to allow us to keep covariance for expressiveness, while removing the dangers.

This technique is not so far from what programmers instinctively do in languages such as C++, Java and C# which enforce novariance. The modeled system, as noted, often cries for covariance. So in the descendant class the programmer will introduce a variable of the new type, the one really desired, and "downcast" (the equivalent of an Object Test) the novariant argument to it. One finds numerous examples of this pattern in practical code from the languages cited. The above rule leads us to a similar solution, but it is more explicit and, one may argue, better for modeling realism: the programmer specifies, in the redefinition, the "true" new type of the argument (like *TRUCKER*); the type system accepts his covariant behavior, but forces him to recognize the risk to of that behavior to others around him, specifically to "polymorphic perverts" (callers of the original routine which, through polymorphism, actually use the new argument type disguised under the old one), and to handle that risk by checking explicitly for the type of the actual objects received through the formal argument.

9   An Application to Concurrency

The third major problem to which the ideas discussed here provide a solution is lazy object reservation in concurrent object-oriented programming.

Concurrency is badly in need of techniques that will make concurrent programs (multithreaded, multi-processed, networked, web-serviced...) as clear and trustworthy as those we write for sequential applications. Common concurrent mechanisms, most notably thread libraries, still rely on 1960-era concepts, such as semaphores and locks. Deadlocks and data races are a constant concern and a not so infrequent practical occurrence.

An effort to bring concurrent programming to the same level of abstraction and quality that object technology has brought to the sequential world led to the definition of the SCOOP model of computation (Simple Concurrent Object-Oriented Programming [11], with a first implementation available from ETH). This is not the place to go through the details of SCOOP, but one aspect is directly relevant. If an entity x denotes a "**separate**" object — one handled by a thread of control, or "processor", other than the processor handling calls to the current object — it appears essential to permit a call of the form $x.f$ only if x is an argument of the enclosing routine r. Then a call to r, with the corresponding actual argument a representing a separate object, will proceed only when it has obtained exclusive access to that object, and then will retain that access for the duration of the call. Coupled with the use of preconditions as wait conditions, this is the principal synchronization mechanism, and leads to elegant algorithms with very little explicit synchronization code (see for example the Dining Philosophers in [11]).

The rule then is:

Validity and semantics of separate calls

A call on a separate object is permitted only if the object is known through a formal argument to the enclosing routine.

Passing the corresponding separate actual arguments to the routine will cause a wait until they are all available, and will reserve them for the duration of the call.

A specific consequence of this policy is of direct interest for this discussion:

Object Reservation rule

Passing a separate actual argument a to a routine r reserves the associated object.

The corresponding formal argument *x* in *r* must also be declared as **separate**, so that it is immediately clear, from the interface of *r*, that it will perform an object reservation.

So far this has implied the converse rule: if a is separate, *r* (*a*) will wait until the object is available, and then will reserve it.

But this second part is too restrictive. If *r* doesn't actually include any call *x*. *f* where *x* is the formal argument corresponding to *a*, we don't need to wait, and the policy could actually cause deadlock. For example in

```
keep_it: separate T              -- An attribute

r (x: separate T)
              -- Remember a for later use.
      do
            keep_it := x
      end
```

we just use *x* as source of an assignment. The actual calls will be done later using *keep_it*, which we will have to pass (according to the above validity rule) as actual argument to some other routine, which performs such calls. But in a call to this *r* we don't need to wait on *x*, and don't want to.

This could be treated as a *compiler optimization*: the body of *r* doesn't perform any call on *x*, so we can skip the object reservation. But this is not an acceptable solution, for two reasons:

- The semantics — including waiting or not — should be immediately clear to client programmers. They will see only the interface (signature and contracts), not the **do** clause.
- In a descendant class, we can redefine *r* so that it *now* performs a call of target *x*. Yet under dynamic binding a client could unwittingly be calling the redefined version!

We need a way to specify, as part of the official routine interface, that a formal argument such as *x* above is, although separate, non-blocking.

The solution proposed is: **use a detachable type**, here **? separate** *T*. With the declaration

```
r (x: ? separate T)              -- The rest as above
```

no reservation will occur.

With this policy, whether reservation occurs is part of the routine's specification as documented to client programmers. The rule is consistent with the general property of detachable and attached types: we need *x* to be attached only if we are going to perform a call on it.

In the example, we can only retain the assignment to *keep_it* if this attribute is itself detachable. If it is attached, declared as **separate** *T* rather than **? separate** *T*, we must rewrite the assignment as

```
if {y: separate T} x then
        keep_it := y
end
```

with the obvious semantic rule that **an object test of separate type causes reservation of the object**. Unlike in the case of an argument, this rule is acceptable since no information hiding is involved: we are looking at implementation, not a routine's interface.

The technique also fits well with inheritance. If *r* had an argument of type **? separate** *T*, we cannot of course redefine it as **separate** *T* in a descendant (the reverse is, as always, possible). But if the descendant version does need to perform a call on *x*, whereas the original didn't, it can achieve the result through an Object Test:

```
if {y: separate T} x then
        y. some_operation
end
```

which will cause a wait — not on entry to the routine (which could contradict the semantics advertised to the client) but as part of that routine's implementation.

It appears then that the distinction between attached and detachable types, and the general-purpose Object Test with its semantics adapted to the concurrent (separate) case, solve this particular problem of concurrent object-oriented programming too.

10   Conclusion

It was impossible to resist including the self-citation that opens this article, but hard to resist the temptation of removing the parts that don't quite fit, especially the bit about the two or three minutes. The ideas presented here didn't come with the self-evidence of morning mist; it was more like the icy rain of an endless Baltic winter. Yet the mechanism is indeed a minuscule syntax extension, the **?** symbol (even if used with two slightly different semantics), combined with the replacement of an existing instruction, the assignment attempt, by a simpler and more general mechanism, the Object Test. With a few validity rules that any reasonable program should meet without the programmer thinking much about them — even though the presentation in this article may have appeared long-winded since it took into account many details, special cases, compatibility issues and the rationale for every decision — the result does address several major problems in one sweep; one of these problems, the starting point for the whole effort, is the only remaining source of crashes in typed object-oriented programs, and hence of critical practical importance. The second one has also been the subject of a considerable literature. The third one is less well known, but of importance for concurrent applications. And in passing we have seen that for two issues that had been addressed by previous mechanisms — Run-Time Type Identification, possible in many languages, and "once per object", for which Eiffel already had a solution — the mechanisms allows new techniques that may offer at least an incremental improvement on those already known.

So while it is for the reader to judge whether the citation is arrogant, I do hope that the mechanisms presented above, as available in Standard Eiffel, will have a lasting effect on the quality of software that we can produce, using the best of object technology.

References

[1] Mike Barnett, Rustan Leino and Wolfram Schulte: *The Spec# Programming System*; CAS-SIS proceedings, 2004.

[2] Craig Chambers et al., papers on the Self language at http://research.sun.com/self/papers/papers.html.

[3] Manuel Fähndrich and Rustan Leino: *Declaring and Checking Non-null Types in an Object-Oriented Language*; in OOPSLA 2003, SIGPLAN Notices, vol. 38 no. 11, November 2003, ACM, pp. 302-312.

[4] ECMA Technical Committee 39 (Programming and Scripting Languages) Technical Group 4 (Eiffel): *Eiffel Analysis, Design and Programming Language*, Draft international standard, April 2005.

[5] Erik Meijer and Wolfram Schulte: *Unifying Tables, Objects, and Documents*; in Proc. DP-COOL 2003, also at http://research.microsoft.com/~emeijer/Papers/XS.pdf.

[6] Bertrand Meyer: *Eiffel: The Language*, Prentice Hall 1990 (revised printing 1991). See also **[12]**.

[7] Bertrand Meyer: *Reusable Software: The Base Object-Oriented Component Libraries*, Prentice Hall, 1994.

[8] Bertrand Meyer: *Object-Oriented Software Construction, 2nd edition*, Prentice Hall, 1997.

[9] Bertrand Meyer, reference **[8]**, chapter 17: *"Typing"*.

[10] Bertrand Meyer, *Prelude to a Theory of Void*; in *Journal of Object-Oriented Programming*, vol. 11, no. 7, November-December 1998, pages 36-48.

[11] Bertrand Meyer, reference **[8]**, chapter 30: *Concurrency, distribution, client-server and the Internet*.

[12] Bertrand Meyer, *Standard Eiffel*, new edition of **[6]**, in progress.

The Emergent Structure of Development Tasks

Gail C. Murphy[1], Mik Kersten[1], Martin P. Robillard[2], and Davor Čubranić[3]

[1] Department of Computer Science, University of British Columbia
murphy@cs.ubc.ca, beatmik@acm.org
[2] School of Computer Science, McGill University
martin@cs.mcgill.ca
[3] Department of Computer Science, University of Victoria
cubranic@cs.uvic.ca

Abstract. Integrated development environments have been designed and engineered to display structural information about the source code of large systems. When a development task lines up with the structure of the system, the tools in these environments do a great job of supporting developers in their work. Unfortunately, many development tasks do not have this characteristic. Instead, they involve changes that are scattered across the source code and various other kinds of artifacts, including bug reports and documentation. Today's development environments provide little support for working with scattered pieces of a system, and as a result, are not adequately supporting the ways in which developers work on the system. Fortunately, many development tasks do have a structure. This structure emerges from a developer's actions when changing the system. In this paper, we describe how the structure of many tasks crosscuts system artifacts, and how by capturing that structure, we can make it as easy for developers to work on changes scattered across the system's structure as it is to work on changes that line up with the system's structure.

1   Introduction

The tools that developers use to build a large software system provide an abundance of information about the structure of the system. Integrated development environments (IDEs), for example, include views that describe inheritance hierarchies, that present the results of system-wide searches about callers of methods, and that report misuses of interfaces. These IDEs have made it easier for developers to cope with the complex information structures that comprise a large software system.

However, some of our recent work suggests that the focus on providing extensive structural information may be having two negative effects on development:

- developers may be spending more time looking for relevant information amongst the morass presented than working with it [10], and
- developers may not always be finding relevant information, resulting in incomplete solutions that lead to faults [4, 19].

We believe that these problems can be addressed by considering how a developer works on the system. More often than not, development tasks require changes that are

A.P. Black (Ed.): ECOOP 2005, LNCS 3586, pp. 33–48, 2005.

scattered across system artifacts. For instance, a developer working on a change task might change parts of several classes, may read and edit comments on parts of a bug report, may update parts of a web document, and so on. As a developer navigates to and edits these pieces, a structure of the task emerges.

In this paper, we describe how this structure crosscuts the structures of system artifacts and we explore how the capture and description of task structure can be used to present information and support operations in an IDE in a way that better matches how a developer works. We believe support for task structure can improve the effectiveness of existing tools and can enable support for new operations that can improve a developer's individual and group work.

We begin with a characterization of how tasks crosscut system artifacts, providing data about the prevalence of scattered changes and arguing that the changes have structure that is crosscutting (Sect. 2). We then introduce a working definition of task structure (Sect. 3) and describe what an IDE with task structure might provide to a developer (Sect. 4). We then elaborate on the possibilities, explaining some of our initial efforts in making task structure explicit (Sect. 5), discuss some open questions (Sect. 6), and describe how our ideas relate to earlier efforts (Sect. 7).

2   Tasks Crosscut Artifacts

Building a software system involves many different kinds of tasks. A one-year diary study of 13 developers who were involved in building a large telecommunications system found 13 different kinds of tasks, including estimation, high-level design, code, and customer documentation [15]. In this paper, we focus on *change tasks* that affect the functionality of the system in some way, by fixing bugs, improving performance, or implementing new features. To simplify the discourse in this paper, we use the term *task* to mean change task.

To complete a task, a developer typically has to interact with several kinds of artifacts, including source code, bug descriptions,[1] test cases, and various flavours of documentation. Conceptually, these artifacts form an information space from which an IDE draws information to display to a developer. Since the source code tends to form the majority of the structure, we focus our characterization mainly on it, returning to the more general information space in later sections of the paper.

2.1   Occurrence of Scattered Changes

It has long been a goal of programming language and software engineering research to make it possible to express a system such that most modification tasks require only localized changes to a codebase [14]. To achieve this goal, modularity mechanisms have been introduced into the programming languages we use (e.g., classes in object-oriented languages) and various design practices have evolved (e.g., design patterns [6]). Despite these advances, we contend that the completion of many tasks still requires changes that are scattered across a code base.

---

[1] Bug descriptions, or reports, at least in many open-source projects, are used to track not just faults with the system, but enhancements and other desired changes.

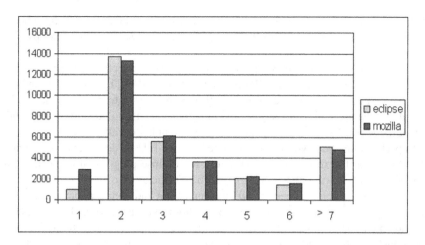

Fig. 1. The number of files (x-axis) involved in check-in transactions (y-axis) for Eclipse and Mozilla

To illustrate that many changes have this property, Fig. 1 shows the number of files checked-in as part of transactions from two large open-source projects — Eclipse and Mozilla.[2] Following a common heuristic used for open-source projects, a transaction is defined as consisting of file revisions that were checked in by the same author with the same check-in comment close in time [13]. For both of these systems, over 90% of the transactions involve changes to more than one file.

To provide some insight into the relationship between the changes and the structure of the system, we randomly sampled 20 transactions that involved four files from the Eclipse data. Of these transactions, fifteen involved changes in multiple classes located close together (i.e., within the same package). These changes are scattered, but it might be considered that they are contained within some notion of module (i.e., a Java package). However, five transactions included changes across packages, and of these five, two included changes across more than one plug-in (a significant grouping of related functionality in Eclipse). Assuming that a transaction roughly corresponds to a task,[3] a reasonable number of tasks (25% of those sampled) involved changes scattered across non-local parts of the system structure.

2.2 Crosscutting Structure of Changes

Are scattered changes simply the result of a bad system structure or is there some structure to the scattering? To provide some insight into these questions, we consider a typi-

---

[2] The Eclipse project can be found at `eclipse.org` and the Mozilla project can be found at `mozilla.org`. The check-in data for Eclipse comes from 2001/04/28 until 2002/10/01 and the check-in data for Mozilla comes from 1998/03/27 until 2002/05/08. Only data for transactions involving 20 or less files is shown.

[3] This is a reasonable assumption because of the work practices used in developing this open-source system.

cal change in the Eclipse code base. We chose to use an example from Eclipse because it is generally considered to be well-designed and extensible. We follow Eclipse documentation guidelines in the approach we take to implementing the change.

The task of interest involves a change to a hypothetical Eclipse plug-in to support the editing and viewing of an HTML document. This HTML plug-in provides an outline view that displays the structure of an HTML document as a tree, where the headings and paragraphs are nodes in the tree. Imagine that your task is to modify the outline view of the HTML plug-in to add nodes that represent hyperlinks.

To perform this task, you need to update both the HTML document model and the view. Assuming the recommended structure for Eclipse plug-ins, this means changing methods in a `ContentProvider`, a `LabelDecorator` and a `Selection-Listener` class. You also need to add a menu action and update appropriate toolbars which requires modifying another class. In addition, you need to declare the new action and any associated icon in an XML file (i.e., `plugin.xml`). In total, this simple change task involves modifications scattered across four Java classes, two parts of an XML file, and an icon resource.

Although these changes are scattered, there is *structure* to the change task; the structure happens to *crosscut* multiple parts of multiple artifacts. In simple terms, two structures crosscut each other if neither can fit neatly inside the structure provided by the other [12]. A developer well-versed in Eclipse plug-in development would be able to explain this structure, and much of it is recorded in the documentation about how to extend Eclipse. The structure of the source code has been chosen to make adding a new listener to a view a change that is localized in the structure, whereas adding a brand-new element (as in our task) is a change that crosscuts the structure.

We believe that many of the tasks involving scattered changes are not ad hoc, but that they do have a crosscutting structure. In our work, we have found that this crosscutting structure emerges from how a developer works with the code base [19, 10]. In the remainder of the paper, we show how this structure, once made explicit, can be used to make IDEs work better for developers.

3   Task Structure

To ground our discussion, we introduce a simple working definition of task structure.

> A **task structure** consists of the parts of a software system and relationships between those parts that were changed to complete the task.

Conceptually, consider forming a graph based on information found in all of the artifacts comprising the system. In this graph, the nodes are structural parts of the artifacts and the edges are relationships between those parts. The structure of a task consists of a collection of subgraphs from this graph. Each node in the graph includes information about the artifact in which it appears, the name of the part, and the type of the part: each kind of artifact will have its own types of parts. For example, the types of parts found in a Java class include method definitions, field definitions, and inner class definitions. As another example, the types of parts found in a bug report include dates when the report is opened or closed, and text fields with discussions about the report. Each edge in the

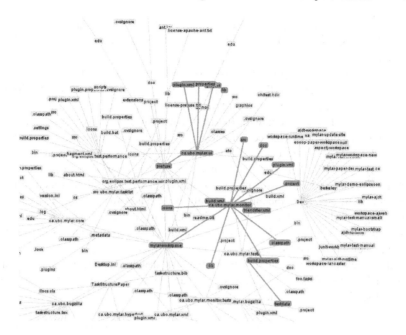

Fig. 2. A graph showing parts of artifacts and relationships between the parts comprising a simple system. The highlighted portions represent the structure of one task performed on the system

graph includes information about the artifact in which it appears (if any) and the type of the relationship. Some relationships will be defined explicitly in a project's artifacts, whereas others may be inferred by tools. For example, a call between two methods in a Java program appears explicitly in the source code, whereas a relationship that indicates a file revision helped solve a particular bug may be inferred by a tool [3].

As a concrete example, we return to the task of adding a new element to an existing view in an Eclipse plug-in. Figure 2 shows a portion of the graph of parts and relationships from artifacts comprising the system.[4] Even though only a fraction of the structure of a small number of artifacts is included in the graph, the amount of information is overwhelming. However, only small parts of the graph relate to the task; the highlighted nodes and edges in Fig. 2 form the structure of the task.

Our definition of task structure is based on completed tasks. An advantage of this definition is that the task structure can be determined with certainty if the time points at which the task started and finished are known. However, we also want to make use of task structure as a task is being performed. We use *task context* as a means of approximating task structure and as a means of describing the subgraphs of the information space of interest when performing a task.

A **task context** consists of parts and relationships of artifacts relevant to a developer as they work on the task.

---

[4] The graph was generated using prefuse [9].

This definition of task context relies on the concept of *relevance* of parts of a system to a task. Relevance can be defined in a number of ways, all of which include some element of cognitive work on the part of a developer [26]. A simple way to determine relevance is for a developer to manually mark the parts and relationships as relevant as they are exploring code [20]. Automatic determinations of relevance are also possible. For example, we are investigating two approaches in which relevance is based on the interaction of the developer with the information in the environment, such as which program elements are selected. In one approach, the interaction information is used to build a model of the degree to which a developer is interested in different parts of the system [10]. This degree-of-interest model is then used to predict interest in other elements and in related project artifacts. In the second approach, relevance is determined by analyzing the interaction information according to the frequency of visits to a program element, the order of visits, the navigation mechanism used to find an element (e.g., browsing, cross-reference search, etc.), and an analysis of the structural dependencies between elements visited [21].

In the rest of this paper, we assume that task structure and task context information is available and focus on providing some examples of how it might be used to improve a developer's work environment.

4   Improving a Developer's Work with Task Structure

Imagine that you are a developer working with an IDE that includes support for capturing, saving and operating on task contexts and task structures. In this section, we describe what it might be like to use this IDE to work on a development task. As we indicate in the scenario, several features we describe have been built or proposed as part of earlier efforts. Task structure enables these operations to be more focused and to provide more semantic information, without any significant input from the developer.

The system on which you are working allows a user to draw points and lines in a window, and to change their colour.[5] The system also has a mode, which when set through a radio button, supports the undo of actions taken by the developer through the user interface.

Your current task involves adding support to enforce the use of a predetermined colour scheme in a drawing. A radio button is to be provided to turn the colour scheme enforcement on and off. When the enforcement is on, the colours of points and lines in the drawing are to be modified to meet the colour scheme and any subsequent request to change a colour will be mapped to the colour scheme.

You start the task by navigating through some of the code attempting to find relevant parts. As you navigate, the IDE is building up your task context based on your selections and edits. After some navigation you determine that you need to add some code in the ButtonsPanel class to add in the necessary radio button. At this point, your task context includes information about several methods you have visited and the constructor in ButtonsPanel. As you add in the call to add a new radio button, a green bug icon

---

[5] This example is based on a simple figure editor used to teach the AspectJ language [11].

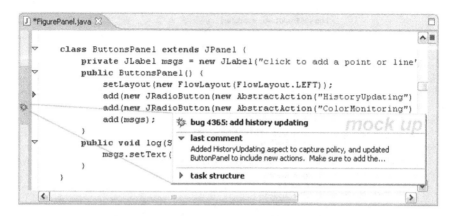

Fig. 3. Based on the task context, a green bug icon appears indicating another bug report may be relevant to the task being performed

appears in the left gutter of the editor (Fig. 3).[6] This icon appears because a tool in the IDE, running in the background, has determined that there is a completed change task whose task structure is similar to your task context.

You decide to click on the bug icon. A popup window appears that describes some information about the bug (Fig 3). You read the description of the bug and you realize that it is similar to the task on which you are working.[7] Since the related bug has been resolved, it has an associated task structure. You expand this task structure and the tree view of the structure shows you which parts overlap with your task context (the highlighted nodes in Fig. 4). You notice the `HistoryUpdating` aspect listed in the task structure that supports the undo functionality. You have not considered whether you will use an aspect to complete your task. However, you look at the code for the aspect and realize that it implements similar functionality to what is needed for your task. After considering the options, you decide to use an aspect-oriented approach and you create a `ColourControl` aspect based on the `HistoryUpdating` aspect. Guided by the previous task context, you also add an image for the new action to the system.

Before you check-in the code for your completed task, you want to ensure your changes will not conflict with concurrent changes being made by other members of your team. As you check-in your code using the facilities of the IDE, you select an option to compare your task structure with any task contexts that your team members have made available (by selecting an option in the IDE). The IDE tool supporting this comparison looks for overlap between your task structure and your team members task contexts and if it finds overlap, it considers any effect, using static analyses, each task has had on the overlapping parts.

---

[6] The user interfaces described are mock-ups of how the described functionality might be provided.

[7] This type of functionality is similar to our Hipikat tool [3]. We sketch the differences between the Hipikat approach and using task structure for this purpose in Sect. 5.

Fig. 4. The task structure of the completed task with highlights indicating overlap with the current task context

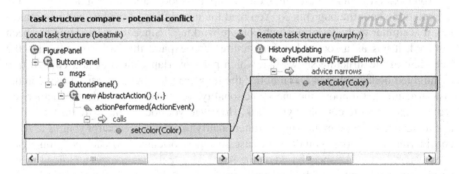

Fig. 5. A comparison of your task structure with a team member's task context identifies a possible conflict. The conflict is determined by statically analyzing the effect of each task context and comparing the results

Figure 5 shows the results of the comparison for the task you are about to complete. It shows that part of your local task structure includes a call to a setColor method (left side of Fig. 5). It also shows that one of your team member's task context's has modified the HistoryUpdating aspect to add advice that narrows setColor [17]. Narrowing advice may result in the setColor method not being called under some circumstances. Given this information, you can contact your colleague to determine how to resolve the conflicts between your changes.[8]

_____

[8] This type of fine-grained conflict determination has similarities to soft locking in Coven [2].

As noted, several of the features that task structure makes possible in this hypothetical scenario have been proposed previously. In comparison to these existing approaches, task structure provides three benefits over existing approaches:

1. it can be determined with minimal effort from the developer as it emerges from how the developer works on the system,
2. it provides a conceptual framework and model that can be built into an IDE to make task-related tools easier to build, and
3. it provides information that may be used to focus views in the IDE, allowing a greater density of relevant information to be displayed.

5   Making Use of Task Structure

The scenario described in the last section illustrates how explicit support of task structure in an IDE can benefit a developer. In this section, we elaborate on these points and describe more possibilities. Through this section, we use the term task structure to simplify the discourse as it should be clear when the use of task context would be more precise.

5.1   Improving IDE Tools

An ideal IDE would present the information a developer needs, when it is needed, and with a minimum of interaction from the developer. Such an IDE would reduce the amount of time a developer spends trying to find relevant information. We outline four ways that an IDE with support for task structure could help move towards this goal.

Reducing Overload in Views and Visualizations. IDEs present system structure mostly in lists and tree views, with some graphical visualizations [24]. When used on large systems, these existing presentation mechanisms tend to overload the developer with information, making it difficult to find the information of interest. For example the Package Explorer, a commonly used tree view in Eclipse which shows the decomposition of Java source into packages, files, classes, and other structural elements, often contains tens of thousands of nodes when used on a moderately-sized system (e.g., see the left-hand side of Fig. 6; notice that the tree structure is not visible). A task's structure can be used to determine what information should be made more conspicuous to a developer. For instance, the task structure can be highlighted [22]. Or, the task structure can be used to filter the view so as to show only task-relevant information as is the case in our Mylar prototype (see the right-hand side of Figure 6; the bolded parts are the elements that are the most important to the task) [10]. Either way, the views can make it clear to the developer the elements important to the task.

Scoping Queries. Task structure can be used to scope the execution of code queries performed by a developer. A default setting, for instance, may be to query code only within one or two relationships in the overall graph of structural information (Sect. 3) from the code on which the query is invoked. Scoping queries with task structure could have two potential benefits: queries may execute more quickly for large systems, and the information returned may be more relevant, reducing the time needed for a developer to wade through search results.

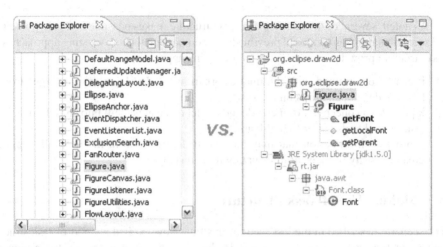

Fig. 6. A view of the containment hierarchy of a system without Mylar active (left-hand side) and with Mylar active (right-hand side). In the Mylar view, the focus provided by task context enables the relevant information to fit on the screen without a scrollbar, and enables the structural relationships to be visible

Performing Queries Automatically. In addition to scoping queries, parts in the task structure can be used to seed queries that run automatically. We call these active queries and they could be used to seed active views [10]. For example, the active search view in the Mylar prototype eagerly finds and displays all Java, XML, and bug reports related to parts in the task structure [10]. This kind of view provides a developer with the structural information they need when it is needed. The result could be a reduction in the number of interruptions a developer must typically make to think about and formulate a query, as the most relevant queries are formulated and executed automatically. Active queries also do away with the need to wait on query execution, since queries are executed automatically in the background.

The concept may also be helpful in the implementation of the IDE. The Eclipse IDE, for instance, requires the Abstract Syntax Tree (AST) for a class to be in memory in order to support features such as semantic highlighting.[9] However, operations that span multiple files, such as the rename method refactoring, are time consuming and require the developer to wait until all related ASTs are loaded into memory. The task structure could be used to define the slices of ASTs that should be kept in memory in order to make common refactorings instantaneous (i.e., as quick for changes across files as they are for changes within the file).

Supporting Task Management. IDEs provide little to no support for managing the tasks a developer is performing. The best support may be an ability to read and manage bug reports within the IDE. Task structure can improve this situation. For example, as part of our Mylar project, we have prototyped support for enabling developers to

---

[9] Semantic highlighting refers to the ability to highlight code according to properties such as whether the code is an abstract method invocation, a reference to a local variable, etc.

associate task structures with specific tasks and to switch between them. Mylar can then filter the views of the system according to the selected task. The task structure can also be attached to a bug report, enabling a developer to re-start if they return to the bug at a later time. The task structure, in effect, is a form of externalization of the developer's memory of the task.

5.2 Improving Collaboration

Over the lifetime of a system many developers work on many tasks. We believe that communicating this structure to other developers as they work, and storing it as the system evolves, can provide collaborative tools with an effective representation of group memory.

Forming and Accessing a Group Memory. It is not uncommon when working on a software development project to come across a problem that is reminiscent of a past problem with the system that has since been solved (Sect. 4). In earlier work, we demonstrated the benefits of processing the artifacts comprising a software system to form a group memory that may then be searched for relevant information as a developer is performing a task [3, 4]. One benefit is that developers may be more aware of subtle, but relevant, information. For example, in an experiment we conducted, newcomers to a project took into account additional information presented from the group memory and finished an assigned task more completely than experts who did not have access to the group memory [4]. Our previous work treated task structure implicitly, forming links automatically between parts of related artifacts. Explicitly stored task structures enable more focused comparisons between a past system and a current system and allow new operations across the group memory, such as an analysis tool that could identify all of the third party APIs involved in commonly reported defects.

Sharing Task Structure. Task structure encapsulates a developer's knowledge about the system. As discussed above, developers may want to store this knowledge in order to access it at a later time. In addition, they may want to share it with others. For example, a developer delegating a task could include the task structure in order to help the team member pick up the task where it was left off. Sharing of task structure could also be done in real-time in order to make developers aware of the activities of their team members. For example, in an open-source project where team members are distributed across time zones, knowing the parts of the system that have been worked on by others can encourage dialog and prevent merge problems. In comparison to existing approaches to providing such awareness [23], task structure can enable a deeper comparison, seeding automated handling by tools or discussions between involved developers with more information.

5.3 Improving the IDE Platform

In addition to improving the developer's experience, task structure may help solve issues related to a number of tools provided by an IDE, and may help simplify the development of tools.

Capturing and Recommending Workflow. In this paper, we have focused on information overload that developers face when working on the content of large systems. These developers also face information overload in the user interfaces of IDEs. Enterprise-application development tools, such as IBM's Rational Software Architect, offer sophisticated support for development across the lifecycle, which results in dozens of views and editors, and hundreds of user interface actions. It can be difficult for developers to know what features exist, let alone try to find them. Adaptive interfaces [7] and Eclipse's capabilities[10] address this in a general way, based on aggregate information about how features are used. We see potential for making the user interface more aware of the task being performed by capturing the task structure of developers who use these tools effectively, and then mining this information for task-specific interaction patterns of the user interface. Mined patterns may suggest ways to focus the user interface on only those tools needed for the completion of a particular task [22].

Simplifying Tool Development. IDE platforms such as Eclipse make it easy to build new tools that expose system structure. For example, a new view that shows all methods overriding the currently-selected method is easy to add. In our experience, it is harder to add tools that depend on some notion of task, and each tool must develop its own ad hoc model of task. While it is possible to layer task information on the models provided by the IDE through an index over existing elements and relationships, we see potential for task information to be more central. For example, it would be beneficial to be able to tag an element as being part of some named task, and to then be able to trigger an action based on when an attempt is made to synchronize that element with the repository. Task structure information could also be used to arbitrate user interface issues; for example, a tool might use a task's structure to determine which of several competing annotations are most applicable to show in the gutter of an editor.

6   Open Questions

Our working definition of task structure is simple and extensional. These characteristics make it easy to describe the possibilities of task structure and do not unduly constrain what a task is or how developers work on tasks. It is an open question as to whether this definition is too simple. It may be that tools built on this definition require information about why artifacts were changed, or the order in which they were changed, to provide meaningful information to a developer. It may also be necessary to include in the definition notions of what constitutes a task, whether a task is worked on in one time period or across various blocks of time, amongst others. These questions will need both empirical and formal investigation.

Regardless of the programming language and software engineering technologies used, we believe many change tasks have an emergent crosscutting structure because it is impossible to simultaneously modularize a system for all kinds of changes that may occur. This statement deserves investigation, such as a characterization of task structure

---

[10] A capability in Eclipse is a feature set that can be enabled or disabled by a user. Capabilities are pre-defined and configured when the IDE is shipped.

for changes performed on systems intended for a variety of domains, written in a variety of languages, of different ages, and so on. It is also an open question as to whether, at this point, more benefit to the developer might result from better support for explicit task structure than new means of expressing sophisticated modularity.

7   Related Work

7.1   Tasks and Desktop Applications

Explicit capture and manipulation of task information has been studied in the domain of desktop applications (e.g., document processors and email clients). Of these, the project most similar to some of our efforts is TaskTracer [5], which is intended to help knowledge workers deal effectively with interruptions, and which seeks to help knowledge workers reuse information about tasks completed in the past. TaskTracer monitors a worker's interaction with desktop application resources, such as mail messages and web documents, attempting to build up a grouping of resources related to a particular task. The worker has to name the task being worked upon when they start the task. Although some of our goals overlap, we differ fundamentally from TaskTracer in our intention to maintain fine-grained structural information across artifacts; TaskTracer works only at the level of resources or files. We believe the collection of fine-grained information provides several benefits. For instance, we can support detailed comparisons about how a current and a past task compare. As a second example, we can trigger the recall of potentially useful information for a task based on the current task context.

7.2   Tasks and Development Environments

In the context of development environments, the term task has largely been used from a tool builder's point of view. For example, the Gandalf project recognized the variety of tasks that needed to be supported by the software development process and created a suite of tools to support the generation of an environment particular to a project [8]. The researchers recognized the need to deal with such issues as expertise of the developer, but focused on the problems that were more important at that time, such as handling the syntax and semantics of the languages being used to develop a system.

More recently, IDEs have introduced user-defined scopes as a way of approximating a concept of task similar to the way that we use the term in this paper. For example, in Eclipse, a developer can define a *working set* which is a set of resources related through the system's containment hierarchy over which queries may be executed and saved. Working sets are more coarse-grained than task structure and a developer must evolve working sets as they change tasks, as opposed to our concept of task structure which evolves from a developer's work.

7.3   Manipulating Program Fragments

The size and complexity of software systems has led to many approaches for extracting and operating on fragments of a system. We describe four approaches that are similar to our idea of task structure as a collection of system fragments. Tarr and colleagues introduced the idea of multi-dimensional software decomposition to support fragments that correspond to concerns [25]. Task structure is similar in cutting across artifacts, but a task need not have the same conceptual coherence that one expects from a concern. In multi-dimensional software decomposition the main operation supported on a fragment is the integration of code into a system, whereas we have considered how task structure supports development-oriented operations, such as work conflicts between team members. Our earlier work on concern graphs is also related to modelling and manipulating fragments of a system's structure that relate to concerns [20]. A main operation supported on a concern graph is the detection of inconsistencies between a version of a system in which a concern graph is defined and an evolved version of the system [18]. The support of inconsistency detection is possible because a concern graph captures more intentional information than task structure. As a third example, virtual source files were proposed to allow a programmer to define an organization for parts of the system appropriate for a task [1]. A virtual source file is defined intentionally based on queries and can be used for such operations as determining conflicting changes between team members (similar to our description in Sect. 4). In contrast to virtual source files, task structure emerges from how a developer works on the system as opposed to requiring the developer to state their intention on a structure of parts of artifacts relevant to a task. Finally, Quitslund's MView source code editor supports the juxtaposition of code elements selected by a query in a single view [16]. Although a fragment in his system is restricted to the results from a set of queries over source code, it shares a similarity with task structure in enabling a development-oriented operation over the fragments, namely enabling editing of the code in a single window. Dealing with fragments in a task-oriented manner may enable better integration of the various fragment ideas into the work environments of developers.

8   Summary

Tools are supposed to make us work more effectively. IDEs have served this purpose for developers in recent years. However, as systems grow more complex, the effectiveness of these development environments is breaking down because they do not adequately support tasks that involve changes to multiple artifacts. In this paper, we have described how many of these tasks do have a structure; the structure emerges from the way in which a developer works with the system. This emergent task structure can be identified and used by an IDE to focus existing views and enable new operations. This support matches the way a developer works, allowing them to modify a system without being overwhelmed by its complexity.

Acknowledgement

Gail Murphy would like to thank AITO for the honour of the Dahl-Nygaard Junior Prize, which made this paper possible. The authors would also like to thank Andrew Black for encouraging a paper to be written, Annie Ying for contributing data and comments, and the inspirational work of Rob Walker, Elisa Baniassad, and Al Lai. The paper is much better for the insightful comments provided by John Anvik, Wesley Coelho,

Brian de Alwis, Jan Hannemann, Gregor Kiczales, and Eric Wohlstadter. Projects contributing to the ideas presented in this paper were funded by NSERC and IBM.

References

1. M. Chu-Carroll and J. Wright. Supporting distributed collaboration through multidimensional software configuration management. In *SCM*, volume 2649 of *LNCS*, pages 40–53. Springer, 2001.
2. M. C. Chu-Carroll and S. Sprenkle. Coven: Brewing better collaboration through software configuration management. In *SIGSOFT '00/FSE-8: Proc. of the 8th ACM SIGSOFT Int'l Symp. on Foundations of Software Engineering*, pages 88–97. ACM Press, 2000.
3. D. Čubranić and G. C. Murphy. Hipikat: Recommending pertinent software development artifacts. In *ICSE '03: Proc. of the 25th Int'l Conf. on Software Engineering*, pages 408–418. IEEE Computer Society, 2003.
4. D. Čubranić, G. C. Murphy, J. Singer, and K. S. Booth. Learning from project history: a case study for software development. In *CSCW '04: Proc. of the 2004 ACM Conf. on Computer Supported Cooperative Work*, pages 82–91. ACM Press, 2004.
5. A. N. Dragunov, T. G. Dietterich, K. Johnsrude, M. McLaughlin, L. Li, and J. L. Herlocker. TaskTracer: A desktop environment to support multi-tasking knowledge workers. In *IUI '05: Proc. of the 10th Int'l Conf. on Intelligent User Interfaces*, pages 75–82. ACM Press, 2005.
6. E. Gamma, R. Helm, R. Johnson, and J. Vlissides. *Design Patterns: Elements of Reusable Object-Oriented Software*. Addison-Wesley, 1995.
7. S. Greenberg and I. H. Witten. Adaptive personalized interfaces – a question of viability. *Behaviour and Information Technology - BIT*, 4:31–45, 1985.
8. A. N. Habermann and D. Notkin. Gandalf: software development environments. *IEEE Trans. Software Engineering*, 12(12):1117–1127, 1986.
9. J. Heer, S. K. Card, and J. A. Landay. prefuse: a toolkit for interactive information visualization. In *CHI '05: Proc. of the SIGCHI Conf. on Human Factors in Computing Systems*, pages 421–430. ACM Press, 2005.
10. M. Kersten and G. C. Murphy. Mylar: a degree-of-interest model for IDEs. In *AOSD '05: Proc. of the 4th Int'l Conf. on Aspect-oriented Software Development*, pages 159–168, 2005.
11. G. Kiczales, E. Hilsdale, J. Hugunin, M. Kersten, J. Palm, and W. G. Griswold. An overview of AspectJ. In *ECOOP '01: Proc. of the 15th European Conf. on Object-Oriented Programming*, pages 327–353. Springer, 2001.
12. H. Masuhara and G. Kiczales. Modular crosscutting in aspect-oriented mechanisms. In *ECOOP '03: Proc. of the 17th European Conf. on Object-Oriented Programming*, pages 2–28. Springer, 2003.
13. A. Mockus, R. T. Fielding, and J. Herbsleb. Two case studies of open source software development: Apache and Mozilla. *ACM Trans. Software Engineering Methodology*, 11(3):309–346, 2002.
14. D. L. Parnas. On the criteria to be used in decomposing systems into modules. *Communications of the ACM*, 15(12):1053–1058, 1972.
15. D. E. Perry, N. Staudenmayer, and L. G. Votta. People, organizations, and process improvement. *IEEE Software*, 11(4):36–45, 1994.
16. P. J. Quitslund. Beyond files: programming with multiple source views. In *Eclipse '03: Proc. of the 2003 OOPSLA Workshop on Eclipse Technology eXchange*, pages 6–9. ACM Press, 2003.
17. M. Rinard, A. Salcianu, and S. Bugrara. A classification system and analysis for aspect-oriented programs. In *SIGSOFT '04/FSE-12: Proc. of the 12th ACM SIGSOFT Int'l Symp. on Foundations of Software Engineering*, pages 147–158. ACM Press, 2004.

18. M. P. Robillard. *Representing Concerns in Source Code*. PhD thesis, University of British Columbia, 2003.
19. M. P. Robillard, W. Coelho, and G. C. Murphy. How effective developers investigate source code: An exploratory study. *IEEE Trans. Software Engineering*, 30(12):889–903, 2004.
20. M. P. Robillard and G. C. Murphy. Concern graphs: Finding and describing concerns using structural program dependencies. In *ICSE '02: Proc. of the 24th Int'l Conf. on Software Engineering*, pages 406–416. ACM Press, 2002.
21. M. P. Robillard and G. C. Murphy. Automatically inferring concern code from program investigation activities. In *ASE '03: Proc. of the 18th Int'l Conf. on Automated Software Engineering*, pages 225–234. IEEE Computer Society Press, 2003.
22. M. P. Robillard and G. C. Murphy. Program navigation analysis to support task-aware software development environments. In *Proc. of the ICSE Workshop on Directions in Software Engineering Environments*, pages 83–88. IEE, 2004.
23. A. Sarma, Z. Noroozi, and A. van der Hoek. Palantír: Raising awareness among configuration management workspaces. In *ICSE '03: Proc. of the 25th Int'l Conf. on Software Engineering*, pages 444–454. IEEE Computer Society, 2003.
24. M.-A. D. Storey, D. Čubranić, and D. M. German. On the use of visualization to support awareness of human activities in software development: A survey and a framework. In *SoftVis '05: Proc. of the 2005 ACM Symp. on Software Visualization*, pages 193–202. ACM Press, 2005.
25. P. Tarr, H. Ossher, W. Harrison, and S. Sutton Jr. N degrees of separation: Multi-dimensional separation of concerns. In *ICSE '99: Proc. of the 21st Int'l Conf. on Software Engineering*, pages 107–119. IEEE Computer Society Press, 1999.
26. D. Woods, E. Patterson, and E. Roth. Can we ever escape from data overload? A cognitive system diagnosis. *Cognition, Technology & Work*, 4(1):22–36, 2002.

Loosely-Separated "Sister" Namespaces in Java

Yo•• i• i S••o* •n• S• i•••• • i••

Dept. of Mathematical and Computing Sciences,
Tokyo Institute of Technology
{yoshiki, chiba}@csg.is.titech.ac.jp

Abstract. Most modern programming systems such as Java allow us
to link independently developed components together dynamically. This
makes it possible to develop and deploy software on a per component
basis. However, a number of Java developers have reported a problem,
ironically called the *version barrier*, imposed by the strict separation of
namespaces. The version barrier prohibits one component from passing
an instance to another component if each component contains that class
type. This paper introduces a novel concept for Java namespaces, called
sister namespaces, to address this problem. Sister namespaces can relax
the version barrier between components. The main purpose of this paper
is to provide a mechanism for relaxing the version barrier, while still
allowing type-safe instance accesses between components with negligible
performance penalties in regular execution.

1 Introduction

P••••i••lly •ll • o•••n ••o•••• • in• •nvi•on• •n•• •llow ••v•lo•••• •o ••ili••
•o• • •in• o• •o• •on•n• •y•••• (•.•., J•v•B••n• [9], • JB [••], ••• BA [•5],
.N• T/D• • M/A••iv•X [••], ••li••• •l••-in• [•9]). A •o• •on•n• •y•••• •llow•
••o•••• • ••• •o ••v•lo• •o• •on•n•-••••• ••• li•••ion, w• i•• ••n ••• •v•lo•••
•n• ••n ••• loy•••• ••• •o• •on•n•. Mo•• o•••• •o• •on•n• •y•••• ••o• J•v• ••o••
• •in•l• •l••• lo•••• ••• •o• •on•n•, •n• ••••••y ••••••• • • ni••• n•• ••••••• •o•
•••• ••• li•••ion •o• •on•n•. A n•• ••••••• i• • • ••• ••o• ••• •l••• n•• ••• •o
••• •l••• ••• ni•ion•. A ••• o• •l••••• in•l•••• in ••• ••• • •o• •on•n• *joins* [1] i••
own n•• •••••• •n• •••• n•• in• •onfli•• •••w••n •o• •on•n•• ••n •• •voi•••.
Mo••ov••, • •o• •on•n• ••n •• •yn•• i••lly •n• in• ivi•••lly •••••••• wi••o••
••••••in• ••• w•ol• •x••••ion •nvi•on• •n•.

• n• •i•ni••n• ••w•••• o•••••• •o• •on•n• •y•••• ••o• J•v• i••• • i• •• l•y
•o• •o• •on•n•• •o •o• • •ni•••• •••o•• •l••• lo•••• •o•n••i•• in ••• J•v• Vi•-
•••l M•••in• (JVM) [13, •0, •, 1•]. In ••••, •••• •o• • •ni•••ion i• w•ll • nown •o
••••••n•ly ••••••• • •••••• ••o• ClassCastException o•• lin• •••o• LinkageError.
Mo•• o• ••• lin• •••o•• ••• j••• •••••; •n •••o• i• •••••• w••n • •l••• i• w•on•ly

---

* Currently, Mitsubishi Research Institute, Inc., Japan.
[1] A class joining a namespace means it is being loaded by the class loader that creates
the namespace.

lo•••• •y • o•• ••••n• •n• •• il• lo••••• [16]. T•••• ••••• ••n •• •••ily •voi•••
i• ••v•lo•••• ••• •••••••l. How•v••, •••• •••o••• ••• •x••••• •ly •i• •• l• •o •voi•
•in•• ••i• ••o•l•• i• •••••••• •y ••• •••i•• •••••••••ion o• n•• •••••••••, i•oni••lly
••ll•• ••• *version barrier*. T•• v•••ion ••••i•• i• • • •••• •ni•• ••••• •••v•n•• •
v•••ion o• • •l••• •y•• ••o• ••in• •onv••••• •o •no•••• v•••ion o• ••••• ••••i••
•l••• •y••. Fo• in•••n••, i• ••••i••• •n in•••n•• o• ••• •o•• •• •y• •o • •••i•n••
•o ••• v••i••l• o• ••• l••••• •y••.

In J•v•, • •l••• •y•• i• •ni••ly i••n•i•••• •• •• n•i• • •y ••• •o• •in••ion o•
• •l••• lo•••• •n• • ••lly •••li••• •l••• n•• •. I• •wo •l••• ••• ni•ion• wi•• •••
••• • •l••• n•• • ••• lo•••• •y •iff••n• lo•••••, •wo v••ion• o• ••••• •l••• •y••
••• •••••••• •n• ••y••n •o-•xi•••, •l••o••• ••y ••• •••••••• ••• •i••in•• •y•••.
T•• v•••ion ••••i•• i• • • •••• •ni•• •o• ••••••n•••in• ••••• •iff•••n• v•••ion• o• •
•l••• ••• •••••••• ••• •iff•••n• •y•••. T• i• •••••n••• i• •i•ni••n• •o• •••o•• •n••
•••••on•. I• •iff••n• v•••ion• o• • •l••• w••• no• ••••••••• •• •iff•••n• •y•••, •••
••v•n••••• o• ••in• • •••i••lly •y••• l•n••••• wo• l• •• lo••. Mo••ov••, i• •••
••• • •l••• ••• ni•ion (i.•., •l••• •l•) i• lo•••• •y •iff•••n• •l••• lo•••••, •iff•••n•
v•••ion• o• ••••• •l••• ••• •••••••• •n• ••••••••• •• •i••in•• •y•••. T••••o••, i•
•wo •o• •on•n•• lo•• ••• •••• • •l••• •l• in•ivi••••lly, on• •o• •on•n••nno••••••
•n in•••n•• o• ••••• •l••• •y•• •o ••• o••••.

T• i• •••••• •••••n•• o• novel •on••• o• n•• ••••••• in J•v•, w•i•• w •••ll
sister namespaces, •n• ••• •••i•n o• ••••• • ••••ni•• . Si•••• n•• ••••••• ••n
••l•x ••• v•••ion ••••i•• •••w••n ••• •li••••ion •o• •on•n••. An in•••n•• ••n ••
••••i•• ••yon• ••• v•••ion ••••i•• •••w••n •i•••• n•• ••••••• i• ••• •y•• o• •••
in•••n•• i• •o• •••i•l• •••w••n ••••• n•• •••••••. T••• •in •••• o•• o• •• i• ••-
••• i• •o ••ovi•• • • •••• •ni•• •o• ••l•xin• ••• v•••ion ••••i•• w il• ••••in•
•y••-••• in•••n•• ••••••••• wi•• n••li•i•l• •••o•• •n•• ••n•l•i•• in ••••l•• •x-
•••ion. T•• • ••••ni•• o• •i•••• n•• ••••••• i• i• •l•• •n••• •y •x••n•in• •••
•y•• •••••••• •n• ••• •l••• lo•••• o• ••• JVM.

T•• ••••• o• •• i• ••••• i• o•••ni••• •• •ollow•. S•••ion • •••••i••• •wo ••o•-
l•• • •••• ••••• ••o•• l• •o• •o• •on•n•-••••• ••• •li••••ion ••v•lo••••. S•••ion 3
••••••n•• ••• •••i•n •n• i• •l•• •n•••ion o• ••• •i•••• n•• ••••••. S•••ion • •i•-
•••••• • ••w i• •l•• •n•••ion i••••. S•••ion 5 ••••••n•• ••• •••• l•• o• o•• •x••-
i• •n••. S•••ion 6 •o• ••••• ••• •i•••• n•• ••••••• • •••••ni•• •o o••••• ••l••••
wo••. S•••ion • •on•l•••• •• i• ••••••.

2   Problems of the Version Barrier

T• i• •••••ion ••••••n•• •wo ••o•l•• • ••••• ••v•lo•••• o•••n •n•o• n••• w••n ••-
v•lo•in• • ••o• •on•n•-••••• •••li••••ion in J•v•. T•••• ••o•l•• • ••• •••••lly
••••••• •y ••• v•••ion ••••i•• •••w••n n•• •••••••.

2.1   J2EE Components

Mo•• J•••• •l•••o•• •, •i•••• •o• • •••i•l (•.•., W•••••••••, W••lo•i•) o• o••n-
•o••••• (•.•., JBo••, To• •••), ••••o•• •o•• ••• ••v•lo•• •n• •n• ••• •••loy• •n•

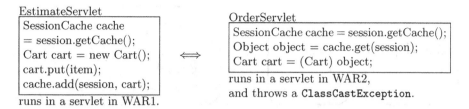

EstimateServlet

SessionCache cache
= session.getCache();
Cart cart = new Cart();
cart.put(item);
cache.add(session, cart);

runs in a servlet in WAR1.

⟺

OrderServlet

SessionCache cache = session.getCache();
Object object = cache.get(session);
Cart cart = (Cart) object;

runs in a servlet in WAR2,
and throws a `ClassCastException`.

Fig. 1. Passing the session cache from one WAR component to another

o•• •l•••••l• •o• •on•n• ••••iv•• (• JB-JA•• •, WA•• •, •n• • A•• •). A W•• A•-•li••ion A•••iv• (WA• •l•) i• •••• •o •••loy • w••-••••• •••li••ion. T• i•
•l• ••n •on••in •••vl•••, HTML •l••, J•v• S••v•• P•••• (JSP•), •n• •ll •••o-•i•••• i• •••• •n• •••o•••• •l••. An • n•••••i•• A••li••ion A•••iv• (• A• •l•)
•• •y •on••in on• o• • o•• • n•••••i•• J•v•B••n• (• JB•) •n• WA•• •. T•• ••n-•ion• li•y o• ••• •o-••ll•• • o• •••loy• •n• •n••l•• •••• J••• •o• •on•n• •o ••
•l••••• •n• •n•l••••• •• ••n•i• • wi••o•• •••••••in• ••• •••li••ion •••v•••.
T•••, • J••• •••li••ion ••n •• •yn• i••lly ••••o• i••• on • •••-•o• •on•n•
•••i•. T• i• •••• ••i••lly i• ••ov•• ••• ••o•••ivi•y o• •o•w••• ••v•lo•• •n•. Fo•
•n••lin• •o• •••loy• •n•, •••• •o• •on•n• join• • i••in•• n•• ••••••, lo•••• •y
• •i••in•• •l••• lo••••.

How•v••, ••• v•••ion •••i•• • •••• i• i• •o••i•l• •o •••• in••n••• o••••• v••-•ion o•• •l••• •••o•• ••• •o•n••y o• J••• •o• •on•n•, o• n•• •••••••. S•••
in•••n••• ••• •y•i••lly •••••, •oo•i••, o• •••ion o• j•••• o• •••n•. Fo• •x•• •l•,
•on•i••• ••• •ollowin• ••n••io. An in•••n•• o• ••• Cart •l••• • ••• •• • •••••••
••w••n •••vl••• in•l•••• in • iff••n• w•• ••• li••ion •••• iv•• (•••• i•, ••o• •••
EstimateServlet in•l•••• in on• w•• ••••iv•, WA• 1, •o ••• OrderServlet
in •no•••• w•• ••••iv•, WA•• •). T•• •l••• •l• o• ••• Cart •l••• i• ••••••••
in•o • J•v• A•••iv• (JA•) •l•, •n• i••n•i••l •o•i•• o• ••• JA• •l• ••i••
in ••• `WEB-INF/lib` •i•••••o•i•• in •••• w•• ••••iv•. T•••, •••• •l••• lo••••
lo••• ••• Cart •l••• •••••••ly. Fi•••• 1 ill•••••••• ••• i• •l•• •n••ion o• •••••
•••vl•••: EstimateServlet •••• •n in•••n•• o• Cart in•o ••• •••ion ••••• •n•
OrderServlet •• ll• •••• in•••n•• o••o••• •••••. W••n •••in• i• ••o• Object
•o Cart, ••• JVM will •••ow • ClassCastException. Sin•• ••• Cart •l••• ••••-•n••• •y ••• EstimateServlet •l••• i• • •i••in• •y• ••o• ••• •y• •••••n•••
•y ••• OrderServlet •l•••, ••• v•••ion •••i•• •••v•n•• ••i•n• •n• o• •••• in-••n•• •o ••• v••i••l• cart in ••• OrderServlet •l••• •y •••owin• • ••••• •••o•
in •• v• n••.

So• • •••••••• • i•••• ••in• ••• ••l•••ion • o••l o• •l••• lo••••• in J•v• i• •
•ol•••ion •o ••• ••o•l•• ••ov•. T•••• WA• •o• •on•n• ••n •••••• ••• ••• • v••-•ion o•• •l••• i• •••y ••l•••••• ••• lo••in• o• •••• •l••• •o •••i• •o• • on •••n•,
•••• •• ••• EAR •l••• lo••••• (Fi•••• •). In ••••, ••• •y•i••l J••• • •l••••••• •••
•••• • •o• • on •••n• lo••••. ••il• •l••• lo••••• ••n ••v• ••i• •••n• lo••••
lo•• • •l••• i• •••y w•n• •o ••••• ••• ••• • v••ion o• •••• •l•••. In ••• •••••
o• J•••, ••• SystemClassLoader i• ••• •••••n• o• •ll • A• •l••• lo••••• •n•
•n • A• •l••• lo•••• i•, in ••n, ••• •••••n• o• •ll WA• •l••• lo••••• in•l•••

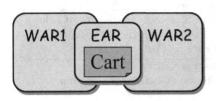

Fig. 2. A parent EAR class loader is used for sharing class types between WAR1 and WAR2. The rounded box represents a namespace for the J2EE component. The overlapping part means the overlapped namespace

Fig. 3. The JBoss application server based on the unified class loader architecture makes a parent-child relationship between the communicating components

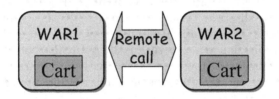

Fig. 4. All inter-component communications are realized by a remote call

in ••••• • A• . How•v••, ••• •ol••ion ••in• • •••••n• •l••• lo•••• •i•••ly •o• •l••
••v•••l i•••l•v•n• J••• •o• •on•n•• •o••••••. S••• •o•••••-•••in•• •o• •o•i•ion
•••••••••• ••• • •in••in••ili•y •n• •v•il••ili•y o••ll ••l•••• •o••w••• •o• •on•n••.
Fo• •x•• • l•, •on•i•• •••• •wo •o• • on•n•• DVDStore •n• Pizzeria: ••• •o•• ••
• o••l• •n onlin• ••-•o• • DVD ••o•• •n• ••• l•••••• o••l• •n onlin• •o• • ••liv-
••y •i••••i• •v•il••l• ••o• •o••• 10 •o •1. I••o•• o• ••••• •o• • on•n•• ••••• •••
•• ov•• •n•ion•• •••li•••ion •o• • on•n• in•l••in• Cart •n• i• ••i• •o• •on•n•
i• ••••••••• in•o Pizzeria, •••n •n•••loyin• Pizzeria •o• • in••n•n•• ••o••
••• •••vi•• •y DVDStore. Sin•• DVDStore • ••• •• n •• •o••• • ••y, i• i• •l• o••
i• •o••i•l• •o •••i•• ••• • •in••n•n•• •••••l• o• Pizzeria.

To •olv• •• i• ••o• l•• , ••• JBo•• ••• li•••ion •••v•• ••ovi•• ••• • ni••• •l•••
lo•••• (U• L) •••• i•••••••• [•1] •o• •••• in• •••o•• •o• • on•n•• •••o•• ••• J•••
•o• • on•n••. A •oll•••ion o• U• L •••• ••• • •in•l• •l••• lo••••, w•i•• • l•••• in•o
• •in•l• n•• •••••• ••ll ••• •l••••• •o •• lo••••. All •l••••• ••• lo•••• in•o •••
••••••• ••• o•i•o•y •n• • •n•••• •y •• i• ••• o•i•o•y. How•v••, ••i• •••• i•••••••
•i•••l•• •iff••n• J••• •o• • on•n•• wi•• ••• ••• • n•• • (Fi•••• 3).

Ano••• •••• ni•••, •on•i••••• • l••• •••o••, i• ••in• ••• J•v• S••i•li•••ion
API •o •x•••n•• o• j•••• •••w••n •iff•••n• J••• •o• • on•n•• •••o••• • • •y••
••••••• , w•i•• i• ••• •••••••• •o •• Call-by-Value (Fi•••• •). Ty•i••l J••• • l••-
•o•• • ••o•• •• i• •••• •o•• •o• in•••-• A• •o• • •ni•••ion•. How•v••, •v•n i• •n
• A• w•n•• •o •••n•••• •n o• j••• •o •no•••• A• •••loy•• in •• •••• • •on••in••
(o• JVM), i• • ••• •x•••• • • ••• o•• ••ll. T•i• ••• o•• ••ll i• • w•••• o• I/• ••-

•o••••• •n• i• •••••••••• ••• ov••ll •••o•• •n••. Al••o••• ••• Lo••l In•••••••
• ••••ni•• in••o••••• in • JB•.0 •llow• •o• • •ni••ion• •••w••n •o• •on•n••
wi••o•• ••• o•• ••ll• (*Call-by-Reference*), •••••• •o• •on•n•• • •••• •• •••••••••
•o••••••• in ••• ••• • •••••iv•.

2.2 Eclipse Plug-in Framework

T•• • •li••• •l•••o•• [3•], •n in••••••••• •••v•lo•• •n• •nvi•on• •n• •o• J•v•, ••n
•• •on•i••••• ••• • •o• •on•n• •y•••• ••• •o i•• ••v•n•••• •l••-in •••• •wo••. A
•l••-in • o••l• ••n •on••in •ll •o••• o•••o••••, in•l••in• •o•• •n• •o••• •n••-
•ion. A • l••-in • o••l• • •••• •l•o •on••in ••• •i•n• in•o•• ••ion •o• ••• • l•••o••
•o in•o•• o••••• ••• •o•• o• •o••• •n••ion in•o i•••l•. T•• • l••-in •••• •wo•• •l-
low• •• •o •••ily •••, •••••• •n• ••• ov• •i•••••• •o••ion• o• ••• •on•n••. In
•••i•ion, •in•• • •••••••• •l••• lo•••• (••ll•• • •l••-in •l••• lo••••) i• ••••••••
•o• ••••• •l••-in • o••l•, •••• •l••-in • o••l• ••• i•• •ni••• n•• •••••• •n• i•
• yn•• i••lly ••• loy•• l•.

How•v••, ••• • •li••• •l••-in •••• •wo•• •••• • •••••••••l ••o•l•• ••• •o •••
v•••ion ••••i••. Fo• •x•• •l•, •on•i•• ••• • •li••• ••l• •y•••• •l••-in • o•-
•l• [1•]. I• i• • •••••l •l••-in • o••l• •••• •llow• ••••• •o • •v•lo• •n• ••-
•loy • •o•••ion•l-••••li•y, •••y-•o-•••, •n• ••••••••l• onlin• •o••• •n••••ion. T••
• •li••• ••l• •y•••• ••n •• •••• •• •n in•o••n••, w•i•• i• •n ••• li•••ion i•-
•l•• •n••• •• • w•• •o• •on•n• •n• •••••••i•l• ••o• • w•• ••ow•••. How•v••,
•o •• •••• •• •n in•o••n••, ••• ••••••n• ••li••• ••l• •y•••• n•••• •o ••n on
• •••••••• ••o•••• ••o• ••• ••o•••• o• ••• w•• •••v•• (Fi•••• 5). T•• w••
•••v•• • •••• • ••• n•w ••o•••••• •o• ••• ••l• •y•••• •n• ••• • ini• •• • •li•••
•y•••• , •n• •••n ••• w•• •••v•• • •••• •i••••• •ll ••••••••• •o ••• ••l• •y-
••• . T•••, •v••y •o• • •ni•••ion •o• •i••••• in• •••••••••• ••o• ••• w•• •••v••
•o ••• ••l• •y•••• i• • ••• o•• ••ll, w•i•• involv•• • •••••llin• •ll •••••••
in•••n•••.

A •••l ••o•l•• o• ••• •x•• •l• ••ov• i• ••••, no • ••••• w•i•• n•• ••••••
••• ••l• •y•••• join•, •ll in•••n••• • •••• •• • •••••l•• •n• •n• •••••l•• wi••
•••o•• •n•• ••n•l•i•• •o •voi• ••o••l• ••• •o ••• v•••ion •••i•• w••n •••y •••
•••••• •••w••n ••• w•• •••v•• •n• ••• ••l• •y•••• . T•i• i• •••• •v•n i• •••
••l• •y•••• i• ••n on ••• ••• • ••o•••• •• ••• w•• •••v••. S•••o•• •••• •••

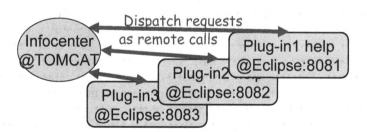

Fig. 5. The Eclipse help system must run as a separate process

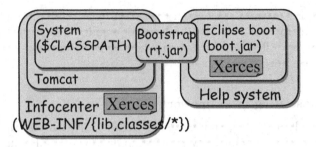

Fig. 6. The Xerces archives are loaded in duplicate for the Eclipse help system and the infocenter

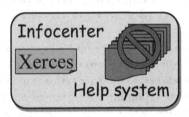

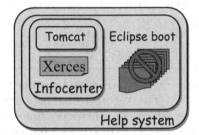

Fig. 7. Loading all components by a class loader breaks the isolation of each namespace

Fig. 8. Delegating the Xerces archives to the web component class loader breaks the isolation of the help system

••]• •y•••• •• n• on ••• ••• • JVM •• ••• in•o••n•••, •n• • o•• ••• ••]• •y•••• •n• ••• in•o••n••• ••• ••• A••••• X••••• [36] •••• iv•, w• i•• •on••in• •n XML •••••• in ••• WEB-INF/lib •i•••o•y. I•••• ••]• •y•••• join• • n•• •••••• in••- ••n••n• o• ••• n•• •••••• o• ••• in•o••n••• (Fi•••• 6), ••• v•••ion ••••i•• •o•• no• •llow ••• in•••n••• o• •n XML ••••• •••• •o •• •x••••n••• •••w••n ••• ••]• •y•••• •n• ••• in•o••n•••, •in•• ••• •o•i•• o• ••• X••••• •••• iv• ••• lo•••• in •••li••••• •n• ••n •iff••n• v•••ion• o• ••• •••••-no•• •]••• •y•• ••• ••••••• •o• •••• •••• iv•. I•••• ••]• •y•••• join• ••• ••• • n•• •••••• •• ••• in•o••n••• •y •••loyin• ••• WA• •l• in•o ••• WEB-INF/lib •i•••o•y (Fi•••• •), ••• XML ••••• •••• ••n •• •x••••n••• •••w••n ••• •wo •o• • on•n••. How•v••, ••i• o•vi- o••ly ••••••• ••• i•ol••ion o• ••• ••]• •y•••• ••o• ••• in•o••n•••. Fo• •x•• •l•, ••v•••l •o•• •o• • on•n•• o• ••• • •li••• •]•••o•• • •••• •]•o •• lo•••• •o••••••• wi•• ••• ••]• •y•••• , •n• ••••• •o•• •o• • on•n•• ••••• n•• in• •onfli••• wi•• ••• in•o••n•••. F••••••• o••, •ll ••• •o• • on•n•• • ••• •• ••••• loy•• •o•••••• w••n •o• • o• ••• •o• • on•n•• ••• ••••• loy•• •o• • in••n•n••. Fin•lly, i• ••• ••]• •y•••• join• • •••••n••n• n•• •••••• o• ••• in•o••n••• (Fi•••• •), ••]••••- in• ••• X••••• •••• iv•• •o ••• •••n• •]••• lo•••• •]•o •llow• ••••in• ••• X••••• •••• iv••. How•v••, i• •n•• •• ••••• in• ••••••••• n•• ••••••••, •oo.

2.3   Extending Assignment Compatibility

T•• ••o• l•• • ill••••••••• •• ov• ••n • • •olv•• i• ••• •l•o•i••• •o• •o• •••in• *as-signment compatibility* in ••• J•v• ••o•••• • in• l•n•••••• i• •x••n••• •o in•l••• v•••ion •onv•••ion• •••w••n •iff•••n• v•••ion• o• • •l••• •y• •. H•••, ••• v•••ion •onv•••ion • ••n• • •onv•••ion ••o• • v•••ion o• • •l••• •y• • •o •ny o•••• v••-•ion o• •••• •l••• •y• •. I• •• i• •onv•••ion i• •• o••n in ••• •on••x• o• •••i•n• •n•, ••••in•, •n• • •••o• invo•••ion •onv•••ion• •••• •• wi••nin• •n• n•••owin• •onv•••ion•, in•••n••• •o• l• •• •••ily •••••• •••o•• ••• v•••ion ••••i•• [2]. Fo• •x•• •l•, •• i• •x••n•ion o• •••i•n• •n• •n• •o• •••i•ili•y wo•l• •llow •••i•n• •n•• •••w••n •iff•••n• v•••ion• o• • •l••• •y• •. T•••, • •o• •on•n• wo•l• •• ••l• •o •••• in•••n••• in•o •n• ••o• •no•••• •o• •on•n•, •v•n i• •o•• •o• •on•n•• lo•• •n• •••n• •••• •l••• •y• • ••••••••ly. T•• `OrderServlet` •l••• in Fi•••• 1 wo•l• no• •••ow • •••• •••o•. Mo••ov••, ••• ••li••• •l••o•• wo•l• no• n••• •o •••• •• o•• w•••• •n• •ow • •ny X••••• li•••i•• ••• •v•il••l• in ••• ••••••n• •x••••ion •nvi•on• •n•.

How•v••, n•iv•ly ••l•xin• ••• v•••ion ••••i•• •y •x••n•in• ••• •••i•n• •n• •o• •••i•ili•y •••••• • •••io• •••••i•y ••o•l••. Fo• •x•• •l•, • ••o•••• • •y •••••• • non-•xi••in• ••l• o• • •••o• •n• ••n •••• ••• JVM. In ••••, ••• v••-•ion ••••i•• o• S•n JDK 1.1 w•• w•on•ly ••l•x••, •n• •••• i• ••• • •••••i•y • ol• •nown •• ••• •y•-••oo•n• ••o•l•• , •••• ••• o•••• •y S•••w•• [•6]. T•i• ••••i•y •ol• ••• ••n •olv•• •y ••• lo•••• •on•••in• •••••• • [1•], w• i•• •••••• ••••n•••n• ••• v•••ion ••••i••. To •voi• •• i• •••••i•y ••o•l•• w•il• ••l•xin• ••• v•••ion ••••i••, i• wo•l• •• n•••••••y •o ••v• •• n•i• • •y•• •••••in•, •• i• •o•n• in •yn•• i••lly •y••• l•n••••••• •••• •• • L• S, S•l•, •n• S• •ll••l•. In •••• l•n•••••••, •in•• • v•••i••l• i• no• ••••i••lly •y•••, •ny •y•• o• in•••n•• ••n •• •••i•n•• •o i•. Fo• •••••i•y, ••v•••l in••••••••• •o• •yn•• i••lly •y•••l•n••••••• •••••o•• ••n•i• • •y•• ••••••, ••ll••• •••••• •••••, •o •••• •n •x•••-•ion ••n •• •••own •• ••n•i• • i• • non-•xi••in• • •••o• o• ••l• i• •••••••••. A •••w•••• o• •• i• ••••o••• i• •••• i• •••• i••• •••••••n• ••n•i• • •y•• •••••, w• i•• i• • li•• non-n••li•i•l• ••••o•• •n•• •••••••••ion, w•••••• ••• JVM •••-•o•• • •••••• •• n•i• • •y•• •••••. Ano•••• •••• ni••• i• •o •••••o• ••n•i• • •y•• •••••• •• •v••y •••i•n• •n• o•••••ion, •••• •• ••• `aastore` J•v• •y•••o• in-••••••ion, w•i•• i• •••• •o• ••o•in• •n o•j••• •••••••n• in •n •••y o• j•••. T•i• o• •••••ion v••i••• •••••• ••• ••o••• o• j••• i• •y•-•••. How•v••, •• i• ••••o••• •l•o •••••• ••••o•• •n•• ••••••••••ion, •in•• ••• JVM • ••• ••••o•• • •y•-•••••• •o• no• only `aastore` ••• •l•o •o• • l•••• n•• ••• o• o•••• •••i•n• •n• in•••••ion•.

3   Sister Namespaces

W• ••o• o•• *sister namespaces*, w•i•• ••n ••l•x ••• v•••ion ••••i•• •••w••n n•• •••••••. Diff•••n• v•••ion• o• • •l••• •y• • •••• join •i•••• n•• ••••••••• ••n ••

---

[2] If two class types have assignment compatibility with each other, one type can be converted to the other type in the context of not only assignment conversions but also casting and method invocation conversions.

•••i•n• •n• •o• •••i•l• wi•• •••• o•••• i• •••••• v•••ion• ••v• •iff•••n••• w•il•
••ill •••••vin• ••• *version compatibility.* ••• ••ll•n•• i• •o ••l•x ••• v•••ion
••••i•• w•il• ••••in• •y••-•••• in•••n•• •••••••• •• •i•n•. In •• i• ••••ion, w•
•••• •••n• •x••n••• •••i•n• •n• •o• •••i•ili•y, w•i•• i• ••••• on J•v• •in••y
•o• •••i•ili•y [•] (S•••ion 3.1). N•x•, w• •• ow ••• •i••••-••••o•••• •y• ••••••••,
w•i•• •••••• •• ••n•••l •ol• in ••l•xin• ••• v•••ion ••••i•• •o• •i•••• n•• ••••••••
(S•••ion 3.3). T•• •y•• •••••••• •lo••• ill•••l o• j•••• w••n •••y • ov• •••o•• •••
v•••ion ••••i••, •n• •••• no •••••••••n• •x••• ••••• i• n•••••• •o• ••••• o•j••••.
T•i• i• •n••l•• •••••••• i• i• ••o•i•i••• •o• • n•• •••••• •o •••o• • • •i•••• o•
i•• ••••n• o• ••il• n•• •••••••. In •••i•ion, w• ••••••n• ••• •i•••• lo•••• •on-
••••in• (S•••ion 3.•) •n• ••n ••• •••••• • •l••• lo••in• •••••• • (S•••ion 3.5).
T••y •••v•n• •••••• •l••• lo••in• •n• •y•• in•on•i••n•i••, •••••••iv•ly.

W• i• •l•• •n••• ••• •i•••• n•• ••••••• on ••• IBM Ji••• • •••••••• Vi••••l
M•••in• (J• VM) [1]. T•• •x••n•ion• •o ••• J• VM ••• only ••• •i••••-n•• •••••••
API, • •i••••-••••o•••• •l••• lo•••••, •n• • •i••••-••••o•••• •y• •••••••. T••
API i• ••ovi••• •• ••n •x••n•ion •o ••• •xi••in• java.lang.ClassLoader in •••
• NU • l•••••••• li•••i••. T•••• •x••n•ion• •on•i•• o• ••v•••l •o•• •l••••• o• •••
J• VM •••• •• •l••• •n• o• j••• ••••••••n•••ion•.

3.1 Version Compatibility

T•i• ••••ion ••ovi••• ••• ••• ••• ni•ion o• v•••ion •o• •••i•ili•y, w•i•• ••••••ly •x-
••n•• ••• •••i•n• •n• •o• •••i•ili•y ••w••n •iff•••n• v•••ion• o• • •l••• •y••.
W• •••n• •wo v•••ion• o• • •l••• •y••, C_{ver1} •n• C_{ver2}, •• •••i•n• •n• •o• •••i-
•l• wi•• •••• o•••• i• C_{ver1} i• v•••ion •o• •••i•l• wi•• C_{ver2} •n• vi•• v••••. A
•l••• •y•• C_{ver2} i• v•••ion •o• •••i•l• wi•• C_{ver1} i• •ll •••• •l••• •y•• •••••• •o•l•
•••vio••ly lin• wi•• C_{ver1} •n• wo••• wi•• •n in•••n•• o• C_{ver1} wi••o•• •••o••
••• ••l• •o •l•o •o•••••ly wo•• wi•• in•••n•• o• C_{ver2} wi••o•• o••••• •••i•n• •n•
•o• •••i•ili•y ••l•• •••• •• • •••••y•in• ••l••ion. T•••, i• C_{ver1} •n• C_{ver2} •••
v•••ion •o• •••i•l•, •••n •n in•••n•• o• C_{ver1} ••n •• •••••ly •onv•••• •o •••
•y•• C_{ver2} w••n i• i• •••i•n•• •o • v••i••l• o• C_{ver2} •n• vi•• v••••. H•••, ••-
in• •••••• • ••n• •••• •v••y o•••••ion on C_{ver2} i• ••• li•••l• •o ••• in•••n•• o•
C_{ver1} wi••o•• •••o••; •ny • •••o• ••ll, ••l• ••••••, o• •y•• •••••in• ••• li••• •o
••• v••i••l• •o•• no• ••il.

T•• •ollowin• ••• ••• •iff•••n••• •••• ••o•••• • ••• ••• •••• i•••• •o • ••••
•••w••n •wo v•••ion• o• • •l••• w•il• ••••••vin• v•••ion •o• •••i•ili•y ••w••n
••• •wo v•••ion•:

- Diff•••n••• o• •••l•••• ••••i• • •• •••• ••• ••• ••• •••••i• ••l•, • ••••i• • •••o•,
  • •on••••••o•, o• •n ini•i• li••••.
- Diff•••n••• o• ••• i• •l•• •n•••ion o• in•••n•• • •• ••••, •••• •• •n in•••n••
  • •••o•.

T•• • iff•••n••• ••• •••iv•• ••o• ••• ••••y o• ••• •in••y •o• •••i•l• ••••n•••
• •n•ion•• in ••• J•v• l•n•••• •••i•••ion [11].

V•••ion •o• •••i•ili•y i• ••••• on ••• i••• o• •in••y •o• •••i•ili•y; i• • ••n•
•••• •n in•••n•• ••••••• •••n • •l••• ••n wo•• wi•• ••• •in••y o• •no•••• v••-

•ion o• ••• •l••• •y••. J•v• •in••y •o• •••i•ili•y •••n•• • ••• o• ••n••• ••••
••v•lo•••• ••• •••• j•••• •o • ••• •o • ••••••• o• •o • •l••• o• in•••••••• •y••
w•il• •••••••vin• ••• •o• •••i•ili•y wi•• ••• ••••xi••in• •in••i••. A •••n•• •o •
•l••• •y•• i• •in••y •o• •••i•l• wi•• ••••xi••in• • in••i• i• ••••xi••in• • in••i••
•••• •••vio••ly lin••• wi••o•• •••o•• will •on•in•• •o lin• wi••o•• •••o• •ilin•.
V•••ion •o• •••i•ili•y •••n•• •iff••n•• •••w••n •wo v•••ion• o• • •l••• •y••
•••• • ••••••v• ••• • in••y •o• •••i•l• ••o• •••y ••w••n •n in•••n•• o• on• v•••ion
•n• ••• • in••y o ••• o••• v•••ion. Unli•• ••• o•i•in•l • in••y •o• •••i•ili•y, •••
v•••ion •o• •••i•ili•y •llow• •ny •••n•• •o ••••i• • •• •••• •in•• ••••i• • •• ••••
•••••••• ••• i•••l•v•n• •o in•••n•••. V•••ion •o• •••i•ili•y •••l• wi•• ••• •o• •••-
i•ili•y •••w••n •n in•••n•• •n• ••• • in••y o• •no••• v•••ion o• •••• •l••• •y••.
T•••••o••, •o •• v•••ion •o• •••i•l•, •wo v•••ion• o• • •l••• •y•• • ••• ••v• •••
••• • ••• o• ••iv•• • •• ••••, •l••o•• ••• i• •l•• •n••ion• o• ••o•• • •• ••••
• •y •iff••. T•i• i• • • •iff•••n•• ••o• ••• • in••y •o• •••i•ili•y, w•i•• •llow• •••
•wo v•••ion• •o ••v• • •iff•••n• ••• o• ••iv•• • •• •••••. Sin•• • ••iv••• • •• ••••
••n •• ••••••••• ••o• no• only this in•••n•• ••• •l•o ••o• o•••• in•••n••• o•
•no•••• v•••ion o• •••• •l••• •y••, v•••ion •o• •••i•ili•y •••• j••• •••• ••• ••wo
v•••ion• ••v• ••• •••• • ••• o• ••iv•• • •• ••••.

3.2 Creating Sister Namespaces

A •j••••• n•• ••••••• i• • ••••-•l••• •n•i•y, ••• i• i• •••••••• i• •li•i•ly w••n • •l•••
lo•••• i• in•••n•i••• wi•• • •l••• lo•••• •iv•n ••• • •••••• ••••. T•• ClassLoader
•l••• ••ovi•• ••• n•w •on••••••o• •• •ollow•:

```
protected ClassLoader(ClassLoader parent, ClassLoader sister)
```

T•• •l••• lo•••• o•••in•• ••o• ••i• •on•••••o• •••o• ••• • *sister class loader* o•
••• •l••• lo•••• •••j••• •y ••• •••••• •••• sister. T•• l••••• •l••• lo•••• •l•o
•••o• ••• •j•••• o• ••• •o•• •• on•. T•••• •wo •i•••• •l••• lo•••• •on•••••• •••i•
own •i•••• n•• •••••••; ••• v•••ion •••j•• •••w••n •••• i• ••l•x•• i••• v•••ion
•o• •••i•ili•y i• •••j••••. T•• •j•••• •l••• lo•••• • ••• no• ••v• • •••••n•-••il•
••l••ion•• i•. T•i• ••l• i• •j•ni••n• •o• ••• •• •i•n• •y• ••••••in• w• ••••j••
l••••. I• ••• •j•••• •l••• lo•••• •••v •••• • ••l••ion•• i•, ••• •on••••••ion o• •••
•j•••• n•• •••••••• ••il•. In •• i• •••••, i• • v•••ion o• • •l••• •y•• i• lo•••• •••li••
(o• l••••) •••n o•••• v•••ion•, i• i• ••ll•• • *younger* (o• *older*) •i•••• v•••ion o•
•••• •l••• •y••. T•i• yo•n•-ol• ••l••ion•• i• i• in•••••n•n• o• ••• •••••ion o•••
o• ••• •j•••• •l••• lo•••••.

In ••• •••• ••••j••• in S•••ion •.1, ••• •••li•••ion ••o•••• • ••• ••n •x-
••n•• in•••n••• •••w••n •wo n•• •••••••• ••o• WA• 1 •n• WA•• i• •••y •••
•j•••• n•• •••••••. •••• n•• •••••• ••n •on••in • •iff•••n• v•••ion o• ••• •y•• o•
••• •x••n••• in•••n••. WA• 1 •n• WA• • • ••• •• lo•••• •y ••• •l••• lo•••••
•••••••• •• •ollow•:

```
ClassLoader ear = new EARClassLoader();
ClassLoader war1 = new WARClassLoader(ear);
ClassLoader war2 = new WARClassLoader(ear, war1);
```

Namespace (class loader)

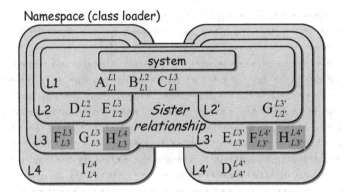

Fig. 9. The notation $C_{L_d}^{L_i}$ represents a class type, where C denotes the name of the class, L_d denotes the class's defining loader, and L_i denotes the loader initiated class loading. An inclusion relation represents a parent-child relationship. For example, the class loader L1 is a parent of both L2 and L2'. And the classes A, B, C, and the system classes are visible in the namespaces L2, L2', L3, L3', L4, and L4'. In this figure, the sister namespace L3 and L3' have a sister relationship

T•• ear, war1, •n• war2 ••• in•••n••• o• ••• ClassLoader •l•••. T•• ••i•• new
o•••••ion ••••••• •i••••• n•• ••••••••• •o• WA• 1 •n• WA• •. Bo•• war1 •n• war2
••v• ••• ••• • ••••n• •l••• lo•••• ear. In ••n•••l, •••li••• ion ••o•••• • ••• o•
•o• • on•n••, •••• •• A••l•••, S••vl•••, ••li••• •l••-in•, •n• • JB, •o no• ••v•
•o •• •w••• o• n•• ••••••• o• •l••• lo••••. T•••• ••• i• • li•i•ly • •n•••• •y •••
••• li••• ion • i• •l•w•••. • ••••in• •i••• • n•• •••••••• •y ••in• ••• ClassLoader
•on•••••o• •• ov• i• ••• wo•• o• • i• •l•w••• ••v•lo• •••. A •i•••• n•• ••••••• ••n
• ••• •no•••• •l• in n•• ••••••• i•• •i•••• on ••• •n• . Sin•• ••• •i••••• ••l••ion•• i•
i• •••n•i•iv•, i•• n•• •••••••• ••o• ••• •i•••• o•• n•• •••••••• •n• •••n i• ••• o• ••
• •i•••• o• •no•••• n•• ••••••, •ll ••••• n•• •••••••••••o• • •i•••• o•••• o•••••.
P•o•••• • ••• ••n in•••• •n••lly ••••• • n•w n•• •••••• •n• • ••• i• •no••••
•i•••• o• ••• o•••• •i••• n•• •••••••. T•i• ••••••• wo•l• •• ••••l in ••••• o•
in•••• •n••l •••v•lo•• •n• ••o•••••• •n• •o••in• • •in••n•n•• wo••.

No•• ••••• •ll •l••• •y••• *defined* • y • •i•••• •l••• lo•••• ••n •• v•••ion •o• •••-
i•l• wi•• ••• •o•••••on• in• •i•••• v•••ion o• •••• •l••• •y••, •v•n i• ••• lo••in•
o• •••••• •l••• •y••• ••• *initiated* •y ••• •• il• •l••• lo••••. An *initiating* •l•••
lo••••, w•i•• ini•i•••• ••• lo••in• o• • •l••• •y••, •o•• no• ••v• •o ••••• lly lo••
• •l••• •l•. In•••••, i• ••n ••l••••• •o ••• ••••n• •l••• lo••••. T•• •l••• lo••••
•••• ••••• lly lo••• • •l••• •l• •n• •••n•• ••••• •y• i• ••ll•• • *defining* •l•••
lo••••• o• ••••• •y••. T•i• ••l••• ion • ••••ni•• i• •••• •o• •••• in• ••• ••• • v••-
•ion o• •l••• •y• • ••w••n ••• ini•i•• in• •n• •••nin• •l••• lo••••. In Fi•••• 9, i•
•wo •i•••• n•• •••••••• ••• •••••• ••w••n •l••• lo••••• L3 •n• L3', ••• •l•••••
F •n• H ••n •• v•••ion •o• •••i•l• wi•• F' •n• H', •••••••iv•ly. T•• ••i•• •
•n• •• ' o• • •n• • ' ••• no• •o• •••i•l• wi•• •••• o•••• •in•• •••y ••• ••• n••
• y o•••• •l••• lo••••.

3.3 Sister-Supported Type Checking

T•• v•••ion ••••i•• i• ••l•x•• • y • •y•• •••••••• •••• •on•i•••• ••• •i•••• n•• ••-
••••••. In J•v• ••o•••• •, • o•• •y•••o•• in••••••ion• •••• •• ••• • •••o• in-
vo•••ion in••••••ion• invokevirtual •n• invokenonvirtual, •n• ••l• •••••••
in••••••ion• •••• •• getfield •n• putfield ••• ••••i••lly •y••• . T•••• in•••••-
•ion• • o no• ••••o•• • yn•• i• •y• • •••••• in•. T•••••o••, ••••• in••••••ion• *as they
are* ••n wo•• •o••••ly wi•• • ny v•••ion o• •l••• •y• • i• •••y ••• v•••ion •o• •••-
i•l•. • n ••• o•••• ••n•, ••v••••l in••••••ion• •••• •• instanceof, checkcast,
invokeinterface, athrow, •n• aastore •n••il •yn•• i• •y• • •••••• in•. T•• •y••
•••••• in• • y •• o•• in••••••ion• • ••• •• ••n••n••• i• ••• v•••ion ••••i•• i• ••l•x••
•o •••• v•••ion •o• •••i•l• in•••n••• ••n •• •••••• • ••w••n •i•••• n•• ••••••••.
T•• •l•o•i••• o• •n••n••• •y• • •••••in• •o• •i•••• n•• ••••••• i• ••own in Fi•-
••• 10. A•••• ••• •••••l•• •y• • •••••• ••• •••••o•• ••, •n• i• •••y ••il (lin• •),
••• •x•••• •••••• ••• •x•••••• (lin•• 3–6). Fi•••, • •i•••• ••l••ion••i• i• •x•• -
in•• (lin• 3). I• ••• l••••-••n• •i•• •l••• •y• • (LHS) •n• ••• •i•••-••n• •i•• •l•••
•y• • (RHS) ••v• • •i•••• ••l••ion••i•, ••• n ••• •y• • •••••••• ••••• in•• w•••••
on• •l••• •y• • •••• •n•••on• ••• •••••• • •o• •••i•l• lo••in• ••o•••• ••• in•• •••
o••••• •y• • (lin• •). S•••• • •o• •••i•l• lo••in• i• in••o••••• l••••.

No•• •••• •••••• •x•••• •••••• •o• •i•••• n•• •••••••• ••• •x•••••• only •••••
••• ••••l•• •y• • •••••••• ••il. Sin•• •y•i••l ••o•••• • •o no• •••••••n•ly ••••• •y••
•••o••, ••i• •n••n••• •n• •o• ••• ••il•-in •y• • •••••••• i• •li•• no •••o•• •n••
••n•l•i•• •• lon• •• in•••n••• ••• no• •••••• ••w••n •i•••• n•• ••••••••.

T•• •i••••-••• o•••• •y• • •••••••• only ••o•i•i•• • v•••ion in•o• •••i•l• in-
•••n•• ••o• ••in• •••••• ••w••n •i•••• n•• ••••••. A v•••ion in•o• •••i•l•
•l••• ••n join •••• o• ••• •i•••• n•• ••••••• i• •n in•••n•• o• •••• v•••ion •••y
wi•• in ••• n•• ••••••. To •voi• ••• •••••i•y ••o•l•• ••••••i••• in S••ion •.3
(n••iv•ly ••l•xin• ••• •••i• n• •n• •o• •••i•ili•y), •i•••• n•• •••••••• • ••• ••••••
• v•••ion in•o• •••i•l• in•••n•• ••in• •••••• ••w••n •i•••• n•• ••••••••. T•i•
•••••••ion i• •x••••••• • y only ••• checkcast in••••••ion. In o•••• wo•••, ••• ••-
••••ion i• no• •x•••••• • y o•••• in••••••ion• •o• • •••o• invo•••ion, ••l• •••••••,

```
1: if LHS is a subtype of RHS  then true
2: else if LHS is not a subtype of RHS  then
3:    if LHS is a sister type of RHS &&
4:       LHS is version compatible with RHS then true
5:    else false
6:    end
7: end
```

Fig. 10. Pseudo code for enhanced type checking for sister namespaces. A type check is
the determination of whether a value of one type, hereafter the right-hand side (RHS)
type , can legally be converted to a variable of a second type, hereafter the left-hand
side (LHS) type. If so, the RHS type is said to be a subtype of the LHS type and the
LHS type is said to be a supertype of the RHS type

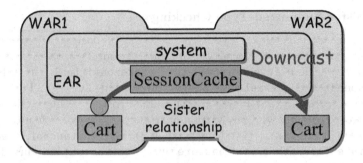

Fig. 11. Downcast enforced by the bridge-safety property satisfied between namespaces

•n• •••i•n• •n•. T•i• i• • •inly ••• •o ••• •••i•n o• •i•••• n•• •••••••, w•i••
• ••• no• ••y• • ••••n•-•• il• ••l•• ion••i• ••w••n •••• . T•i• ••l• ••in•• •••
bridge-safety [•6] ••o•••y •o •ll •l••••• in•l•••• in ••• •i•••• n•• •••••••. T•i•
••o•••y ••••• n•••• •••• •n in••• n•• o• •l•••• •y•• i• •lw•y• •x•• in•• •y •••
checkcast in••••• ion w••n i• i• ••••••• •••w••n •i•••• n•• •••••••. I• • ••• ••
•••• •••••• •o • •y• lo•••• •y ••• •o• • on •••n• •l••• lo•••• o• ••• •wo •i••••
•l••• lo••••, •n• ••n i• • ••• •• •own•••• •••o•• i• i• •••i•n•• •o ••• •l•••
•y• lo•••• •y ••• •i•••• •l••• lo•••• •• ••• •••• in••ion. Fo• •x•• •l•, w••n •n
in••• n•• o• Cart i• •••••••, i• will •• ••••• •••••• •o • •••••• •l••• o• Cart, ••••
•• ••• Object •l•••, •n• ••n •own•••• •o •no•••• v••ion o• ••• Cart •l•••
(Fi•••• 11). T•••••o••, ••• checkcast in••••• ion i• •lw•y• •x••••••• w••n •••
in••• n•• i• •own•••• •o Cart.

To i• •l•• •n• ••• •i••••-••••o•••• •y•• •••••, w• • o•i•••• •••
VM_DynamicTypeCheck •l••• in ••• J• VM. W• •x••n••• ••••• •l••• •n• ••• TIB
(Ty•• In•o•• ••ion Blo••) •o• •••• •y•• •••••• in• •o •on•i••• •i•••• ••l•• ion••i••.
T•• o•i•in•l TIB •ol•• ••v•••l ••••y• o• •y•• i• •n•i•••. Fo• •x•• •l•, ••• ••••y•
o••x••n••• •••••• •l••• •y••• •n• o•i• •l•• •n••• in••••••• •y•• ••• ••••o••• in •••
TIB •o• •••• •y•• ••••• in• wi••o•• loo•in• •• ••• w•ol• •y•• •i•••••• y [3][•].
Si• il••ly, ••• •x••n••• TIB •ol•• •wo ••••y• o• sid•. T•• sid i• •• i••n•i•• o•
• •i•••• ••l•• ion••i•. T•• •wo ••••y• ••• o•••• sid• o• ••• •x••n••• •••• ••l•••••
•n• ••• sid• o• ••• i• •l•• •n••• in•••••••. T•• sid o• • •l••• •n • o•••in••
••o• • VM_Class o• j••• •••••• n•in• •••• •l•••. W• •x••n••• ••• VM_Class •l•••
•o • ol• ••• sid o• ••• •l•••.

3.4   Sister Loader Constraint

A ••••i••••o•w••• i• •l•• •n••ion o• ••• •i••••-••••o•••• •y•• •••••••• •••• j•••
••••• •l••• lo••in•. • v•n i• ••• •i••••-••••o•••• •y•• ••••••• v••i••• ••••• •••
•y• o••n in••• n•• i• v••• ion •o• •••i•l•, •••• in••• n•• ••nno• •• •• lly *trusted.*
T•• in••• n•• • •y •on••in • v••• ion in•o• •••i•l• in••• n•• •• • ••l• v•l•• o•
••••• n i• ••• ••••l• o• • ••• o• •x•••• ion. T••• i•, ••• *untrusted* in••• n•• • •y
relay •n in•o• •••i•l• in••• n••. Sin•• •n in••• n•• i• •y•• ••••••• only w••n i•
i• •own••••, ••• •y•• o• ••• in••• n•• ••••• • •y •• ••l•y•• •••• •l•o •• •y••

•• •••••• •• ••• ••• • •i• •. T••••o••, ••• •y• • •••••••• v••i••• •ll ••• •l••• •y• ••
o•••••in• in ••• •l••• ••• ni•ion o• •••• in•••n••, •••• •• •••••• •••• •y• ••[3], ••-
••n •y•••, •n• ••l• •y•••. I• •l•o •••••••iv•ly v••i••• ••• •l••• •y• •• o•••••in•
in ••• ••• ni•ion• o• •• o•• •y•••. How•v••, i• •• i• •••••••iv• •y• • •••••• i• n•iv•ly
i• •l•• •n•••, •ll ••• ••l•••• •l••••• wo•l• ••v• •o •• •••••ly lo••••. T•i• ••••••
lo••in• i• •••••i••lly •n••••••••l•, •in•• ••• ••v•n••••• o• ••• •yn•• i• •••-
•••••• o• J•v• wo•l• •• lo••. T•• •i••••-•••• o••••• •y• • •••••••• • ••• •• •• •l• •o
wo•• wi•• ••• •••••• • o• l••y •l••• lo••in•. No•• •••••• ••• o•i•in•l •l••• lo••in•
• ••••ni•• o• J•v• i• •••••• on l••y •l••• lo••in•.

To •x•• in• v•••ion •o• •••i•ili•y w•il• •n••lin• l••y •l••• lo••in•, ••• JVM
• •in••in• • ••• o• *sister loader constraints,* w•i•• ••• •yn•• i••lly •••••••• w••n
••• •i••••-•••• o••••• •y• • •••••••• wo•••. I• ••• •y• • ••••••• •n• • •l••• •y• •
•••• • ••• •• v••i••• ••••••• no• ••n lo•••• y••, ••• JVM •o•• no• •••••ly lo••
•••• •l•••; in••••, i• •••o••• • •i•••• lo•••• •on••••in•. Fo• •x•• •l•, i• ••• •y• •
•••••••• ••••• ••• •o v••i•y •••• • v•••ion o• •l••• C i• v•••ion •o• •••i•l• wi••
•no•••• v•••ion C', ••• C o• C' ••• no• ••n lo•••• y••, ••• JVM •••o••• •• •
•on••••in• •••• C • ••• •• v•••ion •o• •••i•l• wi•• C'. T•i• •on••••in• i• l••••
v••i••• w••n C o• C' i• lo••••. I• ••• •y• • •••••••• •••••••• ••• •• i• •on••••in• i•
no• •••i••••, i• ••••ow• • LinkageError. W•il• ••• •y• • •••••••• i• v••i•yin• ••••
•on••••in•, i• i• •n•• •no•••• •l••• •y• •••• • ••• •• v••i••• ••• i• no• lo••••,
• n•w •i•••• lo•••• •on••••in• i• •••o••••. I• ••• •y• • ••••••• •n• • •l••• •y• •
•••• • ••• •• v••i••• •n• ••• ••n •l••••y lo••••, i• •••••iv•ly v••i••• ••••
•l••• •y• • •• ••• ••• • •i• •. No•• •••••• •v••y •on••••in• i• v••i••• only on••. T••
••••l• o• ••• v••i•••••ion i• •••o•••• •o •voi• •••••• v••i•••ion.

In ••• • ••y, ••• JVM n•••• •o • •in••in ••• inv••i•n•: *Each class type co-
existing in the namespace satisfies all the sister loader constraints.* T•• inv••i• n•
i• • •in••in•• •• •ollow•:

*Every time a new class joins a sister namespace, the JVM verifies whether that
class type will violate an existing sister loader constraint.*

I• ••• •l••• •y• • ••in• lo•••• viol•••• •n •xi••in• •i•••• lo•••• •on••••in•,
lo••in• •••• •l••• •y• • ••il• •in•• •••• •l••• •y• • i• •n••••••• in ••• n•• ••••••.
I• •••••• i• no •on••••in• ••••••in• •o •••• •l••• •y••, ••• JVM lo••• •••••• •l•••
•y• •, •l••o••• •••••• •l••• •y• • • i•••• •• v•••ion in•o• •••i•l•. I• i• v••i••• l••••
w••n • n•w •on••••in• ••••••in• •o •••• •l••• •y• • i• •••o••••.

*Every time a new sister loader constraint is recorded, the JVM verifies whether
that constraint is satisfied with the class types that have been already loaded.*

I•• •l••• •y• • •••••• ••• •l•••• y • ••n lo•••• • •o•• no• ••• i••y • n•wly •••o••••
•on••••in•, lo••in• ••• •l••• •y• • ••••••••••• ••• •y• •••••• in• ••o••••••o••• in•
••• n•w •on••••in• i• •n••••••• •n• ••n•• ••• lo••in• i• •• o••••. I• • ny •l•••
•y• •• n•••••• •o• v••i•yin• •••• •on••••in• ••v no• ••n lo••••, ••• v••i••••ion

---

[3] If a parameter type is not version compatible, an incompatible instance may be sent
back without type checking to the namespace that has sent the instance of the class
type including that parameter type.

i• •o••• on•• •n•il ••o•• •l••••• ••• lo••••. • •••wi••, i• •ll ••• •l••• •y•• n••••• •o• ••• v••i•••ion ••v• •••n lo•••• •n• ••• •on••••in• i• •••••••••lly v••i••, ••• •on••••in• i• ••• ov•• ••o• ••• •••o••.

Fo••• •i•n• v••i•••ion o• •on••••in•, w ••••• •n •••• y o•fl•••• •o VM_Class. ••••• fl•• in•i••••• w•••••• ••• v••ion o• ••• •l••• •y•• •••••••••n••• •y • VM_Class o•j••• ••• •••n ••••••iv•ly •y•• •••••••• wi•• •no••• •i•••• v••ion. T•• fl•• i• •••• only i• ••• •wo v••ion• o• ••• •l••• •y•• ••• v••ion •o• •••i• l• •n• i• ••• •y•• ••••••••• v••i••• ••• •• o•• •wo v••ion• n•v• *relay* • v••ion in•o• •••i• l• in•••n••. Sin•• ••••• • i••••••• •l•i• l• •i•••••, ••• VM_Class o•j••• •ol•• •n ••••y o• ••• fl•••, •••• o• w•i•• in•i••••• ••• ••••l• o• ••• •y•• •••••• wi•• •••• •i•••• v••ion. T•• JVM •••• ••••• fl•••• •o• •x•••in• • •••••••iv• •y•• ••••• only on••.

3.5   Schema Compatible Loading

• v•n i• •wo v••ion• o• • •l••• •y•• •••i••y ••• v••ion •o• •••i• ili•y, ••••• in•••n••• • •y ••v• ••••• • in•o• •••i• ili•y. T•i• • ••n• ••••• ••• l•yo•• o• ••• in•••n•l •y•• in•o• ••ion •lo•• (TIB•) • •y no• •• i••n•i••l ••w••n ••• •wo v••ion• o• ••• •l••• •y••. T•• TIB •ol•• ••l•• •n• ••n••ion •oin•••• •o • •o•••••on• in• • ••• •o• • •o•y. T•• o•••• o• ••• TIB •n••i•• •••n•• on ••• JVM o• •o• •il••; i• •o•• no• ••••n• on ••• o•••• o• ••• • ••• ••• •••l•••ion• in • •o•••• •l• o• • •l••• •l•. T•••, •v•n i• •wo v••ion• o• • •l••• •y•• ••v• v••ion •o• •••i• ili•y, ••• l•yo•• o• ••• TIB• • •y no• •• i••n•i••l.

T•• •i••••-•••• o•••• •l••• lo•••• ••••n•••• •••• l•yo•• o• ••• TIB• ••• i••n•i••l ••w••n •wo v••ion• o• • •l••• •y•• i• ••• •l••• •y•• ••• v••ion •o• -•••i• l•. Sin•• ••• JVM •••• • •on•••n in••x in•o ••• TIB w••n i• •••••••• • ••l• o• • • •••o•, ••• JVM ••nno• •o••••ly •x••••• ••• •y•••o•• i• ••• l•y-o••• o• ••• TIB• ••• no• i••n•i••l ••w••n •o• •••i• l• v••ion• o• ••• •l••• •y••. T••••o••, w••n ••• •l••• lo•••• lo••• • yo•n••• v••ion o• • •l••• •y••, ••• JVM •on••••••• ••• TIB o• •••• v••ion o• ••• •l••• •o •••••• l•yo•• o• ••• TIB i• i••n•i••l •o •••• o• ••• TIB o• •n ol••• v••ion o• ••• •l•••. T•i• lo••in• ••o•••• i• ••ll•• *schema compatible loading*. No•• ••••• •• i• •• •o•••• i• •iv•n •• •••in•• ••• in•o• •••i• l• •l••• •y•• ••••• ••• no •in••y •o• •••i• ili•y wi•• ••• ol••• •i•••• v••ion o• •••• •l••• •y••. T•i• •••• l• i• ••• •loy•• •y ••• JVM •o ••i••ly •x•• in• w•••••• • •l••• •y•• i• ••••••• o• no•.

In ••• J• VM, • TIB i• •on•••••••• • ••in• ••• •x••• ion o• ••• resolve • •••o• in VM_Class. T•• resolve • •••o• i• invo••• •••in• ••• •l••• •••ol••ion ••o•••• •y ••• VM_ClassLoader •l•••, •n in••••n•• o• w•i•• ••••••••n•• •l••• lo••••. T•• resolve • •••o• •••••••n •x••n••• •o •••••o•• ••• •••••• • •o• •••i• l• lo••in•.

4   Discussion

4.1   Canceling JIT Compilations

J•••-In-Ti• • (JIT) •o• •il•• •o•• •o• ••i• •• n•••• •o •• ••n••l•• •in•• • ••-vi•••li••• • •••o• ••ll •o•• no• •o••••ly ••••• •o • • •••o• •••l•••• in • •i•-

••• v•••ion o• ••• •l••• •y• •. • ••••n• o••i• i•in• JIT •o• •il••• [15, 3•] •••o••
••• ••vi•••li••ion o••i• i••ion •••• •••n••o•• • no• only • •n•l •n• • ••••i•
• •••o• ••• •l•o • vi•••l • •••o• ••ll •o • ••••i• • •••o•. Fo• • •iv•n vi•••l
••ll, ••• •o• •il•• •••••• in•• w••••• o• no• ••• ••ll ••n •• ••vi•••li••• •y
•n•ly•in• ••• •••••n• •l••• •i••••••y. I•••• • •••o• ••n ••• •vi•••li••• •n• i••
•o•• •i•• i• •• •ll •no•••, ••• •o• •il•• inlin•• ••• • •••o•. T••••o••, i••• •y••
o• •n in•••n•• i• •onv••••• •o • •i•••• v•••ion o• •••• •l••• •y••, ••• JVM wo• l•
•on•in•• •o invo•• ••• o•i•in•l inlin•• •o•• in••••• o• ••• •••l • •••o• o• ••••
in•••n••. T•i• i• •••••••• ••• JIT •o• •il•• •o•• no• •on•i••• •i•••• n•• •••••••;
• •••o• •o•i•• • i••• •• •iff•••n• •• on• •i•••• v•••ion• o• ••• ••• • •l••• •y••.

To •voi• ••i• ••o•l•• , ••• JIT •o• •il•• • ••• ••n••l ••vi•••li••ion w••n
• n•w •i•••• v•••ion o• • •l••• •y•• i• lo••••. Fo••• n•••ly, • o•• o••i• i•in• JIT
•o• •il••• ••y• •n •• •i•n• ••n••ll••ion • •••ni•• •o• •yn•• i• •l•• lo••in•.
Sin•• • w•ol• •l•• •i•••••y ••nno• •• ••••i••lly •••••• in•• in J•v•, JIT •o• -
•il••• ••n •yn•• i••lly ••• l••• [3•] o• ••w•i•• [15] inlin•• •o••. T•i• i• •••o•• ••
w••n • n•w •••l•• i• lo•••• •n• ••• •••l•• ov••i• • • •••o• •••• ••• no•
•••n ov••i•••n •y ••• o•••• ••• •l•••. T•• JIT •o• •il•• •••• ••• •o••• •i••••
n•• •••••••• •l•o ••n••l• ••vi•••li••ion w••n v•••ion •o• •••i•ili•y i• v••i•••
•n• • n•w •i•••• v•••ion o•• •l••• •y•• i• •v•il••l•.

4.2   Eager Notifications of Version Incompatibility

V•••ion in•o• •••i•ili•y •••••• •••w••n •i•••• v•••ion• o• • •l•• •y•• • •y ••-
•••ly •••ow • •••• •••o• •••o•• •ny in•o• •••i•l• •l••• •y••• •••••lly •o-•xi••
in on• n•• •••••••. Fo• •x•• •l•, i• ••• •y•• •••••••• •••••••• ••••• • •l••• •y••
••y ••l•y • v•••ion in•o• •••i•l• in•••n••, i• ••ow• • •••• •••o•. T•i• ••••••
no•i•••ion •••••••y i• •i• il•• •o ••• lo•••• •on•••in •••••• • [1•]. T•• JVM
••o•i•i•• •iff•••n• v•••ion• o• • •l••• •y•• ••o• •v•n ••in• lo•••• i• ••• JVM
•n•o• n•••• •n o••••ion •••• ••l•y in•••n••• ••o• on• n•• •••••• •o ••• o•••.
I• ••• JVM ••• •l••••y lo•••• ••••• v•••ion o• ••• •l•••, ••• JVM •••ow•
• lin• •••o•. How•v••, •x•••• •o• ••• lo•••• •on•••in •••••• •, v••i•••ion o•
•o• •••i•ili•y •n• •••o• no•i•••ion ••• no• •••••o•• •• •• lo••in• •i• • ••• •••
•on• l•••• •y ••• lin•••, w•il• ••• lin••• •••olv•• ••• •on••••n• •ool i••• • (•.•.,
NoSuchMethodError, IllegalAccessError, IncompatibleClasChangeError).
I• • J•v• ••o•••• in•l•••• •in••y in•o• •••i•ili•y, i• •on•in•• •o ••n •n•il i•
•••••lly •x••••• •n ill•••l o•••••ion •••••• •y •••• in•o• •••i•ili•y. T•i• l••y
v••i•••ion •n• no•i•••ion ••• •••••l in ••••••i••.

How•v••, w• ••v• ••o•••• •• ••••• •••••••y •o• •voi•in• •••••o•• •n•• ••n•l-
•i•• •••• •o v•••ion •o• •••i•ili•y ••••••. To ••l•y no•i•••ion• o• in•o• •••i•ili•y
•• lon• •• ••• ••o•••• •on•in•• •o ••n wi••o•• ••••o••, • n•• ••• o•••••• ••••••
• •••• •• •• •••••• in•o ••• in•o• •••i•l• •l•••. In J•v•, on•• ••• JVM •x••••••
• • •••o• invo•••ion o• • ••l• ••••••, ••• o•••••ion i• lin••• wi•• ••• ••ll •i••
•n• •••l•••• wi•• •• •i•n• •o•• ••• •o•• no• •••••o•• •y•• •••••in• •ny• o••.
T•••••o••, ••• •••••• ••••• • ••• •• ••••••• ••••••• •o• v••i•yin• v•••ion •o• •••i•ili•y
•••••• ••• v•••ion in•o• •••i•ili•y i• •o• n•. I• •••• i•••• ••• JIT •o• •il•• •o •••o• -
•il• ••• •o•• •••• •••••• ••• in•o• •••i•l• •l••• •y••. Mo••ov••, ••• •••••• ••••••

i•• •ly ••• non-n••li•i• l• •••o•• •n•• ov•••••• • •n•ion•• in S•••ion •.3; ••••,
w•• •o no• ••l•y ••• no•i•••ion• o• in•o• •••i• ili•y.

5 Experimental Results

T• i• •••ion ••• o••• ••• •••• l•• o• o• • •••o•• •n•• • ••••• ••• •n••. W• •••o•• ••
•ll ••• •x•••i• •n•• on ••• IBM Ji••• • •••••••• Vi•••l M•••in• •.3.• wi•• Lin• x
•••n•l •.•.•5, w• i•• w••• ••nnin• on • P•n•i•• • 1.9• H• ••o•••o• wi•• 1• B
• •• o•y. Bo•• ••• Ji••• • VM •n• o•• • o•i••• • VM w••• •o• •il•• •o •••
••• •••lin• •o• •il•• •o• ••il•in• ••• •oo• i• ••• wi•• ••• ••• i-••••• •••••••
•oll•••o•.

Baseline Performance. To • •••••• ••• ••••lin• •••o•• •n••, w• ••n •••
SP• • jv• 9• [31] ••n••• •••• on •o•• o•• JVM •n• ••• •n• o•i••• JVM. T••
••o•l•• •i••• o• •ll ••• ••n••• •••• w•• 100 (• •xi• ••). T••l• 1 li••• •••
••••l••. T•• n•• ••••• ••• ••• •v••••• •x•••ion •i• • •o• •0 ••••i•ion•. T••
••••lin• ov••••••• ••• •o ••• •i•••• n•• ••••••• w•• n••li•i•l•.

Cost of Loading Classes Into Sister Namespaces. W• • •••••••• ••• •i• •
•o• lo••in• •l••••• wi•• • •l•in •l••• lo•••• o• • •i•••• •l••• lo••••. T• i• •x• ••-
i• •n• •• ow• ••• •••o•• •n•• ••n•l•y in•••••• •y ••• •i•••• •l••• lo••••, w• i••
•x•••••• •••••• • •o• •••i•l• lo••in• •n• v••i••• ••• v••ion •o• •••i•ili•y ••-
•w••n •l•••••. W• •oo• nin• ••• li•••ion ••o•••• •, li•••• in T••l• •, •o • •••••••
••• •o••l lo••in• •i• •. T•• lo••in• ••o•••• in•l•••• ••l•••in• •o ••• ••••n•
•l••• lo••••, •••••• in• •o• • •l••• •l• in • ••••i••• •l••••••, •n• •••olvin•, ini-
•i•li•in•, •n• in•••n•i••in• •••• •l••• •y•• in ••• JVM. All lo••in• ••o••••• •••
i•••••••• •0 •i• ••. T•• •••• l•• •• ow •••• ••• •••o•• •n•• ••n•l•y v••i•• •• on•
•• o•• ••• li•••ion• ••o• ••o•n• 1•% •o 6•%. T•• ••n•l•i•• • o••ly •••n••• on
••• n•• ••• o• •••l•••• • •••o••• •n• ••l••. T•••, ••• l•••••• ••• li•••ion •• ow••
••• l•••••• ov•••••• .

Table 1. SPECjvm98 benchmark results on both our JVM and the unmodified JVM

Benchmark Program	Jikes RVM (JRVM)	Sister-supported JRVM (SVM)	SVM /JRVM
_201_compress	47.293 ms	46.218 ms	97.7%
_202_jess	40.258 ms	38.726 ms	96.2%
_205_raytrace	22.704 ms	23.404 ms	103.1%
_209_db	65.628 ms	67.075 ms	102.2%
_213_javac	54.698 ms	57.759 ms	105.6%
_222_mpegaudio	29.344 ms	29.210 ms	99.5%
_227_mtrt	25.812 ms	24.563 ms	95.2%
_228_jack	28.372 ms	28.047 ms	98.9%
Total	314.109 ms	315.002 ms	100.3%

Table 2. Total loading time using an ordinary class loader and a sister class loader. All classes are sequentially loaded by the `loadClass()` method

Program (No. of classes)	Total loading time		sister /plain
	plain namespace	sister namespace	
JDOM (72 classes)	328 ms	382 ms	116.5%
Crimson (144 classes)	569 ms	696 ms	122.3%
jaxen (191 classes)	802 ms	919 ms	114.6%
dom4j (195 classes)	1,308 ms	1,487 ms	113.7%
SAXON (351 classes)	1,749 ms	2,113 ms	120.8%
XT (466 classes)	1,223 ms	1,422 ms	116.3%
XercesJ 1 (579 classes)	2,495 ms	3,046 ms	122.1%
XercesJ 2 (991 classes)	4,144 ms	6,177 ms	149.1%
XalanJ 2 (1,548 classes)	12,884 ms	15,290 ms	166.6%

JDOM [38] : A simple Java representation of an XML document, version 1.0
Crimson [34] : A Java XML parser included with JDK 1.4 and greater, version 1.1.3
jaxen [39] : An XPath engine, version 1.0.
dom4j [23] : The flexible xml framework for Java, version 1.5.2
SAXON [17] : An XSLT and XQuery processor, version 6.5.3
XT [19] : A fast, free implementation of XSLT in java, version 20020426a
XercesJ 1 : The Xerces Java Parser 1.4.4.
XercesJ 2 : The Xerces2 Java Parser 2.6.2.
XalanJ 2 [35] : An XSLT processor for transforming XML documents, version 2.6.0.

Cost of the `Checkcast` Instruction. Fin•lly, w• • •••••••• ••• •x•••ion •i• • •o• •y•• • ••••• in•. T•• •i••••-••••o•••• •y•• • ••••• in• in•l•••• no• only ••• o•- • in••y checkcast o•••••ion ••• •l•o ••• ••••• in• o• ••••••• in•••n•••. W• ••n • ••o•••• •••• •x•••••• ••• checkcast in•••••ion •o• •v••y •l••• in•l•••• in • •iv•n •••li•••ion, •n• ••• n w• • •••••••• ••• •o••l •x•••••ion •i• • o• •ll ••• checkcast in•••••ion•. Bo•• •x•••i• •n• ••o•••• • ••n ••••• •ll ••• •l••••• ••• ••• n lo•••• •n• ••• n ••• v•••ion •o• •••i• ili•y o• •ll ••• •l••••• w•• v••i•••. W• ••••••••iv•ly ••n ••• ••o•••• •wi••; ••• •x•••ion •i• • o• ••• •••on• ••n in•i- ••••••• ••• •x•••ion •i• • o• checkcast ••••• ••• v•••ion •o• •••i• ili•y o• •ll ••• • o••i•ly ••l•y•• •l••••• i• v••i••• •••in• ••• • ••••• ••n. So• • o•••• •••• ••••••• •l•o • •••• ••• o• ••• ••••l•• o• •••vio•• v••i•••ion•.

T•• l• 3 li•••• ••• ••••l••. T•• •••• l•• ••• ••• •v••••• o• 10,000 i•••••ion•. T•• •o••l •x•••ion •i• • o• ••• •••• •••••• w•• ••o• ••o•• 10 •o •0 •i• •• •low•• ••n ••• o• in••y checkcast o•••••ion. T•i• i• •••••••• ••• •i••••-••••o•••• •y•• •••••••• •••v••••• •ll • o••i• ly ••l•y•• •l••• •y•••. Sin•• ••••• •••li•••ion ••• • •iff•••n• n• • ••• o• •o••i• ly ••l•y•• •l•••••, ••• ••l••iv• •••• o•• •n•• v••i•• •o• •••• ••• li•••ion. • n ••• o•••• ••n•, ••• •••on• •••••• in•l•••• only ••o•n• 160% ov•••••• •o• •••••• •o ••• o• in••y checkcast o•••••ion. No•• ••••• ••i• ov•••••• i• in•••••• only w••n checkcast •x•• in•• ••• •y•• o• •n in•••n•• •o• in• ••o• •no•••• •i•••• n•• •••••••. T•• ov•••••• i• n••li•i•l• in ••••l•• ••••••.

W• •l•o •o• ••••• ••• •x•••ion •i• • o•••• •y•• •••••• wi•• ••• •i• • •o• • ••- •••llin• •n• •n• ••••• llin• ••v•••l XML •••• o• j•••. • •• •• • •• ••••• • ••• • o•• •••• l••• ••••••i•• •o• ••• in•••-•o• • on•n• •o• • •ni•••ion •••••i• •• in S•••ion •

Table 3. Total execution time of the type check by `checkcast`

Program (No. of classes)	checkcast	Sister namespaces		Relative performance	
		first	second	first	second
JDOM (72 classes)	33.3 us	1,205.7 us	53.7 us	3,721%	261.3%
Crimson (144 classes)	69.0 us	1,659.7 us	112.6 us	2,505%	263.1%
jaxen (191 classes)	89.2 us	1,573.1 us	139.8 us	1,864%	256.7%
dom4j (195 classes)	109.7 us	4,371.7 us	185.8 us	4,085%	269.3%
SAXON (351 classes)	295.7 us	5,141.3 us	499.8 us	1,839%	269.0%
XT (466 classes)	381.5 us	4,505.8 us	698.7 us	1,281%	283.1%
XercesJ 1 (579 classes)	644.4 us	7,824.3 us	1,041.3 us	1,314%	261.5%
XercesJ 2 (991 classes)	1,158.6 us	11,534.6 us	1,798.0 us	1,096%	255.1%
XalanJ 2 (1,548 classes)	1,650.6 us	22,627.8 us	2,696.2 us	1,471%	263.3%

i• ••in• • ••• o•• ••ll, w•i•• •••••• •n o•j••• •y • ••n• o• ••• ••ll-•y-v•l••. T•i• ••••i•• l••• •• •voi• ••• ••o•l•• o• ••• v••ion ••••i••, ••• i• i• •li•• ov•••••• ••• •o ••• • •••••llin• •n• •n• ••••llin• •o• ••••• •••• •••in•. • n ••• o•••• ••n•, •i•••• n•• •••••••• •l•o l•• ••• •voi• ••• ••o•l•• , •n• i• i• •li•• •x••• ov•••••• only ••• •o ••• •y•• •••••. W• •••••••• ••• •x•••ion •i• • •o• • •••••llin• •n• •n• ••••llin• D• M o•j••••• •••••• •y X••••J •.6.• ••o• 33 XML •l•• ••••n ••o• ••• ••li••• ••l• •y••••• , w•i•• in•l•••• ••• Pl••o•• , Wo••••n••, JDT, Pl••-in •n• PD• •o••• •n• •l••-in•. T•• ov•••ll •l• •i•• w•• ••o••·00KB. T•• • •••••••• •x•••ion •i• • w•• 3 • illion •i• •• l•••• •••n ••• •x•••ion •i• • o• ••• o••in•·y `checkcast` o••••••ion. • • •o••••, •••••l in•••-•o• • on•n• •o• • • ni••••ion ••in• • ••• o•• ••ll wo•l• •••n• • •••• • o•• •i• • •o• ••• n••wo•• •••• •••n•• o••••ion•. T•••••o••, •• i• •••• l• •• ow• ••• •i•••• n•• ••-•••• i• • •i•ni••n•ly •••••• •ol••ion •o• ••••• •o ••• •ol••ion o••••in• o•j•••• •y • ••• o•• ••ll.

6   Related Work

In ••• o•j••• •••••••• •o• • •ni•y, ••v••l ••••• • •vol••ion ••••ni••• ••••• •• •••••• • o• •l••• v••ionin• [5, 30] ••v• ••n ••••i••. T•••• •••• ni• ••• •llow • •l•i•l• •o-•xi••in• v••ion• o• • ••••• • o• • •l•••. In•••n••• ••• •volv•• w••n ••••in• ••o•• ••• v••ion ••••i•• in•o ••• • o•i•• •••li•••ion o• o•••• ••-•li••ion•. U•in• ••••• •volv••l• o•j••• •••••••• i• • wo••••l• •l•••n••iv• •o• •o• •on•n•-•••••• •••li••ion•. How•v••, o•• wo•• •on••n•••••• on ••o•••• • in• •nvi•on• •n••, •••••i•lly w•••• ••n•i• • ov••••••••• •o •••••• • •vol••ion • ••• •• ••v••ly • ini• i•••.

T•••• ••v• ••n o•••• •••••••• •••ivi•i•• •••• lin• ••• v••ion ••••i•• ••o•l•• in ••• ••o••••• • in• l•n••••• •n• •nvi•on• •n• •o• • •ni•y. Mo• o• ••• ••••vi-o•• •••••••• •••••••• ••• v••ion ••••i•• ••• • ••• •o••l •o•n••y ••w••n *old* •n• *new* •o• •on•n• •n• ••••• •o••••• on •yn•• i• •o•w••• ••••••• o• •vol•-•ion. T••• i•, • •l•i•l• v••ion• o• ••• ••• • •l••• •y•• •o•l• no• •i• •l••n•o• •ly •o-•xi•• in ••• •• nnin• ••o•••• . T•••••o••, o•• ••o•l•• • w••• no• •i•••ly ••-

•••••••. In •• i• •••••••• ••••, ••• • •in •o• i• i• w• i•• •xi••in• o• j••• •• o• l• ••
••••••• •o •n ••••••• v••ion o• ••• •l•••• •y•• •n• •ow •n• w••n. Fo• •x•• -
• l•, ••• wo•• on ••• •o••w•••in• o• •l••••• ••ll• in•o •• i• •••••o•y. M•l•••••• *et
al.* [•0] • o• i••• ••• JVM •o• •••• • •l••• ••lo•••• l• ••• ••n•i• ••o •••• ••ll •xi••-
in• o• j•••• ••n •• •••••••• in•••• •n••lly. T•• JPDA (J•v• Pl••o•• D•••••••
A•••i••••••••) [33] •n• ••• `java.lang.instrument` •••••••• o• ••• J•v•• SDK5.0
••ovi•• ••• •••••j•••• • o••w•• • n••ion• li•y, w•••••y •xi••in• in••n••• ••n ••
•on•i••••• •• ••• n•w v••ion o• ••• •l••• •y•• wi•• o•• ••in• •••••••. Hj•l• -
•y••on •n• • ••y [13] i• •l•• •n••• •yn•• i• •l••••• in • ++ •y ••in• ••• •l••••.
U•••• ••n ••l•••iv•ly •••••• •o• •••• no• •ll o• j•••• wi•• ••• ••l• o• w••••••
(o• ••oxy) •l••••• •n• •••• o••. Hn••yn•• *et al.* [1•] ••o• o••• ••• ••n•• in• ••-
••o••• ••in• • •y•••o•• • •ni••l••ion •ool. A •l••• lo•••• ••in• ••i• ••n•• in•
•••••o••• •llow• ••• ••lo••in• o• •l•••, •l••o••• i• ••n•• •• •••• •l•••.

• •• wo•• • • inly •o••••• on ••• •••••i•l v••ion ••••i••• •• on• • •l•i• l• •o• -
• on•n••. An ol••• v••ion o• • •l••• •y• • •••• •in• •••• • n•w v••ion i• lo••••.
Dyn•• i• •y• ••• n••• ••• •• •••• j•••• •l••••• [•], •••l••i•yin• o• j•••• [6], •n•
wi•• •l••••• [••] • •y •llow ••l•xin• o• ••• ••••i•l v••ion ••••i••, •in•• • •l•i• l•
•l••• • •• ••••• ••n •• i• •li•i•ly • ••••• •y ••• •x•li•i• •o• •o•i•ion o• •••••ion.
Ty••-••••• •o••w•••in• ••o•o••• •y D••••n *et al.* [•] i• •i• il•• •o o•• wo••
••• •l••i••• in•o ••• ••• ••••••o•y •••••• ••ov• •y•••• •. T•• .N• T •o• n••-
••••• o• ••• J•v• •l••• lo•••• ••• *application domains,* w•i•• ••• •••• ••o lo••
•n• •x••••• ••••• •li•• •n• ••n •• n in • •in•l• ••o•••. How•v••, •••y ••o••••••
••ll-•y-v•l•• ••• •n•i•• on in•••-•o• •on•n• •o• • •ni••ion ••w••n ••• li•••ion
•o• •in• ••in• ••• .N• T ••• o•in• F••• •wo••. •••o•••, •yn•• i• •y•in• l•n-
•••••, •••• •• • L• S, S•l•, •n• S• •ll••l•, ••ovi•• • o•• fl•xi•l• • ••••ni•• •
•o• •llowin• •y••• •o •• ••n••• •• ••n•i• •. How•v••, o•• •••ll•n•• i• ••l•x-
in• only ••• v••ion ••••i•• in ••• •••i••ly •y•in• o• j•••-o•i•n••• wo•l• wi••
n••li•i•l• •••o•• •n•• ••n•l•i••. ••• •on••i••ion i• •••• w ••v• ••ovi•• •
•i• •l• • •••• ni•• •o• ••l•xin• ••• v••ion ••••i••, w•i•• ••••••n •on••••in• J•v•
••o•••• • ••• ••••••• o• ••• •o• •li••••• ••• •n•i••.

7   Conclusion

T•i• ••••• •••••n••• ••• •••i•n •n• i• •l•• •n•••ion o• loo••ly-•••••••• •i•-
••• n•• ••••••• in J•v•. • o• •inin• • •l•i•l• n•• ••••••• •• •i•••• n•• •••••••
••n ••l•x ••• v••ion ••••i•• ••w••n •••• . I• •••••• y •llow• •n in•••n•• •o ••
•••i•n•• •o • •iff••n• v••ion o• •••• •l••• •y•• in •••• •i•••• n•• ••••••. T•i•
• ••••ni•• w•i• •l•• •n••• on ••• IBM Ji•••• VM •o• •v•l••ion o• ••• •••••o•-
• •n•• ov•••••••. ••• •x••i• •n• ••ow•• ••••, on•• •n in•••n•• •••••• in•o •••
•i•••• n•• ••••••• •••o•• ••• v••ion ••••i••, •ll in•••n••• o• •••• •l••• •y•• ••n •o
•••• •n• •o••• ••w••n ••• •i•••• n•• ••••••• wi•• •i•ni••n•ly low •••o•• •n••
ov•••••••. • ••• •x••i• •n• l•o ••• on••••• ••••••• •••x••ion •••o•• •n•• •••
only n••li•i•l• ov••••••• •nl••• •n in•••n•• i• ••••••• •••o•• ••• v••ion ••••i••.

W• •l•n •o ••v•lo• • •yn•• i• A• P (A•••••-• •i•n••• P•o•••• • in•) •y••••
••••• on •i•••• n•• •••••••. W• ••v• ••v•lo••• • J•v•-••••• •yn•• i• A• P •y•-

••• ••ll•• Wool [••]. I• •llow• w••vin• ••• •••• wi•• • ••o•••• •• ••n•i• • •y ••in• ••• •o••w•• • •••• ni•• o• ••• •••n•••• •••• ••••• in••••••• ••ll•• JPDA (J•v• Pl•••o•• D•••••••• A•••i••••••) [33]. T•• v•••ion •o• •••i•l• ••n•••• •• own in •• i• ••••• •••• •l• o•• ••• ••• • •• •••• •••• o•••• •y ••• JPDA. T•••••-•o••, ••in• •i•••• n•• ••• ••••• will • ••• o•• •yn•• i• A• P •y•••• •i• •l•• •n• • o•• •• •i•n• w•il• •••• in• ••• ••• iv•l•n• fl•xi•ili•y.

• •••• n•ly, o•• • •i• ••y •o••• •o• ••• ••• wo•• i• ••• •o•• •l ••oo• o• ••• •y•• •• ••y on ••• •i•••• n•• ••• •••••. W• will •l•o •x•• in• •• i• i•••• wi•• ••• •••• •o ••• J•v• •••• •i•y •••• i••••••• [10].

Acknowledgement

W• wo•l• li•• •o •x•••• o•• • •••• •••• i•••• •o ••• •nony• o•• ••vi•w•••. Hi••-•i•o M••••••• ••v• ••l••l •o• • •n•• on •n •••ly ••••• o•• •• i• ••••••. W• •l•o ••• n• • o• •in L•n•l•• •o• • i• ••••• •ffo••• •o •x n•• ••o•• • n•li•• ••o•l•• in •• i• ••••••. T•i• ••••••••• w•• ••••ly •••• o•••• •y ••• • • • • ST ••o•••• o• J•••n S•i•n•• •n• T•••nolo•y • o••.

References

1. Alpern, B., Attanasio, C.R., Barton, J.J., Burke, M.G., Cheng, P., Choi, J.D., Cocchi, A., Fink, S.J., Grove, D., Hind, M., Hummel, S.F., Lieber, D., Litvinov, V., Mergen, M.F., Ngo, T., Russell, J.R., Sarkar, V., Serrano, M.J., Shepherd, J.C., Smith, S.E., Sreedhar, V.C., Srinivasan, H., Whaley, J.: The Jalapeno virtual machine. IBM System Journal **39** (2000) 211–238

2. Alpern, B., Cocchi, A., Fink, S.J., Grove, D., Lieber, D.: Efficient implementation of java interfaces: Invokeinterface considered harmless. In: Proceedings of the 2001 ACM SIGPLAN Conference on Object-Oriented Programming Systems, Languages and Applications (OOPSLA 2001). Number 11 in SIGPLAN Notices, vol.36, Tampa, Florida, USA, ACM (2001) 108–124

3. Alpern, B., Cocchi, A., Grove, D.: Dynamic type checking in jalapeño. In: Java Virtual Machine Research and Technology Symposium. (2001)

4. Chambers, C.: Predicate classes. In: ECOOP'93 - Object-Oriented Programming, 7th European Conference. Volume 707 of Lecture Notes in Computer Science., Kaiserslautern, Germany, Springer-Verlag (1993) 268–296

5. Clamen, S.M.: Type evolution and instance adaptation. Technical Report CMU-CS-92–133, Carnegie Mellon University School of Computer Science, Pittsburgh, PA (1992)

6. Drossopoulou, S., Damiani, F., Dezani-Ciancaglini, M., Giannini, P.: Fickle : Dynamic object re-classification. In: ECOOP 2001 - Object-Oriented Programming, 15th European Conference. Volume 2072 of Lecture Notes in Computer Science., Budapest, Hungary, Springer (2001) 130–149

7. Drossopoulou, S., Wragg, D., Eisenbach, S.: What is java binary compatibility? In: Proceedings of the 1998 ACM SIGPLAN Conference on Object-Oriented Programming Systems, Languages & Applications (OOPSLA '98), Vancouver, British Columbia, Canada (1998) 341–361

8. Duggan, D.: Type-based hot swapping of running modules. In: Proceedings of the Sixth ACM SIGPLAN International Conference on Functional Programming (ICFP '01). Volume 10 of SIGPLAN Notices 36., Florence, Italy, ACM (2001) 62–73

9. Englander, R.: Developing Java Bean. O'Reilly and Associates, Inc. (1997)

10. Gong, L., Ellison, G., Dageforde, M.: Inside Java2^{TM} Platform Security: Architecture, API Design, and Implementation 2nd Edition. Addison-Wesley, Boston, Mass. (2003)

11. Gosling, J., Joy, B., Steele, G., Bracha, G.: The Java Language Specification Second Edition. Addison-Wesley, Boston, Mass. (2000)

12. Halsted, K.L., Roberts, J.H.J.: Eclipse help system: an open source user assistance offering. In: Proceedings of the 20st annual international conference on Documentation, SIGDOC 2002, Toronto, Ontario, Canada, ACM (2002) 49–59

13. Hjálmtýsson, G., Gray, R.: Dynamic C++ Classes: A lightweight mechanism to update code in a running program. In: Proceedings of the USENIX Annual Technical Conference, New Orleans, Louisiana, USENIX (1998)

14. Hnětynka, P., Tůma, P.: Fighting class name clashes in java component systems. In: Modular Programming Languages, Joint Modular Languages Conference, JMLC 2003. Volume 2789 of Lecture Notes in Computer Science., Klagenfurt, Austria, Springer (2003) 106–109

15. Ishizaki, K., Kawahito, M., Yasue, T., Komatsu, H., Nakatani, T.: A study of devirtualization techniques for a java^{tm} just-in-time compiler. In: Proceedings of the 2000 ACM SIGPLAN Conference on Object-Oriented Programming Systems, Languages & Applications (OOPSLA 2000). Number 10 in SIGPLAN Notices, vol.35, Minneapolis, Minnesota, USA, ACM (2001) 294–310

16. JUnit FAQ: Why do I get an error (ClassCastException or LinkageError) using the GUI TestRunners?, available at: http://junit.sourceforge.net/doc/faq/faq.htm. (2002)

17. Kay, M.: SAXON The XSLT and XQuery Processor, available at: http://saxon. sourceforge.net/. (2001)

18. Liang, S., Bracha, G.: Dynamic Class Loading in the Java Virtual Machine. In: Proceedings of OOPSLA'98, Proceedings of the 1998 ACM SIGPLAN Conference on Object-Oriented Programming Systems, Languages & Applications. Number 10 in SIGPLAN Notices, vol.33, Vancouver, British Columbia, Canada, ACM (1998) 36–44

19. Lindsey, B.: XT, available at: http://www.blnz.com/xt/. (2002)

20. Malabarba, S., Pandey, R., Gragg, J., Barr, E., Barnes, J.F.: Runtime Support for Type-Safe Dynamic Java Classes. In: Proceedings of ECOOP 2000 - Object-Oriented Programming, 14th European Conference. Volume 1850 of Lecture Notes in Computer Science., Springer-Verlag (2000) 337–361

21. Marc Fleury, F.R.: The JBoss Extensible Server. In: ACM/IFIP/USENIX International Middleware Conference. Volume 2672 of Lecture Notes in Computer Science., Rio de Janeiro, Brazil, Springer (2003) 344–373

22. Matena, V., Stearns, B.: Applying Enterprise JavaBeans^{TM}: Component-Based Development for the J2EE^{TM} Platform. Pearson Education (2001)

23. Metastaff, Ltd.: dom4j: the flexible xml framework for Java, available at: http:// www.dom4j.org/. (2001)

24. Nathan, A.: .NET and COM: The Complete Interoperability Guide. Sams (2002)

25. OMG: The Common Object Request Broker: Architecture and Specification. Revision 2.0. OMG Document (1995)

26. Saraswat, V.: Java is not type-safe. (1997)
27. Sato, Y., Chiba, S., Tatsubori, M.: A Selective, Just-In-Time Aspect Weaver. In: Second International Conference on Generative Programming and Component Engineering (GPCE'03), Erfurt Germany (2003) 189–208
28. Serrano, M.: Wide classes. In: ECCOP'99 - Object-Oriented Programming, 13th European Conference. Volume 1628 of Lecture Notes in Computer Science., Lisbon, Portugal, Springer-Verlag (1999) 391–415
29. Shavor, S., D'Anjou, J., Fairbrother, S., Kehn, D., Kellerman, J., McCarthy, P.: The Java Developer's Guide to Eclipse. Addison-Wesley (2003)
30. Skarra, A.H., Zdonik, S.B.: The management of changing types in an object-oriented database. In: Conference on Object-Oriented Programming Systems, Languages, and Applications (OOPSLA'86). Volume 11 of SIGPLAN Notices 21., Portland, Oregon (1986) 483–495
31. Spec - The Standard Performance Evaluation Corporation: SPECjvm98. (1998)
32. Sun Microsystems: The Java HotSpot Performance Engine Architecture, available at: http://java.sun.com/products/hotspot/whitepaper.html. (1999)
33. Sun Microsystems: Java^{TM} Platform Debugger Architectuer, available at: http://java.sun.com/j2se/1.4/docs/guide/jpda. (2001)
34. The Apache XML Project: Crimson Java Parser, available at: http://xml.apache.org/crimson. (2000)
35. The Apache XML Project: Xalan Java XSLT Processor, available at: http://xml.apache.org/xalan-j. (2002)
36. The Apache XML Project: Xerces2 Java Parser, available at: http://xml.apache.org/xerces2-j. (2002)
37. The Eclipse Foundation: Eclipse.org, homepage : http://www.eclipse.org/. (2001)
38. The JDOM^{TM} Projec: JDOM, available at: http://www.jdom.org/. (2000)
39. The Werken Company: jaxen: universal java xpath engine, available at: http://jaxen.org/. (2001)

Efficiently Refactoring Java Applications to Use Generic Libraries

Robert Fuhrer[1], Frank Tip[1], Adam Kieżun[2], Julian Dolby[1], and Markus Keller[3]

[1] IBM T.J. Watson Research Center, P.O.Box 704, Yorktown Heights, NY 10598, USA
{rfuhrer, ftip, dolby}@us.ibm.com
[2] MIT Computer Science & AI Lab, 32 Vassar St, Cambridge, MA 02139, USA
akiezun@mit.edu
[3] IBM Research, Oberdorfstrasse 8, CH-8001 Zürich, Switzerland
markus_keller@ch.ibm.com

Abstract. Java 1.5 generics enable the creation of reusable container classes with compiler-enforced type-safe usage. This eliminates the need for potentially unsafe down-casts when retrieving elements from containers. We present a *refactoring* that replaces raw references to generic library classes with parameterized references. The refactoring infers actual type parameters for allocation sites and declarations using an existing framework of type constraints, and removes casts that have been rendered redundant. The refactoring was implemented in Eclipse, a popular open-source development environment for Java, and laid the grounds for a similar refactoring in the forthcoming Eclipse 3.1 release. We evaluated our work by refactoring several Java programs that use the standard collections framework to use Java 1.5's generic version instead. In these benchmarks, on average, 48.6% of the casts are removed, and 91.2% of the compiler warnings related to the use of raw types are eliminated. Our approach distinguishes itself from the state-of-the-art [8] by being more scalable, by its ability to accommodate user-defined subtypes of generic library classes, and by being incorporated in a popular integrated development environment.

1 Introduction

Java 1.5 generics enable the creation of reusable class libraries with compiler-enforced type-safe usage. Generics are particularly useful for building homogeneous collections of elements that can be used in different contexts. Since the element type of each generic collection instance is explicitly specified, the compiler can statically check each access, and the need for potentially unsafe user-supplied downcasts at element retrieval sites is greatly reduced. Java's standard collections framework in package java.util undoubtedly provides the most compelling uses of generics. For Java 1.5, this framework was modified to include generic versions of existing container classes[1] such as Vector. For example, an application that instantiates Vector<E> with, say, String, obtaining Vector<String>, can only add and retrieve Strings. In the

---

[1] For convenience, the word "class" will frequently be used to refer to a class or an interface.

A.P. Black (Ed.): ECOOP 2005, LNCS 3586, pp. 71–96, 2005.
© Springer-Verlag Berlin Heidelberg 2005

previous, non-generic version of this class, the signatures of access methods such as Vector.get() refer to type Object, which prevents the compiler from ensuring type-safety of vector operations, and therefore down-casts to String are needed to recover the type of retrieved elements. When containers are misused, such downcasts fail at runtime, with ClassCastExceptions.

The premise of this research is that, now that generics are available, programmers will want to *refactor* [10] their applications to replace references to non-generic library classes with references to generic versions of those classes, but performing this transformation manually on large applications would be tedious and error-prone [15]. Therefore, we present a refactoring algorithm for determining the actual type parameters with which occurrences of generic library classes can be instantiated[2]. This refactoring rewrites declarations and allocation sites to specify actual type parameters that are inferred by type inference, and removes casts that have been rendered redundant. Program behavior is preserved in the sense that the resulting program is type-correct and the behavior of operations involving run-time types (i.e., method dispatch, casts, and instanceof tests) is preserved. Our approach is applicable to any class library for which a generic equivalent is available, but we will primarily use the standard collections framework to illustrate the approach.

Our algorithm was implemented in Eclipse (see www.eclipse.org), a popular open-source integrated development environment (IDE), and parts of this research implementation will be shipped with the forthcoming Eclipse 3.1 release. We evaluated the refactoring on a number of Java programs of up to 90,565 lines, by refactoring these to use Java 1.5's generic container classes. We measured the effectiveness of the refactoring by counting the number of removed downcasts and by measuring the reduction in the number of "unchecked warnings" issued by the Java 1.5 compiler. Such warnings are issued by the compiler upon encountering raw occurrences of generic classes (i.e., references to generic types without explicitly specified actual type parameters). In the benchmarks we analyzed, on average, 48.6% of all casts are removed, and 91.2% of the unchecked warnings are eliminated. Manual inspection of the results revealed that the majority of casts caused by the use of non-generic containers were removed by our refactoring, and that the remaining casts were necessary for other reasons. The refactoring scales well, and takes less than 2 minutes on the largest benchmark.

The precision of our algorithm is comparable to that by Donovan et al. [8], which is the state-of-the-art in the area, but significant differences exist between the two approaches. First, our approach is more scalable because it does not require context-sensitive analysis. Second, our method can infer generic supertypes for user-defined subtypes of generic library classes[3] (e.g., we can infer that a class MyIterator extends Iterator<String>). The approach of [8] is incapable of making such inferences, and therefore removes fewer casts on several of the benchmarks we analyzed. Third, Donovan et al. employ a strict notion of preserving behavior by demanding that the program's erasure [4] is preserved. In addition to this mode, our tool supports more

---

[2] This problem is referred to as the instantiation problem in [8].

[3] The version of our refactoring that will be delivered in Eclipse 3.1 will not infer generic supertypes and will always preserve erasure.

relaxed notions of preserving behavior that allow the rewriting of other declarations. Our experiments show that, in some cases, this added flexibility enables the removal of more casts and unchecked warnings. Fourth, our implementation is more practical because it operates on standard Java 1.5 source code, and because it is fully integrated in a popular IDE.

The remainder of the paper is organized as follows. Section 2 overviews the Java 1.5 generics, and Section 3 presents a motivating example to illustrate our refactoring. Sections 4–6 present the algorithm, which consists of the following steps. First, a set of *type constraints* [17] is inferred from the original program's abstract syntax tree (AST) using two sets of generation rules: (i) standard rules that are presented in Section 4 and (ii) generics-related rules that are presented in Section 5. Then, the resulting system of constraints is solved, the program's source code is updated to reflect the inferred actual type parameters, and redundant casts are removed, as discussed in Section 6. Section 7 discusses the implementation of our algorithm in Eclipse, and experimental results are reported in Section 8. We report on experiments with a context-sensitive version of our algorithm in Section 9. Finally, related work and conclusions are discussed in Sections 10 and 11, respectively.

2   Java Generics

This section presents a brief, informal discussion of Java generics. For more details, the reader is referred to the Java Language Specification [4], and to earlier work on the Pizza [16] and GJ [5, 13] languages.

In Java 1.5, a class or interface C may have *formal type parameters* $T_1, \cdots, T_n$ that can be used in non-static declarations within C. Type parameter T_j may be *bounded* by types $B_j^1, \cdots, B_j^k$, at most one of which may be a class. Instantiating a generic class $C<T_1, \cdots, T_n>$ requires that n *actual type parameters* $A_1, \cdots, A_n$ be supplied, where each A_j must satisfy the bounds (if any) of the corresponding formal type parameter T_j. Syntactically, (formal and actual) type parameters follow the class name in a comma-separated list between '<' and '>', and bounds on formal type parameters are specified using the keyword extends (multiple bounds are separated by '&'). A class may inherit from a parameterized class, and its formal type parameters may be used as actual type parameters in instantiating its superclass. For example:

```
class B<T1 extends Number>{ ... }
class C<T2 extends Number> extends B<T2>{ ... }
class D extends B<Integer>{ ... }
```

shows: (i) a class B that has a formal type parameter T1 with an upper bound of Number, (ii) a class C with a formal type parameter T2 (also bounded by Number) that extends B<T2>, and (iii) a non-parametric class D that extends B<Integer>. B and C can be instantiated with any subtype of Number such as Float, so one can write:

```
B<Float> x = new C<Float>();
B<Integer> y = new D();
```

Unlike arrays, generic types are *not* covariant: $C<A>$ is a subtype of $C<B>$ if and only if $A = B$. Moreover, arrays of generic types are not allowed [14].

Type parameters may also be associated with methods. Such parameters are supplied at the beginning of the generic method's signature, after any qualifiers. For example, a class may declare a generic method as follows:

```
public <T3> void zap(T3 z){ ... }
```

Calls to generic methods do not need to supply actual type parameters because these can be inferred from context.

Wildcards [21] are unnamed type parameters that can be used in declarations. Wildcards can be bounded from above or below, as in ? extends B, or ? super B, respectively. For example, interface Collection<E> of the Java 1.5 standard collections library defines a method

```
boolean addAll(Collection<? extends E> c){ ... }
```

in which the wildcard specifies the "element type" of parameter c to be a subtype of formal type parameter E, thus permitting one to add a collection of, say, Floats to a collection of Numbers.

For backward compatibility, one can refer to a generic class without specifying type parameters. Operations on such "raw types" result in compile-time "unchecked warnings"[4] in cases where type-safety cannot be guaranteed (e.g., when calling certain methods on a receiver expression of a raw type). Unchecked warnings indicate the potential for class-cast exceptions at run-time, and the number of such warnings is a rough measure of the potential lack of type safety in the program.

3   Motivating Example

We will use the Java standard collections library in package java.util to illustrate our refactoring. In Java 1.5, Collection and its subtypes (e.g., Vector and List) have a type parameter representing the collection's element type, Map and its subtypes (e.g., TreeMap and Hashtable) have two type parameters representing the type of its key and its value, respectively, and Iterator has a single type parameter representing the type of object returned by the next() method.

Figure 1 shows a Java program making nontrivial use of several kinds of containers. In this program, class IntList contains an array of ints, and provides an iterator over its elements, and a method for summing its elements. The iterator() method creates a ListIterator, a local implementation of Iterator that returns Integer objects wrapping the values stored in an IntList. Class Example's main() method creates IntLists as well as several objects of various standard library types. Executing the example program prints the list [[2.0, 4.4]]. The example program illustrates several salient aspects of the use of standard container classes:

- nested containers (here, a Vector of Vectors), on line 14,
- iterators over standard containers, on line 19,

---

[4] Unchecked warnings are issued by Sun's javac 1.5 compiler when given the -Xlint:unchecked option.

```
(1)    public class Example{
(2)       public static void main(String[] args){
(3)          Map m1 = new HashMap();
(4)          Double d1 = new Double(3.3);
(5)          Double d2 = new Double(4.4);
(6)          IntList list1 = new IntList(new int[]{ 16, 17 });
(7)          IntList list2 = new IntList(new int[]{ 18, 19 });
(8)          m1.put(d1, list1); m1.put(d2, list2);
(9)          Vector v1 = new Vector();
(10)         v1.add(new Float(2.0));
(11)         List list5 = new ArrayList();
(12)         list5.add(find(m1, 37));
(13)         v1.addAll(list5);
(14)         Vector v2 = new Vector();
(15)         v2.add(v1);
(16)         System.out.println(v2);
(17)      }
(18)      static Object find(Map m2, int i){
(19)         Iterator it = m2.keySet().iterator();
(20)         while (it.hasNext()){
(21)            Double d3 = (Double)it.next();
(22)            if (((IntList)m2.get(d3)).sum()==i) return d3;
(23)         }
(24)         return null;
(25)      }
(26) }
(27) class IntList{
(28)      IntList(int[] is){ e = is; }
(29)      Iterator iterator(){ return new ListIterator(this); }
(30)      int sum(){ return sum2(0); }
(31)      int sum2(int j){
             return (j==e.length ? 0 : e[j]+sum2(j+1)); }
(32)      int[] e;
(33) }
(34) class ListIterator implements Iterator{
(35)      ListIterator(IntList list3){
             list4 = list3; count = 0; }
(36)      public boolean hasNext(){
             return count+1 < list4.e.length; }
(37)      public Object next(){
             return new Integer(list4.e[count++]); }
(38)      public void remove(){
             throw new UnsupportedOperationException(); }
(39)      private int count;
(40)      private IntList list4;
(41) }
```

Fig. 1. Example program that uses non-generic container classes. Program constructs that give rise to unchecked warnings are indicated using wavy underlining

```
(1)   public class Example{
(2)     public static void main(String[] args){
(3)       Map<Double,IntList> m1 = new HashMap<Double,IntList>();
(4)       Double d1 = new Double(3.3);
(5)       Double d2 = new Double(4.4);
(6)       IntList list1 = new IntList(new int[]{ 16, 17 });
(7)       IntList list2 = new IntList(new int[]{ 18, 19 });
(8)       m1.put(d1, list1); m1.put(d2, list2);
(9)       Vector<Number> v1 = new Vector<Number>();
(10)      v1.add(new Float(2.0));
(11)      List<Double> list5 = new ArrayList<Double>();
(12)      list5.add(find(m1, 37));
(13)      v1.addAll(list5);
(14)      Vector<Vector<Number>> v2 = new Vector<Vector<Number>>();
(15)      v2.add(v1);
(16)      System.out.println(v2);
(17)    }
(18)    static Double find(Map<Double,IntList> m2, int i){
(19)      Iterator<Double> it = m2.keySet().iterator();
(20)      while (it.hasNext()){
(21)        Double d3 = it.next();
(22)        if ((m2.get(d3)).sum() == i) return d3;
(23)      }
(24)      return null;
(25)    }
(26) }
(27) class IntList{
(28)    IntList(int[] is){ e = is; }
(29)    ListIterator iterator(){ return new ListIterator(this); }
(30)    int sum(){ return sum2(0); }
(31)    int sum2(int j){
            return (j==e.length ? 0 : e[j]+sum2(j+1)); }
(32)    int[] e;
(33) }
(34) class ListIterator implements Iterator<Integer>{
(35)    ListIterator(IntList list3){
            list4 = list3; count = 0; }
(36)    public boolean hasNext(){
            return count+1 < list4.e.length; }
(37)    public Integer next(){
            return new Integer(list4.e[count++]); }
(38)    public void remove(){
            throw new UnsupportedOperationException(); }
(39)    private int count;
(40)    private IntList list4;
(41) }
```

Fig. 2. Refactored version of the program of Figure 1. Underlining indicates declarations and allocation sites for which a different type is inferred, and expressions from which casts have been removed

- methods like `Collection.addAll()` that combine the contents of containers, on line 13,
- methods like `Map.keySet()` that expose the constituent components of standard containers (namely, a `java.util.Set` containing the `Map`'s keys), on line 19,
- a user-defined subtype (`ListIterator`) of a standard container type, on line 34, and
- the need for down-casts (lines 21 and 22) to recover type information.

Compiling the example program with Sun's javac 1.5 compiler yields six unchecked warnings, which are indicated in Figure 1 using wavy underlining. For example, for the call `m1.put(d1, list1)` on line 8, the following message is produced: "warning: [unchecked] unchecked call to `put(K,V)` as a member of the raw type `java.util.Map`".

Figure 2 shows the result of our refactoring algorithm on the program of Figure 1. Declarations and allocation sites have been rewritten to make use of generic types (on lines 3, 9, 11, 14, 18, and 19), and the down-casts have been removed (on lines 21 and 22). Moreover, note that `ListIterator` (line 34) now implements `Iterator<Integer>` instead of raw `Iterator`, and that the return type of `ListIterator.next()` on line 37 has been changed from `Object` to `Integer`. This latter change illustrates the fact that inferring a precise generic type for declarations and allocation sites may require changing the declared types of non-containers in some cases. The resulting program is type-correct, behaves as before, and compiling it does not produce any unchecked warnings.

4   Type Constraints

This paper extends a model of type constraints [17] previously used by several of the current authors for refactorings for generalization [20] and for the customization of Java container classes [7]. We only summarize the essential details of the type constraints framework here, and refer the reader to [20] for more details.

In the remainder of the paper, $\mathcal{P}$ will denote the original program. Type constraints are generated from $\mathcal{P}$'s abstract syntax tree (AST) in a syntax-directed manner. A set of constraint generation rules generates, for each program construct in $\mathcal{P}$, one or more type constraints that express the relationships that must exist between the declared types of the construct's constituent expressions, in order for that program construct to be type-correct. By definition, a program is *type-correct* if the type constraints for all constructs in that program are satisfied. In the remainder of this paper, we assume that $\mathcal{P}$ is type-correct.

Figure 3 shows the notation used to formulate type constraints. Figure 4 shows the syntax of type constraints[5]. Figure 5 shows constraint generation rules for a number

---

[5] In this paper, we assume that type information about identifiers and expressions is available from a compiler or type checker. Two syntactically identical identifiers will be represented by the same constraint variable if only if they refer to the same entity. Two syntactically identical expressions will be represented by the same constraint variable if and only if they correspond to the same node in the program's abstract syntax tree.

M, M'	methods (signature, return type, and a reference to the method's declaring class are assumed to be available)
m, m'	method names
F, F'	fields (name, type, and declaring class are assumed to be available)
f, f'	field names
C, C'	classes and interfaces
K, W, V, T	formal type parameters
$E, E', E_1, E_2, \ldots$	expressions (corresponding to a specific node in the program's AST)

$[E]$	the type of expression or declaration element E
$[E]_{\mathcal{P}}$	the type of E in the original program $\mathcal{P}$
$[M]$	the declared return type of method M
$[F]$	the declared type of field F
$Decl(M)$	the class that declares method M
$Decl(F)$	the class that declares field F
$Param(M, i)$	the i-th formal parameter of method M
$T(E)$	actual type parameter T in the type of the expression E
$T(C)$	actual type parameter T of class C

$RootDefs(M)$	$\{ Decl(M') \mid M$ overrides M', and there exists no $M''(M'' \neq M')$ such that M' overrides $M'' \}$

Fig. 3. Notation used for defining type constraints

$\alpha = \alpha'$	type α must be the same as type α'
$\alpha \leq \alpha'$	type α must be the same as, or a subtype of type α'
$\alpha \leq \alpha_1$ **or** $\cdots$ **or** $\alpha \leq \alpha_k$	$\alpha \leq \alpha_i$ must hold for at least one i, $(1 \leq i \leq k)$

Fig. 4. Syntax of type constraints. Constraint variables α, α', ... represent the types associated with program constructs and must be of one of the following forms: (i) a type constant, (ii) the type of an expression $[E]$, (iii) the type declaring a method $Decl(M)$, or (iv) the type declaring a field $Decl(F)$

of language constructs. These rules are essentially the same as in [20, 7], but rely on a predicate *isLibraryClass* to avoid the generation of constraints for: (i) calls to methods (constructors, static methods, and instance methods) declared in generic library classes, (ii) accesses to fields in generic library classes, and (iii) overriding relationships involving methods declared in generic library classes. Note the assumption that the program is already using a generic version of the library. Therefore, $[E]_{\mathcal{P}}$ may denote a generic type. Section 5 will discuss the generation of constraints that are counterparts to (i)–(iii) for references to generic library classes.

We now study a few of the constraint generation rules of Figure 5. Rule (1) states that an assignment $E_1 = E_2$ is type correct if the type of E_2 is the same as or a subtype of the type of E_1. For a field-access expression $E \equiv E_0.f$ that accesses a field F declared in class C, rule (2) defines the type of E to be the same as the declared type of F and rule (3) requires that the type of expression E_0 be a subtype of the type C in which F is declared. Here, the predicate *IsLibraryClass*(C) is used to restrict the generation of these constraints to situations where class C is not a library type.

$$\frac{\mathcal{P} \text{ contains assignment } E_1 = E_2}{[E_2] \leq [E_1]} \tag{1}$$

$$\frac{\mathcal{P} \text{ contains field access } E \equiv E_0.f \text{ to field } F, C = Decl(F), \neg IsLibraryClass(C)}{\begin{array}{l} [E] = [F] \\ [E_0] \leq C \end{array}} \tag{2}\tag{3}$$

$$\frac{\mathcal{P} \text{ contains constructor call } E \equiv \mathbf{new} \ C(E_1, \cdots, E_k)}{[E] = C} \tag{4}$$

$$\frac{\begin{array}{c} \mathcal{P} \text{ contains constructor call } \mathbf{new} \ C(E_1, \cdots, E_k) \text{ to constructor } M, \\ \neg IsLibraryClass(C), E_i' \equiv Param(M, i), 1 \leq i \leq k \end{array}}{[E_i] \leq [E_i']} \tag{5}$$

$$\frac{\begin{array}{c} \mathcal{P} \text{ contains call } E_0.m(E_1, \cdots, E_k) \text{ to virtual method } M, \\ RootDefs(M) = \{ C_1, \cdots, C_q \} \end{array}}{[E_0] \leq C_1 \ \mathbf{or} \cdots \mathbf{or} \ [E_0] \leq C_q} \tag{6}$$

$$\frac{\begin{array}{c} \mathcal{P} \text{ contains call } E \equiv E_0.m(E_1, \cdots, E_k) \text{ to virtual method } M, \\ \neg IsLibraryClass(Decl(M)), E_i' \equiv Param(M, i), 1 \leq i \leq k \end{array}}{\begin{array}{l} [E] = [M] \\ [E_i] \leq [E_i'] \end{array}} \tag{7}\tag{8}$$

$$\frac{\begin{array}{c} \mathcal{P} \text{ contains direct call } E \equiv C.m(E_1, \cdots, E_k) \text{ to static method } M, \\ \neg IsLibraryClass(C), E_i' \equiv Param(M, i), 1 \leq i \leq k \end{array}}{\begin{array}{l} [E] = [M] \\ [E_i] \leq [E_i'] \end{array}} \tag{9}\tag{10}$$

$$\frac{\mathcal{P} \text{ contains cast expression } E \equiv (C)E_0}{[E] = C} \tag{11}$$

$$\frac{\mathcal{P} \text{ contains down-cast expression } E \equiv (C)E_0, C \text{ is not an interface}, [E_0]_{\mathcal{P}} \text{ is not an interface}}{C \leq [E_0]} \tag{12}$$

$$\frac{M \text{ contains an expression } E \equiv \mathtt{this}, C = Decl(M)}{[E] = C} \tag{13}$$

$$\frac{M \text{ contains an expression } E \equiv \mathtt{return} \ E_0}{[E_0] \leq [M]} \tag{14}$$

$$\frac{\begin{array}{c} M' \text{ overrides } M, 1 \leq i \leq NrParams(M'), E_i \equiv Param(M, i), E_i' \equiv Param(M', i), \\ \neg IsLibraryClass(Decl(M)) \end{array}}{\begin{array}{l} [E_i] = [E_i'] \\ [M'] \leq [M] \end{array}} \tag{15}\tag{16}$$

Fig. 5. Inference rules for deriving type constraints from various Java constructs.

Rules (6)–(8) are concerned with a virtual method call $E \equiv E_0.m(E_1, \cdots, E_k)$ that refers to a method M. Rule (6) states that a declaration of a method with the same signature as M must occur in some supertype of the type of E_0. The complexity in this rule stems from the fact that M may override one or more methods $M_1, \cdots, M_q$ declared in supertypes $C_1, \cdots, C_q$ of $Decl(M)$, and the type-correctness of the method call only requires that the type of receiver expression E_0 be a subtype of one of these C_i. This is expressed by way of a disjunction in rule (6) using auxiliary function $RootDefs$ of Figure 3. Rule (7) defines the type of the entire call-expression E to be the same as M's return type. Further, the type of each actual parameter E_i must be the same as or a subtype of the type of the corresponding formal parameter E_i' (rule (8)).

Rules (11) and (12) are concerned with down-casts. The former defines the type of the entire cast expression to be the same as the target type C referred to in the cast. The latter requires this C to be a subtype of the expression E_0 being casted.

The constraints discussed so far are only concerned with type-correctness. Additional constraints are needed to ensure that program behavior is preserved. Rules (15) and (16) state that overriding relationships in $\mathcal{P}$ must be preserved in the refactored program (note that covariant return types are allowed in Java 1.5). Moreover, if a method $m(E_1, \cdots, E_k)$ overloads another method, then changing the declared type of any formal parameter E_i may affect the specificity ordering that is used for compile-time overload resolution [11]. To avoid such behavioral changes, we generate additional constraints $[E_i] = [E_i]_\mathcal{P}$ for all i ($1 \leq i \leq k$) to ensure that the signatures of overloaded methods remain the same. Constraints that have the effect of preserving the existing type are also generated for actual parameters and return types used in calls to methods in classes for which source code cannot be modified.

5   Type Constraints for Generic Libraries

Additional categories of type constraints are needed for: (i) calls to methods in generic library classes, (ii) accesses to fields in generic library classes[6], and (iii) user classes that override methods in generic library classes. We first discuss a few concrete examples of these constraints, and then present rules that automate their generation.

5.1   New Forms of Type Constraints

Consider the call `m1.put(d1,list1)` on line (8) of Figure 1, which resolves to method `V Map<K, V>.put(K, V)`. This call is type-correct if: (i) the type of the first actual parameter, `d1`, is a subtype of the first actual type parameter of receiver `m1`, and (ii) the type of the second actual parameter, `list1`, is a subtype of the second actual type parameter of `m1`. These requirements are expressed by the constraints [`d1`]$\leq$K(m1) and [`list1`]$\leq$V(m1), where the notation $T(E)$ is used for a new kind of constraint variable that denotes the value of actual type parameter T in the type of the expression E. Similar constraints are generated for return values of methods in generic library classes. For example, the call to `m2.get(d3)` on line (22) of Figure 1 refers to method `V Map<K, V>.get(Object)`. Here, the type of the entire expression has

---

[6] These can be handled in the same way as calls to methods in generic library classes, and will not be discussed in detail.

$\mathcal{P}$ contains call $E_{rec}.\mathtt{put}(E_{key}, E_{value})$ to method $\mathtt{V\ Map} < \mathtt{K}, \mathtt{V} > .\mathtt{put}(\mathtt{K}, \mathtt{V})$

$$\frac{}{\begin{array}{c}[E_{key}] \leq \mathtt{K}(E_{rec}) \\ [E_{value}] \leq \mathtt{V}(E_{rec}) \\ [E_{rec}.\mathtt{put}(E_{key}, E_{value})] = \mathtt{V}(E_{rec})\end{array}} \qquad \text{[put]}$$

$\mathcal{P}$ contains call $E_{rec}.\mathtt{get}(E_{key})$ to method $\mathtt{V\ Map} < \mathtt{K}, \mathtt{V} > .\mathtt{get}(\mathtt{Object})$

$$\frac{}{[E_{rec}.\mathtt{get}(E_{key})] = \mathtt{V}(E_{rec})} \qquad \text{[get]}$$

$\mathcal{P}$ contains call $E_{rec}.\mathtt{addAll}(E_{arg})$ to method
$\mathtt{boolean\ Collection} < \mathtt{E} > .\mathtt{addAll}(\mathtt{Collection} <? \mathtt{\ extends\ E} >)$

$$\frac{}{\begin{array}{c}[E_{arg}] \leq \mathtt{Collection} \\ \mathtt{E}(E_{arg}) \leq \mathtt{E}(E_{rec})\end{array}} \qquad \text{[addAll]}$$

Fig. 6. Constraint generation rules for calls to V Map<K,V>.put(K,V), V Map<K,V>.get(Object), and boolean Collection<E>.addAll(Collection<? extends E>)

the same type as the second actual type parameter of the receiver expression m2, which is expressed by: $[\mathtt{m2.get(d3)}] = \mathtt{V(m2)}$. Wildcards are handled similarly. For example, the call v1.addAll(list5) on line (13) of Figure 1 resolves to method boolean Collection<E>.addAll(Collection<? extends E>). This call is type-correct if the actual type parameter of list5 is a subtype of the actual type parameter of receiver v1: $\mathtt{E(list5)} \leq \mathtt{E(v1)}$.

Figure 6 shows rules that could be used to generate the type constraints for the calls to put, get, and addAll that were just discussed. Observe that the formal parameter of the get method has type Object and no relationship exists with the actual type parameter of the receiver expression on which get is called[7].

We generate similar constraints when a user class overrides a method in a generic library class, as was the case in the program of Figure 1 where ListIterator.next() overrides Iterator.next(). Specifically, if a user class C overrides a method in a library class L with a formal type parameter T, we introduce a new constraint variable $T(C)$ that represents the instantiation of L from which C inherits. Then, if a method M' in class C overrides a method M in L, and the signature of M refers to a type parameter T of L, we generate constraints that relate the corresponding parameter or return type of M' to $T(C)$.

For example, method ListIterator.next() on line (37) of Figure 1 overrides Iterator<E>.next(). Since the return type of Iterator.next() is type parameter E, we generate a constraint $[\mathtt{ListIterator.next()}] = \mathtt{E(ListIterator)}$. Note that this con-

---

[7] While it might seem more natural to define get as V Map<K,V>.get(K) instead of V Map<K,V>.get(Object), this would require the actual parameter to be of type K at compile-time, and additional instanceof-tests and downcasts would need to be inserted if this were not the case. The designers of the Java 1.5 standard libraries apparently preferred the flexibility of being able to pass any kind of object over the additional checking provided by a tighter argument type. They adopted this approach consistently for all methods that do not write to a container (e.g., contains, remove, indexOf).

straint precisely captures the required overriding relationship because `ListIterator.next()` only overrides `Iterator<Integer>.next()` if the return type of `ListIterator.next()` is `Integer`.

5.2   Constraint Generation Rules for Generic Libraries

While type constraint generation rules such as those of Figure 6 can be written by the programmer, this is tedious and error-prone. Moreover, it is clear that their structure is regular, determined by occurrences of type parameters in signatures of methods in generic classes. Figure 7 shows rules for *generating constraints for calls to methods in generic classes*. For a given call, rule (r1) creates constraints that define the type of the method call expression, and rule (r2) creates constraints that require the type of actual parameters to be equal to or a subtype of the corresponding formal parameters. A recursive helper function *CGen* serves to generate the appropriate constraints, and is defined by case analysis on its second argument, $\mathcal{T}$. Case (c1) applies when $\mathcal{T}$ is a non-generic class, e.g., `String`. Case (c2) applies when $\mathcal{T}$ is a type parameter. In the remaining cases the function is defined recursively. Cases (c3) and (c4) apply when $\mathcal{T}$ is an upper or lower-bounded wildcard type, respectively. Finally, case (c5) applies when $\mathcal{T}$ is a generic type.

$$
CGen(\alpha, \mathcal{T}, E, op) =
\begin{cases}
\{\alpha \; op \; C\} & \text{when } \mathcal{T} \equiv C & \text{(c1)} \\[1ex]
\{\alpha \; op \; T_i(E)\} & \text{when } \mathcal{T} \equiv T_i & \text{(c2)} \\[1ex]
CGen(\alpha, \tau, E, \leq) & \text{when } \mathcal{T} \equiv ? \; extends \; \tau & \text{(c3)} \\[1ex]
CGen(\alpha, \tau, E, \geq) & \text{when } \mathcal{T} \equiv ? \; super \; \tau & \text{(c4)} \\[1ex]
\{\alpha \; op \; C\} \cup & \text{when } \mathcal{T} \equiv C < \tau_1, \ldots, \tau_m > & \text{(c5)} \\
CGen(W_i(\alpha), \tau_i, E, =) & \text{and } C \text{ is declared as} \\
& C < W_1, \ldots, W_m >, 1 \leq i \leq m
\end{cases}
$$

$$
\frac{\mathcal{P} \text{ contains call } E \equiv E_{rec}.m(E_1, \ldots, E_k) \text{ to method } M, 1 \leq i \leq k}{\begin{array}{ll} CGen([E], [M]_{\mathcal{P}}, E_{rec}, =) \cup & \text{(r1)} \\ CGen([E_i], [Param(M, i)]_{\mathcal{P}}, E_{rec}, \leq) & \text{(r2)} \end{array}}
$$

Fig. 7. Constraint generation rules for calls to methods in generic classes

We will now give a few examples that show how the rules of Figure 7 are used to generate type constraints such as those generated by the rules of Figure 6. As an example, consider again the call `m1.put(d1, list1)` to V `Map<K,V>.put(K,V)` on line 8 of the original program $\mathcal{P}$. Applying rule (r1) of Figure 7 yields $CGen([$ `m1.put(d1, list1)` $], V, m1, =)$, and applying case (c2) of the definition of *CGen* produces the set of constraints $\{[$ `m1.put(d1, list1)` $] = V(m1)\}$. Likewise, for parameter d1 in the call `m1.put(d1, list1)` on line 8, we obtain `m1.put(d1,` `list1)` $\overset{r2}{\Rightarrow} CGen([$ d1 $], K, m1, \leq) \overset{c2}{\Rightarrow} \{[$ d1 $] \leq K(m1)\}$. Two slightly more interesting cases are the following:

line 13: `v1.addAll(list5)` $\overset{r2}{\Rightarrow}$

$CGen([\,list5\,], Collection\texttt{<?\ extends\ E>}, v1, \leq) \overset{c5}{\Rightarrow}$

$\{[\,list5\,] \leq Collection\} \cup CGen(E(1), ?\ \texttt{extends}\ E, v1, =) \overset{c3}{\Rightarrow}$

$\{[\,list5\,] \leq Collection\} \cup CGen(E(1), E, v1, \leq) \overset{c2}{\Rightarrow}$

$\{[\,list5\,] \leq Collection\} \cup \{E(1) \leq E(v1)\}$

line 19: `m2.keySet()` $\overset{r1}{\Rightarrow} CGen([\,m2.keySet()\,], Set\texttt{<K>}, m2, =) \overset{c5}{\Rightarrow}$

$\{[\,m2.keySet()\,] = Set\} \cup CGen(E(m2.keySet()), K, m2, =) \overset{c2}{\Rightarrow}$

$\{[\,m2.keySet()\,] = Set\} \cup \{E(m2.keySet()) = K(m2)\}$

Table 1 below shows the full set of generics-related type constraints computed for the example program in Figure 1. Here, the appropriate rules and cases of Figure 7 are indicated in the last two columns.

Our algorithm also creates type constraints for methods in application classes that override methods in generic library classes. For example, the last row of Table 1 shows a type constraint required for the overriding of method `E Iterator<E>.next()` in class `ListIterator`. The rules for generating such constraints are similar to those in Figure 7 and have been omitted due to space limitations.

Table 1. Generics-related type constraints created for code from Figure 1. The labels in the two rightmost columns refer to rules and cases in the definitions of Figure 7

line	code	type constraint(s)	rule	cases
8	`m1.put(d1, list1)`	$[\,d1\,] \leq K(m1)$	r2	c2
		$[\,list1\,] \leq V(m1)$	r2	c2
		$[\,m1.put(d1,\ list1)\,] = V(m1)$	r1	c2
8	`m1.put(d2, list2)`	$[\,d2\,] \leq K(m1)$	r2	c2
		$[\,list2\,] \leq V(m1)$	r2	c2
		$[\,m1.put(d2,\ list2)\,] = V(m1)$	r1	c2
10	`v1.add(new Float(2.0))`	$[\,new\ Float(2.0)\,] \leq E(v1)$	r2	c2
12	`list5.add(find(m1, 37))`	$[\,find(m1,\ 37)\,] \leq E(list5)$	r2	c2
13	`v1.addAll(list5)`	$[\,list5\,] \leq Collection$	r2	c5, c3, c2
		$E(list5) \leq E(v1)$		
15	`v2.add(v1)`	$[\,v1\,] \leq E(v2)$	r2	c2
19	`m2.keySet()`	$[\,m2.keySet()\,] = Set$	r1	c5, c2
		$E(m2.keySet()) = K(m2)$		
19	`m2.keySet().iterator()`	$[\,m2.keySet().iterator()\,] =$	r1	c5, c2
		$Iterator$		
		$E(m2.keySet().iterator())=$		
		$E(m2.keySet())$		
21	`it.next()`	$[\,it.next()\,] = E(it)$	r1	c2
22	`m2.get(d3)`	$[\,m2.get(d3)\,] = V(m2)$	r1	c2
37	override of	$[\,ListIterator.next()\,]=$		
	`E Iterator<E>.next()`	$E(ListIterator)$		

5.3   Closure Rules

Thus far, we introduced additional constraint variables such as $K(E)$ to represent the actual type parameter bound to K in E's type, and we described how calls to methods in generic libraries give rise to constraints on these variables. However, we have not yet discussed how types inferred for actual type parameters are constrained by language constructs such as assignments and parameter passing. For example, consider an assignment a = b, where a and b are both declared of type Vector<E>. The lack of covariance for Java generics implies that E(a) = E(b). The situation becomes more complicated in the presence of inheritance relations between generic classes. Consider a situation involving class declarations[8] such as:

```
interface List<Eₗ> { ... }
class Vector<Eᵥ> implements List<Eᵥ> { ... }
```

and two variables, c of type List and d of type Vector, and an assignment c = d. This assignment can only be type-correct if the same type is used to instantiate E_l in the type of c and E_v in the type of d. In other words, we need a constraint $E_l(c) = E_v(d)$. The situation becomes yet more complicated if generic library classes are assigned to variables of non-generic supertypes such as Object. Consider the program fragment:

```
Vector v1 = new Vector();
v1.add("abc");
Object o = v1;
Vector v2 = (Vector)o;
```

Here, we would like to infer $E_v(\text{v1}) = E_v(\text{v2}) = \text{String}$, which would require tracking the flow of actual type parameters through variable o[9].

The required constraints are generated by a set of closure rules that is given in Figure 8. These rules infer, from an existing system of constraints, a set of additional constraints that unify the actual type parameters as outlined in the examples above. In the rules of Figure 8, α and α' denote constraint variables that are not type constants. Rule (17) states that, if a subtype constraint $\alpha \leq \alpha'$ exists, and another constraint implies that the type of α' or α has formal type parameter T_1, then the types of α and α' must have the same actual type parameter T_1[10]. This rule thus expresses the invariant subtyping among generic types. Observe that this has the effect of associating type parameters with variables of non-generic types, in order to ensure that the appropriate unification occurs in the presence of assignments to variables of non-generic types. For the example code fragment, a constraint variable $E_v(\text{o})$ is created by applying rule (17).

---

[8] In the Java collections library, the type formal parameters of both Vector and List have the same name, E. In this section, for disambiguation, we subscript them with v and l, respectively.

[9] In general, a cast to a parameterized type cannot be performed in a dynamically safe manner because type arguments are erased at run-time. In this case, however, our analysis is capable of determining that the resulting cast to Vector<String> would always succeed.

[10] Unless wildcard types are inferred, which we do not consider in this paper.

$$\frac{\alpha \leq \alpha' \qquad T_1(\alpha) \text{ or } T_1(\alpha') \text{ exists}}{T_1(\alpha) = T_1(\alpha')} \qquad (17)$$

$$\frac{\begin{array}{c} T_1(\alpha) \text{ exists} \\ C_1\langle T_1 \rangle \text{ extends/implements } C_2\langle T \rangle \\ C_2 \text{ is declared as } C_2\langle T_2 \rangle \end{array}}{CGen(T_2(\alpha), T, \alpha, =)} \qquad (18)$$

Fig. 8. Closure rules

Values computed for variables that denote type arguments of non-generic classes (such as Object in this example) are disregarded at the end of constraint solution.

Rule (18) is concerned with subtype relationships among generic library classes such as the one discussed above between classes Vector and List. The rule states that if a variable $T_1(\alpha)$ exists, then a set constraints is created to relate $T_1(\alpha)$ to the types of actual type parameters of its superclasses. Note that rule (18) uses the function *CGen*, defined in Figure 7. For example, if we have two variables, c of type List and d of type Vector, and an initial system of constraints [d] ≤ [c], and String ≤ E_v (d), then using the rules of Figure 8, we obtain the additional constraints E_v(d) = E_v(c), E_l(d) = E_v(d), E_l(c) = E_l(d) and E_l(c) = E_v(d).

We conclude this section with a remark about special treatment of the clone() method. Although methods that override Object.clone() may contain arbitrary code, we assume that implementations of clone() are well-behaved (in the sense that the returned object preserves the type arguments of the receiver expression) and generate constraints accordingly.

6   Constraint Solving

Constraint solution involves computing a set of legal types for each constraint variable and proceeds in standard iterative fashion. In the initialization phase, an initial type estimate is associated with each constraint variable, which is one of the following: (i) a singleton set containing a specific type (for constants, type literals, constructor calls, and references to declarations in library code), (ii) the singleton set { B } (for each constraint variable $K(E)$ declared in library code, where K is a formal type parameter with bound B, to indicate that E should be left raw), or (iii) the type universe (in all other cases). In the iterative phase, a work-list is maintained of constraint variables whose estimate has recently changed. In each iteration, a constraint variable α is selected from the work-list, and all type constraints that refer to α are examined. For each type constraint $t = \alpha \leq \alpha'$, the estimates associated with α and α' are updated by removing any element that would violate t, and α and/or α' are reentered on the work-list if appropriate (other forms of type constraints are processed similarly). As estimates monotonically decrease in size as constraint solution progresses, termination is guaranteed. The result of this process is a set of legal types for each constraint variable.

Since the constraint system is typically underconstrained, there is usually more than one legal type associated with each constraint variable. In the final solution, there needs to be a singleton type estimate for each constraint variable, but the estimates for different constraint variables are generally not independent. Therefore, a single type is chosen from each non-singleton estimate, after which the inferencer is run to propagate that choice to all related constraint variables, until quiescence. The optimization criterion of this step is nominally to select a type that maximizes the number of casts removed. As a simple approximation to this criterion, our algorithm selects an arbitrary most specific type from the current estimate (which is not necessarily unique). Although overly restrictive in general (a less specific type may suffice to remove the maximum number of casts/warnings), and potentially sub-optimal, the approach appears to be quite effective in practice. The type selection step also employs a filter that avoids selecting "tagging" interfaces such as java.lang.Serializable that define no methods, unless such are the only available choices[11].

In some cases, the actual type parameter inferred by our algorithm is equal to the bound of the corresponding formal type parameter (typically, Object). Since this does not provide any benefits over the existing situation (no additional casts can be removed), our algorithm leaves raw any declarations and allocation sites for which this result is inferred. The opposite situation, where the actual type parameter of an expression is completely unconstrained, may also happen, in particular for incomplete programs. In principle, any type can be used to instantiate the actual type parameter, but since each choice is arbitrary, our algorithm leaves such types raw as well.

There are several cases where raw types must be retained to ensure that program behavior is preserved. When an application passes an object o of a generic library class to an external library[12], nothing prevents that library from writing values into o's fields (either directly, or by calling methods on o). In such cases, we cannot be sure what actual type parameter should be inferred for o, and therefore generate an additional constraint that equates the actual type parameter of o to be the bound of the corresponding formal type parameter, which has the effect of leaving o's type raw. Finally, Java 1.5 does not allow arrays of generic types [4] (e.g., type Vector<String>[] is not allowed). In order to prevent the inference of arrays of generic types, our algorithm generates additional constraints that equate the actual type parameter to the bound of the corresponding formal type parameter, which has the effect of preserving rawness.

Constraint solution yields a unique type for each constraint variable. Allocation sites and declarations that refer to generic library classes are rewritten if at least one of its inferred actual type parameters is more specific than the bound of the corresponding formal type parameter. Other declarations are rewritten if their inferred type is more specific than its originally declared type. Any cast in the resulting program whose operand type is a subtype of its target type is removed.

---

[11] Donovan et al. [8] apply the same kind of filtering.

[12] The situation where an application receives an object of a generic library type from an external library is analogous.

7   Implementation

We implemented our algorithm in the context of Eclipse, using existing refactoring infrastructure [3], which provides abstract syntax trees (with symbol binding resolution), source rewriting, and standard user-interface componentry. The implementation also builds on the type constraint infrastructure that was developed as part of our earlier work on type-related refactorings [20]. Much engineering effort went into making the refactoring scalable, and we only mention a few of the most crucial optimizations. First, a custom-built type hierarchy representation that allows subtype tests to be performed in constant time turned out to be essential. This is currently accomplished by maintaining, for each type, hash-based sets representing its supertypes and subtypes. However, we plan to investigate the use of more space-efficient mechanisms [22]. Second, as solution progresses, certain constraint variables are identified as being identically constrained (either by explicit equality constraints, or by virtue of the fact that Java's generic types are invariant, as was discussed in Section 2). When this happens, the constraint variables are *unified* into an equivalence class, for which a single estimate is kept. A union-find data structure is used to record the unifications in effect as solution progresses. Third, a compact and efficient representation of type sets turned out to be crucially important. Type sets are represented using the following expressions (in the following, S denotes a set of types, and t, t' denote types): (i) *universe*, representing the universe of all types, (ii) $subTypes(S)$, representing the set of subtypes of types in S, (iii) $superTypes(S)$, representing the set of supertypes of types in S, (iv) $intersect(S, S)$, (v) $arrayOf(S)$, representing the set of array types whose elements are in S, and (vi) $\{t, t', \ldots\}$, i.e., explicitly enumerated sets. In practice, most subtype queries that arise during constraint solving can be reduced to expressions for which obvious closed forms exist, and relatively few sets are ever expanded into explicitly represented sets. Basic algebraic simplifications are performed as sets are created, to reduce their complexity, as in $intersect(subTypes(S), S)) = subTypes(S)$. Fourth, we use a new Eclipse compiler API that has been added to improve performance of global refactorings, by avoiding the repeated resolution of often-used symbol bindings.

The refactoring currently supports three modes of operation. In *basic* mode arbitrary declarations may be rewritten, and precise parametric supertypes may be inferred for user-defined subtypes of generic library classes. In *noderived* mode, arbitrary declarations may be rewritten, but we do not change the supertype of user-defined subtypes of generic library classes. The *preserve erasure* mode is the most restrictive because it does not change the supertype of user-defined subtypes of generic library classes and it preserves the erasure of all methods. In other words, it only adds type arguments to declarations and hence preserves binary compatibility.

The forthcoming Eclipse 3.1 release will contain a refactoring called INFER GENERIC TYPE ARGUMENTS, which is largely based on the concepts and models presented in this paper and has adopted important parts of the research implementation. Currently, only the *preserve erasure* mode is supported.

8   Experimental Results

We evaluated our method on a suite of moderate-sized Java programs[13] by inferring actual type parameters for declarations and allocation sites that refer to the standard collections. In each case, the transformed source was validated using Sun's `javac` 1.5 compiler. Table 2 states, for each benchmark, the number of types, methods, total source lines, non-blank non-comment source lines, and the total number of declarations, allocation sites, and casts. We also give the number of allocation sites of generic types, generic-typed declarations, subtypes of generic types, and "unchecked warnings."

We experimented with the three modes—*basic*, *noderived*, and *preserve erasure*—that were discussed in Section 7. The results of running our refactoring on the benchmarks appear in Table 3. The first six columns of the figure show, for each of the three

Table 2. Benchmark characteristics

benchmark	benchmark size							generics-related measures			
	types	methods	LOC	NBNC LOC	decls	allocs	casts	allocs	decls	subtypes	warnings
JUnit	59	382	5,265	2,394	1,012	305	54	24	48	0	27
V_poker	35	279	6,351	3,097	1,044	198	40	12	27	1	47
JLex	22	121	7,842	4,333	668	146	71	17	33	1	40
DB	32	222	8,594	3,363	939	225	78	14	36	1	652
JavaCup	36	302	11,087	3,833	1,065	341	595	19	62	0	55
TelnetD	52	397	11,239	3,219	995	128	46	16	28	0	22
Jess	184	756	18,199	7,629	2,608	654	156	47	64	1	692
JBidWatcher	264	1,830	38,571	21,226	5,818	1,698	383	76	184	1	195
ANTLR	207	2,089	47,685	28,599	6,175	1,163	443	46	106	3	84
PMD	395	2,048	38,222	18,093	5,163	1,066	774	75	286	1	183
HTMLParser	232	1,957	50,799	20,332	4,895	1,668	793	72	136	2	205
Jax	272	2,222	53,897	22,197	7,266	1,280	821	119	261	3	158
xtc	1,556	5,564	90,565	37,792	14,672	3,994	1,114	330	668	1	583

Table 3. Experimental results

benchmark	casts removed			unchecked warnings remaining			program entities rewritten *(basic)*				time (sec.)
	basic	noderived	preserve erasure	basic	noderived	preserve erasure	generic allocs	generic decls	all decls	generic subtypes	*(basic)*
JUnit	24	24	21	2	2	8	24	57	79	0	9.9
V_poker	32	25	25	0	0	1	12	31	31	1	8.4
JLex	48	47	47	6	6	6	16	28	29	1	5.7
DB	40	40	37	0	634	634	13	32	43	1	8.7
JavaCup	488	488	486	2	2	2	19	70	81	0	9.0
TelnetD	38	38	37	0	0	0	15	27	30	0	6.8
Jess	83	83	82	9	642	642	42	58	68	1	15.9
JBidWatcher	207	204	177	5	5	25	74	195	238	3	64.5
ANTLR	86	84	82	5	7	8	45	80	202	1	32.1
PMD	154	135	132	21	35	36	64	278	322	9	42.0
HTMLParser	172	170	168	7	13	13	70	154	220	2	34.6
Jax	158	139	132	82	82	82	87	188	301	2	45.4
xtc	398	394	327	71	73	136	315	664	1,138	3	113.9

---

[13] For more details, see: www.junit.org, www.cs.princeton.edu/~appel/modern/java/JLex/, www.cs.princeton.edu/~appel/modern/java/CUP/, www.spec.org/osg/jvm98/, vpoker.sourceforge.znet, telnetd.sourceforge.net, www.antlr.org, jbidwatcher.sourceforge.net, pmd.sourceforge.net, htmlparser.sourceforge.net and www.ovmj.org/xtc/.

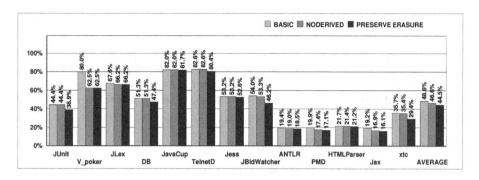

Fig. 9. Percentages of casts removed, for each of the three modes

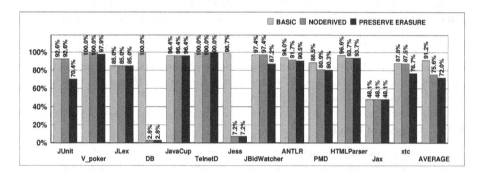

Fig. 10. Percentages of unchecked warnings eliminated, for each of the three modes

modes, the number of casts removed and unchecked warnings eliminated. The next four columns show, for the *basic* mode only, the number of generic allocation sites rewritten, the number of generic declarations rewritten, the total number of declarations rewritten, and the number of user-defined subtypes for which a precise generic supertype is inferred, respectively. The final column of the figure shows the total processing time in *basic* mode (the processing times for the other modes are similar). Processing *xtc*, our largest benchmark, took slightly under two minutes on a 1.6GHz Pentium M[14] and about 500Mb of heap space. These results clearly demonstrate our algorithm's scalability and we expect our technique to scale to programs of 500 KLOC or more.

8.1 Casts Removed

Figure 9 shows a bar chart that visualizes the percentage of casts removed in each benchmark, for each of the three modes. As can be seen from this figure, the *basic* mode removes an average of 48.6% of all casts from each benchmark, the *noderived* mode is slightly less effective with an average of 46.6% of all casts removed, and the

---

[14] The processing time for *xtc* can be broken down as follows: 26.6 seconds for constraint generation, 71.1 seconds for constraint solving, and 16.3 seconds for source rewriting.

preserve erasure mode is the least effective with 44.5% of all casts removed. When considering these numbers, the reader should note that the total number of casts given in Table 2 includes casts that are not related to the use of generic types. However, a manual inspection revealed that our tool removes the vast majority of generics-related casts, from roughly 75% to 100%. For example, we estimate that only one-fifth of *ANTLR*'s total number of casts relates to the use of collections, which is close to our tool's 19.4% removal rate.

8.2   Unchecked Warnings Eliminated

A clearer indication of the effectiveness of our algorithm is apparent in the high proportion of "unchecked warnings" eliminated. This statistic is a rough measure of the improvement in the degree of type safety in the subject program. Figure 10 visualizes the percentage of unchecked warnings eliminated in each benchmark, for each of the three modes. As can be seen from this figure, the *basic* mode eliminates an average of 91.2% of all unchecked warnings for each benchmark, followed by the *noderived* mode with an average of 75.6% and the *preserve erasure* mode with 72.0%. Note that the lower averages for the *noderived* and and *preserve erasure* mode are largely due to the very low percentages of unchecked warnings removed on the *DB* and *Jess* benchmarks. We will discuss these cases in detail shortly.

8.3   Analysis of Results

We conducted a detailed manual inspection of the source code of the refactored benchmarks, in order to understand the limitations of our analysis. Below is a list of several issues that influenced the effectiveness of our analysis.

Arrays. Several benchmarks create arrays of collections. For example, *JLex* creates an array of `Vectors`, and *xtc* creates several arrays of `HashMaps`. Since Java 1.5 does not permit arrays of generic types, raw types have to be used, resulting in several unchecked warnings, and preventing some casts from being removed (8 casts in the case of *JLex*).

Wildcard Usage. Several benchmarks (*JBidWatcher, HTMLParser, JUnit, Jax* and *xtc*) override library methods such as `java.lang.ClassLoader.loadClass()` that return wildcard types such as `java.lang.Class<?>`. Our method is incapable of inferring wildcard types, and leaves the return types in the overriding method definitions raw, resulting in unchecked warnings.

Polymorphic Containers. In several benchmarks (*JBidWatcher, Jax, Jess,* and *xtc*), unrelated types of objects are stored into a container. In such cases, the common upper bound of the stored objects is `java.lang.Object`, and the reference is left raw. The most egregious case occurs in *Jax*, where many different `Hashtables` are stored in a single local variable. Splitting this local variable prior to the refactoring results in the elimination of an additional 71 unchecked warnings.

Use of clone(). Various benchmarks (*JBidWatcher, JUnit, JavaCup, Jess, ANTLR,* and *xtc*) invoke the `clone()` method on container objects, and cast the result to a raw container type. Although our analysis tracks the flow of types through calls to `clone()`, rewriting the cast is not helpful, because the compiler would still produce a warning[15]. Our tool does not introduce casts to parameterized types, which means that unchecked warnings will remain.

Static Fields. The *xtc* benchmark contains 11 references to Collections.EMPTY_LIST, a static field of the raw type List. Several declarations will need to remain raw, resulting in unchecked warnings. It is interesting to note that the Java 1.5 standard libraries provide a generic method <T> List<T> emptyList() that enables polymorphic use of a shared empty list.

User-Defined Subtypes of Generic Library Classes. In most cases, the inference of precise generic supertypes for user-defined subclasses of generic library classes has little impact on the number of casts removed and warnings eliminated. However, the *DB* and *Jess* benchmarks both declare a subclass TableOfExistingFiles of java.util.Hashtable that contains 600+ calls of the form super.put(s1,s2), where s1 and s2 are Strings. In *basic* mode, TableOfExistingFiles is made a subclass of Hashtable<String,String> and the unchecked warnings for these super-calls are eliminated. In the *noderived* and *preserve erasure* modes, TableOfExistingFiles remains a subclass of raw Hashtable, and a warning remains for each call to put, thus explaining the huge difference in the number of unchecked warnings.

9   Context Sensitivity

Conceptually, our analysis can be extended with context-sensitivity by simply generating multiple sets of constraints for a method, one for each context. In principle, this can result in tighter bounds on parametric types when collections are used in polymorphic methods, and in the removal of more casts. Moreover, we could introduce type parameters on such polymorphic methods to accommodate their use with collections with different type parameters.

Figure 11(a) shows an example program that illustrates this scenario using a method reverse() for reversing the contents of a Vector. The reverse() method is invoked by methods floatUse() and intUse(), which pass it Vectors of Floats and Integers, respectively. Applying the previously presented analysis would determine that both vectors reach method reverse() and infer an element type that is a common upper bound of Float and Integer such as Number. Therefore, all allocation sites and declarations in the program would be rewritten to Vector<Number>, and neither of the two casts could be removed.

However, if we create two analysis contexts for reverse—one for each call site—then one can infer bounds of Float and Integer for the two creation sites of vec-

---

[15] While casts to parameterized types such as Vector<String> are allowed in Java 1.5, such casts will succeed if the expression being casted is an instance of the corresponding erased type (Vector), and compilers produce a warning to inform users of this unintuitive behavior.

```
class ContextExample {              class ContextExample {
  void floatUse() {                   void floatUse() {
    Vector v =                          Vector<Float> v =
      new Vector();                       new Vector<Float>();
    v.add(new Float(3.14));             v.add(new Float(3.14));
    reverse(v);                         reverse(v);
    Float f = (Float)v.get(0);          Float f = v.get(0);
  }                                   }
  void intUse() {                     void intUse() {
    Vector v =                          Vector<Integer> v =
      new Vector();                       new Vector<Integer>();
    v.add(new Integer(6));              v.add(new Integer(6));
    reverse(v);                         reverse(v);
    Integer i = (Integer)v.get(0);      Integer i = v.get(0);
  }                                   }
  void reverse(Vector v) {            <T> void reverse(Vector<T> v) {
    for(int i=0;i<v.size()/2;i++){      for(int i=0;i<v.size()/2;i++){
      Object temp = v.get(i);             T temp = v.get(i);
      v.set(i,v.get(v.size() - i));       v.set(i,v.get(v.size() - i));
      v.set(v.size() - i,temp);           v.set(v.size() - i,temp);
    }                                   }
  }                                   }
}                                   }
```

| (a) | (b) |

Fig. 11. Example program that illustrates the need for context-sensitive analysis

tors. Conceptually, this is equivalent to analyzing a transformed version of the program that contains two clones of the `reverse()` method, one of which is called from `intUse()`, the other from `floatUse()`. The two contexts of `reverse` would receive different type estimates for parameter `v`, and our code transformation could exploit this information by transforming `reverse()` into a generic method, and remove both casts. This result is shown in Figure 11(b).

We implemented a context-sensitive version of the previously presented algorithm, in which we used a low-cost variant of Agesen's Cartesian Product Algorithm [1, 2] to determine when different contexts should be created for a method, and reported the results in a previous technical report [19]. To our surprise, we could not find any non-synthetic benchmarks where the use of context-sensitive analysis resulted in the removal of additional casts. We believe that there are two major reasons why context-sensitive analysis was not useful. The first is that the standard libraries already provide a rich set of functionality, and there is relatively little need for writing additional helper methods. Second, the relatively few applications that do define helper methods that operate on collections tend to use these methods monomorphically. An investigation of larger applications might turn up more opportunities for context-sensitive analysis, but it is our conjecture that there will be relatively few such opportunities.

10   Related Work

The work most closely related to ours is that by Donovan et al. [8], who also designed and implemented a refactoring for migrating an application to a generic version of a class library that it uses. Like us, Donovan et al. evaluate their algorithm by inferring generic types for occurrences of the standard collections in a set of Java benchmarks, and measure their success in terms of the number of casts that can be removed. There are a number of significant differences between the two approaches.

First, the approach by Donovan et al. relies on a context-sensitive pointer analysis[16] based on [24, 1] to determine the types stored in each allocation site for a generic library class. Moreover, Donovan et al. create "guarded" constraints that may or may not be applied to the type constraint system depending on the rawness of a particular declaration, and their solving algorithm may require (limited) backtracking if such a rawness decision leads to a contradiction later on. Our approach is simpler because it requires neither context-sensitive analysis nor backtracking, and therefore has greater potential for scaling to large applications. The differences in observed running times seem to bear this out (Donovan et al. report a running time of 462 seconds on the ~27 KLOC *HTMLParser* using a 3GHz Pentium 4 with 200Mb heap, while our tool requires 113.9 seconds on a ~90 KLOC program using a 1.6GHz Pentium M using 512Mb heap).

Second, there are several differences in the kinds of source transformations allowed in the two works: (i) Donovan et al. restrict themselves to transformations that do not affect the erasure of a class, while our approach allows the modification of declarations, (ii) Donovan's work was done prior to the release of Java 1.5 and their refactoring tool conforms to an earlier specification of Java generics, which does not contain wildcard types and which allows arrays of generic types, and (iii) our method is capable of inferring precise generic supertypes for subtypes of generic library classes that are defined in application code (see, e.g., Figure 2 in which we infer that class `MyIterator` extends `Iterator<String>`). Third, our tool is more practical because it is fully integrated in a popular integrated development environment.

For a more concrete comparison, we manually inspected the source generated by both tools for 5 of the 7 benchmarks analyzed in [8]: *JLex*, *JavaCup*, *JUnit*, *V_poker* and *TelnetD*. A head-to-head comparison on *ANTLR* and *HTMLParser* was impossible due to differences in the experimental approach taken[17].

In most cases, our tool was able to remove the same or a higher number of generics-related casts than did Donovan's, in a small fraction of the time. The differences in casts removed derive from several distinct causes. First, our tool's ability to infer type parameters for user-defined subtypes of parametric types permits the removal of additional casts (e.g., 6 additional casts could be removed in *V_poker* in clients of a local class extending `Hashtable`). Second, Donovan's tool was implemented before the final Java 1.5 specification was available and conforms to an early draft, in which parameterized types were permitted to be stored in arrays; the final specification, however, requires that such generic types be left raw. As a result, Donovan's tool infers non-raw types for certain containers in *JLex* that our tool (correctly) leaves raw, preventing the

---

[16] The context-sensitive variant of our algorithm [19] discussed in Section 9 is also based on the Cartesian Product Algorithm, but it uses context-sensitivity for a different purpose, namely to identify when it is useful to create generic methods.

[17] Donovan et al. identified classes in these benchmarks that could be made generic, manually rewrote them accordingly, and treated them as part of the libraries. As a result, the number of removed casts that they report cannot be directly compared to ours, as it includes casts rendered redundant by the generics that they manually introduced.

removal of certain casts. Third, our algorithm models `Object.clone()` so that type parameter information is not lost across the call boundary. As a result, our tool removes all 24 generics-related casts from *JUnit*, while Donovan's tool only removes 16.

Von Dincklage and Diwan [23] address the problems of converting non-generic Java classes to use generics (parameterization) and updating non-generic usages of generic classes (instantiation). Their approach, like ours, is based on constraints. Von Dincklage's tool employs a suite of heuristics that resulted in the successful parameterization of several classes from the Java standard collections. However, the code of those classes had to be manually modified to eliminate unhandled language constructs before the tool could be applied. The tool's correctness is based on several unsound assumptions (e.g., public fields are assumed not to be accessed from outside their class, and the type of the argument to `equals` is assumed to be identical to the receiver's type), and it can alter program behavior by modifying virtual method dispatch due to changed overriding relationships between methods. No results are given about how successful the tool is in instantiating non-generic classes with generic information.

The problem of introducing generic types into a program to broaden its use has been approached before by several researchers. Siff and Reps [18] focused on translating C functions into C++ function templates by using type inference to detect latent polymorphism. In this work, opportunities for introducing polymorphism stem from operator overloading, references to constants that can be wrapped by constructor calls, and from structure subtyping. Duggan [9] gives an algorithm (not implemented) for genericizing classes in a small Java-like language into a particular polymorphic variant of that language. This language predated the Java 1.5 generics standard by several years and differs in a nontrivial number of respects. Duggan does not address the problem of migrating non-generic code to use generics. The programming environments CodeGuide [6] and IntelliJ IDEA [12] provide "Generify" refactorings that are similar in spirit to ours. We are not aware of the details of these implementations, nor of the quality of their results.

11   Conclusions and Future Work

We have presented a refactoring that assists programmers with the adoption of a generic version of an existing class library. The method infers actual type parameters for declarations and allocation sites that refer to generic library classes using an existing framework of type constraints. We implemented this refactoring in Eclipse, and evaluated the work by migrating a number of moderate-sized Java applications that use the Java collections framework to Java 1.5's generic collection classes. We found that, on average, 48.6% of the casts related to the use of collections can be removed, and that 91.2% of the unchecked warnings are eliminated. Our approach distinguishes itself from the state-of-the-art [8] by being more scalable and by its ability to accommodate user-defined subtypes of generic library classes. The "Infer Generic Type Arguments" in the forthcoming Eclipse 3.1 release is largely based on the concepts presented in this paper, and has adopted important parts of our implementation.

Plans for future work include the inference of wildcard types. As indicated in Section 8.3, doing so will help remove additional casts and unchecked warnings.

Acknowledgments

We are grateful to Alan Donovan and Michael Ernst for many useful discussions about comparisons between our two algorithms, and for sharing information about the benchmarks used in [8]. The anonymous ECOOP reviewers, Michael Ernst, and Bartek Klin provided many helpful comments and suggestions.

References

1. AGESEN, O. The cartesian product algorithm: Simple and precise type inference of parametric polymorphism. In *Proc. of ECOOP* (1995), pp. 2–26.
2. AGESEN, O. *Concrete Type Inference: Delivering Object-Oriented Applications.* PhD thesis, Stanford University, December 1995.
3. BÄUMER, D., GAMMA, E., AND KIEŻUN, A. Integrating refactoring support into a Java development tool. In *OOPSLA'01 Companion* (October 2001).
4. BRACHA, G., COHEN, N., KEMPER, C., ODERSKY, M., STOUTAMIRE, D., THORUP, K., AND WADLER, P. Adding generics to the Java programming language, final release. Tech. rep., Java Community Process JSR-000014, September 2004.
5. BRACHA, G., ODERSKY, M., STOUTAMIRE, D., AND WADLER, P. Making the future safe for the past: Adding genericity to the Java programming language. In *Proc. of OOPSLA* (1998), pp. 183–200.
6. Omnicore codeguide. http://www.omnicore.com/codeguide.htm.
7. DE SUTTER, B., TIP, F., AND DOLBY, J. Customization of Java library classes using type constraints and profile information. In *Proc. of ECOOP* (2004), pp. 585–610.
8. DONOVAN, A., KIEŻUN, A., TSCHANTZ, M., AND ERNST, M. Converting Java programs to use generic libraries. In *Proc. of OOPSLA* (Vancouver, BC, Canada, 2004), pp. 15–34.
9. DUGGAN, D. Modular type-based reverse engineering of parameterized types in Java code. In *Proc. of OOPSLA* (1999), pp. 97–113.
10. FOWLER, M. *Refactoring. Improving the Design of Existing Code.* Addison-Wesley, 1999.
11. GOSLING, J., JOY, B., STEELE, G., AND BRACHA, G. *The Java Language Specification (3rd Edition).* Addison-Wesley, 2000.
12. JetBrains IntelliJ IDEA. http://www.intellij.com/idea/.
13. IGARASHI, A., PIERCE, B. C., AND WADLER, P. Featherweight Java: a minimal core calculus for Java and GJ. *ACM TOPLAS 23*, 3 (2001), 396–450.
14. LANGER, A., AND KREFT, K. Arrays in Java Generics. Manuscript http://www.langer.camelot.de.
15. MUNSIL, W. Case study: Converting to Java 1.5 type-safe collections. *Journal of Object Technology 3*, 8 (2004), 7–14.
16. ODERSKY, M., AND WADLER, P. Pizza into Java: Translating theory into practice. In *Proc. of POPL* (1997), pp. 146–159.
17. PALSBERG, J., AND SCHWARTZBACH, M. *Object-Oriented Type Systems.* John Wiley & Sons, 1993.
18. SIFF, M., AND REPS, T. W. Program generalization for software reuse: From C to C++. In *Foundations of Software Engineering* (1996), pp. 135–146.
19. TIP, F., FUHRER, R., DOLBY, J., AND KIEŻUN, A. Refactoring techniques for migrating applications to generic Java container classes. Tech. Rep. Research Report RC 23238, IBM Research, June 2004.
20. TIP, F., KIEŻUN, A., AND BÄUMER, D. Refactoring for generalization using type constraints. In *Proc. of OOPSLA* (Anaheim, CA, 2003), pp. 13–26.

21. TORGERSEN, M., HANSEN, C. P., ERNST, E., VON DER AHÉ, P., BRACHA, G., AND GAFTER, N. M. Adding wildcards to the Java programming language. In *Proc. of ACM Symposium on Applied Computing (SAC)* (Nicosia, Cyprus, 2004), pp. 1289–1296.

22. VITEK, J., HORSPOOL, R. N., AND KRALL, A. Efficient type inclusion tests. In *Proc. of OOPSLA* (1997), pp. 142–157. *SIGPLAN Notices* 32(10).

23. VON DINCKLAGE, D., AND DIWAN, A. Converting Java classes to use generics. In *Proc. of OOPSLA* (Vancouver, BC, Canada, 2004), pp. 1–14.

24. WANG, T., AND SMITH, S. Precise constraint-based type inference for Java. In *Proc. of ECOOP* (2001), pp. 99–117.

Sharing the Runtime Representation of Classes Across Class Loaders

L•••n• D•yn•• •n• • ••••o•• • ••j•ow••i

Sun Microsystems Laboratories
{Laurent.Daynes, Grzegorz.Czajkowski}@sun.com

Abstract. One of the most distinctive features of the Java^{TM} programming language is the ability to specify class loading policies. Despite the popularity of class loaders, little has been done to reduce the cost associated with defining the same class by multiple loaders. In particular, implementations of the Java virtual machine (JVM^{TM}) create a complete runtime representation of each class regardless of how many class loaders already define the same class. This lack of sharing leads to poor memory utilization and to replicated run-time work. Recent efforts achieve some degree of sharing only when dynamic binding behaves predictably across loaders. This limits sharing to class loaders whose behavior is fully controlled by the JVM. As a result applications that implement their own class loading policies cannot enjoy the benefit of sharing.

We present a novel technique for sharing the runtime representation of classes (including bytecodes and, under some conditions, compiled code) across arbitrary user-defined class loaders. We describe how our approach is applied to the multi-tasking virtual machine (MVM). The new multi-tasking virtual machine retains the fast start-up time of the original MVM while extending the scope of footprint savings to applications that exploit user-defined class loaders.

1 Introduction

• n• o• ••• • o•• • i••in••iv• •••••••• o• ••• J•v•^{TM} ••o•••• • in• l•n••••• [10] i• ••• •• ili•y •o •••n• •l••• lo••in• • oli•i•• [13]. • l••• lo••••• ••• •x• loi••• in • wi•• ••n•• o• ••• li••ion•, •••• •• •••i••in• •nvi•on• •n••, ID•• •, ••n•i• • •o•• inj•••ion •ool•, ••••••-o•i•n••• ••o•••• • in• •l•••o•• •, w•• ••ow••••, •••vl•• •n•in••, •n• •••li••ion •••v•••.

• l••• lo••••• ••• • o••l•• •o• ••v•••l ••••on•. T••y ••ovi•• •••••••••• n•• ••- •••••, w•i•• •llow• • ••o•••• •o lin• •o• •on•n•• ••••••l••• o• w••••••• •••y in•l••• • iff•••n• v•••ion• o• ••• ••• • •l••••• o• •iff•••n• •l••••• wi•• ••• •••• • n•• •. T•i• •••••••• •n••l••••• i• •l•• •n••ion o• •o•• o•i•ol••ion, w•••• •••••• •• lly •••••••• •o••w••• • o••l•• ••n •• lo•••• • •l•i•l• •i• •• wi••o•• in••••••in• wi•• on• •no••••• [•]. • l••• lo••••• •l•o •iv• ••o•••• • •on••ol ov•• ••• lo•••ion w••••• •l•••••• ••• lo••••• ••o• , •n• •n o••o•••ni•y •o •••n••••••n•ly •n••n•• •• i••-•••••y •o•• • y ••ovi• in• • •••• ni•• • •o• i•• in••••••••ion •n• • o•i•••••ion

(vi• • y•••o•• •••n••o•• ••ion•) •••o•• i• i• lin••• wi•• ••• •••• o• ••• • •n••••
•x•••ion •nvi•on• •n•.

U•in• •l••• lo••••• •o• •• ••• •o••, •ow•v••. JVM i• • l•• •n••ion• •y• i••lly
•••li••••• ••• •n•i•• •• n•i• • •••••••n••ion o• • •l••• in • •• o•y •o• •••• •l•••
lo••••• •••• ••• n•• ••• •l•••[1]. D••nin• • •l••• • •l•i•l• •i• •• •l•o •••li•••••
••• •ffo•• •o •••••• •n o••i• i••• •• n•i• • •••••••n••ion, •y •••••in• •l••• •l•
•••in•, •on••••ion o• • •in-• •• o•y •••• •••••••••, •y•••o•• v••i•••ion,
(o•• •ion•l) •y•••o••• ••i•••nin•, •••ol••ion o• •on•••n••, •n• i••n•i•••ion •n•
•••o• • il••ion o• •••••n•ly •••• • •••o••.

T•• ••• o• ••l•••ion ••l••ion•• i• •••w••n •l••• lo•••••, w••• on• •l•••
lo••••• ••n ••l•••••• ••• ••• ni•ion o•• •l••• •o •no••••, ••l•• •o li• i• •••••• ••o•-
l•• • •••• ••n •••i•ly •••o• • •••o• ••on• •• ••• •o• •l•xi•y o• ••• ••l•••ion
••l••ion•• i•• in••••••••. B••i•••, no• •ll •••• o• •l••• lo••••• ••n •• •••o• • o-
••••• wi•• ••l•••ion. Fo• •x•• •l•, ••l•••ion i• in•••••••• w••n • •l•i•l• in-
•••n••• o• ••• ••• • •o••w••• •o• • •on•n• • • ••• •• lo••••• •n• i•ol•••• ••o• on•
•no••••.

T•• ••o•• o• ••••-••• n•• •l••• lo•••••• i• • •on•••••n•• o• ••• in••ili•y o•
••••••n• JVM i• •l•• •n••ion• •o ••••• ••• • •in-• •• o•y ••••••n••ion o• •
•l••• •••w••n • •l•i•l• ••• ni•ion• o• ••••• •l•••. JVM• •y•i••lly •on•••••• •••
•x•••••l• i• ••• o• ••o•••• •• •• n•i• • in ••v•••l in•••• •n••l •••••: •••• •y
lo••in• •l••• •l•• ••o• lo••ion• •••i••• •y ••i• lo••••• •n• ••il•in• •o•••-
•• on•in• • •in • •• o•y ••••••n••ion•, •••n •y lin•in• •••• •o o•••• •l•••••
•• •y• •oli• ••••••n••• ••• •n•o• n••••• •••in• •••o• •x•••ion, •n• •v•n•••lly
•y •o• •ilin• •••o•• •n••-••i•i••l • •••o••. T•i• •vol••ion o• • ••o•••• i• •••
i• • •on•••••n•• o• •yn•• i• •in•in• •n• o• ••• ••• o• •n •••• i••••••-n•••l
•o•• •• o• •l••• •l••, •• •••• i••• •y ••• •••i•••ion o• ••• J•v• ••o•••• • in•
l•n••••• [10] (JLS). Bo•• • ••• ••• ••il•in• o• ••••••l• i• ••• •• ••n•i• • •i-
•••l• •n• •••v•n• •••lyin• w•ll-••••li•••• •••••• li•••y •••• ni•••• •••• •o•
l••• •yn•• i• ••o•••• • in• l•n••••• (•.•. [3]).

S•v•••l ••••n• •ffo••• ••v• •••i•v•• •o• • •••••• o• •••in• o• ••• •• n•i• •
••••••••n••ion o• •l••••• •••w••n •x•••in• ••o•••• • [5, 6, 19, •]. How•v••, •••y
••n only •o •o w••n •yn•• i• •in•in• ••• • •••• i•••• l• •••• vio• •••o• lo••••,
•.•., w••n • •y• •oli• lin• ••o• • •l••• A •o • •l••• B i• •••••n•••• •o •••olv•
i••n•i••lly •••o• •ll •l••• lo•••••. T•••, •••• in• i• only •••• o•••• •o• •• o••
•l••• lo••••• w•o•• ••••vio• i• •• lly •on••oll•• •y ••• JVM. S•••in• i• no•
••••o•••• w••n •l••••• ••• ••• n•• •y ••••-••• n•• lo•••••. Sy•••• • ••••• on
•••i• •o• •il••ion (•.•., [•0]) •••• •i• il•• i••••• (••• S••ion 6).

T•i• •••••• ••••n•• • nov•l •••• ni••• •o• ••••in• ••• •• n•i• • ••••••••n••ion
o• •l•••••• •••w••n • •l•i•l• •••i•••y •••nin• •l••• lo•••••, •n• ••••••i••• i••
••• li•••ion •o ••• M•l•i-T••in• Vi•••l M•••in• (o• MVM) [5]. T•i• n•w i• -
•l•• •n••ion o• MVM i• ••ll•• •••••••••• • LSVM (*Class Loader Sharing Virtual
Machine*). • LSVM i• • •i•ni••n• •••• •o•w••• in ••• •••• nolo•y o• •••n••••-

---

[1] The character strings representing symbols are usually shared across representations
of all classes though.

•n• •••in• o• •••• l•n••••• • •••-•••, •n• i• ••ov•• on MVM •y ••in•in• •••
••n•••• o• •••in• •o ••••-••n•• •l••• lo•••••.

• LSVM' ••••in• o• ••• ••n•i• • •••••••n••ion o• • •l••• i• o•••o•on•l •o
•••••in• •y ••l•••ion. S•••in• •y ••l•••ion • ••••• • •l••• •y•• vi•i•l• •o • •l-
•i•l• lo••••• •n• ••• •n i• •••• on ••o•••• ••• •n•i••, w•il• •••in• o• ••
•• n•i• • •••••••n••ion o• •l••••• i• •••n••••n•ly •n• •••o• ••i••lly •••o•• ••
•y ••• JVM, ••• no i• •••• on ••o•••• •••vio•, •n• •o•• no• viol••• o• i• ••••
•y•• ••••y.

In • LSVM, ••••in• i• •••i•v•• •y ••li••in• ••• ••n•i• • •••••••n••ion o•
• •l••• in•o lo••••-•••n••n• •n• lo••••-in•••n••n• •••••, •n• •y • ••in•
•y•••o•• in•••••••••ion *loader re-entrant* •o •••• ••• •y•••o••• o•• •••o•• •••
••••••l• •••o••• • •l•i•l• lo•••••. T•• lo••••-•••n••n• •••• i• •••li••••• •o• •••••
lo•••• •••• ••• n•• ••• •l•••. • l••••• lo•••• •y ••• •oo•••••• lo•••• •••• •••••••
••••i•lly in o•••• •o •x• loi• ••• ••••i••••ili•y o• •y• •oli• lin• •••ol••ion •n•
•on••••n•ly •o • •xi• i•• •••••in•.

A •on••••n•• o•••••• • •••i•n i• •••• •o• • o•••• •l••• lo••in• •n• ••n-•i• •
•o• • il••ion ffo•• i• •••••• •••o•• • •l•i•l• •l••• lo•••••. In •••i••l••, •l••• •l•
•••••in•, •n• • o•• o• ••• ••il•in• o• • • •in-• •• o•y ••n•i• • •••••••n••ion o•
••• •l••• i• •on• only on••. Po•••••o••••in• o••y•••o••• ••••• • •y ••••• •l••• ••
lin• •i• • i• •l•o • on• on••.

• LSVM' •yn•• i• •o• •il•• •ix•• •wo •••••••i•• •o •••••••• ••• ov••••••
o• •yn•• i• •o• •il••ion. W••n•v•• •o••i•l•, ••• •o• •il•• ••••• ••• •o •••••
•o• •il•• •o•••••o•• • •l•i•l• ••• nin• lo•••••. W••n •••in• i• no• •o••i•l•, •••
•o• •il•• •on•••••••• • n•w v••ion o• ••• •o• •il•• •o••. •v•n in ••i• •i•••ion
o••o•••ni•i•• •o• •o• •il••ion •i• • ••vin• ••i••: only i• ••• • •••o• ••• no•
•••n •o• •il•• •• •ll i• i• •o• •il•• ••o• i•• •y•••o••. • •••••wi••, in••••• o•
•••o• •ilin• ••• • •••o•, ••• •o• •il•• •lon•• ••• •o• •il•• •o•• •n• • o•i•• i••
lo••••-•••n••n• •••••.

T•• •••• o••• i• ••••• i• o•••ni••• ••ollow•. S••ion • ••••i••• ••in•i•l•• •o•
•••in• ••w••n • •l•i•l• lo•••••. S••ion 3 ••••il• • ••o•o•y•• i• •l•• •n••ion
o•• LSVM ••••• on MVM, w•i•• in ••n •x••n• ••• J•v• Ho•S• o•*TM* vi•••l
• ••• in• [16] (••••••• •o •• HSVM). S••ion • •i•••••• •ow •yn•• i• •o• •il•-
•ion• •••• ••v•n•••• o• •••in• •••o•• lo•••••. S••ion 5 ••• o••• • ••• n•i••iv•
••••••• •n• o• ••• i• •••• o• •••in• on ••• •••••o•• •n•• •n• • •• o•y •oo••in•
o• ••o••••• • w•i••n in ••• J•v• ••o•••• • in• l•n••••• (o• *Java program•*). • •-
l•••• wo•• i• •i••••••• in S••ion 6. S••ion • •••• • ••i••• ••• •on••i••ion• o•
•• i• wo••.

2   Design Overview

S••in• •n •l•• •n• o•••• •• n•i• • •••••••n••ion o•• •l••• •••w••n •l••• lo•••••
i• •o••i•l• w••n ••• •l•• •n• i• in•••n••n• o• i•• ••• nin• lo•••••. Lo•••• •••n-
••n•i•• ••i•• ••o• •y• oli• lin•• •o o•••• •l•••••, w•i•• • •y •••olv• •• ••n•i• •
•o •iff••n• •l•• •••ni•ion• ••o• on• lo•••• •o •no•••, •n• ••o• •••••••n••
••o• • •l•••'• ••n•i• • •••••••n••ion •o •••• ••• •••• •••iv•• •o • lo••••, ••••

•• in•••n••• o• java.lang.Class o• ••••i• v••i••l••. A• •••• •i•••, • •i•ni••n• •• o•n• o•••• •• n•i• •••••••••n••ion o•• •l••••••••••• in•••• n•• n• o•••• lo•••• •••• ••• n•• i•. In ••••i••l••, i• •• o•l• •• • o••i•l• •o ••••• •••o•• •wo lo•••••, •••• ••• nin• • •l••• ••••i•• • •y ••• ••• • •l••• •l•, ••• • •y•••o••• o• ••••• •l•••, ••• •on•••n• •••• o• i•• •on•••n• • ool (i.•., ••• •••• •••• ••• n n n•v•• •••olv• •o • i- •••n• o•j••••••• n•i• •, •••• •• •on•••n• v•l•••), •n• • •••-•••• ••••i• in• ••• •l••• i•••l• (•.•., ••• l•• •ol• in• ••••i••ion o• •l••, • •••o••, •n• •x•••••ion•).

How•v••, ••v•••l o•••••l•• • ••• •••••in• •••o•• • •l•i•l• lo••••• •i• ••l•. Fi•••, lo••••• • •y •••olv• ••• ••••• •l••• o• ••• ••• • •l••• •iff•••n•ly. T•i• • •y ••••l• in •iff•••n• o•j••• l•yo••• (•in•• on• ••••••-•l••• • •y •••l••• • o•• ••l•• •••n ••• o••••, •n• o• •iff•••n• •y•••), •n• •iff•••n• vi•••••l •••l•• (•in•• on• ••••••-•l••• • •y •••l••• • •iff•••n• n• • ••• o• • •••o••, wi•• •iff•••n• •i- n••••••, •n• •iff•••n• • •••o•• • •y •• ov•••i••n). S••on•, in•••••••• o•••n •x•loi• •••olv•• •y• •oli• lin•• •o ••w•i•• •y•••o••• in•o ••••• v••ion• •••• n••• no• •••• w•••••• lin•• •• o•l• •• •••olv•• o• w••••• •l••••• •• o•l• •• ini•i•li•••. S••• *quickened* •y•••o••• •••o• •, in •ff•••, lo•••-•••••n•n•. T•• • yn•• i• •o• •il•• •l•o •x•loi• in•o•• ••ion •••iv•• ••o• •••olv•• •y• •oli• lin•• •n• • ••••• •o• •il•• •o•• lo••••• ••n••n•. T•••• o•••••l•• •••••n •o••••••• •••• •o •on•••i•• ••• • •••• in••i•ion ••••• • •i•ni••n• •• o•n• o• • •••-•••• ••n •• •••••••• •••o•• lo••••••.

• •••••i•n ov•••o• •• ••••• ••o•l•• ••• •ollow•. Fi•••, ••••in• i• •llow•• only i• •o• • •on• i•ion• on in••i••n•• ••• • ••, •o •• •o •voi• •••lin• wi•• ••••• w•••• o•j••• l•yo••• •n• vi•••••l •••l•• wo•l• •• •iff•••n•. S••on•, ••• in••••••••ion o• •y•••o••• i• • ••• lo•••• ••-•n•••n• •y ••-o•••ni•in• ••• ••n•i• • •••••••••n••ion o••l••••• •o ••• •o •• •i•n•ly ••••• •••• lo••••'• ••iv•• ••••, •n• •y ••• in• *barriers* •o •••••n••• •••• lin• •••ol••ion• •n• •l••• ini•i•li••ion• ••• •••o•• •• •• on •••i• •••• ••• •y • lo••••. T•i••, ••• •yn•• i• •o• •il•• • •in••in• in•o•- • ••ion •o ••l• •••••• in• i• n••iv• •o•• ••n •• ••••• •••w••n lo••••, •n• i• no•, •o ••l• ••il• • n•w v••ion o• •o• •il•• •o•• wi••o•• ••yin• ••• •o•• o•• •• ll-•lown •o• •il••ion ••o• ••• • •••o•'• • •y•••o•••.

2.1   Terminology and Notation

W• ••• ••• •••• inolo•y •n• no•••ion o• [13] •o •••••i• ••l••ion• ••w••n •l••••• •n• •l••• lo•••••. N•• •ly, • •l••• •y•• i• ••no••• •• $< C, L_d >^{L_i}$, w•••• C ••no••• ••• n•• • o• ••• •l•••, L_d ••no••• ••• •l•••'• *defining* lo•••, •n• L_i ••no••• i•• *initiating* lo••••. T•• ini•i••in• lo•••• o• • •l••• (i.•., ••• lo•••• invo••• •o lo•• ••• •l•••) i• no• n•••••••ily ••• lo•••• •••• ••• n•• ••• •l•••, ••• •o ••• API o• •l••• lo•••••• •••• •n••l•• on• lo•••• •o ••l••••• ••• • ••• ni•ion o•• •l••• •o •no••••. T•• •i• •li••• no•••ion $< C, L_d >$ i• ••• w••n ••• ini•i•••in• lo•••• o• • •l••• i• no• ••l•v•n•. Si• il••ly, C^{L_i} ••no••• • •i•••••ion w••n ••• •••nin• lo•••• i• no• ••l•v•n•. By ••• ni•ion $< C, L_1 > = < C, L_2 > \Rightarrow L_1 = L_2$.

W• •x••n• ••i• no•••ion wi•• ••• • ~ o• •••••o• •o ••no•• ••••• •wo •l••• •y•• •••i••y ••• *same sharing conditions* (••• S••••ion •.•) •n• •• n ••••••o•• ••••• ••••i• ••n•i• • •••••••••n••ion. By ••• ni•ion $< C, L_1 > ~ < C, L_2 > \Rightarrow < C, L_1 > \neq < C, L_2 >$ (•• i• •••••i••ion •i• •li••• •i•••••ion •••• •ollow•). Fo• •onv•ni•n••, w•

in••o•••• ••• •ollowin• no•••ion: $< C, L_1 > \;\cong\; < C, L_2 > $ •o • •no•• $< C, L_1 > \sim <$
$C, L_2 > \lor < C, L_1 > = < C, L_2 >$.

2.2   Sharing Conditions

L•• •• •on•i••• •wo •i••in•• lo••••• L_1 •n• L_2, •••• •••nin• • •l••• C. T••
•on•i•ion• •••• •n••l• $< C, L_1 > \sim < C, L_2 >$, •••• i•, ••• •••in• o••• •• •n•i• •
••• ••••n••ion• o• $< C, L_1 > $ •n• $< C, L_2 >$, ••• ••• n•• ••low.

T•• •••• •on•i•ion •o• $< C, L_1 > \sim < C, L_2 >$ i• •••• ••• •l••• •l•• •••• i•-
••• •o ••• JVM •y L_1 •n• L_2 • ••• •• i• •n•i••l. Fo• •i• •li•i•y, •wo •l••• •l••
(•i••• •••i•in• on • •i•• o• •yn•• i••lly ••n•••••) ••• •on•i•••• i• •n•i••l i•
••• •l••••• ••• •y••-•••-•y•• ••••l, •l••o••• ••i• i• • ••i•ly •o•••• • ••• o•• •o•
•••••• inin• i• •wo •l••• •l•• •n•o••• ••• ••• • •l••• •••ni•ion. A • o•• ••••i••
i• •l•• •n••ion wo•l• ••••i•• •••in• ••• •l••• •l•• •n• •••••• inin• •••iv•-
l•n•• o••• •••l•••ion•. T•i• •••o••• i• •••••••n•i•lly • o•• •x••n•iv• •n•, in
•••••i••, i• •nli••ly •o •• • •••• • o•• •ff••iv•.

T•• •••on• •on•i•ion ••••i••• ••• ••• ••• ••••••-•l••••• S^{L_1}, S^{L_2} o• $< C, L_1 >$
•n• $< C, L_2 >$ •••• •••iv•ly ••• •• •••• •••• $S^{L_1} \cong S^{L_2}$.

T•• ••i•• •on•i•ion i• •••• $< C, L_1 > $ •n• $< C, L_2 >$ ••v• ••• ••• • •••••••••
• ••• o••. No•• •••• ••i• ••o••• •y •ol• i• ••• •wo ••••in• •on•i•ion• •• ov• •••
•••i••• •n• i• C •o•• no• i• •l•• •n• •ny in••••••. T•• ••i•• •on•i•ion i•
•••• i••lly •i•••••• ••• •l••••• •••• i• •l•• •n• in••••••. I• ••••n•••• •••• •ll
•l••••• •••• ••••• ••i• ••n•i• • •••••••n••ion ••v• ••• ••• • *unimplemented*
method•, •••• i•, • •••o••••••••• no••• n•• •y ••• •l••• •• y•• ••• •••l•••• in
•n in••••••. Fo• •x•• •l•, l•• •• •on•i••• •l••• C •••• i• •l•• •n•• •n in••••••
I •••• •••l•••• • •in•l• • •••o• m. M•••o• m i• •ni• •l•• •n••• i• n•i•••• C
no• •ny o• i•• •••••-•l•••• i• •l•• •n• m. In ••i• ••••, m • ••• •• •••••••• ••• •
••• li• •••••••• • •••o• o• C.

T•• ••••in• •on•i•ion• •••••n••• ••v•••l ••o•••i•• •••• •i• •li•y •••in•.
Fi•••, •••y ••••n••• •••• $< C, L_1 > $ •n• $< C, L_2 >$ ••v• ••• ••• • n•• ••• o•
••••i• v•i••l••, •••• ••i• •••••••iv• in••n••• ••v• ••• ••• • n•• ••• o• ••l••
(w• •••• •i•••ly ••n•• •y ••• •l•• o• in••i•••), •n• •••••l• wi•• ••• ••• •
n•• • ••v• ••• ••• • •i•n••• •n• will •• •• ••• ••• • off•••. T•i• ••o•••y
•llow• ••• JVM •o l•y o•• i• •n•i••lly ••• in••n••• o• •l••••• w•o•• ••n•i• •
•••••••n••ion i• ••••••, •o ••••• ••••n•• • ••• •••• •o• ••••••• •oll••ion•,
•n• •o ••••• ••• ••••i•ion• o• ••l••. S••on•, ••• •••in• •on•i•ion• ••••n•••
•••• ••• • •••o•• o• $< C, L_1 > $ •n• $< C, L_2 >$, w• •••• •••l•••• •i•••ly •y
•••• •l•••• o• in••i•••, ••v• ••• ••• • n•• •, •i•n••••, •••••ion l•v•l, •n•
•y•••o•••, •n• •••• •••y ••n •• •••i•n•• ••• ••• • in••x in • vi•••l • •••o•
•••l• (••• J•v• ••o•••• • in• l•n••••• in••i•n•• • o••l •n••l•• •••l•-••iv•n
i• •l•• •n••ion o• vi•••l • •••o• •i•••••).

Al••o••• ••• ••••in• •on•i•ion• •••••n••• •••• $< C, L_1 > $ •n• $< C, L_2 >$
i• •l•• •n• ••• ••• • n•• ••• o• in••••••, •n• ••v• ••• ••• • ni• •l•• •n•••
• •••o••, ••y •o no• • •n•••• •••• ••••• in••••••• •••l••• •x••ly ••• ••• •
• •••o••. • on•i••• ••• •x•• •l• in Fi•••• 1. In ••i• ••••, ••• ••••in• •on•i•ion•
•llow ••• ••n•i• • •••••••n••ion o• C •o •• •••••• •••o•• L_1 •n• L_2, •l••o•••
•••y i• •l•• •n• •iff•••n• in••••••••.

```
interface A { // In L₁          interface A { // In L₂
    int foo(int i);                 Integer foo(Integer i);
    long foo(long l);               void bar(int i);
    void bar(int i);
}                               }
abstract class C implements A { // Defined by both L₁ and L₂
    int foo(int i){...}
    Integer foo(Integer i){...}
    long foo(long l){...}
} // bar is the only unimplemented method in both L₁ and L₂
```

Fig. 1. The sharing conditions can be satisfied despite different interface definitions

3   The Design of CLSVM

• LSVM •x••n•• MVM, ••• • •l•i-•••, • •l•i-••••in• vi•••l • ••• in• [5,•] wi••
••• •• ili•y •o •••••• • •••-•••• •••o•• ••••-••• n•• •l••• lo•••••. T•• •••• o• ••••
•••i•n o• MVM ••l•v•n• •o • LSVM ••• ••i•fly ••vi•w•• •••o•• •i••••in• •••
•••••l •••i•n o•• • LSVM.

3.1   Background on MVM

MVM i•• •n i• •l•• •n•••ion o•••• JVM •••• •o-lo••••• ••• •x•••ion o•• •l•i•l•
••o••••• • in • •in•l• o•••••in• •y•••• ••o•••••. ••••• ••o•••• •x•••ion i•••••i••
o•••y •n isolate [11]. I•ol•••• ••ovi•• • ••o•••• wi•• ••• ill••ion o•• •••n• •lon•
JVM: ••o•••• •••y• ••• ••• • ••••vio• •• i•••y w••• •• nnin• on • JVM o••••i•
own. •••• i•ol••• ••• i•• own ••i• o••i•l lo•••• •n• •i•••••y o• •l••• lo•••••.
No ••••in• o• o• j•••• ••n •••• •l••• •••w••n i•ol••••• •n• ••• JVM ••••••••••
•••in•• • o•• •y••• o• in••••-i•ol••• in•••••••n••.

   MVM •••••••n•i•lly ••••••• ••• •oo••in• o• ••o•••• • •y i• •l•• •n•in• •
•o•• o•••••in• •••• w• ••ll task re-entrance. T•• ••-•n•••n•• i• ••••o•••• only
•o• •l•••• ••• n•• •y •l••• lo•••• w•o•• •••••vio• i• •• lly •on••oll•• • y MVM,
•••• i•, ••• primordial •n• system lo•••• o• •••• i•ol•••.

   T•• ••i• o•• i•l lo•••• i• ••••i•l •l••• lo•••• ••••• •oo•••••• ••• •l••• lo••-
in• • ••••ni•• . I• i• •••• •o lo•• ••• base •l••••• •••• ••• in•i• •••ly •••o•i••••
wi•• • JVM i• •l•• •n•••ion •n• ••• ••••n•i•l •o i•• •• n••ionin.• (•••• •• •l••••
o• ••• java.* •••••••). T•• •y•••• lo•••• i• ••• lo•••• •••••• ••• n•• ••• • •in
•l••• o• ••o•••• . I• •y•i••lly o••in• •l••• •l•• ••o• ••• lo••l •l• •y•••• ••• •
•x• lo••ion ••••i•• •••o•••• ••••••-•. MVM •o•••• ••i• lo••ion •o •• •••
••• • •o• •ll ••o•••• • i•• x••••••, •n• •••• i••• ••••• •l•••• •l•• ••o••• •••• ••• •in
• n••• n••• •o• ••• •••••ion o• i•• •x••••ion. T•• •y•••• lo•••• •••y•• •l••• lo••-
in• •••••••• •y •••• •l•••in• •••• •o ••• ••i• o••i•l lo••••, •n• only ••• n••
•l•••• •••• ••• ••i• o••i•l lo•••• ••il•• •o •••n•. T•i• ••••vio• i• ••••i•i•l•,
•n• • •l••• lo•••• •y • ••i• o••i•l o• •y•••• lo•••• o• ny •••• i• •lw•y• ••il•
••o• ••• ••• • •l••• •l•. F••••••, •y• • oli• ••••n••• ••o• •l•••• •••n•• •y •
••i• o••i•l o• • •y•••• lo•••• •lw•y• •••olv• i• n•i••lly •••o•• •ll •••••.

T• i• •llow• •o• • •i• •li••• •o•• o• ••••in• w•••• only ••• • •••• l• ••••• •••• o• ••• •• n•i• • •••••••••n••ion o• • •l••• (•.•., ••••i• v••i••l••, •l••• ini•i•l-i••••ion ••••••, ••o••••ion •o• •in, in•••n•• o• java.lang.Class •••.) n•••• •o •• ••• li••••• ••• lo•••••. In •••• i••l••, in•o•• ••ion •••iv•• ••o• •••olv•• •y• •oli• lin••, ••••• •• ••l• off••••, vi••••l •••l• in••x••, ••••i• • •••o• ••••••••, •••., ••n •• ••••••• •••o•• lo••••• •••••• in••••in• ••• •• o•n• o• •••• in•. In MVM no •o•• o• •••• in• i• •••• o••••• •o• •l••••• ••• n•• •y ••o•••• -•••n•• lo•••••.

Li•• MVM, • LSVM i• •l•• •n•• ••••• ••-•n•••n•• •o• •l••••• lo•••• •y ••i- • o••i•l lo•••••. Fo• •ll ••••-•••n•• lo•••••• • LSVM i• •l•• •n•• *loader re-entrance,* w•i•• •llow• •••• in• o• ••• ••n•i• • •••••••••n••ion o• • •l••• wi•• •ny o•••• •l••• •••• •••i••••• ••• •••• in• •on•i•ion• ••••i••• •••li••. T•• •y• • o• ••-•n•••n•• i• •l•• •n••• •o• •y•••• lo••••• ••n • •••o••n •• •••••• -•• •i• •: •y ••••• l•, • LSVM ••••• ••••• ••-•n•••n••, li•• in MVM. All o••••• •••••• o• MVM, ••••• •• i•ol•••• • •n•••• •n• •n• •••• in••ion, •••-i•ol••• ••••••• •oll•••ion, •n• •••• in•••-i•ol••• •o• • •ni••••ion, ••• l••• •n•••n••• in • LSVM.

T•• •••• o• ••i• ••••ion •o••••• on ••• •ollowin• •••••• o• lo•••• ••-•n•••n••: (i) •ow •o o•••ni•• ••• •• n•i• • •••••••••n••ion o• • •l••• •o •• •o • •xi• i•• ••••in• w•il• • ini• i•in• i•• ov••••••, (ii) •ow •o •• •i•n•ly ••••i•v• lo•••••-••iv••• in•o•• ••ion ••o• •••••• •o••, •n• (iii) •ow •o • ••• ••• in•••••••••••ion o• ••••••• •y•••o••• lo•••• ••-•n•••n•.

3.2   Runtime Representation of Classes

T•• ••n•i• • •••••••••n••ion o• • •l••• •on•i••• o• •••• ••••••••• ••••• • i••o• ••• •••• i••••••••-n••••l •in••y •••••••n••ion o• •••• •l•••, in • • •in • •• o•y •o•• •• o••i• i••• •o• ••• v••io•• •••-•y•••• • o• ••• JVM.

In • LSVM, ••• ••n•i• • •••••••••n••ion o• • •l••• i• ••li• in • lo•••••-in•••n•••n• •n• • lo•••••-•••n• •n• •••••••n••ion (*LIR* •n• *LDR*, •••••••iv•ly). Lo••••• •••• •••i••y ••• ••••in• •on•i•ion• •o• • •l••• •••••• ••• •••• • LI• , ••• •••• ••• i•• own LD• •o• ••• •l•••. LI• • in•l•••• • •••••••n•• •o • LD• *template.* T•• •••• •l••• •••v•• •wo •• n••ion•: i• i• • • l•••• in• •o• •on•••• •in• •n LD• , •n•, •o • ini• i•• ••••• ov••••••, i• i• •lw•y• •••• •• ••• LD• o• on• lo•••.

Fi•••• • ill•••••••• ••i• o•••ni••••ion. I• ••• i••• ••• •• n•i• • •••••••••n••ion o• •wo •l••••• •••i••yin• ••• ••• • •••• in• •on•i•ion•: $< B, L_1 >$, w•o•• LD• •••• •• • •••• •l•••, •n• $< B, L_2 >$ •••• w•• •il• ••in• $< B, L_1 >$.

T•• LI• •on••in• • o•• o••••• ••n•i• • •••••••••n••ion o• • •l•••. I• •on•i••• o• • sharedRep o• j••• w•i•• in•l•••• • •••••••n•• • •• •o• ••••••• •oll•••ion, •••-•••n••• •o •n •••• y o• ••l• ••l•••• •y ••• •l•••••• • •l•••, •o • ••••••• •on•••n• •ool, •n• •o ••• LD• ••••••n•ly •••• ••• •• ••• •l•••.

• ••• sharedRep o• • LI• S •l•o in•l•••• • •••••••n•• •o ••• *super* shared-Rep o• ••• LI• ••••••• •y ••• ••n•i• • •••••••••n••ion o• ••• •••••-•l•••• o• •ll •l••••• ••••• ••v• S •o• •••i• LI• . ••••ll ••••• ••• •••on• ••••in• •on•i•ion ••••j••• ••••• ••• ••••••-•l••••• o• •wo •l••••• $< C, L_1 >$ •n• $< C, L_2 >$ •••• ••••• $< C, L_1 >\sim< C, L_2 >$ ••• •i•••• ••• ••• • •l••• o• ••••• ••i• •• n•i• • •••••••n••ion. In •i•••• ••••, ••i• • ••n• •••• ••• sharedRep• o• ••• ••••••-•l••••• o• $< C, L_1 >$ •n• $< C, L_2 >$ ••• ••• ••• •.

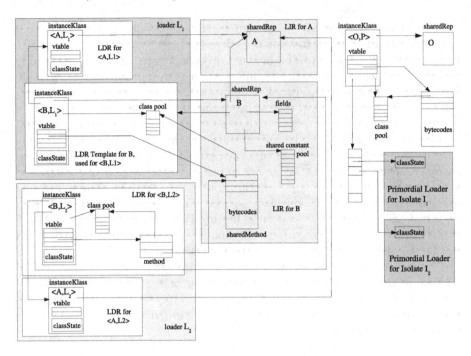

Fig. 2. CLSVM runtime representation of classes

T•• LD• o•• •l••• •on•i••• o• •n instanceKlass o•j•••, w•i•• in•l••••
••o•••• •o• i•• vi••••l • •••o• •••l• (v•••l•) •n• i•• in•••••••• •••l• (i•••l•),
•n• • ••••••n•• •o ••• sharedRep o•j••• i• w•• ••il• ••o• . T•• ••n•i• • •••-
••••n••ion o• •l••••• •••• ••• •••• ••-n•••n• i• ••••••••• •li•••ly •iff••n•ly
in •••• • o•• o• ••• LD• i• •l•o •••••• •••o•• ••• •••• ••-n•••n• lo•••••, •x-
•••• •o• non-••-•n•••n• •••••, •••• •• ••• •l•••'• ••••i• v•i•• l••, ••• in•••n•• o•
java.lang.Class •n• java.lang.ClassLoader •o• ••• •l•••, •n• i•• ini•i•li••-
•ion •••••. T•i• non-••-•n•••n• ••••• i• •• •••••• in ••• instanceKlass o•j•••
•o• lo•••• ••-•n•••n• •l••••. T•i• ••••n••• •n• i• no• • o••i•l• •o• •••• ••-•n•••n•
•l••••• •in•• ••• w•ol• instanceKlass o•j••• i• ••••••• •• on• •ll i•ol•••. In-
•••••, ••• non-••-•n•••n• ••••• o• •••• i•ol••• ••••in• ••• instanceKlass i•
••o••• in • ••••••• o•j••• •••••i•l• vi• • •••l• in••x•• •y i•ol••• i••n•i•••;
••• •••••n•• •o ••• •••l• i• ••o••• in ••• instanceKlass.

An •x•• • l• o•• •i• i• •• own on Fi•••• •: • •l•••• i• •••• n•• •y •••• •i• o•• i•l
lo••••• o• •wo i•ol••••, I_1 •n• I_2. T• ••••l•in• •l•••y•• < O, P > i• ••••••••n•••
•y ••• •••• • instanceKlass •o• • o•• I_1 •n• I_2, •n• only •••••-••••n••n• •••••
i• •••• li••••• •o• •••• ••••. • ••••••l••• o•w••••• •••i• •l••• i• •••• ••-•n•••n• o•
no•, •l••• in•••n••• (i.•., J•v• o•j••••) •on•• in in •••i• ••••••• • •oin••• •o •••
instanceKlass •••• •••••••n•• •••i• •l•••.

A• • •n•ion•• •••li••, ••• •••••in• •on•i•ion• •••••n••• •••• ••• v•••l• in-
••x•• ••• ••• ••• • •••o•• •ll lo••••• •••• •••i•y ••••. T••y •l•o •••••n•••
•••• • •••o•• ••• in••i••• •n• ov•••i••n in •x••ly ••• •••• • w•y ••o•• •l•••

lo••••. How•v••, •n••i•• in v•••l•• • ••• ••••• •o lo••••-•••n••n• • •••o• ••••-
••••n••ion•. M•••o•••v• •wo•• n•i• • ••••••••n••ion•: • lo••••-•••n••n• •••-
••••n••ion, ••ll•• • • •••o• o•j•••, •n• • ••••••• • •••o• o•j•••. M•••o• o•j••••
•on•i•• o• •n invo••ion •o•n••• •n• •••••n••• •o • •••••• • •••o• o•j•••, •o
• •l••• •ool, •n• •o n••iv• •o•• ••o••••• •y ••• •yn•• i• •o• •il••, i• •ny (•••
S•••ion •). S••••• • •••o• o•j•••• •n••••l••• ••• •••l• o•• • •••o• •••ni•ion,
• o•• no•••ly, ••• • •••o• •y•••o•••. All o••• •••••• • •••o• o•j••• i• lo••••-
in•••n••n•, •x•••• •o• • lo••••-••••i•• ••••••. T•i• ••••••• •o• ••i••• ••• •
in•o•• ••ion •• in • •••o• o•j••••, •x•••• •o• ••• •••••• • •••o• o•j•• ••••••n••.
T•i• o•••ni••ion •llow• on• instanceKlass (•y•i••lly, ••• LD• ••• •l•••') •o
••• ••• ••••••• • •••o•• •i••••ly (li••< B, L_1 > on Fi•••• •), •••• •voi•in•
••• ••••• ov•••••• o• •y•••• ••i••lly ••li••in• ••• ••n•i• • •••••••n••ion o• •
• ••• o•.

T•• in•••••••••• •n• ••• •o• •il•• •yn•• i••lly •••olv• lin•• ••in• ••• •l•••
• ool, ••• ••••••• •on•••n• •ool, •n• ••• •on•••n• •ool ••••• o• ••• •l••• •••••
•••n•• ••• • •••o• ••in• •x••••••. T•• •l••• •ool •n• ••• •••••• •on•••n• •ool
••• ••il• •i••••ly ••o• ••• •on•••n• •ool •••n•• in • •l••• •l•. T•• •l••• •ool
i• •ll•• only wi•• •y• •oli• lin•• •o •l•••••. All o•••• •on•••n• •ool •n••i•• •••
•n•••••• in•o ••• •••••••• •on•••n• •ool, w•i•• •on••in• only lo••••-in•••n••n•
in•o•• ••ion, n•• •ly in••x•• •o •l••• •ool o• •••••• •on•••n• •ool •n••i••, •on-
•••n• n•• ••i••l •n• •••in• v•l•••, o• •y• •ol•. Lo••••-•••n••n• in•o•• ••ion,
o•••• •••n •y• •oli• lin•• •o •l•••••, i• •on• n•• •o ••• •on•••n• •ool •••••, •on-
••••••••• •• •l••• lin• •i• •. I• •on••in• in•o•• ••ion ••il• ••o• •••olv•• •y• •oli•
lin•• •o ••l••, • •••o••, •n• in•••••••• •o •n••l• •••••• in•••••••••ion o• •o• •
• y•••o•••.

3.3   Class Loading

• l••••• lo•••• •y ••• JVM ••• •••o•••• in • *system dictionary* •••• • •••
••y• •o• •o••• o• • ••lly •••li••• •l••• n•• • •n• • •l••• lo••••• •••••••n•• •o
•n instanceKlass. M•l•i•l• •n••i•• in ••• •i••ion••y ••n ••••• •o ••• ••• •
instanceKlass ••• • ••••l• o• ••l•••••ion •••w••n lo••••.

A *shared class repository* • ••• lin••• li••• o• sharedRep o•j•••• •o •ni•••
•n••••in•• •o• ••••• ov•••• ••y••• o• •l••• •l••. All sharedRep• in • •iv•n
lin••• li•• ••• •on•••••••• ••o• •l••• •l•• ••••• •ll ••v• ••• ••• • •n••••in•
v•l••. H•vin• • o•• •••n on• ••••• ••n•i• • •••••••n••ion o• • •l••• •o• •••
••• • •l••• •l• ••n o•••• •••••• o• •o••i• l• viol••ion• o• ••• •••in• •on•i•ion•
•••w••n ••• nin• lo••••• (•.•., i•••• •••••• ••••••••n••ion o••• ••••• •l••• o•
••• •••n•• •l••••• ••• •iff••n•). Fin•••• •in• ••• •o• •••••• •• SHA-1 • i•••• [1•]
o• •l••• •l••.

T•• •l••• lo••in• • ••• in••y •••• ••• •y•••• • i••ion••y •n• ••• •••••• •l•••
••• o•i•o•y •o •••••• in• w•••••• • lo•••'• ••••••• •o• ••• nin• • •l••• ••n •••
•n •xi••in• •••••• ••n•i• • •••••••n••ion •o• ••• n•wly ••• n•• •l•••. W••n
in•••••••• •y • lo•••• •o •••n• • •l•••, • LSVM ••••••• • •l••• •l• ••o• •••
•••••i••• in••• •••••• •n• •o• ••••• i• SHA-1 • i•••. T•• •i•••• i• ••••• •o
••••i•v• •ll ••• •••••• •••••••n••ion• o• •l••••• •••• w••• ••il• wi•• • •l••• •l•

o• ••••l v•l••. No•• •••• ••• •o•• •• o• ••• •l••• •l• •o•• no• n••• v••i•••ion
•••o•• •o• •••in• ••• SHA-1 •i••••, •in•• i• ••• •••••i••• •l••• •l• •o•• no•
•on•o•• •o • v•li• •l••• •l• •o•• ••, i•• •i•••• ••nno• • •• •o •n •xi••in• •n••y
o•••• •••••• •l••• ••• o•i•o•y. I• ••• •i•••• •o•• no• • •• •o •ny sharedRep, •••
•o•• •• o• ••• •l••• •l• i• v••i••• •n• •••••• •o •••••• • n•w sharedRep o• j•••,
w•i•• i• •••n •n••••• in•o ••• ••• o•i•o•y.

I• • lin••• li•• o• sharedRep o• j•••• i• •o•n• in ••• ••• o•i•o•y, •n •l•• •n•
•••• •••i••• •• •• •••in• •on•i•ion• •o• ••• ••• nin• lo•••• i• loo••• •••. L•• L ••
•••• lo•••••, •n• $< C, L >$ ••• •l••• •y•• ••in• ••• •n••. T•• •••• o• ••• •••in•
•on•i•ion• •l••••y •ol•• •in•• •ll sharedRep• ••o• ••• li•• ••v• • •i•••• ••••l
•o •••• o• ••• •l••• •l• •••• i•••• •y ••• lo••••. To •••• ••• •••on• •on•i•ion,
••• •y•••• •i••ion••y i• •••••••• •o• ••• instanceKlass o• $< C, L >$' ••••••
•l•••. I•••• •••••• i• no• •••••••••l, •l••• lo•• in• ••o••••• •••••••iv•ly •o lo•• •••
•••••-•l•••. • n•• ••• instanceKlass o••• •••••• •l••• i• •••i•v••, i•• ••••••n••
•o i•• sharedRep i• •o• ••••• wi•• ••• super •••••n•• o• ••• sharedRep • n•••
•v•l••ion. T•• •••on• •••in• •on•i•ion •ol•• i•••• •wo ••••••n••• ••• ••••l.

L•••ly, $< C, L >$ • ••• •••n• ••• ••• • •ni• •l•• •n••• • •••o•• •• o••••
•l••••• •l••••y •••in• ••• •v•l••••• sharedRep. B••••••• ••• ••••• •wo •••in•
•on•i•ion• •l••••y •ol•, only •ni• •l•• •n••• • •••o•• o• $< C, L >$' •••l••••
in••••••• n••• •o •• v••i••. H•n•• ••• ••i•• •on•i•ion i• •••o• ••i••lly ••i•••
i• $< C, L >$ •o•• no• •••l••• •ny in•••••••. I• i• •o••, •••n • ni• •l•• •n•••
• •••o•• ••• loo••• •• in ••• sharedRep •n• •o• ••••• •o ••o•• o• $< C, L >$.
T•• ••i•• •on•i•ion •ol•• i•••• n• ••• o• •ni• •l•• •n••• • •••o•• •n• •••i•
n•• •• •n• •y••• ••• ••• •.

I• non• o•••• •xi••in• sharedRep• •••i•••••• •• •••in• •on•i•ion •o• $< C, L >$,
• n•w on• • ••• •• •••••••. • •••in• • n•w sharedRep in •• i• •••• •o•• no• ••-
••i•• ••••in• ••• •l••• •l•. In•••••, •n •xi••in• sharedRep i• •lon•• •n• •••n•••
only in ••o•• •l•••• •••••n• on ••• ••••• •l••• •n• ••• •ni• •l•• •n••• ••-
••••••• • •••o••, •in•• • viol••ion o•••• •••in• •on• i•ion• •o••••• on•• •o ••vin•
• iff•••n• v•l••• •o• •o• • o• ••••••.

3.4   Sharing Bytecodes

T•• ••n•i• • •••••••••n••ion o• •l••••• •••••i••• ••ov• i• no• ••• •i•n• •o •l-
low •••in• o• •••o••. By••o•• in••••••••ion • ••• •l•o •• • ••• lo••• ••-
•n••n•. T•i• •••• i••• •• •i•n• •••••• •o • •l••• lo•••'• •o•y o••••i• v••i••l••,
•n• ••o••• ••i•••in• o• lin• •••ol••ion •n• •l••• ini•i•li••ion on•• •o• ••••
lo•••• •••• •••••• ••• •y••o•••. Bo•• ••• ••• i•v•• •y ••in• ••• •on•••n• •ool
••••• •••o•i•••• wi•• ••• ••iv•• •••••••n••ion o• ••• *current class*, i.•., •••
•l••• ••••••••• n••• •• • •••o• ••in• •x••••••. T• ••••••n•• •o ••• •••••n• •l••• i•
••o•••, •• on • ••• o• invo•••ion, in • ••i•••• lo•••ion on ••• invo••• • •••o• '•
•••••• •••• •. S•o• ••••••n••• o• in••••••ion• •ll•• •••i•••• ••i•••• lin• •••ol••ion
•n• •l••• ini•i•li••ion.

A lin• •••ol••ion ••••i•• (L•B) i• •••i••• •o• •ll •y••o••• ••• ••••• •o •
lo•••-•••n•n• •y• •oli• lin•. In • LSVM, ••• •y••o••• in •• i• •••••o•y •••
••••i••n•• v••ion• o• getfield, putfield, invokevirtual, invokespecial,

invokeinterface. L• B• ••• •••• •n•• •n• in ••••• n•• o• •l••• ini•i•li•••ion ••••i-
•••, •o ••• •o•• •• i• no• n•••••••y i• ••• l••••• i• •l••••y •••• i•••. A •l••• ini-
•i•li•••ion ••••i•• (• IB) i• n••••• w••n in•••••••in• ••• ••i•••n•• v•••ion• o•
••• •o•• •y•••o•• in••••••ion• ••••• • i••• ••i•••• •l••• ini•i•li•••ion: getstatic,
putstatic, invokestatic •n• new.

Bo•• L• B• •n• • IB• wo•• •lon• ••• ••• • ••in•i•l•: ••• o• •••n• o• • ••i••-
•n•• •y•••o•• i• •n in••x •o •n •n••y o• ••• •••••n• •l•••'• •on•••n• • ool •••••
••••• •ol• in•o•• ••ion n•••••••y •o in••••••••• ••• •y•••o•• (•.•., • ••l• off•••, •
v••• l• in••x, •••.). T•• in•o•• ••ion i• ini•i•li••• wi•• • •i•in••i••••l• • ••••••
•••• i• •••••• •y ••• in•••••••••. • n SPA• • ® ••o•••o••, ••••• ••••i•• ••••••
••• only • •in•l• •••n•• on •••i•••• v•l••. Fo• in•••n••, off•••• •n• v••• l• in••x
in•o•• ••ion ••• •y•i••lly ini•i•li••• •o • n••••iv• v•l•• •o •••• L• B• j••• •on•i••
o• • •in•l• •••n•• on n••••iv• v•l••, •• •• own ••low:

```
ld        [Rcache + // Retrieve offset to field
              (header_size + 2*wordSize)], Roffset
brgz,pt   Roffset, resolved // LRB
ld        [ Robject + Roffset], Rvalue // load field
```

U• on ••••••in• ••• • •••••• •y • •••i••, •x••••ion i• •o•••• •o • •••• ••••• ••ll•
••• •• n•i• • •o •••o•• ••• •••ion •••o•i•••• wi•• ••• •••••i•• (lin• •••ol••ion
o• •l••• ini•i•li•••ion). B••o•• ••••• in• in••••••••• •x••••ion, ••• • ••••• i• ••-
•l•••• wi•• ••• in•o•• ••ion n••••• •y ••• in•••••••••• in ••• •on•••n• • ool •n••y,
•o •••••••••••••n• in••••••••ion o• •y•••o•• in••xin• ••••• •n••y wi•• ••• ••• •
•l••• lo••••• will no• ••i•••• lin• •••ol••ion. T•• •••• in••••••••ion o• ••• ••• •
•y•••o•• in••••••ion, ••• on ••••l• o• • •iff•••n• lo••••, will ••i•••• ••• ••••i••
•••in •in•• •••• lo••••• •••• • •i••in•• •on•••n• • ool •••••.

4   Impact on Dynamic Compilation

HSVM • ix•• •y•••o•• in•••••••••ion wi•• •yn•• i• •o• •il••ion •o ••• i•v• •i••-
•••o•• •n••. M•••o• ••• ini•i•lly in••••••••. P•••- •••o• invo•••ion •o• n••••
••• in•••• •n••• on •••• invo•••ion •o •••••• •••••• n•ly ••ll•• • ••• o••. M•••o••
•••• ••••• • •iv•n •••••• ol• o• in••••••••• invo•••ion• ••• •o• •il••. S•••••• •n•
invo•••ion• ••••l• in •x••••in• •••i• •o• •il•• •o••.

T• i• ••••o••• ••n •• i• ••ov•• •o •••• ••• •ffo•• o• •o• •ilin• ••• • •••o••
o• • •l••• i• •• o••i••• •••o•• ••• lo••••• ••••• •••n• i•. • n• •o••i•l• ••••••••y
i• •o •••• ••• •o•• ••o•••• •y ••• •yn• i• •o• •il•• lo•••• ••-•n•••n•, •o
•••• •iff•••n• ••• nin• lo••••• o• ••• ••• • • •••o• always ••••• ••• ••• • n••iv•
•o••. T• i• •••••••y ••• ••v•••l • •v•n••••. Fi•••, •o• •il••ion •o••• ••• ••i• only
on•• ••• ••••••• •••••••n•••ion o• • ••••o•, no • ••••• •ow • •ny lo••••• •••n•
•••• • •••o•, ••n•• ••• •o•• o• •o• •il••ion i• •• o••i••• •••o•• lo•••••. S••on•,
•••••••• ••• •o•• i• ••-n•••n•, i• ••n • • •••• i• • ••i•••ly • y •ny lo••••• ••• nin•
••• • •••o•, •li• in••in• •y•••o•• in••••••••ion. T• i••, • •• o•y •oo•••in• i•
•••••••• •y •••in• ••• •o• •il•• •o•• •••o•• lo•••••.

How•v••, • ••in• •o• •il•• •o•• lo•••• ••-•n•••n• in••o••••• •o• • ov•••••• o•••wi•• •li• in•••• •y • •yn•• i• •o• •il••. Dyn•• i• •o• •il••ion •x• loi•• ••• •• n•i• • •nowl•••• o• •••olv•• lin•• •o ••• ov• ••• ov•••••• o• •yn•• i• lin•in•. Fo• •x•• •l•, •• •yn•• i• •o• •il•• ••n •••••• in• ••• off••• o• • •l• o••n o• j••• •n• ••n••••• • •i• •l• lo•• in••••ion •••• •o•• no• ••• •ny • •••-in•o•• ••ion (•••• •• ••• ••n•i• • •on•••n• •ool •••••) •• ••n•i• •. S••• o••i• i••ion• ••• no• •o••i• l• wi•• lo•••• ••-•n•••n• •o•• ••••••• • l•v•l o• in• i••••ion i• •••• •i••• w•••v•• • •y• •oli• lin• •o •no•••• •l••• i• ••••. So, •o• in•••n••, lo••in• • ••l• o••n o• j••• •••• i••• •••••• inin•, •••• n•i• •, ••• •••••n• lo••••n• •••n•n•in• o•• ••• off••• •o ••• ••l• in ••• •on••x• o• •••• lo••••. W•••••• ••• i• •••• o• •••• in• i••••ion • •y •• ••ni•n •o ••• ••••o•• •n•• o• in•••••••• • •••o••, i• • •y •• ••o• i• i•iv• in •o• •il•• •o••.

• LSVM ••• •loy• • ••••••-••on••• •••••••y •o• •yn•• i• •o• •il••ion •••• • ix•• •••• ••-•n•••n••, •lonin•, •n• •••in• o• lo•••-•••n••n• •o••.

A• in MVM, • •••o•• o• •••• ••-•n•••n• •l••••• ••• •o• •il•• in•o •••• ••-•n•••n• •o••. S••• •o•• i• ••o••••• •y •••in• •l••• ini•i•li••ion •••i••• ••o•• •v••y •o••i• l• •••• ••• o•• •l•••, •n• ••n•••in• •o•• •o ••••••• •••i• v•i•• l•• in • •••• ••-•n•••n• w•y. T••• i•, ••••i• v•i•l•• ••• ••••i•v•• ••o• ••• •l•••'• ••• l• o• •••-i•ol•• •l••• •••• ••in• •n i•ol••• i••n•i••• ••o••• in • ••••••n• ••••••'• •••••i••o• (••• [5] •o• •••••il•). P••• •x••i•n•• wi•• MVM •• ow•• ••••••• ••• i• ••••• o•••• ••-•n•••n•• on •••o•• •n•• i• n••li•i•l• •o• ••••• wi•• ••• ••n••• o•••••in• •o• •il•• •o•• •o• • •••o• o••l••••• •••n•• •y •••• ••-•n•••n• lo••••.

Fo•• •••o••o•lo••••••-•n•••n• •l•••••, •••o• •il••••o•••••o••o••i• i••• •o• • •••••i••l•• ••• o• lo••• •••••n••n•i••, i.•., ••in• in•o•• ••ion •••iv•• ••o• •y• •oli• lin•••• •••olv•• •y •••••i••l•• lo••••. T•••o•• i• •nno••••• •lon• ••• w•y wi•• in•o•• ••ion i••n•i•yin• ••• lo•••-•••n•n• •••• •n••• o• in••••ion• •n• w•••••y •••n• on. T•• •nno••ion• ••• ••n •••• •o ••••••• in• i• ••• •o••••n ••••••• •• i• •y o•••• lo••••, o• i• • n•w v••ion ••o•l• ••••o••••• •••o••in• •o • n•w ••• o••••n•n•i••. In ••• l••••• ••••, in•••• o••o• •ilin• ••• • •••o• •o•••• •••nin• lo•••• ••o• ••••••••, ••• •o• •il•• •lon•• •n •xi••in• v••ion o• i•, •n• • o•i•• i•• lo•••-•••n•n• •••• only. T•i• • ••••• ••n•••ion o• n••iv• •o••• •••••• •• ••••• •o• •••in• •y••o•••, ••il• in• •n in••••• ••i••• ••••••••n••ion, •••o•• in• o••i• i••ion, •n• ••n•••in• •o•• ••• •voi•••.

Lo••••-•••n•n• •o•• ••••in• i• ••••• on ••• o••••v••ion ••••• ••• lo••••-••••n••n• in•o•• ••ion •••iv•• ••o• •y• •oli• lin••• •y •• •on•••n• •••o•• lo••-••• •••• ••• ••n•i• • ••••••••n••ion o•••• •l••• •••• ••• n•• ••• •o• •il•• • •••o•. Fo• •x•• •l•, ••• off••• •o •n in•••n•• v••i••l• o• • •l••• B i• •on•••n• •••o•• •ll ••• nin• lo•••• o• B •••••••i••y••• •••• • •••in• •on•i•ion. In o•••• wo••, • •y• •oli• lin• •o •n in•••n•• v••i••l• o• B ••o• • •l••• A i• •on•••n• •••o•• •wo lo•••• L_1 •n• L_2 •••• ••• ••• n•i• • •••••••n••ion o• A (i.•., $< A, L_1 >\sim< A, L_2 >$) i• $B^{L_1} \cong B^{L_2}$. T•••, i• ••• only •y• •oli• lin•• •••• in • • •••o• m o• A ••• •o in•••n•• v••i•• l•• o• B, ••• •o• •il•• •o•• •o• m ••n •• ••••••• •••w••n $< A, L_1 >$ •n• $< A, L_2 >$. In ••i• •••••••y • • •••o• i• •o• •il•• ••o• •y••o••• only on••, no • •••••• •ow • •ny lo••••• •••n• i•• •l•••. • n•• •o• •il••, n••iv• •o•• •o• ••• • •••o• i• o••in•• •••o••• •lonin• o• •••in•.

T•• •o• •il•• ••••• •• ••• lin••••• o• ••• lo•••• •••• ••j•••••• ••• •o• •il•-
•ion, •n• •x• loi•• in•o•• ••ion o••• in•• ••o• •••olv•• lin••, •ff••iv•ly • ••in•
••• n••iv• •o•• •••• n••n• on • (• o••n•i•lly •• ••y) ••• o• •••olv•• lin••. To
•n••l• ••••in• •n• •lonin•, ••• lo•••ion o• •••• lo••••-•••n•• n• •••••n•• o•
n••iv• in••••• ion• i• •••o•••• •lon• wi•• ••• • o•i•ion o• ••• •o•••• on• in• •y••-
•o•• in••••• ion. T• i• • o•i•ion off••• • •o• •••• •n• lo••••-in••• n••n• w•y o•
•o••• •n•in• • •••• n••n•y: •iv•n • •y•••o•• • o•i•ion •n• • lo•••• -•••• n••n•
• ••• o• •••••• n•• ion, on• ••n •••• i•v• ••• •y•• o• i•• ••• n••n•y (•.•., off•••
o• •n in•••n•• ••l•), •n• ••• •l••• ••• ••• n••n•y •••••• •o (•••o••• ••• •l•••
• ool o• ••• • ••• o•'• •l•••). T•••, •o•• •nno••ion• •on•i•• o• •• i•• o• off••••:
•n off••• •o ••• •••• in••••• ion o• • lo••••-•••n••n• •••• n•• o• n••iv• •o••,
•n• •no•••• off••• •o • •y•••o•• in••••• ion. T•••• ••j•• ••• •••o••• • in • •••l•
o• •••• n••n•i••.

T•• •••l• o• •••• n••n•i•• i• •••• •o •••••• in• i• n••iv• •o•• li•••• in •••
•••••• • •••o•, •n• ••o••••• •o• • ••••i••l•• lo••••, ••n •• •••• •y •no••••
lo•••• •••• ••••••• ••• ••n•i• • •••••••• n•• ion o• ••• • •••o•. S••in• o• n••iv•
•o•• i• •o••i•l• i• •••••• ••• no •••n••n•i••, o• i• lo•••• ••v• •x••ly ••• ••• •
••• •n••n•i••. Fo• •x•• •l•, • • •••o• •••• only • •ni•• l•••• in••• n•• v••i••l••
o• i•• •l••• i• lo•••• -in••• n••n• •in•• ••• ••••in• •on•i•ion• ••••• n••• •••••
off•••• •o ••••• ••l•• ••• ••• ••• • ••• o•• lo•••• ••• ••j••y ••• ••• • ••••in•
•on•i•ion•. In •no•••• •x•• •l•, • • •••o• • •y ••••• only •o •y• •ol• o• •l•••••
••• n•• •y •••••i• o••i•l lo•••• in •ll lo•••••. In •• i• ••••, ••• n••iv• •o•• •o• •••
• ••• o• ••n •• ••••••• •••w••n lo•••• •in•• •y• •oli• lin•• •o • ••• o•• •n• v••i-
••l•• o•••• ••-n••• n• •l••••• will ••••• •o •x••ly ••• ••• • i••• in •ll lo•••••.

T•• ••••in• o• •o• •il•• •o•• ••n • •••••• i•••• •v•n i•••• •l••••• ••••••• •o
•y ••• •o•• ••• no• ••• ••• •. Fo• •x•• •l•, l•• ••• •on•i••• •l••••• A •n• B:

```
class A {                          class B {
  private int x;                     static int Y = 94;
  private static int X;            }
  int getx(){ return x;}
  int getxX(){ return x * X;}
  int foo(C c){ return x * c.z;}
  int bar(){ return x * B.Y;}
}
```

L•• •• •••••••• ••••• • ••••• •l••• A ••• ••n ••• n•• •y •wo lo••••• L_1 •n• L_2
•••• •••• • •••• $< A, L_1 > \sim < A, L_2 >$. Al••o••• $< A, L_1 > \neq < A, L_2 >$, ••• n••iv•
•o••••o•••• •o•• ••• o• getx ••n •••••••• •••w••n $< A, L_1 >$ •n• $< A, L_2 >$
•in•• ••• only •••• n••n•y o• ••• •o• •il•• •o•• i• ••• off••• •o ••• in••• n••
v••i••l• x, w•i•• i• ••••• n•••• •y ••• ••••in• •on•i•ion• (••• S••ion •.•) •o
•• ••• ••• • •o• •o•• lo••••. S••• •y• •oli• lin• ••••• n••• •o no• n••• •o ••
•••o•••• in ••• ••••n••n•y •••l•. By •on••••, ••• n••iv• •o•• ••o•••• •o•
••• getxX • •••o• ••nno• •• •••••• •••w••n ••• lo•••• •• i• •••• n•• on •••
••••••• o• ••• •••• i• v••i••l• X w•i•• •iff••• •o• •••• •••nin• lo••••. T•• ••••
•o• foo i• • o•• ••••l•: i• $C^{L_1} \cong C^{L_2}$, •••n ••• n••iv• •o•• ••n •• ••••••• •in••

Table 1. Modifications required for each type of dependencies to adapt a clone of a compiled method to a new loader L_r is the requesting loader, L_u is an owner of the original compiled code

Type of symbolic link	Conditions for leaving code unchanged	What to change if condition is false
instance variable	$C^{L_r} \cong C^{L_u}$	offset in load/store instruction
dynamically bound method	$C^{L_r} \cong C^{L_u}$	reset inline cache for virtual method/interface invocation
static variable	$C^{L_r} = C^{L_u}$	address of static variable
class	$C^{L_r} = C^{L_u}$	class address and instance size in immediate value register load
statically bound method	$C^{L_r} = C^{L_u}$	address of method entry point in call instruction

z •••olv•• •o ••• ••• • off••• •o• • o•• lo•••••, •i•••• •••••••• $C^{L_1} = C^{L_2}$, o• ••••••• ••• •••••in• •on• i•ion• ••••n••• •• i•. • ••••wi••, ••• • •••o• ••nno•• •• •••••••. Si• il••ly, ••• n••iv• •o•• •o• ••• bar • •••o• ••n •• •••••• ••w••n L_1 •n• L_2 i• $B^{L_1} = B^{L_2}$. Mo•• ••n•••lly, l•• L_r ••• lo•••• •••• •••••••• n••iv• •o•• •o•• • • •••o• m o••l••• A, L_u ••• lo•••• o•on• o•••• ••••• o• n••iv• •o•• o• • •••o• m, •n• C • •l••• on w• i•• m ••••n••. T••l• 1 li•••, •o• •••• •••n••n•y •y••, ••• •on• i•ion• •o• l••vin• ••• •o••••• on• in• in••••••ion• •n•••n•••, •n• w•••• •••n••• ••• ••••i••• o••••wi••. I• no •on• i•ion i• viol••••, no •••n•• i• n•••••, •n• ••• •o•• ••n •• •••••• •y L_u •n• L_r.

To •••••• in• w•••••• •ny •••n•••• •o ••• •o•• ••• •••• i•••, ••• •o• • il•• i•••-•••• ov•• ••• •••• •n••n• •l••• li•••• in ••• ••••n••n•y ••• l•. Fo•••• •••n••n• •l••• C, ••• •o• • il•• •••• •••••• in•• i• ••• lin• •o C^{L_r} ••• ••n •••olv••, • y •x•• inin• ••• •n••y in L_r' •l••• • ool •• ••• in••x •••o••••• in ••• ••••n••n•y •••l•. I• ••• lin• •o C^{L_r} i• no• •••olv••, ••• •••••• in••ion •o• •o• •••••in• ••n-no• ••• • •••, •n• ••••in• i• •o• i•i•••. T•• •o• • il•• ••n ••l•••• ••• •on• i•ion •••• •••••• in•• i• •o•• •••n•• i• n•••••• ••••• on ••• ••••n••n•i•• •o• •l••• C (••• •l•o T••l• 1). I• ••• •on• i•ion $C^{L_r} = C^{L_u}$ i• •••• i•••, ••• •o• • il•• •o• -•••••• ••• •••••••n••• •o C^{L_r} •n• C^{L_u} o•••in•• ••o• ••• •l••• • ool o• $< A, L_r >$ •n• $< A, L_u >$ ••••••••iv•ly, •• ••• in••x •••o••••• in ••• ••••n••n•y •••l•. I• ••• •on• i•ion $C^{L_r} \sim C^{L_u}$ i• •••• i•••, ••• •o• • il•• •o• •••••• ••• ••••••n••• •o ••• sharedRep o• j•••• ••o• C^{L_r} •n• C^{L_u}.

To •lon• ••• n••iv• •o•• o• • • •••o•, ••• •o• • il•• •••• •o• i•• ••• n••iv• •o•• •n• w•l•• ov•• ••• ••••n••n•y •••l• •o i••n•i•y •l••••• •o• w• i•• •••n••• ••• ••••i••• in ••• n••iv• •o••. Fo•••• •••• •l•••, ••• •o• • il•• i•••••••• ov•• ••• •o•••••on•in• •••••n••n•i••• ••••ion. U•in• ••• • y•••o•• • o•i•ion •••o•••• •••••• i• ••••i•v•• ••• •o••••••on•in• • y•••o•• ••o• ••• • •••o• ••• •l•••, •••• •••• • y•••o•• • • ••• •o • ••n••ion •••• i• •l•• •n•• ••• lo•i• •o• • o•i•yin• ••• ••••••n•• o• n••iv• •o•• •••o•• in• •o ••• o• •••n•• o• ••• • y•••o•• in••••••ion •n• ••• •l••• • ool o• ••• •••i•i•n• o• ••• •lon•.

Sin•• n••iv• •o•• •lonin• o• •••in• i• •••••• •••n •o• •il••ion ••o• •y••
•o•••, •wi••in• ••o• •y••o•• in••••••••ion •o n••iv• •o•• •x•••ion •••••
•l••• •••li•• •o• • ••• o•• •••• ••v• ••n •l•••• y •o• •il•• .

5 Experiments

T• i• ••••ion •o• ••••• MVM •n• • LSVM wi•• •••••• •o • •• o•y •oo••in•,
••o•••• ••••-•• •i• •, •n• •••li••ion •x•••ion •i• •.

T•••i• o••••••••n••• •••• ni•••• i••o•••••••• ••••oo••in• o••o•••• •••••
•x••n•iv•ly••ly on ••••-••• n•• •l••lo•••, •y•••in• ••••• n•i• ••••••••n••ion
o• •l••••• •••o•• lo••••• o• ••• ••• • o• o• •iff•••n• ••o••••. Ano•••• ••••lly
i• •o•••n• •o•l i• •o •voi• •••o•• •n•• •n• •••••-•• •i• •••••••••ion wi•• •••••••
•o MVM. ••• ••o•o•y• o• • LSVM i• •l•• •n•• •••• ••-•n•••n•• •o• •o•• •••
••i• o••i•l •n• •y•••• lo•••••, •n• lo•••• ••-•n•••n•• •o• ••••-••• n•• lo•••••.

• LSVM i• • •••iv•iv• o• MVM, w•i•• in •••n •••iv•••o• HSVM (••• J•v•
Ho•S• o•^{TM} vi••••l • •••in• [16]) v•••ion 1.3.1 wi•• ••• •li•n• •o• •il••. All ••
•• l•• ••• •••o•••• ••l••iv• •o HSVM. T•• •x••i• •n•• w••• •••o•• •• on • S• n
Bl••• 1000^{TM} •••i•••• wi•• • • B o•• •in • •• o•y •n• •wo Ul•••SPA• • ®
III+ ••o••••o•• •lo•••• •• 1015 MH•, ••nnin• ••• Sol••i•^{TM} 10 • •••••in•
• nvi•on• •n•.

5.1 Start-Up Time

In • o•• MVM •n• • LSVM ••o•••• • ••n •• •••••••• •i•••• ••o• ••• •o• • •n•
lin• o• •i••••ly (••o•••• • ••i••lly) •y •n i•ol•••. T•• •o•• •• o••ion involv••
••• •••••ion o• • ••o•••• •••• •o• • • ni••••• wi•• • *login* i•ol••• •o •••••••• •••
l••n••in• o• • n•w i•ol••• •n• •o •••••li•• in•••/o••••• •in•in• •••w••n •••
i•ol••• •n• ••• ini•i••in• ••o•••• (••• [•] •o• •••••• ••••il•).

S•••••-•• •i• ••n •• ••••oxi• •••• •y •nnin• •n •• ••y ••o•••• (i.•., on•
w•o•• main() • •••o•• •on•i•• o• j••• • return •••••• •n•). T••l• • •••o•••
••• ••••l•• •o• • LSVM •n• MVM, •o• •o•• w•y• o• ••••in• • ••o•••• (*cli* •o•
•o• • •n• lin• •••••-••, •n• *java* •o• •••••-•• ••o• wi•• in •n i•ol•••). T••••• l••
••• •x••••••• •• ••••-•• wi•• •••• ••• •o ••• •i• • •o •x••••• ••• •• ••y ••o••••
wi•• HSVM (•.•., in *cli*, MVM •••••• • ••o•••• 1.•• •i• •• •••••• •••n HSVM).
T••y in•i•••• •••• ••••o•• •o• lo•••• ••-•n•••n•• ••• no n•••iv• i• •••• on
•••••-•• •••o•• •n••. T•i• i• •x•••••• •in•• non• o• ••• •••••••• o• lo•••• ••
•n•••n•• ••• •x•••i••• •• •••••-•• .

Table 2. Start-up improvements relative to HSVM

	cli	java
MVM	1.84	26.82
CLSVM	1.85	26.21

5.2   Footprint

To ••• n•i•y ••• i• •••• o• ••• •••i•n o• • LSVM on • •• o•y •••••, w• •x• ••-
i• •n••• wi•• •wo •o• •l•• •••l-wo•l• •••li•••ion•: A••••• An• (v•••ion 1.6.•),
•n• A••••• To• ••• •••vl•• •n•in• (v•••ion •.•.1). T•• l••••• w•• ••••• •o •• n
JSPWi•i [•], • Wi•i •lon• i• •l•• •n••• wi•• J•v• S••v•• P•••• [1]. To• •••
• •in••in• • •i••••••y o• •l••• lo••••• •o •llow i•• •o• •on•n•• •n• ••• li•••ion•
i• •o••• •o ••••••• •iff•••n• ••• o•i•o•i•• o• •v•il••l• •l••••• •n• •••o••••. An•
•••• •l••• lo••••• in • •i• il•• ••••ion, •o •••••o• i•• •••-•••• ••••••• •o • iff••n•
li•••i•• •n• •••o••••.

Ano•••• •o• • on ••• o• •l••• lo••••• i• •o ••• n•••••n•ly inj••• •o•• •• •• n-
•i• •, •i•••• •o• ••o• lin• •••• o••• o• •o •n•n•• ••• li•••ion •o•• wi•• •n •••••
(•.•., •••i••n••). Ty•i••lly • lo•••• •••• • •y•••o• •• i•in• li•••y •o •••n•-
•o•• ••• •on•n•• o• ••••••• •l••• •l•• •n• •••• i•• ••• • o•i••• •y•••o••• •o
•••n• ••• •l•••. ••• ••i•• •x••i• •n•, ••••••• •o •• ••• *bytecode transforma-*
tion workload, •• •l•••• ••i• ••••vio• •in• A•••••'• B• • L •ool• i•. W• ••• li••
i• •o ••o••••• • ••o• ••• SP•• jv• 9• ••i••. T•• •••n••o•• ••ion w•• ••l••iv•ly
•i• •l•: •o•n•in• ••• n•• ••• o• •yn•• i• (•• n-•i• •) •••••••• •o ••••i• v•i••l••
•y ••• li•••ion •o••.

M•• o•y •oo••in• • ••••••• •n•• w••• o••in•• wi•• ••• ••l• o• ••• pmap
•o• • •n• ••o• ••• Sol••i• •••••in• • nvi•on• •n••n• •••n •o•••l••• wi•• •••
JVM-•••i• •• n•i• • in•o•• ••ion •••••in• i•• ••• o• vi•••l • •• o•y •••ion•.
M•• o•y •••o•n•in• w•• •••• ••••••• •o• •ll • •• o•y •••ion•, •••• •• ••• ••••
•••• •••• •o• ••• li•••ion ••••, •• n•i• • •••••••n••ion• o• •l••••, •n• •o• •il••
•o•• ••••. T•• n•• ••••• •••o•••• •x•l••• • •• o•y •••ion• ••••••• •••o•• ••o-
••••••, •••• •••••• -only ••••• o••••••• li•••i•• •n• ••••-only • •• o•y- •••••
j•• •l••.

T•••••• in ••• •ollowin• ••••••• w••• o••in•• •• •ollow•. Fo• non-•••v•• ••••••
(An•, SP•• jv• 9• ••n••• ••••), • •l•i•l• in•••n••• o• • iv•n ••o•••• w••• •x-
••••••• in ••••n••. •••• ••o•••• in•••n•• w•• •••i••i•lly •••• •liv• ••o•• •
•••••own •oo•. •••• •oo• wo•l• ••n• • no•i•••ion •o n •x•••n•l •••••vi-
in• ••o•••• ••n w•i• •o• •n •n•w•• •••o•• •xi•in•. U•on ••••ivin• • ••••••own
•oo• no•i•••ion, ••• ••••••vi•in• ••o•••• wo•l• o•••in • •• o•y ••••• ••o••
••••••in• ••• n•x• ••o•••• in•••n••. •o• • •n•• •o •xi• w••• ••n• •o ••• ••••-
•own •oo•• only on•• •ll ••o•••• •••• •••n •x•••••• •n• •••i• • •• o•y •••••
••••••••.

• ••o•••• •o ••••••own •oo•• •o • •in••in Wi•i •••v••• •liv• i• •nn••••••y
•in•• •••••• •••y •• •n• ••nnin• •n•il •x•li•i•ly in•••••••• •o •••• in•••. T••••-
•o••, ••• •x••i• •n• ••o••••• •y ••••in• on• Wi•i •••v••, •••• i••in• 100 ••-
••••••, •n• •••••in• • •• o•y ••••• ••o•• •••••in• ••i• ••••n•• •• •o •••
••i•• n•• ••• o• •••v•••. T• ••• • • ix o• 100 •••••••• w••••n• •o •••• •••v••.
I• •on•i•••• o• •••••••• •o• ••••••' •on••n•, •o•• ••i•in• •••• , •n• •i•••• ••vin• o•
••n••llin• ••• ••i••.

Fi•••• 3 ••ow• ••• •••• o••in•• •o• An• (•• •o 5 in•••n•••) •n• To• -
•••/JSPWi•i (•• •o 5 •••v•••). T•• l•••-••n• ••••• o• ••• ••••• •• •ow• • •• o•y

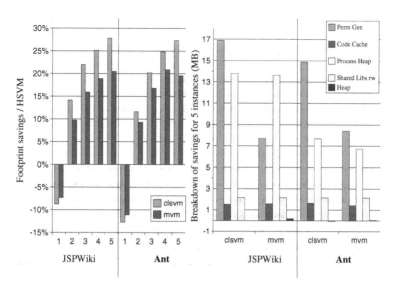

Fig. 3. Footprint savings for JSPWiki on Tomcat and for Ant. The left-hand part shows savings relatively to HSVM as the number of program instance grows. The right-hand part shows the breakdown of savings for 5 running programs

•oo••• •in• •••• ••ion ••l••iv• •o HSVM; ••• •i•••-••n• •••• •• ow• • •••••• own o•• ••• ••vin•• •o• 5 in•••n••• o• ••• • •••••• ••o•••• •.

W••n •x•••• in• • •in•l• ••o•••• , •o•• MVM •n• • LSVM •••• wo••• ••• n HSVM, •••••••• ••• • •• o•y ov••••••• o• ••• lo•in i•ol••• i• no• •• o••i•••. T• i• •••• l•• in •oo••• in• in••••••• ••n•in• ••o• ••.•% •o 1•.•%. T•• ov••••• •o• • LSVM i• l••••• ••• n •o• MVM, •••••• o• (i) ••• ••• i•ion•l •••• ••••••••• •••• i••• •o• lo••• ••-n•••n•• (•.•., ••• •••••• •l••• ••• o•i•o•y, SHA • i••••), w• i•• ••• no• •• o••i••• ••• •o ••• •••n•• o• •••• in•; (ii), ••• •x••• ov••••• ••• •o ••• •l••••• •••• •y • LSVM •o •o• •••• SHA • i••••• o• •l••• • l•• (•.•., `java.security.MessageDigest`); •n•, (iii), ••• •y•••• ••i• •••o• • o•i•ion o••• •• n•i• • ••••••••n•••ion o• *all* •l•••••, in•l• • in• •••• ••-n•••n• on••, in•o lo•••• •••• •n••n• •n• lo••••-in••• •n••n• •••••, w• i••, in ••• ••••n•• o• lo•••• ••-•n•••n• •••• in•, ••in•• no ••n•••••.

A• •oon ••• o•• •••n on• •••li••• ion i• •x••••••, ••• ••n•••• o• ••••in• o• •w•i•• ••• ov••••••• o• ••• lo•in i•ol•••, •n• •o•• MVM •n• • LSVM •••••• ••• •••••••••• •oo••• in• o• ••o•••• • w••n •o• ••••• •o HSVM. T•• ••vin•• in••••••• wi•• ••• n•• ••• o• ••nnin• ••o•••• •, •n• in•••••• •••••• wi•• • LSVM ••• n wi•• MVM. T•• ••••••• own o• ••vin•• •• own in ••• •i•••-••n• •••• o• Fi•••• 3 off••• in•i••• in•o ••• ••••on• •o• •• i• ••••vio•. T•••• ••• •o•• •o•••• o• ••vin••: ••• •••• •n•n• ••n•••• ion (• •••••••• •oll••••• •••• •••• •ol••• • o•• o• ••• •• n•i• • •••••••• n•••ion o• •l•••••); ••• •o•• ••••• (w•••• ••• •o• •il•• •o•• ••o••••• •y ••• •yn•• i• •o• •il•• •••i•••); ••• JVM'• ••o•••• • -•••• (w• i•• ••o••• •o• • o•••• •yn•• i• •••• •••••••••• o•••• JVM); •n• ••• ••iv••• •••• •n•• o• ••• ••••• li•••i•• •••• •y ••• JVM.

Table 3. Population of classes for the programs used in the experiments

defining loader(s)	Ant	Tomcat	db	javac	mpegaudio	jack
Primordial	343	476	316	316	315	316
System	149	14	256	269	263	260
User-defined	540	806	9	149	57	60

T•• •••• •n•n• ••n•••ion •n• ••• ••o••••'• •••• ••• ••• • •in •on••i• ••o•• •o • •• o•y •oo•• •in• •••••••ion. • o•• ••••• ••n •l•o •on••i• ••• •o ••vin••, ••- ••n• in• on ••• •• o•n• o• ••-•n•••n• •o• •il•• • •••o••. S••in• ••• ••n•i• • •••••••n••ion o• •l••••• •••o•• ••••-••• n•• lo••••• • o••ly •ff•••• ••• • •••• •- n•n• ••n•••ion. Fo• •o•• An• •n• To• •••/JSPWi• i, ••• • •••• •n•n• ••n•••ion o• • LSVM ••ow• ••••• •i• •• •low•• ••• n •••• o• MVM wi•• ••••• •••i•ion•l ••o•••• in•••n••. All o••••• • •• o•y ••••• ••ow ••• •l• o•• ••• •••• • •••••.

T•• •• ov• ••• on••••••• ••••• • LSVM ••n ••in• ••n•••• •o ••••• •••li•• •ion• ov•• •n• ••yon• w••• MVM •l••••y ••ovi•••. • LSVM'• ••in•, ••l••iv• •o MVM'•, •••••n• on ••• •••io o• ••• n•• ••• o• •l••••• ••• n•• •y ••o•••• - •••n•• lo••••• (•n• •••i• •i••) •o ••• n•• ••• o• o•••• •l•••••. Bo•• An• •n• To• •••/JSPWi• i •••vily •x• loi• ••••-••• n•• lo••••••: ov•• 50% o• •l••••• ••• •••n•• •y •••• (••• T••l• 3).

T•• •y•••o•• •••n••o•• ••ion wo•• lo•• •iv•• • • o•• •on••••••• •i••••• ••• •o ••• • ••• •• •ll•• ••o• o••ion o• •l•••••• ••• n•• •y ••••-••• n•• lo•••••[2]: •••o•• ••• SP• • jv• 9• ••o••••• •, ••• • o•• •l••ion o• ••••-••• n•• •l••••• (i.•., ••• •l••••• ••• j•••••• •o ••n•i• • •y•••o•• •••n••o•• ••ion) i• ••w••n • (javac) •o 60 (db) •i• •• •• •ll•• ••• n ••• • o•• •l••ion o• o•••• •l•••••. T•• •y•••o•• •••n••o•• ••ion •ool •lon• •••o• n•• •o• •••w••n 35% •o ••% o• ••• •o••l •o••l••ion o• lo•••• •l•••••. D•••i•• ••i• ••• ••••in• •••o•• lo••••• o•• LSVM ••in• vi•i•l• ••n•••••.

T•• l••••-••n• ••••• o• Fi•••• • •o• ••••• ••• •oo•••in• ••vin•• ••o• MVM •n• • LSVM •o• • •••• • l• o• ••• SP• • jv• 9• ••o••••• •. T•• •••• • l• i• ••o••n •o• i•• • iff••in• •oo••• in• ••••••••••i••i••: javac (••••• •••iv•ly, db) •••••• l•••••• (••••• ••- •iv•ly, •• •ll•••) • o•• •l••ion o• •l••••• ••• n•• •y ••••-••• n•• lo••••; megpaudio •n• jack••v• •l• o•• ••• ••• • • o•• •l••ion o• lo•••• •l•••••, ••• ••• •y v••ly • iff•• in ••••• • o•• •• o•y •••••, •• ••own on ••• •i•••-••n• •••• o• Fi•••• •: w••n ••n wi•• HSVM, ••• ••••• in jack •••o• n•• only •o• 30% o• ••• •o••l •oo••in•, •o• ••••• •o 50% •o• mpegaudio, •n• ov•• 60% •o• •o•• javac •n• db. A•• ••••• l•, ••• • •n•••• o• ••• •in• ••• • o•• ••ono• n••• •o• jack••• n •o• ••• o••• ••o•••• •. Li•• •••o••, ••• ov•••••• o• ••• lo• in i•ol••• i• ••l• •o• ••• • •••• ••o•••• invo- •••ion, •n• ••••••• •• •oon ••• • o•• ••• n on• ••o•••• i• ••n. T•• •oo•••in• o• db i• ini•i•lly wo••• wi•• • LSVM •••n MVM ••••••• o• ••• v••y •• •ll n•• •••• o• lo•••• ••-•n•••n• •l•••••. In ••i• ••••, ••• ov•••••• o• ••• •y•••• ••i• ••-

---

[2] The bytecode editing loader rewrites only the classes from the SPECjvm98 programs, not the JDK classes these programs use.

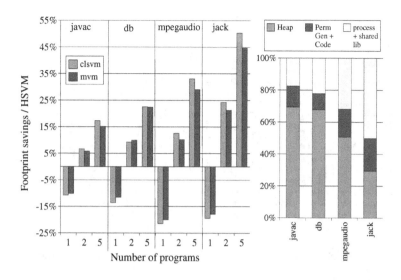

Fig. 4. Footprint savings for the bytecode transformation workload

•o• • o•i•ion o• ••• ••n•i• • •••••••n••ion o• •l••••• in•o lo•••••-•••n••n• •n•
lo•••••-in•••n••n• •••••• •li••ly • i•••v•n•••••• • LSVM.

Li••wi••, w••n ••••-•••n•• lo•••••• ••• no• •••• •y ••o••••• •, ••i• •••o• -
•o•i•ion ••••• n •l• o•• nno•i••••l• ••••••••ion in •oo•••in• •o• •••••• •o MVM
(l••• •••n 0.3% •••o•• •ll ••• SP• • jv• 9• ••o•••• •).

5.3   Performance

• n• o• o•• •o•l• i• •o •n•••• •••• lo•••• ••-•n•••n•• •o•• no• n••••iv•ly i• ••••
•••• o•• •n•• w••n ••••-•••n•• •l••• lo•••••• ••• no• ••••, o• w••n •••••• ••• no
o••o•••ni•i•• •o• •••••in•. T•• l•••-••n• •••• o• Fi•••• 5 ••ow• ••• •••• o•• •n••
i• ••ov•• •n• ••l••iv• •o HSVM on • •••• •l• o• ••• SP• • jv• 9• ••n••• ••••.

Bo•• • LSVM •n• MVM i• ••ov• ••••o•• •n•• no•i••••ly w••n •o• •••••
•o HSVM. T•i• i• ••• •o •wo ••••o••. Fi•••, • •••o•• o• •l••••• •••n•• •y •••
••i• o••i•l •n• •y•••• lo••••• ••• •o• •il•• in•o •••• ••-•n•••n• •o• •••• i•
•••••• •••o•• • •l•i•l• ••o•••• •, w•••••• •••• •x•••• •on••••n•ly o• •••i•lly.
T•••, ••o•••• • ••n••• ••o• ••• •li• in••ion o• •yn•• i• •o• •il••ion •n• in•••-
•••••••ion •o•••. S••on•, ••• invo•••ion •o•n•••• o• • •••o•• ••• •••••• •••o••
••o•••• •x••••ion, w•i•• •llow• i••n•i•yin• •n• •o• •ilin• • o•• •o• •••o••
•••• w•••••n •• i••n•i••• wi•• • •in•l• ••o•••• •x••••ion. A• • ••••l•, • l•••••
••• o••o• •il•• • •••o•• i• •v•il••l• •o• ••o•••• • in MVM •n• • LSVM •••n in
HSVM.

• LSVM •li••ly •••••••• •••• o•• •n•• •o• •••••• •o MVM on •••••• ••n••-
• ••••. W• ••••i• ••• •• i• •o ••• ov•••••• o• •••lin• wi•• •wo • •••o• •••••••n••-
•ion•, w• i•• •••••• •• n•i• • •••••• •o ••• ••llin• •onv•n•ion o• in•••••••••• • •••o••
in • LSVM.

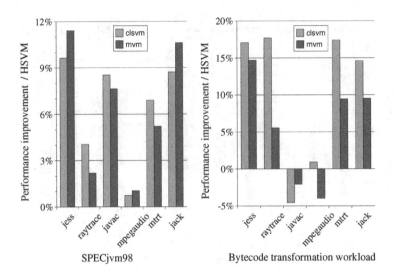

Fig. 5. Performance with respect to HSVM. The right-hand part shows performance improvement with programs from the SPECjvm98 programs. The left-hand part show performance improvement with the bytecode transformation workload

• LSVM ••• ••••• ••••• ••• •o ••• •• •o• •il•• •o•• •••o•• •••-••• n•• lo••-
••• o• •o ••o•••• n•w •o•• •y •lonin• •xi••in• •o•• •n• ••n•in• i•• lo•••-
••••n••n• ••••. T•• •ff••• o• ••i• •••••••y ••n •• o•••v•• on ••• •i•••-••n•
•••• o• Fi••• 5, w•i•• ••ow• ••• ••••o•• •n•• o• ••• •y•••o•• •••n••o•• ••ion
wo••lo•• •••li•• •o • ••• •l• o• ••• SP• • jv• 9• ••i••. • LSVM'• •••••••y •o•
•• o••i•in• ••• •o•• o• •yn•• i• •o• •il••ion •••o•• •••-••• n•• •l••• lo••••• i• -
••ov•• •••o•• •n•• ••l••iv•ly •o MVM. T•• i• •••• ••••n•• on ••• ••o• o••ion
o• lo•••-••••n••n• •o• •il•• • •••o•• •o ••• •o••l n•• ••• o••o• •il•• • •••o••,
•n• •o ••• •• o•n• o• lo•••-•••n••n• •o•• •••• ••n •• •••••. Fo• •x•• •l•,
••% o• •o• •il•• • •••o•• •••••in• •o •l••••• •••n•• •y ••••-•••n•• lo••••• in
jess •n• 30% •o• *raytrace.* How•v••, only 1•% o• ••••• ••• •••••• •••o•• lo••-
••• •o• *jess,* w•••••• n•••ly •5% ••• •••••• •o• *raytrace.* T••• *raytrace* ••n••••
• ••• • o•• ••o• • LSVM. T•• •••••n• ••o•o•y•• o• LSVM i• no• •••••l• o•
••••in• o• •lonin• •o•• •••• inlin•• lo•••• ••-•n•••n• • •••o••. In ••i• ••••, •••
• •••o• n•••• •o •• •••o• •il••. T•i• li• i••ion i• ••••• •i••••ly *jess, javac,* •n•
mpegaudio, •in•• ••••• ••v• • •••••n•i•l •• o•n•[3] o••o• •il•• lo•••• ••-•n•••n•
• •••o•• •••• inlin•• o•••• lo•••• ••-•n•••n• • •••o••.

• LSVM o••••••o•• • MVM on *mpegaudio* •••••• o••iff•••n••• in • ow •••i•
••l•• •••• ••••••••• in • o••.

T•• •••••••n•y o• *mpegaudio'•* •••••••• •o •••i• ••l•• i• ••o•• •wo o•••••
o• • ••ni•••• •i•••• •••n •o• o•••• SP• • jv• 9• ••n••• •••. T•• •iff•••n•• in
• ow •••i• ••l•• ••• ••••••••• in • o•• vi•••l • •••in•• •x•l•in• w•y • LSVM

---

[3] 31%, 14% and 11% for, respectively, *jess, javac* and *mpegaudio.*

o•••••o•• • MVM on ••i• ••n••• •••, •n• •l•o w•y MVM •••o•• • wo••• •••n HSVM. S•••i•••lly, MVM in•••• ••• •o•• o• •n •••i•ion•l l•v•l o• in•i••••ion w••n ••••••in• •••i• ••|••, ••••••|••• o• w••••••• ••• •|••• ••• nin• ••• v••i••|• i• •••• ••-•n•••n• o• no•.

P•••o•• •n•• •••• o•••in•• wi•• An• (no• ••own ••••) in•i•••• 3.3% i• -••ov•• •n• o• • LSVM ov•• MVM, ••in•in• •••o•• •n•• ••|••iv• •o HSVM ••o• •6.•% •o ••.•%.

6   Related Work

• •• wo•• ••|•••• •o ••••n• •ffo••• •o •••••• ••• • • •in-• •• o•y •• n•i• • •••••••n-•••ion o• •|•••• •••w••n ••o••• •. T• i• •o•• o• ••••in• ••n •••••• • o•• ••• •oo•••in• o• J•v• ••o•••• • •n• •••o• o• ••• •• n•i• • •o••• o• •••n••o•• in• •|••• • l• •o •n o••i• i•••, •••• i•••••••-••••i• • •|••• •y• •••••••••n••ion.

• n• •••••o••• •o ••••in• •on•i••• o• l••n••in• •o• •••• J•v• ••o•••• • •••-•••••• • S ••o•••• •o •x•••••• •n in•••n•• o• ••• JVM, •n• •o ••o•• ••• ••••••|• •••• o• ••• ••n•i• • ••••••••n••ion o• •|•••• in •n •••• o• • •• o•y •••••• •y ••• JVM ••o•••••• [6, •]. W••• i• • ••• ••••••|• v••i• •••o••in• •o i• •|•• •n-•••ion•: •• ••• • ini• •• , ••• •y••o•• o•• •••o••, w•i• ••• •y ••• ••• |•••••• •••• o• ••• •• n•i• • ••••••••n••ion o• •|•••••, •••• •• •y• •ol •on•••n•• •n• •o• • o• ••• • •••-•••••i••ion o• • •••o•• •n• ••|••, ••n •l•o •• • •••••• [6]. A••i•ion•l in•o•• ••ion n•••••••y •o ••••on•••••••• • •••• |• •••• o•••• •• n•i• • ••••••n••-•ion o• • •|••• ••n •l•o •• ••o••• in ••• •••••• ••••, •o •voi• •••• in• ••• o•i•in•l •|••• •|• w••n •on••••in• ••• ••o••••-•iv••• •••• o• ••• •|•••'• •••••••n••ion. S• MVM-• [6] •o•• on• •••• ••••••• •y •|•o • •• in• ••• o•••• o• ••• • yn•• i• •o• • il•• ••o•••• ••-•n•••n• •o •••• • •|•i•|• JVM ••o•••••• ••n ••••• i•.

An •|•••n••iv• •o ••o•in• ••• ••••••|• •••• o•• •|••• in •••••• • •• o•y i• •o •n•o•• ••• w•ol• •• n•i• • •••••••n••ion o• •|••••• in • •in••y •o•• •• n••iv•ly •••••o•••• •y ••• •o•• S' •••••• li•••i• • ••••ni•• . Fo• in•••n••, SLVM [19] •n•o•• ••• ••• • •in-• •• o•y ••••••n••ion o• •|•••• in ••• • LF •o•• ••. T•• ••-••|•in• • in••i•• ••• ••|o••••|•. Lo••in• •n• ••|o••ion ••• ••••o•• •• •y ••• lin•••. B•••••• • •• o•y ••ili••ion ••n ••••|• ••o• ••i• ••••o••••, ••• •o ••• •y•-••• ••i• •o•y-on-w•i•• •oli•y i• •|•• •n••• •y ••• lin••• on •ny •••• o• • ••••|• •••ion• o• ••• •••••• li•••y.

Ano••••• ••••o••• •o •••n••o•• in• J•v• •|••••• in•o •••••• li•••i• •i •x•• -•li••• •y • • J [9], • •o••••|•, o••i• i•in•, •••••-o•-•i• • •o• •il•• •o• ••• J•v• ••o•••• • in• l•n•••••. T•• •n-•i• • •y•••• o• • • J ••••o••• ••o•••• -••• n•• •|••• lo•••••• •n• •yn•• i• •|••• lo••in•, ••• •o•• lo•••• ••i• w•y ••n only •• in••••••••••. [•0] •••••i•••• •n •x•n•ion •o • • J •••• ••••o••• ••••in• o• •o•• •o• •il•• •••••• o• •i• • •••o•• ••o•••• •v•n i• •••• •|••• i• no• lin••• •o •|•••••

---

[4] The implementation of class data sharing in the Java HotSpot Virtual machine 1.5.0 is a variant of this, where method bytecodes of boot classes are stored in a file that is memory-mapped at program startup [17].

wi•• ••• ••• • ••• ni•ion in •••• ••o•••• . To •• i• •n• [•0] ••-in••o••••• •• n•i• •
•• n••ion• •n• •••• •••••••••• ••o• • only •o• n• in •••n•••• vi•••1 • •••in• (•.•.,
v•••1•• ••• •on•••••••• •• ••n•i• • •n• •••• •1••• i• •••o•i•••• wi•• • •••1• o•
lin•• •o •x•••n•1 •y• •ol• •••• •••• •ll•• •• •• •1••• lo••-•i• •).

MVM [5] ••••1•• ••• • •• o•y •oo•••in• ••o•1•• •y •ollo•••in• • •1•i•1• J•v•
••o•••• • in ••• ••• • • S ••o••••, •n• •x•••in• •••• wi•• in • •in•1• JVM ••-
•••1• o•• • •1•i-••••in•. Mo•• o• ••• •• n•i• • ••••••••n••ion o• •1•••••, in•1••in•
•o• •il•• •o••, i• •••• ••o•••• ••-•n•••n• •n• •••••• •••o•• •ll •••••. In••••••-
•n•• •• on• ••o•••• • i• •••v•n••• •y •••li••in• ••• ••o•••• -•••n••n• ••••
o• ••• •• n•i• • ••••••••n••ion o• •1•••••.

Non• o• ••• •y•••• • • •n•ion•• •• ov• i• •••••1• o• •••••in•, •i•••• wi•• in •••
••• • ••o•••• o• •••o•• ••o•••• •, ••• •• n•i• • ••••••••n••ion o• •1••••• ••• n••
•y •••i•••y ••••-•••n•• •1••• lo•••••, •••••i•lly w••n •••y ••i• •y•••o••• o•
••n••••• •1••• •1• •• ••n•i• •.

Li•• MVM •n• • LSVM, Mi••o•o••'• .N• T •llow• •o• i•ol•••• •x•••ion o•
• •1•i•1• •••li••ion• in ••• ••• • ••o•••• [1•]. T•• •1•••o•• ••n •• •on••••••
•o •••n••••n•ly ••••• •o• • • •••-••••, •1••o••• no• ••••••••••iv•ly ••• LSVM.
D••i•ion• •on••nin• ••• •••••-off ••w••n • •• o•y •oo•••in• •n• •••••o•• •n••
••n •• • ••• •• •••loy• •n• •i• •. *Domain-neutral* ••• loy• •n•• ••••1• in •low••
•x•••ion •• non-••••i• • •••-••••• i• •••••• w•il• ••••i• •••• •n• •••i• •o••
••• •••li••••. T•• ••• i•ion•1 lo•i• •••• •i••••• ••ll••• •o ••• •••••o•i••• ••••i•
•o•• o• ••••• i• •••• n•••••• •o ••ovi• •••• li•••ion i•ol••ion. T•• •••n•••• •o••
o• •••• li•••ion ••• loy• •n• in .N• T •o•• no• ••v• ••i• •••••••, •••• • o••n•i•lly
••ovi• in• •••••• •••o•• •n•• •• ••• •x•n•• o• • •• o•y •oo••••in•.

• • i•• Silv•• [15] •• o••i••• ••• ••o•• o• ••o••in• • •i••-•••o• •n•• ••n•i• •
i• ••• o•• ••o•••• •y•o• •ilin• ••• • •••o•• o•• •1••• in•o •••lo••••1• •o•• ••
•n• ••o•in• ••• ••••1• o• ••• ••o• •il••ion in •1••. • o• •il•• • •••o• •1•• ••n •
••n•••••• off-lin•, o• w••n •n in•••n•• o• ••• JVM •xi••. S•••••••n• •x•••ion•
o• ••• ••o•••• lo•• ••• ••o• •il•• • •••o• •1••, i••v•il••1•, •• on ••• •1••• ••• ni-
•ion. B••o•• i•• •••, ••• ••o• •il•• •o•• i• ••• j••••• •o v•li••ion •••••• ••••••-
• in• i• ••• ••o•• ••n •• ••-•••• •y ••• ••nnin• ••o•••• . I• v•li••ion ••••••••,
••• ••o•• i• *"stitched"* •••o••in• •o ••• ••••• o• ••• •• nnin• JVM. • ••••wi••, •••
•o•• •n•••o•• •••n•••• •yn•• i• •o• •il••ion. In i•• l••••• v•••ion [1•], • •i••-
Silv•• ••n••••••• •o•• ••••• •••• •n in•i••••ion • ••••ni•• in o••••• •o • ••• • o••
o•••• ••o• •il•• •o•• o• ••• o• ••••-only, •••• •••••in• ••• ••••••••• •oo•••in•
o•• •1•i•1• JVM in•••n•••. How•v••, ••• in•i••••ion • ••••ni•• • •••••••• ••o••
•••••n••n• on ••• ••••••• o••n in•i••••ion •••1• •••••i•• •o on• •1••• lo•••••. A•
• ••••1•, •o•• ••nno• •• ••••••• •••o••• • •1•i•1• •1••• lo•••••• wi••in ••• •••• •
JVM in•••n••. T•i• li• i•• ••• • ••••ln••• o• ••i• •••••o••••, •••••i•lly •o• •••••v••
•nvi•on• •n•• w••••• •1••• lo••••-••••• •on••in••• ••• o•••n ••••.

7   Conclusions

D••nin• •1••• lo••in• • oli•i•• i• ••o• • only •••• •••••••• o• ••• J•v• ••o•••• -
• in• 1•n••••••. T•• ••li••n•• on •1••• lo••••• i• li••ly •o ••ow, •••ly ••• •o •

••owin• •o••l••i•y o• lo••-•i• ••y•••o•• •••n••o•• ••ion• •••li•••l• •o ••••••-
o•i•n••• ••o•••• • in•. How•v••, •xi••in• i• •l•• •n••ion• o• ••• JVM • oo•ly
•••• o•• •l••• lo•••• wi•• •••••• •o •••o•••• •ili••ion.

T• i• •••••• ••••••i• ••• LSVM, •••l•i-••••in• i• •l•• •n••ion o• ••• JVM
•••••l• o• •••n••••n•ly •••in• ••••• n•i• •••••••••n••ion o• •l••••, in•l••in•
••i• •y•••o••• •n• •o• •il•• •o••, •••o•• • •l•i•l ••• nin• lo••••. S••in• i•
•••i•v•• •y ••••••••in• o•••••••• o• ••• ••n•i• •••••••••n••ion o• • •l•••
•••••••• •n•• on •y• • oli• lin• •••ol••ion •n• •y ••in• •y•••o•• in•••••••••ion
lo•••• ••-•n•••n•. • •-•n•••n•• i• i• •l•• •n••• •y ••• ••• i•ion o• •l••• •••ol••ion
•n• ini•i•li••ion •••i•••• •n• •y•• •i•n• •••••••o lo••••-••••• n••n• •o• • on•n••
o• ••• •• n•i• •••••••••n••ion o• •l••••. T•• •yn•• i• •o• •il•• •x• loi•• •••in•
•y • •in••inin• lo•••• ••••n••n•i•• •n• ••in• •••• •o •••••• in• w••n •••in•
o••o• •il•• • •••o•••••o•• lo••••• i• •o••i•l•. I•••• ••••i••• •••in• •on•i•ion•
••• no• • ••, ••• •o•• i• •lon•• •o •voi• i•• •o• •il••ion ••o• •y•••o•••.

T•• •••••n••• •••• ni•••• •n• •n•• MVM •o•• •o •x••n• ••• ••o••n• ••n••••
o••o• •••in• •o •l••••• ••n•• •y ••• i••••y •l••• lo••••, •••••• l••• o• w•••••
•••••• lo••••• •••••in •o •iff•••n• ••o•••• • o• ••• ••• • on•. F••••••, •l••••• •••-
j•••• •o •y•••o•• •••n••o•• ••ion ••••n•i• ••l•o •n••• ••o• •••in•.

T•• i• •••• o•••• ••••• ni•• • i• •l•• •n••• •y • LSVM on •n•-•o-•n• ••-
•li••ion •••o•• •n•• i• •i••ly •••n••n• on ••• ••o• o••ion o• •o• •il•• lo••••
••-•n•••n• • ••• o•••••••n • •••••••. P•••o•• •n•• ••l••iv• •o MVM v••i•• ••-
•w••n −3% •o +1•.•%, ••• •i••••• i• ••ov•• •n•• •o••••• on•in• •o ••••• w••n
••••in• o• lo•••-•••n•••n• •o• •il•• ••••o•• ••n•• •x• loi•••. W••n •o• ••••••
•o ••• J•v• Ho•S•o• vi•••l • •••in•, ••••• in• ••• ••w••n 0.9% •o 1•%. A••li-
••ion •••••-•• •i• • i• •l• o•• i••n•i••l•o• •o•• • LSVM •n• MVM, •n• •••w••n
1.•5 (••o• • •n•-lin• l••n••in• o••••li•••ion•) •n• •6 (••o••••• •••i• l••n••in•
o• ••• •li••ion•) •i• •• ••••••• •••n •o• ••• J•v• Ho•S•o• vi•••l • •••in•.

Alon• wi•• no• •••••• in• •••••-•• •i• • •n• ••in•in• ••o•• • • o•••• i• -
••ov•• •n• in •n•-•o-•n• •••o•• •n•• •o• ••••• •o MVM, ••• • •in • o•iv••ion
•o• ••i• wo••, w•• •o •••••••• • •• o•y •oo••in• o••• li••ion ••••• •x• loi ••••-
••• n•• •l•• lo••in•. T•i• •o•l••••n •••i•v••: •o• •x•• •l•, •o• ••• li••ion•
li•• An• •n• To• ••• LSVM i• ••ov•• ••• • •• o•y ••vin• •l•••• y •••i•v••
•y MVM •y ••w••n 15% •o •0%, ••in•in• •o••l • •• o•y •oo••in• •own •y
11.6% •o ••% wi•• ••••••• •o ••• J•v• Ho•S•o• vi•••l • •••in•. W••n •l•••
lo••in• • ••••ni•• • ••• no• ••••, • •• o•y ov•••••• ••l••iv• •o MVM ••• •in•
••low 3%.

References

1. http://java.sun.com/products/jsp.
2. http://www.jspwiki.org.
3. J. Arnold. Shared Libraries on UNIX System V. In *Summer USENIX Conference*, Atlanta, GA, 1986.
4. D. Balfanz and L. Gong. Experience with Secure Multi- Processing in Java. Technical Report 560-97, Department of Computer Science, Princeton University, Sept. 1997.

5. G. Czajkowski and L. Daynès. Multitasking without Compromise: A Virtual Machine Evolution. In *ACM OOPSLA'01*, Tampa, FL, Oct. 2001.
6. G. Czajkowski, L. Daynès, and N. Nystrom. Code Sharing among Virtual Machines. In *ECOOP'02*, Malaga, Spain, June 2002.
7. G. Czajkowski, L. Daynès, and B. Titzer. A multi-user virtual machine. In *USENIX*, San Antonio, TX, 2003.
8. D. Dillenberger, R. Bordawekar, C. W. Clark, D. Durand, D. Emmes, O. Gohda, S. Howard, M. F. Oliver, F. Samuel, and R. W. S. John. Building a Java^{TM} Virtual Machine for Server Applications: The JVM on OS/390. *IBM Systems Journal*, 39(1), 2000.
9. Free Software Foundation (FSF). GCJ: The GNU Compiler for Java., 2003.
10. J. Gosling, B. Joy, G. Steele, and G. Bracha. *The Java^{TM} Language Specification.* The Java^{TM} Series. Addison Wesley, second edition edition, Sept. 2000.
11. Java Community Process. JSR 121: Application Isolation API., 2003.
12. P. G. Joisha, S. P. Midkiff, M. J. Serrano, and M. Gupta. A framework for efficient reuse of binary code in java. In *International Conference on Supercomputing*, pages 440–453, 2001.
13. S. Liang and G. Bracha. Dynamic Class Loading in the Java Virtual Machine. In *ACM OOPSLA'98*, Oct. 1998.
14. Microsoft Corp. *Programming with Application Domains and Assemblies.* http://msdn.microsoft.com/library/default.asp?url=/library/en-us/cpguide/html/cpconprogrammingwithapplicationdomainsassemblies.asp, 2005.
15. M. J. Serrano, R. Bordawekar, S. P. Midkiff, and M. Gupta. Quicksilver: a Quasi-Static Compiler for Java. In *ACM OOPSLA'00*, Oct. 2000.
16. Sun Microsystems Inc. The Java HotSpot Performance Engine Architecture. http://java.sun.com/products/hotspot/whitepaper.html, 1999.
17. Sun Microsystems Inc. Class Data Sharing. http://java.sun.com/j2se/1.5.0/docs/guide/vm/class-data-sharing.html, 2004.
18. US Department of Commerce. Secure hash standard, Apr. 1995.
19. B. Wong, G. Czajkowski, and L. Daynès. Dynamically loaded classes as shared libraries. In *Proceedings of IEEE International Parallel and Distributed Processing Symposium (IPDPS)*, Nice, France, 2003.
20. D. Yu, Z. Shao, and V. Trifonov. Supporting binary compatibility with static compilation. In *2nd Java Virtual Machine Research and Technology Symposium (JVM'02)*, pages 165–180, 2002.

Aspect-Oriented Programming Beyond Dependency Injection

Shigeru Chiba and Rei Ishikawa

Dept. of Mathematical and Computing Sciences,
Tokyo Institute of Technology

Abstract. Dependency injection is a hot topic among industrial developers using component frameworks. This paper first mentions that dependency injection and aspect-oriented programming share the same goal, which is to reduce dependency among components for better reusability. However, existing aspect-oriented programming languages/ frameworks, in particular, AspectJ, are not perfectly suitable for expressing inter-component dependency with a simple and straightforward representation. Their limited kinds of implicit construction of aspect instances (or implementations) cannot fully express inter-component dependency. This paper points out this fact and proposes our aspect-oriented programming system named *GluonJ* to address this problem. GluonJ allows developers to explicitly construct and associate an aspect implementation with aspect targets.

1   Introduction

A key feature of the new generation of component frameworks like the Spring framework [10] is dependency injection [6]. It is a programming technique for reducing the dependency among components and thereby improving the reusability of the components. If a component includes sub-components, reusing only that component *as is* independently of those sub-components is often difficult. For example, if one of those sub-components is for accessing a particular database, it might need to be replaced with another sub-component for a different database when the component is reused. The original program of that component must be edited for the reuse since it includes the code for instantiating the sub-component. The idea of dependency injection is to move the code for instantiating sub-components from the program of a component to a component framework, which makes instances of sub-components specified by a separate configuration file (usually an XML file) and automatically stores them in the component.

Dependency injection is a good idea for reducing inter-component dependency. However, since existing component frameworks with dependency injection are implemented with a normal language, mostly in Java, the independence and reusability of components are unsatisfactory. For example, the programs of components depend on a particular component framework and thus they must be modified when they are reused with a different framework.

A.P. Black (Ed.): ECOOP 2005, LNCS 3586, pp. 121–143, 2005.

This paper mentions that dependency injection and aspect-oriented programming (AOP) share the same goal from a practical viewpoint. Hence introducing the ideas of aspect-oriented programming into this problem domain provides us with better ability for reducing dependency among components. However, existing aspect-oriented systems used with component frameworks are mostly based on the architecture of AspectJ [12] and thus their design has never been perfectly appropriate for reducing inter-component dependency. In fact, aspect-oriented programming and dependency injection have been regarded as being orthogonal and used for different applications and purposes. Otherwise, aspect-oriented programming is just an implementation mechanism of dependency injection.

This paper presents our aspect-oriented programming framework named *GluonJ*, which we designed for dealing with dependency among components in Java. Although the basic design of GluonJ is based on that of AspectJ, GluonJ allows developers to explicitly associate an aspect implementation with aspect targets. The aspect implementation is a component implementing a crosscutting concern and the aspect targets are components that the concern cuts across. Existing aspect-oriented systems only allow implicit association and hence they cannot fully express inter-component dependency as an aspect.

The organization of the rest of this paper is followings. In Section 2, we discuss dependency injection and problems of the current design. Section 3 presents our aspect-oriented programming framework named GluonJ. Section 4 mentions comparison between GluonJ and AspectJ. Section 5 briefly describes related work and Section 6 concludes this paper.

2   Loosely Coupled Components

This section first overviews the idea of dependency injection. Then it mentions that dependency injection makes components dependent on a particular component framework and a naive aspect-oriented solution is not satisfactory.

2.1   Dependency Injection

Dependency injection enables loosely-coupled components, which are thereby highly reusable. If a component contains a sub-component, it will be usually difficult to reuse without the sub-component since these two components will be tightly coupled. For example, suppose that the program of that component is as following (Figure 1):

```
public class MyBusinessTask {
  Database db;

  public MyBusinessTask() {
    db = new MySQL();
  }
}
```

```
  public void doMyJob() {
    Object result = db.query("SELECT USER.NAME FROM USER");
    System.out.println(result);
  }
}
```

Note that this component contains a MySQL object as a sub-component. MySQL is a class implementing a Database interface. Since MyBusinessTask is tightly coupled with MySQL, the constructor of MyBusinessTask must be modified if MyBusinessTask is reused with another database accessor, for example, a PostgreSQL object. The new constructor would be:

```
public MyBusinessTask() {
  db = new PostgreSQL();     // not new MySQL()
}
```

Dependency injection loosens the connection between MyBusinessTask and MySQL. It enables us to reuse MyBusinessTask without modification even if we must switch a database accessor from MySQL to PostgreSQL. The program of MyBusinessTask would be changed into this:

```
public class MyBusinessTask {
  Database db;

  public void setDb(Database d) {
    db = d;
  }

  public void doMyJob() {
    Object result = db.query("SELECT USER.NAME FROM USER");
    System.out.println(result);
  }
}
```

Now, no constructor in MyBusinessTask initializes the value of the db field. It is initialized (or injected) by a factory method provided by the framework

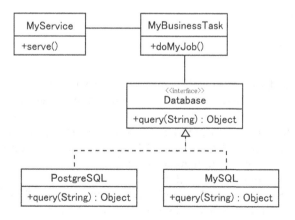

Fig. 1. Class diagram for our example scenario

supporting dependency injection. Thus, a MyBusinessTask object must not be constructed by the new operator but the factory method (or, otherwise, a My-BusinessTask object constructed by the new operator must be explicitly passed to a method provided by the component framework for performing dependency injection). For example, the code snippet below constructs a MyBusinessTask object:

```
XmlBeanFactory factory = new XmlBeanFactory(
    new InputStreamResource(new FileInputStream("beans.xml")));
MyBusinessTask myTask = (MyBusinessTask)factory.getBean("myTask");
```

Here, XmlBeanFactory is a factory class provided by a component framework. The getBean method constructs an instance of MyBusinessTask and initializes the value of the db field. It constructs a MySQL object and assigns it to the db field. This initialization is executed according to an XML configuration file beans.xml. The parameter to getBean is a key to find a configuration entry for MyBusinessTask in beans.xml.

Reusing MyBusinessTask with not MySQL but PostgreSQL is easy. We do not have to modify the program of MyBusinessTask but we have only to modify the configuration file beans.xml, which specifies how the db field is initialized. According to the configuration file, the getBean method will construct a PostgreSQL object and assign it to the db field.

However, using a factory method is annoying. Furthermore, if the hierarchy of components is more complicated, the program of the components depends on a particular component framework. Suppose that MyBusinessTask is a sub-component of another component MyService. The program of MyService would be something like this:

```
public class MyService {
  MyBusinessTask task;

  public MyService(XmlBeanFactory factory) {
    task = factory.getBean("myTask");
  }

  public void serve() {
    task.doMyJob();
  }
}
```

MyService and MyBusinessTask do not require to be modified when they are reused with either MySQL or PostgreSQL. Only the configuration file must be modified.

However, the program above includes XmlBeanFactory, which is a class provided by the component framework. MyService and MyBusinessTask, therefore, depend on the component framework. We cannot reuse them *as is* with another component framework. If we switch component frameworks, we also have to modify the MyService class. This problem can be avoided if we also construct a MyService object through an XmlBeanFactory object. Since the component

framework constructs a MyBusinessTask object for injecting it into the task field
in a MyService object, the constructor of MyService does not have to explicitly
call the getBean method on factory. We can write the program of MyService without referring to XmlBeanFactory. However, this solution requires all components
to be constructed through an XmlBeanFactory object. For example, MyService
might be always reused with MyBusinessTask since these two components are
tightly coupled. If so, dependency injection is not necessary for MyService but we
must write a configuration file for MyService and construct the MyBusinessTask
component through an XmlBeanFactory object. This programming convention is
somewhat awkward.

2.2   Aspect-Oriented Programming

The programming problem of dependency injection mentioned above is that
the programs of components depend on a particular component framework; we
cannot switch component frameworks without modifying the programs of the
components. We must stay with a particular component framework. As we develop a larger collection of useful components, switching component frameworks
becomes more difficult.

   This problem can be easily solved if we accept aspect-oriented programming.
Since the source of this problem is that we cannot intercept object construction
within confines of regular Java, we can solve the problem by using aspect-oriented
programming for intercepting object creation. For example, if we use AspectJ,
we can intercept construction of MyBusinessTask by the following program:

```
privileged aspect DependencyInjection {
  after(MyBusinessTask s):
     execution(void MyBusinessTask.new(..)) && this(s) {
    s.db = new MySQL();
  }
}
```

This aspect corresponds to an XML configuration file of the component framework shown in the previous subsection. If we define this aspect, the definition of
MyService can be written without a factory method:

```
public class MyService {
  MyBusinessTask task;

  public MyService() {
    task = new MyBusinessTask();
  }

  public void serve() {
    task.doMyJob();
  }
}
```

If this class is compiled with the aspect, the construction of MyBusinessTask is intercepted and then a MySQL object is assigned to the db field in MyBusinessTask.

Although this solution using AspectJ requires our development environments to support a new language — AspectJ, we can use a Java-based aspect-oriented framework such as JBoss AOP[9] and AspectWerkz [1] if we want to stay with regular Java.

The solution with aspect-oriented programming enables reusable components that are even independent of component frameworks. We can switch component frameworks and aspect-oriented programming systems without modifying the definition of MyService. Only the DependencyInjection aspect must be rewritten if the aspect-oriented programming system is changed.

2.3   Is This Really a Right Solution?

Although AspectJ could make a MyService component independent of a component framework, this solution would not be a good example of aspect-oriented programming. This solution uses AspectJ only as an implementation mechanism for intercepting object construction. It can be implemented with not only AspectJ but another mechanism such as a metaobject protocol [11, 3, 7, 20], which also enables intercepting object construction. In fact, the description in the DependencyInjection aspect does not directly express the dependency relation among components. It is procedural and includes implementation details. The level of abstraction is relatively low.

However, we mention that aspect-oriented programming is a right approach to solve the problem illustrated above, and more generally, to reduce dependency among components. In other words, aspect-oriented programming and dependency injection share the same goal, which is to reduce inter-component dependency for better component reusability. Aspect-oriented programming is known as a paradigm for implementing a crosscutting concern as an independent and separated component. A concern is called crosscutting if the implementation of that concern in a non aspect-oriented language is tangled with the implementation of other components. Another interpretation of this definition is that aspect-oriented programming is a paradigm for separating tightly coupled components so that they will be less dependent on each other and hence easily reusable. This is the same goal of dependency injection although dependency injection can reduce only a particular kind of dependency while aspect-oriented programming covers a wider range of dependency.

Unfortunately, existing aspect-oriented programming systems represented by AspectJ are not perfectly suitable to reduce inter-component dependency. A main problem is that they implicitly associate an aspect implementation with an aspect target. Here, the aspect implementation is a component implementing a crosscutting concern and the aspect target is a component that the concern cuts across. If program execution reaches a join point specified by a pointcut, an advice body is executed on the aspect implementation associated with the aspect target including that join point. In AspectJ, an aspect implementation is not a regular Java object but an instance of aspect. Thus we cannot use an existing component written in Java as an aspect implementation. To avoid this problem, several frameworks such as JBoss AOP and AspectWerkz allow using a regular object as an aspect implementation. Pointcuts are described in an aspect-binding file, that is, an XML file. However, such a regular object is *implicitly* constructed and associated with the aspect target. An aspect instance of AspectJ is also implicitly constructed and associated.

This implicit association between an aspect implementation and an aspect target has two problems. First, expressing dependency injection is made difficult. Dependency injection can be regarded as associating a component with another. An injected component corresponds to an aspect implementation. If developers do not have full control of the association, they cannot naturally express dependency injection with aspect-oriented programming.

The other problem is that the implicit association does not provide sufficient expressive power enough to express various relations of inter-component dependency as aspects. Although AspectJ lets developers select a scheme from issingleton, perthis, and so on, these options cover only limited kinds of relations among components. Developers might want to associate an aspect implementation with a group of aspect targets. AspectJ does not support this kinds of association. The relations among components in general do not always form a simple tree structure. Hence an aspect implementation is not always a sub-component owned by a single aspect target. It may be referred to by several different aspect targets. It may be a singleton and hence shared among all aspect targets. Existing aspect-oriented programming systems allow only selecting from limited types of the relation and they implicitly construct an aspect implementation and associate it with the aspect target according to the selected option. Therefore, developers must often redesign the relations among components so that the relations fit one of the types provided by the system.

3   GluonJ

This section presents *GluonJ*, which is our new aspect-oriented programming framework for Java. The design of GluonJ is based on the pointcut-advice architecture of AspectJ. However, this architecture has been restructured for GluonJ to provide a simpler programming model for reducing inter-component dependency.

GluonJ separates aspect bindings from aspect implementations. Aspect implementations are regular Java objects, which implement a crosscutting concern. They corresponds to an aspect instance in AspectJ. Aspect binding is the *glue* code described in XML. It specifies how an aspect implementation is associated with aspect targets, which the aspect implementation cuts across, at specified join points. The aspect binding includes not only pointcuts but also code fragments written in Java. These code fragments *explicitly* specify which aspect implementation is associated with the aspect targets. If program execution reaches a join point specified by a pointcut, then the code fragment is executed. It can explicitly construct an aspect implementation and call a method on that aspect implementation to execute a crosscutting concern. Since GluonJ was designed for reducing inter-component dependency, GluonJ lets developers to describe

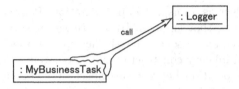

Fig. 2. The aspect of GluonJ is *glue*, which connects two components. Unlike the aspect of AspectJ, the aspect of GluonJ is not part of the Logger component or the MyBusinessTask component

the code fragments in the aspect binding to explicitly express various relations between aspect targets and aspect implementations.

3.1   Logging Example

To illustrate the usage of GluonJ, we below show the implementation of a logging concern in GluonJ. The logging concern is a well-known crosscutting concern, which is often used for showing the usage of an aspect-oriented programming system. The goal of this example is to extend the behavior of MyBusinessTask so that a log message will be printed when a method in MyBusinessTask is executed. However, we cannot modify the program of MyBusinessTask for this extension since modifying that program means that MyBusinessTask includes part of the implementation of the logging concern. The logging concern must be implemented as an independent component separated from the other components.

In GluonJ, we first define a Logger class in Java:

```
public class Logger {
  public void log() {
    System.out.println("method execution");
  }
}
```

Logger is a class for the logging concern. Unlike AspectJ, GluonJ uses a regular Java object as an aspect implementation, which is a component implementing a crosscutting concern such as the logging concern.

In GluonJ, an aspect means the aspect binding written in XML, for example, for describing the dependency between a Logger object and other objects. It glues a Logger object to the objects that must produce log messages (Figure 2). The aspect does not include an aspect implementation, which is the Logger class. For example, the following aspect specifies that a log message is printed just after a method in MyBusinessTask is executed:

```
<aspect>
  <injection>
    Logger MyBusinessTask.aspect = new Logger();
  </injection>
  <advice>
    <pointcut>
```

```
      execution(* MyBusinessTask.*(..))
    </pointcut>
    <after>
      Logger.aspectOf(this).log();
    </after>
  </advice>
</aspect>
```

This aspect makes it possible to keep the two components MyBusinessTask and Logger loosely coupled with low dependency on each other. The GluonJ compiler automatically transforms the program of MyBusinessTask according to this aspect at compilation time. Thus, we can change the behavior of MyBusinessTask without manually modifying the program of MyBusinessTask.

The statement surrounded with the injection tag specifies a connection between a MyBusinessTask object and a Logger object. It means that, when a MyBusinessTask is constructed, a Logger object is also constructed and then associated with that MyBusinessTask object. The syntax of this statement is the same as the intertype field declaration in AspectJ except aspect is not a field name but a special keyword.

The elements surrounded with the advice tag are pointcut and after advice. The pointcut is surrounded with the pointcut tag. It is the almost same language element as AspectJ's pointcut except the syntax. In the aspect shown above, the pointcut picks out as join points method execution on MyBusinessTask objects. The code snippet surrounded with the after tag is an advice body, which is executed just after a thread of control reaches the execution point specified by the pointcut. The code snippet is written in regular Java except that a special form aspectOf is available in that code snippet. In the aspect shown above, Logger.aspectOf(this) is used to obtain the Logger object associated with the MyBusinessTask object referred to by this. aspectOf is a special form that is used in the following form:

$<class\ name>$.aspectOf($<object>$)

This special form is used to obtain an object associated with another object by the injection tag. It returns the object that is of the $<class\ name>$ type and is associated with the given $<object>$.

The advice body, which is the code snippet surrounded with the after tag, is executed in the context of the join point picked out by a pointcut. In the case of our example, the advice body is executed on an MyBusinessTask object since the join points picked out are the execution points when a method is executed on that object. Therefore, this appearing in the advice body refers to that MyBusinessTask object although it refers to an aspect instance in AspectJ. If needed, the advice body can access private fields and methods in MyBusinessTask. This is not allowed in AspectJ unless the aspect is privileged. On the other hand, the advice body in GluonJ cannot access private fields or methods in Logger. The visibility scope is determined by the execution context of the advice body. In AspectJ, it is an instance of the aspect while it is the same context as the join point in GluonJ.

A unique feature of GluonJ is that an aspect implementation must be explicitly constructed in the aspect. In our example, a Logger object was constructed in the statement surrounded with the injection tag. Then it is associated with the MyBusinessTask object and used in the advice body. If program execution reaches a join point specified by a pointcut, the advice body is executed and it explicitly calls a method on the associated aspect implementation, that is, the Logger object. Note that GluonJ never instantiates an aspect since the aspect is glue code in GluonJ. From the implementation viewpoint, the code snippet in the aspect is merged into the methods of the aspect target, that is, MyBusinessTask.

3.2   Using the injection Tag for Dependency Injection

An advice body in GluonJ can be any Java code. It does not have to call aspectOf. For example, if a MyBusinessTask object had a field and that field refers to a Logger object, an advice body could call the log method on the object referred to by that field instead of the object returned by aspectOf.

The special form aspectOf and the injection tag are provided for adding a new field to an existing class while avoiding naming conflict. An aspect can give a specific name to an added new field, for example, by the following description:

```
<injection>
  Logger MyBusinessTask.link = new Logger();
</injection>
```

This adds a new field named link to the MyBusinessTask class and it initializes the value of that field so that it refers to a Logger object. The type of that field is Logger. However, this may cause naming conflict if another aspect adds a link field to the MyBusinessTask class.

If a special keyword aspect is specified as the name of the added field, this field becomes an anonymous field, that is, a field that has no name. An anonymous field can be accessed only through the special form aspectOf. For example, Logger.aspectOf(p) represents the anonymous field that is Logger type and belongs to the object p. We do not have to manually choose a unique field name for avoiding naming conflict.

There is also another rule with respect to the name of a newly added field. If the specified field name is the same as an already existing field in the same class, a new field is never added to the class. The initial value specified in the block surrounded with injection is assigned to that existing field with the same name.

This rule allows us to describe dependency injection with a simple aspect. For example, the example shown in the previous section can be described with the following aspect:

```
<aspect>
  <injection>
    Database MyBusinessTask.db = new MySQL();
  </injection>
</aspect>
```

This aspect specifies that a MySQL object is constructed and assigned to the db field in MyBusinessTask when an MyBusinessTask object is constructed. Since the db field already exists, no new field is added to MyBusinessTask. The aspect does not have to include a pointcut for picking out the construction of a MyBusinessTask object.

Although the block surrounded with the injection tag is similar to the inter-type field declaration of AspectJ, it is not the same language element as the intertype field declaration. The added fields in GluonJ are private fields only accessible in the class to which those fields are added. On the other hand, private fields added by intertype field declarations of AspectJ are not accessible from the class to which those fields are added. They are only accessible from the aspect (implementation) that declares those fields.

3.3   Dependency Reduction

GluonJ was designed particularly for addressing inter-component dependency, which is a common goal to aspect-oriented programming and dependency injection. Thus GluonJ provides mechanisms for dealing with the two sources of the dependency: connections and method calls among components.

A component depends on another component if the former has a connection to the latter (i.e. the former has a reference to the latter) and/or the former calls a method on the latter. This dependency becomes a problem if the latter component implements a crosscutting concern. Let us call the former component *the caller* and the latter one *the callee*. In the example in Section 3.1, the caller is MyBusinessTask and the callee is Logger.

The inter-component dependency makes it difficult to reuse the caller-side component *as is*. If the callee is a crosscutting concern, it is not a sub-component of the caller; it is not contained in the caller or invisible from the outside of the caller. Therefore, those components should be independently reused without each other. For example, since Logger is a crosscutting concern and hence it is not crucial for implementing the function of MyBusinessTask, MyBusinessTask may be reused without Logger. Reusing the callee without the caller is easy; the program of that component can be reused *as is* for other software development. On the other hand, in regular Java, reusing the caller without the callee, for example, reusing MyBusinessTask without Logger needs to edit the program of the caller-side component MyBusinessTask since it includes method calls to the callee. These method calls must be eliminated from the program before the component is reused.

Connections Among Components: For reducing dependency due to connections among components, GluonJ provides the block surrounded with the injection tag. Although this dependency can be reduced with the technique of dependency injection, GluonJ enables framework independence discussed in Section 2.2 since it is an aspect-oriented programming (AOP) system. Furthermore, GluonJ provides direct support for expressing this dependency although in other AOP systems this dependency is indirectly expressed by advice intercepting object creation. We adopted this design of GluonJ because addressing the dependency due to inter-component connections is significant in the application domain of GluonJ.

Method Calls Among Components: For reducing dependency due to method calls, GluonJ provides the pointcut-advice architecture. For example, as we showed in Section 3.1, the dependency between MyBusinessTask and Logger due to the calls to the log method can be separately described in the block surrounded with the advice tag. This separation makes the method calls *implicit* and *non-invasive* and thus MyBusinessTask will be reusable independently of Logger. The reuse does not need editing the program.

Note that the method call on the Database object within the body of MyBusinessTask in Section 2.1 does not have to be implicit by being separately described in XML. This call is a crucial part of the function of MyBusinessTask and hence MyBusinessTask will never be reused without a component implementing the Database interface. We do not have to reduce the dependency due to this method call.

Since the pointcut-advice architecture of GluonJ was designed for reducing dependency due to method calls, the aspect implementation that a method is called on is explicitly specified in the advice body written in Java. That aspect implementation can be any regular Java object. It can be an object constructed in the block surrounded with injection but, if needed, it can be any other object. It is not flexible design to enable calling a method only on the aspect implementation that the runtime system implicitly constructs and associates with the aspect target. We revisit this issue in Section 4.

3.4   The Tags of GluonJ

A block surrounded with the aspect tag may include blocks surrounded with either the injection tag or the advice tag. We below show brief overview of the specifications of these tags.

Injection Tag: In a block surrounded with the injection tag, an anonymous field can be declared. For example, the following declaration adds a new anonymous field to the MyBusinessTask class:

```
<injection>
  Logger MyBusinessTask.aspect = new Logger(this);
</injection>
```

The initial value of the field is computed and assigned right after an instance of MyBusinessTask is constructed. The expression computing the initial value can be any Java expression. For example, it can include the this variable, which refers to that MyBusinessTask object in the example above.

If the declaration above starts with static, then a static field is added to the class. The initial value is assigned when the other static fields are initialized.

The field added by the declaration above is accessible only in the aspect. To obtain the value of the field, the special form aspectOf must be called. For example, Logger.aspectOf(t) returns the Logger object stored in the anonymous field of the MyBusinessTask object specified by t. If the anonymous field is static, then the parameter to aspectOf must be a class name such as MyBusinessTask.

A real name can be given to a field declared in an injection block. If an valid field name is specified instead of aspect, it is used as the name of the added field. That field can be accessed with that name as a regular field in Java. If there already exists the field with that specified name, a new field is not added but only the initial value specified in the injection block is assigned.

An anonymous field can be added to an object representing a control flow specified by the cflow pointcut designator. This mechanism is useful to obtain similar functionality to a percflow aspect instance in AspectJ. To declare such a field, the aspect should be something like this:

```
<injection>
  Logger Cflow(call(* MyBusinessTask.*(..)).aspect
      = new Logger();
</injection>
```

An anonymous field is added to an object specified by Cflow. It represents a control flow from the start to the end of the execution of a method in MyBusinessTask. It is automatically created while the program execution in that control flow. To obtain the value of this anonymous field, aspectOf must be called with the thisCflow special variable. For example,

```
Logger.aspectOf(thisCflow).log();
```

aspectOf returns the Logger object stored in thisCflow. thisCflow refers to the Cflow object representing the current control flow.

An anonymous field can be used to associate a group of objects with another object. This mechanism provides similar functionality to the association aspects [17]. For example,

```
<injection>
  Logger MyBusinessTask.aspect(Session) = new Logger(this, args);
</injection>
```

This declaration associates multiple Logger objects with one MyBusinessTask. this and args are special variables. These Logger objects are identified by a Session object given as a key. The type of the key is specified in the parentheses following aspect. Multiple keys can be specified. The associated objects are obtained by aspectOf. For example,

```
Logger.aspectOf(task, session).log();
```

This statement calls the log method on the Logger object associated with a combination of task and session. aspectOf takes two parameters: the first parameter is a MyBusinessTask object and the second one is a Session object. aspectOf returns an object associated with the combination of these objects passed as parameters. If any object has not been associated with the given combination, aspectOf constructs an object and associates it with that combination. In other words, an associated object is never constructed until aspectOf is called. In the case of the example above, a Logger object is constructed with parameters this and args. this refers to the first parameter to AspectOf (*i.e.* the MyBusinessTask object) and args refers to an array of Object. The elements of this array are the parameters to aspectOf except the first one. In this example, args is an array containing only the Session object as an element.

Advice Tag: A block surrounded with the advice tag consists of a pointcut and an advice body. The pointcut is specified by the pointcut tag. The syntax of the pointcut language was borrowed from AspectJ although the current implementation of GluonJ does not support the if and adviceexecution pointcut designators. Although && and || must be escaped, AND and OR can be used as substitution. The current implementation of GluonJ has neither supported a named pointcut. A pointcut parameter is defined by using the param tag. For example, the following aspect uses an int parameter i as a pointcut parameter. It is available in the pointcut and the advice body.

```
<advice>
  <param><name>i</name><type>int</type></param>
  <pointcut>
    execution(* MyBusinessTask.*(..)) AND args(i)
  </pointcut>
  <after>
    Logger.aspectOf(this).log(i);
  </after>
</advice>
```

An advice body can be before, after, or around. It is executed before, after, or around the join point picked out by the pointcut. Any Java statement can be specified as the advice body although the < and > operators must be escaped since an advice body is written in an XML file. A few special forms aspectOf(), thisCflow, and thisJoinPoint are available in the advice body. The thisCflow variable refers to a Cflow object representing the current control flow. The thisJoinPoint variable refers to an object representing the join point picked out by the pointcut. If the proceed method is called on thisJoinPoint, it executes the original computation at the join point. The return type of proceed() is Object. The proceed method is only available with around advice.

Reflection: Although aspectOf is available only in a advice body, GluonJ provides a reflection mechanism [18] for accessing anonymous fields from regular Java objects. Table 1 lists the static methods declared in Aspect for reflective accesses.

4   Comparison to AspectJ

Although GluonJ has borrowed a number of ideas from AspectJ, there are a few significant differences between them. The first one is the visibility rule. The

Table 1. The static methods in the Aspect class

void add(Object target, Object aspect, Class clazz)
assigns aspect to an anonymous field of target. clazz represents the type of the anonymous field.
void add(Object target, Collection aspects, Class clazz)
associates all the elements in aspects with target. clazz represents the class of the associated elements.
Object get(Object target, Class clazz)
obtains the value of an anonymous field of target. clazz represents the type of the anonymous field.
Collection getAll(Object target, Class clazz)
obtains the collection associated with target. clazz represents the type of the collection elements.
void remove(Object target, Object aspect, Class clazz)
unlinks aspect associated with target. clazz represents the type of the anonymous field.
void remove(Object target, Collection aspects, Class clazz)
unlinks all the elements in aspects associated with target. clazz represents the type of the collection elements.

advice body in GluonJ can access private members of the aspect target since it is glue code. On the other hand, the advice body in AspectJ cannot access except the members added by the intertype declarations. This is because the advice body in AspectJ belongs to the aspect implementation.

Another difference is how to specify which aspect implementation is associated with an aspect target. This section illustrates comparison between GluonJ and AspectJ with respect to this issue. Although GluonJ is similar to JBoss AOP and AspectWerkz rather than AspectJ, we compare GluonJ to AspectJ since the readers would be more familiar to AspectJ. In fact, AspectJ, JBoss AOP, and AspectWerkz are based on the same idea with respect to the association of aspect implementations. Note that, like GluonJ, JBoss AOP and AspectWerkz separate aspect bindings in XML from aspect implementation in Java. Although their aspect implementations are Java objects, they are implicitly constructed and associated as in AspectJ. On the other hand, an aspect implementation in GluonJ is explicitly constructed and associated.

4.1   Example

To illustrate that explicit association of aspect implementations in GluonJ enables a better expression of inter-component dependency than AspectJ, we present an implementation of simple caching mechanism in AspectJ and GluonJ. If a method always returns the same value when it is called with the same arguments, the returned value should be cached to improve the execution performance. Suppose that we would like to cache the result of the doExpensiveJob method in the following class:

```
public class MyTask {
  private int sessionId;
  public MyTask (int id) {
    sessionId = id;
  }
  public String doExpensiveJob(String s) {
    // the execution of this method takes a long time.
    // the result is computed from s and sessionId.
  }
}
```

Note that the returned value from doExpensiveJob depends only on the parameter s and the sessionId field. Thus we share cache memory among MyTask objects with the same session id.

We below see how GluonJ and AspectJ express the dependency between MyTask and the caching component. The goal is to implement the caching component to be independent of MyTask and naturally connect the two components by an aspect.

4.2   GluonJ

We first show the implementation in GluonJ (Figure 3). The following is the class for a caching component:

```
public class Cache {
  private HashMap cache = new HashMap();
  public Object getValue(JoinPoint thisJoinPoint, Object arg) {
    Object result = cache.get(arg);
    if (result == null) {
      try {
        result = thisJoinPoint.proceed();
        cache.put(arg, result);
      } catch (Throwable e) {}
    }
    return result;
  }
  // create a cache for each session.
  private static HashMap cacheMap = new HashMap();
  private static Cache factory(int sessionId) {
    Integer id = new Integer(sessionId);
    Cache c = (Cache)cacheMap.get(id);
    if (c == null) {
      c = new Cache();
      cacheMap.put(id, c);
    }
```

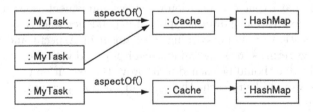

Fig. 3. The caching component in GluonJ

```
      return c;
  }
}
```

This component holds a hash table for caching the value returned from a method. factory is a factory method for constructing a Cache object for each session.

The Cache component is associated with a MyTask object. This association is described in the following aspect:

```
<aspect>
  <injection>
    Cache MyTask.aspect = Cache.factory(this.sessionId);
  </injection>
  <advice>
    <param><name>s</name> <type>String</type></param>
    <pointcut>
      execution(String MyTask.doExpensiveJob(..)) AND args(s)
    </pointcut>
    <around>
      return (String)Cache.aspectOf(this)
                          .getValue(thisJoinPoint, s);
    </around>
  </advice>
</aspect>
```

This aspect adds an anonymous field to MyTask. The value of this field is a Cache object for the session that the MyTask object belongs to. Then, if the doExpensiveJob method is executed, this aspect calls the getValue method on the associated Cache object.

Note that a Cache object is explicitly constructed in the aspect by calling a factory method. It is thereby associated with multiple MyTask objects belonging to the same session. The resulting object graph in Figure 3 naturally represents that the caching concern is per-session cache.

4.3   AspectJ (Using Intertype Declaration)

The caching mechanism can be also implemented in AspectJ. However, since AspectJ does not allow us to associate an aspect instance with a group of MyTask objects belonging to the same session, we must implement the per-session cache with a little bit complex programming. This is an example of the inflexibility for the implicit association of aspect instances in AspectJ. The following is an implementation using a singleton aspect and intertype field declaration (Figure 4):

```
privileged aspect CacheAspect {
  private HashMap MyTask.cache;      // intertype declaration

  after(MyTask t): execution(MyTask.new(..)) && this(t) {
    t.cache = factory(t.sessionId);
  }

  String around(MyTask t, String s): this(t) && args(s)
                 && execution(String MyTask.doExpensiveJob(..)) {
```

```
  String result = (String)t.cache.get(s);
  if (result == null) {
    result = proceed(t, s);
    t.cache.put(s, result);
  }
  return result;
}

// create a cache for each session.
private static HashMap cacheMap = new HashMap();
private static HashMap factory(int sessionId) {
  Integer id = new Integer(sessionId);
  HashMap map = (HashMap)cacheMap.get(id);
  if (map == null) {
    map = new HashMap();
    cacheMap.put(id, map);
  }
  return map;
}
}
```

Although the CacheAspect looks similar to the implementation in GluonJ, the resulting object-graph is different. It is far from the natural design. A single caching component, which is an instance of CacheAspect, manages the hash tables for all the sessions while each caching component in GluonJ manages a hash table for one session. Since there is only one caching component in AspectJ, a hash table for each MyTask object is stored in the cache field of the MyTask object. cache is the field added by intertype declaration. Hence the implementation of the caching concern is not only encapsulated within CacheAspect but also cutting across MyTask. Since AspectJ is a powerful aspect-oriented language, the implementation is not cutting across multiple components at the source-code level; it is cleanly modularized into CacheAspect. However, at the design level, the implementation of the caching concern involves MyTask. The developer must be aware that a hash table is contained in not CacheAspect but MyTask.

Another problem is that the caching concern is not really separated from other components since the dependency description (i.e. pointcut and advice) is

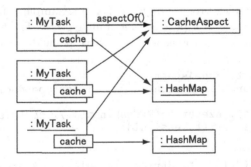

Fig. 4. The caching aspect using intertype declaration

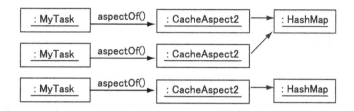

Fig. 5. The caching aspect using perthis

contained in the caching component. The caching component depends on My-Task since the class name MyTask is embedded in the intertype declaration in CacheAspect. If we reuse CacheAspect with another class other than MyTask, we must modify the definition of CacheAspect so that the cache field is added to that class. Although AspectJ provides abstract pointcut for parameterizing a class name occurring in a pointcut definition, it does not provide such a parameterization mechanism for intertype declarations.

Finally, since this aspect must access the sessionId field, which is private, it is declared as being privileged. A privileged aspect is not subject to the access control mechanism of Java. Thus, this implementation violates the encapsulation principle.

4.4   AspectJ (Using perthis)

The caching concern can be implemented with a perthis aspect (Figure 5). In the following implementation, an instance of CacheAspect2 is constructed for each MyTask object. This policy of aspect instantiation is specified by the perthis modifier. See the following program:

```
privileged aspect CacheAspect2 perthis(execution(* MyTask.*(..)) {
  private HashMap cache;     // aspect member

  after(MyTask t) : execution(MyTask.new(..)) && this(t) {
    cache = factory(t.sessionId);
  }

  String around(String s)
    : execution(String MyTask.doExpensiveJob(..)) && args(s) {
    String result = (String)cache.get(s);
    if (result == null) {
      result = proceed(s);
      cache.put(s, result);
    }
    return result;
  }

  // create a cache for each session.
  //       :
  // (the same as the factory method in CacheAspect)
}
```

Note that the hash table is stored in the cache field of the aspect instance. This aspect does not include intertype declaration. The cache field is a member of this aspect itself.

This implementation is simpler than the previous one since an instance of CacheAspect2 manages only one hash table stored in a field of that instance. CacheAspect2 does not have to access a field in MyTask. However, this implementation produces redundant aspect instances. The role of each aspect instance is merely a simple bridge between a MyTask object and a hash table. It has nothing elaborate. This is not appropriate from the viewpoint of either program design or efficiency.

Note that, in this implementation, both the caching component and the dependency description (with pointcuts and advice) are also tangled in CacheAspect2. However, separating the dependency description from the program of the caching component is not difficult if abstract pointcuts are used. We can define an aspect only for the caching mechanism and then define another aspect that extends the former aspect and implements the abstract pointcut for describing the dependency. The perthis modifier must be defined in the latter aspect.

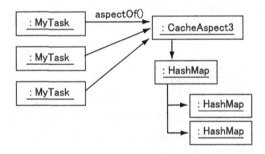

Fig. 6. The caching aspect using a hash table

4.5   AspectJ (Using a Hash Table)

The implementation we finally show uses a singleton aspect but it does not use an intertype field declaration or an aspect member field. In this implementation, either MyTask or CacheAspect3 do not include the cache field. The hash table is obtained from the factory method when the around advice is executed (Figure 6):

```
privileged aspect CacheAspect3 {
  String around(MyTask t, String s): this(t) && args(s)
              && execution(String MyTask.doExpensiveJob(..)) {
    HashMap cache = factory(t.sessionId); // obtain from factory()
    String result = (String)cache.get(s);
    if (result == null) {
      result = proceed(t, s);
      cache.put(s, result);
    }
    return result;
  }
```

```
// create a cache for each session.
//     :
// (the same as the factory method in CacheAspect)
}
```

This would be the best implementation among the three AspectJ-based ones. The caching aspect is separated and independent of MyTask. No redundant aspect instance is produced. However, it is never highly efficient to call the factory method whenever the doExpensiveJob method is executed. Furthermore, this centralized design of caching mechanism is implementation-oriented. It would not be the design easily derived after the modeling phase. The easily derived design would be something like Figure 3 achieved by GluonJ. Figure 6 shown here would be the design that we could obtain by modifying that easily derived design to be suitable for implementation in a particular language.

Note that, in the implementation shown above, the dependency description (with pointcuts and advice) is also tangled with the caching component. However, separating the dependency description from the program of the caching component is possible by using abstract pointcuts.

5   Related Work

There are a number of aspect-oriented languages and frameworks that separate aspect binding and aspect implementation. Like GluonJ, JBoss AOP [9] and AspectWerkz [1] uses XML for describing aspect binding while Aspectual Components [13], Caesar [14] and JAsCo [19] uses extended language constructs. JAC [16] uses a programming framework in regular Java. Even AspectJ provides abstract aspects for this separation [8]. However, these systems allow only implicit association of an aspect implementation and hence they have a problem discussed in this paper. An aspect implementation is automatically constructed and implicitly associated with the aspect target in the specified scheme such as issingleton and perthis of AspectJ. Although JBoss AOP provides customization interface in Java for extending the behavior of perthis, it complicates the programming model.

The dynamic weaving mechanism of Caesar [14] allows associating an aspect implementation at runtime when the developers specify. It provides better flexibility but an aspect implementation is still automatically constructed and implicitly associated with the aspect target.

Association aspect [17] allows implementing a crosscutting concern by an explicitly constructed instance of an aspect. It is an extension to AspectJ and it is a language construct focusing on associating an aspect instance to a tuple of objects. GluonJ can be regarded as a framework generalizing the idea of association aspect and applying it to dependency reduction among components.

The implicit association of an aspect implementation (and an aspect instance in AspectJ) might be the ghost of the metaobject protocol [11], which is one of the origins of aspect-orientated programming. Although this design is not a problem if an aspect crosscuts only a single other concern, it should be revised to fully bring out the power of aspect orientation. Otherwise, advantages of aspect-oriented programming might be small against metaobject protocols.

AspectJ2EE [4] is an aspect-oriented programming system for J2EE. It restricts an aspect implementation to being associated with only a single aspect target. Therefore, it has the problem discussed in this paper.

Alice [5], JBoss AOP [9], and AspectWerkz [1] allow pointcuts that capture Java 5 annotations. This feature can be used for performing dependency injection on the fields annotated with @inject. Although this provides better syntax support, the developers must still define an aspect like DependencyInjection shown in Section 2.2.

The branch mechanism of Fred [15] provides basic functionality of aspect-oriented programming. It is similar to GluonJ since both of them provide only a dispatching mechanism based on pointcut and advice but they do not allow instantiation of aspects unlike AspectJ. However, Fred is a very simple Scheme-based language and it provides only a limited mechanism for dealing with dependency among components.

6   Conclusion

Reducing inter-component dependency is the goal of dependency injection but aspect-oriented programming can give a better solution to this goal. However, existing aspect-oriented programming systems have a problem. They can express only limited kinds of dependency relation since they implicitly associate an aspect implementation with an aspect target. The developers cannot fully control this relation.

To address this problem, this paper proposed *GluonJ*, which is our aspect-oriented framework for Java. A unique feature of GluonJ is that an aspect implementation is explicitly associated with aspect targets. An aspect in GluonJ consists of pointcuts and glue code written in Java. This glue code explicitly constructs an aspect implementation and associates it with appropriate aspect targets. The aspect implementation in GluonJ is a regular Java object.

We have implemented a prototype of GluonJ as a bytecode translator built on top of Javassist [2]. It supports most pointcut designators of AspectJ except cflow, which will be implemented in near future.

References

1. Boner, J., Vasseur, A.: AspectWerkz 1.0. http://aspectwerkz.codehaus.org/ (2002)
2. Chiba, S.: Load-time structural reflection in Java. In: ECOOP 2000. LNCS 1850, Springer-Verlag (2000) 313–336
3. Chiba, S., Masuda, T.: Designing an extensible distributed language with a meta-level architecture. In: Proc. of the 7th European Conference on Object-Oriented Programming. LNCS 707, Springer-Verlag (1993) 482–501

4. Cohen, T., Gil, J.Y.: AspectJ2EE = AOP + J2EE : Towards an aspect based, programmable and extensible middleware framework. In: Proceedings of the European Conference on Object-Oriented Programming. Number 3086 in LNCS (2004) 219–243
5. Eichberg, M., Mezini, M.: Alice: Modularization of middleware using aspect-oriented programming. In: Software Engineering and Middleware (SEM) 2004. (2004)
6. Fowler, M.: Inversion of control containers and the dependency injection pattern. http://www.martinfowler.com/articles/injection.html (2004)
7. Golm, M., Kleinöder, J.: Jumping to the meta level, behavioral reflection can be fast and flexible. In: Proc. of Reflection '99. LNCS 1616, Springer (1999) 22–39
8. Hannemann, J., Kiczales, G.: Design pattern implementation in java and aspectj. In: Proc. of ACM Conf. on Object-Oriented Programming Systems, Languages, and Applications. (2002) 161–173
9. JBoss Inc.: JBoss AOP 1.0.0 final. http://www.jboss.org/ (2004)
10. Johnson, R., Hoeller, J.: Expert One-on-One J2EE Development without EJB. Wrox (2004)
11. Kiczales, G., des Rivières, J., Bobrow, D.G.: The Art of the Metaobject Protocol. The MIT Press (1991)
12. Kiczales, G., Hilsdale, E., Hugunin, J., Kersten, M., Palm, J., Griswold, W.G.: An overview of AspectJ. In: ECOOP 2001 – Object-Oriented Programming. LNCS 2072, Springer (2001) 327–353
13. Lieberherr, K., Lorenz, D., Mezini, M.: Programming with Aspectual Components. Technical Report NU-CCS-99-01, College of Computer Science, Northeastern University, Boston, MA (1999)
14. Mezini, M., Ostermann, K.: Conquering aspects with caesar. In: Proc. of Int'l Conf. on Aspect-Oriented Software Development (AOSD'03), ACM Press (2003) 90–99
15. Orleans, D.: Incremental programming with extensible decisions. In: AOSD '02: Proceedings of the 1st international conference on Aspect-oriented software development, ACM Press (2002) 56–64
16. Pawlak, R., Seinturier, L., Duchien, L., Florin, G.: Jac: A flexible solution for aspect-oriented programming in java. In: Metalevel Architectures and Separation of Crosscutting Concerns (Reflection 2001). LNCS 2192, Springer (2001) 1–24
17. Sakurai, K., Masuhara, H., Ubayashi, N., Matsuura, S., Kimoya, S.: Association aspects. In: Aspect-Oriented Software Development. (2004) 16–25
18. Smith, B.C.: Reflection and semantics in Lisp. In: Proc. of ACM Symp. on Principles of Programming Languages. (1984) 23–35
19. Suvée, D., Vanderperren, W., Jonckers, V.: Jasco: An aspect-oriented approach tailored for component based software development. In: Proc. of Int'l Conf. on Aspect-Oriented Software Development (AOSD'03), ACM Press (2003) 21–29
20. Welch, I., Stroud, R.: From dalang to kava — the evolution of a reflective java extension. In: Proc. of Reflection '99. LNCS 1616, Springer (1999) 2–21

Open Modules: Modular Reasoning About Advice

Jonathan Aldrich

Carnegie Mellon University, Pittsburgh, PA 15213, USA
jonathan.aldrich@cs.cmu.edu

Abstract. Advice is a mechanism used by advanced object-oriented and aspect-oriented programming languages to augment the behavior of methods in a program. Advice can help to make programs more modular by separating crosscutting concerns more effectively, but it also challenges existing ideas about modularity and separate development.

We study this challenge using a new, simple formal model for advice as it appears in languages like AspectJ. We then add a module system designed to leave program functionality as open to extension through advice as possible, while still enabling separate reasoning about the code within a module. Our system, Open Modules, can either be used directly to facilitate separate, component-based development, or can be viewed as a model of the features that certain AOP IDEs provide. We define a formal system for reasoning about the observational equivalence of programs under advice, which can be used to show that clients are unaffected by semantics-preserving changes to a module's implementation. Our model yields insights into the nature of modularity in the presence of advice, provides a mechanism for enforceable contracts between component providers and clients in this setting, and suggests improvements to current AOP IDEs.

1 Modularity and Advice

The Common Lisp Object System introduced a construct called *advice*, which allows a developer to externally augment the behavior of a method [2]. Advice comes in at least three flavors: *before* advice is run before the execution of a method body, *around* advice wraps a method body, and *after* advice runs after the method body. In general, advice can view or change the parameters or result of a method, or even control whether the method body is executed, allowing a rich set of adaptations to be implemented through this mechanism.

This paper examines advice in the context of Aspect-Oriented Programming (AOP), the most widely-used application of advice today [12]. The goal of AOP is to modularize concerns that crosscut the primary decomposition of a software system. AOP systems allow developers to modularize these *crosscutting concerns* within a single, locally-defined module, using an advice mechanism to allow definitions in that module to affect methods defined elsewhere in the system.

A.P. Black (Ed.): ECOOP 2005, LNCS 3586, pp. 144–168, 2005.

Although AOP in general and advice in particular provide many benefits to reasoning about concerns that are scattered and tangled throughout the code in conventional systems, questions have been raised about the ability to reason about and evolve code that is subject to advice. Advice appears to make reasoning about the effect of calling a method more challenging, for example, because it can intercept that call and change its semantics. In turn, this makes evolving AOP systems without tool support error-prone, because seemingly innocuous changes to base code could break the functionality of an aspect that advises that code.

For example, an important issue in separate development is ensuring that improvements and bug-fixes to a third-party component can be integrated into an application without breaking the application. Unfortunately, however, because the developer of a component does not know how is deployed, any change she makes could potentially break fragile pointcuts in a client [13] Although we could solve the problem by prohibiting all advice to third-party components, we would prefer a compromise that answers the research question:

1. *How can developers specify an interface for a library or component that permits as many uses of advice as possible, while still allowing the component to be changed in meaningful ways without affecting clients?*

Another important issue is protecting the internal invariants of component implementations in the presence of advice. For example, consider the Java standard library, which is carefully designed to provide a "sandbox" security model for running untrusted code. In general, it is unsafe for a user to load any code that advises the standard library, because the advice could be used by an attacker to bypass the sandbox.

One possible solution to ensuring the security of the Java library is to prohibit all advice to the standard library. Unfortunately, this rule would prohibit many useful applications of advice. A better solution to the problem would allow as much advice as possible, while still preserving the internal invariants of the Java standard library. We thus use our formal model of modularity to address a second research question:

2. *How can developers specify an interface for a library or component that permits as many uses of advice as possible, while still ensuring correctness properties of the component implementation?*

The research questions above imply a solution that prohibits certain uses of advice in the case of separate development. However, in practice, some applications may only be able to reuse a library or component if they can get around these prohibitions. We think this should be an option for developers, but it should be a conscious choice: a developer should know when she is writing an aspect that may break when a new version of a component is released, and when she is writing an aspect that is resilient to new releases. Similarly, a user uploading code should know whether that code only includes advice that is guaranteed not to violate the Java sandbox, or whether the code contains advice that might violate the sandbox, and therefore ought to be signed by a trusted principal. Our research is aimed at providing developers and users with these informed choices.

1.1   Outline and Contributions

The next section of the paper describes *Open Modules*, a novel module system for advice that provides informal answers to the research questions. Open Modules is the first module system that supports many beneficial uses of advice, while still ensuring that security and other properties of a component implementation are maintained, and verifying that advice to a component will not be affected by behavior-preserving changes to the component's implementation.

We would like to make these answers precise, and to do so, Section 3 proposes TinyAspect, a novel formal model of AOP languages that captures a few core advice constructs while omitting complicating details. Section 4 extends TinyAspect with Open Modules, precisely defining the semantics and typing rules of the system.

Section 5 describes a formal system for reasoning about the observational equivalence of modules in the presence of advice. This is the first result to show that complete behavioral equivalence reasoning can be done on a module-by-module basis in a system with advice, providing a precise answer to research question 2. It also precisely defines what changes can be made to a component without affecting clients, answering research questions 1.

Section 6 discusses lessons learned from our formal model. Section 7 describes related work, and Section 8 concludes.

2   Open Modules

We propose Open Modules, a new module system for languages with advice that is intended to be *open* to extension with advice but *modular* in that the implementation details of a module are hidden. The goals of openness and modularity are in tension (at least in the case of separate development), and so we try to achieve a compromise between them.

In AOP systems, advice is used as a way to reach across module boundaries to capture crosscutting concerns. We propose to adopt the same advice constructs, but limit them so that they respect module boundaries. In order to capture concerns that crosscut the boundary of a module, we use AOP's *pointcut* abstraction to represent abstract sets of events that external modules may be interested in advising. As suggested by Gudmundson and Kiczales [9], exported pointcuts form a contract between a module and its client aspects, allowing the module to be evolved independently of its clients so long as the contract is preserved.

Figure 1 shows a conceptual view of Open Modules. Like ordinary module systems, open modules export a list of data structures and functions such as moveBy and animate. In addition, however, open modules can export pointcuts denoting internal semantic events. For example, the moves pointcut in Figure 1

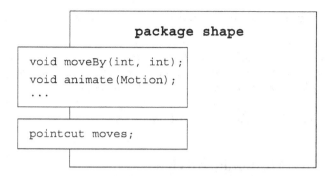

Fig. 1. A conceptual view of Open Modules. The **shape** module exports two functions and a pointcut. Clients can place advice on external calls to the exported functions, or on the exported pointcut, but not on calls that are internal to the module

is triggered whenever a shape moves. Since a shape could move multiple times during execution of the **animate** function, clients interested in fine-grained motion information would want to use this pointcut rather than just placing advice on calls to **animate**.

By exporting a pointcut, the module's maintainer is making a promise to maintain the semantics of that pointcut as the module's implementation evolves, just as the maintainer must maintain the semantics of the module's exported functions.

Open Modules are "open" in two respects. First, their interfaces are open to advice; all calls to interface functions from outside the module can be advised by clients. Second, clients can advise exported pointcuts.

On the other hand, open modules encapsulate the internal implementation details of a module. As usual with module systems, functions that are not exported in the module's public interface cannot be called from outside the module. In addition, in the case of separate development, calls between functions within the module cannot be advised from the outside—even if the called function is in the public interface of the module. For example, a client could place advice on external calls to **moveBy**, but not calls to **moveBy** from another function within the **shape** module.

In concurrent work, Kiczales and Mezini propose the notion of Aspect-Aware Interfaces, which are ordinary functional interfaces augmented with information about the advice that applies to a module. They point out that in a local development setting, analysis tools such as the AspectJ plugin for Eclipse (AJDT) [4] can compute aspect-aware interfaces automatically given whole-program information. Their work shows that in the case of local development and tool support, the benefits of Open Modules can be attained with no restrictions on the use of aspects. Instead, whenever an aspect that depends on internal calls is defined, the tools simply add a new pointcut to the module's aspect-aware interface, so that the new aspect conforms to the rules of Open Modules.

We now provide a canonical definition for Open Modules, which can be used to distinguish our contribution from previous work:

Definition [Open Modules]: *Open Modules describes a module system that:*

- *allows external advice to interactions between a module and the outside world (including external calls to functions in the interface of a module)*
- *allows external advice to pointcuts in the interface of a module*
- *does not allow external modules to directly advise internal events within the module, such as calls from within a module to other functions within the module (including calls to exported functions).*

3   Formally Modeling Advice

In order to reason formally and precisely about modularity, we need a formal model of advice. The most attractive models for this purpose are based on small-step operational semantics, which provide a very simple and direct formalization and are amenable to standard syntactic proof techniques.

Jagadeesan et al. have proposed an operational semantics for the core of AspectJ, incorporating several different kinds of pointcuts and advice in an object-oriented setting [10]. Their model is very rich and is thus ideal for specifying the semantics of a full language like AspectJ [11]. However, we would like to define and prove the soundness of a strong equivalence reasoning framework for the language, and doing so would be prohibitively difficult in such a complex model.

Walker et al. propose a much simpler formal model incorporating just the lambda calculus, advice, and labeled hooks that describe where advice may apply [19]. As a foundational calculus, their model is ideal for studying compilation strategies for AOP languages. However, because their model is low-level, it lacks some essential characteristics of advice in AOP, including the obliviousness property since advice applies to explicit labels [8]. The low-level nature of their language also means that certain properties of source-level languages like AspectJ—including the modularity properties we study—do not hold in their calculus. Thus, previous small-step operational models of aspects are inappropriate for our purposes.

Names	$n ::= x$
Expressions	$e ::= n \mid \mathtt{fn}\ x{:}\tau \mathrel{=\!\!>} e \mid e_1\ e_2 \mid ()$
Declarations	$d ::= \bullet \mid \mathtt{val}\ x = e\ \ d \mid \mathtt{pointcut}\ x = p\ \ d \mid \mathtt{around}\ p(x{:}\tau) = e\ \ d$
Pointcuts	$p ::= n \mid \mathtt{call}(n)$
General exp.	$E ::= e \mid d \mid p$
Types	$\tau ::= \mathtt{unit} \mid \tau_1 \rightarrow \tau_2$
Decl. Types	$\beta ::= \bullet \mid x{:}\tau, \beta \mid x{:}\pi, \beta$
Pcut. types	$\pi ::= \mathtt{pc}(\tau_1 \rightarrow \tau_2)$
General types	$T ::= \tau \mid \beta \mid \pi$

Fig. 2. TinyAspect Source Syntax

3.1   TinyAspect

We have developed a new functional core language for aspect-oriented programming called `TinyAspect`. The `TinyAspect` language is intentionally small, making it feasible to rigorously prove strong properties such as the soundness of logical equivalence in Section 5. Although `TinyAspect` leaves out many features of full languages, we directly model advice constructs similar to those in AspectJ. Thus our model retains the declarative nature and oblivious properties of advice in existing AOP languages, helping to ensure that techniques developed in our model can be extended to full languages.

Because our paper is focused on studying modular reasoning for advice, we omit many of the powerful pointcut constructs of AOP languages like AspectJ. We do include simple pointcuts representing calls to a particular function in order to show how pointcuts in the interface of a module can contribute to separate reasoning in the presence of advice. Our system can easily be extended to other forms of static pointcuts, but an extension to a dynamic pointcut language with constructs like `cflow` [11] is beyond the scope of this work.

Figure 2 shows the syntax of `TinyAspect`. Our syntax is modeled after ML [18]. Names in `TinyAspect` are simple identifiers. Expressions include the monomorphic lambda calculus—names, functions, and function application. To this core, we add a primitive unit expression, so that we have a base case for types. We could add primitive booleans and integers in a completely standard way, and constructs like let can be encoded using lambdas. Since these constructs are orthogonal to aspects, we omit them for simplicity's sake.

In most aspect-oriented programming languages, including AspectJ, the pointcut and advice constructs are second-class and declarative. So as to be an accurate source-level model, a `TinyAspect` program is made up of a sequence of declarations. Each declaration defines a scope that includes the following declarations. A declaration is either the empty declaration, or a value binding, a pointcut binding, or advice. The `val` declaration gives a static name to a value so that it may be used or advised in other declarations.

The `pointcut` declaration names a pointcut in the program text. A pointcut of the form `call(n)` refers to any call to the function declaration n, while a pointcut of the form n is just an alias for a previous pointcut declaration n. The `around` declaration names some pointcut p describing calls to some function, binds the variable x to the argument of the function, and specifies that the advice e should be run in place of the original function. Inside the body of the advice e, the special variable `proceed` is bound to the original value of the function, so that e can choose to invoke the original function if desired.

`TinyAspect` types τ include the unit type and function types of the form $\tau_1 \rightarrow \tau_2$. We syntactically distinguish pointcut types π and declaration types β in order to enforce the second-class nature of these constructs (e.g., they cannot be computed by functions, nor can they be used to simulate fully general references).

3.2   Fibonacci Caching Example

We illustrate the language by writing the Fibonacci function in it, and writing a simple aspect that caches calls to the function to increase performance. While this is not a compelling example of aspects, it is standard in the literature and simple enough for an introduction to the language.

Figure 3 shows the TinyAspect code for the Fibonacci function. Integers, booleans, and if statements have been added to illustrate the example.

TinyAspect does not include a fixpoint operator for defining recursion, but advice can express the same thing. In the fib function above, we define the base case as an ordinary function definition, returning 1. We then place around advice that intercepts calls to fib and handles the recursive cases. The body of the advice checks to see if the argument is greater than 2; if so, it returns the sum of fib(x-1) and fib(x-2). These recursive calls are intercepted by the advice, rather than the original function, allowing recursion to work properly. In the case when the argument is less than 3, the advice invokes proceed with the original number x. Within the scope of an advice declaration, the special variable proceed refers to the advised definition of the function. Thus, the call to proceed is forwarded to the original definition of fib, which returns 1.

In the lower half of the figure is an aspect that caches calls to fib, thereby allowing the normally exponential function to run in linear time. We assume there is a cache data structure and three functions for checking if a result is in the cache for a given value, looking up an argument in the cache, and storing a new argument-result pair in the cache.

So that we can make the caching code more reusable, we declare a cacheFunction pointcut that names the function calls to be cached—in this case, all calls to fib. Then we declare around advice on the cacheFunction pointcut which checks to see if the argument x is in the cache. If it is, the advice gets the result from the cache and returns it. If the value is not in the cache, the advice calls proceed to calculate the result of the call to fib, stores the result in the cache, and then returns the result.

```
val fib = fn x:int => 1
around call(fib) (x:int) =
    if (x > 2)
        then fib(x-1) + fib(x-2)
        else proceed x

(* advice to cache calls to fib *)
val inCache = fn ...
val lookupCache = fn ...
val updateCache = fn ...

pointcut cacheFunction = call(fib)
around cacheFunction(x:int) =
    if (inCache x)
        then lookupCache x
        else let v = proceed x
            in updateCache x v; v
```

Fig. 3. The Fibonacci function written in TinyAspect, along with an aspect that caches calls to fib

In the semantics of `TinyAspect`, the last advice to be declared on a declaration is invoked first. Thus, if a client calls `fib`, the caching advice will be invoked first. If the caching advice calls `proceed`, then the first advice (which recursively defines `fib`) will be invoked. If that advice in turn calls `proceed`, the original function definition will be invoked. However, if the advice makes a recursive call to `fib`, the call will be intercepted by the caching advice. Thus, the cache works exactly as we would expect—it is invoked on all recursive calls to `fib`, and thus it is able to effectively avoid the exponential cost of executing `fib` in the naïve way.

3.3   Operational Semantics

We define the semantics of `TinyAspect` more precisely as a set of small-step reduction rules. These rules translate a series of source-level declarations into the values shown in Figure 4.

Expression-level values include the unit value and functions. In `TinyAspect`, advice applies to declarations, *not* to functions. This is crucial for the modular reasoning result described later, as declarations can be hidden behind a module interface but first-class functions cannot. We therefore need to keep track of declaration usage in the program text, and so a reference to a declaration is represented by a label ℓ. In the operational semantics, below, an auxiliary environment keeps track of the advice that has been applied to each declaration.

A pointcut value can only take one form: calls to a particular declaration ℓ. In our formal system we model execution of declarations by replacing source-level declarations with "declaration values," which we distinguish by using the $\equiv$ symbol for binding.

Figure 4 also shows the contexts in which reduction may occur. Call-by-value reduction proceeds first on the left-hand side of an application, then on the right-hand side. Reduction occurs within a value declaration before proceeding to the following declarations. Pointcut declarations are atomic, and so they only define an evaluation context for the declarations that follow.

Figure 5 describes the operational semantics of `TinyAspect`. A machine state is a pair (η, e) of an advice environment η (mapping labels to values) and an expression e. Advice environments are similar to stores, but are used to keep track of a mapping from declaration labels to declaration values, and are modified by advice declarations. We use the $\eta[\ell]$ notation in order to look up the value of a label in η, and we denote the functional update of an environment as

Expression values $v ::= ()\ |\ \mathtt{fn}\ x{:}\tau \Rightarrow e\ |\ \ell$

Declaration values $d_v ::= \bullet\ |\ \mathtt{val}\ x \equiv \ell\ \ d_v\ |\ \mathtt{pointcut}\ x \equiv \mathtt{call}(\ell)\ \ d_v$

Evaluation contexts $C ::= \square\ e_2\ |\ v_1\ \square\ |\ \mathtt{val}\ x = \square\ \ d$
$\qquad\qquad\qquad\quad |\quad bind\ x \equiv V\ \ \square\ |\ \mathtt{pointcut}\ x = \square\ \ d$

General values $V ::= v\ |\ d_v\ |\ \mathtt{call}(\ell)$

Fig. 4. `TinyAspect` Values and Contexts

$$\frac{}{(\eta, \ (\texttt{fn } x{:}\tau \texttt{ => } e) \ v) \mapsto (\eta, \ \{v/x\}e)} \ \textit{r-app} \qquad \frac{\eta[\ell] = v_1}{(\eta, \ \ell \ v_2) \mapsto (\eta, \ v_1 \ v_2)} \ \textit{r-lookup}$$

$$\frac{\ell \notin domain(\eta) \quad \eta' = [\ell{\mapsto}v] \ \eta}{(\eta, \ \texttt{val } x = v \ d) \mapsto (\eta', \ \texttt{val } x \equiv \ell \ \{\ell/x\}d)} \ \textit{r-val}$$

$$\frac{}{\begin{array}{c} (\eta, \ \texttt{pointcut } x = \texttt{call}(\ell) \ d) \mapsto \\ (\eta, \ \texttt{pointcut } x \equiv \texttt{call}(\ell) \ \{\texttt{call}(\ell)/x\}d) \end{array}} \ \textit{r-pointcut}$$

$$\frac{\begin{array}{c} v' = (\texttt{fn } x{:}\tau \texttt{ => } \{\ell'/\texttt{proceed}\}e) \\ \ell' \notin domain(\eta) \qquad \eta' = [\ell{\mapsto}v', \ell'{\mapsto}\eta[\ell]] \ \eta \end{array}}{(\eta, \ \texttt{around call}(\ell)(x{:}\tau) = e \ d) \mapsto (\eta', \ d)} \ \textit{r-around} \qquad \frac{(\eta, \ e) \mapsto (\eta', \ e')}{(\eta, \ C[e]) \mapsto \eta', \ C[e'])} \ \textit{r-ctx}$$

Fig. 5. TinyAspect Operational Semantics

$\eta' = [\ell{\mapsto}v] \ \eta$. The reduction judgment is of the form $(\eta, e) \mapsto (\eta', e')$, read, "In advice environment η, expression e reduces to expression e' with a new advice environment η'."

The rule for function application is standard, replacing the application with the body of the function and substituting the argument value v for the formal x. We normally treat labels ℓ as values, and there is no rule $\ell \mapsto \eta[\ell]$ because we want to avoid "looking them up" before they are advised. However, when we are in a position to invoke the function represented by a label, we use the rule *r-lookup* to look up the label's value in the current environment.

The next three rules reduce declarations to "declaration values." The val declaration binds the value to a fresh label and adds the binding to the current environment. It also substitutes the label for the variable x in the subsequent declaration(s) d. We leave the binding in the reduced expression both to make type preservation easier to prove, and also to make it easy to extend TinyAspect with a module system which will need to retain the bindings. The pointcut declaration simply substitutes the pointcut value for the variable x in subsequent declaration(s).

The around declaration looks up the advised declaration ℓ in the current environment. It places the old value for the binding in a fresh label ℓ', and then re-binds the original ℓ to the body of the advice. Inside the advice body, any references to the special variable proceed are replaced with ℓ', which refers to the original value of the advised declaration. Thus, all references to the original declaration will now be redirected to the advice, while the advice can still invoke the original function by calling proceed.

The last rule shows that reduction can proceed under any context as defined in Figure 4.

3.4   Typechecking

Figure 6 describes the typechecking rules for TinyAspect. Our typing judgment for expressions is of the form $\Gamma; \Sigma \vdash e : \tau$, read, "In variable context Γ and

$$\frac{x{:}\tau \in \Gamma}{\Gamma; \Sigma \vdash x : \tau} \ \textit{t-var} \qquad\qquad \frac{\Gamma; \Sigma \vdash n : \tau_1 \to \tau_2}{\Gamma; \Sigma \vdash \mathtt{call}(n) : \mathtt{pc}(\tau_1 \to \tau_2)} \ \textit{t-pctype}$$

$$\frac{\ell{:}\tau \in \Sigma}{\Gamma; \Sigma \vdash \ell : \tau} \ \textit{t-label} \qquad\qquad \frac{}{\Gamma; \Sigma \vdash () : \mathtt{unit}} \ \textit{t-unit}$$

$$\frac{\Gamma, x{:}\tau_1; \Sigma \vdash e : \tau_2}{\Gamma; \Sigma \vdash \mathtt{fn} \ x{:}\tau_1 \ \texttt{=>} \ e : \tau_1 \to \tau_2} \ \textit{t-fn} \qquad \frac{\Gamma; \Sigma \vdash e_1 : \tau_2 \to \tau_1 \quad \Gamma; \Sigma \vdash e_2 : \tau_2}{\Gamma; \Sigma \vdash e_1 \ e_2 : \tau_1} \ \textit{t-app}$$

$$\frac{}{\Gamma; \Sigma \vdash \bullet : \bullet} \ \textit{t-empty} \qquad \frac{\Gamma; \Sigma \vdash v : T \quad \Gamma; \Sigma \vdash d : \beta}{\Gamma; \Sigma \vdash bind \ x \equiv v \ \ d : (x{:}T, \beta)} \ \textit{t-vdecl}$$

$$\frac{\Gamma; \Sigma \vdash e : \tau \quad \Gamma, x{:}\tau; \Sigma \vdash d : \beta}{\Gamma; \Sigma \vdash \mathtt{val} \ x = e \ \ d : (x{:}\tau, \beta)} \ \textit{t-val} \quad \frac{\Gamma; \Sigma \vdash p : \pi \quad \Gamma, x{:}\pi; \Sigma \vdash d : \beta}{\Gamma; \Sigma \vdash \mathtt{pointcut} \ x = p \ \ d : (x{:}\pi, \beta)} \ \textit{t-pc}$$

$$\frac{\begin{array}{c} \Gamma; \Sigma \vdash p : \mathtt{pc}(\tau_1 \to \tau_2) \qquad \Gamma; \Sigma \vdash d : \beta \\ \Gamma, x{:}\tau_1, \mathtt{proceed}{:}\tau_1 \to \tau_2; \Sigma \vdash e : \tau_2 \end{array}}{\Gamma; \Sigma \vdash \mathtt{around} \ p(x{:}\tau_1) = e \ \ d : \beta} \ \textit{t-around}$$

$$\frac{\forall \ell \in domain(\Sigma) \ . \ \ \bullet; \Sigma \vdash \eta[\ell] : \Sigma[\ell])}{\Sigma \vdash \eta} \ \textit{t-env}$$

Fig. 6. `TinyAspect` Typechecking

declaration context Σ expression e has type τ." Here Γ maps variable names to types, while Σ maps labels to types (similar to a store type).

The rules for expressions are standard. We look up the types for variables and labels in Γ and Σ, respectively. Other standard rules give types to the () expression, as well as to functions and applications.

The interesting rules are those for declarations. We give declaration signatures β to declarations, where β is a sequence of variable to type bindings. The base case of an empty declaration has an empty signature. For `val` bindings, we ensure that the expression is well-typed at some type τ, and then typecheck subsequent declarations assuming that the bound variable has that type. Pointcuts are similar, but the rule ensures that the expression p is well-typed as a pointcut denoting calls to a function of type $\tau_1 \to \tau_2$. When a val or pointcut binding becomes a value, the typing rule is the same except that subsequent declarations cannot see the bound variable (as it has already been substituted in). The around advice rule checks that the declared type of x matches the argument type in the pointcut, and checks that the body is well-typed assuming proper types for the variables x and `proceed`.

Finally, the judgment $\Sigma \vdash \eta$ states that η is a well-formed environment with typing Σ whenever all the values in η have the types given in Σ. This judgment, used in the soundness theorem, is analogous to store typings in languages with references.

3.5   Type Soundness

We now state progress and preservation theorems for `TinyAspect`. The theorems quantify over both expressions and declarations using the metavariable E, and quantify over types and declaration signatures using the metavariable T. The progress property states that if an expression is well-typed, then either it is already a value or it will take a step to some new expression.

Theorem 1 (Progress). *If* $;\Sigma \vdash E : T$ *and* $\Sigma \vdash \eta$, *then either* E *is a value or there exists* η' *such that* $(\eta, E) \mapsto (\eta', E')$.

Proof. By induction on the derivation of $;\Sigma \vdash E : T$.

The type preservation property states that if an expression is well-typed and it reduces to another expression in a new environment, then the new expression and environment are also well-typed.

Theorem 2 (Type Preservation). *If* $;\Sigma \vdash E : T$, $\Sigma \vdash \eta$, *and* $(\eta, E) \mapsto (\eta', E')$, *then there exists some* $\Sigma' \supseteq \Sigma$ *such that* $;\Sigma' \vdash E' : T$ *and* $\Sigma' \vdash \eta'$.

Proof. By induction on the derivation of $(\eta, E) \mapsto (\eta', E')$. The proof relies on standard substitution and weakening lemmas.

Together, progress and type preservation imply type soundness. Soundness means that there is no way that a well-typed `TinyAspect` program can get stuck or "go wrong" because it gets into some bad state.

Our type soundness theorem is slightly stronger than the previous result of Walker et al., in that we guarantee both type safety and a lack of run time errors. Walker et al. model **around** advice using a lower-level exception construct, and so their soundness theorem includes the possibility that the program will terminate with an uncaught exception [19].

4   Formalizing Modules

We now extend `TinyAspect` with Open Modules, a module system that allows programmers to enforce an abstraction boundary between clients and the implementation of a module. Our module system is modeled closely after that of ML, providing a familiar concrete syntax and benefiting from the design of an already advanced module system. In a distributed development setting, our module system places restrictions on aspects in order to provide the strong reasoning guarantee in Section 5. In a local development setting, however, our "module interfaces" could be computed by tools, and place no true restrictions on developers.

Figure 7 shows the new syntax for modules. Names include both simple variables x and qualified names $m.x$, where m is a module expression. Declarations can include structure bindings, and types are extended with module signatures of the form $\text{sig } \beta$, where β is the list of variable to type bindings in the module signature.

Names	$n ::= \dots \mid m.x$
Declarations	$d ::= \dots \mid \texttt{structure } x = m \; d$
Modules	$m ::= n \mid \texttt{struct } d \texttt{ end} \mid m \texttt{ :> } \sigma \mid \texttt{functor}(x{:}\sigma) \texttt{ => } m \mid m_1 \; m_2$
Decl. types	$\beta ::= \dots \mid x{:}\sigma, \beta$
Module types	$\sigma ::= \texttt{sig } \beta \texttt{ end} \mid \sigma_1 \rightarrow \sigma_2$
Module values $m_v ::= \texttt{struct } d_v \texttt{ end} \mid \texttt{functor}(x{:}\sigma) \texttt{ => } m$
Contexts	$C ::= \dots \mid \texttt{structure } x = \Box \; d \mid \texttt{struct } \Box \texttt{ end}$
	$\mid \quad \Box \texttt{ :> } \sigma \mid \Box \; m_2 \mid m_v \; \Box$

Fig. 7. Module System Syntax, Values, and Contexts

```
structure Cache = functor(X : sig f : pc(int->int) end) =>
    struct
        around X.f(x:int) = (* same definition as before *)
    end

structure Math = struct
    val fib = fn x:int => 1
    around call(fib) (x:int) =
        if (x > 2)
            then fib(x-1) + fib(x-2)
            else proceed x

    structure cacheFib =
        Cache (struct pointcut f = call(fib) end)

end :> sig
    fib : int->int
end
```

Fig. 8. Fibonacci with Open Modules

First-order module expressions include a name, a `struct` with a list of declarations, and an expression m `:>` σ that seals a module with a signature, hiding elements not listed in the signature. The expression `functor` $x{:}\sigma$ `=>` m describes a functor that takes a module x with signature σ as an argument, and returns the module m which may depend on x. Functor application is written like function application, using the form $m_1 \; m_2$.

4.1   Fibonacci Revisited

Figure 8 shows how a more reusable caching aspect could be defined using functors. The `Cache` functor accepts a module that has a single element `f` that is a pointcut of calls to some function with signature `int->int`. The `around` advice then advises the pointcut from the argument module `X`.

The `fib` function is now encapsulated inside the `Math` module. The module implements caching by instantiating the `Cache` module with a structure that binds the pointcut `f` to calls to `fib`. Finally, the `Math` module is sealed with a signature that exposes only the `fib` function to clients.

4.2   Sealing

Our module sealing operation has an effect both at the type system level and at the operational level. At the type level, it hides all members of a module that are not in the signature σ—in this respect, it is similar to sealing in ML's module system. However, sealing also has an operational effect, hiding internal calls within the module so that in a distributed development setting, clients cannot advise them unless the module explicitly exports the corresponding pointcut.

For example, in Figure 8, clients of the `Math` module would not be able to tell whether or not caching had been applied, even if they placed advice on `Math.fib`. Because `Math` has been sealed, external advice to `Math.fib` would only be invoked on external calls to the function, not on internal, recursive calls. This ensures that clients cannot be affected if the implementation of the module is changed, for example, by adding or removing caching.

4.3   Exposing Semantic Events with Pointcuts

Figure 9 shows how the shape example described above could be modeled in `TinyAspect`. Clients of the shape library cannot advise internal functions, because the module is sealed. To allow clients to observe internal but semantically important events like the motion of animated shapes, the module exposes these events in its signature as the `moves` pointcut. Clients can advise this pointcut without depending on the internals of the shape module. If the module's implementation is changed, the `moves` pointcut must also be updated so that client aspects are triggered in the same way.

Explicitly exposing internal events in an interface pointcut means a loss of some obliviousness in the distributed development case, since the author of the module must anticipate that clients might be interested in the event. On the other hand, we are still better off than in a non-AOP language, because the interface pointcut is defined in a way that does not affect the actual implementation of the module, as opposed to an invasive explicit callback, and because external calls to interface functions can still be obliviously advised.

Thus, sealing enforces the abstraction boundary between a module and its clients, allowing programmers to reason about and change them independently. However, our system still allows a module to export semantically important

```
structure shape = struct
    val createShape = fn ...
    val moveBy = fn ...
    val animate = fn ...
    ...
    pointcut moves = call(moveBy)
end :> sig
    createShape : Description -> Shape
    moveBy      : (Shape,Location) -> unit
    animate     : (Shape,Path) -> unit
    ...
    moves       : pc((Shape,Location)->unit)
end
```

Fig. 9. A shape library that exposes a position change pointcut

$$\frac{bind\ x \equiv v \in d_v}{(\eta,\ \texttt{struct}\ d_v\ \texttt{end}.x) \mapsto (\eta,\ v)}\ \textit{r-path}$$

$$\frac{}{\begin{array}{c}(\eta,\ \texttt{structure}\ x = m_v\ \ d) \mapsto \\ (\eta,\ \texttt{structure}\ x \equiv m_v\ \ \{m_v/x\}d)\end{array}}\ \textit{r-struct}$$

$$\frac{}{\begin{array}{c}(\eta,\ (\texttt{functor}(x{:}\sigma)\ \texttt{=>}\ m_1)\ m_v) \\ \mapsto (\eta,\ \{m_v/x\}m_1)\end{array}}\ \textit{r-fapp}$$

$$\frac{seal(\eta, d_v, \beta) = (\eta', d_{seal})}{\begin{array}{c}(\eta,\ \texttt{struct}\ d_v\ \texttt{end}\ \texttt{:>}\ \texttt{sig}\ \beta\ \texttt{end}) \\ \mapsto (\eta',\ \texttt{struct}\ d_{seal}\ \texttt{end})\end{array}}\ \textit{r-seal}$$

$$\frac{}{seal(\eta, \bullet, \bullet) = (\eta, \bullet)}\ \textit{s-empty}$$

$$\frac{seal(\eta, d, \beta) = (\eta', d')}{seal(\eta, bind\ x \equiv v\ \ d, \beta) = (\eta', d')}\ \textit{s-omit}$$

$$\frac{seal(\eta, d, \beta) = (\eta', d')\quad \eta'' = [\ell{\mapsto}\ell']\ \eta'\quad \ell \notin domain(\eta')}{seal(\eta, \texttt{val}\ x \equiv \ell'\ \ d, (x{:}\tau, \beta)) = (\eta'', \texttt{val}\ x \equiv \ell\ \ d')}\ \textit{s-v}$$

$$\frac{seal(\eta, d, \beta) = (\eta', d')}{seal(\eta, \texttt{pointcut}\ x \equiv \texttt{call}(\ell)\ \ d, (x{:}\texttt{pc}(\tau), \beta)) = (\eta', \texttt{pointcut}\ x \equiv \texttt{call}(\ell)\ \ d')}\ \textit{s-p}$$

$$\frac{seal(\eta, d_s, \beta_s) = (\eta', d_s')\quad seal(\eta', d, \beta) = (\eta'', d')}{\begin{array}{c}seal(\eta, \texttt{structure}\ x \equiv \texttt{struct}\ d_s\ \texttt{end}\ \ d, (x{:}\texttt{sig}\ \beta_s\ \texttt{end}, \beta)) \\ = (\eta'', \texttt{structure}\ x \equiv \texttt{struct}\ d_s'\ \texttt{end}\ \ d')\end{array}}\ \textit{s-s}$$

$$\frac{seal(\eta, d, \beta) = (\eta', d')}{\begin{array}{c}seal(\eta, \texttt{structure}\ x \equiv \texttt{functor}(y{:}\sigma_y)\ \texttt{=>}\ m\ \ d, (x{:}\sigma, \beta)) \\ = (\eta', \texttt{structure}\ x \equiv \texttt{functor}(y{:}\sigma_y)\ \texttt{=>}\ m\ \ d')\end{array}}\ \textit{s-f}$$

Fig. 10. Module System Operational Semantics

internal events, allowing clients to extend or observe the module's behavior in a principled way.

4.4   Operational Semantics

Figure 10 shows the operational semantics for Open Modules. In the rules, module values m_v mean either a struct with declaration values d_v or a functor. The path lookup rule finds the selected binding within the declarations of the module. We assume that bound names are distinct in this rule; it is easy to ensure this by renaming variables appropriately. Because modules cannot be advised, there is no need to create labels for structure declarations; we can just substitute the structure value for the variable in subsequent declarations. The rule for functor application also uses substitution.

The rule for sealing uses an auxiliary judgment, $seal$, to generate a fresh set of labels for the bindings exposed in the signature. This fresh set of labels insures that clients can affect external calls to module functions by advising the new labels, but cannot advise calls that are internal to the sealed module.

At the bottom of the diagram are the rules defining the sealing operation. The operation accepts an old environment η, a list of declarations d, and the sealing

$$\frac{\Gamma;\Sigma \vdash m : \text{sig } \beta \text{ end} \quad x{:}\tau \in \beta}{\Gamma;\Sigma \vdash m.x : \tau} \; t\text{-}name \qquad \frac{\Gamma;\Sigma \vdash m : \sigma \quad \Gamma, x{:}\sigma;\Sigma \vdash d : \beta}{\Gamma;\Sigma \vdash \text{structure } x = m \;\; d : (x{:}\sigma, \beta)} \; t\text{-}str$$

$$\frac{\Gamma;\Sigma \vdash d : \beta}{\Gamma;\Sigma \vdash \text{struct } d \text{ end} : \text{sig } \beta \text{ end}} \; t\text{-}struct \qquad \frac{\Gamma;\Sigma \vdash m : \sigma_m \quad \sigma_m <: \sigma}{\Gamma;\Sigma \vdash m :> \sigma : \sigma} \; t\text{-}seal$$

$$\frac{\Gamma, x{:}\sigma_1;\Sigma \vdash m : \sigma_2}{\Gamma;\Sigma \vdash \text{functor}(x{:}\sigma_1) \Rightarrow m : \sigma_1 \to \sigma_2} \; t\text{-}ftor \qquad \frac{\Gamma;\Sigma \vdash m_1 : \sigma_1 \to \sigma \quad \Gamma;\Sigma \vdash m_2 : \sigma_2 \quad \sigma_2 <: \sigma_1}{\Gamma;\Sigma \vdash m_1 \; m_2 : \sigma} \; t\text{-}fapp$$

Fig. 11. Open Modules Typechecking

$$\frac{}{\sigma <: \sigma} \; sub\text{-}reflex \qquad \frac{\sigma <: \sigma' \quad \sigma' <: \sigma''}{\sigma <: \sigma''} \; sub\text{-}trans$$

$$\frac{\beta <: \beta'}{\text{sig } \beta \text{ end} <: \text{sig } \beta' \text{ end}} \; sub\text{-}sig \qquad \frac{\beta <: \beta'}{x : T, \beta <: \beta'} \; sub\text{-}omit$$

$$\frac{\beta <: \beta' \quad \sigma <: \sigma'}{x : \sigma, \beta <: x : \sigma', \beta'} \; sub\text{-}decl \qquad \frac{\sigma_1' <: \sigma_1 \quad \sigma_2 <: \sigma_2'}{\sigma_1 \to \sigma_2 <: \sigma_1' \to \sigma_2'} \; sub\text{-}contra$$

Fig. 12. Signature Subtyping

declaration signature β. The operation computes a new environment η' and new list of declarations d'. The rules are structured according to the first declaration in the list; each rule handles the first declaration and appeals recursively to the definition of sealing to handle the remaining declarations.

An empty list of declarations can be sealed with the empty signature, resulting in another empty list of declarations and an unchanged environment η. The second rule allows a declaration *bind* $x \equiv v$ (where *bind* represents one of val, pointcut, or struct) to be omitted from the signature, so that clients cannot see it at all. The rule for sealing a value declaration generates a fresh label ℓ, maps that to the old value of the variable binding in η, and returns a declaration mapping the variable to ℓ. Client advice to the new label ℓ will affect only external calls, since internal references still refer to the old label which clients cannot change. The rule for pointcuts passes the pointcut value through to clients unchanged, allowing clients to advise the label referred to in the pointcut. Finally, the rules for structure declarations recursively seal any internal struct declarations, but leave functors unchanged.

4.5   Typechecking

The typechecking rules, shown in Figure 11, are largely standard. Qualified names are typed based on the binding in the signature of the module m. Structure bindings are given a declaration signature based on the signature σ of the bound module. The rule for struct simply puts a sig wrapper around the declaration signature. The rules for sealing and functor application allow a module to be passed into a context where a supertype of its signature is expected.

Figure 12 shows the definition of signature subtyping. Subtyping is reflexive and transitive. Subtype signatures may have additional bindings, and the signatures of constituent bindings are covariant. Finally, the subtyping rule for functor types is contravariant.

4.6   Type Soundness

When extended with Open Modules, `TinyAspect` enjoys the same type soundness property that the base system has. The theorems and proofs are similar, and so we omit them.

5   Reasoning About Equivalence

The example programs in Section 4 are helpful for understanding the benefits of `TinyAspect`'s module system at an intuitive level. However, we would like to be able to point to a concrete property that enables separate reasoning about the clients and implementation of a module.

Asking whether the implementation of a module is correct, or whether changes can be made to the module without affecting clients, is asking about the equivalence between a module implementation and a specification or between two module implementations. For the purposes of this paper, we assume that a specification is given as a reference implementation, reducing both questions to comparing two implementations. This definition is limited, since many specifications are intended to leave some behavior up to the implementor, but we leave a more flexible definition to future work.

A natural definition of equivalence is called *observational equivalence* [17] or *contextual equivalence*, meaning that no client context can distinguish two different implementations of a component. A simple way to define contextual equivalence is to use program termination as the observable variable: two expressions in a program are contextually equivalent if, for all client contexts, the client will either terminate when linked to both implementations of a component, or will run forever when linked to both implementations. We formalize this as follows:

Definition [Contextual Equivalence]: *Two expressions E_1 and E_2 are contextually equivalent, written $E_1 \equiv E_2$, if and only if for all contexts C such that $;\vdash C[E_1] : \tau$ and $;\vdash C[E_2] : \tau$ we have $(,E_1) \mapsto^* (\eta_1, V_1) \iff (,E_2) \mapsto^* (\eta_2, V_2)$.*

By definition, two contextually equivalent modules cannot be distinguished by any client.[1] Thus, contextual equivalence is adequate to answer whether a

---

[1] Note that since our formal system only models functional behavior, it cannot distinguish implementations with different performance characteristics.

$$\frac{(\bullet, E_1) \; diverges \qquad (\bullet, E_1) \; diverges}{E_1 \cong E_2}$$

$$\frac{(\bullet, E_1) \mapsto^* (\eta_1, V_1) \qquad (\bullet, E_2) \mapsto^* (\eta_2, V_2) \qquad \Lambda, \Sigma \vdash (\eta_1, V_1) \simeq (\eta_2, V_2) : T}{\Lambda = (domain(\eta_1) \cup domain(\eta_2)) - (fl(V_1) \cup fl(V_2)) \qquad \Lambda, \Sigma \vdash \eta_1 \simeq \eta_2}{E_1 \cong E_2}$$

Fig. 13. Logical Equivalence for Program Text

change to a module might affect clients, or whether an optimized implementation of a module is semantically equivalent to a reference implementation.

5.1 Logical Equivalence

Although contextual equivalence intuitively captures the semantics of equivalence, it is not very useful for actually proving that two modules are equivalent, because it requires quantifying over all possible clients. Instead, we give a more useful set of *logical equivalence* rules that can be used to reason about a module in isolation from possible clients. We then prove that these rules are sound with respect to the more natural, but less useful, contextual equivalence semantics. Finally, we briefly outline how the logical equivalence rules can be used to prove that two different implementations of a module are observationally equivalent.

Figure 13 defines logical equivalence for `TinyAspect` expressions. If two expressions diverge, they are logically equivalent. Otherwise, two expressions are equivalent if, in the empty context, they both reduce to environment-value pairs that obey a value equivalence relation, defined below. Note that these equivalence rules apply only to closed expressions; this is not a significant limitation, as expressions with free variables can easily be re-written as functions or functors.

The equivalence relation for values is somewhat more complex, because whether two values are equivalent depends both on the environment bindings for free labels in the value, and on which labels clients can advise. For example, the `Math` module in Figure 8 is equivalent to the same module without caching if clients cannot advise the internal recursive calls to `fib`, but would not be equivalent if clients can advise these calls.

We define an value equivalence judgment of the form $\Lambda, \Sigma \vdash (\eta, V) \simeq (\eta', V') : T$. Here, Λ represents a set of hidden labels that a client cannot advise. Σ is the type of labels that the client can advise (i.e., those not in Λ). The equivalence judgment includes both values and their corresponding environments, because whether two values are equivalent may depend on how they each use their private labels in Λ. A similar judgment, $\Lambda, \Sigma \vdash \eta_1 \simeq \eta_2$, used in the second logical equivalence rule and defined in Figure 14, verifies that two environments map all labels not in Λ to logically equivalent values.

The second rule in Figure 13 sets Λ to be all of the labels in the two environments that are not free in the values being compared (the set of free labels in V is written $fl(V)$). For the `Math` module in Figure 8, only the label generated for the `fib` function as part of the module sealing operation is free in the module value; all other labels, including the one that captures advice on

$$\frac{}{\Lambda, \Sigma \vdash (\eta_1, ()) \simeq (\eta_2, ()) : \text{unit}} \qquad \frac{\ell \notin \Lambda}{\Lambda, \Sigma \vdash (\eta_1, \ell) \simeq (\eta_2, \ell) : \Sigma[\ell]}$$

$$\frac{\ell \in \Lambda \qquad \Lambda, \Sigma \vdash (\eta_1, \eta_1[\ell]) \simeq (\eta_2, v) : \tau}{\Lambda, \Sigma \vdash (\eta_1, \ell) \simeq (\eta_2, v) : \tau} \qquad \frac{\ell \in \Lambda \qquad \Lambda, \Sigma \vdash (\eta_1, v) \simeq (\eta_2, \eta_2[\ell]) : \tau}{\Lambda, \Sigma \vdash (\eta_1, v) \simeq (\eta_2, \ell) : \tau}$$

$$\frac{\ell \notin \Lambda \qquad \Lambda, (\Sigma, \ell{:}\tau') \vdash (\eta_1, (\text{fn } x{:}\tau' \text{ => } e_1) \ \ell) \cong (\eta_2, (\text{fn } x{:}\tau' \text{ => } e_2) \ \ell) : \tau}{\Lambda, \Sigma \vdash (\eta_1, \text{fn } x{:}\tau' \text{ => } e_1) \simeq (\eta_2, \text{fn } x{:}\tau' \text{ => } e_2) : \tau' \to \tau}$$

$$\frac{}{\Lambda, \Sigma \vdash (\eta, \bullet) \simeq (\eta', \bullet) : (\bullet)} \qquad \frac{\ell \notin \Lambda \qquad \Lambda, \Sigma \vdash (\eta, d_v) \simeq (\eta', d_v') : \beta}{\Lambda, \Sigma \vdash (\eta, \text{val } x \equiv \ell \ \ d_v) \simeq (\eta', \text{val } x \equiv \ell \ \ d_v') : (x{:}\Sigma[\ell], \beta)}$$

$$\frac{\ell \notin \Lambda \qquad \Lambda, \Sigma \vdash (\eta, d_v) \simeq (\eta', d_v') : \beta}{\Lambda, \Sigma \vdash (\eta, \text{pointcut } x \equiv \text{call}(\ell) \ \ d_v) \simeq (\eta', \text{pointcut } x \equiv \text{call}(\ell) \ \ d_v') : (x{:}\text{pc}(\Sigma[\ell]), \beta)}$$

$$\frac{\Lambda, \Sigma \vdash (\eta, m_v) \simeq (\eta', m_v') : \sigma \qquad \Lambda, \Sigma \vdash (\eta, d_v) \simeq (\eta', d_v') : \beta}{\Lambda, \Sigma \vdash (\eta, \text{structure } x \equiv m_v \ \ d_v) \simeq (\eta', \text{structure } x \equiv m_v' \ \ d_v') : (x{:}\sigma, \beta)}$$

$$\frac{\Lambda, \Sigma \vdash (\eta, d_v) \simeq (\eta', d_v') : \beta}{\Lambda, \Sigma \vdash (\eta, \text{struct } d_v \text{ end}) \simeq (\eta', \text{struct } d_v' \text{ end}) : \text{sig } \beta \text{ end}}$$

$$\frac{\forall m^3, m^4 \quad \emptyset \vdash (\bullet, m^3) \cong (\bullet, m^4) : \sigma' \implies \Lambda, \Sigma \vdash (\eta_1, m_v^1 \ m^3) \cong (\eta_2, m_v^2 \ m^4) : \sigma}{\Lambda, \Sigma \vdash (\eta_1, m_v^1) \simeq (\eta_2, m_v^2) : \sigma' \to \sigma}$$

$$\frac{\forall \ell \ . \ \ell \in (domain(\eta_1) \cup domain(\eta_2)) \land \ell \notin \Lambda \implies \Lambda, \Sigma \vdash (\eta_1, \eta_1[\ell]) \simeq (\eta_2, \eta_2[\ell]) : \Sigma[\ell]}{\Lambda, \Sigma \vdash \eta_1 \simeq \eta_2}$$

Fig. 14. Logical Equivalence for Machine Values

recursive calls to `fib`, are hidden in Λ. This is the technical explanation for why the special semantics of `TinyAspect`'s sealing operation are important; without it, all internal calls to the public functions of a module would be available to advice.

This rule also shows the critical importance of keeping advice second-class in `TinyAspect`. In a system with second-class advice, clients can only advise the free labels in a module value, as shown in the rule. If pointcuts and advice were first-class, a function could compute a pointcut dynamically, return it to clients, which could then advise the pointcut. Keeping track of which functions clients could advise would be extremely difficult in this setting.

The rules for logical equivalence of value/environment pairs are defined in Figure 14. In these rules, we consider machine configurations to be equivalent up to alpha-conversion of label names in the environment.

Our rules are similar to typical logical relations rules, but have one important difference. Because `TinyAspect` supports a limited notion of state through the advice mechanism, logical equivalence is defined as a bisimulation [17]. That is, equivalent functions must not only produce equivalent results given equivalent arguments, they must *also* trigger advice on client-accessible labels in the same sequence and with the same arguments. Another way of saying this is that all possibly-infinite traces of pairs of (client-accessible label, argument value) triggered by logically equivalent functions must be themselves equivalent.

This bisimulation cannot be defined inductively on types as is usual for logical relations, because a function of type $\tau \rightarrow \tau'$ may trigger advice on labels whose types are themselves bigger than τ or τ'. Instead, the rules in Figure 14 should be interpreted coinductively for ordinary types–and thus all the rules for ordinary types τ are designed to be monotonic to ensure that the greatest fixpoint of the equivalence relation exists. We can still use an inductive definition of equivalence for module types σ, since module definitions cannot be advised To the best of our knowledge, this coinductive interpretation of logical equivalence rules is novel.

The first rule states that all unit values are equivalent. The second states that we can assume that any non-private label (i.e., one not in Λ) is equivalent to itself. Other labels can be judged equivalent to another value by looking up the label in the environment.

Two functions are equivalent if, when invoked with a fresh label, they execute with that label in a bisimilar way (using the machine expression equivalence judgment from Figure 15). We cannot use the usual logical relations rule for function equivalence, because this rule quantifies over logically equivalent pairs of arguments and is thus non-monotonic and incompatible with our co-inductive definition of equivalence.

Two empty declarations are equivalent to each other. Two `val` declarations are equivalent if they bind the same variable to the same label (since labels are generated fresh for each declaration we can always choose them to be equal when we are proving equivalence). Since the label exposed by the `val` declaration is visible, it must not be in the private set of labels Λ. Pointcut and structure declarations just check the equality of their components. All three declaration forms ensure that subsequent declarations are also equivalent. Two first-order modules are equivalent if the declarations inside them are also equivalent.

For functors, we use the usual logical relations rule: two functors are equivalent if they produce logically-equivalent module results for any logically-equivalent, closed module arguments. This definition is well-formed because equivalence for module types σ is defined inductively rather than coinductively, using the coinduction only for the base case of functions within modules.

Figure 15 shows the rules for logical equivalence of expression/environment pairs. These rules enforce bisimilarity with respect to values returned by a function or functor, or values passed to a non-private label. Our definitions are similar to weak bisimilarity in the π-calculus, with ordinary reductions or lookups of private labels corresponding to τ-transitions in the standard notion of weak bisimilarity.

The first rule states that two expressions are equivalent if they take any number of non-observable steps (written $\mapsto_\Lambda^*$) to reduce to values that are also equivalent. The non-observable step relation $\rightarrow_\Lambda$ is equivalent to ordinary reduction $\rightarrow$, except that the *r-lookup* rule may only be applied to labels in Λ (i.e., those that cannot be advised by clients).

$$\frac{(\eta_1, E_1) \mapsto_\Lambda^* (\eta_1', V_1) \qquad (\eta_2, E_2) \mapsto_\Lambda^* (\eta_2', V_2) \qquad \Lambda, \Sigma \vdash (\eta_1', V_1) \simeq (\eta_2', V_2) : T}{\Lambda, \Sigma \vdash (\eta_1, E_1) \cong (\eta_2, E_2) : T}$$

$$\frac{(\eta_1, E_1) \mapsto_\Lambda^+ (\eta_1', E_1') \qquad (\eta_2, E_2) \mapsto_\Lambda^+ (\eta_2', E_2') \qquad \Lambda, \Sigma \vdash (\eta_1', E_1') \cong (\eta_2', E_2') : T}{\Lambda, \Sigma \vdash (\eta_1, E_1) \cong (\eta_2, E_2) : T}$$

$$\frac{\ell, \ell' \notin \Lambda \qquad \Lambda, \Sigma \vdash (\eta_1, v_1) \simeq (\eta_2, v_2) : \tau}{\Sigma[\ell] = \tau \to \tau' \qquad \Lambda, (\Sigma, \ell':\tau') \vdash (\eta_1, C_1[\ell']) \cong (\eta_2, C_2[\ell']) : T}{\Lambda, \Sigma \vdash (\eta_1, C_1[\ell\ v_1]) \cong (\eta_2, C_2[\ell\ v_2]) : T}$$

Fig. 15. Logical Equivalence for Machine Expressions

The second rule allows two expressions to each take one or more non-observable steps (indicated by the + superscript instead of the * superscript for zero or more steps), resulting in observationally-equivalent expressions. Finally, the last rule states that if two equivalent expressions are both at the point where they need to look up a label that is *not* in Λ in order to continue, we must verify that the values to which the labels are applied are also equivalent, and that the contexts are equivalent once a fresh label (representing the result of the application, which is unknowable due to client advice) is substituted into the contexts. Since our definition of equivalence is coinductive, we can use an infinite sequence of the second and third rules to conclude that two non-terminating expressions are logically equivalent.

Now that we have defined logical equivalence, we can state a soundness theorem relating logical and contextual equivalence:

Theorem 3 (Soundness of Logical Equivalence). *If $E_1 \cong E_2$ then $E_1 \equiv E_2$.*

For space reasons, we give only a brief sketch of the proof of soundness. More details are available in a companion technical report [1]. The proof proceeds by establishing a bisimulation between two programs that consist of the same context with logically equivalent embedded values. The bisimulation invariant states that the two programs are structurally equivalent except for embedded closed values, which are themselves logically equivalent. The key lemma in the theorem states that the bisimulation is sound; that is, the bisimulation invariant is preserved by reduction.

We then observe that the logically equivalent expressions E_1 and E_2 either both diverge, or both reduce to logically equivalent values. In the former case, any context surrounding the expressions will also diverge, so the expressions are contextually equivalent in this case. In the latter case, the expressions will both reduce to values in the same context, which will then obey the bisimulation invariant described above. The soundness of bisimulation implies that these expressions will either both diverge or will reduce to logically equivalent values. Thus, the expressions are contextually equivalent in this case as well.

5.2   Applying Logical Equivalence

The definition of logical equivalence can be used to ensure that changes to the implementation of one module within an application preserve the application's semantics. For example, consider replacing the recursive implementation of the Fibonacci function in Figure 8 with an implementation based on a loop. In AspectJ, or any module system that does not include the dynamic semantics of our sealing operation, this seemingly innocuous change does not preserve the semantics of the application, because some aspect could be broken by the fact that fib no longer calls itself recursively.

Open Modules ensure that this change does not affect the enclosing application, and the logical equivalence rules can be used to prove this. When the module in Figure 8 is sealed, fib is bound to a fresh label that forwards external calls to the internal implementation of fib. We can show that the two implementations of the module are logically equivalent by showing that no matter what argument value the fib function is called with, the function returns the same results and invokes the *external* label in the same way. But the external label is fresh and is unused by either fib function, so this reduces to proving ordinary function equivalence, which can easily be done by induction on the argument value. We can then apply the abstraction theorem to show that clients are unaffected by the change.

6   Discussion

In this section, we reconsider the research questions from the introduction in light of the formal model of Open Modules and the logical equivalence definition. Since the formal model can be used to represent the tool support provided by IDEs like the AJDT, we consider how these tools might be enhanced in light of the model.

1. *How can developers specify an interface for a library or component that permits as many uses of advice as possible, while still ensuring critical properties of the component implementation?*
They can do so by declaring explicit pointcuts in the interface of the component that describe "supported" internal events. These pointcuts form a contract between a component provider and a client: The provider promises that if the client obeys the rules of the Open Module system, then the system will have the desired properties, and upgrades to the component will preserve client functionality. The client's side of the contract can be enforced by a compiler, while the component provider's side can be verified using the logical equivalence rules (and their principled extension to a full AOP language)

Once the proper interface has been declared, our logical equivalence rules show how to prove the full functional correctness of a module in a completely modular way, given that an aspect-aware interface has been computed and that an appropriate specification (e.g., in the form of a reference implementation) is available.

Of course, this answer is also limited: we give formal rules for a core language, and full languages are far more complex. However, our system could be used to prove the correctness of compiler optimizations for the constructs that are expressed in the core language. Our system may also be the foundation for a richer set of equivalence rules that can be applied to a full system. Finally, the formal rules in our system may be most helpful by showing engineers how to reason *informally* about the correctness of changes to an aspect-oriented program. Our system yields strong theoretical support to the intuitive notion that changes to a module will not affect clients as long as functions compute the same result and trigger pointcuts in the same way as the original module does.

2. How can developers specify an interface for a library or component that permits as many uses of advice as possible, while still allowing the component to be changed in meaningful ways without affecting clients?

The same kind of interface can be defined as in the question above. In the context of software evolution, however, the logical equivalence rules can be used to ensure that a proposed change to a module cannot affect that module's clients, even if the clients themselves are unknown. As long as the client code obeys the Open Module interface, it cannot be broken by an upgraded version of a third-party component.

Note that the client is free to choose to bypass the Open Module rules; a future compiler for Open Modules might issue a warning but compile the code anyway. In this case the client would lose the guarantee that upgrades would preserve the correctness of client code, but gain the ability to reuse or adapt the component in more flexible ways than are permitted by the Open Module system. Depending on the precise circumstances, the reuse benefits might outweigh the potential costs of fixing code that breaks after an upgrade.

Tool Support. As Parnas argued, the primary goal of modularity is to ease software evolution. The model we have developed shows that evolving a module's implementation might also involve changing the pointcuts that act on the module, so that they capture events in the new module's implementation that correspond to the events captured by the original pointcut in the original module specification. Currently the AJDT IDE aids this process by identifying what these pointcuts are, but the pointcuts must still be changed at their definition points, making the implementation task non-local. Our model suggests an improvement to IDEs: providing an editable view of the portion of each pointcut that intersects with a module's source code would allow many changes to be made in a more local way.

Language Design. Our modularity result suggests a number of guidelines for AOP language designers who want to preserve modular reasoning. First, declarative, second-class advice (as in **TinyAspect**) is easier to reason about than first-class advice. Second, in a language with first-class functions, advice should affect function declarations, not the functions themselves, again because this allows a module system to scope the effect of advice. Finally, languages should distinguish advice that affects only the interface of a module from more invasive forms of advice that affect a module's implementation.

7 Related Work

Formal Models. The most closely related formal models are the foundational calculus of Walker et al. [19], and the model of AspectJ by Jagadeesan et al. [10], both of which were discussed in the beginning of Section 3. In other work on formal models of AOP, Lämmel provides a big-step semantics for method-call interception in object-oriented languages [15]. Wand et al. give an untyped, denotational semantics for advice and dynamic join points [20].

Aspects and Modules. Dantas and Walker have extended the calculus of Walker et al. to support a module system [7]. Their type system includes a novel feature for controlling whether advice can read or change the arguments and results of advised functions. In their design, pointcuts are first-class and advice applies to functions, providing more flexibility compared to TinyAspect, where pointcuts are second-class and advice applies to declarations. This design choice makes it much more difficult to prove logical equivalence properties, however, because either making pointcuts first-class or tying advice to functions allows join points to escape from a module even if they are not explicitly exported in the module's interface. In their system, functions can only be advised if the function declaration explicitly permits this, and so their system is not oblivious in this respect [8]. In contrast, TinyAspect allows advice on all function declarations, and on all functions exported by a module, providing significant "oblivious" extensibility without compromising modular reasoning.

Lieberherr et al. describe Aspectual Collaborations, a construct that allows programmers to write aspects and code in separate modules and then compose them together into a third module [16]. Since they propose a full aspect-oriented language, their system is much richer and more flexible than ours, but its semantics are not formally defined. Their module system does not encapsulate internal calls to exported functions, and thus does not provide as strong an abstraction boundary as Open Modules does.

Other researchers have studied modular reasoning without the use of explicit module systems. For example, Clifton and Leavens propose engineering techniques that reduce dependencies between concerns in aspect-oriented code [5]. Other work has studied analyzing base code and advice separately using interfaces similar to those of Open Modules [14], and analyzing what advice might be affected by a change to code [13].

Our module system is based on that of standard ML [18]. TinyAspect's sealing construct is similar to the freeze operator that is used to close a module to future extensions in module calculi such as Jigsaw [3].

The name Open Modules indicates that modules are open to advice on functions and pointcuts exposed in their interface. Open Classes is a related term indicating that classes are open to the addition of new methods [6].

8   Conclusion

This paper described `TinyAspect`, a minimal core language for reasoning about aspect-oriented programming systems. `TinyAspect` is a source-level language that supports declarative aspects. We have given a small-step operational semantics to the language and proven that its type system is sound. We have described a proposed module system for aspects, formalized the module system as an extension to `TinyAspect`, and proved that the module system enforces abstraction. Abstraction ensures that clients cannot affect or depend on the internal implementation details of a module. As a result, programmers can both separate concerns in their code and reason about those concerns separately.

Acknowledgments

I thank Gregor Kiczales, Mira Mezini, Shriram Krishnamurthi, Ralf Lämmel, Mitch Wand, Karl Lieberherr, David Walker, Tim Halloran, Curtis Clifton, Derek Dreyer, Todd Millstein, Robert Harper, and anonymous reviewers for comments on this material. This work was supported by the High Dependability Computing Program from NASA Ames cooperative agreement NCC-2-1298, NSF grant CCR-0204047, and the Army Research Office grant number DAAD19-02-1-0389 entitled "Perpetually Available and Secure Information Systems."

References

1. J. Aldrich.   Open   Modules: Modular   Reasoning   about   Advice. Carnegie   Mellon   Technical   Report   CMU-ISRI-04-141,   available   at http://www.cs.cmu.edu/~aldrich/aosd/, Dec. 2004.
2. D. G. Bobrow, L. G. DiMichiel, R. P. Gabriel, S. E. Keene, G. Kiczales, and D. A. Moon. Common Lisp Object System Specification. In *SIGPLAN Notices 23*, September 1988.
3. G. Bracha. The Programming Language Jigsaw: Mixins, Modularity and Multiple Inheritance. Ph.D. Thesis, Dept. of Computer Science, University of Utah, 1992.
4. A. Clement, A. Colyer, and M. Kersten. Aspect-Oriented Programming with AJDT. In *ECOOP Workshop on Analysis of Aspect-Oriented Software*, July 2003.
5. C. Clifton and G. T. Leavens. Observers and Assistants: A Proposal for Modular Aspect-Oriented Reasoning. In *Foundations of Aspect Languages*, April 2002.
6. C. Clifton, G. T. Leavens, C. Chambers, and T. Millstein. MultiJava: Modular Open Classes and Symmetric Multiple Dispatch for Java. In *Object-Oriented Programming Systems, Languages, and Applications*, October 2000.
7. D. S. Dantas and D. Walker. Aspects, Information Hiding and Modularity. Princeton University Technical Report TR-696-04, 2004.
8. R. E. Filman and D. P. Friedman. Aspect-Oriented Programming is Quantification and Obliviousness. In *Advanced Separation of Concerns*, October 2000.
9. S. Gudmundson and G. Kiczales. Addressing Practical Software Development Issues in AspectJ with a Pointcut Interface. In *Advanced Separation of Concerns*, July 2001.

10. R. Jagadeesan, A. Jeffrey, and J. Riely. An Untyped Calculus of Aspect-Oriented Programs. In *European Conference on Object-Oriented Programming*, July 2003.
11. G. Kiczales, E. Hilsdale, J. Hugunin, M. Kersten, J. Palm, and W. G. Griswold. An Overview of AspectJ. In *European Conference on Object-Oriented Programming*, June 2001.
12. G. Kiczales, J. Lamping, A. Mendhekar, C. Maeda, C. V. Lopes, J.-M. Loingtier, and J. Irwin. Aspect-Oriented Programming. In *European Conference on Object-Oriented Programming*, June 1997.
13. C. Koppen and M. Stoerzer. PCDiff: Attacking the Fragile Pointcut Problem. In *European Interactive Workshop on Aspects in Software*, September 2004.
14. S. Krishnamurthi, K. Fisler, and M. Greenberg. Verifying Aspect Advice Modularly. In *Foundations of Software Engineering*, Nov. 2004.
15. R. Lämmel. A Semantical Approach to Method-Call Interception. In *Aspect-Oriented Software Development*, Apr. 2002.
16. K. Lieberherr, D. H. Lorenz, and J. Ovlinger. Aspectual Collaborations: Combining Modules and Aspects. *The Computer Journal*, 46(5):542–565, September 2003.
17. R. Milner. *Communicating and Mobile Systems: The π-Calculus*. Cambridge University Press, 1999.
18. R. Milner, M. Tofte, R. Harper, and D. MacQueen. *The Definition of Standard ML (Revised)*. MIT Press, Cambridge, Massachusetts, 1997.
19. D. Walker, S. Zdancewic, and J. Ligatti. A Theory of Aspects. In *International Conference on Functional Programming*, 2003.
20. M. Wand, G. Kiczales, and C. Dutchyn. A Semantics for Advice and Dynamic Join Points in Aspect-Oriented Programming. *Transactions on Programming Languages and Systems*, 26(5):890–910, September 2004.

Evaluating Support for Features in Advanced Modularization Technologies

Roberto E. Lopez-Herrejon, Don Batory, and William Cook

Department of Computer Sciences, University of Texas at Austin,
Austin, Texas, 78712, U.S.A
{rlopez, batory, wcook}@cs.utexas.edu

Abstract. A *software product-line* is a family of related programs. Each program is defined by a unique combination of features, where a *feature* is an increment in program functionality. Modularizing features is difficult, as feature-specific code often cuts across class boundaries. New modularization technologies have been proposed in recent years, but their support for feature modules has not been thoroughly examined. In this paper, we propose a variant of the expression problem as a canonical problem in product-line design. The problem reveals a set of technology-independent properties that feature modules should exhibit. We use these properties to evaluate five technologies: AspectJ, Hyper/J, Jiazzi, Scala, and AHEAD. The results suggest an abstract model of feature composition that is technology-independent and that relates compositional reasoning with algebraic reasoning[1].

1 Introduction

A *feature* is an increment in program functionality [53]. Researchers in software product-lines use features as a defacto standard in distinguishing the individual programs in a product-line, since each program is defined by a unique combination of features [24]. Features are the semantic building blocks of program construction; a product-line model is a set of features and constraints among features that define legal and illegal combinations. Product-line architects reason about programs in terms of features.

Despite their crucial importance, features are rarely modularized. The reason is that feature-specific code often cuts across class and package boundaries, thus requiring the use of preprocessors to wrap feature-specific code fragments in `#if-#endif` statements. While the use of preprocessors works in practice, it is hardly an adequate substitute for proper programming language support. Among the important properties sacrificed are: static typing of feature modules, separate compilation of feature modules, and specifications of feature modules that are independent of the compositions in which they are used (a property critical for reusability). This sacrifice is unacceptable.

In recent years, new technologies have been proposed that have the potential to provide better support for feature modularity. These technologies have very different

---

[1] This research is sponsored in part by NSF's Science of Design Project #CCF-0438786.

A.P. Black (Ed.): ECOOP 2005, LNCS 3586, pp. 169–194, 2005.

notions of modularity and composition, and as a consequence are difficult to compare and unify. Thus it is increasingly important to advance standard problems and metrics for technology evaluation. A few attempts have been made to compare technologies and evaluate their use to refactor and re-implement systems that are not part of a product family [13][19][30][37]. But for a few studies [16][52][35], the use of new technologies to modularize features in a product line is largely unexplored.

In this paper we present a standard problem that exposes common and fundamental issues that are encountered in feature modularity in product-lines. The problem reveals technology-independent properties that feature modules should exhibit. We use these properties to evaluate solutions written in five novel modularization technologies: AspectJ [1][25], Hyper/J [41][48], Jiazzi [31][32][52], Scala [45][38][39][40], and AHEAD [2][6]. The results suggest a technology-independent model of software composition where the definition and composition of features is governed by algebraic laws. The model provides a framework or set of criteria that a rigorous mathematical presentation should satisfy. Further, it helps reorient the focus on clean and mathematically justifiable abstractions when developing new tool-specific concepts.

2   A Standard Problem: The Expressions Product-Line

The *Expressions Product-Line (EPL)* is based on the extensibility problem also known as the "expression problem" [15][50]. It is a fundamental problem of software design that consists of extending a data abstraction to support a mix of new operations and data representations. It has been widely studied within the context of programming language design, where the focus is achieving data type and operation extensibility in a type-safe manner. Rather than concentrating on that issue, we consider the *design and synthesis* aspects of the problem to produce a family of program variations. More concretely, what features are present in the problem? How can they be modularized? And how can they be composed to build all the programs of the product-line?

2.1   Problem Description

Our product-line is based on Torgersen's expression problem [49]. Our goal is to define data types to represent expressions of the following language:

```
Exp :: = Lit | Add | Neg
Lit :: = <non-negative integers>
Add :: = Exp "+" Exp
Neg :: = "-" Exp
```

Two operations can be performed on expressions of this grammar:

1) `Print` displays the string value of an expression. The expression 2+3 is repre-sented as a three-node tree with an `Add` node as the root and two `Lit` nodes as leaves. The operation `Print`, applied to this tree, displays the string "2+3".
2) `Eval` evaluates expressions and returns their numeric value. Applying the oper-ation Eval to the tree of expression 2+3 yields 5 as result.

We add a class `Test` that creates instances of the data type classes and invokes their operations. We include this class to demonstrate additional properties that are important for feature modules. Figure 1 shows the complete Java code for a program of the product-line that implements all the data types and operations of EPL. Shortly we will see what the annotations at the beginning of each line mean.

```
lp   interface Exp {                   lp   class Lit implements Exp {
lp      void print();                  lp      int value;
le      int eval();                    lp      Lit (int v) { value = v; }
lp   }                                 lp      void print() {
                                       lp         System.out.print(value);
ap   class Add implements Exp {        lp      }
ap      Exp left, right;               le      int eval() { return value; }
ap      Add (Exp l, Exp r) {           lp   }
ap         left = l; right = r; }
ap      void print() {                 lp   class Test {
ap         left.print();               lp      Lit ltree;
ap         System.out.print("+");      ap      Add atree;
ap         right.print();              np      Neg ntree;
ap      }                              lp      Test() {
ae      int eval() {                   lp         ltree = new Lit(3);
ae         return left.eval()          ap         atree = new Add(ltree, ltree);
ae             + right.eval();         np         ntree = new Neg(ltree);
ae      }                              lp      }
ap   }                                 lp      void run() {
                                       lp         ltree.print();
np   class Neg implements Exp {        ap         atree.print();
np      Exp expr;                      np         ntree.print();
np      Neg (Exp e) { expr = e; }      le         System.out.println(ltree.eval());
np      void print() {                 ae         System.out.println(atree.eval());
np         System.out.print("-(");     ne         System.out.println(ntree.eval());
np         expr.print();               lp      }
np         System.out.print(")");      lp   }
np      }
ne      int eval() {
ne         return expr.eval() * -1;
ne      }
np   }
```

Fig. 1. Complete code of the Expressions Product Line

From a product-line perspective, we can identify two different feature sets [17]. The first is that of the operations {`Print`, `Eval`}, and the second is that of the data types {`Lit`, `Add`, `Neg`}. Using these sets, it is possible to synthesize all members of the product-line described in Figure 2 by selecting one or more operations, and one or more data types. For instance, row 4 is the program that contains `Lit` and `Add` with operations `Print` and `Eval`. As with any product-line design, in EPL there are constraints

	Operations		Data types		
Program	Print	Eval	Lit	Add	Neg
1	✓		✓		
2	✓	✓	✓		
3	✓		✓	✓	
4	✓	✓	✓	✓	
5	✓		✓		✓
6	✓	✓	✓		✓
7	✓		✓	✓	✓
8	✓	✓	✓	✓	✓

Fig. 2. Members of the EPL

on how features are combined to form programs. For example, all members require Lit data type, as literals are the only way to express numbers.

A common way to implement features in software product-lines is to use preprocessor declarations to surround the lines of code that are specific to a feature. If we did this for the program in Figure 1, the result would be unreadable. Instead, we use an annotation at the start of each line to indicate the feature to which the line belongs. This makes it easy to build a preprocessor that receives as input the names of the desired features and strips off from the code of Figure 1 all the lines that belong to unneeded features. As can be imagined, this approach is very brittle for problems of larger scale and complexity. Never the less, the approach can be used as a reference to define what is expected from feature modules in terms of functionality (classes, interfaces, fields, methods, constructors), behaviour (sequence of statements executed), and composition.

2.2 Feature Modularization

A natural representation of the expression problem, and thus for EPL, is a two-dimensional matrix [15][50][22]. The vertical dimension specifies data types and the horizontal dimension specifies operations. Each matrix entry is a *feature module* that implements the operation, described by the column, on the data type, specified by the row. As a naming convention throughout the paper, we identify matrix entries by using the first letters of the row and the column, e.g., the entry at the intersection of row Add and column Print is named ap and implements operation Print on data type Add. This matrix is shown in Figure 3 where module names are encircled.

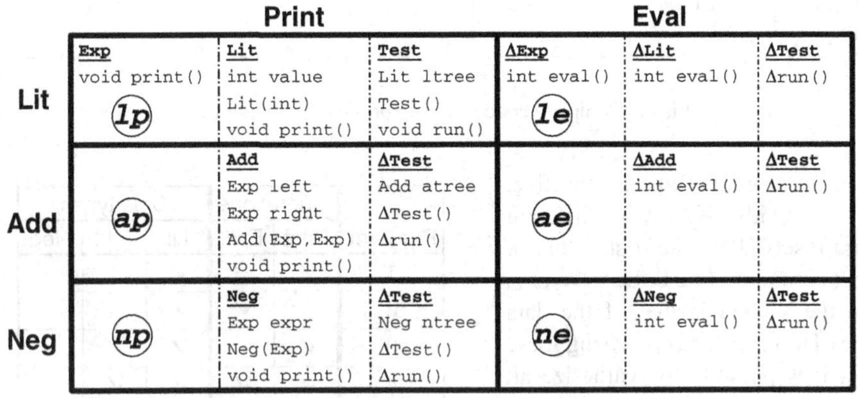

	Print			**Eval**		
Lit (1p)	Exp void print()	Lit int value Lit(int) void print()	Test Lit ltree Test() void run()	ΔExp int eval() (1e)	ΔLit int eval()	ΔTest Δrun()
Add (ap)		Add Exp left Exp right Add(Exp,Exp) void print()	ΔTest Add atree ΔTest() Δrun()	(ae)	ΔAdd int eval()	ΔTest Δrun()
Neg (np)		Neg Exp expr Neg(Exp) void print()	ΔTest Neg ntree ΔTest() Δrun()	(ne)	ΔNeg int eval()	ΔTest Δrun()

Fig. 3. Matrix representation and Requirements

To compose any program from Figure 2, the modules involved are those at the intersection of the selected columns and the selected rows. For example, program number 1, that provides Print operation on Lit, only requires module 1p. Another example is program 6, that implements operations Print and Eval on Lit and Neg data types, requires modules lp, le, np, and ne.

The source code of a feature module are the lines that are annotated with the name of the module. For instance, the contents of feature ap include:

a) Class Add with Exp fields left and right, a constructor with two Exp arguments, and method void print(), and

b) An increment to class Test, because it is adding something to the class as opposed to contributing a brand new class as is the case of class Add. This increment is symbolized by △Test in Figure 3. It adds: field atree, a statement to the body of the constructor expressed with △Test(), and a statement to the body of method run expressed as △run().

For clarity we decided to put the Exp interface inside module lp instead of creating a separate row for it. This decision makes sense since the other data types are built using Lit objects. Also, we put the constructors and fields of the data types in column Print instead of refactoring them into a new column and have columns Print and Eval implement only their corresponding methods. Later we will see an interesting consequence of these two design decisions. Additionally, from the design requirements we can infer dependencies and interactions among the feature modules. For instance, if we want to build a program with module ap, we also need to include module lp because ap increments the Test class which is introduced in lp. Later, we briefly discuss this issue as compositional constraints, which are not the focus of this paper. Constraints are discussed in [2][3][9].

3 Basic Properties for Feature Modularity

To give structure to our evaluation, we identify a set of basic properties about features that can readily be inferred from, illustrated by, and assessed in EPL and its solutions in the five technologies evaluated. Conceivably, there are other desirable properties that feature modules should exhibit such as readability, ease of use, etc. However, for sake of simplicity and breadth of scope, they are not part of this evaluation as their objective assessment would require a larger case study that would prevent us from comparing all five technologies together.

The properties are grouped into two categories, covering the basic definition of features and their composition to create programs. The first properties in each category follow from the structure of EPL, while the others come from the studied solutions to EPL and are desirable from the software engineering perspective.

3.1 Feature Definition Properties

The first category of properties relate to the definition of the basic building blocks of EPL, the representation of each piece, and their organization into features.

Program Deltas. The code in Figure 1 can be decomposed into a collection of *program deltas* or program fragments. The kinds of program deltas required to solve EPL are summarized in Figure 3, and include:

- *New Classes*, for example `Lit` in module `lp`.
- *New Interfaces*, for example `Exp` in module `lp`.
- *New fields* that are added to existing classes, like field `atree` in module `ap` is added to class `Test`.
- *New methods* that are added to existing interfaces, like `eval()` in module `le` is added to interface `Exp`.
- *Method extensions* that add statements to methods. For example, extension to method `run()`, expressed by Δ`run()`, in all modules except `lp`.
- *Constructor extensions* that add statements to constructors. For instance, extensions to constructor `Test()`, expressed by Δ`Test()`, in modules `ap` and `np`.

There are other program deltas, such as new constructors, new static initializers, new exception handlers, etc. that are not needed for implementing EPL and thus are not considered in this paper. Nonetheless, we believe that EPL contains a sufficient set of program deltas for an effective evaluation.

Cohesion. It must be possible to collect a set of program deltas and assign them a name so that they can be identified and manipulated as a cohesive module.

Separate Compilation. Separate compilation of features is useful for two practical reasons: a) it allows debugging of feature implementation (catching syntax errors) in isolation, and b) it permits the distribution of bytecode instead of source code.

3.2   Feature Composition Properties

Once a set of feature modules has been defined, it must be possible to compose them to build all the specific programs in the Expression Product Line.

Flexible Composition. The implementation of a feature module should be syntactically independent of the composition in which it is used. In other words, a fixed composition should not be hardwired into a feature module. Flexible composition improves reusability of modules for constructing a family of programs.

Flexible Order. The order in which features are composed can affect the resulting program. For instance, in EPL, the order of test statements in method `run()` affects the output of the program. The program in Figure 1 is the result of one possible ordering of features, namely (`lp`, `ap`, `np`, `le`, `ae`, `ne`). Another plausible order in EPL is to have expressions printed and evaluated consecutively, as in order (`lp`, `le`, `ap`, `ae`, `np`, `ne`). Hence, feature modules should be composable in different orders.

Closure Under Composition. Feature modules are closed under composition if one or more features can be composed to make a new composite feature. Composite features must be usable in all contexts where basic features are allowed. In EPL, it would be natural to compose the `Lit` and `Neg` representations to form a `LitNeg` feature which represents positive and negative numbers.

Static Typing. Feature modules and their composition are subject to static typing which helps to ensure that both are well-defined, for example, preventing method-not-found errors. We base the evaluation of this property on the availability of a formal typing theory or mechanism behind each technology.

Using these properties we evaluate AspectJ, Hyper/J, Jiazzi, Scala, and AHEAD in the following sections.[2] We use a concrete example to illustrate these alternatives, i.e. the program that supports `Print` and `Eval` operations in `Lit` and `Add` data types (program number 4 in Figure 2). Thus, the program has four modules: `lp`, `ap`, `le`, and `ae` that we compose in this order (the same as in Figure 1). Throughout the paper, we call this program `LitAdd`.

4   AspectJ

An aspect, as implemented in *AspectJ*[3] [1][25], modularizes a *cross-cut* as it contains code that can extend several classes and interfaces.

4.1   Feature Modules and Their Composition

The implementation of module `lp` is straightforward as it consists of Java interface `Exp` and classes `Lit` and `Test`. In AspectJ literature, programs written using only pure Java code are called *base code*. In Figure 4a, the names of files that are base code are shown in italics, while those of *aspect code* are shown in all capital letters.

	Print	Eval
Lit	*Exp, Lit, Test*	LE
Add	*Add, AP*	AE
Neg	*Neg, NP*	NE

(a)

```
public aspect LE {

    // ΔExp interface
    public abstract int Exp.eval();

    // ΔLit class
    public int Lit.eval() { return value; }

    // ΔTest, advice that implements Δrun()
    pointcut LPRun(Test t):
        execution (public void Test.run())
        && target(t);

    void around(Test t) : LPRun(t) {
        proceed(t);
        System.out.println("= "  + t.ltree.eval());
    }
}
```

(b)

Fig. 4. AspectJ Solution

---

[2] For a more detailed description of the implementation see [29].
[3] We used AspectJ version 1.1 for our evaluation.

Alternatively, we could have declared the new classes and interfaces as nested elements of an aspect. However, they would be subject to the instantiation of their containing aspect, and their references would be qualified with the aspect name where they are declared. For these reasons, we decided to implement classes and interfaces in separate files.

From Figure 3, module le:

1) adds method eval() to interface Exp,
2) adds the implementation of eval() to class Lit, and
3) appends a statement to method run() of class Test that calls eval() on field ltree.

The entire code of module le is implemented with the aspect shown in Figure 4b. The first two requirements use AspectJ's *inter-type declaration*, which is part of its *static crosscutting* model [1][25][4]. Method extensions, like that of the third requirement, cannot be implemented as inter-type declarations because members with the same signature can be introduced only once. Hence, to implement the last requirement it is necessary to utilize AspectJ's *dynamic crosscutting* model which permits adding code (*advice*) at particular points in the execution of a program (*join points*) that are specified through a predicate (*pointcut*).

Since it is required to execute an additional statement when method run() is executed, we must capture the join point of the execution of that method. Also, since the statement to add is a method call on field ltree of class Test, we must get a hold of the object that is the target of the execution of method run() to access its ltree field. These two conditions are expressed in pointcut LPRun of Figure 4b, where t is the reference to the target object. Lastly, to add the extension statement we use an around advice. This type of advice executes instead of the join points of the pointcut, but it allows its execution by calling AspectJ's special method proceed. We add the new statement to run() after the call to method proceed(t).[5]

The implementation of feature module ap (not shown in Figure 4) uses two files. The first is a Java class to implement data type Add. The second is an aspect to implement the extensions to class Test. The first extension adds a new field to class Test. This is done also using inter-type declaration in the following way:

```
public Add Test.atree;
```

The other two extensions of module ap, ΔTest() and Δrun(), are implemented in a similar way to those of module le. The other modules ae, np, and ne have an analogous implementation.

To compose program LitAdd, the AspectJ compiler (*weaver*) ajc, requires the file names of the base code and the aspects of the feature modules. The composition is specified as follows, where the order of the terms is inconsequential:

---

[4] We could also implement the first requirement as follows:

```
public int Exp.eval() { return 0; }
```

This alternative defines a default value for the method which can be subsequently overridden by each class that implements Exp.

[5] Method proceed, has the same arguments as the advice where it is used.

```
ajc Exp.java Lit.java Test.java LE.java Add.java AP.java AE.java
    -outjar LitAdd.jar                                          (1)
```

The static crosscutting model of AspectJ has a simple realization that does not depend on order, namely, members can only be introduced once. However, in the case of dynamic crosscutting, i.e. pointcuts and advice, several pieces of advice can apply to the same join point. In such cases, the order in which advice code is executed is in general undefined[6]. This means that a programmer cannot know a priori, by simply looking at the pointcut and advice code, in what order advice is applied. In program LitAdd, this issue is manifested in the order of execution of method run() and its extensions. The order that we want is that of Figure 1, namely, first the statement from lp followed by those of ap, le and ae. However, the order obtained by executing the program is statements from lp, ae, ap, and le[7].

AspectJ provides a mechanism to give precedence to advice, thus imposing an order, at the aspect level. In other words, it can give precedence to all the advice of an aspect over those of other aspects. To obtain the order that we want for method run(), we must define the following aspect:

```
public aspect Ordering {
        declare precedence : AE, LE, AP;
}
```

and add it to the list of files in the specification (1). For further details on how precedence clauses are built, consult [1][26].

4.2 Evaluation

Feature Definition. AspectJ can describe all program deltas required for EPL. However, in cases like module ap which is implemented with class Add and aspect AP, there is no way to express that both together form feature ap. In other words, AspectJ does not have a cohesion mechanism to group all program deltas together and manipulate them as a single module. Nonetheless, this issue can be addressed with relatively simple tool support. Aspects cannot be compiled separately, as they need have base code in which to be woven.

Feature Composition. AspectJ provides flexible composition and order. It can be used to build all members of EPL in the order described in an auxiliary aspect that contains a declare precedence clause. This type of clause can also be used inside aspects that implement feature modules, like LE, but doing that could reduce order flexibility as the order could be different for different programs where LE is used. Feature modules implemented in AspectJ are not closed under composition for two reasons: the absence of a cohesion mechanism and the lack of a general model of aspect composition. The latter is subject of intensive research [18]. Static typing support for AspectJ is also an area of active research [23][51].

---

[6] There are special rules that apply for certain types of advice when advices are defined in either the same aspect or in others [1]. These rules help determine the order in few cases but not in general.

[7] In AspectJ version 1.1.

5 Hyper/J

Hyper/J [48] is the Java implementation of an approach to *Multi-Dimensional Separation of Concerns (MDSoC)* called Hyperspaces [41][47]. A *hyperspace* is a set of units. A unit can be either primitive, such as a field, method, and constructor; or compound such as a classe, interface, and package.

A *hyperslice* is a modularization mechanism that groups all the units that implement a *concern* (a feature in this paper) which consists of a set of classes and interfaces. Hyperslices must be *declaratively complete*. They must have a declaration, that can be incomplete (stub) or abstract, for any unit they reference. Hyperslices are integrated in *hypermodules* to build larger hyperslices or even complete systems.

5.1 Feature Modules and Their Composition

The Hyper/J weaver performs composition at the bytecode level which makes a natural decision to implement each hyperslice (feature module) as a package that can be compiled independently. Hyperslices that contain only new classes and interfaces, like module lp, have a straightforward implementation as Java packages. The interesting case is hyperslices that extend units in other hyperslices. For example, Figure 5a shows the package that implements feature le. It adds method eval() to Exp (new method in an interface), the implementation in Lit (new method in a class), and a call in method run() of class Test (method extension).

interface Exp {	class Lit implements Exp {	class Test {
int eval();	public int value; // stub lp	Lit ltree; // stub lp
}	public Lit (int v) { } // req constructor	public void run() {
	public int eval() { return value; }	System.out.println(ltree.eval());
	}	}
		}

(a) Package LE of feature le

Hyperspace (hs)	Concern Mapping (cm)	Hypermodule (hm)
hyperspace LitAdd	package LP : Feature.LP	hypermodule LitAdd
composable class LP.*;	package LE : Feature.LE	hyperslices:
composable class LE.*;	package AP : Feature.AP	Feature.LP,
composable class AP.*;	package AE : Feature.AE	Feature.AP,
composable class AE.*;		Feature.LE,
		Feature.AE;
		relationships:
		mergeByName;
		end hypermodule;

(b) Composition Specification

Fig. 5. Hyper/J Implementation

However, extra code is required to make a hyperslice declaratively complete so that it can be compiled. For instance, variable `value` that is introduced in feature `lp` is replicated in class `Lit` so that it can be returned by method `eval()`. Something similar occurs with variable `ltree` in `Test`. Additionally, the Hyper/J weaver requires stubs for non-default constructors. When the package is compiled, the references of these variables are bound to the definitions in the package; however, when composed with other hyperslices that also declare these variables, all the references are bound to a single declaration determined by the composition specification. The extension of methods and constructors is realized by appending the code of their bodies one after the other. The rest of the feature modules are implemented similarly.

The `LitAdd` composition is defined by the three files of Figure 5b: hyperspace `Lit-Add.hs`, concern mapping `LitAdd.cm`, and hypermodule `LitAdd.hm`. The hyperspace file lists all the units that participate in the composition. The concern mapping divides the hyperspace into features (hyperslices) and gives them names. Finally, the hypermodule specifies what hyperslices are composed and what mechanisms (operators) to use. Our example merges units that have the same name.

5.2 Evaluation

Feature Definition. Hyper/J's hyperslices can modularize all deltas, treat them as a cohesive unit, and compile them separately. Though, separate compilation requires manual completion of the hyperslices.

Feature Composition. Hyper/J provides flexible composition. The order is specified in the hypermodule and can be done using several composition operators [48], thus composition order is flexible. Hyperslices are by definition closed under composition. To the best of our knowledge there is no theory to support static typing of hyperslices.

6 Jiazzi

Jiazzi [31][32][52] is a component system that implements units [21][22] in Java. A *unit* is a container of classes and interfaces. There are two types of units: *atoms*, built from Java programs, and *compounds* built from atoms and other compounds. Units are the modularization mechanism of Jiazzi. Therefore they are the focus of our evaluation.

6.1 Feature Modules and Their Composition

Jiazzi programs use pure Java constructs. Jiazzi groups classes and interfaces in *packages* that are syntactically identical to Java packages. Implementation of modules like `lp` are thus standard Java packages with normal classes and interfaces. Consider the following code contained in package `le` that implements the feature of the same name[8]:

---

[8] Definition of non-default constructors is required but not shown.

```
public interface Exp extends lp.Exp {
    int eval();
}
public class Lit extends lp.Lit
 implements fixed.Exp {
   public int eval() { return value; }
}
public class Test extends lp.Test {
  public void run() {
    super.run();
    System.out.println(ltree.eval());
  }
}
```

Two important things to note are: a) `Exp`, `Lit` and `Test` *extend* their counterparts of feature `lp`, and b) class `Lit` implements `fixed.Exp` which refers to the version of `Exp` that contains all the extensions in a composition.

Package `le` shows how methods can be added to existing classes and interfaces, and how existing methods can be extended. Jiazzi also supports adding new classes, interfaces, constructor extensions, and fields in a similar way to that of normal Java inheritance. The rest of the feature modules are implemented along the lines of module `le`.

Composition in Jiazzi is elaborate. For simplicity, we illustrate unit composition with units `lp` and `le` instead of `LitAdd`. From this readers can infer what the composition of `LitAdd` entails.

We start with the definition of a *signature* which describes the structure of a package, i.e., the interface it exports. The following code is the signature of package `le`[9]:

```
signature leS = l : lpS + {
  package fixed;
  public interface Exp { int eval(); }
  public class Lit { public int eval(); }
  public class Test { public void run(); }
}
```

Two relevant points are: a) the expression `l:lpS +` indicates that `leS` is an extension of signature `lpS`, meaning that `Exp`, `Lit`, and `Test` of `le` extend their counterparts in `lp`, and b) `fixed` is a *package parameter* that is used, as we have seen, in the implementation of `le`. How this parameter is bound is explained shortly.

A unit definition consists of import and export packages followed (if necessary) by a series of statements that establish relations among the packages which, in the case of compound units, determines the order in which units are composed. Each of the features in our problem is implemented by an atom, and a program in the EPL is expressed by a compound unit. The following code defines unit `le`:

```
atom le {
  import lp : lpS;
  export le extends lp : leS;
  import fixed extends le;
}
```

---

[9] For convention in this section, we form signature names with the names of the packages they described followed by a S.

It asserts that atom le imports package lp with signature lpS and that it exports package le of signature leS which is an extension of lp. It also states that it imports package fixed, an extension of le which is bound, at composition time, to the package parameter of the same name in the signature.

Jiazzi supports composition through the *Open Class Pattern* [31][32]. The key element of this pattern is the creation of a package, called fixed in our example, that contains all the extensions made by the units. This package is imported by the atom units, creating a feedback loop that permits them to refer to the most extended version of the classes and interfaces involved in a composition.

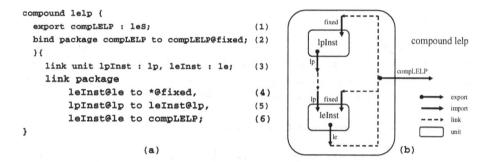

```
compound lelp {
    export compLELP : leS;                      (1)
    bind package compLELP to compLELP@fixed;    (2)
    }{
        link unit lpInst : lp, leInst : le;     (3)
        link package
            leInst@le to *@fixed,               (4)
            lpInst@lp to leInst@lp,             (5)
            leInst@le to compLELP;              (6)
}
```

(a)   (b)

Fig. 6. Jiazzi Composition of le and lp

Figure 6a shows the code that composes these two units. Figure 6b illustrates this composition. Consider the second part of the specification first. It states that the composition contains two units (line 3): lpInst an instance of unit lp, and leInst an instance of unit le. The packages of these two units are linked as follows: a) line 4 states that the exported package le of leInst is bound to all the fixed packages in the compound, b) line 5 sets the link between the export package lp of lpInst to the import package lp of leInst.

To be useful, compound packages must export something, in our case it exports a package that we named compLELP with signature leS (line 1) which is linked to package le of unit leInst in line 6. Since compLELP has signature leS that contains package parameter fixed we must bind it, in this case to itself, as done in line 2.

Signatures allow separate unit compilation. Jiazzi provides a stub generator that uses the unit's signature to create the packages and the code skeletons of the classes and interfaces required to compile the unit. It also provides a linker that checks that the compiled unit conforms to the unit's signature and stores the unit's binaries and signature into a Java archive (jar) file that can be used to compose with other units. For further details on the stub generator and linker refer to [33].

6.2 Evaluation

Feature Definition. Jiazzi units can modularize all program deltas of EPL in a cohesive way. Furthermore, signatures allow separate compilation.

Feature Composition. Jiazzi separates clearly the implementation of features from their composition thus provides a flexible composition. The order of unit composition is determined by the linking statements in compound units and therefore it is flexible. By definition, units are closed under composition. Jiazzi is backed up with a formal theory for type checking units and their compositions [21][22]. This theory permits the linker to statically check and report errors in program composition.

Jiazzi's type checking and separate compilation come with a price. Defining signatures and wiring the relationships between units is a non-trivial task, especially when dealing with multiple units with complex relations among them [52].

7 Scala

Scala is a strongly-typed language that fuses concepts from object-oriented programming and functional programming [45][38]. Though Scala borrows from Java, it is not an extension of it. We included Scala[10] in our evaluation because it supports two nontraditional modularization mechanisms: traits [44] and mixins [10].

7.1 Feature Modules and Their Composition

A trait in Scala can be regarded as an abstract class without state and parameterized constructors. It can implement methods and contain inner classes and traits. We implemented each feature module by a trait. Consider the implementation of feature lp shown in Figure 7a. The trait contains:

- Abstract type exp with upper bound Exp. This means that exp is at least a subtype of Exp and thus it leaves exp open for further extensions by other features.
- Trait Exp declares method print(). A trait is used in this context because it is roughly equivalent to a Java interface, as it declares a type with methods whose implementations are not yet defined.
- Class Lit extends Exp.[11] It has a *primary constructor* (or main constructor) that receives an integer which is assigned to field value. It also provides an implementation for method print() that displays this field.
- Class Test contains abstract field ltree of abstract type exp. Because of this, class Test is also abstract. Test also contains method run() that calls method print() on ltree.

Trait ap is implemented as an extension of trait lp , shown in Figure 7b, that contains:

- Class Add that extends trait Exp of module lp. It has a two parameter constructor to initialize the expression fields and the implementation of method print().

---

[10] We used version 1.3.0.10 for our evaluation.
[11] Scala traits are conceptually not different from classes so that is why we use an extends clause instead of implements.

```
package epl;
trait lp {
  type exp <: Exp;
  trait Exp {
    def print(): unit;
  }
  class Lit(v: int) extends Exp {
    val value = v;
    def print(): unit = System.out.print(value);
  }
  abstract class Test {
    val ltree: exp;
    def run(): unit = { ltree.print(); }
  }
}
                        (a)
```

```
package epl;
trait le extends lp {
  type exp <: Exp;
  trait Exp extends super.Exp {
    def eval(): int
  }
  class Lit(v: int) extends super.Lit(v) with Exp {
    def eval(): int = value;
  }
  abstract class Test extends super.Test {
    override def run(): unit = {
      super.run();
      System.out.println(ltree.eval());
    }
  }
}                       (c)
```

```
package epl;
trait ap extends lp {
  class Add(l: exp, r: exp) extends super.Exp {
    val left = l; val right = r;
    def print(): unit = {
      left.print(); System.out.print("+");
      right.print();
    }
  }
  abstract class Test extends super.Test {
    val atree: exp;
    override def run(): unit = {
      super.run(); atree.print();
    }
  }
}                       (b)
```

```
package epl;
trait ae extends ap with le {
  class Add(l: exp, r: exp) extends super.Add(l, r)
                           with Exp  {
    def eval(): int = left.eval() + right.eval()
  }

  abstract class Test extends super.Test {
    override def run(): unit = {
      super.run();
      System.out.println(atree.eval());
    }
  }
}                       (d)
```

```
package epl;
abstract class Test1 extends lp with ap {
  abstract class Test extends super.Test with super[ap].Test;
}
abstract class Test2 extends Test1 with le {
  abstract class Test extends super.Test with super[le].Test;
}
abstract class Test3 extends Test2 with ae {
  abstract class Test extends super.Test with super[ae].Test;
}
object LitAddObj extends Test3 {
  type exp = Exp;
  class Test  extends super.Test {
    val ltree = new Lit(3);
    val atree = new Add(ltree, new Lit(7));
  }
  def main(args: Array[String]) : unit = {
    var test = new Test();
    test.run();
  }
}                       (e)
```

Fig. 7. Scala Solution

- Extension to class `Test`, that adds field `atree` and extends method `run()` with the call to `print()` on this field[12]. This class is also `abstract` because `atree`'s type is abstract.

---

[12] To prevent inadvertent overriding, Scala requires overriding methods to include an `override` modifier as part of their definitions. Notice also that the overridden method can still be called using super as in Java.

Trait le is also implemented as an extension to trait lp and is shown in Figure 7c. This trait has:

- Trait Exp extends Exp of feature lp by adding method eval().
- Abstract type exp that extends exp of feature lp, meaning that exp is now at least a subtype of Exp that has print() and eval() methods.
- An extension of class Lit. This class uses *mixin composition* (expressed as with Exp in the figure) to indicate that Lit is also a subtype of Exp and thus it must implement both of its methods. Since it inherits print() from trait lp it only needs to implement eval().
- An extension of class Test that modifies run() to invoke eval() on ltree.

Feature ae is implemented as an extension of feature ap and a mixin composition with feature le because it provides an implementation of method eval() for class Add. The code is shown in Figure 7d. Additionally this trait extends method run() of class Test. The other two feature modules of EPL, np and ne, are implemented similarly.

To define program LitAdd is necessary to: a) specify the order in which method extensions are composed, and b) to create an object, a singleton object of a new class, to run the program. Figure 7e illustrates this. For the first part, we use *deep mixin composition* [54] (mixin composition at trait level and nested class level), to establish a linear order of Test classes as they contain extensions of method run(). For the second part, we define LitAddObj that extends Test3 (the most refined abstract Test class), binds abstract type exp to concrete type Exp as defined by Test3, and makes concrete class Test by creating instances for the test objects ltree and atree. The main method creates an instance of Test and calls method run() on it.

7.2 Evaluation

Feature Definition. Scala can implement all program deltas of EPL. Regarding cohesion, traits provide a mechanism to collect program deltas under a single name. Separate compilation in Scala requires traits and classes to be placed in named packages, as it is illustrated by package epl in Figure 7.

Feature Composition. Scala provides flexible composition and flexible order mechanism for implementing EPL. Scala uses inheritance and mixin composition to compose program deltas that add new classes, traits, fields, methods and simple constructor extensions. However, specifying the order of method extensions is a verbose and non-trivial task. Scala traits are closed under composition. Scala is supported by a sophisticated nominal type theory called vObj calculus [40].

8 AHEAD

AHEAD (Algebraic Hierarchical Equations for Application Design) is a feature modularization and composition technology based on step-wise development

[6][4][2]. It was created to address the issues of feature-based development of product-lines.

8.1 Feature Modules and Their Composition

AHEAD partitions features into two categories: *constants* that modularize any number of classes and interfaces, and *functions* that modularize classes, interfaces and their extensions.

AHEAD tools use a language, called *Jak* [4][5], that is a superset of Java. The implementation of constant features like lp, whose elements are standard classes and interfaces, uses pure Java constructs. To distinguish extensions of these elements, Jak provides modifier keyword *refines*. Also, to refer to the method being extended, Jak uses the construct Super.methodName(args). For example, here is the Jak code of feature module le:

```
refines interface Exp { int eval(); }
refines class Lit implements Exp {
  public int eval() { return value; }
}
refines class Test {
  public void run() {
    Super.run();
    System.out.println( ltree.eval() );
  }
}
```

As described in Figure 3, this feature extends interface Exp with method eval(), extends class Lit with the corresponding implementation, and extends class Test by extending method run() with a call to eval() on ltree. Super.run() invokes the previously defined method run(). In the case of LitAdd it calls the run() method of ap. Constructor extensions follow a similar pattern, as illustrated in the following example, which extends the constructor of Test of feature ap by assigning variable atree a value:

```
refines Test() {
  Add atree = new Add( ltree, ltree );
}
```

The remaining feature modules are implemented in a similar way. Each feature is represented by a directory that contains files for each class and interface definition and extension. The command line to compose these directories to form LitAdd is:

```
composer -target=LitAdd lp ap le ae
```

8.2 Evaluation

Feature Definition. AHEAD can modularize all EPL program deltas into a cohesive unit. AHEAD provides tools to compile feature modules to bytecode and compose byte-code representations; however, this is not accomplished by separate compilation. Compilation uses global knowledge of all possible classes, interfaces, and members that can be present in a product-line [2].

Feature Composition. AHEAD feature modules are independent of the composition. The order in which features are composed is the order in which they are listed on the *composer* command line. AHEAD features are by definition closed under composition. A static typing model of feature modules for AHEAD is under development.

9 Perspective Beyond Individual Technologies

Let us step back from these implementation details to assess the fundamental nature of the problems that are being solved. We have seen that all five technologies can be used to implement EPL and how they satisfy, in different degrees, the properties required by feature modules. None of these technologies provide a satisfactory solution to the problem of building product lines, that is, they do not meet all the feature properties or express them in a verbose way. However, many common themes can be identified, even as each technology has particular strengths in meeting one or more of the properties.

In this section we show how the properties of feature definition and feature composition can be understood in terms of an algebra of program deltas. This simple algebra is an abstraction designed to express the underlying structure of feature modularization in product-line development. By hiding the details of particular technologies, this abstraction makes it easier to compare and contrast different technologies and suggests areas where the technologies could be improved or generalized. This discussion will, we hope, help encourage reliance on mathematically justifiable abstractions when developing new tool-specific or language-specific concepts [28].

A fundamental concept of metaprogramming is that programs are data and functions (a.k.a. *transforms*) map programs [7][42]. From this starting point, a program delta can be seen as a function that receives a program as input, adds something to it, and returns the extended program as output. Consider Δrun() of module ap. This delta adds a statement to method run() of class Test of the program received as input. Another example from ap is delta "Add atree", which adds member atree to class Test. For convenience, we refer to functions associated with program deltas by a single name. Thus we omit return types, parameters and their types in our function declarations. Using a mathematical notation, these two deltas are represented as:

```
Δrun(P)-> P' where P' is program with Δrun added to run() of Test of P
atree(Q)->Q', where Q' has field atree added to class Test of Q
```

When viewed in this way, a feature module like lp can be defined by:

$$\text{lp = Test(Lit(Exp(Empty)))} \tag{2}$$

where Empty is the empty program, and Exp, Lit, and Test are program deltas that add a new interface, and two new classes. To simplify notation further, we write expressions like this using the + operation, because it intuitively conveys the notion that we are building programs incrementally by adding program deltas. (2) now becomes:

$$\text{lp = Test + Lit + Exp} \tag{3}$$

where evaluation is from right to left. + denotes function composition; base terms are to the right and extensions are to the left. The choice of operator + was deliberately selected as (we will see) it exhibits composition properties that resemble those of elementary algebra. Next, we examine properties of this operator and relate them to the feature properties of Section 3.

Commutativity and Flexible Order. The order in which program deltas can be composed follows two simple rules. First, a program delta that references a data member or method must be composed *after* (to the left of) the delta that introduces that member or method. (3) is an example: Exp defines an interface, Lit adds a class that references this interface, and Test adds a class that references the class of Lit.

Second, program deltas that extend the same method are not commutative, because if their order is swapped, a different program will result. For example, changing the order in which print methods are added to method run() of class Test alters the output of a program. Summation is *commutative* (A+B=B+A) for arbitrary program deltas A and B if the first rule is not violated and A and B do not extend the same method. The evaluation property of *flexible order* relies on the non-commutativity property of operation +.

Substitution, Cohesion, and Closure. Module ap is defined by:

```
ap = Δrun + ΔTest + atree + Add                              (4)
```

That is, (reading from right to left) it adds class Add, member atree to class Test, extends the Test constructor, and extends method run. When we compose ap with lp, we know the following equality holds because of *substitution* (i.e., replacing equals with equals):

```
ap + lp = (Δrun + ΔTest + atree + Add) + (Test + Lit + Exp)
```

That is, we know that the program produced by adding ap to lp must equal the sum of their deltas. *Cohesion* is the property that we can assign names ap and lp to summation expressions. *Closure* is the property that summation of deltas is itself a delta.[13]

Associativity and Flexible Composition. A common situation in product-line design is not only the addition of new features, but a refactoring of existing features into more primitive features.

Recall that in our EPL design, the Print operation is implemented in the Print column along with the declaration of the data types' fields and constructors. This design prevents, among other things, our ability to build programs without the Print operation. The solution is to refactor the Print column into two columns: Print' that implements operation Print exclusively, and Core that declares the data types with their fields and constructors. Figure 8 shows the refactoring of module lp into its core and non-core parts.

---

[13] Object-oriented classes contain methods that are mutually referential. One can factor each method into an empty (base) method and a program delta that adds the body. In this way, simple algebraic expressions can be written for mutually referential methods.

Class `Test` of module `lp` can be decomposed as:

```
Test = Δrun + run + Testᶜᶜᶜᶜᶜ+ ltree + Testˢ where
Testˢ is class Test { };
ltree is Lit ltree;
Testᶜ is Test() { ltree = new Lit(3); };
run is void run() { };
Δrun is ltree.print();
```
                                                                    (5)

Superscript S stands for skeleton which is the declaration of the class without any members, and superscript C stands for constructor. Class `Lit` has a similar decomposition. Interface `Exp` can be decomposed as:

```
Exp = printᴵ + Expˢ where
Expˢ is interface Exp { };
printᴵ is void print();
```

Our refactoring `lp` in Figure 8 is captured by the following algebraic derivation:

```
1) lp = Test + Lit + Exp
2) lp =(Δrun + run + Testᶜ + ltree + Testˢ) + (print + Litᶜ + value + Litˢ)
      + (printᴵ + Expˢ)
3) lp = (Δrun + print + printᴵ) +
        (run + Testᶜ + ltree + Testˢ + Litᶜ+ value + Litˢ + Expˢ)
4) lp = lp' + lp_Core
```

The first step recites (3). The second step substitutes the definitions of `Test`, `Lit` and `Exp` as in (5) and (6). The third step rearranges terms using the commutativity properties of summations. The last step uses an *associativity* property of summations (whose proof is simple)[14] and cohesion to express `lp` as a sum of `lp'` and lp_{Core} Similar reasoning is applied to the other modules in the `Print` column to refactor them into a core and non-core part. The ability to refactor expressions is the property of *flexible composition*.

(a) lp'

(b) lp_Core

```
// added to Exp          interface Exp { }
void print();
                          class Lit implements Exp {
                            int value;
// added to Lit            Lit (int v) { value = v; }
void print() {            }
     System.out.print(value);
}                         class Test {
                            Lit ltree;
// added to run() of Test    Test() {
ltree.print();              ltree = new Lit(3);
                            }
                            void run() { }
                          }
```

Fig. 8. Refactoring of `lp` to `lp'` + lp_Core

Compositional Reasoning, Static Typing, and Separate Compilation. Compositional reasoning is the ability to prove properties of a program from the properties of its components, which in our case are features, without reference to their

---

[14] + denotes function composition. Function composition is associative.

implementation [36]. By equating program deltas with functions (summations), we are relating *compositional reasoning* with *algebraic reasoning*. Doing so can be a substantial win for several reasons. First, an algebra provides a clean mathematical foundation for compositional reasoning and automation — both of which are needed in product-line development. Second, it changes our orientation on tool development and creation. Instead of inventing new tools with new abstractions and new conceptual models — e.g., the AspectJ, Hyper/J, Jiazzi, Scala, and AHEAD models are hardly similar and are difficult to compare — we have a single simple algebraic model that imposes clean abstractions *onto* tools, so that we can reason about programs in a tool-implementation-independent way.

Jiazzi provides an example of compositional reasoning: each feature module is statically typed. Jiazzi ensures that the composition of statically typed modules is itself a statically typed module. So not only does Jiazzi compose the *code* of individual features, it also computes (or verifies) an important property of a composition. Similar examples can be given from other technologies. All of this can be given an algebraic foundation. If we want property p of a summation, we need a composition operator $+p$ (read p-sum) that tells us how to compose properties of constituent terms. So property p of module $\texttt{lp}$, denoted $\texttt{lp}_p$, is a p-sum of the p properties of its terms:

$$\texttt{lp}_p = \texttt{Test}_p + p \ \texttt{Lit}_p + p \ \texttt{Exp}_p$$

This idea (although not in an algebraic form) is common in the software architecture and product-line communities [46], and has been demonstrated elsewhere [6]. In the product-line and software architecture literature, feature modules map to *functional* requirements, and properties of modules and their compositions (such as the property of being statically typed) correspond to *non-functional* requirements.

The remaining property in our evaluation, *separate compilation*, is not a property of an algebraic model, but rather an engineering requirement of any implementation of the model.

10   Related Work

Relational query optimization is a classic example of the importance that algebra can play in program specification, construction, and optimization. SQL queries are translated to relational algebra expressions (i.e., compositions of relational algebra operators). A query optimizer rewrites the expression into semantically equivalent expressions where the goal is to minimize the expression (program) execution time. Readers will see that this is an example of compositional reasoning: the relational algebra expression defines the program, the optimizer composes a performance model of each operator to produce a performance model of that program [6].

The expression problem originated in the works of Reynolds [43] and Cook [15]. Torgersen [49] presents a concise summary of the research on this problem and four solutions that utilize Java generics. Though extensive, this literature focuses only on programming language design and separate compilation issues, and not about the requirements of feature modularity.

Masuhara et al. describe a framework to model the crosscutting mechanisms of AspectJ and Hyper/J [30]. Both are viewed as weavers parameterized by two input programs plus additional information such as where, what, and how new code is woven. Their focus is on the implementation of crosscutting semantics rather than on the broader software design implications that these mechanisms have.

Murphy et al. [37] present a limited study that uses AspectJ and Hyper/J to refactor features in two existing programs. The emphasis was on the effect on the program's structure and on the refactoring process, not in providing a general framework for comparison. Along the same lines, Driver [19] describes a re-implementation of a web-based information system that uses Hyper/J and AspectJ, but the evaluation is subjective and expressed in terms of factors such as extensibility, plugability, productivity, or complexity. Clarke et al. [13] describe how to map crosscutting software designs expressed as composition patterns (extended UML models) to AspectJ and Hyper/J, and evaluate their crosscutting capabilities to implement such patterns.

Coyler et al. [16] focus on refactoring tangled and scattered code into base code and aspects that could be considered as the features of a product line. They indicate that, based on their experience implementing middleware software, concerns (features) are usually a mixture of classes and aspects; a finding that corroborates the importance of feature cohesion.

For our evaluation we considered MultiJava, an extension of Java that supports symmetric multiple dispatch and modular open classes[11][12]. However, its focus is on solving the *augmenting method problem*, that consists on adding operations (methods) to existing type hierarchies. Given this constraint, it is not possible to implement EPL as it cannot add new fields, add new classes and interfaces, and extend existing methods and constructors. Similarly, *Classboxes* [8] are modules that provide method addition and method replacement (overriding without super reference). However, it is unclear if classboxes can support other program deltas such as adding new fields, or methods and constructor extensions.

The *Concern Manipulation Environment (CME)* [14] is a project that builds on the experience of Hyper/J and MDSoC. Among its goals is to provide support for the identification, encapsulation, extraction, and composition of concerns (features in this paper). CME architecture is geared towards supporting multiple modularization approaches. Thus it would be interesting to evaluate whether the software composition model we propose in this paper can benefit from the tool support that CME provides.

Mezini and Ostermann [35], present a comparison of variability management in product lines between *Feature-Oriented Programing (FOP)*, as in AHEAD, and Aspect-Oriented Programming, as in AspectJ. They identify as weaknesses in these technologies: a) features are purely hierarchical (extensions are made to some base code), b) support for reuse (extensions are tied to names not functionality), c) support for dynamic configuration (in FOP composition is static), and d) support for variability (aspects are either applied or not to an entire composition). They propose

Caesar[34] to address these issues. Caesar relies on Aspect Collaboration Interfaces, or ACIs, which are interface definitions for aspects (Caesar's aspects are similar to AspectJ's) whose purpose is to separate an aspect implementation from its binding. The association between these two is implemented with a *weavelet*, which must be deployed to activate advice either statically, when the object is created, or dynamically, when certain program block is executed. How these ideas could be applied to solve EPL is subject of an ongoing evaluation.

11 Conclusions and Future Work

Features express the kinds of variations product-line developers encounter in program development, because features represent increments in program functionality. Thus, it is natural to consider modularizing features as a way to modularize programs. Unfortunately, the code for features often cuts across classes, and thus traditional modularization schemes do not work well. New program modularization technologies have been proposed in recent years that have shown promise in supporting feature modularity. We have presented a classical problem in product-line design — called the Expressions Product-Line — to identify properties that feature modules should have. We have used these properties to compare and contrast five rather different technologies: AspectJ, Hyper/J, Jiazzi, Scala, and AHEAD. Our results showed that none of these technologies provide a satisfactory solution to the problem of building product-lines.

Instead of debating the merits of particular technologies, we focused on a topic that we believe has greater significance. Namely, product-line architects reason about programs in terms of their features, not in terms of their code or implementing technologies. We proposed an abstract model of features where compositional reasoning was related to algebraic reasoning. We showed how virtually all of the evaluation properties we identified in EPL were actually properties of an algebra. Namely: program deltas are functions that map programs, cohesion and closure under composition are associativity properties of function composition, flexible composition and flexible order is a consequence of the non-commutativity of certain functions, static typing is a property of a function (program delta) and is a property that can be predicted from an expression (i.e., a composition of deltas). Only the property of separate compilation dealt with engineering considerations of the algebra's implementation.

We believe the time has come for programming languages to play a more supportive role in product-lines and feature-based development. A consolidation of different modularization efforts is essential to this objective. We argued that such a consolidation should relate compositional reasoning with algebraic reasoning, because of its clean abstractions, the ability to automate compositional reasoning, and for giving an algebraic justification when adding new modularization concepts.

To continue this effort and because the full potential of the five technologies was not required, we foresee extending EPL and designing other case studies to help derive and illustrate further properties of feature modules (e.g. AOP quantification [28]). We are currently collaborating with proponents of other modularization technologies, such as Composition Filters [20], Caesar [34], and Framed Aspects [27], for this purpose.

Acknowledgments. We thank Sean McDirmid and Bin Xin for their help with Jiazzi, and Martin Odersky for his help with Scala. We are grateful to Axel Rauschmayer and Awais Rashid for their feedback on drafts of the paper, and the anonymous reviewers for their comments.

References

1. AspectJ. Programming Guide. aspectj.org/doc/proguide
2. AHEAD Tool Suite (ATS). www.cs.utexas.edu/users/schwartz
3. Batory, D., Geraci, B.J,: Composition Validation and Subjectivity in GenVoca Generators. IEEE Trans. Soft. Engr., February (1997) 67-82
4. Batory, D., Lopez-Herrejon, R.E., Martin, J.P.: Generating Product-Lines of Product-Families. Automated Software Engineering Conference (2002)
5. Batory, D., Liu, J., Sarvela, J.N.: Refinements and Multidimensional Separation of Concerns. ACM SIGSOFT, September (2003)
6. Batory, D., Sarvela, J.N., Rauschmayer, A.: Scaling Step-Wise Refinement. IEEE Trans. Soft. Engr. June (2004)
7. Baxter, I.D.: Design Maintenance Systems. CACM, Vol. 55, No. 4 (1992) 73-89
8. Bergel, A., Ducasse, S., Wuyts, R.: Classboxes: A Minimal Module Model Supporting Local Rebinding. Joint Modular Languages Conferences JMLC (2003)
9. Beuche, D.:Composition and Construction of Embedded Software Families. Ph.D. Otto-von-Guericke-Universität Magdeburg (2003)
10. Bracha, G., Cook, W.: Mixin-based inheritance. OOPSLA (1990)
11. Clifton, C., Leavens, G.T., Millstein, T., Chambers, G.: MultiJava: Modular Open classes and Symmetric Multiple Dispatch for Java. OOPSLA (2000)
12. Clifton, C., Millstein, T., Leavens, G.T., Chambers, G.: MultiJava: Design Rationale, Compiler Implementation, and User Experience. TR #04-01, Iowa State University (2004)
13. Clarke, S., Walker, R.: Separating Crosscutting Concerns Across the Lifecycle: From Composition Patterns to AspectJ and Hyper/J. Technical Report UBC-CS-TR-2001-05, University of British Columbia, Canada (2001)
14. Concern Manipulation Environment (CME). www.eclipse.org/cme/
15. Cook, W.R.: Object-Oriented Programming versus Abstract Data Types. Workshop on FOOL, Lecture Notes in Computer Science, Vol. 173. Spring-Verlag, (1990) 151-178
16. Coyler, A., Rashid, A., Blair, G.: On the Separation of Concerns in Program Families. TRCOMP-001-2004, Computing Department, Lancaster University, UK (2004)
17. Czarnecki, K., Eisenecker, U.W.: Generative Programming: Methods, Tools, and Applications. Addison-Wesley (2000)
18. Douence, R., Fradet, P., Südholt, M.: Composition, reuse and interaction analysis of stateful aspects. AOSD (2004)
19. Driver, C.: Evaluation of Aspect-Oriented Software Development for Distributed Systems. Master's Thesis, University of Dublin, Ireland, September (2002)
20. Filman, R.E., Elrad, T., Clarke, S., Aksit, M.: Aspect-Oriented Software Development. Addison-Wesley (2004)

21. Flatt, M., Felleisen, M.: Units: Cool modules for HOT languages. PLDI (1998)
22. Findler, R.B., Flatt, M.: Modular Object-Oriented Programming with Units and Mixins. ICFP, (1998) 94-104
23. Jagadeesan, R., Jeffrey, A., Riely, J.: A Typed Calculus of Aspect Oriented Programs. Submitted for publication.
24. Kang, K., et al.: Feature-Oriented Domain Analysis (FODA) Feasibility Study. CMU/SEI-90-TR-21, Carnegie Mellon Univ., Pittsburgh, PA, Nov. (1990)
25. Kiczales, G., Hilsdale, E., Hugunin, J., Kirsten, M., Palm, J., Griswold, W.G.: An overview of AspectJ. ECOOP (2001)
26. Laddad, R.: AspectJ in Action. Practical Aspect-Oriented Programming. Manning (2003)
27. Loughran, N., Rashid, A., Zhang, W., Jarzabek, S.: Supporting Product Line Evolution with Framed Aspects. ACP4IS Workshop, AOSD (2004)
28. Lopez-Herrejon, R.E., Batory, D.: Improving Incremental Development in AspectJ by Bounding Quantification. SPLAT Workshop at AOSD (2005)
29. Lopez-Herrejon, R.E., Batory, D., Cook, W.: Evaluating Support for Features in Advanced Modularization Technologies. Extended Report. The University of Texas at Austin, Department of Computer Sciences, Technical Report TR-05-16, April (2005)
30. Masuhara, H., Kiczales, G.: Modeling Crosscuting Aspect-Oriented Mechanisms. ECOOP (2003)
31. McDirmid, S., Flatt, M., Hsieh, W.C.: Jiazzi: New age components for old-fashioned Java. OOPSLA (2001)
32. McDirmid, S., Hsieh, W.C.: Aspect-Oriented Programming with Jiazzi. AOSD (2003)
33. McDirmid, S., The Jiazzi Manual (2002)
34. Mezini, M., Ostermann, K.: Conquering Aspects with Caesar. AOSD (2003)
35. Mezini, M., Ostermann, K.: Variability Management with Feature-Oriented Programming and Aspects. SIGSOFT04/ FSE-12 (2004)
36. Misra, J.: A Discipline of Multiprogramming. Springer-Verlag (2001)
37. Murphy, G., Lai, A., Walker, R.J., Robillard, M.P.: Separating Features in Source Code: An Exploratory Study. ICSE (2001)
38. Odersky, M., et al.: An Overview of the Scala Programming Language. September (2004), scala.epfl.ch
39. Odersky, M., et al.: The Scala Language Specification. September (2004), scala.epfl.ch
40. Odersky, M., Cremet, V., Röckl, C., Zenger, M.: A nominal theory of objects with dependent types. ECOOP (2003)
41. Ossher, H., Tarr, P.: Multi-dimensional separation of concerns and the Hyperspace approach. In Software Architectures and Component Technology, Kluwer (2002)
42. Partsch, H., Steinbrüggen, R.: Program Transformation Systems. ACM Computing Surveys, September (1983)
43. Reynolds, J.C.: User-defined types and procedural data as complementary approaches to data abstraction. Theoretical Aspects of Object-Oriented Programming, MIT Press, (1994)
44. Schärli, N., Ducasse, S., Nierstrasz, O., Black, A.: Traits: Composable units of behavior. ECOOP (2003)
45. Schinz, M.: A Scala tutorial for Java programmers. September (2004), scala.epfl.ch
46. Software Engineering Institute. Predictable Assembly from Certified Components. www.sei.cmu.edu/pacc
47. Tarr, P., Ossher, H., Harrison, W., Sutton, S.M.: N Degrees of Separation: Multi-Dimensional Separation of Concerns. ICSE (1999) 107-119
48. Tarr, P., Ossher, H.: Hyper/J User and Installation Manual. IBM Corporation (2001)
49. Torgersen, M.: The Expresion Problem Revisited. Four new solutions using generics. ECOOP (2004)

50. `Wadler, P.: The expression problem. Posted on the Java Genericity mailing list (1998)
51. Walker, D., Zdancewic, S., Ligatti, J.: A Theory of Aspects. ICFP (2003)
52. Xin, B., McDirmid, S., Eide, E., Hsieh, W.C.: A comparison of Jiazzi and AspectJ. Technical Report TR UUCS-04-001, University of Utah (2004)
53. Zave, P.: FAQ Sheet on Feature Interaction. www.research.att.com/~pamela/faq.html
54. Zenger, M., Odersky, M.: Independently Extensible Solutions to the Expression Problem. Technical Report TR IC/2004/33, EPFL Switzerland (2004)

Separation of Concerns with Procedures, Annotations, Advice and Pointcuts

Gregor Kiczales and Mira Mezini

University of British Columbia, 201-2366 Main Mall,
Vancouver, BC V6R 1X4, Canada
gregork@acm.org
Technische Universität Darmstadt, Hochschulstrasse 10,
D-64289 Darmstadt, Germany
mezini@informatik.tu-darmstadt.de

Abstract. There are numerous mechanisms for separation of concerns at the source code level. Three mechanisms that are the focus of recent attention – metadata annotations, pointcuts and advice – can be modeled together with good old-fashioned procedures as providing different kinds of bindings: procedure calls bind program points to operations, annotations bind attributes to program points; pointcuts bind sets of points to various descriptions of those sets; named pointcuts bind attributes to sets of points; and advice bind the implementation of an operation to sets of points. This model clarifies how the mechanisms work together to separate concerns, and yields guidelines to help developers use the mechanisms in practice.

1   Introduction

Programming language designers have developed numerous mechanisms for separation of concerns (SOC) at the source code level, including procedures, object-oriented programming and many others. In this paper we focus on three mechanisms – metadata annotations [4], pointcuts [16] and advice [33] – that are currently attracting significant research [9, 10, 19, 34] and developer interest [1, 11, 12, 14, 20].[1]

Our goal is understand what kinds of concerns each mechanism best separates, and how the mechanisms work together to separate multiple concerns in a system. We also seek to provide developers with answers to questions about what mechanism to use in any given situation. To enable this, we study how the three newer mechanisms, along with good old-fashioned procedures, separate concerns in a simple example.

The study is focused on four key design concerns within the example. We present seven implementations of the example that use the mechanisms in different ways. We also present ten change tasks and how they are carried out in each implementation. Based on this, the paper provides:

1. An analysis of the degree to which the different mechanisms are able to separate and clarify the four design concerns in the seven implementations.

---

[1] The paper assumes a reading familiarity with pointcuts and advice as manifested by AspectJ [16] as well as the Java 1.5 metadata facility [4]. Metadata annotations, pointcuts and advice can appear in a wide range of other languages [3, 13, 21, 28, 31] [8, 30], but we do not explicitly discuss that generalization here.

A.P. Black (Ed.): ECOOP 2005, LNCS 3586, pp. 195 – 213, 2004.

2. An analysis of the degree of locality of each change task for each implementation, and a comparison of that locality to the static separation.
3. A unified model of the four mechanisms showing how they work together to separate concerns.
4. An initial set of guidelines for using the mechanisms in development practice.

The paper is structured as follows: Section 2 presents the example, its four key design concerns and the seven implementations. Section 3 analyzes the static locality of the concerns in each implementation, and the locality of the change tasks for each implementation. Section 4 presents the unified model of the mechanisms. Section 5 presents the usage guidelines. We finish with related and future work and a summary.

2 The Example

Our comparison of the mechanisms is based on seven implementations of a simple graphical shapes example [16, 18]. In this example, a number of graphical shapes are shown on a display. Each shape has its own display state, and when that state changes, the display must be signaled so it can refresh itself. This design is shown in Figure 1.

The key objects in the design are the shapes and the display. There is an abstract Shape class, with concrete Point and Line subclasses. (Assume there are other concrete shapes such as Triangle. To save space they are not discussed here.) There is a single Display class, and, for simplicity, there is just a single system-wide display.

2.1 Four Design Concerns

In addition to concerns involving the functionality of the shapes, the design comprises four key design concerns, which are shown as dotted line boxes in Figure 1.

Refresh-Implementation – What is the behavior and implementation of the actual refresh operation?

Context-to-Refresh – What context from the actual display state change points should be available to the refresh implementation?

When-to-Refresh – When should the display be refreshed?

What-Constitutes-Change – What operations change the state that affects how shapes look on the display, i.e. their position?

As is common, these concerns are interconnected. Our design resolves When-to-Refresh by deciding that refresh should happen immediately after each display state changes. This brings What-Constitutes-Change into focus as a concern that must be resolved. One could also argue the causality in the other direction, in that having thought about display state changes one then decides they should cause refreshes.

2.2 Seven Implementations

This rest of this section presents the code for seven implementations of the example. Discussion of the implementations is deferred until Section 3

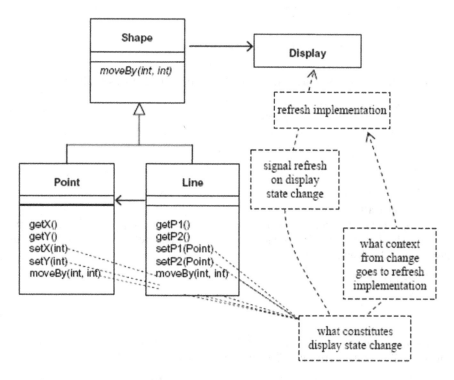

Fig. 1. The design of the graphical shapes program, showing the main classes and two additional design concerns not separated as classes

Straw-Man

The first implementation is a straw man, no good programmer would write this code today. Its purpose is to explicitly introduce procedures into the discussion.

In this implementation all of the methods that change display state directly include several lines of code that implement the actual display refresh. For example, the setX method looks like:

```
void setX(int nx) {
  x = nx;
  Graphics g = Display.getGraphics();
  g.clear();
  for( Shape s : Display.getShapes() ) {
    s.draw(g);
  }
}
```

GOFP

This implementation uses a good old-fashioned procedure (GOFP) to capture the refresh implementation. Each of the methods includes, at the end of the method, a call to a procedure (static method in Java) that refreshes the display.

```
void setX(int nx) {
  x = nx;
  Display.refresh();
}
```

The body of that procedure is the several lines of code that was duplicated in I1.

```
static void refresh() {
  Graphics g = getGraphics();
  g.clear();
  for( Shape s : getShapes() ) {
    s.draw(g);
  }
}
```

Annotation-Call

This implementation uses Java 1.5 metadata annotations [4]. Each method that changes display state has an annotation that says that executing the method should also refresh the display.

```
@RefreshDisplay
void setX(int nx) {
  x = nx;
}
```

A single after advice declaration serves to ensure that execution of methods with this tag calls Display.refresh(). The advice is written as:

```
after() returning: execution(@RefreshDisplay * *(..)) {
  Display.refresh();
}
```

There are other ways to associate run-time behavior with annotations, typically involving ad-hoc post-processors. We use advice in this paper because it is simple and compatible with the rest of the paper.

Annotation-Property

This implementation differs from the previous one only in the name of the annotation. Here the annotation name describes a property of the method – that it changes state that affects the display of the shape – rather than directly saying that executing the method should refresh the display. So the methods look like

```
@DisplayStateChange
void setX(int nx) {
  x = nx;
}
```

Again, a separate advice declaration says that execution of methods with the DisplayStateChange annotation should call Display.refresh().

```
after() returning: execution(@DisplayStateChange * *(..)) {
  Display.refresh();
}
```

Anonymous-Enumeration-Pointcut

This implementation uses an anonymous enumeration-based pointcut to identify method executions that change display state. So the methods have no explicit marking, and simply look like:[2]

```
void setX(int nx) {
  x = nx;
}
```

The entire implementation of signaling a display refresh consists of a single advice on an anonymous pointcut that explicitly enumerates the six methods; the body of the advice calls Display.refresh().

```
after() returning: execution(void Shape.moveBy(int, int)
                 || execution(void Point.setX(int))
                 || execution(void Point.setY(int))
                 || execution(void Line.setP1(Point))
                 || execution(void Point.setP2(Point)) {
  Display.refresh();
}
```

Named-Enumeration-Pointcut

In this implementation the pointcut from the previous implementation is pulled out and given an explicit name. Again, the method bodies require no marking to enable display refresh signaling.

```
void setX(int nx) {
  x = nx;
}
```

The pointcut and advice are:

```
pointcut displayStateChange():
  execution(void Shape.moveBy(int, int)
  || execution(void Point.setX(int))
  || execution(void Point.setY(int))
  || execution(void Line.setP1(Point))
  || execution(void Point.setP2(Point));

after() returning: displayStateChange() {
  Display.refresh();
}
```

Named-Pattern-Pointcut

In this implementation only the pointcut differs from the previous implementation. Rather than enumerating the signatures of the methods that change display state, this implementation relies on the naming convention the methods follow to write a more concise pointcut. Again, the method bodies require no marking to enable display refresh signaling.

---

[2] Even though the method is not explicitly marked by the programmer, IDE support such as the ADJT Eclipse plug-in will show that the advice exists, for example with a gutter marker next to the method declaration [27].

```
void setX(int nx) {
    x = nx;
}
```

The pointcut and advice are:

```
pointcut displayStateChange():
    execution(void Shape.moveBy(int, int)
    || execution(void Shape+.set*(..));

after() returning: displayStateChange() {
    Display.refresh();
}
```

The `execution(void Shape+.set*(..))` pointcut means execution of any method defined in Shape or a subclass of Shape, that returns void, has a name beginning with 'set', and takes any number of arguments.

3   Analysis of the Implementations

Our analysis of the different mechanisms is based on assessing the degree to which the seven implementations separate the four design concerns identified in Section 2.1. The assessment uses three criteria: locality of implementation, degree to which the implementation is explicit rather than implicit, and locality of change in a simple evolution experiment. The assessment of locality and explicit implementation is discussed in Section 3.1. The locality of change assessment is covered in Section 3.2. All three assessments are summarized in Table 1.

3.1   Locality and Explicit Representation

One way to compare how the implementations separate these design decisions is whether the code that implements the decision is localized. Another criterion is the degree to which the implementation of the decision is captured explicitly as opposed to implicitly. This analysis is summarized in the top part of Table 1.

The capture of Refresh-Implementation is implicit and non-localized in Straw-Man. There is no single place in the code that explicitly says that display refresh is implemented by the several lines of code. Instead, each method that the developer decided constitutes a display state change includes code that implements refresh. In the GOFP and subsequent implementations, the refresh procedure declaration captures this concern in an explicit and localized way. The declaration is read as saying "this is the refresh implementation – bind Display.refresh() to this code".

The capture of Context-to-Refresh is implicit and non-localized in Straw-Man. No single place in the code explicitly says that no values from the change context are available to the display refresh implementation. In GOFP, the procedure declaration and every call to the procedure explicitly say that no arguments are passed, so this concern is explicit. But because this is expressed in the procedure and all the calls to it, it is non-localized. In the Annotation implementations there is a single call to the procedure, so this concern is captured explicitly and in two places. The same is true for the

Anonymous-Enumeration-Pointcut implementation. In the last two implementations the named pointcut also expresses this concern, so it is captured explicitly in three places.

The capture of the When-to-Refresh is implicit and non-localized in Straw-Man, GOFP and Annotation-Call. It is localized but implicit in Anonymous-Enumeration-Pointcut. No single place in these implementations explicitly says that execution of methods that change display state should cause a display refresh. In GOFP the scattered calls to Display.refresh() are implicitly about the fact that the affected methods change display state and so must refresh; but all they say explicitly is that the affected methods call Display.refresh(). The same is true for the scattered RefreshDisplay tags in Annotation-Call. In Anonymous-Enumeration-Pointcut, the pointcut localizes the description of what constitutes change, but because no name is given to it, the binding of when to refresh is not to a clear notion of on display state changes, but instead to an enumerated set of conditions. In the other implementations, this concern is explicit and localized in the after advice declarations, which say that any display state change should cause a refresh.

The capture of the What-Constitutes-Change is implicit and non-localized in Straw-Man, GOFP and Annotation-Call – no single place in these implementations explicitly says that execution of the four setter methods and the two moveBy methods changes display state. In Annotation-Property, the DisplayStateChange annotations capture this concern in an explicit, but non-localized way. In Anonymous-Enumeration-Pointcut, this concern is localized, but implicit. In the two named pointcut implementations this concern is localized and explicit. The Named-Pattern-Pointcut captures the decision about what methods change display state, as well as a rule for what methods are considered to change display state. The variation among the pointcut based implementations is discussed in more depth in Section 5.

Names Matter

The two annotation-based implementations differ only in the name of the annotation, but come out significantly different in our separation of concern analysis. Annotation-Call has the same properties as GOFP with regard to When-to-Refresh and What-Constitutes-Change. This should not be surprising since in Annotation-Call the annotation name makes it feel like alternate syntax for a procedure call, or a syntactic macro [6, 7]. So, like GOFP, Annotation-Call, is conflating these two concerns and simply saying to call refresh at certain points.

On the other hand, in Annotation-Property, When-to-Refresh is captured explicitly and in just one place in the code; What-Constitutes-Change is captured explicitly but is not localized. The different annotation name causes both concerns to be explicit. That names matter is not surprising to programmers, but it is important to note its significance in this case. We return to this issue in Section 5.

3.2 Ease of Evolution

This section analyzes the implementations in terms of how well they fare when performing a set of ten representative change tasks. Most tasks affect just a single concern, reflecting a good modularity in the concern model itself. The question we explore now is what must be done to the code to perform each task – how many edits and how localized are they. The analysis is summarized in the lower part of Table 1 by showing, for each change and each implementation, how many places in each implementation have to be visited and possibly edited by the programmer.

Double-buffering – changes the refresh implementation to use double buffering. So it is a change to just the Refresh-Implementation concern. In Straw-Man, the programmer must edit the refresh implementation code that appears in all the display state change methods. For GOFP and all other implementations only the Display.refresh() procedure must be edited. In Table 1, the Double-Buffering row shows 'n' in the first column and 1 in the remaining columns. This is one of the reasons we have learned to introduce a procedure in such cases.

Pass-Changed-Object – provides the actual shape that has changed to the refresh implementation, so that it can optimize refresh based on that information. This constitutes a change to both Refresh-Implementation and Context-to-Refresh. In Straw-Man, this change task involves editing all the state change methods. In GOFP it involves editing the procedure declaration and the call sites in all the state change methods. In the remaining implementations this involves editing the procedure, advice and pointcut declarations. The procedure is edited to accept the shape as an argument, the call sites are edited to pass the current object, and the pointcuts are edited to make the current object accessible.

Disable-Refresh – simply disables activation of display refresh when the state of shapes changes. So this is a change to just When-to-Refresh. In Straw-Man this change requires editing all the state change methods to delete the refresh implementation. GOFP and Annotation-Call require editing all the methods to remove the call to the refresh procedure or the refresh annotation respectively. In the last four implementations this change can be accomplished by removing the aspect containing the advice from the system, or by editing the aspect to delete the advice if for some reason the aspect should remain. The Disable-Refresh table row shows 'n' in the first 3 columns and '1' in the last four.

One might argue that GOFP and Annotation-Call can accommodate Disable-Refresh more expeditiously – for GOFP, one could simply "comment out" the body of the refresh procedure declaration, and for Annotation-Call one could delete the advice declaration. But these alternatives are problematic. There may be other callers of the refresh procedure (or clients of the tag), since nothing has marked the procedure or the tag as particular to handling this kind of refresh activation. Even if there are no other callers, the expeditious changes make the code confusing – the reader sees a call to refresh (or the annotation), but must learn elsewhere that they do not do anything.

A programmer might deal with this by introducing an additional procedure, perhaps called Shape.fireDisplayStateChange(), and have that procedure call Display.refresh(). Then this change can be easily accommodated by making the body of the new procedure empty. This has the same effect of introducing the intermediate annotation, and has the same separation properties as Annotation-Property. Other more elaborate rendezvous mechanisms could be used as well. Having this extra procedure vs. not having it is similar to the difference between the two annotation-based implementations.

Reuse-What-Constitutes-Change adds logging of display state changes. So it reuses What-Constitutes-Change, but does not actually change any of the design concerns. In Straw-Man all the state change methods are edited to add logging code. In GOFP all the state change methods are edited to add a call to a logging operation. In Annotation-Call, each method gets an annotation and a new advice is defined. In the last four implementations, a new advice is defined; in Annotation-Property it references the @DisplayStateChange annotation, in the anonymous pointcut it duplicates the anonymous enumeration-based pointcut, and in the named pointcut implementations it references the displayStateChange pointcut. For all but Straw-Man the table includes an extra count assuming the logging operation must be defined as a procedure.

Again, one might argue that this can be accomplished more expeditiously in GOFP and Annotation-Call, simply by directly editing the refresh procedure or the advice to do the logging. This however, associates the logging with the activation of the refresh, rather than directly with the state changes.

Refresh-Top-Level-Changes-Only ensures that in recursive state change methods (e.g. moveBy on Line calls moveBy on Point, which calls setX and setY on Point) only the top-level display state change method causes a refresh. This prevents multiple refreshes for such methods. So it is a change to the When-to-Refresh concern. In Straw-Man and GOFP this change requires editing all the state change methods, to introduce some mechanism that can detect recursive state change method calls and prevent the sub-calls from calling refresh. A common pattern for doing this is to add a second parameter to all the state change methods, indicating whether they are part of a recursive call. Often a second overloaded method is introduced to handle this. In Java the programmer can use thread local state to do this in a more elegant way.

In the implementations that use pointcuts (all after GOFP), this can be done by editing the pointcut to use the cflowbelow primitive to filter out recursive calls; in the named pointcut implementations the AspectJ code for this would involve modifying the advice to be:

```
after() returning: displayStateChange()
                && !cflowbelow(displayStateChange()) {
    Display.refresh();
}
```

which is read as saying to call refresh after any display state change that is not itself within the control flow of another display state change.

The next five changes all affect What-Constitutes-Change in different ways.

Add-Related-Class adds a new Circle subclass of Shape. The new class has setX, setY, setRadius and moveBy methods that constitute display state changes. This represents a modification of the What-Constitutes-Change concern. Straw-Man, GOFP and both annotation-based implementations each require that all the new state change methods be appropriately edited. The two enumeration-based pointcut implementations require that the pointcut be edited. The pattern-based pointcut does not need to be edited, but it must be at least examined to ensure that the new methods are covered by the pointcut.

The next two changes have the same implications for all implementations as Add-Related-Class. They are included nonetheless because they are typical changes to expect in such a system.

Add-Related-Method adds a new Line.setColor(Color) method that should be considered to change display state.

Table 1. Analysis of the seven implementations. The top part of the table shows many places in the code implement the concern, and whether the implementation is Explicit or Implicit; 'n' means each of the display state change methods. The bottom part of the table summarizes the change task analysis, showing the number of places each implementation must be edited for each change. The 'n' notation indicates that the number goes up as the number of shape classes increases, whereas other numbers are constant. The '*' indicates that the code is only examined, not edited. In this part of the table the first column shows what concerns each tasks changes

Implementations		Straw-Man	GOFP	Annotation-Call	Annotation-Property	Anonymous-Enumeration-Ptc.	Named-Enumeration-Ptc.	Named-Pattern-Ptc.
Design Concerns								
Refresh-Implementation		I, n	E, 1					
Context-to-Refresh		I, n	E, n+1	E, 2 / 3				
When-to-Refresh			I, n		E, 1	I, 1	E, 1	
What-Constitutes-Change			I, n		E, n	I, 1	E, 1	
Change Tasks	*Concerns*							
Double-Buffering	RI	n	1					
Pass-Changed-Object	RI, CtR	n	n+1	2		3		
Disable-Refresh	WtR	n		1				
Reuse-What-Constitutes-Change	WCC	n	n+1	n+2	2			
Refresh-Only-Top-Level-	WtR	n		1		1 + 1		
Add-Related-Class	WCC	each new method					1	1*
Add-Related-Method	WCC	each new method						
Rename-Methods	WCC	0						
Add-Unrelated-Class	WCC	0						
Add-Unrelated-Method	WCC	0						1

Rename-Methods renames the Line.setP1(Point) and Line.setP2(Point) methods to Line.setEnd1(Point) and Line.setEnd(2).

Add-Unrelated-Class adds an entirely unrelated class to the system. It does not change any of the four concerns. None of the implementations require any editing or examination to perform this change.

Add-Unrelated-Method adds a new Shape.setOwner(Owner) method that has nothing at all to do with display state. This change also does not change any of the four concerns. The first six implementations require no editing, but the pattern-based pointcut must be edited to exclude the new setOwner method.

4   Uniform Characterization of Mechanisms

The above analysis suggests that one useful way to characterize the four mechanisms is as establishing different kinds of bindings along a path from points in a program to the implementation of an operation that must execute at those points. As shown in Figure 2, each mechanism introduces an explicit intermediate step along the path, and makes an explicit binding between those steps. These explicit steps and bindings work together to separate larger, higher-level concerns such as the four discussed here.

In these terms, a procedure call binds a point in the program to an operation – it says call this operation at this point in the program execution. A procedure declaration binds the operation to an implementation. So the effect of using a procedure – a declaration and one or more calls to it – is to introduce an explicit operation (the procedure), bindings from points in the program to the operation (calls), and a binding from the operation to the implementation (the declaration).[3] Annotations, pointcuts and advice introduce other explicit intermediate elements and bindings.

In discussing the relation between annotations and pointcuts, we use the following terminology: *Annotations* are the syntactic identifiers described by JSR-175 [4] that the programmer places in the program (i.e. @DisplayStateChange). Properties are the characteristics of points on which pointcuts can match, including class and method names, access modifiers etc. *Pointcut names* are the programmer defined names for pointcuts. We use the term *attribute* to include both annotations and pointcut names. In other words, attributes are user-defined names that can be attached to program points.

Annotations bind attributes to program points. An annotation such as @DisplayStateChange binds the DisplayStateChange attribute to the program point.

There are several different kinds of pointcuts. Enumeration-based pointcuts make a set of points explicit, and establish a binding between the set and each of the points.

Pattern based pointcuts make a set of points and the fact that they conform to a common pattern explicit; they also establish a binding between the set and the points. Property-based pointcuts, such as 'execution(public com.acme.*.*(..))' do the same for properties instead of patterns. Annotation-based pointcuts do this for annotations.

Named pointcut declarations establish a binding between an attribute (the pointcut name) and a (possibly singleton) set of points.

---

[3] We use the term *procedure declaration* to refer to a construct that defines both signature and implementation, such as a static method declaration within a class in Java, as opposed to a construct that just declares the procedure's signature.

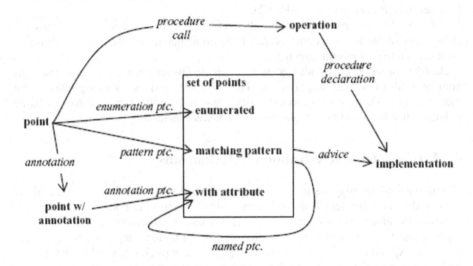

Fig. 2. Intermediate elements and bindings established by the mechanisms. Elements are shown in boldface, the mechanisms are in italics

Advice can be used with any kind of pointcut to bind between the intermediate step that pointcut makes explicit and the implementation of an operation to execute at those points.

This characterization provides an interesting perspective on one difference between AspectJ and AspectWerkz [5]. In AspectJ, the body of an advice is a code block. But in AspectWerkz, advice has no code block; instead it is written as a method, with an annotation that contains the kind of advice and the pointcut.[4] In terms of our model, this means that in AspectWerkz, the advice construct binds to an operation, whereas in AspectJ it binds to an operation implementation. So AspectWerkz provides an extra binding step. In AspectJ the programmer can achieve the extra binding step simply by having the advice body call a procedure.

5 Usage Guidelines

Our model of how the different mechanisms serve to separate concerns suggests a way to approach the process of deciding which mechanism(s) to use in a given situation. The following guidelines are organized around the binding steps in Figure 2 and work to help the programmer decide which path through the figure is most appropriate in a given situation. For each guideline, we discuss how it is validated from by the study described above.

Procedures
If an operation is needed at a given point, then using a procedure (call and declaration) serves to make the operation explicit and local, and to make the binding

---

[4] AspectJ 5 includes both alternatives.

from the point to the operation explicit. This can improve comprehensibility of both the operation and the context, enable reuse of the operation in other contexts, and facilitate later change to the operation.

Comparing Straw-Man to the subsequent implementations, we see that the use of a procedure makes Refresh-Implementation explicit and local. Separating this concern explicitly makes its implementation more clear, and also clarifies the contexts where the operation is invoked (e.g. the setX method). The refresh procedure can easily be called from other points (reused). When Refresh-Implementation changes in the Double-Buffering and Pass-Changed-Object tasks the implementations that use the procedure fare better. None of this is a surprise; we are all familiar with these properties of using procedures. We are elaborating this here only to show how this set of guidelines encompasses the familiar case of procedures and to lay a foundation for discussion guidelines regarding annotations, pointcuts and advice.

Advice and Pointcuts

If an operation is needed at a given set of points then using advice and pointcuts serves to make the binding from the set to the operation explicit and local, which can improve comprehensibility and evolvability in some cases. In particular, consider using advice and pointcut rather than multiple procedure calls if: (i) more than a small number of points must invoke the operation, (ii) the binding between the points and the operation may be disabled or otherwise be context-sensitive, or, (iii) the calling protocol to the operation may change.

All the implementations that use advice and pointcuts (Annotation-Property and on) make the calling protocol to Display.refresh explicit and localized. So they support part iii of this guideline.

But in this regard it is worth looking carefully at the way the implementations that use advice and pointcuts enhance the capture of When-to-Refresh (WtR) and What-Constitutes-Change (WCC). Annotation-Call does not improve WtR or WCC over GOFP. Annotation-Property makes WtR explicit and local and makes WCC explicit but non-local. With Anonymous-Enumeration-Pointcut both concerns are local, but are once again implicit. In the named pointcut implementations both concerns are local and back to being explicit. Since all these implementations use advice and pointcuts of some form, this suggests an interaction between using advice and the form of the pointcut used in the advice, which leads to the next guideline.

Attributes – Named Pointcuts or Annotations

If a set of points used in an advice has a common attribute, then using a named pointcut or an annotation can make that common attribute explicit. Using named pointcuts makes the attribute explicit and local, annotations make it explicit and non-local. When using named attributes, choose a name that describes what is true about the points, rather than describing what a particular advice will do at those points.

This guideline is supported by the Annotation-Property and the two named pointcut implementations. What-Constitutes-Change is made explicit in all three of these implementations. It is made local in the two named pointcut implementations. In each case, the capture of When-to-Refresh also benefits, which is the link to the previous guideline.

As with procedures, the motivation to make the additional bindings and intermediate steps explicit using advice and named attributes comes from comprehensibility, reuse, evolution and other considerations. Comprehensibility is subjective, but to our eye, Annotation-Property and the two named pointcut implementations are the easiest to understand because they make all the steps leading up to a refresh clear. They clearly say "there is an explicit concept of display state change", "here are points that constitute such changes"; and "call refresh at those points". Straw-Man, GOFP and Annotation-Call make it clear that refresh is happening, but not why. Anonymous-Enumeration-Pointcut makes it clear that there is a general condition that causes refresh to happen, but without a pointcut name the abstraction of the condition is not clear.

In terms of reusability, because Annotation-Property and the two named pointcut implementations make the (d/D)isplayStateChange attribute explicit, they make it easy to reuse What-Constitutes-Change in the change task.

In terms of evolution, making the binding from the (d/D)isplayStateChange attribute to the refresh signaling behavior explicit makes the Disable-Refresh change task easy.

The Annotation-Call and Annotation-Property implementations demonstrate the importance of choosing good annotation names. In Annotation-Call the name of the annotation is such that it fails to introduce the intermediate step and make clear why refresh is happening. A named pointcut with a similar name would have similar problems.

Introducing additional attribute names does not always add value. When writing procedural code, most programmers are unlikely to define a new onePlus procedure for the expression 'x + 1'. They could, but in this case the primitive expression is sufficiently clear that it is usually left in line. Named abstraction has to stop at some point, or else programs would never reach primitives.

The same is true for attributes. The pointcut 'execution(public com.acme.*.*(..))' is sufficiently clear that it usually does not warrant a named pointcut. On the other hand 'execution(* Shape+.set*(..))' probably does warrant the displayStateChange named pointcut.

Enumeration, Property, Pattern-Based Pointcuts and Annotations

The previous guidelines leave open the question of what mechanism to use to establish the binding between the individual point(s) and the actual set of points. The choices are enumeration-based pointcuts, name-pattern based pointcuts, property-based pointcuts or annotations.

Prefer enumeration-based pointcuts when: (i) it is difficult to write a stable property-based pointcut to capture the members and (ii) the set of points is relatively small.

Prefer property- or pattern-based pointcuts when: (i) it is possible to write one that is stable or (ii) the set of points is relatively large (more than ten).

Use annotations to mark points when three things are true: (i) it is difficult to write a stable property-based pointcut to capture the points, (ii) the name of the annotation is unlikely to change, and (iii) the meaning of the annotation is an inherent to the points, rather than a context-dependent aspect of the points only true in some configurations.

In addition, lean towards annotations when the property that defines inclusion in the set is an inherent property of the points, and lean towards other pointcuts when the binding from points to the set might change non-locally, or come into existence non-locally.

The implementations after GOFP provide some support for these guidelines, but the example is too small to fully support them.

The difference between how Named-Enumeration-Pointcut and Named-Pattern-Pointcut fare for Add-Unrelated-Method both shows the concern about pattern-based pointcuts, and also shows that using stable patterns can mitigate that concern.[5] For example 'Shape+.set*(*)' means methods defined on Shape or a subtype of Shape, for which the name begins with set, and that have a single argument. This pattern has good stability both because it is restricted to a small part of the type hierarchy, and because it is based on a well-established Java naming convention. By contrast, 'set*(..)' is less stable, it covers any type of object, and methods with any number of arguments.

Once again, the difference between Annotation-Call and Annotation-Property supports the importance of annotation names. As formulated above, the guideline is intended to reduce the likelihood that the name will need to change, and will make it more natural to reference the same annotation in other aspects or in compositions of pointcuts based on the annotation. For example DisplayStateChange may be reasonable as an annotation. But MakesRemoteCall may not be, because it may depend on a particular deployment configuration rather than always being true of a method.

While the guidelines for preferring property and pattern-based pointcuts when the number of points is large and it is possible to write such pointcuts are not supported by this study, they seem fairly straightforward, although it would be valuable to validate them, and all the other above guidelines, in a larger case study.

6 Related Work

There have been a number of characterizations of aspect-oriented programming (AOP) mechanisms: as a means for modularizing crosscutting concerns [16, 17], in terms of obliviousness and quantification [10], in terms of a common join point model framework [25] and others. By contrast, the focus of this paper is on analyzing the separation of concern properties of annotations, pointcuts and advice, and describing those as binding mechanisms similar to procedures.

The work described in [10] and [24] is closer to this paper in that they characterize AOP mechanisms as a new step in "introducing non-locality in our programs" [10], specifically as a means of binding points in the execution space [24]. But, they do not consider annotations. They also do not focus on the way in which the mechanisms compare for separating different kinds of concern or provide guidelines for choosing among the mechanisms.

The discussion by Lopes et al. [22] shares with this paper the view that pointcuts act as a kind of referencing mechanism. The focus in [22] is more on motivating and

---

[5] Practicing AspectJ developer report that the restrictions that come from the use of name patterns often benefits their code. The patterns force them to regularize the rules they use for naming, and that helps with overall system comprehensibility. Nonetheless, this issue is motivating a variety of important research in more powerful pointcut languages, that make it possible to express pointcuts in terms of properties that are more accurate and robust than name patterns [24, 35].

speculating about future "more naturalistic" referencing mechanisms that go beyond current pointcut mechanisms. On the contrary, our focus is on characterizing and assessing state-of-the-art mainstream pointcut mechanisms and especially on providing guidelines for using them.

Rinard et al. [29] propose a classification and an analysis system for AOP programs that classifies interactions between aspects and methods to identify potentially problematic interactions (e.g., caused by the aspect and the method both writing the same field), and guide the developer's attention to the causes of such interactions. Hence, their focus is different than ours. They also do not discuss annotations, and only indirectly suggest usage guidelines. To the extent they do suggest guidelines there appear to be no conflicts between their work and ours.

Baldwin and Clark have developed a general framework for assessing the value of modularity in technical systems [2]. Sullivan et al. [32] show how this framework can be applied to software systems. Lopes and Bajracharya [23] went on to apply the framework to AOP systems. The Baldwin and Clark framework is more heavy-weight than ours, and seems more suitable for architectural decision making than what we discuss here. But again, there does not appear to be any inherent conflict between the analyses. One interesting next experiment would be to see how the guidelines we develop interact with the analyses and net option value framework used by these researchers.

Our guidelines are 'bottom-up' or in-situ in nature. They are focused on how a developer makes isolated decisions about what mechanism to use guided by design goals. By contrast, Jacobsen and Ng have proposed a methodology for designing systems in an aspect-oriented style [15]. Again, there appears to be no contradictions between our guidelines and their methodology.

The work presented in [26] also involves an assessment of pointcut mechanisms with respect to how well programs using them fare in presence of change, as compared to equivalent OO programs that use method calls only. That assessment does not consider annotations, and is primarily on assessing the need for pointcut mechanisms that refer to more dynamic properties of join points than possible today. The design and implementation of such pointcuts is the main focus of their paper.

7 Future Work

The analysis and guidelines in this paper are based on first-principles analysis with a single small example. Based on this, there are several attractive avenues for future work.

One next step would be large-scale validation of these guidelines. There are (at least) two dimensions of improvement. First, they could be validated against a larger sample of code developed by experts. While attractive, at present there do not appear to be large bodies of suitable open source code to work with, although this appears to be changing rapidly.

A second line of work would be to validate these guidelines in some form of user study in which programmers are asked to work with the guidelines in a controlled experiment.

As discussed in Section 6, it would also be interesting to develop a detailed account of how the guidelines we propose interact with classifications such as in [29], architectural analyses such as in [2], and design methodologies such as in [15].

8 Summary

Metadata annotations, pointcuts and advice are useful techniques for separating concerns in source code. To better understand and be able to work with these mechanisms, we propose a characterization in which each is seen as making a different kind of binding: annotations bind attributes to program points; pointcuts create bindings between sets of points and descriptions of those sets; named pointcuts bind attributes to sets of points; and advice bind the implementation of an operation to sets of points.

This characterization yields insight into how the mechanisms relate and suggests areas for improvement. It also yields guidelines for how to choose among the mechanisms in the course of programming with them. The guidelines can be phrased in terms of deciding which kind of binding is appropriate in a given situation or they can be formulated in more prescriptive terms that may be more appropriate in some contexts.

The model and guidelines proposed here provide a good basis for further research and near-term development. We expect improvements to the model and guidelines as the combined use of annotations, pointcuts and advice grows.

Acknowledgements

The author would like to thank Mik Kersten, Mira Mezini and Gail Murphy for fruitful discussions on the ideas developed in this paper. Thanks also go to Andrew Eisenberg, Mik Kersten, Gail Murphy, Kevin Sullivan and Maria Tkatchenko who provided detailed comments on earlier drafts of the paper.

This work is partially funded by the Natural Sciences and Engineering Research Council of Canada (NSERC), IBM Canada Ltd. and the European Network of Excellence in Aspect-Oriented Software Development (AOSD-Europe).

References

1. The Server Side Symposium: AOP Expert Panel, 2004,
   http://www.theserverside.com/news/thread.tss?thread_id=30564.
2. Baldwin, C.Y. and Clark, K.B. Design Rules: The Power of Modularity. MIT Press, 2000.
3. Bergmans, L. and Aksit, M. Principles and Design Rationale of Composition Filters. in Filman, R.E., Elrad, T., Aksit, M. and Clarke, S. eds. Aspect-Oriented Software Development, Addison Wesley Professional, 2004, 63 - 95.
4. Bloch, J. A Metadata Facility for the Java Programming Language, 2004.
5. Boner, J., AspectWerkz http://aspectwerkz.codehaus.org/.
6. Bryant, A., Catton, A., Volder, K.D. and Murphy, G.C., Explicit programming. Aspect-Oriented Software Development, 2002, ACM Press, 10-18.

7. Cheatham, T.E., JR., The introduction of definitional facilities into higher level programming languages. (AFIPS) Fall Joint Computer Conference, 1966, Spartan Books, 623-673.

8. Coady, Y., Kiczales, G., Feeley, M. and Smolyn, G., Using AspectC to improve the modularity of path-specific customization in operating system code. Foundations of Software Engineering (FSE), 2001, ACM Press, 88 - 98.

9. Elrad, T., Aksit, M., Kiczales, G., Lieberherr, K. and Ossher, H. Discussing aspects of AOP. COMMUNICATIONS OF THE ACM, 44 (10). 33-38.

10. Filman, R.E., Elrad, T., Aksit, M. and Clarke, S. (eds.). Aspect-Oriented Software Development. Addison Wesley Professional, 2004.

11. Gradecki, J. and Lesiecki, N. Mastering AspectJ: Aspect-oriented Programming in Java. Wiley, Indianapolis, Ind., 2003.

12. Group, G., Hype Cycle for Application Development, 2004, http://www4.gartner.com/DisplayDocument?doc_cd=120914.

13. Hirschfeld, R. AspectS - Aspect-oriented programming with squeak. Revised Papers from the International Conference NetObjectDays on Objects, Components, Architectures, Services, and Applications for a Networked World, 2591. 216-232.

14. Jacobson, I. and Ng, P.-W. Aspect-Oriented Software Development with Use Cases. Addison-Wesley, 2003.

15. Jacobson, I. and Ng, P.-W. Aspect-Oriented Software Development with Use Cases. Addison Wesley Professional, 2004.

16. Kiczales, G., Hilsdale, E., Hugunin, J., Kersten, M., Palm, J. and Griswold, W.G., An Overview of AspectJ. European Conference on Object-Oriented Programming (ECOOP), 2001, Springer, 327-355.

17. Kiczales, G., Lamping, J., Mendhekar, A., Maeda, C., Lopes, C., Loingtier, J. and Irwin, J., Aspect-oriented programming. European Conference on Object-Oriented Programming (ECOOP), 1997, 220-242.

18. Kiczales, G. and Mezini, M., Aspect-Oriented Programming and Modular Reasoning. ACM International Conference on Software Engineering, 2005 (to appear).

19. Krishnamurthi, S., Fisler, K. and Greenberg, M. Verifying aspect advice modularly. Foundations of Software Engineering (FSE). 137 - 146.

20. Laddad, R. AspectJ in action: practical aspect-oriented programming. Manning, Greenwich, CT, 2003.

21. Liberty, J. Programming C#. O'Reilly, Sebastopol, CA, 2003.

22. Lopes, C., Dourish, P., Lorenz, D. and Lieberherr, K. Beyond AOP: Toward naturalistic programming. ACM SIGPLAN NOTICES, 38 (12). 34-43.

23. Lopes, C.V. and Bajracharya, S., An Analysis of Modularity in Aspect-Oriented Design. Aspect-Oriented Software Development (AOSD'05), 2005 (to appear).

24. Masuhara, H. and Kawauchi, K., Dataflow Pointcut in Aspect-Oriented Programming. Asian Symposium on Programming Languages and Systems (APLAS), 2003, 105--121.

25. Masuhara, H. and Kiczales, G., Modeling crosscutting in aspect-oriented mechanisms. European Conference on Object-Oriented Programming (ECOOP), 2003, Springer, 2-28.

26. Ostermann, K., Mezini, M. and Bockisch, C., Expressive Pointcuts for Increased Modularity. In Proc. of European Conference on Object-Oriented Programming (ECOOP), 2005, Springer.

27. Project, A., AJDT Demonstration, 2004, http://eclipse.org/ajdt/demos/.

28. Rajan, H. and Sullivan, K., Eos: instance-level aspects for integrated system design. Foundations of Software Engineering (FSE), 2003, ACM Press, 297 - 306.

29. Rinard, M., Salcianu, A. and Suhabe, B., A Classification System and Analysis for Aspect-Oriented Programs. Foundations of Software Engineering (FSE), 2004, ACM Press, 147 - 158.

30. Schutter, K.D., What does aspect-oriented programming mean to Cobol? Aspect-Oriented Software Development, 2005, ACM Press, (to appear).

31. Spinczyk, O., Gal, A. and Schröder-Preikschat, W., AspectC++: an aspect-oriented extension to the C++ programming language. Fortieth International Confernece on Tools Pacific: Objects for internet, mobile and embedded applications, 2002, Australian Computer Society, 53 - 60.

32. Sullivan, K.J., Griswold, W.G., Cai, Y. and Hallen, B., The structure and value of modularity in software design. Foundations of Software Engineering, 2001, ACM Press, 99 - 108.

33. Teitelman, W. PILOT: A Step Toward Man-Computer Symbiosis Department of Electrical Engineering and Computer Science, Massachusetts Institute of Technology, 1966.

34. Walker, D., Zdancewic, S. and Ligatti, J., A theory of aspects. International Conference on Functional Programming, 2003, ACM Press, 127 - 139.

35. Walker, R. and Viggers., K., Implementing protocols via declarative event patterns. ACM Sigsoft International Symposium on Foundations of Software Engineering (FSE-12), 2004.

Expressive Pointcuts for Increased Modularity

Klaus Ostermann, Mira Mezini, and Christoph Bockisch

Darmstadt University of Technology, D-64283 Darmstadt, Germany
{ostermann, mezini, bockisch}@informatik.tu-darmstadt.de

Abstract. In aspect-oriented programming, pointcuts are used to describe cross-cutting structure. Pointcuts that abstract over irrelevant implementation details are clearly desired to better support maintainability and modular reasoning.

We present an analysis which shows that current pointcut languages support localization of crosscutting concerns but are problematic with respect to information hiding. To cope with the problem, we present a pointcut language that exploits information from different models of program semantics, such as the execution trace, the syntax tree, the heap, static type system, etc., and supports abstraction mechanisms analogous to functional abstraction. We show how this raises the abstraction level and modularity of pointcuts and present first steps toward an efficient implementation by means of a static analysis technique.

1 Introduction

In aspect-oriented programming (AOP for short), pointcuts are predicates that identify sets of related points in the execution of a program, where to execute behavior pertaining to crosscutting concerns. Given an aspect that modularizes a crosscutting concern, its pointcuts serve as the interface between the crosscutting concern and the rest of the system. As such, the abstraction level at which these predicates are expressed directly affects the robustness of the design in the presence of change. Separation and localization of concerns into individual units is a major feature of modular design - providing interfaces that absorb local changes is another, equally important, feature.

It has been indicated elsewhere that a pointcut that merely enumerates relevant points in the execution by their syntactic appearance in the program code is fragile w.r.t. changes in the code [15, 20]. In this paper, we investigate the issue in more depth: We compare object-oriented (OO for short) and aspect-oriented (AO for short) designs of an exemplary problem with respect to their capability to remain stable in the presence of change. We observe that with current pointcut languages one can indeed separate crosscutting concerns into their own modular units, but the resulting design does not actually perform much better in terms of absorbing changes than the OO design which does not modularize the crosscutting concerns. This reduces the power of aspects to merely supporting pluggability of crosscutting concerns, leaving out of the reach another important modularity principle: Information hiding [30].

To cope with the problem, this paper proposes a pointcut language that allows to specify pointcuts at a high-level of abstraction by providing (a) different *rich models of the program semantics* and (b) *abstraction mechanisms* analogous to functional abstraction. The key insight is that various models of program semantics are needed to enable

A.P. Black (Ed.): ECOOP 2005, LNCS 3586, pp. 214–240, 2005.

reasoning about program execution. For example, the abstract syntax tree (AST) alone is not a very good basis for high-level pointcuts because it is a very indirect representation of the program execution semantics that makes it intractable to specify dynamic properties.

We propose to base the pointcut language on a *combination* of models of the programm's semantics. In this paper, we concentrate on four such models: The AST, the execution trace, the heap, and the static type assignment; if needed, other models such as a profiling or a memory consumption model could be added. Pointcuts in our approach are logic queries over the aforementioned models.

We have implemented a prototype of this approach as an interpreter for a small statically typed AO language, called ALPHA[1]. Pointcuts in ALPHA are logic queries written in Prolog [36]; they operate on-line over databases representing the aforementioned models of the program semantics. We show how AO designs expressed in this language can be made robust against various kinds of changes.

We also present a technique for an efficient implementation of our approach that is based on the notion of *join point shadows* [17]. The shadow of a dynamic join point is a code structure (expression, statement or block) that statically corresponds to an execution of the dynamic join point. The idea is to compute the shadows of pointcuts off-line by a static analysis of pointcuts and to evaluate or extend dynamic semantic models only at these statically computed shadows. Our analysis is different from previous approaches in this direction [17, 28, 35] in that it works on a much more powerful and open pointcut language.

Some concepts used in our approach have also been discussed elsewhere. For example, logic queries have been used in other approaches [15, 19, 37]. The unique contribution of our proposal compared to related work is twofold. First, we present a detailed study of the disadvantages of most current pointcut languages. Second, the openness of the pointcut language, the ability to combine different program models, and the incorporation of the execution trace and heap together with the abstraction mechanisms of a Prolog-like language is also unique. We will give a detailed account of the contribution of this paper and the relation to other works after the technical presentation.

The remainder of the paper is organized as follows. Sec. 2 motivates the need for better pointcut languages by a study of the robustness of aspect-oriented programs. Sec. 3 introduces the ALPHA programming language. Sec. 4 presents some examples in ALPHA and analyzes them in the light of the problems identified in Sec. 2. Sec. 5 describes the static analysis technique. Sec. 6 elaborates on the contribution of this paper in comparison to related work. Sec. 7 describes future work and concludes. The appendix contains different specifications of Prolog constructs that are used in various places but whose specification is not necessary to follow the paper.

2   Pointcuts and Modularity

In this section, we identify the limitations of current pointcut languages by means of an example problem. We focus on AspectJ's pointcut-advice mechanism [21] first; other

---

[1] Source code is available at [2].

pointcut languages will be discussed in the section on related work. We present an object-oriented (OO) and an aspect-oriented (AO) solution to the problem and compare them w.r.t robustness in the presence of change.

2.1   Example Problem and Its OO and AO Solutions

The example problem is about modeling a hierarchy of graphical objects like points and lines which can be drawn on display objects; each display has a list of figures shown in it. The solution should ensure that the state of figure elements and their corresponding views on active displays is kept synchronized by having displays be updated when the state of figure elements changes.

An OO solution for the problem that applies the observer pattern [14] is schematically shown in Fig. 1[2]. To avoid unnecessary updates, the solution supports what we call *object precision* and *field precision*. By object precision we mean that an update to a figure element triggers a repaint only on those displays on which the figure element is visible; in general, there are multiple different display objects active, whereby every figure element is visible only on a (possibly empty) subset of all displays. For this purpose, each figure in Fig. 1 maintains an observer list with the displays it is shown in, if any; when a figure f is added to a display, the display is added to the list of f's observers as well as to the observer lists of f's children; e.g., showing a line on a display will cause the display to be an observer of the line as well as of its start and end points. If a figure f1 is not anymore a child of another figure, f2, the observers that f1 inherited from f2 are removed from the list of f1's observers[3].

By field precision we mean that only changes of the fields that contribute to the graphical representation of a figure element should trigger display updates. The set of the fields affecting the draw behavior generally depends on the dynamic control flow and cannot be determined statically. Hence, it is not always easy to ensure field precision especially if the system is complex. In the Line class in Fig. 1, it is easy to see that the field name is never involved in the drawing behavior and that enable, start and end are potentially read in the control flow of draw. Of the latter variables, only enabled is always read - hence, a change to it always triggers a notification of the observers; fields start and end are only read if enabled is true. Hence, changes to start or end trigger a notification only if enabled is true (see comments on the methods notifyObserversUnconditional(), notifyObservers() and setEnabled(...) in class FigureElement, and Line.setEnd(...) in Fig. 1).

A functionally equivalent AO solution of the problem is schematically shown in Fig. 2. This solution factors the observer management fields and methods out of the figure element classes into the aspect using the inter-type declaration mechanism of AspectJ[4]. The aspect defines three pointcuts. The pointcut addFigure captures any call

---

[2] Complete code for all examples and our ALPHA interpreter are available at [2].

[3] If figures are shared by several parent-figures, reference counters are associated with observers and an observer is actually removed from an observer list, only if its reference counter is zero.

[4] The observer implementation proposed by Hannemann and Kiczales [16] uses hashtables instead of introductions in order to increase the reusability of aspects, but this does not affect the discussion in this paper.

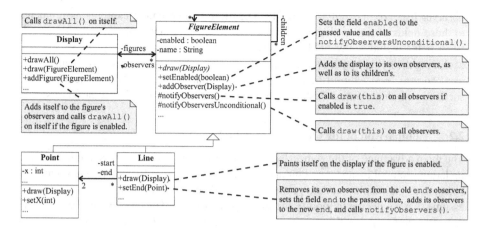

Fig. 1. OO implementation of a precise version of the display updating

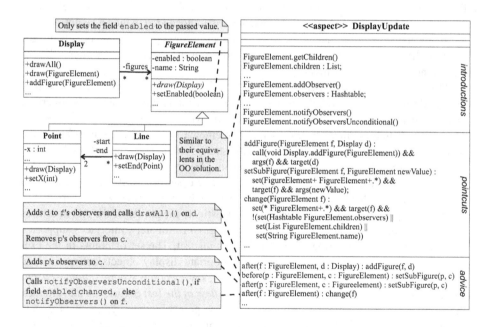

Fig. 2. First AO implementation of the precise display updating

to the method `Display.addFigure(FigureElement)`; the after-advice associated with this pointcut establishes a subject-observer relation between the receiver and the argument.

The `setSubFigure` pointcut captures points in the execution, where parent-child associations are changed - these are assignments on any field of type `FigureElement` or a subtype thereof (denoted by the "+"), declared in `FigureElement` or any of its subclasses. The before and after advice associated with this pointcut make sure that the observer lists are updated accordingly. The `change()` pointcut captures assignments to those fields of figure element objects that affect the draw behavior - the set of relevant fields includes any field declared in `FigureElement` or one of its subclasses, excluding the fields `FigureElement.name`, `FigureElement.observers` and `figureElement.children` (the latter two are introduced by the aspect). The advice associated with this pointcut ensures that notifications are sent to relevant observers.

2.2   Comparison of the OO and AO Solutions

The main advantage of the AspectJ solution over the OO counterpart is that the display updating protocol is made explicit and *localized* in one module. Due to this separation changes to the display update protocol are localized within the aspect. For example, assume that we decide to modify the protocol as follows. The display update signaling currently performed within methods that change the state of figure elements, should happen at caller sites of these methods (e.g., the because the caller object should be logged, which is not possible at execution site). Changes needed to introduce the modified protocol are localized within the aspect code in the AO solution (alternatively a new aspect can be implemented); the same changes are not localized in the OO solution. Furthermore, the separation makes the display updating logic pluggable. The advantages resulting from the separation of crosscutting concerns are discussed elsewhere [22, 16] and are not in the focus of this paper.

Physical separation and localization of concerns, while important, is only one aspect of modularity. Another, equally important aspect of modularity is about the interface that controls the interaction of the separated logic with the rest of the system, thereby employing abstraction mechanisms to hide implementation details. The interface of the separated observer protocol to the rest of the system is defined by pointcuts in the aspect in Fig. 2. A recent paper by Kiczales and Mezini [23] argues that this explicit interface makes modular reasoning in the presence of change easier in an AO setting compared to an OO setting, where there is no explicit interface between these two concerns.

In this paper, we go one step further and investigate the ability of the AO interfaces to absorb change by means of information hiding. Unfortunately, interfaces supported by current pointcut technology fall short in this respect. The set of points in the execution of figure elements where to update appropriate display objects are not defined intentionally by some common semantic property, say, as points where *"changes occur on fields that were previously read in the control flow of the last* `drawAll` *call"*. Rather, the pointcuts in our example mostly describe these points by their syntax, thus, exposing implementation details of the figure element hierarchy to the aspect. The following comparison of the OO and AO solutions from Fig. 1 and Fig. 2 shows that the lack of proper support for information hiding makes the separated display update protocol basically as fragile w.r.t changes as the OO solution. The comparison is organized around the change scenarios presented in Fig. 3, which also summarizes the robustness of the AO and OO solution related to these change scenarios.

First, both scenarios are fragile with respect to scenarios *Ch1* and *Ch3*. In both solutions, moving parts of a figure element's state to a helper class will cause changes to those fields to escape observation, although they might have had effect on the drawing behavior. Hence, they break w.r.t. *Ch1*. Also, renaming the field `enabled`, or adding a

name	description	example	OO	AO
Ch1	Object graph change: Outsource part of the drawing relevant state of a figure element to a class that is not in the `FigureElement` hierarchy.	Use an object of type `Pair` to store the coordinates of a `Point`.	–	–
Ch2	Class hierarchy change: Inserting a new type into the hierarchy of `FigureElements`.	Adding the class `Circle extends FigureElement`.	+/–	+/–
Ch3	Control flow change: Change the condition under which a display update is necessary.	Renaming the field `enabled` to `visible`, or adding a field `hidden`.	–	–
Ch4	Class definition change: Inserting/removing a field whose change makes display update necessary.	Adding the field `color` to the class `FigureElement`.	–	+
Ch5	Class definition change: Inserting/removing a field whose change does not affect display.	Adding the field `changeHistory` to the class `FigureElement`.	+	–

Fig. 3. Change scenarios with comparison of AO and OO solution

new field which also controls when figure elements are displayed, say `hidden`, will break both the AO and OO protocols. This is because the names of such fields are hard-coded in the implementation of `notifyObservers()`, which is the same in both solutions. Hence, both solution fail to absorb *Ch3*.

The AO solution is more robust w.r.t *Ch4*. The OO protocol breaks in the sense that the display update signaling for the field being added, needs to be adopted, respectively encoded anew. The AO protocol that uses wildcards for pattern matching on names of fields that affect drawing behavior carries over automatically. However, the AO solution is less robust than the OO solution w.r.t *Ch5*. This is because the `change` pointcut in Fig. 2 enumerates each field to exclude from the observation explicitly. Adding (or removing) a field which does not influence the graphical representation of a figure will break field precision of the aspect: Changes to these fields will cause the display to be updated.

Finally, with regard to the scenario *Ch2*, we argue that both solutions perform more or less the same under the assumption that the new class, in general, introduces both fields that affect the drawing behavior as well as fields that do not affect drawing. The AO solution performs better for fields that affect drawing: The protocol established by the aspect automatically applies to the new class. This is not true for the OO solution: The whole logic concerning children and field change should be manually coded in the new class. However, the opposite is true for fields that do not affect drawing and, hence, need to be excluded explicitly in the AO solution.

The use of wildcards for pattern matching on names might at first sight appear to support some sort of abstraction by providing a means to identify relevant execution points by some commonality. However, pattern matching on names only allows to abstract over syntax, which is not always sufficient. Our investigation shows that wildcards do not actually increase the ability to absorb change, beyond simple cases, where there are no exceptions to be made from the rule defined by wildcards. As for our example, we could as well have used an AO solution that does not use wildcards but enumerates the relevant points. This solution would exhibit the same robustness w.r.t the change scenarios as the OO solution[5].

The discussion suggests that without more powerful mechanisms for information hiding the potential of AO mechanisms for improving modularity cannot fully be unleashed. This has been the motivation for us to work on a pointcut language that enables better modularity and information hiding. This language will be presented in the following section. Please note that the question is not whether AO mechanisms provide better modularity than OO mechanisms; the question is rather how to further improve the power of the modularity of AO mechanisms. As mentioned in the beginning of this sub-section, AO does support better modularity by separating and localizing the display update logic [22, 16] and by providing an explicit interface [23]. The point we want to improve is that the focus of pointcuts should be *when* (under which conditions) a pointcut should be triggered rather than *where* (lexically) the corresponding places in the code are.

3   The ALPHA Language

ALPHA is an AO extension of a toy OO core language implemented as an interpreter in Java. The OO core of ALPHA is based on L2 [12] - a simple object-oriented language in the style of Java. The formal syntax, semantics, and type system of L2 are described in [12]. Here we present the OO core of ALPHA informally by means of the example in Fig. 4 - a simplified variant of the example from the previous section. ALPHA supports classes and single inheritance and has a standard static type system.

3.1   Pointcuts and Advice

Every class in ALPHA may define fields and methods and may also define pointcuts and associate advice with them. Pointcuts are Prolog queries over a database of both static and dynamic information about the program or program execution. A Prolog query is a sequence of primitive queries combined by the *and* operator " , ". A simple pointcut that denotes "all assignments to fields of objects of type point" is shown in the class DisplayUpdate in Fig. 5.

In contrast to AspectJ and similar to Caesar [29], aspects in ALPHA become effective only after they are *deployed*. Further discussion of this strategy is available at [29]. What matters is to note that the advice of DisplayUpdate will have semantic effect once an instance of DisplayUpdate is deployed. For illustration, consider the use of the aspect DisplayUpdate within the main() method of class Main in Fig. 5 - here, the advice of DisplayUpdate will be effective only during the execution of doSomething().

In order to explain the pointcut in Fig. 5, it is necessary to understand the basic structure of the database. The database contains both static and dynamic information about the program organized in a set of relations. A very simple relation is the unary relation now, denoted now/1. This relation has only one fact that contains the current

---

[5] In [2], the reader can also find code for an AspectJ solution of the example problem that does not uses wildcards.

```
1   class FigureElement extends Object {
2     String name;
3     void draw(Display d) {}
4   }
5   class Point extends FigureElement {
6     int x, y;
7     boolean enabled;
8     void draw(Display d) {
9       if ( this .enabled) d. paintPoint ( this .x,  this .y);
10    }
11  }
12  class Line extds FigureElement {
13    Point  start , end;
14    void draw(Display d) {
15      if ( this .enabled) d. paintLine ( this . start ,  this .end);
16    }
17  }
18  class Display extends object {
19    FigureElement f1, f2;
20    void drawAll() { this .f1.draw(this ); this .f2.draw(this ); }
21    void draw(FigureElement fe) { print (" display  update :"); print (fe ); this .drawAll(); }
22    void paintPoint ( int x, int y) { ... }
23    void paintLine (Point  start , Point end) { ... }
24  }
```

Fig. 4. Figure elements in ALPHA

```
class DisplayUpdate extends Object {
  Display d;
  after  now(ID), set (ID, _, P, _, _),  instanceof (P, 'Point') { this .d.draw(P); }
}

class Main extends Object {
  Display d; DisplayUpdate du;
  void main() {
    this .d = new Display (); this .du = new DisplayUpdate();
    this .du.d = this .d;
    deploy( this .du) { this .doSomething() }
  }
  void doSomething() { ... }
  ...
}
```

Fig. 5. Simple advice in ALPHA

timestamp. These timestamps are necessary in order to reason about temporal relations between events. The query now(ID) in Fig. 5 retrieves the current timestamp and binds it to the variable ID. In Prolog, all names starting with uppercase letters are considered variables, whereas all names starting with lowercase letters or enclosed by single quotes (') are considered constants.

The second part of the query, set(ID, _, P, _, _), queries a relation set/5 that stores all assignments in the current execution. The first element of this relation is the timestamp of this event, the second one is a reference into the syntax tree of the program and denotes the expression in the syntax tree that corresponds to this event. The third element is the object that contains the field, the fourth is the fieldname, and the fifth is the value assigned to the field. By using the name ID for the first element in the query set(ID, _, P, _, _), we specify that this pointcut will match only

```
class DisplayUpdate extends Object {
  Display d; Point p;
  after now(ID), set(ID, _, @this.p, _, _) {
    this.d.draw(this.p);
  }
}
```

Fig. 6. Inserting context into a pointcut

if the assignment has happened right now and not in some time in the past because a variable (ID in this case) must be bound to the same value in all places where it is used. The wildcard "_" is used for anonymous variables that are not interesting; in the set part of the pointcut in Fig. 5 the "_" wildcards are used to denote that the pointcut matches for any expression as well as for any field name and value being assigned. By using the name P for the receiver element of the set/5 relation, we bind the receiver object of each matching assignment to P. In the third part of the pointcut, instanceof(P, 'Point'), we constrain the set of eligible assignments even further by requiring P to be an instance of the class Point.

Variables in a pointcut can be used both as constraints during the unification process and as a means to make context available in the advice. In our example, we use P in the advice body[6]. The form of advice is similar to AspectJ [21].

The kind of data in the database is obviously an important variation point of our approach. In our prototype, the database contains four different program models: a representation of the abstract syntax tree, a representation of the object store (heap), a representation of the static type of every expression in the program, and a representation of the trace of the program execution. These four structures are a natural choice, since they represent the main entities used for interpreting a program. However, it would not invalidate our approach to add or remove other entities, e.g., add a model about resource consumption or remove the object store model. In the example above, the set/5 relation belongs to the execution trace model, whereas the instanceof/2 relation belongs to the object store model and the static type model. A full reference of the relations in the database is available in the appendix in Fig. 14. The basic idea is that each of these models represents a partial view of the program semantics. By making as much information available to the pointcut programmer as possible, the programmer can choose the program model to be used to express his intention as directly and conveniently as possible.

The escape symbol @ can be used to evaluate an expression inside a query, such that object-specific constraints involving values from the enclosing object can be expressed. Fig. 6 shows a refined version of the display update aspect whose pointcut will match only if the target of the assignment is this.p.

3.2   Pointcut Abstraction and Pointcut Libraries

The expressiveness of our pointcut language is due to the rich program models *and* its abstraction mechanisms. Due to Prolog, it is easy to define new predicates that abstract

---

[6] We use type inference to determine a static type for every variable inside a query, which is used to type-check the advice body. We elaborate on this in Sec. 5.

over the primitive generated predicates. Fig. 7 shows an excerpt of the standard pointcut library building on this feature. Line 3 shows - by the example of the primitive `set` predicate - how to define convenient abbreviations of the generated primitive execution trace predicates for the case that we are not interested in past events or in the syntactic location of the event. With these abbreviations the pointcut in Fig. 6 can be written more conveniently as `set(@this.p,_,_)`.

Lines 6-9 demonstrate the usefulness of having the complete history of execution[7]. The `cflow` query specifies under which conditions a join point `ID0` is or has been in the control flow of another join point `ID1`. Reasonably, this other join point may only be a method call. Thus, `ID1` must be the timestamp of a method call. Method calls are stored in the database as pairs of `calls/5` and `endcall/3` facts denoting the beginning respectively the end of a method call. The `before/2` relation is a part of the execution trace model and can be used to compare events w.r.t. their temporal order. The first rule of the `cflow` query, applies when the `ID1` call has completed (i.e., a corresponding `endcall` fact is available). The second rule applies when `ID1` is still on the call stack; it uses the special control predicate `\+`, which succeeds, if the goal cannot be proven (a.k.a. *negation as failure*).

Please note that this `cflow` construct is much more powerful than the AspectJ pointcut designator with this name, since the AspectJ variant can only be used to refer to control flows that are currently on the call stack (corresponding to our second `cflow` rule), whereas our `cflow` also applies to control flows in the past[8].

The pointcut library contains a set of other pointcut predicates that are only sketched in Fig. 7. We have defined predicates to determine whether an object is reachable from another object following a path of links in the object graph (`reachable/2`) and to determine the class of an object (`instanceof/2`). Other predicates provide convenient access to the AST (`class/2`, `method/3`, `field/3`, `within/3`, `subtype-eq/2`).

The `pcflow/3` predicate predicts the control flow of a method based on the AST, basically building the call graph of the method. This is achieved by computing the transitive hull of all outgoing method calls, whereby all method implementations in all subtypes are considered in order to take late binding into account.

The `mostRecent/2` predicate finds the most recent occurence of an event pattern. We will use this predicate to express things like "find the most recent occurence of a call to `draw`".

A very convenient property of Prolog is that these predicates can be used with arbitrary instantiation patterns. This means that the predicates can be used in any direction. For example, the `within/3` predicate can be used to find an expression within a given method and class, or the other way around, to find a class and a method that lexically contain an expression.

---

[7] Due to the optimizations discussed in sec. 5 only parts of the execution history are recorded that are relevant for the pointcuts in the program.

[8] Note, however, that the main purpose of this paper is *not* to propose new control flow pointcut designators. The `cflow` pointcut designator is just an illustration of the extensibility of our pointcut language.

```
1  % abbrevations if we are only interested in the current event
2  set(Receiver, Field, Val) :- now(ID), set(ID, _, Receiver, Field,
3  Val).
4  % abbreviations for new, calls, get similarly
5
6  % is ID0 in the control flow of ID1?
7  cflow(ID0, ID1) :- calls(ID1, _, _, _, _), before(ID1, ID0),
8
9                      endcall(ID2, _, ID1, _), before(ID0, ID2).
10 cflow(ID0, ID1) :-
11    calls(ID1, _, _, _, _),  before(ID1, ID0), \+ encall(_, _, ID1, _).
12
13 % is Obj2 reachable from Obj1 in the object graph?
14 reachable(Obj1,Obj2) :- ...
15
16 % is Obj an instance of C?
17 instanceof(Obj, C) :- ...
18
19 % convenient access to AST: query classes, methods, and fields
20 class(Name, CDef) :- ...  meth(CName, MName, MDef) :- ...
21 field(CName, FName, FDef) :- ...
22
23 % is Expr within method MName of class CName
24 within(Expr, CName, MName,) :- ...
25
26 % is C1 subtype of C2?
27 subtypeeq(C1, C2) :- ...
28
29
30 % is Expr in the statically predicted control flow of CName.MName?
31 pcflow(CName, MName, Expr) :- ...
32
33 % find the most recent event matching a pattern X
34 mostRecent(ID,X) :- ...
```

Fig. 7. Excerpts of the pointcut library

The full definition of these predicates can be found in Fig. 15 in the appendix. For the purpose of this work, the details of their definition are not very important. The interesting point is that ALPHA has an *open* pointcut language, whereby new pointcuts can be added on-demand in a *declarative* way. Simple pointcuts can be combined to more powerful pointcuts, so we have the same kind of abstraction mechanism for pointcuts that functional abstraction provides for functions.

We have developed a rudimentary module mechanism for pointcut libraries. Currently, we have a standard pointcut library, that is always available, and user-defined pointcut libraries, that must have the same file name as the source file. A pointcut library can import other libraries using Prolog's own module mechanism. It would be a straightforward extension to make this a full-fledged module mechanism with explicit imports and exports, namespaces, etc.

4   Programming with ALPHA

In this section, we demonstrate how information from different program models can be combined to increase the abstraction level of pointcuts. Furthermore, we discuss the implications of our pointcut language on the programming model.

4.1   Expressiveness of Pointcuts

The class `DisplayUpdate` in Fig. 8 shows six different ways to specify a display update pointcut in ALPHA, using different models of the program. We use these six diferents pointcuts in order to show how we can gradually increase the abstraction level of the pointcuts by exploiting the available information in the database. The resulting pointcuts differ in their support for *robustness* and *precision*, as discussed below and summarized in Fig. 9.

```
 1   class DisplayUpdate extends Object {
 2     Display d;
 3
 4     // enum pointcut
 5     after  set (P, x, _); set (P, y, _); set (P, ' start ', _); set (P, 'end', _),
 6           instanceof (P, 'FigureElement') { this .d.draw(P); }
 7
 8     // set * pointcut
 9     after  set (P, _, _), instanceof (P, 'FigureElement') { this .d.draw(P); }
10
11     // pcflow pointcut
12     after  now(ID), set (ID, ExpID1, P, F, _), instanceof (P, 'FigureElement'),
13           pcflow(Display, 'drawAll', (_, get ((ExpID2, _), F ))),
14           hastype (ExpID2, 'FigureElement') { this .d.draw(P); }
15
16     // cflow  pointcut
17     after  set (P, F, _), get(T1, _, P, F, _), mostRecent(T2, calls (T2, _, @this.d,'drawAll', _)),
18           cflow(T1, T2), instanceof (P, 'FigureElement') { this .d.draw(P); }
19
20     // cflowreach  pointcut
21     after  set (P, F, _), get(T1, _, P, F, _), mostRecent(T2, calls (T2, _, @this.d,'drawAll', _)),
22           cflow(T1, T2), reachable (Q, P), instanceof (Q, 'FigureElement') { this .d.draw(P); }
23   }
```

Fig. 8. Six display update pointcuts

The `enum` pointcut (line 5, Fig. 8) enumerates[9] all assignments to fields that potentially effect drawing behavior, namely to fields `x`, `y`, `start`, or `end` of any object `P` of type `FigureElement`. It uses the names of the fields to identify the relevant assignments. By precisely enumerating the fields potentially involved with drawing, the pointcut supports some sort of static field precision: It makes at least sure that changes to fields that are never read in any control flow of `drawAll()` do not trigger display updates. However, it requires the programmer to explicitly encode this knowledge. Furthermore, it does not take into account the actual control flow of the concrete program execution and, hence, cannot avoid e.g., updates after assignments to fields of disabled points. Also, object precision is not supported. Precision w.r.t. fields involved in the drawing behavior only under certain dynamic conditions - for convenience let us call this dynamic field precision - and object precision require knowledge from dynamic program models, which this pointcut does not make use of. With respect to robustness, the `enum` pointcut exhibits the same behavior as the OO solution in Sec. 2.

The `set*` pointcut (line 9) is triggered by assignments to *any* field of a `FigureElement` object. Due to the use of the _ wildcard this pointcut may cover too many execu-

---

[9] A semicolon denotes "or" in Prolog

criteria	enum	set*	pcflow	cflow	cflowreach
static field precision	+	-	+	+	+
dynamic field precision	-	-	-	+	+
object precision	-	-	-	+	+
Ch1	-	-	-	-	+
Ch2	+/-	+/-	+	+	+
Ch3	-	-	+	+	+
Ch4	-	+	+	+	+
Ch5	+	-	+	+	+

Fig. 9. Evaluation of pointcuts w.r.t. change scenarios from Fig. 3

tion points whose signature matches the pattern by accident [15, 20, 13]. As a result, the pointcut performs poorly w.r.t. field precision: Any assignment to the field name which is not at all involved with drawing will also trigger a display update. Similar to enum, set* uses only static information, hence, it supports neither dynamic field precision nor object precision. As far as robustness is concerned, set* exhibits the same behavior as the AO solution in Sec. 2.

The pcflow pointcut (line 12) uses the pcflow predicate to approximate the control flow of Display.drawAll() based on the AST model and selects field read expressions in the approximated control flow; only assignments to such fields match the pcflow pointcut. Similar to enum, this pointcut ensures that changes to fields that are never read in the control flow of drawAll() do not trigger display updates. However, neither object nor dynamic field precision is supported, since the pointcut only makes use of the AST and not of the dynamic models of the program. The pointcut is not robust in the case of scenario *Ch1* - outsourcing part of figure element state to external objects. The pointcut explicitly requires P to be a FigureElement in order to be able to pass it to the draw() method call. So, state outsourced to non FigureElement objects escape the observation by this pointcut.

Note that while supporting the same precision as enum, pcflow is much more robust. This is due to the abstraction capabilities of the pointcut language (including functional composition and higher-order pointcuts), which allows us to compose primitive pointcuts into more powerful ones, such as pcflow. With a pointcut language that does not support such abstraction mechanisms, e.g., AspectJ's pointcut language that only provides operations on sets - union (||), intersection (&&), negation (!) -, the programmer cannot express the intention to "first identify all field accesses in the control flow of a certain method and than select set operations to these fields" in terms of a generic description, if this functionality is not available as a primitive pointcut designator. (S)he is basically left with the explicit enumeration of such field accesses, as in enum; the only alternative to enumeration is to describe general rules by wildcards, which is actually not better with regard to robustness.

The cflow pointcut (line 17) is similar to pcflow in that this pointcut also selects field reads in the control flow of drawAll. The crucial difference is that cflow is based on the actual control flow at runtime rather than on a conservative static approximation of it. As a result, cflow performs better than pcflow. It supports both dynamic and static field precision as well as object precision: Only assignments to a field F of an object P that are read in the control flow of the particular display object denoted by this.d (see the expression @this.d in the pcflow pointcut) trigger an update. Changes of any field of any figure element that is not referred to by our active display denoted by this.d do not trigger updates. By its use of the dynamic execution model of the program, cflow significantly improves over pcflow. Note that it would not be possible to express something similar with the AspectJ cflow construct because the drawAll method call is in the past and not on the call stack. The only problem with cflow is lack of robustness w.r.t. *Ch1*.

The cflowreach pointcut (line 21) solves the robustness problem of cflow w.r.t *Ch1*. This pointcut composes the cflow pointcut with the reachable predicate from Fig. 7/Fig. 15. That is, in addition to assignments to objects of type FigureElement, it also captures assignments to any object that is reachable in the object graph from an instance of FigureElement. The use of the object graph model makes cflowreach robust against *Ch1*. Since it also inherits all features of the cflow pointcut, cflowreach fulfills the precision requirements and is robust w.r.t. all change scenarios *Ch1* to *Ch5*.

The foregoing analysis demonstrates how our approach enables robust and precise pointcuts. The pointcuts cflow and cflowreach above encode minimal knowledge about implementation details of the crosscutting structure they describe. They directly express the semantic properties of the display update structure rather than relying on implementation details of how the latter syntactically appears in the program code (the names of the variables involved with drawing are irrelevant for the display update behavior).

This is due to the rich models of program semantics underlying these pointcuts as well as the abstraction mechanisms of the pointcut language. In our approach, the programmer can, however, choose which models of the program (s)he wants to use to express a pointcut: from pure syntactic to very dynamic, operational properties, whichever describe the crosscutting best. In this context, please also note the role of unification in elegantly expressing relations between join points. This is illustrated e.g., by the cflow pointcut, where unification together with the cflow predicate is crucial in expressing the temporal relation between points where variables are read respectively written in the execution flow of drawAll.

4.2   Expressive Power, Openness, and Simplicity

In this section, we reason about the complexity of the programming model of our pointcut language. We argue that in addition to increasing the expressiveness of the language, the rich models of program semantics and the powerful abstraction mechanisms such as Prolog's unification also decrease the complexity of the programming model.

First, consider the version of ALPHA, call it Fixed-ALPHA with a fixed pointcut language, including e.g., only the predicates defined in our standard library. The expressiveness of this language is increased as compared to AspectJ - all pointcuts in Fig.8 are written in this language. Nonetheless, the programming model is not more complex than that of AspectJ-like languages [21]. Similar to AspectJ, the programmer needs to understand the meaning of some predefined pointcuts, such as cflow, within, etc., as well as the semantics of Prolog operators/unification for composing them.

Now let us consider the full ALPHA language, in which (domain-specific) pointcut libraries can be defined as outlined in Sec. 3.2. One may argue that this introduces the complexities of full meta-programming into AOP. Similar to [15], we argue that the problems with full meta-programming occur only in an imperative type of language where the programmer is directly involved with some sort of program transformation.

With ALPHA, the programmer only specifies where and what behavioral effect to apply and is not concerned with how this effect is achieved in terms of operational details. To support our argumentation, two examples are discussed in the following which demonstrate that richer program models and more powerful abstraction mechanisms decrease rather than increase the complexity of the programming model.

First, we review the pointcuts `cflow` and `pcflow` from Fig. 8. They both identify assignments involved in the display update crosscutting by their property of accessing variables previously read in the control flow of `drawAll`. However, the models they use are different. The `cflow` predicate uses a richer model that includes the execution trace; `pcflow`'s model is the AST on top of which it approximates the dynamics. We already argued in Sec. 4.1 that `cflow` specifies the crosscutting structure more precisely. Nonetheless, `cflow` is less complex and easier to understand than `pcflow` (see respective definitions in Fig. 15); The approximation of the dynamics of execution based on the AST model adds accidental complexity to `pcflow`'s definition.

Second, we compare the ALPHA implementation of display updating using the `cflow` pointcut in Fig. 8, with the AspectJ solution shown in Fig. 10. The latter is operationally equivalent to the former: it tries to express the rule *"whenever changes are performed on fields that were previously read in the control flow of the last `drawAll` call, make an update"* by quantifying over the dynamic control flow. However, to compensate for the lack of the needed information about the dynamic execution trace, a model of the latter is constructed and managed by the programmer within the aspect. Especially, in lack of more powerful abstraction mechanisms beyond operations on sets, building this model employs the imperative Turing-completeness of Java.

Concretely, the aspect administers observer lists for individual fields rather than for whole objects; an instance field of type `Hashtable` is added into the class `FigureElement`, whose keys are field names and whose values are the corresponding lists of observers, i.e., `Display` objects. A display is made an observer of those fields that have been read during the last execution of its `drawAll()` method (see the after advice associated with the pointcut `reads` in Fig. 10). The pointcut `change` captures assignments to fields of figure elements binding the receiver object to `f`; the after advice associated with it uses `f` together with the name of the assigned field to retrieve displays that observe the field, if any. Before calling `draw` on each observer display, the latter is removed from all observer lists it is in, since different fields might get read during the next draw (field precision).

Like the `cflow`-based solution in ALPHA, the implementation in Fig. 10 is robust w.r.t. all change scenarios (but *Ch1*). However, the aspect schematically shown in Fig. 10 is very complex as compared to the pointcut-advice `cflow` in Fig. 8. Instead of declaratively defining the crosscutting structure employing functional abstraction, as its ALPHA counterpart does, the aspect employs the imperative Turing-completeness

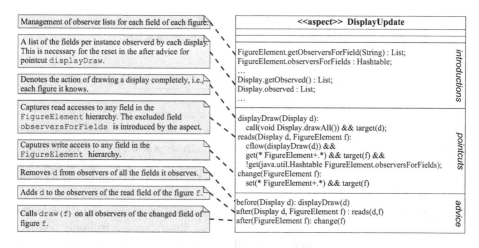

Fig. 10. More robust AO implementation of the precise display updating

of Java to build up a complex infrastructure to basically reverse-engineer the dynamic execution; trying to make it robust w.r.t *Ch1* will further increase the complexity.

All the above said on the decreased rather than increased complexity of the programming model, we would like to add that further investigation is still in place to judge whether the Turing completeness of Prolog is actually needed. It would clearly be desirable to have a simpler, but still sufficiently expressive, pointcut language, both for further decreasing the complexity of the programming model as well as for making an efficient implementation of the language simpler. We did not, however, want to restrict the expressiveness of our language from the very beginning and will consider this issue in future investigation.

5   Abstract Interpretation of Pointcuts

A naive implementation of our approach that extends the Prolog database and evaluates all pointcuts after *every* computation step is obviously not acceptable from both *time* and *space* perspectives.

In this section, we present a new static analysis technique that evaluates pointcuts statically in order to compute (a) a (small) set of expressions in the AST (i.e., join point shadows) that will potentially influence the result of a pointcut, and (b) the *lifetime* of facts that are generated at these shadows. The interpreter can take advantage of this information by extending the database and evaluating the pointcuts only if an expression from the aforementioned pre-computed set is evaluated, and by discarding data in the database if its lifetime is over. A side-effect of the static analysis is that it also infers static types for query variables used to type check advice bodies.

Our optimization is based on an abstract interpretation [8] of the pointcuts. Abstract interpretation of a program uses its denotation to make computations in a universe of abstract objects so that the result of an abstract execution gives some information on the actual computation [8].

Domain	Static abstraction
Time stamps	{now,past}× Expression IDs
Values	Types
Execution Trace	Virtual Trace
Object Store	Virtual Store

Fig. 11. Runtime domains and their static abstractions

In our case, we approximate the runtime domains shown in Fig. 11. The interpretation is done by a special Prolog interpreter (written in Prolog itself) that evaluates pointcut queries based on our abstract domains and collects data about join point shadows and lifetime during the interpretation.

The virtual trace defines all predicates from the execution trace as rules over the abstract syntax tree and the static type model. For illustration we will only consider the calls/5 predicate. In a similar way, all other predicates of the execution trace are approximated statically. Their exact definition can be found in the appendix in Fig. 16 and on the project website [2]. The call/5 predicate is defined as follows:

```
1  absval(RecTypeC), MName, absval(ArgTypeC)) :-
2     within((ExprID, calls((Rec, _), MName, _)), _, _),
3     stype(Rec, RecType),
4     subtypeeq(RecTypeC, RecType),
5     meth(RecType, MName, meth(_, MName, ArgType, _)),
6     subtypeeq(ArgTypeC, ArgType),
7     addshadow((Time, ExprID)).
```

This rule uses the abstractions defined in Fig. 11 in order to create the virtual trace. Timestamps are represented by a pair (Time, ExprID), whereby Time is either the constant now or it is unbound. To achieve this, we fix the now predicate to the definition now((now,_)). This means that all queries getting the timestamp via the now/1 predicate will have their timestamp in the abstraction fixed to the constant now. All other queries will have an unbound variable in the first position of the timestamp; an unbound variable in the first position denotes a query that might refer to the past.

Instead of values, the execution trace uses types of the form absval(SomeType). All method calls (found in the AST via within) imply a corresponding calls predicate, whereby the information from the static type system (stype/2 predicate) is used in order to infer the type of the receiver. Subtyping is taken into account by corresponding subtypeeq constraints.

Of particular interest is the addshadow part of the rule. This is a special predicate that is intercepted by our static analysis. Whenever an addshadow goal is encountered, the interpreter adds the corresponding join point shadow (i.e., ExprID) and its lifetime (Time) to a list of shadows for the pointcut that is currently analyzed.

The definition of the virtual store is relatively straightforward: It defines the store and classOf predicate in terms of types instead of values. The situation becomes a bit complicated by taking subtype polymorphism into account. We deal with this by letting store range over all possible combinations of types in an object – we ignored performance and favored simplicity in our prototype analysis. The definition of the virtual store is also available in the appendix (Fig. 16).

```
subtypeeq(D, display ),
shadows(
  ( set (P, F, _), get(T1, _, P, F, _),  calls (T2, _, absval (D), draw, _),
    cflow (T1, T2),  instanceof (P,  figureElement )),  ,S)
```

Fig. 12. Query for shadows of `cflow` pointcut (line 17, Fig. 8)

```
 1 | class  Point  extends  FigureElement {
 2 |    void  draw(Display  d) {
 3 |       if ( this.enabled ) d. paintPoint ( this.x , this.y );
 4 |    }
 5 | }
 6 | class  Line  extends  FigureElement {
 7 |    void  draw(Display  d) {
 8 |       this . foo ( true );
 9 |       if ( this.enabled ) d. paintLine ( this.start , this.end );
10 |    }
11 | }
12 | class  Main  extends  Object {
13 |    ...
14 |    void  writeSomething () {
15 |       this . p2.y := false ; this .p1.x := true ;
16 |       this .p1.enabled := false ;
17 |    }
18 |    void  main () {
19 |       this .p1 := new Point ();   this .p2 := new Point ();
20 |       this .p2.enabled := true ;
21 |       this . l1 := new Line ();  this . l1 . start := this .p1;
22 |       this . l1 .end := new point;
23 |       this .d := new Display ();  this .d.f1 := this . l1 ;
24 |       this .d.f2 := this .p2;  this .du = new Displayupdate ();
25 |       this .du.d := this .d;
26 |       deploy ( this .du) { this.d.drawAll() ;  this . writeSomething (); }
27 |    }
28 | }
```

Fig. 13. The result of abstract interpretation

Our pointcut interpreter is implemented as a meta-interpreter in Prolog. Meta-interpreters are a common technique for abstract interpretation of logic programs [7]. Our meta-interpreter is basically the so-called *vanilla* meta-interpreter [36–Program 17.5] extended by a loop detection mechanism and an additional parameter that collects shadows. In order to invoke the pointcut interpreter we first have to substitute the dynamic values in the pointcut expressions with their static abstraction. By evaluating the pointcuts over the abstracted domains with our pointcut interpreter we basically perform a constant propagation analysis through the control flow of a pointcut. The code of the meta-interpreter is available in the appendix (`shadows` predicate in Fig. 16). We do not want to discuss its implementation here in detail because it uses some very Prolog-specific mechanisms.

For illustrating the abstract interpretation process, the query to compute the shadows for the *cflow* pointcut from line 17, Fig. 8 is shown in Fig. 12. The program expressions inside the pointcut (e.g., the @this.d expression in Fig. 8) are replaced by an abstract value that is constrained by its static type via a subtype constraint.

The meta-interpreter computes *all* solutions of the query on top of the virtual execution trace and virtual store (thereby collecting shadows triggered by addshadow goals). It is important that *all* solutions are computed such that the back-tracking evaluation of queries covers all possible evaluation scenarios at runtime. The abstract values (i.e., types) returned by the pointcut interpreter are also used to get a bound for the static type of pointcut variables, which is then used to type-check advice bodies.

Fig. 13 illustrates the result of computing the shadows for the aforementioned cflow pointcut (Fig. 8) in terms of the code from Fig. 4 and a sample main class. The shadows identified by the pointcut-interpreter are framed in Fig. 13. If the lifetime of the produced facts is indefinite (i.e., constant now has not been found in the timestamp, the expressions are also underlined, otherwise the lifetime is immediate.

For example, the call to draw and the field reads are marked as "indefinite lifetime" because they could be relevant as past events in the evaluation of the get goal in line 17 of Fig. 8. The lifetime of the field assignments is marked as immediate because they are only relevant for this query if they are the current now event.

5.1   Results and Limitations

The results of the static analysis are directly used in our interpreter in that Prolog facts/ queries are only evaluated at marked shadows. Also, events for shadows that are marked with lifetime immediate are discarded immediately after the evaluation of the corresponding query. Our interpreter can be run both with and without this optimization. The performance gain depends directly on the relation between marked shadows and unmarked shadows. The example in Fig. 8 runs approximately 4 times faster with the abstract interpretation optimization turned on. In a different example, where the percentage of marked shadows to unmarked shadows is smaller, the program runs 300 times faster. This result is not surprising because extending the database and evaluating queries is very expensive, but it indicates that it is possible to have a very expressive pointcut language that is expensive only if pointcuts are used that cannot be projected on a small set of shadows.

Our analysis technique still has several important limitations, though. First, the analysis itself, as it is presented here, is very slow and would not scale to real systems. It is also hard to guarantee termination of the static analysis in all cases; a typical problem of static analysis by meta-circular interpreters [7]. Our primary goal was to show the feasibility of a static analysis only, so we favored simplicity over performance and completeness. We think that our analysis can be embedded into the conceptual framework described by Codish and Søndergaard [7]. They use a different meta-interpreter, a so-called "bottom-up" interpreter, that has better performance properties and is guaranteed to terminate. This is part of our future work.

Another limitation is in the existence of the indefinite lifetime because this means that such facts will never be removed from the database. A more fine-grained analysis that computes lifetimes of the kind "this fact can be removed after some event happened" would be desirable in order to remove this limitation. It is of course easy to construct queries that will inherently require indefinite storage of previous events, but in these cases the static analysis could be used to detect those queries and signal an error if the memory requirements cannot be restricted in a reasonable way.

How do we get from our prototype to an efficient implementation in a compiled language? Besides the limitations mentioned above, our representation of the store is not easy to implement efficiently. A trivial solution is to drop the store model from the pointcut language - there are no conceptual dependencies of our approach on the existence of the store (or any other) model. An alternative would be a database-like organization of the store, which is actually part of our future work.

In order to make the evaluation of the queries itself more efficient, we plan to use partial evaluation techniques such as Logen [26] to reduce dynamic pointcut evaluation to a minimum and to inline the remaining dynamic checks at the computed join point shadows.

6   Related Work

6.1   Pointcut Languages

Gybels' and Brichau's proposal [15] is related in several ways. Similar to our approach, they use logic programming and unification for matching pointcuts. The insertion of dynamic context into a pointcut similar to our @expr expressions is possible by means of *linguistic symbiosis* [3]. As in our approach, pointcuts can be made reusable by means of logic rules. The possibility of user-defined pointcut predicates or pointcut libraries is not discussed in [15], but this is no conceptual limitation.

The most important difference to our approach is the data model upon which point-cuts can be expressed. In their approach, the data model consists of a representation of the current join point, syntax tree, and some special object reifying predicates. It is hence not possible to encode queries that refer to the execution history or need access to data from the store. An efficient implementation by computing shadows of pointcuts is also discussed but the addition of the whole execution trace as in our case makes the problem much harder. Other works from the same group [19, 37, 4] also use logic meta-programming but consider only the static syntax of the program as data model.

LogicAJ [32] is an extension to AspectJ that uses logic variables and unification instead of wildcards in order to make pointcuts more expressive. The data model upon which the pointcuts operate is unchanged, though.

We have developed an extension of Alpha with which it is possible to refer to future events [24]. Due to several limitations of the implementation, this extension should be seen as an experiment to explore the limits of pointcuts and not as a proposal for a practical programming language.

Walker et al have developed an extension to AspectJ for expressing temporal relations between join points [38]. These temporal relations can be expressed via context-free grammars. The program trace is then "parsed" by an automaton for the grammar. Information about the history of the execution is stored in the state of these automata, which is an effective solution to reduce the amount of data that has to be stored. This approach would not be directly applicable to our model because our pointcut language is more powerful than context-free grammars.

Douence et al have proposed a special pattern matching language for execution traces based on Haskell [11]. Other models besides the execution trace are not covered. Many of the issues presented in this paper (integration into the language, context passing, efficient implementation) are not discussed.

Josh [5] is an AspectJ-like language with an extensible pointcut mechanism, built on top of Javassist [6]. Josh does not support declarative pointcut specifications. Rather, new PCDs in Josh are implemented as imperative meta-programs on the abstract syntax tree using the Javassist library. Josh basically suffers from the problems of an imperative meta-programming approach, especially with respect to the composability of the PCDs implemented as meta-programs.

Eichberg et al discussed the usage of the functional query language XQuery as an extensible pointcut language [13]. The data model in this approach is an XML representation of the abstract syntax tree. Due to functional abstraction and the module system of XQuery, it is possible to organize reusable pointcuts in libraries. Other data models or the integration into a programming language are not discussed.

Sakurei et al. [34] propose a design to extend AspectJ with object-specific aspects and pointcuts. Our `deploy` statement can be used with a similar effect as the `associate` statement in this approach. Since runtime values can be used directly in our pointcut language, arbitrary object-specific constraints can be expressed and not just those that are defined in a `perObject` clause. On the other hand, the proposal in [34] has a more a efficient implementation if many instances of the same object-specific aspect are active simultaneously.

6.2 Weaving and Static Analysis

Hilsdale and Hugunin have described the weaving mechanism in AspectJ [17]. The AspectJ weaver also computes shadows for dynamic pointcuts. However, AspectJ has only a fixed, predefined set of pointcut operators, hence it is easier to compute the set of join point shadows statically. Due to the structure of pointcuts, only certain dynamic checks that look at the class of objects or operate on special stacks (for `cflow`), are required, such that these dynamic checks can be directly woven into the code.

A more semantics-based compilation model, based on a simplified model of AspectJ, can be found in [28]. Using partial evaluation, their model can explain several issues in the compilation processes, including how to find places in program text to insert aspect code and how to remove unnecessary run-time checks. Sereni and de Moor describe a static analysis technique [35] for an even more simplified version of the AspectJ pointcut language that allows a more efficient implementation of some pointcuts than the implementation proposed in [28].

Douence et al presented an analysis technique for detecting interactions between aspects [10]. This is complementary to our static analysis, because we simply assume a global ordering among aspects and concentrate on computing *shadows* of single pointcuts. Nevertheless, our abstract interpretation implies a primitive interaction analysis for free, namely in that it becomes trivial to detect whether two pointcuts have intersecting shadows. However, this is not in the focus of our work.

Codish and Søndergaard [7] describe the usage of meta-interpreters for different abstract interpretations of Prolog code. In contrast to their "bottom-up" approach, we use a conventional top-down meta-interpreter with loop-detection. We are not aware of other works that use abstract interpretation for computing join point shadows.

6.3   Aspects and Modularity

Lopes et al. [27] motivate and speculate about future "more naturalistic" referencing mechanisms inspired by natural languages, such e.g., *"those (data) read in previous sentence"*, or even *"in this last operation"*. By means of a simple example they illustrate how referencing mechanisms of current programming languages force programmers to circumscribe their intentions in terms of operational details of the underlying machine. They argue that while pointcuts in AOP languages go one important step further in supporting more powerful referencing they do not go far enough, e.g., in that they lack means of temporal referencing. The prototype we presented in this paper provides a very good basis to experiment with programming models that support more naturalistic referencing mechanisms as those envisaged in [27]. Our prototype can be extended to collect more and different kinds of information about the program to support more "types of referencing".

Aldrich [1] proposes module constructs that export pointcuts as part of the module specification. The rationale for this is the lack of modular reasoning if pointcuts depend on implementation details of a module. He shows that the implementation of such modules can be changed without affecting the consistency of the whole system. On the other hand, this approach is also a serious restriction to the programming model because 1) pointcuts of a module have to be anticipated in its design, 2) the existence of these pointcuts in the interface establishes an implicit coupling to the aspects that use the pointcut, and 3) if pointcuts go across modules (as is inherent for crosscutting concerns), the specification of the pointcut interfaces themselves becomes a crosscutting concern. Our approach also tackles this problem, but with very different means, namely by making the pointcut language more powerful, such that pointcut specifications can be made more robust and less dependent on implementation details. On the other hand, we can give no static guarantees because we cannot enforce implementation-independent pointcuts.

6.4   Information Engineering in Program Models

There are also some interesting related works outside the domain of programming language design. Efficient ways to manage and retrieve dynamic data about the execution of a program have been discussed by De Pauw et al [9]. Both the works by Lange and Nakamura [25] and by Richner and Ducasse [33] discuss the design of a static and a dynamic model of the program semantics as well as the use of logic rules to collect and combine information from these models in order to improve program understanding and program visualizations. Abstraction mechanisms to select interesting events in the execution of a program are also used in the domain of *debugging*, for example in the work of Jahier and Ducasse [18]. Reiss and Renieris have developed a framework for processing execution traces by reducing the amount of data as it is collected through mechanisms such as automata or context-free grammars [31]. These techniques may be helpful for us in order to further reduce the amount of collected data.

7   Summary and Future Work

In this paper we have presented an analysis which shows that current pointcut languages support localization of crosscutting concerns but have some problems with respect to information hiding. And we have described a new pointcut language in the form of logic queries over different models of the program semantics. Together with the abstraction facilities of logic programming, it becomes possible to raise the abstraction level of pointcuts and hence increase the software quality of aspect-oriented code. We have also presented a static analysis technique that can be the starting point of an efficient implementation.

Our future work will concentrate on the embedding of our pointcut language into a real compiled programming language and on further research in efficient implementation techniques that eliminate the limitations of our current analysis.

Acknowledgments

We would like to thank Gregor Kiczales, Michael Haupt and Michael Eichberg for comments on drafts of this paper.

This work is partly supported by the European Network of Excellence on Aspect-Oriented Software Development (AOSD-Europe).

References

[1] J. Aldrich. Open modules: Modular reasoning about advice. In *ECOOP'05: European Conference on Object-Oriented Programming*. Springer LNCS, 2005.

[2] Alpha project. http://www.st.informatik.tu-darmstadt.de/pages/projects/alpha/.

[3] J. Brichau, K. Gybels, and R. Wuyts. Towards a linguistic symbiosis of an object-oriented and a logic programming language. In *Proceedings of the Workshop on Multiparadigm Programming with Object-Oriented Languages (MPOOL 2002)*, 2002.

[4] J. Brichau, K. Mens, and K. D. Volder. Building composable aspect-specific languages with logic metaprogramming. In *Generative Programming and Component Engineering (GPCE'02)*. Springer LNCS, 2002.

[5] S. Chiba and K. Nakagawa. Josh: An Open AspectJ-like Language. In *Proceedings of AOSD 2004*, Lancaster, England, 2004. ACM Press.

[6] S. Chiba and M. Nishizawa. An Easy-to-Use Toolkit for Efficient Java Bytecode Translators. In *Proceedings of GPCE '03*, Lecture Notes in Computer Science, pages 364–376. Springer, 2003.

[7] M. Codish and H. Søndergaard. Meta-circular abstract interpretation in Prolog. In T. Mogensen, D. Schmidt, and I. H. Sudburough, editors, *The Essence of Computation: Complexity, Analysis, Transformation*, LNCS 2566. Springer, 2002.

[8] P. Cousot and R. Cousot. Abstract interpretation: a unified lattice model for static analysis of programs by construction or approximation of fixpoints. In *Symposium on Principles of Programming Languages*. ACM Press, 1977.

[9] W. De Pauw, D. Kimelman, and J. M. Vlissides. Modeling object-oriented program execution. In *ECOOP '94: Proceedings of the 8th European Conference on Object-Oriented Programming*, pages 163–182, London, UK, 1994. Springer-Verlag.

[10] R. Douence, P. Fradet, and M. Südholt. A framework for the detection and resolution of aspect interactions. In *Proceedings of the ACM SIGPLAN/SIGSOFT Conference on Generative Programming and Component Engineering (GPCE'02)*, volume 2487 of *LNCS*. Springer-Verlag, 2002.

[11] R. Douence, O. Motelet, and M. Südholt. A formal definition of crosscuts. In *Proc. of the Third International Conference on Metalevel Architectures and Separation of Crosscutting Concerns (Reflection 2001)*, volume 2192 of *LNCS*. Springer-Verlag, 2001.

[12] S. Drossoupolou. Lecture notes on the L2 calculus. http://www.doc.ic.ac.uk/~scd/Teaching/L1L2.pdf.

[13] M. Eichberg, M. Mezini, and K. Ostermann. Pointcuts as functional queries. In *Second ASIAN Symposium on Programming Languages and Systems (APLAS)*. LNCS, 2004.

[14] E. Gamma, R. Helm, R. Johnson, and J. Vlissides. *Design Patterns*. Addison Wesley, 1995.

[15] K. Gybels and J. Brichau. Arranging language features for more robust pattern-based crosscuts. In *Proceedings of the 2nd international conference on Aspect-oriented software development*, pages 60–69. ACM Press, 2003.

[16] J. Hannemann and G. Kiczales. Design pattern implementation in Java and AspectJ. In *Proceedings OOPSLA '02. ACM SIGPLAN Notices 37(11)*, pages 161–173. ACM, 2002.

[17] E. Hilsdale and J. Hugunin. Advice Weaving in AspectJ. In *Proc. of AOSD'04*. ACM Press, 2004.

[18] E. Jahier and M. Ducasse. Generic program monitoring by trace analysis. In *Theory and Practice of Logic Programming Journal*, volume 2(4-5). Cambridge University Press, 2002.

[19] D. Janzen and K. De Volder. Navigating and querying code without getting lost. In *Proceedings of AOSD'03*. ACM Press, 2003.

[20] G. Kiczales. Keynote talk at AOSD '03, 2003.

[21] G. Kiczales, E. Hilsdale, J. Hugunin, M. Kersten, J. Palm, and W. G. Griswold. An overview of AspectJ. In *Proceedings of ECOOP '01*, 2001.

[22] G. Kiczales, J. Lamping, A. Mendhekar, C. Maeda, C. Lopes, J.-M. Loingtier, and J. Irwin. Aspect-oriented programming. In *Proceedings ECOOP'97*, LNCS 1241, pages 220–242. Springer, 1997.

[23] G. Kizcales and M. Mezini. Aspect-oriented programming and modular reasoning. In *Proceedings International Conference on Software Engineering (ICSE) '05*. ACM, 2005.

[24] K. Klose and K. Ostermann. Back to the future: Pointcuts as predicates over traces. In *Workshop on Foundations of Aspect-Oriented Languages (FOAL) at AOSD'05*, 2005.

[25] D. B. Lange and Y. Nakamura. Interactive visualization of design patterns can help in framework understanding. In *OOPSLA '95: Proceedings of the tenth annual conference on Object-oriented programming systems, languages, and applications*, pages 342–357, New York, NY, USA, 1995. ACM Press.

[26] M. Leuschel, J. Jørgensen, W. Vanhoof, and M. Bruynooghe. Offline specialisation in Prolog using a hand-written compiler generator. In *Theory and Practice of Logic Programming*, volume 4, pages 139–191, 2004.

[27] C. V. Lopes, P. Dourish, D. H. Lorenz, and K. Lieberherr. Beyond AOP: Toward naturalistic programming. In *Proceedings Onward! Track at OOPSLA'03*, Anaheim, 2003. ACM Press.

[28] H. Masuhara, G. Kiczales, and C. Dutchyn. A compilation and optimization model for aspect-oriented programs. In *Proceedings of Compiler Construction (CC2003), LNCS 2622*. Springer, 2003.

[29] M. Mezini and K. Ostermann. Conquering aspects with Caesar. In *Proceedings Conference on Aspect-Oriented Software Development (AOSD) '03*, pages 90–99. ACM, 2003.

[30] D. L. Parnas. A technique for software module specification with examples. *Communications of the ACM*, 15(5):330–336, 1972.

[31] S. P. Reiss and M. Renieris. Encoding program executions. In *International Conference on Software Engineering*, Toronto, Ontario, Canada, 2001. IEEE.

[32] T. Rho and G. Kniesel. Uniform genericity for aspect languages. Technical Report IAI-TR-2004-4, Computer Science Department III, University of Bonn, Dec 2004.

[33] T. Richner and S. Ducasse. Recovering high-level views of object-oriented applications from static and dynamic information. In *ICSM '99: Proceedings of the IEEE International Conference on Software Maintenance*, Washington, DC, USA, 1999. IEEE Computer Society.

[34] K. Sakurai, H. Masuhara, N. Ubayashi, S. Matsuura, and S. Komiya. Association aspects. In *Proc. of AOSD'04*. ACM Press, 2004.

[35] D. Sereni and O. de Moor. Static analysis of aspects. In *Proceedings of AOSD'03*. ACM, 2003.

[36] L. Sterling and E. Shapiro. *The Art of Prolog*. MIT Press, 1994.

[37] K. D. Volder and T. D'Hondt. Aspect-Oriented Logic Meta Programming. In *Conf. Meta-Level Architectures and Reflection, LNCS 1616*. Springer, 1999.

[38] R. J. Walker and K. Viggers. Implementing protocols via declarative event patterns. In *Proceedings of the ACM SIGSOFT International Symposium on Foundations of Software Engineering (FSE-12)*, 2004.

A   Appendix

Format	Example

prog(
  [class(ClassName, SuperClass,
   [field(FieldType, FieldName), ...
   [meth(RetType, MethName, ArgType, Expr), ...],
   [advice(before, Expr), ...]
  ] ...
)
where Expr has the form:
(ExprID, if(IfExpr, ThenExpr, ElseExpr)
(ExprID, get(ReceiverExpr, FieldName)
(ExprID, seq(Expr1, Expr2)
  ...
	prog(
	  [class(point, figureElement,
	   [field(bool, xx), field(bool, yy),
	    field(bool, enabled)],
	   [meth(bool, draw, display),
	    ('9:5', if(('9:13', get(('9:8',this),enabled)),
	     ('10:7', '10:15', seq(
	      ('10:13', get(('10:8', this), xx)),
	      ('10:22', get(('10:17', this), yy)))),
	     ('11:10', true))))],
	  []%no advice
	  )%class point
	  ]%classes
	). %prog

stype(ExprID, Type)	stype('2:26', bool)
new(ID, ExprID, ClassName, Obj) calls(ID, ExprID, Receiver, MethodName, Arg) set(ID, ExprID, Receiver, FieldName, Value) get(ID, ExprID, Receiver, FieldName) deploy(ID, ExprID, Obj) endcall(ID, CallID, ReturnValue) pred(ID1, ID2) % event ID1 happened % immediately before event ID2 before(ID1, ID2) % transitive hull of pred now(ID) % gives the current event ID	calls(3, '53:5', iota1, setP1, iota2) set(4, '66:14', iota1, p1, iota2) endcall(5, 3, false)
store(Obj, FieldName, Value) classof(Obj, ClassName)	classof(iota2, point) store(iota2, enabled, false) store(iota2, yy, false) store(iota2, xx, true)

Fig. 14. Format of the four program models (AST, static typing, execution trace, object store) available for pointcuts in Alpha

```
1  % abbrevations if only interested in current event
2  new(ClassName, Obj) :−
3      now(ID), new(ID, _, ClassName, Obj). *
4  calls (Receiver, Method, Arg) :−
5      now(ID), calls (ID, _, Receiver, Method, Arg).
6  set (Receiver, Field, Val) :−
7      now(ID), set (ID, _, Receiver, Field, Val).
8  get (Receiver, Field ) :−
9      now(ID), get (ID, _, Receiver, Field ).
10 deploy (Receiver) :−
11     now(ID), deploy(ID, _, deploy(Receiver )).
12
13 % is ID0 in the control flow of ID1?
14 cflow (ID0, ID1) :−
15     calls (ID1, _, _, _, _), before (ID1, ID0),
16     endcall (ID2, _, ID1, _), before (ID0, ID2).
17 cflow (ID0, ID1) :−
18     calls (ID1, _, _, _, _), before (ID1, ID0),
19     \+ encall (_, _, ID1, _).
20
21 % is Obj2 reachable from Obj1?
22 reachable (Obj1,Obj2) :− reachablevia (Obj1,Obj2 ,[]).
23 reachablevia (Obj1,Obj2,_) :− store (Obj1, _, Obj2).
24 reachablevia (Obj1,Obj2,Via) :−
25     store (Obj1, _, Obj3), \+ member(Obj1,Via),
26     reachablevia (Obj3, Obj2, [Obj3|Via ]).
27
28 % convenient access of AST
29 class (Name, CDef) :−
30     prog(CDefs), member(CDef, CDefs),
31     CDef = class (Name, _, _, _, _).
32 meth(CName, MName, MDef) :−
33     class (CName, class(_, _, _, MDefs, _)),
34     member(MDef, MDefs), MDef = meth(_,
   MName, _, _).
35 field (CName, FName, FDef) :−
36     class (CName, class(_, _, FDefs, _, _ )),
37     member(FDef, FDefs), FDef = field (_, FName).
```

```
1  within ((ExprID, Expr), CName, MName,) :−
2      meth(CName, MName, meth(_, _, _, Body)),
3      subExpr(Body, (ExprID, Expr )).
4  subExpr(E, E).
5  subExpr(X, E) :−
6      X =.. [_|List ], member(E1, List), subExpr(E1, E).
7
8  % static subtype/subclass relation
9  directsubtype (C1, C2) :−
10     class (C1, class (_, C2, _, _, _ )).
11 subtypeeq(bool, bool ).
12 subtypeeq(C, C) :− class (C, _).
13 subtypeeq(C1, C2) :−
14     directsubtype (C1, C3), subtypeeq(C3, C2).
15
16 % add subtyping to static and dynamic types
17 hastype(ExprID, C) :−
18     stype(ExprID, D), subtypeeq(D, C).
19 instanceof (Obj, C) :−
20     classof (Obj, D), subtypeeq(D, C).
21
22 %predicted control flow
23 pcflow(CName, MName, E) :−
24     pcflow1(CName, MName, E, []).
25 pcflow1(CName, MName, E, _) :−
26     within (E, CName, MName).
27 pcflow1(CName, MName, E, V) :−
28     within ((_, calls ((RecID, _), MName1, _)), CName, MName),
29     stype (RecID, CName2),
30     (subtypeeq(CName1, CName2); subtypeeq(CName2, CName1)),
31     meth(CName1, MName1,_),
32     \+ member((CName1, MName1), V),
33     pcflow1(CName1, MName1, E, [(CName1,MName1)|V]). *
34
35 %finding the most recent of an event pattern X
36 mostRecent(ID,X) :−
37     bagof(ID,X,IDs), maxlist (IDs,ID).
```

Fig. 15. Standard pointcut library

```
1  % virtual store
2  store (absval (CName), Field, absval (TypeC)) :−
3      subtypeeq(CName, CSuper),
4      field (CSuper, Field, field (Type, _ )),
5      subtypeeq(TypeC, Type).
6  classof (absval (CName),CName).
7
8  % virtual event trace
9  calls ((Time,ExprID), ExprID,
10     absval (RecTypeC), MName, absval(ArgTypeC))
11 :−
12     within ((ExprID, calls ((Rec, _), MName, _)), _, _), 
13     stype (Rec, RecType),
14     subtypeeq(RecTypeC, RecType),
15     meth(RecType, MName, meth(_, MName, ArgType, _)),
16     subtypeeq(ArgTypeC, ArgType),
17     addshadow((Time, ExprID)).
18 % similarly for set, get,new,deploy, endcall
```

```
1  now(now).
2  before (_, _).
3  pred(_, _).
4  % the meta−interpreter
5  shadows(true, [], _) :− !.
6  shadows((A,B), Shadows, Trail ) :−
7      !, shadows(A, S1, Trail ), shadows(B, S2, Trail ),
8      append(S1, S2, Shadows).
9  shadows(X, [], _) :−
10     predicate_property (X, built_in ), !, X.
11 shadows(addshadow((Time,Token)), S, _) :−
12     var (Time), !, S = [(Token, indefinite )].
13 shadows(addshadow((now,Token)), S, _) :−
14     !, S = [(Token, immediate )].
15 shadows(A, S0, Trail ) :−
16     loop_detect (A, Trail ), !.
17 shadows(A, S0, Trail ) :−
18     clause (A, B), shadows(B, S0, [A|Trail ]).
```

Fig. 16. Meta-interpreter for computing pointcut shadows

Sustainable System Infrastructure and Big Bang Evolution: Can Aspects Keep Pace?

Celina Gibbs, Chunjian Robin Liu, and Yvonne Coady

University of Victoria, British Columbia, Canada
{celinag, cliu, ycoady}@cs.uvic.ca

Abstract. Realistically, many rapidly evolving systems eventually require extensive restructuring in order to effectively support further evolution. Not surprisingly, these overhauls reverberate throughout the system. Though several studies have shown the benefits of aspect-oriented programming (AOP) from the point of view of the modularization and evolution of crosscutting concerns, the question remains as to how well aspects fare when the code that is crosscut undergoes extensive restructuring. That is, when evolution is a big bang, can aspects keep pace? The case study presented here considers several categories of aspects – design invariants, dynamic analysis tools, and domain specific design patterns – and shows the concrete ways in which aspects had positive, negative and neutral impact during the restructuring of the memory management subsystem of a virtual machine. Compared with best efforts in a hierarchical decomposition coupled with a preprocessor, aspects fared better than the original implementation in two out of four aspects, and no worse in the remaining two aspects.

1 Introduction

Legacy systems eventually face upheavals in system structure. The dawn of new system structure, marked by improved separation of concerns, is often preceded by a darkness in which the old structure must be torn down. This explosive, *big bang*, type of evolution forces simultaneous changes throughout the system. Though aspects have been shown to be effective as a locus of control for evolving crosscutting concerns, the fact that they rely on explicit external interaction implies that aspects could have negative impact under these extreme conditions – when the *code that is crosscut*, or the dominant decomposition – is undergoing structural reorganization.

Low level system infrastructures need to be fast yet flexible – traits that are commonly at odds with each other. To reconcile this tension, standard practices within this domain include preprocessor directives and system patch files. These mechanisms are de facto standard in part because they introduce no performance overhead, and in part because they provide at least rudimentary means to achieve better configurability and extensibility than traditional language constructs in C and Java. Though distasteful to many developers due to their lack of semantic levarage, they are a reality in today's system infrastructure software.

In order to test the sustainability of aspects in systems such as these, we conducted an experiment using the rapidly evolving Memory Management Toolkit (MMTk) [2],

A.P. Black (Ed.): ECOOP 2005, LNCS 3586, pp. 241–261, 2005.

within the Jikes Research Virtual Machine (RVM) [15]. The RVM is a unique open source project in Java. A basis for almost 100 publications over the last 5 years and averaging several hundred CVS commits per month, the RVM is host to most of to-day's state-of-the-art java virtual machine technology. Its code-base affords research-ers the opportunity to experiment with a variety of design and implementation alterna-tives within an otherwise stable and consistently well maintained infrastructure. Specifically, MMTk is a framework used within the RVM designed to support re-search in new garbage collection (GC) strategies. MMTk provides a marked depar-ture from traditional monolithic implementations by being both more modular and efficient than its predecessors [2].

In the experiment described here, we compared the evolution of the original system (MMTk) versus one where we introduced aspects (MMTk$_{ao}$). The aspects included representatives from three different categories: design invariants, dynamic analysis tools [29], and domain specific design patterns [2]. In the original implementation, the Jikes RVM relies on preprocessor directives along with hierarchical decomposition to achieve a highly efficient, configurable system. In order to determine if aspects could keep pace with evolution in a system based on this composition, we considered evolu-tionary restructuring tasks over an intensive change period of 10 months (version 2.3.3 from January – October 2004). In total, 12 significant restructurings across four as-pects were considered in the study, where a single restructuring often had impact on multiple aspects. The aspects were programmed using AspectJ [19, 14].

With respect to the impact of the 12 restructuring tasks, the results show that evo-lution of aspects fared better than the original implementation in two of four aspects, and no worse in the remaining aspects. Results from the DaCapo Benchmark for GC [5] show the system sustained a worst-case performance penalty just under an average of 10% as a result of one fine-grained aspect with of millions of advice invocations. This study demonstrates the ways in which existing mechanisms for AOP can support sustainable system infrastructure relative to their preprocessed/hierarchical counter-parts in the somewhat inhospitable domain of system infrastructure software. Further, the resulting system structure is arguably better suited for future trends in evolution.

This paper is organized as follows. After an overview of related work, the imple-mentation and evolution of MMTk is described (section 2), followed by a description of the same evolution applied to MMTk$_{ao}$ (section 3). In terms of analysis, the evaluation of sustainability considers each category of aspect, limitations of the study, and preliminary performance considerations (section 4).

1.1 Related Work

AOP provides linguistic support aimed at improving modularity. The software engi-neering community has repeatedly demonstrated that modularity plays a key role in determining the cost of change [24, 6, 21]. Unfortunately, structural boundaries tend to decay over time due to increasing dependencies between modules [27, 20]. Struc-tural deficiency results in the need for non-local changes that require considerable effort associated with non-local reasoning [32, 25]. Evolution thus becomes im-paired over time, as modularity becomes compromised.

Original case studies involving AOP implementations generally reveal qualities associated with improved separation of concerns [22, 17, 12]. More recently, aspects have been associated with higher quality code refactorings [28, 10], adaptability in middleware [4, 33, 7], configurability in real time systems [30], and autonomic computing in OS kernels [8]. In terms of evolution, Banniassad's results show that the lack of adequate separation of concerns can stand as an obstacle to evolution [1], while Walker's work demonstrates that explicit separation can have mixed results in terms of understanding and evolving systems [31]. Rashid's study of evolution in database systems [26], and our own previous work in operating systems [3], have uncovered some of the benefits of aspects in terms of evolution.

The case study presented here evaluates aspects in the context of a particularly intense evolutionary scenario. The rapid refactoring of the memory management subsystem of the Jikes RVM provides a rich testbed for assessing sustainability in terms of modularity. In particular, the fact that the aspects needed to change in response to changes in the code they crosscut provided an acid test for aspects. That is, we were able to better establish, (1) the value of the internal structure of the aspects alongside, (2) the changes that occurred to the external interaction explicitly defined by pointcuts. This allowed us to view evolution of the dependencies between the concerns from the perspective of the semantics of the woven system as a whole.

2   Evolution of MMTk

The evolution of MMTk reveals a move towards a more portable and manageable subsystem. Portability is necessary as MMTk can now be used in other systems requiring garbage collection, such as the Glasgow Haskell Compiler [13] and OVM [23]. Manageability is necessary as MMTk serves as platform for developers to experiment with new GC strategies. As a result of these two main motivating factors, key evolutionary steps of MMTk include: (1) new adherence to a strict interface for portability, and (2) new hierarchical decomposition and migration of code within (sub)packages to better separate concerns. A high level overview of the extensive nature of this evolution over a 10 month period is provided by Table 1, with more detailed accounting of 12 major restructurings in Table 2.

Table 1. Evolution in MMTk: old and new class sturcture overview

TOP LEVEL PACKAGE	# OF OLD CLASSES	EVOLVED CLASSES
GCspy	14	moved out of MMTk
Plan	22	15 (new hierarchy)
Policy	10	15 (new hierarchy)
Utility	63	14 (+5 new subpackages)
VMInterface	17	redistributed in MMTk

Table 2. Detailed evolution of 12 restructuing tasks of MMTk over 10 months

BETTER SEPARATION OF MMTK FROM JIKES	BETTER SEPARATION OF CONCERNS WITHIN MMTK	GENERAL EVOLUTION AND MAINTENANCE
1.1) Eliminated MMTk and VM_Magic interaction	2.1) Restructured plan package	3.1) One class changed to implement synchronization interface
1.2) Eliminated utility classes	2.2) Restructured policy package	3.2) Eliminated assertion or failure methods
1.3) Relocated and renamed VM_Address class	2.3) Restructured utility package	3.3) Introduced new classes
1.4) Relocated and renamed synchronization interfaces	2.4) Redistristributed and eliminated VM_Interface	3.4) Introduced calls to assertion or failure methods

The 12 restructurings are significant as they form the basis of the experiment for evolution in this study. The columns represent different categories of restructuring. On the left, changes *1.1-1.4* were necessary to make MMTk more portable, and to make its separation from Jikes specific code more hygienic. In the middle, changes *2.1-2.4* supported better separation of concerns within MMTk, making it easier for developers to experiment with GC. The final column, changes *3.1-3.4* represent more generic tasks associated with maintenance and evolution.

2.1 Inheritance and Preprocessing: Structured, Efficient, and Configurable

MMTk supports the selection of one of many different GC strategies or *plans*. In the old implementation there was a package for each GC plan, which contained the implementation of core features in the *Plan* class. The specific Plan class to be include in a particular build of the system is determined by a command line option. In the evolved implementation, these subdirectories were eliminated and each GC strategy has its own distinctly named class (CopyMS.java, SemiSpace.java, etc.). The Plan class was migrated outside of MMTk, and made a subclass of each of these classes mutually exclusively, using preprocessor directives:

```
//-#if RVM_WITH_SEMI_SPACE
public class Plan extends SemiSpace implements Uninterruptible {
//-#elif RVM_WITH_SEMI_SPACE_GC_SPY
public class Plan extends SemiSpaceGCSpy implements Uninterruptible {
//-#elif RVM_WITH_COPY_MS
public class Plan extends CopyMS implements Uninterruptible {
...
(more plan classes)
//-#endif
```

The Plan class highlights another way in which plans in MMTk evolved, further leveraging hierarchical decomposition and this multiplexed approach. *Semi_Space_GC_Spy* uses a different class than the regular *Semi_Space* plan. This better separates instrumentation for the dynamic analysis tool, GCSpy, from the regular plan. *Semi_Space_GC_Spy* and *Semi_Space* are siblings under *Semi_Space_Base*. Shared code is in the base class, functions instrumented for GCSpy are in the *GC_Spy* child, and uninstrumented versions of those functions are in the regular class. Pre-evolution, this separation was not supported by a class hierarchy. Instead, there were two versions of Semi_Space plan, one with instrumentation and the other without. Figure 1 overviews these two implementations.

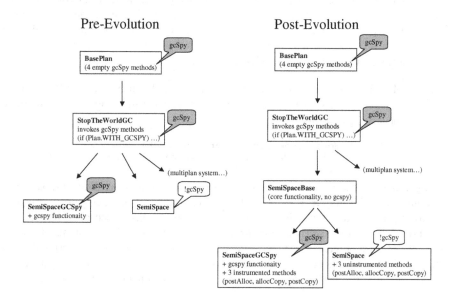

Fig. 1. GCSpy in Pre and Post-evolution in MMTk

2.2 Empty Interfaces: When *Implements* Is a Lower Level Concern

One of the other interesting features of the Jikes system infrastructure is its light-weight leveraging of empty interfaces to flag concerns handled by lower level system code. For example, the majority of the classes in MMTk implement an interface called *VM_Uninterruptible (pre-evolution)* or *Uninterruptible (post-evolution)*. Classes that implement this interface cannot be interrupted. The mechanism to supply the functionality for this concern however, is actually provided by a lower level of the system, outside of the implementation of the Jikes core.

3 Evolution in MMTk$_{ao}$

To build our aspect-oriented version of MMTk, called MMTk$_{ao}$, we took the pre-evolution version of MMTk, before the 10 month evolution period, and factored out aspects for the following four, diverse, crosscutting concerns:

Crosscutting concerns (CCC)	Interacting Concerns (IC) (in terms of packages)
DesignInvariants: VerifyAssertions Synchronization	MMTk.*
GCSpy	plan, policy, utility
Prepare/Release Protocol	plan

Detailed analysis of this original refactoring can be found in previous work [9]. The contribution of the work presented here focuses on the evolution of MMTk$_{ao}$, and the sustainability of these aspects during an intense period of system evolution. An overview of how the evolution of the interacting concerns (i.e., the code that is crosscut by these aspects) impacted each aspect is provided in the subsections that follow.

3.1   Design Invariant: Evolution of Assertions

Jikes RVM uses a boolean field, *VerifyAssertions*, as a global flag to enable assertion checking. The VM class, which originally was home for this flag, has a comment dictating the structure of this design invariant:

```
/* Note: code your assertion checks as
     "if (VM.VerifyAssertions) VM._assert(xxx);"   */
```

During evolution, the *VM_Interface* class was reorganized as several new classes, one of which was the *Assert* class, for better separation of this concern. Further refactoring eliminated a previously core method from this concern. The general structure of the design invariant remains across the evolution of the system, as shown in Table 3 and Figure 2. Since the system is so performance critical, the presence/absense of this code is significant, and evidence that it has been removed for performance but restored for correctness appears in comments in the CVS logs.

Table 3. *VerifyAssertions* across two versions of the *plan* and *policy* packages

OCCURRENCE OF...	PRE-EVOLUTION	POST-EVOLUTOIN
if (verify_assertions)	98 instances, 19 classes	81 instances, 21 classes
call to _assert(..)	75 instances, 25 classes	68 instances, 23 classes
call to sysFail/fail(..)	29 instances, 9 classes	31 instances, 14 classes
call to spaceFailure(..)	14 instances, 8 classes	no longer exists

In terms of accounting for changes inflicted upon this aspect by evolution of the code it crosscuts, this aspect deals with new/removed calls to assert/failure methods without requiring change (Table 2, 3.4), but still had a total of 8 points of change during the evolution. During the separation of MMTk from Jikes, global fields used by MMTk were moved to be within its boundaries (Table 2, 1.2). Cleaning of the

Assert class caused the removal of a method resulting in an obsolete pointcut/advice (Table 2, 2.4, and 3.2). A performance assessment of this aspect is presented in section 4.6.

PRE-EVOLUTION	POST-EVOLUTION

`privileged aspect VerifyingAssertions {`
 	
`    pointcut GCstrategy():`
`        within(org.mmtk. *);`
 	
`    pointcut asserting(boolean condition):`
`        call(void VM_Interface._assert(boolean))`
`        && args(condition)`
`        && GCstrategy();`
 	
`    pointcut failing(String msg):`
`        call(void VM_Interface.sysFail(String))`
`        && args(msg)`
`        && GCstrategy();`
 	
`    pointcut space_failure(VM_Address obj,`
`                    byte space,`
`                String source):`
`        call(void Plan.spaceFailure(VM_Address,`
`                    byte,`
`                        String))`
`        && args(obj, space, source)`
`        && GCstrategy();`
 	
`    void around(boolean b): asserting(b){`
`        if (VM_Interface.VerifyAssertions)`
`            proceed(b);`
`    }`
 	
`    void around(String str): failing(str){`
`        if (VM_Interface.VerifyAssertions)`
`            proceed(str);`
`    }`
 	
`    void around(VM_Address obj, byte space,`
`                String source):`
`        space_failure(obj,space,source) {`
`        if (VM_Interface.VerifyAssertions)`
`            proceed(obj,space,source);`
`    }`
`}`
	`privileged aspect VerifyingAssertions {`
	
	`    pointcut GCstrategy():`
	`        within(org.mmtk.*);`
	
	`    pointcut asserting(boolean condition):`
	`        call(void Assert._assert(boolean))`
	`        && args(condition)`
	`        && GCstrategy();`
	
	`    pointcut failing(String msg):`
	`        call(void Assert.fail(String))`
	`        && args(msg)`
	`        && GCstrategy();`
	
	`    void around(boolean b): asserting(b){`
	`        if (Assert.VerifyAssertions)`
	`            proceed(b);`
	`    }`
	
	`    void around(String str): failing(str){`
	`        if (Assert.VerifyAssertions)`
	`            proceed(str);`
	`    }`
	
	`}`

Fig. 2. *VerifyAssertions* Aspect

3.2 Design Invariant: Evolution of Synchronization

The aspect used for synchronization is very simple. It has a specific set of classes that do *not* need to implement a given interface that flags if the class is uninterruptible. As the majority of the classes in the subsystem cannot be interrupted, this list is of the exceptions to the rule. As previously mentioned, the interface itself is empty, and is used by a lower level concern.

During evolution, new classes added to the system all required the interface. The aspect deals with this correctly (Table 2, 3.3). In total, this aspect underwent two points of change in the evolution: the interface was renamed (Table 2, 1.4), and the BasePolicy class changed status (Table 2, 3.1), such that it required the interface (shown in a comment in Figure 3).

```
privileged aspect Synchronization {

  declare parents:
    (org.mmtk.* || com.ibm.JikesRVM.memoryMangers.mmInterface.*) &&
    !(*Header
      || org.mmtk.utility.alloc.AllocAdvice
      || org.mmtk.utility.TracingConstants
      || org.mmtk.utility.CallSite
  //  || org.mmtk.policy.BasePolicy
      || org.mmtk.vm.ScanStatics
      || org.mmtk.vm.Constants
      || com.ibm.JikesRVM.memoryManagers.mmInterface.MM_Constants
      || com.ibm.JikesRVM.memoryManagers.mmInterface.SynchronizationBarrier
      || com.ibm.JikesRVM.memoryManagers.mmInterface.VM_CollectorThread
      || com.ibm.JikesRVM.memoryManagers.mmInterface.VM_GCMapIteratorGroup
      || com.ibm.JikesRVM.memoryManagers.mmInterface.VM_Handshake)
    implements Uninterruptible;
}
```

Fig. 3. *Synchronization* Aspect

3.3 Evolution of GCSpy

The core implementation of GCSpy, a dynamic analysis tool for GC, involves two parts: (1) gathering of data before and after garbage collection, and (2) connecting to a GCSpy server and client-GUI for heap visualization. In order to instrument MMTk with this code, the configuration of the system with GCSpy requires existing methods to be instrumented, and new methods be added, as outlined in Table 4.

Table 4. Instrumentation of GCSpy

PACKAGE	CLASS	OCCURRENCES OF IF (GCSPY)	NEW METHODS
org.mmtk.plan	Plan (SemiSpace)	5	6
	BasePlan	0	5
	StopTheWorldGC	4	0
org.mmtk.utility	FreeListResource	1	0
	MonoToneVMResource	2	2
com.ibm.JikesRVM. memorymanagers mmInterface	MMInterface	2	0
	Total	*14*	*13*

In the original implementation, part of the configuration strategy for GCSpy involves checking a global flag, *if (VM_Interface.GCSPY)*, before invoking GCSpy functionality (Table 4). The flag is set using preprocessor directives, as follows:

```
public static final boolean GCSPY =
  //-#if RVM_WITH_GCSPY
  true;
  //-#else
  false;
  //-#endif
```

MainThread.java, part of the scheduler package, also uses the directive within its imports and to start the server:

```
//-#if RVM_WITH_GCSPY
import com.ibm.JikesRVM.memoryManagers.mmInterface.MM_Interface;
//-#endif

...
public void run () {
        //-#if RVM_WITH_GCSPY
        MM_Interface.startGCSpyServer();
        //-#endif
```

In *VM_BootRecord.java*, part of the system's runtime support package, 28 fields for GCSpy are declared when this directive is true and *VM_Syscall* contains the methods:

```
//-#if RVM_WITH_GCSPY
    // GCspy entry points
    public VM_Address gcspyDriverAddStreamIP;
    public VM_Address gcspyDriverEndOutputIP;

    ...
    public VM_Address gcspySprintfIP;
//-#endif
```

VM_Syscall.java, has 28 syscall entry points:

```
//-#if RVM_WITH_GCSPY
public static VM_Address
gcspyDriverAddStream (VM_Address driver, int it) {
  return null; }

public static void
gcspyDriverEndOutput (VM_Address driver) {}

...
public static int
gcspySprintf (VM_Address str, VM_Address format,
              VM_Address value) { return 0; }
//-#endif
```

An assortment of several other classes, not in MMTk, use this directive to selectively import and introduce GCSpy functionality. The typical format for these classes is of the form: *#if RVM_WITH_GCSPY, <define method bodies>, #else <provide empty bodies>*. For example, in *ObjectMap.java:*

```
import com.ibm.JikesRVM.VM_SizeConstants;
import com.ibm.JikesRVM.VM_Uninterruptible;
import com.ibm.JikesRVM.VM_Address;

//-#if RVM_WITH_GCSPY
import org.mmtk.plan.Plan;
import org.mmtk.utility.Log;
...
//-#endif

/**
 * THIS CLASS IS NOT A GCSPY COMPONENT
 *
 *   ...
 */

public class ObjectMap
  implements VM_SizeConstants, VM_Uninterruptible {

//-#if RVM_WITH_GCSPY
    private static final int LOG_PAGE_SIZE = 12;
    static final int PAGE_SIZE = 1<<LOG_PAGE_SIZE;
```

```
    ...
    public ObjectMap() { }

    public final void boot() {
       objectMap_ = Util.malloc(OBJECTMAP_SIZE);
       VM_Memory.zero(objectMap_, OBJECTMAP_SIZE);
          ...
    }
    ...
//-#else
    public ObjectMap() {}
    public final void boot() {}

//-#endif
    ...
}
```

Refactoring the portions of GCSpy handled by the preprocessor directives was straightforward. MMTk$_{ao}$ enjoys the added benefit of being able to plug/unplug at build time, instead of requiring the system to be first reconfigured and then rebuilt.

Within MMTk$_{ao}$, as opposed to the strategy of subclassing and introducing redundant code to allow for the GCSpy functionality (Section 2.1 and Figure 1), with minor refactoring of the plan, the aspect provides GCSpy functionality. Thus, the combination of global flags, preprocessor directives, and subclassing leveraged by the original implementation become unnecessary in MMTk$_{ao}$.

As GCSpy was the most thinly scattered concern considered in the study, involving many points in the execution of the system with almost a 1:1 ratio of pointcuts:advice, it was impacted by a majority of the restructuring in Table 2 (9/12 tasks, 1.1-1.3, 2.*, 3.1,2).

3.4 Evolution of Prepare/Release Protocol

To understand how each GC plan is composed one must understand their relationships with the various *policies* supplied in the RVM. Plan and policy are thus two key features of the dominant decomposition of the RVM. Each policy has its own allocation and collection strategies, drawn from basic allocation and collection mechanisms. The memory management GC plans in the RVM are composed of different combinations of these policies. Currently, there are eight different memory management plans available for download in the RVM.

Memory management in the RVM follows a simple algorithm of *prepare, process-all-work*, and *release* for collection. Since each of the GC strategies share the code base for *process-all-work*, the key differences between them are in the *prepare* and *release* phases. With a closer inspection of the original implementation a further breakdown of this design into *global prepare, local prepare, local release* and *global release* can be seen and represented as a simple finite state machine as illustrated in Figure 4. Each of these states is comprised of calls to the various policy mechanisms.

When the relationship between policy and plan is filtered out this way, a clear symmetry between the *prepare* and the *release* phases is uncovered. This symmetry is present in both the *local* and *global* scopes. Each of the policies involved in the *global prepare* are in turn involved in the *global release* and the same is true in the case of the *local* scope.

Blackburn et. al. detail the domain specific design patterns used in the implementation of MMTk, one being the *Prepare/Release* phases involved in garbage collection [2].

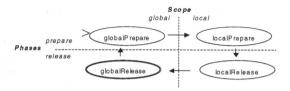

Fig. 4. Finite state machine for prepare/release protocol

```
//handles Prepare/Release of SemiSpace GC plan        //handles Prepare/Release of MarkSweep
privileged aspect PolicyAspect {                       plan
                                                       privileged aspect PolicyAspect {
  private int state = 0;
  private final int GLOBAL_PREPARE = 0;                  private int state = 0;
  private final int LOCAL_PREPARE =  1;                  private final int GLOBAL_PREPARE = 0;
  private final int LOCAL_RELEASE =  2;                  private final int LOCAL_PREPARE =  1;
  private final int GLOBAL_RELEASE = 3;                  private final int LOCAL_RELEASE =  2;
                                                         private final int GLOBAL_RELEASE = 3;
  after(Plan p):target(p)
     && (execution(* Plan.globalPrepare(..))            after(Plan p):target(p)
     || execution(*                                       //same pointcut as SemiSpace
Plan.threadLocalPrepare(..))
     || execution(*                                     {
Plan.threadLocalRelease(..))                                   switch(state){
     || execution(* Plan.globalRelease(..))) {              case(GLOBAL_PREPARE):

         switch(state){                                          Plan.msSpace.prepare();
         case(GLOBAL_PREPARE):                                            Immortal-
             CopySpace.prepare();                       Space.prepare();
             ImmortalSpace.prepare();
             Plan.losSpace.prepare();                           Plan.losSpace.prepare();
             state++;                                                 state++;
             break;                                                   break;

         case(LOCAL_PREPARE):                                 case(LOCAL_PREPARE):
             p.los.prepare();                                     p.ms.prepare();
             state++;                                             p.los.prepare();
             break;                                               state++;
                                                                  break;
         case(LOCAL_RELEASE):
             p.los.release();                                 case(LOCAL_RELEASE):
             state++;                                             p.ms.release();
             break;                                               p.los.release();
                                                                  state++;
         case(GLOBAL_RELEASE):                                    break;
             Plan.losSpace.release();
             CopySpace.release();                             case(GLOBAL_RELEASE):
             ImmortalSpace.release();
             state = GLOBAL_PREPARE;                             Plan.losSpace.release();
             break;
         }                                                      Plan.msSpace.release();
     }                                                                    Immortal-
}                                                       Space.release();
                                                                      state =
                                                        GLOBAL_PREPARE;
                                                                      break;
                                                              }
                                                          }
                                                       }
```

Fig. 5. Pre-evolution version of SemiSpace and MarkSweep aspects

The Prepare/Release aspects for *SemiSpace* and *MarkSweep* GC plans are shown in Figure 5. By looking at the plans in such close proximity, the differences in policy mechanisms employed by the two plans are evident. This same representation is scalable to all plans, providing developers of new plans a clear view of current implementations and a well defined, staged-protocol to follow in the development of new plans.

Pre and post-evolution versions of these plans differ in their pointcuts as result of the combination of hierarchical restructuring and preprocessor directives described in Section 2.1 with respect to Plans (Table 2, 2.1). As a result, the pointcuts move from the generic use of Plan.*<method>*, to the specific use of *SemiSpace.<method>* and *MarkSweep.<method>*.

4 Sustainability Analysis

Table 5 summarizes the findings of this experiment. For each of the 12 restructurings, each of the aspects was forced to change by virtue of the fact that a concern that they interacted with (an interacting concern, *IC*) had changed. That is, while the dominant decomposition of the system is evolving, the core of the aspect's functionality is staying the same – only the explicit interaction must be redefined. Thus,

Table 5. Summary of changes: required change(Δ), change automatically captured (AC)

Aspect / Corresponding IC(s) — Evolutionary Change	GCSpy	IC	Synchronization	IC	Verify Assertions	IC	Prepare/Release	IC
Separation of MMTk								
1.1) Eliminated MMTk and VM_Magic interaction	Δ	Δ						
1.2) Eliminated utility classes	Δ	Δ						
1.3) Relocated and renamed VM_Address class	Δ	Δ						
1.4) Relocated and renamed synchronization interfaces	Δ	Δ	Δ	Δ				
Separation of concerns win								
2.1) Restructured plan package	Δ	Δ					Δ	Δ
2.2) Restructured policy package	AC	Δ					AC	Δ
2.3) Restructured utility package	AC	Δ						
2.4) Redistributed and eliminated VM_Interface class	Δ	Δ			Δ	Δ		
Evolution/ Maintenance								
3.1) Class changed to implement synchronization interface			Δ	AC				
3.2) Eliminated assertion or failure functions					Δ	Δ		
3.3) Introduced new classes	Δ	Δ	AC	Δ			AC	Δ
3.4) Introduced new assertion/failure calls					AC	Δ		

looking at the IC column associated with each aspect, in all but one case, a change occurs. In 3.1 however, no change occurs in the IC, but instead the aspect is changed to flip the status of *BasePolicy* from interruptible to uninterruptible (as indicated by the commented line in Figure 2). The fact that this change is already captured for the IC is marked by the *AC* (*automatically captured*) in the IC column associated with the *Synchronization* aspect.

Looking at the rows associated with the restructurings, 5 change tasks apply to more than one aspect (1.4, 2.1, 2.2, 2.4, 3.3). In 3 of these, changes to ICs force changes in aspects (1.4, 2.1, 2.4), one of them is automatically and completely absorbed by pointcuts (2.2), and the other is automatically absorbed by pointcuts in two out of three aspects involved (3.3). Section 4.4 further considers changes that occur to more than one aspect. However, before considering those, the following subsections consider the positive/negative/neutral impact each of the aspects had on the evolution of the system as a whole. This section concludes with an overview of performance benchmarks on MMTk and MMTk$_{ao}$ respectively.

4.1 Design Invariants: Assertions and Synchronization

In both cases, the aspects that encapsulate design invariants have a positive impact in that they provide a more precise and clearer representation of the internal structure of the crosscutting concerns. Each is in line with growth trends in the system. In the case of assertions, the (un)pluggable application of advice to all/no calls can be concisely and accurately represented. In the case of synchronization however, the pointcut enumerates a relatively long list, as the application of the advice must be selective instead of all/nothing.

In terms of negative impact, checking all assert/failure calls in MMTk$_{ao}$ means there is some (small) amount of redundancy relative to MMTk, where several assertions can be made consecutively in a compound statement. With synchronization, the negative impact stems from the current lack of structure with respect to the otherwise exhaustive list.

Neutral impact, where MMTk and MMTk$_{ao}$ tie in terms of evolvability, stems from the fact that changes to the location and existence of interacting concerns requires cosmetic updating of the objects (MMTk) and aspect (MMTk$_{ao}$) in a similar fashion. Even with the inversion of synchronization status in BasePolicy, there would have to be one change made, either to the aspect or the class. We consider this a tie, with the aspect having the slight edge because the nature of the change arguably falls within the realm of the crosscutting concern and not the interacting concern. Similarly, with respect to the renaming of the *VM_Uninterruptible* interface, in MMTk$_{ao}$ this change was local to the aspect, whereas in MMTk system-wide search and replace would have to be applied throughout the code-base. The redistribution and elimination of the *VM_Interface* class during evolution also affected a design invariant, when the *Assert* class took over this functionality in the utility package, and one of the failure functions was eliminated. This change caused a renaming of all references to the function calls in the aspect in MMTk$_{ao}$, and throughout the code in MMTk.

Overall, however, we found that, though the *Synchronization* aspect does no worse than its scattered counterpart in terms of evolution, the *VerifyAssertions* aspect fares better due to its ability to grow/shrink correctly and precisely with the system.

4.2 GCSpy

Even though the aspect underwent numerous changes, its internal structure and external interaction on the whole was sustained throughout the evolution. In terms of positive impact, it was able to eliminate some redundant code relative to the subclassed *SemiSpace_With_GCSpy* in MMTk (section 2.1), and increase configurability by consolidating what were previously a collection of preprocessor directives coupled with global flags and subclassing.

In terms of negative impact, as a dynamic analysis tool, it is not surprising that GCSpy crosscuts multiple objects across multiple packages of the system. There is very little redundancy in the code captured by the GCSpy aspect, and thus there is a almost a 1:1 ratio of pointcut:advice definitions. Because GCSpy crosses structural and hierarchical boundaries in its interaction, it is subject to evolutionary changes at those interaction points. Among other things, GCSpy interacts with policies, multiple allocators, heap management, and the main collector thread. The evolution of the system caused changes to all of these interacting concerns as well as changes to previously non-interacting concerns. The addition of new policies to the system and the addition/removal of classes dealing with memory management forced changes in interaction.

The GCSpy concern was also affected by the relocation/renaming/redistribution of the VM_* classes, but the impact of this was no worse for the aspect than for the original code. Specifically the redistribution and elimination of the VM_Interface class in the system evolution required changes to all references made to its fields and methods in both MMTk and $MMTk_{ao}$. $MMTk_{ao}$ saw less change of this type due to the elimination of the VerifyAssertion and GCSpy field checks throughout the system. The case was the same for the relocation and renaming of the synchronization classes. This change required seven changes to the aspect across five advice and two inter-type declarations. Those same changes would have also taken place in the corresponding classes in MMTk. In this evolution the *VM_Address* class was also refactored, renamed, relocated changing parameters and return types of functions part of the GCSpy concern. These changes caused a refactoring of these functions and eliminated the use of the VM_Magic class. These changes again would be made in both the $MMTk_{ao}$ and MMTk.

Overall, the GCSpy aspect allows for improved evolution in $MMTk_{ao}$ due to the fact that it (1) sustained no more changes than the original implementation and (2) consolidates and unifies preprocessor directives/global flags/hierarchical decomposition as one manageable, locus of control for this dynamic analysis tool.

4.3 Prepare/Release Protocol

Though the positive impact of the prepare/release protocol aspect is the clarification of the design pattern, and this clarification holds throughout evolution, the negative impact involves the kinds of change that have to be made to the aspect as a result of evolving interacting concerns. The changes to the restructuring of the plan package to facilitate the move to unique naming of classes from the developers perspective had a negative impact on this aspect. Instead of being able to consolidate this combination of compiler directives and hierarchical decomposition, this aspect suffered from it. In

MMTk these changes are limited to the package itself and require no other changes in the system. MMTk$_{ao}$ leveraged the generic Plan.java naming convention in its original design. As a result of this change, the aspect for a given plan requires six occurrences of renaming change across four pointcuts and one advice. In the event that this prepare/release aspect is scaled across all plans, each of the plans would all have to have the corresponding renaming done to their pointcuts and advice.

4. 4 Limitations and Future Work

Constructing MMTk$_{ao}$ allowed us to ask *what-if* with respect to a diverse set of aspects faced with big bang evolution. Future work will consider the costs of an initial refactoring for a system such as MMTk$_{ao}$, and the impact of tool support during the process of evolution. With respect to this case study, changes were performed by a single developer, and evolution of MMTk$_{ao}$ was dictated by the actual evolution of MMTk. It is reasonable to assume that given the original structure of MMTk$_{ao}$, evolution most likely would have played out differently than it did from MMTk. Additionally, the aspects themselves were uncovered by manual inspection of the control flow and the dominant decomposition of the system. Future work includes employing mining tools to identify further aspects.

This study provides a coarse-grained assessment of how a diverse set of aspects can be expected to fare during large-scale change to the system they crosscut. The refactoring in this case study was intentionally done in such a way as to be least invasive to the original system as possible. Based on our experience, we believe that to truly leverage the power of AOP in these examples, a more aggressive refactoring is required. For example, with respect to the semantics encompassed by the synchronization aspect, a stronger naming convention in the interacting concerns could influence the design of this aspect. Naming conventions are currently used within this system to impart design understanding to developers and could easily be used in this case to clarify which classes are in fact uninterruptible. This would facilitate the creation a more property based aspect that would provide a greater understanding of exactly what kind of classes fall into this synchronization family.

A further consideration for future work involves the fact that new concerns simultaneously impact multiple aspects. This confirms that the management issue of compositions of aspects requires a solution before the question of scalability can be more completely resolved.

Table 6 supplies a summary of the positive/negative/neutral effects of these aspects on evolution. The analysis presented here argues that the presence of aspects did not introduce any penalty in terms of the change tasks required, and that two out of four aspects provided evidence of better sustainability in that their structure facilitated evolution and further evolutionary trends.

4.5 Discussion

Although the four examples in this case study are limited, their diversity provides a basis for the categorization of aspect types and how each will hold up under system change. Specifically looking at the example of the dynamic analysis tool GCSpy, characterizations of the underlying nature of these types of tools – having a relatively large number of interaction points within a system that are necessarily scattered across many modules – begin to surface. It provides a general view of how an aspect with many interaction points will react when any or all these points are changed. Though future work includes a more detailed analysis of these and other kinds of characterizations, we begin some of that here.

Table 6. Impact of aspects on system evolution

ASPECT	POSITIVE	NEGATIVE	NEUTRAL
Verify Assertions (BETTER)	internal structure is clear plugability is useful all or nothing – all method calls captured by invariant	some redundant field checking relative to MMTk	change of method name used in a point-cut
Synchronization (no worse)	internal structure is clear and identifies a trend in design invariant, but only to a subset of classes (not all or nothing) localized change of and access to interface	must explicitly specify classes not to be captured in aspect (no dominant pattern can be leveraged)	change in class-concern interaction automatically captures new classes
GCSpy (BETTER)	eliminates redundancy increased configurability	diverse interaction with interacting concerns	evolution of some interacting concerns
Prepare/Release (no worse)	highlights domain specific design pattern clarifies relationship of CCCs and its ICs with finite state machine	one aspect per plan evolution of MMTk yielded a similar result	evolution of interacting concerns

Looking at the results from the view given in Table 6, we can begin to generalize some of our findings and shed some light on what underlying characteristics might predispose certain kinds of aspects to positive/negative/neutral impact. The positive impact of each aspect in this study results from the accepted benefits associated with localization as applied to crosscutting concerns. The more debatable results are summarized in the final two columns detailing the negative/neutral effects.

In the design invariant aspects, the interaction points are numerous, but the behavior at those points is uniform and generalized. In this type of aspect, for example,

Synchronization, the negative impact stems from the weak representation of the invariant, inviting scenarios that may lead to new code unintentionally be encompassed by the aspect. Again, with a more aggressive refactoring this abstraction may be improved and the problem may be alleviated. Additionally, with proper tool support the visibility of aspect interaction can be easily traced.

In the GCSpy and Prepare/Release aspects, the diversity of interaction fuels the negative impact in terms of changes that ripple from interacting concerns to aspects. The GCSpy aspect's diversity is the result of the varied responsibilities at each of its many interaction points, while the Prepare/Release aspect's diversity stems from the leveraging of the generic naming convention which encompasses all plan types. As a result of this diversity, negative/neutral impact encountered is tied to the number of changes that must be made to the aspect when these interacting concerns were renamed/relocated.

4.6 Fear of the Unknown: New Interactions, Multiple Aspects

No one can predict how a system will ultimately evolve. To get a slightly different perspective on the results of this study, we further categorized the changes into 3 groups: modification of interaction, elimination of interaction (where an interacting concern becomes a noninteracting concern, or *NIC*), and new interaction, as shown in the 3 columns in Table 7. Restructurings not listed in the table do not require changes to aspects.

Table 7 demonstrates that one aspect requires changes to existing interactions, two aspects eliminate interactions, and all four aspects deal with new interactions. Furthermore, of these new interactions, two out of four of them impact more than one aspect (2.1, 2.4).

Table 7. Changes by categories per aspect

$IC_{OLD} -> IC_{NEW}$ CHANGE IN INTERACTION OF CCC WITH IC_{OLD}		$IC -> NIC$ ELIMINATION OF INTERACTION OF CCC WITH IC		$NIC -> IC_{NEW}$ INTRODUCTION OF INTERACTION OF CCC WITH PREVIOUSLY NIC	
CCC	Δ	CCC	Δ	CCC	Δ
GCSpy	1.1	GCSpy	1.2	Prepare/Release	2.1
	1.2		1.3	GCSpy	2.1
	1.4	VerifyAssertions	3.2		2.4
	2.1			VerifyAssertions	2.4
	3.3			Synchronization	1.4
					3.1

Arguably, these new interactions that require corresponding changes to multiple aspects potentially pose the biggest threat to developers leery of AOP. The fact that this data shows this kind of change impacts all the aspects in the study, coupled with the fact that these changes simultaneously impact multiple aspects, confirms that this indeed is an intensive, big bang style of evolution. Given that we believe this evolution scenario to be representative, if these kinds of changes cannot be effectively managed, the scalability of collections of aspects in this infrastructure is still an open question, and fertile ground for future work.

4.7 Performance

In the first set of tests considered here, the aspects included in $MMTk_{ao}$ are those that constitute its core functionality – *Prepare/Release* and *Synchronization*. Though the results show some noise (the average of three runs are reported), there is no discernable performance penalty for these aspects. The results of running tests from the DaCapo Benchmark Suite version beta050224 on the Jikes RVM v2.3.3, Linux 2.6.8-1.521smp, gcc-3.3.3-7, AspectJ v1.2, using an AMP Dual Athlon MP 2400+ machine with 1024 MB memory are shown below.

BENCHMARK	MMTK	$MMTk_{ao}$
Antlr	40708 ms	40937 ms (+0.56%)
Bloat	39752 ms	39550 ms (-0.51%)
Fop	14720 ms	14744 ms (0.16 %)
Jython	94148 ms	92297 ms (-1.97 %)
Pmd	42516 ms	43087 ms (1.34%)
Ps	87286 ms	86806 ms (-0.55%)

In order to stress-test a large, fine-grained aspect, we did a separate analysis of the *VerifyAssertions* aspect. In its current incarnation, these tests hammer the code within the aspect with 10s-100s of million invocations of assertion code, as reported below.

BENCHMARK	INVOCATIONS OF ASSERTION CODE
Antlr	74781288
Bloat	86211537
Fop	35325811
Jython	217938922
Pmd	99554310
Ps	100534321

Results from the fast path (assertions turned off) and the slow path (assertions turned on) introduces just under a 10% penalty[1]. In a future refactoring of the system

---

[1] An alternative implementation that could be effective at providing lighter weight support for this design invariant would be to rely on the *declare warning* construct in AspectJ to identify infractions at compile time, and at no cost.

we plan to move all assertion checking into a composition of aspects, so that when assertions are not required, the overhead would be removed.

Table 8. Fast path for assertions (off)

	ASSERTIONS OFF		
	MMTk (ms)	MMTk$_{ao}$ (ms)	Increase (%)
Antlr	37114	39824	7.3
Bloat	34346	37779	10
Fop	12794	14232	11.24
Jython	81689	88987	8.93
Pmd	38419	41460	7.92
Ps	78867	81020	2.73

Table 9. Slow path for assertions (on)

	ASSERTIONS ON		
	MMTk (ms)	MMTk$_{ao}$ (ms)	Increase (%)
Antlr	40708	46281	13.69
Bloat	39799	44183	11.02
Fop	14720	16787	14.04
Jython	93373	103508	10.85
Pmd	42516	47945	12.77
Ps	87286	91116	4.39

5 Conclusions

When evolution is a big bang, can aspects keep pace? This work provides a real world study comparing four crosscutting concerns in the original versus aspect-oriented implementation of the memory management subsystem within the Jikes RVM. One period of intense 10 month evolution of the dominant decomposition of the system is considered. This comparison highlights specific ways in which representative aspects have positive/negative/neutral impact on evolution. Given that aspects here did no harm in terms of a coarse-grained assessment of change tasks, and half of them did better than the original implementation, the study provides compelling evidence that aspects can indeed keep pace, and provide a means of better sustaining separation of concerns in system infrastructure software.

References

[1] E. Baniassad, G. Murphy, C. Schwanninger, and M. Kircher. Managing crosscutting concerns during software evolution tasks: an inquisitive study. In the Proceedings of the International Conference on Aspect-Oriented Software Development (AOSD), 2002.

[2] S. Blackburn, P. Chung and K. McKinley, Oil and Water? High Performance Garbage Collection in Java with MMTK, In the Proceedings of the International Conference on Software Engineering (ICSE), 2004.

[3] Y. Coady and G. Kiczales. A retroactive study of aspect evolution in operating system code. In the Proceedings of International Conference on Aspect-Oriented Software Development (AOSD), 2003.

[4] A. Colyer, A. Clement, Large-scale AOSD for Middleware. In the Proceedings of International Conference on Aspect-Oriented Software Development (AOSD), 2004.

[5] Dacapo Benchmarks, http://www-ali.cs.umass.edu/DaCapo/

[6] E. W. Dijkstra, A Discipline of Programming, Englewood Cliffs, United States: Prentice Hall, 1976.

[7] G. Duzan, J. Loyall, R. Schantz, Building Adaptive Distributed Applications with Middleware and Aspects. In the Proceedings of International Conference on Aspect-Oriented Software Development (AOSD) 2004.

[8] M. Engel, B. Freisleben, Supporting Autonomic Computing Functionality via Dynamic Operating System Kernel Aspects, In the Proceedings of the International Conference on Aspect-Oriented Software Development (AOSD), 2005.

[9] C. Gibbs and Y.Coady, *Aspect of Memory Management*, Hawaiin International Conference On System Sciences (HICSS), 2005.

[10] M.E. Fiuczynski, R. Grimm, Y.Coady, D. Walker, patch(1) Considered Harmful, The Tenth Annual Workshop on Hot Topics on Operating Systems (HotOS), 2005.

[11] B. Goetz, How does garbage collection work?, Developerworks, www-106.ibm.com/developerworks/java/library/j-jtp10283/, 2003.

[12] J. Hannemann and G. Kiczales. Design pattern implementations in Java and AspectJ. ACM Conference on Object-Oriented Programming, Systems, Languages and Applications (OOPSLA), 2002.

[13] Haskell Compiler, http://www.haskell.org/ghc/

[14] IBM, AspectJ Project, http://eclipse.org/aspectj/, 2004.

[15] IBM, Jikes Research Virtual Machine, www-124.ibm.com/developerworks/oss/jikesrvm/, 2004.

[16] IBM, Jikes Research Virtual Machine User's Guide, www-124.ibm.com/developerworks/oss/jikesrvm/user-guide/HTML/userguide.html, 2004.

[17] M. Kersten and G. Murphy. Atlas: A case study. ACM Conference on Object-Oriented Programming, Systems, Languages and Applications (OOPSLA), 1999.

[18] G. Kiczales, J. Lamping, A. Mendhekar, C. Maeda, C. Videira Lopes, J.-M. Loingtier and J. Irwin, Aspect-Oriented Programming. In the Proceedings of the 11th European Conference on Object-Oriented Programming (ECOOP), 1997.

[19] G. Kiczales, E. Hilsdale, J. Hugunin, M. Kersten, J. Palm and W. G. Griswold, An overview of AspectJ. In the Proceedings of 15th European Conference on Object-Oriented Programming (ECOOP), 2001.

[20] L.L. Lehman and L.A. Belady, Program Evolution, APIC Studies in Data Processing, Volume 3, 1985.

[21] Gail C. Murphy, Lightweight Structural Summarization as an Aid to Software Evolution, Computer Science, University of Washington, PhD Thesis, 1996.

[22] G. Murphy, A. Lai, R. Walker, and M. Robillard. Separating features in source code: An Exploratory Study. In the Proceedins of the International Conference on Software Engineering (ICSE), 2001.

[23] OVM, http://www.ovmj.org/

[24] D.L. Parnas, On the Criteria To Be Used in Decomposing Systems into Modules, Communications of the ACM, 15(12), 1972.

[25] D.L. Parnas and P.C. Clements, Software State-of-the-Art: Selected Papers, in T. DeMarco and T. Lister, eds., A rational design process: How and why to fake it., Dorset House Publishing., 1990.

[26] A. Rashid, N.A. Leidenfrost: Supporting Flexible Object Database Evolution with Aspects. Generative Programming and Component Engineering (GPCE) 2004.

[27] W.P. Stevens, G.J. Meyers and L.L. Constantine, Structured Design, IBM Systems Journal, Volume 13, 1974.

[28] D. Sabbah, Aspects - from Promise to Realitys, Keynote, International Conference on Aspect-Oriented Software Development (AOSD), 2004.

[29] Sun, GCspy: A Generic Heap Visualisation Framework, research.sun.com/projects/GCSpy, 2004.

[30] A. Tesanovic, M. Amirijoo, M. Björk, J. Hansson, Empowering Configurable QoS Management in Real-Time Systems, International Conference on Aspect-Oriented Software Development (AOSD), 2005.

[31] R. Walker, E. Baniassad, and G. Murphy, An Initial Assessment of Aspect-Oriented Programming. In the Proceedings of the International Conference on Software. Engineering (ICSE), 1999.

[32] W. Wulf and Mary Shaw, Global variable considered harmful. SIGPLAN Notices, 8(2), 1973.

[33] C. Zhang, G. Gao, H.A. Jacobsen, Towards Just-in-time Middleware Architectures. In Proceedings of the International Conference on Aspect-Oriented Software Development (AOSD), 2005.

First-Class Relationships in an Object-Oriented Language

• •vin Bi••• •n[1] •n• Ali••i• W••n[2]

[1] Microsoft Research, Cambridge
gmb@microsoft.com
[2] University of Cambridge Computer Laboratory
Alisdair.Wren@cl.cam.ac.uk

Abstract. In this paper we investigate the addition of first-class relationships to a prototypical object-oriented programming language (a "middleweight" fragment of Java). We provide language-level constructs to declare relationships between classes and to manipulate relationship instances. We allow relationships to have attributes and provide a novel notion of relationship inheritance. We formalize our language giving both the type system and operational semantics and prove certain key safety properties.

1 Introduction

• • j•••-o•i•n••• ••o•••• • in• l•n••••••, •n• o•j••• • o••llin• •••• ni•••• • o•• ••n••lly, ••ovi•• •o••w••• •n•in•••• wi•• •••••l ••••••••••ion• •o ••••••• l•••• •o••w••• •y••••• •. T•• ••o••in• o• o•j•••• in•o •l••••• •n• ••o•• •l••••• in•o •i••••••i•• ••ovi•••• ••• •o••w••• •n•in••• wi•• •n •x••••• •ly fl•xi•l• w•y o• •••••••••n•in• •••l-wo•l• ••• •n•i• no•ion• • i••••ly in •o••.

How•v••, w•il•• o• j•••-o•i•n••• l•n••••••• •••ily ••• ••••n• •••l-wo•l• •n•i•i•• (•.•. •••• ••n••, l•••••••, ••il• in••), ••• ••o•••• • •• i• •oo•ly ••••v•• w••n ••yin• •o ••••••••n• ••• • •ny n•••••l *relationships* •••w••n ••o•• •n•i•i•• (•.•. '••••n•• l•••••••', 'i• ••••••• in').

• •l••ion•• i• •l•••ly ••n • ••• ••• •••••n••• in o• j•••-o•i•n••• l•n••••••—in••• •• •••••••n• ••y• •••n ••••• li•••• •o• ••• •••••• o•• [10]—•••••i• i• • o•••n• •••••••-•ion ••n ••• lo•• in ••• i• •l•• •n••ion •••• i• •o•••• •• on ••• ••o•••• • ••• •y ••• l••• o• •••••-•l••• •••• o••. Diff•••n• •••••••• o•••• ••l••ion•• i• ••n •• i• •l•-• •n••• •y ••l•• •n• • ••• o•• o• ••• ••••i•i••in• •l•••••, ••• •• i• •i•••i• •••• in•o••• ••ion •• o•• ••• ••l••ion•• i• •••o•• v••io•• •l••••• . Al••n••iv•ly, •• •ll •l••••• ••n •• ••• n•• •o •on•• in •••••n••• •o ••• •wo ••l•••• o•j•••• •lon• wi•• •ny •••i• •••• o•••• ••l••ion•• i• . In •o•• •••••, wi• o••• •••••••••• •••• •••••• ••n •••o• • in••n•lly in•on•i••n•, •••••i•lly in ••• •••••n•• o• •li••in•. F••-•••• o••, w• •••••• •••• ••• ••• li•••ion o• •••n•••• •l•••-•••• in••i••n•• •o ••••• '••l••ion•• i• •l••••' •o•• no• •••••••ly •••••••• ••• in••i•iv• ••• •n•i•• o• ••l••ion•• i• in••i•n••, w•i•• • ••• o•••wi•• •• •n•o••• in •••n•••• J•v•.

A.P. Black (Ed.): ECOOP 2005, LNCS 3586, pp. 262–286, 2005.

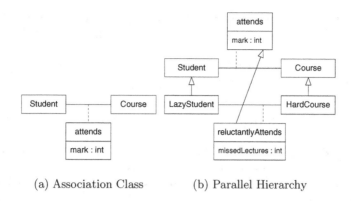

(a) Association Class   (b) Parallel Hierarchy

Fig. 1. Relationships represented as UML *association classes*

S••• •n •n•o•in• ••n only l••• •o ••••••• •o• •l•xi•y •n• • o•• o••o•••ni•i•• •o• in•on•i•••n•y.

T•• i• •o•••n•• o• ••l••ion••i•• i• •l•••ly ••fl•••• •y ••i• ••o• in•n•• in •l• o••ll • o••llin• l•n•••••: ••o• (• x••n•••) •n•i•y-••l••ion••i• Di••••• • (•• -•i••••• •) [5] •o Uni••• Mo••llin• L•n••••• (UML) [9]. In Fi•••• 1 w• •iv• •o• • •x•• •l•• o••l••ion•• i• •x••••••• in UML (w• ••• •••••• •• •• nnin• •x•• •l•• ••o••• o•• ••i• ••••••).

W• ••••• •••• •••• i• •o•••n• •••••••ion• •••••v• ••••-•l••• •••• •o•• ••o• ••o•••• • in• l•n•••••. W• ••• ••• no• ••• •••• •o •o •o; ••• ••••• •l•o • oin••• o•• ••• i• •o•••n•• o• •••-•l••• l•n•••• •••• •o•• •o• ••l••ion•• i• [13]. No•l• •n• • ••n•y •l•o ••o• o••• •••• ••l••ion•• i• ••o•l• ••••i•• ••o• ••• • o•-•llin• •o ••• i• •l•• •n••ion ••••• o• ••o•••• ••v•lo•• •n• [11]. Al• •no •• •l. ••o• o••• •i• il••• x••n•ion •o • l•n•••• •o•• •n••in• o• j•••-o•i•n••• •••••••••• (•• DB) [1], ••• •o •o in • •••• •i•••• ••••• • o• •l •n• •o no• •iv• • •• ll •• •••i• •ion o• •••i• l•n•••••.

In •on••••• •o ••••• wo•••, o•• •••••o••• i• • o•• •o•• •l. W• ••li•v• •••• •••• • •o•• •l, • ••••• ••i•• l ••• •o••• i• •••• n•i• l •o ••• • ••• •o• n••ion •o• ••••••••••••, ••••• •n• i• •l•• •n•o•• o• ••v•n••• ••o•••• • in• l•n•••••. To •••• •n•, o•• • •in •on••i••ion i• • ••••i•• •••••i••ion o• •ow J•v• (o• •ny o••••• •l•••-•••••, •••on•ly-y••• , o• j•••-o•i•n••• l•n•••••) ••n •• •x••n•• •o •••• o•• •••-•l••• ••l••ion•• i•. ••• •ool i• •• ••ll •o•• l•n•••••, RelJ, w i•• i• • ••••••• o• J•v• (• ••• li•• Mi••l•w•i•• J•v• [•]) wi•• ••i••• l• •x••n•ion• •o• ••• ••••• o•• o••l••ion•• i••. RelJ ••ovi••• ••n• •o ••• n• ••l••ion••i• ••w••n o• j•••, •o •••••i•y ••••i••••• •••o•i•••• wi•• ••o•• ••l••ion•• i••, •n• •o •••••• •i•••••• i•• o• ••l••ion••i••. RelJ i• in••n••• •o •••••••• ••• •••••n•• o• •••••• ••x-••n•ion• •o J•v•, y•• i• •• •ll •no••• •o •o•• •li•• •o• •l•••ly. • ••••• •••••••• •o•l• •• ••••••• •o RelJ •o • ••• i• • • o•• •o• •l••• l•n•••••, ••• •••••• wo•l• no• i• •••• on ••• •x••n•ion• •o• ••l••ion••i••.

T•• •••• •in••• o• ••• •••••• i• o•••ni••• •• •ollow•. In S•••. • w• in••o•••• o••••l••l••• •n• •iv• • •••• • ••. T•• •y•• •y••••• o• RelJ i• •••n•• in S•••. 3, w•••• ••• •o•• •l no•ion o• ••••y in• i• •i••••••• •n• w•ll-•y••• RelJ ••o••• •

••• ••••••••••i•••. S•••ion • •iv•• ••• •yn•• i•• o• RelJ wi•• • •• •ll-•••• o•-
••••ion•l ••• •n•i••. W• o••lin• • ••oo• o• •y•• •o•n•n••• •o• RelJ in S•••. 5.
S•••ion 6 ••••i• •• •n •x••n•ion •o RelJ w•i•• •llow• ••• •••i•ion o• UML-••yl•
• •l•i•li•i•y ••••i••ion• •o ••l••ion••i••. Fin•lly, in S•••. •, w• •on•l••• •n•
•on•i•• ••••••• •n• ••l•••• wo••.

2 The RelJ Calculus

A• • •n•ion•• •••li••, ••• •o•• o• RelJ i• • ••••• o• J•v•, •i• il•• •o o•••• ••••-
• •n•• o• J•v•-li•• l•n••••• [•,•,•]. T•• ••••• •n• w• ••• •on•i••• o• •i• •l•
•l••• •••l•••ion• •••• •on••in • n•• ••• o• ••l• •••l•••ion• •n• • •••o• •••-
l•••ion•. T•• •x••• •o•• o• ••• •l••• •••l•••ion• will •• • •••• • o•• ••••i••
l••••.

2.1 Relationship Model

T•• • •in ••••••• o• RelJ i• i•• •••• •o•• •o• ••••-•l••• ••l••ion•• i••. In ••• i•ion •o
•l••• •••l•••ion•, ••••••o••, • RelJ ••o•••• •on•i••• o• • n•• ••• o• ••l••ion•• i•
•••l•••ion•, w• i•• ••• w•i•••n:

relationship r extends r' $(n,\ n')$ { FieldDecl* MethDecl* }

T• i• ••• n••• ••l•••ion•• i•, r, wi•• • n•• ••• o••y••/••l• n•• • ••i••, FieldDecl*
•n• • •••o• •••l•••ion•, MethDecl*. T•• ••l•••ion•• i• i• ••w••n n •n• n' w••••
n, n' ••n•• ov•• •l••••• *and* ••l•••ion•• i••. T• i• ••ovi•• • • ••n• •o• ••l•••ion• i•
in•••n••• •o ••••i•i••• in ••••••• ••l•••ion•• i••. T• i• ••••••• i• •nown •• *aggregation* in • • -• o••llin• [1•]. An •x•• •l• i• ••own in Fi•. •: ••• Recommends
••l•••ion•• i• •••i••• ••••• Tutor • •y •••o• • •n• • Student •o ••••n• • •••-
•i•• l•• Course •y ••l••in• •n in•••n•• o• Tutor •o •n in•••n•• o• Attends, •••
••l•••ion•• i• •••• ••••i••• w•i•• ••••n•• •••n• w•i•• •o•••••. • •l••ion•• i••
••• •i•••••• (on•-w•y) •n• • •ny-•o-• •ny— o•• on •• i• in S•••. 6.

W• ••l••• •wo o• j••••, o_1 •n• o_2, wi•• • ••l•••ion•• i•, r, •y ••••••in• •n in-
•••n•• o• r, w•i•• •••n •xi••• *between* o_1 •n• o_2, •n• ••o•••• ••• v•l••• •o• r'•
••l••. • •l••ion•• i• in•••n••• ••• ••••-•l••• ••n•i• • o• j•••• in RelJ •n• •o ••n,
•o• •x•• • •l•, •• ••o••• in v••i••l••• •n• ••l••. T• i• i• • ••i•••ly in••o•••• ••••i•n
i••••• ••l••in• •o ••• ••• ov•l o• ••l••ion•• i• in•••n••• •n• •on••••n• ••••ion
(o• no•) o• ••n•lin• •oin••••: ••••• ••• •i••••••• l••••.

W• •l•o •••• •o•• ••l•••ion•• i• in••i••n••, w•i•• i• ••no••• i•io• ••i••lly in
UML •• in••i••n•• ••••w•n •••o•i•ion •l••••• (Fi•. 1•). To ••• •••• o• o••
•nowl••••, o•• ••••o•• •o• •• •i• in••i••n•• i• nov•l •n•, •• w• will ••••il l••••,
i• •i•ni••••n•ly •iff•••n• ••o• ••• •••n•••• •l•••-•••• in••i••n•• • o••l.

2.2 Class Inheritance vs Relationship Inheritance

W•il• •l••• in••i••n•• in RelJ i• i••n•i••l •o •••• in J•v•, RelJ'• ••l•••ion•• i•
in••i••n•• i• ••••• on • ••••i••• •o•• o• ••l•••ion, •• •o•n• in l•n••••••
••••• •• S•l• [16] •n•, • o•• •••n•ly, δ [•]. • on•i••• ••• RelJ •o•• •o• • •i• •l•
•x•• •l•, ••••••• ••o• Pool•y •n• S••v•n• [15], w•i•• i• ••own in Fi•. •.

```
class Student {
   String name;
}
class LazyStudent extends Student {
   int    hoursOfSleep;
}
class Course {
   String title;
}
class Tutor {
   String name;
}
relationship Attends (Student, Course) {
   int mark;
}
relationship ReluctantlyAttends extends Attends
                             (LazyStudent, Course) {
   int missedLectures;
}
relationship CompulsorilyAttends extends Attends
                             (Student, Course) {
   String reason;
}
relationship Recommends (Tutor, Attends) {
   String reason;
}
...
alice = new LazyStudent();
programming = new Course();
typeSystems = new Course();
Attends.add(alice, programming);          // Alice attends Programming
ReluctantlyAttends.add(alice, typeSystems);
                             // Alice reluctantly attends Type Systems
for (Course c : alice.Attends) {
  print "Attends: " + c.title;
};                                        // Prints:
                                          //    Attends: Programming
                                          //    Attends: Type Systems
```

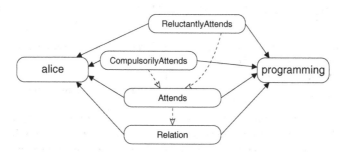

Fig. 2. Example RelJ code and possible instantiation

W••n alice •n• programming ••• •l•••• in ••• Attends ••l••ion•• i•, •n in•••n•• o• Attends i• •••••••• •••w••n •• o•• o• j••••. S•••••••n•ly, w••n alice •n• programming ••• •••••••• •l•••• in ReluctantlyAttends, •n in•••n•• o• ReluctantlyAttends i• •••••••• •••w••n alice •n• programming, ••• •on••in• *only* ••• missedLectures ••l•. I••••• ReluctantlyAttends in•••n•• ••••iv•• • ••l• loo•-•• ••••••• •o• mark, i• ••••••—*delegates*—••• •••••••• •o ••• Attends in•••n••—••• *super-instance*—•••• •xi••• •••w••n •• o•• ••• • o• j••••.

To •n••••• •ll in•••n•••• ••• '•o• •l•••', •••••j••••lly •••••••y ••v• •ll••• ••l•• on• wo• l• •x•••• •y in••i••n••, w• i• • o•• ••• •ollowin• inv••i•n•:

Invariant 1. *Consider a relationship r_2 which **extends** r_1. For every instance of relationship r_2 between objects o_1 and o_2, there is an instance of r_1, also between o_1 and o_2, to which it delegates requests for r_1's fields.*

By ••i• inv••i•n•, i• alice •n• programming w••• •l•••• in ••• ReluctantlyAttends ••l••ion••i• wi••o•• •••• ••vin• •••n •l•••• in ••• Attends ••l••ion••i•, •••n •n Attends in•••n•• wo•l• •• i• •li•i•ly •••••••• •••w••n ••••• .

Invariant 2. *For every relationship r and pair of objects o_1 and o_2, there is at most one instance of r between o_1 and o_2.*

A••o••in• •o ••i• •••on• inv••i•n•, i• alice •n• programming w••• l•••• •l•••• in ••• CompulsorilyAttends ••l••ion•• i•, •••n i•• in•••n•• •n• •••• o• ReluctantlyAttends wo•l• •••••• • •o• • on •••••-in•••n••: ••• Attends in•••n•• •••w••n alice •n• programming. T•i• •i••••ion i• •• own ••••• • o••o• o• Fi•. •, wi•• ••• •o•••• lin•• in•i•••in• ••l•••ion o• •l• loo••••.

T••• o•iv••ion •o•••• • • •••••ni•• i• •••••• on w••• on• • i••• in••i•iv•ly •x••••••o• ••l••ion••i••: • l•••ly, i• Ali•• ••l•••n•ly ••••n•• • •o••••, •••n ••• •l•o ••••n•• i• •n• will ••••iv• • • •••, •••• w ••••i•• •••-••l••ion••i• •o •• in•l•••• in ••••i• ••••••-••l••ion••i•, •ivin• •i•• •o Inv••i•n• 1. Al•o, i• Ali•• i• • o•• •o• ••l•o•ily •n• ••l•••n•ly ••••n•in• •o• • •o•••, ••• • ••• will •• ••• ••• • •••••••l••• o• w•••••• on• vi•w• ••• ••••n••n•• •• ••l•••n•, •o• ••l•o•y o• wi••o•• •ny •nno••••ion. T•••, •o• ••••• ••i• o• ••l•••• o• j••••, ••••• ••o•l• •• only on• in•••n•• o• ••••• ••l••ion•i• •o ••••• ••l••ion•• i• ••o•••i•• ••• •on•i•••n•, ••n•• Inv••i•n• •.

RelJ •l•o •llow• ••• ••• ov•l o••l••ion••i• in•••n•••. Fo• •x•• •l•, w• •o•l• •x••n• ••• •o•• o• Fi•. • •o ••• ov• ••• •••• •••• Alice •••n•• programming:

```
...
Attends.rem(alice, programming);   // Remove Alice attends Programming
for (Course c : alice.Attends){
  print "Attends: " + c.title;     // Prints:
}                                  //    Attends: Type Systems
```

In ••••, • o•• ••• ••l••ion••i• •••i•ion •n• ••• ov•l o••••ion• ••• *statement expressions*. W••n •••• ••n •x••••ion, add •••••n• ••• ••l••ion•• i• in•••n•• •••• w•• •••••••: ••i• ••ovi•••• • •onv•ni•n• ••o••-••• •o• ••••in• ••• n•w in•••n••••

••l••. Fo• ••••l••i•y, rem ••••n• ••• in••n•• •••• w•• ••• ov••, o• null i• •••
••l••ion••i• • i• no• •xi•• ••o•• ••• •••••• •••• ••• ov•l.

W• ••••n now •o ••• i•••• ••i••• •••li•• •on••nin• ••l••ion••i• in••n••
••• ov•l. • on•i• •• ••• •ollowin• •o••:

```
bob = new Student();
bob.name = "Bob";
databases = new Course();
databases.title = "DB 101";

bobdb = Attends.add(bob, databases);    // Add bob to databases
bobdb.mark = 99;
for (Course cs : bob.Attends) {
  print cs.title;
};                                        // Prints DB 101

print bobdb.mark;                         // Prints 99

Attends.rem(bob, databases);              // Remove bob from databases

for (Course cs : bob.Attends) {
  print cs.title;
};                                        // Prints nothing
```

T•• •••on• i•••••ion •• ow• •••• ••• ••l••ion••i• ••w••n bob •n• databases
••• ••n •o••••ly ••• ov••. W• • ••• ••n ••oo•• ••• •••• o• ••• ••••••n•• •o
••• Attends-in••n•• ••o••• in bobdb: w•• ••••••n• i•w• ••••n• ••• •••••• •n•
print bobdb.mark;?

T•••• ••• •l•••ly • n•• ••• o• o••ion•: •i•••• ••• in••n•• i• ••• ov••, in
w•i•• •••• w• wo•l• •x•••• • ••n•i• •••o•; o• ••• ••n•i• • • •in••in• •o• •
liv•n••• in•o•• ••ion •o •••• •n ••••••• •o ••• v••i••l• bobdb wo•l• ••n•••• •
••••i• ••l••ion••i• •x••••ion; o• • n•lly, w• •o•l• ••oo•• no• •o ••• ov• •••
••l••ion••i• in••n•• •• •ll, in w•i•• •••• ••• •o•• wo•l• ••in• 99. W• ••v•
••o••n ••• ••i•• o••ion. T•••, in RelJ, ••• ••l••ion••i• in••n•• i••l• i• no•
••• ov•• •• on ••l••ion, ••• •••••• i• •••••• li•• •ny o•••• ••n•i• • v•l•• •n•
i• ••• ov•• •y ••••••• •oll••ion. Mo•• •x••i•n•• in ••l••ion••i• ••o••• • in•
i• n••••• •••o•• w• ••n •••••• in• i• ••i• i• ••• •o••••• •••i•n •••i•ion.

2.3   Language Definition

W• •iv• ••• •••• • •• •o• RelJ ••o•••• • •n• •y••• in Fi•. 3.

T•• J•v• •y••• •••• in RelJ ••• •l••• n•• •• •n• • •in•l• ••i• i•iv• •y••,
boolean (••• in•l••ion o• ••••••• ••i• i•iv• •y••• •o•• no• i• •••• on ••• •o•-
• •li••ion). A• •i•••••••, w• ••ovi•• ••l••ion••i• n•• •• •• •y•••. To •llow
••l••ion••i• ••o•••in• RelJ ••• • (••n••i•) ••• •y•• set<n>, •••• ••no••• • •••
o• v•l••• o• •y•• n. T•i• ••• •y•• i• no• • *reference* •y••, ••• i• • *primitive*

$$p \in \text{Program} ::= \text{ClassDecl}^* \ \text{RelDecl}^*$$

$$\text{ClassDecl} ::= \text{class } c \text{ extends } c'$$
$$\{ \ \text{FieldDecl}^* \ \text{MethDecl}^* \ \}$$

$$\text{RelDecl} ::= \text{relationship } r \text{ extends } r' \ (n, \ n')$$
$$\{ \ \text{FieldDecl}^* \ \text{MethDecl}^* \ \}$$

$$n \in \text{NominalType} ::= c \mid r$$

$$t \in \text{Type} ::= \text{boolean} \mid n \mid \text{set<}n\text{>}$$

$$\text{FieldDecl} ::= t \ f;$$

$$\text{MethDecl} ::= t \ m(t' \ x) \ mb$$

$$mb \in \text{MethBody} ::= \{ \ s \ \text{return } e; \ \}$$

$$v \in \text{Value} ::= \text{true} \mid \text{false} \mid \text{null} \mid \text{empty}$$

$$l \in \text{LValue} ::= x \mid$$

$e.f$	field access
$e \in \text{Expression} ::= v \mid$	value
$l \mid$	l-value
$e_1 \ \text{==} \ e_2 \mid$	equality test
$e_1 \ \text{+} \ e_2 \mid e_1 \ \text{-} \ e_2 \mid$	set addition/removal
$e.r \mid e{:}r \mid$	relationship access
$e.\text{from} \mid$	relationship source
$e.\text{to} \mid$	relationship destination
se	statement expression
$se \in \text{StatementExp} ::= \text{new } c() \mid$	instantiation
$l \ \text{=} \ e \mid$	assignment
$r.\text{add}(e,e') \mid r.\text{rem}(e,e') \mid$	relationship addition/removal
$e.m(e')$	method call
$s \in \text{Statement} ::= \epsilon \mid$	empty statement
$se; \ s_1 \mid$	expression
$\text{if } (e) \ \{s_1\} \ \text{else } \{s_2\}; \ s_3 \mid$	conditional
$\text{for } (n \ x : e) \ \{s_1\}; \ s_2$	set iteration

Fig. 3. The grammar of RelJ types and programs

(v•l••) •y••, • ••• li•• ••• ••n••i• li••••l •y••• ••••• •y ••• • DM• [1•].[1] RelJ •o•• no• ••••o•• n••••• ••••—•••• o• •••• ••• no• •••• i••••. RelJ off••• • for i••••o• ov•• ••• v•l••• (w• ••o•• ••• ••• • •yn••x •• J•v• 5.0 •o• i••••in• ov•• •oll••ion•). W• •l•o ••ovi•• o••••o•• •o• •x•li•i•ly •••in• •n •l•• •n• •o • ••• (+), •n• •o• ••• ovin• •n •l•• •n• (-).

---

[1] Having sets as a generic value type allows us to soundly support covariance—this is discussed in more detail in Sect. 3.

$\mathcal{C} \in$ ClassTable : ClassName $\rightarrow$ ClassName $\times$ FieldMap $\times$ MethMap

$\mathcal{R} \in$ RelTable : RelName $\rightarrow$ RelName $\times$ NominalType $\times$ NominalType $\times$
$$\text{FieldMap} \times \text{MethMap}$$

$\mathcal{F} \in$ FieldMap : FldName $\rightarrow$ Type

$\mathcal{M} \in$ MethMap : MethName $\rightarrow$ VarName $\times$ LocalMap $\times$ Type $\times$ Type $\times$ MethBody

$\mathcal{L} \in$ LocalMap : VarName $\rightarrow$ Type

Fig. 4. Signatures of class and relationship tables

Fo• •i• • li•i•y, w• •••• i•• •o• • •••• l••i•y in ••• •l••• (•n• ••l••ion•• i•) •••-
l•••ion• o• RelJ ••o•••• •: (1) w• in•i•• •••• •ll •l••• •••l•••ion• in•l••• •••
•••••y• •; (•) w• w•i•• o•• • ••• ••••iv•• o• ••l• •••••• o• • ••• o• invo••ion in
•• ll; (3) •ll • ••• o•• •••• j••• on• ••••• •n•; (•) •ll • ••• o• •••l•••ion• •n•
wi•• • return •••••• •n•; •n• (5) w• ••••• • •••• in • RelJ ••o•••• •x••ly on•
•l••• ••••o••• • main • •••o•. To •• •on•i••, w• •o no• •on•i•• •on•••••o•
• ••• o••; ••l• ini•i•li•••ion, o•••• •••n ••• ••ovi•ion o• •y•-••••o••i•• ini•i•l
v•l•••, i• ••••o•• •• •x• li•i•ly.

T••• ••• •v••i••l• c ••n••• ov•• ••• ••• o• •l••• n•• ••, ClassName; r ••n•••
ov•• ••• ••• o• ••l••ion•• i• n•• ••, RelName; n ••n••• ov•• • o•• ClassName •n•
RelName; f ••n••• ov•• ••• ••• o• ••l• n•• ••, FldName; m ••n••• ov•• •••
••• o• • •••o• n•• ••, MethName; •n• x ••n••• ov•• ••• ••• o• v••i••l• n•• ••,
VarName, w•i•• w• ••••• • •on••in• ••• •l•• •n• this, w•i•• ••nno• •• on •••
l•••-••n• •i•• o••n •••i•n• •n•. M•••v••i••l••• • •y no• ••••• ••• •n•• •n•• v•l••.

A• ••••l •o• •••• l•n••••• •o•• •li•••ion•, w• ••••• • ••••• iv•n • RelJ ••o-
•••• , P, ••• •l••• •n• ••l••ion•• i• •••l•••ion• •iv• •i•• •o •l••• •n• ••l••ion•• i•
••• l•• •••• ••• ••no••• •y $\mathcal{C}_P$ •n• $\mathcal{R}_P$, ••••••iv•ly [6]. (W• will ••o• ••• •••-
••i•• w••n i• i• •n•• •i••o••.) A •l••• (••l••ion•• i•) ••• l• i• •••n • ••• ••o• •
•l••• (••l••ion•• i•) n•• • •o • •l••• (••l••ion•• i•) ••• ni•ion. Si• n••••• •o• •••••
• ••• ••• •o •• •o• n• in Fi•. •.

A •l••• ••• ni•ion i• • •••l•, $(c, \mathcal{F}, \mathcal{M})$, w•••• c i• ••• •••••••l•••; $\mathcal{F}$ i• •
• •• ••o• ••l• n•• •• •o ••l• •y••; •n• $\mathcal{M}$ i• • • ••• ••o• • •••o• n•• •• •o
• •••o• ••• ni•ion•. M•••o• •••ni•ion• ••• •••l•• $(x, \mathcal{L}, t_1, t_2, mb)$ w•••• x i•
••• •••••• ••••; $\mathcal{L}$ i• • • ••• ••o• lo••l v••i••l• n•• •• •o •••i• •y••; t_1 i• •••
•••••• •••• •y• •; t_2 i• ••• •••••n •y• •; •n• mb i• ••• • • •••o• •o• y. Fo• •••vi•y,
w• w•i•• $\mathcal{F}_c$ •n• $\mathcal{M}_c$ •o• ••• ••l• •n• • •••o• •••ni•ion ••• • o• •l••• c.

• •l••ion•• i• •••ni•ion• ••• •••l•• $(r', n, n', \mathcal{F}, \mathcal{M})$ w•••• r' i• ••• •••••-
••l••ion•• i• ; n •n• n' ••• ••• •y••• ••w••n w•i•• ••• ••l••ion•• i• i• •o•• ••
(••• *source* •n• *destination* •••••••iv•ly); •n• $\mathcal{F}$, $\mathcal{M}$ ••• ••• ••l• • ••• •n•
• •••o• • •• •••••••••iv•ly, •• •o•n• in •l••• •••ni•ion•. A• •o• •l•••••, w• w•i••
$\mathcal{F}_r$ •o• r' ••l• •••ni•ion • ••• •n• $\mathcal{M}_r$ •o• r'• • •••o• • ••.

In ••• • ••y, RelJ off••• ••• •ollowin• o• •••ion• •o • •ni•• l••• ••l••ion•• i•:
$e.r$ •n•• ••• o• j•••• ••l•••• •o ••• ••••l• o• e ••o••• ••l••ion•• i• r; $e{:}r$ •n••
••• in•••n••• o• r •••• •xi•• •••w••n ••• ••••l• o• e •n• ••• o• j•••• •o w•i••
i• i• ••l••••; •n• ••• •••••o-••l• from •n• to ••• • ••• •v•il••l• on ••l••ion-
•• i• in•••n•••, •n• •••••n ••• •o•••• •n• •••in••ion o• j•••• ••w••n w•i•• •••
in•••n•• •xi••• (o• •xi••••). T•••• ••• ••••••• •••••i•• in ••• •ollowin• ••••ion•.

3   Type System

W• ••ovi•• Object •o• ••• •oo• o• ••• •l••• •i•••••••y •• ••••l, •n• Relation •• i•• •o• n•••••••• in ••• ••l••ion•• i• •i•••••••y, •n• ••••• • •••••o••i••• •n••i•• in $\mathcal{C}$ •n• $\mathcal{R}$ •••• ••iv•ly. W• ••• n• ••• ••••l •••••y• in• ••l••ion $P \vdash t \leq t'$ w•••• t i• • •••••y•• o• t', •i••••ly •o••l•••• wi•• ••• in•o•• ••ion •• o•• i• • ••i••• •••••••-•y••• ••ovi••• ••y $\mathcal{C}$ •n• $\mathcal{R}$, •••n •lo••• •n••• •••n•i•ivi•y •n• ••fl•xivi•y. P i• o• i••••• w••••• ••• ••on••x• • •••• i• •n•• •i••o••.

W• l••v• ••• l••• i• •o•••n• •y• in• ••l•• •o A••••n• ix A, ••• •wo ••l•• wo••• ••••i••l•• no•• ••• •• own ••••:

<table>
<tr><td style="text-align:center">(STCov)</td><td style="text-align:center">(STObject)</td></tr>
<tr><td style="text-align:center">$\dfrac{\vdash n_1 \leq n_2}{\vdash \mathtt{set}{<}n_1{>} \leq \mathtt{set}{<}n_2{>}}$</td><td style="text-align:center">$\vdash \mathtt{Relation} \leq \mathtt{Object}$</td></tr>
</table>

STCov • •••• ••• •y••• •ov••i•n• wi•• •••i• •on••in•• •y••. I• $\mathtt{set}{<}-{>}$ w••• • •••••••n•• •y••, ••• n ••i• •in• o••ov••i•n•• wo•l• •••n•o•n•. How•v••, $\mathtt{set}{<}-{>}$ i• • v•l•• •y••, •••• •••• v•l••• ••• no• •••••• n••• o• • •••••••, only •o•i••.

To •ni•y ••• ••l••ion•• i• •n• •l••• •i•••••• i•••—••i••l• in ••• ••••• n•• o• ••n••i••—w•••• Relation ••• ••••y•• o• Object in ••l• STObject.[2]

W•il• $\mathcal{F}_c$ •n• $\mathcal{M}_c$ •iv• •• ••• ••l•• •n• • •••o•• •••l••• •i•••ly in c, w• ••• n• $\mathcal{FD}_c$ •n• $\mathcal{MD}_c$ •o ••ovi••• •• wi•• •ll ••• ••l•• •n• • •••o•• ••v•il••l• •o• c'• in••• n•••, in•l••in• ••o•• in••i••• ••o• i•• ••••• ••l••••, •o •••• ••i• •y•••• i••• •• ••••••• in ••• l•••• •y• •• l••:

$$\mathcal{FD}_c(f) = \begin{cases} \mathcal{F}_c(f) & \text{if } f \in \mathrm{dom}(\mathcal{F}_{P,c}) \text{ or } c = \mathtt{Object} \\ \mathcal{FD}_{c'}(f) & \text{if } f \notin \mathrm{dom}(\mathcal{F}_{P,c}) \text{ and } \mathcal{C}(c) = (c', \_, \_) \end{cases}$$

$\mathcal{MD}$ i• ••• n•• •i• il••ly •o••l••• ••• •o••, •••• ••• $\mathcal{FD}$ •n• $\mathcal{MD}$ •o• ••l••ion•• i••.

W• •y• •x•••••ion• •n• ••••••• •n•• in ••• •••••n••• o• ••y• in• •nvi•on• •n•, Γ, w•i•• •••i•n• •y••• •o v••i••l• n•• ••. S•l••••• •y• in• j••••• •n•• •o• RelJ •x• ••••ion• ••• ••iv•n ••low:

<table>
<tr><td style="text-align:center">(TSRelObj)</td><td style="text-align:center">(TSRelInst)</td></tr>
<tr><td style="text-align:center">$\dfrac{\Gamma \vdash e : n_1 \quad \mathcal{R}(r) = (\_, n_2, n_3, \_, \_) \quad \vdash n_1 \leq n_2}{\Gamma \vdash e.r : \mathtt{set}{<}n_3{>}}$</td><td style="text-align:center">$\dfrac{\Gamma \vdash e : n_1 \quad \mathcal{R}(r) = (\_, n_2, \_, \_, \_) \quad \vdash n_1 \leq n_2}{\Gamma \vdash e{:}r : \mathtt{set}{<}r{>}}$</td></tr>
</table>

TSRelObj •y••• ••• loo••• o• o• j•••• ••l•••• •••o••• r •o ••• ••••l• o• e. A• o•• ••l••ion••i•• ••• i• • li•i•ly • •ny-•o-• •ny, ••• ••••l• o• ••i• loo••• i• • ••• o• r'• ••••in••ion •y••, n_2. T•• ••l••ion•• i• in•••n••• •••• •i• ••w••n ••• ••••l• o• e •n• ••• ••••l• o• $e.r$ ••• •••••••• •••o••• $e{:}r$. T•• ••••l• o• •••• • loo••• i• • ••• o• r-in•••n•••, •• •••i••• in TSRelInst. T•••• i• • •i•• ••• ••••w••n ••• •o••• •n• ••••in••ion o•• • ••l••ion•• i•: ••• ••l••ion•• i• in•••n••• • •y only •• •••••••• ••o• ••• •o•••• o• j•••. I• i• no• •i• ••l• •o •x••n• ••• l•n••••• •o •••• ••••••• ••o• ••• ••••in••ion o• j•••• i• •l•o •o••i•l•.

---

[2] If we added generics to RelJ it would be possible to remove this typing rule.

$$\frac{\text{(TSFROM)}}{\begin{array}{c}\Gamma \vdash e : r \\ \mathcal{R}(r) = (\_, n, \_, \_, \_) \\ \hline \Gamma \vdash e.\texttt{from} : n\end{array}} \qquad \frac{\text{(TSTO)}}{\begin{array}{c}\Gamma \vdash e : r \\ \mathcal{R}(r) = (\_, \_, n, \_, \_) \\ \hline \Gamma \vdash e.\texttt{to} : n\end{array}}$$

• iv•n •n r-in•••n••, ••• o• j•••• ••w••n w•i•• i• •xi••• (o• ••w••n w•i•• i• on•• •xi••••) ••n • • •••••••• wi•• ••• from •n• to ••o•••i••. TSFROM •n• TSTO •••i•n •y•• •••o•• in• •o ••• ••l••ion•• i• ' • ••l•••ion—••••••o••, •••••• ••• •y••• •ov•i•n•ly wi•• ••• ••l••ion•• i• •y••, ••• ••i• i• •o•n• •• •••y ••• i• • ••••l• •o• •ll in•••n••• o• •••• • ••l••ion•• i•.

$$\begin{array}{c}\text{(TSRELADD)} \\ \mathcal{R}(r) = (\_, n_1, n_2, \_, \_) \\ \Gamma \vdash e_1 : n_3 \\ \Gamma \vdash e_2 : n_4 \\ \vdash n_3 \le n_1 \\ \vdash n_4 \le n_2 \\ \hline \Gamma \vdash r.\texttt{add}(e_1, e_2) : r\end{array} \qquad \begin{array}{c}\text{(TSRELREM)} \\ \mathcal{R}(r) = (\_, n_1, n_2, \_, \_) \\ \Gamma \vdash e_1 : n_3 \\ \Gamma \vdash e_2 : n_4 \\ \vdash n_3 \le n_1 \\ \vdash n_4 \le n_2 \\ \hline \Gamma \vdash r.\texttt{rem}(e_1, e_2) : r\end{array}$$

Fin•lly, TSRELADD •n• TSRELREM •••i•y •y•in• o• ••• o••••o•• ••••• ••l••• •n• •n••l••• o• j••••. In •o•• •••••, e_1 •n• e_2 • ••• •• o• ••• •o•••• •n• •••in••ion •y••, ••••••iv•ly, o• ••l••ion•• i• r. T•• ••••l• o• •i•••• o• ••••ion will •• •n in•••n••• o• r; •••• w•i•• w•• •••••••• o• ••• ov••. A ••• ov•l • •y •v•l•••• •o null w•••• ••• ••••l•• o• e_1 •n• e_2 w•••• •n••l•••• •y r.

T•• •y••-••••••in• ••l••ion •o• •••••• •n•• i• o• ••• •o•• $\Gamma \vdash s$, ••• ••l•• •o• w• i•• ••• l••••ly •o••in•. W• •• ow •o• • •x•• • l••, •ow•v••:

$$\begin{array}{cc} & \text{(TSFOR)} \\ & \Gamma \vdash e : \texttt{set<}n_1\texttt{>} \\ \text{(TSEXP)} & \Gamma[x \mapsto n_2] \vdash s_1 \\ \Gamma \vdash se : t & \vdash n_1 \le n_2 \\ \cline{1-1}\cline{2-2} \Gamma \vdash s & \Gamma \vdash s_2 \\ \hline \Gamma \vdash se;\, s & \Gamma \vdash \texttt{for } (n_2\ x : e)\ \{s_1\};\, s_2 \end{array} \quad x \notin \mathsf{dom}(\Gamma)$$

TSEXP •llow• •y••-•o•••••• •••••• •n• •x•••••ion• •o • • •••• •• ••••••• •n••, w• il• TSFOR •••••• ••• ••• ••• for •on•••••• i• only ••••• •o i•••••• ov•• • ••• o• o•j••• •••••n•••. No•• ••••, •o • • •on•i•••n• wi•• ••• J•v• 5.0 •yn••x, w• ••••i•• •n •x•li•i• •y•• •o• ••• i•••••in• v••i••l•, •l••o••• ••••• i• no ••••on w•y •• i• •y•• •o•l• no• •• in•••••. W• •l•o ••••i•• ••••• ••• i•••••ion v••i••l• i• no• •l•••• y in ••o••.

T•• ••• validTypes$_P$ •••i•• ••• •y••• •••• • •y •• •••i•n•• •o ••l•• •n• v••i•l••:

$$\mathsf{validTypes}_P = \{\texttt{boolean}\} \cup \mathsf{dom}(\mathcal{C}_P) \cup \mathsf{dom}(\mathcal{R}_P) \cup \{\texttt{set<}n\texttt{>} \mid n \in \mathsf{dom}(\mathcal{C}_P) \cup \mathsf{dom}(\mathcal{R}_P)\}$$

In ••• •ollowin• •wo ••l••, w• ••••• ••l•• •n• • •••o•• in ••• •••••••n•• o• •••i• •n•lo•in• •l••• o• ••l••ion•• i•:

$$\text{(TSFIELD)}$$

$$\begin{array}{c}
\mathcal{C}(n) = (n', \_, \_) \ \vee \ \mathcal{R}(n) = (n', \_, \_, \_, \_) \\
1. \quad f \notin \mathsf{dom}(\mathcal{FD}_{n'}) \\
2. \quad \mathcal{F}_n(f) \in \mathsf{validTypes}_P \\
3. \quad \mathcal{R}(f) = (\_, n_1, n_2, \_) \Rightarrow \not\vdash n \leq n_1 \\
\hline
P, n \vdash f
\end{array}$$

TSFIELD •••••• •••• f i• • •oo• ••l• •o• •l••• o• ••l••ion•• i• n •y v••i•yin• (1) •••• f i• no• •••n•• in •ny •••••-y•• o• n; (•) •••• f'• •y•• i• v•li• in • w•ll-•y••• ••o•••• •n• (3) •••• ••••• i• no ••l••ion•• i• wi•• ••• ••• • n•• • ••• f ••••• i•••• ••• •••••n••• •o f •• •i••o••.

$$\text{(TSMETHOD)}$$

$$\begin{array}{c}
\mathcal{C}_P(n) = (n', \_, \mathcal{M}_n) \vee \mathcal{R}_P(n) = (n', \_, \_, \_, \mathcal{M}_n) \\
\mathcal{M}_n(m) = (x, \mathcal{L}, t_1, t_2, \{\ s \ \mathsf{return}\ e;\ \}) \\
1. \quad t_1 \in \mathsf{validTypes}_P \\
2. \quad \mathbf{this}, x \notin \mathsf{dom}(\mathcal{L}) \\
3. \quad \{x \mapsto t_1, \mathbf{this} \mapsto n\} \cup \mathcal{L} \vdash s \\
4. \quad \{x \mapsto t_1, \mathbf{this} \mapsto n\} \cup \mathcal{L} \vdash e : t_2' \\
5. \quad \vdash t_2' \leq t_2 \\
6. \quad \mathcal{MD}_{n'}(m) = (\_, \_, t_3, t_4, \_) \Rightarrow \vdash t_3 \leq t_1 \ \wedge \ \vdash t_2 \leq t_4 \\
\hline
P, n \vdash m
\end{array}$$

TSMETHOD ••••••• (1) •••• ••• in••• •y•• o• • •••o• m in •l•••/••l••ion•• i• n i• v•li•; (•) •••• ••• ••••• •••• n•• • •n• this •o no• •l••• wi•• •ny lo••l v••i••l••; (3) •••• ••• • •••o• • o•y i• w•ll-•y••• w••n ••• ••••• ••••, this •n• ••• lo••l v••i••l•• ••• •••i•n•• ••• •y••• •••i••• in ••• •l•••' • •••o• •••l•; (•, 5) •••• ••• return •x•••••ion ••• • •••y•• o••• • •••o• '• ••l•••• ••••• •n •y••; •n• (6) •••• ••• in••• •y•• o••• i• • •••o• i• • ••••••y•• o• •ny •••vio•• •••l•••ion o• m in • ••••••-y•• o• c, •n• •••• ••• ••••• n •y•• o• m i•• ••••y•• o• •ny •••vio•• • •••o• •••l•••ion: •••• i•, •••• ••i• •••ni•ion o• m • •y •• •••• •nyw•••• • ••••••y••'• v•••ion o• m ••n •• •••••. W• •••n ••••i•y ••• v•li•i•y o• •l••••• •n• ••l••ion•• i••:

$$\text{(TSRELATIONSHIP)}$$

$$\begin{array}{c}
\mathcal{R}_P(r) = (r' \neq r, n_1, n_2, \mathcal{F}, \mathcal{M}) \\
r' \in \mathsf{validTypes}_P \\
1. \quad \mathcal{R}_P(r') = (\_, n_1', n_2', \_, \_) \\
2. \quad \vdash n_1 \leq n_1' \\
3. \quad \vdash n_2 \leq n_2' \\
\forall f \in \mathsf{dom}(\mathcal{F}) : P, r \vdash f \\
\forall m \in \mathsf{dom}(\mathcal{M}) : P, r \vdash m \\
\hline
P \vdash r
\end{array}$$

$$\text{(TSCLASS)}$$

$$\begin{array}{c}
\mathcal{C}(c) = (c' \neq c, \mathcal{F}, \mathcal{M}) \\
P \vdash c' \\
\forall f \in \mathsf{dom}(\mathcal{F}) : P, c \vdash f \\
\forall m \in \mathsf{dom}(\mathcal{M}) : P, c \vdash m \\
\hline
P \vdash c
\end{array}$$

TSCLASS •••i•• •••••• •l••• •y•• i• w•ll-•o•• •• i•i•• ••••••l••• i• w•ll-•o•• ••, •n• i•••ll o• i•• • •••o•• •n• ••l•• ••• w•ll-•y•••. TSRELATIONSHIP i• •o••• • •ny o• ••• ••• • ••••i••ion•• •• TSCLASS, wi•• ••• ••••i•ion o• •on•i•ion• 1–3, w•i•• •••••• ••• •y••• ••l•••• •y r'• •••••-••l•••ion•• i• ••• •••••••y•• o• ••o•• •••• r ••l•••.

4   Semantics

W• •••••i•y •v•l•••ion ••l•• •o• • •• •ll-•••• ••• •n•i••. W• ••• •v•l•••ion •on-••x•• •o •••••i•y •v•l•••ion o•••• [1•], •n• ••• v••i••l• ••n•• in• •o •voi• ••• n••• •o• •n •x• li•i• •••• • ••••• [•].

T••• •••-v••i••l••• •••• in ••• ••• •n•i•• ••n•• ov•• ••••••••, v•l• ••, •••o••, o• j•••• •n• ••o••• •• •ollow•:

$$\iota \in \mathsf{Address}$$
$$\iota^{\mathtt{null}} \in \mathsf{Address} \cup \{\mathtt{null}\}$$
$$u \in \mathsf{DynValue} = \{\mathtt{null}, \mathtt{true}, \mathtt{false}\} \cup \mathsf{Address} \cup \mathcal{P}(\mathsf{Address})$$
$$w \in \mathsf{Error} ::= \mathsf{NullPtrError} \mid \mathcal{E}_e[w] \mid \mathcal{E}_s[w] \mid \{ \ w \ \mathtt{return} \ e; \ \}$$
$$o \in \mathsf{Object}$$
$$\sigma : \mathsf{Address} \rightarrow \mathsf{Object}$$
$$\rho : (\mathsf{Address} \times \mathsf{Address} \times \mathsf{RelName}) \rightarrow \mathsf{Address}$$
$$\lambda : \mathsf{VarName} \rightarrow \mathsf{DynValue}$$

• • j••••, ••n••• ov•• •y o, ••• •i•••• •l••• in•••n••• o• ••l••ion•• i• in•••n•••. W• w•i•• •l••• in•••n••• •• •n •nno•••• ••i•, $\langle\!\langle c \| f_1 : v_1, \ldots, f_i : v_i \rangle\!\rangle$, •on•• inin• • • ••• in• ••o• ••l• n•• •••o v•l••, •n• ••• o• j••••• •yn•• i• •y••, c. • •l••ion-•• i• in•••n••• ••• w•i•••n •• •n •nno•••• 5-••• l•, $\langle\!\langle r, \iota^{\mathtt{null}}, \iota_1, \iota_2 \| f_1 : v_1, \ldots, f_i : v_i \rangle\!\rangle$, •on•• inin• ••• ••• ili•••l• v•l•• • •• •n• •yn•• i• •y••, •• w•ll ••••• o•-j•••• •••••••••• ••• in•••n•• ••l•••, ι_1 •n• ι_2, •n• • ••••••n•• •o ••• ••l••ion•• i• in•••n••'• *super-instance*, $\iota^{\mathtt{null}}$; ••••i••lly, ••• in•••n•• o• r'• •••••-••l••ion•• i• w• i•• ••l•••• ••• ••• • o• j••• ••••••••• ι_1 •n• ι_2. W•••• $r = \mathsf{Relation}$, ••••• i• no ••••••-••l••ion•• i• •n• ••i• •••••n•• i• null. Fo• • o•• •y•• o• o• j•••, w• •••• $o(f)$ •n• dom(o) •• i• •••y w••• •••li•• •o o'• ••l• v•l•• • •••.

Dyn•• i• v•l••• (•• o••o••• •o •yn••••i• v•l•• li•••l•), ••n•• ov•• •y u, ••• •i•••• ••••••••, ••n••• ov•• •y ι, •••• o•••••••••, o• true, false o• null. A •• •ll-•••• ••• •n•i•• • ••n• •••• •x••••ion• • •y •• •i• •• •• only ••••i•lly •v•l••••, •o w• in•l••• •••• ••n-•i• • v•l••• •n• ••••i•lly-v•l••••• • ••• o• • o• i•• in l•n••••• •x••••ion• •y •x••n•in• Expression •• •ollow•:

$$e \in \mathsf{DynExpression} ::=$$

$u \mid$	dynamic values
$mb \mid$	method body
$\ldots$	terms from Expression grammar

DynLValue •n• DynStatement ••• ••n••••••• ••o• LValue •n• Statement in ••• o•vio•• w•y, •n• e, l •n• s will ••n•• ov•• ••••• n•w ••• ni•ion• ••o• ••i• • oin• onw•••.

A ••o••, σ, i• • • •• ••o• •••••••••• •o o• j••••, w•il• lo••l v••i••l•• ••• •iv•n v•l••• •y • lo••l• ••o••, λ. A ••l••ion•• i• ••o••, ρ • ••• ••l••ion•• i• •••l•• •o ••••••••• •••• •••• $\rho(r, \iota_1, \iota_2)$ in•i•••• ••• ••••••• o• ••• in•••n•• o• r w•i•• •xi••• •••w••n ι_1 •n• ι_2.

D••in• •x••••ion, ••• ••o•• •n• i•• •on••i••••n• o• j•••• ••• • o• i••• •y ••-•••in• ••• ••l•v•n• • ••. U•••• o• •o• • • •• f i• w•i•••n $f[a \mapsto b]$ •••• ••••

$\mathcal{E}_e \in$ ExpContext ::=

	$\bullet$	hole
	$\mathcal{E}_e.f$	field lookup
	$\mathcal{E}_e$ == $e \mid u$ == $\mathcal{E}_e$	equality test
	$\mathcal{E}_e$ + $e \mid u$ + $\mathcal{E}_e$	set addition
	$\mathcal{E}_e$ – $e \mid u$ – $\mathcal{E}_e$	set removal
	$\mathcal{E}_e.r \mid \mathcal{E}_e{:}r$	relationship access
	$\mathcal{E}_e.\texttt{from} \mid \mathcal{E}_e.\texttt{to}$	relationship from/to
	{ $\mathcal{E}$ return e; } | { return $\mathcal{E}_e$; }	method body
	$\mathcal{E}_e.f$ = $e \mid x = \mathcal{E}_e \mid u.f = \mathcal{E}_e$	assignment
	$\mathcal{E}_e.m(e') \mid u.m(\mathcal{E}_e)$	method call
	$r.\texttt{add}(\mathcal{E}_e,e') \mid r.\texttt{add}(u,\mathcal{E}_e)$	relationship addition
	$r.\texttt{rem}(\mathcal{E}_e,e') \mid r.\texttt{rem}(u,\mathcal{E}_e)$	relationship removal

$\mathcal{E}_s \in$ StatContext ::=

	$\mathcal{E}_e$; s	expression
	for $(n\ x : \mathcal{E}_e)$ $\{s_1\}$; s_2	set iteration
	if $(\mathcal{E}_e)$ $\{s_1\}$ else $\{s_2\}$; s_3	conditional

Fig. 5. Grammar for evaluation contexts

$f[a \mapsto b](a) = b$ •n• $f[a \mapsto b](c) = f(a)$ w•••• $a \neq c$. S••• •••••i•••ion• •••
•o• • only ••• li•• •o ••o••• $(\sigma[\iota \mapsto o])$ •n• •o o• j•••• $(o[f \mapsto v])$.

S•••i•••ion o• v••i••l•• in ••o•••• •yn••x •••• ••• •••n•••• no••ion,
$e[x'/x]$, •o• ••• •••l•••• •n• o• •ll v••i••l•• x in e wi•• x', •n• •i• il••ly wi••
•••••• •n••, $s[x'/x]$.

Fi•••• 5 •iv•• ••• •v•l••ion •on••x•• •o• RelJ •x•••••ion• •n• ••••• •n••.
All •on••x•• $\mathcal{E}$ •on••in • •ol•, ••no•••• •, w•i•• in•i••••• ••• •o•i•ion o• •••
•••-•x•••ion •o •• •v•l••••• ••••—in ••i• •••• ••• l•••-• o••, inn••-• o••. An
•x•••••ion • •y ••• •l•••• in • •on••x•'• •ol• •o•i•ion •y •••••i•••ion, ••no•••
$\mathcal{E}_e[e]$. No•i•• •••• w• no lon••• •i••in••i•• ••w••n •• o•• •x•••••ion• ••••• • •y
o• • •y no•• •• •••• in ••••••• •n• •o•i•ion.

A *configuration* in ••• ••• •n•i•• i• • 5-••••l• o• •y• in• •nvi•on• •n•, ••••,
••l••ion••i• ••o••, lo••l• • ••, •n• • ••••••• •n•: $\langle \Gamma, \sigma, \rho, \lambda, s \rangle$. An *error configuration* i• • •on•••••••ion $\langle \Gamma, \sigma, \rho, \lambda, w \rangle$, wi•• •n •••o• in •l••• o• • ••••••• •n•. Γ
i• in•l•••• •o• ••• ••oo• o• •y•• •o• n• n•••.

• x•••••ion •x•••••ion ••o••••• w••n • •••-•x•••••ion in • ol• •o•i•ion • •y ••
••••••••, ••••••i••• ••y OSCONTEXTE. W• •li•• •••• •i• il••• •l• •o• •x•••••ion•
in ••••••• •n• •on••x•:

$$(\text{OSCONTEXTE})\quad \frac{\langle \Gamma, \sigma, \rho, \lambda, e \rangle \overset{P}{\rightsquigarrow} \langle \Gamma', \sigma', \rho', \lambda', e' \rangle}{\langle \Gamma, \sigma, \rho, \lambda, \mathcal{E}_e[e] \rangle \overset{P}{\rightsquigarrow} \langle \Gamma', \sigma', \rho', \lambda', \mathcal{E}_e[e'] \rangle}$$

W• •l•o •x•••••• •••••• •n•• in•i•• • •••i• lly-•x••••• • •••o• • o• i••:

$$(\text{OSINBODY})\quad \frac{\langle \Gamma, \sigma, \rho, \lambda, s \rangle \overset{P}{\rightsquigarrow} \langle \Gamma', \sigma', \rho', \lambda', s' \rangle}{\langle \Gamma, \sigma, \rho, \lambda, \{\ s\ \texttt{return}\ e;\ \} \rangle \overset{P}{\rightsquigarrow} \langle \Gamma', \sigma', \rho', \lambda', \{\ s'\ \texttt{return}\ e;\ \} \rangle}$$

I• ••• •in• now •o ••• n• ••• •••• •••••• •o• ••• o••••••ion••l ••• •n•i••. W•
•••in wi•• RelJ'• •wo ••l••ion••i• o•••••ion• on •n o• j•••• •••••••, ι: •••ly, •••

$$\mathsf{newPart}_P(r, \iota^{\mathtt{null}}, \iota_1, \iota_2) = \langle\!\langle r, \iota^{\mathtt{null}}, \iota_1, \iota_2 \| f_1 : \mathsf{initial}_P(\mathcal{F}_{P,r}(f_1)), \dots, f_i : \mathsf{initial}_P(\mathcal{F}_{P,r}(f_i)) \rangle\!\rangle$$
$$\text{where } \{f_1, f_2, \dots, f_i\} = \mathsf{dom}(\mathcal{F}_{P,r})$$

$$\mathsf{addRel}_P(r, \iota_1, \iota_2, \sigma_1, \rho_1) = \begin{cases} (\sigma_1, \rho_1) & \text{if } \rho(r, \iota_1, \iota_2) = \iota'' \\ (\sigma_1[\iota \mapsto \mathsf{newPart}_P(r, \mathtt{null}, \iota_1, \iota_2)], \rho_1[(r, \iota_1, \iota_2) \mapsto \iota]) & \\ & \text{if } r = \mathtt{Relation} \\ (\sigma_3, \rho_3) & \text{otherwise} \end{cases}$$
$$\text{where } \iota \notin \mathsf{dom}(\sigma_1) \text{ or } \mathsf{dom}(\sigma_2)$$
$$r \neq \mathtt{Relation} \Rightarrow \mathcal{R}_P(r) = (r', \_, \_, \_)$$
$$(\sigma_2, \rho_2) = \mathsf{addRel}_P(r', \iota_1, \iota_2, \sigma_1, \rho_1)$$
$$\sigma_3 = \sigma_2[\iota \mapsto \mathsf{newPart}_P(r, \rho_2(r', \iota_1, \iota_2), \iota_1, \iota_2)]$$
$$\rho_3 = \rho_2[(r, \iota_1, \iota_2) \mapsto \iota]$$

$$\mathsf{remRel}_P(r, \iota_1, \iota_2, \rho) = \rho \setminus \{((r', \iota_1, \iota_2) \mapsto \iota) \mid \; \vdash r' \leq r\}$$

$$\mathsf{fldUpd}(\sigma, f, \iota, u) = \begin{cases} \sigma[\iota \mapsto \sigma(\iota)[f \mapsto u]] & \text{if } f \in \mathsf{dom}(\sigma(\iota)) \\ \mathsf{fldUpd}(\sigma, f, \iota', u) & \text{if } \sigma(\iota) = \langle\!\langle r, \iota', \_, \_\| \dots \rangle\!\rangle \end{cases}$$

Fig. 6. Definitions of auxiliary functions for creating relationship instances (newPart), for putting objects in relationships (addRel) and for removing objects from relationships (remRel). fldUpd demonstrates delegation of field updates to super-relationship instances

o• j•••• ••l•••• •o ι •y ••l••ion••i• r • •y •• ••••••••• ••in• $e.r$; •••on• ly, ••• in•••n••• o• r •••• ••l••• ••o•• o• j•••• •o ι •y •• ••••••••• wi•• $e:r$ •o •••• ••l••ion•• i• ••••i• •••• • •y •• •••• o• • o•i••• :

OSRELOBJ: $\langle \Gamma, \sigma, \rho, \lambda, \iota.r \rangle \overset{P}{\leadsto} \langle \Gamma, \sigma, \rho, \lambda, \{\iota' \mid \exists \iota'' : \rho(r, \iota, \iota') = \iota''\}\rangle$

OSRELOBJN: $\langle \Gamma, \sigma, \rho, \lambda, \mathtt{null}.r \rangle \overset{P}{\leadsto} \langle \Gamma, \sigma, \rho, \lambda, \mathsf{NullPtrError}\rangle$

OSRELINST: $\langle \Gamma, \sigma, \rho, \lambda, \iota{:}r \rangle \overset{P}{\leadsto} \langle \Gamma, \sigma, \rho, \lambda, \{\iota'' \mid \exists \iota' : \rho(r, \iota, \iota') = \iota''\}\rangle$

OSRELOBJ •n• OSRELOBJN •iv• ••• ••• •n•i•• •o• o•••inin• ••• o• j•••• ••l•••• •o ι •••o••• r. No•i•• •••• ••• ••••l• i• no• j••• • • ••••• o• loo•in•-•• ••• ••••l• in • •••l•; ••• o• j•••• ••• •o•n• •y •••yin• ρ. I• $\mathtt{null}$ i• ••• ••••••• o• ••• loo••••, • n•ll-•oin••• •••o• o•••••. Si• il•• ••l•• ••• l••• •o• ••• •••• •n•ix.

T•• •••••o-••l•• $\mathtt{from}$ •n• $\mathtt{to}$ ••ovi•• ••••••• •o ••• o• j•••• •••w••n w•i•• • ••l••ion•• i• in•••n•• •xi•••, ••••• •nin• ••• •o• ••• •n• ••••in••ion o• j•••• ••- •• ••••iv• ly:

OSFROM: $\langle \Gamma, \sigma, \rho, \lambda, \iota.\mathtt{from} \rangle \overset{P}{\leadsto} \langle \Gamma, \sigma, \rho, \lambda, \iota' \rangle$ where $\sigma(\iota) = \langle\!\langle \_, \_, \iota', \_\|\_\rangle\!\rangle$

OSTO: $\langle \Gamma, \sigma, \rho, \lambda, \iota.\mathtt{to} \rangle \overset{P}{\leadsto} \langle \Gamma, \sigma, \rho, \lambda, \iota' \rangle$ where $\sigma(\iota) = \langle\!\langle \_, \_, \_, \iota'\|\_\rangle\!\rangle$

OSRELADD •n• OSRELREM •iv• ••• •n•i•• •o ••• ••l••ion•• i• •••i•ion •n• ••• ov••l o•••••o•• $\mathtt{add}$ •n• $\mathtt{rem}$ ••••••iv•ly, •n• ••• ••••• •n•i••ly on addRel •n• remRel ••o• Fi•. 6:

OSRELADD: $\langle \Gamma, \sigma_1, \rho_1, \lambda, r.\mathtt{add}(\iota_1, \iota_2) \rangle \overset{P}{\leadsto} \langle \Gamma, \sigma_2, \rho_2, \lambda, \iota_3 \rangle$
  where $(\sigma_2, \rho_2) = \mathsf{addRel}_P(r, \iota_1, \iota_2, \sigma_1, \rho_1)$ and $\iota_3 = \rho_2(r, \iota_1, \iota_2)$

OSRELREM1: $\langle \Gamma, \sigma, \rho_1, \lambda, r.\mathtt{rem}(\iota_1, \iota_2)\rangle \overset{P}{\leadsto} \langle \Gamma, \sigma, \rho_2, \lambda, \rho_1(r, \iota_1, \iota_2)\rangle$
        where $(r, \iota_1, \iota_2) \in \mathsf{dom}(\rho_1)$ and $\rho_2 = \mathsf{remRel}_P(r, \iota_1, \iota_2, \rho_1)$

OSRELREM2: $\langle \Gamma, \sigma, \rho, \lambda, r.\mathtt{rem}(\iota_1, \iota_2)\rangle \overset{P}{\leadsto} \langle \Gamma, \sigma, \rho, \lambda, \mathtt{null}\rangle$
        where $(r, \iota_1, \iota_2) \notin \mathsf{dom}(\rho)$

addRel •••• •n in•••n•• o• r •••w••n ι_1 •n• ι_2 i• •••• •n in•••n•• •o•• no•
•l•••• y •xi••. Wi•• • •••••iv• ••ll, i• •l•o •n••••• •••• in•••n••• o• r' ••••••-
••l••ion•• i• •xi•• •••w••n ι_1 •n• ι_2, •n•••in• Inv••i•n• 1 i• • •in••in••.

remRel ••• ov••• •n in•••n•• o• r ••o• •••w••n ι_1 •n• ι_2, ••• •o•• *not* •l••• •••
••••, only ••• ••l••ion•• i• ••o••, ρ. A••in, •o • •in••in Inv••i•n• 1, •ll in•••n•••
o• ••• -••l••ion•• i• •o r ••• •i• il••ly ••• ov•• ••o• •••w••n ι_1 •n• ι_2.

In ••• • •••• o• • ••l••ion•• i• •••i•ion in •x••••ion •on••x•, • •••••••n•• i•
••••••n•• •o ••• ••l••ion•• i• in•••n•• •••• w•• ••••••. • ••l••ion•• i• ••• ov•l •v•l-
•••••• •o ••• in•••n•• •••• w•• ••• ov••, i• •ny. W•••• no •••• in•••n•• •xi•••,
null i• ••••• •n••.

Fi•l• •••••• i• •••••o•• •• wi•• •n ••xili••y •• n••ion fldUpd, •l•o •o• n• in
Fi•. 6, w•i•• ••• on••••••• ••• ••l•••••ion o•• ••l• loo••• •o ••••••-••l••ion•• i•
in•••n•••:

OSFLDASS: $\langle \Gamma, \sigma, \rho, \lambda, \iota.f = u\rangle \overset{P}{\leadsto} \langle \Gamma, \mathsf{fldUpd}(\sigma, \iota, f, u), \rho, \lambda, u\rangle$

W• •on•l••• o•• •i•••••ion o•• ••• o•••••ion•l ••• •n•i•• wi•• ••• •wo •i•-
••• •••n••• in w•i•• v••i•• l•• ••• ••o••• —• •••o• ••ll, •n• ••• for i••••o•.

T•• ••• •n•i•• •o• • •••o• ••ll i• •iv•n in OSCALL. A•••••• •o ••• •o•• •l
••••• ••••, x, lo••l v••i•• l••, $x_{1..i}$, •n• this • ••• •• ••o••• wi••in ••• • o• y
o• m, •o w• •••••• n ••••• •yn•••• i• n•• ••• •o x', $x'_{1..i}$ •n• x'_{this} in ••• ••yl• o•
D•o••o• o• lo• ••• •l. [•].

OSCALL: $\langle \Gamma_1, \sigma, \rho, \lambda_1, \iota.m(u)\rangle \overset{P}{\leadsto} \langle \Gamma_2, \sigma, \rho, \lambda_2, \{ s_2\ \mathtt{return}\ e_2; \}\rangle$
        where
            $\sigma(\iota) = \langle\!\langle n \| \ldots \rangle\!\rangle$ or $\sigma(\iota) = \langle\!\langle n, \_, \_, \_ \| \ldots \rangle\!\rangle$
            $\mathcal{MD}_{P,n}(m) = (x, \mathcal{L}, t_1, \_, s_1\ \mathtt{return}\ e_1;)$
            $\mathsf{dom}(\mathcal{L}) = \{x_1, \ldots, x_i\}$
            $x', x'_{\mathsf{this}}, x'_1, \ldots, x'_i \notin \mathsf{dom}(\lambda_1)$
            $\Gamma_2 = \Gamma_1[x' \mapsto t_1][x'_{\mathsf{this}} \mapsto n][x'_{1..i} \mapsto \mathcal{L}(x_{1..i})]$
            $\lambda_2 = \lambda_1[x' \mapsto u][x'_{\mathsf{this}} \mapsto \iota][x'_{1..i} \mapsto \mathsf{initial}(\Gamma_2(x'_{1..i}))]$
            $s_2 = s_1[x'/x][x'_{1..i}/x_{1..i}][x'_{\mathsf{this}}/\mathtt{this}]$
            $e_2 = e_1[x'/x][x'_{1..i}/x_{1..i}][x'_{\mathsf{this}}/\mathtt{this}]$

W• •x••n• ••• •y•in• •nvi•on• •n•, Γ_2, wi•• n•w lo••l v••i•• l• •y•• • in• in••
•o• ••• •••••• n•• ••• (•• w•ll •• ••o•• •o• ••• •o•• •l •••••• •••• •n• this), •n•
in•l••• ••••o••i••• ini•i•l v•l••• in ••• lo••l• ••o••, λ_2. Fin•lly, ••• ol• •yn-
••••i• n•• ••• ••• ••••••• in ••• • •••o• •o•y, s, •n• return •x••••ion, e, •y
••• ••i••ion.

A •i• il•• ••••••••y i• •••• •o •voi• •in•in• •l••••• •o• ••• for i••••o•:

OSFOR1: $\langle \Gamma, \sigma, \rho, \lambda, \mathtt{for}\ (n\ x : \emptyset)\ \{s_1\}; s_2\rangle \overset{P}{\leadsto} \langle \Gamma, \sigma, \rho, \lambda, s_2\rangle$

OSFOR2: $\langle \Gamma_1, \sigma, \rho, \lambda_1, \text{for } (n\ x\ :\ u)\ \{s_1\}; s_2 \rangle \overset{P}{\rightsquigarrow}$

$\langle \Gamma_2, \sigma, \rho, \lambda_2, s_3\ \text{for } (n\ x\ :\ (u \setminus \iota))\ \{s_1\}; s_2 \rangle$

where

$\iota \in u, x \neq x' \notin \text{dom}(\lambda_1)$

$\Gamma_2 = \Gamma_1[x' \mapsto x], \lambda_2 = \lambda_1[x' \mapsto \iota], s_3 = s_1[x'/x]$

I•••••ion o• ••• •• ••y ••• •v•l••••• i• • ••i•••ly •o '••i• ', w• il• i••••••ion ov••• ••• non-•• ••y ••• •i••• •n •l•• •n• ••o• ••• •••, •••i•n• •• i• •o ••• i•••••o• v••i••l•, •n• •n•ol•• ••• ••••••• •n• •lo••, in w•i•• ••• • •o•n• i•••••o• v••i••l• i• •••••••n••. W• •o no• •••i•y ••• o•••• in w•i•• ••• •l•• •n•• o• u ••• •o•n• •o x.

5   Soundness

In •• i• ••••ion w• o• •lin• • •oo••• o• •wo ••y •••••y ••o• •••i••: ••• • no •y• •-•o••••• ••o••• will ••• '••••••'—•x•••• in • w•ll-••••n•• •••o• •••••—•n• •••• •y••• ••• • ••••••y•• ••• •in• ••o•••• •x•••••ion.

Fi••••ly, •ow•v••, w• •••n• •o• • w•ll-•o••• ••n••• ••o••••i•• o• ••o•••• •n• v•l•••, •o •••• w• ••n ••••• •y•• ••••••••v••ion •••o••• ••• j••• •••••••••ion.

Value Typing and Well-Formedness

W• •••••n• o• • •y• in• ••l••ion •o in•l••• ••• ••o••, σ, •o •••• v•l••• • •y •• •y• ••• —••••i•• l••ly i• • o•••n• •o• •• owin• ••• j••••-•••••••ion. Ty• in•• o• true •n• false wi•• boolean, •n• o• null wi•• •ny v•li• no• in•l •y• • ••• •li•••.

Fi••••ly, •n ••••••• ••• • •y••, n, i• ••• o• j••• •• •••• • •••• •••• in ••• ••o•• ••• • •yn•• i• •y•• (w•i••n $\text{dynType}(\sigma(\iota))$) ••• o•• in••• •o n. T•i• •on• i•ion i• •••n • ••••• ov•• ••• • •• •••• o• • ••• o• •• • ••••••• in DTSET:

(DTADDR)

$$\frac{\vdash \text{dynType}(\sigma(\iota)) \leq n}{P, \Gamma, \sigma \vdash \iota : n}$$

(DTSET)

$$\frac{P \vdash n \qquad \forall j \in 1..i : P, \Gamma, \sigma \vdash \iota_j : n}{P, \Gamma, \sigma \vdash \{\iota_1, \ldots, \iota_i\} : \text{set<n>}}$$

W• •l•o ••ovi••• • •y• in• ••l• •o• ••• • ••• o• •o•y •on••••••ion in••o••••• in Fi•. 5:

(DTMETHBODY)

$$\frac{P, \Gamma, \sigma \vdash s \qquad P, \Gamma, \sigma \vdash e : t}{P, \Gamma, \sigma \vdash \{\ s\ \text{return }e;\ \} : t}$$

W• • ••• ••• o• • 'w•ll-•o••• •• o• j•••' ••l••ion, $P, \sigma \vdash o \diamond_{\text{inst}}$, w••n o i• • w•ll-•o••• •• o• j••• in •o• • ••o••, ••• ••l•• •o• w•i•• •ollow:

(WFFIELD)

$$\frac{\text{dynType}(o) = n \qquad \mathcal{FD}_{P,n}(f) = t \qquad P, \emptyset, \sigma \vdash o(f) : t}{P, \sigma, o \vdash f \diamond_{\text{fld}}}$$

WFFIELD •••••• •••• ••• ••|• f ••○••• • v•|•• ○• •••••○••i••• •y•• •○• i••
••• ni•ion in •|••• ○• ••|••ion••i• n, •••○•• in• ••• • yn•• i• •y• in• ••|••ion •iv•n
•• ○v•. T•i• ••|••ion i• • •••••• •••○•• ••• ••|•• ○• •|••••• •n• ••|••ion••i•• in
••• •ollowin• ••|••:

$$\text{(WFOBJECT1)} \qquad\qquad \text{(WFRELINST1)}$$
$$\frac{}{P, \sigma \vdash \langle\!\langle \mathtt{Object} \| \rangle\!\rangle \diamond_{\mathsf{inst}}} \qquad \frac{\iota_1, \iota_2 \in \mathsf{dom}(\sigma)}{P, \sigma \vdash \langle\!\langle \mathtt{Relation}, \mathtt{null}, \iota_1, \iota_2 \| \rangle\!\rangle \diamond_{\mathsf{inst}}}$$

$$\text{(WFRELINST2)}$$
$$\mathcal{R}_P(r) = (\mathsf{dynType}(\sigma(\iota)), n_1, n_2, \mathcal{F}, \_)$$
$$\{f_1, \ldots, f_i\} = \mathsf{dom}(\mathcal{F})$$
$$\forall j \in 1..i : P, \sigma, o \vdash f_j \diamond_{\mathsf{fld}}$$
$$\vdash \mathsf{dynType}(\sigma(\iota_1)) \leq n_1$$

$$\text{(WFOBJECT2)}$$
$$\vdash \mathsf{dynType}(\sigma(\iota_2)) \leq n_2$$
$$\{f_1, \ldots, f_i\} = \mathsf{dom}(\mathcal{FD}_{P,c})$$
$$\frac{\forall j \in 1..i : P, \sigma, o \vdash f_j \diamond_{\mathsf{fld}}}{P, \sigma \vdash \langle\!\langle c \| f_1 : v_1, \ldots, f_i : v_i \rangle\!\rangle \diamond_{\mathsf{inst}}} \qquad \frac{}{P, \sigma \vdash \langle\!\langle r, \iota, \iota_1, \iota_2 \| f_1 : v_1, \ldots, f_i : v_i \rangle\!\rangle \diamond_{\mathsf{inst}}}$$

WFOBJECT1 •n• WFRELINST1 ••••i•y •••• in•••n••• ○• Object •n•
Relation, ••••••iv•ly, ••• v•li•. WFOBJECT2, ••••i••• ••••• •|| ••|•• ••• w•ll-
•○•• •• •n• •••• ••• •|••• in•••n•• ••• ••••i••ly ••○•• ••|•• ••••• w••• •••|••••
○• in••i•••. WFRELINST2, •••••• •••• only ••○•• ••|•• immediately •••|••••
in r ••• •••••n• in ••• ••|••ion••i• in•••n••; •••• ••○•• ••|•• ••• w•ll-•○•• ••;
••• ••• ••• •••••-in•••n••, •• ι, i• •••••n•, •n• •••• • yn•• i• •y• ••••|•○ r'• ••-
•••y• •; •n• •••• ••• r-in•••n•• •i•• •••w••n •wo in•••n••• ○• •••••○••i••• •y••
•••○••in• •○ r' ••• ni•ion.

W• •••••• •••• ••• ••|••ion••i••• ••• ••○••ly •••i••• in ρ •••○••in• •○ •••
•ollowin• •wo ••|••:

$$\text{(WFRELATION1)}$$
$$\frac{\sigma(\rho(\mathtt{Relation}, \iota_1, \iota_2)) = \langle\!\langle \mathtt{Relation}, \mathtt{null}, \iota_1, \iota_2 \| \rangle\!\rangle}{P, \sigma, \rho \vdash (\mathtt{Relation}, \iota_1, \iota_2) \diamond_{\mathsf{rel}}}$$

$$\text{(WFRELATION2)}$$
$$\mathcal{R}_P(r) = (r', \_, \_, \_, \_)$$
$$(r', \iota_1, \iota_2) \in \mathsf{dom}(\rho)$$
$$\frac{\sigma(\rho(r, \iota_1, \iota_2)) = \langle\!\langle r, \rho(r', \iota_1, \iota_2), \iota_1, \iota_2 \| \ldots \rangle\!\rangle}{P, \sigma, \rho \vdash (r, \iota_1, \iota_2) \diamond_{\mathsf{rel}}}$$

WFRELATION2 •n••••• •••• ••• ••• r-in•••n•• •••w••n ι_1 •n• ι_2 •••• • ••••••-
in•••n•• •••• •|•○ •i•• •••w••n ι_1 •n• ι_2. WFRELATION1 •••• ••• • •••••-•••• •○•
Relation, in•••n••• ○• w•i•• •○ no• •••• • •••••-in•••n••.

W• •••n • ••• ••• •on•i•ion• •○• w•ll-•○•• •• in•••n•••, ••|••ion• •n• lo••l
v•i•• •|•• ov•• ••• ••••, σ, ••• ••|••ion••i• ••••, ρ, •n• ••• lo••l• • ••, λ:

$$\text{(WFHEAP)} \qquad\qquad \text{(WFRELHEAP)}$$
$$\frac{\forall \iota \in \mathsf{dom}(\sigma) : P, \sigma \vdash \sigma(\iota) \diamond_{\mathsf{inst}}}{P \vdash \sigma \diamond_{\mathsf{heap}}} \qquad \frac{\forall (r, \iota_1, \iota_2) \in \mathsf{dom}(\rho) : P, \sigma, \rho \vdash (r, \iota_1, \iota_2) \diamond_{\mathsf{rel}}}{P, \sigma \vdash \rho \diamond_{\mathsf{relheap}}}$$

(WFLocals)
$$\frac{\forall x \in \mathsf{dom}(\Gamma) : P, \Gamma, \sigma \vdash \lambda(x) : \Gamma(x)}{P, \Gamma, \sigma \vdash \lambda \diamond_{\mathsf{locals}}}$$

W• •on•i••• • •on•••••••ion $\langle \Gamma, \sigma, \rho, \lambda, s \rangle$ •o •• w•ll-•o•• •• w••n σ, ρ •n• λ ••• w•ll-•o•• ••, •n• w•••• s i• •y••-•o•••••. • ••o• •on•••••••ion•, $\langle \Gamma, \sigma, \rho, \lambda, w \rangle$, ••• w•ll-•o•• •• • n••• •i• il•• •on• i•ion•.

Safety

Ty•• ••••y i• •• own •y • ••• j••• ••••••••ion •••o••• , ••n•••l •o w• i•• i• ••• i••• ••••• •on••x• ••••••i••• •ion •••• •••• •y• ••:

Lemma 1 (Substitution). *For expressions e_1 and e_2, which are typed t_1 and t_2 respectively, where t_2 is a subtype of t_1 and where $\mathcal{E}_e[e_1]$ is typed t_3, then $\mathcal{E}_e[e_2]$ has a subtype of t_3.*

T•• • •oo• •ollow•• •y in• •••ion on ••• ••••• •••• •• o•••• •y• in• •••iv••ion. N•x•, w• •• ow •y• • • •••••••v••ion, w• i•• •ollow• n•••••lly ••o• ••• • •••vio••l•• • •, •n• • y in• •••ion on ••• •••••• •••• •• o•••• •••iv••ion o• •x••• •ion:

Theorem 1 (Subject Reduction). *In a well-typed program, P, where $\langle \Gamma_1, \sigma_1, \rho_1, \lambda_1, s_1 \rangle$ executes to a new configuration $\langle \Gamma_2, \sigma_2, \rho_2, \lambda_2, s_2 \rangle$, that configuration will be well-formed. Furthermore, $\Gamma_1 \subseteq \Gamma_2$ and all objects in σ_1 retain their dynamic type in σ_2.*

Similarly where the original configuration executes to an error configuration.

Fin• lly, w• •• ow ••••• w•ll-•y••• ••o•••• • •y • lw•y• •••o•• •n •x••• •ion •••• :

Theorem 2 (Progress). *For all well-typed programs, P, all well-formed configurations $\langle \Gamma_1, \sigma_1, \rho_1, \lambda_1, s_1 \rangle$ execute to either:*

i. an error configuration $\langle \Gamma_2, \sigma_2, \rho_2, \lambda_2, w \rangle$, or
ii. a new statement configuration $\langle \Gamma_2, \sigma_2, \rho_2, \lambda_2, s_2 \rangle$

By T••o••• • 1 •n• •, •ny w•ll-•y••• ••o•••• ••n • •••• • •••• •o • n•w w•ll-•o•• •• •on•••••••ion: w•ll-•y••• ••o•••• • •o no• •o w•on•.

6   Restricting Multiplicities

In UML, •••o•i••ion•• •n •• •nno••••• wi•• *multiplicities*, w• i•• •••••i•• ••• n•• ••• o• in•••n••• •••• • •y •••• •••• in •ny •iv•n ••l••ion. Fo• •x•• •l•, i• •o•l• •• ••••• •v••y •••• •n• ••••n•• •x••ly •i••• •o•••••, ••• •••••• •o•••• • •y ••v• •ny n•• ••• o• ••••••n••:

Mo•• •xo•i• • •l•i• li•i•i•• ••n in•l••• ••n••• ('1..•'), •n• •o• • •-••••••••• ••n••• ('1..•, 10..*'). T•••• ••• • n•• ••• o• w•y• in w• i•• •••• •••••i••ion• •o• l• •• •x• ••••••• in RelJ. W• ••••••i•• •••low •o•• • fl•xi•l•, ••• •yn•• i••lly •••••••• •••••o•••, •• w•ll ••• • • o•• •••••i••••, ••••i••lly ••••••• •••••o•••.

6.1   Dynamic Approach

T•• ••• o• • •• n-•i• • •••••• •• •v••y ••l••ion•• i• •••i•ion wo• l• • llow •• •o
•••••••n• • o•• o• ••• • o••i• l• • • l•i• li•i•i•• •••• ••n •• •x••••••• in UML.
W••n, ••y, •oo • •ny •o•••• ••• •••••• •o ••• Attends ••l••ion•• i• , •n •x••• •ion
•o• l• •• ••i•••:

```
relationship Attends (many Student, 2 Course) { int mark; }
...
Attends.add(alice, programming);
Attends.add(alice, semantics);
Attends.add(alice, types);        // Exception!
```

W• ••vi••• ••o• UML •li•••ly: •n •••o•i••ion •nno••••• •• on• •n• wi•• '•'
wo• l• •lw•y• ••v• •x•••ly •wo •••o•i•••• in•••n•••. In•••••, w• in•••••• o•• 2
•nno•••ion on Course •• '0..•' in UML no••ion: •••• i•, •o••••• ••••• wi••o••
•ny •••• •n••.

6.2   Static Approach

• ••• ••••••••n••, •ow•v••, i• •o• • ••••i• •••••o••• •o ••• •x•••••ion o• • •l•i-
•li•i•i•. W•il• l••• fl•xi•l•, w• n••• no• ••n••••• •on•••• in-•••••• in• •o•• •o•
••l••ion•• i• •••i•ion•, •n• w• ••ovi•• • o•• •o•••• ••••n••••• ••• ••• • •l•i-
•li•i•y •on•••• in•• ••• ••i••••. • ••••• ••n •iv• ••• •o•• •l ••••il•, w• ••• ll •iv•
•n ov••vi•w o• ••i• •x••n•ion •o RelJ.

    W• only •llow one •n• many •nno•••ion•. T•• •o•• •• i• ••• iv•l•n• •o '0..1'
in UML, ••• l••••• •o '0..*':

```
relationship Attends (many Student, many Course);
relationship Failed (many PassedStudent, one Course);
```

In ••• •••l•••ion• •• ov•, w• ••• •••• •••• ••n••' •o•••• ••••n••n•• i• •n••••i••••,
••• •••• • PassedStudent • •y ••v• ••il•• ••• • o•• on• •o••••.

    W• •• ••••• ••••••i•• ••l••ion•• i• in••i••n•• •o ••••• • • •ny-•o-on• ••l••ion-
•• i• • •y only in••i• ••o• • • • •ny-•o-on• o• • • •ny-•o- •ny ••l••ion•• i•. W•
i• • •o•• •i• il•• ••••••i••ion• on • •ny-•o- •ny •n• on•-•o- •ny ••l••ion•• i• •••-
ini•ion•. W• •••n ••• •o ••• inv••i•n•• o• S•••. •.

Invariant 3. *For a relationship r, declared "relationship r (n_1, n_2)",
where n_1 is annotated with **one**, there is at most one n_1-instance related through
r to every n_2-instance. The converse is true where n_2 is annotated with **one**.*

    T•••• i• • ••n•ion ••w••n Inv••i•n•• 1 •n• 3. • on•i••• ••• •ollowin• ••l•-
•ion•• i• ••• ni•ion•, w•••• • •o•••• ••n only •• •••••• ••y • •in•l• l•••••••, •n•
w•••• l••••••••• •njoy ••••• in• •••• •o••••, ••• ••••• •••• •lowly:

```
relationship Teaches (one Lecturer, many Course);
relationship ExcitedlyTeaches extends Teaches
                        (one Lecturer, many HardCourse);
```

```
relationship SlowlyTeaches extends Teaches
                        (one Lecturer, many HardCourse);

charlie = new Lecturer();
deirdre = new Lecturer();
advancedWidgets = new HardCourse();
```

S••• o•• •••• charlie ExcitedlyTeaches advancedWidgets, •••n •y Inv••i-
•n• 1, charlie •l•o Teaches advancedWidgets.

Now ••••o•• •••• deirdre i• •o •lowly ••••• advancedWidgets:

```
SlowlyTeaches.add(deirdre, advancedWidgets);
```

By Inv••i•n• 1, deirdre • ••• •l•o •• ••l•••• •o advancedWidgets vi•
Teaches. How•v••, •y Inv••i•n• 3, charlie •n• deirdre ••nno• *both* Teach
advancedWidgets. In o•• •o•• •li••• ••• •n•i••, w• ••• ov• charlie ••o•
Teaches wi•• advancedWidgets: ••• add •••o• •• •n •••i•n• •n•, •••••• •••n
•n ••• i•ion, in ••i• ••••. F•••••• o••, •y Inv••i•n• 1, charlie ••nno• •• in
ExcitedlyTeaches wi•• advancedWidgets on•• •• ••• •••n ••• ov•• ••o•
Teaches—••••••o••, •• i• •l•o ••• ov•• ••o• ExcitedlyTeaches.

T• i• •••• vio••, w•••• no• only •••-••l••ion•• i• o• r •••• •l••••• •y • ••• n••
•o r'• •on••n••, •••• o••i•ly •l•o ••• •on••n•• o••••n•• •n• •i• lin•• o• r, • i•••
•••• • n•x• •••••. A••• ••• • •i• •, •••y • ••• ••n•• w••n •x•• inin• •x•• •l••,
•n• ••ovi•• • • ••n• •o• •voi• in• ••n-•i• • •••••••.

7   Conclusion

In ••i• •••••, w• ••v• •••••n••• RelJ, • •o•• ••••• •n• o• J•v• •••• off••• ••••-
•l••• •••• o•• •o• •••••l••• ••l••ion•• i••. Unli•• o•••• wo••, w• ••v• •o•• •lly
••••i••• o•• l•n•••••; •ivin• • ••••• ••i••l ••• ni•ion• o• i•• •y•• •y•••• •n•
o••••••ion•l ••• •n•i••. • iv•n •••• ••• ni•ion• w• ••• ••l• ••ov• •n i• •o•••n•
•o•••••n••• ••o• •••y o• o•• l•n•••••.

7.1   Related Work

Mo••llin• l•n••••••• li•• UML [9] •n• • • -•i••••• • [5] ••ovi•• •••o•i••ion• •n•
••l••ion•• i• ••• •o•• •••••••••ion•. S•v•••l ••••••• •y•••• •, •o• •x•• •l• o• j•••
••••••••• ••••••in• •o ••• • DM• •••n•••• [1•], •l•o ••ovi•• ••l••ion•• i• ••
••i• i•iv••. Un•o••• n•••ly, ••o•••• • in• l•n•••••• ••ovi•• no ••••-•l••• •••••••
•o •••• ••i• i•iv••, •o w••• API• • ••• •• •••• in•••••.

A• w• • •n•ion•• •••li••, ••• ••••• [13] w•• ••• •••• •o • oin• o• •••••
••l••ion•• i• ••v• •n i• •o•••n• •ôl• •o •l•y in ••n•••l o• j•••-o•i•n••• l•n•••••,
•n• ••v• •n in•o•• •l ••••i••ion o• l•n••••• ••••• on S• •ll••l•. How•v••, •••
• ••••• o• ••l••ion•• i• in••i••n•• w•• • •n•ion•• only •• •n •n•lo••• •o •l•••
in••i••n••, •n• ••••• w• no •o•• •l•••••• •n• o•••i• o•••• l•n••••••••• w•ol•.

No• l• •••• ••••••n••• •o• • •••••••n• •o• ••o•••• • in• wi•• ••l••ion•• i•• [10].
In ••••, • •ny o• •••••• •••••••n• •o•l• •• ••••• in •••n•l••in• RelJ ••o•••• • •o

'•••' J•v•. No• l• •n• • ••n• y •l•o •••••••••• ••••• ••l••ion•• i•• ••• o• l• ••• • •••
•x• li•i• in o• j•••-o•i•n••• ••o•••• [11]. A••in, n•i•••• wo•• ••ovi••• •ny •on-
••••• ••••il• o• l•n••••• •••••o•• •o• ••l••ion•• i••.

A•••• •o• •l••in• ••• •••• ••••• o• ••i• wo•• w• •i••ov•••• ••• •••••• •y
Al••no, ••lli•n• • ••ini [1], w•i•• ••••i••• • l•n••••• ••••• on •••o•i••ion•
(••l••ion•• i••) •o• ••• in •n o• j•••-o•i•n••• •••••••• •nvi•on• •n•. T••i• ••••
• o••l i• ••i•• •iff•••n• ••o• o•••; •o• •x•• •l•, •••y •••• •l••••• •• •on••in•••,
o• •x••n•• [1•]. T••• v•l••• ••n in••i• • •l•i•l• •l••••, •n• •l••••• •l•o ••• •o••
• • •l•i•l• in••i••n••. In ••••, •l••••• ••n o•• •o ••• •n••y •••o•i••ion•, w•i•• i•
••• •o•• •••••••••ion in Al••no ••• •l.'• • o••l.

T••i• • o••l •l•o ••ovi•• • •i•• ••n•• o• •on•••in••; •o• •x•• •l•, •••j••-
•ivi•y •n• ••••in•li•y •on•••in•• •o• •••o•i••ion•, •n• •i•join•n••• •on•••in••
on •l••••. T•••• ••• •o• •il•• •o ••• ••••o•i••• ••n•i• • •••••••. (T••y ••••
••v•n•••• o• ••• • •n••lyin• •••••••• in•••••••••• •n• ••ili•• ••i••••• •n•
•••n•••ion•.) Fin•lly, •••y •iv• no •o•• •l ••••i••ion o•••• l•n•••••.

• •• wo••, in •on•••••, •••••• •• i•• •••••in• •oin• ••• J•v• o• j••• • o••l •n•
••n•• • ••• o•••• •o• •l•xi•y o• Al••no ••• •l.'• • o••l i• •i• •ly no• •v•il••l•.
How•v••, • no•ion o• '•on••in••' ••n •• ••ily •o••• ••. Fi••• •••• • • •l•••
Singleton •n• • •in•l• o• j••• o• ••••• •l•••, ••ll•• default. W ••n ••n ••• •n•
•on••in•• •o• ••• Person •n• Student •l••••• o• Fi•. • •• •ollow• (w•••• w•
•••••• • • •••••-••l••ion•• i• Extent •••w••n Singleton •n• Object •l•••••).

```
relationship Persons extends Extent
                  (Singleton, Person) {
}
relationship Students extends Persons
                  (Singleton, Student) {
}
```

So •o •l••• Tom in ••• Persons •on••in•• w• •i• •ly w•i••
Persons.add(default, Tom). Si• il••ly Students.add(default, Jerry)
wo•l• ••• ••• o• j••• Jerry •o ••• Students •on••in••, •n• •y ••l•••ion •l•o
in ••• Persons •on••in••. T•• •x••••ion default.Persons wo•l• •••••n •••
••••••n• •on••n•• o• ••• Persons •on••in••. (Syn•••i• ••••• •o•l• •••ily ••
•••••• •o • ••• ••i• •o•• • li••l• • o•• •o• ••••.)

In•••••• in ••l••ion•• i•• i• no• •••••i••• •o • o••llin• •n• ••o•••• • in• l•n-
•••••••. In ••• •i• •••••• • o• ••• n•x• ••n••••ion o• Mi••o•o•• Win• ow•, •o••-
n•• •• 'Lon••o•n', ••• Win• ow• ••o•••• •••y•••• will •• ••l•••• wi•• • n•w
•y•••• ••ll•• *WinFS*. WinFS ••ovi•••• • •••••••-li••• •l• ••o••, ••• •o•• o•w•i••
i•• •oll•••ion o• *items*, li•• o• j••••, w•i•• ••••••••n• •••• •••• •• i• ••••, • ••loo•
•on•••••, •n• ••••-•••n•• i••• •. T•• o•••• ••y •o• •on•n• o• ••• WinFS ••••
• o••l i• ••l••ion•• i••, w•i•• ••• ••• n•• ••w••n i••• •. WinFS •••• •••••••n••
•• • ov• •w•y ••o• ••• ••••i•ion•l ••••-••••• •l• •y•••• •i••••••y •o •n •••i-
•••••y •••••-••••• •l• •y•••• , w•••• ••• ••y •••••••••ion i• ••• ••l••ion•• i•. A•
••• •i• • o• w•i•in•, ••••il• o• ••• API •o• WinFS ••• •••••••, ••• i• i• •l••••••
• l•n••••• •••• •• RelJ wo•l• ••ovi••• • o•• •i•••• ••o•••• • in• •••• •wo••,
w•••• v••io•• •o• •il•-•i• • ••••••• •n• o••i• i••ion• wo•l• ••• •o••i•l•. W••n

••• ••••il• o• WinFS ••• •n•li••• •n• • ••• •••li•, i• wo• l• •• in•••••in• •o
•o• •••• v••io•• •y•••• • •o••in•• w•i•••n in • l•n•••••• ••• •• RelJ wi•• ••o••
w•i•••n ••in• ••• API•.

7.2   Further Work

• l•••ly RelJ i• j••• • •••• •••• in ••ovi•in• •o• ••••n•iv• ••••-•l••• •••• •o•• o•
••l••ion•• i•• in •n o• j•••-o•i•n••• l•n•••••. T•••• ••• ••v•••l ••••••• ••• •v•il••l•
in • o••llin• l•n••••••, •••• •• UML, •••• ••nno• ••••••n•ly •• •x•••••• in
RelJ; no•••ly, w• only •••• o•• ••l••ion•• i• •••• ••• on•-w•y. W• •o•• •o •••
••l••ion•• i•• •••• • •y •• •••v••••• in •o•• •i•••ion• ••••ly, •• w•ll •• •••••••
inv•••i•••in• • • l•i•li•i•i••.

In •• i•••••• w• ••v• no• •iv•n •••il• o•• ow RelJ ••n • i• •l•• •n•••. To •••-
• o•• i• •i••••ly in ••• •• n•i• • wo• l• •••• i•• •on•i•••• l• •x••n•ion o• ••• JVM.
T•••••i•n •n• •v•l••ion o••••• •n •x••n•ion i• in•••••in• •••••• wo••. A••n•l-
•••n••iv•, w• ••v• in•o•• •lly •••i•• • •y•••• ••i• •••n•l••ion o• RelJ in•o '••••'
J•v•. In ••• •••••, w• •l•n •o •o•• •li•• •• i• •••n•l••ion •n• ••ov• i• •o•••••.

Ano•••• •i••••ion w• wi•• •o •on•i•• i• •x••n•in• RelJ wi•• • o•• ••••y-li••
•••ili•i•• (in • ••yl• •i• il•• •o • ω [3]). Fo• •x•• •l•, on• • i••• ••• • •i• •l•
• l••• •••ili•y, •.•. ••• •x••••ion alice.Attends[it.title.matches("*101")]
wo• l• ••••n ••• •••inn•••' •o•••• •••• alice i• •••••n•ly ••••n•in•. (T••
••••x••••ion in •••••• •••••••• i• • •i• •l• •ool••n-v•l••• •x••••ion, w••••
it i• •o•n• •o •••• •l•• •n• o• ••• ••l••ion•• i• in ••n.)

Fin•lly, w• •on•l••• •y •••o••in• o•• •o•• •••• o•• l•n•••••• • •y ••ovi•• •
•••• •••• in ••• ••o•••• o• ••in•i•l•• •ni•••ion o• •o••llin• l•n•••••• (UML,
•• -•i••••• •), ••o•••• • in• l•n•••••• (J•v•, • ♯), •n• •••• •••y •n• •••i•-
•••ion l•n•••••• (S• L, ••••• • •••i•n).

Acknowledgments

M••• o•• •• i• wo•• w•• •o• •l•••• w•il•• Bi••• •n w•• •• ••• Univ••i•y o• ••• -
••i••• • o• ••••• L••o•••o•y •n• ••••o•••• •y • U •••n•• A••••• -II •n• ••
F• T-• • ••oj••• IST-•001-33•3• P••i•o. W••n i• ••••••n•ly •••• o•••• •y •n
• PS•• • •••••n•••i•. W• ••• •••••••l •o So••i• D•o••o•o•lo• •n• ••• ••o•• •o•
•••••l •o• • •n•• on •• i• wo••, •• w•ll •• •o M••••w F•i••i•n, • io••io • ••lli,
Al•n My••o••, J•• •• No• l•, M••••w P•••in•on, An••w Pi•••, P•••• S•w•ll
•n• ••• ••••n•••• o• F• • L •005.

References

1. A. Albano, G. Ghelli, and R. Orsini. A relationship mechanism for a strongly typed object-oriented database programming language. In *Proceedings of VLDB*, 1991.
2. C. Anderson and S. Drossopoulou. δ: An imperative object-based calculus with delegation. In *Proceedings of USE*, 2002.
3. G. Bierman, E. Meijer, and W. Schulte. The essence of Cω. In *Proceedings of ECOOP*, 2005.

4. G. Bierman, M. Parkinson, and A. Pitts. MJ: A core imperative calculus for Java and Java with effects. Technical Report 563, University of Cambridge Computer Laboratory, 2003.

5. P. P.-S. Chen. The entity-relationship model – toward a unified view of data. *ACM Transactions on Database Systems*, 1(1):9–36, 1976.

6. S. Drossopoulou. An abstract model of Java dynamic linking and loading. In *Proceedings of Types in Compilation (TIC)*, 2000.

7. S. Drossopoulou, T. Valkevych, and S. Eisenbach. Java type soundness revisited, September 2000.

8. M. Flatt, S. Krishnamurthi, and M. Felleisen. Classes and mixins. In *Proceedings of POPL*, pages 171–183, 1998.

9. I. Jacobson, G. Booch, and J. Rumbaugh. *The unified software development process*. Addison-Wesley, 1999.

10. J. Noble. Basic relationship patterns. In *Pattern Languages of Program Design, vol. 4*. Addison Wesley, 1999.

11. J. Noble and J. Grundy. Explicit relationships in object-oriented development. In *Proceedings of TOOLS*, 1995.

12. R.G.G. Cattell et al. *The Object Data Standard: ODMG 3.0*. Morgan Kaufmann, 2000.

13. J. Rumbaugh. Relations as semantic constructs in an object-oriented language. In *Proceedings of OOPSLA*, pages 466–481, 1987.

14. J. Smith and D. Smith. Database abstractions: Aggregation and generalizations. *ACM Transactions on Database Systems*, 2(2):105–133, 1977.

15. P. Stevens and R. Pooley. *Using UML: software engineering with objects and components*. Addison-Wesley, 1999.

16. D. Ungar and R. B. Smith. Self: The power of simplicity. In *Proceedings of OOPSLA*, pages 227–242. ACM Press, 1987.

17. A. K. Wright and M. Felleisen. A syntactic approach to type soundness. *Information and Computation*, 115(1):38–94, 1994.

A   Details of Type System and Semantics

T• i• •••• •n• ix •on••in• ••• ••••il• o• ••• ••• •n•i•• no• •ov•••• in ••• • •in • o• y o• ••• ••••••.

A.1   Typing Rules

In ••• i•ion •o ••• •••••y• in• ••l•• •iv•n in S•••. 3, ••• •ollowin• ••l•• •o••l••• ••• •••••y• in• ••l••ion wi•• ••• i• • ••i••• ••••••y• •• ••ovi••• •y ••• l•n••••• •yn••x, •n• •iv• ••• ••fl•xiv•, •••n•i•iv• •lo••••:

$$(\text{STREF}) \quad (\text{STTRANS}) \quad (\text{STCLASS}) \quad (\text{STREL})$$

$$\frac{P \vdash t}{\vdash t \leq t} \quad \frac{\vdash t_1 \leq t_2 \quad \vdash t_2 \leq t_3}{\vdash t_1 \leq t_3} \quad \frac{\mathcal{C}(c_1) = (c_2, \_, \_)}{\vdash c_1 \leq c_2} \quad \frac{\mathcal{R}(r_1) = (r_2, \_, \_, \_, \_)}{\vdash r_1 \leq r_2}$$

T•• •y• in• ••l•• •o• ••• RelJ •••••• •n•• •n• •x• •••ion• no• •y• ••• in S•••. 3 ••• •• own in Fi•. •.

W• o• i• ••• •y• in• o• li••••l v•l••• true, false, null •n• empty, w•i•• ••• •y• •• in ••• o•vio•• w•y – boolean, n •n• set<n> ••••••••iv•ly. V••i•• l••

$$
\begin{array}{cc}
\text{(TSVar)} & \text{(TSNew)} \\
\dfrac{\Gamma(x) = t}{\Gamma \vdash x : t} & \dfrac{P \vdash c}{\Gamma \vdash \text{new } c() : c}
\end{array}
\qquad
\dfrac{\begin{array}{c}\text{(TSEq)}\\ \Gamma \vdash e_1 : n \\ \Gamma \vdash e_2 : n'\end{array}}{\Gamma \vdash e_1 \;\texttt{==}\; e_2 : \texttt{boolean}}
\qquad
\dfrac{\begin{array}{c}\text{(TSFld)}\\ \Gamma \vdash e : n \\ \mathcal{FD}_n(f) = t\end{array}}{\Gamma \vdash e.f : t}
$$

$$
\dfrac{\begin{array}{c}\text{(TSAdd)}\\ \Gamma \vdash e_1 : \texttt{set<}n_1\texttt{>} \\ \Gamma \vdash e_2 : n_2 \\ \vdash n_1 \leq n_3 \\ \vdash n_2 \leq n_3\end{array}}{\Gamma \vdash e_1 \;\texttt{+}\; e_2 : \texttt{set<}n_3\texttt{>}}
\qquad
\dfrac{\begin{array}{c}\text{(TSSub)}\\ \Gamma \vdash e_1 : \texttt{set<}n_1\texttt{>} \\ \Gamma \vdash e_2 : n_2 \\ \vdash n_1 \leq n_3 \\ \vdash n_2 \leq n_3\end{array}}{\Gamma \vdash e_1 \;\texttt{-}\; e_2 : \texttt{set<}n_3\texttt{>}}
\qquad
\dfrac{\begin{array}{c}\text{(TSAss)}\\ x \neq \texttt{this} \\ \Gamma \vdash x : t_1 \\ \Gamma \vdash e : t_2 \\ \vdash t_2 \leq t_1\end{array}}{\Gamma \vdash x \;\texttt{=}\; e : t_2}
$$

$$
\dfrac{\begin{array}{c}\text{(TSFldAss)}\\ \Gamma \vdash e_1 : n \\ \Gamma \vdash e_2 : t_1 \\ \mathcal{FD}_n(f) = t_2 \\ \vdash t_1 \leq t_2\end{array}}{\Gamma \vdash e_1.f \;\texttt{=}\; e_2 : t_1}
\qquad
\dfrac{\begin{array}{c}\text{(TSCall)}\\ \Gamma \vdash e_1 : n \\ \Gamma \vdash e_2 : t_1 \\ \mathcal{MD}_n(m) = (x, \mathcal{L}, t_2, t_3, \_) \\ \vdash t_1 \leq t_2\end{array}}{\Gamma \vdash e_1.m(e_2) : t_3}
\qquad
\dfrac{\begin{array}{c}\text{(TSCond)}\\ \Gamma \vdash e : \texttt{boolean} \\ \Gamma \vdash s_1 \\ \Gamma \vdash s_2 \\ \Gamma \vdash s_3\end{array}}{\Gamma \vdash \texttt{if } (e) \; \{s_1\} \texttt{ else } \{s_2\}; \, s_3}
$$

$$
\begin{array}{c}\text{(TSSkip)}\\[4pt] \dfrac{}{\Gamma \vdash \epsilon}\end{array}
$$

Fig. 7. The remaining type rules of RelJ

••• •y••• • y TSVar •i• • ly • y loo•-•• in ••• •y•in• •nvi•on• •n•. No•• ••••
TSVar •ov••• ••• •y• o• this •y i•• in•l••ion in VarName. N•w •l•••-in•••n••
•llo••tion i• •y••• in ••• o• vio•• w•y. T•• ••••li•y •••• i• v•li• •• lon• ••• o••
•x•••••ion• ••• •••••••••. (Si• il•• ••l••• ••• ••••j••• •o• e_1 •n• e_2 •• set<–>o•
boolean •y•••, ••• •••••• ••• o•vio•• •n• o• i•••••.) Fi•l• loo•-•• i• •y••• ••o•
••• ••l• •••l• o• ••• ••••iv•••'• ••••i• •y••. • •l•• TSVarAdd •o TSFldSub
••• on••••••• o• j••• •••i•ion •n• ••• ov•l ••o• ••• v•l•••. In •ll •••••, ••• •i•••-
••n• o•••n• • •••• •• ••• ••••••• o• •n o•j••• wi•• • •y•• •••o••in••• •o
••• •••'• ••••i• •y••. T•• •n•i•• •x••••ion •••••• ••• •i•••-•••n• o•••••n• '• •y••.
V••i••l•• •n• ••l•• • •y •• •••i•n•• v•l••• ••• o•• in••• •o ••• l•••-••n• •i•••'•
•••l•••• •y••. M•••o• ••ll i• •y••• •i••••ly ••o• ••• • •••o• loo•-•• •••l•. T••
for •••••• •n• w•• •y••• in ••• • o•y o• ••• ••••••. T•• •on•i•ion•l'• •y•in•-
•••••in• i• •••n••••, ••••llin• •••• w• •o no• •••i•n •y••• •o •••••• •n••. All
•••••• •n•• •••• •i•• •••• •••i• •on•in••ion ••••• •n• i• •l•o w•ll-•y•••, •n• w•
•x• li•i•ly •y• ••• ••• ••y ••••• •n• (ϵ), w• i•• i• ••••lly o• i•••• in ••o•••• ••x•.

Fin•lly, • ••o•••• i• w•ll-•y••• i• •ll o• i•• •l••••• •n• ••l••ion•• i• ••• w•ll-
•y•••, i• •l••••• •n• ••l••ion•• i• ••• •i•join•, •n• i• ••• •••••y•in• ••l••ion•• i•
i• •n•i•y• • •••i•:

$$
\begin{array}{c}\text{(TSProgram)}\\[4pt]
\forall n \in \mathsf{dom}(\mathcal{C}_P) \cup \mathsf{dom}(\mathcal{R}_P) : P \vdash n \\
\forall n_1, n_2 : P \vdash n_1 \leq n_2 \wedge P \vdash n_2 \leq n_1 \Rightarrow n_1 = n_2 \\
\hline
\vdash P
\end{array}
$$

A.2   Operational Semantics

Fi•••, w• •iv• •• ll ••• ni•ion• o• new, w•i•• ••••••n• •n ini•i•li••• •l••• in•••n••;
initial, w•i•• ••••••n• •n •••••o••i••• ini•i•l v•l•• •o•• v••i••l• o••y•• t; dynType,
w•i•• ••••••n• ••• •yn•• i• •y•• o• •n •••••••• in ••• ••o••; •n• o• fld, w•i••
••••••n• ••• v•l•• o• ••l• f in ••• o•j••• •• ι in ••o•• σ, ••l•••in• ••• ••l•
loo•••• •o ••• •••••in•••n•• •• •••••o••i•••.

$$\mathsf{new}_P(c) = \begin{cases} \langle\!\langle \texttt{Object}\| \rangle\!\rangle & \text{if } c = \texttt{Object} \\ \langle\!\langle c\| f_1 : \mathsf{initial}_P(\mathcal{FD}_{P,c}(f_1)), \ldots, f_i : \mathsf{initial}_P(\mathcal{F}_{P,c}(f_i)) \rangle\!\rangle & \text{otherwise} \end{cases}$$
$$\text{where } \{f_1, f_2, \ldots, f_i\} = \mathsf{dom}(\mathcal{FD}_{P,c})$$

$$\mathsf{initial}_P(t) = \begin{cases} \texttt{null} & \text{if } t = n' \\ \texttt{false} & \text{if } t = \texttt{boolean} \\ \emptyset & \text{if } t = \texttt{set<n>} \end{cases}$$

$$\mathsf{dynType}(o) = n \text{ where } o = \langle\!\langle n\| \ldots \rangle\!\rangle \ \vee \ o = \langle\!\langle n, \_, \_, \_\| \ldots \rangle\!\rangle$$

$$\mathsf{fld}(\sigma, f, \iota) = \begin{cases} \sigma(\iota)(f) & \text{if } f \in \mathsf{dom}(\sigma(\iota)) \text{ or} \\ \mathsf{fld}(\sigma, f, \iota') & \text{if } f \notin \mathsf{dom}(\sigma(\iota)) \ \wedge \ \sigma(\iota) = \langle\!\langle r, \iota', \_, \_\| \ldots \rangle\!\rangle \end{cases}$$

T•• ••• •inin• •• l•• o• ••• o• •••••ion ••• •n•i•• ••• •••n •• •ollow•:

OSEmpty: $\langle \Gamma, \sigma, \rho, \lambda, \texttt{empty} \rangle \overset{P}{\leadsto} \langle \Gamma, \sigma, \rho, \lambda, \emptyset \rangle$

OSVar: $\langle \Gamma, \sigma, \rho, \lambda, x \rangle \overset{P}{\leadsto} \langle \Gamma, \sigma, \rho, \lambda, \lambda(x) \rangle$

OSFldN: $\langle \Gamma, \sigma, \rho, \lambda, \texttt{null}.f \rangle \langle \Gamma, \sigma, \rho, \lambda, \mathsf{NullPtrError} \rangle$

OSFld: $\langle \Gamma, \sigma, \rho, \lambda, \iota.f \rangle \overset{P}{\leadsto} \langle \Gamma, \sigma, \rho, \lambda, \mathsf{fld}(\sigma, \iota, f) \rangle$

OSRelInstN: $\langle \Gamma, \sigma, \rho, \lambda, \texttt{null}{:}r \rangle \overset{P}{\leadsto} \langle \Gamma, \sigma, \rho, \lambda, \mathsf{NullPtrError} \rangle$

OSEq: $\langle \Gamma, \sigma, \rho, \lambda, u \mathrel{\texttt{==}} u \rangle \overset{P}{\leadsto} \langle \Gamma, \sigma, \rho, \lambda, \texttt{true} \rangle$

OSNeq: $\langle \Gamma, \sigma, \rho, \lambda, u \mathrel{\texttt{==}} u' \rangle \overset{P}{\leadsto} \langle \Gamma, \sigma, \rho, \lambda, \texttt{false} \rangle$ where $u \neq u'$

OSNew: $\langle \Gamma, \sigma, \rho, \lambda, \texttt{new } c() \rangle \overset{P}{\leadsto} \langle \Gamma, \sigma[\iota \mapsto \mathsf{new}_P(c)], \rho, \lambda, \iota \rangle$ where $\iota \notin \mathsf{dom}(\sigma)$

OSBody: $\langle \Gamma, \sigma, \rho, \lambda, \{ \texttt{ return } u; \ \} \rangle \overset{P}{\leadsto} \langle \Gamma, \sigma, \rho, \lambda, u \rangle$

OSAdd: $\langle \Gamma, \sigma, \rho, \lambda, u + \iota \rangle \overset{P}{\leadsto} \langle \Gamma, \sigma, \rho, \lambda, u \cup \{\iota\} \rangle$

OSAddN: $\langle \Gamma, \sigma, \rho, \lambda, u + \texttt{null} \rangle \overset{P}{\leadsto} \langle \Gamma, \sigma, \rho, \lambda, \mathsf{NullPtrError} \rangle$

OSSub: $\langle \Gamma, \sigma, \rho, \lambda, u - \iota \rangle \overset{P}{\leadsto} \langle \Gamma, \sigma, \rho, \lambda, u \setminus \{\iota\} \rangle$

OSSubN: $\langle \Gamma, \sigma, \rho, \lambda, u - \texttt{null} \rangle \overset{P}{\leadsto} \langle \Gamma, \sigma, \rho, \lambda, \mathsf{NullPtrError} \rangle$

OSVarAss: $\langle \Gamma, \sigma, \rho, \lambda, x = u \rangle \overset{P}{\leadsto} \langle \Gamma, \sigma, \rho, \lambda[x \mapsto u], u \rangle$

OSFldAssN: $\langle \Gamma, \sigma, \rho, \lambda, \texttt{null}.f = u \rangle \overset{P}{\leadsto} \langle \Gamma, \sigma, \rho, \lambda, \mathsf{NullPtrError} \rangle$

OSRelAddN: $\langle \Gamma, \sigma, \rho, \lambda, r.\texttt{add}(\iota_1^{\texttt{null}}, \iota_2^{\texttt{null}}) \rangle \overset{P}{\leadsto} \langle \Gamma, \sigma, \rho, \lambda, \mathsf{NullPtrError} \rangle$
    where $\iota_1^{\texttt{null}} = \texttt{null}$ or $\iota_2^{\texttt{null}} = \texttt{null}$

OSRelRemN: $\langle \Gamma, \sigma, \rho, \lambda, r.\texttt{rem}(\iota_1^{\texttt{null}}, \iota_2^{\texttt{null}}) \rangle \overset{P}{\leadsto} \langle \Gamma, \sigma, \rho, \lambda, \mathsf{NullPtrError} \rangle$
    where $\iota_1^{\texttt{null}} = \texttt{null}$ or $\iota_2^{\texttt{null}} = \texttt{null}$

OSCallN: $\langle \Gamma, \sigma, \rho, \lambda, \texttt{null}.m(u) \rangle \overset{P}{\leadsto} \langle \Gamma, \sigma, \rho, \lambda, \mathsf{NullPtrError} \rangle$

OSStat: $\langle \Gamma, \sigma, \rho, \lambda, u; s \rangle \overset{P}{\leadsto} \langle \Gamma, \sigma, \rho, \lambda, s \rangle$

OSCondT: $\langle \Gamma, \sigma, \rho, \lambda, \texttt{if (true) } \{s_1\} \texttt{ else } \{s_2\}; s_3 \rangle \overset{P}{\leadsto} \langle \Gamma, \sigma, \rho, \lambda, s_1\, s_3 \rangle$

OSCondF: $\langle \Gamma, \sigma, \rho, \lambda, \texttt{if (false) } \{s_1\} \texttt{ else } \{s_2\}; s_3 \rangle \overset{P}{\leadsto} \langle \Gamma, \sigma, \rho, \lambda, s_2\, s_3 \rangle$

The Essence of Data Access in Cω

The Power is in the Dot!

Gavin Bierman[1], Erik Meijer[2], and Wolfram Schulte[3]

[1] Microsoft Research, UK
gmb@microsoft.com
[2] Microsoft Corporation, USA
emeijer@microsoft.com
[3] Microsoft Research, USA
schulte@microsoft.com

Abstract. In this paper we describe the data access features of Cω, an experimental programming language based on C[♯] currently under development at Microsoft Research. Cω targets distributed, data-intensive applications and accordingly extends C[♯]'s support of both data and control. In the data dimension it provides a type-theoretic integration of the three prevalent data models, namely the object, relational, and semi-structured models of data. In the control dimension Cω provides elegant primitives for asynchronous communication. In this paper we concentrate on the data dimension. Our aim is to describe the *essence* of these extensions; by which we mean we identify, exemplify and formalize their essential features. Our tool is a small core language, FCω, which is a valid subset of the full Cω language. Using this core language we are able to formalize both the type system and the operational semantics of the data access fragment of Cω.

1 Introduction

Programming languages, like living organisms, need to continuously evolve in response to their changing environment. These evolutionary steps are typically quite modest: most commonly the provision of better or reorganized APIs. Occasionally a more radical evolutionary step is taken. One such example is the addition of generic classes to both Java [6] and C[♯][25].

We should like to argue that the time has come for another large evolutionary step to be taken. Much software is now intended for distributed, web-based scenarios. It is typically structured using a three-tier model consisting of a *middle tier* containing the business logic that extracts relational data from a *data services tier* (a database) and processes it to produce semi-structured data (typically XML) to be displayed in the *user interface tier*.

It is the writing of these middle tier applications that we should like to address. These applications are most commonly written in an object-oriented language such as Java or C[♯] and have to deal with relational data (essentially SQL tables), object graphs, and semi-structured data (XML, HTML).

In addition, these applications are fundamentally concurrent. Because of the inherent latency in network communication, the more natural model of concurrency is

A.P. Black (Ed.): ECOOP 2005, LNCS 3586, pp. 287–311, 2005.
© Springer-Verlag Berlin Heidelberg 2005

asynchronous. Accordingly, Cω provides a simple model of asynchronous (one-way) concurrency based on the join calculus [12]. For the rest of this paper, we shall focus exclusively on the data access aspects of Cω; the concurrency primitives have been discussed elsewhere [3]. Thus when we write Cω, we mean the language excluding the concurrency primitives.

Unfortunately common programming practice, and native API support for data access (e.g. JDBC and ADO.NET) leave a lot to be desired. For example, consider the following fragment taken (and mildly adapted) from the JDBC tutorial to query a SQL database (a user-supplied country is stored in variable input).

```
Connection con = DriverManager.getConnection(...);
Statement stmt = con.createConnection();
String query = "SELECT * FROM COFFEES WHERE Country='"+input+"'";
ResultSet rs = stmt.executeQuery(query);
while (rs.next()) {
  String s = rs.getString("Cof_Name");
  float n = rs.getFloat("Price");
  System.out.println(s+" - "+n);
}
```

Using strings to represent SQL queries is not only clumsy but also removes any possibility for static checking. The impedance mismatch between the language and the relational data is quite striking; e.g. a value is projected out of a row by passing a string denoting the column name and using the appropriate conversion function. Perhaps most seriously, the passing of queries as strings is often a security risk (the "script code injection" problem—e.g. consider the case when the variable input is the string "' OR 1=1; --") [17].

Unfortunately API support in both Java and C$^\sharp$ for XML and XPath/XQuery is depressingly similar (even those APIs that map XML values tightly to an object representation still offer querying facilities by string passing).

Our contention is that object-oriented languages need to evolve to support data access satisfactorily. This is hardly a new observation; a large number of academic languages have offered such support for both relational and semi-structured data (see, e.g. [1, 2, 20, 19, 15, 4]). In spite of the obvious advantages of these languages, it appears that their acceptance has been hampered by the fact that they are "different" from more mainstream application languages, such as Java and C$^\sharp$. For example, HaskellDB [19] proposes extensions to the lazy functional language, Haskell; and TL [20] is a hybrid functional/imperative language with advanced type and module systems. We approach this language support problem from a different direction, which is to extend the common application languages themselves rather than creating another new language.

Closer to our approach is SQLJ [24]. This defines a way of embedding SQL commands directly in Java code. Moreover the results of SQL commands can be stored in Java variables and *vice versa*. Thus SQL commands are statically checked by the SQLJ compiler. SQLJ compilation consists of two stages; first to pre-process the embedded SQL, and second the 'pure Java' compilation. Thus the embedded SQL code is not part of the language *per se* (in fact all the embedded code is prefixed by the keyword #sql).

The chief difference is that Cω offers an integration of both the XML and relational data models with an object model.

Design Objectives of Cω. The aim of our project was to evolve an existing language, C$^\sharp$, to provide first-class support for the manipulation of relational and semi-structured data. (Although we have started with C$^\sharp$, our extensions apply equally well to other object-oriented languages, including Java.)

Addressing the title of our paper, the essence of the resulting language, Cω, is twofold: its extensions to the C$^\sharp$ type system and, perhaps more importantly, the elegant provision of query-like capabilities (the sub-title of our paper). Cω has been carefully designed around a set of core design principles.

1. Cω is a coherent extension of (the safe fragment of) C$^\sharp$, i.e. C$^\sharp$ programs should be valid Cω programs with the same behaviour.
2. The type system of Cω is intended to be both as simple as possible and closely aligned to the type system in the XPath/XQuery standard. Our intended users are C$^\sharp$ programmers who are familiar with XPath/XQuery.
3. From a programming perspective, the real power of Cω comes from its query-like capabilities. These have been achieved by generalizing member access to allow simple XPath-like path expressions.

Paper Organization. The rest of the paper is organized as follows. In §2 we give a comprehensive overview to the Cω programming language.[1] In §3.1 we identify and formalize FCω, a core fragment of Cω. In §3.2 we detail a simpler fragment, ICω, and in §3.4 show how FCω can be compiled to ICω. Using this compilation, we are able to show a number of properties of FCω in §3.5, including a type soundness theorem. We briefly discuss some related work in §4 and conclude in §5.

2   An Introduction to Cω

Our design goal was to evolve C$^\sharp$ to provide an integration of the object, relational and semi-structured data models. One possibility would be to add these data models to our programming language in an orthogonal way, e.g. by including new types XML<S> and TABLE<R>, where S and R are XML and relational schema respectively. We have sought to integrate these models by *generalization*, rather than by ad-hoc specializations. In the rest of this section we shall present the key ideas behind Cω, and give a number of small programs to illustrate these ideas. This section should serve as a programmer's introduction to Cω. We assume that the reader is familiar with C$^\sharp$/Java-like languages.

2.1   New Types

Cω is an extension of C$^\sharp$, so the familiar primitive types such as integers, booleans, floats are present, as well as classes and interfaces. In this section we shall consider

---

[1] An preliminary version of Cω was (informally) described in [22]. We have subsequently simplified the language, and our chief contribution here is a formalization (§§3–4).

in turn the extensions to the type system—streams, anonymous structs, discriminated unions, and content classes—and for each consider the new query capabilities.

Streams. The first structural type we add is a stream type; streams represent ordered homogeneous collections of zero or more values. For example, int* is the type for homogeneous sequences of integers. Streams in Cω are aligned with iterators, which will appear in C$^\sharp$ 2.0. Cω streams are typically generated using iterators, which are blocks that contain yield statements. For example, the FromTo method:

```
virtual int* FromTo(int b, int e){
  for (i = b; i <= e; i++) yield return i;
}
```

generates a finite, increasing stream of integers. Importantly, it should be noted that, just as for C$^\sharp$, invoking such a method body does *not* immediately execute the iterator block, but rather immediately returns a closure. (Thus Cω streams are essentially lazy lists, in the Haskell sense.) This closure is consumed by the foreach statement, e.g. the following code fragment builds a finite stream and then iterates over the elements, printing each one to the screen.

```
int* OneToHundred = FromTo(1,100);
foreach (int i in OneToHundred) Console.WriteLine(i);
```

A vital aspect of Cω streams is that they are always *flattened*; there are no nested streams of streams. Cω streams thus coincide with XPath/XQuery sequences which are also flattened. This alignment is a key design decision for Cω: it enables the semantics of our generalized member access to match the path selection of XQuery. We give further details later.

In addition, flattening of stream types also allows us to efficiently deal with recursively defined streams. Consider the following recursive variation of the function FromTo that we defined previously:

```
virtual int* FromTo2(int b, int e){
  if (b>e) yield break;
  yield return b;
  yield return FromTo2(b+1,e);
}
```

The statement yield break; returns the empty stream. The non-recursive call yield return b yields a single integer. The recursive call yield return FromTo2 (b+1,n); yields a stream of integers. As the type system treats the types int* and int** as equivalent this is type correct.

Without flattening we would be forced to copy the stream produced by the recursive invocation, leading to a quadratic instead of a linear number of yields:

```
virtual int* FromTo3(int b, int e){
  if (b>e) yield break;
  yield return b;
  foreach (int i in FromTo3(b+1,e))  yield return i;
}
```

Note that Cω's flattening of stream types does *not* imply that the underlying stream is flattened via some coercion; every element in a stream is yield-ed at most once. As we will see in the operational semantics (§3.3), iterating over a stream will effectively perform a depth-first traversal over the n-ary tree produced by the iterator.

Cω offers a limited but extremely useful form of *covariance* for streams. Covariance is allowed provided that the conversion on the element type is the identity; for example Button* is a subtype of object* whereas int* is *not* (as the conversion from int to object involves boxing). This notion is a simple variant of the notion of covariance for arrays in C$^\sharp$, although it is statically safe (unlike array covariance) as we can not overwrite elements of streams.

The rationale for this is that implicit conversions should be limited to constant-time operations. Coercing a stream of type Button* to type object* takes constant-time, whereas coercing int* to object* would be linear in the length of the stream, as the boxing conversion from int to object is not the identity.

A key programming feature of Cω is generalized member access; as the subtitle suggests the familiar 'dot' operator is now much more powerful. Thus if the receiver is a stream the member access is mapped over the elements, e.g. OneToHundred.ToString() implicitly maps the method call over the elements of the stream OneToHundred and returns a value of type string*. This feature significantly reduces the burden on the programmer. Moreover, member access has been generalized so it behaves like a *path expression*. For example, OneToHundred.ToString().PadLeft(10) converts all the elements of the stream OneToHundred to a string, and then pads each string, returning a stream of these padded strings.

Sometimes one wishes to map more than a simple member access over the elements of a stream. Cω offers a convenient shorthand called an *apply-to-all expression*, written $e.\{\overline{s}\}$, which applies the block $\{\overline{s}\}$, where $\overline{s}$ denotes a sequence of statements, to each element in the stream e.[2] The block may contain the variable it which plays a similar role as the implicit receiver argument this in a method body and is bound to each successive element of the iterated stream. (Such expressions are reminiscent of Smalltalk do: methods.) For example, the following code first creates the stream of natural numbers from 1 to • 56, converts each of the elements to a hex string, converts each of these to upper case, and then applies an apply-to-all expression to print the elements to the screen:

```
FromTo(1,256).ToString("x").ToUpper().{ Console.WriteLine(it); };
```

Anonymous Structs. The second structural type we add are anonymous structs, which encapsulate heterogeneous ordered collections of values. An anonymous struct is like a tuple in ML or Haskell and is written as struct{int i; Button;} for example. A value of this type contains a member i of type int and an unlabelled member of type Button. We can construct a value of this type with the expression: new{i=42, new Button()}.

To access components of anonymous structs we (again) generalize the notion of member access. Thus assuming a value x of the previous type, we write x.i to ac-

---

[2] We shall adopt the FJ shorthand [18] and write $\overline{x}$ to mean a sequence of x.

cess the integer value. Unlabelled members are accessed by their position; for example x[1] returns the Button member. As for streams, member access is lifted over unlabelled members of anonymous structs. To access the BackColor property of the Button component in variable x we can just write x.BackColor, which is equivalent to x[1].BackColor.

At this point we can reveal even more of the power of Cω's generalized member access. Given a stream friends of type struct{string name; int age;}*, the expression friends.age returns a stream of integers. The member access is over *both* structural types. The following query-like statement prints the names of one's friends:

```
friends.name.{ ConsoleWriteLine(it);};
```

Interestingly, Cω also allows repeated occurrences of the same member name within an anonymous struct type, even at different types. For example, assume the following declaration: struct{int i; Button; float i;} z; Then z.i projects the two i members of z into a new anonymous struct that is equivalent to new{z[0],z[2]} and of type struct{int;float;}.

Cω provides a limited form of covariance for anonymous structs, just as for streams. For example, the anonymous struct struct{int;Button;} *is* a subtype of struct{int; Control;}. However it is *not* a subtype of struct{object; Control;} since the conversion from int to object is not an identity conversion. Cω does not support width subtyping for anonymous structs.

Choice Types. The third structural type we add is a particular form of discriminated union type, which we call a choice type. This is written, for example, choice{int; bool;}. As the name suggests, a value of this type is either an integer or a boolean, and may hold either at any one time. Unlike unions in C/C++ and variant records in Pascal where users have to keep track of which type is present, values of a discriminated union in Cω are implicitly tagged with the static type of the chosen alternative, much like unions in Algol68. In other words, discriminated union values are essentially a pair of a value and its static type.

There is no syntax for creating choice values; the injection is implicit (i.e. it is generated by the compiler).

```
choice{int;Button;} x = 3;
choice{int;Button;} y = new Button();
```

Cω provides a test, e was τ, on choice values to test the value's *static* type. Thus x was int would return true, whereas y was int would return false.

Assuming that an expression e is of type choice{τ̄}, the expression e was τ is true for *exactly one* τ in τ̄. This invariant is maintained by the type system. The only slight complication arises from subtyping, e.g.

```
choice{Control; object;} z = new Button();
```

As Button is a subtype of both Control and object, which type tag is generated by the compiler? A choice type can be thought of as providing a *family* of overloaded constructor methods, one for each component type. Just as for standard object creation in Java/C♯, the *best* constructor method is chosen. In the example above, clearly

Control is better than object. Thus z was Control returns true. The notion of "best" for Cω is the routine extension of that for C$^\sharp$.

As the reader may have guessed, member access has also been generalized over discriminated unions. Here the behaviour of member access is less obvious, and has been designed to coincide with XPath. Consider a value w of type choice{char; Button;}. The member access w.GetHashCode() succeeds irrespective of whether the value is a character or a Button object. In this case the type of the expression w.GetHashCode() is int.

However the member may not be supported by all the possible component types, e.g. w.BackColor. Classic treatments of union types would probably consider this to be type incorrect [23–p.207]. However, Cω's choice types follow the semantics of XPath where, for example, the query foo/bar returns the bar nodes under the foo node if any exist, and *the empty sequence* if none exist. Thus in Cω, the expression w.BackColor is well-typed, and will return a value of type Color?. This is another new type in Cω and is a variant of the nullable type to appear in C$^\sharp$ 2.0. A value of type Color? can be thought of as a singleton stream, thus it is either empty or contains a single Color value (when w contains a Button). Again, we emphasize that this behaviour precisely matches that of XPath.

Cω follows the design of C$^\sharp$ in allowing all values to be boxed and hence all value types are a subtype of the supertype object. Thus both anonymous structs and choice types are considered to be subtypes of the class object.

Content Classes. To allow close integration with XSD and other XML schema languages, we have included the notion of a *content class* in Cω. A content class is a normal class that has a single *unlabelled* type that describes the content of that class, as opposed to the more familiar (named) fields. The following is a simple example of a content class.

```
class friend{
  struct{ string name; int age; };
  void incAge(){...}
}
```

Again we have generalized member access over content classes. Thus the expression Bill.age returns an integer, where Bill is a value of type friend.

From an XSD perspective, classes correspond to global element declarations, while the content type of classes correspond to complex types. Further comparisons with the XML data model are immediately below, but a more comprehensive study can be found elsewhere [21].

2.2   XML Programming

It should be clear that the new type structures of Cω are sufficient to model simple XML schema. For example, the following XSD schema

```
<element name="Address"><complexType><sequence>
  <choice>
    <element name="Street" type="string"/>
    <element name="POBox" type="int"/>
```

```
    </choice>
    <element name="City" type="string"/>
  </sequence></complexType></element>
```

can be represented (somewhat more succinctly!) as the Cω content class declaration:

```
class Address {
  struct{
    choice{ string Street; int POBox; };
    string City;
  };
}
```

The full Cω language supports XML literals as syntactic sugar for serialized object graphs. For example, we can create an instance of the Address class above using the following literal:

```
Address a = <Address>
              <Street>13 Elm St</Street>
              <City>Hollywood</City>
            </Address>;
```

The Cω compiler contains a validating XML parser that deserializes the above literal into normal constructor calls. XML literals can also contain typed holes, much as in XQuery, that allow us to embed expressions to compute part of the literal. This is especially convenient for generating streams.

The inclusion of XML literals and the semantics of the generalized member access mean that XQuery code can be almost directly written in Cω. For example, consider one of the XQuery Use Cases [9], that processes a bibliography file (assume that this is stored in variable bs) and for each book in the bibliography, lists the title and authors, grouped inside a result element. The suggested XQuery solution is as follows.

```
for $b in $bs/book
  return <result>{$b/title}{$b/author}<result>
```

The Cω solution is almost identical:

```
foreach (b in bs.book)
  yield return <result>{b.title}{b.author}</result>;
```

The full Cω language adds several more powerful query expressions to those discussed in this paper. For instance, filter expressions $e[e']$ return the elements in the stream e that satisfy the boolean expression e'. As labels can be duplicated in anonymous structs and discriminated unions, the full language also allows type-based selection. For example, given a value x of type struct{ int a; struct{string a;};} we can select only the string member a by writing x.string::a.

Transitive queries are also supported in the full Cω language: the expression $e...\tau::m$ selects all members m of type τ that are transitively reachable from e. Transitive queries are inspired by the XPath descendant axis.

2.3   Database Programming

Relational tables are merely streams of anonymous structs. For example, the relational table created with the SQL declaration:

```
CREATE TABLE Customer (name string, custid int);
```

can be represented in Cω: `struct{string name; int custid}* Customer;`

In addition to path-like queries, the full Cω language also supports familiar SQL expressions, including `select-from-where`, various joins and grouping operators. Perhaps more importantly, these statements can be used on *any* value of the appropriate type, whether that value resides in a database or in memory; hence, one can write SQL queries in Cω code that does not access a database! One of the XQuery use-cases [9] asks to list the title prices for each book that is sold by both booksellers A and BN. Using a `select` statement and XML-literals, this query can be written in Cω as the following expression:

```
select <book-with-prices>
          <title>{a.title}</title>
          <price-A>{a.price}</price-A>
          <price-BN>{bn.price}</price-BN>
        </book-with-prices>
from book a in A.book, book bn in BN.book
where a.title == bn.title
```

Note the use of XML placeholders {a.title} and {bn.price}: when this code is evaluated new titles and new prices are computed from the bindings of the `select-from-where` clause.

So far we have shown how we can query values using generalized member and SQL expressions, but as Cω is an imperative language, we also allow to perform updates. This paper, however, focuses on the type extensions and generalized member access only.

3   The Essence of Cω

In the rest of this paper we study formally the essence of Cω, by which we mean we identify its essential features. We adopt a formal, mathematical approach and define a core calculus, Featherweight Cω, or FCω for short, similar to core subsets of Java such as FJ [18], MJ [5] and ClassicJava [11]. This core calculus, whilst lightweight, offers a similar computational "feel" to the full Cω language: it supports the new type constructors and generalized member access. FCω is a completely valid subset of Cω in that every FCω program is literally an executable Cω program.

The rest of this section is organized as follows. In §3.1 we define the syntax and type system for FCω. Rather than give an operational semantics directly for FCω we prefer to first "compile out" some of its features, in particular generalized member access. This both greatly simplifies the resulting operational semantics and demonstrates that Cω's features do not require extensive new machinery. Thus in §3.2 we define a target language, Inner Cω, or ICω, for this "compilation". ICω is essentially the same language, but for a handful of new language constructs and a much simpler type system. In §3.3 we give an operational semantics for ICω programs. In §3.4 we specify the compilation of FCω programs into ICω programs. This translation is, on the whole, quite straightforward. We conclude the section in §3.5 by stating some properties of our calculi and the compilation. Most important is the type-soundness property for ICω. Space prevents us from providing any details of the proofs, but they are proved using standard techniques and are similar to analagous theorems for fragments of Java [18, 5].

3.1 A Core Calculus: FCω

Syntax An FCω program consists of one or more class declarations. Each class declaration defines zero or more methods and contains exactly one unlabelled type that we call the *content type*. (We can code up a conventional C#/Cω class declaration with a number of field declarations using an anonymous struct.) FCω follows C# and requires methods to be explicitly marked as virtual or override. Given a program we assume that there is a unique designated method within the class declarations that serves as the entry point.

Program	$p ::= \overline{cd}$	
Class Definition	$cd ::= $ class $c : c \{\tau ; \overline{md}\}$	
Method Definition	$md ::= $ virtual $\tau\, m(\overline{\tau}\,\overline{x})\{\overline{s}\}$	
	$\mid$ override $\tau\, m(\overline{\tau}\,\overline{x})\{\overline{s}\}$	

FCω supports two main kinds of types: *value types* and *reference types*. As usual, the distinguished type void is used for methods that do not return anything; null is only used to type null references, as with C#. Value types include the base types bool and int and the structural types: anonymous structs and discriminated unions. Reference types are either class types or streams. As usual only reference types have object identity and are represented at runtime by references into the heap. We assume a designated special class object.

Types

$\tau ::= \gamma$	Value types	**Reference Types**		
$\mid \rho$	Reference types	$\rho ::= c$	Classes	
$\mid$ void $\mid$ null	Void and null types	$\mid \sigma*$	Stream types	
Value Types		$\mid \sigma?$	Singleton stream type	
$\gamma ::= b$	Base types			
$\mid$ struct$\{\overline{fd}\}$	Anonymous structs	**Field Definition**		
$\mid$ choice$\{\overline{\kappa}\}$	Choice types	$fd ::= \tau\, f;$	Named member	
Base Types		$\mid \tau;$	Unnamed member	
$b ::= $ bool $\mid$ int				

We employ the shorthand κ and σ to denote any type *except* a choice type and stream type (singleton or non-singleton), respectively. As Cω flattens stream types, we have made the simplification to FCω of removing nested stream types altogether from the type grammar. We have also simplified FCω choice types so that the members are unlabelled and we also exclude (for simplification) nested choice types. These can be coded up in FCω using unlabelled anonymous structs.

FCω expressions, as for C$^\sharp$, are split into ordinary expressions and promotable expressions. Promotable expressions are expressions that can be used as statements. We assume a number of built-in primitive operators, such as ==, || and &&. In the grammar we write $e \oplus e$, where $\oplus$ denotes an instance of one of these operators. We do not formalize these operators further as their meaning is clear.

Expression

$e ::= b \mid i$	Literals
$\mid e \oplus e$	Built-in operators
$\mid x$	Variable
$\mid$ null	Null
$\mid (\tau) e$	Cast
$\mid e$ is τ	Dynamic typecheck
$\mid e$ was κ	Static typecheck for choice values
$\mid$ new $\tau(e)$	Object creation
$\mid$ new $\{\overline{be}\}$	Anonymous struct creation
$\mid e.f$	Field access
$\mid e[i]$	Field access by position
$\mid pe$	Promotable expression

Promotable expression

$pe ::= x = e$	Variable assignment
$\mid e.m(\overline{e})$	Method invocation
$\mid e.\{e\}$	Apply-to-all

Binding expression

| $be ::= f = e$ | Named binding |
| $\mid e$ | Unnamed binding |

We have made a simplification in the interests of space to restrict apply-to-all expressions to contain an expression rather than a sequence of statements. This simplifies the typing rules, but as apply-to-all expressions can be coded using foreach loops it is not a serious restriction.

Statements in FCω are standard. As mentioned earlier we have adopted the yield statement that will appear in C$^\sharp$ 2.0 to generate streams.

Statement $s ::= $;	Skip
$\mid pe$;	Promoted expression
$\mid$ if (e) s else s	Conditional
$\mid \tau x = e$;	Variable declaration
$\mid$ return e;	Return statement
$\mid$ return;	Empty return
$\mid$ yield return e;	Yield statement
$\mid$ yield break;	End of stream
$\mid$ foreach $(\sigma x$ in $e)$ s	Foreach loop
$\mid$ while (e) s	While loop
$\mid \{\overline{s}\}$	Block

In what follows we assume that FCω programs are well-formed, e.g. no cyclic class hierarchies, correct method body construction, etc. These conditions can be easily formalized but we suppress the details for lack of space.

Subtyping. Before we define the typing judgements for FCω programs we need to define a number of auxiliary relations. First we define the subtyping relation. We write $\tau <: \tau'$ to mean that type τ is a subtype of type τ'. The rules defining this relation are as follows.

$$\frac{}{\tau <: \tau}\ \text{[Refl]} \quad \frac{\tau <: \tau' \quad \tau' <: \tau''}{\tau <: \tau''}\ \text{[Trans]} \quad \frac{}{\gamma <: \text{object}}\ \text{[Box]} \quad \frac{\text{class } c : c'}{c <: c'}\ \text{[Sub]}$$

$$\frac{}{\text{null} <: \rho}\ \text{[Null]} \quad \frac{\tau <: \tau' \quad f = f'}{\tau f <: \tau' f'}\ \text{[FD]} \quad \frac{\sigma <: \sigma' \quad IdConv(\sigma, \sigma')}{\sigma*/? <: \sigma'*/?}\ \text{[Stream]}$$

$$\frac{}{\sigma* <: \text{object}}\ \text{[SBox]} \quad \frac{}{\sigma? <: \sigma*}\ \text{[SSub]} \quad \frac{}{\sigma <: \sigma?}\ \text{[Sing]}$$

$$\frac{\overline{fd} <: \overline{fd'} \quad IdConv(\overline{fd}, \overline{fd'})}{\text{struct}\{\overline{fd}\} <: \text{struct}\{\overline{fd'}\}}\ \text{[Struct]} \quad \frac{}{\kappa <: \text{choice}\{\kappa;\ \overline{\kappa'}\}}\ \text{[SubChoice]}$$

$$\frac{}{\text{choice}\{\overline{\kappa}\} <: \text{choice}\{\overline{\kappa}\ \overline{\kappa'}\}}\ \text{[Choice]}$$

Most of these rules are straightforward. The rule [Stream] contains notation $(\sigma*/?)$ that we use throughout this paper. It is uses to denote two instances of the rule, one where we select the left of the '/' in all cases (in this case $\sigma*$) and one where we select the right in all cases. It does *not* include cases where we individually select left and right alternatives. The rules [Stream] and [Struct] make use of a predicate *IdConv*, which relates two types τ and τ' if there is an identity conversion between them. Thus $IdConv(\text{Button}, \text{object})$ but not $IdConv(\text{int}, \text{object})$. In this short paper we shall not give its straightforward definition.

Generalized Member Access. As we have seen a key programming feature of Cω is generalized member access. Capturing this behaviour in the type system can be tricky, but we have adopted a rather elegant solution, whereby we define two auxiliary relations. The first, written $\tau.f : \tau'$, tells us that given a value of type τ accessing member f will return a value of type τ'. We define a similar relation for function member access, written $\tau.m(\overline{\tau'}) : \tau''$. Having generalized member access captured by a separate typing relation greatly simplifies the typing judgements for expressions. As generalized member access is a key feature of Cω, we shall give it in detail.

The definition of this relation over stream types is as follows.

$$\frac{\sigma.f : \sigma'}{\sigma*.f : \sigma'*} \quad \frac{\sigma.f : \sigma'*/?}{\sigma*.f : \sigma'*} \quad \frac{\sigma.m(\overline{\tau}) : \sigma'}{\sigma*.m(\overline{\tau}) : \sigma'*} \quad \frac{\sigma.m(\overline{\tau}) : \sigma'*/?}{\sigma*.m(\overline{\tau}) : \sigma'*} \quad \frac{\sigma.m(\overline{\tau}) : \text{void}}{\sigma*.m(\overline{\tau}) : \text{void}}$$

The first two rules map the member access over the stream elements, making sure that we do not create a nested stream type. The next two rules for function member access are similar. The last rule captures the intuition that mapping a void-valued method over a stream, forces the evaluation of the stream and does not return a value.

Before defining the rules for member access over anonymous structs, we need to define rules for member access over named field definitions. This is pretty straightforward and as follows.

$$\frac{}{\tau f.f : \tau} \quad \frac{\tau.m(\overline{\tau'}) : \tau''}{\tau f.m(\overline{\tau'}) : \tau''}$$

Now we consider the rules for generalized member access over anonymous structs. First we give the degenerate cases where only one component supports the member access.

$$\frac{\exists! k \in \{1 \ldots n\}.\, fd_k.f : \tau_k}{\texttt{struct}\{fd_1;\ldots fd_n;\}.f : \tau_k} \qquad \frac{\exists! k \in \{1 \ldots n\}.\, fd_k.m(\overline{\tau'}) : \tau''}{\texttt{struct}\{fd_1;\ldots fd_n;\}.m(\overline{\tau}) : \tau''}$$

The non-degenerate cases are then as follows.

$$\frac{\exists S \subseteq \{1 \ldots n\}.|S| \geq 2 \wedge p = |S| \wedge \forall k \in [1..p].\, fd_{S_k}.f : \tau_k}{\texttt{struct}\{fd_1;\ldots fd_n;\}.f : \texttt{struct}\{\tau_1;\ldots \tau_p;\}}$$

$$\frac{\exists S \subseteq \{1 \ldots n\}.|S| \geq 2 \wedge p = |S| \wedge \forall k \in [1..p].\, fd_{S_k}.m(\overline{\tau}) : \tau'_k}{\texttt{struct}\{fd_1;\ldots fd_n;\}.m(\overline{\tau}) : \texttt{struct}\{\tau'_1;\ldots \tau'_p;\}}$$

Thus a subset, S, of the components support the member, and we map the member access over these components in order. The overall return type is an anonymous struct of the component return types.

We now consider the rules for generalized member access over choice types. Again we consider these rules depending on how many components support the member access. First we give the simple case when *all* possible components support the member access.

$$\frac{\forall k \in \{1 \ldots n\}.\, \kappa_k.f : \tau}{\texttt{choice}\{\kappa_1;\ldots \kappa_n;\}.f : \tau} \qquad \frac{\forall k \in \{1 \ldots n\}.\, \kappa_k.m(\overline{\tau}) : \tau'}{\texttt{choice}\{\kappa_1;\ldots \kappa_n;\}.m(\overline{\tau}) : \tau'}$$

We also have the case when only one of the possible components supports the member access. These rules are as follows (we omit the nested cases).

$$\frac{\exists! k \in \{1 \ldots n\}.\, \kappa_k.f : \sigma \quad n > 1}{\texttt{choice}\{\kappa_1;\ldots \kappa_n;\}.f : \sigma?} \qquad \frac{\exists! k \in \{1 \ldots n\}.\, \kappa_k.m(\overline{\tau}) : \sigma \quad n > 1}{\texttt{choice}\{\kappa_1;\ldots \kappa_n;\}.m(\overline{\tau}) : \sigma?}$$

The reader will recall that the return type of this generalized member access involves a singleton stream type. Finally we give the cases where more than one of the possible components supports the member access.

$$\frac{\exists S \subseteq \{1 \ldots n\}.|S| \geq 2 \wedge p = |S| \wedge \forall k \in [1..p].\, \kappa_{S_k}.f : \kappa'_k}{\texttt{choice}\{\kappa_1;\ldots \kappa_n;\}.f : \texttt{choice}\{\kappa'_1;\ldots \kappa'_p;\}?}$$

$$\frac{\exists S \subseteq \{1 \ldots n\}.|S| \geq 2 \wedge p = |S| \wedge \forall k \in [1..p].\, \kappa_{S_k}.m(\overline{\tau}) : \kappa'_k}{\texttt{choice}\{\kappa_1;\ldots \kappa_n;\}.m(\overline{\tau}) : \texttt{choice}\{\kappa'_1;\ldots \kappa'_p;\}?}$$

Generalized member access over singleton streams is relatively straightforward; the only complication being again to ensure that no nested streams are generated.

$$\frac{\sigma.f : \sigma'}{\sigma?.f : \sigma'?} \qquad \frac{\sigma.f : \sigma' {*}/?}{\sigma?.f : \sigma' {*}/?} \qquad \frac{\sigma.m(\overline{\tau}) : \sigma'}{\sigma?.m(\overline{\tau}) : \sigma'?} \qquad \frac{\sigma.m(\overline{\tau}) : \sigma' {*}/?}{\sigma?.m(\overline{\tau}) : \sigma' {*}/?}$$

Finally we need to define rules for generalized member access over classes. Clearly these need to reflect the standard C$^\sharp$ semantics: function member access on classes searches the class hierarchy until a matching method is found. If we find a matching method $\tau'm(\overline{\tau''})$ in class c, we need to check the actual types of the arguments to the types expected by m. This behaviour is given by the following two rules.

$$\frac{\texttt{class } c\!:\!c'\{\tau;\overline{md}\} \quad \tau'm(\overline{\tau''}) \in \overline{md} \quad \overline{\tau} <: \overline{\tau''}}{c.m(\overline{\tau})\!:\!\tau'}$$

$$\frac{\texttt{class } c\!:\!c'\{\tau;\overline{md}\} \quad \tau'm(\overline{\tau''}) \notin \overline{md} \quad c'.m(\overline{\tau})\!:\!\tau'}{c.m(\overline{\tau})\!:\!\tau'}$$

Next we consider the rules for generalized field access. There is a small subtlety here concerning recursive class definitions; consider the following recursive class List of lists of integers: `class List { struct{ int head; List; } }`

Given an instance `xs` of type List, we do not want `xs.head` to recursively select all `head` fields in `xs`. However simply unfolding the content type and using the rules given earlier for generalized access over anonymous structs that is precisely what would happen!

There are a number of solutions, but in order to make the Cω type system as simple as possible, we follow e.g. Haskell and SML and break recursive cycles at nominal types. In our setting that means that we simply do not perform member lookup on nominal members of the content of nominal types. Using these refined rules, the result type of `xs.head` is `int`.

Formalizing this is trivial but time-consuming. We define another family of generalized member access judgements, written $\tau \bullet f : \tau'$, which is identical to the previous rules except they are not defined for nominal types. We elide the definitions here.

To define field access on nominal types, we first define formally the content type of a class, written $content(c)$ for some class c, as follows.

$$\frac{\texttt{class } c\!:\!\texttt{object}\{\tau;\overline{md}\}}{content(c) = \tau} \qquad \frac{\texttt{class } c : c'\{\tau;\overline{md}\} \quad content(c') = \tau'}{content(c) = \texttt{struct}\{\tau';\tau;\}}$$

The rule for generalized member access over classes simply searches for the member f on the content type of class c, and is given by the following rule.

$$\frac{content(c) = \tau \quad \tau \bullet f : \tau'}{c.f\!:\!\tau'}$$

Generalized Index Access. As we mentioned earlier, elements of anonymous structs can be accessed by position. This is captured by the following rule.

$$\frac{type(fd_i) = \tau_i}{\texttt{struct } \{fd_1;\dots fd_n;\}[i]\!:\!\tau_i}$$

As the reader might have expected, this index access is generalized over the other types; the rather routine details are omitted.

Typing Judgements. We are now able to define typing judgements for FCω. We define three relations corresponding to the three syntactic categories of expressions, promotable expressions and statements. For all three judgements we write Γ to mean a partial function from program identifiers to types. The judgements for expressions and promotable expressions are written $\Gamma \vdash e : \tau$ and $\Gamma \vdash pe : \tau$, respectively. These are given in Fig. 1.

Most of these rules are routine; we shall discuss a few of the more interesting details here. In the rule [TStruct], we have made use of a typing judgement for a binding expression. This is defined as follows:

$$\frac{\Gamma \vdash e : \tau}{\Gamma \vdash f = e : \tau\, f}$$

The compactness of the rules [TField], [TIndex] and [TMeth] shows the elegance of having captured generalized member access with auxiliary relations.

The rules [TAAExp1] and [TAAExp2] ensure that the return type of an apply-to-all expression is not nested. The rule [TAAExp3] ensures the appropriate mixed flattening of streams. The rule [TAAExp4] captures the intuition that applying a void-typed expression to a stream forces the evaluation of that stream and hence the overall type is also void.

The typing judgement for FCω statements is written $\Gamma ; \tau \vdash s$ and is intended to mean that a statement s is well-typed in the typing environment Γ. If it returns a value (either via a normal return or a yield return) then that value is of type τ.

The rules [TForeach1] and [TForeach2] reflect the fact that the type of the stream elements can be cast to the type of the bound variable. This can be either via an upcast ([TForeach1]) or a downcast ([TForeach2]) (again this matches C$^\sharp$ 2.0).

3.2   An Inner Calculus: ICω

Rather than consider further our featherweight calculus FCω, we shall in fact define another core calculus for Cω. This inner calculus, called ICω, is intended to be similar but lower-level than FCω; it can be thought of as the internal language of a compiler.

The chief simplification in ICω is that its type system does *not* support generalized member access. The intention is that we compile out generalized member access when translating FCω programs into ICω programs. We give some details of this compilation in §3.4. Apart from a simplified type system, we can define quite simply an operational semantics for ICω; this is given in §3.3.

The grammar of ICω is then a simple varianr of the grammar for FCω. Some extra expression and statement forms are added (which reflects the lower-level nature of ICω) and likewise a couple are removed from the grammar as they are redundant. We do not expect these new syntactic forms to be made available to the Cω programmer (although they could be). The extensions are as follows:

Expression

$e ::= \ldots$

$\mathtt{new}\ \tau\,(\overline{s})$	Closure creation
	$\mathtt{new}\ (\kappa, e)$	Choice creation
	$e\,.\,\mathtt{Content}$	Class content
	$e\ \mathtt{at}\ \kappa$	Choice content

Promotable expression

$pe ::= \ldots$

| | $\tau\,(\{\overline{s}\})$ | Block expression |

Statement

$s ::= \ldots$

| | $\mathtt{yield\ return}\ (\tau, e)\,;$ | Typed yield |

$$\boxed{\Gamma \vdash e : \tau \text{ and } \Gamma \vdash pe : \tau}$$

$$\frac{}{\Gamma \vdash i : \texttt{int}} \text{[TInt]} \quad \frac{}{\Gamma \vdash b : \texttt{bool}} \text{[TBool]} \quad \frac{}{\Gamma, x : \tau \vdash x : \tau} \text{[TId]} \quad \frac{}{\Gamma \vdash \texttt{null} : \texttt{null}} \text{[TNull]}$$

$$\frac{\Gamma \vdash e : \tau' \quad (\tau' <: \tau) \vee (\tau <: \tau')}{\Gamma \vdash (\tau)\, e : \tau} \text{[TSub]} \qquad \frac{\Gamma \vdash e : \tau' \quad (\tau' <: \tau) \vee (\tau <: \tau')}{\Gamma \vdash e \text{ is } \tau : \texttt{bool}} \text{[TIs]}$$

$$\frac{\Gamma \vdash e : \texttt{choice}\{\overline{\kappa'}\ \kappa; \overline{\kappa''}\}}{\Gamma \vdash e \text{ was } \kappa : \texttt{bool}} \text{[TWas]} \qquad \frac{\Gamma \vdash \overline{be} : \overline{fd}}{\Gamma \vdash \texttt{new } \{\overline{be}\} : \texttt{struct}\{\overline{fd}\}} \text{[TStruct]}$$

$$\frac{\Gamma \vdash e : \tau \quad \tau <: content(c)}{\Gamma \vdash \texttt{new } c(e) : c} \text{[TNew]} \qquad \frac{\Gamma \vdash e : \tau \quad \tau . f : \tau'}{\Gamma \vdash e . f : \tau'} \text{[TField]}$$

$$\frac{\Gamma \vdash e : \tau \quad \tau[i] : \tau'}{\Gamma \vdash e[i] : \tau'} \text{[TIndex]} \qquad \frac{\Gamma \vdash x : \tau \quad \Gamma \vdash e : \tau' \quad \tau' <: \tau}{\Gamma \vdash x = e : \tau} \text{[TAss]}$$

$$\frac{\Gamma \vdash e : \tau \quad \Gamma \vdash \overline{e'} : \overline{\tau'} \quad \tau . m(\overline{\tau'}) : \tau''}{\Gamma \vdash e . m(\overline{e'}) : \tau''} \text{[TMeth]} \qquad \frac{\Gamma \vdash e : \sigma * / ? \quad \Gamma, \texttt{it} : \sigma \vdash e' : \sigma'}{\Gamma \vdash e . \{e'\} : \sigma' * / ?} \text{[TAAExp1]}$$

$$\frac{\Gamma \vdash e : \sigma * / ? \quad \Gamma, \texttt{it} : \sigma \vdash e' : \sigma' * / ?}{\Gamma \vdash e . \{e'\} : \sigma' * / ?} \text{[TAAExp2]} \qquad \frac{\Gamma \vdash e : \sigma * / ? \quad \Gamma, \texttt{it} : \sigma \vdash e' : \sigma' ? / *}{\Gamma \vdash e . \{e'\} : \sigma' *} \text{[TAAExp3]}$$

$$\frac{\Gamma \vdash e : \sigma * / ? \quad \Gamma, \texttt{it} : \sigma \vdash e' : \texttt{void}}{\Gamma \vdash e . \{e'\} : \texttt{void}} \text{[TAAExp4]}$$

$$\boxed{\Gamma; \tau \vdash s}$$

$$\frac{}{\Gamma; \tau \vdash \texttt{;}} \text{[TSkip]} \quad \frac{\Gamma; \tau \vdash \overline{s}}{\Gamma; \tau \vdash \{\overline{s}\}} \text{[TNest]} \quad \frac{\Gamma \vdash pe : \tau}{\Gamma; \tau' \vdash pe \texttt{;}} \text{[TProm]} \quad \frac{}{\Gamma; \texttt{void} \vdash \texttt{return;}} \text{[TRetV]}$$

$$\frac{\Gamma \vdash e : \texttt{bool} \quad \Gamma; \tau \vdash s}{\Gamma; \tau \vdash \texttt{while } (e)\ s} \text{[TWhile]} \qquad \frac{\Gamma \vdash e : \texttt{bool} \quad \Gamma; \tau \vdash s_1 \quad \Gamma; \tau \vdash s_2}{\Gamma; \tau \vdash \texttt{if } (e)\ s_1 \texttt{ else } s_2} \text{[TIf]}$$

$$\frac{\Gamma \vdash e : \tau' \quad \tau' <: \tau}{\Gamma; \tau \vdash \texttt{return } e\texttt{;}} \text{[TRet]} \qquad \frac{}{\Gamma; \sigma * \vdash \texttt{yield break;}} \text{[TYieldB]}$$

$$\frac{\Gamma \vdash e : \sigma' \quad \sigma' <: \sigma}{\Gamma; \sigma * \vdash \texttt{yield return } e\texttt{;}} \text{[TYield1]} \qquad \frac{\Gamma \vdash e : \sigma' * / ? \quad \sigma' <: \sigma'' \quad \Gamma, x : \sigma''; \tau \vdash s}{\Gamma; \tau \vdash \texttt{foreach } (\sigma''\ x \text{ in } e)\, s} \text{[TForeach1]}$$

$$\frac{\Gamma \vdash e : \sigma * \quad \sigma * <: \sigma' *}{\Gamma; \sigma' * \vdash \texttt{yield return } e\texttt{;}} \text{[TYield2]} \qquad \frac{\Gamma \vdash e : \sigma' * / ? \quad \sigma'' <: \sigma' \quad \Gamma, x : \sigma''; \tau \vdash s}{\Gamma; \tau \vdash \texttt{foreach } (\sigma''\ x \text{ in } e)\, s} \text{[TForeach2]}$$

Fig. 1. Typing judgements for FCω expressions, promotable expressions and statements

Thus ICω includes expressions to create closure and choice elements. We include an operator e.Content to extract the content element from an object e. Given an element e of a choice type, we add an operation e at κ to extract its κ-valued content. (If it is of another type, this will raise an exception.) We add (typed) block expressions to ICω, and in addition we provide a typed yield statement.

The two syntactic forms that we removed from the grammar of FCω are: (1) We remove field accesses $e.f$ completely; they are replaced by positional access, i.e. $e[i]$; and (2) We remove the untyped yield statement; all yields in ICω are explicitly typed.

We can define typing judgements for ICω expressions and statements, which are written $\Gamma \triangleright e : \tau$ and $\Gamma ; \tau \triangleright s$, respectively. Most of these rules are identical to those for FCω; we shall just give the rules for the new syntactic forms. The rules for creating closure and choice elements are as follows:

$$\frac{\Gamma ; \sigma * / ? \triangleright \overline{s}}{\Gamma \triangleright \text{new } \sigma * / ? (\overline{s}) : \sigma * / ?} \qquad \frac{\Gamma \triangleright e : \kappa' \quad \kappa' <: \kappa}{\Gamma \triangleright \text{new } (\kappa, e) : \text{choice}\{\kappa ; \}}$$

The typing rules for extracting the content of content class and choice elements are as follows:

$$\frac{\Gamma \triangleright e : c}{\Gamma \triangleright e.\text{Content}: content(c)} \qquad \frac{\Gamma \triangleright e : \text{choice}\{\kappa ; \overline{\kappa'}\}}{\Gamma \triangleright e \text{ at } \kappa : \kappa}$$

The typing rule for block expressions and yield statements are as follows:

$$\frac{\Gamma ; \tau \triangleright \overline{s} \quad \tau \neq \text{void}}{\Gamma \triangleright \tau(\{\overline{s}\}) : \tau} \qquad \frac{}{\Gamma ; \sigma * / ? \vdash \text{yield break;}}$$

$$\frac{\Gamma \triangleright e : \sigma' \quad \sigma' <: \sigma}{\Gamma ; \sigma * / ? \triangleright \text{yield return } (\sigma', e);} \qquad \frac{\Gamma \triangleright e : \sigma * / ? \quad \sigma * / ? <: \tau \quad \tau \neq \text{object}}{\Gamma ; \tau \triangleright \text{yield return } (\sigma * / ?, e);}$$

3.3   Operational Semantics for ICω

In this section we formalize the dynamics of ICω by defining an operational semantics. We follow FJ [18] and MJ [5] and give this in the form of a small-step reduction relation, although a big-step evaluation relation can easily be defined. Hence we use evaluation contexts to encode the evaluation strategy in the now familiar way [11]—the definition of ICω evaluation contexts is routine and omitted. First we define the value forms of ICω expressions and statements (where bv is the value form of a binding expression):

Expression values		Statement values	
$v ::= b \mid i \mid \text{null} \mid \text{void}$	Basic values	$sv ::= \text{;}$	Skip
$\mid r$	Reference	$\mid \text{return } v;$	Return value
$\mid \text{new } \{\overline{bv}\}$	Struct value	$\mid \text{return};$	
$\mid \text{new } (\kappa, v)$	Choice value	$\mid \text{yield return } (\tau, v);$	Typed yield value
		$\mid \text{yield break};$	End of stream value

Evaluation of ICω expressions and statements takes place in the context of a state, which is a pair (H, R), where H is a heap and R is a stack frame. A heap is represented as a finite partial map from references r to runtime objects, and a stack frame is a finite partial map from variable identifiers to values. A runtime object, as for $C^\sharp$, is a pair (τ, cn) where τ is a type and cn is a canonical, which is either a value or a closure. A closure is the runtime representation of a stream and is written as a pair $(R, \overline{s})^\alpha$ where R is a stack frame and $\overline{s}$ is a statement sequence. The superscript flag α indicates whether the closure is fresh or a clone. We will explain this distinction later. In what follows we assume that expressions and statements are well-typed.

In Fig. 2 we define the evaluation relation for ICω expressions, written $S, e \rightarrow S', e'$, which means that given a state S, expression e reduces by one or possibly more steps to e' and a (possibly updated) state S'. (We use an auxiliary function $value$ defined as follows: $value(f = v) \overset{\text{def}}{=} v$, $value(v) \overset{\text{def}}{=} v$.) These rules are routine.

As is usual we have a number of cases that lead to a predicable error state, e.g. following a dereference of a null object. These errors in ICω are $CastX$, $ChoiceX$, $NullX$ and $NullableX$. We say that a pair S, e is *terminal* if e is one of these errors, or it is a value.

The evaluation relation for ICω promotable expressions is written $S, pe \rightarrow S', pe'$ and is also given in Fig. 2. The rules for method invocation deserve some explanation: they are differentiated according to whether the method is void-returning. If it is not then the method body is unfolded, and executed until it is of the form return v; where v is a value. This value is then the result of the method invocation. If the method is void-valued, then we unfold the method body and execute it until it is of the form return;. The result is the special value void.

The evaluation relation for statements is written $S, s \rightarrow S', s'$ and in Fig. 3 we give just some of the interesting cases, which are those dealing with foreach loops. As we have mentioned, Cω streams are aligned with C$^\sharp$ 2.0 iterators: there the foreach loop is actually syntactic sugar: first of all an IEnumerator<T> is obtained from the iterator block (which should be of type IEnumerable<T>) using the GetEnumerator method. This is walked over using MoveNext and Current members. Semantically important is that GetEnumerator actually copies the enumerable object. In our semantics we faithfully encode this by tagging closures, and creating clones as appropriate. Thus whilst iterating over a stream we update the reference in place (rules [FVC], [FSC] and [FNC]), but every foreach creates its own copy from a fresh original (rules [FVF], [FSF] and [FNF]). In rule [FBr] we write α to range over both clone and fresh.

Rules [FSF] and [FSC] embody the flattening of streams. To evaluate a foreach loop we first evaluate the stream until it yields a value. If that value is itself a stream, then we should first execute the foreach loop on this stream.

3.4   Compiling FCω to ICω

In this section we give some details of the compilation of FCω into ICω. Much of this compilation is routine, so in the interests of space we shall concentrate only on the most interesting aspect: generalized member access.

We employ a "coercion" technique, in that we translate the *implicit* generalized member access of FCω into an *explicit* ICω code fragment. This can be expressed as an inductively defined relation, written $|\tau.f : \tau'| \rightsquigarrow g$ and $|\tau.m(\overline{\tau'}) : \tau''| \rightsquigarrow g$ for member and function member access respectively. A judgement $|\tau.f : \tau'| \rightsquigarrow g$ is intended to

Expressions

$$\frac{}{(H,R), x \to (H,R), R(x)}$$

$$\frac{H(r) = (\tau', cn) \qquad \tau' <: \tau}{(H,R), (\tau)r \to (H,R), r}$$

$$\frac{H(r) = (\tau', cn) \qquad \tau' \not<: \tau}{(H,R), (\tau)r \to (H,R), CastX}$$

$$\frac{H(r) = (\tau', cn) \qquad \tau' <: \tau}{(H,R), r \text{ is } \tau \to (H,R), \text{true}}$$

$$\frac{H(r) = (\tau', cn) \qquad \tau' \not<: \tau}{(H,R), r \text{ is } \tau \to (H,R), \text{false}}$$

$$\frac{}{S, \text{new } (\kappa, v) \text{ was } \kappa \to S, \text{true}}$$

$$\frac{\kappa \neq \kappa'}{S, \text{new } (\kappa, v) \text{ was } \kappa' \to S, \text{false}}$$

$$\frac{r \notin dom(H)}{(H,R), \text{new } c(v) \to (H[r \mapsto (c, v)], R), r}$$

$$\frac{r \notin dom(H)}{(H,R), \text{new } \sigma*/?(\overline{s}) \to (H[r \mapsto (\sigma*/?, (R, \overline{s})^{\text{fresh}})], R), r}$$

$$\frac{H(r) = (c, cn)}{(H,R), r.\text{content} \to (H,R), cn}$$

$$\frac{}{S, \text{null.content} \to S, NullX}$$

$$\frac{0 \le i \le n}{S, \text{new } \{bv_0, .., bv_n\}[i] \to S, value(bv_i)}$$

$$\frac{}{S, \text{new } (\kappa, v) \text{ at } \kappa \to S, v}$$

$$\frac{\kappa \neq \kappa'}{S, \text{new } (\kappa, v) \text{ at } \kappa' \to S, ChoiceX}$$

Promotable expressions

$$\frac{}{(H,R), x = v \to (H, R[x \mapsto v]), v}$$

$$\frac{(H,R), \overline{s} \to^* (H', R'), \text{return } v; \overline{s'}}{(H,R), \tau(\{\overline{s}\}) \to (H', R'), v}$$

$$\frac{}{S, \text{null}.m(\overline{v}) \to S, NullX}$$

$$\frac{H(r) = (c, \_) \quad method(m, c) = \tau'(\overline{\tau}\,\overline{x})\{\overline{s}\} \quad \tau' \neq \text{void}}{(H, []), \{c \text{ this } = r; \overline{\tau}\,\overline{x} = \overline{v}; \overline{s}\} \to^* (H', R'), \text{return } v'; \overline{s'}}{(H,R), r.m(\overline{v}) \to (H', R), v'}$$

$$\frac{H(r) = (c, \_) \quad method(m, c) = \text{void } (\overline{\tau}\,\overline{x})\{\overline{s}\}}{(H, []), \{c \text{ this } = r; \overline{\tau}\,\overline{x} = \overline{v}; \overline{s}\} \to^* (H', R'), \text{return }; \overline{s'}}{(H,R), r.m(\overline{v}) \to (H', R), \text{void}}$$

Fig. 2. Evaluation rules for ICω expressions and promotable expressions

mean that if invoking a member f on an element of type τ returns an element of type τ', then g is the ICω coercion that encodes the explicit access of the appropriate member. In Fig. 4 we give some details of the compilation of generalized member access (GMA) for members, i.e. the $|\tau.f : \tau'| \rightsquigarrow g$ relation. (The version for function members

$$\frac{}{S, \texttt{foreach}\ (\sigma\ x\ \texttt{in null})\,s \to S, ;}\ \text{[FNull]}$$

$$\frac{H(r) = (\tau', (R', \overline{s'})^{\alpha}) \quad (H, R'), \overline{s'} \to^* (H', R''), \texttt{yield break}\ ; \overline{s''}}{(H, R), \texttt{foreach}\ (\sigma\ x\ \texttt{in}\ r)\ s \to (H', R), ;}\ \text{[FBr]}$$

$$\frac{\begin{array}{cc} H(r) = (\tau', (R', \overline{s'})^{\text{fresh}}) & r' \notin dom(H') \\ (H, R'), \overline{s'} \to^* (H', R''), \texttt{yield return}\ (\sigma', v)\,; \overline{s''} & v \neq \texttt{null} \end{array}}{\begin{array}{c} (H, R), \texttt{foreach}\ (\sigma\ x\ \texttt{in}\ r)\ s \to \\ (H'[r' \mapsto (\tau', (R'', \overline{s''})^{\text{clone}})], R), \{\{\sigma\ x = v; s\}\,\texttt{foreach}\ (\sigma\ x\ \texttt{in}\ r')\ s\} \end{array}}\ \text{[FVF]}$$

$$\frac{\begin{array}{c} H(r) = (\tau', (R', \overline{s'})^{\text{clone}}) \\ (H, R'), \overline{s'} \to^* (H', R''), \texttt{yield return}\ (\sigma', v)\,; \overline{s''} \quad v \neq \texttt{null} \end{array}}{\begin{array}{c} (H, R), \texttt{foreach}\ (\sigma\ x\ \texttt{in}\ r)\ s \to \\ (H'[r \mapsto (\tau', (R'', \overline{s''})^{\text{clone}})], R), \{\{\sigma\ x = v; s\}\,\texttt{foreach}\ (\sigma\ x\ \texttt{in}\ r)\ s\} \end{array}}\ \text{[FVC]}$$

$$\frac{\begin{array}{cc} H(r) = (\tau', (R', \overline{s'})^{\text{fresh}}) & r' \notin dom(H') \\ (H, R'), \overline{s'} \to^* (H', R''), \texttt{yield return}\ (\sigma'*, v)\,; \overline{s''} & v \neq \texttt{null} \end{array}}{\begin{array}{c} (H, R), \texttt{foreach}\ (\sigma\ x\ \texttt{in}\ r)\ s \to \\ (H'[r' \mapsto (\tau', (R'', \overline{s''})^{\text{clone}})], R), \{\texttt{foreach}\ (\sigma\ x\ \texttt{in}\ v)\ s\ \texttt{foreach}\ (\sigma\ x\ \texttt{in}\ r')\ s\} \end{array}}\ \text{[FSF]}$$

$$\frac{\begin{array}{c} H(r) = (\tau', (R', \overline{s'})^{\text{clone}}) \\ (H, R'), \overline{s'} \to^* (H', R''), \texttt{yield return}\ (\sigma'*, v)\,; \overline{s''} \quad v \neq \texttt{null} \end{array}}{\begin{array}{c} (H, R), \texttt{foreach}\ (\sigma\ x\ \texttt{in}\ r)\ s \to \\ (H'[r \mapsto (\tau', (R'', \overline{s''})^{\text{clone}})], R), \{\texttt{foreach}\ (\sigma\ x\ \texttt{in}\ v)\ s\ \texttt{foreach}\ (\sigma\ x\ \texttt{in}\ r)\ s\} \end{array}}\ \text{[FSC]}$$

$$\frac{\begin{array}{cc} H(r) = (\tau', (R', \overline{s'})^{\text{fresh}}) & r' \notin dom(H') \\ (H, R'), \overline{s'} \to^* (H', R''), \texttt{yield return}\ (\tau, \texttt{null})\,; \overline{s''} \end{array}}{\begin{array}{c} (H, R), \texttt{foreach}\ (\sigma\ x\ \texttt{in}\ r)\ s \to \\ (H'[r' \mapsto (\tau', (R'', \overline{s''})^{\text{clone}})], R), \texttt{foreach}\ (\sigma\ x\ \texttt{in}\ r')\ s \end{array}}\ \text{[FNF]}$$

$$\frac{\begin{array}{c} H(r) = (\tau', (R', \overline{s'})^{\text{clone}}) \\ (H, R'), \overline{s'} \to^* (H', R''), \texttt{yield return}\ (\tau, \texttt{null})\,; \overline{s''} \end{array}}{(H, R), \texttt{foreach}\ (\sigma\ x\ \texttt{in}\ r)\ s \to (H'[r \mapsto (\tau', (R'', \overline{s''})^{\text{clone}})], R), \texttt{foreach}\ (\sigma\ x\ \texttt{in}\ r)\ s}\ \text{[FNC]}$$

Fig. 3. Evaluation rules for ICω `foreach` loops

(methods) is similar and omitted.) In the definition we have employed a function-like syntax for coercions, although they are really contexts, and we have dropped the types from various block expressions. We have used the shorthand `yield return`$'(\tau, \texttt{e})$`;` to mean the statement sequence `yield return`$(\tau, \texttt{e})$`;yield break;` and have also used two functions: `Value` that returns the element of a singleton stream or raises an exception if it empty, and `HasValue` that returns a boolean depending on whether the singleton stream has an element or not. These can be coded directly and their definitions are omitted.

Compiling GMA over streams

$$\frac{|\sigma.f:\sigma'| \rightsquigarrow g}{|\sigma*.f:\sigma'*| \rightsquigarrow z \mapsto z.\{g(\texttt{it})\}}$$

Compiling GMA over anonymous structs

$$\frac{\exists S \subseteq \{1\ldots n\}.|S| \geq 2. \wedge p = |S| \wedge \forall k \in [1..p].\, |fd_{S_k}.f : \tau_k| \rightsquigarrow g_k}{|\texttt{struct}\{fd_1;\ldots fd_n;\}.f:\texttt{struct}\{\tau_1;\ldots\tau_p;\}| \rightsquigarrow z \mapsto \texttt{new}\{g_1(z\texttt{[1]}),\ldots,g_p(z\texttt{[p]})\}}$$

$$\frac{\exists!k \in \{1\ldots n\}.\, |fd_k.f : \tau_k| \rightsquigarrow g}{|\texttt{struct}\{fd_1;\ldots fd_n;\}.f:\tau_k| \rightsquigarrow z \mapsto g(z\texttt{[k]})}$$

Compiling GMA over choice types

$$\exists S \subseteq \{1\ldots n\}.|S| \geq 2 \wedge p = |S| \wedge \forall k \in [1..p].\, |\kappa_{S_k}.f : \kappa'_k| \rightsquigarrow g_k$$

$|\texttt{choice}\{\kappa_1;\ldots\kappa_n;\}.f : \texttt{choice}\{\kappa'_1;\ldots\kappa'_p;\}?|$
$\rightsquigarrow z \mapsto$

```
({if(z was κ_S_1)
 {return new choice{κ'_1;...κ'_p;}?(yield return'(κ_S_1,new(κ_S_1,g_1(z at κ_S_1))););}
··· if(z was κ_S_p)
 {return new choice{κ'_1;...κ'_p;}?(yield return'(κ_S_p,new(κ_S_p,g_p(z at κ_S_p))););}
 else return null;})
```

$$\frac{|\kappa_k.f : \tau| \rightsquigarrow g_k \quad \forall k.1 \leq k \leq n}{|\texttt{choice}\{\kappa_1;\ldots\kappa_n;\}.f : \tau| \rightsquigarrow z \mapsto (\{\ \texttt{if}(z\ \texttt{was}\ \kappa_1)\ \texttt{return}\ g_1(z\ \texttt{at}\ \kappa_1);\cdots}$$
$$\texttt{if}(z\ \texttt{was}\ \kappa_n)\ \texttt{return}\ g_n(z\ \texttt{at}\ \kappa_n);\})$$

$$\exists!k \in \{1\ldots n\}.\, |\kappa_k.f : \sigma| \rightsquigarrow g \quad n > 1$$

$|\texttt{choice}\{\kappa_1;\ldots\kappa_n;\}.f : \sigma?|$
$\rightsquigarrow z \mapsto (\{\texttt{if}(z\ \texttt{was}\ \kappa_k)\ \texttt{return new}\ \sigma?(\texttt{yield return}'(\sigma,g(z\ \texttt{at}\ \kappa_k))\,;)\,;$
$\qquad\qquad \texttt{else return null;})$

Compiling GMA over singleton streams

$$|\sigma.f:\sigma'| \rightsquigarrow g$$

$|\sigma?.f:\sigma'?| \rightsquigarrow z \mapsto (\{\texttt{if}\ (\texttt{HasValue}(z))\ \texttt{return new}\ \sigma'?(\texttt{yield return}'(\sigma',g(\texttt{Value}(z)))\,;)\,;$
$\qquad\qquad \texttt{else return null;})$

$$|\sigma.f:\sigma'*/?| \rightsquigarrow g$$

$|\sigma?.f:\sigma'*/?| \rightsquigarrow z \mapsto (\{\texttt{if}\ (\texttt{HasValue}(z))\ \texttt{return}\ g(\texttt{Value}(z))\,;$
$\qquad\qquad \texttt{else return null;})$

Fig. 4. Compilation of Generalized Member Access

For example, we can compile an instance of member access in FCω, $e.f$, as follows: we first compile the expression e into ICω, yielding e', and also generate a coercion, g, corresponding to the member access. The result of the compilation of $e.f$ is then simply $g(e')$. We write the compilation of, e.g. an expression, e, as $|\Gamma \vdash e:\tau| \rightsquigarrow e'$.

Incoherence by Design. Java and C$^\sharp$ are by design incoherent [7]. Both languages use a notion of "best" conversion when there is more than one conversion between two types. If there does not exist a best conversion, a compile-time error is generated. In compiling FCω to ICω we use this notion of a best conversion when dealing with rules that use subtyping. We do not formalize this notion of "best" here; both the Java and C$^\sharp$ language specifications give precise details. The new types in Cω do not complicate this notion greatly: For example, there are two conversions between int and object: one using the rule [Box], the other using the rules [SubChoice] and [Box] along with [Trans] (i.e. int <: choice{int;string;} <: object). It is clear that the first conversion is better. The other critical pairs are similarly easy to resolve.

3.5   Properties of FCω and ICω

In this section we briefly mention some properties of FCω and ICω and the compilation. We do not give any details of the proofs, as they are standard and follow analogous theorems for Java [18, 5]; details will appear in a forthcoming technical report.

Our main result is that ICω is type-sound, which is captured by the following properties. (We use generalized judgements, e.g. $\Gamma \rhd (S, e):\tau$ to mean that the expression e is well-typed and also that the state S is well-formed with respect to Γ, in the familiar way. As is usual [18] we also need to add "stupid" typing rules for the formal proof.)

Theorem 1 (Type soundness for ICω).

1. *If $\Gamma \rhd (S, e):\tau$ and $(S, e) \rightarrow (S', e')$ then $\exists \tau'$ such that $\Gamma \rhd (S', e'):\tau'$ and $\tau' <: \tau$.*
2. *If $\Gamma;\tau \rhd s$ and $(S, s) \rightarrow (S', s')$ then $\exists \tau'$ such that $\Gamma;\tau' \rhd (S', s')$ and $\tau' <: \tau$.*
3. *If $\Gamma \rhd (S, e):\tau$ then either (S, e) is terminal or $\exists S', e'$ such that $(S, e) \rightarrow (S', e')$.*
4. *If $\Gamma;\tau \rhd (S, s)$ then either (S, s) is terminal or $\exists S', s'$ such that $(S, s) \rightarrow (S', s')$.*

We can also prove that our compilation of FCω to ICω is type-preserving, i.e. if an FCω expression e in environment Γ has type τ, then there is a compilation of e resulting in an ICω expression e', such that e' in Γ also has type τ.

Theorem 2 (Type preservation of compilation).

1. *If $\Gamma \vdash e:\tau$ then $\exists e'$ such that $|\Gamma \vdash e:\tau| \rightsquigarrow e'$ and $\Gamma \rhd e':\tau$.*
2. *If $\Gamma;\tau \vdash s$ then $\exists s'$ such that $|\Gamma;\tau \vdash s| \rightsquigarrow s'$ and $\Gamma;\tau \rhd s'$.*

4   Related Work

Numerous languages have been proposed for manipulating relational and semi-structured data. For reasons of space we focus here only on those for semi-structured data (some of the languages for relational data were cited in §1).

A number of special-purpose functional languages [15, 4, 10] have been proposed for processing XML values. This stands in contrast to our approach, which aims at extending an existing widely-used object-oriented programming language.

The languages most similar to Cω are XJ [14] and Xtatic [13]. XJ adds XML and XPath as a first-class construct to Java, and uses logical XML classes to represent XSDs. In this way XJ allows compile time checking of XML fragments; however since the impedance mismatch between XML and objects is quite large, it does not deal with a mix of data from the the object and the XML world. One consequence is, for example, that XPath queries are restricted to work on XML data only.

Xtatic extends C♯ with a separate category of regular expression types [16]. Subtyping is structural. While this gives a lot of flexibility this neither conforms with XML Schema, where subtyping is defined by name through restrictions and extensions, nor does it allow a free mix of objects and XML. Further, Xtatic uses pattern matching for XML projections, which fits well with the chosen type system but lacks first-class queries.

In contrast to XJ and Xtatic, Cω does not treat XML as a distinct and separate class. Its ingenuity lies in the uniform integration of the new stream, choice and struct types into the existing types and the generalization of member access— "the power is in the dot". In fact, generalized member access in Cω achieves many of the benefits that other type systems try to solve. For example, a long standing problem is how to write a query over data that comes from two sources that are similar, modulo some distribution rules, but not the same [8]. The type algebra of regular expression types often allows a factorization which makes this scenario possible. Generalized member access, on the other hand, handles this problem itself, without the need for distribution rules at the type level.

Another popular approach to deal with XML in an object-oriented language is by using so called data-bindings. A data-binding generates some strongly typed object representation from a given XML schema (XSD). JAXB for Java and xsd.exe in the .NET framework generate classes from a given XSD. However, it is often impossible to generate reasonable bindings, since the rich type system of XSDs cannot adequately be mapped onto classes and interfaces. As a consequence the resulting mappings are often weakly typed.

Cω takes a different but simpler view: XML is considered to be a serialization syntax for the rich type system of Cω. We are not tied to a particular XML data model. While Cω by design doesn't support the entirety of the full XML stack, in our experience Cω's type system and language extensions are rich enough to support realistic scenarios. We have written a large number of applications, including the complete set of XQuery Use Cases, several XSL stylesheets, and a substantial application (50KLOC) to manage TV listings.

5   Conclusions and Future Work

In this paper we have considered the problem of manipulating relational and semi-structured data within common object-oriented languages. We observed that existing methods using APIs provide poor support for these common application scenarios.

Therefore, we have proposed a series of elegant extensions to $C^\sharp$ that provides type-safe, first-class access to, and querying of, these forms of data. We also have built a full compiler that implements our design. In this paper we have studied these extensions formally.

This work represents an industrial application of formal methods; on the whole, we found the process of formalizing our intuitions extremely useful, and indeed we managed to trap a number of subtle design flaws in the process. (In addition we had to formalize a fragment of $C^\sharp$, which was a little subtle in places. For example, we believe that this paper gives the first formal operational semantics for iterators.) That said, we also found it useful to be simultaneously developing a compiler. On a small number of occasions we found that our formalization was too high-level, in that it failed to capture some lower-level issues. Also whilst FCω is small enough to prove theorems about by hand, we should have liked to formalized a larger fragment of the language. At the moment, this seems unrealistic without more highly developed machine assistance.

One aspect of this project that we should like to consider further is the compilation. The Common Type System (CTS) for the Common Language Runtime (CLR) whilst general, lacks support for structural types. As our current compiler targets .NET 1.1, this means that the choice and anonymous structs types have to be "simulated". In future work, we plan to study extending the CLR with structural types. This would also enable more effective compilation of other languages that offer structural types, such as functional languages. It would also be interesting to study whether the lightweight covariance of $C\omega$ could be added to the CTS and other languages.

Implementation Status. A prototype $C\omega$ compiler is freely available. It covers the entire safe fragment of $C^\sharp$ and includes all the data access features described in this paper (and more) and also the "polyphonic" concurrency primitives [3]. (Available from http://research.microsoft.com/comega.)

References

1. A. Albano, G. Ghelli, and R. Orsini. Types for databases: the Galileo experience. In *Proceedings of DBPL*, 1989.
2. A. Albano, G. Ghelli, and R. Orsini. Fibonacci: A programming language for object databases. *Journal of Very Large Data Bases*, 4(3):403–444, 1995.
3. N. Benton, L. Cardelli, and C. Fournet. Modern concurrency abstractions for $C^\sharp$. *TOPLAS*, 26(5):769–804, 2004.
4. V. Benzaken, G. Castagna, and A. Frisch. CDuce: An XML-centric general-purpose language. In *Proceedings of ICFP*, 2003.
5. G.M. Bierman, M.J. Parkinson, and A.M. Pitts. MJ: An imperative core calculus for Java and Java with effects. Technical Report 563, University of Cambridge, 2003.
6. G. Bracha, M. Odersky, D. Stoutamire, and P. Wadler. Making the future safe for the past: Adding genericity to Java. In *Proceedings of OOPSLA*, 1998.
7. V. Breazu-Tannen, T. Coquand, C.A. Gunter, and A. Scedrov. Inheritance as implicit coercion. *Information and computation*, 93(1):172–221, 1991.
8. P. Buneman and B.C. Pierce. Union types for semistructured data. In *Proceedings of IDPL*, 1998.
9. D. Chamberlin et al. XQuery use cases. http://www.w3.org/TR/xquery-use-cases/.

10. S. Boag et al. XQuery. `http://www.w3.org/TR/xquery`.

11. M. Flatt, S. Krishnamurthi, and M. Felleisen. Classes and mixins. In *Proceedings of POPL*, 1998.

12. C. Fournét and G. Gonthier. The reflexive chemical abstract machine and the join-calculus. In *Proceedings of POPL*, 1996.

13. V. Gapeyev and B.C. Pierce. Regular object types. In *Proceedings of ECOOP*, 2003.

14. M. Harren, M. Raghavachari, O. Shmueli, M. Burke, V. Sarkar, and R. Bordawekar. XJ: Integration of XML processing into Java. Technical report, IBM Research, 2003.

15. H. Hosoya and B.C. Pierce. XDuce: A typed XML processing language. In *Proceedings of WebDB*, 2000.

16. H. Hosoya, J. Vouillon, and B.C. Pierce. Regular expression types for XML. In *Proceedings of ICFP*, 2000.

17. M. Howard and D. LeBlanc. *Writing Secure Code*. Microsoft Press, 2003.

18. A. Igarashi, B.C. Pierce, and P. Wadler. Featherweight Java: A minimal core calculus for Java and GJ. *ACM TOPLAS*, 23(3):396–450, 2001.

19. D. Leijen and E. Meijer. Domain Specific Embedded Compilers. In *Proceedings of Conference on Domain-Specific Languages*, 1999.

20. F. Matthes, S. Müßig, and J.W Schmidt. Persistent polymorphic programming in Tycoon: An introduction. Technical report, University of Glasgow, 1994.

21. E. Meijer, W. Schulte, and G.M. Bierman. Programming with circles, triangles and rectangles. In *Proceedings of XML*, 2003.

22. E. Meijer, W. Schulte, and G.M. Bierman. Unifying tables, objects and documents. In *Proceedings of DP-COOL,*, 2003.

23. B.C. Pierce. *Types and programming languages*. MIT Press, 2002.

24. J. Price. *Java programming with Oracle SQLJ*. O'Reilly, 2001.

25. D. Yu, A. Kennedy, and D. Syme. Formalization of generics for the .NET common language runtime. In *Proceedings of POPL*, 2004.

Prototypes with Multiple Dispatch:
An Expressive and Dynamic Object Model

L•• S•l•• •n •n• Jon•••n Al••i••

Carnegie Mellon University, Pittsburgh, PA 15217, USA
lsalzman@alumni.cmu.edu
jonathan.aldrich@cs.cmu.edu

Abstract. Two object-oriented programming language paradigms—dynamic, prototype-based languages and multi-method languages—provide orthogonal benefits to software engineers. These two paradigms appear to be in conflict, however, preventing engineers from realizing the benefits of both technologies in one system. This paper introduces a novel object model, prototypes with multiple dispatch (PMD), which seamlessly unifies these two approaches. We give formal semantics for PMD, and discuss implementation and experience with PMD in the dynamically typed programming language Slate.

1 Overview

W• •••in ••• •••••• •y ••••i• in• • • o•iv••in• •x•• •l• •••• •• ow• ••• li• i••-•ion• o• •••••n•, •o••l•• o• j•••-o•i•n••• l•n••••••• •o• ••••••in• • ow • •••o• ••••vio• •••• •n•• on ••• in••••••ion ••w••n o•j•••• •n• •••i• ••••••. T•• •x-•• •l• ••ow• ••••• • •l•i-• ••• o•• ••n •l••nly ••••••• •ow ••••vio• ••••n•• on ••• in••••••ion ••w••n o•j••••, w•il• •yn•• i•, ••o•o•y•-•••••• l•n•••••• ••n •l••nly ••••••• •ow ••••vio• ••••n•• on o•j••• ••••••. Un•o••• n•••ly, •ni•yin• •i••ly •yn•• i•, ••o•o•y••-••••• l•n••••• wi•• • •l•i-• ••• o•• i• ••••, •••••••• ••••i•ion•l • •l•i-• ••• o•• •••••• • • ••••i• •l••• •i••••••y •••• i• no• •••••n• in •yn•• i• ••o•o•y••-••••• l•n••••••.

In ••••ion 3 w• ••••i• • P•o•o•y• •• wi•• M• l•i•l• Di•••••• (PMD), •n o• j••• • o••l •••• •o• •in•• ••• ••n•••• o• •yn•• i•, ••o•o•y•-••••• l•n••••• wi•• • •l•i-• ••• o••. PMD ••••o••• •o•• •••••i•• • •y in••o••in• • •ol• •on•••• •••• lin•• • •lo• wi••in •n o•j••• •o • •i•••••• •o•i•ion on • • •••o•, •n• •••nin• • •yn•• i• • •l•i-• ••• o•• •i•••••• • ••••ni•• ••••• •••v••••• ••• ••••• o• o• j••••, • •••o••, •n• •ol•• •o •n• ••• • o•• •••i•• • •••o• i• •l•• •n••ion •o• • •iv•n ••• o• •••••iv•• o• j••••.

S•••ion • •••n•• ••• PMD • o••l • o•• •••••i••ly ••in• o• •••••ion•l ••• •n•i••. S•••ion 5 ••• on••••••• ••• •x•••••iv•n••• o• PMD •••o••• ••• •••n•••• li•••y o• Sl•••, • •yn•• i••lly-•y••• l•n••••••• ••i• •l•• •n•• ••• PMD o•j•••• o••l. S•••ion 6 •••••i••• •n •• •i•n• •l•o•i••• •o• i• •l•• •n•in• •i•••••• in Sl•••. S•••ion • •••••i••• ••l•••• wo••, •n• ••••ion • •on•l••••.

A.P. Black (Ed.): ECOOP 2005, LNCS 3586, pp. 312–336, 2005.
© Springer-Verlag Berlin Heidelberg 2005

2   Motivating Example

In •• i• ••••ion, w• ••• • •i• • l• •• nnin• •x•• • l• •o •x•• in• ••• ••n•••• •n•
li• i•••ion• o• •wo •••••n• •••n•• in o• j•••-o•i•n••• ••o•••• • in•: ••o•o•y•-
••••• l•n•••••• •n• • •l•i-• •••o• l•n••••••. • • j•••• w••• o•i•in•lly inv•n•••
•o• • o••lin• •n• •i• •l••ion •••• o•••, •n• o••x•• •l• •ollow•• i• ••••i•ion •y
• o••lin• • •i• • l• o•••n ••o•y•••• .

Fi•••• 1 •••••n•• ••• •• nnin• •x•• • l• in • •onv•n•ion•l •l•••-••••• l•n••••••
li•• J•v• o• • #. T•• in•••i•n•• •i•••••• y i• • ••• •• o• •n •••••••• Animal
••••••l••• •n• •wo •on•••• •••l•••••, Fish •n• Shark. An •ni• •l'• ••••vio•
i• •••n•• •y ••• encounter • •••o•. Fi•• •wi• •w•y ••o• •••l••y •••••••, •••
i•no•• o•••• •ni• •l•. I• • ••••• i• •••l••y, i• will ••• •ny ••• i• •n•o•n••••
•n• •••• o•••• ••••••; i• ••• ••••• i• no• •••l••y i• will •wi• •w•y ••o• o••••
•ni• •l•. W••n • •••••• •••••, i• •••o• •• •n•••l••y.

T•i• •x•• •l• ill•••••••• ••••vio• •••• •••••n•• on •o•• •n o•j•••'• •l••
•n• i•• •••••, •••oin• • •ny i• •o•••n• •••l-wo•l• ••o•••• • in• •i•••ion•. Fo•
•x•• •l•, • ••• '• ••••vio• ••••n•• on ••• •y•• o• •ni• •l •••• i• •n•o•n••••.
A •••••'• ••••vio• •••••n•• •o•• on ••• •y•• o• •ni• •l i• •n•o•n••• •n• i••
••••n• •••l•• .

```
class Animal {
    abstract method encounter (other : Animal);
    method swimAway () { ... }
}

class Fish inheriting Animal {
    method encounter (other : Animal) {
        if (other.isShark())
            if (other.isHealthy())
                swimAway();
    }
}

class Shark inheriting Animal {
    variable healthy : boolean;
    method isHealthy() {
        return healthy;
    }
    method swallow (other : Animal) { ... }
    method encounter (other : Animal) {
        if (isHealthy())
            if (other.isFish())
                swallow (other);
            else if (other.isShark())
                fight (other);
        else
            swimAway();
    }
    method fight (other : Shark) {
        healthy := False;
    }
}
```

Fig. 1. A simple inheritance hierarchy modeling an ocean ecosystem. The encounter method illustrates behavior that depends both on an object's class (Shark or Fish) and its state (healthy or not). In conventional class-based languages, the behavior specification is complex, imperative, and hard to extend with additional classes

In •• i• •x•• • l•, o• j•••-o•i•n••• ••o•••• • in• i• ••n•••i•l in •••• i• •llow•
•• •o •n••••• l••• • •••••• '• •••• vio• wi•• in ••• ••••• ••o•• •n• • •••• '• •••• vio•
wi•• in ••• •••• '• •o••. How•v••, i• •l•o ••ow• ••o•l•• • wi•• ••••••n• o• j•••-
o•i•n••• l•n••••••. T•• ••••i•••ion o••••vio• i• •o• •w••• •o• •l•x•n• • ••••
•o • n• ••••• n•–v•n •o• •• i• •i• • l• •x•• • l•–•••••• •• ••• ••on••ol ••••• •• ••• wi•• in
••• encounter • •••o••••n•••• on • •ny •on• i•ion•. T•• ••o•••• i• •l•o ••l•-
•iv•ly •••• •o •x••n• wi•• n•w •in•• o••ni• •l•, ••••••• in •••i•ion •o •••nin•
• n•w ••••l•••• o• Animal, ••• ••o•••• • •• • ••• ••• •••••o••i••• ••••• •o •••
encounter • •••o•• in Fish •n• Shark •o •• ow • ow •••••• •ni• •l• ••••v• w••n
•••y •n•o• n••• ••• n•w •y•• o• •ni• •l.

2.1   Multiple Dispatch

A l•n•••••• wi•• • •l•i-• •••o•• •i•••••••• on ••• •l••••• o• •ll ••• •••••• •n•
o• j•••• •o • • •••o•, •••••• •••n on j••• ••• •l••• o• ••• ••••iv••. M•l•i•l•
•i•••••• i• •••••l •o•• o••lin• •• n••ion•li•y ••••••••••n•• on ••• •y•• o•• •l•i•l•
in••••••in• o• j••••.

Fi•••• • •• ow• ••• o•••n ••o•y•••• • o••l•• ••in• • •l•i-• •••o••. In••••• o•
••in• w•i•••n •• ••••• o• •••• •l•••, • •l•i-• •••o•• ••• •••l•••• •• ••• •o• l•v•l

```
class Animal { }
    method swimAway (animal : Animal) { ... }

class Fish inheriting Animal { }
    method encounter (animal : Fish, other : Animal) { }
    method encounter (animal : Fish, other : Shark) {
        if (other.isHealthy())
            swimAway(animal);
    }

class Shark inheriting Animal {
    variable healthy : boolean;
}
    method isHealthy (animal : Shark) {
        return animal.healthy;
    }
    method swallow (animal : Shark, other : Animal) { ... }
    method encounter (animal : Shark, other : Fish) {
        if (animal.isHealthy())
            swallow (animal, other);
        else
            swimAway(animal);
    }
    method encounter (animal : Shark, other : Shark) {
        if (animal.isHealthy())
            fight (animal, other);
        else
            swimAway(animal);
    }
    method fight (animal : Shark, other : Shark) {
        animal.healthy := False;
    }
```

Fig. 2. Modeling the ocean ecosystem using multi-methods. Here, the encounter method dispatches on both the first and second arguments, simplifying the control structure within the methods and making the system more declarative and easier to extend

•n• •x• li•i•ly in•l••• ••• • •••• (o• ••••iv••) ••••• •n•. M•l•i-• •••o•• •i••••••
on •ll ••••• •n• •o•i•ion•, •o •••• on• o••o•• encounter • •••o•••n • •••ll••,
•••••n•in• on w••••••••••• •wo •ni• •l• ••• •o•• ••••••, •o•• •••, o• on• o••••••
in •i•••• o••••.

Ty•i••lly, • •l•i•l• •i•••••• i• •••olv•• •y •i••in• ••• • o•• •••••i•• • •••o•
•••• i• ••• li•••l• •o •ll o•••• ••••• •n•, wi•• • •••y• ••l••ion •• on• •l•••••
•••••• inin• •• i• •••i••i••y. Fo• •x•• •l•, i• • ••• •n•o•n•••• • •••••, •• l••••
•wo • •••o•• ••• •••li•••l•: ••• •••• • •••o• •••n•• ••••••• • ••• in ••• •••••
• o•i•ion •n• •ny •ni• •l in ••• •••on• •o•i•ion, ••• ••• •••on• i• • o•• •••-
•i••, •••••in• • ••• in ••• •••• •o•i•ion ••• only •••••• in ••• •••on• •o-
•i•ion. In ••i• •••• ••• •••on• • •••o• wo•l• •• invo••• ••••••• i• i• • o••
•• ••i••.

In ••••• w•••• •wo • •••o•• ••• •••lly •• ••i••, l•n•••••• • iff••. L•n••••••
li•• • ••il •••• ••• •y• • •••i• •i•••••• wo•l• •i•n•l • *message ambiguous* ••-
•o• [5], w•il• l•n•••••• li•• • L• S •n• Dyl•n wo•l• ••oo••• • • •••o• •y •ivin•
••• l•••• o•••••••• •n•• •••••••• •io•i•y w••n•v•• ••• •••i••i•i•• o••wo• •••o••
••• •o• ••••• [•, 9].

T•• •x•• •l• ••ow• ••••• • •l•i•l• •i•••••• ••• • n•• ••• o• ••v•n•••• ov••
•in•l• •i•••••. I• i• • o•• •••l•••iv•, •on•i••, •n• ••y •o •n•••••n•, •••••••
••• •on••ol-flow •••n••• wi••in ••• encounter • •••o• ••v• ••n •••l•••• wi••
•••l•••iv• o•j•••-o•i•n••• •i••••••. I• i• • o•• •x••n•i•l•, •••••••• •••y••••
••n •• •x••n••• wi•• n•w o•j•••• •n• n•w • •••o•• wi••o•• •••n•in• •xi••in•
o•j•••• •n• • •••o••. T•••• ••v•n•••• ••• ••i• il••• •o••• ••v•n••••••••• o•j•••-
o•i•n••• ••o•••• • in• ••in•• ••l••iv• •o •o•••••l ••o•••• • in•.

How•v••, •••••• ••• •in ••o•l•• • wi•• ••• •x•• •l•, •• •x•••••••. I• i• ••ill
•w•w••• •o •x••••• •••••••l • •••vio•; ••i• i• ••ill •••••••n••• •y ••• •on••ol
flow •••n•••• in•i•• encounter • •••o••. F•••••• o••, ••• •o•• •••••i• in• ••••
•n•••l••y •••••• •wi• •w•y ••o• •ll o•••• •ni• •l• i• ••• li•••• in •wo • iff•••n•
encounter • •••o••. T•i• •••• •n••n••y • •••• ••• ••o•••• •••••• •o •n•••••n•,
•n• •••••••• ••• • o••i•ili•y •••• •••o•• • •y •• in••o••••• i• ••• •••li•••• •o••
i• •volv•• in in•on•i•••n• w•y•.

2.2 Prototype-Based Languages

P•o•o•y••-••••• l•n•••••••, •ion•••• •y ••• l•n••••• S•l• [1•], •i• •li•y •••
••o••••• • in• • o••l o• o•j•••-o•i•n••• l•n•••••• •y •••l••in• •l••••• wi•• ••o-
•o•y• o• j•••. In•••• o•••••••in• • •l•••• o•••••••n•• •on•••, ••• ••o•••• • ••
•••••••• •n o•j••• •••• ••••••••n•• •••• •on••••. W••n•v•• ••• ••o•••• n••••• •n
in•••n•• o• •••• •on••••, ••• ••o•o•y• o•j••• i• •lon•• •o •o•• • n•w o•j•••
•••• i• i••n•i••l in •v••y w•y •x•••• i•• i••n•i•y. S••••••••n• • o•i••ion• •o
••• •lon• •iv•••• ••o• ••• o•i•in•l n• vi•• v••••.

P•o•o•y••-••••• l•n••••• •l•o •• •••••i•• ••• •••• -wi•• •on••••ion o• o•-
j•••• ov•• • •••••i• •n• •o• •l•• ••••••i••ion. M•••o•• • •y •• •••••• •• n•w
"•lo••" o• •n o•j•••• •• •ny •i• •, •n• in l•n••••• li•• S•l•, in••i••n•• ••l••ion-
••i•• • •y •l•o • •••n••• •• •ny •i• •. T•i• •• •••••i• on in•••• •n••l •on•••••-
•ion o•••••• ••••••• o•j•••• ••• now ••l•-••• •i•n• •n•i•i•• •••• •on••in ••• •vio•

```
object Animal;
object Fish;
object Shark;
object HealthyShark
object DyingShark

addDelegation (Fish, Animal);
addDelegation (Shark, Animal);
addDelegation (Shark, HealthyShark);

method Animal.swimAway () { ... }

method Fish.encounter(other) {
   if (other.isHealthyShark())
      swimAway();
}

method HealthyShark.swallow (other : Fish) { ... }
method HealthyShark.fight (other : Shark) {
   removeDelegation(HealthyShark);
   addDelegation(DyingShark);
}

method HealthyShark.encounter (other) {
   if (other.isFish())
      swallow (other);
   else if (other.isShark())
      fight (other);
}
method DyingShark.encounter (other) {
   swimAway();
}
```

Fig. 3. Modeling the ocean ecosystem using a prototype-based language. Here, the health of a shark is modeled by delegation to either the HealthyShark or the Dying-Shark. These abstractions represent behavior more cleanly and declaratively compared to the solutions described above

•• • ••n• in• •o• • on•n• o• •••i• •••••, •••••• •••n ••in• in•••n••• o• • •l••• w•i•• • •••ly •••••j••• •••i• ••••vio• •o• •••• .

Fi•••• 3 •• ow• •ow ••• o•••n ••o•y•••• ••n •• •x••••••• in • ••o•o•y••- ••••• l•n•••••. T•• ••o•••• • •• •••• ••••••• • ••o•o•y•• Ani• •l o• j•••, •••n ••••••• ••o•o•y•• S•••• •n• Fi•• o• j•••• •••• ••l••••• •o ••• Ani• •l.

T•• •••l•• o•• S•••• i• •••••••n••• •y ••l••••ion •o •i•••• • H••l••yS•••• o• j••• o• • Dyin• S•••• o• j•••. T•••• o• j•••• •n•••••l••• ••• ••••vio• o• ••• ••••• w••n i• i• •••l••y o• •yin•, •••••••iv•ly. S••••• •••in in ••• •••l••y •••••, ••l••••in• •o ••• H••l••yS•••• o• j••• •n• •••• in•••i•in• i•• encounter • •••o• . W••n • H••l••yS•••• •••••, ••• •••••n• o• j•••'• ••l••••ion i• •••n••• ••o• H••l••yS•••• •o Dyin• S••••, •n• ••o• •••• • oin• on ••• ••••• in•••i•• ••• encounter • •••o• ••o• Dyin• S••••.

T• i• •x•• •l• •• ow• • ••••n••• o• ••o•o•y••-•••• l•n••••••: ••l••••ion ••n •••ily •• •••• •o •••••••n• ••• •yn•• i• ••••vio• o• •n o• j•••. T•• ••••vio• ••n •• •••n••• •yn•• i••lly w••n •o• • •v•n• o••••• •i• •ly •y •••n•in• ••• o• j•••'• ••l••••ion. Al••o••• w• ••• •yn•• i• in•••i••n•• •• •n ill••••••ion o• •••• • •ll•••ili•y ••ovi•• •y ••o•o•y••-••••• l•n••••••, o•••• ••••••• o• •••••• l•n•••••• ••ovi•• •x••••iv•n••• ••n•• •• •• w•ll. Fo• •x•• •l•, w• •o• l• j•• ••

•••ily ••v• •••••n•• S••••'• encounter • •••o• in ••• fight • •••o• •o • o••l ••n••• in •••l••.

D•••i•• ••• ••v•n•••••• •••• ••o•o•y••• ••in•, •o• • ••o•l•• • ••• •in. Li•• ••• o•i•in•l •l•••-••••• •o••, ••• ••o•o•y••-••••• i• •l•• •n••ion o• ••• encounter • •••o• •••n•• •x•li•i•ly on ••• •y• • o• ••• o•j•••••in• •n•o•n-••••••. A• •i••••••• •••li••, ••i• • •••••• •••• •o•• • o•• •i• ••l• •o •n••••••n• •n• •••••• •o •x••n• wi•• n•w •in•• o• •ni• •l•.

2.3 Discussion

T•• ••v•n•••••• o• • •l•i•l• •i•••••• •n• ••o•o•y•• •• ••• •l••ly •o• •l•• •n••y. M• l•i•l• •i••••••• •llow ••o•••• • ••• •o • o•• •••l••••iv•ly ••••i•• •••vio• •••• ••• ••n•• on • •l•i•l• in•••••in• o•j••••. P•o•o•y••• •llow ••o•••• • ••• •o • o•• •l••nly •••••i•• • ••••••l ••••vio•, in •••i•ion •o o•••• ••n•••• ••••••• •y • o•• • •ll•••l• o•j•••• •••• ••• • o•• •••••i•l• o•j•••••••••n••ion, •n••-•••in•• • •••o• •••ni•ion, •n• •••i••••y o•j••• •x••n•ion.

B••••••• o• •••••• •o• •l•• •n••y •v•n••••, i• i• n••••l •o •••••••• •o• •in-in• ••• •wo • o••l•. S••• • •o• •in••ion i• •i• ••l•, •ow•v••, ••••••• • •l•i•l• •i••••••• •••n•• on • •••••••• in•• •i•••••y o• •l••••, w• il• ••o•o•y••• ••n-•••lly •llow • ••l•••••ion •i••••••y •o •••n•• •••i••••ily •• •ny •i• •.

T•••• •vio• l•n•••••••••• ••• •••il •••••o• •in•• •••• •wo • o••l ••••••i•• ••l••••ion •n• • •••o• •••ni•ion •o••• •l••iv•ly •x•• ••• •lo••l••o• ••••• • •y •• •••ily •n•ly••• [5]. Un•o••• n••ly, •••••i••in• •••• • •ni• •l••ion o•o•j•••• •n• • •••o••, wi••o•• •o• ••n•••in• wi•• •••i•ion•l •••••ni•• •, •l•o •li• in•••• • ••y ••v•n•••• o• ••o•o•y••: ••• •l•v••ion o• •••vio• •o ••••••. T• i• •x•• ••l••••ion •i••••••y •n• • •••o• •••ni•ion •••o• •• •••• ini••••n• o••l••••• w• i•• •l•o, in ••n•••l, •• ••••i•• ••i• •x•• in•••i••n•• •n• •on••••••ion.

W• il• o•••• ••••ni••• •o• •••l••••iv•ly ••••i•yin• ••• ••• •n••n•• o•o•j•••• •••vio• on ••••• •o •xi••, [6,•,13], •••y ••• • o•• •o• •l•x •n• •••••i•••• •••n •yn•• i• in••i••n•• •n• • •••o• •••••• • ••••ni•• • in S•l•.

3   Prototypes with Multiple Dispatch

T•• •on••i••ion o• •i• ••••• i• •••••i•in• •ow • •yn•• i•, ••o•o•y••-••••• o•j••• • o••l in ••• ••yl• o• S•l• ••n •• •••on•il•• wi•• • •l•i•l• •i••••••. • •• o•j••• • o•l, P•o•o•y••• wi•• M• l•i•l• Di••••••• (PMD), •o• •in••• ••• ••n•••• o• •••••• •wo •••vio• o•j••• • o••l•.

Fi•••• • •• ow• ••• ••o•••• •••'• vi•w o• PMD. T•• ••o•••• • ••• •••••••• •n o•j••• •••••••••• •••• • i••o•• ••• ••o•o•y•• •o•• •iv•n •••li••. W••n ••• n-in• • •••o••, •ow•v••, ••• ••o•••• • ••• ••••l•••• •ll ••••• •n•• (in•l• •in• ••• •••••iv••) •x•li•i•ly, •• in ••• • •l•i-•••o• •o•• •iv•n ••li••. In••••• o• •ivin• ••• •l••• •••• ••••• ••••• •n• •i•••••••• on, • •••o•o•y•• •o•j••• i• •iv•n.

T•• •o•• in Fi•••• • •o• •in•• ••• ••••• o• •o•• ••o•o•y•• ••n• • •l•i•l• •i•-••••••. A• in ••• ••o•o•y•• ••••, ••• ••••vio•l •••n••n•• on ••• •••l•• o•••• •••••• i• • o••l•• •••l••••ion •o H••l••yS•••• o• • Dyin•S•••• o•j••. T•i• ••l••••ion ••n •• •••n•••, •o• •x•• •l•, i•••• •••••• i• inj•••• in • ••••. A• •••

```
object Animal;
object Fish;
object Shark;
object HealthyShark;
object DyingShark;

addDelegation (Fish, Animal);
addDelegation (Shark, Animal);
addDelegation (Shark, HealthyShark);

method swimAway (animal : Animal) { ... }

method encounter(animal : Fish, other : Animal) /* A */ { }
method encounter(animal : Fish, other : HealthyShark) /* B */ {
   swimAway(animal);
}

method swallow (animal : Shark, other : Fish) { ... }
method fight (animal : HealthyShark, other : Shark) {
   removeDelegation(animal, HealthyShark);
   addDelegation(animal, DyingShark);
}

method encounter (animal : HealthyShark, other : Fish) /*C*/ {
   swallow (animal, other);
}
method encounter (animal : HealthyShark, other : Shark) /*D*/ {
   fight (animal, other);
}
method encounter (animal : DyingShark, other : Animal) /*E*/ {
   swimAway(animal);
}
```

Fig. 4. Modeling the ocean ecosystem in Prototypes with Multiple Dispatch (PMD). PMD combines multiple dispatch with a dynamic, prototype-based object model, leading to a declarative treatment of both state and dispatch

••• • •i• •, •••vio••l •••n••n•• on • •l•i•l• in•••••in• o• j•••• i• •x•••••• •••o••• • •l•i•l• • •••o• •••l•••ion•, on• •o• •••• ••l•v•n• ••••. In • ••n••, ••• •o•• i• •• •l••n •n• •••l•••iv• •• i• •o•l• • o••i•ly ••: no ••••• v••i••l•• o• •on••ol-flow •••n•••• ••• •in.

3.1 Dispatch Model

T•• ••y in•i••• ••••• •••• PMD wo•• i• ••••• • •l•i-• •••o•• • ••• •• in••n•l-i••• in•o o• j••••, •••••• •••n •••••••• •• •x•••n•l •n•i•i• •••• • i•••••• •••o•• • • x•• in••i••n•• •i•••••y. • •••inin• • l•••ly •x••in•i• •i•••••• ••o••••, •• in •••vio••• • •l•i-• ••o• l•n•••••, in•vi••ly ••••i•••• ••• •••••••ili•y o• ••v•l-o•• ••• •o • •ni••l••• ••• • ••••vio• o• •n o• j••• •••o••• •yn•• i• in••i••n•• o• • •••o• •••••••.

In S•l•, • •••o•• ••• in••n•li••• •y ••o•in• •••• in •lo•• o• ••• ••••iv•• o• j•••. PMD ••nno• ••• •• i• •••••••y, • ow•v••, •••••••• • • •l•i-• •••o• • ••• o•••••• on • •l•i•l• o• j••••; ••••• i• no •i••in••i•••• ••••iv••.

W•• •olv• ••i• •••ll•n•• •y in••o••in• ••• •on•••• o• ••• *role* •l•y•• •y • ••••i••l•• o• j••• in •n in••••••ion •••n•• •y • • •l•i-• •••o•. •••• • •l•i-• ••••o• ••• n•• • •ol• •o• •••• o• i•• ••••• •n• •o•i•ion•. Fo• •x•• • l•, in ••• l•••

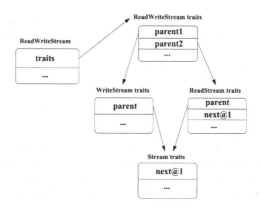

Fig. 5. A conceptual view of prototypes with multiple dispatch

• ••• o• o• Fi•••• •, ••• encounter • •••o•'• •••• •ol• i• •l•y•• •y • Dyin•S•••• o• j•••, w• il• ••• •••on• •ol• i• •l•y•• •y •n Ani• •l o•j•••.

• ••• o•j••• ••••• ••••• o• w•i•• •ol•• i• •l•y• •o• w•i•• • •l•i-• •••o••. Fi-••• 5 •• ow• ••• •ol•• ••••• •iff•••n• o•j••••• •l•y in •iff•••n• encounter • •••o••. Ani• •l •l•y• ••• •••on• •ol• in •wo •iff•••n• encounter • •••o• •o•i••: ••• on•• • •••••• A •n• • in ••• •o•• •• ov•. Fi•• •l•y• ••• • •••• •ol• in ••• • •••• •wo • •••o•• (•in•• •••i• •••• ••••• •••• •i•••••••• on Fi••) •n• ••• •••on• •ol• in • •••o• • .

Di•••••• o•••••• •y •••••• in• ••• ••l•••ion •i•••••y •o• in••i••• • •••o•• wi•• ••• •i••• n•• • •n• •••o•i••• •ol•• •o• •••• o• ••• •••••• •n••. Fo• •x•• -•l•, •on•i••• w••• •••••n• w••n • ••• •n•o•n•••• • ••••• •••• i• •••l••y (i.•., ••ill i• ••l••••in• •o ••• H••l••yS•••• o•j•••). Fi•• ••n •l•y ••• "•n•o• n•••••" •ol• (•ol• #1) in •o•• • •••o•• A •n• B. T•• •••••• ••n •l•y ••• "•n•o• n•••••" •ol• (•ol• #•) in • •••o•• A •n• •, in••i••• ••o• Ani• •l, • •••o• B, in ••-i••• ••o• H••l••yS••••, •n• • •••o• D, ••• n•• in ••• S•••• o•j••• i•••l•. • nly • •••o•• A •n• B will wo•• •o• •o•• •ol••. W• •• oo•• ••• • •••o• •o invo•• •y o•••in• ••• ••l•••ion• •o• • •iv•n o•j•••, in •••• •••••• ••• • •l•i•l• •••• ••l••••ion•.

A n•• ••• o• ••• •n•i•• ••• •o••i•l• •o• •••••• inin• ••• •••••••n•• o• •iff••-•n• ••• li••• l• • •••o••. T•• ••• •n•i•• w• •• o•• i• •l•• •n•• • •o••l o•••in• o• • •••o•• •y •on•i••in• (••••) ••••• •n•• •••••• •o ••• l••• •o •••• •••••••n•• ov•• •••••• •n•• •o ••• •i•••, (•••on•) • •l•i•l• ••l•••ion• wi•• in • •in•l• o•j•••• •o•• o•••••• •••o••in• •o ••• • o•• ••••n• •i• • o•••• ni•ion, •n• (••i••) • ••• -o•• •lo••• in ••• ••l••••ion •i••••••y •o ••• ••••li•• • •••o• ••••• •n•• •o •• • o•• ••••i••.

W• •• o•• • •o••l o•••• ••••••• •••n • ••••i•l o••••, •• in • ••il [5], •o •voi• ••• •o••i•ili•y o• •• •i••i•y in •i•••••. A l•••-•o-•i••• o•••in• i• •••n•••, •• i• ••• ••i•••i• o• •lo••n••• in ••• •i•••••• •i•••••y. W• •• o•• •o ••io•i•i•• • o•• ••••n• ••l•••ion• ••••••• •• i• •iv•• •••v•lo•••• • o•• fl•xi•ili•y •o •ff•• ••• ••••vio• o• o•j•••• •y •••in• • n•w ••l•••ion. W• ••io•i•i•• •••• on ••• ••••• •n• •o•i•ion, •••n on ••• o•••in• o• ••l•••ion•, •••n on ••• •i••n•• in

••• ••l•••ion •i••••••y, •••••••• ••i• •iv•• •• • •onv•ni•n• •••••-•••• •••••••
•l•o•i••• •o •n• ••• •••o••i••• • •••o• (S•••ion 6.1). T•i• •l•o•i••• i• •o••
• o•• •• •i•n• •n• ••i•• •o• • ••o•••• ••• •o •n•••••n• ••n • ••••••••-••••
•l•o•i••• •••• wo•l• o•••wi•• •• ••••i•••.[1]

4   Formal Model

T•i• ••••ion ••ovi••• • •o•• •l • o••l o• ••o•o•y•• wi•• • •l•i•l• •i••••••
•••o••• • n•w o•j•••••l••l••, • •••l••l••• • o••ow• i•••• ••o• ••v•••l •••vio••
o•j•••••l••li, •••••• • iff•••n••• •••w••n PMD •n• •••vio• o•j•••• o••l• •••
•oo •••••• •o ••• • ••••i•••o•w•• •x••n•ion o•• •••vio••••l••l••. Fo• •x•• •l•,
only on• •••vio••••l••l••••• w• •now o•••• •o••• i• ••••iv••••••• o•• •••-
o•• [1]. How•v••, ••i• ••l••l••, li•• • o•• o•••• [3], •o• •il••w•y••l•••ion •y
•i• •ly •o•yin• • •••o•• ••o• ••• ••l••••• in•o ••• ••l•••o•. T•i• •••••••y
••nno• •o••i•ly wo•• in PMD ••••••• ••l•••ion ••n •••n•• ••••• •n o•j•••
i• ••••••••. T•••, ••• •••••••n••ion o• o•j•••• in ••• ••l••l•• • •••• • •in••in
in•o••• ••ion •• o•• ••l•••ion •o •••• o•• ••i• ••o••ly.

T•• • o•• •i•ni••n• •iff•••n• wi•• •ll •••vio••••l••li i• o•• • o••lin• o•
••l•i•l• •i•••••• •••o••• •ol•• on o•j••••; ••i• • ••••••••• ••o• • on •••••o•••
o•• • o••lin• o•j•••• •• •••o••• o• • •••o•• in••••o••i••• [10,1,3]. Al••o••• •
••w o•j•••••l••li • o••l • •l•i-• •••o•• [1•,•], •••y •ll • o••l • •l•i-• •••o••
•• •x•••n•l ••n••ion• •••• • i•••••• ov•• • •x•• •i•••••• •i••••••y, w••il• PMD
•llow• ••• ••v•lo••• •o •••n•• ••• • •••o•• ••••• ••• •••li•••l• •o •n o•j•••, ••
w•ll •• •o • o•i•y ••• in••i••n•• •i••••••y •• ••n •i• •.

W• in••••• ••••••• •n •n•y•••, i• •••••iv• o•j•••••l••l••, PMD (P•o•o•y••
wi•• M•l•i•l• Di••••••), •••• •••i••ly •••••i•••• ••• ••• •n•i•• o• o•• ••o•o•••
o•j•••• o••l. T•••• •in •on••i••ion• o•••• • o••l••• •o•• •li•in• • •l•i-• ••• o•
•i•••••• ••••• on •ol••, •n• •x•o•in• ••• ••oi••• l•n•••••• •••i•n••• ••v• •o•
•••••• inin• •i•••••in• ••••••••i••. W• •o•• •••• ••• ••l••l•• ••n •• •x••n•••
wi•• • •y•• •y•••• , ••• ••i• ••• •in• •••ll•n•in• •••••• wo••.

4.1   Syntax

Fi•••• 6 •x•l•in• •yn••x o• PMD. T•i• •yn••x ••ovi••• l•• ••• •x•••••ion• •o•
•••nin• • •••o• •o•i••, o•j••• •on••••••ion •••o••• o••••••• ••l•••ion •n•
• •••o• •••ni•ion, •n• •ol•• •••• •••n• ••• v••io•• •onn••••ion• •••w••n o•-
j•••••. A• in S• •ll••l• [11], • •••o• ••l•••o•• ••• •••• ••lv•• o•j•••• •n• ••n ••
•o• ••••••.

A• PMD i••n i• ••••••iv••••l••l••, •••• • o••l••••••••••• ••• •••o•• • •••in•
• ••o•• lo•••ion, •••• •o •••••••n• o• j••• i••n•i•y, •o •n o•j•••'• •••••••n••ion.
T•• o•j••• •••••••n••ion •on•i••• •••• o• • •••••n•• o• lo•••ion• ••no•in• •••

---

[1] If depth in the delegation hierarchy were considered first, for example, then simply
adding an extra layer of delegation would affect dispatch, which seems extremely
counterintuitive.

$l \in locations$ possible object identities in the store

$f ::= \lambda \overline{x}.e$ lambda expressions defining a method body

$e ::= x$ bindings

    $\mid l$ locations that the store maps to objects

    $\mid e_s(\overline{e})$ invokes method identified by selector e_s upon arguments $\overline{e}$

    $\mid e_s(\overline{e}) \leftarrow f$ defining a method at selector e_s with body f, dispatching on $\overline{e}$

    $\mid clone(e)$ copies an object

    $\mid e \triangleright e_d$ updates e to delegate to e_d

    $\mid e \not\triangleright$ removes the last delegation that was added to e

$v ::= l$ reduced values

$d ::= l$ delegations

$r ::= (l, i, f)$ roles contain a method selector, a method parameter index, and a method body

$O ::= (\langle \overline{d} \rangle, \{\overline{r}\})$ objects contain a list of delegations and set of roles

$S ::= l \mapsto O$ store mapping object identity to representation

Fig. 6. The syntax of PMD. The notation $\overline{z}$ denotes a syntactic sequence of z

$$Animal \stackrel{def}{=} clone(Root)$$
$$Fish \stackrel{def}{=} clone(Root)$$
$$Shark \stackrel{def}{=} clone(Root)$$
$$HealthyShark \stackrel{def}{=} clone(Root)$$
$$DyingShark \stackrel{def}{=} clone(Root)$$
$$Fish \triangleright Animal$$
$$Shark \triangleright Animal$$
$$Shark \triangleright HealthyShark$$
$$encounter(Fish, HealthyShark) \leftarrow \lambda xy.swimAway(x)$$
$$encounter(Fish, Animal) \leftarrow \lambda xy.x$$
$$fight(HealthyShark, Shark) \leftarrow \lambda xy.x \not\triangleright \triangleright DyingShark$$
$$encounter(HealthyShark, Fish) \leftarrow \lambda xy.swallow(x, y)$$
$$encounter(HealthyShark, Shark) \leftarrow \lambda xy.fight(x, y)$$

Fig. 7. The example scenario represented in the formal model

o• j•••• ••• ••••j•• l•• o• j••• ••l•••••• •o • n• ••n • ••• o• •ol•• i••n•i•yin• •••
• ••• o•• •onn••••• •o ••• ••••j•• l•• o• j•••.

T•• no•••ion $S[l]$ will • • ••••• •o ••no•• o• j••• ••• •••••n••ion •o••••• on• in•
•o ••• lo•••ion l in ••• ••o•• S, •n• ••• no•••ion $S[l \mapsto O]$ will •• ••••• •o ••no••
••• ••o•• S ••j••••• •o • •• ••• lo•••ion l •o ••• o• j••• •••••••••n••ion O.

4.2   Example

Fi•••• • ••••n•• ••• •• nnin• •x•• • l• in ••• PMD ••l••l••. I• ••ill ••••in• • ll o•
••• •on•i••n••• • n• •••••i••iv•n••• •• ••• o•i•in•l PMD-in••i••• •x•• • l• •n•
• iff••• li••l• ••o• i•, ••••i•• ••in• •••• •• in •••• • o•••• low••-l•v•l ••l••l••. T••

PMD ••• •n•i•• ••• •i•n•ly ••••••••• ••• • ••••ni•• • ••••• l••• •o ••• • ini• •l ••••o•in• o• ••• •• nnin• •x•• • l•.

T•• •x•• • l• ••••• •• ••• •xi••n•• o•• •i••in•• i•••• •• ••y o•j•••• •• oo• ••o• w•i•• •l•n• o•j••••• •y•• •lon•• •• w•ll •• ••• •i•n• •ni••• o•j•••• ••• n•• •o •ov•• •ll • •••o• ••l•••o•• •••• in ••• •x•• • l•. • ••••wi••, ••• •x•• • l• ••• •in• • •••• i•••-•o•w•• •••n•l••ion o• ••• •••li•• in•o•• •l PMD •x•• • l•.

4.3   Dynamic Semantics

Fi•••• • •••••n•• ••• •o•• •yn• i• ••• •n•i•• o• PMD. T•••• •••••••ion ••l•• •••• ••• •o•• $S \vdash e \hookrightarrow e', S'$, •o•• ••••• •• "wi•• ••••••• •o • ••o•• S, ••• •x•••••ion e ••••••• in on• •••• •o e', yi•l•in• • n•w ••o•• S'''. T•• •••••••ion ••l•• ••• n• • •••o• invo•••ion, • •••o• •••ni•ion, o•j•••lonin•, •n• ••l•••ion •••i•ion •n• ••• ov•l. T•• •on•••n•• ••l•• ••• n• ••• o•••• o• •v•l••ion in ••• •••n•••• w•y.

T•• ••l• **R-Invoke** loo•••• ••• ••• •o•y o•••• • o•• •••li•••l• • •••o•, wi•• •••••• •o • • •••o• ••l•••o• •n• • ••••••n•• o• • •••o• ••••• •n••, •iv•n •y ••• *lookup* •• n••ion (•••n•• ••low in Fi•••• 9). T•• • •••o• ••••• •n•• ••• •••n ••••••i•••• in•o ••• l•• ••• •x•••••ion/• •••o• •o•y w•i•• i• ••• •••• l•. S•••i••ion o•••••• •• in ••• l•• ••• ••l••l••.

T•• ••l• **R-Method** •••n•• • n•w • •••o• •o•y, •o•• invo••• wi•• • •iv•n ••l•••o•, •n• •i••••••in• on ••• •iv•n ••• o•o•j••••. A n•w •ol• i• •••••• •o •••• o•j•• v_i, •••in• •••• ••• o•j••• (o• •ny o•j•• ••••• ••l•••••• •o i•) ••n •l•y ••• i•• •ol• in • •i••••• on • •••o• ••l•••o• v_s •o • •••o• •o•y f. T•• o•j••• •••••••n••ion• ••• ••••••• in ••• ••o•• •o ••fl••• •• i•, yi•l•in• • n•w ••o••. T•• •••• •on•i•ion •n••••• •• i• •••ni•ion i• •ni••• •o ••• ••••i••l•• • •••o• ••l•••o• •n• ••••• •n••; ••••• i• no o•••• • •••o• •o•y ••• n•• •• on •• i• •x••• invo•••ion. T•• •x•••••ion ••••••• •o ••• •••• ••••• ••n• •••• only •o •i• • li•y •••••n••ion. W• o• i• • ••l• •o• • •••o• ••• ov•l•o• •••vi•y'• ••••, w•i•• wo•l• •• • ••••i•••-•o•w••• inv••ion o• ••• i• ••••i••l•• ••l•.

No•• ••••• • •••o• •••ni•ion •••• •ff•••• in••in•i• ••o•••i•• o• ••• •••• li•• ••••• •n• o•j••••' ••••••n••ion•, ••••• ••• n ••••• lin• •o •o• • •x••in•i• ••- • •n•i• ••vi••. T• i• •••o• •• •i•ni••n• in ••• ••l• **R-Clone**, w•i•• ••ovi••• ••• • •i••i•o•• •o•yin• o•••••ion •o•n• in ••o•o•y•-••••• l•n••••••. To •n- •••• ••••• ••• •o•i• o•j••••, w•i•• ••••• • n•w lo•••ion •n• •••••••n••ion in ••• ••o••, •••• on•• •o •ll • •••o• invo•••ion• in •i• il•• •••• ion ••• ••• o•i•in•l o•j•••, ••• ••l• only n•••• •o •o ••• li•••• ••• li•• o• ••l•••ion• •n• ••• o• •ol••. T• i• •i• •l• •••li•••ion o• ••l•v•n• •i••••• in•o•• ••ion in ••n •i• •li•• ••• i•• •l•• •n••ion o• •••••• ••• •n•i••.

T•• ••l•• **R-AddDelegation** •n• **R-RemoveDelegation** •o•••••• • •ni•- •l••• ••• o•••••• li•• o• ••l•••ion• o• •n o•j••• in •••••-li•• ••••ion. T•• ••l• **R-AddDelegation** ••••• • ••••• o•j••• •• • ••l•••ion •o ••• •o• o• ••• o•- •••• li•• o• ••l•••ion• o• ••• o•i•in o•j••. T•• ••l• **R-RemoveDelegation** ••• ov•• ••• •o• o• •i• o•••••• li•• •n• ••••n• ••• ••• ov•• ••l•••ion •••- •••. T•••• •wo ••••i••l•• ••l•• w••• • •••ly ••o••n •o •i• • li•y ••••n••ion, •n• o•••• •l••n•iv• ••l•• •llowin• •o• ••• i•••y • o• i••••ion o• ••• li•• ••• ••••• inly • o••i• l•.

Reduction Rules

$$\frac{lookup(S, v_s, \overline{v}) = \lambda \overline{x}.e}{S \vdash v_s(\overline{v}) \hookrightarrow [\overline{v}/\overline{x}]\, e, S'} \text{ R-Invoke}$$

$$\frac{\nexists f'\, (\forall_{0 \leq i \leq n}\, (S_0\,[v_i] = (\langle \cdots \rangle, \{\cdots, (s, i, f')\})))}{\forall_{0 \leq i \leq n} \left(\begin{array}{c} S_i\,[v_i] = (\langle \overline{d} \rangle, \{\overline{r}\}) \\ \wedge\, S_{i+1} = S_i\,[v_i \mapsto (\langle \overline{d} \rangle, \{\overline{r}, (v_s, i, f)\})] \end{array} \right)}{S_0 \vdash v_s(v_0 \cdots v_n) \leftarrow f \hookrightarrow v_0, S_{n+1}} \text{ R-Method}$$

$$\frac{S\,[v] = O \qquad l \notin dom(S) \qquad S' = S\,[l \mapsto O]}{S \vdash clone(v) \hookrightarrow l, S'} \text{ R-Clone}$$

$$\frac{S\,[v_o] = (\langle \overline{d} \rangle, \{\overline{r}\}) \qquad S' = S\,[v_o \mapsto (\langle \overline{d}, v_t \rangle, \{\overline{r}\})]}{S \vdash v_o \triangleright v_t \hookrightarrow v_o, S'} \text{ R-AddDelegation}$$

$$\frac{\begin{array}{c} S\,[v] = (\langle d_0 \cdots d_n \rangle, \{\overline{r}\}) \qquad n \geq 0 \\ S' = S\,[v \mapsto (\langle d_0 \cdots d_{n-1} \rangle, \{\overline{r}\})] \end{array}}{S \vdash v \not\triangleright \hookrightarrow d_n, S'} \text{ R-RemoveDelegation}$$

Congruence Rules

$$\frac{S \vdash e_s \hookrightarrow e_s', S'}{S \vdash e_s(\overline{e}) \hookrightarrow e_s'(\overline{e}), S'} \qquad\qquad \frac{S \vdash e_s \hookrightarrow e_s', S'}{S \vdash e_s(\overline{e}) \leftarrow f \hookrightarrow e_s'(\overline{e}) \leftarrow f, S'}$$

$$\frac{S \vdash e_i \hookrightarrow e_i', S'}{S \vdash v_s(v_0 \cdots v_{i-1}, e_i, e_{i+1} \cdots e_n) \hookrightarrow v_s(v_0 \cdots v_{i-1}, e_i', e_{i+1} \cdots e_n), S'}$$

$$\frac{S \vdash e_i \hookrightarrow e_i', S'}{S \vdash v_s(v_0 \cdots v_{i-1}, e_i, e_{i+1} \cdots e_n) \leftarrow f \hookrightarrow v_s(v_0 \cdots v_{i-1}, e_i', e_{i+1} \cdots e_n) \leftarrow f, S'}$$

$$\frac{S \vdash e_o \hookrightarrow e_o', S'}{S \vdash e_o \triangleright e_t \hookrightarrow e_o' \triangleright e_t, S'}$$

$$\frac{S \vdash e_t \hookrightarrow e_t', S'}{S \vdash v \triangleright e_t \hookrightarrow v \triangleright e_t', S'} \qquad\qquad \frac{S \vdash e_o \hookrightarrow e_o', S'}{S \vdash e_o \not\triangleright \hookrightarrow e_o' \not\triangleright, S'}$$

Fig. 8. The dynamic semantics of PMD

4.4   Dispatch Semantics

Fi•••• 9 •••••n•• •••• •j•••••• ••• •n•i•• ••ovi•••• •y ••• *lookup* ••n••ion. T••
•• l• **R-Lookup** i• • ••••i•••-•o•w••• •••n•••i••ion o• ••• i••• o• • •l•i•l• •i•-
••••••. I• ••••••• ••••• • • •••o• •o•y ••o•l• ••• •i••••••••• i• i• i• •••li•••l• - •
• •• ••• o• ••• ••• o•••li•••l• • •••o•• - •n• i• i• •••• • o•• ••••i•• o• •ll ••••
• •••o• •o•i••, o• •••••••, i• •••• l•••• • •••o• •o•y •••o••in• •o •n o••••••o•
••••••o• •••••• ••• •••• li•••l• • •••o• •o•i••. T•• *rank* ••n••ion •n• ≺ o•••••o•
•o•••••• i• •l•• •n• ••i• •o• •••i•on o• ••••o•.

$$\frac{f \in applic(S, v_s, \overline{v}) \quad \forall_{f' \in applic(S, v_s, \overline{v})} \left(f = f' \bigvee rank(S, f, v_s, \overline{v}) \prec rank(S, f', v_s, \overline{v}) \right)}{lookup(S, v_s, \overline{v}) = f} \textbf{ R-Lookup}$$

$$applic(S, v_s, v_0 \cdots v_n) \stackrel{def}{=} \left\{ f \middle| \forall_{0 \leq i \leq n} \left(\begin{array}{c} delegates(S, v_i) = \langle d_0 \cdots d_m \rangle \wedge \\ \exists_{0 \leq k \leq m} \left(S\left[d_k\right] = (\langle \overline{d'} \rangle, \{\cdots, (v_s, i, f)\}) \right) \end{array} \right) \right\}$$

$$rank(S, f, v_s, v_0 \cdots v_n) \stackrel{def}{=} \prod_{0 \leq i \leq n} \min_{0 \leq k \leq m} \left\{ k \middle| \begin{array}{c} delegates(S, v_i) = \langle d_0 \cdots d_m \rangle \\ \wedge S\left[d_k\right] = (\langle \overline{d'} \rangle, \{\cdots, (v_s, i, f)\}) \end{array} \right\}$$

Fig. 9. The dispatch semantics of PMD

W• •••n •••n• ••• *applic* ••• o• • •••o•• •• ••o•• • •••o•• •o• w•i•• •v••y ••••• •n• •i•••• •on••in• • •••i•••••o•y •ol• •o• ••• • •••o•, o• ••l•••••• •o •n o•j••• wi•• ••••• • •ol•. A •ol• •••• i• •••i•••••o•y i• in••x o• ••• • •••o• ••••• •n• on w•i•• i• i• •o•n• • •••••••••• in ••• •ol•, •n• ••• • •••o• ••l•••o• • •••••• •••• in ••• •ol• •• w•ll. T•i• ••• ni•ion ••li•• on ••• *delegates* •• n••ion, w•i• ••••• •n• •n o••••• li•• o••ll ••l•••••-•o o•j••• •••n•i•iv•ly ••••••• •l• • •y •••••l•••••ion li••• in o•j••••, •n• in•l••in• ••• o•i•in• l ••• o• ••••• •n• i•••l•. In ••• •••• o• • •••i••lly-•x•• ••l•••••ion •i••••••y, •• i• ••l• •x••ly• i••o•• ••• ••• li•••ili•y ••i•••i• in •••vio•• • •l•i-• •••o• l•n••••••• ••••• •• • ••il, Dyl•n •n• • L• S.

No•• ••••• •••••••• o•••• ••••• •on•i•ion o• **R-Method**, only on• • •••o• • o• y ••n ••• •i••••ly •••n•• on • •••l• o• o•j•••• ••• • •••••i••l•• ••l•••o•. T•••, in ••• ••••n•• o••••l•••••ion, •i•••••• i• ••ivi•l •in•• ••• ••• li•••l• ••• o• • •••o•• •on••in• ••• o•• • •in•l• • •••o• • o• y. • •n•in• ••• ••• li•••l• ••• o•• i• •••• • n••••••••y •on•••• •n•• o• ••l•••••ion.

Fin•lly, ••• *rank* •• n••ion, •on••••••lly, • n••, •• on• ••o•• • •••o•• in ••• *applic* •••, ••• •i•••n•• •• w•i•• ••• •ol•• •o••••••on•in• •o •o• • • •••o• ••- •••••••. • iv•n ••• o••••••• li•• o• *delegates* •o• •n ••••• •n• •••••i••• ••• ov•, i• ••••••• in••••• • ini• •l •o•i•ion •• w•i•• • • •l•••••••-•o o•j•••• •on••in• • •••i•- •••••o•y •ol• •o••••• •on•in• •o •••• • •••o•. T•• ∏ o• ••••o•, w•i•• •l•o •••• ••••- i••• ••• *rank* •• n••ion, •o• • in•• ••••• • ini• •l •o•i•ion• •o•••••• •••••• •n• • n• ••o••••• • •in•l• ••n• v•l•• - •on••••••lly, • n-•i• •n•ion• l •oo•• in••• in ••• ••n•in•. T•• •o••l o•••• in• •iv•n • y ••• *delegates* •• n••ion •••ili••••• ••• o•••••- in• •••• *rank* ••ovi•••, wi••o•• w•i•• ••••• ••• •n•i•• wo• l• • ••••i••i•• •o ••• n•.

W• ••••• • •••• •••• • ••••i••l•• • •••o• • o• y i• •ni••• •o • •in•l• • •••o• ••• ni•ion. So, in ••• •••••n•• o•••• ••l• **R-Clone**, •o• • •••••i• • • •••o• ••l•••o• •n• ••••• •••• in••x, ••••• ••n only •xi•• • •in•l• •••i•••••o•y •ol• •o••••• •on•- in• •o •••• ••••i••l•• • •••o• • o• y. How•v••, •in•• w• •o in•l••• **R-Clone**, •n• • •ol• • •y ••••••• ••o• i•• •o •no•••• o• j•••, • •l•i•l• •••i•••••o•y •ol•• •o•- •••• •on•in• •o ••• • •••o• • o• y •xi•• •n• ••• •lo•••• •ol• •• on• •••• in ••• *delegates* o•••in• i• •• o••n.

W• l••v• ••• *delegates* •• n••ion, ••• ≺ o••••o•, •n• ••• ∏ o• •••• o• •n- •••n••. T•• ••••••• • •y ••• n• ••••• •••i••••ily •o •• i• •••i• in••n••• • i•••••••

••• •n•i••. Sl•••'• ••• •n•i•• •o• ••••• o••••o•• ••• •••n•• •lon• wi•• Sl•••'•
•i•••••• •l•o•i••• in S••ion 6.1.

5   Slate

P•o•o•y••• wi•• M• l•i• l• Di•••••• ••••••n i• •l•• •n••• in Sl••• [16], • •yn•• -
i••lly •y••• ••o•••• • in• l•n••••••. S•l• [1•], ••il [5], •n• • L• S [•] •i••••ly
in••i••• ••• •••i•n o• Sl••• •n• ••• PMD • o••l on w•i•• i• i• ••••••. How-
•v••, ••• •o ••• ••••in•• fl•xi•ili•y o• ••o•o•y••• in PMD, Sl••• • o•• •••on•ly
••••• •l•• S•l• •n• ••••in• • ••• o• i•• l•n•••••• o•••ni••ion wi••o•• •••••ly
•o• ••o• i•in• i•• •i• •l• o• j••• • o••l.

T•• •ollowin• ••••ion ••ovi••• • ••••• o•••• Sl••• l•n•••••• •••o••• •x•• •l••
••o• ••• Sl••• •••n•••• li•••y ill•••••in• ••• ••n•••• o• ••• PMD • o••l.

5.1   Brief Overview

T•• •yn••x •n• •y•••• o•••ni••ion o• Sl••• •••on•ly ••••• •l•• •••• o• S•l•
•n• S• •ll••l• [11]. D•• •o ••••• li• i•••ion•, w• o• i• • ••••il•• •i••••ion o•
Sl•••'• •yn••x, w• i•• •o•l• ••• •n••••••n•••l• •o ••• •••••••• ••• ili• wi• •••••
l•n••••••; ••• •yn••x i• •l•o •o••• •n••• in ••••il l••w•••• [16].

W• ••i•fly ••••••i•• Sl•••'• • ••o• •••ni•ion •yn••x, w•i•• i• ••• ••i• ••y
•yn••••i• •iff•••n•• •••w••n Sl••• •n• S•l• o• S• •ll••l•. A • •••o• •••ni•ion
loo•• li•• • • •••o• ••n• in S•l• o• S• •ll••l•, •x••••• •••• on• o• • o•• o• •••
••••• •n••2 i• •••li••• •y ••• o•j••• on w•i•• ••• • •••o• •i••••••••. T••
•••li•••• ••••• •n• •yn••x i• o• ••• •o•• "parameterName @ roleArgument",
wi•• "roleArgument" i••n•i•yin• ••• o•j••• •••o•i•••• wi•• ••i• •ol• o• ••i•
• •••o• •o•y, •n• "parameterName" ••in• • v••i••l• •o•n• in ••• •o•y o•
••• • •••o•. T•• "roleArgument" ••n •• o• i•••, in w•i•• •••• ••• • •••o•
•i•••••••• on ••• •i••in••i•••• o•j••• "Root" •o w•i•• • o•• o•••• o•j•••• in
Sl••• ••l••••. T•• •••••n•• o• •• l•••• on• ••••• ••••• wi•• • •ol• ••••• •n•
•••li••• i• w••• •i•n•l• • • •••o• •••ni•ion in ••• •••• • •• (•• o••o••• •o •
• •••o• invo•••ion).

So• i• •o•••n• • ••••••• •o •• ••••• in ••• •••••••••n• •x•• •l•• in•l•••:

resend • •••n•• ••• • •••••• •••• invo••• ••• •••••n• • •••o• w•il• i•no•in•
    •ny • •••o•• o• •••••••• o• ••••l ••••••n•• in ••• •i••••• o•••• ••n •••
    ••••••n• • •••o• •••in• •i••••••.
prototype clone • ••••n• • n•w •o•y o• "prototype" •••• •on••in• •ll •••
    ••• • •lo•, ••l•••ion •lo••, •n• •ol••.
object addSlot: name valued: initialValue A••• • n•w •lo• •o "object"
    •n• •••n•••••• •••o• "name" wi•• w•i•• •o•••••• i•• v•l•••n• •••• •••o•
    "name:" wi•• w•i•• •o ••• i•. "name" • ••• •v•l•••• •o • •y• •ol. T•• •lo•'•
    v•l•• i• ini•i•lly "initialValue".

---

2 Note that in a language with multiple dispatch, the "arguments" to a method include
the receiver.

object addDelegate: name valued: initialValue T• i• • •••o• ••••v•• •x-
•••ly li•• "addSlot:valued:", •x•••• only •••• ••• •lo• i• •••••••• ••• • ••l-
•••ion •lo•. T•• v•l•• o• ••• ••l•••ion •lo• i• •••••••• •• •n o•j••• •••••
"object" ••l••••••• •o.

object traits A•••••o• • •••••• •o• ••• "traits" ••l•••ion •lo•, w• i•• •ol•••
•l•••-li•• o•j••• •••••in• • •••o• •ol•• •o• w•ol• ••• ily o• "•lon•"-• o•j••••.

block do • v•l••••• "block".

collection do: block • v•l••••• "block" wi•• •••• •l•• •n• o• •oll•••ion
"collection" ••••li•• in ••n •• •n ••••• •n•.

cond ifTrue: trueBlock ifFalse: falseBlock • v•l••••• "trueBlock" i•
"cond" •v•l••••• •o "True", o• in••••• "falseBlock" i• i• •v•l••••• •o
"False".

5.2   Example: Instance-Specific Dispatch

In•••n••-•••••i•• • i•••••• i• •n •x••n•iv•ly •••• i•io• in Sl•••, ••n••in• •••o•
i•• ••o•o•y•-••••• • o••l. W••n •o• •in•• wi•• • •l•i•l• •i••••••, i• •••in•
•o •••on•ly ••••• •l• •••••••n-• ••••in• [15] w•il• ••ill wi•• in •n o•j•••-o•i•n•••
•••• •wo••. Fo• •x•• •l•, • ••• o• ••• •ool••n lo•i• •o•• in Sl••• i• w•i•••n in •
•••i•in•ly •••l••••iv• •o•• ••in• in•••n••-•••••i•• • i•••••••:

```
_@True and: _@True [True].
_@(Boolean traits) and: _@(Boolean traits) [False].
_@False or: _@False [False].
_@(Boolean traits) or: _@(Boolean traits) [True].
```

T•• •o•• •i••••••••• •i•••ly on "True" •n• "False" •o••n•l• •••i•• •••••.
I• •••n ••• n•• • •••o•• on "Boolean traits" •o••n•l• ••• ••• •inin• ••••l•
•••••.

5.3   Example: Eliminating Double Dispatch

S• •ll••l• [11] •n• •i• il•• l•n••••••• ••••• on •in•l• •i••••••• •y•i•lly ••ly on
•n i•io• ••ll•• "•o••l• •i••••••" •o wo•• ••o•n• ••• li• i•••ion• ••i• • o••l
i• • o•••. In ••i• i•io• , • • •••o• •i••••••• on ••• ••••iv•• ••••, ••n invo•••• •
••l•••• •••o• (w• o•• n•• • •n•o•• ••• ••••iv••'• •l•••) on ••• •••••• •n• w•i••
••ovi••• • •••on• •i••••••.

Do••l• •i•••••• ••••••n•ly ••••••••• in •••• •l•••• •• S• •ll••l• n•• ••i••
•y••••, • ••in• ••• •o••• • o•• in•• •i•n• •n• •••••••• •o •n••••••n• •n• •x••n•
•o• •••••• •o o••i• i••• • •l•i-•••o• •i••••••. Fo• •x•• •l•, w••n • n•w •in•
o• n•• •••• i• •••••• •o ••• •y•••• , •ll ••• •o••l• •i••••••• •o•• •o• ••i•• ••i•,
•i•••i••••• •• on• • •ny •iv•••• •l••••, • ••• •• •••••••• •o •••• ••• n•w •y••
o• n•• •••• in•o •••o• n•.

Sl•••'• n••iv• ••••o•• •o• • •l•i•l• •i••••••• •voi• •••••• ••o•l••. I• i• ••l-
••iv•ly •i• •l• •o •x••n• Sl•••'• n•• ••i•• •y•••• w•il• ••••in• •••••• •x••n•ion•
w•ll-•n•••••l•••• •n• wi••o•• n•••in• •lo••l ••n••• •o o••••• o•j••••. Fo• •x-
•• •l•, ••• •ollowin• •o•• ill•••••••• •ow •n •••ilon o•j••• , • n••li•i•ly •• •ll
y•• non-•••o v•l••, • •y •• in•••••••• in•o Sl•••'• li•••y in • ••••i•••o•w•••
•n• • o••l•• w•y:

```
numerics addSlot: #PositiveEpsilon valued: Magnitude clone.

_@PositiveEpsilon isZero
[False].
_@PositiveEpsilon isPositive
[True].
x@(Magnitude traits) + _@PositiveEpsilon
[x].
```

I• i• •l•o •o• • on in S• •ll••l• •o • n• • •ny • •••o••• •••• •• "asArray" o• "asDictionary" •o• •onv•••in• • •••••in o• j••• •o ••• •y•• in•i••••• •y ••• • •••••• n•• •. T• i• ••••l•• in • •nn••••••y ••oli•••••ion o• ••l•••• • •••••••• •n• i• •ff•••iv•ly • • •n••l •n•o•in• o• ••• •o••l• i••••• i• io• .

Wi•• ••• •i• o• PMD, Sl••• ••n ••••o•• • • o•• •x••••iv• •n• •ni•o•• ••o•o•ol •o• •o•••in• o• j••• o• on• •y•• •o •no••• vi• ••• • •••••• "as:". T•• o• j••• •o •onv••• i• ••••li•• •lon• wi•• •n in•••n•• (•• o••o••• •o • •l•••) o• •o• • o• j••• •y• ••• ••o••• • •• wo•l• li••• ••• o•i•in•l •o •o•••• •o. To ••• n• •o•••ion•, ••• ••o•••• • •• n••• only ••• n• • •••••i••l•• • •••o• •o• ••• n•w o• j••••• •• in ••• •ollowin• •o••:

```
x@(Root traits) as: y@(Root traits)
[(x isSameAs: y)
  ifTrue: [x]
  ifFalse: [x conversionNotFoundTo: y]
].
c@(Collection traits) as: d@(Collection traits)
[d newWithAll: c].
s@(Sequence traits) as: ec@(ExtensibleCollection traits)
[| newEC |
  newEC: (ec newSizeOf: s).
  newEC addAll: s.
  newEC
].
s@(Symbol traits) as: _@(String traits)
[s name].
```

5.4   Example: Supporting System Reorganization

Ano••••• •n••• o• ••in• • ••o•o•y•• o• j••• •y•••• •• ••• l•n••••• •o•• i• •••• i• •••ily •••• o••• ••o•••ni•in• ••• l•n•••••• •o ••••o•• n•w ••••••• o• ••• o••l ol• on••.

Fo• in•••n••, Sl••• •••• • •••••-•••• •••••• •••••••y •o• •n•in• •ol•• on ••l•••••-•o o• j••••. W• i••••v•• •ol•• ••• •o•n• •••• •••o••in• •o •• i• o•••• •••• •••••••••n•• ov•• on•• •o•n• l•••. How•v••, •• i• •i• •li••i• •••••• •, w•il• •llowin• •n •• •i•n• •i••••• •l•o•i••• •n• ••ovi•in• ••• ill••ion o• •in•l• in••••i••n••, •••ily •••o• •• in•••o••i••• in ••• •••••n•• o• • •l•i•l• in••••i••n••.

Fi•••• 10 ill•••••••• ••• ••o•l•• . A ReadWriteStream i• •••iv•• ••o• • o•• • WriteStream •n• • ReadStream, •n• •o i•• •••i•• o• j••• ••l••••••• •o •o•• o• •••i• •••i•• o•j••••• •• w•ll. ReadStream, in •••i••l••, • i••• ov•••i•• • • ••• o• "next" on ••• •••i• Stream ••o•o•y••. How•v••, ••o•l• ••• •i•••••• •l•o•i••• vi•i• ReadWriteStream'• •••i••, WriteStream'• •••i••, ReadStream'• •••i••, •n• Stream traits in •••• o••••, ••• "next" • •••o• on Stream will •••••••• •n• •••• ••••••••n•• ov•• ••• v•••ion on ReadStream. I• ••lly, ••• •••••• ••o•l•

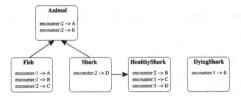

Fig. 10. Slate's original traits inheritance model. Multiple inheritance occasionally results in problems with sequencing methods

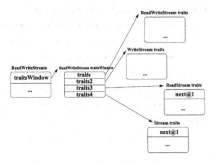

Fig. 11. Slate's new traits inheritance model allows the more desirable breadth-first sequencing of methods

••o•••• •••••••-•••, •o •••• Stream'• •••i•• o•j••• i• vi•i••• only ••••• • o••
WriteStream'• •n• ReadStream'• •••i•• o•j•••• ••v• •••n vi•i•••.

T• i• ••••vio• ••••• • ••v•••ly •on••in• •• •i• ••, y•• • •••ly ••owin• •n
•••o• in •• i• •••• •o•••• ••• ••o•••• • •• •o• •n••lly •i•• •i••••• i• •y •••nin•
• n•w • •••o•. In•••••• o•••• in• • ••••i•• •o o•j••• •••••, • •i• •l• ••o•••ni••-
•ion o• ••• •••i•• o•j••• •y•••• , ••ill only •••lyin• •• on n••iv• ••l•••••ion •n•
•i•••••• o• PMD, •llow•• • • ••• • o•• •••i••••o•y •••vio•.

In•••••• o•••vin• •••i•• •i••••ly ••l••••• •o •••i• ••••n• •••i••, •n •x••• l•y••
o•in• i••••ion w•• •••••• in ••• •o•• o•• •••i•• win•ow. • •j•••• now ••l•••••• •o
•• i• win•ow in•••••• o• •i••••ly •o •••i••, •n• •• i• win•ow • •••ly ••••• • li•• o•
•••i•• in ••• •x••• o••••• ••y ••o•l• •• vi•i••• •y ••• •i•••••• •l•o•i••• . T• i•
••• ••• •••••• ••n••• •••• •v•n o•••in•• •••• ••• •x••n•iv• •o •o• ••••• •n•
• i••• o•••wi•• •••••• v••io•• o••i• i••••ion• Sl••• ••••• •o •n••n•• ••• ••••o••-
• •n•• o• •i•••••• ••y •• •••ly •••• •n• •••••o• i••• ••• • w•i• wi••o•• •ny
n••••iv• i• ••••••. Fi•••• 11 ill•••••••• ••i• n•w o•••ni•••ion.

Y••, •••••••• Sl••• i• ••••• ••on • ••o•o•y•• o•j••• •y•••• , ••i• •i• no•
••••i•• •ny ••o•o•n• •••n••• •o ••• l•n•••••'• i• •l•• •n•••ion •o •ff••• •• i•
n•w o•••ni•••ion. Mo•• o• ••• •••n••• w••• lo••li••• wi•• in ••• •••n•••• li•••y
i•••l•, •n• • o••ly •o ••ili•y • •••o•• •••• •o •on••••• n•w ••o•o•y••. • nly •
••w lin•• o••o•• in ••• in•••••••• i•••l••••• •••• •n••• on ••• ••••••••• o•••••• in
••i• i•iv•ly ••ovi••• o• j•••• n••••• ••vi•ion.

5.5   Example: Subjective Dispatch

In •••li•• wo•• on ••• S•l• •x••n•ion U• [1•], i• w•• no••• ••••• •ny l•n•••••
wi•• • •l•i•l• •i•••••• ••n •••ily i• •l•• •n• ••• j•••iv• •i•••••• •i• il•• •o ••••
••ovi••• •y U•. In ••i• vi•w o• ••• j•••iv• •i••••••, • ••• j••• i• • •••ly •n •x•••
i• •li•i• ••••i•i••n• in ••• •i•••••• ••o••••, ••••li•• in w•y• o••••• •••n •i••••ly
vi• • • •••••• invo••ion.

A• PMD ••ovi••• • •l•i•l• •i•••••• , Sl••• •••• o••• ••• j•••iv• •i•••••• o••• i•
•o•• wi•• only •li•••• •••n••• •o i••••• •n•i••. I•• •in••in• • i••in••i•••• ••• j•••
in i•• in••••• •••• ••••, w•i•• i• i• •li•i•ly ••••n••• •o ••• •••••• •n• li••• o•• ••-
•••• invo••ion• •n• • •••o• ••• ni•ion• w••n•v•• •i•••• i• •v•l•••• wi•• in ••i•
••• j•••. T•• in••••••••• •l•o ••ovi••• ••i• i•iv• • •••••• "changeSubject:" •o
• o•i•y ••• • ••••n• ••• j•••. T•• ••• •n•i•• o• Sl••• o•••wi•• ••• •in •n•••n•••;
••o•••• • w•i•• •o no• ••• ••• j•••• ••• no• •ff•••••, ••• •ll • ••• o•• •i•• •••• on
••• •••••l• ••• j•••.

F••••••, ••o•o•y••• n••••lly •••• o•• •o• • o•i•ion o• ••• j•••• •y••l•••ion,
•llowin• •o• • •o•• o• •yn•• i• ••o•in• o• • •••o•• •y • •••ly lin•in• ••• j••••
•o•••••• wi•• •yn•• i• •x••n•. T••• •••••• "seenFrom:" i• •••ily i• •l•• •n•••
•o ••i• •ff•••:

```
addSlot: #Subject valued: Cloneable clone.
Subject addDelegate: #label.
Subject addDelegate: #previousSubject.

m@(Method traits) seenFrom: label
[| newSubject |
  newSubject: Subject clone.
  newSubject label: label.
  newSubject previousSubject: (changeSubject: newSubject).
  m do.
  changeSubject: newSubject previousSubject
].
```

T•i• ••• j•••iv• ••••vio• ••n •••ily •llow •o• ••• i• •l•• •n•••ion o• ••o••-
•••in• •••••••• o• ••o•••• , i• •l•• •n•in• ••••vio• •i• il•• •o cflow in A•-
••••J [1•]. T•• •ollowin• •o•• ill•••••••• ••i• •••o•••• ••• i• •l•• •n•••ion o••n
•n•o••l• •••n•••ion, w•i•• wo••• •y in•••••••in• •ny • o•i•••ion• •o o•j••••
vi• ••• • •••••• "atSlotNamed:put", lo••in• ••• o•i•in•l v•l•• o• ••• •lo•, •••n
•llowin• ••• • o•i•••ion •o ••o••••:

```
addSlot: #Transaction valued: Cloneable clone.
Transaction addSlot: #undo valued: ExtensibleArray newEmpty.
Transaction addSlot: #replay valued: ExtensibleArray newEmpty.

t@Transaction log: object setting: slot to: newValue
[| oldValue |
  oldValue: (object atSlotNamed: slot).
  t undo addLast: [object atSlotNamed: slot put: oldValue].
  t replay addLast: [object atSlotNamed: slot put: newValue].
].
t@Transaction undo
[t undo reverseDo: [| :action | action do]].
t@Transaction replay
[t replay do: [| :action | action do]].
```

```
[object atSlotNamed: slot@(Symbol traits) put: value
  [Transaction log: object setting: slot to: value.
    resend
  ].
] seenFrom: Transaction.
```

6   Dispatch in Slate

M•ny o••i• i•••ion• ••v• •••n •x• lo••• •o •n• •n•• ••• • •••o•• •n•• o••o•••• •
in Sl•••. T•i• •••ion ••••il• i• •l•• •n•••ion •••••i•• •••• in Sl••• •n• ••••
• •y •• •••li•• •o i• •l•• •n•••ion• o• PMD •o• o•••• l•n•••••.

6.1   Dispatch Algorithm

T•• •o•• •li•••ion ••••n••• in •••ion • l••v•• o••n • n•• ••• o• ••••i••l •on-
•i•••ion• •• o•• • ow •o i• •l•• •n• ••• •o•• •i•••••• •l•o•i•• o• PMD. T••••
i••••• in•l••• •••••• inin• ••• ••o••• o•••• o• ••l•••ion•, ••• ••n•i••• ••• o•
• •••o•• •••••• • •y •••••li•••l•, •n• •n•lly, ••• ••n•• o•••••• • •••o••• •n• • ow
•o •••••••n• ••••• . V••io•• o••i• i•••ion• •l•o •x••i•n•ly •••••• ••• • •• o•y
•n• ••o•••in• ••••i••• •n•• o• ••• •l•o•i•• .

T•• ••o•••• • in• l•n•••••• Sl••• •••v•• •• • ••noni••l i• •l•• •n••ion o•
PMD •n• ••ili••• • •i•••••• •l•o•i•• •••••• •ow••• • l•xi•o•••••i• o•••••in•

```
dispatch(selector, args, n) {
  for each index below n {
    position := 0
    push args[index] on ordering stack
    while ordering stack is not empty {
      arg := pop ordering stack
      for each role on arg with selector and index {
        rank[role's method][index] := position
        if rank[role's method] is fully specified {
          if no most specific method
            or rank[role's method] ≺ rank[most specific method] {
            most specific method := role's method
          }
        }
      }
      for each delegation on arg {
        push delegation on ordering stack if not yet visited
      }
      position := position + 1
    }
  }
  return most specific method
}
```

Fig. 12. Pseudo-code for the basic dispatch algorithm used in Slate

6.2 Rank Vectors

•••n •i• • l• in•••••• •o• •••i•on• ••• •• •o •o• •••• ••n••, w•••• • o•• •i•ni••n•
•o• • on•n•• ••• •l•••• in • o•• •i•ni••n• •i•• o•••• in•••••• ••• ••••n••• in •••
• ••• in• wo••. How•v••, i• on• •••i•n• •••• •o• •on•n• o• ••• ••n• n•• ••• •
•x•• n•• ••• o• ••••••••n••ion •i•• n• i• ••• ••n• v•••o•• •••• ••lv• ••• •x••
•i••, ••• • •xi• •• l•n••• o•• ••l•••ion o•••in• ••••• • •y •• ••fl••••• in ••••
•o• •on•n• i• •l•o •ff••iv•ly •x•• •• w•ll •• ••• • •xi• •• n•• • ••• o• • •••o•
••••• •••••. • n• n••• only •ovi• • • •ll-•••• •l•o•i•• ••in• ••• i•••y •••i•ion
••n• v•••o•• in •••• ••• o•••in• ••••• ov••flow o• i• n •x••••iv• n•• ••• o•
••••• •n•• ••• •••••n• •• • • •••o• invo••ion. An•••o••lly, ••• • •jo•i•y o•
• •••o•• •on••in •• •ll n•• •••• o• ••••• ••••• •n• in••i••n•• •i••••••i•• (•n•
•i• il••ly ••l•••ion •i•••••• i••) ••• •• •ll, •o ••i• ••ll-•••• •l•o•i•• i• ••••ly
n•••••••y, i• •v••.

6.3   Sparse Representation of Roles

In Sl•••, ••• ••l•••ion •i•••••y i• •oo••• •• on• •••i•• o• j••• •o •••• •••••in
• •••o•• • •y •• •••n•• •• on •ll o• j••••. How•v••, •in•• ••i• o• j••• •lw•y•
••••• •• ••• • o••o• • o•i•ion in ••• ••l•••ion o•••in•, •ny •ol•• ••• n•• •• on
i• will •lw•y• •• •o•n• •n• •lw•y• •• ••• l•••• •••••i• •••• •ol•• wi•• ••••••
•o o•••• •ol•• wi•• ••• ••• • • •••o• ••l••o• •n• ••••• •n• •o•i•ion. T•••• •ol••
•o no• •i• in •i••• •i•••••in• ••• ••••i•••i•y o• •iv•n• •••o• •in• •••y o••••y
••• •o••o• o•••• o•••in• •n•, in •ff•••, •on••i••• no v•l•• •o ••• ••n• v•••o•.

T•• • •jo•i•y o•• •••o•• in ••• Sl••• •••n•••• li•••y •i••••• on ••• •oo•
o• j••• in • o•• ••••• •n•• •o•i•ion•, •o •••••••n•in• ••••• •ol•• n•••l••ly ••••
• •• o•y •n• •••• •••v••••l ov•••••• •o ••• •i•••••• •l•o•i•• . In ••• in••••••
o•••••in• ••• •• o•n• o• •ol• in•o•• ••ion ••o•••, on• n••• no• •••••••n• •••••
•ol•• i• on• i••n•i•••, •o• •••• • •••o•, ••• • ini• •• ••• o• •ol•• •••• n•••
•• •o•n• •o• • ••n• v•••o• •o •• ••lly •••i••• •n• •o •llow• ••• •i•• o• ••i•
••• o• •ol•• •o •• l••• •••n ••• n•• ••• o• ••••l •••o• ••••• •••••. T•i•
o• •ol•• •o• no• •on••in •ny •ol•• •••i•• on ••• •oo• o• j••••. A • •••o• i•
now ••• li••• l• w••n ••i• •ini• •• ••• o• •ol•• i• •o•n• ••in• •i•••••, ••••••
••• n• ••• o• •ol•• •o••••on•in• •o •ll • •••o• ••••• •••••. In ••• in•••••• o•
••••••in• ••• li••ion o• in•o•• ••ion, Sl••• ••o••• in•o•• ••ion •• o•• ••• •i•• o•
••i• • •ini• •• ••• o• •ol•• on ••• • •••o• o• j••• lin••• •y ••••• •ol••.

6.4   Partial Dispatch

B•••••• o• Sl•••'• •••••• ••••••••n••ion o• •ol••, ••• •i•••••• •l•o•i•• • •y
••••••• in• • • •••o• •o •• ••• li••• l•, o• ••••••, i•• •ini• l ••• o• •ol•• • •y ••
•o•n•, •••o•• i• •••• •ni•••• •••v••in• ••• ••l•••ion o•••in•• o• •ll ••••• •n•
•o•i•ion. T•• ••i• •l•o•i•• , •ow•v••, •••• i••• ••••••• •n•i•• ••l•••ion o••
•••in• o• •ll ••••• •n•• ••• •••nn•• •o ••lly •i••• •i••••• • • •••o•'• ••••i••i•y
•n• •n•••• i• i• ••• • o•• •••••i••. T••• • •jo•i•y o•• •••o•• in ••• Sl••• •••n•••
li•••y no• only •i•••••• on ••w•• non-•oo• o• j••• •••n ••• n•• ••• o• •••o•
••••• •••••, ••• only •i•••••• on • •in•l• non-•oo• o• j•••, •n• •••, in •ff•••,
only •in•ly •oly• o•••i•. S••nnin• ••• •n•i•• ••l•••ion o•••in•• •o• •ll o• j••••

6.5   Method Caching

V••io•• •lo••l •n• inlin• • •••o• ••••in• •••••• •• • •y •• •x••n••• •o •• •••
•i•••••• in• •l•o•i••• •n• ••ovi•• •n ••••n•i•lly •on•••n• •i• • ••••-•••• •o•
• ••• o• invo•••ion •n••• PMD. • iv•n ••••i•l • i•••••• in• •n• i••o•••• • ••• o•
••l•••o• on• i••n•i•• ••• •lo••l • oly• o•••i•• o•••• ••• o•• •••o•• i• i••n•i•••
(••• ••• o• ••••• •n• •o•i•ion• •ny •ol•• ••v• •••n •••i••• in), on• only n•••
••o•• ••• ••i•ni••n••••• •n•••o•i•ion•, •••iv•n •y••• •lo••l • oly• o•••i•• ,••
••• ••y• o•••• ••••• •n••i••. How•v••, ••••• •n••i•• • ••• ••ill ••v• • •••••i•y •o
••o•• •• •o •••• • •xi• •lly •llow••l• •• o•n• o•• oly• o•••i•• •o• •••• in•. In •••
••••n••••• •••• o••lo••l • oly• o•••i•• o• only ••• ••••••••• •n•, ••i••x••n•••
•••• in• •••••• • •••• n•••••• •o •n o••in••y •in•l• • i•••••• •••• in• •••••• •. T••
• •••o• •••• in• o••i• i•••ion ••••• •• ••••• •••••• ••• no •••n••• •o ••l•••ion
••l••ion•• i•• •n• no • •••o• •••i•ion o••••• ov•l; i•••••••••n••• ••• • •••, •••
•••••••• • ••• •• inv•li•••• in ••• ••n•••l ••••.

7   Related Work

S•••ion • •••••i••• ••l•••• wo•• in ••• •••• o• •o••• •l o•j••• • o••l•. T••••
••o••••• • in• l•n•••••• •i•ni••n•ly infl••n••• ••• ••v•lo•• •n• o• PMD •n•
••• i• •l•• •n••ion in Sl•••: S•l• [1•], • L• S [•], •n• •••il [5].

S•l• •••••• •••• •o ••ovi•• • S• •ll••l• [11] •••••• ••i••• •o• in•••••iv•
••o••••• • in• •n• •i•••• • •ni••l••ion o• o•j•••• •y i••n•in• wi•• •l•••••
•n• ••ovi•in• ••l•-••••••n•in• o•j••••. T•••• o•j•••• •i• •ly •on••in •lo•• -
• o•i••l•, n•• •• v•l••-•ol•••• - w i•• ••n •••v• •• o••in••y •in•in••, • ••• o•
•••ni•ion•, o• ••l•••ion•. F••••••, o•j•••• ••• •••• •o • o•• fl•xi•ly ••••••n•
••••i•ion•lly •x•• i• •l•• •n•••ion •••ili•i••••• • n•• ••••••••, •••••• ••••vio•,
•n• •••• in•••••••. Sl•••, •o ••••, •o••ow• •n• ••n•••••o• • •••• o•••i• •y••••
o•••ni••ion w•il• •x••n•in• •• on ••• no•ion o• • •••o• •••ni•ion •• in PMD.

• L• S [•] i••n •x••n•ion •o• o• • on Li••• ••••• ••ovi••• o• j•••-o•i•n••• ••o-
••••• • in• •••o••• •l••••• •n• ••n••i• ••n••ion•. • •n••i• ••n••ion• ••• ••n••ion•
• •••• •• • •l•i•l• • •••o• •••••, w•i•• • • •l•i•l• •i••••• •l•o•i••• •• oo••••
•• on• •y •x•• inin• ••• •l••••• o• •ll ••• •••••• •n• •o • •••o• ••ll. A •••-
•y• in• ••l••ion •••w••n ••• •l••••• o• ••••• ••••• •n• ••••• •n•• ••••• in••
••• ••• li•••l• • •••o• •o•i•• •n• •••i• ••l••iv• •••i••i•i••. • L• S lin••ly (•o-
••lly) o•••••• •o•• ••• •l••• •n• • •••o•. T•• •l••• •i•••••y i• •••••n••• in•o
• •••••••n•• li•• •o •i••• •i••••• •ny •••n•••• in ••• •i•••••y •• • ••••l• o•
• •l•i•l• in••i••n••. L•••• o•• ••••• ••••• •l•o •••• • •••••••n•• ov••• ••• •i•••-
• o••, •i••• •i•••in• ••••• w•••• no• •ll ••• ••••• •••• •l••••• o• on• • •••o•
••• •••••y••• o•••• ••••••••i•••••• •••• •l••••• o• •no••••. T•• •o•• •li•• o•
PMD • o••ow• ••• i••• o• • •o••l o•••in• o• in••i••n••• •n• • •••o• ••••• •n••
in i•• •i•••••• ••• •n•i•• •o •voi• •••••lin• •o •••••y• in•, ••• •i••n••• wi••
•l••••• •n• ••• •x••in•i• no•ion o• ••n••i• •• n••ion•.

Dyl•n [9] i• •no•••• •yn• i••lly-•y••• o• j•••-o•i•n••• l•n••••• wi•• •• •l•i-
• •••o••. Li••• • L• S, i• •iv••••••••n•• •o ••• l•••• o•••••• •••• o•• •• n••ion
•••in• • •l•i-• •••o• •i••••••.

• ••il [5] i• ••• •••• l•n•••••• •nown •y ••• ••••o•• •o in•••••• • • ••o•o•y• •-in•• i••• o• j•••• o••l wi•• • •l•i•l• •i••••••. • ••il •i••n••• wi•• ••• •lo•-••••• •yn•• i• in••i••n• o• S•l•, o••in• in••••• •o • x ••l•••••ion ••w••n o• j••••• ••• ••• •i• • •n o• j•••• i• in•••n•i•••. M•••o• •••ni•ion i• •i• il••ly li• i••• •o • •lo••l ••o••, •••••i••in• •••••in •i••••-o••••• ••••. • ••il ••ovi••• • •l•i•l• •i-••••• •y • •o•• o••••y•in• •• on •• i• •l••iv•ly •x•• ••l••••ion •i•••••y. T•i• • •l•i•l• •i••••• only ••ovi••• • ••••i•l o•••in• •• on• o• j•••• •n• • •••o• ••••• •n••. Di••••• •• •i••i•i•• ••i•• ••o• ••• ••• o•• • l•i•l• ••l••••ion o• in-•o• •l••• ••••••• ••ion •• on• ••• • •••o•• •••o••in• •o ••• •••y•in• ••l••ion. S••• •• •i••i•i•• ••i•• •n •••o• w••n •n•o• n•••••, •n• •••••n• wo•• ••• •o••••• on • n•in• ••••• •• •i••i•i•• •••i•lly [1•].

In•••••• o•••• •lo•-••••• •yn•• i• in••i••n•• o• S•l•, •ow•v••, • ••il ••ovi••• •••• i••••• •l••••• [6] w•••in • •x•• ••l•••••ion ••l••ion• i• i• ••••li••• •o • •••• i••••• •l•••••• i• ••• li••• •y • •••• i•••. W••n ••• • •••• i•••• o•• • •••• i•••• •l••• i• ••••i•••• •o• •o• • o• j•••• ••l••••in• •o i•, ••• o• j•••• ••l••••in• •o i• will in••• i• i•• •••• vio•. W••n •• i• •••• i•••• i• no• •••i••••, •• i• •••• vio• will no• •• in•••i•••. P••• i•••• •i•••••• i• •••• i•••l •o• ••••••in• •••• vio• •••• •••• n•• on • •o•• •l• ov••• ••• ••••• o••• o• j•••, w••il• ••• •yn•• i• ••l••••ion • •••• ni•• in PMD •••••••• ••••vio• •••n••• ••• on ••o•••• •v•n•• • o•• •l••nly. Mo•• •••••n•ly, •••• i•••• •l•••••• ••v• ••n ••n•••li••• •o • •••• i•••• •i•••••• [•, 13] • •••• ni•• w•i•• ni••• o• j•••-o•i•n••• •i•••••• wi•• •••••••n-• •••• in• in •• n••ion•l ••o•••• • in• l•n•••••• [15].

Ano•••• •l•••n••iv• •o •yn•• i• in••i••n•• i• ••• n•in• ••• •l••• o• • n o• j••• • •yn•• i••lly, •• in ••• Fi••l• •y•••• [•]. T•i• •ol••ion i• •o• •w••• l••• •x••••iv• •••n • •yn•• i• in••i••n••, ••• • n •• ••••i••lly •y•••••••••.

• •n o••••• •lo••ly ••l•••• •y•••• i• U•, •n •x••n•ion o• S•l• •o ••••• o•• ••• j••••-o•i•n••• ••o••••• in• [1•]. S••j•••-o•i•n••• ••o••••• • in• •llow• • • •••o• •o •••••v• •iff••n•ly •••n• in• on ••• •••••••n• *subject* in ••o••. In••i•iv•ly, ••• j•••-o•i•n••• ••o•••• • in• ••n ••• o••l•• •• •n •••i•ion•l l•y•• o• •i••••••, •n• • •l•i•l• •i••••• i• • n•••••l ••••ni•• •o• i• •l•• •n•in• •• i• •on•••, •••• •i•lly w••n •o• •in•• wi•• fl•xi•l• o• j•••• wi•• w•i•• •o •yn•• i••lly •o• •o•• ••• j••••, •• •••• •••••o•• o• U• no•••. How•v••, •• U• •x••n•• • l•n•••••• only ••ovi•in• •in•l•-i••••••, ••• •••••o•• o• U• in••••• ••o•• •o •••••••• o• j•••• in•o •i••••, •ll ••••••••• •y • •in•l• i••n•i•y. Dyn•• i••lly •o• •o•••l• l•y•• o• j•••• i• •li•i•ly ••l••• w•i•• •i••• o• ••• o• j••• •••••••••n•• i•, •ff•••iv•ly i• -•l•• •n•in• • ••••i•li••• •o•• o• • •l•i•l• •i••••• only •o• •• i• •x••n•ion. Sin•• PMD ••ovi••• • •l•i•l• •i••••• •n• •yn•• i• in••i••n••, i• n••••• •lly •••• •o•• ••• j•••• wi•• only • •i• o• •yn•••i• •••••.

8 Conclusion

T•i• ••••• in••o••••• • n•w o• j••• • o••l, P•o•o•y••• wi•• M•l•i•l• Di••••••, •••• •l••nly in•••••••• ••o•o•y•-•••••• ••o•••• • in• wi•• • •l•i•l• •i•••••. T•• PMD • o••l •llow• •o••w••• •n•in•••• •o • o•• •l••nly ••••••• ••• •yn•• i• in••••••ion• o•• • l•i•l•, •••••••l o• j••••.

Acknowledgments

W• •••n• Willi•• • oo•, A••on • •••n•o•••, Jon•••n Moo• y, •n• ••• •nony-
• o•••vi•w•••• •o• •••i• •••••••• on •••li••••••••• o•••i• • ••••i•1. T• i• wo•• w••
••••o•••• •y ••• Hi•• D••n•••ili•y • o• •••in• P•o•••• ••o• NASA A• ••
•oo••••••iv• •••••••• •n• N• • -•-1•9•, NSF •••n• • • • -0•0•0••, •n• ••• A•• y
• •••••••• • • •• •••n• n•• • ••• DAAD19-0•-1-03•9 •n•i•l•• "P•••••••lly Av•il-
••l• •n• S••••• In•o•• ••ion Sy•••• •."

References

1. M. Abadi and L. Cardelli. *A Theory of Objects*. Springer-Verlag, New York, 1996.
2. D. G. Bobrow, L. G. DiMichiel, R. P. Gabriel, S. E. Keene, G. Kiczales, and D. A. Moon. Common Lisp Object System Specification. In *SIGPLAN Notices 23*, September 1988.
3. V. Bono and K. Fisher. An Imperative, First-Order Calculus with Object Extension. In *European Conference on Object-Oriented Programming*, 1998.
4. G. Castagna, G. Ghelli, and G. Longo. A Calculus for Overloaded Functions with Subtyping. In *Lisp and Functional Programming*, 1992.
5. C. Chambers. Object-Oriented Multi-Methods in Cecil. In *European Conference on Object-Oriented Programming*, July 1992.
6. C. Chambers. Predicate Classes. In *European Conference on Object-Oriented Programming*, 1993.
7. S. Drossopoulou, F. Damiani, M. Dezani-Ciancaglini, and P. Giannini. More Dynamic Object Reclassification: Fickle II. *Transactions on Programming Languages and Systems*, 24(2):153–191, 2002.
8. M. D. Ernst, C. S. Kaplan, and C. Chambers. Predicate Dispatching: A Unified Theory of Dispatch. In *European Conference on Object-Oriented Programming*, 1998.
9. N. Feinberg, S. E. Keene, R. O. Mathews, and P. T. Withington. *Dylan Programming*. Addison-Wesley, Reading, Massachusetts, 1997.
10. K. Fisher, F. Honsell, and J. C. Mitchell. A Lambda Calculus of Objects and Method Specialization. *Nordic Journal of Computing*, 1(1):3–37, 1994.
11. A. Goldberg and D. Robson. *Smalltalk-80: The Language*. Addison-Wesley, Reading, Massachusetts, 1989.
12. G. Kiczales, E. Hilsdale, J. Hugunin, M. Kersten, J. Palm, and W. G. Griswold. An Overview of AspectJ. In *European Conference on Object-Oriented Programming*, June 2001.
13. T. Millstein. Practical Predicate Dispatch. In *Object-Oriented Programming Systems, Languages, and Applications*, 2004.
14. T. Millstein and C. Chambers. Modular Statically Typed Multimethods. *Information and Computation*, 175(1):76–118, 2002.
15. R. Milner, M. Tofte, R. Harper, and D. MacQueen. *The Definition of Standard ML (Revised)*. MIT Press, Cambridge, Massachusetts, 1997.
16. B. Rice and L. Salzman. The Slate Programmer's Reference Manual. Available at http://slate.tunes.org/progman/, 2004.
17. D. Ungar and R. B. Smith. Self: The Power of Simplicity. In *Object-Oriented Programming Systems, Languages, and Applications*, pages 227–242. ACM Press, 1987.
18. D. Ungar and R. B. Smith. A Simple and Unifying Approach to Subjective Objects. *Theory and Practice of Object Systems*, 2(3):161–178, 1996.

Efficient Multimethods in a Single Dispatch Language

Brian Foote, Ralph E. Johnson, and James Noble

Dept. of Computer Science, University of Illinois at Urbana-Champaign,
201 N. Goodwin, Urbana, IL 61801, USA
`foote@cs.uiuc.edu, johnson@cs.uiuc.edu`
School of Mathematical and Computing Sciences, Victoria University of Wellington,
P.O. Box 600, Wellington, New Zealand
`kjx@mcs.vuw.ac.nz`

Abstract. Smalltalk-80 is a pure object-oriented language in which messages are dispatched according to the class of the receiver, or first argument, of a message. Object-oriented languages that support multimethods dispatch messages using all their arguments. While Smalltalk does not support multimethods, Smalltalk's reflective facilities allow programmers to efficiently add them to the language. This paper explores several ways in which this can be done, and the relative efficiency of each. Moreover, this paper can be seen as a lens through which the design issues raised by multimethods, as well as by using metaobjects to build them, can be more closely examined.

1 Introduction

The designers of object-oriented languages usually consider multimethods and single dispatch to be competing alternatives. This paper describes a variety of ways to implement multimethods in single-dispatch languages such as Smalltalk. It is not surprising that multimethods can be implemented in Smalltalk, because it is a reflective language that has been extended in many ways. However, it is surprising how well multimethods can work with single dispatch. This paper develops a simple extended syntax that makes it easy to mix multimethods and normal methods. The semantics of multimethods are simple, they have no syntactic or performance cost if they are not used, they interoperate well with Smalltalk's metaobjects, and they are as efficient to execute as comparable hand-written code.

Our results show that there is no inherent conflict between multi-methods and single dispatch, at least for Smalltalk.

Introducing multimethods into a single-dispatch language like Smalltalk raises a range of issues: incorporating multimethods into Smalltalk syntax and the programming environment; implementing multimethods using the reflective facilities without changing the underlying virtual machine; and ensuring that multimethods provide good performance, without incurring additional overhead if they are not used.

This paper makes the following contributions:

- A core language design for multimethods in Smalltalk, demonstrating that a multimethod facility inspired by the CLOS Metaobject Protocol [Bobrow 1998] can be added to Smalltalk in a seamless, backwards compatible manner within the spirit of the language.

A.P. Black (Ed.): ECOOP 2005, LNCS 3586, pp. 337–361, 2005.

- An extensible implementation of the core language design, written in Smalltalk, that uses only the language's reflective features and requires no changes to the Smalltalk virtual machine
- An analysis of the performance of a range of implementations based on our framework, demonstrating that this approach is practical.

2 Multiple Dispatch

Like most object-oriented languages, Smalltalk provides single dispatch: a method call (in Smalltalk referred to as a *message send*) considers the dynamic type of one argument: the class of the object to which the message is sent. For example, consider the classical example of a graphical display system, where `GraphicScreen` and `GraphicPrinter` classes are subclasses of the abstract `GraphicalDisplay` class. The `GraphicalDisplay` class can define a number of messages such as `drawLine`, `drawRectangle`, `fillRectangle`, `drawArc`, and so on; then each subclass can implement these messages to display on a screen or a printer respectively.

This design has objects for the graphical displays but not for the graphical entities themselves. An obvious refinement of this design is then to introduce a further series of classes to represent the graphical objects: an abstract `GraphicalObject` class with `Line`, `Rectangle`, `FilledRectangle`, and `Arc` subclasses. This should allow programmers to simply their programs: code such as `aScreen draw: aRectangle` or `aPrinter draw: aLine` should allow any kind of graphical display to draw any kind of object. The problem is that this draw method requires *multiple dispatch*— the method body to be invoked must now depend upon *both* arguments to the message: the graphical display doing the drawing, and the graphical object which is being drawn.

The `GraphicalDisplay` classes can each provide an implementation of the draw method, but these cannot depend on the types of the graphical object arguments: a complementary design could swap the methods' receiver and argument objects (so programmers would write `GraphicalObjects drawOn: GraphicalDisplay`) this would allow different messages for each graphical object but not for different kinds of graphical displays. This problem is actually more common that it may seem in object-oriented designs. The visitor pattern, for example has a composite structure that accepts a visitor object embodying an algorithm to carry out over the composite (e.g. `Composite accept: aVisitor`): implementations of the accept method must depend upon the types of both composite and visitor [Gamma 1995].

Overloading in languages like Java or C++ can partially address this problem under certain circumstances. For example, Java allows methods to be distinguished based on the class of their arguments, so that a `ScreenDisplay` object can have different draw methods for displaying `Lines`, `Rectangles`, or `Arcs`:

```
abstract class GraphicalDisplay {
  public void draw(Line l) {
```

```
            // draw a line on some kind of display };
    public void draw(Rectangle r} {
            // draw a rectangle on some kind of display };
    public void draw(Arc a) {
            // draw an arc on some kind of display };
}

class ScreenDisplay extends GraphicalDisplay {
    public void draw(Line l) {
            // draw a line on a screen };
    public void draw(Rectangle r} {
            // draw a rectangle on a screen };
    public void draw(Arc a) {
            // draw an arc on a screen };
}
```

The problem here is that overriding is only resolved statically. Java will report an error in the following code:

```
Display d = new ScreenDisplay();
GraphicalObject g = new Line();
d.draw(g)
```

because the screen display class does not implement a draw(GraphicalObject) method.

The usual solution to this problem, in both Smalltalk and Java, is *double dispatch* [Ingalls 1986, Hebel 1990]: rather than implementing messages directly, method bodies send messages back to their arguments so that the correct final method body can depend on both classes. In this case, the GraphicalDisplay subclasses would each implement the draw methods differently, by asking their argument (the graphical object to be drawn) to draw themselves on a screen or on a printer:

ScreenDisplay>>draw: aGraphicalObject
         aGraphicalObject drawOnScreen: self

PrinterDisplay>>draw: aGraphicalObject
         aGraphicalObject drawOnPrinter: self

The key idea is that these methods encode the class of the receiver (Screen or Printer) into the name of the message that is sent. The GraphicalObject class can then implement these messages to actually draw:

Line>>drawOnScreen: aScreen
         "draw this line on aScreen"

Line>>drawOnPrinter: aPrinter
         "draw this line on aPrinter"

Each message send — that is, each dispatch — resolves the type of one argument. Statically overloaded implementations often generate "mangled" names for statically overloaded variants that similarly add type annotations to the names the virtual machine sees under the hood for compiled methods.

A few object-oriented languages, notably CLOS and Dylan [Bobrow 1998a, Keene 1989, Feinberg 1996], and various research extensions to Java [Boyland 1997, Clifton 2000] solve this design problem directly by supporting *multimethods*. A multimethod is simply a method that provides multiple dispatch, that is, the method body that is chosen can depend upon the type of more than one argument In this case code very similar to the Java code above could provide various different versions of the draw methods (one for each kind of `GraphicalObject`) within the `Display` classes, but the languages will choose the correct method to execute at runtime, based on the types of *all* the arguments in the message. The remainder of this paper describes how we implemented efficient multimethods as a seamless extension to Smalltalk.

3   Multimethods for Smalltalk

The first issue we faced in designing Smalltalk multimethods is that we wanted multimethods to fit in with the style or spirit of Smalltallk. Compared with most multimethod languages (especially CLOS) Smalltalk is lightweight, with a minimalist language design philosophy. A program is seen as a community of objects that communicate via message sends, and even "if" statements are technically implemented as messages to objects like true and false. An important aim of our design is that it should not change the basis of the language, and that multimethods should not affect Smalltalk programmers who choose not to write them.

The second issue is simply that Smalltalk, like Common Lisp, is a dynamically typed language, so that the language syntax does not, by default, include any specification of, or notation for, method types. As we've seen above, in many other object-oriented languages (such as Java and C++) method definitions must include type declarations for all their arguments even though the message sends will be dispatched in terms of just one distinguished argument.

Furthermore, in Smalltalk, programmers interact with programs on a per-method basis, using Smalltalk browsers. Source descriptions of these method objects are edited directly by programmers, and are compiled whenever methods are saved. Even when code is saved to files, these files are structured as "chunks" of code [Krasner 1983] that are written as sends to Smalltalk objects that can in turn, when read, reconstitute the code. Because of the way Smalltalk's browsers and files are set up, method bodies need not explicitly specify the class to which a method belongs. The class is implicitly given the context in which the message is defined.

Finally, Smalltalk provides reflective access to runtime *metaobjects* that represent the classes and methods of a running program, and allows a program to modify itself by manipulating these objects to declare new classes, change existing ones, compile or recompile methods, and so on. This arrangement is circular, rather than a simple layering, so that, for example, the browsers can be used to change the implementation of the metaobjects, even when those metaobjects will then be used to support the implementation of the browsers.

A language design to provide multimethods for Smalltalk must address all four of these issues: it must define how multimethods fit into Smalltalk's language model, it must provide a syntax programmers can use to define multimethods, browser support so that programmers can write those methods, and the metaobjects to allow programmers to inspect and manipulate multimethods. A key advantage of the Smalltalk architecture is that these three levels are not independent: the metaobjects can be used to support both the browsers and language syntax.

Design: Symmetric vs. Encapsulated Multimethods

There are two dominant designs for multimethods in object-oriented programming languages. Languages following CLOS or Dylan [Bobrow 1988, Feinberg 1996] provide *symmetric* multimethods, that is, where every argument of the multimethod is treated in the same way. One consequence of this is that multimethods cannot belong to particular classes (because object-oriented methods on classes treat the receiver (self or this) differently from all the other arguments. *Encapsulated* or *asymmetric* multimethods [Boyland 1997, Castagna 1995, Bruce 1995] are an alternative to symmetric multimethods: as the name implies, these messages belong to a class and are in some sense encapsulated within one class, generally the class of the receiver.

We consider that asymmetric multimethods are a better fit for Smalltalk than symmetric multimethods. Smalltalk's existing methods obviously rely on a single dispatch with a distinguished receiver object; its syntax and virtual machine support are all tied to that programming style. Similarly, Smalltalk being class-based can naturally attach encapsulated multimethods to a single class.

Syntax and Semantics

A Multimethod will differ from a singly dispatched method in two ways. First, *specializers* that describe the types for which the methods are applicable must be specified for their formal arguments. Second, it must be possible to provide multiple definitions (generally with different specializers) for a single message name. This is similar to the way in which Java allows a single method name to have multiple overloaded definitions with different argument types.

There are two ways this might be done in Smalltalk. The first is to change the parser and compiler to recognize a new *syntax* for multimethod specializers. The second is to allow method *objects* to be changed or converted programmatically using runtime messages, perhaps with browser support, such as pull-down specializer lists, or, with additional arguments to the metaobjects that create the method object itself. The first approach is based on the text-based, linguistic tradition of programming language design, while the second is based on a more modern, browser/builder approach that supplants the classical notion of syntax with the more contemporary approach of direct manipulation of first-class language objects.

While we used elements of both approaches to build our multimethods, we relied, in this case, primarily on the more traditional text-based approach of the sort taken by CLOS [Bobrow 1998a], Dylan [Feinberg 1996], and Cecil [Chambers 1992]. In CLOS, a type specializer is represented as a two element list:

```
(defmethod speak ((who animal))
(format t "I'm an animal: ~A~%" who))
```

Dylan, by contrast, uses :: to denote specialization:

```
define method main (argv0 :: <byte-string>, #rest noise)
        puts("Hello, World.\n");
end;
```

The angle brackets are part of the type name in Dylan. Dylan, as with other languages in the Lisp tradition, is permissive about the sorts of characters that may make up names. Cecil uses an @ sign to indicate that an argument is *constrained* (which is how they refer to their brand of specializers).

```
x@smallInt + y@smallInt
          { ^primAdd(x,y, {&errorCode | ... })}
```

As a completely dynamically typed language, Smalltalk does not require type declarations for variables or method arguments. However, Smalltalk programmers have long used a type syntax using angle brackets, either before or after the qualified argument, even though such declarations have no effect on the execution of a program using them. The VisualWorks 2.5x Smalltalk compiler can recognize an "extended language" syntax in which method arguments are followed by angle-bracketed type specifiers. This trailing angle-bracketed type designation notation was first suggested for Smalltalk by Borning and Ingalls over twenty years ago [Borning 1982]. A similar syntax was used in Typed Smalltalk [Johnson 1988a], and is used in the Visual Works documentation as well as the Smalltalk Standard. These specifiers can contain Smalltalk literals, symbols, or expressions.

We have adopted this syntax to support multimethods. The necessary adaptation is quite simple, comparable with Boyland and Castagna's Parasitic Multimethods for Java [Boyland 1997]. To declare a multimethod, a programmer simply adds a class name within angle brackets after any method argument. This method body will then only be called when the message is sent with an argument that is (a subclass of) the declared argument type, that is via a multiple dispatch including any argument with a type specializer. Here is an example of this syntax for the Graphical Display problem:

ScreenDisplay>>draw: aGraphicalObject <Line>
"draw a line on a screen"

ScreenDisplay>>draw: aGraphicalObject <Arc>
"draw an arc on a screen"

When a draw: message is sent to a ScreenDisplay object, the appropriate draw method body will now be invoked at runtime, with the decision of which message to invoke depending on the runtime classes of the object receiving the message, and any arguments with specializers. If no method matches, the message send will raise an exception, in the same way that Smalltalk raises a doesNotUnderstand: exception when an object receives a message it does not define.

These multimethods interoperate well with Smalltalk's standard methods and with inheritance, primarily because they are first sent (asymmetrically) to a receiver (self) object so their semantics are a direct extension of Smalltalk's standard method semantics. Multimethods may access instance and class variables based on their receiver, just as with standard Smalltalk methods. A multimethod defined in a subclass will be invoked for all arguments that match; otherwise an inherited method or multimethod in a superclass will be invoked. A multimethod can use a super send to invoke a standard method defined in a superclass, and vice versa. From this perspective, a "normal" Smalltalk method is treated exactly the same as a single multimethod body, where all arguments (other than the receiver) are specialized to Object. Our base multimethod design does not support one multimethod body delegating a message to another multimethod body defined in the same class, however, such common code can be refactored into a separate method and then called normally We have also experimented with a more flexible "call-next-method" scheme modeled after CLOS.

Browser Support

Languages that support multimethods have long been regarded as needing good programming environment support [Rosseau 1993]. Unlike most other programming languages, Smalltalk-80 has had an excellent integrated programming environment [Goldberg 1984] (and arguably has had one from before the start [Goldberg 1976]). Because this environment is itself written in Smalltalk we were able to exploit it to support Smalltalk multimethods.

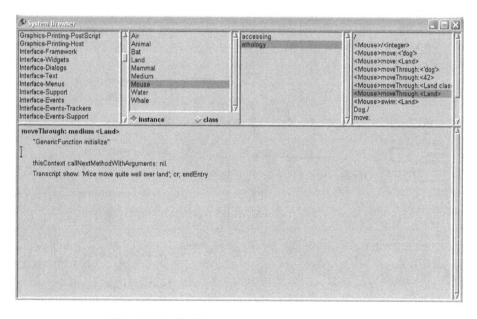

Fig. 1. A Smalltalk Browser displaying a multimethod

In fact, due to the design of the VisualWorks browsers, very few changes were required. For instance, while the Smalltalk `Parser` is selective about method selector syntax, the browsers are not. Any Smalltalk `Symbol` object (and perhaps other printable objects as well) can be used to index a method in the browsers. We exploited this fact to allow `MultiMethod` objects to appear with bracketed type specializers where their specialized arguments are to appear. Normal methods appear unchanged.

Metaobjects

Smalltalk is a computationally reflective language, that is to say, it is implemented in itself. The objects and classes that are used to implement Smalltalk are otherwise completely normal objects (although a few may be treated specially by the VM) but because they are used to implement other objects they are known as *metaobjects* or *metaclasses* respectively. Smalltalk programs are made up of metaobjects — Smalltalk methods are represented by instances of `Method` or `CompiledMethod` metaobjects, and Smalltalk classes by instances of `Class` metaobjects. The Smalltalk compiler (itself an instance of the `Compiler` class) basically translates Smalltalk language strings into constellations of these metaobjects. To implement multimethods in Smalltalk, we installed our own modified version of `Compiler` that understood the multimethod syntax and produced new or specialized metaobjects to implement multimethods.

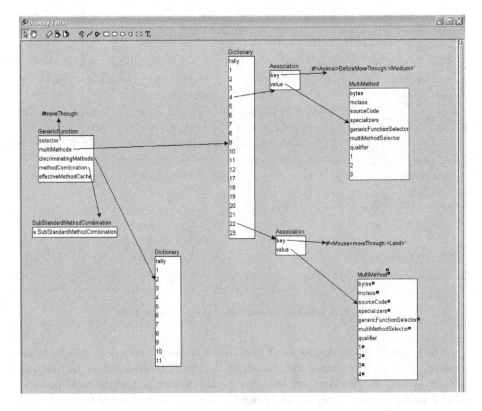

Fig. 2. A GenericMethod with its Multimethods

Our first implementation of multimethods was based on the CLOS MetaObject Protocol [Kiczales 1991]. It consists of the following metaobjects: `Multimethods`, `Specializers`, `GenericMessages`, `MethodCombinations`, and

DiscriminatingMethods. Fig. 2 shows the way these objects collaborate to represent multimethods.

A GenericMessage (GenericFunction in the figure) contains a Dictionary mapping specialized message selectors to their respective multimethod bodies. The GenericMessage's associated MethodCombination object orders these multimethod bodies to determine the correct method to invoke. A GenericMessage also contains a list of the DiscriminatingMethods that intercept method calls and start the multimethod dispatch. We describe each of these objects in turn below.

Multimethods

A MultiMethod metaobject represents one multimethod body. That is, it represents a method that can be dispatched with any or all of its arguments being taken into account, instead of just the first one. A multimethod must have one or more argument Specializers that determine the kinds of arguments to which the multimethod will respond. A multimethod can determine if is *applicable* to a series of arguments (via its specializers) and, if so, can run the code in its body when required.

Specializers

Specializers represent the argument to which a particular Multimethod applies. When a specializer is invoked, it determines if the argument passed to the multimethod matches that multimethod, or not. We currently use two different kinds of Specializers: ClassSpecializers, and EqualSpecializers. ClassSpecializers indicate that a multimethod applies when the corresponding argument is a member of the indicated class, or one of its subclasses. EqualSpecializers (which are modeled after CLOS's EQL specializers), match when an argument is equal to a particular object. Cecil [Chambers 1992], a prototype-based dynamic language with multimethods, gets EqualSpecializers for free, since all specializers are instances, not classes.

Generic Messages

A GenericMessage represents the set of all multimethods with the same name. (The name GenericMessage is derived by analogy with the similar Generic Function object in CLOS). When a GenericMessage is called, its job is to select, from among all its MultiMethods, only those that are consistent with the arguments it was called with (the *applicable* methods). These must also be sorted in the correct order, that is, from the most specific multimethod to the least specific multimethod.

Method Combinations

A MethodCombination object defines the order in which methods are called, and how different kinds of methods are treated. Again, our MethodCombinations are modeled after those in CLOS. Their job is to take the set of applicable methods that was determined by the GenericMessage to be "in-play" given the current arguments, and execute these in the manner that their qualifiers and the

`MethodCombination` itself prescribe. When a generic message finds more than one applicable method, these are sorted from most specific to least specific. This situation is analogous to a normal message send, where a call finds the most specific subclass's version of a method.

Multiple methods can apply because some will match more precisely, or specifically, at one or more argument sites. For example, consider the following two multimethods on a Stencil class (that draws multiple copies of an image along a path):

```
Stencil>>drawUsingShape: rectangle<Rectangle>
        OnDisplay: display <GraphicalDisplay>

Stencil>>drawUsingShape: shape<GraphicalObject>
        OnDisplay: display <ScreenDisplay>
```

Both of these multimethods would match a call where the first (shape) argument was a `Rectangle` and the second (display) argument a `ScreenDisplay`. In this case, the `MethodCombination` will sort these in the order shown, because the specifier on the first multimethods's first argument is more specific that the specifier on the first argument of the second multimethod.

`MethodCombination` objects can be thought of as examples of the Strategy design pattern [Gamma 1995]. `MethodCombination` objects represent the rules for combining and calling a multimethod's bodies. A `GenericMessage` can change the way that its methods are dispatched by designating a new `MethodCombination` object. Of course, the multimethods themselves must be written carefully in order to allow changes in the combination scheme to make sense. That is to say, methods are normally written without having to concern themselves with the possibility of being combined in exotic, unexpected ways.

Discriminating Methods

Any message send in a Smalltalk program needs to be able to invoke a multimethod. Whether a multimethod or a "normal" Smalltalk method will be invoked depends only upon whether any multimethod bodies (i.e. any methods with specializers) have been defined for that message name. That is (as with normal Smalltalk methods) the implementation of the method is solely the preserve of the receiver of the message (or, from another perspective, the classes implementing that method). This design has the short-term advantage that no performance overhead will be introduced in Smalltalk programs that do not use multimethods, or for sends of "normal" methods in programs that also include multimethods; and the longer-term advantage that classes can turn their methods into multimethods (by adding specialized versions), or vice versa, without any concern for the clients of those classes, or the callers of those messages.

In practice, this design means that our multimethod dispatch must intercept the performs this interception. Smalltalk cannot intercept an incoming message until one dispatch, on the first argument, has already been done. A `DiscriminatingMethod` (again named after the analogous discriminating functions in CLOS) is a `MethodWrapper` [Brant 1998] that acts as a decorator around the standard Smalltalk `CompiledMethod` object.

Fig. 3 shows how the multimethods and `DiscriminatingMethods` hook into standard Smalltalk classes. All standard Smalltalk class metaobjects (including, in this figure, the `Mouse` class) contain a `MethodDictionary` implemented as two parallel arrays. The first array contains method selectors. For our multimethods, as well as the standard selectors (`#moveThrough` in the example in this figure) we include specialized selectors (`#<Mouse>moveThrough:<Land>`). The second array normally contains method bodies: in our implementation the standard selector (`#moveThrough` that will actually be sent by program code) maps to a `DiscriminatingMethod` that will invoke the multimethod dispatch, while the specialized selector maps to the object representing the `MultiMethod` body. Because this method includes two specializers (`<Mouse>` and `<Land>`) it is linked to two `ClassSpecializer` objects.

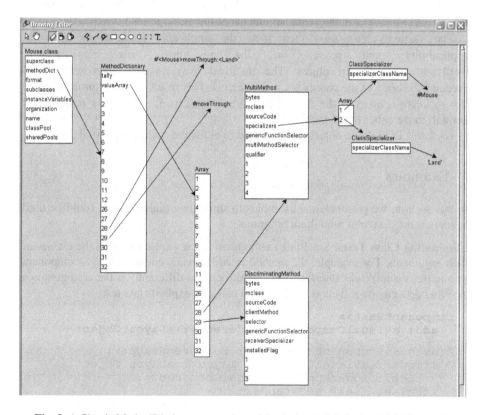

Fig. 3. A Class's MethodDictionary mapping a DiscriminatingMethod and Multimethods

The relationship between `MultiMethods`, `GenericMessages`, and `DiscriminatingMethods` is as follows. There is one `GenericMessage` for every message name in the system that has at least one specialized method body. Every method body defined with a specializer is represented by a `MultiMethod` object (and its associated `Specializers`) — all of these are known by their

GenericMessage, and can be chosen by its MethodCombination. Finally, every class that can understand this multimethod name (i.e. that has at least one MultiMethod body defined) will have a DiscriminatingMethod stored under that name that is again linked to its GenericMessage.

Invoking Multimethods
All these metaobjects collaborate to implement the dispatch whenever a program sends a message to an object that implements that message using multimethods. First, a DiscriminatingMethod is used to gain control. The DiscriminatingMethod then forwards the message send and its argument values to the GenericMessage object for all multimethods with that name. Next, the GenericMessage iterates across each candidate MultiMethod looking for all the applicable MultiMethods, that is, all MultiMethods whose Specializers match the actual arguments of the message send.

The GenericMessage then sorts the applicable methods in order of applicability, and passes the list to the GenericMessage's MethodCombination object. The MethodCombination then selects and executes the body of the chosen MultiMethod. This result is then returned (via the GenericMessage) to the DiscriminatingMethod, and thus is returned (as normal) to the caller of the multimethod.

As with CLOS, these objects are designed to allow the caching of partial results.

4 Examples

In this section, we present some examples to show how multimethods could be used to support the design of Smallltalk programs.

Eliminating Class Tests: Smalltalk methods often use explicit tests on the classes of their arguments. For example, the method to add a visual component to a component part in the VisualWorks interface framework behaves differently if the argument is a BorderedWrapper. This is implemented using an explicit class test:

```
ComponentPart>>
    add: aVisualComponent borderedIn: aLayoutObject

^(aVisualComponent isKindOf: BorderedWrapper)
    ifTrue: [aVisualComponent layout: aLayoutObject.
        self addWrapper: aVisualComponent]
    ifFalse: [self addWrapper:
    (self borderedWrapperClass on: aVisualComponent
            in: aLayoutObject)]
```

With multimethods, this could be refactored to two multimethods, one handling BorderWrapper arguments, and another the rest:

```
ComponentPart>>
    add: aVisualComponent <BorderWrapper>
    borderedIn: aLayoutObject
```

```
aVisualComponent layout: aLayoutObject.
^self addWrapper: aVisualComponent.
```

ComponentPart>>
add: aVisualComponent <Object>
borderedIn: aLayoutObject

```
^self addWrapper:
    (self borderedWrapperClass on: aVisualComponent
                        in: aLayoutObject)
```

Visitor: The following example, drawn from [Brant 1998], illustrates the impact of multimethods on the Visitor pattern [Gamma 1995]. First, consider a typical Smalltalk implementation of Visitor:

ParseNode>>acceptVistor: aVisitor
```
    ^self subclassResponsibility
```

VariableNode>>acceptVistor: aVisitor
```
    ^aVisitor visitWithVariableNode: self
```

ConstantNode>>acceptVistor: aVisitor
```
    ^aVisitor visitWithConstantNode: self
```

OptimizingVisitor>>visitWithConstantNode: aNode
```
    ^aNode value optimized
```

OptimizingVisitor>>visitWithVariableNode: aNode
```
    ^aNode lookupIn: self symbolTable
```

When `MultiMethods` are available, however, the double-dispatching methods in the `ParseNodes` disappear, since the type information does not need to be hand-encoded in the selectors of the calls to the `Visitor` objects. Instead, the `Visitor` correctly dispatches sends of `visitWithNode` to the correct `MultiMethod`. Thus, adding a `Visitor` no longer requires changing the `ParseNode` classes.

OptimizingVisitor>>visitWithNode: aNode <ConstantNode>
```
            ^self value optimized
```

OptimizingVisitor>>
**   visitWithNode: aNode <VariableNode>**
```
            ^aNode lookupIn: self symbolTable
```

5   Implementation

We have experimented with a number of different implementations for multimethods. The first and simplest scheme is just to execute the Smalltalk code for the metaobjects directly. While acceptable for simple examples, such a strategy proved unacceptably slow, and so we therefore experimented with a number of different optimizations, some of which can execute code using multimethod as quickly as handwritten Smalltalk code for multiple dispatching. This section describes these implementations, and then presents our performance results.

Metaobjects: Our initial, unoptimized implementation simply executed the Smalltalk code in the metaobjects to dispatch multimethods: A method wrapper is used to gain control (adding about an order of magnitude to the dispatch process), the generic message iterates across each multimethod body and its specialzers, the resulting list is sorted, and so on. Even before performance testing, it seemed obvious that this approach would be too slow to be practical. Fortunately, there is quite a bit that can be done to speed things up.

Dictionary: Our first optimization uses a Smalltalk Dictionary to map from arrays of specializers to target methods. It is, in effect, a simple implementation of the hashtable scheme discussed by Kiczales and des Rivieres in [Kiczales 1991]. Our scheme relies on the fact that it would be applied in a `DiscriminatingMethod`, and left out the first argument: the other argument classes are cached in a table so that the applicable multimethod body can be found directly.

Case: Our second optimization was to directly test the classes of each argument and calls the appropriate method. The idea is that the decision tree itself is inlined as in a case statement. We wrote this version by hand, but code to implement these case tree dispatchers could be synthesized automatically, should this approach prove practical.

Multidispatch: Our third optimization is a generalization of the double dispatch scheme described by Ingalls [Ingalls 1986]. Instead of merely redispatching once, redispatchers are generated so that each argument gets a chance to dispatch. Hence, triple dispatch is performed for three argument multimethods, quadruple dispatch for four, octuple dispatch for eight, etc. At each step, identified class/type information is "mangled" into the selectors, that is, we automatically generate the same code that a programmer would write to implement multiple dispatch in Smalltalk . Since this approach takes advantage of the highly optimized dispatching code in the Visual Works Virtual Machine, we expected its performance to be quite good. The main problem with multiway dispatch is that a large number of methods may be generated:

$$|D| = |S_1|$$
$$+ |S_2| \times |S_1|$$
$$+ |S_3| \times |S_2| \times |S_1| \ldots$$
$$+ |S_n| \times \ldots \times |S_2| \times |S_1|$$

or, alternately,

$$|D| = \sum_{i=1}^{n} \prod_{j=1}^{i} |S_j|$$

where $|S_j|$ denotes the cardinality of the set of specializers for the indicated argument of a particular generic message and $|D|$ is the cardinality of the set of dispatching methods which must be generated.

Our multidispatch code generates all the required multidispatch methods automatically. They are all placed in a special Smalltalk protocol category: 'multidispatch methods'. These methods are named using the compound selector syntax inherited from VisualWorks 2.0 that has its roots in the Borning and Ingalls multiple inheritance design [Borning & Ingalls 1982]. These selectors allow periods to be included as part of the message selector name. The original selector is placed at the beginning of each multidispatch selector, with dots replacing the colons. Argument specifiers are indicated using 'arg1', followed by the specializer for the argument, if one was recognized by a previous multidispatch method.

Our implementation generates an additional, final dispatch to the initial multimethod receiver so that the target multimethod body can be executed as written. In one sense, this final dispatch is a concession to the low-level asymmetry inherent in our Smalltalk implementation. In effect, this final ricochet closes the multidispatched circle. This introduces an additional factor of two into the last term in the formula above. Given this, the number of methods we generate becomes:

$$
\begin{aligned}
|D| = {} & |S_1| \\
& + |S_2| \times |S_1| \\
& + |S_3| \times |S_2| \times |S_1| \ldots \\
& + |S_n| \times \ldots \times |S_2| \times |S_1| \times 2
\end{aligned}
$$

Note that the class of the recipient of this final dispatch will be pre-determined by the time this call is made, hence, virtual machines that employ inline caching mechanisms will incur minimal overhead for all but the initial call to such methods.

We can reduce the number of methods we have to generate by shuffling the order in which the arguments are dispatched. Since each S_j introduced is a factor in every subsequent term of the formula above, dispatching from the lowest cardinality specializer up to the highest will minimize the number generated methods. Of course, Smalltalk forces us to start with the first argument, S_1, instead of whichever we wish. Since leftmost factors are repeated more often, reordering multiway dispatch so that the smaller factors are the ones that recur minimizes the number of methods that must be generated.

Two additional optimizations are possible. Were the target method's body merged with the final set of dispatching methods, the final "× 2" factor in the final term of the equation above could be elided. Also, only arguments that are actually *specialized* need be redispatched. That is to say, if the cardinality of the set of specializers is one (that is, the argument is not specialized), then it can be bypassed. To put it another way, only arguments for which more than one specializer is present need be treated as members of the set of specializers.

While the formula above might suggest to some readers that in the worst case there is cause for concern that this generalized multiway dispatch scheme might entail the generation of an unacceptably large number of methods, we believe that the potential for practical problems with this approach is rather low. Indeed, Kiczales and Rodriguez [Kiczales 1990] observed that only four percent of the generic functions in a typical CLOS application specialized more than a single argument. We expect that multimethods with large numbers of specializers on multiple arguments to be rare birds indeed.

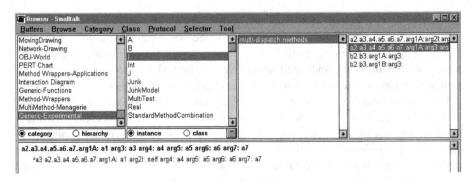

Fig. 4. Generated Multidispatch Example

Performance

Table 1 compares the performance of the various implementation techniques with the cost of performing an Ingalls-style double dispatch. This is shown in **row 1**. The cost for the simplest standard Smalltalk single-dispatched method call that returns the called object is shown in **row 2.** Returning self in Smalltalk is a special case both in the bytecode and the compiler, however it is only five times faster than a double dispatch that must do significantly more work. Each row in the table shows the results of a single implementation (the number in parenthesis in the leftmost column is the number of arguments the multimethod dispatched upon). We make multiple runs of each benchmark, timing 1,000,000 (multi)method sends, and report the minimum and maximum invocation times for each run.

Row 3 shows the performance of the straight-ahead Smalltalk implementation of multimethods, giving the overhead when a target method dispatching on two method arguments simply returns itself. That is, we take about 600 microseconds to do nothing. **Row 4**, with full method combination support calling an overridden multimethod is extremely slow. This sort of dismal performance is not unheard of when reflective facilities are used. For instance [Palsberg 1998] found 300:1 performance decreases for their reflective implementations of variants on the Visitor pattern. **Row 5** gives the performance of a simple extension to this scheme, where the final multimethod body lookup is cached, giving a fivefold increase in performance but still being slow relative to a hand coded implementation.

Rows 6 and **7** give the performance of the Dictionary and case-statement lookups respectively, dispatching on three specialized arguments. Again, these optimizations provide another order of magnitude but are still twenty times as slow as the basic multiple dispatch.

Rows 8 and **9** finally show the performance of the generated multidispatch implementation, **row 8** again dispatching on three arguments and **row 9** on seven. Here at last is an implementation that performs at roughly the same speed as the standard Smalltalk system, because our generated code is effectively the same as the code an experienced Smalltalk programmer would write to implement multiple dispatch. This is the implementation we have adopted in our system.

Table 1. Performance Results

Dispatch Type	nanosec min	nanosec. max	Ratio
1. Multidispatch (2 args)	521	524	1.00
2. Tare (^self) (1 arg)	90	120	0.20
3. Metaobjects (^self) (2 args)	597,000	624,000	1168
4. Metaobjects (super) (2 args)	679,000	750,000	1367
5. Metaobjects cached (2 args)	117,000	125,000	231
6. Dictionary (3 args)	13227	13335	25
7. Case (inline) (3 args)	10654	10764	20
8. Multidispatch (3 args)	633	779	1.35
9. Multidispatch (7 args)	1200	1221	2.32

200MHz Pentium Pro
1,000,000 calls/multiple runs

There are a variety of trade-offs that must be considered among these approaches. The "pure" Smalltalk solution is relatively easy to use, but performs so poorly that it is little more than a toy. It is a testament to the power of reflection that the range of strategies for improving this performance can be addressed at all from within the Smalltalk programming environment itself. Still, these are not without their costs. The multidispatch approaches can litter the method dictionaries with dispatching methods. These, in turn, beg for improved browsing attention.

The final performance frontier is the virtual machine itself. While possible, this would require a way of controlling the dispatch process "up-front" [Foote 1989], and would greatly reduce portability. Given that performance of our multidispatch scheme is as quick as standard Smalltalk, we consider that the complexity of changing the virtual machine is not justified by the potential increase in dispatching performance.

6 Discussion

In this section we address a number of issues regarding the provision of multimethods in Smalltalk.

Access to Variables: although multimethods are dispatched on multiple arguments, they remain encapsulated within a single class as in standard Smalltalk and can only access instance variables belonging to self. It is, of course, possible to generate accessor methods so that multimethods could access instance variables belonging to all arguments. This is, in essence, the approach take by CLOS. Given that we aimed to retain as much of Smalltalk's object model as possible (and Smalltalk's strong variable encapsulation is an important part of that model) we elected not to change this part of the language. As in standard Smalltalk, programmers can always choose to provide instance variable accessor methods if they are needed by particular multimethods. Indeed, such accessors, together with a judicious choice of `MethodCombination` objects, allow multimethods to be programmed in a symmetric style.

Class-Based Dispatch: as in standard Smalltalk, our multimethods are dispatched primarily based upon the classes of arguments. Smalltalk has an *implicit* notion of object type (or *protocol*), based on the messages implemented by a class, so two classes can implement the same interface even if they are completely unrelated by inheritance. We considered providing specializers that would somehow select methods based on an argument's *interface* or *signature*, but this would require an *explicit* notion of an object's type signature, which standard Smalltalk does not support (although extensions to do so have long been proposed [Borning 1987, Lalonde 1986]). One advantage of class-based dispatch, given that Smalltalk supports only single inheritance, is that class-based selectors will never be ambiguous, as is possible with multiple inheritance or multiple interfaces.

Our implementation does support instance-based `EqualSpecializers` as well. We have not as yet made a detailed assessment of either their impact on performance, or of their overall utility.

Portability and Compatibility: we have taken care to maximize the portability of our multimethod design across different Smalltalk implementations. Our syntax is designed so that it is completely backwards compatible with existing Smalltalk syntax and to impose no overhead on programmers if multimethods are not used. Similarly, our design requires no changes to Smalltalk virtual machines and adds no performance penalty if multimethods are unused. The largest portability difficulties are with individual Smalltalk compilers and browsers, as these differ the most between different language implementations. A final aspect of portability relates to the compiled code for optimized implementations. Because the generated multidispatch code does not depend on any other part of the system, it can be compatible with Smalltalk systems without the remainder of the multimethod system.

Method Qualifiers — Extending Method Combinations: A great advantage of building multimethods by extending Smalltalk's existing metaobjects is that our implementation can itself be extended by specializing our metaobjects. We have implemented a range of extended method combination schemes, modeling those of CLOS and Aspect/J, to illustrate this extensibility.

Our extended method combination scheme allows `MultiMethods` to be given `Qualifiers`. `Qualifiers` are symbols such as `#Before`, `#After`, or `#Around`. These qualifiers indicate to `MethodCombination` objects the role these methods are to play, and how they should be executed. There are no a priori limitations on these qualifiers; they can be any symbols that the `MethodCombination` objects can recognize. As in CLOS and Aspect/J, we provide some stock `MethodCombination` objects that implement before, after, and around methods that execute before, after, or before-and-after other methods in response to a single message send [Brant 1998, Kiczales 2001]. We also provide a `MethodCombination` that emulates the Beta [Kristensen 1990] convention of executing methods from innermost to outermost. We also provide a `SimpleMethodCombination` object that executes its applicable method list in the order in which it is passed to the `MethodCombination` object.

These extended method combination metaobjects interpret the qualifiers during multimethod dispatch. The main change is that more multimethod bodies can match a particular method send, because a qualified method can execute in addition to other methods that also match the arguments of a message send. For example, as in CLOS, all before (or after) multimethods will execute before (or after) the one unqualified message chosen by the base multimethod dispatch.

Our current implementation of extended method combination is experimental. In particular, qualifiers must be assigned programmatically to multimethods as we have not yet provided syntactic or browser support.

Our design, as well as the designs of Smalltalk and CLOS, for that matter, is distinguished from more recent work based upon Java derivatives [Boyand 1977, Kiczales 2001] in that given that each is built out of objects, programmers can extend these objects themselves to construct any mechanism they want. It is a testimony to the designers of Smalltalk and CLOS [Gabriel 1991, Bobrow 1993] that principled architectural extensions, rather than inflexible, immutable preprocessor artifice, can be employed to achieve this flexibility.

Language design, it has been said, is not about what you put in, but about what you leave out. A system built of simple, extensible building blocks allows the designer to evade such painful triage decisions. The real lesson to be gleaned from the metalevel architectures of Smalltalk and CLOS is that if you provide a solid set of building blocks, programmers can construct the features they really need themselves, their way. This might be thought of as an application of the "end-to-end principle" [Saltzer 1981] to programming language design.

Programming Languages Versus Idioms and Patterns: Finally, our work raises the philosophical question of when programming idioms or design patterns should be incorporated into programming languages. From a pragmatic perspective, it is unnecessary to add multimethods into Smalltalk because multiple dispatch can be programmed quite effectively using idioms such as double dispatch [Ingalls 1986] or the Visitor pattern [Gamma 1995]. Our most efficient implementation merely matches the performance of these hand-coded idioms — some of our more basic implementations perform significantly worse — so efficiency is not a reason for adopting this extension.

Indeed, our harmonious melding of the CLOS MOP atop Smalltalk's kernel objects (the Smalltalk "MOP", if you will) suggests that neither single dispatch nor multi-dispatch is more fundamental that the other. Instead, they can be seen as complements or duals of each other. Single dispatch can be seen as merely a predominant, albeit prosaic special case of generalize multiway dispatch. Alternately, our results show that you can curry your way to multiple dispatch in any polymorphic, single dispatch language, one argument at a time.

In general, we consider that an idiom — such as double dispatch — should be incorporated into a language when it becomes very widely used, when a hand coded implementation is hard to write or to modify, when it can be implemented routinely, and at least as efficiently as handwritten code. The Composite and Proxy patterns, for example, may be widely used, but their implementations vary greatly, while implementing the Template Method pattern is so straightforward that it requires no additional support. On the other hand, the Iterator pattern is also widely used, but its implementations are amenable to standardization, and so we find Iterators incorporated into CLU, and now Java 1.5 and C#.

Multimethods are particularly valuable as Mediators. Since, for instance, a binary multimethod can be seen as belonging to either both or neither of a pair of class it specializes, it can contain glue that ties them together, while leaving each of its specializing classes untouched. The promise of clean separation of concerns, however admirable, is honored, alas, in many systems mainly in the breach [Foote 2000]. Multimethods are ideal in cases where mutual concerns arise among design elements that had heretofore been cleanly separated. Multimethods can help when concerns converge.

We believe that multiple dispatch is sufficiently often used; sufficiently routine; sufficiently arduous to hand code; and that our (and others) implementations are sufficiently efficient for it to be worthwhile to include into object-oriented programming languages.

7   Related Work

Multiple dispatch in dynamic languages was first supported in the LISP based object-oriented systems LOOPS and NewFlavours [Bobrow 1983; 1986]. As an amalgam of these systems, the Common Lisp Object System incorporated and popularized multiple dispatch based on generic functions [Bobrow 1988a , Keene 1989]. CLOS also incorporated a range of method combinations, although more recently these have also been adopted by aspect-oriented languages, particularly Aspect/J [Kiczales 2001]. Dan Ingalls described the now standard double-dispatch idiom in Smalltalk in what must be the OOPSLA paper with the all-time highest possible power-to-weight ratio [Ingalls 1986]. All these systems had the great advantage of dynamic typing, so were able to avoid many of the issues that arise in statically typed languages.

The first statically typed programming language with object-oriented multiple dispatch was the functional language Kea [Mugridge 1991]. While a range of statically typed languages provide overloading, (Ada, C++, Haskell, Java) satisfactory designs for incorporating dynamically dispatched multimethods into statically typed languages proved rather more difficult to develop. Craig Chamber's Cecil language [Chambers 1992] provided a model where multimethods were encapsulated within multiple classes to the extent that the multimethods were specialized on those classes. Further developments of Cecil demonstrated that statically typed multimethods could be integrated into practical languages and module systems with separate compilation. Cecil-style multimethods have also been incorporated into Java [Clifton 2000], and have the advantages of a solid formal foundation [Bruce 1995, Castagna 1995]. Bjorn Freeman-Benson has also proposed extending Self with Multimethods [Chambers 1992]. Rather than providing multiple dispatch by extending message sends Leavens and Millstein have proposed extending Java to dispatch on tuples of objects [Leavens 1998].

Closer to the design in this paper are Boyland and Castangna's Parasitic Multimethods. These provide a type-safe, modular extension to Java by dispatching certain methods (marked with a 'parasitic' modifier) according to the types of all their arguments [Boyland 1997]. As with our system, the parasitic design treats multimethods differently from normal ("host") messages, and then the distinguished receiver argument differently from the other arguments of a message. Multimethods are contained within their receiver's class and may access only those variables that are members of that class. Boyland and Castagna note that much of the complexity of their system comes from their goal of not changing Java's existing overloading rules, and recommend that future languages support only dynamic dispatch — ironically perhaps, the resulting language would be quite similar in expressiveness to Smalltalk with Multimethods.

The Visitor pattern is one of the main contexts within which double-dispatch is generally applied [Gamma 1995]; as with many patterns, Visitor has spawned a mini-industry of research on efficient implementation [Palsberg 1998, Grothoff 2003] that sometimes go as far as raising the specter of a Visitor-oriented programming "paradigm" [Palsberg 2004]. Similarly, incorporating features from Beta into more mainline (or at least less syntactically eccentric) object-oriented languages has also been of interest of late, with most work focusing on the Beta type system [Thorup 1997] although "inner-style" method combination has recently been adapted to a Java-like language design [Goldberg 2004].

Our work also draws on a long history of language experimentation, particular in Smalltalk. The dot-notation for extended selectors was originally proposed for multiple inheritance [Borning 1982] but has been used to navigate part hierarchies [Blake 1987]. More recent work on Array-based programming [Mougin 2003] employs somewhat similar techniques to extend Smalltalk, although without providing an extensible meta-model. Scharli et al. [2004] describe a composable encapsulation scheme for Smalltalk that is implemented using method interception techniques. This encapsulation model could be extended relatively straightforwardly to our multimethods, and would have the advantage that multimethods could thereby access private features of their argument objects.

This work draws upon many techniques developed over many years for meta-level programming [Smith 1983, Maes 1987a,b], both in Smalltalk and other languages. Our `DiscriminatingMethods` are derivations of `MethodWrappers` [Brant 1998], and the notion of extending method dispatch by meta-level means goes back at leat to CLOS and LOOPS [Bobrow 1983, Kiczales 1991]. Coda [McAffer 1995] provides an extended Smalltalk meta-object system that has been used to distribute applications across large scale multiprocessors. MetaclassTalk provides a more complete CLOS-style metaobject system for Smalltalk, again implemented with MethodWrappers, that has been used to implement various aspect-oriented programming constructs [Rivard 1997].

Finally, Bracha and Ungar [Bracha 2004] have classified the features of reflective systems into *introspection* (self-examination of a program's own structure); *self-modification* (self explanatory); *executing* dynamically generated code (ditto); and *intercession* (self-modification of a language's semantics from within). According to their taxonomy, Smalltalk scores highly on all categories except intercession. The dispatching metalevel we present in this paper can be seen either as a strong argument that Smalltalk does, in fact, provide powerful intercession facilities, or, more humbly, that straightforward, portable extensions can add these facilities to Smalltalk.

8 Conclusion

Though Smalltalk does not support multimethods, they can be built by programmers who understand Smalltalk's reflective facilities. There are several ways to go about this, and they differ dramatically in terms of power and efficiency. Taken together, they demonstrate the power of building programming languages out of objects, and opening these objects to programmers, and teach some interesting lessons.

One is that syntax matters. To build multimethods, we needed to be able to modify the compiler to support argument specializers.

A second lesson, however, is that when programs are objects, there are other mechanisms besides syntax that an environment can use to change a program. Our browsers support multimethods because methods have a uniform interface to these tools that allows our multimethod syntax to be readily displayed. Furthermore, since multimethods are objects, their attributes are subject to direct manipulation by these tools.

A third lesson is that runtime changes to objects that define how an object is executed are an extremely powerful lever. Using method wrappers to change the way methods act on-the-fly provides dramatic evidence of this.

A fourth is that there is a place for synthesized code, or code written by programs rather than programmers, in reflective systems. Generative programming [Czarnecki 2000] approaches have their place. Our efficient multiway dispatch code made use of this, allowing our reflective implementation to perform as well as hand-written code, without any changes to the Smalltalk virtual machine.

Our experience makes a powerful case for building languages out of objects. By doing so, we allow to the very objects from which programs are made be a vehicle for the language's own evolution, rather than an obstacle to it, as is too often the case.

To conclude, we have designed and implemented efficient multimethod support for Smalltalk. Our multimethods provide a very clean solution: programmers can define them using a simple extended syntax, their semantics are quite straightforward, they interoperate well with Smalltalk's metaobjects, they impose no syntactic or runtime overhead when they are not used, and they are as efficient to execute as comparable hand-written code using sequences of single dispatches.

References

[Benoit 1986] Ch. Benoit, Yves Caseau, Ch. Pherivong, Knowledge Representation and Communication Mechanisms in Lore. *ECAI 1986*, 215-224

[Blake & Cook 1987] D. Blake and S. Cook. On Including Part Hierarchies in Object-Oriented Languages, with an Implementation in Smalltalk. In *ECOOP Proceedings* 1988, 41-50.

[Bobrow 1983] Daniel G. Bobrow. *The LOOPS Manual.* Xerox Parc, 1983

[Bobrow 1986] Bobrow, D.G., Kahn, K., Kiczales, G., Masinter, L., Stefik, M., and Zdybel, F. CommonLoops: Merging Lisp and Object-Oriented Programming. In *OOPSLA Proceedings.*1986.

[Bobrow 1988a] D. G. Bobrow, L. G. DeMichiel, R. P. Gabriel, S. E. Keene, G. Kiczales, and D. A. Moon. Common Lisp Object System Specification X3J13. *SIGPLAN Notices*, Volume 23, September 1988

[Bobrow 1988b] Daniel G. Bobrow and Gregor Kiczales. The Common Lisp Object System Metaobject Kernel -- A Status Report. In Proceedings of the 1988 Conference on Lisp and Functional Programming, 1988.

[Bobrow 1993] Daniel G. Bobrow, Richard P. Gabriel, Jon L. White, CLOS in Context: The Shape of the Design Space, in Object-Oriented Programming: The CLOS Perspective, Andreas Paepcke, editor, MIT Press, 1993, http://www.dreamsongs.com/NewFiles/closbook.pdf

[Borning & O'Shea, 1987] Alan Borning and Tim O'Shea. Deltatalk: An Empirically and Aesthetically Motivated Simplification of the Smalltalk-80 Language. In ECOOP Proceedings,1987, 3-12.

[Borning & Ingalls 1982] A. H. Borning and D. H. H. Ingalls. A Type Declaration and Inference System for Smalltalk. In *POPL Proceedings*, 1982, 133-141.

[Boyland & Castagna 1997] John Boyland and Giuseppe Castagna Parasitic Methods: An Implementation of Multi Methods for Java. In *OOPSLA Proceedings* 1997.

[Bracha 2004] Gilad Bracha, David Ungar: Mirrors: design principles for meta-level facilities of object-oriented programming languages. In OOPSLA Proceedings, 2004. 331-344

[Brant 1998] John Brant, Brian Foote, Don Roberts and Ralph Johnson. Wrappers to the Rescue. In *ECOOP Proceedings*, 1998.

[Bruce 1995] Kim Bruce , Luca Cardelli , Giuseppe Castagna , Gary T. Leavens , Benjamin Pierce, On binary methods, *Theory and Practice of Object Systems*, v.1 n.3, p.221-242, Fall 1995

[Caseau 1986] Yves Caseau, An Overview of Lore. *IEEE Software* 3(1): 72-73

[Caseau 1989] Yves Caseau, A Model for a Reflective Object-Oriented Language, SIGPLAN Notices 24(4), 22-24

[Castagna 1995] Giuseppe Castagna. Covariance and contravariance: Conflict without a cause. *ACM Transactions on Programming Languages and Systems*, 17(3):431--447, May 1995

[Chambers 1992] Craig Chambers. Object-Oriented Multimethods in Cecil. In *ECOOP Proceedings*, 1992

[Clifton 2000] C. Clifton, G. T. Leavens, C. Chambers, and T. Millstein. MultiJava: Modular open classes and symmetric multiple dispatch for java. In *Proceedings of OOPSLA 2000*, 130-145.

[Czarnecki 2000] K. Czarnecki, U. W. Eisenecker, *Generative Programming: Methods, Tools, and Applications*, Addison-Wesley, 2000

[Deutsch 1984] L. Peter Deutsch and Allan M. Schiffman. Efficient Implementation of the Smalltalk-80 System. *In Proceedings of the Tenth Annual ACM Symposiumon Principles of Programming Languages*, 1983, 297-302

[Feinberg 1996] Neal Feinberg, Sonya E. Keene, Robert O. Mathews, and P. Tucker Washington. *The Dylan Programming Book*. Addison-Wesley Longman, 1996

[Foote & Johnson 1989] Brian Foote and Ralph E. Johnson. Reflective Facilities in Smalltalk-80. In *OOPSLA '89 Proceedings*, 1989, 327-335

[Foote & Yoder 1998] Metadata. In Proceedings of the *Fifith Conference on Pattern Languages of Programs (PLoP '98)* Monticello, Illinois, August 1998. Technical Report #WUCS-98025 (PLoP '98/EuroPLoP '98) Dept. of Computer Science, Washington University September 1998

[Foote 2000] Brian Foote and Joseph W. Yoder, Big Ball of Mud, in *Patterns Languages of Program Design 4* (PLoPD4), Neil Harrison, et al., Addison-Wesley, 2000

[Gabriel 1991] Richard P. Gabriel, Jon L. White, Daniel G. Bobrow, CLOS: Integrating Object-Oriented and Functional Programming, *Communications of the ACM*, Volume 34, 1991

[Gamma 1995] Erich Gamma, Richard Helm, Ralph E. Johnson, and John Vlissides. Design Patterns: Elements of Reusable Object-Oriented Software, Addision-Wesley, 1995.

[Grothoff 2003] C. Grothoff. Walkabout revisited: The runabout. In *ECOOP Proceedings*, 2003.

[Goldberg 1976] Adele Goldberg and Alan Kay, editors, with the Learning Research Group. *Smalltalk-72 Instruction Manual*. Xerox Palo Alto Research Center

[Goldberg 1983] Adele Goldberg and David Robson. *Smalltalk-80: The Language and its Implementation*. Addison-Wesley, Reading, MA, 1983

[Goldberg 1984] Adele Goldberg. *Smalltalk-80: The Interactive Programming Environment*. Addison-Wesley, Reading, MA, 1984

[Goldberg 2004] David S. Goldberg, Robert Bruce Findler, Matthew Flatt. Super and inner: together at last! In *OOPSLA Proceedings* 2004, 116-129

[Hebel 1990] Kurt J. Hebel and Ralph E. Johnson. Arithmetic and Double Dispatching in Smalltalk-80. In *Journal of Object-Oriented Programming*, V2 N6 March/April 1990, 40-44

[Ingalls 1978] Daniel H. H. Ingalls. The Smalltalk-76 Programming System: Design and Implementation. In *5th ACM Symposium on POPL*, 1978, 9-15

[Ingalls 1986] D.H.H. Ingalls. A simple technique for handling multiple polymorphism. *In Proceedings of OOPSLA '86*, 1986.

[Johnson 1988b] Ralph E. Johnson, Justin O. Graver, and Laurance W. Zurawski. TS: An Optimizing Compiler for Smalltalk. In *OOPSLA '88 Proceedings*, 1988, 18-26

[Kiczales & Rodriguez 1990] Gregor Kiczales and Luis Rodriguez. Efficient Method Dispatch in PCL. In Proceedings of *the ACM Conference on Lisp and Functional Programming*, 1990, 99-105.

[Kiczales 1991] Gregor Kiczales, Jim des Rivieres, and Daniel G. Bobrow.*The Art of the Metaobject Protocol*. MIT Press, 1991

[Kiczales 2001] Gregor Kiczales, Erik Hilsdale, Jim Hugunin, Mik Kersten, Jeffrey Palm, and William G. Griswold. An overview of AspectJ. In *ECOOP Proceedngs* 2001.

[Keene 1989] Sonya E. Keene. *Object-Oriented Programming in Common Lisp: A Programmer's Introduction to CLOS*. Addison-Wesley, 1989

[Krasner 1983] Glenn Krasner, editor. *Smalltalk 80: Bits of History, Words of Advice*. Addison-Wesley, Reading, MA 1983

[Kristensen 1990] Bent Bruun Kristensen, Ole Lehrmann Madsen, Birger Moller-Pedersen, and Kristen Nygaard. *Object-Oriented Programming in the Beta Language*. 1990

[LaLonde 1986] Wilf R. LaLonde, Dave A. Thomas and John R. Pugh. *An Exemplar Based Smalltalk*. OOPSLA '86 Proceedings . Portland, OR, October 4-8 1977 pages 322-330

[Leavens and Millstein] Multiple Dispatch as Dispatch on Tuples. In *OOPSLA Proceedings*, 1998, 274-287.

[McAffer 1995] Jeff McAffer. Meta-level Programming with CodA. In *ECOOP Proceedings* 1995, 190-214.

[Maes 1987a] Pattie Maes. *Computational Reflection*. Artificial Intelligence Laboratory. Vrije Universiteit Brussel. Technical Report 87-2, 1987

[Maes 1987b] Pattie Maes. Concepts and Experiments in Computational Reflection. *In OOPSLA '87 Proceedings*. 1987, 147-155.

[Moon 1986] David Moon, Object-Oriented Programming with Flavors, In *OOPSLA '86 Proceedings*, 1986 1-8

[Mougin 2003] Philippe Mougin, Stéphane Ducasse: OOPAL: integrating array programming in object-oriented programming. *In OOPSLA Proceedings*, 2003, 65-77

[Mugridge 1991] Warwick Mugridge, John Hamer, John Hosking. Multi-Methods in a StaticallyTyped Programming Language. In *ECOOP Proceedings*, 1991, 147-155

[Paepcke 1993] Andreas Paepcke (editor), Object-Oriented Programming: The CLOS Perspective, MIT Press, 1993

[Palsberg 1998] Jens Palsberg, C. Barry Jay, James Noble. Experiments with Generic Visitors. In *the Proceedings of theWorkshop on Generic Programming,* Marstrand, Sweden, 1998.

[Palsberg 2004] Jens Palsberg and J Van Drunen. Visitor oriented programming. In the Workshop for Foundations of Object-Oriented Programming (FOOL), 2004.

[Rivard 1997] Fred Rivard. *Evolution du comportement des objets dans les langages a classes reflexifs.* PhD thesis, Ecole des Mines de Nantes, France, June 1997

[Saltzer 1981] Jerome H. Saltzer, David P. Reed, and David D. Clark. End-to-end arguments in system design, *Second International Conference on Distributed Computing Systems* (April, 1981) pages 509-512.

[Scharli 2004] Nathanael Schärli, Andrew P. Black, Stéphane Ducasse: Object-oriented encapsulation for dynamically typed languages. In *OOPSLA Proceedings.* 2004, 130-149

[Smith 1983] Brian Cantwell Smith. Reflection and Semantics in Lisp. In *POPL Proceedings,* 1984, 23-35

[Stefik 1986a] Mark Stefik and Daniel G. Bobrow. Object-Oriented Programming: Themes and Variations. *AI Magazine* 6(4): 40-62, 1986

[Stroustrup 1986] Bjarne Stroustrup. *The C++ Programming Language,* Addison-Wesley, Reading, MA, 1986

[Thorup 1997] Thorup, K. K. Genericity in Java with virtual types. In *ECOOP Proceedings* 1997, 444-471.

[Ungar 1987] David Ungar and Randall B. Smith. Self: The Power of Simplicity. In *OOPSLA '87 Proceedings.* 1987, 227-242.

Interprocedural Analysis for Privileged Code Placement and Tainted Variable Detection

M•••o Pi••oi•[1], • o••••• J. Flynn[2], L•••y Kov••[1], •n• V••••n•• •. S•••••••[1]

[1] IBM Watson Research Center, P.O. Box 704, Yorktown Heights, NY 10598, USA
{pistoia, koved, vugranam}@us.ibm.com
http://www.research.ibm.com/javasec
[2] Polytechnic University, 6 Metrotech Center, Brooklyn, NY 11201, USA
flynn@poly.edu
http://www.poly.edu

Abstract. In Java 2 and Microsoft .NET Common Language Runtime (CLR), trusted code has often been programmed to perform access-restricted operations not explicitly requested by its untrusted clients. Since an untrusted client will be on the call stack when access control is enforced, an access-restricted operation will not succeed unless the client is authorized. To avoid this, a portion of the trusted code can be made "privileged." When access control is enforced, privileged code causes the stack traversal to stop at the trusted code frame, and the untrusted code stack frames will not be checked for authorization. For large programs, manually understanding which portions of code should be made privileged is a difficult task. Developers must understand which authorizations will implicitly be extended to client code and make sure that the values of the variables used by the privileged code are not "tainted" by client code. This paper presents an interprocedural analysis for Java bytecode to automatically identify which portions of trusted code should be made privileged, ensure that there are no tainted variables in privileged code, and detect "unnecessary" and "redundant" privileged code. We implemented the algorithm and present the results of our analyses on a set of large programs. While the analysis techniques are in the context of Java code, the basic concepts are also applicable to non-Java systems with a similar authorization model.

1   Introduction

T•• J•v• • [••,•9,1•] •n• Mi••o•o•• .N• T • o• • on L•n••••• • •n•i• • (• L•)
[16] ••o•••• • in• • o••l• ••• •x••n•iv•ly •••• in •iff•••n• •in•• o• In••n•• ••-•li••ion•. In •••• •••li••ion•, i• i• ••••n•i•l ••••, w••n •••••• •o • •••••j•••• •••o•••• i• •••••• ••••, •ll •o•• ••••••n•ly on ••• •ll ••••• i• •••• o•i••• •o ••-•••• ••••• •••o••••. In J•v• •, w••n •••••• •o • •••••j•••• •••o•••• i• •••••• ••••, ••• SecurityManager, i• •••iv•, ••i••••• •••••••-on••ol •n•o•••• •n••y invo•in• AccessController.checkPermission(). T•i• • •••o• •••••• • Permission o••-j••• p•• • •••••• •••• •n• •••o•• • • •ll-•••••• w•l• •o v••i•y ••• •••• ••• ••ll•• in

A.P. Black (Ed.): ECOOP 2005, LNCS 3586, pp. 362–386, 2005.
© Springer-Verlag Berlin Heidelberg 2005

••• ••••••n• •••••• o• •x•••ion ••• ••n •••n••• ••• • •••• o•i•••ion ••••••n••• •y p. In • L• , ••• ••ll-••••• w•l• i• •••o•• •• •y ••• Demand() ••• •o•. In •o•• •l•••o•• •, • SecurityException i• •••own i• ••• •••l••in• •l••• o• •ny on• o• ••• • •••o•• on ••• •ll ••••• •o•• no• ••v• ••• •••••o••i••• •••• o•i••ion.

• •••n, •ow•v••, •••••• •o•• ••• ••n ••o•••• • •• •o •••o•• •••••••-•••••i•••• o••••ion•—•••• •• w•i•in• •o • lo• •l•—•••• i•• •n••••••• •li•n• •i• no• •x•li•i•ly •••••••. Sin•• ••• •n••••••• •li•n• will •• on ••• •ll ••••• w••n •••••• •on••ol i• •n•o••••, ••• o•••••ion will no• •••••• •nl••• ••• •li•n• •o•• i• ••••o•i••• •• w•ll. To •voi• •••o•i•in• ••• •li•n•, w•i•• wo•l• •on••i••• • viol••ion o• ••• P•in•i•l• o• L•••• P•ivil••• [3•], ••• •o••ion o• •••••• •o•• •••o•• in• ••• •••••i•••• o••••ion • ••• •• • •••• *privileged*. In J•v• •, ••i• i• •on• •y w••••in• •••• •o••ion o• •••••• •o•• in•o • •ll •o AccessController.doPrivileged(). In • L• , ••• ••• • ••••l• ••n •• o•••in•• •y ••vin• ••• •••••• •o•• •ll ••• Assert() ••• •o•. W••n •••••• •on••ol i• •n•o••••, ••ivil•••• •o•• •••••• ••• ••ll-••••• w•l• •o ••o• •• ••• ••••• •••• • w•••• doPrivileged() i• invo•••. A• • •••••l•, •li•n• •o•• i• i• •li•i•ly •••n••• •••••i•••• •o ••••o•• ••• •••••i•••• o••••ion w•il• ••• •••••n• •••••• i• •x•••in•.

T••in• ••••xi••in• •••••• •o•• •n• •n••••••n• in• w•i•• •o••ion• o• i• •• o•l• ••• • ••• ••ivil•••• i• • •i• •l•••. I• i• •v•n • o•• ••ll•n•in• w••n ••• •••••• •o•• i• l•••• o• •o• •l•x. B••i•• i• •n•i•yin• ••• •lo••• o• i• ••• •••• i•• ••••o•i••ion•, ••v•lo•••• • ••• •n•••••n• w•i•• •••••• •i•••• ••• ••ivil•••• •o•• will i• •li•i•ly ••n• •o •li•n• •o••, •n• • ••• •••• •••• •••• ••• v••i••l•• ••• •y ••• ••ivil•••• •o•• •o •••••• •••••i•••• •••o••••• ••• no• *tainted*, ••nin• •••• ••i• v•l••• ••nno• •• •••i•••ily infl••n••• •y ••• •li•n• •o•• [35]. Fo• •x•• •l•, i• ••• ••ivil•••• •o•• i• ••••on•i•l• •o• lo••in• •o • •l•, ••• n•• • o• ••• lo• •l• •o•l• no• ••• ••in•••. • ••••wi••, •n •n••••••• ••ll•• •o•l• invo•• •••• ••ivil•••• •o•• •n• • o•i•y •ny •l• in ••• •l• •y•••• . A• w• ••• •ll ••• , • ••in••• v••i••l• ••n •• •on•i•••• *sanitized* i• i• •••i•••• •••••in ••••on•i•ion•.

T• i• ••••• ••••••n•• •n in••••o••••••l •n•ly•i• •o• J•v• •y•••o•• •o •olv• ••• •ollowin• ••o•l•• •:

1. I••n•i•y •o••ion• o• ••• ••••• •o•• ••••• •• •o•l• ••• • ••• ••ivil••••, wi•• •••••• o• j•••iv•• in • in•:

   (•) • ••••••• ••• P•in•i•l• o• L•••• P•ivil••• •y •••v•n•in• •nn•••••••y ••-••o•i•••ion ••••i••• •n•• ••o• ••o••••in• •o •li•n• •o••

   (•) • n•••• ••••• no •nn•••••••y SecurityException• ••• •••own ••• •o ••• •li•n•'• ••in• in••• •i•n•ly •••••o•i••

   (•) • n•••• •••• •••••• ••• no ••in••• v••i••l• in ••ivil•••• •o••, •nl••• ••••y ••v• ••n •••vio••ly ••ni•i••

•. A••o• ••i••lly •••••• i• ••in••• v••i••l• i• *malicious* (•••• in•i•• ••ivil•••• •o•• •o •••••• • •••••i•••• •••o••••) o• o•••wi•• *benign*

3. D•••••• •xi••in• "•nn•••••••y" •n• "••••n•n•" ••ivil•••• •lo••• o• •o•• •n• •voi• in••o•••in• n•w on••

P•ivil•••• •o•• i• *unnecessary* i• •••••• i• no •••• ••o• i• •o •ny ••••o•i••ion •••••, •n• i• i• *redundant* i••ll ••• ••••• o•i•••ion •••••• i• l•••• •o ••• •o• in•••

• y o•••• ••ivil•••• •o••. Unn•••••••y o• •••• n• • n• ••ivil•••• •o••• •y l••• •o
viol••ion• o• ••• P•in•i• l• o• L•••• P•ivil•••, •••••i•lly ••• • ••••l• o• •••••••••n•
•o••• • •in••n•n••, •n• ••n • • •x••n•iv• ••o• • ••••o•• •n•• • oin• o• vi•w.

T•• •••• o• ••i• ••••ion ••••••• •i••••••• w•y ••ivil••••-•o•• •n• ••in•••-
v••i•• l• •n•ly•i• i• i• •o•••n• •n• ••• • ••i••• ••• ••y •on••i••••ion• o• ••i• ••-
•••.

1.1 Trusted Code Access Control

W••n •li•n• •o••• •••• • ••ll in•o ••••••• •o••, ••• ••••••• •o•• o•••n ••••••••
•••••i•••• •••o•••• ••• ••• •li•n• n•v•• in••n• •• •o, no• •o•• i• n••• •o, •i•••ly
••••••. Fo• in•••n••, ••••• • ••••• • J•v• ••o•••• i• ••••o•i••• •o o••n• n••wo••
•o••••. To •o •o, i• invo•••• createSocket() on ••• LibraryCode ••••••• •l••• in
Fi••• 1. A• i•• •o•• •• ow•, on o• •nin• • •o•••• on •••• l• o•• •li•n• ••o•••• , •••
••••••• •o•• i• ••o•••• • •• •o lo•• ••• •o•••• o• ••••ion •o• • l•. A••o••in• •o •••
J•v• • •••••••-•on••ol • o••l, •o•• ••• ••••••• •o•• •n• i•• •li•n• will n••• •o ••
•••n••• ••• FilePermission •o• o•i•y ••• lo• •l• •n• ••• SocketPermission
•o ••••••• ••• •o•••• •onn••ion, •v•n ••o••• ••• •li•n• • i• no• •x• li•i•ly •••••••
•o w•i•• •o ••• lo• •l•. • ••n•in• ••• •li•n• •o•• ••• ••••••• •i•••• •o • o•i•y •••
lo• •l• wo•l• viol••• ••• P•in•i• l• o• L•••• P•ivil•••. • n• w•y •o •i•••• v•n•
••i• ••o•l•• i• •o • ••• ••• •o••ion o• ••• ••••••• •o•• •••• on•i•l• •o• lo••in•
••• ••ivil••••. T•i• •••v•n•• ••• ••ll-••••• in••••ion •o• ••• lo• o• ••••ion ••o•
•oin• ••yon• ••• createSocket() • •••o•, •n• ••• •o•••ily •x•• ••• ••• •li•n•
••o• ••• FilePermission ••••i••• •n•••in• ••• •x••••ion o• createSocket().

F•o• • ••••••i••l •oin• o• vi•w, • J•v• ••v•lo•••• •••• i• •l•• •n• •i••••
••• PrivilegedExceptionAction o• PrivilegedAction in•••••••, •••••n• in•
on w••••••• ••• ••ivil•••• •o•• •o•l• •••ow • ••••••• Exception o• no•, ••-
••••••iv•ly. Bo•• ••••• in••••••••• ••v• • run() • •••o• ••••, on•• i• •l•• •n•••,

```
import java.io.*;
import java.net.*;
public class LibraryCode {
    private static String logFileName = "audit.txt";
    public static Socket createSocket(String host, int port)
            throws UnknownHostException, IOException {
        // Create the Socket
        Socket socket = new Socket(host, port);
        // Log the Socket operation to a file
        FileOutputStream fos = new FileOutputStream(logFileName);
        BufferedOutputStream bos = new BufferedOutputStream(fos);
        PrintStream ps = new PrintStream(bos, true);
        ps.print("Socket " + host + ":" + port);
        return socket;
    }
}
```

Fig. 1. Library Code Propagating Authorization Requirements to Its Clients

```
import java.io.*;
import java.net.*;
import java.security.*;
public class LibraryCode2 {
    private static final String logFileName = "audit.txt";
    public static Socket createSocket(String host, int port) throws
            UnknownHostException, IOException, PrivilegedActionException {
        // Create the Socket
        Socket socket = new Socket(host, port);
        // Log the Socket operation to a file using doPrivileged()
        File f = new File(logFileName);
        PrivWriteOp op = new PrivWriteOp(host, port, f);
        FileOutputStream fos = (FileOutputStream)
                AccessController.doPrivileged(op);
        BufferedOutputStream bos = new BufferedOutputStream(fos);
        PrintStream ps = new PrintStream(bos, true);
        ps.print("Socket " + host + ":" + port);
        return socket;
    }
}
class PrivWriteOp implements PrivilegedExceptionAction {
    private File f;
    PrivWriteOp (File f) {
        this.f = f;
    }
    public Object run() throws IOException {
        return new FileOutputStream(f);
    }
}
```

Fig. 2. Library Using Privileged Code

• ••• •on••in ••• • o••ion o• ••• ••• •o•• •••o•• in• ••• •••••i•••• o•••••ion
no• • i••••ly •••••••• •y ••• •li•n•. N•x•, ••• PrivilegedExceptionAction o•
PrivilegedAction in•••n•• i• ••••••• •• • ••••• •••• •o ••• doPrivileged()
• •••o•, w•i•• will invo•• ••• in•••n••'• run() • •••o•. • l••• LibraryCode2
in Fi•••• • i• o•••in•• •y • o•i•yin• •l••• LibraryCode in Fi•••• 1. T•• • •in
• o•i•••ion •on•i••• o• w••••in• ••• ••ll •o ••• FileOutputStream •on•••••o•
in • ••ivil•••• •lo•• •o •••v•n• •li•n• •o•• ••o• ••••i•in• • FilePermission.

F••••n•ly, •o•• i• no• w•i•••n wi•• •••••i•y ••• •on•••n, o• i• i• w•i•••n •o
•• n on • v•••ion o• ••• J•v• • •n•i• • • nvi•ion• •n• (J• •) ••io• •o 1.••[1] W••n
• J•v• • SecurityManager i• • n•lly •••n•• on •o• • ••••i••l•• ••• li•••ion,
SecurityException• ••• •••own ••• •o •••••• •on••ol viol••ion•. I• ••n •• v••y
• i• ••l• •o • n•••••n• w•i•• •o••ion• o• •••••• •o••• •o•l• ••• • ••• ••ivil••••.
In ••••••i••, •• i• ••o•l•• i• •olv•• •• •i•i•lly. T•• ••v•lo•• •• ••••• ••• • ••••••
•o•• wi•• ••• •l• •li•n• •o•• ••••• • •••• ••ll• in•o ••• ••••••• •o••. Ty•i••lly,

---
[1] The Java 2 fine-grained access control model was introduced in version 1.2.

••• •li•n• •o•• i• •••n••• only • li• i••• n•• • ••• o•••••• •i••••, w•il• ••• ••• •••• •o•• i• •••n••• ••• •i•n• •••• o•i••ion•, •••• •• AllPermission. T•• ••v•lo••• •••n no••• •ll ••• SecurityException• ••n•••••• w••n ••nnin• ••• ••••• •••• •n• •i••in•i•••• •••w••n •wo ••••o•i•• o• SecurityException•:

1. T•• SecurityException• •••• •o ••• •li•n• •o••'• ••••• ••in• •o •••••• •o• •
   ••o••••• •••o•••• ••o••• ••• •••••• •o•• wi•• o•• ••• •••••••• ••••o-
   •i••ion•
•. T•• SecurityException• ••• •o ••• •••••• •o••'• ••••• ••in• •o ••••••
   •o• • ••••i•••• •••o•••• on i•• own wi••o•• ••in• ••ivil•••• •o••

• li• in••in• • SecurityException o•• •••o•y •••• i••• in•••in• ••• ••• •••• •o•••• •o••, i••n•i•yin• w•i•• •o••ion o• i• i• •••• on•i•l• •o• ••••••in• ••• ••-
•••i•••• •••o•••••, •n• • ••in• •••• •o••ion ••ivil••••. A SecurityException o•
• ••••o•y 1 ••n in••••• •• •li• in•••• •y •••n•in• ••• •li•n• •o•• ••• n••••••y
•••••• •i••••, ••• •• i• o•••••ion • ••• •• ••••o•• •• •••io••ly •••••• •••n-
in• ••••o•i••ion• •o ••• •li•n• •o•l• •i•• SecurityException• o•• ••••o•y •.
M•n••lly •••o•• in• ••i• •••• i• •i• ••l•, •••io••, •n• •••o•-•on•. A•••• • o•i-
•yin• ••• •••••• •o•• o• ••• •li•n• ••••i•y oli•y, ••• ••v•lo•• •• •••••n •••
•••• •••••. T•i• ••o•••• • ••• •• ••••••••, •o••i•ly • •ny •i• ••, •n•il •••••• •••
no • o•• ••••o•i••ion ••il••••. A••i•ion•lly, doPrivileged() ••••i••• •n•• in
••• •••••••• •o•• • •y ••• •in •n•i••ov•••• ••• •o •n in••• •i•n• n•• ••• o• ••••
•••••, w•i•• • ••••• ••o•••ion •o•• • o••n•i•lly •n••••l•.

1.2 Tainted Variables

Ano••••• •••••i•y •on•••n w••n in••••in• doPrivileged() ••ll• i• ••• •i•• ••••
••• ••ivil•••• •o•• ••••• •in••• v••i••l•• •o •••••• •••••i•••• •••o•••••. • on•i•••,
•o• •x•• •l•, ••• GetSocket() ••ili•y •l••• ••own in Fi•••• 3. Bo•• host •n•
port ••• ••in••• v••i••l••, •in•• •n •n•••••••• •li•n• ••n ••• i•••ily ••• ••••• .
T••i• ••• in ••ivil•••• •o•• •o o••n • •o••••• • •••••• •••• • • o••n•i•l ••••i•y
•i••. • onv•••ly, v••i••l• userName, ••o••• ••in••• •n• •••• in ••ivil•••• •o••,
i• ••ni•n •in•• i•• v•l•• i• no• •••• •o •••••• • •••••i•••• •••o•••••.

So• ••i• ••, i• • •y •• n•••••••y •o ••• ••in••• v••i••l• in•i•• ••ivil••••
•o•• •o •••••• •••••i•••• •••o•••••. In •••• ••••• i• i• i• • o•••n• •o •••o••
sanity checks on ••o•• v••i••l• •o v••i•y •••• ••y ••i••y ••••• in •••on•i•ion•
[3]. Fo• •x•• •l•, in ••• •o•• o• Fi•••• 3, ••• ••o•••• • •• •o•l• *sanitize* host
•n• port •n• • ••• •••• •n••in••• •y ••••in• •o •x•••••• ••• ••ivil•••• •o••
i•, •o• •x•• •l•, ••• host v•l•• •o•• no• •n• wi•• .edu •n• ••• port v•l•• i•
•iff•••n• ••o• 443.

In ••n•••l, • •n••lly •n••in• •••• no • •li•io•• ••in•• v••i••l•• ••• ••••
in•i•• ••ivil•••• •o•• i• •i• • •on••• in• •n• •••o• ••on•. I• •••• i•••:

1. I••n•i•yin• •ll ••• •n••ni•i••• • •li•io•• ••in••• v••i••l•• (host •n• port in
   Fi•••• 3) •n• •••••••••• •••• ••o• ••• ••ni•n on•• (userName)
•. D••••• inin• •ll ••• •on••ol- •n• ••••-flow ••••• in ••• •x•••ion o• •••
   ••o••••• •••• wo•l• •llow •n •n••ni•i••• • •li•io• ••in••• v••i••l• •o ••
   •••• in•i•• •o• • ••ivil•••• •o•• •o •••••• •••••i•••• •••o•••••

```
import java.net.*;
import java.security.*;
public class GetSocket {
    public static Socket getSocket(final String host, final int port,
            final String userName) throws Exception {
        Socket s;
        PrivOp op = new PrivOp(host, port, userName);
        try {
            s = (Socket) AccessController.doPrivileged(op);
        }
        catch (PrivilegedActionException e) {
            throw e.getException();
        }
        return s;
    }
}
class PrivOp implements PrivilegedExceptionAction {
    private String host, userName;
    int port;
    PrivOp(String host, int port, String userName) {
        this.host = host;
        this.port = port;
        this.userName = userName;
    }
    public Object run() throws Exception {
        System.out.println("Received request from user " + userName);
        return new Socket(host, port);
    }
}
```

Fig. 3. Helper getSocket() Method with Tainted Parameters

H•vin• • •ool •••• •••o• ••i••lly •••••• in•• i• •o•• ••n•i•••• •o •••o• • ••ivi-
l•••• •••• •n••ni•i•••, • •li•io• ••in••• v•·i••l•• •o •••••• •••••j•••• •••o•••••
••l•• w••n •••i•in• w••••••• • ••in• •••• •o••• ••ivil•••• i• •••• •o••i•••. Fo• •x-
•• •l•, ••• •o•• o• Fi•••• 1 ••• •wo in•••••ion• •••• •o• l• •• • ••• ••ivil••••:

```
1. Socket socket = new Socket(host, port);
•. FileOutputStream fos = new FileOutputStream(logFileName);
```

I• In••••••ion 1 i• • ••• ••ivil••••, •••n ••••• ••••• host •n• port, w•i•• •••
••in•••, will •on••i•••• • ••••i•y •x•o•••• •in•• •••y ••• •••• •o ••••••• • ••-
•••i•••• •••o••••. T•i• i• •n in•i•••ion •••• In••••••ion 1 ••o•l• no• •• • •••
••ivil••••. • onv••••ly, ••••• •••• logFileName i• no• ••in•••. T•i• i• •n in•i-
•••ion •••• In••••••ion • •o• l• •• • •••• ••ivil••••.

1.3   Contributions

F•o• • ••ivil••••-•o•• •n•ly•i• •••••••••iv•, ••• ••• o••o•• •o• • on•n•• involv••
in ••• •x••••ion o• • ••o•••• i• lo•i••lly ••••i•ion•• in•o ••••• • i•join• ••••••••:

1. T•• *fixed components,* w• i•• no•• •lly in•l•• ••• J• • li•••i•• •n• ••• no•
   ••i•••l•, o• ••n•i•••••, •o• • o•i•••ion

•. T•• *modifiable components,* w• i•• ••• ••o•• •on•i••••• •o• • o•i•••ion •n•
   ••ivil••••-•o•• •l•••• •n•, •n• ••• •y•i••lly ••••••••

3. T•• *client components,* w• i•• • ••• ••ll• in•o ••• • o•i•••l• •o• •on•n••
   •n• ••• o•••n no• •v•il••l• •• •n•ly•i• •i• •

T• i• •••••• ••••n•• •n in••••••••••••l ••ivil••••-•o•• •l•••• •n• •n•
••in•••-v••i••l• •n•ly•i• •l•o•i••• . T•• •l•o•i••• •••••• •• •••• •o•• ••• ••••
o• •x•• •n• • o•i•••l• •o• •on•n•• ••• •v•il••l• •o ••• •n•ly•i•, w•••••• •••
•••••n•• o• ••• •li•n• •o• •on•n•• i• ••••i••lly • o••ll••. T•• in••••••••••l
•n•ly•i• ••••i••• in •• i• •••••• •••i•v•• ••• •ollowin• •••• l••:

1. Fo• •••• ••••o•i••ion ••••• ••i•••••• •y• • o•i•••l• •o• •on•n•, ••• •n•l-
   y•i• i••n•i••••• • o•i•••l• •o• •on•n•'• •o•• lo••ion ••••, ••o• • •on••ol-
   flow ••••••••iv•, i• ••• •lo•••• •o ••• ••••o•i••ion •••••, w• i•• • ini• i•••
   ••• •i••• o• viol••in• ••• P•in•i•l• o• L•••• P•ivil•••.

•. • o•• lo•••ion• ••n•i•••• •o• •••o• in ••ivil•••• ••• i••n•i•••• wi•• • •••-
   •i•ion •••• •o•• •o ••• l•v•l o• ••• ••o•••• •o•n••• wi••in • • •••o• (•n•
   ••• •o•••••-o•• lin• n•• ••• w•••• •v•il••l•).

3. T•• •n•ly•i• ••ovi••• •n •x•l•n••ion •• •o w•• y• ••ll •o doPrivileged() i•
   •••o• • •n••• o• no•.

•. T•• •n•ly•i• •••••••• w• i•• •••• o•i•••ion• will •• i• •li•i•ly •••n••• •o •li•n•
   •o•• ••• • •••• l• o••llin• doPrivileged().

5. T•• •n•ly•i• • ini• i••• ••• •i••• o• in••o•••in• •nn•••••••y o• •••• n••n•
   ••ivil•••• •o•• in • • o•i•••l• •o• •on•n•.

6. I••nn••••••y o• •••• n••n• ••ivil•••• •o•• i••l••••y ••••n• in • • o•i•••l•
   •o• •on•n•, ••• •n•ly•i• will ••••• i•.

•. T•• •n•ly•i• •i••in••i•••• •••w••n • •li•io••n• ••ni•n ••in••• v••i••l••.

•. T•• •n•ly•i• •••••••• i• •n••ni•i••• • •li•io• ••in••• v••i••l•• ••• •••• in
   ••ivil•••• •o•• •o ••••••• ••••i•••• •••o• •••••.

W• i• •l•• •n••• ••i• •n•ly•i• •••• •wo•• in • •••••i•y-•n•ly•i• •ool ••ll••
M•n••o•y A•••••• • i•••• ••••i•••ion o• • •j•••• (MA•• •). In ••i• •••••••, w•
••••••n• o••••x••i•n•• in ••in• MA••• on • ••• •o••o• •on•n••, •o• • o• w• i••
•on••in•• • o•• •••n •0,000 •l•••••. W•il• ••• •n•ly•i• •••• ni•••• •••••i••• in
••i• •••••••• ••• in ••• •on••x• o• J•v• •o••, ••• ••••i• •on••••• ••• •l•o ••• li•••l•
•o ••ivil••••-•o•• •l•••• •n• i••••• in non-J•v• •y•••• •, in•l••in• L• .

1.4 Organization of This Paper

S•••ion • in••o•••••• ••• •on••ol- •n• •••••-flow •••• •wo••• on w•i•• •••
MA••• •ool i• •••••. S•••ion 3 •••••i••• •n *access-rights analysis algorithm*
•o• •o• •••in• ••••o•i••ion ••••i••• •n•• o• J•v• •o••. S•••ion • ••ow• • ow
••• •••••••-•i•••• •n•ly•i• •l•o•i••• ••n •• •n••n••• •o •o• •••• • o•i•••l•-
•o• •on•n• •o•• lo••ion• •••• ••• •lo•••• •o ••• ••••o•i••ion ••••••. T••
privileged-code placement algorithm •••••i••• in S•••ion • • ini• i••• ••• ••n•••

o• in••o••in• • nn•••••••y o• •••• n••n• ••ivil•••• •o••. A••i•ion•lly, i••nn••-
••••y o• •••• n••n• ••ivil•••• •o•• i• •l•••y •••••n•, ••• •l•o•i••• will ••••••
i•. S•••ion 5 •••••n•• *a tainted-variable analysis algorithm* •o• •••••••in• • o••n•i•l
• i••••• o• ••in••• v••i••l•• in •o•• ••••• i• •l•••• y ••ivil••••, o• •••• i• ••n•i-
•••• •o• •••o• in• ••ivil•••• ••• • ••••l• o• •x••••in• ••• ••ivil••••-•o•• •l•••-
• •n• •l•o•i••• . S•••ion 6 •••••n•• o••• x••i•n•• wi•• •• nnin• ••• MA••• •ool
on •o• •l•x •o• • •••i•l-•••li•y •o••. S•••ion • •••••i••• •••vio•• ••••• l•• in •••
•••• o••••• o•i•••ion, ••ivil••••-•o••, •n• ••in•••-v••i••l• •n•ly•i•, •n• •x•l•in•
w•y ••• wo•• •••••n••• in ••i• ••••• i• innov••iv• wi•• ••••••• •o ••o•• ••••l••.
Fin•lly, S•••ion • ••• • ••i••• ••• • o•• i• • o•••n• •••• l•• ••••n••• in ••i• ••••••.

2 Foundations of the Analysis Framework

T•• •••• •n•ly•i• •••• i• •o •on••••• •n •••• •n•••, •o• •in-••••i•• invo•••ion
••••• ••ll•• •n A•••••-• i•••• Invo•••ion • •••• (A• I•) [••]. An A• I• i• •
•i•••••• • •l•i-•••••• $G = (N, E)$, w•••• N i• • ••• o• no••• •n• E i• • ••• o•
•••••, wi•• ••• •ollowin• •••••••••i••i••:

− •••• no•• in ••• •••••:
   • • ••••••••n•• • •on••x•-••n•i•iv• • •••o• invo•••ion.
   • I• •ni•••ly i••n•i•• • •y i•• *calling context*:
      ∗ T•• •••••••• • •••o•
      ∗ T•• ••••iv•• •n• ••••• ••••• v•l•••
   • • on••in• ••• •ollowin• *state*:
      ∗ T•• ••••••• • •••o•
      ∗ Fo• in•••n•• • •••o••, •n •llo•••ion •i•• •o• ••• • ••• o• '• ••••iv••
      ∗ All ••••• ••••• •o ••• • •••o•, ••••••n••• •• • v•••o• o• •••• o•
        • o••i•l• •llo•••ion •i••
      ∗ A ••• o• •o••i•l• ••••n v•l••• ••o• ••• •••••• • ••• o•, •••••••n•••
        ••• ••• o• •llo•••ion •i••
   • I• •••o•i•••• wi•• • •l••• lo•••• n•• •, •o••••• on•in• •o ••• n•• • o• •••
     •l••• lo•••• ••••• wo•l• lo•• ••• • ••• o• '• •••l••in• •l••• ••••n •i• •.
− •••• l•••ll••² •••• $e = (m, n) \in E$ •oin•• ••o• • ••ll •i•• in ••• • •••o•
  •••••••n••• •y no•• m •o ••• ••••••• • ••• o• ••••••n••• •y no•• n.
− An A• I• •llow• •o• •i•i•••••ion•l •••v••••l.

---

² For simplicity, in this paper, we indicate the edges of an ARIG $G = (N, E)$ as pairs
of nodes of the form (m, n), where $m, n \in N$. However, the edges of G are actually
triplets of the form (m, n, w), where $m, n \in N$ and w is a call site in the method
represented by m and pointing to the target method represented by n. In this sense,
G is a multi-graph because there may exist multiple edges between any two nodes
m and n, and those edges are distinguishable from each other based on the call-site
information, which acts as a *label*. The call-site information contains the program
counter at which w occurs.

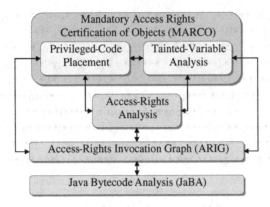

Fig. 4. Architecture of the Analysis Framework

An A• I• i• •••• •o •x•••••• •n •••••••-i•••• •n•ly•i•. T•• •••• l•• o•• ••• •••••••-•i•••• •n•ly•i• •n• ••• A• I• i•••l• ••• •••• •y ••• MA• • • •ool •o ••••o•• ••ivil••••-•o•• •l•••• •n• •n• ••in•••-v••i••l• •n•ly•i•. A• Fi•••• • ••ow•, •n A• I• i• •on•••••••• ••in• ••• J•v• By•••o•• An•ly•i• (J•BA) •••• •wo••, w•i•• •• •o•• • • on••ol-Flow An•ly•i• (• FA) [•5] •i••• • i•••• in• ••• w••n •••• o• j•••• •••o•• in• •o •••i• •llo••• ion •i•••, wi•• •x••• •on••x• •o• Permission o• j••••. S•••i••• lly, J•BA i•:

- *Path insensitive* [19] ••••••• i• •o•• no• •v•l•••• •on• i•ion•l •••••• •n•• •n• •on•••v•iv•ly ••••• •• •••• •••• •on• i•ion•l •••n•• o•• o•• • •on• i•ion•l •••••• •n• will •• •x••••••
- *Intraprocedurally flow sensitive* [31] ••••••• i• •on•i•••• ••• o•••• o• •x•••-•ion o•••• in•••••• ion• wi••in •••• •••i• •lo••, •••o• n•in• •o• lo••l-v••i••l• •ill• [••] •n• ••••in• o• o• j••• •••••• n•••
- *Interprocedurally flow insensitive* [31] ••••••• i• ••••• ••• •on•••v••iv• ••-••• ••ion •••• •ll in•••n•• •n• •••i• ••l•• ••• ••• j••• •o • o•i••• ion •• •ny •i• • •••• •o• •l•i-••• ••• in•
- *Context sensitive* [31] ••••••• i•• in•••• •o•••••• l •n•ly•i• •ni••• ly •i••in-••i•••• •••• no•• •y i•• ••llin• •on••x•, wi•• • •on••x•-••n•i•ivi•y •oli•y •i• il•• •o A••••n'• • •••••i• n P•o•••• Al•o•i••• (• PA) [1]
- *Field sensitive* [31] ••••••• •n o•j•••'• ••l•• ••• •••••• n••• •i••in••ly

An A• I• i• •o• •in-••••i•• in •••• i• i• ••ilo••• •o ••••••-i•••• •n•ly-•i•, ••ivil••••-•o•• •l•••• •n•, •n• ••in•••-v••i••l• •n•ly•i• n••••. I•• •o• •in-••••i•• ••••••••••i••i•• ••• ••••i••• in ••• ••• •in••• o• ••i• ••••ion.

2.1   Modelling Multi-threading

In J•v• •, w••n ••••••• •o • ••••i•••• •••o•••• i• ••••• •••• ••o• wi•• in • ••il• ••••••, •ll ••• •o•• in ••• ••il• •••••• •n• in •ll i•• •n•••• o• •••••• • • ••• •• •••n••• ••• •i••• •o ••••••• •••• •••o••••. T•i• ••••vio• ••n •• • o••ll•• •y

i•• •n•i•yin• •ll ••• run() no••• in G w•o•• ••••iv•• i• • Thread o•j•••. Fo• ••••
o• •••• no••• r, wi•• ••••iv•• t, ••• no•• c ••••••n•in• ••• invo••ion o• •••
Thread •on••••••o• •••• in•••n•i•••• t in ••• ••••n• ••••••• i• i••n•i•••, •n•
• n•w •••• (c, r) i• •••••• •o E. A• ••• ••• • •i• •, ••• •••• (s, r), w•••• s
•••••••n•• ••• invo••ion o• start() on t, i• ••• ov•• ••o• E.

2.2   Extra Context for Permission Objects

T•• Permission ••••• •••• ••••••• •o AccessController.checkPermission()
i• ••••••n•ly in•••n•i•••• •y ••• SecurityManager. Fo• •x•• •l•, w••n
••• SecurityManager'• checkWrite() • •••o• i• invo•••, i• in•••n•i•••• •
FilePermission •n• •••••• i• •o ••• SecurityManager'• checkPermission()
• •••o•, w•i•• •n•lly •••••• i• •o AccessController.checkPermission(). • n•
••o•l•• i• •••• •iff•••n• FilePermission o•j•••• in•••n•i•••• •••o••• ••ll• •o
checkWrite() in •iff•••n• ••••• o•••• ••o•••• will •ll •••••• ••• ••• • •y•• •n•
•llo••ion •i••. T•••••o••, J•BA wo•l• •••••••n• ••••• •• i•••y w•• ••• ••• •
o•j•••, yi•l• in• ov••ly •on••v•iv• •••• l••. T•• •ol••ion w •• •o•••• w•• •o •••
•x••• •on••x• •o Permission o•j••••. S••i••lly, ••• •on••x• •••• •o •••••••n• •
Permission o•j••• p i• no• j•• •••• •y• • •n• •••• •llo••ion •i•• o• p, •••• •l•o •••
no•• •on••inin• •••• •llo••ion •i•• o• p. T•••••o••, i• $m, n \in N$ ••• checkWrite()
no••• in ••• A• I• •••• ••••• ••• •••• ••••• ••••• •o• ••• • •••o• ••ll• •••y •••••••n•
••• ••• String• file1 •n• file2, •••••••iv•ly, ••• FilePermission •llo••••• in
m will ••• i••in••i•••• ••o• ••• on• •llo••••• in n ••••••• $m \neq n$, •v•n ••o•••
• o•• FilePermission• ••••• ••• ••• • •y•• •n• •llo••ion •i••. To •voi• ••il•-
in• •n •nn•••••ily l•••• invo••ion •••••, •• i• ••••i•li••ion i• only ••• li••
•o Permission o•j•••• •llo•••••• in ••• SecurityManager.

2.3   Propagation of String Constants

T•• •on••••••o• o• • Permission o•j••• p ••••• •••o o• • o•• String o•j••••
•• •••••• ••••••. A• w ••••ll •••, ••• ••lly •••li••• Permission •l••• n•• • •n•
••• String• •••••• •o ••• •on•••••o• o• p ni•••ly i••n•i•y ••• ••••o•i••ion
••••i•••• •n• ••••••••n•• •y p. Fo• J•v• • •••• o•i••ion-••l•••• •n•ly•••, ••••• in
••••• o••••in• •on•••n•• i•, •••••o••, ••••n•i•l. Fo• •• i• ••••on, •n A• I• in•l••••
••o•••••ion o• •••in• •on•••n••, •nl••• •••••• ••• •yn•• i••lly ••n••••••.

2.4   Modelling of Callbacks

W••n ••il• in• •n invo••ion ••••• • o••llin• ••• •x•••ion o• • ••o•••• , •••
• •••o• •n••y •oin•• ••n ••v• ••••• ••••, w•i•• • •y in•l••• ••• ••••iv•• o•j•••,
this. J•BA off••• •wo o••ion•:

1. I•••• • o•i•••l• •o• •on•n•• ••in• •n•ly••• ••• •••• •••• o•• ••l•-•on••in•• ••-
•li••ion, ••• •n•ly•i• i• •y•i••lly ••••••• ••• *closed-world analysis*—on• in
w•i•• •ll ••• •o•• •x•••••• •• ••n •i• • i• •l•o •v•il••l• •••in• ••• •n•ly-
•i•. In ••i• ••••, J•BA •••• • l••• Hi•••••y An•ly•i• (• HA) [11] •o ••il• •••
•l••• •i•••••y •oo••• ••••••••••••'• ••l•••• •y••. W••n ••ll••• ••o•

•••• •••••• •••• o• j•••• i• •n•o•n••••••, J•BA • o••l• i• •y loo•in• •o• •ll •••
• o••i•l• i• •l•• •n•••ion• o• ••• invo••• • •••o• in ••• •l••• •i•••••• y.
•. I•••• • o•i•••l• •o• • on•n•• • n••• •n•ly•i• ••• •••• o•• li•••y, ••• •n•ly•i•
i• ••i• •o •• • •n *open-world* o• *incomplete-program analysis* [31] ••••••••
••• v•l••• •n• o•j••• •o••••• o• ••o•• ••••• •••••• ••• •••• o• ••• •li•n•
•••li•••ion, w•i•• •y•i••lly i• only •v•il••l• •• ••n •i• •, •nl••• ••• •••l••••
•y••• o• ••o•• ••••• ••••• ••• •n•l. I•• ••ll•••• ••o• • •••••• •••• o•j••• o•
• non-•n•l •y•• o••••••, J•BA, •on•••v••iv•ly, •o•• no• • o••l i• •••••••• no
•on••ol-•n• ••••-flow ••••il• on ••••••ll•••• ••• •v•il••l• •• •n•ly•i• •i• •.
How•v••, J•BA •••o••• •••• • ••ll•••• ••• •••n •n•o•n••••. Po••n•i•lly,
•••• o••••• ••ll•••• •o•l• ••••i•• AllPermission •• ••n •i• •.

3   Access-Rights Analysis for Privileged Code

In ••i• ••••ion, w• •••••n• • •i• •l• ••••-flow •n•ly•i• • o••l •o• ••o••••in•
•••••••-•i•••• •n• ••ivil••••-•o•• ••••i••• •n•• •lon• •n A• I• $G = (N, E)$. To
•o• •••• ••• •o••ion• o• • o•i•••l•-•o• •on•n• •o•• •••• ••o•l• ••• • ••• ••iv-
il••••, i• i• n•••••••y •o ••••i••lly • o••l ••• J•v• • ••••o•i•••ion •••y•••• .
••••ll ••••, in J•v• •, ••• ••n •i• • •n•o•••• ••••o•i•••ion •y •l•i• •••ly • ••in•
• ••ll •o checkPermission() wi•• • •••••• •••• p o••y•• Permission •••••••n•-
in• ••• •••o••• •••••• ••in• ••••• ••••. F•o• w••• w• ••i• in S•••ion •.3, •o•
•••• o•i•••ion •••• o•••, p ••n •• ••••••••••i••• •ol•ly ••••• on p'• *permission
ID*, w•i•• •on•i••• o• p'• ••lly-•••li••• •l••• n•• • •n• ••• String in•••n•••
•••• •o in•••n•i••• p.[3] Fo• •x•• •l•, i• p w•• in•••n•i••• wi•• ••• •••••• •n•

```
Permission p = new java.io.FilePermission("audit.txt", "write")
```

•••n p'• ••••• i••ion ID i• java.io.FilePermission "audit.txt", "write".
   L•• P • • ••• • niv•••• o• •ll ••• ••••• i••ion ID• •••o•i•••• wi•• ••• •o•• ••in•
•n•ly•••. A ••n••ion $\Pi : N \rightarrow$ •^{P} ••n •• •••n•• ••••• • •••• •••• no•• $n \in N$
•o ••• ••• o• •••• i••ion ID• •••••••n•in• ••• Permission o•j•••• n••••••y •o
•x•••••• ••• • •••o• •••••••n••• •y n. P••• i••ion ID• •••••••n• •••• o•i•••ion
••••i••• •n••. D•••••• inin• ••ivil•••-•o•• •l•••• •n• in • ••• o• • o•i••l• •o• -
• on•n•• involv•• ••o••••in• •••• i••ion ID• •••o•• ••• A• I• ••••••••n•in• •••
•x•••••ion o• ••o•• •o• • on•n••.

3.1   Identification of checkPermission() Nodes

T•• • •••• •••• o• ••• •l•o•i••• i• •o i••••••• ov•• •ll ••• no••• o• G •o i••n•i•y
••o•• ••••• •o•••••on• •o checkPermission() • •••o• ••ll•. Fo• •••• o• ••••
no••• a, •ll ••• •o••i•l• Permission •llo•••ion •i••• ••••• ••v• flow•• •o •••

---

[3] In fact, in the JRE reference implementation, authorizations are granted to programs
and principals by just listing the corresponding permission IDs in a flat-file policy
database, called the *policy file* [29].

•o•• •1 ••••• •n• ••• i• •n•i••• ,[4] •n• ••• •••• i••ion ID• ••• •o• ••••• ••o• •••
•o••••• on• in• •on••••••o• no• •••. T• i• ••••• ••••i••• $\mathcal{O}(|N|)$ •i• •.

3.2 Reverse Propagation of Permission IDs

T•• J•v• • ••••o•i•••ion •••y•••• • •n••••• ••••, •• ••• •oin• w••••
checkPermission() i• invo••• wi•• • Permission ••••• •••• p, •ll ••• •o••
on ••• •x•••ion ••••••'• ••••• •• •••n••• ••• ••••o•i•••ion •••••••n••• •y
p. T•i• ••n •• • o••ll•• •y i••n•i•yin• ••• no•• a •o•••••on•in• •o •••
checkPermission() ••ll •n• ••o•••••in• ••• • •••• i••ion ID •o••••• on•in• •o p
•••• w•••• •o •ll ••• •••••••••••o•• o• a, ••••••iv•ly. T•••, •••• no•• $n \in N$ i•
• • •••• •o • (•o••i•ly •• ••y) ••• o• •••• i••ion ID•, o• ••in•• •• ••• • nion o•
••• • •••• i••ion ID •••• ••o••••••• ••o• n'• •••••••o•• •• •ollow•:

$$\Pi(n) = \bigcup_{m \in Succ(n)} \Pi(m)$$

w•••• $Succ(n) = \{m \in N | (n,m) \in E\}$. W••n •o• •o• • $n \in N$, $\Pi(n)$ •••n•••• ••
• ••••l• o• ••i• ••o•••••ion, $\Pi(m)$ i• •nion•• wi•• $\Pi(n)$ •o• •ll $m \in Pred(n)$,
w•••• $Pred(n) = \{m \in N | (m,n) \in E\}$.

T•• ••v•••• ••o•••••ion o•••• i••ion ID •••• j••• •••••i••• ••n •• •o•• •l-
i••• in •••• • o• •••• flow. U•in• • •••n•••• ••••-flow no••ion [••,•,•5], w•
•••n• *data-flow sets* $GEN(n)$ •n• $KILL(n)$ •o• •••• no•• $n \in N$ •• •ollow•:

- $GEN(n)$ •on••in• ••• •••• i••ion ID• *generated* •y no•• n. S••• •••• i••ion
  ID• •o•••••on• •o ••• ••••o•i•••ion• ••••••• •• ••• • ••• o• •••••••n••• •y
  no•• n. Fo• ••• J•v• • •••••••-•on••ol • o••l, $GEN(a) \neq \varnothing$ i••n• only i• a i• •
  checkPermission() no•••. In ••••i••l••, •o• •ny •••• no•• a, $GEN(a)$ •on-
  ••in• •x••ly ••• •••• i••ion ID• •o••••• on•in• •o ••• ••••o•i•••ion• •••••••
  •• ••• • •••o• •••••••n••• •y a in ••• A• I• .
- $KILL(n)$ •on••in• ••• • •••• i••ion ID• *killed* •y no•• n. S••• •••• i••ion ID•
  •o••••• on• •o ••••o•i•••ion •••••i••• •n•• w•o•• ••o•••••ion• on ••• ••ll
  ••••• ••o• •• ••• ••••••••••o•• o• no•• n. A••o••in• •o ••• J•v• • ••••••-
  •on••ol • o••l, i• $d \in N$ •••••••n•• • doPrivileged() • •••o• invo••••ion,
  $KILL(d)$ i• ••• •niv•••• P o• •ll ••• • •••• i••ion ID• •••n•• in ••• A• I• .
  T•i• i• ••••••••, in J•v• •, • ••ll •o doPrivileged() •o•• no• •x••n• ••••o-
  •i•••ion• •o •li•n• •o•• ••l••••iv•ly, in • •n•-••••in•• •••• ion, ••• •o•• i• in •
  •o••••-•••in•• •••• ion.[5] Fo• •ny o•••• no•• $n \in N$, $KILL(n) = \varnothing$.

---

[4] Even though `checkPermission()` takes only one `Permission` parameter, that parameter may correspond to more than one object in the ARIG model, since JaBA is path insensitive and interprocedurally flow insensitive.

[5] Unlike the Java 2 `doPrivileged()` method, the CLR `Assert()` method shields client code from authorization requirements in a fine-grained fashion [7]. Library code can assert a specific `IPermission` object, and only the authorization represented by that object will be implicitly granted to the client code currently on the stack. To model this behavior correctly, the *KILL* set of the asserting method's node would only have to contain the permission IDs of the asserted `IPermission` objects.

I• i• •••••o•• •onv•ni•n• •o in••o•••• • ••n••ion $NodeType$: $N \rightarrow$ $\{check, grant, other\}$. Fo• •••• $n \in N$, $NodeType(n)$ i• ••• n•• •• •ollow•:

$$NodeType(n) = \begin{cases} check, & \text{i• } n \text{ i• • checkPermission() no••;} \\ grant, & \text{i• } n \text{ i• • doPrivileged() no••;} \\ other, & \text{o•••••wi••.} \end{cases}$$

T•• $check$ no••• ••• ••o•• •••••••n•in• checkPermission() • •••o• ••ll•, w•i•• ••i•••• •••o•i••ion ••••••, w• il• ••• $grant$ no••• ••• •• o•• •••••••••n•in• ••ll• •o doPrivileged(), •••o••• w•i•• ••• ••ll••• on ••• ••••••• •••••• ••• i• •li•i•ly •••n••• ••••o•i••ion•. T•• $other$ no••• •o no• •ff••• ••• •••• flow. T•• •ollowin• ••••• o-•o•• •o•• •li••• ••• •••i•n• •n• o• ••• ••••-flow ••••:

1:    •o• •••• no•• • n {
2:       •wi••• ($NodeType(n)$) {
3:          •••• $check$:
4:             $GEN(n) = \{p \in P | p$ i• •••••••• •• $n\}$
5:             $KILL(n) = \varnothing$
6:          •••• $grant$:
7:             $GEN(n) = \varnothing$
8:             $KILL(n) = P$
9:          •••• $other$:
10:            $GEN(n) = \varnothing$
11:            $KILL(n) = \varnothing$
12:      }
13:   }

T•• •••••-flow ••••••ion• •o• •••• no•• • $n \in N$ ••• •••n•• in ••• ••••l w•y •• •ollow•:

$$OUT(n) = (IN(n) \cup GEN(n)) - KILL(n)$$
$$IN(n) = \bigcup_{m \in Succ(n)} OUT(n)$$

w•••• $OUT(n)$ •n• $IN(n)$ ••• ••• •••• o• •••• i••ion ID• ••o•••••• ••o• n •n• ••••• in• n, ••••••iv•ly. T•• •••••-flow •n•ly•i• j••• •••••i• •• •onv•••••• •o • •x•• • oin• in $\mathcal{O}(|E||P|)$ •i• • •in•• ($\bullet^P, \subseteq$) i• • •ni•• l•••i•• •n• ••• $data\text{-}flow$ $functions\ OUT, IN : N \rightarrow \bullet^P$ ••• • ono•oni• wi•• ••••• ••• •o ••• l•••i••'• ••••i•l o••••, $\subseteq$ [1•].

3.3   Permission ID Propagation from doPrivileged() Nodes

A••o••in• •o ••• J•v• • ••••o•i••ion •••y•••• , ••••o•i••ion ••••i••• •n•• ••o•••••••• ••w•••• vi• • doPriviledged() no•• • ••• no• ••o••••• ••yon• ••• ••••••••••o•• o• ••• doPrivileged() no••. T•i• ••n ••• • o•••ll•• •• •ollow•: W••n • doPrivileged() no•• d i• •n•o• n••••• •••in• ••• ••v•••• ••o••••ion

o•••• i••ion ID• •••••i••• in S•••ion 3.•, i•• •••• i••ion ID •••, $\Pi(d)$, i• ••o•-
••••• •o d' •••••••••o•• only ••••• ••• ••o•••••ion •l•o•i••• •o• •ll ••• o••••
no••• ••• •••• in••••. T•••o•••••ion o• $\Pi(d)$ ••w•••• ••• no••• ••••o•• ••
•••• ••iv•ly. I• n i• • no•• in $Pred(d)$ •n• $\Pi(n)$ •••n••• ••• • •••• l• o• ••• ••o•-
••••ion o• $\Pi(d)$ ••o• d, $\Pi(n)$ i• no• •••n•• i•••• •o ••• no••• in $Pred(n)$. • n•
••••-flow ••••••ion i••• •i•n• •o ••••i• •• i• on•-•••• ••o•••••ion:

$$IN(n) = IN(n) \cup \bigcup_{\substack{d \in Succ(n) \\ NodeType(d)=grant}} IN(d)$$

T•i• ••••••ion ••• •n •ff••• only •o• ••o• no••• ••••• ••v• • *grant* no•• ••• •
•••••••o•. T•• •i• • •o• •l•xi•y o• ••i• on•-•••• ••o••••ion i• $\mathcal{O}(|E|)$.

3.4 Complexity

T•• ••••••-•i•••• •n•ly•i• •onv••••• in $\mathcal{O}(|E||P|)$ •i• •. W••n ••• •n•ly•i• •••-
• in••••, •o• •••• no•• $n \in N$, ••• ••••-flow ••• $IN(n)$ will •• ••••l •o •••
••• $\Pi(n)$ •n• will ••••••n• ••• ••••o•i••••ion• •••• i••• •o •x••••• ••• • •••o•
••••••n••• •y n wi•• n' ••llin• •on••x•.

4 Privileged-Code Placement

T•i• ••••ion ••••i••• •ow ••• ••o•••••ion •l•o•i••• •••••i••• in S•••ion 3 ••n
•• ••••• •n••• •o •••o• ••i••lly •••••• w•i•• •o••ion• o• • o•i••l•-•o• •on•n•
•o•• ••o•l• ••• • ••• ••ivil•••• w•il• • ini• i•in• ••• •i••• o• viol••in• ••• P•in-
•i•l• o• L•••• P•ivil•••, wi•• • ••••i•ion •••• •o•• •o ••• l•v•l o• ••• ••o••••
•o•n••• wi••in • • •••o•. Fo• •••• ••ivil••••-•o• lo••ion i• •••o• • •n••, •••
•l•o•i••• ••ovi••• •n •x•l•n•ion. A••i•ion•lly, ••i• •••••ion •• ow• •ow •o •o• -
•••• ••• ••••o•i•••ion• •••• ••ivil•••• •o•• will i• • li•i•ly •••n• •o •li•n• •o••.
Fin•lly, ••i• ••••ion ••••i••• •ow ••• •l•o•i••• ••••••• •xi••in• •nn••••••y
o• ••••n••n• ••ivil•••• •o••, •n• •voi•• in•••in• n•w ••ivil•••• •o•• •••• i•
•nn•••••••y o• •••• n••n•.

4.1 Insertion of doPrivileged() Calls

In J•v• •, •l••• lo••••• ••• o•••ni••• ••• •••• T, ••ll•• ••• *class-loading delegation tree* [••]. J•BA • o••l• ••• •l•••-lo••in• •y•••• •n• •••o•i•••• • •l•••
lo•••• n••• • wi•• •v••y no•• in •n A• I• . T••• ••ivil••••-•o•• •l•••• •n• ••o••••
i• •on••••••• •y ••••• in• •••• •ll ••• •l•••• in ••• • o•i••l• •o• •on•n•• will
•• lo••••• •y • •••i•n•••• •l••• lo••••, ••ll•• ••• *component loader*. A *boundary
edge* in G i• •ny •••• $e = (m, n) \in E$ •••• •••• m i• •••o•i•••• wi•• ••• •o• •o-
n•n• lo•••• •n• n i• •••o•i•••• wi•• • •iff•••n• •l••• lo•••• in T. I• $\Pi(n) \neq \varnothing$,
•••n ••• ••ll •••••••n••• •y e i• •••••n•••• •o l••• •o ••• J•v• • •••• o•i••ion
••••y•••• . S••• • ••ll i• • ••n•i•••• •o• •••o• in• ••ivil••••. Fo• •x•• •l•, e
• •y •• ••• ••••• ••••l•in• ••o• ••llin• ••• •on••••o• o• FileOutputStream

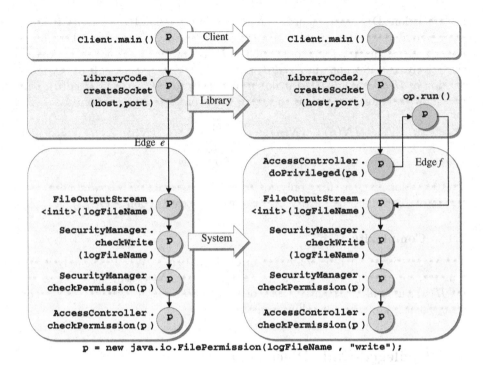

Fig. 5. Changes in the ARIG after Making Library Code Privileged

••o• • •••o• createSocket() in Fi•••• 1. Fi•••• • ••ow• •ow •o w••• •••
FileOutputStream •on•••••••o• ••ll in•o • ••ivil•••• •lo••, •n• Fi•••• 5 ••ow•
••• •o•••••on•in• A• I• •. No•i•• •ow ••• A• I• on ••• •i••• in Fi•••• 5 ••-
fl•••• ••• •••••n•• o• doPrivileged() •y no• ••o•••••in• ••• FilePermission
••••i••• •n• ••yon• ••• invo•••ion o• createSocket(), •x•• ••in• •li•n• •o••
••o• ••• FilePermission ••••i••• •n•, •• ••••i•••.

T•• •l•o•i••• •••••i••• in S•••ion 3 ••n •• •••• •n••• •o i••n•i•y •ny
•o•n••y •••• $e = (m, n)$ •••• •••• $\Pi(n) \neq \varnothing$. T•• in•o•• ••ion •on••in• in e
•n• $\Pi(n)$ i• ••• •i•n• •o •••••• in• ••• •x••• •o••ion o• • o•i••• l•-•o• •on•n•
•o•• •••• i• • ••n•i•••• •o• •••o• in• ••ivil•••• •lon• wi•• •n •x•l•n••ion, •n•
•o i••n•i•y ••• •••••o•i•••ion• •••• ••• ••ivil•••• •o•• will i• •li•i•ly •••n• •o
•li•n• •o••:

1. T•• •l••• n•• •, • •••o• •i•n••••••, •n• ••o•••• •o•n••• •••• •on••i••• •
   • o••i•l• doPrivileged() lo•••ion ••n •• o•••in•• ••o• no••• m •n• •••
   ••ll •i•• in e. Sin•• e i• • •o•n••y ••••, ••o• • •on••ol-flow •••••••iv• •••
   lo•••ion •o• •••••• •y ••i• •l•o•i••• i•, in ••• • o•i•••l•-•o• •on•n• •o••,
   ••• •lo•••• •o ••• ••••o•i•••ion ••••. T• i• •n•••••• •••• only ••• •o••ion o•
   • o•i•••l•-•o• •on•n• •o•• •ff•••iv•ly l•••in• •o•n ••••o•i•••ion ••••• will
   ••• • •••• ••ivil••••, w•i•• • ini• i••• ••• •i••• o• viol••in• ••• P•in•i•l• o•
   L•••• P•ivil•••.

•. T•• ••••o•i•••ion• i• • li•i•ly •••n••• •o •li•n•• i• ••ll •o doPrivileged()
i• in•••••• ••• ••••••••n••• •y ••• • •••• i••ion ID• in $\Pi(n)$.

3. A• •n •x•l•n••ion, ••• •• lly •••li••• •i•n••••• o•••• • •••o• ••in• invo•••
•• no•• n •n• •••in• ••• • ••••o•i••ion •••• i••• •n•• in $\Pi(n)$ ••n •• o•-
••in•• ••o• no•• n i•••l•. I•• • o•• ••••il•• •x•l•n••ion i• ••i•••, •ll •••
••••• ••o• n •o ••• checkPermission() no••• in ••• A• I• •••••••• •oo•••
•• n ••n •• ••• o••••. S••• •••• •••• ••• •• o•• ••o••• w•i•• ••• •••• o•i•••ion
•••• i••• •n•• in $\Pi(n)$ ••v• ••o••••••• •• •o n.

T•• ••ivil••••-•o•• •l•••• •n• •l•o•i•• ••n •• ••••o• i•••. In•••• o••••-
o• • •n• in• ••• ••ivil••••-•o•• lo••ion• ••••, in ••• • o•i•••l• •o• •on•n••,
••• ••• •lo•••• •o ••• ••••o•i••ion ••••••, ••• •l•o•i•• ••o•l•, •o• •x•• •l•,
i••n•i•y ••• ••ivil••••-•o•• lo••ion• •lo•••• •o •• o•• •o• •on•n••' •n••y • oin••.
Wi•• •• i• •••o•••, •ow•v••, •o•• no• •••• i•in• •••• o•i•••ion• • •y •••o• •
• nn•••••••ily ••ivil••••.

4.2 Detecting Unnecessary or Redundant Privileged Code

An •nn•••••••y doPrivileged() ••ll • •y ••••l• ••o• •••n••• • ••• •o
• o•i•••l•-•o• •on•n• •o• •••in• •o•• ••v•lo•• •n• o• • •in••n•n••. A ••ll
•o doPrivileged() •••• w•• o•i•in•lly •on•i•••• n•••••••y no lon••• ••i••••
•n •••• o•i••ion ••••• •••• ••• ••• •••n••. A •••• n••n• doPrivileged() ••ll • •y
••••l• ••o• •oo• •o• •••i•n o• ••o• in•••••in• •iff••n• •o• •on•n• •o ••••
• ••ll •o doPrivileged() •••• w•• on•• •on•i•••• n•••••••y •••••• i• l•• •o
•n •••• o•i••ion ••••• •••o• •• •••• n••n• ••••••• o•••• doPrivileged() ••ll•
now •o• in••• ••• ••••o•i•••ion ••••••. A• w• o•••v•• in S••ion 1, •nn•••••
•••y o• •••• n••n• ••ivil•••• •o•• ••o•l• ••• • ••• •n••ivil•••• •o• ••••i•y •n•
••••o•• •n•• ••••on•. T•• •l•o•i•• ••••i••• in S••ion 3 ••n • •• •••• •n••• •o
i••n•i•y •nn•••••••y o• •••• n••n• ••ll• •o doPrivileged() •y •i• •ly ••••••in•
•ny doPrivileged() no•• d in ••• ••••• •••• •••• $\Pi(d) = \varnothing$.

I•• •o•• in••••••ion •o•• no• •••• i•• •••• o•i•••ion•, i• i• • • •oo• ••••••i•y
••••••i•• •o• ••• i• ••ivil•••• [35]. T•• •ollowin• in••••••ion in ••• run() • •••o•
o• Fi•••• 3 ••• •••n• • •••• ••ivil•••• •v•n •• o••• i• •o•• no• ••••••• • ••••••i••••
•••o••••:

```
System.out.println("Received request from user " + userName);
```

S••• •n in•••••ion ••o•l• •• • ••• •n••ivil•••• •v•n ••o•••, in ••i• ••••,
$\Pi(d) \neq \varnothing$. T•• ••ivil••••-•o•• •l•••• •n• •l•o•i•• ••n •••ily ••••••• •nn••-
•••••ily ••ivil•••• in••••••ion•. L•• d •• • doPrivileged() no•• •n• r i••
PrivilegedAction o• PrivilegedExceptionAction run() •••••••o•. I• $\Pi(r) \neq$
$\varnothing$ •n• •••• •xi••• $n \in Succ(r)$ •••• •••• $\Pi(n) = \varnothing$, •••n ••• • •••o• invo••ion
••••••n••• •y n ••o•l• ••• • ••• •n••ivil••••.

4.3 Avoiding Unnecessary or Redundant Privileged Code

T•• •••• i••ion ID ••• $\Pi(n)$ •••o•i•••• wi•• ••• ••••• no•• n o• • •o•n••y
•••• $e = (m, n)$ • •••• • non-•• ••y •o• ••• ••ivil••••-•o•• •l•••• •n• •l•o•i••

•o •••o• • •n• • ••ll •o doPrivileged(). T•••••o••, •x•••• •o• ••o•• ••••• in
w•i•• ••• •••••••-•i•••• •n•ly•i• •on••v•iv•ly ••• o••• •n•••li••• l• ••••o•i••ion
••••i••• •n••, non• o•••• doPrivileged() ••ll• •••o• • •n••• •y••• ••ivil••••-
•o•• •l•••• •n• •l•o•i••• ••• •nn••••••y o• •••• •n••n•. F••••••• o••, •in•• •••
••ivil••••-•o•• •l•••• •n• •l•o•i••• ••••i••ly i••n•i••• ••• • •••o• invo•••ion•
•••• ••o•l• ••• • •••• ••ivil••••, no •o•• in•••••ion will •••o• • • •nn•••••••ily
o•••••n••n•ly ••ivil•••• ••• • ••••l• o• •x•••in• ••• •l•o•i•• , •x••••, •••in,
•o• ••• • ••••• o• •on•••v••iv•n••.

How•v••, i••• o•l• •• o•••v•• ••••, i• ••• •n•ly•i• i• •••o•• •• ••••• • ••ll
•o doPrivileged() •••••n in•••••, •ny •••• ••o• ••• PrivilegedAction o•
PrivilegedExceptionAction'• run() no•• in•o • •iff•••n• •l••• lo•••'• n•• •
••••• will •l•o••, •y•••ni•ion, ••o•n••y••••. Fo••x•• •l•, in Fi•••• 5, •••••
••• FileOutputStream •on••••••o• •••••n w••••••• in • ••ivil•••• •lo••, •••
•••• f ••o• ••• op.run() no•• •o ••• FileOutputStream.<init>() no•• i•
••o•n••y ••••, •n• ••• •••• i••ion ID ••• •••o•i•••• wi•• ••• •••• no•• i•
non-•• ••y. ••• o••in• • ••ivil••••-•o•• ••••i••• •n• wo•l• • ••• ••• ••xi••in•
••ll •o doPrivileged() ••••n••n•. To •voi• ••i• •i•••ion, •ny •o•n••y ••••
o•i•in••in• ••o• • PrivilegedAction o• PrivilegedExceptionAction'• run()
no•• •••• •••• ••• only ••••••••••o•• o• ••• run() no•• ••• doPrivileged()
no••• i• •••o• ••i••lly •x•l•••• • ••n•i•••• •o• doPrivileged().

4.4   Complexity

T•• ••ivil••••-•o•• •l•••• •n• •l•o•i••• i• o•••in•• •y •••• •n•in• ••• •••••••-
•i•••• •n•ly•i• •l•o•i••• in • w•y•••••o•• no• •ff••• ••• •l•o•i••• '••o• •l•xi•y
•n• •onv••••n•• •x•••• •o• • •on•••n• •••••o•. T••••o••, •x•••in• •••••ivil••••-
•o•• •l•••• •n• •l•o•i••• ••ill •••• i••• $\mathcal{O}(|E||P|)$ •i• •.

5   Tainted-Variable Analysis

W• •••••• •o ••• ••••• •••• •i•••• o•i•in••• ••o• •n •n•••••• •o•••• o• ••••
••n •• •••iv•• ••o• •n •n••••••• •o•••• •• ••in• *tainted* [••]. T•in••• ••••
•n• ••• v••i••l•• •••• •ol• o• ••••••n•• i• ••n •• •••• •o• •••••in •in•• o•
ov••w•i•• •••••••• [••], •••• •• ov••w•i•in• ••• n•• • o• • •l• o• j•• • •••••••.
So• ••i• ••, •ow•v••, i• •y•• n•••••••y •o ••• • ••in••• v••i••l• w••n ••••••in•
•••••j•••• •••o• •••. In •••• •••••, ••• •••• ••n •• *sanitized* •n• • •••• •n••in•••
•y ••••o•• in• ••ni•y ••••• on i• •••o•• ••in• i• in •••••i•••• o•••••ion• [3].
S•ni•y ••••••• ••• ••••lly •o• •in o• •o• •on•n• ••••i••. W• ••••• • ••••, •o• •
••••i•• •••li•••ion, ••••• i• •n •••o•i•••• li•••y •on••inin• ••• ••ni•y ••••••
on •••• ••• li•••ion'• ••in••• v••i••l••.

A ••in•••• v••i••l• i• no• n•••••••ily • •••••i•y ••o•l•• . I• • •y •on••i•••
• •••••i•y ••o•l•• i• i• i• •l•o • *privileged* v••i••l•, • ••nin• •••• i• i• ••••
in•i•• ••ivil•••• •o•• [35]. • v•n • ••ivil•••• ••in••• v••i••l• i• no• n•••••••ily •
••••i•y ••o•l•• . In ••••, w• i••in•i•• •wo •y•• o• ••ivil•••• ••in••• v••i••l••:
i•• ••ivil•••• ••in••• v••i••l• i• •••• •o ••••••• • •••••j•••• •••o• •••, w• will ••ll

i• *malicious*, o•••••wi•• w• will ••ll i• *benign*. Sin•• ••••o•i•••ion •••••• ••• no•
•••••o•• •• ••yon• ••• •••••• •••• • invo•in• doPrivileged(), •n • n••••••• •li•n•
•••li•••ion •o•l• •x•loi• • • •li•io•• v••i••l• •o ••v• ••• ••ivil•••• •o•• •••••••
•••••i•••• •••o••••• on i•• ••••l•.

In Fi•••• •, v••i••l• logFileName i• no• ••in••• •••••••• i•• v•l•• ••nno• ••
••• • y • •li•n• ••• li•••ion. In Fi•••• 3, ••• host •n• port ••••• •••••• ••• • o••
••in••• •••••••• •••i• v•l••• ••n • • ••• ••y •ny •li•n• ••• li•••ion •n• no ••ni•y
••••• i• ••••o•• •• on •••• . A••i•ion•lly, •••y ••• •o•• •ivil•••• ••••••• •••y
••• •••• in•i•• ••ivil•••• •o••, •n• ••y ••• • •li•io•• •••••••• •••y ••• ••• ••••
•o ••••••• • •••••i•••• •••o••••. An •n••••••• •li•n•, wi•• no SocketPermission,
••n invo•• getSocket() on ••• ••••••• li•••y •n• ••v• ••• li•••y o••n •n
••• i•••y •o•••• •onn••ion on i•• ••••l•. V••i••l• userName, ••o••• ••in••• •n•
••ivil•••, i• ••ni•n • ••••••• i• i• no• •••• •o •••o•• •ny ••••i•••• o•••••ion.

T•i• •••ion • ••••n•• • •i• •l• in•••••o••••••l ••in•••-v••i••l• •n•ly•i• •l-
•o•i••• •••• •••• •n•• ••• ••ivil•••-•o•• •l•••• •n• •l•o•i••• •••••i••• in
S•••ion •. T•• o• j••••iv• o••• ••in•••-v••i••l• •n•ly•i• i• •o•• •o ••••••• •xi••-
in• • •li•io•• v••i••l•• •n• •o •voi• ••• in••o••••ion o• n•w • •li•io•• v••i••l••
w••n • ••in• n•w •o•• ••ivil••••.

T•• ••••• •••• o• ••• ••in•••-v••i••l• •n•ly•i• •l•o•i••• i• •o •o• ••••• •••
ini•i•l ••• *S* o••in••• v••i••l••, w••i•• i• ••• •nion o• ••• •ollowin• •wo ••••:

- S•• S_1, •on••inin• ••• • o•i•••l•-•o• •on•n• in•••n•• •n• •••••i• ••l•• ••••
  ••n ••• • o•i••• •y •li•n• •o••
- S•• S_2, •on••inin• ••ll ••• •••••• ••••• •o ••• • o•i•••l• •o• •on•n••' •••li•
  •n• ••o•••••• •n••y • •••o••, in•l••in• ••• ••••iv•• o• j•••• •o• non-••••i•
  • •••o••

S•• S_2 ••n • ••o• ••••• ••••ily. How•v••, i• ••o•l• ••o•••v•• •••• i• •••••••• in
•• o•i•••l• •o• •on•n• i• no• •••l•• [•9], •••n S_2 ••o•l• •on••in ••••••• •••••
•o ••• •••••••••'• ••••l•••o• • ••• o••• •• w•ll.

A ••in••• v••i••l• ••n, •i•••ly o• in•i•••ly, ••in o••• v••i••l••, •o• •x•• •l•
••••o••• •••i•n• •n••. T•• ••••on• •••• o••• ••in•••-v••i••l• •n•ly•i• •l•o•i••
•on•i••• o• i••n•i•yin• •xi••in• ••ivil•••• v••i••l•• in ••• • o•i•••l• •o• •on•n••
•n• •••••• i• ••y ••• ••in•••. Any ••n••••• in••••o••••••l ••o•••• -•li•in•
•n•ly•i• •l•o•i•• [36] ••n •• ••••• •o ••••••• v•l•• flow• ••o• ••in••• v••i••l••
•o ••ivil•••• v••i••l••. • ••• •l•o•i••• ••••• ••••o•••• -•li•in• •l•o•i••• ••••, •o•
•ny ••ivil•••• v••i••l• x, •on••••••• • •li•• o• x •n• ••n •••••• i• ••• •li••
•on••in• v••i••l•• in ••• S. I• •o, x i• •o••n•i•lly ••in••• •• w•ll. I• •••• •in• •o ••
•••n w•••••• x i• ••ni•n o• • •li•io••. T•• •••••••-•i•••• •n•ly•i• •l•o•i•• •iv••
•• ••• •n•w••. Sin•• x i• ••ivil••••, x ••••• •• •••• in •• l•••• on• ••ivil••••
in•••••ion. Fo• x •o • • • •ni•n, i• • • •••• $\Pi(n) = \varnothing$ •o• •ny no•• n ••••••••n•in•
• • •••o• •x•••in• •ny ••ivil•••• in•••••ion •••• •on••in• x. I• ••••• •xi••• •
no••• n •••••••••n•in• • • •••o• in w•i•• • ••ivil•••• in•••••ion •on••inin• x i•
•x••••••, •••• •••• $\Pi(n) \neq \varnothing$, ••n w• •on•••v••iv•ly ••••• • ••••• x i• •li•io••,
in w•i•• ••••• w• loo• •o• • ••ni•y ••••• on x. I• • ••ni•y ••••• •o• x •xi••• •n•
i• ••n • • •••••• in•• ••••• x ••••• i•, ••n x i• •on•i••••• ••ni•i•••. • ••••wi••,
••• ••in•••-v••i••l• •n•ly•i• ••• o••• • • •o••n•i•l ••••i•y •i••.

I• x i• no• •n •xi••in• ••ivil•••• v••i••l•, ••• i• wo•l• •••o• • •o •y • ••-
in• n•w •o•• ••ivil•••• •• • ••••l• o• •x•••in• ••• ••ivil••••-•o•• •l•••• •n•
•l•o•i•• , ••• ••in•••-v••i••l• •n•ly•i• ••o••••• •x••ly •• ••o••. T•• only • i-
••••n•• i• •••• i• will ••• o•• •••• ••• •o•• •on••inin• x ••n •• • ••• ••ivil••••
only i• x i• ••ni•n o• ••ni•i••l•.

6   Experimental Results

• on••x•- •n• in••••o•••••lly flow-••n•i•iv• ••••i• •n•ly•i• ••• • ••••••••ion
•o• ••••i•in• •i•ni••n• ••o•••in• • ow•• •n• • •• o•y. W• ••v• ••••o•• ••
••ivil••••-•o•• •n• ••in•••-v••i••l• •n•ly•i• on ••••• o• rt.jar, l•••• •o• • ••-
•i•l • i••l•w•••, •n• ••• S••n•••• P•••o•• •n•• •v•l••ion •o••o••ion J•v•
B••in••• B•n••• ••• •000 (SP•• j•••000) ••o•••• [3•]. T•• •i• •l••• li•••y
•••• w• •n•ly••• i• ••• LibraryCode •l••• in Fi•••• 1. Fi•••• 6 ••ow• ••• Hy-
•••T•x• M••••• L•n••••• (HTML) o•••••••o••••• •y ••• MA••• •ool. Fo•
•••••• ••••ili•y, ••• HTML o•••• •••• lin•• •o ••• •o•••• •o•• •n••o••• •o •••
lin• n•• •••• w•••• • •ll •o doPrivileged() ••o•l• •• in•••••••. A• •x• •••••,
••• •ool ••• o•••• •wo • o••i• l• ••ivil••••-•o•• •l•••• •n••, •••••••••• ••••• o••
••• •••••• ••••• •o ••• Socket •on••••••o• w••• ••in•••. T•i• w•• •n in•i••ion
•••• only ••• •ll •o ••• FileOutputStream •on••••••o• •o•l• •• ••••ly • •••
••ivil••••. T•• ••••l•• •••o•••• •y ••• MA••• •ool on •ll ••• o•••• ••n••-
• •••• w••• •l•o •o•••••••••• on •o•••••-•o••• •n••l in•••••ion •n• ••••••••n•
••••in•. In ••••i••l••, ••• •ool •••••••• w••n •xi••in• ••ivil•••• •o•• w•• •n-
n•••••••y o• ••••n••n•, •n• ••••o••i••ly •i••in••i•••• •••w••n • •li•io••n•
••ni•n •• in••• v••i••l••.

Mo•• ••••n•ly, w• •n•ly••• ••li••• V3.0 [13] •o i••n•i•y w•i•• •o••ion• o•
••• •l••-in •o•• ••o•l• •• •••• ••ivil•••• in o•••• •o •n••l• ••li••• •o ••n

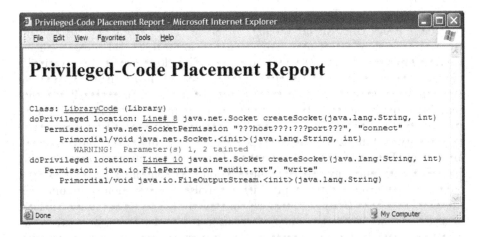

Fig. 6. Privileged-Code Placement Report on LibraryCode

Table 1. Analysis Results

Eclipse Plug-in	Classes	Methods	Time (sec)	Nodes	Edges	Instr. (bytes)	doPriv.
ant	2245	14799	4668	169539	1833305	818342	1908
core.runtime	1265	7233	1379	59771	134191	421094	353
osgi	1069	6091	814	62031	141397	362482	256
tomcat	2804	19885	5793	197709	471957	1066369	2011
ui	2910	16299	11254	191752	1843518	891270	150
ui.forms	972	4497	4430	29199	59605	286739	14

wi•• • J•v• • SecurityManager •n••l••. T•• ••••l•• ••• o•••• in T••l• 1 •••
••o• ••nnin• ••• MA••• •ool on •n IBM P•••on•l • o• ••••• wi•• •n In••l
1.6 • H• P•n•i•• M ••o•••o• •n• 1 • B o••n•o• A••••• M•• o•y (• AM),
•n• wi•• o•••••in• •y•••• Mi••o•o•• Win•ow• XP SP•. T•• MA••• •ool •••
•••n i• •l•• •n••• in J•v•. W• •n i• • o•• ••• • •••n•-•lon• •••li••ion •n• in-
•i•• • •li••• V3.0 ••in• S•n Mi••o•y•••• •' J•• V1.•.•_0•. J•• •• n••ion•li•y
w•• • •••• ••• o• ••• •n•ly•i• ••o•• •y in•l••in• ••• J•• V1.•.•_0• •y••••
•n• •x••n•ion li••••i••. To •••••• ••• •i•• o• ••• •n•ly•i• ••o••, ••• MA•••
•ool w•• ••••o• i••• •o ••il• ••• •n•ly•i• ••o•• ••••• on ••• •l••-in •••n••n-
•i••. T•• n•• ••• o• •l•••• in ••• •n•ly•i• ••o•• w•• ••ill •••••• •••n •0,000.
T••l• 1 •• ow•, •o• •o• • • •li••• •l••-in•, •ow • •ny •l••••• •n• • •••o•• w•••
in•l•••• in ••• A• I• , ••• •i• • ••• •loy•• •o ••n ••• w•ol• •n•ly•i• (in•l••in•
••• A• I• •on••••••ion, w• i•• on •v•••••••••• 96% o•••• •o••l •i• •), ••• n•• -
••• o• no••• •n• ••••• in ••• A• I• , ••• in••••••ion• •o•n•, •n• ••• n•• ••• o•
doPrivileged() lo•••ion• •••••••••• •y ••• •ool. • n •v•••••, 50% o•••• •o••
• o••ion• ••n• i•••• •o •••o• • ••ivil•••• •on••in•• • •li•io•• ••in••• v•i••l••—
•n in•i•••ion •••• doPrivileged() ••o•l• no••• ••••. T•• osgi •l••-in w••
••• only on• ••••• l••••y •on••in•• ••ll• •o doPrivileged(). T•• •o••l n•• •••
w•• •9, •n• • o•• •o•• w••• •nn••••••y o• •••• n••n•.

• •••• •n•ly••• w••• •••o•• •• on l•••• •o• • •••i•l ••o••••• (ov•• •0,000
•l••••• in ••• •n•ly•i• ••o••), ••••• on ••• J•• V1.1 •••••••on••ol • o••l.
T•• •o•l w•• •o i••n•i•y •••i• ••ivil••••-•o•• ••••i••• •n•• •o •llow •••• •o
•••••••••lly •• n wi•• ••• J•v• • •••••••on••ol • o••l •n••l••.

7 Related Work

P•ivil•••• •o•• •••• i••o•i• •oo•• in ••• 19•0'•. T•• Di•i••l ••• i•• •n• • o••o-
•••ion (D••) Vi••••l A•••••• • x••n•ion/Vi••••l M•• o•y Sy•••• (VAX/VMS)
o•••••in• •y•••• ••• • •••••• •i• il•• •o ••• doPrivileged() • •••o• in J•v•
• •n• ••• Assert() • •••o• in • L•. T•• VAX/VMS •••••• w•• ••ll•• *privileged images.* P•ivil•••• i• •••• w••• •i• il•• •o UNIX setuid ••o•••• •, •x••••
•••• ••ivil•••• i• •••• ••n in ••• ••• • ••o•••• •• •ll ••• ••••'• o•••• •n••ivi-
l•••• ••o•••• •. T•i• • ••n• •••• •••y w••• •on•i•••• ly •••i•• •o ••••••• •••n
UNIX setuid ••o•••• • •••••••• •••y l••••• ••• ••••l •••••••••• ••o•••/••••••••

•••••••• ••••• ••o•••ion•. • n• •x•• •l• o• •n •••••• on ••ivil•••• i• •••• i•
••• on•••••••• in • •••••• •y Ko•••l, Ko•••l, Li, •n• Mi•••• [•3].[6]

Mo•• •••••n•ly, •••i• •n• •yn•• i• •n•ly•i• ••••ni•••• ••v• •o•• •••n ••••
•o• • o••llin• ••••o•i•••ion •l•o•i•• •. M••• o• •• wo•• ••• •o••••• on •••-
•o•• •n•• o••i• i•••ion• o• on ••ovi•in• •l•••n••iv• •o ••• •xi••in• ••••o••••
•• •loy•• •y J•v• [•9,••] •n• • L• [16]. Po••i•, S••l••, •n• S• i•• [30] •x-
••n• •n• •o•• •li• W•ll•••'• ••••i•y ••••in• ••yl• [•1] vi• •y•• •••o•y ••in•
• λ-••l••l••, ••ll•• λsec. How•v••, •••i• ••••o••• •o•• no• • o••l •ll o• J•v•'•
••••o•i•••ion •••••••••i•i••, in•l••in• • •l•i-•••••••• •o•• •n• •n•ly•i• o• in-
•o• •l••• ••o•••• • [31], no• •o•• i• •o• •••• ••• ••••o•i•••ion o•j•••, w•i••
o•••n in•l•••• i••n•i•yin• ••• String ••••• ••••• •o ••• Permission o•j•••'•
•on•••••o•. B••ol•••i, D•••no, •n• F••••i [5] ••• in•••••••• in o••i• i•in• •••-
•o•• •n•• o• •• n-•i• • ••••o•i•••ion ••••in•. T•i• i• •on• •y •li• in•in• ••••n-
••n• ••••• •n• ••lo•••in• o•••• •• i• n•••••. A••i•ion•lly [6], •••y inv•••i••••
w•y• in w•i•• ••o•••• •••n••o•• ••ion• ••n ••••••v• ••••••i•y ••o•••i•• in •x-
i••in• •o••, ••••i••l••ly in ••• •on••x• o• J•v•. S••i••lly, ••• •••n••o•• ••ion•
•••y •••• y in•l••• •••••n••n• ••••o•i•••ion ••••• •li• in••ion, •••• •o•• •li• i-
n••ion, • •••o• inlinin•, •n• •n ••••• •v•l••ion ••••••y •o• ••••• in••••••ion.
W•il• •••i• • o••l ••••• ••ivil•••• •o•• in•o •••o• n•, •••y ••••• • ••••• ••ivi-
l•••• •o•• •••• •l•••• y ••n in••••••, •n• •o no• •olv• ••• ••o•l•• o••••••in•
w•i•• •o••ion• o• li•••y •o•• ••o•l• •• • •••• ••ivil••••. B••••j•• •n• N••-
••nn [•] •••ly ••no•••ion•l ••• •n•i•• •o ••ow ••• •••iv•l•n•• o• eager •n•
lazy •••• •n•i•• •o• ••••• in•••••ion, ••ovi•• • •••i• •n•ly•i• o• safety, •n• i••n-
•i•y ••• n••o•• ••ion• ••••• ••n ••• ov• •nn•••••••y •••• o•i•••ion •••••. Si•ni••• n•
li• i•••ion• •o •• i• ••••o•••• ••• •••• •••• •n•ly•••• li• i••• •o • •in•l• •••••••,
•n• in•o• •l•••-••o•••• •n•ly••• ••• no• ••••o••••. J•n••n, L• M•••y••, •n•
T•o•n [•0] •o••• on ••ovin• •••• •o•• i• •••••• wi•• •••••••• •o • •lo••l ••••••i•y
•oli•y. T••i• o••l ••o••• o••••ion•l ••• •n•i•• •o ••ov• ••• ••o•••i••, ••in• •
•wo-l•v•l ••• •o••l lo•i•, •n• ••ow• ow •o •••••• •••• •n••n• •••• o•i••ion •••••.
T••y ••••• • •ll o•••• •o•• i• •v•il••l• •o• •n•ly•i•, •n• ••••• • ••ll ••••• ••n
•• ••on•••••••• •o• ••• •o••. F•l••n, W•ll•••, D••n, •n• B•l••n• ••v• ••••i••
• n•• •••• o• •••••i•y ••o•l•• • ••l•••• •o • o•il• •o•• [39,1•,•1,•,•0,10,9]. In
•••i••l••, •••y •••••n• • •o•• •li••ion o• ••••• in••o••••ion, w•i•• •x•• in••
••••• o•i•••ion ••••• on ••• ••in•i••l• •••••n•ly ••iv• in • •••••••• ••••• •• ••n
•i• • (security state). An ••••o•i•••ion o••i• i•••ion ••••ni•••, ••ll•• security
passing style, •n•o••• ••• •••••i•y ••••• o• •n •••li•••ion w•il• ••• ••• li•••ion
i• •x•••in• [•1]. ••••• • •••o• i• • o•i••• •o ••••• i• •••••• • ••••••i•y •o••n ••
•••• o• ••••• invo•••ion. T•• •o••n ••••••••n•• •n •n•o•in• o• ••• •••••i•y ••••••
•• ••••• ••••• •••• •, •• w•ll •• ••• ••••l• o• •ny ••••o•i•••ion •••• •n•o•n••••.
By •• nnin• ••• ••• li•••ion •n• •n•o•in• ••• •••••i•y •••••, ••• •••••i•y •••in•

[6] In a private communication with Dr. Paul A. Karger [21], he indicated that privileged
images had been a very significant source of security attacks in the VAX/VMS
operating system, and required many patches and updates over the years. He did
extensive work on resolving those problems at DEC in the 1979-1980 timeframe.

••yl• •x•lo••• ••••••••• o•• ••• •o• •••••l• invo••ion •••••, •n• •i••ov••• •••
•••o•i•••• •••••i•y ••••••• •n• ••••o•i••ion•. T•• ••••o•• o• •••i• wo•• i• •o
o••i• i•• ••• •••••o•i••ion •••o•• •n••, w•il• o••• i• •o i••ov•• w•i•• • o••ion•
o• li•••y •o••••o• l• ••• • ••• •••ivil••••. •••••••o••• •n•ly••• •ll ••• • o••i•l•
•x•••ion •••••, •v•n ••o•• ••••• •y no• ••• •i••ov•••• •y • li• i••• n•• ••• o•
•••• •••••. ••••••••n •n•ly•in• ••••i•y •oli•i•• •••• •o•i•• •y •xi••in• •o••,
• •lin••on •n• S••n•i••• [1•] ••••i•• • •y•••• •••• inlin•• •••••n•• • oni•o••
in•o ••• •o•• •o •n•o••• •••i•• •••••i•y •oli•i••. T••i• o•j••iv• i• •o •••n• •
••••••i•y • oli•y •n• •••n inj•••••• o•i••ion •oin•• in•o ••• •o••. T•i• •••o•••
••n •••••• o• •li• in•• ••• •n•n• ••••o•i••ion •••••. Kov••, Pi••oi•, •n• K••-
••n•••• [••] •••••i•• •n •l•o•i••• •n• •y•••• •o• •o• •••in• J•v• • •••••i•y
••••o•i••ion ••••i••• •n•• •o• •xi••in• J•v• •o••. T••i• •l•o•i••• , w•i•• i• •••
•••••in• • oin• •o• ••i• •••••, •ov••• • •ny o•••• •••••l• ••••••• o• J•v• • •••••-
•i•y, in•l••in• ••••o•i••ion ••••i••• •n•• •o• • •l•i-•••••••• •••li••ion• •n•
•n•ly•i• o• in•o• •l••• ••o•••• • [31], •o• ••• •o• ••••••ion o••n A• I• .

T•• no•ion o••in••• v••i••l••••••• • • nown wi•• ••• P••l l•n••••. In P••l,
••in• ••• -T o••ion •llow• ••••••in• ••in••• v••i••l•• [3•]. S••n•••, T•lw••, Fo•-
•••, •n• W••n•• •••••n• • ••in•••-v••i••l• •n•ly•i• •o• •••• l ••in• •on•••in•
•••••• • [33]. To •n• •o•• •• •••in• ••••, ••• •l ••••• •y•-••li••• •y•••• [15]
wi•• •wo •••li••••: *tainted* •n• *untainted*. T•• •y••• o• v•l••• ••••• ••n •• •on-
••oll•• •y •n •n••••••• ••v•••••y ••• •••li••• •• ••in• ••in•••, •n• ••• •••• o•
••• v••i••l•• ••• •••li••• •• •n••in•••. A •on•••in• ••••• i• •on•••••• •o•
• • • ••l ••o•••• . I•••••• i• • •••• ••o• • ••in••• no•• •o •n •n••in••• no••
in ••• •••••, •n •••o• i• fl••••. N•w•o• • •n• Son• [••] ••o•o•• • •yn•• i•
••in•••-v••i••l• •n•ly•i• •••• •••••o•• •y • oni•o•in• ••in••• v••i••l•• ••
••n •i• •. D••• o•i•in••in• o• ••i••• ••i••lly ••iv•• ••o• •n•••••• •o•••••,
•••• •• ••• n••wo••, ••• • •••••• •• ••in•••. T•in•• v••i••l•• ••• •••••• •• ••n
•i• •, •n• w••n••y••• •••• in • •n•••o•• w•y •n •••••• i• ••••••••. Vol••no,
I•vin•, •n• S• i•• [3•] ••l••• ••in•••-v••i••l• •n•ly•i• •o •n•o••in• in•o•• ••ion
flow • oli•i•• •••o••• •y•in•. A•••••• •n• • n•l• [3] •l•o ••• ••in•••-v••i••l•
•n•ly•i• •o •••••• •o••w•• ••••••• •• •o ••in••• v••i••l••. T••i• •••o••• ••o-
vi•• •••••-••• n•• ••ni•y •••••• •o •n••in• •o••n•i•lly ••in••• v••i••l••. In J•v•
•, • n••••i•• ••i•ion (J•••), ••••• •i•••• ••• •••n•• in •••• • o• o•••••ion•
on •o• •on•n••, in••••• o• ••• ••••• •n••••l•••• •n• •••• •y ••• •o• •on•n••.
N••• ovi•• •n• • •n•on•• [•6] ••••••• ••• n••• •o• ••••i•yin• ••••••• •i•••• on
••••. A•••••• •i•••• ••••o•• •o• ••••• •n •i• •li•y ••ni•y •••••• •o• ••in••• v••i-
••l••. Fo• in•••n••, • ••in••• v••i••l• i• ••ni•n •o••••o•• •li•n•• w•o ••v• •••••••
•i•••• ov•• ••• •••• •••••n••• •y ••• ••in••• v••i••l•.

8 Conclusion

In ••i• •••••, w• •••••n••• •n in•••• •o•••••l •n•ly•i• •o• •••ly •••in• ••iv-
il•••• •o•• in o•••• •o •n•••• •••• no •nn••••••y •••••• •i•••• ••• •••n•••
•o •li•n• •o••, •n• ••••••in••• v••i••l•• ••• no• •x•loi•••. •••••••o••• •o•
••ivil•••-•o•• •n• ••in•••-v••i••l• •n•ly•i• i• ••il• on •o• o• •n •••••••-i•••

•n•ly•i• •n• •••• •n A•••••-• i•••• Invo•••ion • •••• (A• I•). A• •••• o• •••
•n•ly•i•, w• •olv• • n•• ••• o• o•••• ••l•••• ••o•l•• •, in•l••in• i••n•i•••ion
o••nn••••••y •n• •••n••n• ••ivil•••• •o•• •n• fl•••in• w••n ••in••• v••i-
••l•• ••• ••ni•n o• • •li•io••. W• ••v• i• •l•• •n••• ••• •n•ly•i• ••••i• •• in
•• i• •••••• •n• ••• •••••n•ly ••in• i• •o i••n•i•y ••••i•y viol••ion• ••• •o ••ivi-
l•••• •o•• in l•••• li•••i•• •n• •••li••ion•. • •••n•ly•i• •••• ni••• •••l•• w•ll
•no••• •o ••o•••• ••••l• ••••l•• on l•••• •••li••ion• •n• li•••i••. W•il• •••
•n•ly•i• •••• ni•••• ••••i• •• in •• i• •••••• ••• in ••• •on••x• o• J•v• •o••, •••
•••i• •on••••• ••• •••li•••l• •o ••ivil••••-•o•• •l•••• •n• •n• ••in•••-v••i••l•
•n•ly•i• i••••• in non-J•v•-••••• •y•••• • •• w•ll.

Acknowledgments

T•• ••••o•• wo•l• li•• •o •••n• •••i• •oll•••••• •• ••• IBM T. J. W•••on
• •••••••• • •n•••: J•li•n Dol•y, T•• H••••••, P••l K•••••, A••on K••••n•••• ,
Mi•••l S••in••, S•• W••••, •n• Xi•ol•n •••n• •o• •••i• inv•l•••l• ••••ni••l
•on••i••••ion• •o •• i• ••••••. T••n•••l•o •o •••••••• P •005 ••vi•w••• •o• •••i•
in•i••••l •o• • •n•• •n• ••••••••••ion•, w•i•• ••l••• •o i• ••ov• •• i• ••••••.

References

1. Ole Agesen. The Cartesian Product Algorithm: Simple and Precise Type Inference Of Parametric Polymorphism. In *Proceedings of the 9th European Conference on Object-Oriented Programming*, pages 2–26. Springer-Verlag, August 1995.
2. Alfred V. Aho, Ravi Sethi, and Jeffrey D. Ullman. *Compilers: Principles, Techniques, and Tools*. Addison-Wesley, Reading, MA, USA, January 1986.
3. Ken Ashcraft and Dawson Engler. Using Programmer-Written Compiler Extensions to Catch Security Holes. In *Proceedings of the 2002 IEEE Symposium on Security and Privacy*, pages 143–159, Oakland, CA, USA, May 2002. IEEE Computer Society.
4. Anindya Banerjee and David A. Naumann. A Simple Semantics and Static Analysis for Java Security. Technical Report CS2001-1, Stevens Institute of Technology, Hoboken, NJ, USA, July 2001.
5. Massimo Bartoletti, Pierpaolo Degano, and Gian Luigi Ferrari. Static Analysis for Stack Inspection. In *Proceedings of International Workshop on Concurrency and Coordination, Electronic Notes in Theoretical Computer Science*, volume 54, Amsterdam, The Netherlands, 2001. Elsevier.
6. Massimo Bartoletti, Pierpaolo Degano, and Gian Luigi Ferrari. Stack Inspection and Secure Program Transformations. *International Journal of Information Security*, 2(3):187–217, August 2004.
7. Frédéric Besson, Tomasz Blanc, Cédric Fournet, and Andrew D. Gordon. From Stack Inspection to Access Control: A Security Analysis for Libraries. In *Proceedings of the 17th IEEE Computer Security Foundations Workshop*, pages 61–75, Pacific Grove, CA, USA, June 2004. IEEE Computer Society.
8. Drew Dean. The Security of Static Typing with Dynamic Linking. In *Proceedings of the 4th ACM conference on Computer and Communications Security*, pages 18–27, Zurich, Switzerland, 1997. ACM Press.

9. Drew Dean, Edward W. Felten, and Dan S. Wallach. Java Security: From HotJava to Netscape and beyond. In *Proceedings of the 1996 IEEE Symposium on Security and Privacy*, pages 190–200, Silver Spring, MD, USA, 1996. IEEE Computer Society Press.

10. Drew Dean, Edward W. Felten, Dan S. Wallach, and Dirk Balfanz. Java Security: Web Browsers and Beyond. Technical Report 566-597, Princeton University, Princeton, NJ, USA, February 1997.

11. Jeffrey Dean, David Grove, and Craig Chambers. Optimization of Object-Oriented Programs Using Static Class Hierarchy Analysis. In *Proceedings of the 9th European Conference on Object-Oriented Programming*, pages 77–101, Aarhus, Denmark, August 1995. Springer-Verlag.

12. Richard Drews Dean. *Formal Aspects of Mobile Code Security*. PhD thesis, Princeton University, Princeton, NJ, USA, January 1999.

13. Eclipse Project, http://www.eclipse.org.

14. Úlfar Erlingsson and Fred B. Schneider. IRM Enforcement of Java Stack Inspection. In *Proceedings of the 2000 IEEE Symposium on Security and Privacy*, pages 246–255, Oakland, CA, USA, May 2000. IEEE Computer Society.

15. Jeffrey S. Foster, Tachio Terauchi, and Alex Aiken. Flow-Sensitive Type Qualifiers. In *Proceedings of the 2002 ACM SIGPLAN Conference on Programming Language Design and Implementation*, pages 1–12, Berlin, Germany, June 2002.

16. Adam Freeman and Allen Jones. *Programming .NET Security*. O'Reilly & Associates, Inc., Sebastopol, CA, USA, June 2003.

17. Li Gong, Gary Ellison, and Mary Dageforde. *Inside Java 2 Platform Security: Architecture, API Design, and Implementation*. Addison-Wesley, Reading, MA, USA, second edition, May 2003.

18. George Grätzer. *General Lattice Theory*. Birkhäuser, Boston, MA, USA, second edition, January 2003.

19. Sumit Gulwani and George C. Necula. Path-sensitive Analysis for Linear Arithmetic and Uninterpreted Functions. In *11th Static Analysis Symposium*, volume 3148 of *LNCS*, pages 328–343. Springer-Verlag, August 2004.

20. Thomas P. Jensen, Daniel Le Métayer, and Tommy Thorn. Verification of Control Flow Based Security Properties. In *Proceedings of the 1999 IEEE Symposium on Security and Privacy*, pages 89–103, Oakland, CA, USA, May 1999.

21. Paul A. Karger, IBM Thomas J. Watson Research Center, Yorktown Heights, NY, USA. Private communication, 17 December 2004.

22. Gary A. Kildall. A Unified Approach to Global Program Optimization. In *Proceedings of the 1st Annual ACM SIGACT-SIGPLAN Symposium on Principles of Programming Languages*, pages 194–206, Boston, MA, USA, 1973. ACM Press.

23. John F. Koegel, Rhonda M. Koegel, Zhiming Li, and Dattaram T. Miruke. A Security Analysis of VAX VMS. In *ACM '85: Proceedings of the 1985 ACM Annual Conference on the Range of Computing: Mid-80's Perspective*, pages 381–386. ACM Press, 1985.

24. Larry Koved, Marco Pistoia, and Aaron Kershenbaum. Access Rights Analysis for Java. In *Proceedings of the 17th ACM SIGPLAN Conference on Object-Oriented Programming, Systems, Languages, and Applications*, pages 359–372, Seattle, WA, USA, November 2002. ACM Press.

25. Steven S. Muchnick. *Advanced Compiler Design and Implementation*. Morgan Kaufmann Publishers Inc., San Francisco, CA, USA, June 1997.

26. Gleb Naumovich and Paolina Centonze. Static Analysis of Role-Based Access Control in J2EE Applications. *SIGSOFT Software Engineering Notes*, 29(5):1–10, September 2004.

27. James Newsome and Dawn Song. Dynamic Taint Analysis for Automatic Detection, Analysis, and Signature Generation of Exploits on Commodity Software. In *Proceedings of the 12th Annual Network and Distributed System Security Symposium*, San Diego, CA, USA, February 2005. IEEE Computer Society.

28. Marco Pistoia, Nataraj Nagaratnam, Larry Koved, and Anthony Nadalin. *Enterprise Java Security*. Addison-Wesley, Reading, MA, USA, February 2004.

29. Marco Pistoia, Duane Reller, Deepak Gupta, Milind Nagnur, and Ashok K. Ramani. *Java 2 Network Security*. Prentice Hall PTR, Upper Saddle River, NJ, USA, second edition, August 1999.

30. François Pottier, Christian Skalka, and Scott F. Smith. A Systematic Approach to Static Access Control. In *Proceedings of the 10th European Symposium on Programming Languages and Systems*, pages 30–45. Springer-Verlag, 2001.

31. Barbara G. Ryder. Dimensions of Precision in Reference Analysis of Object-Oriented Languages. In *Proceedings of the 12th International Conference on Compiler Construction*, pages 126–137, Warsaw, Poland, April 2003. Invited Paper.

32. Jerome H. Saltzer and Michael D. Schroeder. The Protection of Information in Computer Systems. In *Proceedings of the IEEE*, volume 63, pages 1278–1308, September 1975.

33. Umesh Shankar, Kunal Talwar, Jeffrey S. Foster, and David Wagner. Detecting Format String Vulnerabilities with Type Qualifiers. In *Proceedings of the 10th USENIX Security Symposium*, Washington, DC, USA, August 2001.

34. Standard Performance Evaluation Corporation Java Business Benchmark 2000 (SPECjbb2000), http://www.spec.org.

35. Sun Microsystems, Security Code Guidelines, http://java.sun.com.

36. Frank Tip and T. B. Dinesh. A Slicing-based Approach for Locating Type Errors. *ACM Transactions on Software Engineering and Methodology*, 10(1):5–55, 2001.

37. Dennis Volpano, Cynthia Irvine, and Geoffrey Smith. A Sound Type System for Secure Flow Analysis. *Journal of Computer Security*, 4(2-3):167–187, January 1996.

38. Larry Wall, Tom Christiansen, and Jon Orwant. *Programming Perl*. O'Reilly & Associates, Inc., Sebastopol, CA, USA, third edition, July 2000.

39. Dan S. Wallach. *A New Approach to Mobile-Code Security*. PhD thesis, Princeton University, Princeton, NJ, USA, January 1999.

40. Dan S. Wallach, Dirk Balfanz, Drew Dean, and Edward W. Felten. Extensible Security Architectures for Java. In *Proceedings of the 16th ACM Symposium on Operating Systems Principles*, pages 116–128, Saint Malo, France, 1997. ACM Press.

41. Dan S. Wallach and Edward W. Felten. Understanding Java Stack Inspection. In *Proceedings of the IEEE Symposium on Security and Privacy*, pages 52–63, Oakland, CA, USA, May 1998.

State Based Ownership, Reentrance, and Encapsulation

Anindya Banerjee[1,*] and David A. Naumann[2,**]

[1] Kansas State University, Manhattan KS 66506 USA
ab@cis.ksu.edu
[2] Stevens Institute of Technology, Hoboken NJ 07030 USA
naumann@cs.stevens.edu

Abstract. A properly encapsulated data representation can be revised for refactoring or other purposes without affecting the correctness of client programs and extensions of a class. But encapsulation is difficult to achieve in object-oriented programs owing to heap based structures and reentrant callbacks. This paper shows that it is achieved by a discipline using assertions and auxiliary fields to manage invariants and transferrable ownership. The main result is representation independence: a rule for modular proof of equivalence of class implementations.

1   Introduction

You are responsible for a library consisting of many Java classes. While fixing a bug or refactoring some classes, you revise the implementation of a certain class in a way that is intended not to change its observable behavior, e.g., an internal data structure is changed for reasons of performance. You are in no position to check, or even be aware of, the many applications that use the class via its instances or by subclassing it. In principle, the class could have a full functional specification. It would then suffice to prove that the new version meets the specification. In practice, full specifications are rare. Nor is there a well established logic and method for modular reasoning about the code of a class in terms of the specifications of the classes it uses, without regard to their implementations or the users of the class in question [20] (though progress has been made). One problem is that encapsulation, crucial for modular reasoning about invariants, is difficult to achieve in programs that involve shared mutable objects and reentrant callbacks which violate simple layering of abstractions. Yet complicated heap structure and calling patterns are used, in well designed object-oriented programs, precisely for orderly composition of abstractions in terms of other abstractions.

There is an alternative to verification with respect to a specification. One can attempt to prove that the revised version is behaviorally equivalent to the original. Of course their behavior is not identical, but at the level of abstraction of source code (e.g., modulo specific memory addresses), it may be possible to show equivalence of behavior. If any specifications are available they can be taken into account using assert statements.

There is a standard technique for proving equivalence [18, 24]: Define a *coupling relation* to connect the states of the two versions and prove that it has the *simulation*

---

* Supported in part by NSF grants CCR-0209205, ITR-0326577, and CCR-0296182.
** Supported in part by NSF grants CCR-0208984, CCF-0429894, and by Microsoft Research.

A.P. Black (Ed.): ECOOP 2005, LNCS 3586, pp. 387–411, 2005.

property, i.e., it holds initially and is preserved by parallel execution of the two versions of each method. In most cases, one would want to define a *local coupling* relation for a single pair of instances of the class, as methods act primarily on a target object (self) and the *island* of its representation objects; an *induced coupling* for complete states is then obtained by a general construction. A language with good encapsulation should enjoy an *abstraction* or *representation independence* theorem that says a simulation for the revised class induces a simulation for any program built using the class. Suitable couplings are the identity except inside the abstraction boundary and an *identity extension lemma* says simulation implies behavioral equivalence of two programs that differ only by revision of a class. Again, such reasoning can be invalidated by heap sharing, which violates encapsulation of data, and by callbacks, which violate hierarchical control structure.

There is a close connection between the equivalence problem and verification: verification of object oriented code involves object invariants that constrain the internal state of an instance. Encapsulation involves defining the invariant in a way that protects it from outside interference so it holds globally provided it is preserved by the methods of the class of interest. Simulations are like invariants over two copies of the state space, and again modular reasoning requires that the coupling for a class be independent from outside interference. *The main contribution of this paper is a representation independence theorem using a state-based discipline for heap encapsulation and control of callbacks.*

Extant theories of data abstraction assume, in one way or another, a hierarchy of abstractions such that control does not reenter an encapsulation boundary while already executing inside it. In many programming languages it is impossible to write code that fails to satisfy the assumption. But it is commonplace in object oriented programs for a method m acting on some object o to invoke a method on some other object which in turn leads to invocation of some method on o —possibly m itself— while the initial invocation of m is in progress. This makes it difficult to reason about when an object's invariant holds [20, 25]; we give an example later.

There is an analogous problem for reasoning with simulations. In previous work [2] we formulated an abstraction theorem that deals with sharing and is sound for programs with reentrant callbacks, but it is not easy to apply in cases where reentrant callbacks are possible. The theorem allows the programmer to assume that all methods preserve the coupling relation when proving simulation, i.e., when reasoning about parallel execution of two versions of a method of the class of interest. This assumption is like verifying a procedure implementation under the assumption that called procedures are correct. But the assumption that called methods preserve the coupling is of no use if the call is made in an uncoupled intermediate state. For the examples in [2], we resort to ad hoc reasoning for examples involving callbacks.

In a recent advance, [6, 21] reentrancy is managed using an explicit auxiliary (or *ghost*) field *inv* to designate states in which an object invariant is to hold. Encapsulation is achieved using a notion of ownership represented by an auxiliary mutable field *own*. This is more flexible than type-based static analyses because the ownership invariant need only hold in certain flagged states. Heap encapsulation is achieved not by disallowing boundary-crossing pointers but by limiting, in a state-dependent way, their use.

Reasoning hinges on a global *program invariant* that holds in all states, using *inv* fields to track which object invariants are temporarily not in force because control is within their encapsulation boundary. When *inv* holds, the object is said to be *packed*; a field may only be updated when the object is unpacked.

In this paper we adapt the *inv/own* discipline [6, 21][1] to proving class equivalence by simulation. The *inv* fields make it possible for an induced coupling relation to hold at some pairs of intermediate states during parallel execution of two alternative implementations. This means that the relation-preservation hypothesis of the abstraction theorem can be used at intermediate states even when the local coupling is not in force. So per-method modular reasoning is fully achieved. In large part the discipline is unchanged, as one would hope in keeping with the idea that a coupling is just an invariant over two parallel states. But we have to adapt some features in ways that make sense in terms of informal considerations of information hiding. The discipline imposes no control on field reads, only writes, but for representation independence we need to control reads as well. The discipline also allows ownership transfer quite freely, though it is not trivial to design code that correctly performs transfers. For representation independence, the transfer of previously-encapsulated data to clients (an unusual form of controlled "rep exposure" [16]) is allowed but must occur only in the code of the encapsulating class; even then, it poses a difficult technical challenge. The significance of our adaptations is discussed in Section 7.

A key insight is that, although transferring ownership and packing/unpacking involve only ghost fields that cannot affect program execution, it is useful to consider them to be observable. It is difficult to reason about two versions of a class, in a modular way, if they differ in the way objects cross the encapsulation boundary or in which methods assume the invariant is in force. The requisite similarity can be expressed using assert statements so we can develop a theory based on this insight without the need to require that the class under revision has any specifications.

Contributions. The main contributions are (a) formulation of a notion of instance-based coupling analogous to invariants in the *inv/own* discipline; (b) proof of a representation independence theorem for a language with inheritance and dynamic dispatch, recursive methods and callbacks; mutable objects, type casts, and recursive types; and (c) results on identity extension and use of the theorem to prove program equivalence. Together these constitute a rule by which the reasoner considers just the methods of the revised class and concludes that the two versions yield equivalent behavior for any program context.

The theorem allows ownership transfers that cross encapsulation boundaries: from client to abstraction [16], between abstractions, and even from abstraction to client [29, 4]. The theorem supports the most important form of modularity: reasoning about one method implementation (or rather, one corresponding pair) at a time —on the assumption that all methods preserve the coupling (even the one in question, modulo termination). Our theorem also supports local reasoning in the sense that a single instance

---

[1] Called the "Boogie methodology" in the context of the Spec# project [7] at Microsoft Research, which implements the discipline as part of a comprehensive verification system inspired by the ESC projects.

(or pair of instances) is considered, together with the island comprised of its currently encapsulated representation objects.

The discipline can be used in any verification system that supports ghost variables and assertions. So our formalism treats predicates in assertions semantically, avoiding ties to any particular logic or specification formalism.

Related Work Besides the inv/own Discipline. Representation independence is needed not only for modular proof of equivalence of class implementations but also for modular reasoning about improvements (called data refinement). Such reasoning is needed for correctness preserving refactoring. The refactoring rules of Borba et al. [10] were validated using the data refinement theory of Cavalcanti and Naumann [13] which does not model sharing/aliasing. We plan to use the present result to overcome that limitation. Representation independence has also been used to justify treating a method as pure if none of its side effects are visible outside an encapsulation boundary [8, 26].

Representation independence is proved in [2] for a language with shared mutable objects on the basis of ownership confinement imposed using restrictions expressed in terms of ordinary types; but these restrictions disallow ownership transfer. The results are extended to encompass ownership transfer in [4] but at the cost of substantial technical complications and the need for reachability analysis at transfer points, which are designated by explicit annotations. Like the present paper, our previous results are based on a semantics in which the semantics of primitive commands is given in straightforward operational terms. It is a denotational semantics in that a command denotes a state transformer function, defined by induction on program structure. To handle recursion, method calls are interpreted relative to a *method environment* that gives the semantics of all methods. This is constructed as the limit of approximations, each exact up to a certain maximum calling depth. This model directly matches the recursion rule of Hoare logic, of which the abstraction theorem is in some sense a generalization.

For simple imperative code and single-instance modules, O'Hearn *et al.* [29, 23] have proved strong rules for local reasoning about object invariants and simulations using separation logic which, being state based, admits a notion of ownership transfer.

Confinement disciplines based on static analysis have been given with the objective of encapsulation for modular reasoning, though mostly without formal results on modular reasoning [14, 11]. Work using types makes confinement a *program invariant*, i.e., a property required to hold in every reachable state. This makes it difficult to transfer ownership, due to temporary sharing at intermediate states. Most disciplines preclude transfer (e.g., [15, 11]); where it is allowed, it is achieved using nonstandard constructs such as destructive reads and restrictive linearity constraints (e.g., [12, 30]).

Outline. Sect. 2 sketches the *inv/own* discipline. It also sketches an example of the use of simulation to prove equivalence of two versions of a class involving reentrant callbacks, highlighting the problems and the connection between our solution and the *inv/own* discipline. Sect. 3 formalizes the language for which our result is given and Sect. 4 formalizes the discipline in our semantics. Sect. 5 gives the main definitions— proper annotation, coupling, simulation—and the abstraction theorem. Sect. 6 connects simulation with program equivalence. Sect. 7 discusses future work and assesses our adaptation of the discipline. For lack of space, all proofs are omitted and can be found in the companion technical report, which also treats generics [5].

2   Background and Overview

2.1   The *inv/own* Discipline

To illustrate the challenge of reentrant callbacks as well as the state based ownership discipline, we consider a class Queue that maintains a queue of tasks. Each task has an associated limit on the number of times it can be run. Method Queue.runAll runs each task that has not exceeded its limit. For simplicity we refrain from using interfaces; class Task in Fig. 1 serves as the interface for tasks. Class Qnode in the same Figure is used by Queue which maintains a singly linked list of nodes that reference tasks. Field count tracks the number of times the task has been run. For brevity we omit initialization and constructors throughout the examples.

Fig. 2 gives class Queue. One intended invariant of Queue is that no task has been run more times than its limit. This is expressed, in a decentralized way, by the invariant declared in Qnode. Some notation: we write $\mathscr{I}^{Qnode}(o)$ for the predicate o.tsk$\neq$null and o.count$\leq$o.limit.

Another intended invariant of Queue is that runs is the sum of the count fields of the nodes reached from tsks. This is the declared $\mathscr{I}^{Queue}$ of Fig. 2. (The reader may think of other useful invariants, e.g., that the list is null-terminated.) Note that at intermediate points in the body of Queue.runAll, $\mathscr{I}^{Queue}$ does not hold because runs is only updated after the loop. In particular, $\mathscr{I}^{Queue}$ does not hold at the point where p.run() is invoked.

```
class Task {    void run(){ }    }
class Qnode {
    Task tsk;    Qnode nxt;    int count, limit;
    invariant tsk ≠ null ∧ 0≤count≤limit;
    ... // constructor elided (in subsequent figures these ellipses are elided too)
    void  run() { tsk.run(); count := count+1; }
    void  setTsk(Task t, int lim) {
        tsk := t; limit := lim; count := 0; pack self as Qnode; }    }
```

Fig. 1. Classes Task and Qnode. The pack statement is discussed later

```
class Queue {
    Qnode tsks;    int runs := 0;
    invariant runs = (Σp ∈ tsks.nxt* | p.count);
    int getRuns() { result := runs; }
    void  runAll() {
        Qnode p := tsks; int i := 0;
        while p ≠ null do {
            if p.getCount() < p.getLimit() then p.run(); i := i+1; fi; p := p.getNxt(); }
        runs := runs+i; }
    void  add(Task t, int  lim){
        Qnode n := new  Qnode; n.setTsk(t,lim); n.setNxt(tsks); tsks := n; } }
```

Fig. 2. Class Queue

For an example reentrant callback, consider tasks of the following type.

class RTask extends Task { Queue q;   **void** run(){q.runAll(); } ... }

Consider a state in which o points to an instance of Queue and the first node in the list, o.tsks, has count=0 and limit=1. Moreover, suppose field q of the first node's task has value o. Invocation of o.runAll diverges: before count is incremented to reflect the first invocation, the task makes a *reentrant call* on o.runAll —in a state where $\mathscr{I}^{Queue}$ does not hold. In fact runAll again invokes run on the first task and the program fails due to unterminating recursion.

As another example, suppose RTask.run is instead   **void** run(){q.getRuns();} . This seems harmless, in that getRuns neither depends on $\mathscr{I}^{Queue}$ nor invokes any methods —it is even useful, returning a lower bound on the actual sum of runs. It typifies methods like state readers in the observer pattern, that are intended to be invoked as reentrant callbacks.

The examples illustrate that it is sometimes but not always desirable to allow a reentrant callback when an object's invariant is violated temporarily by an "outer" invocation. The ubiquity of method calls makes it impractical to require an object's invariant to be reestablished before making *any* call —e.g., the point between n.setTsk and n.setNxt of method add in Fig. 2 — although this is sound and has been proposed in the literature on object oriented verification [17, 22].

A better solution is to prevent just the undesirable reentrant calls. One could make the invariant an explicit precondition, e.g., for runAll but not getRuns. This puts responsibility on the caller, e.g., RTask.run cannot establish the precondition and is thus prevented from invoking runAll. But an object invariant like $\mathscr{I}^{Queue}$ involves encapsulated state not suitable to be visible in a public specification.

The solution of the Boogie methodology [6, 21] is to introduce a public ghost field, *inv*, that explicitly represents whether the invariant is in force. In the lingo, o.*inv* says object o is *packed*. Special statements **pack** and **unpack** set and unset *inv*.

A given object is an instance not only of its class but of all its superclasses, each of which may have invariants. The methodology takes this into account as follows. Instead of *inv* being a boolean, as in the simplified explanation above, it ranges over class names C such that C is a superclass of the object's allocated type. That is, it is an invariant (enforced by typing rules) that o.*inv* $\geq type(o)$ where $type(o)$ is the dynamic type of o. The discipline requires certain assertions preceding pack and unpack statements as well as field updates, to ensure that the following is a *program invariant* (i.e., it holds in all reachable states).

$$o.inv \leq C \Rightarrow \mathscr{I}^C(o) \qquad (1)$$

for all C and all allocated objects o. That is, if o is packed at least to class C then the invariant $\mathscr{I}^C$ for C holds. Perhaps the most important stipulated assertion is that $\mathscr{I}^C(o)$ is required as precondition for packing o to level C.

Fig. 3 shows how the discipline is used for class Queue. Assertions impose preconditions on runAll and add which require that the target object is packed to Queue. In runAll, the **unpack** statement sets *inv* to the superclass of Queue, putting the task in a position where it cannot establish the precondition for a reentrant call to runAll, although it can still call getRuns which imposes no precondition on *inv*. After the update

```
void  runAll() {     assert self.inv = Queue && ! self.com;
   unpack self from Queue;
   Qnode p := self.tsks; int  i := 0;
   while p ≠ null do  {
      if  p.getCount() < p.getLimit() then   p.run(); i := i+1; fi; p := p.getNxt(); }
   self.runs := self.runs + i;
   pack self as Queue; }
void  add(Task t, int  lim){     assert  self.inv = Queue && ! self.com;
   unpack self from Queue;
   Qnode n := new  Qnode; setown n to (self,Queue);
   n.setNxt(tsks); n.setTsk(t,lim); self.tsks := n;
   pack self as Queue; } }
```

Fig. 3. Methods of class Queue with selected annotations

Table 1. Stipulated preconditions of field update and of the special commands

assert $e_1.inv > C$;   /* where C is the class that declares f; i.e., $f \in dom(dfields\,C)$ */
$e_1.f := e_2$

assert $e.inv = super\,C \wedge \mathscr{I}^C(e) \wedge \forall p \mid p.own = (e,C) \Rightarrow \neg p.com \wedge p.inv = type\,p$;
pack e **as** C /* sets $e.inv := C$ and $p.com := true$ for all p with $p.own = (e,C)$ */

assert $e.inv = C \wedge \neg e.com$;
unpack e **from** C /* sets $e.inv := super\,C$ and $p.com := false$ for all p with $p.own = (e,C)$ */

assert $e_1.inv = $ Object $\wedge (e_2 = $ **null** $\vee e_2.inv > C)$;
setown e_1 **to** (e_2,C) /* sets $e_1.own := (e_2,C)$ */

to runs, $\mathscr{I}^{Queue}$ holds again as required by the precondition (not shown) of **pack**. The ghost field *com* is discussed below.

In order to maintain (1) as a program invariant, it is necessary to control updates to fields on which invariants depend. The idea is that, to update field f of some object p, all objects o whose invariant depends on $p.f$ must be unpacked. Put differently, $\mathscr{I}(o)$ should depend only on state encapsulated for o. The discipline uses a form of ownership for this purpose: $\mathscr{I}(o)$ may depend only on objects transitively owned by o. For example, an instance of Queue owns the Qnodes reached from field tsks.

Ownership is embodied in an auxiliary field *own*, so that if $p.own = (o,C)$ then o directly owns p and an admissible invariant $\mathscr{I}^D(o)$ may depend on p for types D with $type(o) \leq D \leq C$. The objects transitively owned by o are called its *island*. For modular reasoning, it is not feasible to require as an explicit precondition for each field update that all transitive owners are unpacked. A third ghost field, *com*, is used to enforce a protocol whereby packing/unpacking is dynamically nested or bracketed (though this need not be textually apparent).

In addition to (1), two additional conditions are imposed as program invariants, i.e., to hold in all reachable states of all objects. The first may be read "an object is committed to its owner if its owner is packed". The second says that a committed object is fully packed. These make it possible for an assignment to $p.f$ to be subject only to the precondition $p.inv > C$ where C is the class that declares f.

The invariants are formalized in Def. 3 in Sect. 4. The stipulated preconditions appear in Table 1, which also describes the semantics of the pack and unpack statements in detail.[2] The diligent reader may enjoy completing the annotation of Fig. 3 according to the rules of Table 1. Consult [6, 21] for more leisurely introductions to the discipline.

2.2   Representation Independence

Consider the subclass AQueue of Queue declared in Fig. 4. It maintains an array, actsks, of tasks which is used in an overriding declaration of runAll intended as an optimization for the situation where many tasks are inactive (have reached their limit). We've dropped runs and getRuns for brevity. Method add exhibits a typical pattern: unpack to establish the condition in which a super call can be made (since the superclass unpacks from its own level); after that call, reestablish the current class invariant. (This imposes proof obligations on inheritance, see [6].)

The implementation of Fig. 4 does not set actsks[i] to null immediately when the task's count reaches its limit; rather, that situation is detected on the subsequent invocation of runAll. An alternative implementation is given in Fig. 5; it uses a different data structure and handles the limit being reached as soon as it happens. Both implementations maintain an array of Qnode, but in the alternative implementation, its array artsk is accompanied by a boolean array brtsk. Instead of setting entry i null when the node's task has reached its limit, brtsk[i] is set false.

We claim that the two versions are equivalent, in the context of arbitrary client programs (and subclasses, though for lack of space we do not focus on subclasses in the sequel). We would like to argue as follows. Let $filt1(o.\text{actsks})$ be the sequence of non-null elements of $o.$actsks with count $<$ limit. Let $filt2(ts, bs)$ take an array ts of tasks and a same-length array bs of booleans and return the subsequence of those tasks n in ts where bs is true and $n.$count $< n.$limit. Consider the following relation that connects a state for an instance o of the original implementation (Table 4) with an instance o' for the alternative: $filt1(o.\text{actsks}) = filt2(o'.\text{artsk}, o'.\text{brtsk})$. The idea is that methods of the new version behave the same as the old version, modulo this change of representation. That is, for each method of AQueue, parallel execution of the two versions from a related pair of states results in a related pair of outcomes. (For this to hold we need to conjoin to the relation the invariants associated with the two versions, e.g., the second version requires artsk.length=brtsk.length.)

The left side of the picture below is an instance of some subclass of AQueue, sliced into the fields of Queue, AQueue, and subclasses; dashed lines show the objects encapsulated at the two levels relevant to reasoning about AQueue —namely the Qnodes reached from tsks and the array actsks.

---

[2] We omit the preconditions $e \neq$ **null** and "e not error" that are needed for the rest of the precondition to be meaningful. Different verification systems make different choices in handling errors in assertions. Our formulation follows [28] and differs superficially from [6, 21].

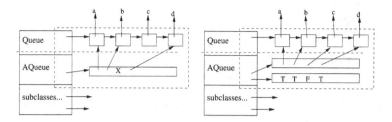

On the right is an instance for the alternate implementation of AQueue. It is the connection between these two islands that is of interest to the programmer. The "a"..."d" of the figure indicate that both versions reference the same sequence of tasks, although those tasks are not part of the islands.

In general, a *local coupling* is a binary relation on islands. It relates the state of an island for one implementation of the class of interest with an island for the alternative.

A local coupling gives rise to an *induced coupling* relation on the complete program state: Two heaps are related by the induced coupling provided that (a) they can be partitioned into islands and (b) the islands can be put into correspondence so that each corresponding pair is related by the local coupling. Moreover, the remaining objects (not in an island) are related by equality. (More precisely, equality modulo a bijection on locations, to take into account differences in allocation between the two versions.) The details are not obvious and are formalized later.

The point of the abstraction theorem is to justify that it is sufficient to check that the induced coupling is preserved by methods of AQueue, assuming the changed data structure is encapsulated and can neither affect nor be affected by client programs. At first glance one might expect the proof obligation to be that each method of AQueue preserves the local coupling, and indeed this will be the focus of reasoning in practice. But in general a method may act on more than just the island for self, e.g., by invoking

```
class AQueue extends Queue {
    private Qnode[ ] actsks;    private int alen;
    void add(Task t, int lim) {    assert self.inv= AQueue && ! self.com;
        unpack self from AQueue;
        super.add(t,lim); actsks[alen] := self.tsks; self.alen := self.alen+1;
        pack self as AQueue; }
    void runAll() {    assert self.inv= AQueue && ! self.com;
        unpack self from AQueue;
        int i := self.alen - 1;
        while i ≥ 0 do {
            Qnode qn := self.actsks[i];
            if qn ≠ null then if qn.getCount() < qn.getLimit()
                              then qn.run(); else self.actsks[i] := null; fi; fi;
            i := i - 1; }
        pack self as AQueue; } }
```

Fig. 4. First version of Class AQueue. An invariant: actsks[0..alen-1] contains any n in tsks with n.count $< n$.limit, in reverse order. (There may also be nulls and some n with n.count $= n$.limit). The elided constructor allocates actsks and we ignore the issue of the array becoming full

```
class AQueue extends Queue {
    private Qnode[ ] artsk;
    private boolean[ ] brtsk;
    private int  len;
    void  add(Task t, int  lim) {
        assert self.inv= AQueue && ! self.com;
        unpack self from AQueue;
        super.add(t,lim); self.artsk[alen] := self.tsks; self.brtsk[len] := true; self.len := len+1;
        pack self as AQueue; }
    void  runAll() {
        assert self.inv= AQueue && ! self.com;
        unpack self from AQueue;
        int  i := self.len - 1;
        while i ≥ 0 do {
            if self.brtsk[i] then  Qnode n := self.artsk[i];  int  diff := n.limit - n.count;
                                   if  diff ≤ 1 then  self.brtks[i] := false; fi;
                                   if  diff ≠ 0 then  n.run(); fi; fi;
            i := i - 1; }
        pack self as AQueue; } }
```

Fig. 5. Alternative implementation of AQueue

methods on client objects or on other instances of AQueue. So the proof obligation is formalized in terms of the induced coupling.

In fact the proof obligation is not simply that each corresponding pair of method implementations preserves the coupling, but rather that they preserve the coupling *under the assumption that any method they invoke preserves the coupling*.[3] There is also a proof obligation for initialization but it is straightforward so we do not discuss it in connection with the examples.

For example, in the case of method runAll, one must prove that the implementations given in Fig. 4 and in Fig. 5 preserve the coupling on the assumption that the invoked methods getCount, getLimit, Qnode.run, etc. preserve the coupling. The assumption is not so important for getCount or getLimit. For one thing, it is possible to fully describe their simple behavior. For another, the alternative implementation of runAll does not even invoke these methods but rather accesses the fields directly.

The assumption about Qnode.run is crucial, however. Because run invokes, in turn, Task.run, essentially nothing is known about its behavior. For this reason both implementations of runAll invoke run on the same tasks in the same order; otherwise, it is hard to imagine how equivalence of the implementations could be verified in a modular way, i.e., reasoning only about class AQueue. But here we encounter the problem with simulation based reasoning that is analogous to the problem with invariants and reentrant callbacks. There is no reason for the coupling to hold at intermediate points of the methods of AQueue. If a method is invoked at such a point, the assumption that the

---

[3] The reason this is sound is similar to the justification for proof rules for recursive procedures: it is essentially the induction step for a proof by induction on the maximum depth of the method call stack.

called method preserves the coupling is of no use —just as the assumption of invariant-preservation is of no use if a method is invoked in a state where the invariant does not hold.

The Boogie discipline solves the invariant problem for an object o by replacing the declared invariant $\mathscr{I}(o)$ with an implication —see (1)— that is true in all states. As with invariants, so too with couplings: It does not make sense to ask a coupling to hold in every state, because two different implementations with nontrivial differences do not have lockstep correspondence of states. (For example, imagine that in the alternative version, the arrays are compressed every 100th invocation of runAll.) Our generalization of the Boogie idea is that the local coupling relation for a particular (pair of) island(s) is conditioned on an inv field so that the local coupling may hold in *some pairs of states* at intermediate points —in particular, at method calls that can lead to reentrant callbacks.

Consider corresponding instances o, o' of the two versions of AQueue. The local coupling serves to describe the corresponding pair of islands when o and o' are packed. So the induced coupling relation on program states requires corresponding pairs of islands to satisfy the local coupling just when they are packed. Because inv is part of the behavior observable at the level of reasoning, we can assume both versions follow the same pattern of packing (though not necessarily of control structure) and thus include $o.inv = o'.inv$ as a conjunct of the induced coupling.

Consider the two implementations of runAll. To a first approximation, what matters is that each updates some internal state and then both reach a point where run is invoked. At that point, the *local* coupling does not hold —but the *induced* coupling relation can and does hold, because the island is unpacked. This parallels the way $\mathscr{I}^C(o)$ can be false while $o.inv \leq C \Rightarrow \mathscr{I}^C(o)$ remains true, recall (1). So we can use the assumption about called methods to conclude that the coupling holds after the corresponding calls to run.

The hardest part of the proof for runAll is at the point where the two implementations pack self to *AQueue*. Just as both implementations invoke run (and on the same queue nodes), both need to pack in order to preserve the coupling. And at this point we have to argue that the local coupling is reestablished. To do so, we need to know the state of the internal structures that have been modified. We would like to argue that the only modifications are only those explicit in the code of runAll, but what about the effect of run? Owing to the preconditions on add and runAll, the only possible reentrant callbacks are to getRuns and this does no updates. (In other examples, modifies specifications would be needed at this point for modular reasoning.)

This concludes the sketch of how our abstraction theorem handles reentrant callbacks and encapsulation using the inv/own discipline. Several features of the discipline need to be adapted, in ways which also make sense in terms of informal considerations of information hiding. The additional restrictions are formalized in Section 5 and their significance discussed in Section 7. As a preview we make the following remarks, using "*Abs*" as the generic name for a class for which two versions are considered.

The discipline does not constrain field access, as reading cannot falsify an invariant predicate. Of course for reasons of information hiding one expects that visibility and alias confinement are used to prevent most or all reads of encapsulated objects. Information hiding is exactly what is formalized by representation independence and indeed the abstraction theorem fails if a client can read fields of encapsulated objects. So every field access $e.f$ is subject to a precondition: If e is transitively owned by some instance o of the class, *Abs*, under revision, then either self is o or else self is transitively owned by o.

Another problematic feature is that "**pack** e **as** C" can occur in any class, so long as its preconditions are established. This means that, unlike traditional theories, an invariant is not simply established at initialization. In our theory the local coupling must be established preceding each "**pack** e **as** *Abs*". We aim for modular reasoning where only *Abs* needs to be considered, so we insist that **pack** e **as** C with $C = Abs$ occurs only in code of *Abs*.

Although the discipline supports hierarchical ownership, our technical treatment benefits from heap partitioning ideas from separation logic (we highlight the connections where possible, e.g., in Proposition 1). For this reason and a more technical one, it is convenient to prevent an instance of *Abs* from transitively owning another instance of *Abs* (lest their islands be nested). This can be achieved by a simple syntactic restriction. It does not preclude that, say, class AQueue can hold tasks that own AQueue objects, because an instance of AQueue owns its representation objects (the Qnodes), not the tasks they contain. Nor does it preclude hierarchical ownership, e.g., *Abs* could own a hashtable that in turn owns some arrays.

Finally, consider ownership transfer across the encapsulation boundary. The hardest case is where a hitherto-encapsulated object is released to a client, e.g., when a memory manager allocates nodes from a free list [29, 4]. This can be seen as a deliberate exposure of representation and thus is observable behavior that must be retained in a revised version of the abstraction. Yet encapsulated data of the two versions can be in general quite different. To support modular reasoning about the two versions, it appears essential to restrict outward transfer of objects encapsulated for *Abs* to occur only in code of *Abs*, where the reasoner can show that the coupling is preserved.

3   An Illustrative Language

Following [6, 21], we formalize the *inv/own* discipline in terms of a language in which fields have public visibility, to illuminate the conditions necessary for sound reasoning about invariants and simulations. In practice, private and protected visibility and perhaps lightweight alias control would serve to automatically check most of the conditions. This section formalizes the language, adapting notations and typing rules from Featherweight Java [19] and imperative features and the special commands from our previous papers [2, 28].

A complete program is given as a *class table*, CT, that maps class name C to a declaration $CT(C)$ of the form **class** C **extends** $D \{ \bar{T} \bar{f}; \bar{M} \}$. The categories T, M are given by the grammar in Table 2. Barred identifiers like $\bar{T}$ indicate finite lists, e.g., $\bar{T} \bar{f}$ stands for a list $\bar{f}$ of field names with corresponding types $\bar{T}$.

Well formed class tables are characterized using typing rules which are expressed using some auxiliary functions that in turn depend on the class table, allowing classes to make mutually recursive references to other classes, without restriction. In particular, this allows recursive methods (so we omit loops). For a class C, *fields*(C) is defined as the inherited and declared fields of C; *dfields*(C) is the fields declared in C; *super*(C) is the direct superclass of C. For a method declaration, $T m(\bar{T}_1 \bar{x}) \{S\}$ in C, the method type *mtype*(m, C) is $\bar{T}_1 \rightarrow T$ and parameter names, *pars*(m, C), is $\bar{x}$. For m inherited

Table 2. Grammar

$C \in ClassName \quad m \in MethName \quad f \in FieldName \quad x, \mathsf{self}, \mathsf{result} \in VarName$

$T ::= $ **bool** $\mid$ **void** $\mid C$	data type
$M ::= T\ m(\bar{T}\ \bar{x})\ \{S\}$	method declaration
$S ::= x := e \mid e.f := e$	assign to local var. or param., update field
$\mid \quad x := $ **new** $C \mid x := e.m(\bar{e})$	object creation, method call
$\mid \quad T\ x := e$ **in** $S \mid S; S \mid$ **if** e **then** S **else** S **fi**	local variable, sequence, conditional
$\mid \quad$ **pack** e **as** $C \mid$ **unpack** e **from** C	set *inv* to C, set *inv* to super$C$
$\mid \quad$ **setown** e **to** (e', C)	set $e.own$ to (e', C)
$\mid \quad$ **assert** $\mathscr{P}$	assert (semantic predicate $\mathscr{P}$)
$e ::= x \mid$ **null** $\mid$ **true** $\mid$ **false**	variable, constant
$\mid \quad e.f \mid e = e \mid e$ **is** $C \mid (C)\ e$	field access, ptr. equality, type test, cast

Table 3. Typing rules for selected expressions and commands

$$\frac{\Gamma \vdash e : C \quad (f : T) \in fields(C)}{\Gamma \vdash e.f : T} \qquad \frac{\Gamma \vdash e_1 : D_1 \quad \Gamma \vdash e_2 : D_2 \quad D_2 \leq C}{\Gamma \vdash \mathbf{setown}\ e_1\ \mathbf{to}\ (e_2, C)}$$

$$\frac{\Gamma \vdash e : D \quad D \leq C}{\Gamma \vdash \mathbf{pack}\ e\ \mathbf{as}\ C} \qquad \frac{\Gamma \vdash e : D \quad D \leq C}{\Gamma \vdash \mathbf{unpack}\ e\ \mathbf{from}\ C}$$

$$\frac{\Gamma \vdash e : D \quad mtype(m, D) = \bar{T} \to U \quad x \neq \mathsf{self} \quad \Gamma \vdash \bar{e} : \bar{U} \quad \bar{U} \leq \bar{T} \quad U \leq \Gamma x}{\Gamma \vdash x := e.m(\bar{e})}$$

in C, $mtype(m, C) = mtype(m, D)$ and $pars(m, C) = pars(m, D)$ where D is the direct superclass of C.

For use in the semantics, $xfields(C)$ extends $fields(C)$ by assigning "types" to the auxiliary fields: com : **bool**, own : owntyp, and inv : (invtyp C). (These are not included in *FieldName*.) Neither invtyp C nor owntyp are types in the programming language but there are corresponding semantic domains and the slight notational abuse is convenient.

A *typing context* Γ is a finite function from variable names to types, such that $\mathsf{self} \in dom\ \Gamma$. Selected typing rules for expressions and commands are given in Table 3. A judgement of the form $\Gamma \vdash e : T$ says that expression e has type T in the context of a method of class $\Gamma\ \mathsf{self}$, with parameters and local variables declared by Γ. A judgement $\Gamma \vdash S$ says that S is a command in the same context. A class table CT is well formed if each method declaration $M \in CT(C)$ is well formed in C; this is written $C \vdash M$ and defined by the following rule:

$$\frac{\bar{x} : \bar{T}, \mathsf{self} : C, \mathsf{result} : T \vdash S}{\quad \text{if } mtype(m, superC) \text{ is defined then } mtype(m, superC) = \bar{T} \to T \text{ and } pars(m, superC) = \bar{x} \quad}{C \vdash T\ m(\bar{T}\ \bar{x})\{S\}}$$

To formalize assertions, we prefer to avoid both the commitment to a particular formula language and the complication of an environment for declaring predicate names to be interpreted in the semantics. So we indulge in a mild and commonplace abuse of notation: the syntax of **assert** uses a semantic predicate. We say $\Gamma \vdash$ **assert** $\mathscr{P}$ is well

Table 4. Semantic categories θ and domains $[\![\theta]\!]$. (Readers familiar with notation for dependent function spaces might prefer to write $[\![\text{pre-heap}]\!] = (o : Loc \rightharpoonup [\![\text{state}\,(type\,o)]\!])$ and similarly for $[\![\text{state}\,C]\!]$ and $[\![\Gamma]\!]$.)

$$\theta ::= T \mid \Gamma \mid \theta_\perp$$

$\mid$ owntyp $\mid$ invtyp C $\mid$ state C	*own* and *inv* val., object state
$\mid$ pre-heap $\mid$ heap $\mid$ heap $\otimes \Gamma$ $\mid$ heap $\otimes T$	heap fragment, closed heap, state, result
$\mid$ $(\Gamma \vdash \text{cmd}) \mid (\Gamma \vdash T) \mid (C, \bar{x}, \bar{T} {\rightarrow} T_1) \mid$ menv	command, expr., method, method envir.

$[\![C]\!] = \{nil\} \cup \{o \in Loc \mid type\,o \leq C\}$ $[\![\textbf{bool}]\!] = \{true, false\}$ $[\![\textbf{void}]\!] = \{it\}$

$$
\begin{aligned}
[\![\text{invtyp}\,C]\!] &= \{B \mid C \leq B\} \\
[\![\text{owntyp}]\!] &= \{(o, C) \mid o = nil \vee type\,o \leq C\} \\
[\![\text{state}\,C]\!] &= \{s \mid dom\,s = dom(xfields\,C) \wedge \forall (f : T) \in xfields\,C \mid s\,f \in [\![T]\!]\} \\
[\![\text{pre-heap}]\!] &= \{h \mid dom\,h \subseteq_{fin} Loc \wedge \forall o \in dom\,h \mid h\,o \in [\![\text{state}\,(type\,o)]\!]\} \\
[\![\text{heap}]\!] &= \{h \mid h \in [\![\text{pre-heap}]\!] \wedge \forall s \in rng\,h \mid rng\,s \cap Loc \subseteq dom\,h\} \\
[\![\Gamma]\!] &= \{s \mid dom\,s = dom\,\Gamma \wedge s\,\text{self} \neq nil \wedge \forall x \in dom\,s \mid s\,x \in [\![\Gamma\,x]\!]\} \\
[\![\text{heap} \otimes \Gamma]\!] &= \{(h, s) \mid h \in [\![\text{heap}]\!] \wedge s \in [\![\Gamma]\!] \wedge rng\,s \cap Loc \subseteq dom\,h\} \\
[\![\text{heap} \otimes T]\!] &= \{(h, v) \mid h \in [\![\text{heap}]\!] \wedge v \in [\![T]\!] \wedge (v \in Loc \Rightarrow v \in dom\,h)\} \\
[\![\Gamma \vdash \text{cmd}]\!] &= [\![\text{heap} \otimes \Gamma]\!] \to [\![(\text{heap} \otimes \Gamma)_\perp]\!] \\
[\![\Gamma \vdash T]\!] &= \{v \mid v \in ([\![\text{heap} \otimes \Gamma]\!] \to [\![T]\!]_\perp) \wedge \forall h, s \mid v(h, s) \in Loc \Rightarrow v(h, s) \in dom\,h\} \\
[\![(C, \bar{x}, \bar{T} {\rightarrow} T_1)]\!] &= [\![\text{heap} \otimes (\bar{x} : \bar{T}, \text{self} : C)]\!] \to [\![(\text{heap} \otimes T_1)_\perp]\!] \\
[\![\text{menv}]\!] &= \{\mu \mid \forall C, m \mid \mu Cm \text{ is defined iff } mtype(m, C) \text{ is defined,} \\
&\quad\quad \text{and } \mu Cm \in [\![C, pars(m, C), mtype(m, C)]\!] \text{ if } \mu Cm \text{ defined }\}
\end{aligned}
$$

formed provided that $\mathcal{P}$ is a set of program states for context Γ. This treatment of assertions is also convenient for taking advantage of a theorem prover's native logic.

Semantics. Some semantic domains correspond directly to the syntax. For example, each data type T denotes a set $[\![T]\!]$ of values. The meaning of context Γ is a set $[\![\Gamma]\!]$ of stores; a *store* $s \in [\![\Gamma]\!]$ is a type-respecting assignment of locations and primitive values to the local variables and parameters given by a typing context Γ. The semantics, and later the coupling relation, is structured in terms of category names θ given in Table 4 which also defines the semantic domains.

A *program state* for context Γ is a pair (h, s) where s is in $[\![\Gamma]\!]$ and h is a *heap*, i.e., a finite partial function from locations to object states. An *object state* is a type-respecting mapping of field names to values. A command typable in Γ denotes a function mapping each program state (h, s) either to a final state (h_0, s_0) or to the distinguished value $\perp$ which represents runtime errors, divergence, and assertion failure. An *object state* is a mapping from (extended) field names to values. A *pre-heap* is like a heap except for possibly having dangling references. If h, h' are pre-heaps with disjoint domains then we write $h * h'$ for their union; otherwise $h * h'$ is undefined. Function application associates to the left, so $h\,o\,f$ is the value of field f of the object $h\,o$ at location o. We also write $h\,o.f$. Application binds more tightly than binary operator symbols and ",".

We assume that a countable set *Loc* is given, along with a distinguished value *nil* not in *Loc*. We assume given a function *type* from *Loc* to non-primitive types distinct from Object, such that for each C there are infinitely many locations o with $type\,o = C$. This is used in a way that is equivalent to tagging object states with their type.

Table 5. Semantics of selected expressions and commands. To streamline the treatment of $\perp$, the metalanguage expression "let $\alpha = \beta$ in ..." denotes $\perp$ if β is $\perp$. We use function extension notation $[h \mid o \mapsto st]$ for h extended or overridden at o with value st. For brevity the nested function extension for field update is written $[h \mid o.f \mapsto v]$

$\llbracket \Gamma \vdash e.f : T \rrbracket(h,s) \quad = $ let $o = \llbracket \Gamma \vdash e : C \rrbracket(h,s)$ in if $o = nil$ then $\perp$ else $h\,o.f$

$\llbracket \Gamma \vdash x := e.m(\bar{e}) \rrbracket \mu(h,s) = $ let $o = \llbracket \Gamma \vdash e : T \rrbracket(h,s)$ in if $o = nil$ then $\perp$ else

$\qquad$ let $\bar{v} = \llbracket \Gamma \vdash \bar{e} : \bar{U} \rrbracket(h,s)$ in let $\bar{x} = pars(m,T)$ in

$\qquad$ let $s_1 = [\bar{x} \mapsto \bar{v}, \mathsf{self} \mapsto o]$ in

$\qquad$ let $(h_1, v_1) = \mu(type\,o)m(h, s_1)$ in $(h_1, [s \mid x \mapsto v_1])$

$\llbracket \Gamma \vdash \mathbf{assert}\ \mathscr{P} \rrbracket \mu(h,s) \ = $ if $(h,s) \in \mathscr{P}$ then (h,s) else $\perp$

$\llbracket \Gamma \vdash \mathbf{pack}\ e\ \mathbf{as}\ C \rrbracket \mu(h,s) = $

$\quad$ let $q = \llbracket \Gamma \vdash e : D \rrbracket(h,s)$ in if $q = nil$ then $\perp$ else

$\quad$ let $h_1 = \lambda p \in dom\,h \mid$ if $h\,p.own = (q, C)$ then $[h\,p \mid com \mapsto true]$ else $h\,p$ in $([h_1 \mid q.inv \mapsto C], s)$

$\llbracket \Gamma \vdash \mathbf{unpack}\ e\ \mathbf{from}\ C \rrbracket \mu(h,s) = $

$\quad$ let $q = \llbracket \Gamma \vdash e : N \rrbracket(h,s)$ in if $q = nil$ then $\perp$ else

$\quad$ let $h_1 = \lambda p \in dom\,h \mid$ if $h\,p.own = (q, C)$ then $[h\,p \mid com \mapsto false]$ else $h\,p$ in

$\quad ([h_1 \mid q.inv \mapsto super\,C], s)$

$\llbracket \Gamma \vdash \mathbf{setown}\ e_1\ \mathbf{to}\ (e_2, C) \rrbracket \mu(h,s) = $

$\quad$ let $q = \llbracket \Gamma \vdash e_1 : N_1 \rrbracket(h,s)$ in if $q = nil$ then $\perp$ else

$\quad$ let $p = \llbracket \Gamma \vdash e_2 : N_2 \rrbracket(h,s)$ in $([h \mid q.own \mapsto (p, C)], s)$

The meaning of a derivable command typing $\Gamma \vdash S$ will be defined to be a function sending each method environment μ to an element of $\llbracket \Gamma \vdash \mathsf{cmd} \rrbracket$. (The keyword "cmd" just provides notation for command meanings.) That is, $\llbracket \Gamma \vdash S \rrbracket \mu$ is a state transformer $\llbracket \mathsf{heap} \otimes \Gamma \rrbracket \to \llbracket (\mathsf{heap} \otimes \Gamma)_\perp \rrbracket$. The method environment is used only to interpret the method call command. Meanings for expressions and commands are defined, in Table 5, by recursion on typing derivation. The semantics is defined for an arbitrary location-valued function $fresh$ such that $type(fresh(C,h)) = C$ and $fresh(C,h) \notin dom\,h$.

The meaning of a well typed method declaration M, of the form $M = T\ m(\bar{T}\ \bar{x})\{S\}$, is the total function in $\llbracket \mathsf{menv} \rrbracket \to \llbracket (C, \bar{x}, \bar{T} \to T) \rrbracket$ defined as follows: Given a method environment μ, a heap h and a store $s \in \llbracket \bar{x} : \bar{T}, result : C \rrbracket$, first execute S to obtain the updated heap h_0 and the updated store s_0; then return $(h_0, s_0(result))$. A method environment μ maps each C, m to a meaning obtained in this way or by inheritance. For well formed class table CT, the semantics $\llbracket CT \rrbracket$ is defined as the least upper bound of an ascending chain of method environments—the approximation chain—with method declarations interpreted as above and a suitable interpretation for inherited methods. Details omitted.

A *predicate* for state type Γ is just a subset $\mathscr{P} \subseteq \llbracket \mathsf{heap} \otimes \Gamma \rrbracket$. For emphasis we can write $(h,s) \models \mathscr{P}$ for $(h,s) \in \mathscr{P}$. Note that $\perp \notin \mathscr{P}$. We give no formal syntax to denote predicates but rather use informal metalanguage for which the correspondence should be clear. For example, "self.$f \neq \mathbf{null}$" denotes the set of (h,s) with $h(s\,\mathsf{self}).f \neq nil$. and "$\forall o \mid \mathscr{P}(o)$" denotes the set of (h,s) such that $(h,s) \models \mathscr{P}(o)$ for all $o \in dom\,h$. Note that quantification over objects (e.g., in Table 1 and Def. 3) is interpreted to mean quantification over allocated locations; the range of quantification can include unreachable objects but this causes no problems.

By contrast with [6, 21], we have taken care to separate the annotations required by the *inv*/*own* discipline from the semantics of commands. The invariants encoded in the semantic domains (e.g., the value in a field has its declared type and there are no dangling pointers) depend in no way on assertions, only on typing. A similar semantic model has been machine checked in PVS [27].

4 The *inv*/*own* Discipline

The discipline reviewed in Sect. 2.1 is designed to make (1) a program invariant for every object. This is achieved using additional program invariants that govern ownership. We formalize this as a global predicate, *disciplined*, defined in three steps.

Definition 1 (transitive C- and $C\!\uparrow$-ownership). For any heap h, the relation $o \succ^h_C p$ on $dom\, h$, read "o owns p at C in h", holds iff either $(o,C) = h\, p.own$ or there are q and D such that $(o,C) = h\, q.own$ and $q \succ^h_D p$. The relation $o \succ^h_{C\uparrow} p$ holds iff there is some D with $C \leq D$ and $o \succ^h_D p$.

Definition 2 (admissible invariant). A predicate $\mathscr{P} \subseteq [\![heap \otimes (self : C)]\!]$ is *admissible as an invariant for C* provided that it is not falsifiable by creation of new objects and for every (h,s) and o,f such that $\mathscr{P}$ depends on $o.f$ in (h,s), field f is neither *inv* nor *com*, and one of the following conditions holds: $o = s(\mathsf{self})$ and f is in $dom(xfields\, C)$ or $s(\mathsf{self}) \succ^h_{C\uparrow} o$.

For dependence on fields of self, the typing condition, $f \in dom(xfields\, C)$, prevents an invariant for C from depending on fields declared in a subclass of C (which could be expressed in a formula using a cast). An invariant can depend on any fields of objects owned at C or above. We refrain from introducing syntax for declaring invariants. In the subsequent definitions, an admissible invariant $\mathscr{I}^C$ is assumed given for every class C. We assume $\mathscr{I}^{Object} = \mathbf{true}$.

Definition 3 (disciplined, $\mathscr{J}$). A heap h is *disciplined* if $h \models \mathscr{J}$ where $\mathscr{J}$ is defined to be the conjunction of the following: $\forall o,C \mid o.inv \leq C \Rightarrow \mathscr{I}^C(o)$

$$\forall o,C,p \mid o.inv \leq C \wedge p.own = (o,C) \Rightarrow p.com$$
$$\forall o \mid o.com \Rightarrow o.inv = type(o)$$

A state (h,s) is *disciplined* if h is. Method environment μ *is disciplined* provided that every method maintains $\mathscr{J}$ (i.e., for any C,m,h,s, if $h \in \mathscr{J}$ and $\mu\, C m\, (h,s) = (h_0,v)$— and thus $\mu\, C m\, (h,s) \neq \bot$— then $h_0 \in \mathscr{J}$).

Lemma 1 (transitive ownership). Suppose h is disciplined and $o \succ^h_C p$. Then (a) *type* $o \leq C$ and (b) $h\, o.inv \leq C$ implies $h\, p.com = true$.

Corollary 1. If h is disciplined, $o \succ^h_C p$, and $h\, p.inv > type\, p$ then $h\, o.inv > C$.

Partitioning the Heap. We partition the objects in the heap in order to formalize the encapsulation boundary depicted in Sect. 2.2. Given an object $o \in dom\, h$ and class name

A with $type\,o \leq A$ we can partition h into pre-heaps Ah (the A-object), Rh (the representation of o for class A), Sh (objects owned by o at a superclass), and Fh (free from o) determined by the following conditions: Ah is the singleton $[o \mapsto ho]$, Rh is h restricted to the set of p with $o \succ^h_A p$, Sh is h restricted to the set of p with $o \succ^h_C p$ for some $C > A$, and Fh is the rest of h. Note that if $o \succ^h_B p$ for some proper subclass $B < A$ then $p \in dom\,Fh$. A pre-heap of the form $Ah * Rh * Sh$ is called an *island*. In these terms, dependency of admissible invariants is described in the following Proposition. As an illustration, here is the island for the left side of the situation depicted in Sect. 2.2:

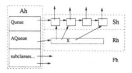

Proposition 1 (island). Suppose $\mathscr{I}^C$ is an admissible invariant for C and $o \in dom\,h$ with $type\,o \leq C$. If $h = Fh * Ah * Rh * Sh$ is the partition defined above then $Fh_0 * Ah * Rh * Sh \models \mathscr{I}^C(o)$ iff $h \models \mathscr{I}^C(o)$, for all Fh_0 such that $Fh_0 * Ah * Rh * Sh$ is a heap.

The Discipline. To impose the stipulated preconditions of Table 1 we consider programs with the requisite syntactic structure (similar to formal proof outlines).

Definition 4 (properly annotated). The *annotated commands* are the subset of the category of commands where each **pack**, **unpack**, **setown**, and field update is immediately preceded by an **assert**. A *properly annotated command* is an annotated command such that each of these assertions is (or implies) the precondition stipulated in Table 1. A *properly annotated class table* is one such that each method body is properly annotated.

For any class table and family of invariants there exists a proper annotation: just add **assert** commands with the stipulated preconditions. For practical interest, of course, one wants assertions that can collectively be proved correct. The abstraction theorem depends on proper annotation but does not depend on the invariants themselves; one may take $\mathscr{I}^C = $ **true** for all C. What matters is ownership structure and the use of *inv*. We use the following [6, 21, 28].

Proposition 2. If method environment μ is disciplined then any properly annotated command S maintains $\mathscr{J}$ in the sense that for all (h,s), if $h \models \mathscr{J}$ and $(h_0,s_0) = [\![\Gamma \vdash S]\!]\mu(h,s)$ then $h_0 \models \mathscr{J}$. If CT is a properly annotated class table then the method environment $[\![CT]\!]$ is disciplined.

5   The Abstraction Theorem

5.1   Comparing Class Tables

We compare two implementations of a designated class *Abs*, in the context of a fixed but arbitrary collection of other classes, such that both implementations give rise to a well formed class table. The two versions can have completely different declarations, so long as methods of the same signatures are present — declared or inherited — in both. To simplify the additional precondition needed for reading fields, we consider programs desugared into a form like that used in Separation Logic.

Definition 5 (properly annotated for _Abs_). The _annotated commands for Abs_ are those of Def. 4 with the additional restriction that no expression of the form $e.f$ occurs except in commands of the form **assert** $\mathscr{P}; x := e.f$ (in particular, no field access appears in this e). The _properly annotated commands for Abs_ are those that are properly annotated according to Def. 4 and moreover

- fields of _Abs_ have private visibility (i.e., if $f \in dfields\,Abs$ then accesses and updates of f only occur in code of class _Abs_)
- If $\Gamma\,\text{self} \neq Abs$ then field access $\Gamma \vdash x := e.f$ is subject to stipulated precondition $(\forall o \mid o \succ_{Abs} e \Rightarrow o \succ_{Abs} \text{self})$
- if $\Gamma\,\text{self} \neq Abs$ then $\Gamma \vdash$ **pack** e **as** _Abs_ is not allowed
- if $\Gamma\,\text{self} \neq Abs$ then $\Gamma \vdash$ **setown** e_1 **to** (e_2, C) is subject to an additional precondition: $(\exists o \mid o \succ_{Abs} e_1) \Rightarrow C = Abs \vee (\exists o \mid o \succ_{Abs} e_2)$

The effect of the last precondition is that if e_1 is initially owned at _Abs_ then after a transfer (that occurs in code outside class _Abs_) it is still owned at _Abs_.

In order to work with heap partitions, along the lines of Prop. 1, it is convenient to have notation to extract the one object in a singleton heap. We define _pickdom_ by $pickdom(h) = o$ where $dom\,h = \{o\}$; it is undefined if $dom\,h$ is not a singleton.

Prop. 1 considers a single object together with its owned representation; now we consider all objects of a given class.

Definition 6 (_A_-decomposition). For any class A and heap h, the _A-decomposition_ of h is the set $Fh, Ah_1, Rh_1, Sh_1 \ldots, Ah_k, Rh_k, Sh_k$ (for some $k \geq 0$) of pre-heaps, all subsets of h, determined by the following conditions:

- each $dom\,Ah_i$ contains exactly one object o and $type\,o \leq A$
- every $o \in dom\,h$ with $type\,o \leq A$ occurs in $dom\,Ah_i$ for some i;
- $dom\,Rh_i = \{p \mid o \succ_A^h p\}$ where $pickdom\,Ah_i = o$;
- $dom\,Sh_i = \{p \mid o \succ_{(super\,A)\uparrow}^h p\}$ with $pickdom\,Ah_i = o$;
- $dom\,Fh = dom\,h - (\cup i \mid dom(Ah_i * Rh_i * Sh_i))$

We say that _no A-object owns an A-object in_ h provided for every o, p in $dom\,h$ if $type\,o \leq A$ and $o \succ_{(type\,o)\uparrow}^h p$ then $type\,p \not\leq A$. Def. 8 in the sequel imposes a syntactic restriction to maintain this property as an invariant, where A is the class for which two representations are compared. A consequence is that there is a unique decomposition of the heap into separate islands of the form $Ah * Rh * Sh$. We use the term "partition" even though some blocks can be empty.

Lemma 2 (_A_-partition). Suppose no _A_-object owns an _A_-object in h. Then the _A_-decomposition is a partition of h, that is, $h = Fh * Ah_1 * Rh_1 * Sh_1 * \ldots * Ah_k * Rh_k * Sh_k$.

To maintain the invariant that no _Abs_-object owns an _Abs_-object, we formulate a mild syntactic restriction expressed using a static approximation of ownership.

Definition 7 (may own, $\succ^{\exists}$). Given well formed CT, define $\succ^{\exists}$ to be the least transitively closed relation such that

- $D_2 \succ^{\exists} D_1$ for every occurrence of **setown** e_1 **to** (e_2, D) in a method of CT, with static types $e_1 : D_1$ and $e_2 : D_2$
- if $C \succ^{\exists} D$, $C' \leq C$ and $D' \leq D$ then $C' \succ^{\exists} D'$

If $Abs \not\succ^{\exists} Abs$ then it is a program invariant that no Abs-object owns an Abs-object (recall the definition preceding Lemma 2). This is a direct consequence of the following.

Lemma 3. It is a program invariant that if $o \succ^{h}_{C} p$ then $type\, o \succ^{\exists} type\, p$.

Definition 8 (comparable class tables). Well formed class tables CT and CT' are *comparable* with respect to class name Abs ($\neq$ Object) provided the following hold.

- $CT(C) = CT'(C)$ for all $C \neq Abs$.
- $CT(Abs)$ and $CT'(Abs)$ declare the same methods with the same signatures and the same direct superclass.
- For every method m declared in $CT(Abs)$, m is declared in $CT'(Abs)$ and has the same signature; *mutatis mutandis* for m declared in CT'.
- CT and CT' are properly annotated for Abs.
- $Abs \not\succ^{\exists} Abs$ in both CT and CT'

The last condition ensures that the Abs-decomposition of any disciplined heap is a partition, by Lemmas 2 and 3. We write $\vdash, \vdash'$ for the typing relation determined by CT, CT' respectively; similarly we write $[\![-]\!], [\![-]\!]'$ for the respective semantics.

5.2   Coupling Relations

The definitions are organized as follows. A *local coupling* is a suitable relation on islands. This induces a family of *coupling relations*, $\mathscr{R}\beta\,\theta$ for each category name θ and typed bijection β. Each relation $\mathscr{R}\beta\,\theta$ is from $[\![\theta]\!]$ to $[\![\theta]\!]'$. Here β is a bijection on locations, used to connect a heap in $[\![heap]\!]$ to one in $[\![heap]\!]'$. The idea is that β relates all objects except those in the Rh_i or Rh'_i blocks that have never been exposed. Finally, a *simulation* is a coupling that is preserved by all methods of Abs and holds initially.

Definition 9. A *typed bijection* is a bijective relation, β, from Loc to Loc, such that $\beta\, o\, o'$ implies $type\, o = type\, o'$ for all o, o'. A *total bijection* on h, h' is a typed bijection with $dom\, h = dom\, \beta$ and $dom\, h' = rng\, \beta$. Finally, β *fully partitions* h, h' *for Abs* if, for all $o \in dom\, h$ (resp. $o \in dom\, h'$) with $type\, o \leq Abs$, o is in $dom\, \beta$ (resp. $rng\, \beta$).

Lemma 4 (typed bijection and Abs-partition). Suppose β is a typed bijection with $\beta \subseteq dom\, h \times dom\, h'$ and β fully partitions h, h' for Abs. If h, h' are disciplined and partition as $h = Fh * \ldots Ah_j * Rh_j * Sh_j$ and $h' = Fh' * \ldots Ah'_k * Rh'_k * Sh'_k$ then $j = k$.

Definition 10 (equivalence for Abs modulo bijection). For any β we define a relation $\sim_\beta$ for data values, object states, heaps, and stores, in Table 6.

Table 6. Value equivalence for the designated class *Abs*. The relation for heap is the same as for pre-heap. For object states, $\sim$ is independent from the declared fields of $CT(Abs)$ and $CT'(Abs)$

$o \sim_\beta o'$	in $[\![C]\!]$	$\Leftrightarrow \beta\, o o' \vee o = nil = o'$
$v \sim_\beta v'$	in $[\![T]\!]$	$\Leftrightarrow v = v'$ for primitive types T
$s \sim_\beta s'$	in $[\![\text{state}\,C]\!]$	$\Leftrightarrow \forall (f : T) \in xfields\,C \mid sf \sim_\beta s'f \vee (f : T) \in dfields\,Abs$
$s \sim_\beta s'$	in $[\![\Gamma]\!]$	$\Leftrightarrow \forall x \in dom\,\Gamma \mid sx \sim_\beta s'x$
$h \sim_\beta h'$	in $[\![\text{pre-heap}]\!]$	$\Leftrightarrow \forall o \in dom\,h, o' \in dom\,h' \mid \beta\, o o' \Rightarrow ho \sim_\beta h'o'$
$(h, s) \sim_\beta (h', s')$	in $[\![\text{heap} \otimes \Gamma]\!]$	$\Leftrightarrow h \sim_\beta h' \wedge s \sim_\beta s'$
$v \sim_\beta v'$	in $[\![\theta_\perp]\!]$	$\Leftrightarrow v = \perp = v' \vee (v \neq \perp \neq v' \wedge v \sim_\beta v' \text{ in } [\![\theta]\!])$
$(o, C) \sim_\beta (o', C')$	in $[\![\text{owntyp}]\!]$	$\Leftrightarrow (o = nil = o') \vee (\beta\, o o' \wedge C = C')$
$B \sim_\beta B'$	in $[\![\text{invtyp}\,C]\!]$	$\Leftrightarrow B = B'$

Equivalence hides the private fields of *Abs*. In the identity extension lemma, it is used in conjunction with the following which hides objects owned at *Abs*.

Definition 11 (encap). Suppose no A-object owns an A-object in h. Define *encap A h* to be the pre-heap $Fh * Ah_1 * Sh_1 * \ldots * Ah_k * Sh_k$ where the A-partition of h is as in Lemma 2.

The most important definition is of local coupling, which is analogous to an object invariant but is a relation on pairs of pre-heaps. In Def. 2, we take an invariant $\mathscr{I}^C$ to be a predicate (set of states) and the program invariant $\mathscr{I}$ is based on the conjunction of these predicates for all objects and types —subject to *inv*, see Def. 3). By contrast, we define a local coupling $\mathscr{L}$ in terms of pre-heaps. And we are concerned with a single class, *Abs*, rather than all C. We impose the same dependency condition as in Def. 2, but in terms of pre-heaps of the form $h = Ah * Rh * Sh$. (Recall Proposition 1.)

Definition 12 (local coupling, $\mathscr{L}$). Given comparable class tables, a *local coupling* is a function, $\mathscr{L}$, that assigns to each typed bijection β a binary relation $\mathscr{L}\beta$ on pre-heaps that satisfies the following. First, $\mathscr{L}\beta$ does not depend on *inv* or *com*. Second, $\beta \subseteq \beta_0$ implies $\mathscr{L}\beta \subseteq \mathscr{L}\beta_0$. Third, for any β, h, h', if $\mathscr{L}\beta\, hh'$ then there are locations o, o' with $\beta\, o o'$ and $type\, o \leq Abs$ such that the *Abs* partitions of h, h' are $h = Ah * Rh * Sh$ and $h' = Ah' * Rh' * Sh'$ with

- $pickdom\,Ah = o$ and $pickdom\,Ah' = o'$
- $o \succ^h_{Abs} p$ for all $p \in dom(Rh)$ and $o' \succ^{h'}_{Abs} p'$ for all $p' \in dom(Rh')$
- $o \succ^h_{(superAbs)\uparrow} p$ for all $p \in dom(Sh)$ and $o' \succ^{h'}_{(superAbs)\uparrow} p'$ for all $p' \in dom(Sh')$
- If $\mathscr{L}\beta$ depends on f then f is in $xfields\,Abs$

The first three conditions ensure that $\mathscr{L}$ relates a single island, for an object of some subtype of *Abs*, to a single island for an object of the same type. Although $\mathscr{L}$ is unconstrained for the private fields of $CT(Abs)$ and $CT'(Abs)$, it may also depend on fields inherited from a superclass of *Abs* (but not on subclass fields). The induced coupling relation, defined below, imposes the additional constraint that fields of proper sub- and super-classes of *Abs* are linked by equivalence modulo β. Although superficially different, the notion of local coupling is closely related to admissible invariant.

Table 7. The induced coupling relation for Def. 13

$$\mathscr{R}\,\beta\,\theta\,\alpha\,\alpha' \qquad\qquad\qquad \Leftrightarrow \alpha \sim_\beta \alpha' \text{ if } \theta \text{ is } \mathbf{bool}, C, \Gamma, \text{ or state} C$$

$$\mathscr{R}\,\beta\,(\mathsf{heap}\otimes\Gamma)\,(h,s)\,(h',s') \Leftrightarrow \mathscr{R}\,\beta\,\mathsf{heap}\,h\,h' \wedge \mathscr{R}\,\beta\,\Gamma\,s\,s' \wedge disciplined(h,s) \wedge disciplined(h',s')$$

$$\mathscr{R}\,\beta\,(\mathsf{heap}\otimes T)\,(h,v)\,(h',v') \Leftrightarrow \mathscr{R}\,\beta\,\mathsf{heap}\,h\,h' \wedge \mathscr{R}\,\beta\,T\,v\,v'$$

$$\mathscr{R}\,\beta\,(\theta_\perp)\,\alpha\,\alpha' \qquad\quad \Leftrightarrow (\alpha = \perp = \alpha') \vee (\alpha \neq \perp \neq \alpha' \wedge \mathscr{R}\,\beta\,\theta\,\alpha\,\alpha')$$

$$\mathscr{R}\,\beta\,(\Gamma \vdash T)\,v\,v' \qquad\quad \Leftrightarrow \forall h,s,h',s' \mid \mathscr{R}\,\beta\,(\mathsf{heap}\otimes\Gamma)\,(h,s)\,(h',s')$$
$$\Rightarrow \mathscr{R}\,\beta\,T_\perp\,(v(h,s))\,(v'(h',s'))$$

$$\mathscr{R}\,\beta\,(C,\bar{x},\bar{T}{\to}T_1)\,v\,v' \Leftrightarrow \forall h,s,h',s' \mid \mathscr{R}\,\beta\,(\mathsf{heap}\otimes\Gamma)\,(h,s)\,(h',s')$$
$$\Rightarrow \exists \beta_0 \supseteq \beta \mid \mathscr{R}\,\beta_0\,(\mathsf{heap}\otimes T_1)_\perp\,(v(h,s))\,(v'(h',s'))$$
$$\text{where } \Gamma = [\bar{x}:\bar{T}, \mathbf{self}:C]$$

$$\mathscr{R}\,\mathsf{menv}\,\mu\,\mu' \qquad\qquad \Leftrightarrow \forall C,m,\beta \mid \mathscr{R}\,\beta\,(C,\bar{x},\bar{T}{\to}T)\,(\mu Cm)\,(\mu'Cm)$$
$$\text{where } mtype(m,C) = \bar{T}{\to}T \text{ and } pars(m,C) = \bar{x}$$

In applications, $\mathscr{L}\,\beta\,h\,h'$ would be defined as something like this: h and h' partition as islands $Ah * Rh * Sh$ and $Ah' * Rh' * Sh'$ such that $Ah * Rh * Sh \models \mathscr{I}^{Abs}$ and $Ah' * Rh' * Sh' \models \mathscr{I}'^{Abs}$ and some condition links the data structures [18]. The bijection β would not be explicit but would be induced as a property of the formula language.

A local coupling $\mathscr{L}$ induces a relation on arbitrary heaps by requiring that they partition such that islands can be put in correspondence so that pairs are related by $\mathscr{L}$.

Definition 13 (coupling relation, $\mathscr{R}$). Given local coupling $\mathscr{L}$, we define for each θ and β a relation $\mathscr{R}\,\beta\,\theta \subseteq [\![\theta]\!] \times [\![\theta]\!]'$ as follows.

For heaps h, h', we define $\mathscr{R}\,\beta\,\mathsf{heap}\,h\,h'$ iff h, h' are disciplined, $\beta \subseteq dom\,h \times dom\,h'$, and β fully partitions h, h' for Abs; moreover, if the Abs-partitions are $h = Fh * Ah_1 * Rh_1 * Sh_1 \dots Ah_k * Rh_k * Sh_k$ and $h' = Fh' * Ah'_1 * Rh'_1 * Sh'_1 \dots Ah'_k * Rh'_k * Sh'_k$ then (recall Lemma 4) (a) β restricts to a total bijection between $dom(Fh)$ and $dom(Fh')$; (b) $Fh \sim_\beta Fh'$; and (c) for all i, j, if $\beta\,(pickdom\,Ah_i)\,(pickdom\,Ah'_j)$ then

- β restricts to a total bijection between $dom(Sh_i)$ and $dom(Sh'_j)$
- $(Ah_i * Sh_i) \sim_\beta (Ah'_j * Sh'_j)$
- $h(pickdom\,Ah_i).inv \leq Abs \Rightarrow \mathscr{L}\,\beta\,(Ah_i * Rh_i * Sh_i)\,(Ah'_j * Rh'_j * Sh'_j)$

For other categories θ we define $\mathscr{R}\,\beta\,\theta$ in Table 7.

The third item under (c) is the key connection with the inv/own discipline.

Under the antecedent in the definition, $(Ah_i * Sh_i) \sim_\beta (Ah'_j * Sh'_j)$ is equivalent to the conjunction of $Ah_i \sim_\beta Ah'_j$ and $Sh_i \sim_\beta Sh'_j$. And $Ah_i \sim_\beta Ah'_j$ means that the two objects o, o' agree on superclass and subclass fields (but not the declared fields of Abs); in particular, $type\,o = type\,o' \leq Abs$ and $Ah_i\,o.inv = Ah'_j\,o'.inv$.

The gist of the abstraction theorem is that if methods of Abs are related by $\mathscr{R}$ then all methods are. In terms of the preceding definitions, we can express quite succinctly the conclusion that all methods are related: $\mathscr{R}\,\mathsf{menv}\,[\![CT]\!]\,[\![CT']\!]'$. We want the antecedent of the theorem to be that the meaning $[\![M]\!]$ is related to $[\![M']\!]'$, for any m with declaration M in $CT(Abs)$ and M' in $CT'(Abs)$. Moreover, $[\![M]\!]$ depends on a method environment. Thus the antecedent of the theorem is that $[\![M]\!]\mu$ is related to $[\![M']\!]'\mu'$ for all related μ, μ'. (It suffices for μ, μ' to be in the approximation chains defining $[\![CT]\!]$ and $[\![CT']\!]'$).

5.3   Simulation and the Abstraction Theorem

Definition 14 (simulation). A simulation is a coupling $\mathscr{R}$ such that the following hold.

- ($\mathscr{L}$ is initialized) For any $C \leq Abs$, and any o, o' with $\beta\, o\, o'$ and $type\, o = C$ we have $\mathscr{L}\,\beta\, h h'$ where $h = [o \mapsto [dom(xfields\, C) \mapsto defaults\, C]]$ and $h' = [o' \mapsto [dom(xfields'\, C) \mapsto defaults'\, C]]$.
- (methods of Abs preserve $\mathscr{R}$) For any disciplined μ, μ' such that $\mathscr{R}$ menv $\mu\ \mu'$ we have the following for every m declared in Abs. Let $\bar{U} \to U = mtype(m, Abs)$ and $\bar{x} = pars(m, Abs)$. For every β, we have $\mathscr{R}\,\beta\ \theta\ (\llbracket M \rrbracket \mu)\ (\llbracket M' \rrbracket' \mu')$ where $\theta = (Abs, \bar{x}, \bar{U} \to U)$. where M (resp. M') are as above. (We omit the similar condition for inherited methods.)

Lemma 5 (preservation by expressions). For all expressions $\Gamma \vdash e : T$ that contain no field access subexpressions, and all β, we have $\mathscr{R}\,\beta\ (\Gamma \vdash T)\ (\llbracket \Gamma \vdash e : T \rrbracket)\ (\llbracket \Gamma \vdash e : T \rrbracket')$.

Lemma 6 (preservation by commands). Let μ, μ' be disciplined method environments with $\mathscr{R}$ menv $\mu\ \mu'$. If $\Gamma \vdash S$ is a properly annotated command for Abs, with Γ self $\neq Abs$, then for all β we have the following. If $\mathscr{R}\,\beta$ (heap $\otimes \Gamma$) (h, s) (h', s') and $\neg(\exists o \mid o \succ^h_{Abs} s(\text{self}))$ and $\neg(\exists o' \mid o' \succ^{h'}_{Abs} s'(\text{self}))$ then there is $\beta_0 \supseteq \beta$ such that $\mathscr{R}\,\beta_0$ (heap $\otimes \Gamma)_\perp$ $(v(h, s))\ (v'(h', s'))$.

Our main result says that if methods of Abs preserve the coupling then all methods do.

Theorem 1 (abstraction).
If $\mathscr{R}$ is a simulation for comparable class tables CT, CT' then $\mathscr{R}$ menv $\llbracket CT \rrbracket\ \llbracket CT' \rrbracket'$.

6   Using the Theorem

A complete program is a command S in the context of a class table. To show equivalence between CT, S and CT', S, one proves simulation for Abs and then appeals to the abstraction theorem to conclude that $\llbracket S \rrbracket$ is related to $\llbracket S \rrbracket'$. Finally, one appeals to an *identity extension lemma* that says the relation is the identity for programs where the encapsulated representation is not visible. We choose simple formulations that can also serve to justify more specification-oriented formulations. We say that a state (h, s) is *Abs-free* if $type\, o \not\leq Abs$ for all $o \in dom\, h$.

Lemma 7 (identity extension). If $\mathscr{R}\,\beta$ (heap $\otimes \Gamma$) (h, s) (h', s') then $encap\, Abs\,(h, s) \sim_\beta encap\, Abs\,(h', s')$.

Lemma 8 (inverse identity extension). Suppose (h, s) and (h', s') are Abs-free. If $(h, s) \sim_\beta (h', s')$ and β is total on h, h' then $\mathscr{R}\,\beta$ (heap $\otimes \Gamma$) (h, s) (h', s').

Definition 15 (program equivalence). Suppose programs $CT, (\Gamma \vdash S)$ and $CT', (\Gamma \vdash' S')$ are such that CT, CT' are comparable and properly annotated, and moreover S, S' are properly annotated. The programs are *equivalent* iff for all disciplined, *Abs*-free (h, s) and (h', s') in $[\![\text{heap} \otimes \Gamma]\!]$ and all β with β total on h, h' and $(h, s) \sim_\beta (h', s')$, there is some $\beta_0 \supseteq \beta$ with $encapAbs([\![\Gamma \vdash S]\!]\mu(h, s)) \sim_{\beta_0} encapAbs([\![\Gamma \vdash' S']\!]'\mu'(h', s'))$ where $\mu = [\![CT]\!]$ and $\mu' = [\![CT']\!]'$.

Proposition 3 (simulation and equivalence). Suppose programs $CT, (\Gamma \vdash S)$ and $CT', (\Gamma \vdash' S)$ are properly annotated and $\mathscr{R}$ is a simulation from CT to CT'. If Γ self $\neq$ *Abs* then the programs are equivalent.

7   Discussion

Adaptations of the inv/own Discipline. As compared with previous work on the discipline, we have imposed some additional restrictions to achieve sufficient information hiding to justify a modular rule for equivalence of class implementations. We argue that the restrictions are not onerous for practical application, though further practical experience is needed with the discipline and with our rule.

The first restriction is on field reads. Code in a client class cannot be allowed to read a field of an encapsulated representation object, although the discipline allows the existence of the reference; otherwise the client code could be representation dependent. On the other hand, a class such as *Hashtable* might be used both by clients and in the internal representation of the class *Abs* under revision; certainly the code of *Hashtable* needs to read its own fields. A distinction can be made on the basis of whether the current target object, i.e., self, is owned by an instance o of *Abs*. If it is, then we do not need the method invocation to preserve the coupling and we can allow reading of objects owned by o. If the target object is not owned by an instance of *Abs* then it should have no need to access objects owned by *Abs*. This distinction appears in the statement of Lemma 6 and it is used to stipulate a precondition for field access (see Def. 5).[4]

Because the coupling relation imposes the user-defined local coupling only when an *Abs*-object is packed, it appears necessary to restrict **pack** e **as** *Abs* to occur only in code of *Abs* in order for simulation to be checked only for that code. In the majority of known examples, packing to a class C is only done in code of C, and this is required in Leino and Müller's extension of the discipline to handle static fields.

Similar considerations apply to **setown** o **to** (p, C): care must be taken to prevent arbitrary code from moving objects across the encapsulation boundary for *Abs* in ways that do not admit modular reasoning. One would expect that code outside *Abs* cannot move objects across the *Abs*-boundary at all, but it turns out that the only problematic case is transfer out from an *Abs* island. In the unusual case that **setown** o **to** (p, C) occurs in code outside *Abs* but o is initially inside the island for some *Abs*-object, then

---

[4] This is unattractive in that the other stipulated preconditions mention only direct ownership whereas this one uses transitive ownership. But in practical examples, code outside *Abs* rarely has references to encapsulated objects. We believe such references can be adequately restricted using visibility control and/or lightweight confinement analyses, e.g., [31, 2].

o must end up in the island for some *Abs*-object. Our stipulated precondition says just this. In practice it seems that the obligation can be discharged by simple syntactic considerations of visibility and/or lightweight alias control.

The last restriction is that an *Abs* object cannot own other *Abs* objects. This does not preclude containers holding containers, because a container does not own its content (e.g., AQueue owns the Qnodes but not the tasks). It does preclude certain recursive situations. For example, we could allow Qnode instances to own their successors but then we could not instantiate the theory with *Abs*:=Qnode. This does not seem too important since it is Queue that is appropriate to view as an abstraction coupled by a simulation. The restriction is not needed for soundness of simulation. But absent the restriction, nested islands would require a healthiness condition on couplings (similar to the healthiness condition used by Cavalcanti and Naumann [13–Def. 5]); e.g., coupling for an instance of Qnode would need to recursively impose the same predicate on the nxt node. We disallow nested islands in the present work for simplicity and to highlight connections with separation logic.

Future Work. The discipline may seem somewhat onerous in that it uses verification conditions rather than lighter weight static analysis for control of the use of aliases. (We have to say "use of", because whereas confinement disallows certain aliases, the invariant discipline merely prevents faulty exploitation of aliases.) The Spec# project [7] is exploring the inference of annotations. For many situations, simple confinement rules and other checks are sufficient to discharge the proof obligations and this needs to be investigated for the additional obligations we have introduced. The advantage of a verification discipline over types is that, while simple cases can be checked automatically, complicated cases can be checked with additional annotations rather than simply rejected.

The generalization to a small group of related classes is important, as revisions often involve several related classes. One sort of example would be a revision of our Queue example that involves revising Qnode as well. If nodes are used only by Queue then this is subsumed by our theory, as we can consider a renamed version of Qnode that coexists with it. The more interesting situations arise in refactoring and in design patterns with tightly related configurations of multiple objects. The friend and peer dependencies of [21, 9, 28], and the flexible ownership system of Aldrich and Chambers [1] could be the basis for a generalization of our results.

References

1. J. Aldrich and C. Chambers. Ownership domains: Separating aliasing policy from mechanism. In *ECOOP*, 2004.
2. A. Banerjee and D. A. Naumann. Ownership confinement ensures representation independence for object-oriented programs. *Journal of the ACM*, 2002. Accepted, revision pending. Extended version of [3].
3. A. Banerjee and D. A. Naumann. Representation independence, confinement and access control. In *POPL*, 2002.
4. A. Banerjee and D. A. Naumann. Ownership transfer and abstraction. Technical Report TR 2004-1, Computing and Information Sciences, Kansas State University, 2003.

5. A. Banerjee and D. A. Naumann. State based encapsulation and generics. Technical Report CS Report 2004-11, Stevens Institute of Technology, 2004.
6. M. Barnett, R. DeLine, M. Fähndrich, K. R. M. Leino, and W. Schulte. Verification of object-oriented programs with invariants. *Journal of Object Technology*, 3, 2004.
7. M. Barnett, K. R. M. Leino, and W. Schulte. The Spec# programming system: An overview. In *CASSIS post-proceedings*, 2004.
8. M. Barnett, D. A. Naumann, W. Schulte, and Qi Sun. 99.44% pure: useful abstractions in specifications. In *ECOOP workshop on Formal Techniques for Java-like Programs*, 2004.
9. M. Barnett and D. A. Naumann. Friends need a bit more: Maintaining invariants over shared state. In *Mathematics of Program Construction*, 2004.
10. P. H. M. Borba, A. C. A. Sampaio, and M. L. Cornélio. A refinement algebra for object-oriented programming. In *ECOOP*, 2003.
11. C. Boyapati, B. Liskov, and L. Shrira. Ownership types for object encapsulation. In *POPL*, 2003.
12. J. Boyland, J. Noble, and W. Retert. Capabilities for sharing: A generalisation of uniqueness and read-only. In *ECOOP*, 2001.
13. A. L. C. Cavalcanti and D. A. Naumann. Forward simulation for data refinement of classes. In *Formal Methods Europe*, 2002.
14. D. Clarke and S. Drossopoulou. Ownership, encapsulation and the disjointness of type and effect. In *OOPSLA*, 2002.
15. D. G. Clarke, J. Potter, and J. Noble. Ownership types for flexible alias protection. In *OOPSLA*, 1998.
16. D. L. Detlefs, K. R. M. Leino, and G. Nelson. Wrestling with rep exposure. Research 156, DEC Systems Research Center, 1998.
17. J. V. Guttag and J. J. Horning, editors. *Larch: Languages and Tools for Formal Specification*. Texts and Monographs in Computer Science. Springer-Verlag, 1993.
18. C. A. R. Hoare. Proofs of correctness of data representations. *Acta Inf.*, 1, 1972.
19. A. Igarashi, B. Pierce, and P. Wadler. Featherweight Java: A minimal core calculus for Java and GJ. *ACM Trans. Prog. Lang. Syst.*, 23, 2001.
20. B. Jacobs and E. Poll. Java program verification at Nijmegen: Developments and perspective. In *International Symposium on Software Security*, 2003.
21. K. R. M. Leino and P. Müller. Object invariants in dynamic contexts. In *ECOOP*, 2004.
22. B. Meyer. *Object-oriented Software Construction*. Second edition, 1997.
23. I. Mijajlovic, N. Torp-Smith, and P. O'Hearn. Refinement and separation contexts. In *Foundations of Software Technology and Theoretical Computer Science (FST&TCS)*, 2004.
24. J. C. Mitchell. Representation independence and data abstraction. In *POPL*, 1986.
25. P. Müller, A. Poetzsch-Heffter, and G. Leavens. Modular invariants for object structures. Technical Report 424, ETH Zürich, Oct. 2003.
26. D. A. Naumann. Observational purity and encapsulation. In *FASE*, 2005.
27. D. A. Naumann. Verifying a secure information flow analyzer. To appear in *TPHOLS*, 2005.
28. D. A. Naumann and M. Barnett. Towards imperative modules: Reasoning about invariants and sharing of mutable state (extended abstract). In *LICS*, 2004.
29. P. O'Hearn, H. Yang, and J. Reynolds. Separation and information hiding. In *POPL*, 2004.
30. F. Smith, D. Walker, and G. Morrisett. Alias types. In *ESOP*, 2000.
31. J. Vitek and B. Bokowski. Confined types in Java. *Software Practice and Experience*, 31, 2001.

Consistency Checking of Statechart Diagrams
of a Class Hierarchy

Vi••• S.W. L•• •n• J•li•n P•••••

Department of Computer Science, University of Bath
{lsw, jap}@cs.bath.ac.uk

Abstract. One of the limitations of UML is it lacks a systematic way for verifying consistency within and between models. This paper explores the intra-model consistency problem in the context of statechart diagrams. We propose an algebraic approach for determining whether the statechart diagrams of a superclass and its subclass are consistent with respect to their behaviour. The statechart diagrams are first translated into the π-calculus and then verified automatically using the Mobility Workbench.

1 Introduction

T•• P•in•i•l• o• S•••••i•••••ili•y [1] ••i••l•••• •••• •n in•••n•• o• ••• •••••-•y•• ••n •lw•y• •• •••l•••• wi•• •n in•••n•• o• ••• •••••y••. In ••• •on••x• o• ••• o• j•••-o•i•n••• •••• nolo•y, ••• •o••••• on• in• no•ion •o• •••••y•• ••l••ion ••w••n • •••••••y•• •n• i•• •••••y•• i• in•••i••n••.

In ••• Uni••• Mo••lin• L•n•••••• (UML) [•], • ••n•••li••ion ••l••ion•• i• •••••i••• •••• • •••• •l••• in•••i•• ••o• • •••••••l•••. T•• ••••vio•• o• ••• o•-j•••• (in•••n•••) o• ••• ••••l••• •n• ••••••l••• i• no•• •lly •••••••n••• ••in• •••••••••• •i•••• •, ••• ••••••• ••• ••••••••• •i•••• •••• •••wn ••••••••ly, • •i•o•o•• •••••o••• •o• v••i•yin• •on•i•••n•y ••w••n ••• ••••••••• •i•••• • •n• •••••i•••••ili•y o• •n o• j••• o• ••• ••••••l••• •y •n o• j•• o• ••• ••••l••• i• n•••••. In ••i• ••••••, w• ••• w••• o• •n •i•i• •l••ion o• ••• π-••l••l•• [3, •] •o• ••••••in• in•on•i•••n•y ••w••n ••••••••• •i•••• • o• • ••••••l••• •n• i•• ••••l•••. T•• •on•i•••n•y ••••• in• o• ••••••••• •i•••• • i• ••••i•• o•• •••o-••i••lly ••in• ••• Mo•ili•y Wo•••••n•• (MWB) [5, 6].

T•• ••• o• ••• •••• i• o•••ni••• •• •ollow•. S•••ion • •••••i• ••• •io• wo•• in ••• •••••. S•••ion 3 ••ovi••• •n ov••vi•w o• ••• • •in •••••••• o• UML •••••••••• •i•••• • •n• ••• π-••l••l••. T•• •n•o•in• o• • ••••••• o• •••••••••• •i•••• • in ••• π-••l••l•• i• ••••n••• in S•••ion •. S•••ion 5 •i•••••••• ••• •on••••• o• •••••i•••••ili•y •n• •••vio••l •on•i•••n•y. S•••ion 6 •x•• in•• ••• •on•i•••n•y ••••• in• o• •••••••••• •i•••• • o• •l••••• lin••• wi•• • ••n•••li••••ion ••l••ion-••i• ••in• ••• MWB. • on•l••ion• ••• •iv•n in S•••ion •.

2 Related Work

T•• •on•i•••n•y ••••• in• o• ••• ••••••••••• •i•••• • o• •l••••• w•i•• ••• lin••• wi•• • ••n•••li••ion ••l••ion•• i• ••• no• ••••n •• lly •x•loi••• in ••• vio•• ••••-i•• [•, •, 9, 10].

A.P. Black (Ed.): ECOOP 2005, LNCS 3586, pp. 412–427, 2005.

In [•], So•••o• ill• •••n•l•••• ••••••••••• •i••••• • in•o •n o• j•••-o•i•n••• l•n-•••••• •n• •x• lo••• ••• •on•••• o• ••••vio•• in••i••n•• •n• ••••••i••••ili•y. In •on•••••, w• •••n•l••• ••••••••••• •i••••• • in•o ••• π-••l••l•• •n• •••••• in•• ••• •••••i••••ili•y o• ••••••••••• •i••••• • ••in• ••• w••• o••n •i•i• •l••ion o• ••• π-••l••l••. F••••••• o••, o•••••••o••• i• •••••• on • •o•• •l• •••o• in••••• o•• ••o•••• • in• l•n•••••. So•••o• ill• [•] ••••• •i• •li••• •o•• o•••n•i•ion•, w••••••• o•• •••••o••• ••••o•••• •••••• ••••i••• •v•n••, •••••• •on•i•ion• •n• ••-•ion• • i••••ly.

In [•], •wo •y••• o• •••••i••••ili•y ••• ••• n••. Lin••• ••• ••••i••••ili•y •••••• •••• •v••y ••••• in • ••••••l••• i• • ••••• o• i•• ••••l•••••. B••n•• in• •••-••i••••ili•y ••i••l•••• ••••• •ny •••vio•• in • ••••••l••• i• •i• •l•••• •y i•• •••••l•••••. B••n•• in• ••••i••••ili•y i• •n•• •••n lin••• ••••i••••ili•y. Any ••••••l••• C_1 w• i•• i• •••n•• in• ••••i••••l• •y • ••••l••• C_2 i• lin••• •••••i-••••l• •y ••• ••••l••• C_2.

Unli•• [•] w• i•• •••n•• ••••i••••ili•y in ••••• • o• •••••• •on••in• •n• •n• •i• •l••ion, w• •••n• ••••i••••ili•y ••in• ••• w••• o••n •i•i• •l••ion o• ••• π-••l••l••. • ••••••o••• ••• •o• •••v•n•••• ov•• [•] •• (i) i• ••••o••• ••••• •-••••i••• •v•n••, •••••• •on•i•ion• •n• •i••••••i••l ••••••••••• •i••••• •; •n• (ii) i• •••o• •••• ••• •••••in• o• ••••i••••ili•y ••o••• ••• ••• o• ••• MWB.

S••• ••n•• •n• S•••fl [9] v••i•y •on•i•••n•y ••w••n ••• ••o•i••• ••••••-•••••• •i••••• • o•• ••••••l••• •n• i•• ••••l••• ••in• ••• •on•••• o• o•••v••ion •on•i•••n•y •n• invo••ion •on•i•••n•y •• w•ll ••• ••• o• ••l••. W••n •o• ••••• wi•• [9], o•••••••o••• ••••o•••• •••••• ••••i••• •v•n••, •••••• •on•i•ion• •n• ••-•ion•, •n• •••in ••• •on•i•••n•y •••••in• i• ••••o••• •• ••o• ••i••lly.

In [10], •on•i•••n•y •••w••n ••• ••o•i••• ••••••••••• •i••••• • o•• ••••••l••• •n• i•• ••••l••• i• v••i••• ••in• • o• • •ni••in• S•••n•i•l P•o••••• (• SP). T•• •••n••o•• ••ion ••o• ••••••••••• •i••••• • in•o • SP i• ••••• on • •••-• o••l •• •l••. In •on•••• •o o•• •••••o•••, ••• •••n••o•• ••ion i• no• ••••• on UML ••• •n•i•• •n• •o•• no• •••••o••• •••••• ••••i••• •v•n••, •••••• •on•i•ion•, •••ion• •n• •on•••••n• •o• •o•i•• ••••••. T•• •••••o••• o• [10] ••ovi•• ••• only • w•y •o v••i•y •on•i•••n•y •••w••n ••••••••••• •i••••• •, w••••• o•• •••••o••• ••ov••• •on•i•••n•y •••••in•, ••• iv•l•n•• •••••in• [11] •n• • o••l •••••in• [1•, 13] o• ••••••••••• •i••••• •.

• ••••• ••l•••• ••••i•• on •on•i•••n•y •••••in• in•l••• [1•, 15, 16, 1•]. • n••l• •• •l. [1•] ••o• o•• •n •••o•••• •o• •••••in• •on•i•••n•y •••w••n (i) ••••• l• •••••-•••••• •••• •n• (ii) ••••l• •••••••••• •n• ••o•o•ol •••••••••. Li••wi••, • n••l• •• •l. in [15] •••••• in• ••• •on•i•••n•y •••w••n •n ol• •••••l• •••••••••• •n• • n•w •••••l• •••••••••• o• UML-• T • o••l• •y v••i•yin• ••••• ••• ol• •••••l• ••••••••••• i• • •••n•• •n• o•••• n•w •••••l• ••••••••••. In [16], ••• •••••••v••ion o• •vol••ion •on•i•••n•y o• ••• UML-• T • o••l• i• ••••••••• ••in• • ••l•-•••••• •••n••o•• ••ion •••••o•••. T•• wo••• o• [1•] •••••i••• • •o•• •l ••• •n•i•• w• i•• •••••••••••• ••• •on•••••n• •x•••••ion o• • •l•i•l• o•••••ion• on • n o• j•••. P•••••i-••l •••li•••ion• o• ••• •o•• •l ••• •n•i•• in•l••• •••••in• ••o•••i•• o• • o••l•, •• owin• in•••-• o••l •on•i•••n•y •n• •••••••o•in• o• • o••l•. ••• •••••••o•••, •n-li•• [1•, 15, 16, 1•] w•i•• •o••• on UML-• T • o••l• •n• v••io•• •y••• o• UML

•ı•••• •, •• ••••ı••• UML ••••••••••• •ı••••• • •n• •on•ı•••n•y ••••w••n UML
••••••••••• • ı••••• • o•• •l••• • ı••••••y.

3 Basic Concepts

In ••ı• ••••ion, w• in••o••••• ••• no•ion• •n• no•••ion• •••• •••o••••o•• •••
••••••.

3.1 Statechart Diagrams

A ••••••••••• • ı•••••• o• UML •••ı•••• •ow •n o• j••• o•• •l••• •••• on•• •o v••io••
•v•n•• ••• •o••• o•• ı•• li•••ı• •. T•• •wo •••ı• •n•ı•ı•• o•• ••••••••••• • ı••••• •••
•••••• •n• •••n•ı•ion.

Fi•••• 1 ••ow• ••• ••••••••••• ı••••• o•• •l••• C_2 w• ı•• •on•ı••• o••n ini•i•l
•••••• o•••••• •n• •o•• •••ı• •••••• S_1, S_2, S_3 •n• S_4. T•• ini•i•l •••••o••••• ı•
•••••••n••• •• • •• •ll •ll•• •ı••l• wi•• •n o••ioin• •••n•ı•ion •o ••• •••••l•
•••••• S_1. U•on ••••ı•• o••n •v•n• E_2, ••• •••n•ı•ion w• ı•• •onn•••• •••••• S_1
•n• S_2 i• ••••, ••••• S_1 i• •xi•••• •n• ••••• S_2 i• •n•••••. Unli•• •v•n• E_2,
•v•n• $E_1(p_1, p_2)$ i• • •••••• •••ı••• •v•n• wi•• ••••• ••••• p_1 •n• p_2. B••i•••• •n
•v•n•, • •••n•ı•ion i• o••ion•lly l•••ll•• wi•• • ••••••-•on•i•ion •n• •n •••ion.
T•• •••n•ı•ion w• ı•• •onn•••• •••••• S_3 •n• S_4 i• •••• w••n ••• •v•n• E_4 o•••••
•n• ••• •• ••••• -•on•i•ion $cond_1$ • ol••. T•• •••ion i• •x•••••• •n• •n •v•n• E_5 i•
••n• •o •n o• j••• o.

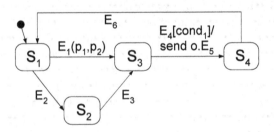

Fig. 1. Statechart diagram of class C_2

In Fi•••• •, ••••• S_2 o••l••• C_1 i• • non-•on•••••n• •o• •o•i•• ••••• in w• ı••
only on• o• ı•• ••••••••• V_1 o• V_2 i• •••iv• •• •ny •oin• o• •x•••• ion.

T•• •l••• •ı••••• o••l••••• C_1 •n• C_2 i• ••own in Fi•••• 3. T•• •l•••
C_1 in••ı•• ••o• ••• •l••• C_2 •n• •x••n•• ••• •l••• C_2 •y •o•• n•w • •••o••
E_7, E_8, E_9 •n• E_{10}.

3.2 The π-Calculus

T•• π-••l••l•• i• • ••o••••• •l•••••• •o• •••i•yin• •on•••••n• •y••••• • in w• ı•• •••
••o•••••• •o• • •ni•••• ov•• •••nn•l•. A• • •ny v••i• n•• o• ••• π-••l••l•• l• ••v•

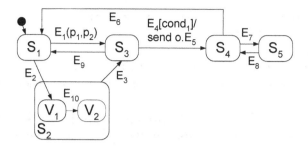

Fig. 2. Statechart diagram of class C_1

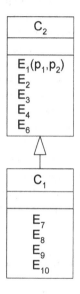

Fig. 3. Class hierarchy

•••n •• o• o•••, w• ••i•fly ••vi•w ••• •yn••x •n• ••• •n•i•• o• ••• π-••l••l•• in •• i• •••••••ion. T•• •••••• i• •••••••• •o [1•, 19] •o• ••••il•.

W•• l•• $\mathcal{A}$ ••• ••• o••o•••••• ••n••• ov•• •y $P, Q, R, \mathcal{N}$ ••• ••• o••••nn•l• (n•• ••) ••n••• ov•• •y x, y •n• $\Im$ ••• • ••• o• ••o•••• i••n•i•••. T•• •yn••x •n• ••• •n•i•• o• π-••l••l•• ••o•••• •x••••ion• ••• ••• n•• •• •ollow•:

$x(\bar{y}).P$: i•• •n in•• • •••• x w•i•• •••iv•• ••nn•l• •lon• ••• nn•l x •n• •on•in•• •••••o•••• P wi•• $y_1, y_2, \ldots, y_n$ ••• l•••• •y ••• ••••iv•• ••• nn•l•. T•• in•• •••• x $x().P$ i• •••••vi•••• •• $x.P$.

$\bar{x}\langle\bar{y}\rangle.P$: i••n o•••• ••••x w•i•• ••n•• ••• nn•l• $y_1, y_2, \ldots, y_n$ •lon• ••• nn•l x •n• •on•in•• •• •• •o•••• P. T•• o•••• • ••••x $\bar{x}\langle\rangle.P$ i• ••••••vi•••• •• $\bar{x}.P$.

$P|Q$: •••••••••n•• •on•• •••n• ••o••••• P •n• Q ••• •x••••in• in ••••ll•l.

$P + Q$: ••• •••••n•• • non-•••••• ini••i• •• oi•• w•i•• •i•••• ••o•••• P o• Q ••o- •••••. $\Sigma_{i=1}^{n} P_i$ ••••vi•••• $P_1 + \ldots + P_n$.

$(\boldsymbol{\nu}\vec{x})P$: i• • •••••i••ion w• i•• •••• •••• n•w •••nn•l• $x_1, x_2, \ldots, x_n$ •••• •o• •o• -
• •ni•••ion in ••o••••• P.

$[x = y]P$: i• • • •••• in• •on•••••• w• i•• ••o•••••• •• ••o••••• P i• •••nn•l• x
•n• y ••• i•n•i••l; o•••wi••, •••••v•• li•• • n•ll ••o••••.

$\tau.P$: i••n •no••••v••l• •••• x w• i•• •••o••• ••n in•••n•l •••ion τ •n• •on•in••
•• ••o••••• P.

$A(x_1, x_2, \ldots, x_n) \stackrel{\text{def}}{=} P$: ••no••• • ••o•••• i••n•i••• A w• i•• •••••• n ••••••• ••••••
•n• •••••v•• li•• ••o••••• P. P•o••••• P • •y •on••in o••••••n••• o• A.

T•• in••• ••••x $x(\vec{y}).P$ •n• •••••i••ion o•••••o• $(\boldsymbol{\nu}\vec{x})P$ •in• $\vec{y}$ •n• $\vec{x}$ in P,
••••••iv•ly. Unli•• ••• in•••••••x, ••••••nn•l• $\vec{y}$ in o••••••••••x $\overline{x}\langle\vec{y}\rangle.P$ •••
••••. T•• •o•n• n•• ••••n• •••• n•• ••o• P •••••••n•• •• $bn(P)$ •n• $fn(P)$. T••
•x•••••ion $fn(P) \cup fn(Q)$ i• •••••vi•••• •• $fn(P, Q)$.

In ••• π-••l••l••, ••• no•ion o• o••n •i•i• •l••ion i• •••• •o• •••••• inin•
w•••••• •wo π-••l••l•• ••o•••••• ••• •••iv•l•n•. W• ••v• ••o•••• o••n •i•i• -
•l••ion in ••i• ••••• •••••• •••n •••ly •n• l••• •i•i• •l••ion •• o••n •i•i• •l•-
•ion i• • •on•••n••. I• •••••v•• •ll π-••l••l•• o• •••••o••. In ••• i•ion, ••• n•• •
in•••n•i••ion o• o••n •i•i• •l••ion ••• ••o•••• • ••ll-•y-n••• ••••o••• w• i••
••••ly ••••••• ••• n•• ••• o• •••••i••ion• •n• ••ovi••• •n •• •i•n• •••• •o•
•ool ••v•lo•• •n•.

D••n• in• on ••• •••••• •n• o• ••• in•••n•l •••ion•, o••n •i•i• •l••ion i•
•l••i••• in•o •••on• o••n •i•i• •l••ion •n• w••• o••n •i•i• •l••ion. W••• o••n
•i•i• •l••ion i• •o••••• •• i• •o•• no• •iff•••n•i••• •••w••n •wo π-••l••l•• ••o-
•••••• w• i•• •iff•• ••o• •••• o•••• in ••••n••• o• in•••n•l •••ion•.

4   Translation of Statechart Diagrams into the π-Calculus

T•i• •••ion •••• •••ll• • ••••••• o• •••n•l••ion ••l•• •n• •••ni•ion• ••o•o•••
in [•0]. T•• • ••• in• o• •••••••••• •i••••• • •o ••• π-••l••l•• i• li• i••• •o
no•••ion•l •l•• •n•• w• i•• ••• ••l•v•n• •o ••i• ••••••. T•••• in•l••• •v•n••,
••••••, •••••-•on• i•ion•, •••ion•, ••••• •••i••• •v•n••, non-•on••••n• •o• •o•-
i•• •••••• •n• •on••••n• •o• •o•i•• ••••••. T••n •n ••• li•••ion o•••• •••n•l••ion
••l•• i• ill•••••••• ••in• Fi••••• 1 •n• •. T•• •o•• •li••• •x•••••ion ••• •n•i••
in ••i• •••••ion •x••n•• ••• ••l•-••••• • •••in• o• o•• •••vio•• wo•• [•0] •y
••ovi•• in• • w•y •o• •••n•o•• in• • •••••• ••••i••• •v•n•• ••••••••n•in• • • •••o•
invo•••ion in•o • π-••l••l•• •x•••••ion.

4.1   Translation Rules

W• •••n• $\mathcal{SC}$ ••• ••• o• •••••••••• •i••••• • ••n••• ov•• •y $F, G, H, \mathcal{ST}$ •••
••• o• ••••••• ••n••• ov•• •y $S, T, V, W, \mathcal{E}$ ••• • ••• o• •v•n•• ••n••• ov•• •y $E, \mathcal{E}_p$
•• • ••• o• •••••• ••••i•• •v•n•• ••n••• ov•• •y $E(p_1, \ldots, p_n)$ •n• $\mathcal{TR}$ ••• •••
o• •••n•i•ion• ••n••• ov•• •y t. In ••• i•ion, •n in•ni•• ••• o• n•••••l n•• •••• $\mathbb{N}$
i• ••••• ••.

T•• •••n•l••ion o• •••••••••• •i•••••• • in•o ••• π-••l••l•• i• ••••• on •••
o• •i•l UML ••• •n•i•• •iv•n in [•1,••] •n• • ••• o• ••l•• w•i•• ••• •o•• •li•••
•• •ollow•:

Rule 1. *The function* $\phi_{event} : \mathcal{E} \to \mathcal{N}$ *maps each event in a statechart diagram to a channel in the* π-*calculus.*

Rule 2. *The function* $\phi_{state} : \mathcal{ST} \to \Im$ *returns a unique process identifier for each state. Each process identifier* $S_1(event, \vec{e}, \ldots) \in \Im$ *is defined as*

$$event(x).([x = e_1] \ldots + \ldots + [x = e_n] \ldots)$$

where $\vec{e}$ *stands for* $e_1, \ldots, e_n$ *and* $\forall a \in \{\vec{e}\}.\phi_{event}^{-1}(a) \in \mathcal{E}.$

• •l• 1 ••••i•• •••• •n •v•n• i• • o••ll•• ••• • •••nn•l in ••• π-••l••l••. T••
inv•••• o• ϕ_{event} ••no••• •y ϕ_{event}^{-1} i• • •• n••ion ••o• $\mathcal{N}$ •o $\mathcal{E}$. • •l• • ••i••l••••
••••• • •••••• i• •n•o••• in ••• π-••l••l•• ••• • ••o••••. T•• ••o•••• i• ••••••••
•• •n •v•n• ••o•••o• o• ••• •••••••••• •i••••• w•i•• ••n•l•• ••••• •i••••••••
•v•n• •••o••in• •o ••• UML ••• •n•i••. I• •••••• in•• w••• ••• •v•n• i• •y ••in•
• n•• ••• o• • •••• in• •on•••••••.

W• •••n• $\mathcal{A}_{in} = \{x(\vec{y})|x, \vec{y} \in \mathcal{N}\}$ •o • • • ••• o• in••• •••ion• •n• $\mathcal{A}_{out} = \{\overline{x}\langle\vec{y}\rangle|x, \vec{y} \in \mathcal{N}\}$ •o • • ••• o• o•••• •••ion•.

Definition 1. *The function* ••i•y: $(\mathcal{A}_{in} \cup \mathcal{A}_{out}) \to \mathbb{N}$ *returns the number of channels which an input or output action takes as parameters.*

Rule 3. *A mapping between guard-conditions and output actions is defined as* $\phi_{guard} : GCond \to \{\alpha|\alpha \in \mathcal{A}_{out} \wedge arity(\alpha) = 1\}$ *where GCond is a set of guard-conditions. The Boolean value of a guard-condition is tested by*

$$\overline{g}\langle x\rangle.x(y).([y = true] \cdots + [y = false] \cdots)$$

where $g, x, y, true, false \in \mathcal{N}$ *and* $\phi_{guard}^{-1}(\overline{g}\langle x\rangle) \in GCond.$

Rule 4. *Each action representing the invocation of an operation or the sending of a signal to an object is related to an output action in the* π-*calculus by* $\phi_{action} : Act \to \mathcal{A}_{out}$ *where Act is a set of actions.*

• •l•• 3 •n• • ••y •••• ••• ••••••-•on• i•ion •n• •••ion o• • •••n•i•ion •••
• o•• ••••••••n••• •• •n o•••• •••ion. • •l• 3 ••• n•• • ow • •••••-•on• i•ion •n•
i•• •v•l••ion ••• •o•• •li•••. T•• •n•o• in• •••• •wo • •••• in• •on••••••• •o
• i••in•• i•• ••• w••n ••• •wo ••••• v•l•••.

Rule 5. *The function* $\phi_{pevent} : \mathcal{E}_p \to \mathcal{N}$ *maps a parameterized event to a channel.*

Rule 6. *The receipt of a parameterized event* $E_1(p_1, \ldots, p_n) \in \mathcal{E}_p$ *is encoded as:*

$$event(x).([x = e_1]x(p_1, \ldots, p_n). \cdots + \cdots + [x = e_n] \cdots)$$

• •l• 5 •••••• •••• • ••••• ••••i••• •v•n• i• •••n•l•••• in•o • •••nn•l. T•• ••- ••• ••••• $p_1, \ldots, p_n$ o• ••• ••••• ••••i••• •v•n• E_1 ••• ••••iv•• •lon• ••• •v•n• •••nn•l e_1 •• •••n•• •y • •l• 6.

Definition 2. *The function* ••• •••••••: $ST \to {}^{\bullet ST}$ *returns the direct substates that are directly contained in a composite state.*

Rule 7. *A non-concurrent composite state* S_1 *and its active substate* V_1 *are denoted as* $\phi_{state}(S_1)|\phi_{state}(V_1)$ *where* $V_1 \in substates(S_1)$ *and* $\phi_{state}(S_1)$ *and* $\phi_{state}(V_1)$ *are defined by:*

$$S_1(step, event_S, \vec{e}, event_V, pos, neg) \stackrel{\text{def}}{=}$$
$$event_S(x).(\boldsymbol{\nu}ack)$$
$$\overline{event_V}\langle x\ ack \rangle.ack(y).([y = pos]\overline{step}. \cdots + [y = neg]\overline{step}. \cdots)$$

$$V_1(event_V, \vec{e}, pos, neg) \stackrel{\text{def}}{=}$$
$$event_V(x\ ack).$$
$$([x = e_1]\overline{ack}\langle value_1 \rangle. \cdots + \cdots +$$
$$[x = e_n]\overline{ack}\langle value_n \rangle. \cdots)$$

where $value_i \in \{pos, neg\}$ *for* $i = 1, \ldots, n$.

Rule 8. *A concurrent composite state* S_1 *and its active substates* $V_1, \ldots, V_n$ *which are located in* n *different orthogonal regions are represented in the* π-*calculus as* $\phi_{state}(S_1)| \phi_{state}(V_1)| \ldots | \phi_{state}(V_n)$ *where* $\bigwedge_{i=1}^n V_i \in substates(S_1)$ *and* $\phi_{state}(S_1), \phi_{state}(V_1), \ldots, \phi_{state}(V_n)$ *are defined by:*

$$S_1(step, event_S, \vec{e}, event_{V_1}, \ldots, event_{V_n}, pos, neg, \ldots) \stackrel{\text{def}}{=}$$
$$event_S(x).(\boldsymbol{\nu}\overrightarrow{ack})\overline{event_{V_1}}\langle x\ ack_1 \rangle. \cdots .$$
$$\overline{event_{V_n}}\langle x\ ack_n \rangle.ack_1(y_1). \cdots .ack_n(y_n). \cdots$$

$$V_i(event_{V_i}, \vec{e}, pos, neg, \ldots) \stackrel{\text{def}}{=}$$
$$event_{V_i}(x\ ack).$$
$$([x = e_1]\overline{ack_i}\langle value_1 \rangle. \cdots + \cdots +$$
$$[x = e_n]\overline{ack_i}\langle value_n \rangle. \cdots)$$

where $1 \leq i \leq n$ *and* $value_i \in \{pos, neg\}$ *for* $i = 1, \ldots, n$.

• •l••• • •n• • •••i•y •••••• •o• • o•i•• ••••• •n• i•• •••iv• •i•••• ••• •••••• [•1] ••• ••no••• •• ••o••••••• w• i•• ••• •• nnin• in ••••ll•l. A non-•on•• •••n• •o• - • o•i•• •••••• i• •••••••••• ••• • •••i•l •••• o•• •on•• •••n• •o• • o•i•• ••••• in w• i••

•• •• • i• only on• o••• o• on•l •••ion. T•• •o• • o•i•• •••• • •o•• •••• •ny •••iv••
•v•n•• •o i•• ••• ••••••. A• ••• ••• •••••• • •o•••• ••• ••••iv•• •v•n• ••o•• •••
•o• • o•i•• ••••, ••• low•••-• ••• ••in• ••io•i•y o• UML ••• •n•i•• i• •••••v•• in
o•• ••• n•l••ion. T•• •n• o• • •• n-•o-•o• •l••ion •••• [•1,••] i• •n•o••• •• •n
o•• •• • •••ion $\overline{step}$ (•• •l• •).

4.2   Application of the Translation Rules

An ill•• •••• •ion o• • ow v••io•• no•••ion•l •l•• •n•• in•l••in• • •••i• •••••, •n
•v•n•, • ••••• •••i••• •v•n•, • ••••••-•on• i•ion, •n •••ion, • non-•on•••••n•
•o• • o•i•• ••••, • ••••••• ••n• •n in•••l•v•l ••• n•i•ion ••• ••••••••n••• in ••• π-
••l••l• i• •• own ••••. To i• ••ov ••• •••••• ili•y o•••• π-••l••l•• ••••i•••ion•,
•o• • ••••••vi••ion• ••• ••• n•• •• •ollow•:

$$\widetilde{e_{C_2}} = e_1, e_2, e_3, e_4, e_5, e_6$$

$$\widetilde{e_{C_1}} = e_1, e_2, e_3, e_4, e_5, e_6, e_7, e_8, e_9, e_{10}$$

$$\widetilde{ack} = pos, neg$$

A••o•• in• •o • •l•• 1, •, 5 •n• 6, ••• •••i• ••••• S_1, ••• •v•n• E_2 •n• •••
••••• •••i••• •v•n• $E_1(p_1, p_2)$ o• •l••• C_2 in Fi•••• 1 ••• • o••ll•• in ••• π-
••l••l• • ••:

$$S_1^{C_2}(step, events, \widetilde{e_{C_2}}, cond_1, ins_0) \stackrel{\text{def}}{=}$$
$$events(x).$$
$$([x = e_1]x(p_1, p_2).\overline{step}.$$
$$\qquad S_3^{C_2}(step, events, \widetilde{e_{C_2}}, cond_1, ins_0) +$$
$$[x = e_2]\overline{step}.S_2^{C_2}(step, events, \widetilde{e_{C_2}}, cond_1, ins_0) +$$
$$\Sigma_{i \in \{3,...,6\}}[x = e_i]\overline{step}.S_1^{C_2}(step, events, \widetilde{e_{C_2}}, cond_1, ins_0))$$

T•• ••o•••• $S_1^{C_2}$ ••••iv•• •n •v•n• •lon• $events$ •n• •••••• in•• w••• •••
••••iv•• •v•n• i•. I•••• •v•n• E_1, • o••ll•• •• •••nn•l e_1, i• ••••iv••, i• in•••
•wo ••••• ••••• p_1 •n• p_2 •lon• e_1, ••n•• • •i•n•l on •••nn•l $step$ •n• •on•in••
•• ••o•••• $S_3^{C_2}$. U•on ••••i•• o• ••• •v•n• E_2, i• ••n••• • •i•n•l on •••nn•l $step$
•n• •volv•• •o ••• ••o••••• $S_2^{C_2}$. • ••••wi••, i• o•••• ••• • •i•n•l on •••nn•l $step$
•n• •on•in•• •• •• i•••l•.

B•••• on • •l•• 1–•, ••• •••i• ••••• S_3 •n• ••• ••• n•i•ion l•• •ll•• wi•• •n •v•n•
E_4, • •••••••-•on• i•ion $cond_1$ •n• •n •••ion $send o.E_5$ (Fi•••• 1) ••• ••• •••••n••• ••:

$$S_3^{C_2}(step, events, \widetilde{e_{C_2}}, cond_1, ins_0) \stackrel{\text{def}}{=}$$
$$events(x).$$
$$([x = e_4](\boldsymbol{\nu}true\ false)\overline{cond_1}\langle true\ false\rangle.$$
$$(true.\overline{ins_0}\langle e_5\rangle.\overline{step}.$$
$$\qquad S_4^{C_2}(step, events, \widetilde{e_{C_2}}, cond_1, ins_0) +$$
$$false.\overline{step}.S_3^{C_2}(step, events, \widetilde{e_{C_2}}, cond_1, ins_0)) +$$
$$\Sigma_{i \in \{1,2,3,5,6\}}[x = e_i]\overline{step}.S_3^{C_2}(step, events, \widetilde{e_{C_2}}, cond_1, ins_0))$$

T•• ••o••••• $S_3^{C_2}$ w•i•• on •••nn•l $event_S$ •o• ••• •v•n• E_4, •••••••• • ••i• o• •••nn•l• $true$ •n• $false$ •n• o•••••• •••• on •••nn•l $cond_1$. • n ••••ivin• • •i•n•l •lon• $true$, i• ••n•• ••• •v•n• E_5 on •••nn•l ins_0, o•••••• • •i•n•l on •••nn•l $step$ •n• ••o••••• •• ••o••••• $S_4^{C_2}$. U• on ••••i•• o• •i•n•l •lon• $false$, i• o•••••• • •i•n•l on •••nn•l $step$ •n• ••o••••• •• i•••l•.

A••lyin• • •l•• 1, •, 5, 6 •n• •, ••• •••i• ••••• S_1, ••• non-•on••••n• •o• - •o•i•• ••••• S_2, ••• •••••••• V_1 •n• ••• in•••l•v•l •••n•i•ion ••w••n S_1 •n• V_1 in Fi•••• • ••• •••n•l•••• in•o • π-••l••l•• ••••i•••ion ••• n•• ••low:

$$S_1^{C_1}(step, events, \widetilde{e_{C_1}}, cond_1, ins_0, \widetilde{ack}) \stackrel{\text{def}}{=}$$
$$events(x).$$
$$([x = e_1]x(p_1, p_2).\overline{step}.S_3^{C_1}(step, events, \widetilde{e_{C_1}}, cond_1, ins_0, \widetilde{ack}) +$$
$$[x = e_2]\overline{step}.(\nu event_{sub})(S_2^{C_1}(step, events, \widetilde{e_{C_1}}, cond_1, ins_0, event_{sub}, \widetilde{ack})|$$
$$V_1^{C_1}(event_{sub}, \widetilde{e_{C_1}}, cond_1, ins_0, \widetilde{ack})) +$$
$$\Sigma_{i \in \{3,...,10\}}[x = e_i]\overline{step}.S_1^{C_1}(step, events, \widetilde{e_{C_1}}, cond_1, ins_0, \widetilde{ack}))$$

• n ••••ivin• ••• •v•n• E_2, ••• ••o••••• $S_1^{C_1}$ o•••••• • •i•n•l •lon• $step$ •n• •on- •in•• •• •wo •on••••n• ••o••••• $S_2^{C_1}$ •n• $V_1^{C_1}$ •••••••n•in• ••• non-•on••••n• •o• • o•i•• ••••• •n• ••• •••iv• ••••••••.

U•in• • •i• il•• ••••o•••, o•••• ••••• o• Fi••••• 1 •n• • ••• •••n•l•••• in•o •••i• •••iv•l•n• π-••l••l•• ••••••••n••ion•. Fo• ••••on• o• •••••, w• o• i• ••• ••••il• •••••.

5   Substitutability and Behavioural Consistency

T• i• ••••ion •••• in••o•••••• ••• no•ion• o• •x••n•ion, ••••••i•••• ili•y o• o• j•••••, •••••i•••• ili•y o• •••••••••• •i••••• ••n• •••vio••l •on•i••n•y o• •••••••••• •i••••• •. T••n w• •i••••• •ow ••• •••vio••l •on•i••n•y o• •••••••••• •i- •••• • o•• •l•• •i••••••y i• •••••••• ••in• w••• o• •n •i•i• •l••ion.

W• •••n• C ••• • ••• o• •l••••• ••n••• ov•• •y C •n• •••••i•• now • •o•• •l ••• ni•ion o• •l•••.

Definition 3 (Class). *Given a class $C \in \mathcal{C}$, the class C is a 2-tuple $C = (\Omega_A^C, \Omega_M^C)$ where (i) Ω_A^C is a set of attributes and (ii) Ω_M^C is a set of methods.*

W• l•• Ω_A^C •• • ••• o• ••••i••••• •n• Ω_M^C ••• • ••• o• •••o•• o• • ••••l••• $C \in \mathcal{C}$. T•• •••• o• n•w ••••i••••• •n• n•w • •••o•• •••n•• in ••• ••••l•••• C ••• ••no••• •• Δ_A^C •n• Δ_M^C w•••• $\Delta_A^C \subseteq \Omega_A^C$ •n• $\Delta_M^C \subseteq \Omega_M^C$.

Definition 4. *The function $\delta : \mathcal{C} \to SC$ maps each class to an associated statechart diagram.*

Definition 5. *The function S•••••: $SC \to \bullet^{ST}$ defined by States(F) = \{S \mid S$ is a state of the statechart diagram F\} returns the set of states of a statechart diagram $F \in SC$.*

Definition 6. *The function* $\gamma : \mathcal{ST} \rightarrow \bullet^{\Omega_A^C}$ *where* $S_i \in \mathcal{ST}$ *for* $i = 1, \ldots, n$ *such that* $States^{-1}(\bigcup_{i=1}^{n}\{S_i\}) = F$ *and* $\delta^{-1}(F) = C$ *returns a set of attributes which are grouped together as a state of the statechart diagram* F *of a class* C.

Definition 7 (Extension). *Given* $C_1, C_2 \in \mathcal{C}$ *and* C_1 *is a subclass of* C_2, *the class* C_1 *extends the class* C_2, *written* $C_1 \Rightarrow_E C_2$, *iff (i)* $\Omega_A^{C_2} \subseteq \Omega_A^{C_1}$; *(ii)* $\Omega_M^{C_2} \subseteq \Omega_M^{C_1}$; *(iii)* $\Delta_A^{C_1} \cap \Omega_A^{C_2} = \emptyset$; *and (iv)* $\Delta_M^{C_1} \cap \Omega_M^{C_2} = \emptyset$.

Corollary 1. *The relation* $\Rightarrow_E$ *is transitive.*
Proof. Let $C_1, C_2, C_3 \in \mathcal{C}$. Suppose $C_1 \Rightarrow_E C_2$ and $C_2 \Rightarrow_E C_3$. Since $C_1 \Rightarrow_E C_2$ and $C_2 \Rightarrow_E C_3$, it follows that $\Omega_M^{C_2} \subseteq \Omega_M^{C_1}$ and $\Omega_M^{C_3} \subseteq \Omega_M^{C_2}$. Since $\subseteq$ is transitive, we get $\Omega_M^{C_3} \subseteq \Omega_M^{C_1}$. Since $\Omega_M^{C_3} \subseteq \Omega_M^{C_2}$ and $\Delta_M^{C_1} \cap \Omega_M^{C_2} = \emptyset, \Delta_M^{C_1} \cap \Omega_M^{C_3} = \emptyset$. A similar argument holds for attributes. Thus, $\Rightarrow_E$ is transitive.

Definition 8 (Generalization). *Given* $C_1, C_2 \in \mathcal{C}$ *and* C_1 *is a subclass of* C_2, *the class* C_1 *generalizes the class* C_2, *written* $C_1 \Rightarrow_G C_2$, *iff (i)* $\Omega_A^{C_2} \subseteq \Omega_A^{C_1}$; *(ii)* $\Omega_M^{C_2} \subseteq \Omega_M^{C_1}$; *(iii)* $(\Delta_A^{C_1} \cap \Omega_A^{C_2} = \emptyset) \vee (\Delta_A^{C_1} \cap \Omega_A^{C_2} \neq \emptyset)$; *and (iv)* $(\Delta_M^{C_1} \cap \Omega_M^{C_2} = \emptyset) \vee (\Delta_M^{C_1} \cap \Omega_M^{C_2} \neq \emptyset)$.

Proposition 1. *Let* $C_1, C_2 \in \mathcal{C}$. *If* $C_1 \Rightarrow_E C_2$ *then* $C_1 \Rightarrow_G C_2$.
Proof. Let C_1 and C_2 be arbitrary classes. Suppose $C_1 \Rightarrow_E C_2$. Since $C_1 \Rightarrow_E C_2$, it follows that $\Omega_A^{C_2} \subseteq \Omega_A^{C_1}, \Omega_M^{C_2} \subseteq \Omega_M^{C_1}, \Delta_A^{C_1} \cap \Omega_A^{C_2} = \emptyset$ and $\Delta_M^{C_1} \cap \Omega_M^{C_2} = \emptyset$. Consider the clause $\Delta_A^{C_1} \cap \Omega_A^{C_2} = \emptyset$. Then clearly C_1 and C_2 also satisfy the clause $(\Delta_A^{C_1} \cap \Omega_A^{C_2} = \emptyset) \vee (\Delta_A^{C_1} \cap \Omega_A^{C_2} \neq \emptyset)$. A similar argument holds true for the clause $\Delta_M^{C_1} \cap \Omega_M^{C_2} = \emptyset$. Since $C_1 \Rightarrow_G C_2$ satisfies the other two clauses $\Omega_A^{C_2} \subseteq \Omega_A^{C_1}$ and $\Omega_M^{C_2} \subseteq \Omega_M^{C_1}$ according to the definition of $\Rightarrow_G$, we can conclude that if $C_1 \Rightarrow_E C_2$ then $C_1 \Rightarrow_G C_2$.

• •l••ion•• i• • •• • • •y •xi•• •••w••n •l• •••• in•l• •• •x••n•ion (D•• ni•ion •)
•n• ••n•••li•••ion (D•• ni•ion •). Unli•• •n •x••n•ion [• 3] w•i•• only • •• • • o••
•••• i• •• •• • n• • •••o•• •o • •••••• l•••, • ••n••• li•••ion •llow• •••• i• •••• •n•
• ••• o• ov••• i• in•. An •x••n•ion i• • n•• •••n • ••n••• li•••ion •• •••• i• •• in
P•o• o•i•ion 1.

Definition 9 (Substitutability of Objects). *Given* $C_1, C_2 \in \mathcal{C}$, *any object* o_1 *of the class* C_1 *is substitutable for an object* o_2 *of the class* C_2, *written* $o_1 \preceq_{obj} o_2$, *iff* $C_1 \Rightarrow_E C_2$ *or* $C_1 \Rightarrow_G C_2$ *holds.*

Definition 10 (Substitutability of Statechart Diagrams). *Given* $C_1, C_2 \in \mathcal{C}, C_1 \Rightarrow_E C_2, \delta(C_1) = F_1$ *and* $\delta(C_2) = F_2$, *the statechart diagram* F_1 *which is associated with the class* C_1 *is substitutable for the statechart diagram* F_2 *which is associated with the class* C_2, *written* $F_1 \preceq_{sc} F_2$, *if the extra attributes and methods declared in the class* C_1 *are specified as invisible.*

S• • ••i• •••• ili•y [•, •, 10, •3] o• o• j•••• (D••ni•ion 9) i• •n i• •o•••n• •on-
•••• in o• j•••-o•i•n••• •••• nolo• y w• i•• •n••••• •••• •n o• j••• o• • ••••l•••
i• •o• •••i• l• wi•• •n o• j••• o• • ••••••l•••. Si• il••ly, w• in••o•••• ••• •on-
•••• ••••••i•••• ili•y o• •••••••••• •i•••••• • (D••ni•ion 10) •o• ••••i•yin• •••
•o• •••i• ili•y ••w••n ••• •••••••••• •i•••••• • o• • ••••l••• •n• i•• ••••••l•••
••• •o •n •x••n•ion. Hi• in• ••• •x••n•• ••••i•••• •n• • •••o•• in • ••••l•••
••••••n•••• ••• ••••••i•••• ili•y o• •••••••••• •i•••••• •. Bo•• •x••n•ion •n• ••n-
•••li••••ion i• • ly ••• •••••i••••• ili•y o• o• j••••, w•••••• •x••n•ion i• • li•• •••
••••••i•••• ili•y o• •••••••••• ••• •i•••••• •.

Definition 11. (Behavioural Consistency of Statechart Diagrams) *Given*
$C_1, C_2 \in \mathcal{C}, C_1 \Rightarrow_E C_2, \delta(C_1) = F_1$ *and* $\delta(C_2) = F_2$, *the statechart diagram* F_1 *is*
behaviourally consistent with the statechart diagrams F_2, *written as* $F_1 \precsim_{sc} F_2$, *iff*
$F_1 \preceq_{sc} F_2$.

T•• •••• vio•• o• F_1 •n• F_2 i• •on•i•••n• •• •x••n••• ••••i•••• •n• • •••o••
o• F_1 ••• •i••• n •••o•• in• •o ••• ••• ni•ion o• ••• •••••i•••• ili•y o• ••••••••••
•i•••••• •.

Corollary 2. *The relation* $\preceq_{sc}$ *is transitive.*
Proof. Let $\delta(C_1) = F_1, \delta(C_2) = F_2$ *and* $\delta(C_3) = F_3$. *Suppose* $F_1 \preceq_{sc} F_2$ *and*
$F_2 \preceq_{sc} F_3$. *Since* $F_1 \preceq_{sc} F_2$ *and* $F_2 \preceq_{sc} F_3$, *it follows that* $C_1 \Rightarrow_E C_2$ *and*
$C_2 \Rightarrow_E C_3$. *Since* $\Rightarrow_E$ *is transitive, we get* $C_1 \Rightarrow_E C_3$ *and we can conclude that*
$F_1 \preceq_{sc} F_3$. *Thus,* $\preceq_{sc}$ *is transitive.*

Corollary 3. *The relation* $\precsim_{sc}$ *is transitive.*
Proof. By Definition 11 and Corollary 2.

T•• •••••i•••• ili•y •n• •••vio•••l •on•i•••n•y o• •••••••••• •i•••••• • •••
•••n•i•iv• •n• •ny ••••• •••••••••• •i•••••• • •••l•••• •y •x••n•ion• ••• •o• •••i-
•l•.

Proposition 2. *Consider two objects* o_1 *and* o_2 *of classes* C_1 *and* C_2 *and the*
respective statechart diagrams F_1 *and* F_2 *of the two classes. If* $F_1 \preceq_{sc} F_2$ *then*
$o_1 \preceq_{obj} o_2$.

Proof. Suppose $F_1 \preceq_{sc} F_2$. *Since* $F_1 \preceq_{sc} F_2$, *it follows that* $C_1 \Rightarrow_E C_2$. *Therefore,*
$o_1 \preceq_{obj} o_2$. *Thus, if* $F_1 \preceq_{sc} F_2$ *then* $o_1 \preceq_{obj} o_2$.

Proposition 3. *Consider two objects* o_1 *and* o_2 *of classes* C_1 *and* C_2 *and the*
respective statechart diagrams F_1 *and* F_2 *of two classes. If* $F_1 \precsim_{sc} F_2$ *then* $o_1 \preceq_{obj}$
o_2.

Proof. Follows directly from Definition 11 and Proposition 2.

P•o• o•i•ion • ••y• •••• •n o• j••• o_1 i• ••••••i••••l• •o• •n o• j••• o_2 w••n-
•v•• ••• •••o•i•••• •••••••••• •i•••••• F_1 o• ••• o• j••• o_1 i• ••••••i••••l• •o•
••• •••o•i•••• •••••••••• •i•••••• F_2 o•••• o• j••• o_2. Si• il••ly, ••• •••• vio• ••l

•on•i•••n•y o• ••••••••••• •i•••••• • i• •li•• ••• •••••i•••• ili•y o• •••i• •o•••-
•• on• in• o• j•••• •• ••••••• in P•o• o•i•ion 3.

N•x•, w• •••n• ••• n•• • •••••i••ion •• n••ion [3,•,19] •n• • n•• ••• o•
•••••x•• [5,19]. T••n w• ••••ll ••• no•ion o• w••• o••n •i•i• •l••ion [6,19,••,•5]
in ••• π-••l••l••.

Definition 12. *The name substitution function* $\sigma : \mathcal{N} \to \mathcal{N}$, *written* $\{\vec{x}/\vec{y}\}$,
replaces each $y_i \in \mathcal{N}$ *by* $x_i \in \mathcal{N}$ *for* $1, \ldots, n$.

T•• •yn••x •n• ••• •n•i•• o• •••x•• •••• in ••• •••ni•ion o• w••• o••n
•i•i• •l••ion ••• •iv•n ••low:

$P \xrightarrow{\alpha} P'$: ••• •x•••ion o• •••ion α •n• ••o•••• P •••o• •• P'.

$P \Longrightarrow P'$: ••o•••• P •••o• •• P' ••••• •••o o• • o•• in•••n•l •••ion•.

$P \xRightarrow{\alpha} P'$: i• •••iv•l•n• •o $P \Longrightarrow \xrightarrow{\alpha} \Longrightarrow P'$.

$P \xRightarrow{\hat{\alpha}} P'$: $\begin{cases} P \xRightarrow{\alpha} P' \text{ if } \alpha \neq \tau \\ P \Longrightarrow P' \text{ if } \alpha = \tau \end{cases}$

Definition 13 (Weak Open Bisimulation [19]). *A symmetric binary relation* $\mathcal{R}$ *on processes is a weak open bisimulation if* $(P, Q) \in \mathcal{R}$ *implies* $\forall \sigma$ *whenever* $P\sigma \xrightarrow{\alpha} P'$ *where* $bn(\alpha) \cap fn(P\sigma, Q\sigma) = \emptyset$ *then,* $\exists Q' : Q\sigma \xRightarrow{\hat{\alpha}} Q'$ $\wedge (P', Q') \in \mathcal{R}$. *P is weakly open bisimilar to Q, written* $P \approx_o Q$, *if they are related by a weak open bisimulation.*

Definition 14. *The translation of statechart diagrams into the* π-*calculus is defined by the function* $\phi : \mathcal{SC} \to \bullet^{\Im}$ *which represents a group of translation functions as specified by Rules 1–8.*

Proposition 4. *Let* $\delta(C_1) = F_1, \delta(C_2) = F_2, \mathcal{MC}$ *be a set of matching constructs and* $\mathbb{Z}^+$ *be a set of positive integers. If* $C_1 \Rightarrow_E C_2$ *and* $\phi(F_2) \dot{\approx}_o (\boldsymbol{\nu}\phi(m_1)$ $\phi(m_2) \ldots \phi(m_n)) \phi(F_1)$ *then* $F_1 \precsim_{sc} F_2$ *where* $\bigcup_{i=1}^n \{m_i\} = \Delta_M^{C_1}$ *and the execution of the* π-*calculus expression* $event_S(x).[x = \phi(m_i)]\overline{step}$ *becomes* $\phi(S_i)$ *for* $i = 1, \ldots, n$ *such that (i)* $event_S(x) \in \mathcal{A}_{in}$, *(ii)* $[x = \phi(m_i)] \in \mathcal{MC}$, *(iii)* $\overline{step} \in \mathcal{A}_{out}$, *(iv)* $S_i \in \mathcal{ST}$, *(v)* $\gamma(S_i) = \{a_j | a_j \in \Delta_A^{C_1} \wedge j \in \mathbb{Z}^+\}$ *and (vi)* $\bigcup_{i=1}^n \{S_i\} \subseteq States(\delta(C_1))$.
Proof. By Definitions 10 and 11.

P•o• o•i•ion • ••i• •l•••• •••• •o •••••• in• ••• ••••vio•••l •on•i•••n•y o•
••••••••••• •i•••••• •, w• •••n•l••• ••• •••••••••• •i•••••• • in•o π-••l••l•• ••••i-
••••ion• •n• •i•• ••• •x••n••• • •••o•• •x•li•i•ly •n• •x••n••• ••••i•••• i• -
•li•i•ly ••in• • •••••i••ion. T••n w• •••• w••••••••• •wo π-••l••l•• ••••i•••ion•
••• w•••ly o••n •i•i• il••.

6   Consistency Checking Using the MWB

T•• MWB i• •n •••o• •••• •o••w••• •ool •o• ••• π-••l••l••. I• ••ovi••• •n •nvi•on• •n• •o• •n•ly•in• •on••••n• •y•••• • w• i•• ••v• •yn•• i••lly •volv-in• •o• • •ni•••ion •o• olo• i••. • •• iv•l•n••-•••••in• •o• • •n•• •o• •••••• inin• w••••••• •wo ••o•••••• •••j••• in ••• π-••l••l•• ••• ••l•••• •y v••io•• w••• o• •n •i•i• •l••ion• ••• •••• o••••.

T•• •yn•••••i••l •iff•••n••• •••w••n ••• MWB •n• ••• π-••l••l•• ••• • ino•. T•• •••••i••ion o• •••o• ν •n• o••••• •••ion $\overline{x}$ ••• ••••••••n••• in ••• MWB •• ˆ •n• 'x, ••••••iv•ly. In ••• MWB, • ••o•••• i• •••n•• in ••• ••• • w•y •• in ••• π-••l••l•• •x•••• •••• i• i• •••••••• •y ••• ••ywo•• *agent*.

To ••••• w••••••• ••• •••••••••• •i••••• o• •l••• C_1 i• ••••vio•••lly •on-•i•••n• wi•• ••• ••••••••••• •i••••• o• •l••• C_2 (Fi•••••• 1 •n• •), ••• •••nn•l• e_7, e_8, e_9 •n• e_{10} •••••••n•in• •x•••n••• • ••• o•• ••l•••• in •l••• C_1 ••• •i•••n ••in• • •••••i••ion •• •ollow•:

$$(\boldsymbol{\nu} e_7 \ e_8 \ e_9 \ e_{10} \ \widetilde{ack})$$
$$S_1^{C_1}(step, event_S, \widetilde{e_{C_1}}, cond_1, ins_0, \widetilde{ack})$$

W• •••n ••o•••• •o v••i•y w•••••• $S_1^{C_2}(step, event_S, \widetilde{e_{C_2}}, cond_1, ins_0)$ ••• •i•-•••••• in S•••ion • i• w•••ly o••n •i•i• il•• •o $(\boldsymbol{\nu} e_7 \ e_8 \ e_9 \ e_{10} \ \widetilde{ack}) S_1^{C_1}(step, event_S, \widetilde{e_{C_1}}, cond_1, ins_0, \widetilde{ack})$ i.•. w••••••• ••• ••• iv•l•n••

$$S_1^{C_2}(step, event_S, \widetilde{e_{C_2}}, cond_1, ins_0) \dot{\approx}_o$$
$$(\boldsymbol{\nu} e_7 \ e_8 \ e_9 \ e_{10} \ \widetilde{ack})$$
$$S_1^{C_1}(step, event_S, \widetilde{e_{C_1}}, cond_1, ins_0, \widetilde{ack})$$

•ol••••in• ••• MWB.

A• ••own in Fi•••• •, ••• MWB •o• • •n• *input* i• •o••• ••• π-••l••l•• •••••i•••ion• o• ••• ••••••••••• •i••••• • o• •l••••• C_1 •n• C_2 ••o• ••• •l• *stat-echarts_of_C1_C2.pi* •n••• ••• •i••••o•y *inheritance*. T•• ••o••••••

$$S\_1\_C^{\bullet}(step, event\_S, e\_1, e\_^{\bullet}, e\_3, e\_^{\bullet}, e\_5, e\_6, \\ cond\_1, ins\_o)$$

•n•

$$(\hat{}e\_^{\bullet})(\hat{}e\_^{\bullet})(\hat{}e\_9)(\hat{}e\_10)(\hat{}pos)(\hat{}neg)$$
$$S\_1\_C1(step, event\_S, e\_1, e\_^{\bullet}, e\_3, e\_^{\bullet}, e\_5, e\_6, \\ e\_^{\bullet}, e\_^{\bullet}, e\_9, e\_10, cond\_1, ins\_o, pos, neg)$$

••• •••••n•in•

$$S_1^{C_2}(step, event_S, \widetilde{e_{C_2}}, cond_1, ins_0)$$

•n•

$$(\nu e_7 \; e_8 \; e_9 \; e_{10} \; \widetilde{ack})$$
$$S_1^{C_1}(step, event_S, \widetilde{e_{C_1}}, cond_1, ins_0, \widetilde{ack})$$

••• ••• n ••••••• w•••••• •••y ••• w•••ly o••n •i•i• il•• •iv•n •••• •••nn•l• $step, event_S, e_1, e_2, e_3, e_4, e_5, e_6, cond_1$ •n• ins_o ••• •i••in•••in• ••• MWB •o• - ••n• $weqd$.

T•• •wo ••o•••••• (•••n••) ••• ••l•••• •y • w••• o••n •i•i• •l••ion •n• ••• •i•• o•••• w••• o••n •i•i• •l••ion i• 19. T•• •i• • ••••n •o• ••• •on•i••n•y ••••• w•• 0.0•• •••on••. T•• •••l •i• • •l••••• w•• • •••••• ••in• ••• MWB $time$ •o• • •n•. T•• •••• w•• •••o•• •• ••in• MWB 3.1•• •• nnin• •n••• Win•ow• XP P•o•••ion•l o••••in• •y•••• on • •.• • H• P•n•i•• P• wi•• 51•MB o• • AM.

```
The Mobility Workbench
(MWB'97, polyadic version 3.122, built Mon Apr 21 23:02:07 2003)

MWB>input "inheritance\statecharts_of_C1_C2.pi"
MWB>weqd \
(step,event_S,e_1,e_2,e_3,e_4,e_5,e_6,cond_1,ins_o) \
S_1_C2(step,event_S,e_1,e_2,e_3,e_4,e_5,e_6,cond_1, \
       ins_o) \
((^e_7)(^e_8)(^e_9)(^e_10)(^pos)(^neg) \
S_1_C1(step,event_S,e_1,e_2,e_3,e_4,e_5,e_6,e_7,e_8, \
       e_9,e_10,cond_1,ins_o,pos,neg))
The two agents are related.
Relation size = 19.
```

Fig. 4. Consistency checking of statechart diagrams

7   Conclusions

• n•• •in• ••• •on•i••n•y o•• o••l• i• • non-••ivi•l ••• ll•n•• •o• ••• •o••w••• •n- •in•••in• ••l•. T•i• ••••••••• •x•• in•• ••• •on•••• •••••i•••• ili•y o• o• j••••, •••••i•• •••• ili•y o• ••••••••••• •i••••• • •n• •••• •vio••l •on•i••n•y o• ••••••••• •i•••••• •. W• ••v• ••••n••• • n•w •l••••i• • •••o• olo•y •o• v••i•yin• w•••••• ••• •••••••••• •i••••• • o• •l••••• lin••• wi•• • ••n•••li••ion ••l••ion•• i• ••• •on•i••n•. T•• •••••••••• •i••••• •••• •n•o••• in ••• π-••l••l•• •n• ••• •on- •i•••n•y o• ••• ••••••••••• •i••••• • i• v••i•• ••in• ••• MWB. W• ••v• •l•n• •o •x••n• ••• • ••• o• olo•y •o• ••••• in• ••• •••••••v••ion o• •on•i•••n•y • ••w••n • iff•••n• •y••• o• UML • o••l•.

References

1. P. Wegner and S.B. Zdonik. Inheritance as an incremental modification mechanism or what like is and isn't like. In *ECOOP '88*, LNCS 322, pages 55–77, 1988.
2. OMG. OMG Unified Modeling Language specification version 1.5, March 2003. http://www.omg.org; accessed January 20, 2005.
3. R. Milner, J. Parrow, and D. Walker. A calculus of mobile process (Parts I and II). *Information and Computation*, 100:1–77, 1992.
4. R. Milner. The polyadic π-calculus: A tutorial. In *Logic and Algebra of Specification, Proceedings of International NATO Summer School*, volume 94, pages 203–246. Springer-Verlag, 1993.
5. B. Victor and F. Moller. The mobility workbench: A tool for the π-calculus. In *CAV '94*, LNCS 818, pages 428–440, 1994.
6. B. Victor. *A Verification Tool for the Polyadic π-Calculus*. Department of Computer Systems, Uppsala University, 1994. Licentiate thesis.
7. J.L. Sourrouille. UML behaviour: Inheritance and implementation in current object-oriented languages. In *UML '99*, LNCS 1723, pages 457–472, 1999.
8. D. Harel and O. Kupferman. On the behavioral inheritance of state-based objects. In *TOOLS 34*, pages 83–94. IEEE Computer Society, 2000.
9. M. Stumptner and M. Schrefl. Behaviour consistent inheritance in UML. In *ER2000*, LNCS 1920, pages 527–542, 2000.
10. G. Engels, R. Heckel, and J.M. Küster. Rule-based specification of behavioural consistency based on the UML meta-model. In *UML 2001*, LNCS 2185, pages 272–286, 2001.
11. V.S.W. Lam and J. Padget. Analyzing equivalences of UML statechart diagrams by structural congruence and open bisimulations. In *Proceedings of 2003 IEEE Symposium on Human Centric Computing Languages and Environments*, pages 137–144. IEEE Computer Society, 2003.
12. V.S.W. Lam and J. Padget. Symbolic model checking of UML statechart diagrams with an integrated approach. In *Proceedings of Eleventh IEEE International Conference and Workshop on the Engineering of Computer-Based Systems*, pages 337–346. IEEE Computer Society, 2004.
13. V.S.W. Lam and J. Padget. Formal specification and verification of the SET/A protocol with an integrated approach. In *Proceedings of 2004 IEEE International Conference on E-Commerce Technology*, pages 229–235. IEEE Computer Society, 2004.
14. G. Engels, J.M. Küster, R. Heckel, and L. Groenewegen. A methodology for specifying and analyzing consistency of object-oriented behavioral models. In *ESEC/SIGSOFT FSE*, pages 186–195. ACM Press, 2001.
15. G. Engels, J.M. Küster, R. Heckel, and L. Groenewegen. Towards consistency-preserving model evolution. In *Proceedings of the International Workshop on Principles of Software Evolution*, pages 129–132. ACM Press, 2002.
16. G. Engels, R. Heckel, J.M. Küster, and L. Groenewegen. Consistency-preserving model evolution through transformations. In *UML 2002*, LNCS 2460, pages 212–226, 2002.
17. J. Davies and C. Crichton. Concurrency and refinement in the Unified Modeling Language. *Formal Aspects of Computing*, 15(2–3):118–145, 2003.
18. R. Milner. *Communicating and Mobile Systems: the π-Calculus*. Cambridge University Press, 1999.

19. J. Parrow. An introduction to the π-calculus. In A. Bergstra, J.A. Ponse and S.A. Smolka, editors, *Handbook of Process Algebra*, chapter 8, pages 479–543. Elsevier Science, 2001.
20. V.S.W. Lam and J. Padget. On execution semantics of UML statechart diagrams using the π-calculus. In *Proceedings of the International Conference on Software Engineering Research and Practice*, pages 877–882. CSREA Press, 2003.
21. OMG. OMG Unified Modeling Language specification version 1.5, March 2003. http://www.omg.org; accessed January 20, 2005.
22. OMG. UML 2.0 superstructure specification, August 2003. http://www.omg.org; accessed January 20, 2005.
23. J. Ebert and G. Engels. Structural and behavioural views on OMT-classes. In *Object-Oriented Methodologies and Systems*, LNCS 858, pages 142–157, 1994.
24. D. Sangiorgi. A theory of bisimulation for the π-calculus. In *CONCUR '93*, LNCS 715, pages 127–142, 1993.
25. P. Quaglia. The π-calculus: Notes on labelled semantics. *Bulletin of the EATCS*, 68, June 1999.

Towards Type Inference for JavaScript[*]

Christopher Anderson[1], Paola Giannini[2], and Sophia Drossopoulou[1]

[1] Department of Computing, Imperial College London,
180 Queen's Gate, London SW7 2BZ, U.K
[2] Dipartimento di Informatica,
Università del Piemonte Orientale,
Via Bellini 25/G, Alessandria, Italy

Abstract. Object-oriented scripting languages like JavaScript and Python are popular partly because of their dynamic features. These include the runtime modification of objects and classes through addition of fields or updating of methods. These features make static typing difficult and so usually dynamic typing is used. Consequently, errors such as access to non-existent members are not detected until runtime.

We first develop a formalism for an object based language, JS_0, with features from JavaScript, including dynamic addition of fields and updating of methods. We give an operational semantics and static type system for JS_0 using structural types. Our types allow objects to evolve in a controlled manner by classifying members as *definite* or *potential*.

We define a type inference algorithm for JS_0 that is sound with respect to the type system. If the type inference algorithm succeeds, then the program is typeable. Therefore, programmers can benefit from the safety offered by the type system, without the need to write explicitly types in their programs.

1 Introduction

The popularity of scripting languages stems from the flexible programming features they support. These include the runtime modification of objects through addition of fields or updating of methods. These features make static typing difficult and so usually dynamic typing is used. Consequently, errors such as access to non-existent members are not detected until runtime, or, as in JavaScript, not detected at all which can result in a web browser reporting an error when viewing a web page containing JavaScript code.

We introduce JS_0, a formalism of JavaScript[16]. JS_0 supports the standard JavaScript flexible features, e.g. functions creating objects, and dynamic addition/reassignment of fields and methods. We also introduce $JS_0^\top$, an explicitly typed version of JS_0. Types in $JS_0^\top$ comprise object types, function types, and

---

[*] Work partly supported by EU within the FET - Global Computing initiative, project DART IST-2001-33477,MURST Cofin'02 project McTati, and MIUR Prin'04 project EOS

A.P. Black (Ed.): ECOOP 2005, LNCS 3586, pp. 428–452, 2005.

Int (the type of integers). Object types list the methods and fields present in the object, $\mu\,\alpha.[m_1 : (t_1, \psi_1) \cdots m_n : (t_n, \psi_n)]$. We use the μ-binder to allow a type to refer to itself. Our type system permits objects to evolve in a controlled manner by allowing members to be added to an object after it has been created. This is achieved by annotating with ψ, each member of an object type as either *potential* '○' or *definite* '●'.

Function types have the form, $t = \mu\,\alpha.(O \times t_1 \rightarrow t_2)$, where O is the type of the receiver, t_1 is the type of the formal parameter and t_2 is the return type. As for object types, the bound variable α allows references to t within O, t_1, and t_2. Thus, $\mu\,\alpha.(\_ \times \_ \rightarrow \alpha)$ is a function that returns a value of the same type as the function itself.

A function can be used as a *global function* if its type does not make any requirements of its receiver. The type system is rich enough to allow typing of many JavaScript programs, and at the same time prevents runtime errors such as access to non-existing members of objects.

We develop a sound type inference algorithm to automatically translate JS_0 code to $JS_0^\top$ code. The algorithm uses *type variables* which represent the type of expressions. Constraints are generated between the type variables. If there is a solution to the constraints this can be used to translate code from JS_0 to $JS_0^\top$. We define a translation between constraints and types that provides the types for the typed version of the code.

In [6] we introduced the language JS_0 and its type system. In this paper we have simplified the presentation of $JS_0^\top$ and its type system and defined a sound type inference algorithm.

This paper is organized as follows. In Section 2 we define the syntax of JS_0 and its operational semantics, and in Section 3 we give $JS_0^\top$. Properties of the type system for $JS_0^\top$ are outlined in Section 4. In Section 5 we show type inference for JS_0, and in Section 6 we show how to turn constraints into types. In Section 7 we compare our work with others. In Section 8 we draw conclusions and outline our future directions. The proofs and a prototype implementation can be found at http://www.binarylord.com/work/js0/.

2 JS_0

We have developed JS_0 a subset of JavaScript. Figure 1 gives an example JS_0 program that describes an implementation of the JavaScript Date object[1]. We define functions Date and addFn. The code preceded by the comment //Main is the entry point into the program. Although the syntax of JS_0 requires all code to be within a function body to aid presentation we allow a main body of code and the declaration of local variables x and y. The example demonstrates the *core* JavaScript features we have included:

---

[1] For more information on the Date object see [15]. We give a simplified version and allow the adding of one date to another, with add.

```
1  function Date(x) {
2    this.mSec = x;
3    this.add = addFn;
4    this
5  }
6  function addFn(x) {
7    this.mSec = this.mSec + x.mSec; this
8  }
9  //Main
10 x = new Date(1000);
11 y = new Date(100);
12 x.add(y);
```

Fig. 1. Untyped JS_0 Date Example

1. creating objects using functions (line 10 and 11),
2. implicit creation of members in objects through assignment (lines 2 and 3), and
3. acquiring methods through assignment of a function to a member (line 3).

We chose these features because, (1) represents the way objects are created in JavaScript, (2) and (3) represent the way objects acquire fields and methods thus giving flexibility to the programmer. JS_0 does not include the following JavaScript features: member names as strings, functions as expressions, dynamic removal of members, automatic conversions, and delegation. We omitted the first three as we believe they are not essential in supporting flexible object-oriented programming. The last two while useful can complicate static typing and type inference. We can write the introductory examples from [15] in JS_0 assuming libraries of functions, and predefined types *e.g.* floats, strings, etc.

The syntax of JS_0 is given in Figure 2. Note that, in the syntax of JS_0 we omitted conditional expressions, which were present in [6]. Their presence does not produce conceptual difficulties regarding the type system and type inference. A program is a sequence of function declarations. In JS_0 functions may have only one formal parameter. The extension to functions with multiple parameters is trivial, whereas going to a variable number of parameters, as in JavaScript, is an interesting possible future extension.

For a program P, we use $P(f)$ as a shorthand for looking up the definition of function f in P.

2.1   Operational Semantics

We give a structural operational semantics for JS_0 that rewrites tuples of expressions, heaps and stacks into tuples of values, heaps and stacks in the context of a program. The signature of the rewriting relation $\twoheadrightarrow$ is:

$$\twoheadrightarrow \; : \; Program \; \rightarrow \; Exp \; \times \; Heap \; \times \; Stack \rightarrow (Val \cup Dev) \times \; Heap \times \; Stack$$

$$
\begin{array}{lll}
\mathsf{P} \in \textit{Program} & ::= \mathsf{F}^* & \\
\mathsf{F} \in \textit{FuncDecl} & ::= \texttt{function f (x) \{ e \}} & \\
\mathsf{e} \in \textit{Exp} & ::= \texttt{var} & \text{locals} \\
& \quad\; \texttt{f} & \text{function identifier} \\
& \quad\; \texttt{new f(e)} & \text{object creation} \\
& \quad\; \texttt{e; e} & \text{sequence} \\
& \quad\; \texttt{e.m(e)} & \text{member call} \\
& \quad\; \texttt{e.m} & \text{member select} \\
& \quad\; \texttt{f(e)} & \text{global call} \\
& \quad\; \texttt{lhs = e} & \text{assignment} \\
& \quad\; \texttt{null} & \text{null} \\
& \quad\; \texttt{n} & \text{integer} \\
\texttt{var} \in \textit{EnvVars} & ::= \texttt{this} \mid \texttt{x} & \\
\texttt{lhs} \in \textit{LeftHandSide} & ::= \texttt{x} \mid \texttt{e.m} & \\
\end{array}
$$

Identifiers

$$
\begin{array}{ll}
\mathsf{f} \in \textit{FuncID} & ::= \mathsf{f} \mid \mathsf{f}' \mid \ldots \\
\mathsf{m} \in \textit{MemberID} & ::= \mathsf{m} \mid \mathsf{m}' \mid \ldots \\
\end{array}
$$

Fig. 2. Syntax of JS_0

where:

$$
\begin{array}{lll}
\mathsf{H} \in \textit{Heap} = \textit{Addr} \to_{\text{fin}} \textit{Obj} \\
\chi \in \textit{Stack} = \{\texttt{this}, \texttt{x}\} \to \textit{Val} \quad \text{such that} \quad \chi(\texttt{this}) \in \textit{Addr} \\
\mathsf{v} \in \textit{Val} \; = \{\texttt{null}\} \cup \textit{FuncID} \cup \textit{Addr} \cup \textit{Int} \\
\mathsf{dv} \in \textit{Dev} = \{\texttt{nullPntrExc}, \texttt{stuckErr}\} \\
\mathsf{o} \in \textit{Obj} \; = \textit{MemberID} \to_{\text{fin}} \textit{Val} \\
\end{array}
$$

The heap maps addresses to objects, where addresses, *Addr*, are $\iota_0, ..\iota_n...$ We use $\to_{\text{fin}}$ to indicate a finite mapping. As usual, the notation $\mathsf{f}[\mathsf{x} \mapsto \mathsf{y}]$ denotes updating function f to map x to y. Thus, the meaning of heap update $\mathsf{H}[\iota \mapsto \mathsf{v}]$ and stack update $\chi[\mathsf{x} \mapsto \mathsf{v}]$ is clear. The stack maps this to an address and x to a value, where values, *Val*, are function identifiers (denoting functions), addresses (denoting objects), null , or integers. Finally objects are finite mappings from member identifiers to values. With $\ll \mathsf{m}_1 : \mathsf{v}_1 ... \mathsf{m}_n : \mathsf{v}_n \gg$ we denote the object mapping m_i to v_i for $i \in 1 \cdots n$.

A full description of the rules is given in [6]. In JavaScript access to non-existent members result in an undefined value not a runtime error[2]. This may cause errors later on in the code. We consider accesses to non-existent members a runtime error and our type system prevents them. Below we give two of the

---

[2] For some interesting insights into issues surrounding JavaScript's treatment of undefined members see [24].

more interesting rules, $(memAdd)$ for adding/updating members and $(memCall)$ for calling methods:

$$\frac{\begin{array}{c}e_1, H, \chi \twoheadrightarrow \iota, H_1, \chi_1 \\ e_2, H_1, \chi_1 \twoheadrightarrow v, H_2, \chi' \\ H' = H_2[\iota \mapsto H_2(\iota)[m \mapsto v]]\end{array}}{e_1.m = e_2, H, \chi \twoheadrightarrow v, H', \chi'} \ (memAdd) \qquad \frac{\begin{array}{c}e_1, H, \chi \twoheadrightarrow \iota, H_1, \chi_1 \\ e_2, H_1, \chi_1 \twoheadrightarrow v', H_2, \chi' \\ H_2(\iota)(m) = f \\ P(f) = \texttt{function } f(x) \ \{e'\} \\ \chi_2 = \{\texttt{this} \mapsto \iota, x \mapsto v'\} \\ e', H_2, \chi_2 \twoheadrightarrow v, H', \chi''\end{array}}{e_1.m(e_2), H, \chi \twoheadrightarrow v, H', \chi'} \ (memCall)$$

In rule $(memAdd)$ we express how objects obtain new members. We first evaluate the receiver, then the right hand side. Using heap update we add/update member m in the receiver. Returning to the example in Figure 1, executing $\texttt{this.mSec} = x$ from Date with $\chi_0(\texttt{this}) = \iota_0, \chi_0(x) = 1000, H_0(\iota_0) = \texttt{«»}$, will produce H_1 with $H_1(\iota_0) = \texttt{«mSec} : 1000\texttt{»}$

In rule $(memCall)$ we first evaluate the receiver and then the actual parameter of the method. We obtain the function definition (corresponding to the method) by looking up the value of member m in the receiver (obtained by evaluation of e) in P[3]. We execute the body with a stack in which this refers to the receiver of the call and x to the value of the actual parameter.

For example, executing the code in Figure 1 in the presence of an empty heap, H_0 and χ_0, mapping x and y to null will result in stack $\chi_1(x) = \iota_0, \chi_1(y) = \iota_1$ and updated heap H_1, $H_1(\iota_0) = \texttt{«mSec} : 1100, \texttt{add} : \texttt{addFn»}, H_1(\iota_1) = \texttt{«mSec} : 100, \texttt{add} : \texttt{addFn»}$. For demonstration purposes the stack contains an extra variable y although the definition of stack allows only this and x.

Note that member add of both ι_0 and ι_1 has value addFn. This indicates that it is an alias of function addFn, which is invoked when $\texttt{x.add(y)}$ is executed.

3   A Type System for JS_0

In this section we introduce $JS_0^\top$ a typed version of JS_0. Figure 3 shows the parts of $JS_0^\top$ that differ from JS_0 along with the definitions of types. Observe that functions are now annotated with a function type G.

Types $t_1, ..., t_n$, comprise object types, function types, or Int (the type of integers). Object types list the methods and fields present in the object. We use the μ-binder to allow a type to refer to itself. So $\mu\ \alpha.M$ where $M = [m_1 : (t_1, \psi_1) \cdots m_n : (t_n, \psi_n)]$, is the type of an object with members $m_1, ..., m_n$ of type $t_1, ..., t_n$, respectively. Figure 4 gives a $JS_0^\top$ version of the Date example from Figure 1. We use t_1 for type $[\texttt{mSec} : (\texttt{Int}, \circ), \texttt{add} : ((t_2 \times t_2 \to t_2), \circ)]$ and t_2 for type $\mu\ \alpha.[\texttt{mSec} : (\texttt{Int}, \bullet), \texttt{add} : ((\alpha \times \alpha \to \alpha), \bullet)]$. To aid the presentation we allow local variable type declarations on lines 10 and 11. These are not part of the syntax of $JS_0^\top$, where type declarations are only allowed for the

---

[3] For clearness of presentation we omit P from the reduction rules.

Syntax

$$P \in Program \qquad ::= F^*$$
$$F \in FuncDecl \qquad ::= \text{function } f(x) : G \ \{ \ e \ \}$$

Types

$$t \in Type \qquad \quad ::= O \ | \ G \ | \ \text{Int}$$
$$tp \in PreType \qquad ::= \alpha \ | \ t$$
$$O \in ObjType \qquad ::= \mu \ \alpha.M \ | \ M$$
$$G \in FuncType \qquad ::= \mu \ \alpha.R \ | \ R$$
$$M \in ObjMembers \ ::= [(m : tm)^*]$$
$$tm \in MemberType ::= (tp, \psi)$$
$$R \in FuncRow \qquad ::= (O \times tp \rightarrow tp)$$

$$\psi \ \in Annotation \ ::= \circ \quad | \ \bullet$$
$$\alpha \in ObjVar \qquad ::= \alpha \ | \ \alpha' \ | \ \alpha'' \ \dots$$

Fig. 3. Syntax of $JS_0^\top$

parameter of a method and `this` and are implicitly given in the function type for a function.

```
1  function Date(x):(t₁ × Int → t₂) {
2    this.mSec = x;
3    this.add = addFn;
4    this
5  }
6  function addFn(x):(t₂ × t₂ → t₂) {
7    this.mSec = this.mSec + x.mSec; this;
8  }
9  //Main
10 t₂ x = new Date(1000);
11 t₂ y = new Date(100);
12 x.add(y);
```

Fig. 4. Typed JS_0 Date Example.

Our type system permits objects to evolve in a controlled manner by allowing members to be added to an object after it has been created. This is achieved by annotating each member of an object type as either *potential* '$\circ$' or *definite* '$\bullet$' e.g. mSec : (Int, $\circ$) in t_1 and mSec : (Int, $\bullet$) in t_2. When a potential member is assigned to, it becomes definite, replacing ○ with •. To keep the type system manageable we only track assignments to variables (formal parameters and this) within the scope of a function. In a well-typed program potential members may not be accessed until they have been assigned to.

Function types, $(O \times t_1 \to t_2)$ or $\mu\, \alpha.(O \times t_1 \to t_2)$, list the type of the receiver, O, which is an object type, the type of the parameter, t_1, and the type of the return value of the function, t_2. As for object types the μ-binder allows a function type to refer to itself, thus $\mu\, \alpha.(\_ \times \_ \to \alpha)$ is a function that returns a function with its type.

If the type of m is an object type, or Int, the member represents a field. If the type of m is a function type, then m represents a method. In case the type of the m is α then if α is bound in an objects type the member is a field, whereas if it is bound in a function type it is a method. An object type is well-formed if it is closed and contains unique member definitions that are themselves well-formed. A function type $G = \mu\, \alpha.R$ (or $G = R$) is well-formed, $\vdash G \diamond$, if the receiver, parameter and return types of $G[\alpha/R]$ (or R) are well-formed.

For a well-formed object type O, define $O(m)$, which selects the annotated type of the member m in O (if it is defined) by first defining selection from $O = [m_1 : (t_1, \psi_1) \cdots m_n : (t_n, \psi_n)]$ as

$$O(m) = \begin{cases} (t_i, \psi_i) & \text{if } m = m_i \text{ for some } i, 1 \le i \le n \\ \mathcal{U}df & \text{otherwise} \end{cases}$$

and then if $O = \mu\, \alpha.M$,

$$O(m) = M[\alpha/O](m)$$

That is, the type is closed by substituting occurrences of α with the enclosing type. Therefore, if O is well-formed, then also $O(m)$ is well-formed.

With $O[m \mapsto (t, \psi)]$ we denote the *updating of the member* m *to type* t *with annotation* ψ *in* O. Note that, if O and t are well-formed, then $O[m \mapsto (t, \psi)]$ is well-formed.

Congruence and Subtyping

Congruence between types is defined in Figure 5. With $t_1[\alpha/t_2]$, we denote the substitution of the free occurrences of α in t_1 with t_2. Object types are congruent up to α-conversion, permutation of their members, and unfolding of the bound variable, and function types are congruent up to α-conversion, and unfolding of the bound variable.

The *subtyping* judgement $t \le t'$, defined in Figure 6, means that an object or function of type t can be used whenever one of type t' is required. For object types we have subtyping in width. If $O \le O'$, then all definite members of O' must be present and congruent with those in O, and all potential members of O' must be present as potential or definite members of O with congruent types. This condition is needed to insure that the addition of a new member to an object does not break compatibility.

Returning to the example in Figure 4 we see that t_2 is a subtype of t_1 because all members of t_1 are also members of t_2, and have congruent types; furthermore, all members of t_2 are definite.

Reflexivity	Unfolding		Transitivity

$$t \equiv t \qquad \dfrac{}{\mu\,\alpha.M \equiv M[\alpha/\mu\,\alpha.M]} \qquad \dfrac{t_1 \equiv t_2 \quad t_2 \equiv t_3}{t_1 \equiv t_3}$$
$$\mu\,\alpha.R \equiv R[\alpha/\mu\,\alpha.R]$$

Alpha – conversion

$$\dfrac{\alpha' \notin \mathcal{FV}(M)}{\mu\,\alpha.M \equiv \mu\,\alpha'.M[\alpha/\alpha']} \qquad\qquad \dfrac{\alpha' \notin \mathcal{FV}(R)}{\mu\,\alpha.R \equiv \mu\,\alpha'.R[\alpha/\alpha']}$$

Reordering **Functions** **Members**

$$\dfrac{\forall m \; : \; M(m) \equiv M'(m)}{M \equiv M'} \qquad \dfrac{M \equiv M' \;\; t_1 \equiv t_1' \;\; t_2 \equiv t_2'}{(M \times t_1 \to t_2) \equiv (M' \times t_1' \to t_2')} \qquad \dfrac{t \equiv t'}{(t,\psi) \equiv (t',\psi)}$$

Fig. 5. Congruence for types

For function types subtyping coincides with congruence. In future versions of this work we may relax this restriction and allow contravariance of the receiver and parameter type and covariance of the return type. However, since type inference was our main aim, we started with the reduced system. Given types t and t' it is decidable whether $t \le t'$ or not.

$$\dfrac{\psi' = \bullet \;\; \Longrightarrow \;\; \psi = \bullet}{\psi \le \psi'} \qquad \dfrac{\begin{array}{c} t \equiv t' \\ \psi \le \psi' \end{array}}{(t,\psi) \le (t',\psi')} \qquad \dfrac{t \equiv t'}{t \le t'}$$

$$\dfrac{\forall m \; : \; O'(m) = (t',\psi') \;\; \Longrightarrow \;\; (O(m) = (t,\psi) \;\wedge\; (t,\psi) \le (t',\psi'))}{O \le O'}$$

Fig. 6. Subtyping

3.1 Typing Expressions

Typing expression e in the context of program P, and environment Γ has form:

$$P, \Gamma \vdash e : t \parallel \Gamma'$$

The environment, $\Gamma = \{\text{this} : O, x : t\}$, maps the receiver, this, to a well-formed object type, and the formal parameter, x, to a well-formed type. The environment on the right hand side of the judgement, Γ', reflects the changes to the type of the receiver or parameter while typing the expression. The only possible difference between Γ and Γ' is that some members that are annotated with $\circ$ in Γ are annotated with $\bullet$ in Γ'. With $\Gamma[\text{var} \mapsto t]$ we denote the *updating of* var *to type* t *in* Γ.

Consider the typing rules of Figure 7. Rules (var), $(func)$, $(const)$, and (seq) are straightforward. Note that null may have any object type.

In rule $(memAcc)$ the expression e must be of an object type in which the member m is definite, i.e. with annotation $\bullet$.

We use the notation $G(\text{this})$, $G(\text{x})$, and $G(\text{ret})$, to denote the types of the receiver, parameter and return value of G. As for member selection, we define for $G = (O \times t_1 \to t_2) : G(\text{this}) = O \qquad G(\text{x}) = t_1 \qquad G(\text{ret}) = t_2$ and for $G = \mu\,\alpha.R$, we define $G(\text{z}) = (R[\alpha/G])(\text{z})$ where $\text{z} \in \{\text{x}, \text{this}, \text{ret}\}$.

Rule $(methCall)$ checks that the type of the receiver is an object type in which the member m has a definite function type. Moreover, the type of the receiver and actual parameter must be subtypes of the declared type of the receiver and formal parameter.

In $(call)$ we consider global calls and constructors, and require that the type of the receiver defined in the function has no definite members. This is consistent with the operational semantics, as in the case of global call and object creation we start with an empty receiver object.

In rule $(assignAdd)$ in Γ'' we ensure that member m (of this or the formal parameter) is definite. From this point onwards, member m of var may be accessed. For example, consider the expression $\text{x.m}_2 = \text{x}$ in the environment Γ, where $\Gamma(\text{x})$ has type $t = \mu\,\alpha.[\text{m}_1 : (\text{Int}, \bullet), \text{m}_2 : (\alpha, \circ)]$. The expression is well-typed in Γ and we have $P, \Gamma \vdash \text{x.m}_2 = \text{x} : t \parallel \Gamma'$ where Γ' maps this to $\Gamma(\text{this})$ and x to $[\text{m}_1 : (\text{Int}, \bullet), \text{m}_2 : (t, \bullet)]$. This reflects the updating of member m_2. Any aliases to this or the formal parameter will not *see* the update of a member. This would require dataflow analysis techniques and is beyond the scope of this work. The fact that the type system requires a member to be *known* (either as potential or definite) for an assignment to succeed is not a limitation. The process of type inference will find all members for a type with their appropriate type and annotation.

Rule $(assignUpd)$ is used when the assignment is to a definite member m. In this case we just check that the type of the expression on the right hand side is a subtype of the type of the member m.

A program P is *well-formed* if all the function declarations in P are well-typed. Figure 7 gives the definition.

4   Formal Properties of the Type System

In this section we give the relevant definitions and the statement that asserts that our type system is sound w.r.t. to the operational semantics given in Section

Typing Expressions

$$\frac{}{\begin{array}{l}P, \Gamma \vdash \text{this} : \Gamma(\text{this}) \parallel \Gamma \\ P, \Gamma \vdash x : \Gamma(x) \parallel \Gamma\end{array}} \ (var)$$

$$\frac{P(f) = \text{function } f(x) : G...}{P, \Gamma \vdash f : G \parallel \Gamma} \ (func)$$

$$\frac{}{\begin{array}{l}P, \Gamma \vdash \text{null} : O \parallel \Gamma \\ P, \Gamma \vdash n : \text{Int} \parallel \Gamma\end{array}} \ (const)$$

$$\frac{\begin{array}{l}P, \Gamma \vdash e_1 : t \parallel \Gamma' \\ P, \Gamma' \vdash e_2 : t' \parallel \Gamma''\end{array}}{P, \Gamma \vdash e_1 ; e_2 : t' \parallel \Gamma''} \ (seq)$$

$$\frac{\begin{array}{l}P, \Gamma \vdash e : O \parallel \Gamma' \\ O(m) = (t', \bullet)\end{array}}{P, \Gamma \vdash e.m : t' \parallel \Gamma'} \ (memAcc)$$

$$\frac{\begin{array}{l}P, \Gamma \vdash e : t \parallel \Gamma' \\ t \leq \Gamma'(x)\end{array}}{P, \Gamma \vdash x = e : t \parallel \Gamma'} \ (varAss)$$

$$\frac{\begin{array}{l}P, \Gamma \vdash e_1 : O \parallel \Gamma' \\ O(m) = (G, \bullet) \\ P, \Gamma' \vdash e_2 : t' \parallel \Gamma'' \\ t' \leq G(x) \\ O \leq G(\text{this})\end{array}}{P, \Gamma \vdash e_1.m(e_2) : G(\text{ret}) \parallel \Gamma''} \ (methCall)$$

$$\frac{\begin{array}{l}P, \Gamma \vdash e : t \parallel \Gamma' \\ P(f) = \text{function } f(x) : G... \\ t \leq G(x) \\ \{t' \mid (G(\text{this}))(m) = (t', \bullet)\} = \emptyset\end{array}}{\begin{array}{l}P, \Gamma \vdash \text{new } f(e) : G(\text{ret}) \parallel \Gamma' \\ P, \Gamma \vdash f(e) : G(\text{ret}) \parallel \Gamma'\end{array}} \ (call)$$

$$\frac{\begin{array}{l}P, \Gamma \vdash e_2 : t \parallel \Gamma' \\ \Gamma'(var) = O \\ O(m) = (t'', \psi) \\ t \leq t'' \\ \Gamma'' = \Gamma'[var \mapsto O[m \mapsto (t'', \bullet)]]\end{array}}{P, \Gamma \vdash var.m = e_2 : t \parallel \Gamma''} \ (assignAdd)$$

$$\frac{\begin{array}{l}P, \Gamma \vdash e_1 : O \parallel \Gamma' \\ P, \Gamma' \vdash e_2 : t \parallel \Gamma'' \\ O(m) = (t'', \bullet) \\ t \leq t''\end{array}}{P, \Gamma \vdash e_1.m = e_2 : t \parallel \Gamma''} \ (assignUpd)$$

Well − formed Programs

$$\forall f : \quad P(f) = \text{function } f(x) : G \ \{e\} \ \wedge \ \vdash G \diamond$$
$$\implies P, \{ \text{ this} : G(\text{this}), x : G(x) \ \} \vdash e : t \parallel \Gamma'' \ \wedge \ t \leq G(\text{ret})$$

$$\frac{}{\vdash P\diamond}$$

Fig. 7. Type Rules for Expressions in $JS_0^\top$

2.1. We assume that types are well-formed. We first define the notion of a value being compatible with a given type. The definition is given co-inductively by first defining the properties that any agreement relation between values and well-formed types should have.

Definition 1. *Given a heap,* H, *and a program,* P, *we say that* $A \subseteq (Val \times Type)$ *is an* agreement relation *if the following conditions are satisfied:*

- *if* $(\texttt{null}, t) \in A$, *then* $t = O$ *for some well-formed* O,
- *if* $(\texttt{n}, t) \in A$, *then* $t = \texttt{Int}$,
- *if* $(\texttt{f}, t) \in A$, *then* $P(\texttt{f}) = \texttt{function } \texttt{f}(\texttt{x}) : G$ *and* $G \equiv t$,
- *if* $(\iota, t) \in A$, *then*
  $t = O$ *for some well-formed* O, $H(\iota) = \langle\!\langle m_1 : v_1 \ldots m_p : v_p \rangle\!\rangle$, *and*
  - $O(\texttt{m}) = (t', \bullet) \implies m = m_i$ *for some* i, $i \in 1...p$, *and* $(v_i, t') \in A$
  - $O(\texttt{m}) = (t', \circ)$ *and* $m = m_i$ *for some* i, $i \in 1...p$, $\implies (v_i, t') \in A$

If A and A' are agreement relations, then $A \cup A'$ is also an agreement relation. Therefore, the union of all agreement relations defines a relation between values and types, which determines when a value has a given type.

Definition 2. Value v is compatible with type t in H

$$P, H \vdash v \blacktriangleleft t$$

if $(v, t) \in A$ *for some agreement relation* A *on* H *and* P.

Note that an address may be compatible with more than one type. In particular, a value compatible with a type is compatible with all its supertypes.

Lemma 1. *If* $t \leq t'$ *and* $P, H \vdash v \blacktriangleleft t$ *then* $P, H \vdash v \blacktriangleleft t'$.

In the following we define when *a stack* χ *and a heap* H *are compatible with an environment* Γ.

Definition 3. $P, \Gamma \vdash H, \chi \diamond$ *holds if* $P, H \vdash \chi(\texttt{this}) \blacktriangleleft \Gamma(\texttt{this})$ *and* $P, H \vdash \chi(\texttt{x}) \blacktriangleleft \Gamma(\texttt{x})$.

We can now state the Soundness Theorem. The theorem asserts that if an expression is well-typed,

$$P, \Gamma \vdash e : t \parallel \Gamma'$$

then the evaluation of the expression starting in a heap and stack that are compatible with Γ will not get stuck. That is, the result of the evaluation is either a value compatible with type t, or it is a nullPntrExc exception. In particular, it is not a stuckErr error. Moreover, the stack and heap produced are compatible with the final environment Γ'.

Theorem 1. *[Type Soundness] For a well-formed program* P*, environment* Γ*, and expression* e*, such that:*

$$P, \Gamma \vdash e : t \parallel \Gamma'$$

If $P, \Gamma \vdash H, \chi \diamond$ *and* $e, H, \chi \twoheadrightarrow w, H', \chi'$, *then either*

- $w = \texttt{nullPntrExc}$, *or*
- $w = v$, $P, H' \vdash v \blacktriangleleft t$, *and* $P, \Gamma' \vdash H', \chi' \diamond$.

5   Type Inference

We show how type inference for JS_0 can be expressed as a finite system of constraints between type variables. Type variables are used to represent the type of an expression. From a JS_0 program, we can generate a set of type variables with constraints between them. Constraints represent the relationships we expect between types in the program. For example, that the actual parameter to a function call should be a subtype of the formal parameter.

If the constraints have a solution we say that they are satisfiable. A solution can be used to translate a JS_0 program into an equivalent $JS_0^{\top}$ program. This involves annotating the JS_0 program with type declarations. We show that the annotated program is well-typed.

5.1   Type Variables

As in [20,3,21,18], we use type variables to express the - yet unknown - types of expressions. Thus, $[\![new\ Date(1000)]\!]$ expresses the type of new Date(1000).

Because the types of this and x differ for different occurrences in the same method body, we use labels to distinguish them, for example, $[\![this\_1]\!]$, $[\![x\_2]\!]$, $[\![this\_3]\!]$, etc.. Labeled type variables[4] $[\![this\_f]\!]$ and $[\![x\_f]\!]$ represent the type of this and x at the beginning of the function f, and $[\![ret\_f]\!]$ represents the return type of the function.

We generate a new label for each method call; this label is used to generate three type variables. These variables denote the type of the receiver, parameter and return type of the method. For example, for x.add(y) we could use label 5 which would generate $[\![call\_this\_5]\!]$, $[\![call\_x\_5]\!]$, and $[\![call\_ret\_5]\!]$. Note that these type variables depend on the label but not on the name of the method.[5] Figure 8 gives the syntax of labeled expressions.

Figure 9 defines type variables. Type variables can be used to describe function types, e.g. $(\tau \times \tau' \to \tau'')$, or object types, e.g. $[m:(\tau,\psi)]$ with the obvious meaning.

5.2   Constraints and Solutions

A solution, S, is a mapping from type variables to types. For the Date example, let t_2 be $\mu\ \alpha.[mSec : (Int, \bullet),\ add : ((\alpha \times \alpha \to \alpha), \bullet)]$, S_0 represents part of a solution, as follows:

$$S_0([\![this\_Date]\!]) = [mSec : (Int, \circ),\ add : ((t_2 \times t_2 \to t_2), \circ)]$$
$$S_0([\![this\_1]\!]) = [mSec : (Int, \bullet),\ add : ((t_2 \times t_2 \to t_2), \circ)]$$
$$S_0([\![ret\_Date]\!]) = t_2 \quad S_0([\![x\_Date]\!]) = Int$$
$$S_0([\![this\_Date.mSec]\!]) = Int \quad S_0([\![this\_5]\!]) = [mSec : (Int, \bullet)]$$

---

[4] In [3] Agesen et al. use a similar labeling, $[\![e]\!]_\tau$, to indicate who the sender, τ, of a method call is.

[5] It is possible to optimize the creation of new variables at the call site, for example by sharing some of them. Refer to Section 7 where we discuss [25] which shows possible optimizations.

$$
\begin{array}{lll}
\text{e} \in \mathit{LabExp} & ::= \text{vor} \mid \text{f} \mid \textbf{new } \text{f}(\text{e}) \mid \text{e; e} \mid \text{e.m}(\text{e}) \mid \\
& \quad\; \text{e.m} \mid \text{f}(\text{e}) \mid \text{lhs} = \text{e} \mid \textbf{null} \mid \text{n} \mid \text{ie} \\
\text{vor} \in \mathit{LabEnvVars} & ::= \text{this\_1} \mid \text{x\_1} \\
\text{lhs} \in \mathit{LeftSide} & ::= \text{x\_1} \mid \text{e.m} \\
\text{ie} \in \mathit{InferExp} & ::= \text{ret\_f} \mid \text{call\_this\_1} \mid \text{call\_x\_1} \mid \text{call\_ret\_1} \\[2mm]
\text{1} \in \mathit{Lab} & ::= 1 \mid 2 \mid \; ... \; \mid \text{f} \mid \text{f}' \mid \; ...
\end{array}
$$

Fig. 8. Syntax of Labeled Expressions

Constraints between type variables express the relationship between the types of expressions, i.e. which members a type must have, how the members of two types may differ and whether a type has any definite members. The syntax of constraints is given in Figure 9. There are three kinds of constraint: $\tau \leq \rho$, $\tau \lhd \tau$, and τ°. We use c to range over constraints and C for a set of constraints.

Figure 10, rule ($solSat$), defines that S satisfies a set of constraints, $S \vdash C$, if it satisfies each constraint. We now discuss each kind of constraint and how it is satisfied by a solution.

- $\tau \leq \rho$ - requires a type variable to be a subtype of ρ: Thus, $\tau \leq \text{Int}$ requires τ to be Int, c.f. rule ($solInt$); while $\tau \leq \tau'$ requires τ to be a subtype of τ', c.f. ($solSub$); while $\tau \leq (\tau_1 \times \tau_2 \to \tau_3)$ requires τ to be the function type composed from τ_1, τ_2 and τ_3, c.f. ($solSubFunc$); finally, $\tau \leq [\text{m} : (\tau', \psi)]$ requires τ to have a member m of type τ' with annotation at least ψ, c.f. ($solMemChange$).
  Thus, $S_0 \vdash [\text{this\_1}] \leq [\text{this\_Date}]$, and $S_0 \vdash [\text{this\_1}] \leq [\text{this\_5}]$, $S_0 \vdash [\text{this\_Date}] \leq [\text{mSec} : ([\text{this\_Date.mSec}], \circ)]$, but $S_0 \not\vdash [\text{this\_Date}] \leq [\text{mSec} : ([\text{this\_Date.mSec}], \bullet)]$.
- $\tau \lhd_{\text{m}} \tau'$ - requires τ and τ' to have the same members with the same types, but member m can be potential in τ' but must be definite in τ, c.f. rule ($solMemChange$).
  For example, $S_0 \vdash [\text{this\_1}] \lhd_{\text{mSec}} [\text{this\_Date}]$, while $S_0 \not\vdash [\text{this\_Date}] \lhd_{\text{mSec}} [\text{this\_1}]$. Also $S_0 \not\vdash [\text{this\_1}] \lhd_{\text{mSec}} [\text{this\_5}]$. Note, however, that $S_0 \vdash [\text{this\_1}] \leq [\text{this\_5}]$ – this should clarify the difference between the two kinds of constraint.
- τ° - requires τ to have no definite members, c.f. rule ($solNoDefs$). This is needed for constructors and global functions whose receiver must have no definite members. For example, $S_0 \vdash [\text{this\_Date}]^\circ$.

5.3 Constraint Generation

Constraint generation for a JS_0 program produces a set of constraints between type variables, and a labeled version of the original expression, e. A

Type Variables

$$\tau ::= [\![\mathrm{e}]\!]$$

Constraints

$$\begin{aligned} \rho \in \mathit{ConstRhs} &::= \tau \mid \sigma \mid [\mathsf{m} : (\tau, \psi)] \\ \sigma \in \mathit{FuncInt} &::= (\tau \times \tau) \to \tau \mid \mathsf{Int} \end{aligned}$$

$$\begin{aligned} \mathsf{c} \in \mathit{Const} &::= \tau \le \rho \mid \tau \lhd_{\mathsf{m}} \tau \mid \tau^{\circ} \\ \mathsf{C} &\in \mathcal{P}(\mathit{Const}) \end{aligned}$$

Fig. 9. Syntax of Type Variables and Constraints

pre-environment, $\gamma = \{$`this : l, x : l'`$,$ `lab : L`$\}$, keeps track of the current labeling of `this` and `x` along with the set of labels used so far, stored in the set `L`. Constraint generation for an expression `e` in the context of a pre-environment, γ, has the form:

$$\gamma \vdash \mathsf{e} : \mathbb{e} \mid\mid \gamma' \mid\mid \mathsf{C}$$

$$\frac{\mathsf{C} = \{\mathsf{c}_1 ... \mathsf{c}_n\} \quad \mathsf{S} \vdash \mathsf{c}_i \ \forall\, i \in 1...n}{\mathsf{S} \vdash \mathsf{C}} \ (solSat)$$

$$\frac{\mathsf{S}(\tau) \le \mathsf{S}(\tau')}{\mathsf{S} \vdash \tau \le \tau'} \ (solSub) \qquad \frac{\mathsf{S}(\tau) \le (\mathsf{S}(\tau_1) \times \mathsf{S}(\tau_2) \to \mathsf{S}(\tau_3))}{\mathsf{S} \vdash \tau \le (\tau_1 \times \tau_2 \to \tau_3)} \ (solSubFunc)$$

$$\frac{\mathsf{S}(\tau) = \mathsf{Int}}{\mathsf{S} \vdash \tau \le \mathsf{Int}} \ (solInt) \qquad \frac{\mathsf{S}(\tau)(\mathsf{m}) \le (\mathsf{S}(\tau'), \psi)}{\mathsf{S} \vdash \tau \le [\mathsf{m} : (\tau', \psi)]} \ (solMember)$$

$$\frac{\forall\, \mathsf{m}' \ne \mathsf{m} : \mathsf{S}(\tau)(\mathsf{m}') \equiv \mathsf{S}(\tau')(\mathsf{m}') \quad \mathsf{S}(\tau)(\mathsf{m}) \le \mathsf{S}(\tau')(\mathsf{m})}{\mathsf{S} \vdash \tau \lhd_{\mathsf{m}} \tau'} \ (solMemChange)$$

$$\frac{\{\mathsf{m} \mid \mathsf{S}(\tau)(\mathsf{m}) = (\mathsf{t}, \bullet)\} = \emptyset}{\mathsf{S} \vdash \tau^{\circ}} \ (solNoDefs)$$

Fig. 10. Solution Satisfaction

where γ' reflects the changes to the labeling of this, x and lab while generating constraints. The constraints generated for an expression consist of the union of the constraints for each subexpression augmented by local constraints.

In (*var*) we generate a labeled expression for this and x by looking in the pre-environment for the current label. No constraints are generated.

In (*funcId*) we require f to have a function type derived from the type of the receiver, parameter and return value of the function. The type variables come from the initial labeled this and x and the labeled return variable ret_f. For example, function identifier addFn produces constraint:

$$[\![addFn]\!] \leq ([\![this\_addFn]\!] \times [\![x\_addFn]\!] \to [\![ret\_addFn]\!])$$

In (*assignAdd*) we use var for this or x, and we model the change of member m of var to definite. var_1 and var_1$'$ represent the type of var *before* and *after* the update, where 1$'$ is fresh. Constraint $[\![var\_1]\!] \leq [m : ([\![var\_1.m]\!], \circ)]$ requires var to have member m with annotation at least $\circ$ before the update, while $[\![var\_1']\!] \leq [m : ([\![var\_1'.m]\!], \bullet)]$ requires var to have member m with annotation definite after the update[6]. The constraint $[\![var\_1']\!] \lhd_m [\![var\_1]\!]$ requires that only member m is affected by the assignment. The remaining constraints require that the type of member m, $[\![var\_1'.m]\!]$, and the overall expression have the type of the right hand side of the assignment. For example, this.add = addFn in a pre-environment $\gamma_2 = \{this : 1, lab : L, ...\}$ where $2 \notin L$, generates the constraints: $[\![this\_1]\!] \leq [add : ([\![this\_1.add]\!], \circ)], [\![this\_2]\!] \leq [add : ([\![this\_2.add]\!], \bullet)], [\![this\_2]\!] \lhd_{add} [\![this\_1]\!], [\![addFn]\!] \leq [\![this\_2.add]\!], [\![addFn]\!] \leq [\![this\_2.add = addFn]\!]$ and the post-environment $\gamma_2[this \mapsto 2, lab \mapsto L \cup \{2\}]$.

In (*new*) a function is used to create an object. The constraint $[\![this\_f]\!]^\circ$ requires the initial this for f to have no definite members. The constraint $[\![e]\!] \leq [\![x\_f]\!]$ requires the actual parameter to have a subtype of the formal parameter, where x_f is the type of the formal parameter at the beginning of the function body. The constraint $[\![ret\_f]\!] \leq [\![new\ f(e)]\!]$ requires the return type of the function to be a subtype of the overall type of the new expression . For example, new Date(1000) generates constraints: $[\![this\_Date]\!]^\circ, [\![1000]\!] \leq [\![x\_Date]\!], [\![ret\_Date]\!] \leq [\![newDate(1000)]\!]$ The rule for global function (*funcCall*) is similar in structure to that for (*new*).

For member access, (*memAcc*), and for assignment where the receiver is not this or x, (*assignUpd*), the receiver must have the definite member. For example, x.mSec, in a $\gamma_1 = \{x : 2, ...\}$, generates constraint: $[\![x\_2]\!] \leq [mSec : ([\![x\_2.mSec]\!], \bullet)]$

For method call, (*methCall*), we consider the label characterizing the occurrence of the call. For a call with label 1 we require the receiver to have a definite member, m, with function type $[\![call\_this\_1]\!] \times [\![call\_x\_1]\!] \to [\![call\_ret\_1]\!]$, as expressed through the con-

---

[6] Using $[\![var\_1]\!] \leq [m : ([\![e]\!], \_)]$ instead of $[\![var\_1]\!] \leq [m : ([\![var\_1.m]\!], \_))]$ would have been too restrictive. Namely, a solution would require the type of m to be the same as the type of $[\![e]\!]$ rather than a supertype.

straint $[\![e_1]\!] \leq [\mathtt{m} : ([\![\mathtt{call\_this\_1}]\!] \times [\![\mathtt{call\_x\_1}]\!] \to [\![\mathtt{call\_ret\_1}]\!], \bullet)]^7$. This will ensure that a solution to the constraints will give a type to the member, that is the least upper bound of all the receivers, parameters and return types at the call sites. For example, $\mathtt{x.add(y)}$ in a pre-environment $\gamma_3 = \{\mathtt{x : Main}, \mathtt{y : Main}, \mathtt{lab : L}, ...\}$ where $5 \notin \mathtt{L}$, generates constraints:

$[\![\mathtt{x\_Main}]\!] \leq [\mathtt{add} : ([\![\mathtt{x\_Main.add}]\!], \bullet)], [\![\mathtt{x\_Main.add}]\!] \leq ([\![\mathtt{call\_this\_5}]\!] \times [\![\mathtt{call\_x\_5}]\!] \to [\![\mathtt{call\_ret\_5}]\!]), [\![\mathtt{x\_Main}]\!] \leq [\![\mathtt{call\_this\_5}]\!], [\![\mathtt{y\_Main}]\!] \leq [\![\mathtt{call\_x\_5}]\!], [\![\mathtt{call\_ret\_5}]\!] \leq [\![\mathtt{x\_Main.add(y\_Main)}]\!]$ and the post-environment $\gamma_3[\mathtt{lab} \mapsto \mathtt{L} \cup \{5\}]$.

For programs, $(Prog)$, we collect the constraints generated for each function with a pre-environment mapping $\mathtt{this}$ and $\mathtt{x}$ to their respective initial versions and $\mathtt{lab}$ to the given set of labels.

5.4   Soundness of the Constraints

We now show that the constraints are sound with respect to the type system. Given a solution, S, and pre-environment, γ, we can generate an environment, Γ, as follows: $\Gamma_{\mathsf{gen}}(\gamma, S) = \{\mathtt{this} \mapsto S(\mathtt{this\_}\gamma(\mathtt{this})), \mathtt{x} \mapsto S(\mathtt{x\_}\gamma(\mathtt{x}))\}$.

Theorem 2 guarantees soundness of the constraints at expression level: Given an expression and its constraints, if there is a solution then the type given by the type system is a subtype of that given in the solution. The environments used for type checking are those produced by Γ_{gen} with pre-environments γ and γ'.

Theorem 2. *If $\gamma \vdash$ e : e $\|$ γ' $\|$ C and $S \vdash C$ and $\Gamma = \Gamma_{\mathsf{gen}}(\gamma, S)$ and $\Gamma' = \Gamma_{\mathsf{gen}}(\gamma', S)$ then $P, \Gamma \vdash$ e : t $\|$ Γ' and $t \leq S([\![e]\!])$.*

Theorem 3 states soundness of the constraints at the program level. Given a program and its constraints, if there is a solution we can use it to generate a well-typed version of the program. Given a JS_0 program and a solution, function $\mathcal{T}(\mathbb{P}, S)$ generates the corresponding typed $JS_0^\top$ program, by using the solution to find the type of the formal parameter, receiver and return type of all the functions and removing the labeling.

Theorem 3. *If $\vdash P : C$ and $S \vdash C$ then $\vdash \mathcal{T}(P, S) \diamond$*

6   From Constraints to Solutions

We now discuss how constraints can be closed to make explicit a solution and how to check that constraints are well-formed. We show how a well-formed set of constraints can be used to generate a solution.

---

[7] Constraint $[\![e_1]\!] \leq [\mathtt{m} : ([\![e_1]\!] \times [\![e_2]\!] \to [\![e_1.m(e_2)]\!], \bullet)]$ would have been too restrictive. Namely, it would require all the receivers of the method to have the same type.

Constraint Generation for Expressions

$$\frac{}{\begin{array}{l}\gamma \vdash \mathtt{null} \;:\; \mathtt{null} \parallel \gamma \parallel \emptyset \\ \gamma \vdash \mathtt{n} \;:\; \mathtt{n} \parallel \gamma \parallel \{[\![\mathtt{n}]\!] \;\leq\; \mathsf{Int}\} \\ \gamma \vdash \mathtt{this} \;:\; \mathtt{this}\_\gamma(\mathtt{this}) \parallel \gamma \parallel \emptyset \\ \gamma \vdash \mathtt{x} \;:\; \mathtt{x}\_\gamma(\mathtt{x}) \parallel \gamma \parallel \emptyset \end{array}} \;(var)$$

$$\frac{C = \{[\![\mathtt{f}]\!] \;\leq\; ([\![\mathtt{this}\_\mathtt{f}]\!] \times [\![\mathtt{x}\_\mathtt{f}]\!]) \rightarrow [\![\mathtt{ret}\_\mathtt{f}]\!]\}}{\gamma \vdash \mathtt{f} \;:\; \mathtt{f} \parallel \gamma \parallel C} \;(funcId)$$

$$\frac{\begin{array}{l}\gamma \vdash \mathtt{e} \;:\; \mathtt{e} \parallel \gamma'' \parallel C' \\ \gamma''(\mathtt{var}) = 1 \\ 1' \notin \gamma''(\mathtt{lab}) \\ \gamma' = \gamma''[\mathtt{var} \mapsto 1', \mathtt{lab} \mapsto (\gamma''(\mathtt{lab}) \cup \{1'\})] \\ C = \{[\![\mathtt{var}\_1]\!] \;\leq\; [m : ([\![\mathtt{var}\_1.\mathtt{m}]\!], \circ)], \\ \quad [\![\mathtt{var}\_1']\!] \;\leq\; [m : ([\![\mathtt{var}\_1'.\mathtt{m}]\!], \bullet)], \\ \quad [\![\mathtt{var}\_1']\!] \;\lhd_m\; [\![\mathtt{var}\_1]\!], \; [\![\mathtt{e}]\!] \;\leq\; [\![\mathtt{var}\_1'.\mathtt{m}]\!], \; [\![\mathtt{e}]\!] \;\leq\; [\![\mathtt{var}\_1'.\mathtt{m} = \mathtt{e}]\!]\}\end{array}}{\gamma \vdash \mathtt{var.m} = \mathtt{e} \;:\; \mathtt{var}\_1'.\mathtt{m} = \mathtt{e} \parallel \gamma' \parallel C \cup C'} \;(assignAdd)$$

$$\frac{\begin{array}{l}\gamma \vdash \mathtt{e} \;:\; \mathtt{e} \parallel \gamma' \parallel C' \\ C = \{[\![\mathtt{this}\_\mathtt{f}]\!]^\circ, \; [\![\mathtt{e}]\!] \;\leq\; [\![\mathtt{x}\_\mathtt{f}]\!], \\ \quad [\![\mathtt{ret}\_\mathtt{f}]\!] \;\leq\; [\![\mathtt{new}\;\mathtt{f}(\mathtt{e})]\!]\}\end{array}}{\gamma \vdash \mathtt{new}\;\mathtt{f}(\mathtt{e}) \;:\; \mathtt{new}\;\mathtt{f}(\mathtt{e}) \parallel \gamma' \parallel C \cup C'} \;(new)$$

$$\frac{\begin{array}{l}\gamma \vdash \mathtt{e} \;:\; \mathtt{e} \parallel \gamma' \parallel C' \\ C = \{[\![\mathtt{this}\_\mathtt{f}]\!]^\circ, \; [\![\mathtt{e}]\!] \;\leq\; [\![\mathtt{x}\_\mathtt{f}]\!], \\ \quad [\![\mathtt{ret}\_\mathtt{f}]\!] \;\leq\; [\![\mathtt{f}(\mathtt{e})]\!]\}\end{array}}{\gamma \vdash \mathtt{f}(\mathtt{e}) \;:\; \mathtt{f}(\mathtt{e}) \parallel \gamma' \parallel C \cup C'} \;(funcCall)$$

$$\frac{\gamma \vdash \mathtt{e} \;:\; \mathtt{e} \parallel \gamma' \parallel C'}{\gamma \vdash \mathtt{e.m} \;:\; \mathtt{e.m} \parallel \gamma' \parallel C \cup \{[\![\mathtt{e}]\!] \;\leq\; [m : ([\![\mathtt{e.m}]\!], \bullet)]\}} \;(memAcc)$$

$$\frac{\begin{array}{l}\gamma \vdash \mathtt{e_1} \;:\; \mathtt{e_1} \parallel \gamma' \parallel C' \\ \gamma' \vdash \mathtt{e_2} \;:\; \mathtt{e_2} \parallel \gamma'' \parallel C'' \\ C = \{[\![\mathtt{e_1}]\!] \;\leq\; [m : ([\![\mathtt{e_1.m}]\!], \bullet)], \; [\![\mathtt{e_2}]\!] \;\leq\; [\![\mathtt{e_1.m}]\!], \; [\![\mathtt{e_2}]\!] \;\leq\; [\![\mathtt{e_1.m} = \mathtt{e_2}]\!]\}\end{array}}{\gamma \vdash \mathtt{e_1.m} = \mathtt{e_2} \;:\; \mathtt{e_1.m} = \mathtt{e_2} \parallel \gamma'' \parallel C \cup C' \cup C''} \;(assignUpd)$$

$$\frac{\begin{array}{l}\gamma \vdash \mathtt{e_1} \;:\; \mathtt{e_1} \parallel \gamma' \parallel C' \\ \gamma' \vdash \mathtt{e_2} \;:\; \mathtt{e_2} \parallel \gamma'' \parallel C'' \\ 1 \notin \gamma''(\mathtt{lab}) \\ C = \{[\![\mathtt{e_1}]\!] \;\leq\; [m : ([\![\mathtt{e_1.m}]\!], \bullet)], \; [\![\mathtt{e_1.m}]\!] \;\leq\; (([\![\mathtt{call\_this\_1}]\!] \times [\![\mathtt{call\_x\_1}]\!]) \rightarrow [\![\mathtt{call\_ret\_1}]\!]), \\ \quad [\![\mathtt{e_1}]\!] \;\leq\; [\![\mathtt{call\_this\_1}]\!], \; [\![\mathtt{e_2}]\!] \;\leq\; [\![\mathtt{call\_x\_1}]\!], \; [\![\mathtt{call\_ret\_1}]\!] \;\leq\; [\![\mathtt{e_1.m}(\mathtt{e_2})]\!]\}\end{array}}{\gamma \vdash \mathtt{e_1.m}(\mathtt{e_2}) \;:\; \mathtt{e_1.m}(\mathtt{e_2}) \parallel \gamma''[\mathtt{lab} \mapsto (\gamma''(\mathtt{lab}) \cup \{1\}] \parallel C \cup C' \cup C''} \;(methCall)$$

$$\frac{\begin{array}{l}\gamma \vdash \mathtt{e_1} \;:\; \mathtt{e_1} \parallel \gamma' \parallel C' \\ \gamma' \vdash \mathtt{e_2} \;:\; \mathtt{e_2} \parallel \gamma'' \parallel C'' \\ C = \{[\![\mathtt{e_2}]\!] \;\leq\; [\![\mathtt{e_1; e_2}]\!]\}\end{array}}{\gamma \vdash \mathtt{e_1; e_2} \;:\; \mathtt{e_1; e_2} \parallel \gamma'' \parallel C \cup C' \cup C''} \;(seq)$$

$$\frac{\begin{array}{l}\gamma \vdash \mathtt{e} \;:\; \mathtt{e} \parallel \gamma' \parallel C' \\ \gamma'(\mathtt{x}) = 1 \\ C = \{[\![\mathtt{e}]\!] \;\leq\; [\![\mathtt{x}\_1]\!], \; [\![\mathtt{e}]\!] \;\leq\; [\![\mathtt{x}\_1 = \mathtt{e}]\!]\}\end{array}}{\gamma \vdash \mathtt{x} = \mathtt{e} \;:\; \mathtt{x}\_1 = \mathtt{e} \parallel \gamma' \parallel C \cup C'} \;(varAss)$$

Constraint Generation for Programs

$$\frac{\begin{array}{l}P = \mathtt{function}\;\mathtt{f_1}(\mathtt{x})\;\{\;\mathtt{e_1}\;\} \cdots \mathtt{function}\;\mathtt{f_n}(\mathtt{x})\;\{\;\mathtt{e_n}\;\} \\ \{\mathtt{this} \mapsto \mathtt{f_i}, \mathtt{x} \mapsto \mathtt{f_i}, \mathtt{lab} \mapsto \gamma'_{i-1}(\mathtt{lab})\} \vdash \mathtt{e_i} \;:\; \mathtt{e_i} \parallel \gamma'_i \parallel C_i \quad 1 \leq i \leq n \;\wedge\; \gamma_0 = \emptyset \\ C = \bigcup_{i \in 1..n} C_i \cup \{[\![\mathtt{e_i}]\!] \;\leq\; [\![\mathtt{ret\_f_i}]\!]\}\end{array}}{\vdash P \;:\; C} \;(Prog)$$

Fig. 11. Constraint Generation

6.1   Constraint Closure

To simplify the extraction of a solution from a set of constraints we apply constraint closure, which makes the solutions (or lack of) explicit. The closing relation, $C \longrightarrow C'$, is defined in Figure 12[8].

In $(closeTrans)$ we add a constraint implied by the transitivity of subtyping.

In $(closeTransMem)$ the type variable τ is required to have the same members as τ' with the same types definite annotation for m (because of $\tau \lhd_m \tau'$); the type variable τ' is required to have member m with type τ'' and annotation ψ (because of $\tau' \leq [m : (\tau'', \psi)]$). Therefore, τ is also required to have the member m with type τ'' and annotation ψ, as expressed by $\tau \leq [m : (\tau'', \psi)]$.

In $(closeBalance)$ the type variable τ is required to be a subtype of τ', and τ is required to be a subtype of a σ, $i.e.$ either of Int, or of a function type. Because the subtype relationship for Int and function types is the identity, it follows that τ and σ will have to be "the same", and therefore, it follows that τ' will have to be a subtype of σ.

In $(closeBalanceMem)$ the type variable τ is required to have member m with type τ'' and annotation ψ. Because τ' is required to have the same members as τ with the same types it follows that τ' will also have the member m with type τ''. The annotation, ψ, depends on whether m $=$ m$'$. If m $=$ m$'$ then ψ can be less defined i.e. $\circ$ otherwise the annotations for m in τ and τ' must be the same.

In $(closeCong)$ the same type variable, τ, is required to contain a member m with type τ' and also with type τ''. It follows that τ' should be "equivalent" with τ''. Similarly, in $(closeCongFunc)$ because τ is required to be a subtype of two function types, it follows that the two function types should be "equivalent", which, because of the subtype rules for function types, implies that the receiver, argument and return types should be "equivalent".

Thus, for $[\![\text{this\_2}]\!] \lhd_{\text{add}} [\![\text{this\_1}]\!]$ and $[\![\text{this\_1}]\!] \leq [\text{mSec} : ([\![\text{this\_1.mSec}]\!], \bullet)]$ application of $(closeTransMem)$ generates $[\![\text{this\_2}]\!] \leq [\text{mSec} : ([\![\text{this\_1.mSec}]\!], \blacklozenge)]$, which ensures that $[\![\text{this\_2}]\!]$ will have member mSec. Also, closing $[\![\text{this\_2}]\!] \lhd_{\text{add}} [\![\text{this\_1}]\!]$ and $[\![\text{this\_2}]\!] \leq [\text{add} : ([\![\text{this\_2.add}]\!], \bullet)]$ with $(closeBalanceMem)$ generates $[\![\text{this\_1}]\!] \leq [\text{add} : ([\![\text{this\_2.add}]\!], \circ)]$. Lastly, $[\![\text{this\_2}]\!] \leq [\text{add} : ([\![\text{this\_1.add}]\!], \circ)]$ and $[\![\text{this\_2}]\!] \leq [\text{add} : ([\![\text{this\_2.add}]\!], \bullet)]$, closed with rule $(closeCong)$ generate $[\![\text{this\_1.add}]\!] \leq [\![\text{this\_2.add}]\!]$, and $[\![\text{this\_2.add}]\!] \leq [\![\text{this\_1.add}]\!]$.

Definition 4. C *is closed,* $\vdash C \diamond_{cl}$, *if for any* C': $C \longrightarrow C'$ *implies that* $C = C'$.

Lemma 2 states that a set of constraints and its closure have the same set of solutions.

Lemma 2. *If* $S \vdash C$ *and* $C \longrightarrow C'$ *then* $S \vdash C'$.

---

[8] We assume the closure of a set of constraints includes the reflexive closure.

$$\frac{\begin{array}{c} c_1,...,c_n \longrightarrow c'_1,...c'_m \\ c_1,...,c_n \in C \end{array}}{C \longrightarrow C \cup \{c'_1,...c'_m\}} \ (closeMany1) \qquad \frac{}{C \longrightarrow C} \ (closeMany2)$$

$$\frac{}{\tau \leq \tau', \tau' \leq \rho \longrightarrow \tau \leq \rho} \ (closeTrans)$$

$$\frac{}{\tau \vartriangleleft_{\_} \tau', \tau' \leq [m:(\tau'',\psi)] \longrightarrow \tau \leq [m:(\tau'',\psi)]} \ (closeTransMem)$$

$$\frac{}{\tau \leq \tau', \tau \leq \sigma \longrightarrow \tau' \leq \sigma} \ (closeBalance)$$

$$\frac{\psi' = \circ \ (if \ m = m') \ \psi' = \psi \ (otherwise)}{\tau \vartriangleleft_{m'} \tau', \tau \leq [m:(\tau'',\psi)] \longrightarrow \tau' \leq [m:(\tau'',\psi')]} \ (closeBalanceMem)$$

$$\frac{}{\tau \leq [m:(\tau',\_)], \tau \leq [m:(\tau'',\_)] \longrightarrow \tau' \leq \tau'', \tau'' \leq \tau'} \ (closeCong)$$

$$\frac{}{\begin{array}{c} \tau \leq (\tau_1 \times \tau_2 \to \tau_3), \tau \leq (\tau'_1 \times \tau'_2 \to \tau'_3) \longrightarrow \\ \tau'_1 \leq \tau_1, \tau_1 \leq \tau'_1, \tau'_2 \leq \tau_2, \tau_2 \leq \tau'_2, \tau_3 \leq \tau'_3, \tau'_3 \leq \tau_3 \end{array}} \ (closeCongFunc)$$

Fig. 12. Constraint Closure

6.2   Well-Formed Constraints

The well-formedness of constraints, $\vdash C\diamond$ (shown in Figure 13), ensures that a set of constraints can be used to create a solution. For a set of constraints, C, to be well-formed they must be closed and all the constraints in C must be well-formed. We define function $\mathcal{A}(C, \tau, m)$ which determines the annotations that any solution satisfying C should give to m in τ. This is done by looking for constraints detailing members: $\tau \leq [m:(\_,\_)]$. A member is annotated with $\circ$ if there are no constraints indicating it should be definite:

$$\mathcal{A}(C, \tau, m) = \begin{cases} \bullet & if \ \tau \leq [m:(\_,\bullet)] \in C \\ \circ & if \ \tau \leq [m:(\_,\circ)] \in C \ and \ \tau \leq [m:(\_,\bullet)] \notin C \\ \mathcal{U}df & otherwise \end{cases}$$

Intuitively, rule $(wlfNoDefs)$ corresponds to the solution satisfaction rule $(solNoDefs)$ in Figure 10. Where $S(\tau)(m)$ is represented by looking for constraints detailing members, $\tau \leq [\mathsf{m} : (\_, \_)]$, with $\mathcal{A}(\mathsf{C}, \tau, \mathsf{m})$ being used to find the appropriate annotation.

Rules $(wlfMix1)$, $(wlfMix2)$ and $(wlfMix3)$ ensure that the constraints cannot mix object types with function types or integers.

$$\frac{\vdash \mathsf{C} \diamond_{cl} \quad \mathsf{C} = \{c_1...c_n\} \quad \mathsf{C} \vdash c_i \quad \forall\, i \in 1...n}{\vdash \mathsf{C} \diamond} \; (wlfAll)$$

$$\frac{\tau \leq [\mathsf{m} : (\_, \bullet)] \notin \mathsf{C}}{\mathsf{C} \vdash \tau^\circ} \; (wlfNoDefs) \qquad \frac{\tau \leq (\_ \times \_ \to \_) \notin \mathsf{C} \wedge \tau \leq \mathsf{Int} \notin \mathsf{C}}{\mathsf{C} \vdash \tau \leq [\mathsf{m} : (\tau', \psi)]} \; (wlfMix1)$$

$$\frac{\tau \leq [\mathsf{m} : (\_, \_)] \notin \mathsf{C} \wedge \tau \leq \mathsf{Int} \notin \mathsf{C}}{\mathsf{C} \vdash \tau \leq (\tau_1 \times \tau_2 \to \tau_3)} \; (wlfMix2)$$

$$\frac{\tau \leq (\_ \times \_ \to \_) \notin \mathsf{C} \wedge \tau \leq [\mathsf{m} : (\_, \_)] \notin \mathsf{C}}{\mathsf{C} \vdash \tau \leq \mathsf{Int}} \; (wlfMix3)$$

Fig. 13. Well-formed Constraints

6.3 From Constraints to Solutions

We now show how well-formed constraints, $\vdash \mathsf{C} \diamond$, can be translated into a solution. We first define a *type variable function*, V, from type variables to variables in the type system, $\alpha_1...\alpha_n \in ObjVar$. We say that V is well-formed for C, i.e. $\mathsf{C} \vdash \mathsf{V} \diamond$, iff $\tau \leq \tau', \tau' \leq \tau \in \mathsf{C}$ and $\mathsf{V}(\tau) = \alpha$ implies $\mathsf{V}(\tau') = \alpha$.

The translation relation, $\mathsf{C}, \mathsf{V}, \tau \to \mathsf{tp}, \mathsf{V}'$, in Figure 14 translates a type variable, τ, into a type. If a type variable has no constraints indicating whether it should be an object, function or integer type, we default to making it an object type with no members. The extension of V, which is denoted by $\mathsf{V} \oplus \tau$, is defined as follows (where α is a fresh variable):

$$(\mathsf{V} \oplus \tau)(\tau') = \begin{cases} \alpha & \text{if } \tau' \notin dom(\mathsf{V}) \text{ and} \\ & \quad (\tau' = \tau \text{ or } (\tau' \leq \tau \in \mathsf{C} \text{ and } \tau \leq \tau' \in \mathsf{C})) \\ \mathsf{V}(\tau') & \text{if } \tau' \in dom(\mathsf{V}) \\ \mathcal{U}df & \text{otherwise} \end{cases}$$

$V \oplus \tau$ extends V with new type variables thus, keeping track of type variables that have already been translated. Because each step of the translation either extends V or finishes when $V(\tau) = \alpha$ (or $\text{tp} = \text{Int}$ or $\text{tp} = \mu\,\alpha.[\,]$) termination is guaranteed.

$$\frac{V(\tau) = \alpha}{C, V, \tau \to \alpha, V} \qquad \frac{\tau \leq \text{Int} \in C}{C, V, \tau \to \text{Int}, V} \qquad \frac{\begin{array}{l} \tau \leq [m:\_] \notin C \\ \tau \leq (\_\times\_\to\_) \notin C \\ \tau \leq \text{Int} \notin C \\ V' = V \oplus \tau \\ V'(\tau) = \alpha \end{array}}{C, V, \tau \to \mu\,\alpha.[\,], V'}$$

$$\frac{\begin{array}{l} n \geq 1 \\ V(\tau) = \mathcal{U}df \\ V_0 = V \oplus \tau \\ V_0(\tau) = \alpha \\ \{m_1...m_n\} = \{m \mid \tau \leq [m:(\_,\_)] \in C\} \\ \tau \leq [m_i:(\tau_i,\_)] \in C \ (for \ i \in 1...n) \\ C, V_{i-1}, \tau_i \to \text{tp}_i, V_i \\ \psi_i = \mathcal{A}(C, \tau, m_i) \end{array}}{C, V, \tau \to \mu\,\alpha.[m_1:(\text{tp}_1, \psi_1)...m_n:(\text{tp}_n, \psi_n)], V_n} \qquad \frac{\begin{array}{l} V(\tau) = \mathcal{U}df \\ V_0 = V \oplus \tau \\ V_0(\tau) = \alpha \\ \tau \leq (\tau_1 \times \tau_2 \to \tau_3) \in C \\ C, V_{i-1}, \tau_i \to \text{tp}_i, V_i \quad (for \ i \in 1...3) \end{array}}{C, V, \tau \to \mu\,\alpha.(\text{tp}_1 \times \text{tp}_2 \to \text{tp}_3), V_3}$$

Fig. 14. Generating the Solution

6.4   Main Result

Lemma 3 states that if two type variables are "equivalent", $\tau \leq \tau', \tau' \leq \tau \in C$, by a set of well-formed constraints, they will translate to congruent types or the same variable.

Lemma 3. *If* $\vdash C\diamond$ *and* $C \vdash V\diamond$ *and* $C, V, \tau \to \text{tp}, V'$ *and* $C, V, \tau' \to \text{tp}', V''$ *and* $\tau \leq \tau', \tau' \leq \tau \in C$ *then* $C \vdash V'\diamond$ *and* $C \vdash V''\diamond$ *and* $(\text{tp} \equiv \text{tp}'$ *or* $\exists\alpha : \text{tp} = \alpha = \text{tp}')$.

Given a well-formed set of constraints and well-formed type variable function we define a generated solution, $S_{C,V}$, such that $S_{C,V}(\tau) = t$ if and only if $C, V, \tau \to t, V'$. Theorem 4 states that a generated solution from a well-formed set of constraints is well-formed.

Theorem 4. *If* $\vdash C\diamond$ *then* $S_{C,\emptyset} \vdash C$.

7   Related Work

Recursive Types and Subtyping Our choice of a recursive types was motivated by the need to allow typing of a large number of JavaScript programs, but at the same time make possible the development of a type inference algorithm. Hence, we have not considered more expressive type systems such as [19].

Type systems for object based languages have been developed mainly in a functional setting, see [1] and [14]. In [22] a type system is defined for the Abadi Cardelli object calculus with concatenation that uses recursive types. The definition of the object types is like ours (without function types) with width subtyping.

Subtyping for recursive function types (that are a subset of our types) has been considered in [4] where subtyping is contravariant on the input types and covariant on the return type. In our paper we have adopted congruence for subtyping between function types, because our aim is not to study the interaction between subtyping and recursive type (as in [4]) but to have a type system allowing type inference.

An imperative, type safe object oriented language, TOIL, was introduced in [8]. Even though the language is class based, its type system does not identify types with classes. This makes the definition of types similar to ours. TOIL, however, does not have extensible objects, so there is no need for identifying potential members.

Dynamic Addition of Members Extensible objects are considered in a functional setting in [13]. An imperative calculus for extensible objects was proposed by Bono and Fisher, in [7]. In their type system there are two types for objects: the *proto*-types that can be extended and the *object*-types that cannot. The type system tracks potential members. The main difference between our type system and their's is that we use recursive types (instead of row types plus universal and existential quantification). This makes it possible to have a decidable type inference algorithm. Note that, Bono and Fisher's aim was to encode classes in their object calculus, not to obtain a type inference algorithm.

In [24] Thiemann gives a type system for a considerable subset of JavaScript. Types are based on discriminative sums with two levels. The outer level determines what kind of base type e.g. number, string, object etc. The inner level determines the features of the type such as the value e.g. the singleton type Number(100). Row types are used to detail the members of an object type. The type system models the automatic conversions that occur in JavaScript through a matching relation. As all conversions are tracked it is possible to flag those which could result in dangerous or unexpected behaviour. Access to a non-existent member does not result in a type error. There are no recursive types and no type inference algorithm is given but there is an implementation.

In the context of type assembly language Morrisett et al. in [17] uses an initialisation flag on the members of type to indicate if they have been assigned to. One could think of the potential and definite annotations of our types as representing the state of initialisation of a member.

Alias types are used in [5] and [9] to track the evolution of objects. In particular, in [9] potential members are used for the same purpose as the current paper. Alias types are, however, very different from the types used in this paper. They are singleton types identified with the address of objects.

Type Inference In [18,21] Palsberg et al. develop a type inference algorithm for a class based language based on flow analysis. The set of types is the class names defined in the program. Each expression, e, is given a type variable, $[\![e]\!]$, that expresses the - yet unknown - type. They employed a novel approach to model late binding through *conditional constraints*. A conditional constraint has the form $t \in [\![e]\!] \implies C$ saying that constraints C are only applicable when t is a possible type for $[\![e]\!]$. In [3] this work is applied to the object based language SELF[12]. Each occurrence of an object is given a unique token ω. Thus, object structure is derived from the program. Our work differs in that we must infer the structure of objects. With StarKiller[23] Salib uses the Cartesian Product Algorithm[2] to infer types for Python programs in order to improve compiled code. Object types maintain a reference to their definition when a member is added or updated new object types are generated and propagated through the system.

In [20] Palsberg considers type inference for the first order type system (with recursive types and subtyping) for the Abadi Cardelli object calculus[1]. The system of constraints is a subset of those used in this paper, with two kinds $\tau \leq \tau'$ and $\tau \leq [m : (\tau, \psi)]$. Furthermore, the Abadi Cardelli calculus does not allow member addition like JS_0. The type system uses a subsumption rule which is encoded in the system by having two type variables for each program point, one before subtyping and one after. For variables there is x and $[\![x]\!]$ and member access, $[\![e.m]\!]$ and $< e.m >$. Instead of a subsumption rule, our type system uses the subtype relation where necessary *e.g.* the actual parameter being a subtype of the formal parameter. Hence, the subtype relation is always used *explicitly* between the types of expressions in the program. Therefore, we don't need to use two type variables to model the application of subsumption. After the constraints are generated a graph is generated and closed. A well-formedness criteria is given to graphs which are then converted to an automata which is used to annotate the program. Our work differs in that we specify closure and well-formedness in terms of constraints rather than convert to a graph.

In [10] Eifrig et al. consider type inference for the class-based language *I-LOOP*. The types are *recursively constrained* in that a type is supplemented with a set of constraints, $\tau \backslash C$. They take a different approach to us by defining type rules that generate constraints and then modifying the rules to make a deterministic and complete inference system. Fields and methods of a type are detailed with constraints of the form $\tau \leq$ **Inst** $m : \tau'$, which states that τ has a field m of type τ'.

In [25], Wang et al. give a type inference system for Java that can statically verify the correctness of downcast. The types used are based on those used in [10] as described above. There are types that describe the structure of objects, **obj** $(\delta, \overline{[1_i : \tau_i]})$ where δ and 1_i are abstract labels for the class name and fields/methods respectively. The structure of the object types is derived from the class structure. Unlike our treatment of method call sites, where we *always* allocate new type variables, they delegates this to closure. By parameterizing closure with a mapping it is possible to *share* type variables between different invocations of a method.

8   Conclusions and Further Work

In this paper a flexible type system for an idealized version of JavaScript is presented, its soundness is outlined, and a type inference algorithm for this type system is defined. The type inference algorithm is sound with respect to the type system. We show how well-formed constraints can be used to generate a solution and annotate an untyped JS_0 program. The main challenges for both the type system and the inference are the imperative nature of the language combined with the possibility of extending objects.

For future work we want to study the completeness of the type inference algorithm, its complexity, and extend the type system to allow more typeable expressions, e.g., allowing a more flexible subtyping for functions. To show completeness we need principality of the type produced, this is quite difficult to achieve for recursive type systems. We would also like to develop a *mixed mode* system where some of the type annotations are already given by the user. For example, we could provide a typing of the Document Object Model[11] and check code in web pages against it.

Acknowledgements

We would like to thank Mario Coppo, Mariangiola Dezani, Matthew Smith and Alex Buckley for their help and insight and our colleagues at Imperial College Department of Computing and Dipartimento di Informatica of Torino University. We would also like to thank the anonymous ECOOP reviewers.

References

1. Martín Abadi and Luca Cardelli. *A Theory of Objects*. Springer-Verlag, New York, NY, 1996.
2. Ole Agesen. The Cartesian Product Algorithm: Simple and Precise Type Inference of Parametric Polymorphism. In *ECOOP*, 2-26, 1995.
3. Ole Agesen, Jens Palsberg, and Michael I. Schwartzbach. Type inference of SELF: Analysis of objects with dynamic and multiple inheritance. *Softw., Pract. Exper.*, 25(9):975–995, 1995.
4. Roberto M. Amadio and Luca Cardelli. Subtyping recursive types. *ACM Transactions on Programming Languages and Systems*, 15(4):575–631, 1993.
5. C. Anderson, F. Barbanera, M. Dezani-Ciancaglini, and S. Drossopoulou. Can addresses be types? (a case study: objects with delegation). In *WOOD '03*, volume 82 of *ENTCS*. Elsevier, 2003.

6. Christopher Anderson and Paola Giannini. Type checking for javascript. In *WOOD '04*, volume WOOD of *ENTCS*. Elsevier, 2004. http://www.binarylord.com/work/js0wood.pdf.

7. V. Bono and K. Fisher. An Imperative, First-Order Calculus with Object Extension. In *Proc. of ECOOP'98*, volume 1445 of *LNCS*, pages 462–497, 1998. A preliminary version already appeared in Proc. of 5th Annual FOOL Workshop.

8. Kim Bruce, A. Schuett, and R. van Gent. Polytoil: A type safe polymorphic object-oriented language. In *Proceedings of the European Conference on Object-Oriented Programming (ECOOP)*, 1995.

9. F. Damiani and P. Giannini. Alias types for environment aware computations. In *WOOD '03*, volume 82 of *ENTCS*. Elsevier, 2003.

10. Jonathan Eifrig, Scott F. Smith, and Valery Trifonov. Sound polymorphic type inference for objects. In *Proc. Object-Oriented Programming Systems, Languages, and Applications (OOPSLA)'95*, pages 169–184, New York, NY, 1995. ACM Press.

11. Arnaud Le Hors et al. Document Object Model (DOM) Level 3 Core Specification. Technical report, 1998. http://www.w3.org/TR/2003/CR-DOM-Level-3-Core-20031107.

12. Ole Agesen et al. The SELF 4.0 Programmer's Reference Manual. http://research.sun.com/self/, 1995.

13. K. Fisher. *Type Systems for Object-Oriented Programming Languages*. PhD thesis, Stanford University, 1996. Available as Stanford Computer Science Technical Report number STAN-CS-TR-98-1602.

14. K. Fisher, F. Honsell, and J. C. Mitchell. A Lambda Calculus of Objects and Method Specialization. *Nordic Journal of Computing*, 1(1):3–37, 1994. A preliminary version appeared in *Proc. of IEEE Symp. LICS'93*.

15. David Flanagan. *JavaScript - The Definitive Guide*. O'Reilly, 1998.

16. ECMAScript Language Specification. ECMA International. ECMA-262, 3rd edition, december 1999. http://www.ecma-international.org/publications/files/ECMA-ST/Ecma-262.pdf.

17. Greg Morrisett, David Walker, Karl Crary, and Neal Glew. From system f to typed assembly language. *ACM Trans. Program. Lang. Syst.*, 21(3):527–568, 1999.

18. Nicholas Oxhoj, Jens Palsberg, and Michael I. Schwartzbach. Making type inference practical. In *ECOOP*, pages 329–349, 1992.

19. W. Hill W. Olthoff P. Canning, W. Cook and J. C. Mitchell. F-bounded polymorphism for object-oriented programming. In *Proc. Conf. on Functional Programming Languages and Computer Architecture*, pages 273–280. ACM Press, 1989.

20. Jens Palsberg. Efficient inference of object types. *Inf. Comput.*, 123(2):198–209, 1995.

21. Jens Palsberg and Michael I. Schwartzbach. Object-oriented type inference. In Norman Meyrowitz, editor, *Proceedings of the Conference on Object-Oriented Programming Systems, Languages, and Applications (OOPSLA)*, volume 26, New York, NY, 1991. ACM Press.

22. Jens Palsberg and Tian Zhao. Type inference for record concatenation and subtyping. *Inf. Comput.*, 189(1):54–86, 2004.

23. Mike Salib. Static Type Inference (for Python) with Starkiller. http://www.python.org/pycon/dc2004/papers/1/paper.pdf, 2004.

24. Peter Thiemann. Towards a type system for analyzing javascript programs. In *ESOP*, pages 408–422, 2005.

25. Tiejun Wang and Scott F. Smith. Precise constraint-based type inference for java. In *ECOOP '01: Proceedings of the 15th European Conference on Object-Oriented Programming*, pages 99–117. Springer-Verlag, 2001.

Chai: Traits for Java-Like Languages

• •••]•• S• i•• •n• So••i• D•o••o• o• lo•

Department of Computing, Imperial College London

Abstract. Traits support the factoring out of common behaviour, and its integration into classes in a manner that coexists smoothly with inheritance-based structuring mechanisms.

We designed the language *Chai*, which incorporates statically typed traits into a simple Java-inspired base language, and we discuss three versions of the language: *Chai$_1$*, where traits are only a mechanism for the creation of classes; *Chai$_2$* where traits are a mechanism for the creation of classes, *and* can also introduce types, and *Chai$_3$* where traits play a role at runtime, and can can be applied to objects, and change the objects' behaviour. We give formal models for these languages, outline the proof of soundness, and our prototype implementation.

1 Introduction

T••i•• w••• •••i•n•• •o •••ili•••• •o•• ••••• •n• •o •••i•• in ••••••••in•]••••
••o••••• •. T••y ••• •on•••••••lly •i• il•• •o •]••••, •x••• • ••••• •••y •on••in no
••••••, only ••• •vio••, •n• ••n •• •o• •in•• ••in• • ••• o• •i• •]• •o• •o•i•ion
•n• • o•i•••ion o••••• o••. •]•• •n•• o• ••••vio•• ••••• n••• •o •• ••••••• in
••v•••] •iff••n• ••••• o•• ••o•••• ••n •• •n•••••]•••• in •••i w•i•• • •y••
••••••n••• w••••• n•••••••y, •voi•in• ••• n••• •o ••• li•••i•• •o••.

T••i•• • ••• • ••• • ••••• in ••• o• j•••-•••••]•n••••• S•]•[••] w••• •••y•oo• •••
•o•• o• •••• •n• o• j•••• •o w•i•• •n o• j••• •• n ••]••••• •o• • o• i•• ••••vio••.
S•••••••n• wo•• on T••i•• w•• ••••• on ••• •]•••-•••••]•n•••••• S• •ll••]•,
•o• w•i•• •n •x••n•ion ••••o••in• T••i•• w•• •••••••• [1•, 19]. U•• o• •••i•• ••n
•i•ni•••n•ly •••••• ••• ov•••ll •i•• o• li•••i••[3].

Mixin•[5, •, 11], M•]•i•]• In•••i••n••[• 1, 1•], F•• ily Poly• o•••i•• [9], D•]•-
•••ion L•y•••, •n• A•••••• • •i•n••• P•o•••• • in• ••••• wi•• T••i•• ••• •i• o•
•o•• •••••. T••i••, li•• Mixin•, •n• •nli•• •]••••• in M•]•i•]• In•••i••n••, ••v
no •••••••]••••, •n• •••• ••• no• •i•• •o ••••i••]•• lo••ion in •n in••i••n••
•i•••••y. T••i•• •n• Mixin• •••• lly •••••••n• •o• • o•i•ion o• in•o• •]••• i• •]•-
• •n••ion•, •n• •••• •••••• o•• •••o• •o•i•ion ••• • •n•• •••in ••• n •]••••. W••n
• •••i• i• •••• •y • •]••• ••y• ••• ••• •n•i•• o•••• •]••• i• ••• ••• • ••• i•••• •••i•
• ••• o•• w••• •••• o• ••• •]••• i•••]• — ••i• i• ••]]•• ••• *flattening* ••o•••y.

S• •ll••]• i• ••• •••• *class based*]•n••••• on w•i•• •••i•• ••v •••n ••-
•li••. W•il• S• •ll••]• i• •yn•• i••lly •y•••, o•• •••• i• w•• •o •••ly •••i•• •o •
••••i••lly •y•••, •]••• •••••]•n•••••. In ••i• ••••• w• •i•••••• ••• •••i•n •n•
i• •]•• •n••ion o• *Chai*, •n •x••n•ion o•• • •• •]] J•v•-li••]•n••••• wi•• •••i••.

A.P. Black (Ed.): ECOOP 2005, LNCS 3586, pp. 453–478, 2005.

W• i••n•i••• ••••• •iff•••n• •ôl•• •o• •••i•• in *Chai*, •n• •o, w• •••i•n•• •• •••
l•n••••••:

Chai$_1$ A l•n••••• li•• J•v•, w•••• •••i•• ••• ••••ly • • ••••ni•• •o •••••••
•l••••••, •n• w•••• ••• •••li•••ion o• • •••i• ••n only •• •y•-••••••• ••-
••• ••• ••••l•in• •l••• ••• •••n "fl•••n••".

Chai$_2$ H••• w• •x••n• ••• ••• i• o• •••i•• •o •••• •••y • •y •• ••• •y•••.
T•i• •••• i•• •••••in• o• •••i•• *before* •••i• ••• li•••ion.

Chai$_3$ Fin•lly, w• •llow •••i•• •o •• ••••••i•••• •o• on• •no•••• •yn•• i••lly,
•••• o••in• •• n•i• • •••n••• in o• j••• •••• •vio••.

In ••••ion • o• ••i• •••••• w• in••o•••• *Chai* •••o••• •x•• •l••. In ••••ion• 3,
• •n• 5 w• •••••n• •o•• •l • o••l• •o• *Chai*$_1$, *Chai*$_2$ •n• *Chai*$_3$. In ••••ion 6 w•
•i••••• • ••o•o•y•• i• •l•• •n•••ion o• ••••• l•n••••••, •n• ••••ion • •on••in•
•on•l••ion• •n• ••••••• wo••.

T•• ••o•o•y•• i• •l•• •n•••ion •n• ••• MS• ••••i• ••• •v•il••l• ••
http://chai-t.sourceforge.net/. An ••••n•ix wi•• •o• •l••• •••ni•ion•
•n• ••n•w•i••n ••oo•• i• •v•il••l• •• http://www.doc.ic.ac.uk/
~scd/ChaiApp.

2   An Example

Fi•••• 1 •iv••n•x•• •l• o• *Chai*$_1$.[1] W• •••n• •o•••i• •l• •••i••: TScreenShape,
TPrintedShape, TEmptyCircle •n• TFilledCircle, w•i•• ••••i• •o••••• on•-
in• •o• •on•n•• in • •i• •l• ••••i•• ••o•••• : w• •n •o•• on •••••n, o• ••in•,
•• ••y •i••l•• o• •ll•• •i••l•• in •ny •o• •in••ion in w•i•• w• ••• in••••••••,
•i• •ly •y ••••in• • ••••l••• o• Circle •••• •••• ••• •••i•• ••ovi•in• ••• ••-
••vio•• w• w•n•. In ••• •x•• •l•, w• •• ow only •wo o••• •o•• •o• •in••ion•,
i.e., •l••••• ScreenEmptyCircle •n• PrintedFilledCircle.

A •••i• T • •y •••l••• *requirements*, *i.e.*, • li•• o• • •••o• •i•n••••••,
•o• • •••o•• •••• • ••• •• ••ovi••• •y •l••••• o• •••i•• ••in• T. H•••, •••i•
TEmptyCircle ••••i•••• • •••o• drawPoint wi•• •••••n •y•• void, •n• •wo int
••••• ••••••, •n• • •••o• getradius wi•• no ••••• ••••••, •n• int ••••n •y••.
• l••• SreenEmptyCircle •••• TScreenEmptyCircle; •••••, ••• •••• • •••o• i•
••ovi••• •y •••i• TScreenShape •n• ••• •••on• •y •l••• Circle.

Fo•• in• ••• •o•• •o• •in••ion• ••in• •in•l• in••i••n•• wo•l• • ••n •on•i-
••••l• •o•• •••li•••ion, •l••o••• i• •o•l• •• i• •l•• •n••• ••in• • •l•i•l• in-
•••i••n•• o• • ixin•. S•• [•0] •o• •x•• •l•• o• •i•••ion• w•••• T•i•• •iv• • o••
•l•••n• •ol••ion• •••n • ixin•, •n• •l•o •o• •x•• •l•• w•••• • ixin• •iv• • o••

---

[1] For the sake of simplicity, *Chai* only allows methods with a single parameter called
x, and does not permit sequences of expressions. These restrictions have minimal
implications for the presentation of the features we are interested in, and are not
adhered to by the examples in this section, nor by the prototype implementation.

```
class Circle {                      trait TScreenShape {
   int radius;                         void drawPoint(int x,int y) {
   int getRadius() { ... }                ...
}                                         }
                                    }
trait TEmptyCircle {
   requires {                       trait TPrintedShape {
      void drawPoint(int x,int y);     void drawPoint(int x,int y) {
      int getRadius();                    ...
   }                                      }
   void draw() { ... }              }
}
                                    class ScreenEmptyCircle
                                       extends Circle
trait TFilledCircle {                  uses TEmptyCircle,TScreenShape { }
   requires {
      void drawPoint(int x,int y);  class PrintedFilledCircle
      int getRadius();                 extends Circle
   }                                   uses TFilledCircle,TPrintedShape
   void draw() { ... }                 { }
}
```

Fig. 1. *Chai*₁ Example

```
class ScreenShapeStack {
   void push(TScreenShape shape) { ... }
   TScreenShape pop() { ... }
   ...
}

ScreenShapeStack stack = new ScreenShapeStack();
stack.push(new ScreenEmptyCircle());
stack.push(new ScreenFilledCircle());
TScreenShape shape = stack.pop();
```

Fig. 2. *Chai*₂ Example

•l•••n• •ol••ion• •••n •••i••. B•••••• ••• •••i• •o• •o•i•ion o••••••o•• ••• •o
fl•xi•l•, *Chai*₁ •llow• • ••• •n•• •o•• ••••• •••n J•v•.

    Fi•••• • •iv•••n •x•• •l• o••• ••••i•ion•l •••••••• o• *Chai*₂, w•••• w• •llow
•••i•• •o • • •••• •• •y•••. Any o•j••• o• • •l••• ••in• ••• •••i• TScreenShape
••n •• •••••••n••• •••o••• • v••i••l• o• •y• • TScreenShape. Allowin• •••i•• •o
••• n• •y••• ••••o••• • o•• •oly• o•••i•• , •n• i• •llow• •• •o •y•• •••••• •••i••
in•••• n••n•ly o• ••• •l••••• •••• ••• ••••.

```
class CircleShape extends Circle uses TEmptyCircle,TScreenShape {}

CircleShape circle = new CircleShape(); circle.draw();
        // draws an empty circle on screen
circle<TEmptyCircle -> TFilledCircle>; circle.draw();
        // draws a filled circle on screen
circle<TScreenShape -> TPrintedShape>; circle.draw();
        //  prints a filled circle
```

Fig. 3. *Chai₃* Example

In ••• • n•l •x•• • l•, in •••• 3, w• •• ow • ow • yn•• i• ••••i•• •ion o• •••i•• ••n •••n•• ••• ••••vio•• o• •n o• j••• •• •• n•i• •. T•• o• j••• circle ••••• o•• •• •n •• ••y •i••l• on •••••n, ••• •y •••••i•• •ion o• TFilledCircle •o• TEmptyCircle w• ••n •••n•• i• •o • •ll•• •i••l•, •n• •••••••••n•ly •y •••••i• ••••in• TPrintedShape •o• TScreenShape w• ••n •••n•• i• •o •••o• • • ••in••• • ll•• •i••l•.

3   The Language *Chai₁*

3.1   Syntax

Fo• *Chai₁* w• •••••••• T••i•• ••o• S• •ll••l• [1•] •o ••• J•v• ••••in•. A• in [1•], •••i•• ••n •• •••• •o ••• ••••vio•• •o •l••••• o• •o o•••• •••i••. T••i•• • •y •on••in • •••o• •••ni•ion•, ••• no ••l•• — •• w• ••i• •••li••, •••i•• ••• *pure behaviour* [1•]. A •••i• ••nno• i•••l• •••• •••• in •x•••ion (i.•. i• ••nno• •• in•••n•i••••) — i• (o• • •••i• ••in• i•) ••n •• *used* •y •o• • •l•••, w•i•• ••n ••n •• in•••n•i••••.

T••i•• ••• no• ••••i••• •o •• •o• •l••• - •••• i•, •••y • •y ••••i•• ••n•-•ion•li•y ••yon• •••i• own •o •• ••ovi•• •y •l••••• o• •••i•• ••in• •••• . T•• ••••i••• •n•• ••• •••l•••• •x•li•i•ly in ••• •o•• o•• ••• o• *required methods*.

A *Chai₁* ••o••••• •on•i••• o• •••i• •n• •l••• •••l•••ion•. A •••i• •••l•••ion •on•i••• o•• n•• • •o• ••• •••i•, •n o••ion• l li•• o• ••••• •••i•• (w• o•• •••• vio•• i• in•o•• o•••••), •n• • •••i• •o• y. T•• •••i• •o• y •on••in• • •••o• •••ni•ion•, •n• "•••i• •l••", *i.e.*, •••l•••ion o• ••••i••• • •••o••, •x•l••• •••l•••ion• (w• i•• •x•l••• • •••o•• •••• wo• l• o•••wi•• •• in•o••o••••• ••o• •••• •••i••) •n• •li•• •••l•••ion• (w• i•• •iv• n•w l•••l• •o • •••o•• in•o••o••••• ••o• • •••• •••i•).

In •on••••• •o ••• l•n••••• in [1•] w•i•• i• •n•y••• •n• w•••• ••••i••-• •n•• ••• in•••••• •••o• ••i••lly, in *Chai₁* ••ovi••• *and required methods* • ••• •• •••l•••• ••in• • •• ll •y•• •i•n•••••.² In •o• • on wi•• [1•], w• •i•-•in••i•• ••••i••• • •••o•• in•o ••o•• •••• • ••• •• ••ovi••• •y • •l••• ••in•

---

² In a related work [17], a typed language with automatic inference of required
  methods is described.

```
program   ::== ( trait | class )*
trait     ::== trait tr [uses tr+] { (trait-glue | meth)* }
field     ::== type f;
meth      ::== meth-sig { exp }
type      ::== cl
exp       ::== exp.f := exp | exp.m(exp) | super.m(exp) |
              new cl | var | this | null | x
trait-glue ::== requires { (meth-sig ; | super-sig ;)* } |
              exclude { (t.m ;)* } |
              alias { (t.m as m ;)* }
meth-sig  ::== type m(type x)
super-sig ::== type super.m(type x)
class     ::== class cl extends cl [uses tr+] { (field | meth)* }
cl,tr,m,f ::== identifiers
```

Fig. 4. *Chai₁* Syntax

••• •••i•, •n• ••o•• •••• • ••• •• ••ovi••• *by the superclass* o• ••• ••in• •l•••. T•·i• w•• n•••••••y ••••••• J•v• •llow• •x•li•i• •••••• •o ••••••l••• • •••o•• (•••o••• ••• super.m(...) •on••••••), •n• •o i• • •••i• tr i• •••• •y • •l••• cl, •••n •••••••l••• • •••o• ••ll• in•i•• • •••o•• o• tr will •••olv• •o • •••o•• ••o• ••• •••••••l••• o• cl.

A •l••• •••l•••ion •on•i••• o•• n•• • •o• ••• •l•••, i•• ••••••l•••, •n o••ion•l li•• o• •••• •••i•• (w•o•• ••••vio•• i• in•o•• o•••••), •n• • •l••• • o• y. T•• •l••• • o• y •on••in• • •••o• ••• ni•ion• •n• ••l••.

Fo• •i• • li•i•y, o••• o••l•o•• no• •••• •o•• • •••o• ov••lo••in• o• ••l• •i•in•, • ow•v•• w• ••li•v• i• ••n ••• •••ily •x••n••• •o •o •o — ••• i• •l•• •n••ion o• *Chai₁* •••• o••• i•.

No••, •••• in *Chai₁* •l••••• •o•• •y••• ••• •••i•• • o no•.

3.2 Basic Lookup Functions

W• •on•i•• •••• • ••o•••• P i• •li•i•ly •••n•• ••• •ollowin• •i••• (••••i•l) loo••• •• n••ion•:

- $P^{sup}(cl)$ •••• •n• ••• •i•••• ••••••l••• o• cl in P.
- $P^{fld}(cl,f)$ •••• •n• ••• •y•• o•••l• f •• ••• n•• in •l••• cl.
- $P^{mth}(cl,m)$ •n• $P^{mth}(tr,m)$ •••• •n ••• (•o••i•ly •• ••y) ••• o•• • •••o•• wi•• i••n•i•••• m •••n•• in •l••• cl o• •••i• tr.
- $P^{use}(cl)$, o• $P^{use}(tr)$ •••• •n ••• ••• o• •••i•• •i•••ly •••• in •l••• cl, o• •••i• tr.
- $P^{excl}(tr)$ •••• •n• ••• ••• o• •••i• •n• • •••o• i••n•i••• ••i•• •x•l•••• ••o• •••i• tr.
- $P^{alias}(tr,m)$ •••• •n• ••• ••• o• •••i• •n• • •••o• i••n•i••• ••i•• w•i•• ••• •li•••• o•• •••o• m in •••i• tr.

— $P^{req}(tr)$ •••••n• ••• ••• o• • •••o• •i•n•••••• • •n•ion•• •• ••••i••• in •••
•••l•••ion o• tr.

— $P^{req\_sup}(tr)$ •••••n• ••• ••• o• • •••o• •i•n•••••• • •n•ion•• •• ••••i••• •o•
••• ••••••l••• (•••o••• t super.m(t'x)) in ••• •••l•••ion o• tr.

No•• ••• ••• •• ov• •• n••ion• •o••••• on• •o *direct* loo•••• in ••• ••o••••
••x•, •n• •o no• •••• •l••• in••i••n•• no• •••i•• ••• in•o •••o• n•. In ••• n•x•
•••ion w• will ••• n• ••• •• n••ion• $\mathcal{F}$, $\mathcal{F}s$, $\mathcal{M}$, $\mathcal{MSig}$, •n• $\mathcal{M}^{orig}$, w•i•• loo•••
••l••, •n• • •••o••, •n• w•i•• *do* •••• •l••• in••i••n•• •n• •••i•• ••• in•o
•••o• n•.

3.3   Method or Field Acquisition Through Traits Use and Inheritance

T•• •• n••ion $\mathcal{F}(P, cl, f)$ loo•••• ••• ••l• f in cl o• i•• ••••••l••••, •n• ••••n•
t w•••• t i• ••• •y•• o• f in cl. T•• •• n••ion $\mathcal{F}_s(P, cl)$ •••••n• ••• ••• o• ••l••
•••n•• in cl, o• in••i••• ••o• cl'• ••••••l•••••. T•• •wo •• n••ion• o• •••••
only on •l••••• (•••i•• ••v• no ••l••).

$$\mathcal{F}(P, \text{Object}, f) = \bot$$
$$\mathcal{F}(P, cl, f) = \begin{cases} P^{fld}(cl, f) & i\bullet\ P^{fld}(cl, f) \neq \bot \\ P^{fld}(P^{sup}(cl), f) & o\bullet\bullet\bullet\bullet wi\bullet\bullet \end{cases}$$
$$\mathcal{F}_s(P, cl) = \{\ f\ |\ \mathcal{F}(P, cl, f) \neq \bot\ \}$$

A •l••• cl •••• •••• • •••i• tr •••• i••• ••• • •••o•• ••o• tr in •••• • w•y
•••• •x•••n•lly ••••• i• no w•y •o ••ll •••• ••• • •••o•• w••• no• •••l•••• •y cl
i•••l•. T•i• •o•• •••• •••i• o• ••• *flattening property* o• •••i•• - • •••i• •o•• •• •y
••in• •xi••in• •••i•• ••n • • vi•w•• •• •i•••• • •o• •o•i•• •n•i•y •o• ••i•in• •••
•••• •••i•• •n• ••• ••• ni•ion• in ••• n•w •••i•, o• ••• fl•••n•• •n•i•y •on••inin•
•ll ••• ••• ni•ion• o• i•• •on••i•• •n••.

W• now ••• n• $\mathcal{M}(P, cl, m)$ •n• $\mathcal{M}(P, tr, m)$, w•i•• •••••••iv•ly ••••••• ••• • ••••
•••i•• •n• ••••••l•••••. In••i•iv•ly, ••••• •• n••ion• •• • o• y •iv• •••••••n•• •o
"lo••l" •••l•••ion•: • •••o•• ••• n•• in • •••i• •o•y ••v• •i•••• •••••••n••,
•n• • •••o•• •••• ••v• ••n •li•••• ••v• •i•••• •••••••n•• •••n • •••o•• ••-
••i••• ••o• •••• •••i••. M•••o•••••n•• in •l••••o•y ••v• •i•••• •••••••n••,
•n• • •••o•• •••• i••• ••o• •••• •••i•• ••v• •i•••• •••••••n•• •••n ••o•• ••-
••i••• ••o• ••••••l•••••.

$$\mathcal{M}: \texttt{program} \times (\texttt{classId} \cup \texttt{traitId}) \times \texttt{methodId} \rightarrow \wp(\texttt{methodBody})$$

I• tr i• • •••i• :

$$\mathcal{M}(P, tr, m) = \begin{cases} P^{mth}(P) & i\bullet\ P^{mth}(P) \neq \emptyset \\ MsAlias & i\bullet\ P^{mth}(P) = \emptyset \neq MsAlias \\ MsUsed & i\bullet\ P^{mth}(P) = \emptyset = MsAlias. \end{cases}$$

w• ••••
$$MsAlias = \bigcup_{tr'.m' \in P^{alias}(tr, m)} \mathcal{M}(P, tr', m')$$
$$MsUsed = \bigcup_{tr'' \in P^{use}(tr),\ tr''.m \notin P^{excl}(tr.m)} \mathcal{M}(P, tr'', m)$$

I• cl i•• •|••• :

$$\mathcal{M}(\mathtt{P}, \mathtt{Object}, \mathtt{m}) = \emptyset$$

$$\mathcal{M}(\mathtt{P}, \mathtt{cl}, \mathtt{m}) \quad = \begin{cases} \mathtt{P^{mth}(cl,m)} & \text{i• } \mathtt{P^{mth}(cl,m)} \neq \emptyset \\ MsUsed & \text{i• } \mathtt{P^{mth}(cl,m)} = \emptyset \neq MsUsed \\ \mathcal{M}(\mathtt{P}, \mathtt{P^{sup}(cl)}, \mathtt{m}) & \text{i• } \mathtt{P^{mth}(cl,m)} = \emptyset = MsUsed, \\ \quad \text{w• •••} \end{cases}$$

$$MsUsed = \bigcup\nolimits_{\mathtt{tr} \in \mathtt{P^{use}(cl)}} \mathcal{M}(\mathtt{P}, \mathtt{tr}, \mathtt{m})$$

B•••••• •• ••• ••• ••v••••l w•y• • •••j• • j••• •••• •j•• • • •••o• (••o• •ny o• ••• •••j•• j• ••••), ••• • •••o• loo•••• •• n••ion• •••••n *sets* o• • •••o••. I• ••• ••••••••n•• ••|•• •o no• •••olv• ••• • •••o• loo•••• •o • •in•l• • •••o•, *i.e.*, i• in • •|••• cl, $|\mathcal{M}(\mathtt{P}, \mathtt{cl}, \mathtt{m})| > 1$ •o• •o• m, •••n • •onfli•• o•••••, [3].

A •l••• i• *complete* i• i• ••• no •onfli•••, •n• i• •ny ••ll •o super in •ny in••••j••• • •••o• •o•y •••olv•• wi••o•• •onfli••:[4]

$$\frac{\forall \mathtt{m}: \quad \text{e •on••in• super.m(...)} \implies |\mathcal{M}(\mathtt{P}, \mathtt{P^{sup}(cl)}, \mathtt{m'})| = 1}{\text{super •••olv•• wi••o•• •onfli•• in e •n• cl}}$$

$$\frac{\begin{array}{l} \forall \mathtt{m}: |\mathcal{M}(\mathtt{P}, \mathtt{cl}, \mathtt{m})| \leq 1 \\ \forall \mathtt{m}, \mathtt{cl'} \quad \mathtt{P} \vdash_1 \mathtt{cl} \leq \mathtt{cl'}, \text{ ...} \{e\} \in \mathcal{M}(\mathtt{P}, \mathtt{cl'}, \mathtt{m}) \implies \\ \qquad \text{super •••olv•• wi••o•• •onfli•• in e •n• cl'} \end{array}}{\mathtt{P} \vdash_1 \mathtt{cl} \diamond_{\mathrm{cmpl}}}$$

Fo• •l••• cl, •n• •••i• tr, w• •••n• ••• •• n••ion• $\mathcal{MSi}\bullet_1(\mathtt{P}, \mathtt{cl}, \mathtt{m})$, $\mathcal{MSi}\bullet_1(\mathtt{P}, \mathtt{tr}, \mathtt{m})$, •n• $\mathcal{MSi}\bullet_1^{\mathrm{sup}}(\mathtt{P}, \mathtt{cl}, \mathtt{m})$ w•i•• •••••n ••• ••• o• •i•n•••••• •o• • •••o• m •• •o•n• in cl, tr o• ••• •••••••l••• o• cl.

$$\mathcal{MSi}\bullet_1(\mathtt{P}, \mathtt{cl}, \mathtt{m}) = \{ \mathtt{t} \ \mathtt{m(t' \ x)} \mid \mathtt{t} \ \mathtt{m(t' \ x)}\{...\} \in \mathcal{M}(\mathtt{P}, \mathtt{cl}, \mathtt{m}) \}$$
$$\mathcal{MSi}\bullet_1(\mathtt{P}, \mathtt{tr}, \mathtt{m}) = \{ \mathtt{t} \ \mathtt{m(t' \ x)} \mid \mathtt{t} \ \mathtt{m(t' \ x)}\{...\} \in \mathcal{M}(\mathtt{P}, \mathtt{tr}, \mathtt{m}) \}$$
$$\mathcal{MSi}\bullet_1^{\mathrm{sup}}(\mathtt{P}, \mathtt{cl}, \mathtt{m}) = \mathcal{MSi}\bullet_1(\mathtt{P}, \mathtt{P^{sup}(cl)}, \mathtt{m})$$

No••, •••• ••• loo• •• •• n••ion• $\mathcal{M}(\mathtt{P}, \mathtt{cl}, \mathtt{m})$ •n• $\mathcal{MSi}\bullet_1(\mathtt{P}, \mathtt{cl}, \mathtt{m})$ ••••••••
••o• ••• ••• o• •••j••. T•••••o••, •• w• will ••• l••••, w• w••• ••l• •o w•i•• ••• o• •••ion•l ••• •n•i•• •n• •y• • •y•••• o• *Chai*$_1$ •n• *Chai*$_2$ wi••o•• •x• li•i• • •n•ion o• •••i••.

W• •••n• ••• •• n••ion $\mathcal{M}^{\mathrm{orig}}$ w•i•• •••••• in••• ••• "o•i•in" o• • • •••o•, *i.e.*, ••• • o•• •••••j•• •••••••l••• o• • •l••• cl w•i•• •on••in• • •o•y •o• m. W• will ••• $\mathcal{M}^{\mathrm{orig}}$ •o • o••l ••• •••••vio•• o• super.m(_).[5]

---

[3] Conflicts can be avoided by overriding the conflicting method in the class where the conflict occurs, or by excluding one of the conflicting methods - in our system without overloading this works only if all conflicting methods have the same signature.

[4] A simpler, but more restrictive, requirement would be to require no conflicts in any of cl's superclasses.

[5] This formalization of **super** has been suggested to us by Andrew Black and Chuan-Kai Lin, and slightly adapted by Rok Strnisa.

$$
\begin{aligned}
\rightsquigarrow \ : \quad & \textbf{program} \quad \rightarrow \quad \textbf{exp} \times \textbf{stack} \times \textbf{heap} \quad \rightarrow \quad (\textbf{val} \cup \textbf{dev}) \times \textbf{heap} \\
\textbf{stack} \ =\ & \textbf{addr} \times \textbf{val} \times \textbf{classId} \\
\textbf{heap} \ =\ & \textbf{addr} \rightarrow \textbf{object} \\
\textbf{val} \ =\ & \{\ \texttt{null}\ \} \cup \textbf{addr} \\
\textbf{object} \ =\ & \{\ [\![\, \texttt{cl} \,\|\, \texttt{f}_1 : \texttt{v}_1, \ldots, \texttt{f}_r : \texttt{v}_r \,]\!]\ \mid\ \texttt{cl} \in \textbf{classId},\ \texttt{f}_{1,\neg}\texttt{f}_r \in \textbf{fldId},\ \texttt{v}_{1,\neg}\texttt{v}_r \in \textbf{val}\ \} \\
\textbf{addr} \ =\ & \{\ \iota_n \mid n \text{ is a natural number}\ \} \\
\textbf{dev} \ =\ & \{\ \texttt{nllPntrExc}, \texttt{stuckExc}\ \}
\end{aligned}
$$

Fig. 5. *Chai*$_1$ Runtime

$$
\mathcal{M}^{\mathrm{orig}}(\mathrm{P}, \mathtt{cl}, \mathtt{m}) = \begin{cases}
\mathtt{cl} & \textbf{i•}\ \mathrm{P}^{\mathtt{mth}}(\mathtt{cl}, \mathtt{m}) \neq \emptyset \quad \textbf{o•}\ \exists \mathtt{tr}\ \text{wi••} \\
& \mathtt{tr} \in \mathrm{P}^{\mathtt{use}}(\mathtt{cl})\ \textbf{•n•}\ \mathcal{M}(\mathrm{P}, \mathtt{tr}, \mathtt{m}) \neq \emptyset, \\
\bot & \textbf{i•}\ \mathtt{cl} = \mathtt{Object}, \\
\mathcal{M}^{\mathrm{orig}}(\mathrm{P}, \mathtt{cl}', \mathtt{m}) & \textbf{o•••••wi••, •o•}\ \mathtt{cl}' = \mathrm{P}^{\mathtt{sup}}(\mathtt{cl}).
\end{cases}
$$

3.4   Operational Semantics

W• •iv• • l•••• •••• ••• •n•i•• •o• *Chai*$_1$, w•••• ••o•••• • • •• •x•••••ion•, •••••• •n• •••••, on•o ••••l•• •n• n•w •••••. A •••••, $\sigma \in$ **stack**, i• • ••i•l• •on•i•in• o•••• •••••••• o••••••••n• ••••iv••, ••• v•l•• o••••••••••l ••••• ••••• •n• ••• •l••• •on•• inin• •••• • •••o• • •o• y•••••n•ly ••in• •x••••••. T•• no•••ion $\sigma(\mathtt{this})$, $\sigma(\mathtt{x})$, •n• $\sigma(\mathtt{this\_class})$ ••l••••• ••• ••••, •••on• •n• ••i•• •o• •on•n• o• σ. A ••••, $\chi \in$ **heap**, • ••• •••••••••• •o o• j••••. • •j•••• •on•• in ••• •l••• o• ••• •o• j••• (cl), •n• v•l•• (v$_i$) •o• ••• o• j•••'• ••l•• (f$_i$).

T•• o•••••ion•l ••• •n•i•• o• *Chai*$_1$ •o•• no• • •n•ion ••••i•• •x• li•i•ly, •n• o•••••••• •n•i••ly in •••• • o• •l••••; •••• i• i• v••y •i• il•• •o •••• o• • •• •ll J•v•-li•• l•n••••• (*e.g.*, CLASSICJAVA[11] o• *Fickle*[•]), •n• i• ••••••• •••n••••. I• i• •iv•n in •••••• 6. T•• ••••iv•• •n• ••• ••••• •••• ••• loo••• •• in ••• •••• (**var**). I• null i• •••••••••n•••, • nullPnterExc •x••••ion i• •••own (**null-exception**). Fi•l• •••••• i• •v•l••••• •y loo•in• •• ••• •••••i••l•• ••l• in ••• o• j••• (**field**). Fi•l• •••i•n• •n• ov••i•• ••• •o••••• on in• ••l• wi•• ••• v•l•• o• ••• •i••• ••n• •i• (**field-assign**). • •j••• •••••ion ••••••• • n•w o• j••• o• ••• ••••o••i••• •l•••, •n• ini•i•li••• •ll i• ••l•• wi•• null (**new**). M•••o• ••ll •v•l••••• ••• • •••o• • o• y •o• n• in ••• *dynamic* •l••• o••• ••••iv••; •v•l••ion •••••• •l••• in • •••••• •on•i••in• o••• ••••iv•• •n• •••••l••••• •••• o• ••• ••ll, •n• ••• i••n•i•• o••• ••l••• •on•• inin• ••• • •••o• •o• y (**method-call**). Fo• ••• ••ll •o super ••• •v•l••ion i• •i• il••, ••• ••• • •••o• i• loo••• •• in ••• *static* ••••••l••• o• •••• •l••• •iv•n • y $\sigma(\mathtt{this\_class})$, *i.e.*, ••• •••••l••• o• •••• •l••• •on•• inin• ••• • •••o• ••••••n•ly ••in• •x•••••• (**super-call**). W• ••••i•• ••• • •••o• loo••• •• n••ion• •o ••••n • •in•l••on •••, *i.e.*, ••••• ••o•l• •• no •onfli••in• • •••o• ••• ni•ion•.

Fo• ••••i•y, w• o• i•••• ••• ••l•• •••owin• stuckErr w••n •onfli••in• • •••-o••• •••• ••ll••, o• non-•xi•••n• ••l•• o• • •••o••• ••• •••••••• o• ••ll••, •• w•ll •• •••• ••l•• ••o••••in• •x•••••ion• stuckExc o• nullPntrExc.

null

$$\frac{}{\texttt{null},\ \sigma,\ \chi \leadsto_{\texttt{P}} \texttt{null}, \chi}$$

null-exception

$$\frac{\texttt{e},\ \sigma,\ \chi \leadsto_{\texttt{P}} \texttt{null}, \chi'}{\begin{array}{l}\texttt{e.f := e}',\ \sigma,\ \chi \leadsto_{\texttt{P}} \texttt{nllPntrExc}, \chi' \\ \texttt{e.f},\ \sigma,\ \chi \leadsto_{\texttt{P}} \texttt{nllPnterExc}, \chi' \\ \texttt{e.m(e}'\texttt{)},\ \sigma,\ \chi \leadsto_{\texttt{P}} \texttt{nllPntrExc}, \chi'\end{array}}$$

field

$$\frac{\texttt{e},\ \sigma,\ \chi \leadsto_{\texttt{P}} \iota, \chi'}{\texttt{e.f},\ \sigma,\ \chi \leadsto_{\texttt{P}} \chi'(\iota)(\texttt{f}), \chi'}$$

var

$$\frac{}{\begin{array}{l}\texttt{x},\ \sigma,\ \chi \leadsto_{\texttt{P}} \sigma(\texttt{x}), \chi \\ \texttt{this},\ \sigma,\ \chi \leadsto_{\texttt{P}} \sigma(\texttt{this}), \chi\end{array}}$$

field-assign

$$\frac{\begin{array}{l}\texttt{e},\ \sigma,\ \chi \leadsto_{\texttt{P}} \iota, \chi'' \\ \texttt{e}',\ \sigma,\ \chi'' \leadsto_{\texttt{P}} \texttt{v}, \chi''' \\ \chi' = \chi'''[\iota \mapsto \chi'''(\iota)[\texttt{f} \mapsto \texttt{v}]]\end{array}}{\texttt{e.f := e}',\ \sigma,\ \chi \leadsto_{\texttt{P}} \texttt{v}, \chi'}$$

new

$$\frac{\begin{array}{l}\mathcal{F}_s(\texttt{P}, \texttt{cl}) = \texttt{f}_1, \ldots \texttt{f}_r \\ \forall \texttt{k} \in 1, \ldots \texttt{r} : \texttt{v}_k = \texttt{null} \\ \iota \text{ is new in } \chi\end{array}}{\texttt{new cl},\ \sigma,\ \chi \leadsto_{\texttt{P}} \iota, \chi[\iota \mapsto [\![\, \texttt{cl} \parallel \texttt{f}_1 : \texttt{v}_1, \ldots \texttt{f}_r : \texttt{v}_r \,]\!]]}$$

method-call

$$\frac{\begin{array}{l}\texttt{e}_r,\ \sigma,\ \chi \leadsto_{\texttt{P}} \iota, \chi_0 \\ \texttt{e}_a,\ \sigma,\ \chi_0 \leadsto_{\texttt{P}} \texttt{v}_1, \chi_1 \\ \chi_1(\iota) = [\![\, \texttt{cl} \parallel \ldots \,]\!] \\ \mathcal{M}(\texttt{P}, \texttt{cl}, \texttt{m}) = \{\ \texttt{t m(t}'\ \texttt{x)}\ \{\ \texttt{e}\ \}\ \} \\ \mathcal{M}^{orig}(\texttt{P}, \texttt{cl}, \texttt{m}) = \texttt{cl}' \\ \sigma' = (\iota, \texttt{v}_1, \texttt{cl}') \\ \texttt{e},\ \sigma',\ \chi_1 \leadsto_{\texttt{P}} \texttt{v}, \chi'\end{array}}{\texttt{e}_r\texttt{.m(e}_a\texttt{)},\ \sigma,\ \chi \leadsto_{\texttt{P}} \texttt{v}, \chi'}$$

super-call

$$\frac{\begin{array}{l}\texttt{e}_a,\ \sigma,\ \chi \leadsto_{\texttt{P}} \texttt{v}_1, \chi_1 \\ \sigma(\texttt{this_class}) = \texttt{cl} \\ \texttt{P}^{sup}(\texttt{cl}) = \texttt{cl}'' \\ \mathcal{M}(\texttt{P}, \texttt{cl}'', \texttt{m}) = \{\ \texttt{t m(t}'\ \texttt{x)}\ \{\ \texttt{e}\ \}\ \} \\ \mathcal{M}^{orig}(\texttt{P}, \texttt{cl}'', \texttt{m}) = \texttt{cl}' \\ \sigma' = (\sigma(\texttt{this}), \texttt{v}_1, \texttt{cl}') \\ \texttt{e},\ \sigma',\ \chi_1 \leadsto_{\texttt{P}} \texttt{v}, \chi'\end{array}}{\texttt{super.m(e}_a\texttt{)},\ \sigma,\ \chi \leadsto_{\texttt{P}} \texttt{v}, \chi'}$$

Fig. 6. *Chai*$_1$ Operational Semantics

$$\frac{\texttt{P} = \ldots\ \texttt{class cl extends cl}'\ \ldots}{\begin{array}{l}\texttt{P} \vdash_1 \texttt{cl} \leq \texttt{cl} \\ \texttt{P} \vdash_1 \texttt{cl} \leq \texttt{cl}' \\ \texttt{P} \vdash \texttt{cl} \diamond_{\text{class}} \\ \texttt{P} \vdash_1 \texttt{cl} \diamond_{\text{type}}\end{array}} \qquad \frac{\begin{array}{l}\texttt{P} \vdash_1 \texttt{cl} \leq \texttt{cl}' \\ \texttt{P} \vdash_1 \texttt{cl}' \leq \texttt{cl}''\end{array}}{\texttt{P} \vdash_1 \texttt{cl} \leq \texttt{cl}''} \qquad \frac{\texttt{P} = \ldots\ \texttt{trait tr}\ \ldots}{\texttt{P} \vdash \texttt{tr} \diamond_{\text{trait}}}$$

Fig. 7. Subclasses and Subtypes in *Chai*$_1$

3.5 Type System

In ••••• • w• •••n• ••• j••••• •n•• $\texttt{P} \vdash \texttt{cl} \leq \texttt{cl}'$ in•i•••in• ••••y•••, •n• $\texttt{P} \vdash \texttt{cl} \diamond_{\text{class}}$ •n• $\texttt{P} \vdash \texttt{tr} \diamond_{\text{trait}}$ in•i•••in• •••• $\texttt{cl}$ i• • •l••• o• $\texttt{tr}$ i• • •••i•. W• •l•o •••n• ••• j••••• •n• $\texttt{P} \vdash \texttt{t} \diamond_{\text{type}}$ in•i•••in• •••• $\texttt{t}$ i• • •y••.

$$\textbf{subsumption} \qquad\qquad\qquad \textbf{var-this}$$

$$\frac{\begin{array}{l} P,\Gamma \vdash_1 e : t \\ P \vdash_1 t \le t' \end{array}}{P,\Gamma \vdash_1 e : t'} \qquad\qquad \frac{P,\Gamma \vdash_1 x : \Gamma(x)}{P,\Gamma \vdash_1 \text{this} : \Gamma(\text{this})}$$

$$\textbf{new} \qquad\qquad\qquad \textbf{null}$$

$$\frac{P \vdash_1 cl \diamond_{cmpl}}{P,\Gamma \vdash_1 \text{new } cl : cl} \qquad\qquad \frac{P \vdash_1 t \diamond_{type}}{P,\Gamma \vdash_1 \text{null} : t}$$

$$\textbf{field} \qquad\qquad\qquad \textbf{field-assign}$$

$$\frac{\begin{array}{l} P,\Gamma \vdash_1 e : cl \\ \mathcal{F}(P,cl,f) = t \end{array}}{P,\Gamma \vdash_1 e.f : t} \qquad\qquad \frac{\begin{array}{l} P,\Gamma \vdash_1 e : cl \\ P,\Gamma \vdash_1 e' : t \\ \mathcal{F}(P,cl,f) = t \end{array}}{P,\Gamma \vdash_1 e.f := e' : t}$$

$$\textbf{method-call} \qquad\qquad\qquad \textbf{super-call}$$

$$\frac{\begin{array}{l} P,\Gamma \vdash_1 e_r : t_r \\ P,\Gamma \vdash_1 e_a : t_a \\ \mathcal{MS}ig_1(P,t_r,m) = \{\, t\ m(t_a\ x)\,\} \end{array}}{P,\Gamma \vdash_1 e_r.m(e_a) : t} \qquad \frac{\begin{array}{l} \Gamma(\text{this}) = t_r \\ P,\Gamma \vdash_1 e_a : t_a \\ \mathcal{MS}ig_1^{sup}(P,t_r,m) = \{\, t\ m(t_a\ x)\,\} \end{array}}{P,\Gamma \vdash_1 \text{super}.m(e_a) : t}$$

Fig. 8. $Chai_1$ Type Rules

Fo• •y•• •••••in• w• ••• • •y• in• •nvi•on• •n• Γ w• i•• • ••• ••• ••••iv••, this, •n• ••• • •••o• ••••• ••••, x, •o • •l••• n•• •.   T•• •y• in• j••••• •n• $P,\Gamma \vdash_1 e : t$ • ••n• •••• in ••• •on••x• o••o•••• P •n• •nvi•on• •n• Γ, in ••• •y•• •y•••• o• $Chai_1$, ••• •x• •••ion e ••• •y•• t. Al••o••• in $Chai_1$ only •l••••• ••n •• •y•••, ••• •y•• •l•• in •••••• • • •n•ion •y••• t ••••••• ••n •l••••• cl; •• i• ••n•••li•y •llow• •• •o ••••• •••••• •y•• •l•• •o• $Chai_2$.

T•• •y•• ••l••, •iv•n in •••••• •, *do not explicitly mention traits*, ••-••••• •••i•• ••v• •l••••y ••n •••• n in•o •••o• n• •••o••• $\mathcal{MS}i•_1(\_,\_,\_)$ •n• $\mathcal{MS}i•_1^{sup}(\_,\_,\_)$. T••y ••• •••n•••• in •ll o•••• •••••••••: An •x• •••ion o• • ••••••in •y•• •l•o ••• •ny o• i•• ••••••y••• (**subsumption**). T•• •y•• o• ••• •o•• •l ••••• ••••• ••n• ••••iv•• ••• loo••• •• in ••• •y•• •nvi•on• •n• (**var-this**). T•• ••••••ion o• • n•w o• j••• ••• ••• •y•• o• ••••• •l•••, ••ovi••• ••••• ••• •l••• i• •o• •l••• (**new**), w• il• null ••• •ny •y•• (**null**). T•• •y•• o• • • •••o• ••ll i• ••• •••••n •y•• o• ••• ••n••ion •o• n• •y loo• in• in ••• •l••• o•••• •••• •x•••-•ion •••o••• $\mathcal{MS}i•_1(P,cl,m)$, ••ovi•• •••• ••• •••on• •x• •••ion ••• ••• •y•• o•••• •o•• •l ••••• •••• •y•• (**method-call**). Si• il••ly •o• (**super-call**), w• ••• ••• • •••o• i• loo••••-•• in ••• ••••••l••• •••o••• $\mathcal{MS}i•_1^{sup}(P,cl,m)$.

$$P^{sup}(cl) = cl'$$
$$\forall f: \quad P^{fld}(cl, f) = t \implies \mathcal{F}(P, cl', f) = \bot, \; P \vdash_1 t \; \Diamond_{type}$$
$$\forall m: \quad t_0 \; m(t_1 \; x)\{e\} \in \mathcal{M}(P, cl, m) \implies$$
$$\qquad P \vdash_1 t_0 \; \Diamond_{type}$$
$$\qquad P \vdash_1 t_1 \; \Diamond_{type}$$
$$\qquad P, t_1 \; x, cl \; \mathtt{this} \vdash_1 e : t_0$$
$$\qquad \mathcal{M}(P, cl', m) = \emptyset \; \lor \; \mathcal{M}(P, cl', m) = \{ \; t_0 \; m(t_1 \; x) \; \{...\} \; \}$$
$$\overline{P \vdash_1 cl}$$

for all classes cl defined in P: $P \vdash_1 cl$
$$\overline{\vdash_1 P}$$

Fig. 9. Well formed classes and programs in *Chai₁*

No•••, •••• ••••i••• • •••o•• •o no• •l•y •ny •ôl• in *Chai₁* •y••-••••••in• (•••y •o •l•y • •ôl• in *Chai₂* •n• *Chai₃* •y•• ••••••in•).

In •••••• 9 w •••n• ••• no•ion o•• w•ll-•o•• •• *Chai₁* •l•••, *i.e.,* P ⊢₁ cl . A •l••• cl i• w•ll-•o•• •• i•:

1. Any ••l• •••n•• in •••• •l••• ••• • v•li• •y••, •n• i• no• •••n•• in i•• ••••••l••• cl';
•. Any • •••o• •••n•• in ••• •l•••, o• ••••i••• ••o••• ••••• o• • •••i• o• in••i••n•• ••o• • •••••l•••, ••• •••••n •n• ••••• ••• •y•• w i•• ••• v•li• •y•••, •n•, in • •y•in• •nvi•on• •n• w•i•• • ••• x •o ••• ••••• •n• •y•• t₁ •n• this •o cl (•••• •n •nvi•on• •n• i• w•i••n•• t₁ x, cl this), ••• • •••o• •o•y ••• ••• ••l•••• ••••n •y•• t₀. A••i•ion•lly, i•••i• • •••o• i• •••••n in ••• •••••••l•••, o• •ny •••• •••i••, •••n i• •••••••••n•• ••••• wi•• ••• ••• • ••••••n •y•• •n• ••••• •••• •y••.

T•• ••••i••• •n••. ••o• •• ov• i• v••y •••on•: I•••••••• *all inherited and acquired* • •••o•• in •l••• - ••••••••nj•••••• • •••o••••n•• in ••• •l••• i•••l•. T•••, • • •••o• •••n•• in ••• i• will •• •y•• •••••••• in •ll •l••••• ••in• •••• •••i•; ••i• i• •n•voi••l•, •••••••• in *Chai₁* • •••o• •o•i•• ••nno• •• •••••••• in ••• •••i••.

A••o•••• i• w•ll-•o•• ••, ⊢₁ P, i••ll i•• •l•••••••• w•ll-•o•• ••. No•• ••••••• •••i••••• no• •••••••. No•• •l•o, •••• w• •o no• •••• i•• ••• in••i••n•• •i•••••y •o •• ••y•li•; •l••o••• •• i• i• •onv•ni•n•, i• i• no• n••••••••y •o• •o• n•n•••; in • ••o•••• wi•• •y•li• in••i••n••, • ••nin• ••n •• •iv•n •o loo••• •• n••ion• (*M*, *M*orig) •••o••• •l•••• •x•• •oin••.

3.6 Type Soundness

T•• j••••• •n• P,σ ⊢v ◁ t in ••••• 10 • ••n• •••• ••• v•l•• v •••••• wi•• ••• •y•• t. In ••••i••l••, i• v i• •n •••••••, i• ••••i••• •••• ••• o•j••• •• v ••lon•• •o • •l••• cl w•i•• i• • •••y•• •o• t, •n• •o• •ll ••l•• •••n•• in cl,

••• o• j••• •on•• in• v• l••• w• i•• ••••• wi•• ••• •y• •• o• ••• ••l•• ••• ••l•••• in cl.[6] T•• j•• ••• •n• P, Γ ⊢₁ σ, χ • ••n• ••• •••• o• j•••• in ••• •••• χ ••••• wi•• •••i• •l•••••, •n• ••lon• •o •o• •l••• •l••••• (*i.e.*, no •onfli•••), •••• •• •••• iv•• o• j••• •n• ••••• •n• v•l•• •••• wi•• •••i• •y• ••• •iv•n in Γ, •n• ••••• •• •l••• •on•• inin• ••• • ••• o• ••••• n•ly •in• •x••••• (σ(this_class)) i• ••• •• •• ••• •y• • o• ••• ••• iv•• in ••• •y• • •nvi•on• •n• (Γ(this)).

$$\frac{P \vdash_1 t \diamond_{type}}{P, \chi \vdash_1 \mathtt{null} \triangleleft t}$$

$$\chi(\iota) = \llbracket \mathtt{cl} \parallel \ldots \rrbracket$$
$$P \vdash_1 \mathtt{cl} \leq t$$
$$\frac{\mathcal{F}(P, \mathtt{cl}, \mathtt{f}) = t' \implies P, \chi \vdash_1 \chi(\iota)(\mathtt{f}) \triangleleft t'}{P, \chi \vdash_1 \iota \triangleleft t}$$

$$\forall \iota: \ \chi(\iota) = \llbracket \mathtt{cl} \parallel \ldots \rrbracket \implies P, \chi \vdash_1 \iota \triangleleft \mathtt{cl}, \text{and } P \vdash_1 \mathtt{cl} \diamond_{cmpl}$$
$$P, \sigma \vdash_1 \sigma(\mathtt{this}) \triangleleft \Gamma(\mathtt{this})$$
$$P, \sigma \vdash_1 \sigma(\mathtt{x}) \triangleleft \Gamma(\mathtt{x})$$
$$\sigma(\mathtt{this\_class}) = \Gamma(\mathtt{this})$$
$$\frac{}{P, \Gamma \vdash_1 \sigma, \chi}$$

Fig. 10. Agreement in *Chai₁*

T•• •ollowin• l•• • • i• •••• i•l in ••• ••oo• o• •o• n• n•••, •n• ••••• n•••• •••• 1-•) ••• •xi••• n•• •n• •y• •• o• ••l•• •n• • ••• o•• i• ••••• v•• •o ••• •l•••••, 3) •••• ••••• ••• no • o•• •••n on• • ••• o• •i•n••••• ••• • ••• o• in • ••••• •l••• o• • •o• •l••• •l••• (•l••o••• ••••• ••n •• ••v••• l • ••• o• •o•i••, •n• •) •••• i• • • ••• o• ••• • ••••• in •i•n••••• in • ••• •••l••• cl′, ••• n • ••• o• loo••• in ••• ••• •l••• cl will ••••• n • • ••• o• •o• y w• i•• •y• • •••••• wi•• ••i• •i•n••••• in ••• •l••• cl″ w• i•• •on•• in• ••i• • ••• o• •o• y (o• in•• •i•• i• ••o• • ••• i•).

Lemma 1. *If* ⊢₁ P *and* P ⊢₁ cl ≤ cl′ *then:*

1. $\mathcal{F}(P, \mathtt{cl}', \mathtt{f}) = t \implies \mathcal{F}(P, \mathtt{cl}, \mathtt{f}) = t$.
2. $\mathcal{MSi}\bullet_1(P, \mathtt{cl}', \mathtt{m}) \subseteq \mathcal{MSi}\bullet_1(P, \mathtt{cl}, \mathtt{m})$.
3. $P \vdash_1 \mathtt{cl} \diamond_{cmpl} \implies |\mathcal{MSi}\bullet_1(P, \mathtt{cl}', \mathtt{m})| \leq 1$.
4. $t \ m(t' \ x) \in \mathcal{MSi}\bullet_1(P, \mathtt{cl}', \mathtt{m}) \implies \exists \mathtt{cl}'', e:$
   - $\mathcal{M}^{orig}(P, \mathtt{cl}, \mathtt{m}) = \mathtt{cl}''$, $\quad t \ m(t' \ x)\{e\} \in \mathcal{M}(P, \mathtt{cl}, \mathtt{m})$,
   - $P \vdash_1 \mathtt{cl} \leq \mathtt{cl}'' \quad P, t' \ x, \mathtt{cl}'' \ \mathtt{this} \vdash_1 e : t.$

W• ••n now ••ov• •o• n• n••• o• ••• •y• • •y•••• :

Theorem 2 (Type Soundness of *Chai₁*). *For program* P, *typing environment* Γ, *expression* e, *so that* super *resolves without conflict in* e *and* Γ(this_class), *stack* σ, *heap* χ, *and type* t:

---

[6] Although the definition of $P, \chi \vdash_1 \iota \triangleleft t$ is recursive, there exists an equivalent non-recursive definition for it.

If

$$\vdash_1 \mathtt{P} \ and \ \mathtt{P}, \Gamma \vdash_1 \mathtt{e} : \mathtt{t} \ and \ \mathtt{P}, \Gamma \vdash_1 \sigma, \chi \ and \ \mathtt{e}, \sigma, \chi \leadsto_P \mathtt{r}, \chi'$$

then:

$$\mathtt{P}, \Gamma \vdash_1 \sigma, \chi' \quad and \quad \mathtt{P}, \chi' \vdash_1 \mathtt{r} \lhd \mathtt{t} \ or \ \mathtt{r} = \mathtt{nllPntrExc}.$$

In o•••• wo•••, •x•••ion o• w•ll •y••• •x•••ion• •••••v•• w•ll •o•• •• n••• o•
••• •••• •n• •••••, •o•• no• ••• ••••• (•in•• r i• •i•••• • v•l•• o• • n•ll • oin•••
•x•••ion), •n• i• i• ••••n• • v•l••, •••n •• i• v•l•• i• o• ••• ••• • •y•• •• •••
o•i• in•l •x• ••••ion.

4 The Language *Chai*$_2$

In *Chai*$_2$ w• •x••n••• ••• ••• i• o• •••i••, •o •••• •••y • •y •• • •••• •• •y•••.
T• i• ••• ••••• i• • o•••n• ••• ••••••ion•:

Fi•••, w• ••n ••••• in • •ni•o•• w•y o• j•••• w•o•• •l••• •••• • •iv•n •••i•,
e.g., w• ••n w•i•• • •••••• •o• •••••n••••••, •• in •••••• •. T•••, •••i•• •••• •o••
• oly• o••• i•• , •l•y ••• •ol• o• in••••••••, •n• in••o•••• • •l•i• l• ••• •••y•••.

S••on•, w• ••n •y••••••• •••i•• in i•ol••ion, •n• ••••••o••, w• will •• ••l•
•o •y• • •••••• • • •••o• ••• n•• in • ••i• only on••, ••••••• ••• n ••vin• •o •••••
i• •••in in •ll ••• •l••••• ••in• •••• •••i•.

T• i••, w• ••n •••• •••• i••• • ••• o•• in•o •••o• n•, •n• ••n •y• • •••••• ••ll•
•o •••• i••• • ••• o•• w•i•• •o no• ••v• • • ••• o• • o• y in ••• ••••iv•'• •l•••
o• •••i•. T• i• i• ••••, ••••••• w• •llow o• j••• ••••ion only •o• *complete* •l•••••,
•n• *Chai*$_2$ •o• • l••• •l••••• ••• •• o•• •••••• ••ovi• •• ••• o• • o•i•• •o• •ll •••• i•••
• ••• o••.

4.1 *Chai*$_2$ Syntax and Operational Semantics

T•• only • iff•••n••• •••w••n ••• •yn••x o• *Chai*$_2$ •n• •••• o• *Chai*$_1$ i• •••• *Chai*$_2$
•llow• •••i•• •o •• •y•••, i.•:

type ::= cl | tr

T•• o•••••ion•l ••• •n•i•• o• *Chai*$_2$ i• i• n•i••l •o •••• o• *Chai*$_1$.

4.2 Required Methods

W• ••• •••n• *indirect use* o• •••i••, w•••• $\mathcal{U}se^*(\mathtt{P}, \mathtt{tr})$ •oll•••• ••• •••n•i•iv•
•lo•••• o• ••• •••i•• •••• in tr, •n• $\mathcal{U}se^*(\mathtt{P}, \mathtt{cl})$ •oll•••• •ll •••i•• in•i•••ly ••••
•y •••i•• •••• in cl, o• in cl'• •••••••l•••••.

$$\mathcal{U}se^*(\mathtt{P}, \mathtt{tr}) \ = \ \bigcup\nolimits_{\mathtt{tr'} \in \mathrm{P}^{\mathrm{use}}(\mathtt{tr})} \mathcal{U}se^*(\mathtt{P}, \mathtt{tr'}) \ \cup \ \{ \ \mathtt{tr} \ \}$$
$$\mathcal{U}se^*(\mathtt{P}, \mathtt{cl}) \ = \ \bigcup\nolimits_{\mathtt{P} \vdash \mathtt{cl} \leq \mathtt{cl'}, \ \mathtt{tr} \in \mathrm{P}^{\mathrm{use}}(\mathtt{cl'})} \mathcal{U}se^*(\mathtt{P}, \mathtt{tr})$$

A •••i• tr • •y •••n• • li•• o• *required* • ••• o••. A •••on• •••i• tr' w•i••
•••• tr in••••i•• tr'• •••• i••• • ••• o•••n• • •y••• n•w •••• i••• •n•• o• i•• own,
••• o••• •x• li•i• •••• i••• •n•• o• •••o••• •x•l••ion. A •l••• ••in• tr in••••i•• •••
•••• i••• •n•• o• tr.

$$\mathcal{MR}^{\bullet\bullet}(P, tr, m) = \bigcup_{tr' \in \mathcal{U}se^*(P,tr)} P^{req}(tr') \cup$$
$$\bigcup_{tr' \in \mathcal{U}se^*(P,tr)} \{ \ t \ m(t' \ x) \mid \exists tr'' : \ (tr'', m) \in P^{excl}(tr'),$$
$$t \ m(t' \ x) \in \mathcal{MSi}^{\bullet}_1(P, tr'', m) \cup \mathcal{MR}^{\bullet\bullet}(P, tr'', m) \ ) \}$$
$$\mathcal{MR}^{\bullet\bullet}(P, cl, m) = \bigcup_{tr \in \mathcal{U}se^*(P,cl)} \mathcal{MR}^{\bullet\bullet}(P, tr, m)$$
$$\mathcal{MR}^{\bullet\bullet\,sup}(P, tr, m) = \bigcup_{tr' \in \mathcal{U}se^*(P,tr)} P^{req\text{-}sup}(tr')$$
$$\mathcal{MR}^{\bullet\bullet\,sup}(P, cl, m) = \bigcup_{tr \in \mathcal{U}se^*(P,cl)} \mathcal{MR}^{\bullet\bullet\,sup}(P, tr, m)$$

No•••, •••• i• i• •o••i••l• •o• • •i•n••••• •o •• ••••i••• in • •••i• tr, •n• •o• ••• •••i• •o ••v• • • •••o• • o•y •o• ••i• •i•n•••••. Si• il••ly •o• •l•••••.

A •l••• w•i•• i• •o• •l••• in ••• ••n•• o• $Chai_1$, •n• w••••• •ll ••••i••• • •••o••••v• • •o•y i• •o• •l••• •o• $Chai_2$:

$$\forall m: \ t \ m(t' \ x) \in \mathcal{MR}^{\bullet\bullet}(P, cl, m) \implies \exists e : \ t \ m(t' \ x) \{e\} \in \mathcal{M}(P, cl, m)$$
$$\forall m: \ |\mathcal{M}(P, cl, m)| \leq 1$$
$$\forall m, cl' \quad P \vdash_1 cl \leq cl', \ ...\{e\} \in \mathcal{M}(P, cl', m) \implies$$
$$\text{super} \ \bullet\bullet\bullet \text{olv}\bullet\bullet \ \text{wi}\bullet\text{o}\bullet\bullet \ \bullet \text{onfli}\bullet\bullet \ \text{in } e \ \bullet n\bullet \ cl'$$
$$\overline{P \vdash_2 cl \ \Diamond_{cmpl}}$$

T•••, • •o• •l••• ••••l••• o• t will ••ovi•• • • •••o• • o•y •o• •ny • •••o• ••••i••• • y t. T•• ••n••ion $\mathcal{MSi}^{\bullet}_2(P, t, m)$ ••••n• ••• •i•n••••• o• ••• • •••o• •••• will •• ••ovi••• •o• m •y • •o• •l••• ••••l••• o• t, w•il• ••• ••n••ion $\mathcal{MSi}^{\bullet\,sup}_2(P, t, m)$ ••••n• ••• •i•n••••• o• •ll • •••o•• •••• will •• ••ovi••• in ••• •• •••l••• o• • •o• •l••• ••••l••• o• t:

$$\mathcal{MSi}^{\bullet}_2(P, tr, m) = \mathcal{MSi}^{\bullet}_1(P, tr, m) \cup \mathcal{MR}^{\bullet\bullet}(P, tr, m)$$
$$\mathcal{MSi}^{\bullet}_2(P, cl, m) = \mathcal{MSi}^{\bullet}_1(P, cl, m) \cup \mathcal{MR}^{\bullet\bullet}(P, cl, m)$$
$$\mathcal{MSi}^{\bullet\,sup}_2(P, tr, m) = \mathcal{MSi}^{\bullet\,sup}_1(P, cl, m) \cup \mathcal{MR}^{\bullet\bullet\,sup}(P, tr, m)$$
$$\mathcal{MSi}^{\bullet\,sup}_2(P, cl, m) = \mathcal{MSi}^{\bullet\,sup}_1(P, cl, m) \cup \mathcal{MR}^{\bullet\bullet\,sup}(P, cl, m)$$

No•i••, •••• $t \in P^{use}(t')$ i• •li•• •••• $\mathcal{MSi}^{\bullet}_2(P, t, m) \subseteq \mathcal{MSi}^{\bullet}_2(P, t', m)$ •o• •ll m, •n• •l••• o• •••i• t, •n• t'.

4.3   Type System

A• w• •••n• in ••••• 11, • •l••• o• •••i• i• • •••y•• o• •ny •••i• •••• i• •••• -•o••i•ly in•i••••ly. T•••, • •l••• cl o• •••i• tr •••• •••• • •••i• tr' i• • •••y• o• tr', •v•n i• tr $requires \ more$ • •••o• •••• n tr'. T•i• • •y •••• ••••i•i•, ••• i• i• •••• •o• ••• ••ollowin• •••on: •v•n ••o••• •••i•• ••• •y••, ••• ••n•i• • •n•i•i•• (i.•. ••• o• j••••) will ••lon• •o $complete$ •l••••, w•i••, • y •••ni•ion, ••ovi•• • • •••o• • o•y •o• •ny ••••i••• • •••o•. T•• •n••in• •••• y•• ••l••ion••i• i• •••n•i•iv•.

No•• •••• $P \vdash_2 t' \leq t$ i• •li•• •••• $\mathcal{MSi}^{\bullet}_2(P, t, m) \subseteq \mathcal{MSi}^{\bullet}_2(P, t', m)$ - w• •o•l• ••v• •••n•• •••y•• in • ••••••••••l, •••••• •••n • no• in•l w•y ••in• ••• •• ov• ••o•••y.

In $Chai_2$ •••i•• ••n •• •y••, ••••••o•• in $Chai_2$ •y•in• •nvi•on•n•• • •y • •• this, •n• x •o • •••i• o• • •l•••. T•• •y•in• ••l•• ••• ••• ••• • •• ••o•• •o• $Chai_1$, wi•• ••••• •x•••••ion•. Fi•••, ••• $subsumption$ ••l• ••••• ••• n•w

$$\frac{P \vdash \mathtt{tr} \diamond_{\mathrm{class}}}{P \vdash_2 \mathtt{cl} \diamond_{\mathrm{type}}} \qquad \frac{P \vdash \mathtt{tr} \diamond_{\mathrm{trait}}}{P \vdash_2 \mathtt{tr} \diamond_{\mathrm{type}}}$$

$$\frac{P \vdash_1 \mathtt{cl} \leq \mathtt{cl}'}{P \vdash_2 \mathtt{cl} \leq \mathtt{cl}'} \qquad \frac{\mathtt{tr} \in \mathcal{U}se^*(P, \mathtt{cl})}{P \vdash_2 \mathtt{cl} \leq \mathtt{tr}} \qquad \frac{\mathtt{tr} \in \mathcal{U}se^*(P, \mathtt{tr}')}{P \vdash_2 \mathtt{tr}' \leq \mathtt{tr}}$$

Fig. 11. Types and Subtypes in *Chai₂*

•••y•• ••l••ion P ⊢₂ t′ ≤ t. S••on•, ••• ••l•• **method-call** •n• **super-call** ••••
••• ••••j••• • •••o• in•o •••o• n•, *i.e.,* ••• $\mathcal{MS}i$•₂(P,t,m) •n• $\mathcal{MS}i$•₂^{sup}(P,t,m).
T•i••, ••• ••l• **new** ••••j••• ••• •l••• •o•• •o• •l••• •••o••in• •o P ⊢₂ cl $\diamond_{\mathrm{cmpl}}$.

A •••i• tr i• w•ll •o•• ••, *i.e.,* P ⊢₂ tr in ••••• 1•, i••• • •••o•• *directly
defined* in •••• •••i• ••• w•ll-•y••, •n• ••v• ••• ••• • •i•n•••••• ••• •ny • •••o•
wi•• ••• ••• • i••n•i••• ••••j••• ••o• • •••• •••j•.

A •l••• cl i• w•ll •o•• ••, *i.e.,* P ⊢₂ cl, i••• ••l•• in •••• •l••• ••v• w•ll-
•o•• •• •y••; •n• i••• • •••o•• *directly defined* in •••• •l••••• w•ll-•y••, •n•
••v• ••• ••• • •i•n•••• ••• •ny • •••o• ••••j••• ••o• • •••• •••j•, o• in••j•••
••o• • •••••••l•••. A ••o•••• i• w•ll •o•• ••, i• •ll i•• •l••••• •n• •••j••• ••• w•ll
•o•• ••.

No•j•• ••••, •o ••••li•• P ⊢₂ t w• only ••••• ••• • •••o•• *directly defined* in
•l••• o• •••j• t; (w• ••• P^{mth}(cl,m) - •• o••o•••• •o $\mathcal{M}$(P,cl,m) in *Chai₁*). Al•o,
P ⊢₁ t •o•• no• *imply* P ⊢₂ t, •n• no• •o•• P ⊢₂ t i• •ly P ⊢₁ t.

4.4   Type Soundness

In *Chai₂* w• ••••in ••• ••• ni•ion o•••••• •n• ••w••n o• j•••• •n• •l••••• ••o•
••••• 10, •••••• ••• •••••y• ••l••ion P ⊢₂ t ≤ t′, •n• ••• ••• ni•ion o••o• •l••
•l••••• P ⊢₂ cl $\diamond_{\mathrm{cmpl}}$ ••o• •• i• ••••ion.

T•••, w• w••• ••l• •o •iv• "•ni•o••" •••ni•ion o• *Chai₁* •n• *Chai₂*, •n•
•i••ill •••i• •i• il••i•i•• •n• •iff•••n•••.

T•• •ollowin• l•• • • i• ••• •o•n••••••• •o l•• • • 1; ••• •iff•••n•• i• ••••
•••• w• ••l• o• •y•• (•n• •••• •l•o o• •••j••) •••••• •••n j••• o• •l•••••, w• •••
••• *Chai₂* •••••y•• ••l••ion•• i• wi•• •l•o in•o•• o•••••• •••j•• •••••, •n• in •••
Chai₂ •i•n••••• loo•••• ••n••ion w• •l•o •••• ••• •••• •••j••• •n•• in•o •••o• n•.

Lemma 3. *If* ⊢₁ P *and classes* cl, cl′ *and types* t *and* t′, *with* P ⊢₂ cl ≤ cl′,
P ⊢₂ t ≤ t′, *and* P ⊢₂ cl ≤ t′, *then:*

1. $\mathcal{MS}i$•₂(P,t′,m) ⊆ $\mathcal{MS}i$•₂(P,t,m).
2. P ⊢₂ cl $\diamond_{\mathrm{cmpl}}$ ⟹ | $\mathcal{MS}i$•₂(P,t′,m) | ≤ 1.
3. P,t$_a$ x, t′ this ⊢₂ e : t″ ⟹ P,t$_a$ x, t this ⊢₂ e : t″.
4. P ⊢₂ cl $\diamond_{\mathrm{cmpl}}$, t″ m(t‴ x) ∈ $\mathcal{MS}i$•₂(P,t′,m) ⟹ ∃cl″,e :
   - $\mathcal{M}^{\mathrm{orig}}$(P,cl,m) = cl″,   t″ m(t‴ x){e} ∈ $\mathcal{M}$(P,cl″,m),
   - P ⊢₁ cl ≤ cl″   P,t‴ x, cl″ this ⊢₂ e″ : t″.

$$\forall m : t_0\ m(t_1\ x)\{e\} \in P^{mth}(P) \implies$$
$$\qquad P \vdash_2 t_0 \Diamond_{type}$$
$$\qquad P \vdash_2 t_1 \Diamond_{type}$$
$$\qquad P, t_1\ x, tr\ this \vdash_2 e : t_0$$
$$\qquad \forall tr' : tr' \in P^{use}(tr) \implies$$
$$\qquad\qquad \mathcal{MS}ig_2(P, tr', m) = \emptyset\ \lor\ \mathcal{MS}ig_2(P, tr', m)\{t_0\ m(t_1\ x)\}$$

$$\overline{P \vdash_2 tr}$$

$$cl' = P^{sup}(cl)$$
$$\forall f: \quad P^{fld}(cl, f) = t \implies P \vdash_2 t \Diamond_{type}\ ,\ \mathcal{F}(P, cl', f) = \bot$$
$$\forall m: \quad t_0\ m(t_1\ x)\{e\} \in P^{mth}(cl, m) \implies$$
$$\qquad P \vdash_2 t_0 \Diamond_{type}$$
$$\qquad P \vdash_2 t_1 \Diamond_{type}$$
$$\qquad P, t_1\ x, cl\ this \vdash_2 e : t_0$$
$$\qquad \mathcal{MS}ig_2(P, cl', m) = \emptyset\ \lor\ \mathcal{MS}ig_2(P, cl', m) = \{t_0\ m(t_1\ x)\}$$
$$\qquad \forall tr \in P^{use}(cl) : \mathcal{MS}ig_2(P, tr, m) = \emptyset\ \lor\ \mathcal{MS}ig_2(P, tr, m) = \{t_0\ m(t_1\ x)\}$$

$$\overline{P \vdash_2 cl}$$

for all classes cl defined in P: $P \vdash_2 cl$
for all traits tr defined in P: $P \vdash_2 tr$

$$\overline{\vdash_2 P}$$

Fig. 12. Well-formed traits, classes and programs in $Chai_2$

Wi•• ••• •• ov• l•• • • w• ••n ••ov• •o• n• n••• •o• ••• •y•• •y•••• o• $Chai_2$:

Theorem 4 (Type Soundness of $Chai_2$). *For any program* P, *environment* Γ, *expression* e *with* **super** *resolves without conflict in* e *and* $\Gamma(this\_class)$, *stack* σ, *type* t, *where* $\vdash_2 P$, *and* P, $\Gamma \vdash_2 e : t$ *and* P, $\Gamma \vdash_2 \sigma$, χ *and* e, σ, $\chi \rightsquigarrow_P r, \chi'$:

$$P, \Gamma \vdash_2 \sigma, \chi' \qquad and \qquad P, \chi \vdash_2 r \lhd t\ or\ r = nllPntrExc.$$

5   The Language $Chai_3$

$Chai_3$ in••o•••••• *dynamic trait substitution.* Sin•• •••i•• ••••i•y •••• • •••vio••, i• ••o•l• •• •o••i•l• •o ••••••i•••• on• •••i• •o• •no•••• •• ••n•i• • in o•••• •o •••n•• ••• ••••vio•• o• •n o•j•••. • ••w•••ly, ••• in•••••••• o• ••• o•j••• wo•l• •••• in ••• ••• •, ••ovi•in• ••• ••• • ••l•••n• • •••o••, ••• in•••n•lly ••• i• •l•• •n•••ion o• v••io•• • •••o•• •o•l• ••• •l•••••.

Al••o••• ••• i••• o• o•j•••• ••• n•in• ••••vio••• • ••n•i• • (•yn•• i• o•j••• •••-•l•••i•••ion) ••• ••n •••••n••• in ••v•••l •iff•••n• •o•• •[•,••], ••• only •i• ••• i• •on••••••••••••n •x•lo••• in ••• •xi••in• li••••••••• on ••• i••7 i• ••l••ion

---

[7] The authors of [18] mention using traits to dynamically change object behaviour as an element of future work.

•o ••• o• j•••-••••• l•n•••••• S• LF[1,••], w•••• •yn•• i• •••n••• in •••vio••
••n •• o•••in•• •y •••n•in• w•i•• o•j••• •••• •• ••• •••••n• o• ••• •••••••n•
o• j•••. W• ••••••n• • • ••••••ni•• •••••o••in• •yn•• i• •••i•• in••i••• •y ••• i••••
••o• S• LF, ••• in • •l•••-••••• l•n••••••.

5.1   Example

• on•i••• • •••••i••l win•owin• •y•••• : A win•ow in ••i• •y•••• • •y •• •n
OpenedWindow o• •n IconifiedWindow. In •••• •••••• ••• win•ow will ••••v•
• iff•••n•ly, •n• • win•ow • •y •••n•• •••w••n ••••• •wo ••••••• •• •ny •i• •.

To i• •l•• •n• ••i• in ••••i•ion•l • •j••• • •i•n••• ••o•••• • in•, w• wo• l•
n••• •o ••• w••••••••, o• •o• • •o•• o•••• ••••• •••••••n.

U•in• •yn•• i• ••••••i•••ion o• •••i••, w• ••n off••• • o•• •l•••n•, •n• •i••••
•ol••ion: w• •••n• • •l••• Window, •n• •wo •••i•• TOpened •n• TIconified,
w•••• TOpened •n• TIconified ••ovi•• •n• ••••j•• ••• ••• • •••• o• • •••o•
•i•n••••••, ••• ••ovi•• •iff•••n• i• •l•• •n••ion• o• ••• • •••o•• •n• •o •i•-
••••n• ••••vio••. W• •••n• ••• •l••• Window •• class Window uses TOpened
... (••• win•ow •••in• in ••• o••n•• •••••). T••n, •o• • Win•ow o•j••• w
(Window w = new Window();) w• ••n •••n•• •o ••• i•oni••• •••••• ••in• •••
•••••• •n• w<TOpened ↦TIconified>. T• i• will ••••l• in ••• ••••••i••• ion o•
••• •••i• TIconified •o• ••• •••i• TOpened in•i•• ••• o•j••• w.

Sin•• ••• •l••• Window w•• •••l•••• •• ••in• ••• •••i• TOpened, ••• l•••l
TOpened •••o• •• • "•l••••ol•••" •o• ••••• •••i• ••••• •y Window, •n• • •••i•
"•o• •••i•l•" wi•• TOpened ••n • •• •••••i•••• •o• TOpened •• •ny •i• •. W• •••
••• l•••l TOpened in •ll •••••• •••••i•••ion• •o• ••••• •••i• "•l••••ol•••" o• w.
Fo• •x•• • l•, •o •wi••• •••• •o ••• o•i•in•l ••••vio• • o• w, w• w•i•• w<TOpened
↦TOpened> (•n• *not*, ••• i•••••• i• ••in••, w<TIconified ↦TOpened>).

5.2   *Chai*₃ Syntax and Operational Semantics

W• •x••n••• ••• •yn••x o• •x••••ion• •o •llow •••i• ••••i••• ion.

$exp ::= exp< \text{tr} \mapsto \text{tr} > \mid ...$

Resolving Method Calls. • on•i••• ••• ••o•••• •iv•n in ••••• 13. I• w•
•••••• •n o•j••• o• •l••• C, •.• C x = new C, •••n o•vio••ly •x•••in• x.m1()
will ••••••n ••• v•l•l• 3, •n• •x•••in• x.m2() will •l•o ••••••n ••• v•l•l• 3.

I• w• •x••••• x < TrtB ↦ TrtB2 > •ollow•• •y x.m1(), •••n ••• v•••ion o•
m1 ••ovi••• •y TrtA will •• • ••••, •in•• ••• • •••o• m1 w•• o•i•in•lly ••ovi••
•o •l••• C •y •••i• TrtA, •n• no •••i• ••• •••l•••• TrtA in c.

I• w• •x••••• x < TrtB ↦ TrtB2 > •ollow•• •y x.m2(), •••n ••• •i••••ion i•
• o•• •o• •l•x. • •vio••ly, ••• • •••o• m2 •••n•• in TrtB2 will •• •x•••••• (•in••
TrtB o•i•in•lly ••ovi•• m2, •n• TrtB ••• ••n •••l•••• •y TrtB2). How•v••,
•••••• ••• •••••• •o••i•ili•i•• •o• ••• •in•in• o• m1 ••o• wi•• in ••• •o•y o• m2:

1. T•• v•••ion o• m1 ••o• TrtA will •• •••••; •••••••• invo•in• • • •••o• ••o•
   wi•• in • •••i• ••o•l• ••v ••• ••• • ••• •n•i•• •• invo•in• i• ••o• wi•• in
   ••• •l••• ••in• ••• •••i•. T•••, w• •••olv• • •••o• •••••• on ••• fl•••n••
   v•••ion o• ••• •l••• ••in• ••• •••i••.

```
trait TrtA { int m1() { 3 } }

trait TrtB {
   requires { int m1(); }
   int m2() { this.m1() }
}

trait TrtB2 {
   int m2() { this.m1() }
   int m1() { 5 }
}

class C uses TrtA,TrtB { }
```

Fig. 13. Resolving Method Calls in *Chai*$_3$

•. T•• v•••ion o• m1 ••o• TrtB2 will •• ••••; •••••• ••• • •••o•• in TrtB2 ••• in•••••l••••, i• i• li••ly ••••• ••• i• •l•• •n•o• o• TrtB2 in••n•• ••• ••ll •o m1 •o •••olv• •o ••• • •••o• in TrtB2. T•••, w• •••olv• • •••o••••••• on ••• •••i• in w•i•• ••• ••ll w•• •o• n••.

3. T•• •i•••ion i• ill•••l; *i.e.*, •••i• TrtB2 ••nno• •• •••••i•••• •o• •••i• TrtB •••••• i• ••••••• ••i• "•• •i••i•y" ••••• in• ••• •••ni•ion o• • •••o• m1.

In •• i• •••••, w• ••o•• o• •ion 1 ••o• ••ov•, •••••• o• i•• •lo•• ••l••ion•• i• •o ••• fl••••nin• ••o••••y w•i•• i• • ••••i•l •l•• •n• o• T••i•• ••ilo•o••y.

Object Representation. S••••i•••ion o• •••i•• •• ••n•i• • i• on • •••-o•j••• •••i• (••••••• ••• n • •••-•l••• ••••i•). T•i• • ••n• •••• w•il• ••• li•• o• •••i•• •••• •y •ny •l••• ••• •in• •on•••n•, •o• •v••y o•j••• o• •••• •l•••, •••• •••• •••i• • •y •• •••o•i•••• wi•• •o• • (• o••i•ly •iff•••n•) •••i•. T•••••o••, w• •x••n• ••• •••••••n•••ion o• j•••• ••o• ••••• 5 wi•• • li•• o• •••i• •••••i•••ion• ••••• ••v• •••n • ••• •o ••• o• j•••.

$$\textbf{object} = \{\ [\![\ \texttt{cl} \parallel \texttt{f}_1 : \texttt{v}_1, ... \texttt{f}_r : \texttt{v}_r \parallel \texttt{tr}_1 : \texttt{tr}'_1, ... \texttt{tr}_n : \texttt{tr}'_n\ ]\!] \quad | \quad \texttt{cl}, \texttt{f}_1, ... \texttt{f}_r, \texttt{tr}_1, ... \texttt{tr}_n, \texttt{tr}'_1, ... \texttt{tr}'_n \text{ i• •n•i• •••; } \texttt{v}_1, ... \texttt{v}_r \in \textbf{val}\ \}$$

To •••••• •n• •••••• ••••• •••i• •••••i•••ion• •o• •n o•j••• $o = [\![\ \texttt{cl} \parallel ... \parallel \texttt{tr}_1 : \texttt{tr}'_1, ... \texttt{tr}_n : \texttt{tr}'_n\ ]\!]$, w• •••n• *trait lookup* $o(\texttt{tr})$ w•i•• •n•• ••• •••••n• •••••i•••ion •o• • •iv•n •••i• n•• •, •n• *object mutation* $o[\texttt{tr} \mapsto \texttt{tr}']$ w•i•• •••l•••• ••• •••i• n•• •• tr •y tr′.

$$o(\texttt{tr}) = \begin{cases} \texttt{tr}'_k & \text{if } \texttt{tr} = \texttt{tr}_k \text{ for some } k \in 1, ...n \\ \bot & \text{otherwise.} \end{cases}$$

$$o[\texttt{tr} \mapsto \texttt{tr}'] = \begin{cases} [\![\ \texttt{cl} \parallel ... \parallel \texttt{tr}_1 : \texttt{tr}'_1 ... \texttt{tr}_k : \texttt{tr}' ... \texttt{tr}_n : \texttt{tr}'_n\ ]\!] & \text{for } \texttt{tr} = \texttt{tr}_k, k \in 1, ..., n \\ \bot & \text{otherwise.} \end{cases}$$

Runtime Method Lookup and Operational Semantics. T••i• •••••i•••ion• • ••• •• •••••n in•o •••o• n• •o• • •••o• ••ll. T•• ••n••ion $\mathcal{M}_3$ •n•• ••• ••••o••i••• • •••o• •o•y, •••in• •o•• ••• •l••• o• ••• o•j•••, •n• ••• o•j••• i•••l• in•o •••o• n• – ••• l••••• i• n•••••, in o•••• •o •n• ••• •••i•• ••••• ••v•

••• l•••• ••• o•i•in•l on••. $\mathcal{M}_3$ •••• •••••• in•• w•i•• •l••• o• •••i• n•• • i• "••_
••on•i•l•" •o• ••• •o••••• on• in• • •••o• •••o••• $\mathcal{M}_3^{\text{resp}}(\text{P},\text{cl},\text{m})$, w•i•• ••••
•••••••• ••• ••••••n• •l••, ••n ••• ••••• •••i••, •n• •••n •on•in••• wi•• ••• ••_
•••••l•••. I• $\mathcal{M}_3^{\text{resp}}(\text{P},\text{cl},\text{m})$ i• • •l••• cl′ •••n ••• • •••o• •o• y i• •o•n• •i••••ly
in cl′. I• $\mathcal{M}_3^{\text{resp}}(\text{P},\text{cl},\text{m})$ i• • •••i• tr •••n ••• • •••o• •o• y i• •o•n• in •••i•
tr′, w•i•• •••l•••• tr in ••• ••••••n• o• j••• (*i.e.*, $o(\text{tr}) = \text{tr}'$).

$$\mathcal{M}_3^{\text{resp}}(\text{P},\text{tr},\text{m}) = \begin{cases} \{\ \text{tr}\ \} & \text{if } \text{P}^{\text{mth}}(\text{tr},\text{m}) \neq \emptyset \\ \bigcup_{\text{tr}' \in \text{puse}(\text{tr})} \mathcal{M}_3^{\text{resp}}(\text{P},\text{tr}',\text{m}) & \text{otherwise.} \end{cases}$$

$$\mathcal{M}_3^{\text{resp}}(\text{P},\text{cl},\text{m}) = \begin{cases} \{\ \text{cl}\ \} & \text{if } \text{P}^{\text{mth}}(\text{cl},\text{m}) \neq \emptyset \\ \textit{Trts} & \text{where } \textit{Trts} = \bigcup_{\text{tr} \in \text{puse}(\text{cl})} \mathcal{M}_3^{\text{resp}}(\text{P},\text{tr},\text{m}) \\ & \text{if } \textit{Trts} \neq \emptyset = \text{P}^{\text{mth}}(\text{cl},\text{m}) \\ \mathcal{M}_3^{\text{resp}}(\text{P},\text{P}^{\text{sup}}(\text{cl}),\text{m}) & \text{otherwise.} \end{cases}$$

$$\mathcal{M}_3(\text{P},\text{cl},\text{o},\text{m}) = \begin{cases} \text{P}^{\text{mth}}(\text{cl}',\text{m}) & \text{if } \mathcal{M}_3^{\text{resp}}(\text{P},\text{cl},\text{m}) = \{\text{cl}'\} \\ \text{P}^{\text{mth}}(\text{tr}',\text{m}) & \text{if } \mathcal{M}_3^{\text{resp}}(\text{P},\text{cl},\text{m}) = \{\text{tr}\}, \text{ and } o(\text{tr}) = \text{tr}' \\ \bot & \text{otherwise.} \end{cases}$$

A •l••• cl i• •o• •l••• in *Chai*$_3$ i• i• ••ovi••• • • •••o• •o• y •o• •ny ••••i•••
• •••o•, i• •••••• ••• no •onfli••• •o• •ny •••••l••• (•• i• •i• •li••• ••• •••••• •n•
o• super), •n• i• $\mathcal{M}_3^{\text{resp}}(\text{P},\text{cl},\text{m})$ i• •• ••y o• • •in•l••on.

$$\frac{\begin{array}{l} \forall \text{m}:\ \text{t m}(\text{t}'\,\text{x}) \in \mathcal{MR}{\bullet}{\bullet}(\text{P},\text{cl},\text{m}) \implies \exists \text{e}:\ \text{t m}(\text{t}'\,\text{x})\{\text{e}\} \in \mathcal{M}(\text{P},\text{cl},\text{m}) \\ \forall \text{m},\text{cl}'\quad \text{P} \vdash_1 \text{cl} \leq \text{cl}', \ |\mathcal{M}(\text{P},\text{cl}',\text{m})| \leq 1 \\ \forall \text{m}:\ |\mathcal{M}_3^{\text{resp}}(\text{P},\text{cl},\text{m})| \leq 1 \end{array}}{\text{P} \vdash_3 \text{cl} \diamond_{\text{cmpl}}}$$

T•• o• ••••ion•l ••• •n•i•• o• *Chai*$_3$ •iff••• ••o• •••• o• *Chai*$_1$ •n• *Chai*$_2$ in
••• ••n• lin• o•• ••••ion, o• j••• •••••ion, •n• • •••o• ••ll, •••••o••, w• •x••n•
••• •••• •n•i•• ••o• •••••• 6. A • ••••• •x••••ion •••••i••••• on• •••i• • y •no••••
(**mutate**). • •j••• •••••ion ini•i•li••• ••• ••l•• *and* ••• li•• o• •••i• ••••••i•••ion•
•o• n•w o•j••• •••o••• ••• i• •n•i•y ••••i•••ion, i.•. •••o•i•••• •ll •••i•• wi••
•••• ••lv•• (**new**).

new

	mutate	**new**

$$\frac{\text{e}, \sigma, \chi \leadsto_P \iota, \chi'' \qquad \chi' = \chi''[\iota \mapsto \chi''(\iota)[\text{tr} \mapsto \text{tr}']]}{\text{e} <\text{tr} \mapsto \text{tr}'>, \sigma, \chi \leadsto_P \iota, \chi'}$$

$$\frac{\begin{array}{c} \mathcal{F}_{\text{s}}(\text{P},\text{cl}) = \{\ \text{f}_1, \ldots, \text{f}_r\ \} \\ \{\ \text{tr}_1, \ldots \text{tr}_n\ \} = \mathcal{U}se^*(\text{P},\text{cl}) \\ \iota \text{ i• n•w in } \chi \\ o = [\![\ \text{cl} \parallel \text{f}_1:\text{null}\ldots\text{f}_n:\text{null} \parallel \\ \text{tr}_1:\text{tr}_1\ldots\text{tr}_n:\text{tr}_n\ ]\!] \end{array}}{\text{new cl}, \sigma, \chi \leadsto_P \iota, \chi[\iota \mapsto o]}$$

In • •••o• ••ll w• ••• ••• n•w • •••o• loo••• ••n••ion $\mathcal{M}_3(\text{P},\text{c},\text{o},\text{m})$
(**method-call**). T•••, i• •••i• i• •••• in •l••• cl •••o••• •wo •iff•••n• ••••••
(*e.g.*, •••• •y cl, •n• •l•o •y cl′, w•••• cl′ i• cl'• ••••••l•••), •••n • ••••ion
o• ••• •••i• will •ff••• ••• ••••vio•• o• i•• • •••o• •••••••l••• o• ••• ••••• ••••
•o •••••• ••• o•j••• (*e.g.*, ••• v•l•• o• •y•• cl, o• cl′) - ••i• i• •on•i•••n• wi••

••• fl•••nin• ••o•••y. • n ••• o••••••n•, i• • •••i• tr w•i•• •••• •••i• tr′ i•
•••l•••• •y tr″, •••n only ••• • •••o•• •i•••ly ••ovi••• •y tr will •• loo•••
•• in •••i• tr″; ••• on•• •••• w••• in•••i••• •y tr′ will ••• •in •n•ff••••• . T•i•
i•, in •o• • ••n••, in•on•i•••n• wi•• ••• fl•••nin• ••o•••y, •n• in ••••••• wo••
w• wo•l• li•• •o inv•••i•••• •l•••n••iv••.

method-call	super-call
$e_r, \sigma, \chi \leadsto_P \iota, \chi_0$	$e_a, \sigma, \chi \leadsto_P v_1, \chi_1$
$e_a, \sigma, \chi_0 \leadsto_P v_1, \chi_1$	$\sigma(\texttt{this\_class}) = \texttt{cl}$
$\chi_1(\iota) = [\![\,\texttt{cl} \parallel \ldots\,]\!]$	$P^{\texttt{sup}}(\texttt{cl}) = \texttt{cl}''$
$\mathcal{M}_3(P, \texttt{cl}, \chi_1(\iota), \texttt{m}) =$	$\mathcal{M}_3(P, \texttt{cl}'', \chi_1(\iota), \texttt{m}) =$
$\quad\{\, \texttt{t m(t}' \texttt{ x) } \{\, \texttt{e} \,\} \,\}$	$\quad\{\, \texttt{t m(t}' \texttt{ x) } \{\, \texttt{e} \,\} \,\}$
$\mathcal{M}^{\texttt{orig}}(P, \texttt{cl}, \texttt{m}) = \texttt{cl}'$	$\mathcal{M}^{\texttt{orig}}(P, \texttt{cl}'', \texttt{m}) = \texttt{cl}'$
$\sigma' = (\iota, v_1, \texttt{cl}')$	$\sigma' = (\sigma(\texttt{this}), v_1, \texttt{cl}')$
$e, \sigma', \chi_1 \leadsto_P v, \chi'$	$e, \sigma', \chi_1 \leadsto_P v, \chi'$
$\overline{e_r.\texttt{m}(e_a), \sigma, \chi \leadsto_P v, \chi'}$	$\overline{\texttt{super.m}(e_a), \sigma, \chi \leadsto_P v, \chi'}$

5.3   Type System

T•• j•••• •n• $P \vdash \texttt{tr}' \lesssim \texttt{tr}$ ••y• •••• •••i• tr′ • •y ••• l••• •no•••• •••i• tr. I•
•••• i••• •••• tr′ ••ovi••• •ll••• • •••o•• •••• tr •o•• (wi•• ••• ••• • •i•n••••••,
•••• •o••i• ly •iff•••n• •o•i••), •n• •••• ••ny • ••• o•• ••ovi••• o• •••• i••• •y tr′
••• •l•o ••ovi••• o• •••• i••• in tr.

$$
\dfrac{
\begin{array}{l}
P \vdash \texttt{tr} \diamond_{\texttt{trait}} \qquad\qquad P \vdash \texttt{tr}' \diamond_{\texttt{trait}} \\
\forall \texttt{m}: \quad \texttt{t}_0 \texttt{ m(t}_1 \texttt{ x)}\{\ldots\} \in P^{\texttt{mth}}(\texttt{tr}, \texttt{m}) \implies \texttt{t}_0 \texttt{ m(t}_1 \texttt{ x)}\{\ldots\} \in P^{\texttt{mth}}(\texttt{tr}', \texttt{m}) \\
\forall \texttt{m}: \quad \mathcal{MS}i\!\cdot_2(P, \texttt{tr}', \texttt{m}) \subseteq \mathcal{MS}i\!\cdot_2(P, \texttt{tr}, \texttt{m})
\end{array}
}{
P \vdash \texttt{tr}' \lesssim \texttt{tr}
}
$$

W• •••• i•• $\mathcal{MS}i\!\cdot_2(P, \texttt{tr}', \texttt{m}) \subseteq \mathcal{MS}i\!\cdot_2(P, \texttt{tr}, \texttt{m})$[8] ••••••• $P \vdash \texttt{tr}' \lesssim \texttt{tr}$ •n•
$P, \texttt{t}' \texttt{ x}, \texttt{tr}'$ this $\vdash_3 e : t$ ••o•l• i• •ly $P, \texttt{t}' \texttt{ x}, \texttt{tr}$ this $\vdash_3 e : t$ – n•• •ly,
i• •n o•j••• •on••in• • •••i• •l••••ol••• tr, w•i•• i• •••l•••• •y tr′,
•••n i• • •y •x••••• • •••o• •o•y e w•i•• w•• •••n•• in tr′. To •••i••y
$P, \texttt{t}' \texttt{ x}, \texttt{tr}$ this $\vdash_3 e : t$ •o• ••• •••• w•••• e=this, w• n••• $P \vdash_3 \texttt{tr} \leq \texttt{tr}'$,
w•i•• •••• i••• $\mathcal{MS}i\!\cdot_2(P, \texttt{tr}', \texttt{m}) \subseteq \mathcal{MS}i\!\cdot_2(P, \texttt{tr}, \texttt{m})$.

In o•• •x•• •l•, _ ⊢ $\texttt{TrtB2} \lesssim \texttt{TrtB}$, •n• _ ⊬ $\texttt{TrtB} \lesssim \texttt{TrtB2}$ – ••••••• TrtB2
••••• • •••o• •o•y •o• m1, •n• TrtB ••• no•.

B••••••• •••i• •••••i••••• ili•y i• •li•• •••• •y••• , in *Chai*$_3$ w• •x••n• ••• ••••-
•y• ••l••ion•• i• ••o• •••••• • •• •ollow•:

---

[8] Andrew Black suggested to us that we could weaken our original requirement of
$\mathcal{MS}ig_2(P, \texttt{tr}', \texttt{m}) = \mathcal{MS}ig_2(P, \texttt{tr}, \texttt{m})$.

$$\frac{P \vdash_2 t' \leq t}{P \vdash_3 t' \leq t} \qquad \frac{P \vdash tr' \lesssim tr}{P \vdash_3 tr \leq tr'} \qquad \frac{P \vdash_3 t' \leq t'' \quad \bullet n \bullet \quad P \vdash_3 t'' \leq t}{P \vdash_3 t' \leq t}$$

T•• •y•• •y•••• o• *Chai₃* i• i••n•i••l •o •••• o• *Chai₂*, •x•••• •o• ••• n•w ••• ni•ion o• ••• •y••• $(P \vdash_3 t' \leq t)$ •n• •o• •l••• •l••••• $(P \vdash_3 cl \diamond_{cmpl})$, •n• ••• ••• i•ion o• ••• ••l• •o• • •••ion •x••••ion•. I• •••• j••• •••••••• •y•• o•e ••o•l• ••• •ny •l••• o• •••i• t, •••• t •• o•l• • •••in• • •••i• tr, •n• •••• tr' • •y •••l••• trin t. T••n, ••• •••••i••ion o• tr •••o••• tr' in e ••• •y•• t:

mutate

$$\begin{array}{c}
P, \Gamma \vdash_3 e : t \\
tr \in \mathcal{U}se^*(P, t) \\
P \vdash tr' \lesssim tr \\
\hline
P, \Gamma \vdash_3 e < tr \mapsto tr' > : t
\end{array}$$

5.4   Type Soundness

A•••• •n• •o• *Chai₃* i• •••n•• in ••• •ollowin•. In •••i•ion •o ••• ••o• •••i•• •o• •••••• •n• in *Chai₂*, •o• *Chai₃* w• ••• ••• n•w •••y•• ••l••ion $(P \vdash_3 cl \leq t)$, •n• •••• i•• •••• •ll •••i•• •••• •y •l••• cl •• o•l• •••••• in ••• ••••••••n••ion o• ••• o• j••••, •n• •••• •ll •••i•• •v• ••n ••• l•••• •y •••••i•••• l• •••i••:

$$\begin{array}{c}
\chi(\iota) = [\![cl \parallel \ldots \parallel tr_1 : tr_1', \ldots, tr_n : tr_n']\!] \\
\{ tr_1 \ldots tr_n \} = \mathcal{U}se^*(P, cl) \\
\forall i \in 1, \ldots, n: \quad P \vdash tr_i' \lesssim tr_i \\
P \vdash_3 cl \leq t \\
\mathcal{F}(P, cl, f) = t' \implies P, \chi \vdash_3 \chi(\iota)(f) \triangleleft t' \\
\hline
P, \chi \vdash_3 \iota \triangleleft t
\end{array}$$

T•• •o• n•••••••• •o ••• ••o•••i•• ••o• l•• • ••• 1 •n• 3 •ol• •o• *Chai₃*.

Lemma 5. *For program* P *with* $\vdash_3 P$, *classes* cl, cl', *types* t, t', t'', *with* $P \vdash_3 cl \leq cl'$, *and* $P \vdash_3 t \leq t'$:

1. $\mathcal{F}(P, cl', f) = t \implies \mathcal{F}(P, cl, f) = t$.
2. $\mathcal{MS}i \bullet_2 (P, t', m) \subseteq \mathcal{MS}i \bullet_2 (P, t, m)$.
3. $P, t_a \; x, \; t' \; this \vdash_3 e : t'' \implies P, t_a \; x, \; t \; this \vdash_3 e : t''$.
4. $P, \sigma \vdash_3 \iota \triangleleft cl$, *and* $P \vdash_3 cl \diamond_{cmpl}$, *and* $\mathcal{M}^{orig}(P, cl', m) = \{ cl'' \}$, *and* $t_0 \; m(t_1 \; x)\{e\} \in \mathcal{M}_3(P, cl, \chi(\iota), m)$, $\implies$
   - $P \vdash_3 cl' \leq cl''$
   - $P, t_1 \; x, \; cl'' \; this \vdash_3 e'' : t_0$.
5. $t_0 \; m(t_1 \; x) \in \mathcal{MS}i \bullet_2 (P, t, m)$, *and* $P, \sigma \vdash_3 \iota \triangleleft cl$, *and* $P \vdash_3 cl' \leq t$, *and* $P \vdash_3 cl \diamond_{cmpl} \implies \mathcal{M}_3(P, cl', \chi(\iota), m) = \{ t_0 \; m(t_1 \; x)\{ \ldots \} \}$.

W• ••n now ••ov• •o• n• n••• •o• ••• •y•• •y•••• o• *Chai*$_3$:

Theorem 6 (Type Soundness of *Chai*$_3$). *For any program* P, *environment* Γ, *expression* e, *stack* σ, *heap* χ, *type* t, *where* $\vdash_3$ P, *and* P, Γ $\vdash_3$ e : t *and* P, Γ $\vdash_3$ σ, χ *and* e, σ, χ $\leadsto_P$ r, χ′:

P, χ′ $\vdash$ r ◁ t   *or*   r = nullPointerExc   *and*   P, Γ $\vdash_3$ σ, χ′.

6   Implementation

T•i• ••••ion ••••i••• ••• •••n•l••ion o• • ••o•••• in *Chai* (••• •o•••• l•n-••••••) •o on• in J•v• (••• •••••• l•n•••••). T•i• i• i• •l•• •n••• •y • • •••in• ••o• •••i•• •n• •l••••• in *Chai* •o •n•i•i•• in J•v• [9] T•••• ••• ••v•••l •o••i•l• • •••in• w• •o•l• ••v• ••o••n •o• ••i• ••••o••; w• •o•l• • ••• • •l••• (•n• •ll ••• • ••••vio•• i• in•l•••• ••o• •••i••) in *Chai* •o • •in•l• •l••• in J•v•. In•••••, w• ••oo•• • •li••ly • o•• •o• •l•x • •••in•, w•i•• •••••••n•• •••i•• in J•v• •y •l••••• w•i•• ••• in•••n•i•••• •o •iv• *proxy objects* •o w•i•• ••••vio•• ••n •• ••l••••• •y • •l••• w•i•• •••• ••o•• •••i••. T•i• •llow• •• •o i• •l•• •n• ••• •yn•• i• •••i• ••••••i•••ion o• *Chai*$_3$.

• v••y •••i• tr i• ••••••••n••• •y •n o•j••• o• •y• tr_impl, •n• •on••in• • ••l• ••ll•• user_proxy o• •y• tr_user. T•• user_proxy ••l• •lw•y• ••o•••• • •••••••n•• •o •n o•j••• o• ••• •••i• o• •l•••• •••• • •••• ••i• •••i•. Al•o, •o• •ny •l••• o• •••i•, •••••• ••• ••l•• tr′_proxy •o• •ll •••i•• tr′ •••• •y ••• •l••• o• •••i•. •••• o• •••••• i• • •••••n•• •o •n o•j••• o• ••• ••l•v•n• •y• tr′_interface

T•••, •o• •x•• •l•, • •l••• D w•i•• •••• • •••i• T3, •n• T3 •••• •••i•• T1 •n• T2. B••••••• T3 ∈ P^{use}(D), ••• D o•j••• •on••in• • ••••••n•• •o • T3_impl o•j•••. Si• il••ly •••••••• T1 ∈ P^{use}(T3) •n• T2 ∈ P^{use}(T3), ••• T3 o•j••• •on••in• •••••••n••• •o T1_impl •n• T2_impl o•j•••.

In o•••• •o• ••i• ••••n••• •n• •o •• •y•• •o•••••, •ll •l••••• tr_impl • •••i• •l•• •n• tr_interface, •n• •l•o tr′_user •o• •ll tr′ •••• •••• tr′ ∈ P^{use}(tr). A••i•ion•lly, •l••••• •••• ••• •••i•• • •••• i• •l•• •n• •••••o••i••• tr_user in•••••••• (in ••• •x•• •l•, T3 ∈ P^{use}(D) •n• •o D • •••• i• •l•• •n• T3_user).

T•• •••••on •••• ••• •y•• o• ••• ••l•• tr_proxy i• tr_interface (•n• no• tr_impl) i• •o •llow •iff•••n• v•l••• ••o••• in ••• ••l• •o ••••• •o •iff•••n• •••i• i• •l•• •n••••ion o•j•••• (••ovi••• •••••••y i• •l•• •n• tr_interface), •n• •••-•o•• •••i• •••••i••ion• (•n••• ••• •••••i••ion• •••••i••• •y *Chai*$_3$).

In • o•• ••••il, •v••y •••i• tr in *Chai* i• • •••••• •o •••••• •n•i•i•• in J•v•:

1. A *trait interface* •on••inin• •ll ••• ••ovi••• • •••o•• o• tr.
•. A *trait-user interface* •on••inin• •ll ••• ••••i••• • •••o• •i•n•••••• (i.•. ••o••.•x•••••• •o • ••ovi••• •y ••• •••• o• ••• •••i• tr), •• w•ll ••• •ll ••• ••ovi••• • •••o• •i•n•••••• o• tr (••• ••low).
3. A *trait implementation class* w•i•• •on••in• ••• ••• ni•ion• •o• ••• ••ovi••• • •••o•• o• ••• •••i•, ••oxy ••l• •o• ••• •••• o• ••• •••i• •n• •ll •••• •••i••,

---

[9] Similarly, Java-mixins were implemented through a mapping from Jam into Java[2].

•• w•ll •• ••l•••ion • •••o• ••••• •o• •••• i••• • •••o••, w• i•• •o•w•••
• •••o• ••ll• •o ••• •••• •••i• ••oxy o• j••••.

A •l••• in *Chai* i• • ••••• •o • •l••• in J•v•, wi•• ••• •••i•ion o• ••oxy ••l••
•o• •••• •••i••, i• •l•• •n•• •••l•••ion• •o• ••• •••i•-•••• in••••••• o• •••i•• ••••
•y ••• •l•••, •n• •••o• ••••• •o• •••• i••• • •••o•• •n• •••••l••• • •••o••
•••• •i••• •y • •••• •••i•.

To •••••v• ••• in••n••• ••• •n•i•• o• ••• fl••••nin• ••o•••y (••• ••••ion
3.3), i• i• n••••••y •••• ••• ••• o• ••• •x••••ion this wi•• in • •••i• ••oxy i•
•••n•l•••• •o •••••• ••• o• j•••••lon•in• •o ••• •l••• w• i•• •••• •• •••i• (no•• ••••
•••••• • •y •• ••v•••l l•v•l• o• in••v•nin• •••i• ••oxi•• ••w••n ••• •••i• ••oxy
•n• ••i• o• j•••). T•• •••on ••••• i• i• n••••••y, i• ••• •• •••l•••ion• o• •••o••
"• o•• lo••l" •o ••• •v•n••l •••• o•• •••i• ••v• •••••• •n••, •••••o•• •o •••••v•
••• fl••••nin• ••o•••y, w• • ••• ••••• ••• •••••• •o• • • •••o• i• •l•• •n••ion
••o• ••i• •••• o• j••• i•••l• •n• wo•• ••w••• in•o •••i•• ••••••••n••• •y ••oxy
o• j••••.

Prototype. T•• ••o•o•y•• i• •l•• •n••ion o• ••• •o• •il•• i• w•i••n in J•v•.
A• ••••••n• i• •••• o••• •ll o•••• •••••••• o• *Chai*$_1$, •n• wo•l• •••ily •••o• • o•••••
•x••n•ion• •o •••• o•• *Chai*$_2$ •n• *Chai*$_3$. T•• •o• •il••, in•l••in• ••ll •o••• •o••,
i• ••v•il••l• ••o• http://chai-t.sourceforge.net/.

7 Conclusions, Related and Further Work

W• ••v• ••v•lo••• ••••• •x••n•ion• •o • • ini••l J•v•-li•• l•n•••• in•o•• o-
••in• •••i••, ••v• ••ov•n •o• n•n••• o• ••• •y• •y•••• •, •n• ••v• o••lin• o••
••o•o•y•• i• •l•• •n••ion.

T•• • •in i••••• w• ••• •o •••••••• •••in• ••• •••i•n o• *Chai* w•••:

– T•• •••i•• ••• •n•i•• o• ••in• • •••i• •• •••• o• • •l••• in J•v•;
– How •o ••••o•• •y•-•••••in• on •••i••, •n• in ••••i•l•• •ow •o •voi•
  ••vin• •o •y•-•••••• ••• ••• • • •••o• • o•y in •••• •l••• ••• •••• •••i•;
– T•• ••fl•••ion o• ••ll• •o super in ••• •••• i••• •n• •••• o• •••i••
– In • ow ••• •l•••• ••v• •o •• •o• •l•••, *i.e.*, ••ovi•• • •••o• • o•i•• •o• •ll
  ••• • •••o• •••• i••• •y ••• •••i•• •••y ••• ••in•;
– S• •y•• ••l••ion•• i• • ••w••n •l•••• •n• •••i••, •• •••• i••• in *Chai*$_2$; in-
  •••••in•ly, • •••i• • •y •••• i•• *more* • •••o• ••• n • •••••••y• •••i••;
– Dyn•• i• ••••i••ion o• •••i••, •n• ••• ••• •n•i• o•• ••• o• loo••• in *Chai*$_3$;
– T•• ••i• •••••i••••ili•y ••l••ion• i• in *Chai*$_3$; in••••••in•ly, •••••i••••ili•y
  in *Chai*$_3$ •o•• no• i• •ly •••y•• in *Chai*$_2$.

• •••n•ly, •n• •••••i•lly ••••• ••• •••li•••ion o• •••i•• •o S• •ll••l• [1•, 19],
••• in•••••• in •••i•• ••• •oo• ••. In [10] • i• ••••iv• ••l••l• •o• •••i•• in
••• l•n••••• Mo•y i• ••v•lo••••. T•• ••••i•i•ion o• • •••o•• ••o••• ••• ••

o• •••i•• i• • o••l•• •••o••• "•l••• •v•l••ion" w•i•• ••••••n• fl•••n•• •l•••••.
A• in o•• wo••, •li•• •n• •x•l••ion o•• •••o•• in [10] i• •••o• ••ni•• •y• •••o•
•i•n••••••; •nli•• o•• wo••, •••i•• in [10] • •y ••••i•• ••• ••••••n•• o••l••.

In FTJ [13] •••i•• •••• •••• •• •o F••••••w•i••• J•v•[1•]; ••• •y•••• i• ••n•-
•ion•l, •n• •••i•• ••• •••••••• •• • •l••• •••••ion • ••••ni•• , •i• il•• •o $Chai_1$.
T•• •• ll ••l••l•• l•• o• FTJ •n• • ••oo• o• •o• n• n••• o•••• •y• •y•••• i• ••••••n•••.

T••i•• ••• •••• o•••• l•n••••• S••l• [15], w•••• •••y •l•y •i• il•• •ôl• •o ••••
o• $Chai_1$ •n• $Chai_2$. S••l• in•o•• o•••••• • •ny •• v•n••• •••••••• e.g., ••n••i••,
•n• •••• •n••n• •y•••; i• i• •n•nown w•••••• i•• •y•• •y•••• i• •••i•••l• [16].

T•• So••w••• • o• •o•i•ion ••o•• •• ••• Univ•••i•y o• B••n• [•] •on••in• •
l•••• ••n••• •o• ••• •••••••• ••o•n• ••• •••i•n, ••• •n•i••, •n• •••li••ion o•
•••i••. Tool• •o• T••i•• •o• S•••••• ••• ••in• ••v•lo••• , •n• Mi••o•o•• •••••••••
i• •• on•o•in• ••• •••i•n •n• i• •l•• •n••ion o• •••i•• •o• • #.

In •••••••• wo••, w• wo•l• li•• •o •••n• o•• • o••l •o ••••o•• ov••lo•• in•.
W• •l•o w•n• •o ••vi•i• •n• •••on•i••• ••• •••i•n •••i•ion• in $Chai_2$ •n• $Chai_3$;
•o ••• •••y w••• ••••n j••• wi•• ••• •i• •o o•••in •y•• •o•n•n•••, ••• w•
••o•l• •x•lo•• ••• •••i•n ••••• •o• •••i••, i•• ••l••ion wi•• ••n••i• •••••••• [6], • o••i• ly
•l•o in•o•• o•••• •oly• o••• i• •••••••• in•o •••i••. W• •l•o wo•l• li•• •o •on•i•••
••n•••li••ion o• ••• l•n••••••, e.g., •llow •l••••• •o ••v• •••i• •l••, o• •llow
•••i• •l•• •o ••••i•• ••l••.

Acknowledgments. W• •••• •••• ly •••••••l •o An•••w Bl•••, Ti• S•••••, •n•
•••i• •••••••• ••o••, •o• in•i••••l ••••••••ion•, ••••in•n• ••••••ion•, •n• ••••il••
•o• • •n•• on •n •••li•• v•••ion o•••i• wo••. T••i• ••••••••• •••••••••ly i• ••ov••
••• •••••••••• l•n••••• •••••••• in $Chai_1$, $Chai_2$ •n• $Chai_3$, ••• •x•l•n••ion•,
•n• •••••n•••ion – w• ••v• no• y•• •••• ••• ••i• • •o in•o•• o••••• •ll o• i•. •••n-
K•i Lin •n• An•••w Bl••• ••••••••• ••• •o••••• •o• •li••ion o• super.

T•• •nony• o•••••• P •••••••, Al•x B••l•y, ••i••o••• An•••on, Ni••
• •• ••on, •n• • o• S••ni•• ••v• •• v•l••l• ••••••••. No•••o Yo••i•• •••••••••
••• •i••ill••ion o• ••• •••••n•i•l ••o•••i•• •••• in ••• ••oo• o• •o•n•n••• •o•
$Chai_1$, $Chai_2$ •n• $Chai_3$, •• in l•• • •• 1, 3 •n• 5.

References

1. Ole Agesen, Lars Bak, Craig Chambers, Bay-Wei Chang, Urs Hölzle, John Maloney, Randall B. Smith, and David Ungar. *The Self 4.0 Programmer's Reference Manual.* Sun Microsystems, Inc., 1995.

2. Davide Ancona, Giovanni Lagorio, and Elena Zucca. Jam - A Smooth Extension of Java with Mixins. In *Proceedings of the 14th European Conference on Object-Oriented Programming*, pages 154–178. Springer-Verlag, 2000.

3. Andrew Black, Nathanael Schärli, and Stéphane Ducasse. Applying Traits to the Smalltalk Collection Hierarchy. pages 47–64. ACM Conference on Object Oriented Systems, Languages and Applications (OOPSLA), October 2003.

4. Gilad Bracha. *The programming language jigsaw: mixins, modularity and multiple inheritance*. PhD thesis, University of Utah, 1992.

5. Gilad Bracha and William Cook. Mixin-Based Inheritance. In Norman Meyrowitz, editor, *Proceedings of the Conference on Object-Oriented Programming: Systems, Languages, and Applications / Proceedings of the European Conference on Object-Oriented Programming*, pages 303–311, Ottawa, Canada, 1990. ACM Press.

6. Gilad Bracha, Martin Odersky, David Stoutamire, and Philip Wadler. Making the Future Safe for the Past: Adding Genericity to the Java Programming Language. In Craig Chambers, editor, *ACM Symposium on Object Oriented Programming: Systems, Languages, and Applications (OOPSLA)*, pages 183–200, Vancouver, BC, 1998.

7. S. Drossopoulou, F. Damiani, M. Dezani-Ciancaglini, and P. Giannini. Fickle: Dynamic object re-classification. In *ECOOP'01*, LNCS 2072, pages 130–149. Springer, 2001.

8. Stéphane Ducasse, Oscar Nierstrasz, Nathanael Schärli, and Roel Wuyts. Traits - Composable Units of Behaviour. University of Berne, Software Composition Group, http://www.iam.unibe.ch/ scg/Research/Traits/index.html.

9. Erik Ernst. Family Polymorphism. In *ECOOP '01: Proceedings of the 15th European Conference on Object-Oriented Programming*, pages 303–326. Springer-Verlag, 2001.

10. Kathleen Fisher and John Reppy. Statically Typed Traits. Technical Report TR-2003-13, Department of Computer Science, University of Chicago, December 2003. presented at FOOL, January 2004.

11. Matthew Flatt, Shriram Krishnamurthi, and Matthias Felleisen. Classes and Mixins. In *Conference Record of POPL 98: The 25TH ACM SIGPLAN-SIGACT Symposium on Principles of Programming Languages, San Diego, California*, pages 171–183, New York, NY, 1998.

12. Atshushi Igarashi, Benjamin Pierce, and Philip Wadler. Featherweight Java: A minimal core calculus for Java and GJ. In Loren Meissner, editor, *Proceedings of the 1999 ACM SIGPLAN Conference on Object-Oriented Programming, Systems, Languages & Applications (OOPSLA'99)*, volume 34(10), pages 132–146, N. Y., 1999.

13. L. Liquori and A.Spiwack. Featherweight-Trait Java, A Trait-based Extension for FJ. 2004, http://www-sop.inria.fr/mirho/Luigi.Liquori/PAPERS/ftj.ps.gz.

14. Bertrand Meyer. *Eiffel: the Language*. Prentice-Hall, 1988.

15. Martin Odersky, Philippe Altherr, Vincent Cremet, Burak Emir, Stéphane Micheloud, Nikolay Mihaylov, Michel Schinz, Erik Stenman, and Matthias Zenge. The Scala Language Specification Version 1.0. Technical report, Programming Methods Laboratory, EPFL, Switzerland, 2004.

16. Martin Odersky, Vincent Cremet, Christine Röckl, and Matthias Zenger. A Nominal Theory of Objects with Dependent Types. In *Proc. ECOOP'03*, Springer LNCS, 2003.

17. Philip J. Quitslund and Andrew P. Black. Java with Traits — Improving Opportunities for Reuse. In *The MASPEGHI Workshop at ECOOP 2004*.

18. Nathanael Schärli, Stéphane Ducasse, Oscar Nierstrasz, and Andrew Black. Traits: Composable Units of Behavior. European Conference on Object-Oriented Programming (ECOOP), Springer LNCS 2743, July 2003.

19. Nathanael Schärli, Oscar Nierstrasz, Stéphane Ducasse, Roel Wuyts, and Andrew Black. Traits: The Formal Model. Technical Report IAM-02-006, Institut für Informatik, Universität Bern, Switzerland, November 2002.
20. Charles Smith. Typed Traits, September. MSc thesis - Department of Computing, Imperial College London, September 2004, http://chai-t.sourceforge.net/.
21. B. Stroustrup. Multiple inheritance for C++. In *Proceedings of the Spring 1987 European Unix Users Group Conference*, Helsinki, 1987.
22. David Ungar and Randall B. Smith. Self: The power of simplicity. In *Conference proceedings on Object-oriented programming systems, languages and applications*, pages 227–242. ACM Press, 1987.

A Type System for Reachability and Acyclicity

Yi L•• •n• Jo•n Po••••

Programming Languages and Compilers Group,
School of Computer Science and Engineering,
The University of New South Wales,
Sydney 2052, Australia
{ylu, potter}@cse.unsw.edu.au

Abstract. The desire for compile-time knowledge about the structure of heap contexts is currently increasing in many areas. However, approaches using whole program analysis are too weak in terms of both efficiency and accuracy. This paper presents a novel type system that enforces programmer-defined constraints on reachability via references or pointers, and restricts reference cycles to be within definable parts of the heap. Such constraints can be useful for program understanding and reasoning about effects and invariants, for information flow security, and for run-time optimizations and memory management.

1 Introduction

Poin•••• •n• •••••••n••• •llow •• n-•i• • •••••in• o• •••• •••••• •••••. In • o•• •o••-
w•••, •••••n••• ••• •n•voi••• l• •o• ••••• ••i• •• •i•n•y ••••on•, •v•n •• o•••
•••y •o• •li•••• ••o•••• ••••onin• •n• ••i• ••••• i• •••o•-••on•. W••n ••••
••••••••• ••• • ••••l•, ••o•l•• • ••• in•vi••• l•. • ••••n•• •y•l••, •i••• • i••••
o• in•i•••, ••n ••••• •••io•• ••o•••• • in• •••o••; • •••••n•• o• • •••o• ••ll•
•ollowin• • •••••••n•• •y•l•, • •y •n•x•••••ly ••••• inv••i•n•• o• lo••l ••••••
o• ••••• non-•••• in••ion. • •••••n•• •y•l•• •l•o •o• •li•••• ••• •••• o• • •• o•y
• •n•••• •n• •n• •lonin•; •o• in•••n••, ••••y o• •x•li•i• • •• o•y •••llo•••ion
• •y •• •i• •• l• in ••• •••••n•• o• ••• i•••y •y•l•• •n• •••o• ••i• ••••••• ••ol-
l•••ion ••nno• ••ly on •••••n•• •o•n•in• •lon• in ••• ••••••n•• o• •y•l••.

• • j•••-o•i•n••• ••o•••• • in• l•n••••• ••• •••••••n•• •••• •n•i•• •o• o•j••••
w•i•, •o•••••• wi•• •••y•in• •n• • ••n••i• •o•in• ••yl•, in••••• ••• li•li•oo•
o• •nin••n•• o• j••• ••••••n•• •y•l••. • o• • on o• j•••-o•i•n••• •••i•n ••••••n•,
li•• ••• •••o•••o•, o••n ••••i•• •n •••n•• o• •••• •y•l••. W•••in• •n o•j•••
wi•• ••l•-y•l• yi•l•• • •••i•n ••o•l•• : ••o•l• ••• ••l•-y•l•• •• ••-•o•••• vi•
••• w•••••• o• no•? W••n i• i• ••••• •o w••• •n o•j•••?

T•• •o••n•i•l •o• •y•l•• li• i•• o• ••ili•y •o ••• •l••• inv••i•n•• in ••••onin•
••o••••• ••••• o••n o• j••• ••••o•• •n• ••••• • •••o• ••ll•. I•• • ••• o• in•i•••ly
••ll• •••• on •n o•j•••, vi• •n in•i•••• •••••n•• •y•l•, ••y, ••n ••• ••ll-••••
• •y •• •n•••in• ••• o•j••• in •n inv•li• •••••, •o ••• ••ll-•••• •o•• • •y ••
wo••in• o• ••i• o• i•• ••••• •• ••••on•i•ion, •n• •••••••• o•• ••• o•i•in•l ••ll
on ••• •o•j•••• •y no• • ••w••• o•••• in• i•••• •ff••• o••••• ••ll-••••, •o i•• •••i•••

A.P. Black (Ed.): ECOOP 2005, LNCS 3586, pp. 479–503, 2005.

• o•••on• i•ion • •y no• • • • ••. Wi•• ••••••n•• •y•l•• w• ••nno• •••••• • ••••• •n
inv••i•n• will •ol• •o• •ll ••ll• on •n o• j•••. T• i• ••o•l•• • •ni••••• i•••l• in •
l•n•••••• li••• iff•l w•i•• •llow• •• n-•i• • •••••••ion •••••in• •o• •l••• inv••i•n•• –
w••n••o•l• ••• inv••i•n• •ol•? T•• ••o•l•• •••••••n •i••li•••• in ••••n• wo••
on v••i•••ion o• o• j•••-o•i•n••• ••o•••• • [3, •1] w•i•• ••••••• •n•i••in• •••
••o•••• •••••• •o ••••• w••n o• j••• inv••i•n•• •ol•; •••y in•o••o•••• • no•ion
o• •yn•• i• own•••• i•.

• ••••••n•• ••o•l•• •••• •i• ••l• •o ••••on ••o•• •••••••• in • o•• •••••• ••ll-
•••••• •n• in•ni•• loo••• •y •• ••••••• •y in•i•••• •••••••n•• w•i•• • ••o•••• -
• ••• • •y •• •n•w••• o•. S•••• •n•ly•i• ••••• ••• •o •••••••••i•• ••• ••••• • o•
•••• •••••••••••• vi• w•ol• ••o•••• •n•ly•i• [•6]. How•v••, ••••• ••••o•••••••-
••• ••o• •x•on•n•i•l •o• •l•xi•y •n• ••nno•••••••••• •••••i•lly in ••• •••••n•
o• •y•li• •••••••n•• ••••••••••. T••y ••• •l•o •••• •o •••l• •o l•••• o• in•o• •l•••
••o•••• • •••••••• o• l••• o• • o• •l••i•y in ••• •n•ly•i• •••• ni•••.

In •• i• ••••••, w• •• •loy • •y•• •y•••• , ••ll•• *Acyclic Region Type Sys-tem*, ••••• •llow• ••o•••• • ••• •o •••i•y ••i••• •••••••ili•y ••l••ion• •••w••n
o•j•••• vi• •••ion•. W• ••• ••• n•• • *ARTS* •o ••••• •o o•• •y• •y•••• , •••
ov•••ll • o••l, •n• •n•••lyin• l•n••••. • ••ion• ••••i•ion ••• ••••• in•o •i••in••
lo•i••l •lo••• o•• •• o•y, •n• •v••y o•j••• liv• in • •x•• •••ion •••••• in•• ••o•
i•• •y••. • •j••• •••••••n•• •y•l•• ••• only •llow•• wi•• in ••• ••• • •••ion, ••••
i•, •••ion• ••• ••••i•lly o••••••• •y ••• o•j••• •••••••ili•y ••l••ion. In •• i• w•y,
••o••••• • ••• ••• ••l• •o •x•••• w•••• •y•l•• ••• •llow••, •y ••••in• o•j••• in
••• ••• • •••ion; •••y ••n •l•o •o•• i• •nw•n••• •y•l•• •y ••in• •iff••n• •••ion•.
A• TS •llow• • o••l•• ••••onin• on • •n• o•n••• n•• ••• o•••ion• •n• •••••••••
••o• •il••ion i• •o••i•l•. W• •l•o •••••n• • •yn•• i• ••• •n•i•• ••••• •llow• •• •o
•o•• •li•• ••• ••y ••••••••l inv••i•n•: o•j••• ••••••n•• ••• ••• ••• •••ion ••••••• il-
i•y, •o •••• o•j••• •y•l•• o•••• only wi•• in •••ion•. B••i•• ••o•••• ••••onin•,
o•• •y•• •y•••• ••• ••o••n•i•l •••li•••ion in • •ny •••••: in•o•• ••ion flow ••-
•••i•y, • •• o•y • •n•••• •n•, •••• •o•yin• o• •lonin•, •••• lo•• •voi••n••, •n•
••••• •n•ly•i• w•••• •y•l•• ••• •in •n o••••l•.

T•i• •••••• i• o•••ni••• •• •ollow•: •n in•o•• •l ov••vi•w o• A• TS i• •iv•n
in ••• n•x• •••ion wi•• •o• • ••o•••• •x•• •l••. T•• •o•• l•n••••• o• A• TS
i• •o•• •li••• in S••ion 3, w•••• •lon• w• •••••n• •••i•• ••• •n•i••. Dyn•• i•
••• •n•i••• •n• •o• •i• •o•••n• ••o•••i•• o•••• •y•• •y•••• ••• •iv•n in S•••ion
•. Di••••ion •n• ••l•••• wo•• ••• •iv•n in S•••ion 5 •n• S••ion 6. S••ion •
••i•fly •on•l•••• ••• •••••• •lon• wi•• •o• • ••o••••• on •••••• •i•••ion•.

2   Overview of the Acyclic Region Type System

A• TS ••••• •••ion-••••• •y•• ••o •••••••••• ••• • o••n•i•l o••n o• j••• •o ••••• o••••
o•j••••, •i•••ly o• in•i•••ly. In •y••• •l•n••••••, ••• o•••••n•• o• • •y•l• in
••• ••n-•i• • o•j••••••• i• •li•• ••••• • •••••• •y•l• in ••• •y•• •••n••n•y
•••••; in o•••• wo•••, i• ••••• i• no •y•l• in ••• •y•• •••n••n•y •••••, ••n
••••• will •• non• in ••• ••n-•i• • o•j••• •••••. I••••••• ••• •y•-l•v•l •y•l••, •••
•y•• •y•••• i• •ow••l••• •o •••v•n• •y•li• •••••••n••, •v•n i•••y ••• •n••i•••l•.

Wi•• o•• ••y•li• •••ion •y•• •y•••• , w• ••n •n•o••• on•-w•y •••••••• ili•y •o• o• j••••, •••• i•, on• o• j••• • •y •••••• •no•••• vi• • •••• •••• i• no•••• o•• •y- •l• in ••• o• j••• ••••••. *Acyclic reachability* •o• •••ion• i• ••• ••y •on•••• in o•• • o••l: i• i• • •••i•• ••••i•l o•••• w•i•• w• ••no•• •y ▷. Un••lyin• ••• •••i•n o• A• TS i• ••• ••y•li• ••••• in•••• •y ••• •••i•ion o• • i••••••• ••••• in•o i•• •••on•ly •onn••••• •o• •on•n•• (*scc*). All •y•l•• wi••in ••• o•i•in•l ••••• • •••• o•••• wi••in ••••• •o• •on•n••. W• ••v• •••i•n•• o• •y•• •y•••• •o •••• •••ion• •n• ••y•li• •••••••ili•y ••ovi•• • •••i• •••••••••ion o• ••• •••on•ly •onn••••• •o• •on•n• o• ••• •yn• i• o• j••• ••••• •n• o• j••• ••••••• ili•y ••- •w••n ••••• . T•• ••y i••• i• •o •o•• •l••• •••i• •on•••in•• on ••• o• j••• •••• •y •••i•yin• •••ion• wi•• in w•i•• •ll ••••••n•• •y•l•• ••• ••••••••. • ••ion• ••• • i•join• •••• o• o• j•••• •n• •v••y o• j••• liv•• in ••• ••• • •••ion •o• i•• li••i• •. W• i• • o•• •on••••in•• on •••ion •••••••ili•y, •n• •••••n••• •••• in•••-o• j••• ••••••n••• ••••• ••• ••••• in•••-••ion•l ••••••• ili•y •on••••in••.

To ••• ••••• • • o••l, ••o•••• • ••• • •••••••• •l• •o •••i• w••n •••y w•n• •o ••n ••• • o••i• ili•y o• •y•l•• o• •li•••• •• •n•in• ••o• •••i••l•• o• j••• ••l••. T• i• will •• •l••••• i• w• loo• •• •n •x•• •l• ill•••••in• • •i• •l• ••• o• A• TS.

```
class A<p>
  r from p;
  B<r> f;
  ...
    // assert a property about this object's fields
    f.m();
    // assert the same property
```

T• i• •o•• ••ow• ••• •i• •l••• •••• o• A• TS. •l••• A i• •••••• •••i••• wi•• • •••ion ••••• •••• p, w•i•• •••••••n•• ••• •••ion ••• ••••••n• o• j••• liv•• in. A •••ion r i• ••• n•• wi••in ••• •l••• wi•• ••• •on••••in• r from p, w•i•• • ••n• p on•-w•y ••••••• r, o• p ▷ r. T• i• i• • li•• •••••• • •y •• • ••••••n•• ••••••n•• ••••••in• in p •••• •n•• in r ••• no• vi•• v••••. T•• ••y• o• ••• ••l• f i• B<r> w•i•• • ••n• f ••••••n••• •n o• j••• livin• in ••• •••ion r. In ••i• ••••, ••• o• j••• ••••••n••• • •y f ••n n•v•• •ol• • •••••••n•• •o ••• ••••••n• o• j••• ••••••• o• ••• o•••• w• •o••• on •••i• •y•••. So •ny • •••o• ••ll • ••• on f ••nno• •••n••• ••• ••••••n• o• j•••. S••• •nowl•••• •llow• ••o ••••••• ••o•••i•• ••• ••• n••••••••ily inv••i•n• •••in• ••• ••ll, ••••• •• ••• •••••••n•• ••o••• in ••• ••l• f.

A• TS ••n •i•ni••n•ly i• ••ov• ••o•••• •n••••••n•in•. P•o•••• • ••• ••• ••l• •o •x••••• •••••••n•• ••••••• ili•y ••••w••n o• j••• vi• •y•••, •n• •now •••• •wo •••••••n•• ••nno• ••• •i•••• •li•••• i• •••i• o• j••• liv• in •iff•••n• •••ion•. T•• n•x• •x•• •l• will ••ow •ow •o •x••••• •o• •l•x ••••• ••••••••••, •••••• •• lin••• li••• wi•• i••••••o••, in A• TS.

2.1   A Linked List Example

Lin••• li••• ••ovi•• • • •o• • on •x•• •l• •o• ••• on•••••in• •x••••iv•n••• o• l•n- ••••• ••••••••• •••lin• wi•• •••••••n•••. ••• li•• •x•• •l• will ••ow • •ow •••ion•

482   Y. Lu and J. Potter

wo•• •n• • ow ••y•li• ••o•••i•• ••• •x•••••• in • ••o•••• . In •••i••l••, ••i•
•x•• •l• ••ow• • ow ••• li•• •••• •••••••• i• ••n•l•• •o •••• • li•• o•j••• ••n
n•v•• •••••• i•••l• vi• i•• •••• o•j••••. In o•••• wo•••, ••• •••• o•j•••• •on••in••
•y • li•• • ••• no• ••••• •n• ••••••y •l••• ••• li••, w•i•• •o•l• ••••• i••••o••
on ••• li•• •o ••il, •o• •x•• •l•. T•• •••• o•j•••• ••••• ••lv•• • •y w•ll •• ••••••
•y o•••• •••• o• ••• ••o•••• .

```
class List<list, data from list>
  link from list to data;
  Link<link, data> head;
  Link<link, data> tail;
  void addElement(Data<data> d)
    head = new Link<link, data>(head, d);
    if (tail == null) tail = head;
    tail.next = head;
  Iterator<list, data> getIterator()
    return new Iterator<list, data>(head);

class Link<link, data from link>
  Link<link, data> next;
  Data<data> d;
  Link(Link<link, data> next, Data<data> d)
    this.next = next;
    this.d = d;

class Iterator<list, data from list>
  Link<List<list, data>.link, data> current;
  Iterator(Link<List<list, data>.link, data> current)
    this.current = current;
  void next()
    current = current.next;
  Data<data> element()
    return current.data;
```

A li•• o•j••• i• i• •l•• •n••• •y • •y•l• o• lin• o•j••••. I••••o• o•j•••• •••
•••••• in•i•• ••• li••'• •••ion, •n• ••• •••• •o •••••• ••• •••• ••o••• in lin•
o•j••••. T••y ••n n•• • ••• link •••ion ••o••• • •••li•••ion ov•• ••• •y•• o•
••• li••. T•i• ••• ov•• ••• n•• in• ••••i••ion in in•••n••-•••• ••••• •••i• •y••
•y•••• • ••••• •• own•••i• •y••• (••• S••ion 6).

T•• ••l••ion• •••w••n ••• •••ion• in ••• •x•• •l• ••• ••own in Fi•••• 1. All
lin• o•j•••• liv• in ••• ••• • •••ion •••n•• in ••• List •l•••, •n• •ll li••, lin•
•n• i•••••o• o•j•••• ••v• •••••• •o ••• •••• o•j•••• in •no••• •••ion •iv•n •y
• ••••• •••• o• ••i• •l••••. T•• •y•• •y•••• •n•o•••• • l••• o• •y•l•• •••w••n
•••ion•. D••• o•j•••• ••n n•v•• •••••n•• ••• li•• o• i••••o• o•j••••; ••••• •••
•• own in ••• •••••• •• '••• •••••n•••'. A• •x••••••, •y•li• •••••n••• ••• •llow••
wi•• in • •••ion. In ••• •x•• •l•, lin• o•j•••• •o•• • •y•l• wi•• in •••i• •••ion.

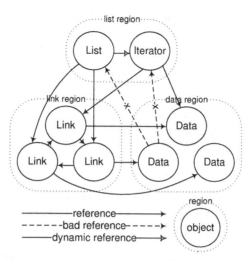

Fig. 1. List Example

3   The Language and Static Semantics of ARTS

In •• i• •••••ion w• •o•• •li•• o•• • o••l, ••ovi•in• •n •••••••• •yn••x w•i••
•• o•n•• •o • •i• •l• J•v•-li•• l•n•••••, •n• • •y•• •y•••• •••• •••••••• •••
•••i••• ••o•••i••. Bo•• ••• l•n••••• •n• ••• •y•• •y•••• ••• •••••i••• in
•o• • ••••il, •n• w• ill••••••• •••i••l•• l•n••••• •••••••• wi•• •• •ll •x•• •l••.

T•• ••y ••••ni••l •on••i••ion o• ••• ••••• i• ••• w•y in w•i•• n•w •••ion
••• ni•ion• •••n• • •••n•• •n• o• ••• ••y•li• ••••••• ili•y o•••in• on •xi••in•
•••ion•. How • o•• •• i• wo••? • on•i•• in••••• • ow ••••l••• ••• ni•ion •x••n••
••• ••y•li• in••i••n•• ••l••ion on •xi••in• •l•••••: ••• ••y •n••in• •••• in•••-
i••n•• i• ••y•li• i• •o •n•••• •••• ••••• i• •n o•••• o• •••ni•ion o• •l••••• in
w• i•• ••••l••••• ••• •••n•• ••••• ••••l•••••. Fo• •••ion •••ni•ion• in A• TS,
w• •l•o ••ly on • •••ni•ion o•••• •o •n•••• ••y•li•i•y. B•• •x••• •••• i• n••••••.
N•w •••ion• no• only •x••n• ••• ••••••• ili•y, ••• •l•o •••n• i• •y •l••in• n•w
•••ion• •••w••n •xi••in• on••. T•• ••l ••i•• •o • ••• ••• •y•••• wo••, i• ••••,
in ••• •••• o• •••ion •••n•• •n•, ••• ••••••• ili•y ••w••n ••• •xi••in• •••ion•
• •••• •l•••• y •• ••iv••l• ••o•• ••• n•w •••ion i• in••o•••••.

3.1   An Abstract Syntax for ARTS

To •i• • li•y ••• •••••••• •yn••x ••••n••• in T••l• 1, w• •••• • •w ••••vi•ion•.
T•• ov•••••• i• •••• •o• • ••••••n•• o• •on•••••••; •o• •x•• •l•, $\overline{\sigma}$ i• •••• •o• •
• o••i•ly •• ••y •••••n•• $\sigma_1 ... \sigma_n$, •• ••• $\overline{p}, \overline{q}, \overline{fd}, \overline{mth}$ •n• $\overline{e}$. Si• il••ly, $\overline{t\,x}$
•••n••••o• • • o••i•ly •• ••y •••••n•• o•••i•• $t_1\,x_1 ... t_n\,x_n$. In ••• •l••• ••o•••-
•ion, $[t]_{opt}$ i• •n o••ion•l •••• o• ••• •l••. In ••• •y•• •y•••• ••• ••• •iv•l•n••
•y• • ol ≡ ••no••• •yn••••i• •••iv•l•n••; i• i• •••• in •••nin• •yn•••i• loo•••
•n• •••••i••ion ••n••ion• in T••l• 3. J••• •• in J•v•, this i• • •i••in••i••••

Table 1. Abstract Syntax

$c \in$ ClassName; $r \in$ RegionName; $x \in$ VarName; $f \in$ FieldName; $m \in$ MethodName

$$
\begin{array}{lll}
cls \in \text{Class} & ::= c\ \overline{p}\ [t]_{opt}\ \overline{q}\ \overline{fd}\ \overline{mth} \\
p,q \in \text{RegionConstraint} & ::= \overline{\sigma} \triangleright \sigma \triangleright \overline{\sigma} \\
t \in \text{Type} & ::= c\langle \overline{\sigma} \rangle \\
\sigma \in \text{Region} & ::= \textsf{base} \mid t.r \mid r \\
fd \in \text{Field} & ::= t\ f \\
mth \in \text{Method} & ::= t\ m(\overline{t\ x})\ e \\
e \in \text{Expression} & ::= x \mid \textsf{new}\ t \mid \textsf{null} \mid e.f \mid e.f = e \mid e.m(\overline{e}) \mid e;e \mid \textsf{if}\ e\ e\ e
\end{array}
$$

v••i••l• n•• • •••• •o ••••n•• ••• ••••• o• j••• •o• ••• •••••n• ••ll, •••• i•, ••• *current object.* In ••• •on••••• •yn••x w• ••• in o•• •x•• •l••, w• ••• ••ywo••• •••• •• class •n• extends •o• •••• o• •••• in•.

Classes and Constrained Formal Parameters. • ••• •yn••x i• •lo•• •o J•v• •x•••• •••• •l••••• ••• ••••• •••i••• wi•• •••ion ••••• •••••• •n• •••ion n•• •• ••• ••• n•• •• • •• •••• wi•• in •l•••••.

T•• ••l••ion•l •y• • ol ▷, in •••ion •on••••in••, ••no••• ••• *acyclic reacha-bility* ••l••ion ••• w••n •••ion•. In ••• •on••••• •yn••x, ••• •••ion •on••••in•• $q \equiv \overline{\sigma} \triangleright r \triangleright \overline{\sigma'}$ ••••• ••• n•• n•w •••ion r i• w•i•••n ••:

$$r\ \textsf{from}\ \sigma_1, ..., \sigma_m\ \textsf{to}\ \sigma_1', ..., \sigma_n'\quad \text{w}••• \quad |\overline{\sigma}| = m\quad •n•\quad |\overline{\sigma'}| = n$$

T•• ••• • •••li•• •o ••• •on••••in•• •o• ••• •o•• •l ••••• ••••• $p \equiv \overline{\sigma} \triangleright r \triangleright \overline{\sigma'}$. T•• •o•• •l •••ion ••••• ••••• o•• •l••• ••• ••••• •• •o •••i••y ••• ••••• ili•y •on-••••in•• •••i••• in ••• from •n• to •l•••• o• •••• ••••• ••••. T••y ••• •••• wi•• in • •l••• •o i••n•i•y •••ion• •o• o• j•••• ••••• •y ••• •l•••. T•• •••• •o•• •l ••••• ••••• ••no••• ••• •••ion w•••• ••• ••••••n• o• j••• (this) liv••. • ••• •yn••x •o• •••ion n•• •• r • o•• no•• •i••in•• i•• •••w••n n•• •• o• •••ion ••••• •••••• •n• lo••lly ••• n•• •••ion•. T•• ••••on •o• ••in• •wo ••y wo••• from •n• to in ••• •on••••• •yn••x in••••• o• on• i• •o • ••• ••• •on••••in•• •l••• − ••• • ••••• •••• o• n•w •••ion •o •• in••o••••• o••••• ••••.

Types. • l••••• ••• •y•• •••••• ••. A •y•• i• •o•• •• •y •in•in• ••• •••ion ••-••• ••••• •o ••••l •••ion• in ••• •nvi•on• •n• w•••• ••• •y•• i• •o•• ••. A •y•• •on•i••• o•• •l••• n•• • •n• ••• •••ion ••••• •n•• •••• j••• • y i•• •l••• ••• ni•ion. T•• ••••• •••ion ••••• •n• i• ••• •••ion w•••• ••• o• j••• o•• •i• •y•• •••i•••. Un-•••••i•in•ly, •o• • •y•• •o •• v•li•, ••• •••••l •••ion ••••• •n•• • ••• •••i••y ••• •l••• •on••••in•• ••• n•• on ••• •o•• •l ••••• ••••.

Regions and Region Definitions. In A• TS, •v••y o• j•••• •lon•• •o • •x•• ••-•ion •o• i•• •n•i•• li•••i• •. • ••ion •x••••ion• ••• •o•• •• ••o• ••• •••••i•l •lo••l •••ion base, ••o• •y••-•••li••• •••ion•, •n• •••ion ••••• ••••. To •n••• ••• ••y•li• ••o• ••y •o• ••• •••ion •••••••ili•y ••l••ion, ••• o•••• o• in••o•••ion o• n•w •••ion• in ••• ni•ion• i• i• • o••••n•. A •••ion ••• ni•ion q in••o••••• • ••••• n•• • •o• i•• •••ion, •o••••• wi•• •on••••in•• •••• •••i••y i•• ••••••• ili•y

Table 2. Static Semantics Given Class Definitions Π

Well-Formed Program and Well-Ordered Class Definitions $\vdash_P e; \ \vdash_c \Gamma; \ \Gamma \vdash_c cls$

[PROGRAM]   [CLS−DEF0]   [CLS−DEFS]

$$\frac{\vdash_c \Pi \quad \Pi \vdash_e e : t}{\vdash_P \Pi \, e}$$

$$\overline{\vdash_c \emptyset}$$

$$\frac{\vdash_c \Gamma \quad \Gamma \vdash_c cls}{\vdash_c \Gamma, cls}$$

[CLS−DEF]

$$\frac{c \notin \Gamma \quad \overline{r} \equiv \mathcal{R}(\overline{p}) \quad E \equiv \Pi, \overline{p}, \mathtt{this} : c\langle \overline{r} \rangle \quad \Pi \vdash_r \overline{p} \quad \Gamma, \overline{p} \vdash_r \overline{q} \quad E \vdash_f \overline{fd} \quad E \vdash_m \overline{mth} \quad [t \equiv c'\langle r_1, ... \rangle \quad E \vdash_t t \quad c' \in \Gamma]_{opt}}{\Gamma \vdash_c c \, \overline{p} \, [t]_{opt} \, \overline{q} \, \overline{fd} \, \overline{mth}}$$

Well-Ordered Region Definitions $E \vdash_r \overline{p}; \ E \vdash_r p$

[REG−DEF0]   [REG−DEFS]

$$\overline{E \vdash_r \emptyset}$$

$$\frac{E \vdash_r \overline{p} \quad E, \overline{p} \vdash_r p}{E \vdash_r \overline{p}, p}$$

[REG−DEF]

$$\frac{r \notin \mathcal{R}(E) \quad E \vdash_\sigma \overline{\sigma}, \sigma' \quad E \vdash_\triangleright \overline{\sigma} \triangleright \overline{\sigma'}}{E \vdash_r \overline{\sigma} \triangleright r \triangleright \overline{\sigma'}}$$

Well-Defined Field and Method $E \vdash_f fd; \ E \vdash_m mth$

[FIELD]

$$\frac{t_o \equiv c_o\langle r, ... \rangle \quad t \equiv c\langle \sigma, ... \rangle \quad E \vdash_e \mathtt{this} : t_o \quad E \vdash_t t \quad E \vdash_\triangleright r \trianglerighteq \sigma}{E \vdash_f t \, f}$$

[METHOD]

$$\frac{E \vdash_t t, \overline{t} \quad E, \overline{x : t} \vdash_e e : t}{E \vdash_m t \, m(\overline{t \, x}) \, e}$$

Well-Formed Region and Type $E \vdash_\sigma \sigma; \ E \vdash_t t$

[REG−BASE]   [REG−NAME]   [REG−QUAL]

$$\overline{E \vdash_\sigma \mathtt{base}}$$

$$\frac{r \in \mathcal{R}(E)}{E \vdash_\sigma r}$$

$$\frac{E \vdash_t t \quad t.r \in \mathcal{R}(t)}{E \vdash_\sigma t.r}$$

[TYPE]

$$\frac{t \equiv c\langle \overline{\sigma} \rangle \quad \mathcal{C}(t) \equiv c \, \overline{p} \, ... \quad c \in E \quad E \vdash_\sigma \overline{\sigma} \quad E \vdash_\triangleright \overline{p}}{E \vdash_t t}$$

Subtype $\vdash_{<:} t <: t'$

[SUBTYPE−REFL]   [SUBTYPE−EXTEND]   [SUBTYPE−TRANS]

$$\overline{\vdash_{<:} t <: t}$$

$$\frac{\mathcal{C}(t) \equiv ... \, t' \, ...}{\vdash_{<:} t <: t'}$$

$$\frac{\vdash_{<:} t <: t' \quad \vdash_{<:} t' <: t''}{\vdash_{<:} t <: t''}$$

Region Reachability $E \vdash_\triangleright \sigma \triangleright \sigma'; \ E \vdash_\triangleright \sigma \triangleright \sigma' \triangleright \sigma''; \ E \vdash_\triangleright \sigma \trianglerighteq \sigma'$

[REACH−ENV]   [REACH−DEF−TO]   [REACH−DEF−FROM]   [REACH−TRANS]

$$\frac{\sigma \triangleright \sigma' \in E}{E \vdash_\triangleright \sigma \triangleright \sigma'}$$

$$\frac{t.r \triangleright \sigma \in \mathcal{Q}(t)}{E \vdash_\triangleright t.r \triangleright \sigma}$$

$$\frac{\sigma \triangleright t.r \in \mathcal{Q}(t)}{E \vdash_\triangleright \sigma \triangleright t.r}$$

$$\frac{E \vdash_\triangleright \sigma \triangleright \sigma' \triangleright \sigma''}{E \vdash_\triangleright \sigma \triangleright \sigma''}$$

[REACH−COMB]   [REACH−REFL]   [REACH−EXT]

$$\frac{E \vdash_\triangleright \sigma \triangleright \sigma' \quad E \vdash_\triangleright \sigma' \triangleright \sigma''}{E \vdash_\triangleright \sigma \triangleright \sigma' \triangleright \sigma''}$$

$$\overline{E \vdash_\triangleright \sigma \trianglerighteq \sigma}$$

$$\frac{E \vdash_\triangleright \sigma \triangleright \sigma'}{E \vdash_\triangleright \sigma \trianglerighteq \sigma'}$$

Well-Formed Expression $E \vdash_e e : t$

[EXPR−VAR]   [EXPR−NEW]   [EXPR−NULL]

$$\overline{E \vdash_e x : E(x)}$$

$$\frac{E \vdash_t t}{E \vdash_e \mathtt{new} \, t : t}$$

$$\frac{E \vdash_t t}{E \vdash_e \mathtt{null} : t}$$

[EXPR−FIELD]   [EXPR−ASSIGN]   [EXPR−CALL]

$$\frac{(t \, f) \in \mathcal{F}(t_o) \quad E \vdash_e e : t_o}{E \vdash_e e.f : t}$$

$$\frac{(t \, f) \in \mathcal{F}(t_o) \quad E \vdash_e e : t_o \quad E \vdash_e e' : t}{E \vdash_e e.f = e' : t}$$

$$\frac{\mathcal{M}(t_o, m) \equiv (\overline{t}, \_, t, \_) \quad E \vdash_e e : t_o \quad E \vdash_e \overline{e : t}}{E \vdash_e e.m(\overline{e}) : t}$$

[EXPR−SEQ]   [EXPR−IF]   [EXPR−SUBSUM]

$$\frac{E \vdash_e e : t \quad E \vdash_e e' : t'}{E \vdash_e e; e' : t'}$$

$$\frac{E \vdash_e e : t \quad E \vdash_e e' : t' \quad E \vdash_e e'' : t'}{E \vdash_e \mathtt{if} \, e \, e' \, e'' : t'}$$

$$\frac{E \vdash_e e : t \quad \vdash_{<:} t <: t'}{E \vdash_e e : t'}$$

Table 3. Auxiliary Lookup Functions for Static Semantics

$$\frac{[\text{LOOKUP–CLASS}]}{t \equiv c\langle\overline{\sigma}\rangle \quad \overline{r} \equiv \mathcal{R}(\overline{p}) \quad \overline{r'} \equiv \mathcal{R}(\overline{q}) \quad \Pi(c) \equiv cls \equiv c\,\overline{p}\,...\overline{q}\,...}{\mathcal{C}(t) \equiv cls[\overline{\sigma/r}, \overline{t.r'/r'}]} \qquad \frac{[\text{LOOKUP–DEF}]}{\mathcal{C}(t) \equiv ...\,\overline{q}\,...}{\mathcal{Q}(t) \equiv \overline{q}}$$

$$\frac{[\text{LOOKUP–FIELD}]}{\mathcal{C}(t_o) \equiv ...\,[t']_{opt}\,...\,\overline{t\,f}}{\mathcal{F}(t_o) \equiv [\mathcal{F}(t')]_{opt}, \overline{t\,f}} \qquad \frac{[\text{LOOKUP–METHOD}]}{\mathcal{C}(t_o) \equiv ...\,t\,m(\overline{t\,x})\,e\,...}{\mathcal{M}(t_o,m) \equiv (\overline{t},\overline{x},t,e)} \qquad \frac{[\text{LOOKUP–METHOD}']}{\mathcal{C}(t_o) \equiv ...\,t\,...\,\overline{mth}\,...}{\mathcal{M}(t_o,m) \equiv \mathcal{M}(t,m)}$$

$$\frac{[\text{LOOKUP–REGION–ENV}]}{\mathcal{R}(\emptyset) \equiv \emptyset \quad \mathcal{R}(E,cls) \equiv \mathcal{R}(E) \quad \mathcal{R}(E,p) \equiv \mathcal{R}(E), \mathcal{R}(p) \quad \mathcal{R}(E,x:t) \equiv \mathcal{R}(E)}$$

$$\frac{[\text{LOOKUP–REGION–DEF}]}{\mathcal{R}(\overline{\sigma} \triangleright \sigma'' \triangleright \overline{\sigma'}) \equiv \sigma'' \quad \mathcal{R}(\overline{q},q) \equiv \mathcal{R}(\overline{q}), \mathcal{R}(q) \quad \mathcal{R}(t) \equiv \mathcal{R}(\mathcal{Q}(t))}$$

••o• •••i•• in •••• • o• •••vio••ly •••n•• •••ion•. F••••••• o•• ••••• •on••••in•• • ••• no• i• • o•• •ny •••••••• ••••i••• •n• on ••• ••••••••ili•y ••l••ion •o• ••• •••vio••ly •••n•• •••ion•. In ••i• w•y w• ••• ••l• •o in•i•i• •y•l•• in ••• ••-•ion ••••••••ili•y ••l••ion. T•i• i• •••••••• •n• •n•o•••• •y ••• •y•• •y•••• •• •o•• •li••• in S•••ion 3.•.

• o• ••••• wi•• •on••••in•• on •o•• •l ••••• •••••, w•i•• j••• i• • o•• •••• i••-• •n•• on ••• •••••l •••ion ••••• •n•• •o• •l•••, •••ion ••• ni•ion• ••••• lly •••••-• in•• ••• •••ion •••••••••• •o• ••• •y•••• . • v••y •l••• ••• n•• • •y• ••••• •, wi•• i•• own lo••lly •••n•• •••ion•. W• •llow •y••• (no• j••• •l••• n•• ••) •o ••• li•y •••ion n•• •• – •v••y •••• •••li••• •••ion $t.r$ •ni••ly •••••• in•• • ••••i••l•• •••ion in ••• •y•••• . To ••••n••• •• i• •ni••n•••, w• •o no• •llow •••ion• •o •• in••• i••• • y •••• •l••••; o•••wi•• ••• ••• • •••ion •o•l• •• i••n•i••• •••o•• •• • ••• •y•• w•i•• in••• i• i•. In •••• i• i• •••• i•••o•w••• •o •llow •••ion in ••i••n••, ••• •• ••• no •x••• •x•••ivi•y, •n• •li••ly •o• • li•••••• ••• •y• •y•••• .

In••••••in•ly, •••ion• •n• •y••• •n• ••••••iv•ly ••• n••: •••ion• ••• ••• n•• wi•• in •l••••• •n• n•• •• vi• •y• •••• li•••ion; •y•• ••••• •o•• •• • y•in• in• •l••• ••••• ••••• wi•• ••••l •••ion•. B••••••• o• •• i• •••••iv• •••••••• •••••• ••• ••• •n •n•o•n••• n•• ••• o• •••ion in ••• •y•••• , •ll •lo••lly •••••••i•l• vi• •••ion •••• •x••••ion•. Fo•••n•••ly ••• ••o••••• • ••• •o•• no• ••v• •o •••l wi•• •lo••l •••ion n•• ••, ••••••• ••• •••ion ••••• ••••• o• • •l••• lo••li•• ••• •x••••ion o• ••• •••ion• ••l•v•n• •o• • •l•••, •o no•• •lly •••ion •x••••ion• •o no• n••• •o •• n••••• •••o••• • o•• •••n on• l•v•l o• •y• •••li•••ion.

T•• ••i• ••y •o•l o• A• TS i• •o •llow ••o•••• • ••• •o ••• n• • •••i• ••o•••• on ••• ••n-•i• • o•j•••• ••••••••• w•i•• in••••• • ••••i•l o••••• on ••• •••'• o• ••• o•j••••, •••••••y ••••i••in• w•••• •y•l•• •• n o•••••. By • ••in• •l••••-••• n•• •••ion n•• •• •••li•ly •••••i•l• w• •••• fl•xi•ili•y in •••• •v••y ••o•n• •••ion •••• • •ni••• •lo••l n•• •. • •o•n• •••ion• ••• ••o•• wi•• no •••• •••ion ••••• -••••: •i•••• base, o• • •••ion $t.r$ •••li••• •y • ••o•n• •y•• t; • ••o•n• •y•• i• on• wi•• no •••• •••ion ••••• ••••. • •j•••• o• ••• ••• • •y••• (not just the same class) •••••• ••• ••• • •••ion; o• j•••• o• •iff•••n• •y•• • •y o••••y ••• ••• • •••ion, ••• ••i• •y••• • ••• •••••• ••• ••• • •••• •••ion ••••• •n• •••••••• i• ••••••• in•• ••• •••ion •n o• j••• liv•• in).

T•• •••i•l •••ion base i• •••-•••n•• •n• i• ••• only •n••li••• ••o•n•
•••ion in ••• •y•••• . An i• •o•••n• no•• •••• i• ••• •••••ion• •o *not* ••v• •o ••
•••••••l• ••o• base o• vi••-v••••; •l•o •ny •oo• o• j••• (o• j•••• ••••••• in •••
• •in • •••o•) •o•• *not* ••v• •o ••• •l•••• in base. base i• j••• ••• • •••• •••ion
•••• •o n•• • •ny o•••• ••o•n• •••ion. T•• •• ili•y •o n•• • • ••• ••ion i• •iff•••n•
••o• ••• •• ili•y •o ••••••• • •••ion, w•i•• i• •••••• in•• •y ••• to •n• from
•l••••• o• ••• •••ion ••• ni•ion•. In ••••, w• •o•l• •llow ••• •x••••ion ••• nin•
•••• • •in • •••o• o•• ••o•••• •o ••• n• i•• own •••ion•, • •in• ••• ••• o••lo••l
•••ion• ••••fl• o••.

All •••ion •on••••in•• ••• ••••i••lly v••i••• •y ••• •y•• •y•••• •o •n•••
•lo••l ••y•li•i•y. Any •••on•ly •onn••••• •o• •on•n• in ••• o• j••• ••••• •••in•
••• •x•••ion o• •n A• TS ••o•••• • ••• o•••• •n•i••ly wi•• in • •••ion. • ••ion•
n••• no• •xi•• •• ••n-•i• • •••••••• ••• •x•••ion l•n•••• only •••• •y••• •o•
o• j••• •llo•••ion, •n• •••ion• ••n •• ••••••• ••o• •••• wi•• no ••n•• in ••-
••vio••. • ••ion• ••• only •••• in •y•• •••••in• •o ••l• o•••ni•• •n• •••••on
•• o•• •y•li •••••••n••• •n• o• j••• •••••••• ili•y.

Fields and Methods. In A• TS, ••• •••••••••• ••l inv••i•n• i• • •in••in•• •y i• -
•o•in• • •••on••• ••••••i•ion on o• j••• ••l•• •••n on o•••• •••••••n••-v•l••• •n-
•i•i••, n•• •ly • •••o• ••••• •n•• •n• ••••l••. • • j••• ••l•• ••• •in•l•• o•• ••o•
••••i•l •••n•ion ••••••• ••• •y ••n •o•• •nw•n••• ••••-•o-•••••• •y•l•• in o• j•••
••••••. T•• •••••••• ••l inv••i•n• •••••• •••• i• •n o• j••• •on••in• • •••••••n•• •o
•no•••• o• j••• ••• •n • o•• o• j•••• • ••• •• in ••• ••• • •••ion o• ••• •••ion o•
••• •o•• •• o• j••• ••••• •• ••l• •o ••••• ••• •••ion o• ••• l••••• o• j••• wi•• no
••••••n ••••••n•• • o••i•l•.

How•v••, w• •o •llow •••o• ••••• •n•• •o ••••• • o• j••• w•i•• ••• no•
••••••i•l• •o ••• •••••n• o• j•••, •••• i•, ••• •••ion• o• • •••o• ••••• ••••• •n•
••••l•• •o no• ••v• •o •• ••••••••l• ••o• ••• •••ion o• ••• this o• j•••. T•i• i• -
•li•• •••• w• ••ill •llow in•••-••ion ••ll•••••, • •• •••• ••• •y o•••• wi••in • •••o•
••o••, •n• ••• • •••o• ' •y• •i•n••• in i•••• w•••••• •ny •••• ••ll-•••• i•
•llow•• o• no•. T•••• •yn•• i• ••••••n••• ••n •• •on•i••••• •••• •••••••• •••y
•• •n••• ••o• ••• ••llin• ••••• •••••• ••• n ••• ••••, w•i•• i• no• •••••n•••l•
••o• ••• ••••• •n• •••llo••••• •• ••• •xi• o• ••• • •••o•.

I• i• wo••• ••• nowl••in• ••• ••i• ••••• •••• o•• •• oi•• o• •••••i••ion• •o• ••l•
•n• • •••o• •••••• i• •o• •w••• •••i•••y. I• i• •••y •o • o•i•y ••• •y•• ••l••
•o •n•o••• •iff•••n• inv••i•n••; •o• •x•• •l•, i• w• wi•• •o •lo•• ••• •o••i•ili•y
o• •y•l•• wi•• •yn•• i• ••••••n••• •• w•ll, ••n w• •o•l• i• •o•• ••• •••••i••ion
•••• •ll •••o• ••••• •n•• •n• •••l•• ••• •••••i•l• ••o• ••• •••ion o• this
j••• li•• w• •o •o ••l••. T•• ••y •oin• o• ••• •y•• •y•••• i• •••• w• ••v• •••
•• ili•y •o inv•n• •••• •y•• ••l••, •••••• w• ••v• • • ••••ni•• •o• ••••i•yin•
•n• ••••i••lly ••••in• ••y•li• •••••••• ili•y o• •••ion•.

3.2   Static Semantics

W• •••••n• •n ov••vi•w o• ••• ••••i• ••• •n•i•• o• A• TS, •lon• wi•• ••••il••
•••••i••ion o• •o• • i• •o•••n• •y•in• ••l••. T•• •o• l••• •y•• •y•••• ••n ••

•o•n• in T••l• •. In •••i•ion •o ••• •y•• •y•••• , w• •••n• ••xili••y ••n••ion• •o loo••• •n• •in• •l•••••, •y••, •••ion•, •••ion •••ni•ion•, ••l••n• •••o••• in T••l• 3. W• in••n•ion•lly • ov• •ll o•••••n••• o• ••••••i•••ion in•o ••• ••x-ili••y ••n••ion• •o •i• •li•y ••• •y•in• ••l••, •o• •x•• •l•, ••• •l••• loo••• •o• • •iv•n •y•• ••••••i•••• •• ••••l •••ion ••••• •n•• in•o ••• •l••• ••• ni•ion, •n• •••li••• •ll o••• lo••l •••ion ••• ni•ion• wi•• ••• •y••.

W• •l•o ••••• • ••••, •o• • ••o•••• •o•• v•li•, no i••n•i••• ••n•• ••• •l•••• • o•• •••n on•• wi•• in ••• ••• ••o••. T••• i•, no •l••• n••• ••n•• ••• •l•••• • o•• •••n on••; no ••l• •n• •••o• n••• • ••n•• ••• •l•••• • o•• •••n on•• wi•• in ••• ••• • •l•••; •••ion n•• ••, in•l••in• •o•• •l ••••• •••••, ••nno• •• •••l•••• • o•• •••n on•• wi•• in ••• ••• • •l•••. In ••••, w• •x• li•i•ly ••••• •• i• in ••• •••• o• •l••• n•• •• •n• •••ion n•• ••, ••••••• w• n••• •o ••••• •••• •••ion •••ni•ion i• w•ll-o••••••• in ••• ••l••.

W• ••• •o• • •yn•••i• ••o•••••. By •••••l• $E \vdash_\sigma \overline{\sigma}$ ••••••n•• • •o••i•ly •• ••y ••••••n•• o• j•••••• •n•• $E \vdash_\sigma \sigma_1 ... E \vdash_\sigma \sigma_n$. T•• ••• • ••••••vi••ion i• •••• •o• j•••••• •n•• involvin• $\overline{fd}, \overline{mth}$ •n• $\overline{t}$. Si• il••ly, $E \vdash_e \overline{e:t}$ •••n•• •o• $E \vdash_e e_1 : t_1 ... E \vdash_e e_n : t_n$, •n• $[\sigma/r]$ ••••vi•••• • •••••n•• o• ••••••i•••ion• $[\sigma_1/r_1] ... [\sigma_n/r_n]$.

A ••o•••• P i• ••i• •on•i••in• • •x•• ••••••n•• o• •l••• •••ni•ion• Π •n• •n •x••••ion e. Γ ••no••• •ny ••••••n•• o• •l••• •••ni•ion•. An •nvi•on• •n• E ••y •x••n• • ••••••n•• o• •l••• •••ni•ion• wi•• •on••••in• on •••ion n•• ••, o• ••• •y•• o• v••i••l••. T•• o•••• o• ••• •l•• •n• in ••• •nvi•on• •n• i• •i•ni••n•.

$$P ::= \Pi\, e \qquad \Pi ::= \Gamma \qquad \Gamma ::= \emptyset \mid \Gamma, cls \qquad E ::= \Gamma \mid E, x : t \mid E, \overline{\sigma} \triangleright r \triangleright \overline{\sigma}$$

B•••••• ••• n•• ••• o• •••••••iv•ly •••n•• •••ion• •n• •y••• i• in•ni••, •o •••i•v• • ••i•• ••••i•l o••••• on• •ll •o••i•l• •••ion•, w• i••n•i•y •wo •••• i••-• •n•• ••••• ••• • ••••i•••• •y ••• •y•• •y•••• . Fi•••ly •ny ••••••ili•y ••• n•• •••w••n •wo •••ion• n•••• •o •• on•-w•y only. S••on• ly, •ny •x••n•ion •o ••• •••••••ili•y ••l••ion ••o•l• no• in••o•••• •ny • o•• •••••••ili•y ••••w••n •xi••-in• •••ion•, ••• ••••••• in••o•••• n•w •••ion •o•••••• wi•• •••i• •••••••ili•y ••l••iv• •o •xi••in• on••.

••• •y•• •y•••• •••i•••• •••••• •wo •••• i••• •n••. To •n•••• on•-w•y ••••••• •ili•y, ••• ••••••••ili•y ••l••ion •••w••n •ny •wo •••ion• ••n •• •••n•• *once* only. T•i• ••n •• ••• i•v•• •y o•••in• ••• •••ion •••ni•ion• •o ••••• ••• l•••• •••ni•ion• ••• •x••••• in •••• • o• ••li•• on••, •• •••••••• •y ••• $\Gamma, \overline{p} \vdash_r \overline{q}$ j•••• •n• in ••• [CLS-DEF] ••l•.

To ••i••y ••• •••on• ••••i••• •n•, ••• •y•• •y•••• •••••••n•••• •••• i•• n•w •••ion li•• •••w••n •xi••in• •••ion•, ••n ••o•• •••ion• w••• •l•••••y ••l•••••. Fo• •x•• •l•, i• $\sigma \triangleright \sigma'$ i• •l••••y •••n••, ••n • n•w •••ion r ••n •• •••n•• vi• $\sigma \triangleright r \triangleright \sigma'$, ••• no• $\sigma' \triangleright r \triangleright \sigma$ ••••••• ••i• wo•l• in••o•••• •y•l•• in•o ••• •••ion ••••••••. Si• il••ly, i• •••••• i• no •xi••in• •••••••ili•y ••••w••n σ •n• σ' ••n •• •••iv••, ••n $\sigma \triangleright r \triangleright \sigma'$ i• inv•li• •oo ••••••• i• i• •li•• $\sigma \triangleright \sigma'$ w•i•• i• •n•••i••• o•i•in•lly. T•i• •on•••in• i• •n•o•••• •y ••• [REG-DEF] ••l• w•i•• •••••n•••• ••••• ••• n•w •••ion v••i••l• •n• ••• ••l••ion• on i• •o no• viol••• ••• •on•i•••n•y o• ••• •••ion o•••••in•.

3.3   Examples

W• •iv• •o• • •oy •x•• •l•• •o ill••••••• ••• •••• o• •••ion•, ••• n •• ow • ow •••ion•
•• n •• • •••• •• ••••• i•y l•v•l• •o ••••••• ••• o••••in• o• in•o•• ••ion flow.

Toy Examples

```
class A<p1, p2 from p1, p3>
  a1 from p1 to p2;          // OK
  a2 from p2 to p1;          // BAD require p2 to p1
  a3 from p1 to p3;          // BAD require p1 to p3
  a4 from base;              // OK

class B<p from base>
  b1 from p;  b2 from b1;  b3 to p;
  A<p, b2, p> f1;            // OK by transitivity
  A<b1, b2, p> f2;           // OK
  A<p, b3, b2> f3;           // BAD require b3 from p
  A<p, base, b1> f4;         // BAD require base from p
  A<p, B<b3>.b2, p> f5;      // BAD require B<b3>.b2 from p

class C<
  p1 from base,              // OK
  p2 from B<p1>.b1,          // OK p1 already introduced
  p3 from B<p3>.b1,          // BAD p3 undefined yet
  p4 to B<base>.b3,          // BAD require base from base
  p5 from p1 to B<p2>.b2     // OK by transitivity
  >
```

• l••• A •• ow• • ow •••ion• ••• ••• n••. T•• ••y •oin• in •••ion •••ni•ion• i•
••••• •ny n•wly in••o••••• •••ion ••nno• •••n•• ••• ••l••ion o• •ny •••vio• ••-
•n•• •••ion. • l••• B •• ow• ••••• v•li• •y•• n•••• •o •••i•y i•• •l••• •on•••• in••.
• l••• C •• ow• v••io•• •l••• •on•••• in•• on •o•• •l •••ion ••••• •••••, •o• • wi••
•••li•• •• •••ion•.

```
class M<p>
  m to N<p>.n;               // BAD require ordering of classes

class M'<p>
  m to p;                    // OK

class M"<p1, p2 to N<p1>.n>   // OK do not require ordering of classes
  m to p2;

class N<p>
  n to M<p>.m;
```

T•• •x•• •l•• •• ov• •• ow ••• i• •o•••n•• o• •l••• o••••in•. • l••• o••••in•
i• no• only i• •o•••n• •o• •o••••• in•••i••n••, •••• •l•o i• •o•••n• in •••• in• •••

o•••in• o• •••ion ••• ni•ion•. In •l••••• M •n• N, ••••• i• • •y•l• •••w••n M<p>.m •n• N<p>.n w••n•v•• •••i• •l••• ••••• •••••• ••• •o•n• •o ••• ••• • •••ion. To •olv• •• i• ••o•l•• , w• •o••i• •••ion• in •••li•• •l••••• •o •• •• n•• •o ••l••• •o •••ion ••• n•• in l•••• •l••••• •o •n•o••• ••• o•••• o• •••ion ••• ni•ion•, •••• i•, •••ion• ••• ni•ion• in •••li•• •l••••• ••• •on•i••••• •o •• •••li•• •••n ••o•• in l•••• •l••••. Sin•• •l••• M i• •••n•• •••li•• •••n •l••• N, •l••• M i• no• v•li• •n• • ••• •• ••w•i•••n •o •l••• M' w•il• l•••• •l••• N i• •lw•y• v•li•. Al•••n••iv•ly, •l••• M ••n •• ••w•i•••n •o •l••• M" w••••• ••• •••ion m ••n •• •••n•• •o ••••• N<p1>.n •••o••• ••• •o•• •l ••••• •••• p2 •in•• •l••• o•••in• •o•• no• ••• ly •o ••• •on•••in•• on •o•• •l •••ion ••••• ••••••.

```
class SubjectFactory<factory, subject>
  Subject<factory> s1;              // OK
  Subject<subject> s2;              // BAD
  Subject<subject> makeSubject()    // OK
    return new Subject<subject>();  // OK
```

A• w• •i•••• ••••li•• o•• ••••••n• v•••ion o• A• TS •llow• •yn•• i• ••••••n••• (• •••o• ••••• •n•• •n• ••••l••) •o •• •••••••• • iff•••n•ly •o ••••i•/••l• ••••••n•••. T•••• i• no ••••i••ion on w••• •••ion• ••n •• •••• •o• •yn•• i• ••••••n•••. Un••••i•••• •yn•• i• ••••••n••• ••• fl•xi•ili•y w•i•• ••n •• •••n in ••• •••••o•y •x•• •l•. T•• SubjectFactory •l••• • o••l• • •••o•y in •••ion factory •o• •••••in• Subject o• j•••• in •••ion subject. B••••••• ••••• i• no •nown ••••••ili•y •••w••n factory •n• subject, ••• •y• •y•••• •••v•n•• ••• SubjectFactory •l••• ••o• • ol•in• ••l• •••••n••• •o o•j•••• in subject. How•v••, •in•• • yn•• i• ••••••n••• ••• no• •o•n• •y •• i• •••••i••ion, n•w o•j•••• ••n •• •••••••• in subject •n• •••••n•• •••o•••• ••• makeSubject • •••o• •o• •li•n•• •o •••.

Type Enforced Security Levels. B••i••• ••in• •••ion• •o •••v•n• ••••••n•• •y•l•• •n• •o •••on ••o•• •li•in•, ••y•li• •••ion• ••n •l•o •• ••••• •• •••••i•y l•v•l• •o •on•ol •••••• •n• ••••• in•o•• ••ion flow in • • •l•i-l•v•l ••••••i•y •y•••• (••• S••ion 6). P•o•••• • ••• ••n •x••••• •••j•••• •••••• •on••ol •n• in•o•• ••ion flow •oli•i•• in ••• •••ion ••••••••• o• • ••o•••• . B••••• ••••• ••••i•y •oli•i•• ••• now •x•••••• in •y•••, •••y ••n •• •n•o•••• ••••i••lly •y ••• •y•• •y••••.

```
class Machine<floor>
  display from floor;
  Display<display> disp;
  Machine()
    disp = new Display<display>();
  adjust()                          // modify the display
    ...
class Operator<skill, floor from skill>
  Machine<floor> mach;
  Display<Machine<floor>.display> disp;
  set(Machine<floor> mach)
```

```
    this.mach = mach;
    this.disp = mach.disp;
  operate()                      // do a job, such as adjust the machine
    ...
class Factory<factory>
  skill1 from factory;
  skill2 from factory to skill1;
  floor1 from skill1;
  floor2 from skill2;
  Machine<floor1> mach1;
  Machine<floor2> mach2;
  Operator<skill1, floor1> op1;
  Operator<skill2, floor2> op2;
  Operator<skill2, floor1> op3;
  Operator<skill1, floor2> op4;  // BAD, not a valid type
  op1.set(mach1);                // OK
  op1.set(mach2);                // BAD, op1 is on wrong floor
```

A ••••o•y•••• • n•• ••• o•o•••••o••• n• • ••• in••. Diff•••n• • ••• in•• •••• •i•• •iff•••n• l•v•l o• ••ill• •o o••••••. In ••i• •x•• •l•, •wo • ••• in•• ••• •l•••• in •iff•••n• floo• •••ion• •n• •o•• o•••••o•• o•••• y •wo ••ill l•v•l •••ion•. T•• •••ion •••••••• o• Operator ••••i••• •n o•••••o• •o ••v• •no••• ••ill •o wo•• on • • ••• in•. T•• ••l••ion• ••w••n •iff•••n• ••ill• •n• floo•• ••• ••• n•• in ••• Factory •l••• - o•••••o•• wi•• skill2 ••n wo•• on ••• • ••• in•• on •ny floo• w•il• o•••••o•• wi•• skill1 ••n only o•••••• ••• • ••• in•• on floor1. Mo••ov••, o•••••o•• wi•• skill1 ••n n•v•• o••• in • •••••• n•• •o • ••• in•• on floor2, w•i•• i• •li• in•o••••ion ••o••• in •••ion floor2 ••n n•v•• flow •o o• j•••• in •••ion floor1.

4   Some Properties and a Dynamic Semantics

In ••i• •••• ion, •••• w• •o•• •li•• •o• • ••••i• ••o•••i•• •• o•• •••ion• •o• • w•ll-•o•• •• ••o•••• : n•• •ly •••• ••• •••ion •••••••ili•y •• l••ion i• ••y•li•. T••n, ••••• ••i•fly in••o••• in• • •o•• •l • i•-•••• ••• •n•i••, w• ••••••••••i•• ••• inv••i•n•• •o• o•j••• ••••••n••• on •oo• ••••• •o• w•ll-•o•• •• ••o•••• •: in•••- o• j••• •••••• n••• •i•••• o•••• wi•• in •••ion• o• •••••••• ••• •••ion ••••••• ili•y ••l••ion. Fin•lly w• •••••• • ••• n•••• ••• j••• •••••••ion •••o••• , ••••, •• on••• o•••• •• in••, •••••• •••• •••• •••• •oo•n••• i• ••••• •v•• ••• •o••• ••••••••ion•.

Fi••• w• •••••••• ••• i••• o• on• •••ion ••in• ••• n•• •••li•• ••n •no••••. A •l••• ••• ni•ion •••• •n•• Γ, •••• i• w•ll-•o•• ••, $\vdash_c \Gamma$, •••••• in•• • ••••• n•• o• •••ion ••• ni•ion•. A •••li••• •••ion $t.r$ •••• i• w•ll-•o•• ••, $\Gamma \vdash_\sigma t.r$, i• •••o•i•••• wi•• • •ni••• in••x in ••• ••• ni•ion •••• •n••, n•• •ly •••• w•i•• ••• n•• ••• •••ion n•• • o• ••• •••li••• •••ion. W• ••ll ••i• ••• $rank$ o• ••• •••ion. W• •l•o ••n• ••• ••n• o• base •o •• 0. A •••ion σ wi•• • ••• •ll•• ••n• ••• n •no•••• σ' i• ••• n•• ••li••; w• will •l•o w•i•• ••i• •• $\sigma \prec \sigma'$. I•• •••ion •••••••• ••• • o• n• in • ••• ni•ion •o• •no••••, ••• n ••• •••ion• • •••• •v• •iff••• n• ••n••; ••••n•i• lly ••i• i• •••••••• o• ••• [REG-DEF] ••l•.

Table 4. Dynamic Features

$$
\begin{aligned}
\iota, \iota_t &\in \text{TypedLocation} \\
e &\in \text{Expression} \quad ::= ... \mid \iota \\
v &\in \text{Value} \quad ::= \iota \mid \texttt{null} \\
obj &\in \text{Object} \quad = \text{FieldName} \longrightarrow \text{Value} \\
H &\in \text{Heap} \quad = \text{TypedLocation} \longrightarrow \text{Object}
\end{aligned}
$$

W• ••• now in • • o•i•ion •o ••••• • •• n••• •n••l ••o•••y o• •••••••ili•y ••oo••: •ny •••••••ili•y •••w••n •wo •••ion• ••n •• •••n•• ••o••• • •••••n•• o• •••ion •••ni•ion•, w•••• ••• ••••••iv• ••n•• ••• •••i••ly •••••••in• •n•il • • ini• •• ••n• i• •••••••, ••••• w•i•• ••• ••n•• ••• •••i••ly in•••••in•.

Lemma 1 (Reachability via Earlier Regions). *Given* $\vdash_c \Gamma$ *and* $\Gamma \vdash_\sigma \sigma, \sigma'$: *If* $\Gamma \vdash_\triangleright \sigma \triangleright \sigma'$ *then* $\exists \sigma_1 ... \sigma_n$ *for* $n > 1$ *such that:*

1. $\sigma \equiv \sigma_1 \triangleright ... \triangleright \sigma_n \equiv \sigma'$, *and*
2. $\sigma_1 \succ \sigma_2 \succ ... \succ \sigma_m \prec ... \prec \sigma_n$ *for some* $m \in 1..n$ *where* $(\sigma_i \triangleright \sigma_{i+1}) \in \mathcal{Q}(t_i)$ *for* $1 \leq i < m$ *(where* $\sigma_i \equiv t_i.r$*), and* $(\sigma_i \triangleright \sigma_{i+1}) \in \mathcal{Q}(t_{i+1})$ *for* $m \leq i < n$.

Proof Outline. Any ••oo• o• •••••••ili•y • ••• •on••••• • ••••••n•• o• on• o• • o•• •••li••ion• o• • •••ni•ion vi• [REACH-DEF-FROM/TO]. So ••• • •••• •••• o• ••• l•• • • •ollow•, wi•• •••••••iv• ••i•• ••lon•in• •o •o• • •••ni•ion. S••• o•• ••• •••on• •••• •o•• no• •ol•. T••n w• ••n • n• $(\sigma_{i-1} \triangleright \sigma_i \triangleright \sigma_{i+1}) \in \mathcal{Q}(t_i)$ wi•• $(\sigma_{i-1} \prec \sigma_i \succ \sigma_{i+1})$. B•• •y ••• ••••i••• •n• o• [REG-DEF] •••• •ny •••••••ili•y o• •on••••in•• ••n •• •••iv••l• ••o• •••li•• •••ni•ion•, w• ••• •••• w• ••n o• i• σ_i ••o• o•• ••oo•. T•• ••••l• •ollow• •y •n in•••ion on ••• • •xi• •• •••ion •••ni•ion ••n• in Γ.

Theorem 1 (Acyclicity of Regions). *Given* $\vdash_c \Gamma$ *and* $\Gamma \vdash_\sigma \sigma, \sigma'$: *if* $\Gamma \vdash_\triangleright \sigma \triangleright \sigma'$ *then* $\Gamma \nvdash_\triangleright \sigma' \trianglerighteq \sigma$.

Proof Outline. S••• o••, •y •on••••i••ion •••• $\Gamma \vdash_\triangleright \sigma \triangleright \sigma'$ •n• $\Gamma \vdash_\triangleright \sigma' \trianglerighteq \sigma$. Wi•• o• • lo•• o• ••n•••li•y, ••••• • •••• $\sigma \prec \sigma'$. By •••n•i•iviy o• $\triangleright$, w• •n• •••• $\Gamma \vdash_\triangleright \sigma \triangleright \sigma$. F•o• L•• • • 1 w• •n ••• •••• w• ••n • n• •wo (• o••i•ly ••• •) •••li•• •••ion• σ_1 •n• σ_2, •••• •••• $\sigma \triangleright \sigma_1 ... \sigma_2 \triangleright \sigma$ •n• $\sigma_1, \sigma_2 \prec \sigma$. B•• ••in, w• • ••• ••v• $(\sigma_2 \triangleright \sigma \triangleright \sigma_1) \in \mathcal{Q}(t)$, •o i• •ollow• •••• $\sigma_2 \triangleright \sigma_1$. T•• ••••l• •ollow• •y •n in•••ion on ••• • ini• •• ••n• o••• •wo •••ion• •n••• •on•i• ••••ion.

L•• • • now •on•i•••••• • •yn•• i• ••• •n•i••. T••l• • •o•• •l•••• •o• • •yn•• i• ••••••• o• A• TS •n• ••• •yn•• i• ••• •n•i•• i• •iv•n in T••l• 5. T••l• 6 ••ow• ••• ••l•• •o• w•ll-•o•• ••n••• o• •••• ••n• •x••••ion in ••• •yn•• i• • o••l.

W• in•o•• o••••• •ll •y• in•o•• ••ion (wi•• •••ion•) wi•• ••• lo•••ion• o• ••• ••••, •••••• •••n in ••• o• j••••. T•••• ••l• •o •i• •li•y ••• ••• •n•i•• •n• ••• ••oo• o• •yn•• i• ••o•••i••. No•• •••• non• o• ••• ••••••ion •••vio•• ••••n•• on ••i• •y•• in•o•• ••ion; ••• new t •••••••ion only •••• ••• ••l• n•• •• o• ••• •l•••; • •••o• •i•••••• only ••••n•• on ••• •l••• •n• no• on ••• •••ion •in• in••

Table 5. Dynamic Semantics

[RED–NEW]
$$\frac{\iota_t \notin dom(H) \quad \mathcal{F}(P,t) = \overline{\_f}}{H, \mathbf{new}\ t \Downarrow \iota_t, H'} \qquad H' \equiv H, \iota_t \mapsto \overline{f \mapsto \mathbf{null}}$$

[RED–FIELD]
$$\frac{H, e \Downarrow \iota, H'}{H, e.f \Downarrow H(\iota)(f), H'}$$

[RED–ASSIGN]
$$\frac{H, e \Downarrow \iota, H' \quad H', e' \Downarrow v, H'' \quad H''' \equiv H''[\iota \mapsto H''(\iota)[f \mapsto v]]}{H, e.f = e' \Downarrow v, H'''}$$

[RED–CALL]
$$\frac{H, e \Downarrow \iota_t, H' \quad H', \overline{e} \Downarrow \overline{v}, H'' \quad \mathcal{M}(P, t, m) = (\_, \overline{x}, \_, e') \quad H'', e'[\iota_t/\mathbf{this}, v/x] \Downarrow v, H'''}{H, e.m(\overline{e}) \Downarrow v, H'''}$$

[RED–SEQ]
$$\frac{H, e \Downarrow \_, H' \quad H', e' \Downarrow v, H''}{H, e; e' \Downarrow v, H''}$$

[RED–IF–LOCATION]
$$\frac{H, e \Downarrow \iota, H' \quad H', e' \Downarrow v, H''}{H, \mathbf{if}\ e\ e'\ e'' \Downarrow v, H''}$$

[RED–IF–NULL]
$$\frac{H, e \Downarrow \mathbf{null}, H' \quad H', e'' \Downarrow v, H''}{H, \mathbf{if}\ e\ e'\ e'' \Downarrow v, H''}$$

Table 6. Auxiliary Rules for Dynamic Semantics

[HEAP–WELLFORMED]
$$\frac{\forall \iota_t \in dom(H)\cdot \quad \Gamma \vdash_t t \quad H(\iota_t) = \overline{f \mapsto v} \quad \mathcal{F}(t) = \overline{t\ f} \quad \Gamma \vdash_e \overline{v : t}}{\Gamma \vdash_H H}$$

[EXPR–LOCATION]
$$\frac{\Gamma \vdash_t t}{\Gamma \vdash_e \iota_t : t}$$

o• ••• •••••• o• j•••. A••in, •o• •i• • li•i•y, w• •o no• ••• lo••l v••i••l•• in o•• • o••l, •o w• ••• ••••i••ion o• • •••o• ••••• •n•• in•o • •••o• •o•i••, •••• •voi•in• ••• •x••• • •••in••y o• • •••••• •••• •. No•• ••••• ••• if •••• •••n•••• on null •••• v•l••.

Now • w•ll-•o•• •• •••• •n••••• ••••• •ny ••l• o••n o•j••• in ••• ••••• ••o•• ••• v•l•• w•o•• •••••l •y•• •••••••••• ••• •••l•••• •y•• o••• ••l• in ••• •y•• o• ••• o•j•••. T•i• l•••• •i•••ly •o ••• •ollowin• •°o•••y •o• •oo• •••••, w•o•• ••oo• •ollow• •i•••ly ••o• ••• ••••i• ••o• •••i•• o• •••ion•. T•i• ••••••••••• o•j••• •••••n••• ••••••• •••ion ••••••• •ili•y. • on••••• •n•ly, •••••n•• •y•l•• • ••• o•••• wi•• in •••ion•.

Lemma 2 (Direct Referenceability). *Given* $\vdash_c \Gamma$ *and* $\Gamma \vdash_H H$: *if* $\iota_{c\langle \sigma...\rangle} \mapsto [... \_ \mapsto \iota'_{c'\langle \sigma'...\rangle} ...] \in H$, *then* $\Gamma \vdash_\triangleright \sigma \unrhd \sigma'$.

Proof. By ••• [HEAP-WELLFORMED] ••l•, $c\langle \sigma...\rangle$ • •••• ••• w•ll-•o•• •• •n• $c'\langle \sigma'...\rangle$ i• ••• •y•• o• on• o••l••• c'• ••l••. By ••• [FIELD] ••l•, $\Gamma \vdash_\triangleright \sigma \unrhd \sigma'$.

Theorem 2 (Reachability and Cycles). *Given* $\vdash_c \Gamma$ *and* $\Gamma \vdash_H H$: *if* $\iota_{c\langle \sigma...\rangle}$ *can reach* $\iota'_{c'\langle \sigma'...\rangle}$ *through a path of direct references in the heap* H, *then* $\Gamma \vdash_\triangleright \sigma \unrhd \sigma'$. *Furthermore, if there is a path in* H *in the reverse direction, then* $\sigma = \sigma'$.

Proof. By L•• • • • •o• •••• •j•••• •••••••n•• in ••• ••••, •n• ••• •••n•i•ivi•y o• ▷, ••• • •••• •••• •ollow•. W•• n ••••• i• • ••v•••• ••••, ••• •••on• •••• •ollow• •y ••• ••y•li•i•y o• ▷, •• in T••o••• 1.

Fin• lly w• •••••n• • •••n•••• ••• j••• ••• ••••ion •••• l•, •o••••••• wi•• • ••••••-• •n• •••• •oo•n••• o• • •••• i• inv••i•n• •••o••• •x••••ion •••••••ion•. T• i• i• • li•• •••• ••• •••• inv••i•n•• ••• • •in••in•• •••o••• ••o•••• •x•••••ion.

Theorem 3 (Preservation). *Given* $\vdash_c \Gamma$, *and* $\Gamma \vdash_H H$:

$$if \begin{cases} \Gamma \vdash_e e : t \\ H, e \Downarrow v, H' \end{cases} \quad then \begin{cases} \Gamma \vdash_e v : t \\ \Gamma \vdash_H H'. \end{cases}$$

Proof Outline. T•• • •oo• •o• •y• • • •••••••v••ion i• •o• • l•••ly •••n••••• • y •••••-••••l in••••ion on ••• •o•• o• •x••••ion• ov•• •••••••ion •• l••. W• • o no• •• ow • ••• •y•• o• *t* •o• *v*, ••••••• i• i• •ov•••• •y ••••••• ••ion.

5   Discussion

5.1   Expressiveness and Limitation

A• TS ••ovi••••• • ow•••• l •••• •wo•• •o• •llowin• • ••••in•• •••••i•••ion o•• •ny •l•••••• o• ••••••• • ili•y ••l••ion. I• •• • loy• •n in••i•iv• no•ion o• •••ion •o •••-•••• ••• •on•••• o• •••on•ly •onn••••• •o• •on•n•• in ••••• •••o•y, w•i•• ••-•••••• •o •• n••••l •n• fl•xi• l• •no•• •o •x•••• v••io• •••• •••••••• in ••o-•••• •. T•• •y•• •••••in• i• •i• • l• y•• ••• •i•n• •n• • ow•••l; i• lo••lly •••••• ••o•••• • ••-•••n•• •••••••ili•y ••l••ion• •o ••••n••• •lo••l ••y•li•i•y •o •••• •••••••• •o• •il••ion ••n •• •llow••. A• TS •llow• ••• ••o••••• • •• •o n•• • •ny • o••i• l• •••ion •v•n ••o••• ••• n•• ••• o• •••ion• • •y •• • n•o•n•••. T•• •• ili•y •o • • l•i• ly in•••n•i••• •••ion ••• ni•ion• ••o•••• •y• • •••li••ion •iv•• ••o••••• • ••• •no•••• •oi•• •o i••n•i•y ••• •ny i••in•• •••ion •• ••y n•••.

A• TS ••n •i•ni••n•ly i• ••ov• ••o•••• • n••••••n•in•. P•o•••• • ••• ••• •• l• •o •••••i•y vi• •y••• w•••••• •y•l•• •••• •llow•• o• •i••llow••. A• TS ••n •l•o •• • •••• •o ••••on ••o•• •li••in• ••••••• •••ion• ••• •i•join• •n• o• j•••• liv• in • •in•l• •••ion •o• •••i• li••i• •. Mo••ov••, A• TS ••n •x••••• •o• • in•o•• ••ion flow • oli•y (••• S••ion 6) •n• •v•n •n••••l•• o• j•••• (••• l•••• ••i• S•••ion). A• TS ••• •i•••• ••• li•••ion in • •l•i-•••••••• ••o••••• •. M• l•i-••••• in• will no• • ff•••• ••• •••••••••• •o•••• o• j•••••••••, •••• •nowl••• o• ••• •••ion •••••••• •llow•, •o• •x••• • l•, o••••• lo••in• ••••••••i•• •o •• i• • o••• [•]. How•v••, in •• i• ••••• w• only •on•i•••••• •••n••• •n••l i••••• in ••••••ili•y •n• ••y•li•i•y in ••• o• j•••••••••, •n• •o no• •ov• ••• i••••• wi• • • l•i-•••••• in•.

• • ••o••••, •• wi•• • ny •y•• •y••••, •••• • i• • ••i• •o ••y •o• ••• i• -••ov•• ••••y off•••• • y •••on• •y•• •••••• in•. Fi•••, ••••• i• ••• •x••• •yn•••i• w•i•••••o•i•••• wi•• • o•• •x•••••iv•n•••; ••• •yn••x ••••••n i• no• •oo •• xin•, •• o• n•in• •o ••• •o•• o• ••••• •••• i••• •y•••. Fo• o•• •••• •o•••, i• i• ••••n•i•l •o • i•••in••i•• •••w••n •y•• (••••• •) •••ni•ion •n• ••• ••• o• • •y•• (in•••n••). Wi•• o•• •• i• • i••in••ion, o•••o• o••l wo• l• ••ovi•• li••l• • o•• ••• n ••• n•• •-••••• •••••• ••••••i••ion• off•••• • y • o••l• o• •••••••-•••••• ••••o•••••. S••on•

•n• • o•• i• •o•••n•ly, w••• ••• ••• •x•••••iv• li• i••ion• o• o•• •••o•••? In •o• • ••n••, non•, ••••••• ••• •y•• •y•••• ••o• o••• in •• i• ••••• •llow• ••o-•••• • ••• •o •o•• wi•• no •••••••••l •on••••in• w•••o•v••, •••• i•, •ll o• j•••• liv• in ••• ••• • •••ion. In S•••ion 5.• w• will •i•••••• ••• ••ili•y •o in•••••••• wi•• •••ion-•••• •o••.

• ••li••i••lly ••o•••, in o••••• •o ••n••• •••o• •••• ••ili•y o• o•• •y•• •y•••• •o in•i• i• •y•l•• •n• /o• •••••in•, i• i• n••••••y •o • ••• in•i•i•in• ••i•n ••i•ion•. ••• •y•• •y•••• will in•i•• •••• ••o•••• • ••• •••i•• w•i•• o• j••• ••l•• • •y •o•• •••• o• • •y•l•, •n• w•i•• • •y no•. I• i• ••l••iv•ly •i• •l• ••n •o •••o•• •y•• w•i•• will ••••• ••• •••i•n •••i•ion •o•• •n•o••••. A••in •• wi•• • ny •y•• •y•••• , ••••• i• • •••••-off ••w••n •x••• •••••y off•••• •y •••on• •y•• ••••••in•, •n• ••• lo•• o• fl•xi• ili•y in ••• ••o•••• • in• • o••l, o• •• l••••• •nnoy•n•• •• ••in• • ••• •o i• •o• ••••••i••ion• •••ly on in • •••i•n. In •••••i•• o•• •y•••• will no• •• •oo •nnoyin•, •••••• w••n ••o•••• • ••• •o no• •••• ••o•• •y•l••, •••y ••n •ff•••iv•ly •llow •••• •o o•••• •nyw••••, •n• ••• •••o••i••• •y••• ••• ••• l••• •o• •l•x •o •x•••••, •o••••• on• in• •x••ly •o ••• • ••••• •• l•••y •o••.

A• TS ••n •x•••• ••••••iv• •••• •••••••••. How•v••, •••• • ••••••• n•••• •o ••v• ••l•• wi•• ••• ••• • •y•• •• ••• ••l• •y••. B•••••• •••y ••v• ••• ••• • •y••, •ll ••• ••••••••••l o• j•••• •o•• in• ••• •••••••iv• •••• ••••••••• • •••• •ll liv• in ••• ••• • •••ion. A• • ••••l•, •ll ••• •••• o• j•••• will •l•o liv• in ••• ••• • •••ion •• •••• o••••. A• TS •llow• ••• ••o•••• • •• •o n•• • •ny •o••i• l• •••ion •v•n •• o••• ••• n•• ••• o• •••ion• i• •n• o• n•••. T•i• fl•xi• ili•y •o• •li•••••• ••• •••• o••y• •••••••in• on ••• ••••••• •ili•y ••l••ion•. In ••• wo••••••, •o ••••••• ••• ••l••ion ••w••n •wo •••ion•, ••• •y•• •••••••• • •y ••v• •o loo• in•o •ll •l••••• in ••• ••••••iv• •y•• ••••li••••ion ••••• •o• •o•• •••ion• •n• •o• •••• •l••• ••• •y•• •••••••• • •y ••v• •o loo• in•o •ll •••ion ••• ni•ion• o• ••• •l•••. How•v••, in •••••i•• •o•• ••• n•• ••• o• •••••••iv• ••••• •o • ••• ••n•i• l• ••• o•• •••ion •n• ••• n•• ••• o• •••ion ••• ni•ion• in • •l••• ••• v••y •• •ll, •o •••• ••• ••n•i• • •o• •y•• ••••••in• ••o•l• no• ••• •i•ni••n•. Mo•••ov••, •ny ••••••••ili•y ••l••ion i• •••i••• l• •••••••• •••• •••ion ••n only ••v• • •ni•• n•• ••• o• •••••••iv• ••••• •n• •••• •l••• ••n only ••v• • •ni•• n•• ••• o• •••ion ••• ni•ion•.

5.2   Extensions to the Core Language

Object Encapsulation with Owned Regions. • •• •y•• • •y•••• ••n ••ovi•• •••ion •xi•••n•i•l •oly• o•••i•• ••• •l• o•• no •o••. • xi•••n•i•l •••ion• ••n ••o-vi•• ••• ••• • l•v•l o• o• j•••n••••l••ion •• own•••i• •y••• •o (••• S••ion 6). In o•• •x••n••• l•n•••••, •••ion ••n •• • i•••n •y ••in• •n owned •••l••••ion; own•• •••ion• ••nno• •• n•• •• vi• • •y•• •••li•••ion •n• ••n•• lo••l •o ••• ••o•• o• ••• •l•••. To •n••l• •y•• •••••in• on own•• •••ion•, w• •i• •ly n••• •o ••• •n o••ion•l ••y wo•• owned in ••on• o• ••• •••ion n•• • in ••• •yn••x w••n • •••ion i• in••o•••••, •n• •i•• •l• •y•• •••li••••ion ov•• own•• •••ion• in ••• •••ion ••l••.

I• i• i• •o•••n• •••• own•• •••ion• ••• in•••n•• l•v•l •n• ••• •n•••••l•••• •y •••i• •••nin• o• j•••• •••••• no on• ••n n•• • ••••• ••o• o••i••. T•i• i•

•i• il•• •o ••• in•••n•l •on••x• this in own••••i• •y•••. An own•• •••ion ••n
only •• n•• •• wi••in ••• •••nin• o•j••• o• ••o•••••••• •o i•• •n•••••l••ion
vi• •••ion ••••• •••••. Unown•• •••ion• ••• •in ••••i• •o •y•••, ••••• •y no• ••
n•• •• •lo••lly i•••i• •y•• ••• ••••• ••••i••• •y •n own•• •••ion. T• i• •••• l••
in own••••i•-li•• ••••• ••• ••• on •o• • ••••• o• ••• DA• ••••• ••• ••• o• o• o• j•••
• o••l. P•o•••• • ••• • •y ••v• •••••• •n•••••n• in• •n• •n•-•••in•• •on••ol
ov•• ••• ••••••n•• ••••• ••••.

Fo• •x•• •l•, own•• •••ion• ••n •• •••• •o •x••••• own••••i•-li•• lin•••
li••• wi••o•• ••ff••in• ••• lon•-•••o•ni••• ••o•l•• o• •x•••••in• i•••••o•• in
own••••i• •y•••. In ••• n•x• •x•• •l•, •v••y li•• o•j••• now ••• i•• own i• •l•-
• •n•••ion •n••••l•••• •y ••• own•• •••ion link. B•••••• own•• •••ion• •••
in•••n••-•••••, •••y ••• no• •••••• •y iff•••n• li•• o•j•••• o• ••• ••• • •y••
(li•• • nown•• •••ion• •••). T•• lin• o•j•••• ••• own•• •y ••• li•• •••••••• no
o•j••• ••o• o••i• o••• li•• ••n n•• • ••• own•• •••ion link. An i•••••o• ••n
•••••• ••• in•••n•l •••• o• ••• li••, •••••• i• i• ••••••• in•i•• ••• li••, ••• ••n
••ill •• ••••• ••o• o••i• •••••• i• liv•• in ••• ••• • •••ion •• ••• li•• o•j•••.
W• ••• •••y• in• •o •i• ••• n•• • o• ••• link •••ion in ••• •y• o• ••• i•••••o•,
•o ••• •li•n• ••n •iv• •y• •o• ••• i•••••o• wi••o•• •nowin• ••• •i••• n•• • •o•
••• link •••ion.

```
class List<list, data from list>
  owned link from list to data;
  Link<link, data> head;
  Link<link, data> tail;
  Iterator<list, data> getIterator()
    return new ListIterator<list, data, link>(head);
  ...
class Iterator<list, data from list>
  ...
class ListIterator<list, data from list, link from list to data>
      extends Iterator<list, data>
  Link<link, data> current;
  Iterator(Link<link, data> current)
    this.current = current;
  ...
```

Default Regions and Interoperability with Legacy Code. T•• •••••n
o• •••ion •nno•••ion• •n• ••• in•••o•••••ili•y wi•• l•••••y •o•• • •y •ff••• •••
•••• o• ••• •o• ••• l•n••••••. In ••••i••, •••ion• ••• only •••• w••n n••••••.
W• •x•••• ••o•••• • ••• •o ••• •••ion• in •o• • ••i•i••l •••ion•, •o• •x•• •l•, •o
• •o•••• •••i•l •l••• inv••i•n•• ••o• • n•x•••••• • •••o• •••n•••n• ••ll•. In • •ny
••••• •••ion• ••n •• •i••• v•n••• w••n ••y ••• no• n•••••• •n• ••o•••• • •••
n••• no• •v•n •• •w••• o• •••ion•. W• •••i•n • ••w •••ion •••••l•• •o ••l•
•••••• ••• n•• •••• o• •••ion •nno•••ion• •n• in••••••• non-•••ion •o•• ••••• ••
l•••••y li•••••y •l•••••. T•• •o• •il•• • •y ••••o• ••i••lly •nno•••• •••ion• wi••
••• ••••••l• • oli••y.

Fo• •l•••••• ••••• •o no• ••v• •o•• •l •••ion ••••• •••••, ••• ••y wo•• here i•
•••• •o ••••• ••• •••ion ••• ••••••n• o• j••• liv•• in. T• i• i• •i• il•• •o this, self

o• me •••• in • •ny o• j•••-o•i•n••• l•n•••••• •o ••••• ••• ••••••n• o• j•••. Fo• •in•in•• o• •••ion• in •y•••, i• •y•• i• •••l•••• wi••o•• •ny •••ion, i.•. only • •l••• n•• •, ••n • •••••l• •••ion i• •o•n• •o •ll •o•• •l ••••• ••••• o• ••• •l•••. In ••• • •in •o•• in•, base ••n •• ••••• •• ••• •••••l• •••ion •o• •y••• w•il• in •l••••• ••• •••• •o•• •l ••••• •••• o• ••• •l••• (o• here i• ••••• i• non•) i• ••• •••••l• •••ion. Fo• l•••• y •o•• •ll •o•• •l •••ion ••••• ••••• •n• •y•• •••l•••- •ion• ••• •••• l••• .

Flexible Class Constraints. ••• l•n••••• ••n •• •••ily •x••n••• wi•• • o•• • o••i•l• ••l••ion• o•••• ••• n ••y•li• ••••••• ili•y. • •o••••, ••••• •o••i•l• ••l- •ion• ••n only •• • •••• •o •on•••• in •o•• •l •••ion ••••• ••••• o• • •l•••, i.•., no• •o ••• •••ion ••• ni•ion•. T••y ••• j••• •l••• •on•••• in•• •o• v•li• •••ion ••••• - •••• •in•in••, •••y ••o•l• no••• •on••••• wi•• ••• ••••••• ili•y ••l••ion ••• n•• ••w••n •••••l •••ion•. T•• •i• •l••• i• •o •llow •••••• ili•y ••o• •on• •••ion ••••• •••• •o •no••• •o •• •••l••• wi••o•• •o•• i• •in• •••• w•••• •••••• ili•y, ••no••• •• ▷ in ••• •y•• •y•••• w•i•• i• • •fl•xiv• •lo•••• o• ••• •y•li• •••••- ••ili•y ▷. W••n •••l•••, i• • ••n• •••• w••n •llow •••••n••• in ••• •i•••ion o• ••• •••l•••• •••••• ili•y, ••• w• ••n •llow •o•• ••••• ••••• •o •• •o•n• •o ••• •••• • •••••l •••ion. T•i• i• •o• •w••• ••ivi•l ••• •••••l •x••n•ion •o• • o•• fl•xi•l• ••o•••• • in•.

6   Related Work

To o• • •nowl••••, ••i• i• ••• •••• ••••• •• •o •••on •• •o•• •y•l•• •n• •••in• in ••o•••• • ••••• on • •y•• •y•••• i• • o•in• ••••••• ili•y •on••••in•• on ••• o•- j••• ••••••. • ••• •y•• •y•••• • •o• ••v• •o• • •i• il••i•i• wi•• o•••• •y•• •y•••• •, •••• •• ••••• •••i• •oly• o•••i•• •n• •xi•••n•i•l •oly• o•••i•• on •••ion•. • •• •y•• •••li••• •••ion• •n• •••ion ••••• •••• i••• •y••• ••ovi•• • nov•l w•y •o ••• •o•• •lo• •l n•• •in• •n• ••••i• ••••onin• on •n •n• o• n••• n•• ••• o• •••ion•.

Ownership Type Systems. M• ny •y•• •y•••• • •o••• on •li•• • •n•••• •n• •n• ••••• •• •o •••••i•• ••••••n••• in•o • li• i••• ••o••. • •ly wo•• li•• I•l•n•• [16] •n• B•lloon• [•] •n•o••••• •• ll •n••••• l••ion on o• j•••• w•i•• •••v•n••• •••- •••n•in• •••o•• ••• •n•••• l••ion. T••y ••• ••n•••lly •oo ••••• i••iv•. Univ••••• [19] i• ••ov•• ••• •x••• •iv•n••• o• •• ll •n••••• l••ion •y in••o••• in• •••• -only •••••• n••• •o ••o••• ••• •o•n••y o• •n••••• l••ion. • wn•••• i• •y••• [•, 6,5] i• - ••ov•• ••• ••• •vio•• wo•• on o• j••• •l•v•l •n••••• l••ion •y •llowin• • n•••• i•••• o• ••• oin• ••••••• n••• ••o• •n •n••••• l••ion w• il• ••ill •••v•n•in• in•o in• •••••- •n•in• in•o •n •n•••• l••ion.

• wn•••• i• •y•• ••• ••••• ••••i••• •y•• •y•••• ••o ••••• ••• n•• •• o•o• j•••• vi• •l••• ••••• ••••. In o•••• •o •••l•••• •y•• •o• • •••••n••, on• • ••••• •••l• •o n•• • ••• 'own••' •••• •n••••• l•••• ••i• o• j•••. • n••••• l••ion i• ••o•••••• ••o• in•o• in• •••••n•in• ••••••• ••• own••• o• o• j•••• in•i•• •n •n••••• l••ion ••nno• •• n•• •• ••o• ••• o••i••. How•v••, o• j•••• in•i•• •n •n••••• l••ion ••• ••l• •o n•• • ••• o• j•••• livin• o• ••i•• •••o••• ••• own•• n•• •• •••••••

in •• •l••• ••••• •••••. ••• •y•• •y•••• i• •lo•• •o own••••i• •y••• •••• •••
••••• ••••i••• •l••••• in • •i• il•• w•y, •n• ••• •••• ••••• •••• i••n•i••• •••
own••/•••ion o• ••• this o•j•••. How•v••, ••• inv••i•n• o• o•• •y•••• i• ••o••
••y•li•i•y •••••• •••n •n•••••l••ion. T•• • •jo• •iff•••n•• •••w••n ••••• •wo
••o•••••i•• i• •••• •n••••l••ion i• in•••n••••••• •n• •n•o•••• •••o••• own••-
••i•, w•i•• i• • lo••l ••o•••y o• •n o•j••• w•••••• ••y•li•i•y i• •lo••l.

A v••i•n• o• own••••i• •y••• ••• ••••n•ly ••n ••o• o••• [1] •o •llow ••o-
•••• • ••• •o •••••i•y •li•in• •oli•y ••w••n own••••i• •o• •in• (w•i•• •••••i•ion
•n own••'• •on••x•) •••••• •••n own••••i• •y•••' own••-••-•o• in••o• ••o• •••y.
T••i• •o• •in• •n• lin• •oli••• ••• •••n•• wi••in •l••••• in • •i• il•• •••ion •o
o•••••ion• •n• •••ion •on••••in•. T••i• •li•in• •oli•i•• •••n• •••••n•••• ili•y,
••• •• ili•y •o •i•••• ly •••••n•• •n o•j•••, •••w••n • •o• •in•. T••y ••• •on•••n••
wi•• n•i•••• ••••••• ili•y – ••• lin• •oli•i•• ••• no• •••n•i•iv•, no• ••y•li•i•y –
i• i• •o••i•l• •o lin• •o• •in• •y•li••lly. In ••••, o•• •••ion• ••n •l•o ••••• •o
•••on •• o•• •li•in• in • •i• il•• w•y ••• wi•• • • iff•••n• •oli•y – w• ••n •n•o•••
• ••••• •••••••• ili•y •oli•y in••••• o• • •••llow •i•••• •••••n•••• ili•y •oli•y.

S• J [•] in•••o••••• • •on••• o• lo•• l•v•l •o ••l• o•••• lo••• ••••i••lly, •x-
••n• in• ••• i••• o• •in• own••••i• •y••• •o i••n•i•y ••o•• o•j••• w•i•• ••• no•
•••••• • •y ••••••• (•o ••••i•• no lo•••). In •••i• l•n•••••, lo•• l•v•l• ••• •••-
•i•lly o•••••• •n• •ll lo••• ••• •••••i•ion•• in•o lo•• l•v•l •n• ••••••o•• o••••••
•••o••in• •o •••i• lo•• l•v•l•. Si• il•• •o own••••i• •o• •in• •n• o•• •••ion•,
•••i• lo•• l•v•l• •n• o•••• in• ••• •••n•• wi•• in •l•••••. How•v•• •••i• lo•• l•v-
•l• ••• ••••i• •o •l••••• w•i•• • ••n• ••• n•• •••• o• •ll lo•• l•v•l• i• li i••• •y
••• n• •••• o• •l••••. Mo••ov••, •••i• ••• li•••• •y• •y•••• •o•• no• •••••••
•o ••••• ••• ••••i•l o•••• in• o• lo•• l•v•l•.

In •on•••••, o•• •y•••• •••• o••• •••ion ••••• •••i• •oly o•••i•• •o• •o••
•••••• •n• •••ion •xi••n•i•l •oly o•••i•• •o• o•j••• l•v•l •n••••l••ion. W•
•l•o ••ovi•• • nov•l •y••-••••• n•• in• • ••••ni•• •o •llow •n •n•o•n••• n•• -
••• o• •••ion• •o •• n•• •• ••••o•••o•• ••• •y••••. Ty•• ••li••• •••ion• •llow
•o• •l•••ly •••i• •••onin• on •ny •o••i•l• •••ion •n• •••i• •on••••in•, •x•l••-
in• own•• •••ion• w•i•• only ••n •• •••••on•• ••o•• lo••lly. T•i• •iv•• • •i••••
• o••l •o• o•• •••ion ••••••••, •n• • ••n••• ••••• ••o•••• •• •• i• ••l• •o ••• •o••
•i•••i• in••in• in •• oo•in• •n •••••o••i••• •••ion •••••••••. W• •••v• ••ov•• ••••
o•• •y•• •y•••• •••••n•••• ••y•li•i•y •• •on••• •n •n•o•n••• n•• •••• o• •••ion•.

Pointer and Shape Analysis. Poin••• •n• ly•i• •••••• ••• •o •••• •i••• •nowl••••
••o•• •n-•i• • •oin•••• vi• w•ol• ••o•••• •n• ly•i• •n• •••• •• i• in•o•• ••ion
•o ••l• ••o•••• •n•••••n•in• •n• o••i• i•••ion [15]. S•••• •n• ly•i• i• ••il•
on ••• ••o• o• • oin••• •n• ly•i• •o i• •n•i•y ••• •••••• o• ••••• ••••••••••• [10,•6].
H••••••• •n• • ••in• ••v• •••n•ly ••o•o••• • ••••• •n• ly•i• •l•o•i•• ••••
••••••• •own •lo••l •n• ly•i• ••o• •n•i•• •••• in•o lo••l •n• ly•i• ••o••• •ll••
• •• o•y ••••••••••ion• w•i•• ••y •l•o •ll •••ion• [1•]. Si• il•• •o o•• •••ion•,
•••i•• ••• •i•join• •••• o• • •• o•y lo••ion•, w• i•• •llow ••• ••••••••••n• ••••••
•n• ly•i• •o •••• ly •on•l••• •••• •n •••••• in on• ••• ion will no• •••n•• •••
v•l•• o• lo•••ion• in o•••• •••ion•. Diff•••n• ••o• o•••, •••i• • •• o•y •••ion•

••• no• ••y•li• •n• •••y •i• • ly i••n•i•y •i•••• *points-to* ••l••ion• •••w••n •••ion•
•••••• •••n •••n•i•iv• •••••••ili•y ••l••ion•.

• o• •••••• •o •y•• •y•••• •, •oin••• •n• •••••• •n•ly•i• •••• i•• li••l• o• no l•n-
•••••• •nno•••ion. P•o•on•n•• o• •• i• •••o••• o•••n •on•i•• •y• •y•••• • •••
•oo •••••i••iv• •n• • •y••l• o••o• ••oo• ••o•••• •• nn••••••ily. How•v••, •x-
••• •oin••• •n• •••••• •n•ly•i• no• only •••• i•• •x•on•n•i•l •i• • •o• v••i•••ion,
•••••• •n••i•• •l•, •o in ••••i••, • •y•• o• ••l••iv•ly low ••••i•ion. T••y •••
•l•o •••• •o •••l• •o l•••• o• in•o• •l••• ••o•••• •. Mo••ov••, • o•• wo•• in •• i•
•••• ••• •••n •on• •o• • -li•• l•n••••••, •n• l••• •o• o• j•••-o•i•n••• l•n•••••••.

In o•••• •o i• ••ov• •••••••y o• ••o•••• •n•ly•i•, '•••n• •o• •n•ly•••ili•y'
•••••o•••••, ••••• •• ADDS •n• ASAP [1•, 1•], ••• ••• ••o•••• • •• •o •x•li•i•ly
•••••i•• •o• • •o• ••i•• o• •••• •••••••••. T••y ••• ••• •on•••• o• • i• •n•ion
w•i•• i• ••l•••• •o ••• ••••• in • lin••• li•• o• • •••••. A• TS' •••ion •on•••• i•
• iff•••n•, ••• ••• • nowl•••• o• •••ion• • •y •l•o •• • ••••l •o •llow • o•• •••••••••
••o•••• •n•ly•i• •n• •••••• •••o•• •n••, •••• i•lly •o• •y•li• •••• •••••••••••.

Type-Based Information Flow Security.

A• TS i• ••i• ••ily •••i•n•• •o
•••• on •• o•• ••••••n•• •••••••ili•y •n• •on•n• •••••••n•• •y•l••. B•• i• ••n•
o•• •o ••v• •i•••• •••li•••ion in ••• •••• o• in•o•• ••ion flow •••••i•y. T•i• i•
•••••••• ••• • ••••i•lly o••••••• ••y•li• •••ion• ••• •on••••• lly ••• • •o ••• •l••i•
l•••i•• • o••l o• in•o•• ••ion flow •on••ol •y D•nnin• •n• D•nnin• [•, 9].

Ty•• •y•••• •••v• •l•••• y •••n •••• •o ••••• in•o•• ••ion flow wi•• in ••o-
•••• • in • ••l•i-l•v•l ••••i•y •y•••• ••••• on ••• l•••i•• • o••l. T•• ••n•••l
i••• i• •••• •v••y •y•• i• •••o•i•••• wi•• • ••••i••l•• ••••i•y •l••• [9, ••, •5].
S•••i•y •l•••••, •o• ••i• ••• •l•o ••ll•• ••••i•y ••o•••, •ol••, ••••• o• ••in•i••l•,
•o•• • l•••i•• w•i•• i• • ••••••• •• •ni•• ••• ••••i•lly o•••••• •y ••• l•v•l o•
••••i•y (•i•• o• low). In•o•• ••ion flow o••••ion•, •••• •• •••i•n• •n••, • •••
•••• ••• ••• o•••• o• ••• •••••i•y •l••••• •••••••• •o •y••••.

So• • •y•• •y•••• •, in••••• o• •••o•i••in• •y••• wi•• • •in•l• ••••i•y •l•••,
•••y •llow • •l•i•l• ••••i•y •l••••• •o •o•• • •••••i•y ••o•••y o• l•••l •o• ••••
•y•• [13, •0]. T•••• •••••• •on••ol li•• li•• ••••i•y l•••l• •llow • o•• •o• •l•x
••••i•y •on••ol •n• •yn• i• • •ni••l••ion. T•• l•••l• ••• •••-o•••••• ••••••
••n ••••i•lly o•••••. T•• •o••••n••• o• in•o•• ••ion flow ••ill ••li•• on •••
o•••• o• ••••• •n•• ••••i•y •l••••.

A• TS i• ••i• il•• •o •••••• •y•• •y•••• • in ••• w•y •y•• ••• •o•• •• wi•• ••-
•ion• •o••••• on•in• ••••i•y •l••••. How•v••, ••• •o•n•n••• o• ••••• •y•••• •
•••n•• on ••• •••••••n•• •ni•• ••••i•y •l••••• w•i•• ••• ••••• •• •o •• •••-
•i•lly o•••••••, i.•., •••y •o no• •••••lly ••••• ••• •o•••••n••• o• ••••i•y •l••••
•n• •••i• o••••in•. T•• •y•• ••••••in• only •n•••••• ••••• ••o•••• • •••••• •••
•••• •i•y •oli•i•• •• ••••••• in ••• •y•••. B••i••• •••• •i• il•••••••• •n• o• •y•••,
A• TS •llow• ••• ••o•••• • •• •o •••••i•y ••• i•• •••••i•y •l••••• •n• ••• •••••i•y
l•v•l ••w••n ••••. T•••• ••o•••• • ••-•••n•• ••••i•y •l••••• ••• in•ni•• •n•
••••••n•••• •o • •••••i•lly o••••••• vi• •y•• •••••in•. T•i• i• ••n•••lly • •••••••
•••• •o• • o••l•• •y•• •••••••••• ••••••• •lo••l ••y•li• inv••i•n• i• •n••••• •y
•••••in• lo••l •••••••• ili•y ••l••ion•. W• ••ov• o•• •y•• •y•••• i• •o•n•.

Mo•• wo•• on in•o•• ••ion flow ••••••i•y ••• •••n •on• in ••o•••••l l•n-
••••••, w•i•• • •inly •••l wi•• ••i• i•iv• •••• •y•••. T••y •llow •••• in • low
••••••i•y •l••• •o •• •••i•n•• •o • v••i•l• in • •i•• •••••i•y •l•••, ••• no• vi••
v••••. In ••• •i• •l• o• j•••-o•i•n••• l•n••••• w• •••••n• in •• i• ••••••, w• only
••v• o• j••• •y•••, •n• •••••i•y •l••••• ••• •o•n• •o •l••• •••••• ••••••. B••••••
o• j••••• ••v• ••l••, ••• •••••i•y •l••• ••• ••• •o inv••i•n• •o• •••i•n• •n••. • ••-
••wi••, w• •o•l• •• •loy •o• • •i• •l• •ov••i•n• • •••••ni•• • ••••• •• •••l••••
•ov••i•n• on •l••• •••••• ••••• li•• JFlow • o•• [•0] o• • o•• • ow•••• l • ••••ni•• •
•••• •• v••i•n• ••••• •••i• •y••• [1•].

Region-Based Memory Management. • •• no•ion o• ••• ion i• •i• il••o ••••
•••• in •••ion-••••• • •• o•y• •n•••• •n• [••,•,3,11] ••••••• •••y • o•• ••••• •o
• ••••i•ion o• •••• o• j••••. • ••ion-••••• • •• o•y • •n•••• •n• •o••••• on •••
••••y •n• •• •i•n•y o• •x• li•i• • •• o•y •llo•••ion •n• •••llo•••ion on ••• •••i•
o• •••ion•. T• • o•••in• ••l••ion on •••ion• i• ••••• on li•••i• ••, •••• i•, on w•i••
•••ion• • •y o• •liv• o•••••. In••••• o•• •••ion• •••••••n• • •••i• •••••••••ion o•
•••on•ly •onn••••• •o• •on•n•• in o• j••• •••••• •n• •o••• on •••••n•• •y•l••.
Al••o••• ••• •••ion ••••••••• ••• •iff•••n•, i• wo•l• •• in•••••in• •o ••• i•
o• j•••• •••• liv• in o•• •••ion• wi•• •y•li• •••••n••• •••••• ••• •••• • li•••i• •.
Mo••ov•• ••• o• •liv• ••l••ion• i• •••w••n •••ion• o•• •• o•y n•••• •o • • ••y•li•
•• w•ll, w•••• o•• •on••• o• •••ion• • •y j••• •• in.

7 Conclusion and Future Work

T• • • •jo• ••••l• o• ••i• ••••• i• • •l•••-••••• •••ion-••••• •••i• •y•• •y••••
••••• •llow• •o•••• • ••• •o •••i•y •••ion• w•i•• •••• •ll o• j••• •••••n•• •y•l••,
•n• •o o•••wi•• •on•ol ••• ••y•li• •••••• ili•y •o• •ll o• j•••. T•i• ••ovi•• •
nov•l •on••i••ion •o on•oin• wo•• inv•••i••in• ••• ••• o• •y•• •y••••• •, •n•
o•••• •o•• •li•• •, •o• ••• in• •••i••••y o• j••• •••••n•• •••••• •••••. T•••• •••
••• i•••l •v•n••• o•• •n•• •• •o• on•oin• •••••••••. Fo• •• ••• • o•• ••o• i•in• •i-
•••ion i• •o inv••i•••• in•o•• o•••in• • o•• •in• • o• •on•••• in••, •••• •• •o••i•l•
•••••in•, non-••••in•, •n• own•••• i• -li•• •on••in• •n• ••o•••i••. I• i• •ill •n-
•l••• •o •• w•••••• ••••• ••in• •o •o• •in• • n•• ••• o• ••••• •in• o• •on•••• in••
will •• in•••••••l•, •o•• in •••• • o• ••• •yn•••i• lo••, •n• ••• ••• •n•i• •o• -
•l•xi•y ••o•••• ••o•• •y ••• in•••••ion• •••w••n v••io•• •in• o• •on•••• in••.
W• ••• •in •o•••l •••• •y ••••in• ••••• i•••• ••o• • •••••• •••o•••i• vi•w-
•oin•, • o•• •••i•••l •n• •x••••iv• ••••o••••• will •••••••.

References

1. J. Aldrich and C. Chambers. Ownership domains: Separating aliasing policy from mechanism. In *European Conference for Object-Oriented Programming (ECOOP)*, July 2004.
2. P. S. Almeida. Balloon types: Controlling sharing of state in data types. *Lecture Notes in Computer Science*, 1241:32–59, 1997.

3. M. Barnett, R. DeLine, M. Fähndrich, K. R. M. Leino, and W. Schulte. Verification of object-oriented programs with invariants. In S. Eisenbach, G. T. Leavens, P. Müller, A. Poetzsch-Heffter, and E. Poll, editors, *Formal Techniques for Java-like Programs (FTfJP)*, July 2003. Published as Technical Report 408 from ETH Zurich.

4. C. Boyapati, R. Lee, and M. Rinard. Ownership types for safe programming: Preventing data races and deadlocks. In *Object-Oriented Programming, Systems, Languages, and Applications (OOPSLA)*, November 2002.

5. D. Clarke. *Object Ownership and Containment*. PhD thesis, School of Computer Science and Engineering, The University of New South Wales, Sydney, Australia, 2001.

6. D. G. Clarke, J. Noble, and J. M. Potter. Simple ownership types for object containment. In *European Conference for Object-Oriented Programming (ECOOP)*, 2001.

7. D. G. Clarke, J. M. Potter, and J. Noble. Ownership types for flexible alias protection. In *Proceedings of the 13th ACM SIGPLAN conference on Object-oriented programming, systems, languages, and applications*, pages 48–64. ACM Press, 1998.

8. D. E. Denning. A lattice model of secure information flow. *Commun. ACM*, 19(5):236–243, 1976.

9. D. E. Denning and P. J. Denning. Certification of programs for secure information flow. *Commun. ACM*, 20(7):504–513, 1977.

10. R. Ghiya and L. J. Hendren. Is it a tree, a dag, or a cyclic graph? a shape analysis for heap-directed pointers in c. In *Proceedings of the 23rd ACM SIGPLAN-SIGACT symposium on Principles of programming languages*, pages 1–15. ACM Press, 1996.

11. D. Grossman, G. Morrisett, T. Jim, M. Hicks, Y. Wang, and J. Cheney. Region-based memory management in cyclone. In *Proceedings of the ACM SIGPLAN 2002 Conference on Programming language design and implementation*, pages 282–293. ACM Press, 2002.

12. B. Hackett and R. Rugina. Region-based shape analysis with tracked locations. In *POPL*, pages 310–323, 2005.

13. N. Heintze and J. G. Riecke. The SLam calculus: programming with secrecy and integrity. In ACM, editor, *Conference record of POPL '98: the 25th ACM SIGPLAN-SIGACT Symposium on Principles of Programming Languages, San Diego, California, 19-21 January 1998*, pages 365–377, New York, NY, USA, 1998. ACM Press.

14. L. J. Hendren, J. Hummel, and A. Nicolau. Abstractions for recursive pointer data structures: Improving the analysis and transformation of imperative programs. In *Proceedings of the Conference on Programming Language Design and Implementation (PLDI)*, volume 27, pages 249–260, New York, NY, 1992. ACM Press.

15. M. Hind. Pointer analysis: haven't we solved this problem yet? In *Proceedings of the 2001 ACM SIGPLAN-SIGSOFT workshop on Program analysis for software tools and engineering*, pages 54–61. ACM Press, 2001.

16. J. Hogg. Islands: aliasing protection in object-oriented languages. In *Conference proceedings on Object-oriented programming systems, languages, and applications*, pages 271–285. ACM Press, 1991.

17. J. Hummel, L. J. Hendren, and A. Nicolau. A language for conveying the aliasing properties of dynamic, pointer-based data structures. In *8th International Parallel Processing Symposium*, pages 208–216, Cancun, Mexico, 1994.

18. A. Igarashi and M. Viroli. On variance-based subtyping for parametric types. In *Proceedings of the 16th European Conference on Object-Oriented Programming*, pages 441–469. Springer-Verlag, 2002.

19. P. Müller and A. Poetzsch-Heffter. Universes: A type system for controlling representation exposure. *Programming Languages and Fundamentals of Programming*, 1999.

20. A. C. Myers. JFlow: Practical mostly-static information flow control. In *Symposium on Principles of Programming Languages*, pages 228–241, 1999.

21. K. Rustan, M. Leino, and P. Müller. Object invariants in dynamic contexts. In *European Conference for Object-Oriented Programming (ECOOP)*, 2004.

22. M. Tofte and J.-P. Talpin. Implementation of the typed call-by-value lambda-calculus using a stack of regions. In *Symposium on Principles of Programming Languages*, pages 188–201, 1994.

23. M. Tofte and J.-P. Talpin. Region-based memory management. *Information and Computation*, 1997.

24. D. Volpano, G. Smith, and C. Irvine. A sound type system for secure flow analysis. *Journal of Computer Security*, 4(3):167–187, 1996.

25. D. M. Volpano and G. Smith. A type-based approach to program security. In *TAPSOFT*, pages 607–621, 1997.

26. R. Wilhelm, S. Sagiv, and T. W. Reps. Shape analysis. In *Computational Complexity*, pages 1–17, 2000.

Eclat: Automatic Generation and Classification of Test Inputs

Carlos Pacheco and Michael D. Ernst

MIT Computer Science and Artificial Intelligence Lab,
The Stata Center, 32 Vassar Street,
Cambridge, MA 02139 USA
{cpacheco, mernst}@csail.mit.edu

Abstract. This paper describes a technique that selects, from a large set of test inputs, a small subset likely to reveal faults in the software under test. The technique takes a program or software component, plus a set of correct executions—say, from observations of the software running properly, or from an existing test suite that a user wishes to enhance. The technique first infers an operational model of the software's operation. Then, inputs whose operational pattern of execution differs from the model in specific ways are suggestive of faults. These inputs are further reduced by selecting only one input per operational pattern. The result is a small portion of the original inputs, deemed by the technique as most likely to reveal faults. Thus, the technique can also be seen as an error-detection technique.

The paper describes two additional techniques that complement test input selection. One is a technique for automatically producing an oracle (a set of assertions) for a test input from the operational model, thus transforming the test input into a test case. The other is a classification-guided test input generation technique that also makes use of operational models and patterns. When generating inputs, it filters out code sequences that are unlikely to contribute to legal inputs, improving the efficiency of its search for fault-revealing inputs.

We have implemented these techniques in the Eclat tool, which generates unit tests for Java classes. Eclat's input is a set of classes to test and an example program execution—say, a passing test suite. Eclat's output is a set of JUnit test cases, each containing a potentially fault-revealing input and a set of assertions at least one of which fails. In our experiments, Eclat successfully generated inputs that exposed fault-revealing behavior; we have used Eclat to reveal real errors in programs. The inputs it selects as fault-revealing are an order of magnitude as likely to reveal a fault as all generated inputs.

1   Introduction

Much of the skill in testing a software artifact lies in carefully constructing a small set of test cases that reveals as many errors as possible. A test case has two components: an *input* to the program or module, and an *oracle*, a procedure that determines whether the program behaves as expected on the input. Many techniques can automatically generate candidate inputs for a program [10, 18, 17, 23, 8, 4, 19, 9, 12], but constructing an oracle for each input remains a largely manual task (unless a formal specification of

A.P. Black (Ed.): ECOOP 2005, LNCS 3586, pp. 504–527, 2005.

the software exists, which is rare). Thus, a test engineer wishing to use automated input generation techniques is often faced with the task of inspecting each resulting candidate input, determining whether it is a useful addition to the test suite, and writing an oracle for the input or somehow verifying that the output is correct. Doing so for even a few dozen inputs—much less the thousands of inputs automated techniques can generate—can be very costly in manual effort.

This paper presents three techniques that help the tester with the difficult task of creating new test cases. The first technique is an input selection technique: it selects, from a large set of test inputs, a small subset likely to reveal faults in the software under test—inputs for which writing full-fledged test cases is worth the effort. The goal of the technique is to focus the tester's effort on inputs most likely to reveal faults. Thus, the technique can also be viewed as an error-detection technique, and we have used it to find real errors in practice.

The input selection technique works by comparing the program's behavior on a given input against an operational model of correct operation. The model is derived from an example program execution, which can be an initial test suite or a set of program runs. If the program violates the model when run on the input, the technique classifies the input as (1) likely to constitute an illegal input that the program is not required to handle, (2) likely to produce normal operation of the program (despite violating the model), or (3) likely to reveal a fault. A second component of the technique (called the reducer) discards redundant inputs—inputs that lead to similar program behavior.

The other two techniques complement the input selection technique, by converting its output (test inputs) into a test suite (consisting of full-fledged test cases), and by providing a source of candidate test inputs for it to operate on.

Converting a test input into a test case requires the addition of an oracle, which determines whether the test succeeds or fails. We use an oracle that checks the properties in the operational model. Since the model was derived from correct executions, those properties are suggestive of correct behavior. By construction, the selected inputs will fail on these oracles. Together, the input selection and oracle generation techniques produce a set of failing test cases. This is a great starting point for the tester, whose job is to inspect each input, determine if its execution is in fact faulty, and determine if the oracle captures the proper behavior of the input. The tester can accept, reject, or modify each test input and test oracle.

The third technique is a generation-guided test input generation technique that makes use of operational-model-based classification to construct legal inputs. The input selection technique requires a set of candidate inputs; this technique provides it, while avoiding the generation of many illegal inputs.

We have implemented these techniques in the Eclat tool, which generates unit tests for Java classes. Eclat's input is a set of classes to test and an example program execution (say, a passing test suite). Eclat's output is a set of JUnit test cases, each containing a potentially fault-revealing input and a set of assertions at least one of which fails. Our experiments show that Eclat reveals real errors in programs, and the inputs it selects are an order of magnitude as likely to reveal a fault as all generated inputs. Eclat is publicly available at http://pag.csail.mit.edu/eclat/.

The rest of the paper is structured as follows. Section 2 introduces the techniques with an example use of Eclat, a tool that implements them. Section 3 describes the techniques in detail. Section 4 describes the Eclat tool. Section 5 details our experimental evaluation of the technique. Section 6 discusses related and future work, and Section 7 concludes.

2   Example: BoundedStack

We illustrate the test generation and selection technique by describing the operation of the Eclat tool, when applied to a bounded stack implementation used previously in the literature [22, 30, 9]. The bounded stack implementation (Figure 1) and testing code were written in Java by two students, an "author" and a "tester." The tester wrote a set of axioms on which the author based the implementation. The tester also wrote two small test suites by hand (one containing 8 tests, the other 12) using different methodologies [22]. The smaller test suite reveals no errors, and the larger suite reveals one error (the method pop incorrectly handles popping an empty stack).

Eclat takes two inputs: the class under test, and a set of correct uses, in the form of an executable program that exercises the class. In this example, the set of correct uses is the 8-test passing test suite.

```
public class BoundedStack {
  private int[] elems;
  private int numElems;
  private int max;

  public BoundedStack() { ... }
  public int getNumberOfElements() { ... }
  public int[] getArray() { ... }
  public int maxSize() { ... }
  public boolean isFull() { ... }
  public boolean isEmpty() { ... }
  public boolean isMember(int k) { ... }
  public void push(int k) { ... }
  public int top() { ... }

  public void pop() {
    numElems --;
  }

  public boolean equals(BoundedStack s) {
    if (s.maxSize() != max)
      return false;
    if (s.getNumberOfElements() != numElems)
      return false;
    int[] sElems = s.getArray();
    for (int j=0; j<numElems; j++)  {
      if (elems[j] != sElems[j])
        return false;
    }
    return true;
  }
}
```

Fig. 1. Class BoundedStack [22] (abbreviated). Methods pop and equals contain errors

Eclat Report

| Input 1 | ```
BoundedStack var8 = new BoundedStack();
var8.push(2);
int var9 = var8.getNumberOfElements();
var8.push(var9);
``` |

The last method invocation violated this property:

On exit: $size(\text{var8.elems}[]) - 1 \neq \text{var8.elems}[\text{var8.max} - 1]$

During execution of the last method invocation, a postcondition was violated. Since no preconditions were violated, this suggests a fault.

| Input 2 | ```
BoundedStack var8 = new BoundedStack();
var8.equals((BoundedStack)null);
``` |

The last method invocation signaled a
`java.lang.NullPointerException.`

There were no violations, but a throwable was signaled. Since the throwable is considered severe, this suggests a fault.

| Input 3 | ```
BoundedStack var8 = new BoundedStack();
var8.pop();
``` |

The last method invocation violated this property:

On exit: $\text{numElems} \geq 0$

During execution of the last method invocation, a postcondition was violated. Since no preconditions were violated, this suggests a fault.

Fig. 2. Eclat's XML output for `BoundedStack` (formatted for presentation). Inputs 2 and 3 expose errors in the code under test. Input 1 is a false report: it merely indicates a deficiency in the original test suite

Eclat's output is a set of 3 new inputs—uses of the stack—that are classified as fault-revealing by the tool because their behavior differs from the provided test suite. Eclat can produce output in text, XML, or a JUnit test suite. Figure 2 shows the output in XML form. Each input is accompanied by an explanation of why the input suggests a fault, including any violated properties. Each violated property was true during execution of the original test suite, but was violated by the new input.

Input 1 violates one property during the call of `var8.push(var9)`. The violated property says that the last element of array `elems` is never equal to its index. This input reveals no fault; Eclat has made a mistake. The input, however, does point out a stack state not covered by the original test suite, so it may be a good addition to the test suite.

Execution of Input 2 violates no properties, but the `equals` method throws an exception. Eclat classifies the input as fault-revealing. The `equals` method (Figure 1) incorrectly handles a `null` argument. This fault went undetected in all previous analyses of the class [22, 30, 9].
```

```
public void test_3_pop() throws Exception {

    ubs.BoundedStack var8 = new ubs.BoundedStack();

    // Check preconditions.
    checkPreconditions_pop(var8);
    checkObjectInvariants(var8);

    var8.pop();

    // Check postconditions.
    checkPostconditions_pop(var8);
    checkObjectInvariants(var8);

}

public static void checkPreconditions_pop(Object thiz) {

    // Check: elems[max-1] >= 0
    junit.framework.Assert.assertTrue(
      eclat.Helper.intArray(this, "elems")[eclat.Helper.intField(this, "max")-1] >= 0);
}

public static void checkPostconditions_pop(Object thiz) {

    // Check: elems[max-1] >= 0
    junit.framework.Assert.assertTrue(
      eclat.Helper.intArray(this, "elems")[eclat.Helper.intField(this, "max")-1] >= 0);
}

public static void checkObjectInvariants(Object thiz) {

    // Check: max == elems.length
    junit.framework.Assert.assertTrue(
      eclat.Helper.intField(thiz, "max")
      == eclat.Helper.intArray(thiz, "elems").length);

    // Check: elems != null
    junit.framework.Assert.assertTrue(
      eclat.Helper.intArray(thiz, "elems") != null);

    // Check: max == 2
    junit.framework.Assert.assertTrue(
      eclat.Helper.intField(thiz, "max") == 2);

    // Check: numElems >= 0
    junit.framework.Assert.assertTrue(
      eclat.Helper.intField(thiz, "numElems") >= 0);
}
```

Fig. 3. JUnit test created by Eclat corresponding to Input 3 of Figure 2. When this JUnit test is executed, the last assertion in checkObjectInvariants fails during the second call (at the end of test_3_pop). This test detects an error in BoundedStack's handling of pop when applied to an empty stack. Fields like this.elems are accessed via reflection, through method calls like eclat.Helper.intArray(this, "elems"). This allows the JUnit test suite to access non-public members of the tested class

Input 3 is classified as fault-revealing because its execution violates the property numElems ≥ 0. The variable numElems becomes negative after a call of pop on an empty stack. Eclat has revealed another true error: the pop method always decrements the top-of-stack pointer, even on an empty stack. This is a subtle error, because it silently corrupts the stack's state, and a fault only arises on a subsequent access to the stack. In particular, Input 3 itself has no user-observable fault; Eclat detects the corrupted stack state before it leads to an observable fault. A more complicated input—for example, an input that attempts to push an element when the stack pointer is negative and leads to an out-of-bounds exception—would probably be harder to understand and less useful for debugging.

Figure 3 shows a portion of Eclat's JUnit output. The figure shows the JUnit test created for Input 3, and its associated helper methods. Each test in the JUnit test suite will fail upon execution, indicating the violated property.

In summary, Eclat creates 3 inputs that quickly lead a user to discover two errors, and provides a JUnit test suite that exhibits the faulty behavior. Behind the curtains, Eclat generates and analyzes 806 distinct inputs. Some are discarded because they violate no properties and throw no exceptions (and thus suggest no faults). Some are discarded because they violate properties but are determined to constitute illegal uses of the class instead of faults. Some are discarded because they violate properties but are considered a new but non-faulty use of the class. Finally, some inputs are discarded because they behave similarly to already-chosen inputs: 5 of the inputs expose the pop-on-empty-stack fault (for example, one input pushes two items and then pops three times) but only one is selected.

3   Selection and Generation via Classification

This section describes the technique for selecting test inputs likely to reveal faults (Sections 3.1–3.3), the use of an operational model to create test cases from test inputs (Section 3.4), and the technique for generating candidate inputs (Section 3.5). We describe the techniques in the context of unit testing in an object-oriented programming language. The techniques can also be applied to non-object-oriented programs and to components larger than methods and constructors (see Section 3.6).

Figure 4 shows the input selection technique. The technique requires three things: (1) the program under test, (2) a set of correct executions of the program (for instance, an existing passing test suite for the program that a user wishes to enhance), and (3) a source of candidate inputs (each candidate may be an illegal input, or cause the program to behave normally, or reveal a fault).

The selection technique has three steps.

- **Model generation.** Observe the program's behavior on the provided correct executions, and create an *operational model* of correct behavior (Section 3.1).
- **Classification.** Classify each candidate as (1) *illegal*, (2) *normal operation*, or (3) *fault-revealing*. Do this by executing each candidate and comparing the program's behavior against the operational model (Section 3.2).
- **Reduction.** Partition the *fault-revealing* candidates based on their *violation pattern*: the set of violated properties. Report one candidate from each partition (Section 3.3).

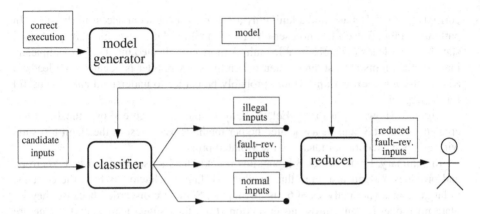

Fig. 4. The input selection technique. Implicit in the diagram is the program under test. Rectangles with rounded corners represent steps in the technique, and rectangles with square corners represent artifacts

3.1   Model Generation

The first step is to generate an operational model of the program. An operational model consists of properties that hold at the boundary of the program's components (e.g., on a

Object invariants (hold on entry and exit of all public methods)
$max = $ `elems.length`
`elems` $\neq$ `null`
$max = 2$
`numElems` ≥ 0

Properties that hold on entry to pop
`elems`$[max - 1] \geq 0$

Properties that hold on exit from pop
`elems`$[max - 1] \geq 0$

Properties that hold on entry to push
`numElems` $\in \{0, 1\}$

Properties that hold on exit from push
`numElems` $\in \{1, 2\}$
$size(\texttt{elems}[]) - 1 \neq \texttt{elems}[max - 1]$

Fig. 5. Part of an operational model for `BoundedStack` with respect to an 8-element test suite, generated by the Daikon [11] tool. An operational model reflects particulars of the test suite used to derive it; for example, the last property states that the last element in array `elems` is never equal to its index

public method's entry and exit). Our techniques impose no constraints on the program behavior captured by a model, but they require that every property can be evaluated at runtime.

The Eclat implementation uses operational abstractions generated by the Daikon invariant detector [11]. There are other techniques for generating models of program behavior based on an example use of the program [14, 26, 1, 16]. The models that these techniques generate vary in the kinds of properties they express, from legal sequences of method calls [26] to algebraic specifications of method behavior [16].

Figure 5 shows a simple operational model for BoundedStack. In this model, properties are observations about the state of the stack at various program points.

3.2   The Classifier

The classifier takes a candidate input and labels it *illegal*, *normal operation*, or *fault-revealing*. The classifier takes three arguments: a candidate input, the program under test, and an operational model. The classifier runs the program on the candidate input and records which model properties are violated during execution.

A violation means that the candidate input's behavior deviated from previous behavior of the program. Since the previously-seen behavior may be incomplete, such a violation does not necessarily imply faulty behavior. Depending on its violation pattern (the set of violated properties), the classifier labels a candidate input as *illegal*, *normal operation*, or *fault-revealing*. Figure 6 shows the decision table.

Executing an input can result in two kinds of violations: entry or exit violations. Entry violations suggest illegal program inputs, and exit violations suggest improper program behavior. The four possible categories of entry/exit violations are:

- **No entry or exit violations.** This category means that according to the operational model, the program received legal inputs and behaved properly. The technique labels the input *normal operation*.
- **No entry violations, some exit violations.** According to the model, a legal program input led to improper program behavior. The technique labels the input *fault-revealing*.
- **Some entry violations, no exit violations.** The program behaved properly on an illegal input. Since the program behaved properly, the technique labels the input *normal operation*. The program's satisfaction of the exit properties means that it is normal behavior; violation of the entry properties man that it is new behavior not seen in the example correct execution from which the model was generated.
- **Some entry and some exit violations.** The program behaved improperly on an illegal input. The technique labels the input *illegal*.

3.3   The Reducer

Section 3.2 described how an input's violation pattern leads to its classification. Violation patterns also induce a partition on all inputs, with two inputs belonging to the same partition if they violate the same properties. Inputs exhibiting the same pattern of violations are likely to be manifestations of the same faulty program behavior. Consider

Entry violations?	Exit violations?	Classification
no	no	*normal operation*
no	yes	*fault-revealing*
yes	no	(new) *normal operation*
yes	yes	*illegal*

Fig. 6. Decision table for classifying a candidate input, based on the model violations that result from its execution

```
BoundedStack var0 = new BoundedStack();
var0.pop();
```
```
BoundedStack var0 = new BoundedStack();
var0.push(3);
var0.pop();
int var1 = var0.top();
var0.pop();
```

Fig. 7. Two Eclat-generated inputs that reveal the same error in the pop method. Both inputs violate the single property numElems $\geq$ 0 on exit from the last pop

Figure 7, which contains two fault-revealing inputs. Both inputs violate the same set of properties—namely, the single property numElems $\geq$ 0—and they uncover the same error in method pop. Presenting only one input will save the user the time to inspect a redundant input.

3.4   Oracle Generation: From Test Input to Test Case

A test engineer's goal is to find errors and to write tests that may find errors in the future. A test consists of an input and an oracle, so providing test inputs, even ones that are likely to be fault-revealing, leaves the test engineer responsible for determining both how the program ought to behave on the input, and how to verify that behavior. This section describes a technique that automatically converts a test input into a test case by proposing an oracle. The human remains the final arbiter of the test suite and should check and/or modify each test case, but the effort can be greatly eased by providing complete test cases rather than partial ones.

The oracle generation technique uses the model described in Section 3.1. Since the properties can be evaluated at run time, they can be converted into assertions and used as test oracles. These oracles check for deviation from previously-observed behavior. In addition to checking behavior, the properties serve as a human-readable explanation of what is being checked, which is important in a test case. Figure 3 shows an example of a test case output by our implementation.

3.5   Classifier-Guided Input Generation

We have presented a technique that selects from a set of candidate inputs a subset likely to reveal faults, and a technique that converts an input into a test case. This section describes a similar methodology to avoid generating illegal inputs in a bottom-up input generation strategy. First we present an unguided strategy for generating inputs, and then we present an enhancement to the strategy that makes use of the classifier from Section 3.2.

We describe input generation in the context of inputs like those in Figure 7, where an input is a sequence of method calls. The last method call is the tested call, with all previous method calls setting up state for the tested call. For example, the second input in Figure 7 has five method calls; the first four are setup, and the fourth one tests the method pop via the method call var0.pop().

Unguided Bottom-up Generation. The unguided bottom-up generation strategy maintains a growing pool of values used to construct new inputs. Every value in the pool is accompanied by a code snippet (usually a sequence of method calls) that can be run to construct the value. Each code snippet can be viewed as a test input.

New values are created by combining existing values through method calls. For example, given stack value s and integer value i, the method call s.isMember(i) creates a new boolean value. Methods that return void are treated as producing a new value for the receiver. For example, method call s.push(i) creates a new stack value.

Bottom-up input generation proceeds in rounds. The pool is initialized with a set of initial values (for example, in Java, a few primitive values and null). In each round, new values are created by calling methods and constructors with values from the pool. Each new value is added to the pool and its code is emitted as a test input. The process is repeated any number of times.

Combining Generation and Classification. The unguided generation strategy is likely to produce both interesting inputs and a large number of illegal inputs, since there are no constraints on the arguments passed to method calls. The guided generation technique takes advantage of the classifier to guide the generation process.

As before, input generation proceeds in rounds. For each round:

1. Construct a new set of candidate values (and corresponding inputs) from the existing pool.
2. Classify the new candidate inputs with the classifier.
3. Discard inputs labeled *illegal*, add the values represented by the candidates labeled *normal operation* to the pool, and emit inputs labeled *fault-revealing* (but do not add them to the pool).

Figure 8 illustrates the process (it also adds the oracle generation technique discussed in Section 3.4, to give a complete view of the multiple techniques in a single framework). In the classifier-guided technique, a set of candidate inputs is no longer a required input—it has been replaced by an input generator that uses the classifier to avoid creating illegal inputs.

This enhancement removes *illegal* and *fault-revealing* inputs from the pool as soon as they are discovered, preventing these inputs from being used as building blocks to new method calls (any input that makes such a call would also be classified *illegal*, and is therefore useless to construct).

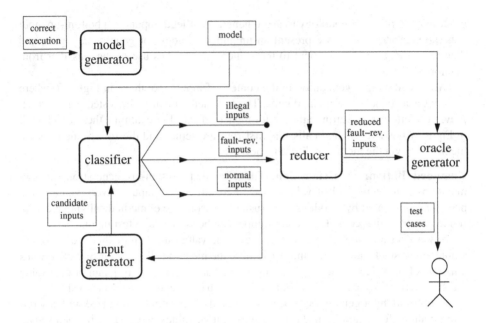

Fig. 8. The input selection technique of Figure 4, augmented with an input generator that uses the classifier to avoid creating illegal inputs, and with an oracle generator that produces test cases from test inputs. This diagram shows all the paper's techniques in a single integrated framework

3.6   Discussion

Applicability. We have presented our test selection technique in the context of an object-oriented programming language. The technique is also applicable in other programming contexts, as long as an operational model can be obtained, the model can be evaluated in the context of new program executions, and the model can be partitioned into entry and exit properties (preconditions and postconditions).

The technique reveals faults that are violations of the model properties. Eclat uses the Daikon invariant detector to infer a model. Daikon infers many kinds of properties about data structures, including heap-based ones, but does not infer, for instance, temporal properties of a program. Thus, one would not expect Eclat to be particularly good at finding faults that have to do with temporal properties.

Integration with manually-written specifications. Our research addresses a testing situation in which the tester has no access to a formal specification, but has a set of correct program executions from which an operational model can be derived. Increasingly, programmers write partial specifications to capture important properties of their software; safety-critical systems, for instance, sometimes contain at least a partial specification of the critical parts of the system. These specifications can be used to generate and classify test inputs. Partial specifications can erroneously classify inputs; for example, an illegal input may be labeled legal because the partially-specified precondition is not strong enough. Our classification technique permits use of manually-written or

Number of rounds	4
Goal number of new invocations per method per round	100
Failed tries after which generation attempts stop for a given method	100
Time limit (generation stops after limit is exceeded)	no limit

Fig. 9. Eclat's default parameters for generating test inputs

mechanically-derived properties, or both. The operational model can be complemented with manually-written specifications that capture important properties not mechanically derived. Conversely, partial specifications can be complemented with inferred properties to improve the input generation and classification process.

4 Implementation: Eclat

We have implemented our input generation, input selection, and oracle generation techniques in Eclat, a tool that automatically creates unit tests for Java classes. Eclat can produce output in text, XML, or a JUnit test suite. Eclat can be used through a command-line interface or as an Eclipse plugin. Eclat is publicly available at http://pag.csail.mit.edu/eclat/.

Eclat takes as input a set of classes to test and a program or test suite P that uses the classes. Eclat performs the following steps.

Deriving an operational model. Eclat uses the Daikon dynamic invariant detector [11] to derive a model of the classes' behavior on P; an example of Daikon's output appeared in Figure 5.

Compiling for runtime property checking. We have implemented a run-time-check instrumenter (distributed as part of Daikon at http://pag.csail.mit.edu/daikon/). The instrumenter takes the source files of the tested classes and the operational model derived by Daikon. It transforms the sources to check model properties during execution. Instrumentation is transparent: a violation does not alter the behavior of the class. Violated properties are recorded in a log.

Generating candidate inputs. Eclat generates candidate inputs using the classifier-guided, bottom-up generation strategy outlined in Section 3.5. Each round, new inputs are created by calling methods of the tested classes, selecting parameters at random from the pool. For each round, Eclat attempts to create a fixed number of new inputs for a given method using existing values from the pool. After a fixed number of failed attempts, it moves on to the next method. Figure 9 gives Eclat's default parameters. Section 5.6 evaluates Eclat's behavior when varying these parameters.

5 Evaluation

We have run a series of experiments to quantify the effectiveness of our test input generation and selection techniques. Section 5.1 introduces the programs and experimental methodology. Section 5.2 evaluates how well Eclat's selected inputs reveal faults.

Program	versions	suites per version	independent components	classes per component	public methods	NCNB LOC
BoundedStack	1	2	1	1	11	88
DSAA	1	1	9	1.5	110	640
JMLSamples	1	1	25	1.9	221	1392
utilMDE	1	2	1	1	69	1832
RatPoly	97	1	1	4	17	512
Directions	80	2	1	6	42	342

Fig. 10. Subject programs. For programs with multiple versions, numbers are average per version. NCNB LOC means non-comment, non-blank lines of code. These numbers do not include testing code

Section 5.3 measures Eclat's effectiveness when supplied small initial test suites. Sections 5.4–5.6 evaluate the classifier, the reducer, and the classifier-guided input generator individually.

5.1   Subject Programs and Methodology

Figure 10 lists our subject programs. The programs encompass 64 distinct interfaces, and a total of 631 implementations of those interfaces in 75,000 non-comment non-blank lines of code. All subject programs implement modestly-sized libraries designed to support larger programs; thus, unit testing is appropriate for them. All errors are real errors inadvertently introduced by the author(s) of the program.

- BoundedStack is the stack implementation discussed in Section 2. We report separately the results of running Eclat with the 8-test suite, and with the 12-test suite (with the one fault-revealing test removed).
- DSAA is a collection of data structures from an introductory textbook [25]. The author of the classes wrote a small set of example uses of the class: they are not exhaustive tests.
- JMLSamples is a collection of 25 classes that illustrate the use of the JML specification language. It is part of the JML distribution (www.jmlspecs.org). The test suites and specifications were written by the authors of the classes.
- utilMDE is a utility package that augments the java.util package. We report two results: one running Eclat with the test suite written by the authors of utilMDE, and the other via the unit tests of an unrelated program (Daikon [11]) that uses part of the utilMDE package.
- RatPoly is a set of student solutions to an assignment in MIT class 6.170, Laboratory in Software Engineering. The RatPoly library implements the core of a graphing calculator for polynomials over rational numbers. The course staff provided a test suite to the students as part of the assignment.
- Directions is a different set of student solutions in MIT class 6.170, written by the same students who wrote the RatPoly solutions. The Directions library is used by a MapQuest-like program that outputs directions for traveling from one location to another along Boston-area streets. For this assignment, students wrote their own

test suites. We report separately the results of running Eclat with the student-written suite, and with the suite used by the staff to grade the assignment, which was not provided to the students.

Eclat assumes a correct set of executions. Before running Eclat on BoundedStack and its 12-test suite, which contains one failing test, we removed the failing test.

For RatPoly, we discarded submissions that did not pass the staff test suite, which was provided as part of the assignment. For both RatPoly and Directions, we also discarded submissions for which Eclat generated more than 10 times the average number of fault-revealing inputs. These were solutions so faulty that finding fault-revealing inputs was not challenging, making input selection techniques unnecessary. The numbers in Figure 10 count only versions we kept.

Measurements. We organized our subject programs into nine experiments, each corresponding to using Eclat with a particular subject program and test suite. For a given experiment, we ran Eclat separately on each independent component (for example, we ran Eclat separately on DSAA's nine components: a binary tree, a disjoint set, a treap, an array-backed stack, a list-backed stack, a queue, a red-black tree, a linked list, and a binary heap). Thus, each experiment consisted of potentially many runs of Eclat: one per ⟨ component, version ⟩ pair. For each experiment, we report results that are the average over all runs.

When computing average results for all experiments, we give the same weight to each experiment, regardless of the number of versions or runs of Eclat that the program represents. We do this to avoid over-representing experiments with multiple versions or components.

We wrote formal specifications for all the subject programs (except for JMLSamples, which already had formal specifications written by its authors). We use the specifications to evaluate the classification technique, with the specification representing an ideal classifier. Of course, in the presence of a formal specification our classification technique is not necessary: the specification indicates whether an input is illegal, normal, or fault-revealing. Our techniques are intended for use when formal specifications are not available, as was the case for most of the programs.

Comparison with other tools. JCrasher [9], Jtest [19], and Jov [30] have the same goals as Eclat: to generate random candidate inputs and select potentially fault-revealing ones. We report results from running JCrasher. We tried the other tools, but Jov and Jtest were unusable in many instances (Jov sometimes exited abnormally, and Jtest sometimes failed to terminate).

5.2 Evaluating Eclat's Output

Figure 11 shows how many inputs per run Eclat generated, how many it selected, and how many of those revealed faults. The figure also shows JCrasher's results on the subject programs. The results for JCrasher are the same for experiments that use the same programs with different test suites because JCrasher does not make use of the test suite. We also executed all the inputs against the formal specifications (using `jmlc` [6]). We

Program	Generated inputs			Selected inputs			JCrasher inputs		
	inputs generated	reveal faults	preci- sion	inputs selected	reveal faults	preci- sion	inputs selected	reveal faults	preci- sion
BoundedStack (8-test suite)	806	13	1.6%	3	2	67%	0	0	—
BoundedStack (12-test suite)	1411	22	1.6%	1	1	100%	0	0	—
DSAA	806	0	0%	1.3	0	0%	0.89	0	0%
JMLSamples	396	0.50	0.13%	0.72	0.061	8.4%	0.12	0	0%
utilMDE (test suite)	1787	92	5.1%	18	4	22%	1	0	0%
utilMDE (sample usage)	1774	63	3.6%	18	2	11%	1	0	0%
RatPoly	2862	29	1.0%	1.5	0.65	42%	4	0.13	3.3%
Directions (student suite)	1099	40	3.6%	1.3	0.081	6.4%	1.6	0.025	1.6%
Directions (staff suite)	1099	41	3.8%	0.45	0.079	18%	1.6	0.025	1.6%
average	1338	33	2.3%	5.0	1.1	30%	1.13	0.02	0.92%

Fig. 11. Summary of Eclat's results. The first three numeric columns represent inputs internally generated by Eclat. The next three columns represent inputs reported to the user (after selection and reduction). The last three columns represent inputs selected as fault-revealing by JCrasher. Precision is the percentage of inputs that are fault-revealing. We calculated the average precision by taking the average of the individual experiments; this gives each experiment equal weight, but is slightly different from dividing the average number of fault-revealing inputs by the average number of selected inputs

true label	inputs generated	inputs selected
normal	74%	31%
illegal	24%	38%
fault	2.3%	30%

Fig. 12. True labels of generated and selected inputs. The entries in each column sum to 100% (modulo rounding imprecision). These results represent a total of 440,000 inputs

considered an input fault-revealing if it satisfied all preconditions of the tested method, and the method invocation caused a postcondition violation.

On average, Eclat selected 5.0 inputs per run, and 30% of those revealed a fault. By comparison, JCrasher selected 1.13 inputs per run, and 0.92% of those revealed a fault.

The inputs that Eclat selects are an order of magnitude as likely to reveal faults as the original candidate inputs (30% vs. 2.3%). Figure 12 shows another view of the results: it gives the true label of the generated and selected inputs, i.e., the label assigned by the formal specification. Selection is effective at improving a set of inputs by increasing the ratio of fault-revealing to non-fault-revealing ones.

5.3   Effectiveness on Small Initial Test Suites

Classification depends on a set of correct program executions to derive an approximate model of correct program behavior. This section measures the effect of the initial test suite on Eclat's fault-finding effectiveness. To evaluate the technique's performance on smaller suites, we artificially reduced the set of correct executions used by Eclat to construct an operational model. We compared our previous results with running Eclat using only the first 10% of the original execution trace (which was itself sometimes quite small). The table below shows the results.

	inputs generated	reveal faults	inputs selected	reveal faults
original trace	1338	33	5.0	1.1
10% of trace	1219	29	5.6	1.2

When given a smaller trace, Eclat selected more inputs (5.6 for the small trace, 5.0 for the original trace). Of those, almost the same percentage were fault-revealing.

Generating inputs based on the full-sized trace yields only slightly better results— fewer inputs to inspect, and almost the same number of fault-revealing ones among them. The technique is still effective with an impoverished trace, which makes it useful in the presence of a small test suite that does not cover all aspects of the program's behavior.

The table below shows the percentage of methods covered per test suite, and average number of calls made to each covered method. The number of calls per method covered does not give the whole story, since the distribution is highly non-uniform: in each case (even when test suites exist), a few methods are called many times and most methods are called very few times.

Program	methods covered	calls per method covered
BoundedStack (8-test suite)	82%	8
BoundedStack (12-test suite)	100%	18
DSAA	90%	679
JMLSamples	84%	102
utilMDE (test suite)	46%	13747
utilMDE (sample usage)	1.5%	4
RatPoly	83%	501
Directions (student suite)	85%	330
Directions (staff suite)	85%	3015

For the programs with multiple test suites (BoundedStack, DSAA, and utilMDE), the difference in coverage and number of calls per method is large, but the difference in Eclat's results is smaller.

5.4   Evaluating the Classifier

Every input has two labels, one assigned by Eclat and the true label assigned by the formal specification. Figure 13 shows the proportion of inputs falling into each ⟨Eclat label, true label⟩ category

The last row in Figure 13 shows the *precision* [21, 24] of Eclat's classifier. Precision is the ratio of correct labelings to the total number of labelings:

$$\text{precision} = \frac{\text{inputs correctly labeled as } L}{\text{inputs labeled as } L}$$

true	Eclat label			
label	normal	illegal	fault	**recall**
normal	0.67	0.045	0.030	90%
illegal	0.057	0.17	0.012	24%
fault	0.013	0.0035	0.0058	59%
precision	90%	78%	12%	

Fig. 13. Each entry shows the average proportion of generated inputs with the given Eclat label and true label. The sum of the nine middle entries is 1. The sum of each row in the nine middle entries yields the percentages in the middle column of Figure 12

The last column in Figure 13 shows the *recall* [21, 24] of the classifier. Recall is the ratio of correct labelings to the total number of inputs that belong to the label:

$$\mathrm{recall} = \frac{\text{inputs correctly labeled as } L}{\text{inputs that are actually } L}$$

In summary, the classifier:

- correctly labels the vast majority of inputs as non-fault-revealing (90% precision, 90% recall for normal inputs),
- recognizes most fault-revealing inputs (59% precision for fault-revealing inputs), but
- labels fault-revealing many inputs that are not (12% precision for fault-revealing inputs).

The degree to which the technique overclassifies normal inputs as illegal depends on the accuracy with which the operational model captures the legality of the program's inputs. An operational model that is out of sync with the true input space of the program can indicate a poor test suite. A good example of this is BoundedStack. This interface permits arbitrary sequences of method calls with arbitrary parameters, so it is impossible to produce an illegal input, but the technique classifies many inputs as such, due to the test suite's poor coverage. When a test engineer inspects an input that is incorrectly classified as fault-revealing, the engineer is likely to find weaknesses in the test suite, permitting the engineer to improve it.

Identifying new behavior. Our technique classifies inputs into one of three labels: *illegal*, *normal operation* and *fault-revealing*. As shown in Figure 6, there are two kinds of normal inputs: those that violate no model properties, and those that violate some preconditions but no postconditions. The latter, called *new* inputs, are inputs that diverge from the original test suite, but the properties they violate are not considered indicative of faults; instead they are considered indicative of an overconstrained model. We experimented with outputting the *new* inputs for user inspection along with the fault-revealing ones, but we found that new behaviors were no more effective in revealing faults than normal behaviors that violate no properties. However, distinguishing new behaviors from old ones might help the programmer improve a test suite's coverage by suggesting normal program operation not already covered by the suite.

5.5   Evaluating the Reducer

The reducer takes the inputs labeled *fault-revealing*, and retains a representative subset. The table below summarizes its behavior. The first numeric column shows the average distribution of all inputs that the classifier labeled *fault-revealing* (the input to the reducer). The next column shows the distribution of inputs selected (the output of the reducer). Each column sums to 100%, modulo rounding imprecision.

true label	inputs labeled as fault by classifier	inputs selected (reduced)
normal	63%	31%
illegal	25%	38%
fault	12%	30%

The reduction step increases the percentage of fault-revealing inputs from 12% to 30%. For these programs (and, we suspect, for programs in general), fault-revealing program behavior is more difficult to produce than illegal or normal behavior, and thus more difficult to produce repeatedly by different inputs. This makes fault-revealing inputs less reducible than other inputs, because there are fewer inputs per partition, resulting in an increased proportion of selected fault-revealing inputs.

5.6   Evaluating the Input Generator

Classifier-guided Input Generation. Section 3.5 describes the use of the classifier in a bottom-up input generation strategy in which only inputs classified as *normal operation* are added to the growing pool of inputs. The first line in Figure 14 shows the results of this strategy (Eclat's default) for the formally-specified programs (this line repeats the averages from Figure 11). The second line shows the result of running Eclat using unguided generation: all inputs from previous rounds are added to the pool regardless of their classification.

Unguided generation leads to a larger number of inputs generated. The reason is that the pool has a larger number of building blocks to create new inputs from. Despite the larger number of inputs generated, fewer of those inputs are fault revealing. This is reflected in the results: with the unguided generation strategy, Eclat reports a larger number of inputs and yet fewer inputs are fault-revealing.

We can gain insight into this difference by looking back at Figure 12, which shows that the input selection technique selects not only more *fault-revealing* inputs, but also more *illegal* inputs. Eclat is most effective at correctly classifying normal inputs, but less so for illegal ones. When we remove the classifier from the generation process, the number of illegal inputs among candidate inputs increases, and Eclat selects more of them as fault-revealing, which decreases the tool's precision. Constraining the building blocks used by the generator to inputs classified as *normal operation* reduces these false positives.

Generation Parameters. This section evaluates Eclat's output under varying parameters. We varied two parameters:

	inputs generated	reveal faults	inputs selected	reveal faults
classifier-guided generation	1338	33	5.0	1.1
unguided bottom-up generation	3217	17	5.3	0.80

Fig. 14. Comparison of unguided and enhanced bottom-up generation. The first line summarizes the results for classifier-guided generation (averages reproduced from Figure 11). The second line uses unguided input generation

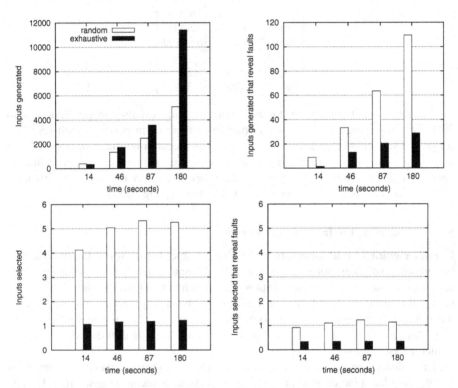

Fig. 15. Number of inputs generated and selected by Eclat, when varying the number of rounds and the generation strategy. The white bars are the results of running Eclat using random generation. The four data points are for the end-to-end time Eclat takes doing 2, 4, 6, and 8 rounds of random generation. The black bars are the results of running Eclat using exhaustive generation. The times shown are averages over all experiments

- The number of rounds of bottom-up generation. Eclat's default is 4 rounds; we also ran the experiments using 2, 6, and 8 rounds of generation.
- The number of new inputs generated per round. Eclat's default is to randomly generate 100 new inputs per method per round. To compare this approach against a more systematic approach, we added exhaustive generation to Eclat: for each round, it exhaustively generates all new inputs that are possible to generate given the current pool of values. To compare this approach against random generation, we mea-

sured how random and exhaustive generation performed given the same amount of time. We measured the time that Eclat spent generating, classifying and reducing inputs using random generation for a given number of rounds, and we ran Eclat again, using exhaustive generation and setting a time limit equal to the time spent by random generation.

Figure 15 shows the results for the eight possible combinations of parameter variations described above. Given the same amount of time, random generation generates fewer candidate inputs (upper-left plot). At every attempt to generate a new input for a method, Eclat's random generation algorithm randomly chooses a set of parameters, and then checks to see if the input has already been generated. This adds two costs to random generation: the cost of comparing a newly-generated random input for membership in the set of existing inputs, and the wasted cost of generating an input that is already in the pool. Exhaustive generation, on the other hand, never re-generates an already-existing input.

Despite creating fewer candidate inputs, random generation produces better-quality candidates—candidates that are fault-revealing (upper-right plot). Exhaustive generation creates many inputs that exercise the class in ways that are indistinguishable for the purpose of fault detection. Random generation produces a more diverse collection of inputs and more fault-revealing inputs than exhaustive generation (bottom plots). In future work, we plan to investigate exhaustive generation combined with techniques for avoiding generation of duplicate inputs [28, 29].

6   Related Work

The most closely related work to ours is the Jov [30] and JCrasher [9] tools, which share the goal of selecting, from a randomly-generated set of candidate inputs, a set most likely to be useful. This reduces the number of test inputs a human must examine.

Our research was inspired by Jov [30]. Jov builds on earlier work [15] that identified a test as a potentially valuable addition to a test suite if the test violates an operational abstraction built from the suite: the test represents some combination of values that differs from all tests currently in the suite. (The DIDUCE tool [14] takes a similar approach, though with the goal of identifying bugs at run time rather than improving test suites: a property that has held for part of a run, but is later violated, is suggestive of an error.) The Jov tool uses the operational abstraction not just to select tests, but also to guide test generation, by iterated use of the Jtest tool [19]. Jov also differs from the previous, automated work on test selection [15] by placing it in a loop with human interaction and iterating as many times as desired:

1. Create an operational model (invariants) from a test suite.
2. Generate test inputs that violate the invariants.
3. A human selects some of the generated tests and adds them to the test suite.

Often, overconstrained preconditions rendered Jtest incapable of producing any outputs, so Xie and Notkin report on the effectiveness of Jov after eliminating all preconditions from the operational model generated in step 1. Essentially, this permitted Jtest to generate any input that violates the postconditions (including many illegal ones), not just inputs similar to the ones in the original test suite. However, the user gets no help in recognizing such illegal inputs. In fact, the majority of errors that Jov finds [30] are illegal inputs and precondition violations, not true errors [27].

Our work extends that of Xie and Notkin in several ways. Our technique explicitly addresses the imperfect nature of a derived operational model. Our technique explicitly distinguishes between illegal and fault-revealing inputs. Our technique is more automated: it requires only one round of examination by a human, rather than multiple rounds. Our technique uses operational abstractions in a different way to direct test input generation. Our implementation is more robust and faster; Eclat takes less than two minutes for a class that took Jov over 10 minutes to process, primarily because the Jtest tool is so slow. We have performed a more extensive experimental evaluation (631 classes rather than 12). Even though we count only actual errors, not illegal inputs, our approach outperforms the previous one.

JCrasher [9], like Eclat, generates a large number of random inputs and selects a small number of potentially fault-revealing ones. An input is considered potentially fault-revealing if it throws an undeclared runtime exception. Inputs are grouped (reduced) based on the contents of the call-stack when the exception is thrown. JCrasher and Eclat have similar underlying generation techniques but different models of correct program behavior, which leads to different classification and reduction techniques. JCrasher's model takes into account only exceptional behavior, and Eclat augments the model with operational behavior, which accounts for its greater effectiveness in uncovering faults.

6.1   Future Work

Future work on this research centers around two themes.

- **Input generation.** While it may not help in establishing the reliability of a program, random testing seems to be remarkably effective in exposing errors and may be as effective as more formally founded techniques [10, 13]. However, it is primarily useful when all inputs are legal, or when a specification of valid inputs is available. Therefore, techniques that make it more effective are valuable contributions. Our technique could be combined with any technique for generating tests [8, 4], in order to filter the tests before being presented to a user. Our technique is attractive because it does not require a human-written formal specification; when one is present, much more powerful testing methodologies are possible [2, 7].
- **Input classification.** Eclat's reduction step clusters test inputs in order to reduce their number, and JCrasher has a similar step. Several researchers have used machine learning to classify program executions as either correct or faulty [20, 5, 3]. It would be interesting to apply such techniques in order to further improve Eclat.

7 Conclusion

We have presented an input selection technique that incorporates a classifier and a reducer, both of which make use of a model of correct program operation. We have combined our input selection technique with two other techniques. One technique uses the classifier to guide input generation towards legal inputs, which improves the efficiency of the input search space by pruning illegal sequences of methods calls as early as they are encountered. The other additional technique uses the operational model to produce oracles for the selected test inputs, which converts the test inputs into full-fledged test cases. Together, these techniques result in an effective test generation and selection methodology.

We have implemented the methodology in Eclat, a tool for Java unit testing, and demonstrated its effectiveness in producing fault-revealing test inputs. The input generation technique creates legal, fault-revealing candidate inputs for the methods in our subject programs, and the input selection technique selects inputs that are an order of magnitude as likely to reveal faults as the candidate inputs. The methodology reveals real, previously unknown errors in the subject programs. When the test inputs fail to reveal faults, the user is not heavily inconvenienced, because only a few inputs are selected.

References

[1] G. Ammons, R. Bodík, and J. R. Larus. Mining specifications. In *Proceedings of the 29th Annual ACM SIGPLAN-SIGACT Symposium on Principles of Programming Languages*, pages 4–16, Portland, Oregon, Jan. 16–18, 2002.

[2] M. J. Balcer, W. M. Hasling, and T. J. Ostrand. Automatic generation of test scripts from formal test specifications. In *Proceedings of the ACM SIGSOFT '89 Third Symposium on Testing, Analysis, and Verification (TAV3)*, pages 210–218, Dec. 1989.

[3] J. F. Bowring, J. M. Rehg, and M. J. Harrold. Active learning for automatic classification of software behavior. In *ISSTA 2004, Proceedings of the 2004 International Symposium on Software Testing and Analysis*, pages 195–205, Boston, MA, USA, July 12–14, 2004.

[4] C. Boyapati, S. Khurshid, and D. Marinov. Korat: Automated testing based on Java predicates. In *ISSTA 2002, Proceedings of the 2002 International Symposium on Software Testing and Analysis*, pages 123–133, Rome, Italy, July 22–24, 2002.

[5] Y. Brun and M. D. Ernst. Finding latent code errors via machine learning over program executions. In *ICSE'04, Proceedings of the 26th International Conference on Software Engineering*, pages 480–490, Edinburgh, Scotland, May 26–28, 2004.

[6] L. Burdy, Y. Cheon, D. Cok, M. D. Ernst, J. Kiniry, G. T. Leavens, K. R. M. Leino, and E. Poll. An overview of JML tools and applications. In *Eighth International Workshop on Formal Methods for Industrial Critical Systems (FMICS 03)*, Trondheim, Norway, June 5–7, 2003.

[7] J. Chang and D. J. Richardson. Structural specification-based testing: Automated support and experimental evaluation. In *Proceedings of the 7th European Software Engineering Conference and the 7th ACM SIGSOFT Symposium on the Foundations of Software Engineering*, pages 285–302, Toulouse, France, Sept. 6–9, 1999.

[8]   K. Claessen and J. Hughes. QuickCheck: A lightweight tool for random testing of Haskell programs. In *ICFP '00, Proceedings of the fifth ACM SIGPLAN International Conference on Functional Programming*, pages 268–279, Montreal, Canada, Sept. 18–20, 2000.

[9]   C. Csallner and Y. Smaragdakis. JCrasher: an automatic robustness tester for Java. *Software: Practice and Experience*, 34(11):1025–1117, Sept. 2004.

[10] J. W. Duran and S. C. Ntafos. An evaluation of random testing. *IEEE Transactions on Software Engineering*, 10(4):438–444, July 1984.

[11] M. D. Ernst, J. Cockrell, W. G. Griswold, and D. Notkin. Dynamically discovering likely program invariants to support program evolution. *IEEE Transactions on Software Engineering*, 27(2):1–25, Feb. 2001. A previous version appeared in *ICSE '99, Proceedings of the 21st International Conference on Software Engineering*, pages 213–224, Los Angeles, CA, USA, May 19–21, 1999.

[12] Foundations of Software Engineering group, Microsoft Research. *Documentation for AsmL 2*, 2003. http://research.microsoft.com/fse/asml.

[13] D. Hamlet and R. Taylor. Partition testing does not inspire confidence. *IEEE Transactions on Software Engineering*, 16(12):1402–1411, Dec. 1990.

[14] S. Hangal and M. S. Lam. Tracking down software bugs using automatic anomaly detection. In *ICSE'02, Proceedings of the 24th International Conference on Software Engineering*, pages 291–301, Orlando, Florida, May 22–24, 2002.

[15] M. Harder, J. Mellen, and M. D. Ernst. Improving test suites via operational abstraction. In *ICSE'03, Proceedings of the 25th International Conference on Software Engineering*, pages 60–71, Portland, Oregon, May 6–8, 2003.

[16] J. Henkel and A. Diwan. Discovering algebraic specifications from Java classes. In *ECOOP 2003 — Object-Oriented Programming, 17th European Conference*, pages 431–456, Darmstadt, Germany, July 23–25, 2003.

[17] B. Korel. Automated test data generation for programs with procedures. In *Proceedings of the 1996 ACM SIGSOFT international symposium on Software testing and analysis*, pages 209–215. ACM Press, 1996.

[18] T. J. Ostrand and M. J. Balcer. The category-partition method for specifying and generating functional tests. *Communications of the ACM*, 31(6):676–686, June 1988.

[19] Parasoft Corporation. *Jtest version 4.5*. http://www.parasoft.com/.

[20] A. Podgurski, D. Leon, P. Francis, W. Masri, M. Minch, J. Sun, and B. Wang. Automated support for classifying software failure reports. In *ICSE'03, Proceedings of the 25th International Conference on Software Engineering*, pages 465–475, Portland, Oregon, May 6–8, 2003.

[21] G. Salton. *Automatic Information Organization and Retrieval*. McGraw-Hill, 1968.

[22] D. Stotts, M. Lindsey, and A. Antley. An informal formal method for systematic JUnit test case generation. In *Proceedings of 2nd XP Universe and 1st Agile Universe Conference (XP/Agile Universe)*, pages 131–143, Chicago, IL, USA, Aug. 4–7, 2002.

[23] N. Tracey, J. Clark, K. Mander, and J. McDermid. An automated framework for structural test-data generation. In *Proceedings of the 13th Annual International Conference on Automated Software Engineering (ASE'98)*, pages 285–288, Honolulu, Hawaii, Oct. 14–16, 1998.

[24] C. J. van Rijsbergen. *Information Retrieval*. Butterworths, London, second edition, 1979.

[25] M. A. Weiss. *Data Structures and Algorithm Analysis in Java*. Addison Wesley Longman, 1999.

[26] J. Whaley, M. Martin, and M. Lam. Automatic extraction of object-oriented component interfaces. In *ISSTA 2002, Proceedings of the 2002 International Symposium on Software Testing and Analysis*, pages 218–228, Rome, Italy, July 22–24, 2002.

[27] T. Xie. Personal communication, Aug. 2003.

[28] T. Xie, D. Marinov, and D. Notkin. Rostra: A framework for detecting redundant object-oriented unit tests. In *ASE 2004: Proceedings of the 20th Annual International Conference on Automated Software Engineering*, pages 196–205, Linz, Australia, Nov. 9–11, 2004.

[29] T. Xie, D. Marinov, W. Schulte, and D. Notkin. Symstra: A framework for generating object-oriented unit tests using symbolic execution. In *Tools and Algorithms for the Construction and Analysis of Systems (TACAS)*, pages 365–381, Edinburgh, UK, Apr. 4–8, 2005.

[30] T. Xie and D. Notkin. Tool-assisted unit test selection based on operational violations. In *ASE 2003: Proceedings of the 18th Annual International Conference on Automated Software Engineering*, pages 40–48, Montreal, Canada, Oct. 8–10, 2003.

Lightweight Defect Localization for Java

Valentin Dallmeier, Christian Lindig, and Andreas Zeller

Saarland University, Saarbrücken, Germany
{dallmeier, lindig, zeller}@cs.uni-sb.de

Abstract. A common method to localize defects is to compare the *coverage* of passing and failing program runs: A method executed only in failing runs, for instance, is likely to point to the defect. However, some failures, occur only after a specific *sequence* of method calls, such as multiple deallocations of the same resource. Such sequences can be collected from arbitrary Java programs at low cost; comparing object-specific sequences predicts defects better than simply comparing coverage. In a controlled experiment, our technique pinpointed the defective class in 39% of all test runs.

1   Introduction

Of all debugging activities, locating the defect that causes the failure is by far the most time-consuming. To assist the programmer in this task, various automatic methods rank the program statements by the *likelihood* that they contain the defect. One of the most lightweight methods to obtain such a likelihood is to compare the *coverage* of *passing* and *failing* program runs: A method executed only in failing runs, but never in passing runs, is correlated with failure and thus likely to point to the defect.

Some failures, though, come to be only through a *sequence* of method calls, tied to a *specific object*. As an example, consider streams in Java: If a stream is not explicitly closed after usage, its destructor will eventually do so. However, if too many files are left open before the garbage collector destroys the unused streams, file handles will run out, and a failure occurs. This problem is indicated by a sequence of method calls: if the last access (say, `read()`) is followed by `finalize()` (but not `close()`), we have a defect.

In this paper, we explore comparing call sequences between program runs for defect localizaton. Specifically, we explore three questions:

1. **Are *sequences of method calls* better defect indicators than single calls?** In any Java stream, calls to `read()` and `finalize()` are common; but the sequence of these two indicates a missing `close()` and hence a defect.
2. **Do method calls indicate defects more precisely when collected *per object*, rather than globally?** The sequence of `read()` and `finalize()` is only defect-revealing when the calls pertain to the same object.
3. **Do missing (or extra) method calls indicate defects in the callee—*or in the caller?*** For any Java stream, a missing `close()` indicates a defect in the caller.

Generalizing to arbitrary method calls and arbitrary defects, we have set up a tool that instruments a given Java program such that sequences of method calls are collected

A.P. Black (Ed.): ECOOP 2005, LNCS 3586, pp. 528–550, 2005.

on a per-object basis. Using this tool, we have conducted two experiments that answer the above questions. In short, it turns out that (1) sequences predict defects better than simply comparing coverage, (2) per-object sequences are better predictors than global sequences, and (3) the caller is more likely to be defective than the callee. Furthermore, the approach is lightweight in the sense that the performance is comparable to coverage-based approaches. All these constitute the contribution of this paper.

2   How Call Sequences Indicate Defects

Let us start with a phenomenological walkthrough and take a look at the AspectJ compiler—more precisely, at its bug #30168. This bug manifests itself as follows: Compiling the AspectJ program in Fig. 1 produces illegal bytecode that causes the virtual machine to crash (run r):

```
$ ajc Test3.aj
$ java test.Test3
test.Test3@b8df17.x

Unexpected Signal : 11 occurred at PC=0xFA415A00
Function name=(N/A)
Library=(N/A)
...
Please report this error at http://java.sun.com/...
$ -
```

As the bug not only affects execution of the Java program per se, but crashes the virtual machine completely, there is no hint to the origin of the problem like for example a stack trace. As the AspectJ compiler has 2,929 classes, finding the location of the defect is a nontrivial task. To ease the task, though, we can focus on *differences* in the program execution, in particular the difference between a passing run (producing valid Java bytecode) and the failing run in question. Since the outcome of passing and failing runs is different, chances are that earlier differences in the program runs are related to the defect. For the AspectJ example in Figure 1, we can easily identify a passing run—commenting out Line 32, for instance, makes AspectJ work just fine (run r).

Since capturing and comparing entire runs is costly, researchers have turned to *abstractions* that summarize essential properties of a program run. One such abstraction is *coverage*—that is, the pieces of code that were executed in a run. Indeed, comparing the coverage of r and r reveals a number of differences. The method getThisJoin-PointVar() of the class BcelShadow, for instance, is only called in r, but not in r, which makes BcelShadow.getThisJoinPointVar() a potential candidate for causing the failure.

Unfortunately, this hypothesis is wrong. In our AspectJ problem, the developers have eventually chosen to fix the bug in another class; therefore, BcelShadow is not the location of the defect. In fact, none of the methods that are called *only* within r contain the defect.

However, it may well be that the failure is caused not by a single method call, but rather by a *sequence of method calls* that occurs only in the failing run r. Such se-

```
1    package test;
2    import org.aspectj.lang.*;
3    import org.aspectj.lang.reflect.*;
4
5    public class Test3 {
6        public static void main(String[] args) throws Exception {
7            Test3 a = new Test3();
8            a.foo(-3);
9        }
10       public void foo(int i) {
11           this.x=i;
12       }
13       int x;
14   }
15
16   aspect Log {
17       pointcut assign(Object newval, Object targ):
18           set(* test..*)  && args(newval) && target(targ);
19
20       before(Object newval, Object targ): assign(newval,targ) {
21           Signature sign = thisJoinPoint.getSignature();
22           System.out.println(targ.toString() + "." + sign.getName() +
23                              ":=" + newval);
24       }
25
26       pointcut tracedCall():
27           call(* test..*(..)) && !within(Log);
28
29       after() returning (Object o):  tracedCall() {
30           // Works if you comment out either of these two lines
31           thisJoinPoint.getSignature();
32           System.out.println(thisJoinPoint);
33       }
34   }
```

Fig. 1. This AspectJ program causes the Java virtual machine to crash

quences can be collected for specific objects. This sequence, for instance, summarizes method calls initiated by an instance of ThisJoinPointVisitor in r :

$$\left\langle \begin{array}{l} \text{ThisJoinPointVisitor.isRef(),} \\ \text{ThisJoinPointVisitor.canTreatAsStatic(),} \\ \text{MethodDeclaration.traverse(),} \\ \text{ThisJoinPointVisitor.isRef(),} \\ \text{ThisJoinPointVisitor.isRef()} \end{array} \right\rangle$$

This sequence of calls does not occur in r —in other words, only in r did an object of the ThisJoinPointVisitor class call these five methods in succession. This difference in the ThisJoinPointVisitor behavior is correlated with failure and thus makes ThisJoinPointVisitor a class that is more likely to contain the defect. And indeed, it turns out that AspectJ bug #30168 was eventually fixed in ThisJoinPointVisitor. Thus, while a difference in coverage may not point to a defect, a difference in call sequences may well.

Comparing two runs usually yields more than one differing sequence. In our case (r vs. r), we obtain a total of 556 differing sequences of length 5. We can determine the originating class for each of these sequences, assign a weight to each sequence, and rank the classes such that those with the most important sequences are at the top. In this ranking, the ThisJoinPointVisitor class is at position 6 out of 542 executed classes—meaning that the programmer, starting at the top, has to examine only 1.1% of the executed classes or 3.2% of the executed code (0.2% of all classes or 0.8% of the entire code) in order to find the defect. (In comparison, if we had compared only the method coverage of r and r, we would have discovered no difference and hence no indication that the defect is located in `ThisJoinPointVisitor`.)

While such anecdotal evidence is nice, we had to evaluate our approach more thoroughly. In the remainder of this paper, we first describe in detail how we collect sequences of method calls (Section 3), and how we compare them to detect likely defects (Section 4). In Section 5, we describe our experiments with the NanoXML parser and AspectJ; the results support our initial claims. Section 7 discusses related work and Section 8 closes with conclusion and consequences.

3   Summarizing Call Sequences

Over its lifetime, an object may receive and initiate millions of method calls. How do we capture and summarize these to characterize normal behavior? These are the highlights of our approach:

- Recording a trace of all calls per object quickly becomes unmanageable and is a problem in itself (Reiss and Renieris, 2001). Rather than recording the full trace, we abstract from it by *sliding a window* over the trace and remembering only the observed substrings of calls in a *call-sequence set*.
- Collecting a sequence set per object is still problematic, as an application may instantiate huge numbers of objects. We therefore *aggregate* sequence sets into *one set per class*, which thus characterizes the behavior of the class.
- An object receives and initiates method calls. The trace of *incoming* (received) calls tells us how an object is *used* by its clients. The trace of *outgoing* (initiated) calls tells us how an object is *implemented*. We consider both types of traces for fault localization.
- We keep the *overhead* for collecting and analyzing traces as low as possible. Overall, the overhead is comparable to measuring coverage—and thus affordable even in the field.

The following sections describe these techniques in detail.

3.1   From Traces to Call Sequences

A *trace* is an observation of events over the lifetime of an objects, class, or program. In order to capture an object's behavior, we can record the calls it initiates or receives. For realistic runs, these traces are very large. Our approach therefore uses a more abstract representation of an object's behaviour. Instead of investigating whole traces, we remember only *characteristic sequences* of calls. This abstraction of a trace works equally well for a trace of initiated or received calls, or any other trace, which is why we talk about traces in general.

When we slide a window over a trace, the contents of the window characterize the trace—as demonstrated in Fig. 2. The observed window contents form a set of short sequences. The wider the window, the more precise the characteristic set will be.

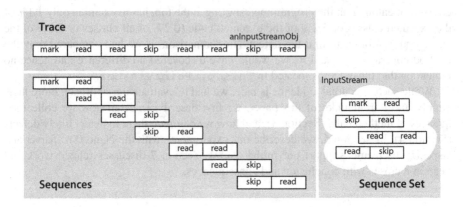

Fig. 2. The call trace of an object is abstracted to a *call-sequence set* using a sliding window

Formally, a trace S is a string of calls: $\langle m_1, \ldots, m_n \rangle$. When the window is k calls wide, the set $P(S, k)$ of observed windows are the k-long substrings of S: $P(S, k) = \{w \mid w$ is a substring of $S \wedge |w| = k\}$. For example, consider a window of size $k = 2$ slid over S and the resulting set of sequences $P(S, 2)$:

$$S = \langle abcabcdc \rangle \qquad P(S, 2) = \{\langle ab \rangle, \langle bc \rangle, \langle ca \rangle, \langle cd \rangle, \langle dc \rangle\}$$

Obviously different traces may lead to the same set: for $T = \langle abcdcdca \rangle$, we have $P(T, 2) = P(S, 2)$. Hence, going from a trace to its sequence set entails a loss of information. The equivalence of traces is controlled by the window size k, which models the context sensitivity of our approach: in the above example a window size $k \geq 3$ leads to different sets $P(S, k)$ and $P(T, k)$. In the remainder of the paper, we use $P(T)$ to denote the sequence set computed from T, not mentioning the fixed k explicitly.

Note that two calls that are next to each other in a sequence may have been far apart in time: between the two points in time when the object received or initiated the calls, other objects may have been active.

If a trace has less entries than the window size, the missing entries are filled up with dummy invocations that can be distinguished from regular entries. Thus, every sequence set for a trace contains at least one entry.

The size of a sequence set may grow exponentially in theory: With n distinct methods, n^k different sequences of length k exist. In practice, sequence sets are small because method calls are induced by code, which is static. Hence, loops in the code lead to reoccuring sequences that make sequence sets a useful and compact abstraction—one could also consider them an *invariant* of program behavior.

Much of the versatility of sequence sets is due to their set nature: this makes it easy to aggregate and compare sequence set, unlike tree- or graph-based representations (Reiss and Renieris, 2001; Ammons et al., 2002).

3.2   From Objects to Classes

Collecting one sequence set per object raises an important issue: In a program with millions of objects, we will quickly run out of memory . As an alternative, one could think about tracing calls at the *class level* to derive one sequence set per class. In an implementation of such a trace, an object adds an entry to the trace of its class every time it receives (or initiates) a call. Sliding a window over this trace results in a sequence set that characterizes the class's behavior.

As an example of sequence sets aggregated at class level, consider the traces X and Y of two objects. Both objects are *live at the same time* and because we are collecting one trace S per class, their calls interleave in this trace:

$$X = \langle\ a\ \ b\ c\ d\ \ \ dc\rangle$$
$$Y = \langle a\ \ a\ b\ c\ ab\ \ \rangle$$
$$S = \langle aaabbccdabdc\rangle$$
$$P(S, 2) = \{\langle aa\rangle, \langle ab\rangle, \langle bb\rangle, \langle bc\rangle, \langle cc\rangle, \langle cd\rangle, \langle da\rangle, \langle bd\rangle, \langle dc\rangle\}$$

The resulting sequence set $P(S, 2)$ characterizes the behavior of the class—somewhat. The set contains sequences like $\langle da\rangle$ or $\langle bb\rangle$ that we never observed at the object level. How objects interleave has a strong impact on the class trace S, and consequently on its sequence set. This becomes even more obvious when a class instantiates many objects and when their interleaving becomes non-deterministic, as in the presence of threads.

We therefore use a better alternative: We trace objects *individually,* but rather than aggregating their traces, we aggregate their *sequence sets.* Previously, we collected all calls into one trace and computed its sequence set. Now, we have individual traces, but combine their sequence sets into one set per class. The result $P(X, 2) \cup P(Y, 2)$ is more faithful to the traces we actually observed—$\langle bb\rangle$ and $\langle da\rangle$ are no longer elements of the sequence set:

$$P(X, 2) = \{\langle ab\rangle, \langle bc\rangle, \langle cd\rangle, \langle dd\rangle, \langle dc\rangle\}$$
$$P(Y, 2) = \{\langle ab\rangle, \langle bc\rangle, \langle ca\rangle, \langle aa\rangle\}$$
$$P(X, 2) \cup P(Y, 2) = \{\langle aa\rangle, \langle ab\rangle, \langle bc\rangle, \langle cd\rangle, \langle dd\rangle, \langle dc\rangle, \langle ca\rangle\}$$

The sequence set of a class is the union of the sequence sets of its objects. It characterizes the behavior of the class and is our measure when comparing classes in passing and failing runs: we simply compare their sequence sets.

3.3   Incoming vs. Outgoing Calls

Any object receives incoming and initiates outgoing method calls. Their traces tell us how the object is used by its clients and how it is implemented, respectively. Both kinds of traces can be used to detect control flow differences between a passing and a failing run. However, they differ in their ability to relate those differences to defects.

As an example, consider object aQueue in Fig. 3. The queue receives calls like enqueue() to add an element, and dequeue() to remove it. These are *incoming* calls to object aQueue.

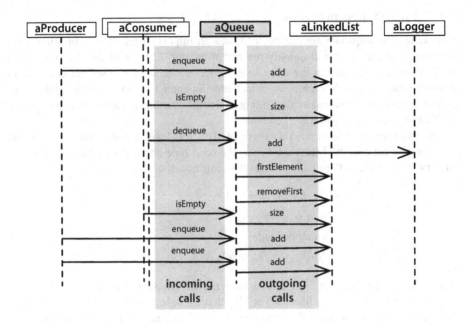

Fig. 3. Traces of *incoming calls* (left) and *outgoing calls* (right) for object aQueue

To implement these methods, the queue object uses another object aLinkedList. It calls add() to add an element at the end of the linked list, firstElement() to obtain the first element, and removeFirst() to remove it from the list. These calls are *outgoing* calls of object aQueue.

Incoming Calls. Inspired by the work of Ammons et al. (2002), we first examined *incoming* calls. The technique of Ammons et al. observes clients that call into a part of the X11 API and learns automatically a finite-state automaton that describes how the API is used correctly by a client: for example, a client must call open() before it may call write(). Such an automaton is an invariant of the API; it can be used to detect non-conforming clients.

By tracing incoming calls, we can also learn this invariant and represent it as a sequence set: each object traces the calls it receives. Since we know the class Queue of the receiving object, we have to remember in a sequence only the names of the invoked methods (and their signatures, to resolve overloading). In our example, the trace of incoming calls for the aQueue object is

$$\langle \texttt{enqueue()}, \texttt{isEmpty()}, \ldots, \texttt{enqueue()}, \texttt{enqueue()} \rangle \ .$$

As discussed in Section 3.2, sequence sets of individual objects are aggregated into one sequence set per class. After training with several passing runs, we can detect when a class receives calls that do not match a learned sequence set.

Learning class invariants from incoming calls is appealing for at least two reasons: First, the number of methods an object can receive is restricted by its class. We thus can expect small traces and may even fine-tune the window size in relation to its number of methods. Second, class invariants could be learned across several applications that use the class, not just one.

Outgoing Calls. In our setting, incoming calls show a major weakness: When we detect a non-conforming usage of a class, it is difficult to identify the responsible client. For example, let us assume we observe a new sequence of incoming calls like $\langle$dequeue(),dequeue(),dequeue()$\rangle$. This sequence could indicate a problem because a consumer should check for an empty queue using isEmpty() before attempting a dequeue(). The sequence could also be harmless, for instance, when the dequeue() calls stem from different objects. In any case, it is not the queue object which is responsible for the new sequence, but the objects that initiated the dequeue() calls. Consequently, we turned from incoming to *outgoing* calls, which summarize the method calls initiated by an object. For aQueue, these are:

$$\langle \texttt{LinkedList.add(),LinkedList.size(),Logger.add(),} \ldots \rangle$$

Because an object may call objects from several classes, method names are no longer unique—witness the different calls to add. We therefore remember the class *and* method name in a trace. Again, we build one trace per object and aggregate the traces of individual queue objects into one sequence per class, which represents its behavior.

When we detect a sequence of outgoing calls that is not in a learned sequence set, we know where to look for the reason: the Queue class. Unlike a trace of incoming calls, the trace of outgoing calls can guide the programmer to the defect.

3.4   Collecting Traces

We trace a Java program using a combination of off-line and on-line methods. Before the program is executed, we instrument its bytecode for tracing. While it is running, the program collects traces, computes the corresponding sequence sets, and emits them in XML format before it quits; analyzing sequence sets takes place offline.

For program instrumentation, we use the Bytecode Engineering Library (BCEL, Dahm (1999)). This requires just the program's class files and works with any Java virtual machine. We thus can instrument any Java application, regardless of whether its source code is available. While this is not a typical scenario for debugging, it allows us to instrument the SPEC JVM 98 benchmark, or indeed any third-party code.

Instrumentation of a class rewrites all call sites and the start of every non-static method. The code injected at call sites is needed to determine the caller of a method invocation: because of dynamic binding, a caller cannot statically know the exact class of the method called, and a method (without inspecting the stack) does not know the calling class.

A call is rewritten such that, before a call occurs, the caller's class and instance identifers are written to a thread-local variable from where they are read by code added to the prolog of the called method (the callee). The callee finally enters the actual call to the trace of the caller (when tracing outgoing calls) or callee (when tracing incoming calls).

```
class Caller extends Object {          class Callee extends Object {
  public void call() {                   public void method() {
    Callee c;                              Tracer.addCall((id for Callee.method>));
    ...                                    ...
    Tracer.storeCaller(this.id);         }
    c.method();                        }
    ...
  }
}
```

Fig. 4. Instrumentation of caller and callee to capture outgoing calls

Each object has its own trace of incoming or outgoing calls, but the trace is not stored within the object. Instead, trace data associated with an object is stored in global hash tables. Since Java's `Object.hashCode()` method is unreliable for object identification, each object creates a unique integer for identification in its constructor. Keeping trace data outside of objects has the advantage that they can be accessed by foreign objects, which is essential for outgoing calls.

For an incoming call, the callee simply adds its name and signature to *its own* trace. But for an outgoing call, the callee must add its name, signature, and class to the trace of the *caller*. To do so, it needs to access the caller's trace using the caller's id.

Fig. 4 presents a small example illustrating instrumentation for tracing outgoing calls. (For the sake of readability, we provide Java code instead of byte code.) Statements added during the instrumentation are shown in bold face. Prior to the invocation of `Callee.method()` in method `Caller.call()`, the id of the caller is stored in the `Tracer`. At the very start of `Callee.method()`, `Tracer.addCall()` adds the method id of `Callee.message()` to the trace of the calling object—the one which was previously stored in the `Tracer`. Hence, `addCall()` only receives the message id—an integer key associated with a method, its class, and signature.

The combined trace of all method calls for all objects quickly reaches Gigabytes in size and cannot be kept in main memory, but writing it to a file would induce a huge runtime overhead. We therefore do not keep the original trace but compute the sequence set for each class online—while tracing. Sequence sets are small (see next Section 3.5 for a discussion of the overhead), kept in memory, and emitted when the program quits.

To compute the sequence set of a class online, each object maintains a window for the last k (incoming or outgoing) calls, which is advanced by code in the prolog of the called method. In addition, a sequence set is associated with every traced class. Whenever a method finds a new sequence—a new window of calls—it adds the sequence to the set of the class. Finally, each class emits its sequence set in XML format.

After the program has quit, we use offline tools to read the sequence sets and analyze them. For our experimental setup, we read them into a relational database.

Computing and emitting sequence sets rather than the original trace has a few disadvantages. To compute sequence sets online, the window size must be fixed for a program run, where sequence sets for many window sizes could be computed offline from a raw trace. While a trace is ordered, a sequence set is not. We therefore lose some of the trace's inherent notion of time.

3.5   Overhead

To validate our claim that capturing call-sequence sets is a lightweight method, we instrumented and traced the programs from the SPEC JVM 98 benchmark suite (SPEC, 1998). We compared the overhead with JCoverage (Morgan, 2004), a tool for coverage analysis that, like ours, works on Java bytecode, and whose results can point to defects.

The SPEC JVM 98 benchmark suite is a collection of Java programs, deployed as 543 class files, with a total size of 1.48 megabytes. Instrumenting them for tracing incoming calls with a window size of 5 on a 3 GHz x86/Linux machine with 1 GB of main memory took 14.2 seconds wall-clock time. This amounts to about 100 kB or 38 class files per second. The instrumented class files increased in size by 26%. Instrumentation thus takes an affordable overhead, even in an interactive setting.

Running an instrumented program takes longer and requires more memory than the original program. Table 1 summarizes the overhead *factors* of the instrumented program relative to the memory consumption and run time of the original program.

The two ray tracers `raytrace` and `mtrt` demonstrate some challenges: tracing them required 380 MB of main memory because they instantiate ten thousands of objects of class `Point`, each of which was traced. This exhausted the main memory, which led to paging and to long run times.

The overheads for memory consumption and runtime varied by two orders of magnitude. At first sight, this may seem prohibitive—even when the overhead was comparable or lower than for JCoverage. We attribute the high overhead in part to the nature of the SPEC JVM 98, which is intended to evaluate Java virtual machines—most programs in the suite are CPU bound and tracing affects them more than, say, I/O-intensive programs.

Table 1. Overhead measured for heap size and time while tracing incoming calls (with window size 5) for the SPEC JVM 98 benchmark. The overhead of our approach (and JCoverage in comparison) is expressed as a factor relative to the original program. The rightmost columns show the number of sequences and the size of their gzip-compressed XML representation

| Program | Memory | | | Time | | | Sequences | |
	original MB	JCoverage factor	**our approach** factor	original seconds	JCoverage factor	**our approach** factor	count	XML KB
check	1.4	1.2	1.1	0.14	10.0	1.5	113	3
compress	30.4	1.2	2.2	5.93	1.7	59.8	85	3
jess	12.1	2.1	17.6	2.17	257.1	98.2	1704	37
raytrace	14.2	1.5	22.7	1.93	380.8	541.6	1489	34
db	20.4	1.4	1.2	11.31	1.5	1.2	127	3
javac	29.8	1.5	1.2	5.46	45.7	31.4	15326	334
mpegaudio	12.8	1.6	1.2	5.96	1.2	27.9	587	13
mtrt	18.4	1.4	18.2	2.06	367.9	574.8	1579	36
jack	13.6	1.7	1.7	2.32	40.5	6.3	1261	28
average		1.5	7.5		122.9	149.2	2477	55
AspectJ	41.8	1.4	1.4	2.37	3.3	3.0	13920	301

The database db and the mpegaudio decoder benchmarks, for instance, show a small overhead. When we traced the AspectJ compiler for the example in Section 1 (with window size 5), we also observed a modest overhead and consider these more typical for our approach.

4   Relating Call Anomalies to Failures

As described in Section 3.2, a program run yields one sequence set per class. These sequence sets now must be compared across multiple runs—or, more precisely, across passing and failing runs. Our basic claim is that a defective class shows a substantially different sequence set in a passing run than in a failing run. We therefore *rank* classes such that classes whose sequence sets differ the most between passing and failing runs get the highest priority.

For ranking classes we consider *one failing* run r and n *passing* runs $r^1, \ldots, r^n$, where $n \geq 1$. We take into account only one failing run because any additional failing run could be caused by a different defect—something we don't know. We do know, however, that all passing runs are equivalent in the sense that they don't reveal the defect.

Each passing and failing run of a class C is a set of call sequences: r is the set of call sequences observed in the failing run, and so on. Since we consider only one class at a time, we don't mention C explicitly and write r instead of $r\,(C)$. As an example, we consider five sequences in three passing runs and one failing run:

$$
\begin{aligned}
r &= \{v, w, y, z\} \qquad r^2 = \{x, y, z\} \\
r^1 &= \{v, y, z\} \qquad\quad r^3 = \{v, w, z\}
\end{aligned}
$$

To characterize an individual sequence s in absolute terms, we define the number of passing runs $\#$ that contain s, and dual to it, the number of failing runs $\#$:

$$
\# (s) = \left| \bigcup_{i=1}^{n} \{r^i \mid s \in r^i\} \right|
$$

$$
\# (s) = |\{r \mid s \in r \}|
$$

In relative terms, a call sequence s is characterized by the fraction $\# (s)/n$ of passing runs where it was observed, and the fraction $\# (s)/1$ of failing runs. These two constitute the *weight* $w(s)$ of a sequence:

$$
w(s) = \left| \frac{\# (s)}{1} - \frac{\# (s)}{n} \right|
$$

The weight of a sequence denotes its responsibility for a fault, expressed as a number in the range 0 to 1. It depends on which sets the sequence is contained in. Figure 5 shows weights for three passing runs and one failing run.

For our example we obtain the counts and weights shown on the right side in Fig. 5. Sequence z is common to all runs and thus has a weight of 0. Sequence w, on the other hand, was observed in the failing run, but only in one out of three passing runs. This earns it a high weight of $2/3$. No sequence was observed only in the failing run. The

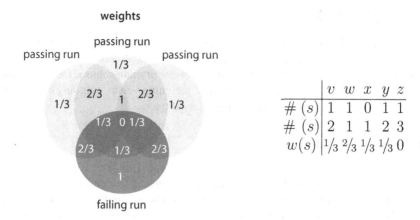

Fig. 5. The weight of a sequence depends on the number of passing and failing runs where it was found. The right side shows the weights for the example of five sequences found in three passing and one failing run

weight of a sequence is high when it is observed in the failing run but in none or few of the passing runs: we then found a "new" sequence in the failing run. Likewise, the weight is high when we find a sequence in many passing runs, but not in the failing run: the sequence is then "missing" in the failing run. A high weight thus is a witness for a different behavior of a class in passing and failing runs. Missing and new sequences are treated dually because a defect could be caused by an extra call, as well as a missing call.

Conversely, the weight of a sequence is low, when it was found in many passing runs as well as in the failing run: we then observed a "common" sequence. It is a witness for similar behavior in passing and failing runs.

Note that the weight of a sequence depends heavily on the number of passing runs. To gain importance, a sequence must be present in many of them. Passing runs thus should be related and show common sequences, but selecting a few unrelated runs does not hurt.

Classes with a similar behavior in passing and failing runs contain mostly light sequences, where the prime suspects are those with many heavy sequences. To identify them, we define the *average sequence weight* for a class:

$$W(C) = \frac{1}{|r|} \sum_{s \in r} w(s) \qquad \text{where } r = r \cup r^1 \cup \cdots \cup r^n$$

In our example, the average sequence weight is $1/3$. Because the average sequence weight is independent from the number of sequences observed for a class, we can compare it across classes. The average sequence weight is thus a measure for the importance of a class. When we rank classes by it, classes ranked to the top have a high average weight and are likely to contain a defect. To validate this claim, we conducted two experiments.

5   A Case Study

As described in Section 4, we rank classes based on their average sequence weight and claim that a large weight indicates a defect. To evaluate our rankings, we studied them in an experiment, with the NanoXML parser as our main subject. Our experiments evaluate class rankings along three main axes: incoming versus outgoing calls, various window sizes, and class-based versus object-based traces.

5.1   Object of Study

NanoXML is a non-validating XML parser implemented in Java, for which Do et al. (2004) provide an extensive test suite. NanoXML comes in five development versions[1], each comprising between 16 and 23 classes, and a total number of 33 known faults (Table 2). These faults were discovered during the development process, or seeded by Do and others. Each fault can be activated individually, such that there are 33 variants of NanoXML with a single fault.

Table 2. Characteristics of NanoXML, the subject of our controlled experiment

				Tests		
Version	Classes	LOC	Faults	All	Failing	Drivers
1	16	4334	7	214	160	79
2	19	5806	7	214	57	74
3	21	7185	10	216	63	76
5	23	7646	9	216	174	76
total		24971	33		474	

Faults and test cases are related by a fault matrix: for any given fault and test case, the matrix tells whether the test case uncovers the fault. Related test cases share the same driver, which provides general infrastructure for a test.

5.2   Experimental Setup

Our experiment simulates the following situation: for a fixed program, a programmer has one or more passing test cases, and one failing test case. Based on traces of the passing and failing runs, our techniques ranks the classes of the program. The ranking aims to place the faulty class as high as possible.

In our experiment, we know the class that contains the defect (our techniques, of course, do not); therefore, we can assess the ranking. We express the quality of a ranking as the *search length*—the number of classes above the faulty class in the ranking. The best possible ranking places the faulty class at the top (with a search length of zero).

---

[1] We could not use Version 4 because it lacks known faults for experiments.

To rank classes, we needed at least one passing run for every failing run. However, we wanted to avoid comparing totally unrelated program runs. For each ranking we therefore selected a set of program runs from the suite of programs that met the following conditions:

- We analyze a version of NanoXML with *one known defect*, which is located in a single class.
- As *failing run*, we used a test case that uncovered the known defect.
- As *passing runs*, we selected *all* test cases that did not uncover the known defect.
- All test cases for passing and failing runs must use the *same test driver*. This limits the number of passing runs to those that are semantically related to the failing run.

Altogether, we had 386 such sets (Table 2). The test suite contains 88 more failing runs for which we could not find any passing run. This can happen, for example, when a fault always causes a program to crash such that no passing run can be established.

For each of the failing runs with one or more related passing runs, we traced their classes, computed their sequence sets, and ranked the classes according to their average sequence weight. The rankings were repeated in several configurations:

- Rankings based on class and object traces (recall Section 3.2)
- Rankings based on incoming and outgoing calls (recall Section 3.3).
- Rankings based on 10 window sizes: 1 to 10.

We compared the results of all configurations to find the one that minimizes the search length, and thus provides the best recommendations for defect localization.

5.3   Threats to Validity

Our experiments are not exhaustive—many more variations of the experiment are possible. These variations include other ways to rate sequences, or to trace with class-specific window sizes rather than a universal size. Likewise, we did not evaluate programs with multiple known defects or defects whose fix affects several classes.

The search lengths reported in our results are abstract numbers that don't make potential mistakes obvious. We validated our methods when possible by exploiting known invariants, for example:

- To validate the bytecode instrumentation, we generated Java programs with statically known call graphs and, hence, known sequence sets. We verified that these were indeed produced by our instrumentation.
- When tracing with a window size of one, the resulting sequences for a class are identical for object- and class-based traces: any method called (or initiated) on the object level is recorded in a class-level trace, and vice versa. Hence, the rankings are the same; object- and class-based traces show no difference in search length.

5.4   Discussion of Results

Table 3 summarizes the average search lengths of our rankings for NanoXML, based on different configurations: incoming versus outgoing calls, various window sizes, and

Table 3. Evaluation of class rankings. A number indicates the average number of classes in atop the faulty class in a ranking. The two rightmost columns indicate these numbers for a random ranking when (1) considering only executed classes, (2) all classes

| | Incoming Calls | | | | | | | | | | | |
| | Window Size | | | | | | | | | | Random Guess | |
Trace	1	2	3	4	5	6	7	8	9	10	Executed	All
Object	3.66	3.74	4.08	4.07	4.10	4.02	3.91	3.67	3.55	3.49	4.78	9.22
Class	3.66	3.71	3.97	4.05	3.97	4.04	3.97	3.90	3.86	3.85	4.78	9.22

| | Outgoing Calls | | | | | | | | | | | |
| | Window Size | | | | | | | | | | Random Guess | |
Trace	1	2	3	4	5	6	7	8	9	10	Executed	All
Object	2.53	2.31	2.19	2.17	2.04	2.00	1.98	2.12	2.15	2.14	4.78	9.22
Class	2.53	2.35	2.22	2.14	2.03	2.04	2.03	2.02	2.22	2.25	4.78	9.22

rankings based on object- and class-based traces. The search length is the number of classes atop of the faulty class in a ranking.

For a ranking to be useful, it must be at least better than a random ranking. Each search length in Table 3 is an average over 386 program runs (or rankings). On average, each run utilizes 19.45 classes from which 10.56 are actually executed (excluding the test driver). Random placing of the faulty class would result in an average search length of $(19.45 - 1)/2 = 9.22$ classes, and 4.78, respectively.

All rankings in our experiment are noticeably better than random rankings. They are better even if a programmer had had the additional knowledge of which classes were never executed.

> *Comparing sequences of passing and failing runs is effective in locating defects.*

Sequences vs. Coverage. Previous work by Jones et al. (2002) has used coverage analysis to rank source code statements: statements more often executed in failing runs than in passing runs rank higher. Since we are ranking classes, the two approaches are not directly comparable.

Ranking classes based on incoming calls with a window size of one is identical to method coverage: the sequence set of a class holds exactly those methods of the class that were called, hence executed. The corresponding search length of 3.66 is the smallest in the table for incoming calls. This suggests that incoming calls perform worse than coverage analysis for defect localization.

The picture is reversed for outgoing calls. Here the search length for a window size of one is the highest in the table. Sequences of calls thus perform better than individual calls.

> *Incoming calls provide no help for finding defects. Comparing sequences of length 2 or greater always performs better than sequences of length 1 for outging calls.*

Classes vs. Objects. Tracing on the object level (rather on the simpler class level) offered no advantage for incoming calls, and only a slight advantage for outgoing calls. We attribute this to the few objects NanoXML instantiates per class and the absence of threads. Both would lead to increased non-deterministic interleaving of calls on the class level, which in turn would lead to artificial differences between runs.

> *Object-based traces are at least slightly better defect locators than class-based traces. For multi-threaded programs, object-based traces should yield a greater advantage.*

Window Size. Incoming calls sequences show no strict relation between window size and search length. There is a trend of an increasing search length when going from a window size of one to 5, and a trend of decreasing search length when moving from 5 to 10.

Outgoing calls show a clear and opposite trend: search lengths are the shortest for window sizes around 7 and increase towards smaller and wider windows. Moving from a window size of one to a window size of 7 reduces the search length by 0.5 classes. This supports our claim that longer outgoing call sequences capture essential control flow of a program. Moving towards wider windows probably does not pay off because increasingly fewer long-living objects actually can fill such windows.

> *Medium-sized windows, collecting 3 to 8 calls, provide the best predictive power.*

Outgoing vs. Incoming Calls. Outgoing calls predict faults better than incoming calls. The search length for rankings based on outgoing calls are smaller than those based on incoming calls. Even the worst result for outgoing calls (2.53 for window size of 1) beats the best result for incoming calls (3.66 for window size of 1). This strongly supports our claim (3): the caller is more likely to be defective than the callee.

The inferiority of incoming calls is not entirely surprising: traces for incoming calls show how an object (or a class) is used. A deviation in the failing run from the passing runs indicates that a class is used differently. But the class is not responsible for its usage—its clients are. Therefore, different usage does not correlate with faults.

This is different for outgoing calls, which show how an object (or a class) is implemented. For any deviation here the class at hand is responsible and thus more likely to contain a fault.

> *Outgoing calls locate defects much better than incoming calls.*

Benefits to the Programmer. Tracing outgoing calls with a window size of 6, the average search length for a ranking was 2.00. On the average, a programmer must thus inspect two classes before finding the faulty class—that is, 18.9% of 10.56 executed classes, or 8.7% of all 23 classes.

Fig. 6 shows a cumulative plot of the search length distribution. Using a window of size 7, the defective class is immediately identified in 39% of all test runs (zero search length). In 47% of all test runs, the programmer needs to examine at most one false positive (search length = 1) before identifying the defect.

Because NanoXML is relatively small, each class comprises a sizeable amount of the total application. As could be seen in the example of AspectJ, large applications

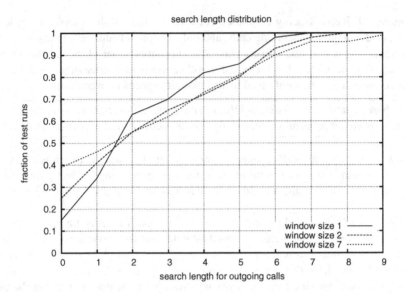

Fig. 6. Distribution of search length for outgoing calls in NanoXML. Using a window size of 7, the defective class is pinpointed (search length 0) in 39% of all test runs

may exhibit vastly better ratios. We also expect larger applications to show a greater separation of concerns, such that the number of classes which contribute to a failure does not grow with the total number of classes. We therefore believe that the results of our controlled experiment are on the conservative side.

> In NanoXML, the defective class is immediately identified in 39% of all test runs. On average, a programmer using our technique must inspect 19% of the executed classes (9% of all classes) before finding the defect.

6   Does it Scale?

We have complemented the evaluation of our method with a study of the AspectJ compiler (Kiczales et al., 2001). It differs from NanoXML mainly in its size: AspectJ 1.1.1 consists of 979 classes, representing 112,376 lines of code. Unlike NanoXML, AspectJ does not come pre-packed with a set of defects, and therefore it was not possible to use AspectJ in a systematic evaluation. However, the AspectJ developers have collected bug reports and provide a source code repository that documents how bugs were fixed. From these repositories, we reconstructed passing and failing test cases for our evaluation.

In order to obtain results comparable with our evaluation using NanoXML, we restricted ourself to bugs whose fixes involved only one Java class. Altogether, there are 6 such bugs in the AspectJ bug database, which are shown in Table 4.

For each bug in Table 4, we constructed one passing and one failing run. We traced them for outgoing calls and ranked their classes accordingly.

Table 4. Bugs in AspectJ used for the evaluation. A *Bug ID* refers to the bug description in the AspectJ bug database at http://bugs.eclipse.org/

			Size (LOC)	
Bug ID	Version	Defective Class	Class	Fix
29665	1.1b4	org.aspectj.weaver.bcel.BcelShadow	1901	20
29691	1.1b4	org.aspectj.weaver.patterns.ReferencePointcut	294	4
29693	1.1b4	org.aspectj.weaver.bcel.BcelShadow	1901	8
30168	1.1b4	org.aspectj.ajdt.internal.compiler.ast.ThisJoinPointVisitor	225	20
43194	1.1.1	org.aspectj.weaver.patterns.ReferencePointcut	299	4
53981	1.1.1	org.aspectj.ajdt.internal.compiler.ast.Proceed	133	19

Table 5. Evaluation of class rankings for AspectJ. A number indicates the average *search length*: the number of classes atop of the faulty class in a ranking. The two rightmost columns indicate these numbers for a random ranking when (1) considering only executed classes, (2) all classes

	Window Size										Random Guess	
	1	2	3	4	5	6	7	8	9	10	Executed	All
Object	32.4	31.8	30.8	10.2	8.6	23.4	22.6	23.8	24.4	24.0	209	272
Class	32.4	32.2	34.8	12.8	12.4	25.2	24.8	25.2	25.2	25.6	209	272

Our results for window sizes up to 10 are shown in Table 5. The results confirm our previous findings for outgoing calls from the evaluation with NanoXML as subject:

– Rankings based on outgoing calls perform better than random rankings.
– Object-based rankings perform slightly better than class-based rankings.
– Medium-sized windows of 4–7 calls performs best; shorter or wider windows lead to an increased search length. Defect localization benefits from the additional context provided compared to a window size of one.

The difference in search length between a random ranking and a ranking produced by our method is much greater for AspectJ than for NanoXML. Therefore, the benefit for the programmer is even greater: Using a window size of 5, our method on average requires the programmer to examine only 9 of 979 classes (i.e. 0.92% of all classes) until spotting the defect. Again, these results do not necessarily generalize to AspectJ, or to other applications, but they indicate the potential of the approach; they also show that the approach indeed can scale to larger applications.

In our evaluation of AspectJ, we did not consider incoming calls, since they did not prove useful for the NanoXML subject. Also, Table 5 does not take into account the ranking for bug #29665. While bug #29665 is a real bug, the call sequence sets of the defective class were identical in passing and failing runs for all window sizes. A closer inspection of the fix for this bug revealed that the defective method incorrectly returns the same value for the passing and failing run, which is why the defect does not induce a different call sequence. Thus, our method is blind to this defect and cannot localize it.

> *Defect localization using call-sequence sets scales well to the AspectJ compiler (with excellent results) and is likely to scale to other real-world applications.*

7   Related Work

We are by no means the first researchers who compare multiple runs, or analyze function call sequences. The related work can be grouped into the following categories:

Comparing Multiple Runs. The hypothesis that a fault correlates with differences in program traces, relative to the trace of a correct program, was first stated by Reps et al. (1997) and later confirmed by Harrold et al. (1998). The work of Jones et al. (2002) explicitly compares coverage and thus is the work closest to ours. Jones et al. try to locate an error in a program based on the statement coverage produced by several passing and one failing run. A statement is considered more likely to be erroneous the more often it is executed in a failing run rather than in a passing run. In their evaluation, Jones et al. find that in programs with one fault the one faulty statement within a program is almost certainly marked as "likely faulty", but so is also 5% to 15% of correct code. For programs with multiple faults, this degrades to 5% to 20% with higher variation. Like ours, this approach is lightweight, fully automatic and broadly applicable—but as demonstrated in the evaluation, sequences have a significantly better predictive power.

Intrusion Detection. Our idea of investigating sequences rather than simply coverage was inspired by Forrest et al. (1997) and Hofmeyr et al. (1998)'s work on *intrusion detection*. They traced the system calls of server applications like `sendmail`, `ftpd`, or `lpd` and used the sliding-window approach to abstract them as sequence sets (n-tuples of system calls, where $n = 6, \ldots, 10$). In a training phase, they learned the set from normal behavior of the server application; after that, an unrecognized sequence indicated a possible intrusion. As a variation, they also learned sequence that did not match the normal behavior and flagged an intrusion if that sequence was later matched by an application. Intrusion detection is considerably more difficult than defect localization because it has to *predict* anomalous behavior, where we *know* that a program run is anomalous after it failed a test. We found the simplicity of the idea, implementation, and the modest run-time cost appealing. In contrast to their work, though, our approach specifically exploits object orientation and is the first to analyze sequences for defect localization.

Learning Automata. Sekar et al. (2001) note a serious issue in Forrest et al. (1997)'s approach: to keep traces tractable, the window size n must be small. But small windows fail to capture relations between calls in a sequence that are n or more calls apart. To overcome this, the authors propose to *learn finite-state automata* from system call sequences instead and provide an algorithm. The interesting part is that Sekar et al. learn automata from traces where they annotate each call with the caller; thus calls by two different callers now become distinguishable. Using these more context-rich traces, their automata produced about 10 times fewer false positives than the n-gram approach. Learning automata from object-specific sequences is an interesting idea for future work.

Learning APIs. While we are trying to locate defects relative to a failing run, Ammons et al. (2002) try to locate defects relative to *API invariants* learned from correct runs: they observe how an API is used by its clients and learn a finite-state automaton that describes the client's behavior. If in the future a client violates this behavior, it is flagged with an error. A client is only required during the learning phase and the learned invariants can later be used to validate clients that did not even exist during the learning phase. However, as Ammons et al. point out, learning API invariants requires a lot of effort—in particular because context-sensitive information such as resource handles have to be identified and matched manually. With object-specific sequences, as in our approach, such a context comes naturally and should yield better automata with less effort.

Data Anomalies. Rather than focusing on diverging control flow, one may also focus on differing data. *Dynamic invariants,* pioneered by Ernst et al. (2001), is a predicate for a variable's value that has held for all program runs during a training phase. If the predicate is later violated by a value in another program run this may signal an error. Learning dynamic invariants takes a huge machine-learning apparatus and is far from lightweight both in time and space. While Pytlik et al. (2003) have not been able to detect failure-related anomalies using dynamic invariants, a related lightweight technique by Hangal and Lam (2002) found defects in four Java applications. In general, techniques that detect anomalies in data can complement techniques that detect anomalies in control flow and vice versa.

Statistical Sampling. In order to make defect localization affordable for production code in the field, Liblit et al. (2003) suggest statistical sampling: Rather than collecting all data of all runs, they focus on exceptional behavior—as indicated by exceptions being raised or unusual values being returned—but only for a *sampled set.* If such events frequently occur together with failures (i.e. for a large set of users and runs), one eventually obtains a set of anomalies that statistically correlate with the failure. Our approach requires just two instrumented runs to localize defects, but can be easily extended to collect samples in the field.

Isolating Failure Causes. To localize defects, one of the most effective approaches is isolating *cause transitions,* as described by Cleve and Zeller (2005). Again, the basic idea is to compare passing and failing runs, but in addition, the delta debugging technique generates and tests *additional runs* to isolate failure-causing variables in the program state (Zeller, 2002). A cause transition occurs at a statement where one variable ceases to be a cause, and another one begins; these are places where cause-effect chains to the failure originate (and thus likely defects). Due to the systematic generation of additional runs, this technique is precise, but also demanding—in particular, one needs an automated test and a means to extract and compare program states. In contrast, collecting call sequences is far easier to apply and deploy.

8   Conclusion and Consequences

Sequences of method calls locate defective classes with a high probability. Our evaluation also revealed that per-object sequences are better predictors of defects than per-class or global sequences, and that the caller is significantly more likely to be defective than the callee. In contrast to previous approaches detecting anomalies in API usage, our technique exploits object orientation, as it collects method call sequences per object; therefore, the approach is fully generic and need not be adapted to a specific API. These are the results of this paper.

On the practical side, the approach is easily applicable to arbitrary Java programs, as it is based on byte code instrumentation, and as the overhead of collecting sequences is comparable to measuring coverage. No additional infrastructure such as automated tests or debugging information is required; the approach can thus be used for software in the field as well as third-party software.

Besides general issues such as performance or ease of use, our future work will concentrate on the following topics:

Further Evaluation. The number of Java programs that can be used for controlled experiments (i.e. with known defects, automated tests that reveal these defects, and changes that fix the defects) is still too limited. As more such programs become available (Do et al., 2004), we want to gather further experience.

Fine-Grained Anomalies. Right now, we are identifying *classes* as being defect-prone. Since our approach is based on comparing *methods,* though, we could relate differing sequences to sets of methods and thus further increase precision. Another interesting option is to identify anomalies in sequences of basic blocks rather than method calls, thus focusing on individual statements.

Sampled Calls. Rather than collecting every single method call, our approach could easily be adapted to *sample* only a subset of calls—for instance, only the method calls of a specific class, or only every 100th sequence (Liblit et al., 2003). This would allow to use the technique in production code and thus collect failure-related sequences in the field.

Exploiting Object Orientation. Our approach is among the first that explicitly exploits object orientation for collecting sequences. Being object-aware might also be beneficial to related fields such as intrusion detection or mining specifications.

Integration with Experimental Techniques. Anomalies in method calls translate into specific objects and specific moments in time that are more interesting than others. These objects and moments in time could be good initial candidates for identifying failure-inducing program state (Zeller, 2002).

An Eclipse Plugin. Last but not least, we are currently turning our prototype into an Eclipse plugin called AMPLE (for "Analyzing Method Patterns to Locate Errors"). As soon as a JUnit test fails, AMPLE displays a list showing the most likely defective classes at the top—as in the AspectJ example (Fig. 7). We plan to make AMPLE publicly available in the second half of this year. For future and related work regarding defect localization, see

http://www.st.cs.uni-sb.de/dd/

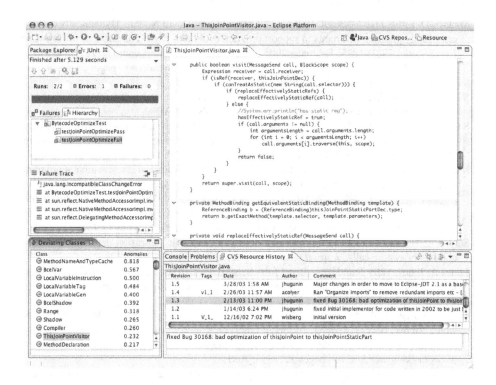

Fig. 7. For the AspectJ bug of Section 2, Eclipse ranks likely defective classes (bottom left)

Acknowledgments. Gregg Rothermel made the NanoXML test suite accessible. Tom Zimmermann provided precious insights into the AspectJ history. Holger Cleve, Stephan Neuhaus, and the anonymous reviewers provided valuable comments on earlier revisions of this paper.

Bibliography

Glenn Ammons, Rastislav Bodík, and Jim Larus. Mining specifications. In *Conference Record of POPL'02: The 29th ACM SIGPLAN-SIGACT Symposium on Principles of Programming Languages*, pages 4–16, Portland, Oregon, January 16–18, 2002.

Holger Cleve and Andreas Zeller. Locating causes of program failures. In *Proc. 27th International Conference of Software Engineering (ICSE 2005)*, St. Louis, USA, 2005. to appear.

Markus Dahm. Byte code engineering with the JavaClass API. Technical Report B-17-98, Freie Universität Berlin, Institut für Informatik, Berlin, Germany, July 07 1999. URL http://www.inf.fu-berlin.de/~dahm/JavaClass/ftp/report.ps.gz.

Hyunsook Do, Sebastian Elbaum, and Gregg Rothermel. Infrastructure support for controlled experimentation with software testing and regression testing techniques. In *International Symposium on Empirical Software Engineering*, pages 60–70, Redondo Beach, California, August 2004.

Michael D. Ernst, Jake Cockrell, William G. Griswold, and David Notkin. Dynamically discovering likely program invariants to support program evolution. *IEEE Transactions on Software Engineering*, 27(2):1–25, February 2001. A previous version appeared in *ICSE '99, Proceedings of the 21st International Conference on Software Engineering*, pages 213–224, Los Angeles, CA, USA, May 19–21, 1999.

Stephanie Forrest, Steven A. Hofmeyr, and Anil Somayaji. Computer immunology. *Communications of the ACM*, 40(10):88–96, October 1997. ISSN 0001-0782.

Sudheendra Hangal and Monica S. Lam. Tracking down software bugs using automatic anomaly detection. In *Proceedings of the 24th International Conference on Software Engineering (ICSE-02)*, pages 291–301, New York, May 19–25 2002. ACM Press.

Mary Jean Harrold, Gregg Rothermel, Rui Wu, and Liu Yi. An empirical investigation of program spectra. In *ACM SIGPLAN-SIGSOFT Workshop on Program Analysis for Software Tools and Engineering (PASTE'98), ACM SIGPLAN Notices*, pages 83–90, Montreal, Canada, July 1998. Published as ACM SIGPLAN-SIGSOFT Workshop on Program Analysis for Software Tools and Engineering (PASTE'98), ACM SIGPLAN Notices, volume 33, number 7.

Steven A. Hofmeyr, Stephanie Forrest, and Somayaji Somayaji. Intrusion detection using sequences of system calls. *Journal of Computer Security*, 6(3):151–180, 1998.

James A. Jones, Mary Jean Harrold, and John Stasko. Visualization of test information to assist fault localization. In *Proc. International Conference on Software Engineering (ICSE)*, pages 467–477, Orlando, Florida, May 2002.

Gregor Kiczales, Erik Hilsdale, Jim Hugunin, Mik Kersten, Jeffrey Palm, and William G. Griswold. An overview of AspectJ. In Jorgen Lindskov Knudsen, editor, *Proceedings of the 15th European Conference on Object-Oriented Programming (ECOOP)*, volume 2072 of *Lecture Notes in Computer Science*, pages 327–353, 2001.

Ben Liblit, Alex Aiken, Alice X. Zheng, and Michael I. Jordan. Bug isolation via remote program sampling. In *Proc. of the SIGPLAN 2003 Conference on Programming Language Design and Implementation (PLDI)*, San Diego, California, June 2003.

Peter Morgan. JCoverage 1.0.5 GPL, 2004. URL http://www.jcoverage.com/.

Brock Pytlik, Manos Renieris, Shriram Krishnamurthi, and Steven Reiss. Automated fault localization using potential invariants. In Michiel Ronsse, editor, *Proc. Fifth Int. Workshop on Automated and Algorithmic Debugging (AADEBUG)*, Ghent, Belgium, September 2003. URL http://xxx.lanl.gov/html/cs.SE/0309027.

Steven P. Reiss and Manos Renieris. Encoding program executions. In *Proceedings of the 23rd International Conference on Software Engeneering (ICSE-01)*, pages 221–232, Los Alamitos, California, May12–19 2001. IEEE Computer Society.

Thomas Reps, Thomas Ball, Manuvir Das, and Jim Larus. The use of program profiling for software maintenance with applications to the year 2000 problem. In M. Jazayeri and H. Schauer, editors, *Proceedings of the Sixth European Software Engineering Conference (ESEC/FSE 97)*, pages 432–449. Lecture Notes in Computer Science Nr. 1013, Springer–Verlag, September 1997.

R. Sekar, M. Bendre, D. Dhurjati, and P. Bollineni. A fast automaton-based method for detecting anomalous program behaviors. In Francis M. Titsworth, editor, *Proceedings of the 2001 IEEE Symposium on Security and Privacy (S&P-01)*, pages 144–155, Los Alamitos, CA, May 14–16 2001. IEEE Computer Society.

SPEC. SPEC JVM 98 benchmark suite. Standard Performance Evaluation Corporation, 1998.

Andreas Zeller. Isolating cause-effect chains from computer programs. In William G. Griswold, editor, *Proceedings of the Tenth ACM SIGSOFT Symposium on the Foundations of Software Engineering (FSE-02)*, volume 27, 6 of *Software Engineering Notes*, pages 1–10, New York, November 18–22 2002. ACM Press.

Extending JML for Modular Specification and Verification of Multi-threaded Programs

•• win • o•• ¶••••• [1], M••••• w Dwy•• [2], • o•• •• Fl• n••• n [3], Jo• n H•• liff [1],
• ••y T. L••v•n• [4], •n• • o•• y [1]

[1] Department of Computing and Information Sciences, Kansas State University
{edwin, hatcliff, robby}@cis.ksu.edu
[2] Department of Computer Science and Engineering, University of Nebraska-Lincoln
dwyer@cse.unl.edu
[3] Computer Science Department, University of California at Santa Cruz
cormac@cs.ucsc.edu
[4] Department of Computer Science, Iowa State University
leavens@cs.iastate.edu

Abstract. The Java Modeling Language (JML) is a formal specification language for Java that allows developers to specify rich software contracts for interfaces and classes, using pre- and postconditions and invariants. Although JML has been widely studied and has robust tool support based on a variety of automated verification technologies, it shares a problem with many similar object-oriented specification languages—it currently only deals with sequential programs. In this paper, we extend JML to allow for effective specification of multi-threaded Java programs. The new constructs rely on the non-interference notion of *method atomicity*, and allow developers to specify locking and other non-interference properties of methods. Atomicity enables effective specification of method pre- and postconditions and supports Hoare-style modular reasoning about methods. Thus the new constructs mesh well with JML's existing features. We validate the specification language design by specifying the behavior of a number of complex Java classes designed for use in multi-threaded programs. We also demonstrate that it is amenable to automated verification using model checking technology.

1 Introduction

T•• ••• o• •i•• •o•••••-l•v•l ••••i•••ion l•n••••••• •o• •x••••in• •o•••••n•••
••o•••i•• o• o• j•••-o•i•n••• ••o•••• • i• ••owin• in ••••i•. S••••i•••ion l•n-
•••••• ••• •• ••• J•v• Mo••lin• L•n••••• (JML) [1,•,3,•] •n• S•••# [5]
••ovi••• • wi•• ••n•• o• li•••-w•i••• •nno••ion• (•.•., ••••i•yin• non-n•lln•••
o• v••i••l•• o• •••••••n•• •y••) •• w•ll •• •on••••••• •o• w•i•in• ••••i•••ion• o•
•• ll •• n••ion•l •••• vio•• o• •l••• i• •l•• •n••ion• •••• ••n •• •••••••• •y • v•-
•i••y o• v••i•••ion •••• nolo•i•• in•l••in• ••••i• •n•ly•i•, ••n-•i• • • oni•o•in•,
• o••l •••••• in•, •n• •••o••• -••ovin•. JML i• • ••••vio••l in••••••• ••••i•••-
•ion l•n••••• ••••• llow• ••v•lo••• •o ••••i•y • o•• ••• •yn•••i• •n• •••• vio••l

A.P. Black (Ed.): ECOOP 2005, LNCS 3586, pp. 551–576, 2005.
© Springer-Verlag Berlin Heidelberg 2005

in•••••••• o•• • o••ion o• J•v• •o••. I• •••• o••• ••• •••i•n • y •on•••• ••••• i••
[6] •y in•l••in• no•••ion •o• •••- •n• • o•••on• i•ion• •n• inv••i•n••. JML ••••
J•v•'• •x• •••ion •yn••x •n• •••• •••••• •••o•: • niv••••l (\forall) •n• •xi••n-
•i•l (\exists) •••n•i•••ion ov•• o• j••• in•••n••• •• w•ll •••••i• •y••, ••••• ••
in••••••, •n• •on•••••• •o• •x••••in• •o•••i•• o••••• •llo••••• •••• (••••• ••
\reach w•i•• ••••n• ••• ••• o• o• j•••• ••••••l• ••o• • •••i••l•• ••••••n••).

JML •••••ov•• •o••• n •ff••iv• v••i•l• •o• •in•in• •o•••••• n•• ••• o•
•••••••• •••• • [1] ••••in• •o (•) •x••n• ••• lo•i•l •o•n••ion• o• •••i•••ion
•o•• •li•• n••••• •o••••••in• ••• •n•i••lly •o• •l•x l•n••••• ••••••• ••••
•• • yn•• i• •i•••••, •x•••ion•, •yn•• i• o• j••• ••••ion, •n• (•) ••il• •ool
•••• o•• •o• •••o• •••• •n• •o• •••••-••i••• ••••onin• •• o•• •••l-wo•l• J•v•
•••li•••ion•. How•v••, ••••i•• ••• •••••• o• JML in •••i•yin• ••o•••• • w•i••n
in ••••n•i•l J•v• •n• i•• J•v• •••• •i•l•••, JML' •••• o•• •o• •on•••••n•y "i•
••ill in i•• in••n•y" [•].

Al••o••• • •ny in•••••in• ••o•••• • ••• ••••••n•i•l, ••• fl•xi•ili•y •••• ••-
•o• ••ni•• •on•••••n• ••o•••• • in• in •••• • o• ••••••• • o••l•i•in• ••• ••-
•i•n (•••••• • o••l••i•y), ••n• •••• • o•• • o•••••ly •o• •l•x •y•••• • •••
••o•••• • •• wi•• •o• • •o•• o• •on•••••n•y • o••li•y (• •l•i-•••••••in•, • •l•i-
••o••••in•, •••.). Mo••ov••, • •l•i-••••••in• ••••••ili•i•• ••• •••o• in• • o•• ••-
••••i•l• •o ••o••••• • •••• •in•• l•n••••• li•• J•v• •n• • # ••ovi•• •i•••• l•n-
•••••• ••••o•• •o• ••••••, w•il• o•••• l•n•••••• ••ovi•• •o••i••i•••• ••••o••
vi• li•••i•• (•.•., P• SIX ••••••).

Mo•• •xi••in• ••••i•••ion •n• •••••in• •ool• •o• • •l•i-••••••• ••o•••• •
•o•••• on ••o•••i•• •••• ••••••n• o••••• •on•i•ion•, •••••li•• in• • ••••l•x•l•-
•ion, •n• •i• •l• •v•n• o•••in• •n• ••• •o••l ••o•••i•• (•.•., •••••••in• ••o••
o•••in• o•••ll• •o API•). How•v••, ••y •y•i••lly i•no•• •••on• •n••ion•l ••o•-
••i•• •n• •o• •l•x •••• •••••••• inv••i•n••. T•••• in••••••i•• ••••• ••o• •••
•••ll•n••• o• •••lin• wi•• •••••• in•••••n•• in ••• • •ni•• l••ion o• ••••••
(••••) •••••. • n• ••nno• •i• •ly ••• ly Ho••••-•yl• lo•i•• ••in• • •••o• •••- •n•
•o•••on•i•ion• •o ••••on • o••l••ly, ••••••• • •••o• •x••••ion i• o••n *non-
serial*—••• •••ion• o• o•••• ••••••• • •y in••••••• wi•• ••• ••••••• •x•••in• •••
••••o• •n• •••• ••n••• inv•li• ••••• ••ion• ••••••• in • •••o• •••on• i•ion•
•n• •••••n•••• •••••••• in • o•••on• i•ion•.

D•• •o ••• •••v••iv•n••• o• • •l•i-••••••in• •n• ••• in••••in• ••• o•• • l•i-
•••••••• o• j••-o•i•n••• •o•• in •• ••••••• •n• • i••ion- •n• •••••y-••i•i••l ••-
•li••ion•, i• i• n•••••••y •o •x••n• ••••n•i•l •••i•••ion l•n••••• li•• JML
•o •••• o•• ••••i•••ion •n• ••••onin• ••o••• • •l•i-••••••• ••o•••• •. F•••••-
• o••, ••••• •x••n•ion• ••o•l• •llow •o•• li••-w•i•• •nno•••ion• •n• • o••
•o• •l•••, ••n••ion•l ••••i•••ion•, •n• ••o•l• wo•• wi•• • •l•i•l• •iff••n• •••-
•onin• •ool•. T•i• •••••• ••v•n••• •ow••• ••••• •o•l• •y ••in• ••• •ollowin•
•on••i••ion•:

– W• i••n•i•y •i•••ion• in w•i•• ••• •••••n• JML ••il• •o •n••l• •ff••iv•
   ••••i•••ion •n• • o••l•• ••••onin• •o• • •l•i-••••••• ••o•••• •.
– W• i••n•i•y ••••i•••ion •o•• • •••• w• •n• o•••• •••••••••••• •••v• •o• n•
   ••••l •o• • •l•i-••••••• ••o••••. T•i• in•l•••• (•) v••io•• li•••-w•i••

•nno••ion• •••• ••n •• l•v•••••• •y ••o• •••• ••••in• •••• nolo•i•• •n•
(•) ••• ••• o••o• i•i•y •••i•••ion• •o •••i•v• • o••l•• •••onin• ••o••
• •••o••.

– W• ••ow •ow •o in•••••• •••• •o•• • in•o JML in • w•y •••• •n••l•• •o••
••••onin• ••o•• •••• v•l••• •n• •on••••n•y •on•••n•.

– W• v•li•••• ••• •••i•n o••• i• •n••n••• v•••ion o• JML •y ••in• i• •o •••••i•y
••o••••i•• o• • n•• ••• o• J•v• li•••i•• •••i•n•• •o• •on••••n•y, in•l••in•
• o•• o•••• •on••••n• •••• •••• •••• •l••••• ••o• java.util.concurrent,
w•i•• in•l•••• •o• • v••y in••i•••• •on••••n• J•v• •o•• (••• •• ll •oll•••ion
o• ••••• •••••i••• •x•• •l•• ••• •o•••• on o•• •oj••• w••-•i•• [•]).

– W• •••••li•• •••• ••••• •••i•••ion •o•• •li•• • ••• •• •n••l• •o •ff•••iv•
•••o• •••• v••i•••ion, •y ••ovi•in• •x••i• •n••l ••••l•• o• •••••in• •••••
••in• • v••i•••ion •••• •wo•• ••il• on •o• o• o• Bo•o• •o•w••• • o••l
••••••• (•x••n••• ••o• o•• ••••vio•• wo•• on • o••l •••••in• JML [•] •n•
••o• i•i•y •••i•••ion• [9]).

• •••••••o••• •o•• no• •x•li•i•ly •••l wi•• J•v•'• ••l•x•• • •• o•y• o••l [10],
•n• in•••••• ••••• •• • •••••n•i•l •on•i•••n• • •• o•y• o••l. T• i• ••••• ••ion i•
•o•n• •o• •o•••• • •••• ••• •••• o• •••• •on•i•ion•, •n• ••••-•••••o• ••n ••
v••i••• vi• ••••••••• •n•ly••• [11].

Al•• o••• w ••v• •••• JML •o••i• wo••, w• ••li•v• ••• i•••• •o•l• •l•o ••
•••••••• •o o•••• •••i•••ion l•n••••••• ••• •• S•••# •n• • iff•l. How•v••, w•
l••v• ••••il•• inv••i•••ion o•••• ••••••••ion •o• •••••• wo••.

In ••• n•x• •••••ion, w• •••••i• ••• •••o•l•• • ••••••••• in ••i• wo••, in •••-
•i••l••, ••• li• i••••ion• o• JML •o• •on••••n• ••o•••• •. S•••ion 3 •iv•• ••••-
••o•n• on ••• •on•••• o• ••o• i•i•y, on w•i• o•• •••••o••• i• •••••. S•••ion •
in••o••••• ••• n•w ••• o• •nno•••ion•, •ivin• •x•• •l•• •n• •n ••••••• •n• o•
••• i••••• •••••••• •y •••• •nno•••ion. S•••ion 5 ••• o••• on •n •v•l•••ion o•
••in• JML •x••n•ion• •o •••••i•y J•v• •l•••• •n• o•••••in• •••• ••••i•••ion•
••in• • •••••o• i••• • o••l ••••••. S•••ion 6 ••v•y• •l•••• wo••, •n• S••. •
•on•l•••.

2   The Problem

In ••i• ••••ion w• •i••••• ••• ••• •n•i•l •n• •x•••••iv•n••• ••o•l•• • ••••• n•••
•o •• •olv•• •o •llow •ff•••iv• •••i•••ion •n• •••onin• ••o••• o•• •••• v•l•••
•n• ••o••• •••••• •••vio• in • • •l•i-••••••• ••o••••.

2.1 Interference

In•••••••n•• ••••••• ••o•l•• ••••• •ff••• • o••l•• ••••onin• ••o••••• v•l••• in
• •l•i-•••••••• ••o•••• •. T•••• ••• •n•i•l •o•l•• • •••• •••• ill••••••• •y •n
•x•• •l•.

• on•i••• ••• • •••o• in Fi•. 1. T•i• i• • • •••o• ••o• • •on••••n• lin•••
••••• •l•••, •n• i• •••••••• ••o• L••'• •oo• [1•]. T•i• • •••o• •x••••• •n •l•-
• •n• ••o• •••••••••. T•• ••••• ••ow• •n inv••i•n• •o•••• •l••• ••• ••• •••innin•

```
public class LinkedQueue {
    protected /*@ spec_public non_null @*/ LinkedNode head;
    protected /*@ spec_public non_null @*/ LinkedNode last;
    //@ public invariant head.value == null;

    /*@ public normal_behavior
      @    requires head == last;
      @    assignable \nothing;
      @    ensures \result == null;
      @ also public normal_behavior
      @    requires head != last;
      @    assignable head, head.next.value;
      @    ensures head == \old(head.next) && \result == \old(head.next.value);
      @*/
    public synchronized Object extract() {
        synchronized (head) {
            Object x = null;
            LinkedNode first = head.next;
            if (first != null) {
                x = first.value;
                first.value = null;
                head = first;
            }
            return x;
        }
    }
}
```

Fig. 1. JML Specification for the method `extract()`

o•••• •]••• •••]•••ion. Inv••i•n•• • •••• •• •••i•••• •y ••• in•••n••• o•••• •]•••
•• •v••y • •••o•'• •••- •n• • o••-•••••. T•• •••••• •]•o •• ow• • •••• vio••] ••••i-
•••ion o•••• • ••• o• w•i•••n in JML, wi•• o•• • •in• •ny o••• •x••n•ion• ••o-
•o••• in •• i• •••••. JML'• •nno•••ion• ••• w•i•••n •••••i•] J•v• •o• • •n•• ••••
••• in wi•• •n ••-•i•n (@). T•• •••i•••ion o•••• extract() • ••• o• ••••••••
j••• •••o•• i•• ••••••. T• i• ••••i•••ion i• •o• ••i••• o• •wo normal_behavior
•••i•••ion •••••, •••• o• w•i•• ••• • requires •]••••, w•i•• •iv•• i•• •••-
•on•i•ion, •n assignable •]••••, w•i•• •iv•• • •••• • •xio• , •n• •n ensures
•]••••, w•i•• •iv•• i•• •o•••on•i•ion. T•• •••• •••• ••• li•• w••n ••• li•• i• •• •y
•• ••• ••• innin• o•••• • ••• o•'• •x•••ion (head == last), •n• ••• o•••• w••n
••• li•• i• non-•• ••y (head != last). In ••• •••• •••• ••• • •••o• • ••• ••••• •n
null, wi•• o•• •••i•nin• •o •ny lo•••ion•. • •••• wi••, ••• • •••o• •••••••• head
•o ••• n•x• no•• in ••• ••••• (head.next), •n• • ••• ••••• •n ••• o• j••• •• •• w••
•on•• in•• in •••• no•• (•in•• head i• • ••n•in•l, •• ••••• i••• •y ••• inv••i•n•).
To •••i••y ••• inv••i•n• ••• • •••o• • •••• •]•o • ••• ••• v•]•• o•••• n•w ••••
null. T•• • •••o• • •y •••i•n •o • o•• head •n• head.next.value •o ••• i•v•
•• i• •••• •vio•.

T•• • ••nin• o•• JML • •••o• •••i•••ion wi•• •wo o• • o•• •••i•••ion
•••••, •o• in•• wi•• "also", i• •••• ••• ••]]•• ••• •o •••i••y ••• •i•j•n••ion o•
••• •••••on• i•ion• in ••• •iv•n ••••i•••ion •••••, •n• ••• i• •]•• •n••ion ••• •o
•••i••y ••• •o•••on•i•ion• o• •]] ••••i•••ion ••••• •o• w•i•• ••• • •••on• i•ion•
••]• [•, 13]. T•••, in Fi••. 1 ••• ••]]•• ••• no o• li•••ion•, •in•• ••• • •i•j•n••ion o•
••• •••••on• i•ion• o•••• •wo •••i•••ion ••••• i• ••• •••olo• y "head == last
|| head != last".

Internal Interference. Al••o••• ••• •••i•••ion •iv•n in Fi•. 1 •••• • ••n-•i•l•, i• i• w•on• •o• • • •l•i-••••••• •nvi•on• •n•, ••••••• i• •o•• no• •••o• n• •o• in••••••n••. An •x•• •l• o• in•••••••n•• i• •••i•••• in Fi• •. T•• •••••• i• •• ••y in ••• • •••o•'• •••-•••••. Sin•• ••i• • •••o• i• synchronized, ••• •••• in•••••ion i• •x•••••• i• •o •••• i•• ••• lo•• on this. T••n, in •• i• ••••••, •no•••• •••••• i• i• • •• i••ly •••••• l•• ••••• •x•••••• • •ll •o• •••o• insert(Object), w• i•• i• •yn•••oni••• on • lo•• o•••• •••n this (•o •llow • • n• •••in•• •••••• o• •on•••••n•y), •n• •x•••••• i• •o •o• • l••ion. W••n ••• extract() ••ll in ••• •••• •••••• •••••• •• ••• ••••• •••• i• no lon••• •• ••y •n• ••• • •••o• will • n• • non-n•ll •l•• •n• •o •x•••••. Sin•• ••• li•• w•• •• ••y in ••• • •••-•••••, ••• • •••• •••i•••ion •••• ••o• l• •••ly, ••• ••• in••••••n•• ••••••• • non-n•ll v•l•• •o •• ••••• •n•• w• i•• viol•••• ••• • •o•••on• i•ion o• ••••• •••••.

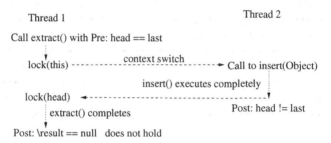

Fig. 2. Execution of extract() call interleaved with a call to insert(Object)

W• ••ll ••• ••o• l•• ill••••••• •y Fi•. • *internal interference.* T• i• ••o• l•• ••i••• w••n •no•••• •••••• •ff•••• ••• ••••••n• ••••••'• •x•••ion o• • • •••o•, •y ••n•in• •••• •••• ••• • •••o• ••n o•••v•. S••n•••• Ho••• lo•i• •o•• no• •llow •o• •••• in••••••n••, •n• •••• w••n •••onin• •• o••••• •o•••••n••• o• ••• i• •l•• •n••ion o• • • •••o• in Ho••• lo•i•, on• ••••• •• ••••• ••o••i••, •••• •• ••• • •••o•'• ••••on•i•ion, •o no• •••n•• •x•••• •y •••ion• o• ••• • •••o• i•••l•.

• •n•i• • •n• ••••i• •n•ly•i• •ool• •o• ••••n•i•l •o•••• • •x• loi• •• i• ••• •n-•i•• w••n •••y wo•• wi•• j••• •wo •••••: ••• *pre-state* (•• ••• ••• innin• o• ••• • •••o•'• •x•••ion) •n• ••• *post-state* (••••• •n•). In • • •l•i-••••••• •••••in•, • ow•v••, •••• •n•ly••• • ••• ••on•i••• •ll •o••i• l• in•••l••vin• •o •••ly •••o• n• •o• • o••i• l• in••••••n••. T• i• i• •on•i•••• ly • o•• •x•n•iv• ••n •••••i••in• •••onin• •o •••- •n• •o••-••••••; ••••••• o••, i• i• non-• o• • l••.

External Interference. *External interference* ••••• n• w••n •no•••• ••••••• • •••• o• •••v•• l• •••••• •••n••• •••w••n • • •••o• ••ll •n• ••• • •••o•'• •n••y, o• • •w••n ••• • •••o•'• •xi• •n• ••• ••ll••'• ••••• ••ion. J•••• • in••n•l in•••-••••n•• ••n inv•li•••• •••n••• Ho•••••yl• ••••onin• •• o••••• •o••••n••• o• • •••o• i• •l•• •n••ion, •x••n•l in••••••n•• ••n i••••• ••••onin• •• o•• ••• •o••••n••• o• •li•n• •o•• ••••• •••ll• ••••• • •••o•.

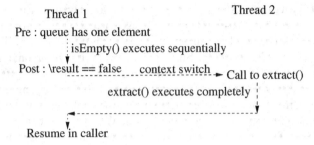

Fig. 3. Execution of extract() call interleaved immediately after call to isEmpty()

Fi•••• 3 ill•••••••• ••• ••o•l•• . S•••o•• ••• •••••• ••• •x••ly on• •l•-
• •n•. T•• isEmpty() •••o• •x•••••• wi••o•• in•••l••vin• •n• ••••n• ••l••.
How•v••, ••w••n ••• ••••n o• isEmpty() •n• ••• •••••• ••ion o• ••• ••ll••,
•no•••• •••••• in•••l••v•• • ••ll •o extract(), w•i•• ••• ov••••• lon• •l•• •n•.
T•• ••••l• i• ••••• ••on ••••• ••ion o• ••• ••ll••'• •••••••, ••• • o•••on•i•ion no
lon••• •••••i•••• ••• •••••• •o•••••ly, •• ••• •••••• i• now •• ••y. Si• il•• in••••••-
••n•• ••n ••••• n wi•• ••••• ••• •o ••• ••••on•i•ion ••••• li••••• •y ••• ••ll•• •n•
o••••v•• ••on • •••o• •n••y. A• ••n •• •••n ••o• ••i• •x•• •l•, •x•••n•l in••••-
••••n•• ••••••• ••• • o••l••i•y o••••onin•, ••••••y ••n••in• •xi••in• ••••• n•i•l
•n•ly•i• ••••ni•••• in•••li•••l•.

Mo•• ••n•••lly, ••••• •y••• o• in••••••n•• • ••n ••••• ••••i•••ion• ••nno•
•••v• •• ••••vio••l ••••••••ion• in ••• ••••• n•• o• •on•••••n•y. T••• i•, on•
••nno• •••• • •••o• •••i•••ion• •o ••••on ••o•• ••• •o•••••n••• o• •n i• •l•-
• •n•••ion wi••o•• •nowin• •o• • ••••il• o• i•• ••llin• •on••x•, o• ••••on ••o••
••ll• •o ••• • •••o• wi••o•• •nowin• •o• • ••••il• o• i•• i• •l•• •n•••ion. To • x
••••• ••o•l•• •, w•il• ••ill •llowin• • o••l•• ••••onin•, ••• •••••i•••ion l•n•••••
• ••• •• •n•i••••.

2.2 Expressing Thread-Safe Behavior

T•• ••• ••• • v••i••y o• w•y• •••• on• • i••• in•o•• o•••• •••••••• in•o • •••• •vio••l
•••• i•••ion l•n••••• •o ••••o•• •••i•••ion in ••• •••••n•• o• •on•••••n•y.
• •• ••••o••• ••• •••n • o•iv•••• ••i• ••ily •y ••• •••• l•• o• • ••v•y o• •xi••-
in• J•v• i• •l•• •n•••ion• •o •n•••••n• ••• • •••• ni•• • •••• •y ••v•lo•••• •o
••••••••o•••on•••• n• •x••••ion, •n• o• •xi••in• •••i•••ion •••••••• in •••
JML l•n••••. W• w•n••• •o • ini••lly •x••n• JML, •n• y••• •n••l• • o••l••
••••vio••l •••• i•••ion o• • wi•• ••n•• o• •xi••in• • •l•i•••••••• J•v• i• •l•-
• •n•••ion•.

• ••• ••n••• •n••l o• •••v••ion i• •••• w•il• ••o•••• • ••• • •y ••• • v••i-
••y o• • •••• ni•• • •o •••i•v• •••••• •••••y, ••• •o•• no•ion o• •••••y i• on• o•
non-in•••••••n••. In••••••n•• ••n •• •voi••• •••o••• ••• ••• o• •yn•••oni••-
•ion, w•i•• •••v•n•• •nw•n••• in•••l••vin•, o• •y •on••ollin• •••••• •o ••••,

w• i•• •••v•n•• • nw•n••• •••••• •o o•••••wi•• •••••• o• j•••••.[1] W••n w• •••••
o• *thread safety*, w• • ••n •i•••• •yn•••oni•••ion o• •on••oll•• •••••••• •o •••••, o•
•o• • •o• • in••ion o• • o••. W• ••v• i••n•i••• ••v•••l ••n••• •n••l no•ion• ••••
• • ••• •• in•l•••• in JML o• •i• il•• l•n•••••••• •o •••• • o•• •••••••• _•••• •••• vio••l
•• ••i•••ion.

Locking Specifications.

P•o•••• • ••• ••• • v••i••y o• lo••in• • i••i•lin•• •n•
••• l•n•••••• • ••• •• •i•• •no••• •o •••••••• •••• v••i••y. I• i• n••••••••y •o •llow
••••i•••ion o•:

– w••• lo•••• • • •••o• will ••••i•• •n• ••l•••• •••in• i•• •x••••ion,
– w••• lo••• ••o•••• ••••i••l•• •••• • o• •n o• j•••'• •••••,
– •••• •o• • o• j•••• ••• •••• •• lo•••, •n• w••n •••• lo•• o• j•••• ••• lo••••,
– ••• ••• o• lo•••••l• •y ••• ••••••n• •••••••, •n•
– •••• •n o• j••• i• ••o•••••• •y •o• • lo•• ••l• •y ••• ••••••n• •••••••.

W• ••v• •l•o •o•n• i• n••••••••y •o •••i•y ••• •on•i•ion• • n••• w• i•• • • •••o•
• •y • lo•• [1•].

Data Confinement Specifications.

• x•••iv• lo••in• ••n •••••• ••••ll•li••
•n• ••n••••••o•• •n••. Fo• •• i• ••••on, • •ny i• •l•• •n••ion• •voi• lo••in• •n•
in••••• ••ly on ••o•••i•• o• • ••o••• '• •••• l•yo•• •o •n•••• •••••• ••••y. I•
i• n••••••••y •o •llow ••••i•••ion o•:

– w•••• •li••in• •n• own••••i• •••••••n• •xi•• •• on• o• j•••• [15, 16, 1•],
– •••• •n o• j••• i• lo••l •o • ••••••, •n•
– ••• •ff••• o• • • •••o• '• •x•••ion on •xi••in• lo•••ion• (*i.e.*, • •••• • •xio•
  [1•]).

Serializability Specifications.

Lo••in• ••n• •••• •on•n•• •n• ••••i•••ion•
••• •••••l in ••••i•yin• ••• •on•i•ion• •n•• w•i•• • •l•i-•••••••• •x•••ion•
••• •••iv•l•n• •o ••••n•i•l •x•••ion•. I• i• n••••••••y •o •llow ••••i•••ion o•
••i• •i••-l•v•l *serializability* ••o•••y o• • •••o••. W• ••v• •o•n• •wo •iff••-
•n• ••••n•••• o• •••• ••••i•••ion •o •• •••••l in •••••i••: ••o• i•i•y •n• in-
••••n••n••. T•••• •on••••• •n• ••• •x••n•ion• •o JML •••• •••• o•• ••••• •••
••••i•• •• in ••• n•x• ••••ion•.

3   Background on Atomicity and Independence

• • ••• ••• •o••• •o ••••••••in• ••• in••••••n•• ••o•l•• ••• ov• i• ••••• on ••• •on-
••••• o• ••o• i•i•y [19, •0] •n• in•••n••n•• [•1]. A •••ion o• •o•• •••••• •n••
(*e.g.*, • • •••o• • o• y) i• ••i• •o • • *atomic* i•••• •••••••• •n•• in ••• •••ion ••• *se-*
rializable—•••• i•, i• •o• •ny •x•••ion ••••• •on••inin• ••• •••ion'• •••••• •n••

---

[1] We do not treat extra-program forms of concurrency control, such as scheduling.

(• o••i• ly in•••l••v•• wi•• •••••• •n•• •x•••••• •y o••••• ••••••••) ••••• i• •n ••••iv•l•n• •x••••ion ••••• w••••• ••• •••ion'• •••••• •n•• ••• •x••••••• ••••••n-•i•lly (*i.e.*, •x•••••• wi••o•• •ny in•••l••vin•• ••o• o••••• ••••••••). I• • •o•• •••ion i• ••o• i•, •••n i• i• •o•n• •o ••••on ••o•• i•• •••ion•• i• ••• y o•••• in • •in•l• ••o• i• ••••—in ••••n••, •llowin• on• •o ••• ••••i•ion•l ••••••n•i•l •••onin• •••• ni•••• on ••• •o•• •••ion. F•o• •no•••• •oin• o• vi•w, in••••• o• ••vin• •o •on•i••• • n•• ••• o• in•••• ••i••• •••••• ••o••••• •y •••••• in-•••l••vin••, •o• •n ••o• i• •••ion i• i• •o•n• •o •on•i••• only •wo •••••: ••• *pre-state* ••o•• ••• •on•••••l •in•l• ••o• i• •••• •••in•, •n• ••• *post-state* ••-••• ••• •on•••••l •in•l• ••o• i• •••• •o• •l••••. T••• i•, •ny in•••••••n•• ••o• ••• o••••• •••••• i• ••ni•n, •ow•v••, ••• •in•l• ••o• i• •••• • •y in•••••• wi•• o••••• ••••••••' •o• •••••ion•.

T•••• ••• • •ny w•y• •o •••••li•• ••• ••o• i•i•y o• • •o•• •••ion. In ••• n•x• •wo •••••••ion• w• •••••i•• •wo • o••l•• •••••o•••••; •••••• •••••o••••• will • o•iv••• ••• JML no•••ion• •••• w• ••v•lo• in ••• •ollowin• ••••ion•.

3.1   Lipton's Reduction Theory

Li••on in••o••••••• ••• •••o•y o• l•••/•i•••• •ov••• •o •i• in ••ovin• ••o•••i•• ••o•• •on•••••n• ••o•••• • [19]. In Li••on'• • o••l, • •o•• •••ion i• ••o•••• o• ••• • •••••••n•• o• ••i• i•iv• •••••• •n•• (*e.g.*, J•v• •y•••o•••), w•i•• •• ••ll•• *transitions*. P•oo•• ••o•• ••• •••n•i•ion• in • ••o•••• ••n ••• ••• ••i• •l•• i• on• i• •llow••• •o ••••• • ••••• • ••••i•• l•• •••••n•• o• •••n•i•ion• i• in•ivi•i• l•. To •on•l•••• ••••• • ••o•••• , P, w•i•• •on••in• • •••••n•• o• •••n•i•ion•, S, i• •••iv•l•n• •o ••• ••••••• ••o•••• , P/S, in w•i•• S i• •o••l•• •• on• in•ivi•i• l• •••n•i•ion, Li••on ••o• o••• ••• no•ion o• • •o• • ••in• •••n•i•ion. A *commuting transition* i• • •••n•i•ion •••• i• •i••••• •i•••• •ov• o• • l••• • ov••. In•• i•iv•ly, • •••n•i•ion, α, i• • *right (left) mover* i•, w••n•v•• α i• •ollow•• (•••••••) •y •no•••• •••n•i•ion, β, o•• iff••n• •••••••, •••n α •n• β ••n • •w••••• wi••o•• •••n•in• ••• •••• l•in• •••••. • on•••ly, • lo•• ••••i••, ••••• •• ••• •••innin• o•• J•v• •yn•••oni••• •lo••, i• •i•••• •ov••, •n• ••• lo•• ••l•••• •• ••• •n• o• ••••• • •lo•• i• • l••• • ov••. Any •••• o• w•i•• •o • v••i••l• o• ••l• •••• i• ••o••ly ••o•••••• •y • lo•• i• •o•• • l••• •n• •i••• • ov••, w•i•• i• •••• •• • *both mover*.

To ill•••••• ••• •••li••ion o• ••••• i•••••, w• •••••• ••• •x•• •l• •iv•n in [•0]. • on•i•••• • •••o• m •••• •••••i•••• lo••, •••••• • v••i••l• x ••o••••• •y •••• lo••, •••••••• x, •n• ••n ••l••••• ••• lo••. S••o•• •••• ••• •••n•i•ion• o• ••i• • •••o• ••• in•••l••v•• wi•• •••n•i•ion• E_1, E_2, •n• E_3 o• o••••• ••••••, •• ••own •• ••• •o• o• Fi•. •. B•••••• •••ion• o• ••• ••••o• m ••• • ov••• (acq •n• rel ••• •i•••• •n• l••• • ov•••, •••••••iv•ly, •n• ••• lo••-••o•••• •••i•n• •n• •n• •o x i• • •o•• • ov••), Fi•. • i• •li•• •••• •••••• •xi••• •n ••• iv•l•n• •x•••ion (•• own •• ••• • o••o• o• ••• • ••••), w••••• ••• o• •••••ion• o• m ••• no• in•••l••v•• wi•• o•••••ion• o• o•••• •••••. T••• i• i• •••• •o ••••on ••o•• ••• • •••o• •• •x•••••in• in • •in•l• ••o• i• •••••.

• n• ••n ••••n• •n *atomic region* •• on• ••••• •••i•••••• ••• •••••••n o• •••••• •n•• R*N?L*, w• •••• R* ••no••• 0 o•• • o•• •i•••• ov•• •••••• •n••, L* ••no••• 0 o•• • o••

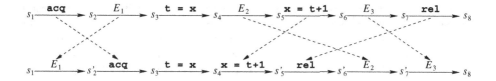

Fig. 4. Left/Right movers and atomic blocks

l••• • ov•• •••••• •n••, •n• N[?] ••no••• 0 o• 1 •••••• •n•• ••• • ••• n•i•••• l••• no•
•i•••• ov•••. T••• i•, •n ••o• i• •••ion ••n •on••in •• • o•• on• non-•o• • • •in•
(*i.e.*, • o••i• ly in••••••in•) •••••• •n•. T•• • lo•• •• own in Fi•. • • •••••• •• i•
•••••• n in ••• •ollowin• w•y: ••• •••••• •n• acq i• •i•••• ov•• (R), ••• •••••• •n•
t = x i• •o•• •i•••• •n• l••• • ov•• •o i• •n •••n •o• •i••• (R), ••• •••••• •n•
x = t+1 i• •o•• •i•••• •n• l••• • ov•• •o i• •n •••n• •o• l•• (L), •n• ••• •••••• •n•
rel i• l••• • ov••. T••• w• ••• RRLL, w•i•• ••• ••• • •••••n.

In o•••• wo•••, •n ••o• i• •••ion ••n ••v• • •in•l• •x•••n•lly-o•••v•• l• •ff•••
in i•• •o•y w•il• i• i• •x•••••. How•v••, no•• ••••• •n ••o• i• • •••o• •n ••v•
• • •l•i•l• •••••••• •o •••• o•j•••• •• lon• •• •••y ••• •i•••• ••••••• lo••l o• lo••-
••o•••••• ••••••••• [••]. T•i• i• •••••••• •••••••• •o o• j•••• lo••l •o • •••••• •n•
•o o•j•••• ••o•••••• •y lo••• ••nno• •• o•••v•• •y o•••• •••••••• •n•il ••••••
o• j•••• •••o• • •••••• o• •n•il ••• lo••• ••• ••l•••••, ••••••iv•ly. Si• il••ly,
lo••-••••i••• •n• lo••-••l••••• on •n o•j••• ••••• i• •l•••• y lo•••• •y • •••••••
••nno• •• o•••v•• •y o•••• •••••••• •n•il •••• lo•• i• ••l•••••.

Li• •on •l•o •••••• •wo •••• ni••l •on•i•ion• n•••••••y •o ••ov• ••••• ••• •••
o•• •n•l ••••••• o• • ••o•••• P ••••l• ••• ••• o• •n•l ••••••• o• ••• ••••••• ••o-
•••• P/S. T•• ••••• o• ••••••, • 1, [19–•• • 19] •••••• ••••• "i• S i• •v•• •n•••••
•••n i• ••o•l• ••• •o••i•l• •o •v•n•••lly •xi• S." T•i• i• • ••i•ly •••on• liv•n•••
••••i••• •n• ••••• ••n •• viol•••• i•, •o• •x•• •l•, S •on••i•••• •o • •••• lo••
o• liv•lo••, o• ••il• •o •o• •l••• •••••••• i• •••o•• • • J•v• wait •n• i• n•v••
no•i•••. • ••••i•ion • • i• •••• "••• •ff••• o• •••••• •n•• in S w••n •o•••••
•n• •••••••••• • ••• •• ••• ••• •." T•i• i• •••n•i•lly •••in• •n in••••••n••-••••
••o••••y ••o• ••• o•••• •••••••• •o• S: •ny in•••l••vin•• •••w••n ••• ••••••• •n••
o• S •o no• •ff••• ••• •n•l ••o•• i• ••o••••••.

3.2 Independent Statements

S••••• •n•• •••• ••• ••• •o•• • ov••• ••• •l•o •••••••• •o •• *independent statements*
•in•• •••y •• n •o• • ••• •o•• •o ••• l••• •n• ••• •i••• o• o•••• ••o•••• •••••-
• •n••. W• ••y ••••• • •o•• •••ion i• *independent* i• •••• •••••• •n• wi•• in •••
•••ion i• in••• •n•• •n•. T•••, •n in••• •n••n• •o•• •••ion •••i•••• ••• ••••••n o•
•••••• •n•• l*, w•••• l* ••no••• 0 o• • o•• •o•• • ov•• •••••• •n••. An in••• •n-
••n• •••ion i• •o••lly non-in••••••in•, •n• ••••• i• ••ivi•lly ••o• i•.

• ••• ••••i•••ion • •••o•olo•y •o• •••••onin• ••o••• ••• •o• ••ll• wi•• in •on-
••x•• will ••ly on ••• •••• ••••• in••• •n••n• •••ion• ••v• •l•••in• •o• •o•••ili•y
••o••••i••. S•••• n•i•lly •o• • o•in• •wo in••• •n••n• •••ion• yi•l•• •n in••• •n-

••n• •••ion, ••• •o• • o•in• •wo ••o• i• •••ion• • • •y no• yi•l• •n ••o• i• •••ion
i• •••• •••ion •on••in• • non-• ov••. Mo••ov••, ••• ••••••n•i•l •o• • o•i•ion o•
•n in•••n••n• •••ion •n• •n ••o• i• •••ion i• •n ••o• i• •••ion (•in•• • o••
• ov••• ••n •••v• •• •i•••• l••• o• •i••• • ov•••). In••i•iv•ly, ••llin• • • •••o•
M_2 ••o• in•i•• o• • • •••o• M_1 ••••••••n•• ••• ••••••n•i•l •o• • o•i•ion o• •••••
•o•• •••ion• (••• •••• o• M_1 ••o•• ••• ••ll, ••• • o• y o• M_2, ••• •••• o• M_1).
T•••, i• on• •••••• •n ••o• i• • •••o•, M_1, •n• in••••• in•o i•• • o• y • ••ll •o •n
in•••n••n• • •••o•, M_2, •••n M_1 ••• •in• ••o• i•. How•v••, i• ••• in•••••• ••ll
i• •o •n ••o• i• • •••o•, M_3, •••n M_1 •o• no• n••••••ily ••• •in ••o• i•.

Fin•lly, w• no•• •••• •o• • •••ion •o •• in•••n••n•, on• •o•• no• ••v• •o
•••••li•• Li••on'• • 1 liv•n••• •on•i•ion •o •n•••• ••• •xi•••n•• o• •n ••• iv•l•n•
•••i•li••• •••••• (i• i• ••• ••y• • •••i• n••••• o• ••• l••• •n• •i••• • ov••• in •••
••i••ion •o• ••o• i• •••ion• •••• n••••i•••• ••• liv•n••• •on• i•ion, • 1).

4 Introducing Concurrency into JML

• ••• ••••o••• •o• in••o•••in• •on•••••n•y in•o JML i• •o •••••••••• ••• •on•••n
o• ••o•••y •••i•••ion •o• • •••o•• in•o •wo •••••: (1) ••o• i•i•y •n• in••-
••n••n•• ••o•••i••, •n• (•) •••i•••ion o• ••••••n•i•l (o• •• n••ion•l) •••vio•.
T•i• i• •n ol• i•••, ••• ••i•• •••••l. W••• w• •l•i• i• n•w i• ••• l•n•••••• ••-
•i•n, w•i•• ••ovi••• n•••••••y •n• ••• •i•n• •on•••••• •o •••••i•y • wi•• ••n••
o• • •l•i-••••••• ••o•••• •.

In w••• •ollow• w• ••••i•• j••• ••• n•w JML •on•••••• ••l••in• •o ••••-
i••••ion o• ••o• i•i•y •n• in•••n••n•• •n• •o •x•••••in• lo••in• •n• o••••
••o• •••i•• •••i• •o • •l•i-•••••••• ••o•••• •. W• ill••••••• ••• n•w •on•••••
••in• •x•• •l• ••o• Do•• L••'• •n• J•v• 1.5'• •on•••••n• li•••i••.

4.1 Locking Notations

Lo••in• i• •n i• • o•••n• •••••• o• •on•••••n• •••••vio••, •in•• i• i• ••• ••••l
• •••• •ni•• •••• •o •••i•v• ••o• i•i•y. So w• n••• ••v••l no•••ion• •••• •llow
•o• ••• •••i••••ion o• lo••in• •••vio••. T•••• no•••ion• •l•o •llow • o••l••
••••••in• o• ••o• i•i•y •••i•••ion• (••••i••• in S••. •.3).

JML •l•••• y ••• ••v••l no•••ion• •••• ••n •• •••• •o ••••i•y in•o•• ••ion
•• o•• lo••in•. T•• monitors_for •l•••• •llow• •••i•yin• ••• lo•••••••• ••o••••
••• •••••• •o • •iv•n ••l•. T•• •yn••x o• •• i• •l•••• i•:

⟨• oni•o••-•o•-•l•••⟩ ::= monitors_for ⟨i••n•⟩ <- ⟨••o••-•••-li••⟩ ;

T••• ••nin• i• •••• •ll o• ••• (non-n•ll) lo•••• n•• •• in ••• ⟨••o••-•••-li••⟩ • •••
•• ••l• •y• ••••••• in o••••• •o ••••••• ••• ••l• ident. (In JML, • ⟨••o••-•••-li••⟩ i•
• •o• • •-••••••••• li•• o••••••• •x•••••ion•, w•i•• in•l•••• i•n•i•••, ••l• •n•
••••y ••••••••, •n• v••io•• •••••••n• [•].) An •x•• •l• in S••. •.• ••• on••••••
••• ••• o••• monitors_for •l•••.

Fin•lly, ••• \lockset() •x•••••ion ••••••n• •n o• j•••, o• •y•• JMLObjectSet,
•••• •••••••n•• ••• ••• o• •ll lo••• ••l• •y ••• •••••n• ••••••.

T•• •••• n•w •on•••••• w• ••• •o JML i• ••• locks •l•••. T• i• •l•••• ••n
•••••• in ••• •o• y o• • •••i•••ion •••• ••••• ••• ••••in• •••• (in w• i•• •••
requires •l•••• ••••••). I•• •yn••x ••••i••• • li•• o• lo•••:

⟨lo•••-•l•••⟩ ::= locks ⟨••o••-•••-li••⟩;

Fi•••• 5 •• ow• ••• ••• o•••• locks •l•••• in ••• • •••o• extract(). T•• locks
•l•••• •••o• • li•••• •wo • iff••n• •••• o•••. Fi•••, i• i• •n •x• li•i• •••••• •n• o•••
lo••• ••• ••• •• ••••n• • •••o• •••• i••• (•n• ••l••••) ••• in• i•• •x•••ion. T••
• ••nin• i• ••••, on •ny •iv•n •x•••ion (w•••• ••• ••• •••on• i•ion i• •••i•••), •••
• •••o• will lo•• •ll ••• lo••• in ••• •iv•n li••. S••on•, ••• locks •l•••• ••••••
•n i• • li•i• •on• i•ion •o• in••• •n••n••. In ••n•••l, • locks •l•••• o• ••• •o•• :

locks $l_1, \ldots, l_n$;

•••••••• •o •n •n•••• •l•••• o• ••• •o•• :

ensures \old(\lockset().has(l_1) && ... && \lockset().has(l_n))
        ==> \independent;

T•••••o••, i• •no••••• •••o• ••ll•••• • •••o• wi•• ••• locks •l•••• in • •on••x•
w••••• •ll ••• lo••• in ••• li•••••• •••l•, •••n ••• ••ll•• • ••••••••••n•••• •o ••
in•••n••n• (••• S••. •.•). In ••i• ••n••, ••• locks •l•••• •iv•• • low•• •o•n•
on ••• ••• o• lo••• •••• ••• • •••••l• •y ••ll••• •o •n•••• in••• •n••n• •x•••ion
w••n ••• • •••o• i• ••ll••. T• i• ••n••l• v••i•y • ••ll••'• ••o• i•i•y ••••i••••ion.
• onv••••ly, ••• locks •l•••• li• i•• ••• lo••• ••••• •n i• •l•• •n••ion o• •••
• •••o• • •y ••y •o ••••i•• (w••n ••• •••••on• i•ion o• ••• •••••i•••ion •••• i•
•••••••• in •ol••); •••• •o• ••• i• •l•• •n••ion ••• locks •l•••• •iv•• •n •••••
•o•n• on ••• ••• o• lo••• •••• ••• • •••o• • •y ••y •o ••••i••.

Fo• •n in•••n•• (••••i•) • •••o•, ••• locks •l•••• ••• • •••••l• v•l•• o•
this (••• •l••• o• j•••) i• ••• • •••o• i• •••••i••• •• synchronized, o•••wi•• i•
•••••l•• •o \nothing. T•• •••••l• •o• •yn••oni••• • •••o• •• i• ••••••l •••••••
• •ny •on••••n• • •••o• •• in J•v• •yn••oni•• on this.

Fin•lly, w• ••• • ••••i••••, \lock_protected, wi•• ••• •ollowin• •yn••x.
⟨lo••-•• o••••••-•x•••ion⟩ ::= \lock_protected(⟨••o••-•••⟩)
An •x••••ion •••• •• \lock_protected(o) •••••• •••• ••• o• j••• •••••••n••• •y
o i• •••••••-••o•••••• •y •o• • non•• ••y ••• o• lo•••, •n• •ll o• ••o•• lo••• •••
••l• •y ••• ••••••n• •••••••. No•i•• ••••••i• i• • v••y •••on• ••o• •••y: ••• •••••••
i• •••••i••• wi•• •••••••• •o ••• o• j•••, no• ••• ••••••n•• v••i•• l•, •••••• o•• i• •••
o• j••• i• •li•••, ••i• ••o••••y •••••• •••• •••••• •o •ll ••• •li•••• i• •••••i•••
•y ••• lo•••-••• o• ••i• o• j•••. T•• i••n•i•i• o• ••••• lo••• ••• no• •••i•••. T• i•
no•••ion •llow• on• •o •••i•y lo••in• ••••vio•, w•il• • i• in• ••• ••••il• o• lo•••
involv••. V••i•••ion o• \lock_protected(x.f) wo•l• ••• ••• \monitors_for
•l•••• •o• f in x'• •l••.

4.2   Heap Restriction Notations

In ••• i•ion •o lo••in•, •••••• ••••y ••n •l•o •• •••i•v•• •y •••••i•ion• on
••••••n•••. JML'• •••• •••••i••ion no•••ion• ••• •i• •• •• ••••i•yin• •ow lo••l

```
public class BetterLinkedQueue {
    protected /*@ spec_public non_null rep @*/ LinkedNode head;
    protected /*@ spec_public non_null rep @*/ LinkedNode last;
    //@ public invariant head.value == null;

    /*@ public normal_behavior
      @   requires head == last;
      @   locks this, head;
      @   assignable \nothing;
      @   ensures \result == null;
      @ also public normal_behavior
      @   requires head != last;
      @   locks this, head;
      @   assignable head, head.next.value;
      @   ensures head == \old(head.next) && \result == \old(head.next.value);
      @*/
    public /*@ atomic @*/ synchronized /*@ readonly @*/ Object extract() {
        synchronized (head) {
            /*@ readonly @*/ Object x = null;
            /*@ rep @*/ LinkedNode first = head.next;
            if (first != null) {
                x = first.value;
                first.value = null;
                head = first;
            }
            return x;
        }
    }
}
```

Fig. 5. Extended JML specification for extract()

v••i••l•• • •y ••••• •o o•j•••• in ••• ••••, •n• •ow ••••• o•j•••• • •y •••••
•o •••• o••••. T••y •llow •••lin• wi•• i••••• li•• ••••••••n••ion •x• o••••• [16]
•n• o••••• •in•• o• •nw•n•••• •li••in• •••• wo•l• o•••wi•• •••v•n• • o••l••ly
•••••in• ••o• i•i•y •••i•••ion. Fo• •x•• • l•, •on•i••• ••• • ••• o• extract()
in Fi•. 1. T•i• • •••o• ••••••••• ••• ••l• head •y •••• ••••i•in• ••• lo•• on •••
o•j•••, •o •• •o •n•••• ••o• i•i•y. How•v••, i• •••••• i• •••••••n••ion •x• o•••••,
in ••••i••l•• i• ••••• i• •no•••• ••••••n•• •o ••• o•j••• •oin••• •o •y head, ••• n
•••• •li•• • i•••• •• ••l• •y •no•••• ••••••. T••• on• wo•l• ••v• •o •x•• in•
o••••• ••o•• in ••• ••o•••• •o ••l• o•• •••••• •y •o• • o••••• •••••• •o ••• •••••
o••••• o•j••• head ••••• •o, in •••i••l•• •o ••• ••l• head.next. In o•••• wo•••,
•••••••n••ion •x• o•••• o• •• i• •o•• wo•l• n••••i••••• • non-lo••l •n•ly•i• o••••
••o•••• •o ••l• o•• ••••• • o••i• l• in••••••n••.

To •••v•n• ••••• ••o• l•• • w• ••••• ••v•n•••• o• ••• Univ•••• •y•• •y••••
[1•], •n own••••i• •y•• •y••••• ••••• •l•••• y •xi••• in •n •x••i• •n••l •o•• in
JML [•3]. T•i• •y•• •y••••• •••••• ••• • o•i•••• rep •n• readonly •o •••l•••-
•ion•.

T•• rep • o•i••••n •• • •••• on ••l• •••l•••ion•. I• •••••• ••• •• ••• o•j•••
•••••••n••• •y ••• ••••i••• ••l• i• •••• o• ••• •••••••n••ion o• ••• • iv•n •l•••.
T•••• ••n •• no ••••••n••• ••o• o••i•• •n o•j••• o• ••• •l••• •o •••• •••••-
••n••ion o•j••••. F•o• o••i•• ••• •l•••, on• ••n only ••••• •o ••• •n•lo•in•
o•j•••, w•i•• i• ••• owner o•••• ••••••••n••ion o•j••••. Fo• •x•• • l•, in Fi•. 5
••• ••l• head •n• last ••• rep ••l••, •••••••o•• ••••• ••n •• no •x•••n•l •li••••
•o ••• o•j••• •o w•i•• ••••• ••l•• •••••, •n• ••n•• no ••••••••n••ion •x• o••••••.
T•i• •n••l•• ••• • o••l•• v••i•••ion o• ••• ••o• i•i•y •••i•••ion.

```
/*@ normal_behavior
  @    requires c != null && \thread_local(c);
  @    assignable elementCount, elementData;
  @    ensures elementCount == c.size() && \fresh(elementData);
  @also
  @ exceptional_behavior
  @    requires c == null;
  @    assignable \nothing;
  @    signals (Exception e) e instanceof NullPointerException;
  @*/
public /*@ atomic @*/ Vector(Collection c) {
  elementCount = c.size();
  elementData = new Object[(int)Math.min((elementCount*110L)/100,Integer.MAX_VALUE)];
  c.toArray(elementData);
}
```

Fig. 6. Extended JML specification for a constructor in `java.util.Vector`

T•• readonly • o•i••• i• • •y••• o•i•••. I•• •••••• •••••••n•• •• ••••-only, • ••nin• •••• ••• o• j••• ••nno• ••• o• i••• ••o••• •••• •••••••n••. • •••-only •••••n••• ••• no• n•••••••ily own•• •y • n o• j••• •on••inin• ••• readonly ••l•, •n• i• i• o•••n ••• •••• •••• •••• •••••••n••• ••• •li•••• •x•••n•lly. T•• i••• i• •••• only ••• i• •n•i•y o• • readonly o• j••• • ••••• •o ••• •••••••• ••••• o• ••• •n•lo•in• o• j•••. (JML will •v•n•••lly •n•o••• v••io•• •••••i••ion• on •••••• •o ••••-only o• j•••• in ••••••ion•.)

T•• no••ion• j••• •i•••••• •••l wi•• own•••• i• •••w••n o•j•••. ••••lly i• •o•••n• in •on••••n• ••o•••• • i• ••• own•••• i• o• o•j••• •y •••••••. An *object o is owned by a thread t* i• only •••••• t ••n ••••• o •y • •••••••n•• •••in. T• i• •on•i•ion •••••n•••• •••• •••• ••nno• ••• • •••• •on•i•ion on o, •••••••• o i• no• •••••••. W• in••o•••• ••• no•••ion \thread_local(o) wi•• ••• • ••nin• •••• o i• own•• •y ••• •••••n• ••••••. T•• ••n•••l •yn••x i• ••• •ollow•.

⟨•••••••-lo••l-•x••••ion⟩ ::= \thread_local (⟨••o•••-••••⟩)

T• i• no•••ion i• ••••l •o•• o••l•• v••i•••ion o• ••o• i•i•y, •••••• • •••••••• •o •••••• lo••l o•j•••• ••• in•••n•••n• (non-in•••••in•).

Fo• •x••• •l•, •on•i••• ••• •on•••••o• ••o• J•v•'• Vector •l••• •• own in Fi•. 6. In ••n•••l, •on•••••o•• ••• in•••n•••n• •••••••• ••• •on••••••• o•j••• i• no• •••••••l• ••o• •ny o•••• •••••••. How•v••, i• ••• •on•••••o• ••••• o•j••• ••••• •n•• •o ini•i•li•• ••• in•••n•l ••••• o• ••• •on•••••• o•j•••, •••n i•• •x•-•••ion • i••• no• ••• ••o• i•. T•• ••o•l•• i• •••••••• •n ••••• •n• o•j••• i••• ••• •on•••••n•ly • o•i••• •y o•••• •••••••. So, in ••i• •x•• •l• ••• •on•••••o•'• ••••on•i•ion ••••i••• •••• ••• •••• ••n•, c, •• •••••• lo••l.

4.3   Atomicity Modifier

W• in••o•••• ••o• i•i•y ••••i•••ion in•o JML wi•• • n•w • •••o• • o•i•••, atomic. T•i• •••••i••• ••••, w••n • • •••o• i• invo••• in • ••••• •••• • •••• i•• ••••on•i•ion, i•• i• •l•• •n•••ion • ••• •n•••• •••• ••• ••••l•in• •x•••ion i• •••i•li••l•. T•i• • o•i••• i• in•••i••• •y ov•••i•in• • ••• ••o••. Fi•. 5 ••ow• • ow w• ••• ••i• n•w • o•i••• •o •••i•y extract() ••o• Fi•. 1.

```
public class ArrayBlockingQueue<E> {
  private /*@ spec_public non_null rep @*/ final E[] items;
  //@ monitors_for items <- lock;
  private /*@ spec_public rep @*/ final ReentrantLock lock;

  /*@ normal_behavior
    @   requires lock.isLocked() && 0 < i && i < items.length;
    @   ensures \result == \old((i + 1) % items.length) && \independent;
    @*/
  final /*@ atomic @*/ int inc(int i) {
    return (++i == items.length)? 0 : i;
  }
```

Fig. 7. Extended JML specification for inc()

• •••• in• •••• • • •••o• •••l•••• •o• • ••o• i• i• ••••lly ••o• i• ••n••• •on•
in • v••i••y o• w•y•. Fo• •x•• •l•, on• •o•l• ••ov •••• ••• •o•• i• ••••i•l•
•y Li••on'• •••o•y [•0,••] o• •y ••in• ••• no•ion o• in•••n••n• •••n•i•ion•.
Ano•••• •••• ni••• i• •••• in ••• A•o• i••• [•5], w•i•• •yn•• i••lly •••••• ••••
lo•• •••• i•i•ion• •n• ••l••••• ••• ••o••ly n••••• •n• ••••• •ll •••••••• •o •••••••
•••• i• lo•• ••o••••••. T•• monitors_for •l•••• wo•l• •• •••• •o ••••• in•
w•••• lo••• ••o•••• w••• •i•••• o• •••••.

By i• • o•in• •n ••• i•ion•l o•li•••ion •o •••••n••• •••i•li•••l• •x•••ion• on
• • •••o•'• i• •l•• •n•••ion, ••• atomic • o•i••• •i• •li•••••• i• •l•• •n••ion'•
••oo•o••• n•••ion•l •o•••••n•••. T•• ••n•••ion•l •o••••n••• ••oo••n ••••• • •••••
••• •x•••ion i• •••i•li•••l•, •••• •voi•in• in•••n•l in••••••n•••. Fo• •x•• •l•, in
••• • •••o• extract() •••i••• in Fi•. 5, ••• • o•••on•i•ion o•••• •••i•••ion
•••• • •••• •ol• only •o• ••••• in w•i•• ••• • •••o• i• •x••••• ••••n•i•lly.
How•v••, w••n •o• • in•• wi•• ••• •••i•ion•l ••oo• o• ••o• i•i•y, on ••ill •••• •
•••on• •o••••n••• •••• n•••• •••• o•• • ••o• •l••• •••• vio o••• i• •l•• •n••ion.
T•i• •ivi•ion o••oo• o• li•••ion• •o• i• •l•• •n•••ion• •llow• ••oo•• o• •• n••ion•l
•o•••••n••• •o • • •••••••• ••o• •yn••oni••ion •••• il•.

Fo• ••• •ll••'• •oin• o• vi•w, ••••• i• no •o••n•i•l •o• in•••n•l in••••••n••
•y ••o• i• • •••o••, •n• •••• ••• ••ll•• only ••• •o wo••y ••o•• •x••n•l in-
••••••n••. To •voi• •x••n•l in••••••n••, ••• ••ll•• • •••• •n•••• •••• o• j••••
n••••• •o •••••••v• ••• ••••• o• •ny •••on•i•ion o• • o•••on•i•ion ••• ••••••
•••• (e.g., lo•••• o• lo••l •o ••• ••ll••'• ••••••• [••]). T• i• ••• i•ion•l •••• i••• •n•
••l•• ••••• o• •yn••oni••ion •••• wi•o•• •••vyw•i••• ••• • o••l lo•i•—•• i•
i• •o• ••• in• •••• ••• no• ••n •x•lo••• in o•••• ••••i•/•yn•• i• •n•ly••• •o•
••o• i•i•y.

I• i• •l•o •o••i•l• •o• •n ••o• i• • •••o• •o •••n•••• •o• • o• i•• o•li•••ion •o
•n•••• ••o• i• •x•••ion •o ••• •ll••, •y ••••in• • ••••on•i•ion involvin• lo•••
o• ••••••• own••••i•. Fo• •x•• •l•, •n ••o• i• • •••o• ••n ••••i•• •o• • lo•••••o
••••l• ••o•• ••in• ••ll••, ••in• • •••on•i•ion •••• •• \lockset.has(lock),
w•i•• ••y• ••••• ••• •••••n• ••••••• •ol•• •••• lo•• n•• •• lock. S••• • ••••on-
•i•ion • •y ••v• ••• ••••• ••n••• o• •••v•n•in• •x••n•l in••••••n••. In•••,
••vin• ••• •l•i• ••• •li•n•• o••in lo••• • •y •• ••n•i•l• ••o• •n ov••ll ••i•n
•••n••oin• (vi• •n •n•-o-•n• ••••• •n• [•6]). Fi•••• • ••ow •n •x•• •l• o• •• i•
••••, in w•i•• ••• • •••o• inc() •••n••••• ••• •••• on•i•ili•y o• •ol•in• ••• lo••

on lock •o ••• ••ll••. (T• i• ••ili•y •o •••n•••• •o• • o•li•••ion •o ••• ••ll•• •• ow•
• ow atomic i• • iff•••n• ••• n J•v•'• synchronized • o•i•••.)

Fin•lly, in • •ny •on•••••n• •l••••, •ll • •••o•• ••o•l• •• ••o• i•. To •llow
• •••i•n•• •o ••••• •• i•, ••• atomic ••ywo•• ••n •• •••• in • •l••• o• in•••••••
•••l•••ion. S••• • • o•i•• ••i• •ly •••••• ••••• •ll ••• • •••o•• •••l•••• in •••
•y••'• •••l•••ion ••• ••o• i•. T•i• •y•• • o•i••• i• in••i••• •y ••• •y••.

4.4 Independent Predicate

A • •••o• •x•••ion i• *independent* i• •ll o• i•• •••n•i•ion• ••• in•••n••n• n•. Fo•
•x•• • l•, •••••••• •o o•j•••• lo••l •o ••• •••••• •n• •••••••• •o o•j••••• •••••
••• ••o•••••• •y lo••• ••• •ll in•••n••n• •••n•i•ion•, •in•• ••• o••••• ••••••••
••nno• o•••v• •••• ••••••••. To •••i•y •• i• ••o•••y o• • • •••o• •x••••ion,
w• in••o•••• • n•w •••i•••ion ••••i••••, \independent. T• i• ••••i•••• ••n
only •• ••••• in • o•••on•i•ion•.

An •x•• • l• •••• •• ow• • ow in•••n••n•• ••n •• •••• •o •voi• •x•••n•l
in•••••••n•• i• java.util.concurrent.ArrayBlockingQueue'• • •••o• inc().
T•i• • •••o• i• •••i••• in Fi•. •. T•• •••on•i•ion •••••• •••• ••• • •••o•
• ••• •• ••ll•• ••o• • •on••x• in w•i•• lock i• lo••••. Sin•• items i• ••o••••••
•y lock, ••• •o ••• monitors_for •••l•••ion, •n• •in•• i i• • •••••• •••• o•
••• • •••o•, no o•••• •••••• ••n •••••• ••• •••• •••• •y inc() •n• •••••• •ny
in•••••••n••. T•••, w••n ••• •••on•i•ion i• • ••, ••i• • •••o•'• •x•••ion• •••
in•••n••n•. F••••••• o••, •in•• ••• ••ll•• • ••• •ol• ••• lo••, •n• •in•• •••
••••l• i• no• •••••i•l• •o o•••• •••••••, ••ll• ••nno• ••ff•• •x•••n•l in•••••••n••.

4.5 Blocking Behavior and Commit Atomicity

In ••i• •••••ion w• •••••i•• no••ion• •o• ••n•lin• • •••o•• ••••• w•i• •o• •o• •
•on•i•ion •o • ••o• • •••• • ••o•• •••y ••o•••• •o •••• •o• • (••o• i•) •••ion. S•••
• •••o•• ••v• w••• w• •ll • *blocking behavior*.

• on•i••• ••• • •••o• take(), ••o• ArrayBlockingQueue in J•v• 1.5, ••
•• own in Fi•. •. T•i• • •••o• •••••• •n •l•• •n• ••o• ••• ••••••, ••• i• ••• li•• i•
•• ••y, i• w•i•• •n•il •••• i• •n •l•• •n• •o ••• ov•.

To •••i•y ••• •lo••in• •••vio• o• • •••o••, w• ••• JML'• when •l••••
(••••••• ••o• L••n••'• wo•• [1•]):

⟨w••n-•l•••⟩ ::= when ⟨•••i••••⟩ ;

I•• • ••nin• i• ••••, i• • • •••o• i• ••ll•• in • ••••• in w•i•• ••• • •••o•'•
when •••• i•••• •o•• no• •ol•, ••• • •••o• •lo••• •n•il •• i• •••• i•••• i• •••i•••
(•••••• •• ly •y •n •••ion o• • •on•••••n• ••••••). T•i• ••••i•••ion •o•• no•
•on••••in w••• ••o•o•ol i• •••• •o w•i• •o• ••• •on•i•ion •o •••o• • ••••; •o•
•x•• • l•, • •••y w•i• loo• • i••• •• •••••. A •lo••in• • •••o• •••i•••ion ••n
•• •o•• •li••• ••• • •••i•l •••ion •••• •o•• no• •x••••• •n•il ••• when •••• i••••
•ol••, •n• ••n ••o• i••lly •••n•i•ion• ••o• ••• •••-•••• •o ••• • o••-•••• (••
••••i••• •y ••• •••-•n• • o•••on•i•ion, *etc*). T•• when •l•••• •y •••••l• •••• •
v•l•• o• true (•o• JML'• •••vyw•i•• ••••i•••ion •••••).

```
/*@ public normal_behavior
  @   locks this.lock;
  @   when count != 0;
  @   assignable items[takeIndex], takeIndex, count;
  @   ensures \result == \old(items[takeIndex]) && takeIndex == \old(takeIndex + 1)
  @         && count == \old(count - 1);
  @*/
public /*@ atomic @*/ E take() throws InterruptedException {
  final ReentrantLock lock = this.lock;
  lock.lockInterruptibly();
  try {
    try {
      while (count == 0)
        notEmpty.await();
    } catch (InterruptedException ie) {
      notEmpty.signal(); // propagate to non-interrupted thread
      throw ie;
    }
    /*@ commit: @*/ E x = extract();
    return x;
  } finally {
    lock.unlock();
  }
}
```

Fig. 8. Extended JML specification for `take()`

To •••• when •l••••, w• ••• • •••i•l •••••• •n• l•• •l, commit. I••• i• l•••l i•
no• •••••n• in • • ••• o•, i• i• i• •li•i•ly •••• •• •• ••• • •••o• • o• y'• •n•. T• i•
l•••l •iv•• • *commit point* •o• ••• • ••• o•; w••n •x•••ion •••••• ••• •o• • i•
• oin•, ••• • •••o• i• no lon••• •lo•••• •n• ••• •••• o• ••• • •••o• '• •x•••ion
• ••• • • ••o• i•. Al•o, ••• ••••i•••• •iv•n in ••• when •l•••• • ••• •ol• •• •••
•o• • i• •oin•, ••• no• n•••••••ily ••in• ••• •••• o• ••• • •••o• '• •x•••ion.
T• i• i••• i• ••l•••• •o ••• •on•••• o• •o• • i•• •n• in •••••••• •••n••••ion• •n•
••• no•ion o• "•o• • i• ••o• i•i•y" in••o••••• •y Fl•n••••n [••].

Fi•••• • ill•••••••• ••• ••• o• ••• when •l•••• •n• ••• commit l•••l. M••• o•
`take()` ••• ov••• n •l•• •n• ••o• ••• •••••, •n• •lo••• i• ••• ••••• i• •• ••y.
T•• when •l•••• in Fi•. • ••y• •••• ••• • •••o• • •y ••o•••• only w• •n count
i• no• •••o. T•• •o• • i• •oin• o• ••i• • •••o• i• w•••• ••• commit l•••l ••••••••,
•i••• ••••• ••• loo• •••• •lo••• •n•il ••• •••••• i• non-•• • •y.

4.6   Notations for Lock Types

Ano•••• i• • o•••n• ••• o• no•••ion• ••• •o • o wi•• i• •n•i•yin• w••• •l•••• •n•
in•••••••• ••v• in•••n••• •••• ••• in••n•• •o • • lo•••. S••• lo•• o• j•••• •••
•n •••i•ion •o ••• i• •li•i• •••n•••n• lo•• in •••• o• j••• •••• ••n •• •••• i•••
••in• J•v•'• `synchronized` •••••• •n•. J•v• 1.5 •••• ••v•••l •••• •y••• o• lo••
o• j••••, w•i•• •••• •o•• n•w •on•••••n•y ••••••n•. An •x•• •l• i• ••• n•w •l•••
`ReentrantLock`, w• o•• in•••n••• ••• ••••i•li••• lo••• •••• ••• • •ni••l•••• • y
• •••o• ••ll•. S••• lo••• ••n • ••• •yn•••oni•••ion • o•• fl•xi•l• •n• •llow •o•
• o•• •• •i•n• •o••. In JDK 1.5, ••••• ••n •l•o •••n• •••i• own lo••• •y i• •l•-
• •n•in• ••• in••••••• `java.util.concurrent.locks.Lock`.

To •••l wi•• •••••• n•w •in•• o• lo•••, JML will •on•i••• • •y•• •o • *lock
type* i• i• i• • •••y•• o• ••• Lock in•••••••. An •x•••••ion w•o•• •••• i• •y•• i•

• lo•• •y•• i• •on•i•••• •o ••no•• • *lock object.* T•••• i• • •o••n•i•l ••• •n•i•
•• •i••i•y •••• ••i••• ••••••• lo•• o•j•••• •l•o •on••in J•v•'• i• •li•i• •yn••o-
ni•••ion lo•••. To •••olv• •• i• •• •i••i•y w• ••••• • •••• w••n lo•• o•j•••• •••
• •n•ion•• in • •on••x• w•••• • lo•• i• •x•••••, ••• •••i••• •lw•y• • ••n• •••
lo•• o•j••• i•••l•, no• ••• i• •li•i• •yn•••oni•••ion lo•• i• •on••in•. Fo• •x•• •l•,
in • `monitors_for` •l•••• • lo•• o•j••• •x•••ion ••••• •o ••• lo•• o•j••• i•••l•.

To •now w••n • lo•• o•j••• i• lo••••, w• in••o•••• • n•w •y••-l•v•l •••l•-
•••ion, ••• `locked_if` •l••••. I•• •yn••x i• •• •ollow•:

⟨lo••••-i•-•l••••⟩ ::= `locked_if` ⟨••••i••••⟩ ;

• ••• •y•• •••• i• • •••y•• o• `java.util.concurrent.locks.Lock` • ••• ••-
•l••• o• in••i• •x••ly on• `locked_if` •l••••. T•i• •l•••• •••••• • •••• j•••• ••••
• ol•• i• •n• only i• ••• •iv•n in•••n•• o• ••• lo•• •y•• i• in ••• *locked* •••••.

So, •o• •x•• •l•, •o• ••• •l••• `ReentrantLock` w• ••v••:

```
package java.util.concurrent;
import java.util.concurrent.locks.Lock;
public class ReentrantLock implements Lock, java.io.Serializable {
    //@ locked_if isLocked();
    /* ... */
}
```

In `ReentrantLock`, `isLocked` i• • (••••) • •••o• •••• •••••n• true i• •••
••••• in•••n•• i• lo••••, •n• false o•••wi••. T•• `locked_if` •l•••• i• •••• in
••• `lockset()` o• •••o•'• ••• •n•i••. Fo• •x•• •l•, i• rl •••y•• ReentrantLock,
••n `\lockset().has(rl)` ••••n• true i••n• only i• `rl.isLocked()` • ol••.

4.7   Revisiting External Interference

In S••. •.3 w• ••••i•• • ow ••• atomic • o•i••• •olv•• ••• in•••n•l in•••••••n••
••o•l•• •y ••ovi•in• •n ••••••••ion in w•i•• o•••• •••••••• •i• no• in•••l••v•
••in• ••• •x•••ion o• ••• • •••o•. Now w• loo• •• •ow ••• •••• o• ••• •n-
no•••ion• ••l• in •olvin• ••• ••o•l•• o• •x•••n•l in•••••••n••. A• ••••••••• in
S••. •.3, ••• •y •o ••v•n•in• •• i• ••o•l•• i• •i••llowin• •••••• ••o• o••••
•••••••• •o ••• o•j•••• • •n•ion•• in •••••- •n• •o•••on•i•ion•.

• x•••n•l in••••••••n• i• ••o•l•• o• in••••••n•• •••w••n •wo • •••o••: on•
• •••o• (••• ••ll••) ••llin• •no•••• •••o• (••• ••ll••) •n• o•••• ••••••• •••••-
in• ••• •on••• ••w••n ••• •wo o•••••. To •••• o•• •on•••• ••• •i•••ion• •••••
•••o• n• •o• •x•••n•l in••••••••n• w• •on•i••• •wo •••••: •n ••o• i• • ••• o• ••llin•
•no•••• ••o• i• • •••o•, •n• • non-••o• i• • ••• o• ••llin• •n ••o• i• • ••• o•.
No••• •••• ••o• i• • •••o•• ••n only ••ll ••o• i• • ••• o••, •n• ••• •••• w•••• •
non-••o• i• • ••• o• ••ll •no••• non-••o• i• • ••• o•, ••i•• ••o• ••in• •n•o• -
• on, wo•l• no• ••••n•l•• •y o•• no•••ion•.

In ••• •••• ••••, i••n ••o• i• • ••• o• ••ll •no•••• ••o• i• • ••• o•, ••n •••
in••••••••n•• •••w••n ••• ••ll•• •n• ••• ••ll•• wo•l• •• in••••n•l in••••••••n•• in
••• ••ll••, w•i• i• •l•••• •y ••n•l•• •y ••• ••o• i•i•y ••••••••ion.

In ••• •••on• ••••, w••n • non-••o• i• • •••o• ••ll• •n ••o• i• • ••• o•, •••
••ll•• n•••• •o •n•••• ••• ••• o•j••• n••••• •o •••••••v• ••• •••••• o• ••• •••-

•n• •o•••on•i•ion ••• *thread safe.* W• ••• n• •••••• ••••y • y in••o•••in• • n•w
o•••••o•, \thread_safe, ••• n•• •••• ••••

$$\text{\texttt{\textbackslash thread\_safe}}(SR) \equiv \text{\texttt{\textbackslash thread\_local}}(SR) \text{ || } \text{\texttt{\textbackslash lock\_protected}}(SR).$$

T••• i•, SR i• ••••••-••• i• i• i• own•• •y ••• •••••n• •••••• o• i• lo•• ••o•••••.
To •voi• •x•••n•l in••••••n••, • •on••••• • ••• •••• i•• ••••• •ll o• j•••• n•••••
•o •••••y• ••• •• ••• o• ••• •••-•n• •o•••on•i•ion ••• •••••••-•••. W• il• •• i•
i• • •••on• •on•i•ion, in o•• •x••i•n•• i• i• ••i••• •y •ll w•ll-w•i•••n • •l•i-
•••••••• •o••.

A• •n •x•• •l• o• •••••• ••••y l•• •• •••• •no•••• loo• •• Fi••. 6. In ••••
•x•• •l•, ••• ••••i•••ion •••• i••• ••• •oll•••ion c •o •• •••••• lo••l, •ow•v••
••i• •on•i•ion i• ••••lly •••on••• ••n w••• i• ••••lly n•••••. T•• ••••l
•••• i••• •n• i• •••• ••• •oll•••ion •• •••• o• in•••••••n••. T•••••o••, w• ••n ••l•x
••• ••••on•i•ion in ••• Vector •on•••••o• •o \thread_safe(c), •••o•n•in•
•o• ••• in•••n••• in w•i•• ••• •on•••••o• i• ••ll•• wi•• •n ••••• •n• •••• i•
•x•••n•lly ••o•••••• •y • lo••.

5   Evaluation

In •• i• ••••ion w• ••••i• o•• •x••i•n••• in ••• lyin• o•• JML •x••n•ion•. W•
•v•l•••• ••i• •••••••y •n• •• •••y •y ••• lyin• •••• in • •oll•••ion o• *speci-*
fication case studies. In •••••• ••• •i••, w• ••••• •• •o w•i•• •o• •l••• •••• vio••l
•••i•••ion• •o• • •oll•••ion o• J•v• •l••••• •••wn ••o• ••• li••••••• ••• w•••
•••i•n•• •x•li•i•ly •o• ••• in • •l•i-•••••••• ••o•••• •. T•••• •l••••• ••• ••i-
ni•••n•ly • o•• •o• •l•x •on••••n•y •oli•i•• ••n •o •y•i••l •l•••••, *e.g.,* J•v•
•on••in•• •l••••. T•••, i• w• ••n ••••o•• ••• ••••i•••ion o• •i•• •• n••ion•l
••o••••i•• •o• ••••• •l•••••, ••n o•• •x••n•ion• will •• ••o••ly ••• li•••l•. W•
•l•o •v•l•••• ••• •••••••• ili•y o• o•• JML •x••n•ion• in • ••• o• *verification case*
studies. In •••••• ••• •i••, w• ••• •l•• ••• •l••••• •n• •••i•••ion• ••o• o••
•••i•••ion •••• i•• •n• •••••••• •••• ••in• •n •x••n•ion o• ••• Bo•o• • o••l
•••• in• •••• •wo•• [••] ••••i•• •• ••low.

T•• n•x• •wo •••ion• ••••n• ••• ••••il• o• ••••• o• •••• ••• •i••, •iv• •••• -
• ••y o• ••• •••l• o••in••, •n• •n ••o•n• o• o•• •on•l••ion•. T•• •o• •l•••
••• o• ••i••• •••• in o•• •••i•• ••• •v•il••l• ••o• ••• w•• [•].

5.1   Specification Case Studies

To •••••• ••• ••••••••y •n• ••••vio• •ov••• o• ••• •x••n•ion• •o JML, w•
i•n•i•• • ••• o• o• •on••••n• J•v• •l••••• •n• w•o•• •••i•••ion• •o• •••i•
• •••o•••in• ••• •x••n••• JML. T•• •l••••• •o• • ••o• • •l•i•l• •o••••• •n•
• o•• ••• i• •l•• •n•••ion• o• •on••••n• •••• ••••••••••:

- A •o• n••• ••ff••, BoundedBuffer (••o• H•••l•y [•9]).
- Dinin• ••ilo•o•••••, DiningPhilosophers (••o• H•••l•y [•9]).
- A lin••• ••••••, LinkedQueue (••o• L•• [1•]).

Table 1. Summary of statistics from specification case studies with the extended JML. The classes marked with a * belong to Java 1.5's package `java.util.concurrent`

Class Name	Number of methods	Frequency of annotations				
		atomic	\independent	locks	\thread_safe	when
BoundedBuffer	3	3	0	2	0	2
DiningPhilosphers	7	7	4	2	0	1
LinkedQueue	7	7	0	7	0	1
RWVSN	8	8	2	4	0	2
java.util.Vector	45	45	4	34	9	0
ArrayBlockingQueue*	19	19	7	15	3	2
CopyOnWriteArrayList*	27	27	6	13	12	0
CopyOnWriteArraySet*	13	13	2	6	5	0
DelayQueue*	17	17	3	14	4	2
LinkedBlockingQueue*	17	17	4	12	1	2
PriorityBlockingQueue*	21	21	4	10	1	1
ConcurrentLinkedQueue*	11	11	2	0	2	4
Total:	195	195	38	119	37	17

— • o•• •o• •••••••-w•i••••, RWVSN (••o• L•• [1•]).
— T•• •l••• java.util.Vector.
— • i••• •on•••••n• •l••••• ••o• java.util.concurrent in J•v• 1.5.

T•• • •l••••• ••o• java.util.concurrent ••• ••••i••l••ly i• •o•••n•, •• •••y ••v• ••i•ly •o• •l•x •n• v••i•• •on•••••n•y •••••••n• •n• •••••••n• ••• n•w J•v• •on•••••n•y ••••• i•• .

T••l• 1 •••••n•• ••••i••i•• on ••• ••••i•••ion• w• ••v•lo•••. T••••• •• own i• only •o• ••• 195 •••li• • •••o•• in ••• ••••i•• •l•••••; in•l• in• ••iv••• • •••- o•• ••in•• ••• •o••l •o ov•• ••0. W• no•• ••••• •o• •ll • •••o•• w• w••• ••l• •o w•i•• •o• •l••• ••••vio••l •••i•••ion•. So, •o• ••i• •••ll•n•in• ••• o•• on•••••n• •l••••, o•• •x••n•ion ••••••• ••• •i•n• •o• ••••••in• •••i• •••• vio•.

T••l• 1 •l•o ••• o••• ••• •••••••n•y wi•• w•i•• w• ••••• •iff•••n• ••o•• o• •x••n••• JML ••i• i•iv••; ••••• ••o••• w••• ••••i••• in ••• •••-•••ion• o• S••.•.• •••• •n••y •• ow••• •n• • ••• o•• •••o•• in ••• •l••• w•o•• ••••i•••ion •••• •n •nno••ion in ••• •iv•n ••o••.

W• o•••v• ••••• •ll o••• • •••o•• ••••i•• ••• •••i•••ion• •••• •••• ••• ••ywo•• atomic, •••• i•, ••• • •••o•• •x•i•i• ••• ••o• i•i•y ••o•••y. T•••• ••••l•• ••• •o •xi••in• •vi••n• [•5] in •••• o•• o•••• •on•l•ion •••• • o•• J•v• • •••o••••• in••n••• •o •x•••••••o• i••lly. T•i• v•li•••• o••••••o••• •o ••in• ••o• i•i•y •• •••• ••n•••l ••••••••ion •o• •x••n•in• JML •o •••• •o•• •on•••••n•y.

T•• ••• o• \independent i• no• ••••i••l••ly •o• • on in ••i• •oll•••ion o• •l•••••. W• ••li•v• ••••• •i• i• •••• •o ••• •••• •••• • •••o•• in •••••• •l••••• ••n- •••lly ••v• •o• •l•x •on•••••n•y •oli•i••. Mo•• •y•i••l •l••••• wi•• get •n• set • •••o•• •o• in•••n•• ••l•• wo•l• ••o•••ly yi•l• l•••• n•• •••• o• in•••••n••n• • •••o••, •••• ••••o•••• •••y o• J•v• •l••••• i• n•••••• •o •on••• ••i• in••i•ion.

T•• ••••y •on••• • ••• • •o••l••i•y o• •yn•••oni•••ion in •n•o••in• •o••••• •••••••-•••• •l••• ••••vio• ••• • o•• •••n 60% o• ••• • •••o•• ••••• ••• lo••in• •x••n•ion•. U•• o•••••• •on•n•• •n• i• • ••• l••• •o• • on in ••i• ••••y wi•• l••• •••n •0% o•••• • •••o•••••in• \thread_safe •nno•••ion•.

Table 2. Summary of statistics from verification case studies with the extended JML. Classes marked with a * belong to Java 1.5's package `java.util.concurrent`

Class Name	Number of Methods	Checkable Atomicity	Checkable Functionality	Coverage Ratio
BoundedBuffer	3	1	3	.67
DiningPhilosphers	7	6	7	.93
LinkedQueue	7	1	7	.57
RWVSN	8	4	8	.75
CopyOnWriteArrayList*	10	5	10	.75
LinkedBlockingQueue*	7	3	7	.71
Total:	42	20	42	.74

W• ••li•v• •••• ••• •••••• ••• o• when •l•••• in •• i• •••• y i• ••• •o ••• ••••
••••• • o•• o• o• •• •l••••• ••• •on••in•• •••• ••••• ••••••. In • o•• •••••, •on••••n•
•••• •••• •••••• ••v• •wo • lo•• in• • •••o••: on• •••• in••••• •l•• •n•• •••• • lo•••
i• ••• •••••••• i• •• ll •n• •no•••• on• •••• ••• ov•• •l•• •n•• •••• • lo••• i• •••
••••• •••• i• •• ••y. Mo•• v••i•• in•••••••• •o• •••••••in• •n• • o• i•yin• ••o•••
•••• will in••••••• ••• n••• •o• •• i• •nno••ion.

T••• o•• i• • o•••n• •••• l• o• ••••• •••• i•• i• ••• ••••• •••• •••• ••o• o••• JML
•x••n•ion• •••••• •o •• • o•• n••••••y (•ll •nno••ion• ••• •••• in ••• ••••y)
•n• ••• •i•n• (•ll • •••o•• in ••• •••• y •o• l• • • ••••i• ••) •o• •••• o••in• •••••••-
•••• •• n••ion•l •• ••i• •••ion.

5.2   Verification Case Studies

In •••vio•• wo•• [••], w• ••ow•• •ow •n •x••n•i•l• • o••l ••••• in• •••• •wo••,
••ll•• Bo•o•, •o• l• •• •x••n•• •o ••••• •o• •l•x JML ••••i•••ion• [•], •n•
•ow •••• •••• •wo•• •o•l• •• in•••n••n•ly •x••n••• •o ••••• ••o• i•i•y ••••-
i•••ion• [9]. W• ••v• in•••••••• •••••• •wo ••••••••• •x••n•ion• •o •x••••• •i-
• •l••n•o••ly •••in• ••••••-••••• •n•ly•i• •o ••••• •x••n••• JML •on••••n•y
••••i•••ion•. T••• • in •••• ni••l nov•l•y o• ••i• in•••••ion i• •••• • o•••on-
•i•ion •n• ••••• • •on•i•ion •••••in• i• •n•o•••• only i• ••• ••••••n• •x•••ion
o• ••• • •••o• w•• •••i•l, •••• i•, i• ••• • •••o• •o•y w•• •x•••••• wi••o••
•ny in•••l••vin• ••o• o•••• •••••••. So •• i• •••••••y • o•• •••••• ••• •• n••ion•l
•••• i•••ion• •n• in••• •n••n•ly •••••• ••••• •ll •on•••••n• •• n• o• ••• • •••o•
•on•o•• •o ••• ••o• i•i•y •••• i•••ion•. I• •i•••• ••• ••o• i•i•y •••i•••ion o•
••• •• n••ion•l ••••i•••ion ••• no• •••i•••, •••n Bo•o• ••• o••• • •• ••i•••ion
viol••ion.

T•• •••• l• o• ••• lyin• ••i• •••i•••ion •••••in• •ool •o • •••••• o• •••
•l••••• li••••• in T••l• 1 ••• ••• • • •i••• in T••l• •. T•• ••••• •ol•• n in •• i• ••• l•
• i•• l•y• ••• •l••• n•• • •o• ••• •••i•• l•• ••••• •••• y. T•• •••on• •ol•• n •• ow•
••• •o••l n•• •••• o•• •••o•• involv•• in ••• •••• ••••y. Fo• •o• • •l•••••, only
• ••••ion o• ••• •o••l • •••o•• in ••• •l••• w••• •••••••. W• ••l••••• • •••o••
wi•• • iv•••• •• n••ion•li•y in••••• o• ••••••in• l•••• n•• •••• o• •i• il••• ••• o••.

T•• •••• o•••• •ol•• n• in ••• ••• l• ••••n• •••• on ••• • ••••• •o w•i•• •••
•ool w•• •••••• l• o• ••••onin• ••o•• •• ••i••• • •••o••. W• • ivi••• ••• •• ••i••-

•ion in•o •wo •••••: ••• ••o• i•i•y ••••i•••ion •n• ••• •• n••ion•l •••i•••ion. T•• ••i•• •ol•• n in ••• •••l• ••ow• ••• n•• ••• o• • •••o•• in ••• •l••• •o• w•i•• ••• ••o• i•i•y ••••i•••ion •o•l• •• • •••••••, •n• ••• n•x• •ol•• n •• ow• ••• n•• ••• o• ••o•• •o• w•i•• ••• •• n••ion•l •••i•••ion •o•l• •• • •••••••. Fin•lly, ••• l••• •ol•• n •iv• • •••io o• •••i•••ion• ••••••• v••••• •o••l ••••-i•••ion• w•i••n •o• •ll • •••o•• in • •l•••.

T••l• • •• ow• •••• ••• •ool •o•l• v••i•y •ll o• ••• •• n••ion•l •••i•••ion• •o• •••• • •••o• in ••• ••••.y. W• no•• •••• •••••• ••• •••on• •••i•••ion• •••• involv• ••• n•i•••ion ov••• ••••• •l•• •n••, ••••in• •••• • •on•i•ion•, ••••• n•••, •••••• ili•y, •n• •• l•• l••in• ••• v•l••• o• • •• o•y lo••ion• in ••• ••••-•••••.

• ••••in• o• ••o• i•i•y i• no• n•••ly •• •o• •l•••. T•• •ool •o•l• v••i•y ••o• -i•i•y •o• only •0 o•• o• ••• •• • •••o••. T•• •••• y in•l•••• •• • •••o••• ••••• •x•i•i• • •in• o• ••o• i•i•y w•i•• Bo•o• ••nno• v••i•y. Bo•o•'• ••o• i•i•y ••••-in• • ••••ni•• i• ••••• on Li••on' •••••••ion [19] •n• •••n•i•ion in•••n••n•• [9], w•••••• ••• •• •n•ov•••• • •••o•• in ••••• •••• •••• i•• •x•i•i• • • iff••n• •y•• o••o• i•i•y. 11 o••o•• ••• • •••o•• •x•i•i• *commit atomicity* •••• n•• •y Fl•n•••n in [••]. In •••• wo••, Fl•n•••n •••••i••• • • o••l •••••in• •l•o•i•• •••• •llow• ••••in• •o• • i• ••o• i•i•y •••i•••ion•. T•i• ••••ni••• •o•l• •• in•••••••• in•o Bo•o•, •n• wo•l• yi•l• • •ov•••• •••io o• .••.

T•• o•••• 11 •n•••••••l• • •••o•• i• •l•• •n• •o• •l•x •on••••n•y •••••n• •••• o•• •ool •o•l• no• ••••••, •v•n i• •n••n••• •o •••••• •o• • i• ••o• i•i•y. T•• • o••l ••••••• •o•l• •• ••••••• •x••n••, o• •o••••, •o in•l••• •••••• •yn-•••oni•••ion ••••••n• •n• ••••••y in••••• ••••••in• ov••••. B••in•• ••••• in• ••o• i•i•y i• •n••i•••l• in ••n•••l, •••• will •lw•y• •• •o• • ••••••n• •••• ••• •ool •o•l• no• ••••••. Fo••• n•••ly, ••• •o• •l•x ••••••n• •n• •••ll•n•in• •on•••-••n•y •l••••• •••• w• ••l••••• •o• o• ••• •y ••• no• •o• • on in •••l ••• li•••ion •o••. In••••, Fl•n•••n •n• F•••n• •o•n• ••••• • o•• ••n 90% o• ••• • •••o•• •••y •n•ly••• [•5] •x•i•i••• ••l••iv•ly •i• •l• •o•• • o• ••o• i•i•y. T••• w ••x-•••• ••••• • •ny ••l ••o•••• • •••i••• wi•• •x••n••• JML will •• ••• •n••l• •o •n•ly•i• vi• • o••l •••••in•. How•v••, • •i•ni••n•ly ••o••••• •v•l•••ion o• ••• ••• o• JML •n• i•• •••••o•• •o• •n•ly•i• will •• n•••••• •o •on••• ••i• •onj•••••••.

6   Related Work

P•••••• ••• •lo•••• ••l•••• wo•• •o o••• i• ••• wo•• on •x••n•in• S•••# •o •••l wi•• • •l•i-•••••••• ••o•••• • [30]. T•• •••i•••ion l•n•••••• •••• o• S•••# [5], i• •i• il•• in • •ny w•y• •o JML, •l••o••• i• i• in•••••••• in•o ••• ••o•••• • in• l•n•••••• (•• in • iff•l [6]). Li•• JML, S•••# •l•o ••• •n •x••n•iv• •ool •••, in-•l••in• •• n•i• • •••••••ion •••••in• •n• • v••i•••ion •n•in•. Al••o••• S•••# i• v••y •i• il•• •o •#, i• i• • n•w ••o•••• • in• l•n••••• ••••• •x••n•• •n• • o•i-•••• • •# in ••v•••l w•y•. T•• • o•• in•••••••in• o• ••••• •••n••• •o • •# •o• • in ••• w•y• ••••• S•••# •••l• wi•• •li•• •on••ol •n• •on••••n•y •on••ol. In •o• o• •••••• •••••, S•••# •••• n•w ••••••• •n• (pack •n• unpack •o• •li•• •on••ol, •n• acquire •n• release ••••• •n•• •o• •on••••n•y •on••ol). T•• ••••••• •n•

o•• •li•• •on••ol i• • o•• •yn•• i• ••• n •••• •o•n• in ••• Univ•••• •y•• •y••••
w•i•• JML ••••, w•i•• • •y• ••• i• • o•• •i• •• l• •o •n•ly•• ••••i••lly. Fo• •on-
••••••n•y •on••ol, S•••# •••l• wi•• •x•••n•l in•••••••n•• in • ••••••i• •••• ion, •y
••vin• acquire ••in •x•l••iv• •••••• •o •n o•j•••, •o •••• i• i• •••••• lo••l. T••
S•••# •i••i•lin• •olv•• ••• in•••n•l •n• •x•••n•l in•••••••n•• ••o•l•• •, •n• •••
• ••oo• o• •o•n•n••. How•v••, ••• •••oo•• only •••li•• •o ••o•••• • ••••• ••n
•• w•i••n •ollowin• •••• •i••i•lin•. T•• •••• o•• li•• •• •••••• wo•• "•x••n• in•
••• ••••o••• •o •••l wi•• o•••• •••i•n ••••••n•" [30–S••. 9]. In •on••••, o••
wo•• •••••• ••• •o •••l wi•• •xi••in• •on•••n• J•v• ••o•••• •, wi•• o••••• i•in•
•••• •••y •ollow • ••••i••l•• ••o•••• • in• •i••i•lin•.

A•••••• *et al.* [31] ••ovi•• • ••oo• •y•••• •o• • •l•i-•••••••• J•v• ••o-
•••• •. T••i• •n•ly•i• i• •o•n• •n• •ool •••• o••••. How•v••, •• •••y ••ly on
w•ol•-••o•••• • wi••i-• •i•• ••yl• •nno••ion• •••y •o no• •••i•v• • o••l••i•y
in ••• ••n•• w• •i• •o• (*i.e.*, •• ••• l•v•l o• in•ivi••l •o• •il••ion • ni••). F•-
•••• o••, •••i• ••oo• •y•••• only •••l• wi•• • oni•o• •yn••oni••ion, w•••••
o••• ••••o••• i• ••• li•••l• •o •ll J•v•, •n• ••••••• • v••y wi•• ••n•• o• •yn••o-
ni••ion •••••••n• •y •••••••in• •w•y ••o• •yn••oni••ion •on•i•ion•. T•••
o••• ••••o••• ••o• i••• •o ••• o•• ••••l •o• •xi••in• J•v• •o••.

• o••y ••• •l. [•] i••n•i••• ••• ••o•l•• o• *internal interference* ••••••i••• in
S••.•. T••y •olv•• i••y •••••••o•in• •••• ••n••ion•l•o•• o••• ••• o•, in•o •no••••
• •••o•, •••••••in• i• ••o• ••• •yn••oni••ion •o••. In ••i• w•y ••y••• ••l• •o
••••• JML •••i••••ion •• on ••• ••••••o••• • •••o• •••• i• •lw•y• ••ll•• wi•• in
•n ••o• i• •on••x•. How•v••, ••i• •••• ni••• i• •o•• li• i••• in i•• ••• li•••ili•y
•n• in•onv•ni•n• •o• •••••.

F•••n• •n• •••••• i• •l•• •n• • • o••l•• •n•ly•i• •o• ••o• i• ••••i•••ion•
on • •l•i-•••••••• •o••w••• [3•]. T•• i••• o• ••in• • l•••l •o • ••• ••• •o• • i•
•oin•• o•• • •••o•, •i• il•• •o ••• commit l•••l in••o•••• in S••. •.5, •o• ••
••o• •••i• wo••. T••y •••i•v• • o••l••i•y •y •nno••in• •••••• v•i••l•• wi••
•n •••••• •••• i•••, •n• •y ••in• ••• •on•••• o• ••••••ion •o lin• ••o•••••
•o i•• ••••i••••ion. T••y •••n•l•• • • •l•i-•••••••• ••o•••• in•o •••••n•i•l
••o•••• in w•i•• ••o• i• ••o••••••••• ••• •x•••••• •••••n•i•lly. How•v••, JML
i• •o•• •x•••••iv• ••n ••• ••••i•••ion l•n••••• •••y••••.

H•••liff •• •l. [9] ••v•lo••• • •••• ni••• •o v••i•y ••o• i•i•y •nno••ion• ••in•
• o••l •••••in•. W•n• •n• S•oll•• [33] ••ovi•• •wo ••o• i•i•y •••••••ion •l•o-
•i••• • ••••• on ••n•i• • •n•ly•i•: on• ••••• on Li••on'• ••••••ion [19] •n• •n-
o••••••••• on • •o••i•i••••• •••••••n • ••••in• • •••• ni•• . How•v••, ••i• •y•-
••• only ••ovi•••• v••i•••ion o• ••o• i•i•y ••••i•••ion•. T•• v••i•••ion •ool
•••••i•••• in S••. 5 ••n • vi•w•• ••• • n•••••l •x••n•ion •o ••••• ••••ni••••,
w•i•• •l•o •••••••• •• n••ion•l ••••i•••ion•.

7   Conclusions and Future Work

W• ••v• •x••n••• JML •y •••in• no••ion• •••• •llow ••• v••i•••ion o•• •l•i-
••••••••• J•v• ••o••••• •. T•• ov••ll ••••o•••• i• •o ••• ••• •on•••• o••o• i•i•y,
••o• Li••on'• •••••••ion ••o•y •o• ••••ll•l ••o•••• •. W• ••v• •• own • ow •••

••••• •nno••••ion• ••••• o•• ••• ••on•••• o• ••o• i•i•y •n• •llow ••• •••••i•••ion
o• lo••in• •••••vio•. In •••i•ion, w• ••v• •• own • ow ••• ••on•••• o• ••o• i•i•y
••n •• ••••• •o •voi• ••• ••o•l•• • o• in•••n•l •n• •x•••n•l in••••••n••, •n•
•••• •o ••••o•• • o••l•• ••••onin•. W• ••v• •••••i••• o•• •••••••• in w•i•in•
•x••n••• JML ••••i•••ion• o• •xi••in• J•v• •l•••••• •n• ••v• •••o•••• ••••l••
on ••• i• •l•• •n••ion o•• •ool •••• l•v••••••••••••• l•n••••• •x••n•ion• •o v••i•y
•••••vio••l ••••i•••ion• o• • •l•i-•••••••• ••o•••• •.

W• ••• •l•nnin• on •x••n• in• •n• •on•in•in• •• i• wo•• •lon• ••v•••l lin••.
• n ••• JML l•n•••••• •i••, w• ••• •l•nnin• •o wo•• on • •o•• •li•••ion o• •ll •••
n•w l•n••••• •on•••••••• •••••n••• in •• i• ••••••, •n• in••o•••• • •o•• •l• o••l••
•n•ly•i• •o• •••••vio••l ••••i•••ion• o• • •l•i-•••••••• ••o•••• •. So• • •••••il•,
•••• •• • ow •o •x••n• JML'• •on•••• o• ••••• • •••o••• •o •llow •o• lo••in•
[3] •l•o n•••• •o •• wo•••• o••. Al•o, w• ••• •••••yin• o•••• w•y• •o i• ••ov•
•on•••••n•y ••••o•• in JML. Fo• •x•• •l•, on• w•y in w•i•• JML •o•l• ••
•••••••• i• ••ov•• i• ••• •••i•ion o•••• •o••l lo•i• ••••i•••ion o••••o•• •••••
on •••i•••ion •••••••n• [3•] •• in BSL (B•n•••• S•••i•••ion L•n•••••) [35].
T•••• ••• •yn••oni••ion ••••••n i• •l•• •n••ion•, •••• •• ••o•• ••••••n••• in
[36], •o• w•i•• i• i• no• •l••• w•••••• •• •••x••n•ion •••••n••• in •• i• wo••
••• ••• ••• •i•n•, •n• •••• • i••• •••••i•• JML •o •• •x••n••• wi•• ••• • o••l lo•i•
•nno••••ion• •o •• ••o••••ly •••i•••.

• n ••• •ool ••••o•• •i••, ••• ••• • •••i• •ivi•ion o• l••o• •••••i••• in S••. 5
•o•• o••l••••••in•, •o•l• ••••••• •o••••• JML'• ••n•i• • ••••••ion ••••• in• •ool
[3•] •o o•• JML •x••n•ion•. T• i• •ool in•••••• •n• J•v• ••o••••• • wi•• •••i•ion•l
in•••••••ion• •••• ••••• • •••o• •••- •n• •o•••on•i•ion•, inv••i•n••, etc. T•• i• ••
wo•l• •• •o ••• •••••• ••o• ••• A•o• i••• •ool [•5], w•i•• ••••••• •••••• ••o••••
•••••• •on•o•• •o Li••on' ••o• i•i•y ••••••n. By •••••••ly ••••in• •o• ••o• i•
•x•••ion•, ••• •• n•i• • ••••••ion ••••••• •o•l• ••••y on •• ••o••, ••••• in•
•••• ••o• i• • ••• o•• w••• •x•••••• ••••n•i•lly.

W• •l•n •o in••••••• •• i• wo•• in•o ••• JML• •li••• •••• •wo•• [3•] w•i•• i•
•n • •li•••-••••• ••on•-•n• •o• JML v••i•••ion •n•in• (in ••••i••l••, i• will ••
••• ••on•-•n• •o• o•• JML • o••l••••••in• •ool). Ano••••• •o••i•l• ••••• •o• ••••••
wo•• i• •o •x••n• o•••• JML •ool•, ••••• ••• S• /J•v•• o• o••••• v••i•••ion •ool•
(e.g., [39]) •o in•o•• o•••• ••• n•w •••••••••.

Acknowledgments

T• i• wo•• w•• •••• •o•••• in ••••• •y: ••• U.S. A•• y • ••••••• • • •• (•n•••••n•
DAAD19011056•), •y DA• PA/IX• '• P•• S ••o•••• (AF• L • on••••• F33615-
00-• -30••), •y NSF (• • F-030660•, • • F-03•11•9, • • F-0•••0••, • • F-0••91•9,
• • F-0••956•, • • F-0••16•), •n• Lo••••••• M•••in. T••n•• •o • ••••i• • li••on,
D•vi• • o•, S••••• J•••nn•••n, Jo• Kini•y, • ••••n L•ino, To•• W•l•n•in•
•n• ••• ••••• • P •••o•••• ••o• • i•••• •o• •o• • •n•• on •••li•• • ••••••.

References

1. Burdy, L., Cheon, Y., Cok, D., Ernst, M., Kiniry, J., Leavens, G.T., Leino, K.R.M., Poll, E.: An overview of JML tools and applications. International Journal on Software Tools for Technology Transfer (STTT) (2004) To appear.
2. Leavens, G.T., Baker, A.L., Ruby, C.: Preliminary design of JML: A behavioral interface specification language for Java. Technical Report 98-06y, Iowa State University, Department of Computer Science (2004) See www.jmlspecs.org.
3. Leavens, G.T., Cheon, Y., Clifton, C., Ruby, C., Cok, D.R.: How the design of JML accommodates both runtime assertion checking and formal verification. Science of Computer Programming **55** (2005) 185–208
4. Leavens, G.T., Poll, E., Clifton, C., Cheon, Y., Ruby, C., Cok, D.R., Kiniry, J.: Jml reference manual. Department of Computer Science, Iowa State University. Available from http://www.jmlspecs.org (2005)
5. Barnett, M., Leino, K.R.M., Schulte, W.: The Spec# programming system: An overview. In: Proceedings of the International Workshop on Construction and Analysis of Safe, Secure and Interoperable Smart Devices. (2004) To appear.
6. Meyer, B.: Object-oriented Software Construction. Second edn. Prentice Hall, New York, NY (1997)
7. SAnToS: SpEx Website. |http://spex.projects.cis.ksu.edu— (2003)
8. Robby, Rodríguez, E., Dwyer, M., Hatcliff, J.: Checking strong specifications using an extensible software model checking framework. In: Proceedings of the 10th International Conference on Tools and Algorithms for the Construction and Analysis of Systems. Volume 2988 of Lecture Notes in Computer Science., Springer (2004) 404–420
9. Hatcliff, J., Robby, Dwyer, M.: Verifying atomicity specifications for concurrent object oriented software using model checking. In: Proceedings of the 5th International Conference on Verification, Model Checking, and Abstract Interpretation. Volume 2937 of Lecture Notes in Computer Science., Springer (2004) 175–190
10. Pugh, W.: Fixing the java memory model. In: Proceedings of the ACM 1999 Conference on Java Grande, New York, NY, USA, ACM Press (1999) 89–98
11. Flanagan, C., Freund, S.N.: Type-based race detection for java. In: Proceedings of the ACM SIGPLAN 2000 Conference on Programming Language Design and Implementation, New York, NY, USA, ACM Press (2000) 219–232
12. Lea, D.: Concurrent Programming in Java: Second Edition. Addison-Wesley (2000)
13. Raghavan, A.D., Leavens, G.T.: Desugaring JML method specifications. Technical Report 00-03d, Iowa State University, Department of Computer Science (2003)
14. Lerner, R.A.: Specifying Objects of Concurrent Systems. PhD thesis, School of Computer Science, Carnegie Mellon University (1991) TR CMU–CS–91–131.
15. Boyland, J., Noble, J., Retert, W.: Capabilities for sharing. In: Proceedings of the 15th European Conference on Object Oriented Programming. Volume 2072 of Lecture Notes in Computer Science., Springer-Verlag (2001) 1–27
16. Noble, J., Vitek, J., Potter, J.: Flexible alias protection. In: Proceedings of the 12th European Conference on Object Oriented Programming. Volume 1445 of Lecture Notes in Computer Science., Springer-Verlag (1998) 158–185
17. Müller, P., Poetzsch-Heffter, A.: Universes: A type system for alias and dependency control. Technical Report 279, Fernuniversität Hagen (2001) Available from www.informatik.fernuni-hagen.de/pi5/publications.html.
18. Borgida, A., Mylopoulos, J., Reiter, R.: On the frame problem in procedure specifications. IEEE Transactions on Software Engineering **21** (1995) 785–798

19. Lipton, R.J.: Reduction: a method of proving properties of parallel programs. Communications of the ACM **18** (1975) 717–721

20. Flanagan, C., Qadeer, S.: Types for atomicity. In: Proceedings of the 2003 ACM SIGPLAN International Workshop on Types in Languages Design and Implementation, ACM Press (2003) 1–12

21. Clarke, E., Grumberg, O., Peled, D.: Model Checking. MIT Press (2000)

22. Dwyer, M.B., Hatcliff, J., Robby, R.Prasad, V.: Exploiting object escape and locking information in partial order reduction for concurrent object-oriented programs. Formal Methods in System Design **25** (2004) 199–240

23. Dietl, W., Müller, P.: Universes: Lightweight ownership for jml. Journal of Object Technology (2005) To appear.

24. Flanagan, C., Qadeer, S.: A type and effect system for atomicity. In: Proceedings of the ACM SIGPLAN 2003 Conference on Programming Language Design and Implementation, ACM Press (2003) 338–349

25. Flanagan, C., Freund, S.N.: Atomizer: a dynamic atomicity checker for multi-threaded programs. In: Proceedings of the 31st ACM SIGPLAN-SIGACT symposium on Principles of programming languages, ACM Press (2004) 256–267

26. Saltzer, J.H., Reed, D.P., Clark, D.D.: End-to-end arguments in system design. ACM Transactions on Computer Systems **2** (1984) 277–288

27. Flanagan, C.: Verifying commit-atomicity using model-checking. In: Proceedings of the 11th International SPIN Workshop on Model Checking of Software. Volume 2989 of Lecture Notes in Computer Science., Springer (2004) 252–266

28. Robby, Dwyer, M.B., Hatcliff, J.: Bogor: An extensible and highly-modular model checking framework. In: Proceedings of the 9th European Software Engineering Conference held jointly with the 11th ACM SIGSOFT Symposium on the Foundations of Software Engineering. Volume 28 number 5 of SIGSOFT Softw. Eng. Notes., ACM Press (2003) 267–276

29. Hartley, S.: Concurrent Programming - The Java Programming Language. Oxford University Press (1998)

30. Jacobs, B., Leino, K.R.M., Schulte, W.: Verification of multithreaded object-oriented programs with invariants. In: Proceedings of The ACM SIGSOFT Workshop on Specification and Verification of Component Based Systems, ACM Press (2004) To appear.

31. Ábrahám, E., de Boer, F.S., de Roever, W.P., Steffen, M.: A tool-supported proof system for multithreaded java. In: Proceedings of the International Symposia on Formal Methods for Components and Objects. Volume 2852 of Lecture Notes in Computer Science., Springer (2002) 1–32

32. Freund, S.N., Qadeer, S.: Checking concise specifications for multithreaded software. Journal of Object Technology **3** (2004) 81–101

33. Wang, L., Stoller, S.D.: Run-time analysis for atomicity. In: Proceedings of the Third Workshop on Runtime Verification (RV). Volume 89(2) of Electronic Notes in Theoretical Computer Science., Elsevier (2003)

34. Dwyer, M.B., Avrunin, G.S., Corbett, J.C.: Property specification patterns for finite-state verification. In: Proceedings of the Second Workshop on Formal Methods in Software Practice. (1998) 7–15

35. Corbett, J.C., Dwyer, M.B., Hatcliff, J., Robby: Expressing checkable properties of dynamic systems: The Bandera Specification Language. International Journal on Software Tools for Technology Transfer **4** (2002) 34–56

36. Deng, X., Dwyer, M.B., Hatcliff, J., Mizuno, M.: Invariant-based specification, synthesis, and verification of synchronization in concurrent programs. In: Proceedings of the 24th International Conference on Software Engineering (ICSE 2002), New York, NY, USA, ACM Press (2002) 442–452
37. Cheon, Y., Leavens, G.T.: A runtime assertion checker for the Java Modeling Language (JML). In: Proceedings of The International Conference on Software Engineering Research and Practice, CSREA Press (June 2002) 322–328
38. SAnToS: JMLEclipse Website. |http://jmleclipse.projects.cis.ksu.edu— (2004)
39. Burdy, L., Requet, A., Lanet, J.L.: Java applet correctness: A developer-oriented approach. In: Proceedings of the 12th International Symposium of Formal Methods Europe. Volume 2805 of Lecture Notes in Computer Science., Springer-Verlag (2003) 422–439

Derivation and Evaluation of Concurrent Collectors

Martin T. Vechev[1], David F. Bacon[2], Perry Cheng[2], and David Grove[2]

[1] Computer Laboratory, Cambridge University,
Cambridge CB3 0FD, U.K
[2] IBM T.J. Watson Research Center,
P.O. Box 704, Yorktown Heights, NY 10598, U.S.A

Abstract. There are many algorithms for concurrent garbage collection, but they are complex to describe, verify, and implement. This has resulted in a poor under-standing of the relationships between the algorithms, and has precluded system-atic study and comparative evaluation. We present a single high-level, abstract concurrent garbage collection algorithm, and show how existing snapshot and incremental update collectors, can be derived from the abstract algorithm by re-ducing precision. We also derive a new hybrid algorithm that reduces floating garbage while terminating quickly. We have implemented a concurrent collector framework and the resulting algorithms in IBM's J9 Java virtual machine prod-uct and compared their performance in terms of space, time, and incrementality. The results show that incremental update algorithms sometimes reduce memory requirements (on 3 of 5 benchmarks) but they also sometimes take longer due to recomputation in the termination phase (on 4 of 5 benchmarks). Our new hybrid algorithm has memory requirements similar to the incremental update collectors while avoiding recomputation in the termination phase.

1   Introduction

The wide acceptance of the Java programming language has brought garbage collected languages into the mainstream. However, the use of traditional synchronous ("stop the world") garbage collection is limiting the domains into which Java and similar lan-guages can expand. The need for concurrent garbage collection is primarily being driven by two trends: the first is increased heap sizes, which make the pauses longer and less tolerable; the second is the increase in the use of, and complexity of, real-time systems, for which even short pauses are often unacceptable. Therefore there is need for rapid improvement in various kinds of incremental and concurrent collector technology.

Unfortunately, concurrent garbage collectors are one of the more difficult concur-rent programs to construct correctly. The study of concurrent collectors began with Steele [27], Dijkstra [14], and Lamport [20].

Concurrent collectors were considered paradigmatic examples of the difficulty of constructing correct concurrent algorithms. Steele's algorithm contained an error which he subsequently corrected [28], and Dijkstra's algorithm contained an error discovered and corrected by Stenning and Woodger [14]. Furthermore, some correct algorithms [9] had informal proofs that were found to contain errors [25].

A.P. Black (Ed.): ECOOP 2005, LNCS 3586, pp. 577–601, 2005.

These problems also manifest themselves in practice because concurrent bugs generally have a non-deterministic effect on the system and are non-repeatable, so that connecting the cause of the error to the observed effect is particularly difficult.

Many incremental and concurrent algorithms have been introduced in the last 30 years [1, 3, 4, 6, 7, 10, 11, 12, 13, 16, 17, 18, 19, 21, 23, 24], but there has been very little comparative evaluation of the properties of the different algorithms due to the complexity of implementing even one algorithm correctly. As noted in [2], because of these constraints, current state-of-the-art concurrent systems are generally not quantitatively compared against each other and the exact relationships among the different concurrent schemes are largely unknown.

For example, early collectors were all examples of *incremental update* collectors which "chase down" modifications to the object graph that are made by the program during collection. Yuasa [29] introduced snapshot collectors, which do not attempt to collect garbage allocated after collection begins, but do not require any rescanning of the object graph. Thus, snapshot collectors trade off reliable termination for a potential increase in floating garbage. However, costs and benefits relative to incremental update techniques have not been systematically studied.

This paper presents a high-level algorithm for concurrent collection that subsumes and generalizes several previous concurrent collector techniques. This algorithm is significantly more precise than previous algorithms (at the expense of constant-factor increases in both time and space), and more importantly yields a number of insights into the operation of concurrent collection. For instance, the operation of concurrent write barriers can be viewed as a form of degenerate reference counting; in our algorithm, we do true reference counting and are thereby able to find live data more precisely.

Existing algorithms can then be viewed as instantiations of the generalized algorithm that sacrifice precision for compactness of object representation and speed of the collector operations (especially the write barriers).

Additionally, we argue that all of the existing concurrent algorithms fundamentally share a deeper structure. And there is a whole continuum of existing algorithms, which we have not yet explored, but could be uncovered if we start from such a structure. Moreover, by having a common abstract algorithm, much of the construction of the practical collector will be simplified.

The contributions of this paper are:

- A generalized, extendable, abstract concurrent collection algorithm, which is more precise than previous algorithms;
- A demonstration of how the abstract algorithm can be instantiated to yield existing snapshot and incremental update algorithms;
- A new snapshot algorithm (derived from the abstract algorithm) that allocates objects unmarked ("white") and reduces floating garbage without re-scanning of the heap required by incremental update algorithms;
- An implementation of four concurrent collectors in a production-quality virtual machine (IBM's J9 JVM product): Snapshot (after Yuasa), two incremental- update (after both Dijkstra and Steele), and our hybrid snapshot algorithm; and
- A quantitative experimental evaluation comparing the performance of the different algorithms.

2   An Abstract Collector

This section presents the abstract collector algorithm. The algorithm is designed for maximum precision and flexibility, and keeps much more information per object than would be practical in a realistic implementation. However, the space overhead is only a constant factor, and thus, does not affect the asymptotic complexity of the algorithm, while the additional information allows a potential reduction in complexity.

Similarly, a number of operations employed by the abstract algorithm also have constant time overheads that would be undesirable in a realistic collector. In particular, there is no special treatment of stack variables: they are assumed to be part of the heap and therefore every stack operation may incur a constant-time overhead for the collector to execute an associated barrier operation. There are a number of collectors for functional languages (such as ML and Haskell) that treat the stack in exactly this way.

Our generalized concurrent collection algorithm makes use of the framework of Bacon et al. [5]: they showed that for synchronous ("stop the world") garbage collection, tracing and reference counting can be considered as dual approaches to computing the reference count of an object. Tracing computes a least fixpoint, and reference counting computes a greatest fixpoint. The difference between the greatest and least fixpoints is the cyclic garbage. In most practical tracing collectors, the reference count is collapsed into a single bit.

Furthermore, they showed that all collectors could be considered as a combination of tracing and reference counting, and that any incrementality is due to the use of a reference counting approach with its write barriers.

This insight is now extended to concurrent tracing collectors: we show that they are also a tracing/reference counting hybrid. The collector traces the original object graph as it existed at the time when collection started, but does reference counting for pointers to live objects that could be lost due to concurrent mutation.

The abstract algorithm makes use of the variables depicted in Table 1. In the discussion that follows, we elaborate more on the semantics of each shared variable.

Table 1. Shared variables, $|N|$ is object size, $|P|$ is maximum number of pointers in the heap and $|H|$ is the number of objects in the heap

Shared Variable	Description	Computed By	Value Domain
Global Variables			
Phase	Current Collector phase	Collector	[Idle, Tracing, Sweeping]
Hue	Scanned Part of the Heap	Collector	$[0, |H|]$
Per-Object Variables			
Marked	Mark flag	Collector	Boolean
SRC	Scanned reference count	Mutator	$[0, |P|]$
Shade	Scanning progress within object	Collector	$[0, |N|]$
Recorded	Recorded in buffer by barrier	Mutator	Boolean
DontSweep	Allocated after Hue	Mutator	Boolean

2.1   Restrictions and Assumptions

The algorithms we discuss are non-moving and concurrent, but not parallel. That is, the collector is single-threaded. The ideas derived from this discussion, however, are easily extendable to algorithms using multiple spaces, such as generational ones.

Furthermore, the algorithm performs synchronization with atomic sections rather than isolated atomic (compare-and-swap) operations. Atomic sections are relatively expensive on a multiprocessor, so that although the algorithm can be executed on a multiprocessor it is better suited to a uniprocessor system based on safe points, in which low-level atomicity is a by-product of the implementation style of the run-time system.

Additionally, we assume that the concurrency between the mutators and the collector is bounded by a single cycle. This is a common underlying assumption in most practical algorithms. Essentially, this means that all mutator operations started in collector cycle N finish in that cycle. They do not carry over to cycle N + 1, for example. No pipelining between the collector phases is assumed: sweeping is followed by marking.

For the sake of presentation, we also make a number of simplifying assumptions about the heap. We assume that all heap objects are the same size S and consist only of collector meta-data and object data fields which are all pointers. The fields of an object X are denoted $X[1]$ through $X[S]$.

2.2   Tracing

The abstract algorithm is shown in Fig 1 and 2. We begin by describing the outer collection loop and the tracing phase of collection cycle.

The Collect() procedure is invoked to perform a (concurrent) garbage collection. When it starts, the Phase of the collector is Idle, and the first thing it does is to atomically mark the root object and set the collector phase to Tracing. Atomicity is required because mutators can perform operations dependent on the collection phase.

Because all variables live in the heap, there is only a single root that must be marked atomically. In a realistic collector that avoided write barriers on stack writes, this single operation would be replaced by atomic marking of all of the roots – which could be on stacks or on global variables.

The core of the algorithm is the invocation of Trace(), which is performed repeatedly until the concurrently executing mutators have not modified the object graph in a way that could result in unmarked live objects.

Tracing in our algorithm is very similar to the tracing in a synchronous collector: it repeatedly gets an object from the mark stack and scans it.

Shades of Grey. In the Scan() procedure the first major difference appears. Like a standard tracing collector, we iterate over the fields of the object and mark them. However, as each field is read, the *Shade* of the object is incremented.

The use of shades is one of the generalizations of our algorithm. Most concurrent collectors use the well-known *tri-color* abstraction: an object is white if it has not been seen by the collector, grey if it has been seen, but all of its fields have not been seen, and black if both it and its fields have been seen.

The color of an object represents the progress of the tracing wavefront as it sweeps over the graph. However, the tri-color abstraction loses information because it does not

```
Collect()
    atomic
        Mark(root);
        Phase = Tracing;

    do
        Trace();
    while (ProcessBarriers());

    atomic
        ProcessBarriers());
        Trace();
        Phase = Sweeping;

    Sweep();
    Phase = Idle;

Trace()
    while(! markStack.empty())
        Obj = markStack.pop();
        Scan(Obj);

Scan(Obj)
    for (field = 1; field <= Obj.Size; field++)
        atomic
            Ptr = Obj[field];
            Obj.Shade = field;
        Mark(Ptr);

Mark(Obj)
    if (! Obj.Marked)
        markStack.push(Obj);
        Obj.Marked = true;

ProcessBarriers()
    retrace = false;
    atomic
        while (true)
            if (barrierBuffer.empty())  return retrace;
            Obj = barrierBuffer.remove();
            Obj.Recorded = false;
            if ((INSTALLATION_COLLECTOR && Obj.SRC == 0) ||
                (DELETION_COLLECTOR && Obj.SRC == 0 && isLeaf(Obj)))
                continue;
            if (! Obj.Marked)
              Mark(Obj);
              retrace = true;
```

Fig. 1. Abstract Collector Code

```
Sweep()
    for (i = 1; i <= Heap.Size; i++)
        Hue = i;
        Obj = Heap[i];
        if (! Obj.Marked && ! Obj.DontSweep)
            FREE(Obj)
        Reset(Obj)

    Hue = 0;

Reset(Obj)
    Obj.Shade = Obj.SRC = 0;
    Obj.Marked = Obj.Recorded = Obj.DontSweep = false;
```

```
atomic WriteBarrier(Obj, field, New, isAllocated)
    if (Phase == Tracing)
        Old = Obj[field];

        if (field < Obj.Shade) // Already scanned by collector
            if (! New.Marked)
                if (DELETION_COLLECTOR)
                    if (isAllocated)
                        Remember(New);
                else
                    if (! New.Recorded)
                        Remember(New);
                New.SRC++;
            if (! Old.Marked)
                Old.SRC--;
        else if (DELETION_COLLECTOR && ! Old.Marked
                && ! Old.Recorded &&
                (!isLeaf(Obj) || (isLeaf(Obj) && Old.SRC > 0)))
            Remember(Old);
    Obj[field] = New;

atomic AllocateBarrier(Obj, field, New)
    Reset(New);
    if (Phase == Sweeping)
        if (Heap.free >= Heap.Hue)
            New.DontSweep = true;
    else
        WriteBarrier(Obj, field, New, true);

Remember(Obj)
    BarrierBuffer.append(Obj);
    Obj.Recorded = true;
```

Fig. 2. Abstract Mutator Code

track the progress of sweeping within the object. Fundamentally, the synchronization between the collector and the mutator depends on whether an object being mutated has been seen yet by the collector. Therefore, by losing information about the marking progress, the precision of the algorithm is compromised.

The *Shade* of an object is simply a generalization of the tri-color abstraction: objects are still white, grey, or black, but there are many shades of grey. The shade represents the exact progress of marking within the object. When *Shade* is 0, the object is white. When it is the same as the number of fields in the object, the object is black. We will describe how the shade information is used when we present the write barrier executed by the mutator.

Once the `Scan()` procedure has updated the shade, it marks the target object. The `Mark()` procedure pushes the object onto the mark stack if it was not already marked.

2.3   Mutator Interaction

We now turn to the interaction between the mutator and collector by considering the actions of the mutator when it changes the object graph. The connectivity graph can be modified by both pointer modification and object allocation.

Write Barrier. The write barrier is depicted by the procedure `WriteBarrier()` in Fig 2. In our presentation of the algorithm, the entire write barrier is atomic. Finer-grained concurrency is possible, but is not discussed in this paper.

The write barrier takes a pointer to the object being modified, the field in the object that is being modified, the new pointer that is being stored into the object, and a flag indicating whether the new pointer refers to an object that was just allocated.

If the collector is not in its tracing phase, it simply performs the write: because it is the tracing phase that determines reachability of objects, only object graph mutations during tracing can affect reachability (object graph additions – via allocation – require some additional synchronization, which is described below).

An object can be protected either (1) when a pointer to it is stored or (2) when a pointer to it is overwritten. We call saving the pointer at 1 an *installation barrier* and saving the pointer at 2 a *deletion barrier*. The Dijkstra-style barrier is an instance of an installation barrier; the Yuasa-style barrier is an instance of a deletion barrier.

Earlier, we described our collector as a combination of tracing and reference counting. The reference counting is done in the write barrier. In particular, we keep a count of the number of references to an unmarked object from scanned portions of the heap. This is called the Scanned Reference Count or *SRC*. The *SRC* is one of the most important aspects of our abstract algorithm and allows for a number of interesting insights.

The SRC allows us to defer reachability decisions from the time of a write barrier to the time when collector tracing is finished. For example, if a pointer to an object is installed into the scanned portion of the heap, and subsequently removed from the scanned portion of the heap, then it can not possibly affect the liveness of the object.

Object Allocation. Besides pointer assignments, the mutator can also add objects to the connectivity graph. Similarly to pointer assignments, the allocation interacts with the tracing phase. In addition, allocation also interacts with the sweeping phase of the collector. This is performed in the procedure `AllocateBarrier()` in Fig 2.

In terms of reachability, if the collector is in its tracing phase, object allocation can be seen as just another pointer modification event. The main difference between allocation and pointer writes is that upon allocation we know that the new pointer is unique. We also know that the new object does not contain any outgoing pointers.

During the sweeping phase, the collector iterates over the heap, reclaims all unreachable objects and resets the state of the live objects. We assume that we can designate which parts of the heap the collector has passed indicated by the variable *Heap.Hue*. The variable is similar to *Shade*, except *Shade* is applied per object while *Hue* is applied per heap. That is, we have one *Hue* variable. Similarly to *Shade*, the variable is monotonic within the same collector cycle.

If the mutator allocates during the collector's sweeping phase, we require a mechanism to protect the object from being collected erroneously. The field *DontSweep* indicates if the object has been allocated in a part of the heap that the collector has yet to reach in its sweeping action.

2.4   Lost Object Problem

In a concurrent interleaving between the application and the collector, the program can accidentally hide pointers during collector heap marking. A mutator can store a pointer into a portion of the heap the collector has already scanned, and subsequently destroy all paths from an unscanned reachable portion of the heap to that object. The problem can be broken down into hiding directly and transitively reachable objects. For illustration purposes an object with a black color is one that the collector has marked reachable and has scanned all of its children. A white-colored object is one that the collector has not yet reached.

The sequence for *directly* hidden objects is depicted in Fig. 3. Each state of the graph is shown in time steps. In the initial state, three are objects: scanned object Y, unscanned but reachable object X and object Z which is not yet marked, but is reachable only from X via pointer *a*. In step D1, a mutator copies pointer *a* and stores it into the scanned object Y resulting in pointer *b*. In step D2, the mutator removes the only pointer to Z from an unscanned but reachable object X. The mutator is then immediately preempted by the collector and in step D3, the collector processes object X, turns it black (scanned) and assumes that its marking phase is completed. Next, in step D4, the collector starts its sweeping phase and erroneously frees object Z, although Z is reachable from Y via pointer *b*. In this case we say that object Z is *directly* hidden from the collector.

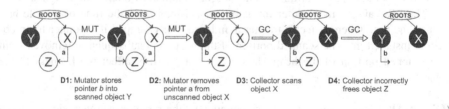

| **D1:** Mutator stores pointer *b* into scanned object Y | **D2:** Mutator removes pointer *a* from unscanned object X | **D3:** Collector scans object X | **D4:** Collector incorrectly frees object Z |

Fig. 3. Erroneous collection of live object Z via deletion of direct pointer *a* from object X

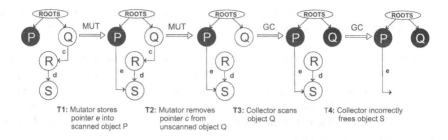

Fig. 4. Erroneous collection of live object S via deletion of pointer c from object Q which transitively reaches S through R

Alternatively, an object can be hidden *transitively*. This case is illustrated in Fig. 4. In the initial state, object P is scanned and Q, R, and S are reachable but not yet seen. Starting from this state, in step T1, the mutator introduces pointer e from a scanned and visited object P to object S. In step T2, the mutator destroys the unscanned pointer c from Q to R, essentially, destroying the only path starting from Q to object S. Next, in step T3, the collector preempts the mutator and scans object Q as shown and assumes to have finished the tracing phase. In step T4, the collector incorrectly frees object S. In this case we say that object S was *transitively* hidden from the collector.

The lost object problem consists of two main events in time: storing a pointer to the particular object to be lost and in a subsequent step destroying all other paths to that object. The two well-known solutions to this problem operate at either of these two steps. They either operate at state D1/T1 or at state D2/T2. Dijsktra's and Steele's solutions operate at states D1/T1 and aim to prevent the un-acknowledged introduction of pointers from scanned portions of the heap to reachable but unmarked objects. They essentially speculate that a pointer destruction will occur sometime in the future, and this will lead to hiding of the object. Alternatively, solutions can operate at steps D2/T2. When a pointer is destroyed as in steps D2 and T2, we reason that a pointer to the object must have been introduced earlier and make the target of the overwritten object reachable. This is the solution chosen by Yuasa. For example, Yuasa would make Z live when pointer a is removed in step D2 or pointer c is removed in step T2. In the transitive case, even though object R might have become unreachable when the pointer is destroyed in step T2, Yuasa's solution requires that object R is kept live as a potential only path left to the hidden object S.

2.5   Design Alternatives

The abstract algorithm maintains rich object and heap-level information. This section attempts to provide an intuitive understanding of the abstract algorithm.

The essence of the abstract algorithm is that it allows for deferring reachability decisions from the mutator to the collector. That is, in the write barrier the mutator detects a potential problem and nominates a candidate pointer for the collector. Subsequently, before the termination of its tracing phase, the collector examines the nominated pointers and optionally discards unnecessary candidates. The specific choices of which pointers are selected by the mutator and which pointers are processed by the collector are discussed in the following sections.

Mutator Selection. When a mutator hits the write barrier, it can protect an object using either the *installation* choice or the *deletion* choice. Intuitively, to protect an object, the mutator speculates about reachability, since it has no knowledge of how the graph changes before the collector has finished tracing. In the abstract algorithm, the mutator detects a potential problem, but does not make explicit decisions whether the object is reachable at the end of tracing.

If the *installation* choice is utilized, the object is nominated by the mutator as soon as the *SRC* becomes > 0, thereby, protecting the object *directly* rather than transitively. The installation choice speculates that right after the *SRC* becomes > 0, the only path to the object from an unscanned, but reachable object will be destroyed. Immediately after nominating the pointer, the SRC could be decremented back to zero effectively undoing the previous operation.

For the *deletion* approach, if a pointer in an unscanned object is overwritten, another object can become hidden either transitively or directly. If the *SRC(X)* is > 0 and a pointer to object X is overwritten from an unscanned portion of the heap, we need to protect object X directly. Therefore, the mutator must nominate this pointer. Alternatively, if the *SRC(X)* is 0, we might need to protect some transitively reachable object from X. The key is to recognize that if X does not contain any outgoing pointers, then no object can be hidden transitively. In such cases, we do not need to nominate X.

Determining whether object X is a leaf can be done by using the type of the object. Examples of acyclic types are scalar arrays as well as newly allocated objects before pointers are stored into them. Objects of acyclic types are leaves for their entire lifetime while newly allocated objects can be leaves only temporarily.

Moreover, even if object X is not a leaf, a write barrier could possibly perform nested checks and determine that at, for example, two-levels deep all objects pointed from X are leaves and their SRC is 0. In this case, we can again refrain from nominating the overwritten X pointer.

In some way, it would be logical to make a conclusion that the deletion choice should be more precise, since it always reasons about an event which has already occurred: the *SRC* of some object has become > 0. The *installation* choice speculates about the future, that may be at some point an unscanned pointer will be destroyed. Although a deletion collectors reasons about past event and should have more information, it has no practical way of determining those transitive objects whose *SRC* > 0. In contrast, the *installation* choice always has an immediate access to the critical object.

Besides pointer events, the mutator can modify the connectivity graph via object allocation. Allocation can be seen as an instance of a write barrier with special knowledge that the target pointer is unique. For installation choice collectors, allocation events are treated exactly as all pointer events. For deletion choice collectors, if the resulting pointer from an allocation request is stored into a scanned portion of the heap, it is possible that the object will be lost. We can then think of allocation as a normal pointer store, except that immediately after the pointer store into a scanned region of the heap, an unscanned virtual pointer to the object is overwritten. Since the virtual event cannot be captured by the barrier, we *simulate* it in the barrier. The flag *isAl-*

located is passed specifically for this reason from the `AllocateBarrier()` to the `WriteBarrier()` procedure.

Characterizing graphs that allow different barrier choices per object is an interesting though primarily theoretical question. It is generally not possible to make that decision arbitrary without some local knowledge of the graph.

Finally, if all barriers occur on leaf objects, the deletion choice will always require us to nominate fewer pointers. Of course, in both barrier choices precisely the same number of objects will be marked live. This can be logically explained by the fact that in both cases, the immediate object is available during the pointer store therefore we can reason locally about reachability. In that case, for leaf objects, the decision of which barrier to use can be made per-object rather than per-collector-cycle. We do not deal with this topic further.

Collector Choice. Once the collector has finished the initial tracing of the heap, there could be a number of unmarked candidates nominated by the mutator. It is possible that in between the time when the mutator has nominated a candidate and the collector sees it, the candidate is no longer necessary.

Similarly to the mutator's pointer selection mechanism, the collector also uses a mechanism to filter out unnecessary candidates. This selection mechanism for the collector is the same as that for the mutator. This can be seen in the write barrier processing phase, the procedure `ProcessBarriers()` in Fig. 1.

Although the collector uses the same mechanism as the mutator, it is possible that candidates nominated by the mutator are ignored by the collector. For example, if the *installation* choice is used and if the object's *SRC* is > 0, when the collector sees such pointers, the corresponding object must be retraced. If the object's *SRC* is 0 however, then the object was recorded by the mutator, but before tracing finished, its *SRC* dropped to 0. Such objects are skipped by the collector in this phase. They have either become garbage or are live but hidden. In the latter case, the object is reachable transitively from a chain of reachable objects starting at an object whose *SRC* is > 0. We therefore only need to re-trace objects whose *SRC* is > 0. Similar reasoning although with a different selection criteria is applied to the deletion choice.

Maintaining an accurate *SRC* has several advantages. First, the SRC prevents us from inducing *floating garbage*. That is because at the time a pointer store occurs, the mutator *nominates* objects that could be *potentially* hidden from the collector. It need not make an explicit decision whether they will actually be reachable once the tracing is complete. The reachability is left to the collector when the barrier tracing phase occurs. It is because of the *SRC* that the mutator does not need to make such explicit decisions about reachability. Secondly, the collector must start re-scanning only from specific objects. For example, for the installation choice it does not need to consider objects whose *SRC* is 0.

3   Transformations: Trading Precision for Efficiency

The abstract algorithm of the previous section provides a much higher degree of precision than previously published and implemented algorithms, but it is also impractical.

In this section we describe how practical collectors can be derived via orthogonal transformations of the abstract collector. Since the transformations are orthogonal, and since the reduction in precision can be modulated, this framework allows the derivation of a much broader set of algorithms than have previously been described, as we will show in the following section.

The transformations presented are (1) reduction in write barrier overhead by treating multiple pointers as roots; (2) reduction in root processing by eliminating re-scanning of the root set; (3) reduction in object space overhead and barrier time overhead by reducing the size of the scanned reference count (SRC); (4) reducing object space overhead by reducing the precision of the per-object shade; (5) conflation of shade and SRC to further reduce object space overhead and speed up the write barrier.

These transformations are not strictly semantics-preserving, since the set of collected objects is changed. However, they are invariant-preserving in that live data is never collected (the collector safety property).

3.1   Root Sets: Eliminating Write Barriers

In the abstract algorithm, all memory is reached from a single root. Thus stacks and global variables are treated as objects like any other. Such an approach is actually used in some implementations of functional programming languages [12]. However, in systems with a significant level of optimization, the cost of such an approach is prohibitive because the mutation rate of the stack is generally extremely high and every stack mutation must include a write barrier.

Therefore, we can transform an abstract algorithm with a uniform treatment of memory into an algorithm which partitions memory into two regions: the roots and the *heap*. The roots generally include the stack and may also contain the static variables and other distinguished pointer data.

In common parlance the static variables are generally considered to be roots, but if they are barriered then they are in effect treated as fields of the "global variable object", and only the pointer to that "object" is a true root. From the point of view of the root transformation, the only issue is that the memory is partitioned into two sets, the roots and the heap, such that there are no pointers from the heap into the roots.

In the abstract collector, there is a single root pointer. Therefore, examining the root is an inherently atomic operation. With the addition of multiple roots, they must either be processed atomically or a further transformation must be applied to incrementalize root processing [15]. In this work we restrict ourselves to algorithms with atomic root processing.

In particular, at the beginning of every collection, we stop the mutators and mark all heap objects directly reachable from roots, placing them on the work queue (mark stack). Subsequently, when the roots are mutated, no write barrier is executed.

Since the roots are processed atomically at the beginning of collection, they are in effect a *scanned object*. However, since we no longer perform a barrier on mutation, the SRC field of objects referenced by mutated roots is no longer guaranteed to be correct and they will not have been placed in the barrier buffer. Therefore, the algorithm must be adjusted to correct or accommodate this imprecision.

The imprecision can be corrected by atomically *re-scanning* the roots before barrier processing. Consider a sequence of stores into a particular root pointer. These stores must be treated like stores into a scanned portion of the heap, so that the SRC of the installed and overwritten pointers must be incremented and decremented, respectively. If we rescan the roots, then any pointers which were scanned previously will have already been marked, and the SRC will be unaffected.

When a pointer to an unscanned object is stored into a root for the first time, the pointer that is being overwritten must point to a marked object, since all direct referents of roots are marked atomically at the start of collection. Thus the SRC of the overwritten pointer would not have changed if the write had been barriered. However, the SRC of the newly installed pointer would have been incremented, but if the roots are rescanned this pointer will be discovered and since it points to an unmarked object it is known to be a new pointer, and the SRC is incremented. Thus in the case of a single store to a root, the SRC is correct.

Inductively, if there are multiple stores to a root, then each subsequent store will cause the SRC of the overwritten pointer to be decremented and the SRC of the installed pointer to be incremented. The decrement will cancel the increment that was performed on the same pointer when it was previously installed. Therefore, a sequence of stores to a particular root pointer will result in the SRC of all objects except the last one to remain unchanged. [1]

Since that object is found by rescanning, rescanning will compute an accurate SRC, and the transformation that separates the memory into roots and heap leaves the precision of the algorithm unchanged.

3.2   Root Rescan Elimination

As we have just shown, the special treatment of roots does not affect the precision of the collector if root re-scanning is used to correct the SRC. However, re-scanning is undesirable because it increases the running time of the algorithm.

If root re-scanning is eliminated, then the SRC values may be under-approximations (because the increment of the final pointer stored in a root will have been missed). Since increments may keep objects live that would otherwise have been collected, this means that any reclamation of an object based on its SRC being 0 is unsafe. Therefore, the algorithm must be conservative in such cases and precision will be sacrificed.

Furthermore, when an installation barrier is used the installation of pointers into the scanned portion of the heap is what causes them to be remembered in the barrier buffer for further tracing during barrier processing. This means that regardless of the imprecision of the SRC, objects that would have had a non-zero SRC must be seen during barrier processing. In effect, this means re-scanning can not be eliminated for algorithms that use the installation barrier.

For algorithms that use the deletion barrier, the only pointers to new objects that are remembered in the write barrier are the newly allocated objects. Therefore, as long

---

[1] This is the same reasoning that was applied by Barth to eliminate redundant reference count updates at compile time [8], and by Levanoni and Petrank to remove redundant reference count updates between epochs in a concurrent reference counting collector [22].

as those objects are placed in the barrier buffer by the allocator, and the SRC-based computation in the barrier processing is eliminated, then the root re-scanning can be safely eliminated.

Since no collector decisions are based on the value of the SRC, it is redundant and can be eliminated. The result is an algorithm with more floating garbage (in particular, all newly allocated objects are considered live), of which Yuasa's algorithm is an example.

3.3   Shade Compression

The shade of an object represents the progress of the collector as it processes the individual pointers in the object. The precision of the shade can always safely be reduced as long as the processing of the pointers in the object in the write barrier treats the imprecise shade conservatively.

In particular, since many objects have a small number of pointers N, it is efficient to treat the shade which originally had the range $[0, N]$ as the set $\{0, [1 \ldots N - 1], N\}$. These three values represent an object for which collector processing has not yet begun, is in progress, or has been completed. This is the standard tri-color abstraction introduced by Dijkstra, where the three values are called white, grey, and black, respectively.

When N is small, the chance is low that the mutator will store a pointer into the object currently being processed by the collector, so the reduction in precision is likely to be low. However, with large objects (such as pointer arrays) the reduction in precision can be more noticeable. Some collectors therefore treat sections of the array independently, in effect mapping equal-sized subsections of the array into different shades.

3.4   Scanned Reference Count Compression

The scanned reference count (SRC) can range from 0 to the number of pointers in the system. However, the number of references to an object is usually small, and the SRC will be even lower (since it only counts references from the scanned portion of the heap to unmarked objects). Therefore, the SRC can be compressed and the loss of precision is likely to be low.

However, the compression must be conservative to ensure that live objects are not collected. This is accomplished by making the SRC into a "sticky" count [26]: once it reaches its maximum value, it is never decremented. As a result, the SRC is an over-approximation, which is always safe since it will only cause additional objects to be treated as live.

An important special case for collectors that use an installation barrier is a one-bit SRC, since in this case the SRC becomes equivalent to the Recorded flag, allowing those two fields to be collapsed.

3.5   Conflation of Shade and Scanned Reference Count

In a collector using an installation barrier with a one-bit sticky SRC and tri-color shade, an object with a stuck SRC must be scanned by the collector. Similarly, a grey object must be scanned by the collector. Thus the meaning of these two states can be collapsed and the grey color can be used to indicate a non-zero (stuck) SRC, which also represents the Recorded flag.

This is in fact the representation used by most collectors that have been implemented. In effect, they have collapsed numerous independent invariants into a small number of states. This helps to understand why such algorithms are bug-prone: collapsing the states corresponding to algorithmic invariants relies on subtle transformations and simultaneously reduces redundancy in the representation.

4   Using Transformations to Derive Practical Collectors

In this section, we derive various practical algorithms by applying the previously discussed transformations to the abstract collector algorithm. Some of the schemes are well-known concurrent algorithms such as Dijkstra and Yuasa, while others are new derivations.

4.1   Derivation of a Dijkstra Algorithm

The Dijkstra algorithm is an instance of an abstract installation collector and to derive it we apply the following transformations:

1. *Root Sets* transformation
2. *Shade compression* to tri-color
3. *SRC compression* to a single sticky bit
4. *Conflation of Shade* and *SRC*

Although at the end of the transformation steps, we arrive at a practical Dijkstra algorithm, the intermediate steps also represent valid algorithms with different precision.

The compressions of *SRC* and *Shade* can lead to floating garbage. However, unlike *Shade* and *SRC* compressions, the *Conflation* transformation does not lead to increased floating garbage. On the other side, it reduces, both, space consumption in the header of the object, and, complexity of the write barrier.

The *Root Sets* transformation also preserves the treatment of allocated objects. When a new object is allocated and stored into the roots, the mutator will not nominate the pointer because the store will occur into a scanned partition (roots) and the write barrier is not active on the roots. If the pointer to the allocated object gets stored in the heap, then it will be processed in the mutator write barrier, similarly to all other objects existing at collection startup. If the allocated object dies before the roots are rescanned, the collector will not mark that object as live.

A Steele-like collector is similar to a Dijkstra collector except that its transformation covers a wider range of rescanning. A Steele algorithm is not limited to rescanning only the roots, but can also rescan heap partitions. However, the barrier processing phase and the selection criteria are exactly the same as in the Dijkstra collector.

4.2   Derivation of a Yuasa Algorithm

Our second derived collector is a Yuasa snapshot algorithm. The Yuasa algorithm is an instance of a deletion collector. The algorithm can be derived by applying the following transformations to the abstract collector:

```
MarkRoots()
    while (! roots.end())
      Obj = roots.get();
      Mark(Obj);

MarkRootsDirect()
    while (! roots.end())
      Obj = roots.get();
      if (Obj.isAllocatedInThisCycle)
          Obj.Color = black;

Collect()
    atomic
        MarkRoots();
        Phase = Tracing;

    do
        Trace();
    while (ProcessBarriers());

    atomic
        MarkRootsDirect();
        ProcessBarriers());
        Trace();
        Phase = Sweeping;

    Sweep();

    Phase = Idle;

atomic WriteBarrier(Obj, field, New)
    if (Phase == Tracing)
        Old = Obj[field];

        if (New.Color == white && New.isAllocatedInThisCycle)
            New.Color = black;

        if (   Obj.Color != black && Old.Color == white
            && !Old.Recorded )
            Remember(Old);
    Obj[field] = New;
```

Fig. 5. Pseudo Code For The Hybrid Collector

1. *Root Sets* transformation
2. *Shade compression* to tri-color
3. *Root Rescan Elimination*

During barrier processing, deletion collectors can skip objects whose *SRC* is 0 and are leafs. However, since *Root Rescan elimination* prevents the roots rescanning process, an accurate *SRC* cannot be computed, and subsequently the collector selection criteria cannot be applied. Therefore, in order to preserve the safety property of the abstract collector, the collector must mark all overwritten pointers and rescan from them. The *SRC* is removed since it cannot serve its primary purpose: a guide for the collector selection criteria.

The Yuasa collector is the most conservative approach to floating garbage. It does not allow any destruction in the connectivity graph once the collector has started and it effectively allocates only reachable object (black).

One fundamental difference between Yuasa and Dijkstra algorithms is that in the presence of a *Root Sets* transformation, installation collectors must never use the *Root Rescan elimination*, while deletion collectors have no requirement to apply it. The rescanning in deletion collectors is done mostly to eliminate floating garbage, albeit, at the expense of triggering work to rescan the roots.

Also, although at the end of our derivation, we arrived at a Yuasa algorithm, the result of every intermediate step is a valid deletion collector.

4.3   Derivation of a Hybrid Algorithm

The third derived practical algorithm is the Hybrid collector. The Hybrid algorithm is an instance of an abstract deletion collector. The Hybrid algorithm can be derived by applying the following transformations:

1. *Root Sets* transformation
2. *Shade compression* to tri-color
3. *SRC compression* to a single sticky bit
4. *Conflation of Shade and SRC*
5. *Root Rescan elimination for existing objects*
6. *Over approximate Shade*

The first two transformation steps are the same as for the Yuasa algorithm. However, in the Hybrid algorithm, we utilize the rescanning of roots only for newly allocated objects. The roots rescan transformation is parameterized to be active only for existing objects. The idea is to obtain a deletion Yuasa algorithm for the existing heap graph while maintaining a less restricted policy for newly allocated objects, similarly to the Dijkstra collector. By eliminating rescanning for existing objects, we can remove the *SRC* for those objects. Whenever the collector encounters an existing object during its barrier processing phase it will always mark the object, without applying any selection criteria.

After step 5 we still have a working deletion algorithm, but we would like to obtain more of the properties of Yuasa, namely, bounded re-tracing of newly allocated objects triggered by roots rescanning. To do that, we perform an additional transformation where if a newly allocated pointer is stored into the heap, the object is marked as reachable for this collection cycle. This simply means that if a newly allocated pointer is stored into the heap, we always increase the *SRC*, ignoring what the color of the destination object is. This is clearly a trivial over-approximation transformation on Shade of the destination object as indicated in step 6. With this, the collector now only needs to trace from existing objects and not from newly allocated objects. Newly allocated objects are essentially allocated white and colored black either during roots rescanning or during a pointer store in the heap.

The *Hybrid* collector is particularly suited for hard real-time applications, where it is desirable to achieve a bound on the roots rescanning work while reducing the floating garbage.

The skeleton code for the algorithm is illustrated in Fig. 5. $MarkRootsDirect$ is the procedure that performs the one-level deep rescanning procedure for the roots partition while the $isAllocatedInThisCycle$ bit is used to differentiate between newly allocated and existing objects.

5   Experimental Evaluation

We have implemented a concurrent collector framework in IBM's J9 virtual machine. The collector supports both standard work-based collection (for every a units of allocation the collector performs ka units of collection work) as well as time-based collection (the collector runs for c out of q time units). This collector has been built as a second-generation Metronome real-time collector [4].

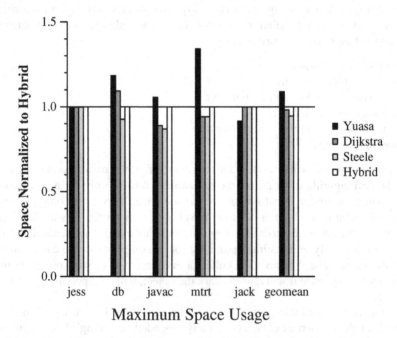

Fig. 6. Summary of the maximal space usage of the four collector algorithms. Data is normalized to the Hybrid algorithm. Shorter bars represent lower space usage

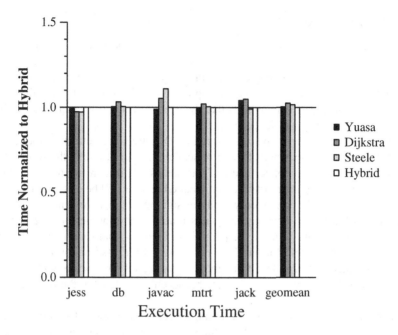

Fig. 7. Summary of overall execution time of the four collector algorithms. Data is normalized to the Hybrid algorithm. Shorter bars represent faster execution time

However, in this paper we will concentrate on work-based collection because its use is more common in more widely used soft real-time systems, and is likely to provide a better basis for comparison with other work. Isolated experiments have shown that the trends we report for work-based collection generally hold for time-based collection as well.

Our collector is implemented in a J2ME-based system that places a premium on space in the virtual machine. Therefore, we use the microJIT rather than the much more resource-intensive optimizing compiler. The microJIT is a high-quality single-pass compiler, producing code roughly a factor of 2 slower than the optimizing JIT.

The system runs on Linux/x86, Windows/x86, and Linux/ARM. The measurements presented here were performed on a Windows/x86 machine with a Pentium 4 3GHz CPU and 500MB of RAM.

The measurements presented all use a collector to mutator work ratio of 1.5, that is, for every 6K allocated by the mutator, the collector processes 9K. Collection is triggered when heap usage reaches 10MB.

We have measured the SPECjvm98 benchmarks, which exhibit a fairly wide range of allocation behavior (with the exception of compress, which performs very little allocation).

Figure 7 summarizes the performance of the four collector algorithms. The left graph shows the maximum heap size, the right graph total execution time. Both graphs are normalized to the Hybrid algorithm, and shorter bars represent better performance (less heap usage or shorter execution times). A geometric mean is also shown. These graphs summarize more detailed performance data which can be found in the Appendix.

5.1   Space Consumption

As expected, the incremental update collectors (Dijkstra and Steele) often require less memory than the snapshot collector (Yuasa). This is because the incremental update collectors allocate white (unmarked) and only consider live those objects which are added to the graph. However, there is no appreciable difference on 2 of the five benchmarks (jess and jack), which confirms that the space savings from incremental update collectors are quite program-dependent.

The use of Steele's write barrier instead of Dijkstra's theoretically produces less floating garbage at the expense of more re-scanning, since it marks the source rather than the target object of a pointer update. This means that if there are multiple updates to the same object, only the most recently installed pointer will be re-scanned.

However, the Steele barrier only leads to significant improvement in one of the benchmarks (db). This is because db spends much of its time performing sort operations. These operations permute the pointers in an array, and each update triggers a write barrier. With a Steele barrier, the array is tagged for re-scanning. But with a Dijkstra barrier, each object pointed to by the array is tagged for re-scanning. As a result, there is a great deal more floating garbage because the contents of the array are being changed over time.

Finally, the hybrid collector which we introduced, a snapshot collector that allocates white (unmarked), significantly reduces the space overhead of snapshot collection: the space overhead over the best collector is at worst 13% (for javac), which is quite reasonable.

5.2   Execution Time

While the incremental update collectors are generally assumed to have an advantage in space, their potential time cost is not well understood. Incremental update collectors may have to repeatedly re-scan portions of the heap that changed during tracing. Termination could be difficult if the heap is being mutated very quickly.

Our measurements show that incremental update collectors do indeed suffer time penalties for their tighter space bounds. The Dijkstra barrier causes significant slowdown in db, javac, mtrt, and jack. The Steele barrier is less prone to slowdown – only suffering on javac – but it does suffer the worst slowdown, about 12%. These measurements are total application run-time, so the slow-down of the collector is very large – this represents about a factor of 2 slowdown in collection time.

Once again, our hybrid collector performs very well – it usually takes time very close to the fastest algorithm. Thus the hybrid collector appears to be a very good compromise between snapshot and incremental update collectors.

Because its only rescanning is of the stack, it suffers no reduction in incrementality from a standard Yuasa-style collector, which must already scan the stack atomically. Its advantage over a standard snapshot collector is that it significantly reduces floating garbage by giving newly allocated objects time to die. But because it never rescans the heap, it avoids the termination problems of incremental update collectors and is still suitable for real-time applications.

As shown by the more detailed graphs in the appendix, the primary reason why the Yuasa and Hybrid algorithms are quicker is that the Dijkstra and Steele collectors both scan significantly more data during barrier buffer processing.

The benchmark with the most unusual behavior is jack, for which the Yuasa snapshot collector uses the *least* memory, while the Steele algorithm uses the least time. We are still in the process of investigating this behavior.

6   Conclusions

We have presented an abstract concurrent garbage collection algorithm and showed how incremental update collectors in the style of Dijkstra, and snapshot collectors in the style of Yuasa, can be derived from this abstract algorithm by reducing precision through various transformations.

We have also used the insights from this formulation to derive a new type of Hybrid snapshot collector which allocates its objects unmarked, and therefore induces less floating garbage.

We have implemented all four collectors in a production virtual machine and compared their time and space requirements. Incremental update collectors do indeed suffer less floating garbage, while the pure snapshot collector sometimes uses significantly more memory. The Hybrid collector greatly reduces the space cost of snapshot collection.

Incremental update collectors can significantly slow down garbage collection, leading to noticeable slow-downs in application execution speed. Our new Hybrid snapshot collector is generally about as fast as the fastest algorithm. For most applications, this collector will represent a good compromise between time and space efficiency, and has the notable advantage of snapshot collectors in terms of predictable termination.

We hope this work will spur further systematic study of algorithms for concurrent collection and further quantitative evaluation of those algorithms.

References

[1] APPEL, A. W., ELLIS, J. R., AND LI, K. Real-time concurrent collection on stock multiprocessors. In *Proceedings of the SIGPLAN'88 Conference on Programming Language Design and Implementation* (Atlanta, Georgia, June 1988). *SIGPLAN Notices, 23*, 7 (July), 11–20.

[2] AZATCHI, H., LEVANONI, Y., PAZ, H., AND PETRANK, E. An on-the-fly mark and sweep garbage collector based on sliding views. In *Proceedings of the 18th ACM SIGPLAN conference on Object-oriented programing, systems, languages, and applications* (Oct 2003), ACM Press, pp. 269–281.

[3] BACON, D. F., ATTANASIO, C. R., LEE, H. B., RAJAN, V. T., AND SMITH, S. Java without the coffee breaks: A nonintrusive multiprocessor garbage collector. In *Proc. of the SIGPLAN Conference on Programming Language Design and Implementation* (Snowbird, Utah, June 2001). *SIGPLAN Notices, 36*, 5 (May), 92–103.

[4] BACON, D. F., CHENG, P., AND RAJAN, V. T. A real-time garbage collector with low overhead and consistent utilization. In *Proceedings of the 30th Annual ACM SIGPLAN-SIGACT Symposium on Principles of Programming Languages* (New Orleans, Louisiana, Jan. 2003). *SIGPLAN Notices, 38*, 1, 285–298.

[5] BACON, D. F., CHENG, P., AND RAJAN, V. T. A unified theory of garbage collection. In *Proceedings of the ACM Conference on Object-Oriented Systems, Languages, and Applications* (Vancouver, British Columbia, Oct. 2004), pp. 50–68.

[6] BAKER, H. G. List processing in real-time on a serial computer. *Commun. ACM 21*, 4 (Apr. 1978), 280–294.

[7] BAKER, H. G. The Treadmill, real-time garbage collection without motion sickness. *SIGPLAN Notices 27*, 3 (Mar. 1992), 66–70.

[8] BARTH, J. M. Shifting garbage collection overhead to compile time. *Commun. ACM 20*, 7 (July 1977), 513–518.

[9] BEN-ARI, M. Algorithms for on-the-fly garbage collection. *ACM Trans. Program. Lang. Syst. 6*, 3 (1984), 333–344.

[10] BOEHM, H.-J., DEMERS, A. J., AND SHENKER, S. Mostly parallel garbage collection. In *PLDI '91: Proceedings of the ACM SIGPLAN 1991 conference on Programming language design and implementation* (1991), ACM Press, pp. 157–164.

[11] BROOKS, R. A. Trading data space for reduced time and code space in real-time garbage collection on stock hardware. In *Conference Record of the 1984 ACM Symposium on Lisp and Functional Programming* (Austin, Texas, Aug. 1984), G. L. Steele, Ed., pp. 256–262.

[12] CHEADLE, A. M., FIELD, A. J., MARLOW, S., PEYTON JONES, S. L., AND WHILE, R. L. Non-stop Haskell. In *Proc. of the Fifth International Conference on Functional Programming* (Montreal, Quebec, Sept. 2000). *SIGPLAN Notices, 35*, 9, 257–267.

[13] CHENG, P., AND BLELLOCH, G. E. A parallel, real-time garbage collector. In *Proceedings of the ACM SIGPLAN 2001 conference on Programming language design and implementation* (Jun 2001), ACM Press, pp. 125–136.

[14] DIJKSTRA, E. W., LAMPORT, L., MARTIN, A. J., SCHOLTEN, C. S., AND STEFFENS, E. F. M. On-the-fly garbage collection: an exercise in cooperation. *Commun. ACM 21*, 11 (1978), 966–975.

[15] DOMANI, T., KOLODNER, E. K., LEWIS, E., SALANT, E. E., BARABASH, K., LAHAN, I., LEVANONI, Y., PETRANK, E., AND YANORER, I. Implementing an on-the-fly garbage collector for java. In *Proceedings of the second international symposium on Memory management* (Oct 2000), ACM Press, pp. 155–166.

[16] DOMANI, T., KOLODNER, E. K., AND PETRANK, E. A generational on-the-fly garbage collector for Java. In *Proc. of the SIGPLAN Conference on Programming Language Design and Implementation* (June 2000). *SIGPLAN Notices, 35*, 6, 274–284.

[17] HENRIKSSON, R. *Scheduling Garbage Collection in Embedded Systems*. PhD thesis, Lund Institute of Technology, July 1998.

[18] HUDSON, R. L., AND MOSS, E. B. Incremental garbage collection for mature objects. In *Proc. of the International Workshop on Memory Management* (St. Malo, France, Sept. 1992), Y. Bekkers and J. Cohen, Eds., vol. 637 of *Lecture Notes in Computer Science*.

[19] JOHNSTONE, M. S. *Non-Compacting Memory Allocation and Real-Time Garbage Collection*. PhD thesis, University of Texas at Austin, Dec. 1997.

[20] LAMPORT, L. Garbage collection with multiple processes: an exercise in parallelism. In *Proc. of the 1976 International Conference on Parallel Processing* (1976), pp. 50–54.

[21] LAROSE, M., AND FEELEY, M. A compacting incremental collector and its performance in a production quality compiler. In ISMM [?], 1–9.

[22] LEVANONI, Y., AND PETRANK, E. An on-the-fly reference counting garbage collector for java. In *Proceedings of the 16th ACM SIGPLAN conference on Object oriented programming, systems, languages, and applications* (Oct 2001), ACM Press, pp. 367–380.

[23] NETTLES, S., AND O'TOOLE, J. Real-time garbage collection. In *Proc. of the SIGPLAN Conference on Programming Language Design and Implementation* (June 1993). *SIGPLAN Notices, 28*, 6, 217–226.

[24] NORTH, S. C., AND REPPY, J. H. Concurrent garbage collection on stock hardware. In *Functional Programming Languages and Computer Architecture* (Portland, Oregon, Sept. 1987), G. Kahn, Ed., vol. 274 of *Lecture Notes in Computer Science*, pp. 113–133.

[25] PIXLEY, C. An incremental garbage collection algorithm for multi-mutator systems. *Distributed Computing 3, 1 6*, 3 (Dec. 1988), 41–49.

[26] ROTH, D. J., AND WISE, D. S. One-bit counts between unique and sticky. In ISMM [?], pp. 49–56.

[27] STEELE, G. L. Multiprocessing compactifying garbage collection. *Commun. ACM 18*, 9 (Sept. 1975), 495–508.

[28] STEELE, G. L. Corrigendum: Multiprocessing compactifying garbage collection. *Commun. ACM 19*, 6 (June 1976), 354.

[29] YUASA, T. Real-time garbage collection on general-purpose machines. *Journal of Systems and Software 11*, 3 (Mar. 1990), 181–198.

Appendix: Detailed Performance Data

This section includes graphs that illustrate for each benchmark, the behavior of the four collectors with respect to space utilization and barrier-induced work.

Figure 8 shows space usage over time by javac. Each data point represents the amount of data in use when the tracing and barrier processing terminated, but before sweeping. This represents the point of maximum memory use. The Yuasa-style collector consistently uses more memory than the others, but it also terminates the quickest (at termination, memory consumption is 0).

The reason why the Yuasa and Hybrid algorithms are quicker can easily be seen in Figure 9: the Dijkstra and Steele collectors both scan significantly more data during barrier buffer processing. Note that barrier-induced scanning is still significant even for the pure snapshot (Yuasa) collector. This is because pointers to some objects that are part of the snapshot may have been overwritten and not discovered during marking. Therefore, the snapshot it "completed" during barrier buffer processing. However, the total work will be based on the live data in the object graph at the time collection began, whereas in the incremental update algorithms it varies.

The rescanning overhead that we observed above for the db benchmark with Dijkstra's barrier can be seen clearly in Figure 11: rescanning typically causes about 20% of the heap to be re-visited, while rescanning for the other three collectors is negligible.

Details for the remaining benchmarks are found in Figures 12 through 17.

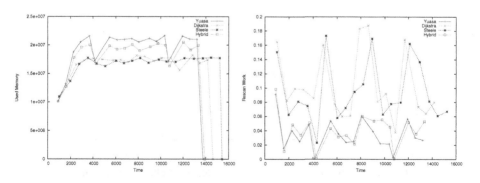

Fig. 8. Space vs. Time: javac   **Fig. 9.** Collector Rescanning Work: javac

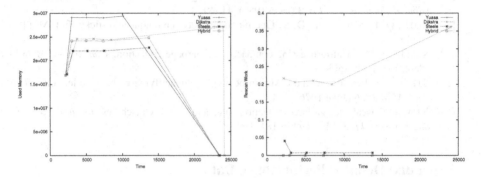

Fig. 10. Space vs. Time: db   **Fig. 11.** Collector Rescanning Work: db

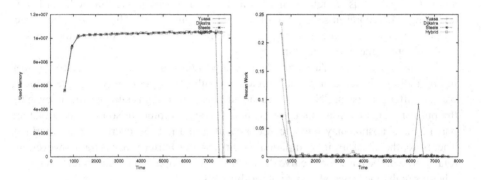

Fig. 12. Space vs. Time: jess   **Fig. 13.** Collector Rescanning Work: jess

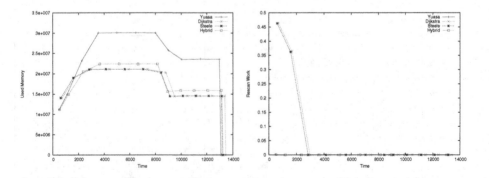

Fig. 14. Space vs. Time: mtrt   **Fig. 15.** Collector Rescanning Work: mtrt

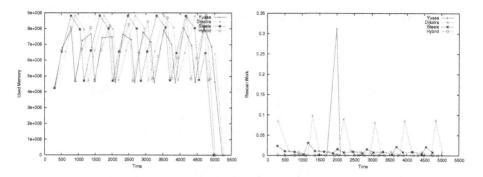

Fig. 16. Space vs. Time: jack   **Fig. 17.** Collector Rescanning Work: jack

Static Deadlock Detection for Java Libraries

A• y Willi•• •, Willi•• T•i••, •n• Mi••••l D. • •n••

Computer Science and Artificial Intelligence Laboratory,
Massachusetts Institute of Technology,
Cambridge, MA 02139 USA
{amy, thies, mernst}@csail.mit.edu

Abstract. Library writers wish to provide a guarantee not only that
each procedure in the library performs correctly in isolation, but also that
the procedures perform correctly when run in conjunction. To this end,
we propose a method for static detection of deadlock in Java libraries.
Our goal is to determine whether client code exists that may deadlock
a library, and, if so, to enable the library writer to discover the calling
patterns that can lead to deadlock.

Our flow-sensitive, context-sensitive analysis determines possible
deadlock configurations using a lock-order graph. This graph represents
the order in which locks are acquired by the library. Cycles in the graph
indicate deadlock possibilities, and our tool reports all such possibilities.
We implemented our analysis and evaluated it on 18 libraries comprising
1245 kLOC. We verified 13 libraries to be free from deadlock, and found
14 distinct deadlocks in 3 libraries.

1 Introduction

D•••lo•• i• • •on• i•ion • n••• w•i•• ••• ••o••••• o•• ••o•••• i• ••l••• •• ••••
•••••• in • ••• ••••• ••• •o ••••i•• • lo•• •l••••y ••l• •y •no••• •••••• in •••
•••. B••••••• ••••lo•• •••v•n•• •n •n•i•• ••o•••• ••o• wo••in•, i• i• • •••io••
••o•l•• .

Fin•in• •n• •xin• ••••lo•• i••i• •• l•. T•••in• •o•• no• •lw•y• •x•o•• ••••-
lo•• •••••••• i• i• in•••i•l• •o •••• •ll •o••i•l• in•••l••vin•• o• • ••o•••• '•
••••••••. In •••i•ion, on•• ••••lo•• i• •x•i•i••• •y • ••o•••• , •••o••in• •••
••••lo•• •••n••io ••n •• ••o•l••o• •, •••• • ••in• ••• •o•••• o• ••• •••• lo••
•i• •• l• •o •••••• in•. • n• • ••• •now • ow ••• ••••••• w••• in••l••v•• •o • now
w•i•• ••• o• lo••• ••• in •on••n•ion.

W• ••o• o•• • • ••• o• •o• ••••i• ••••lo•• ••••••••ion in J•v• li•••i••. •••
• ••• o• ••••••• in•• w•••••• i• i• o••i•l• •o •••• lo•• ••• li•••y •y ••llin• •o• •
••• o• i•• ••• li• • •••o••. I• ••••lo•• i• •o••i•l•, i• ••ovi••• ••• n•• •• o• •••
• ••• o•• •n• v••i••l•• involv••.

To o•• • •nowl•••, ••• ••o•l•• o•••••••in• ••••lo•• in li•••i•• ••• no• •••n
inv•••i•••• •••vio••ly. T•i• ••o•l•• i• i• •o•••n• ••••••• li•••y w•i•••• • •y
wi•• •o •••••n••• •••i• li•••y i• ••••lo••-•••• •o• •ny ••llin• •••••••n. Fo• •x-
•• •l•, ••• •••i•••ion •o• java.lang.StringBuffer in S•n'• J•v• D•v•lo•• •n•
Ki• (JDK) ••••••:

```
class BeanContextSupport {
  protected HashMap children;

  public boolean remove(Object targetChild) {
    synchronized(BeanContext.
                 globalHierarchyLock) {
      ...
      synchronized(targetChild) {
        ...
        synchronized (children) {
          children.remove(targetChild);
        }
        ...
      }
    }
    return true;
  }

  public void
  propertyChange(PropertyChangeEvent pce) {
    ...
    Object source = pce.getSource();
    synchronized(children) {
      if ("beanContext".equals(propertyName)
          && containsKey(source)
          && ((BCSChild)children.get(source)).
             isRemovePending()) {
        BeanContext bc = getBeanContextPeer();
        if (bc.equals(pce.getOldValue())
            && !bc.equals(pce.getNewValue()))) {
          remove(source);
        } else {
          ...
}}}}}
```

Fig. 1. Simplified code excerpt from the `BeanContextSupport` class in the `java.beans.beancontext` package of Sun's JDK

```
Object source
  = new Object();

BeanContextSupport support
  = new BeanContextSupport();

BeanContext oldValue
  = support.getBeanContextPeer();

Object newValue
  = new Object();

PropertyChangeEvent event
  = new PropertyChangeEvent(source,
                            "beanContext",
                            oldValue,
                            newValue);

support.add(source);
support.vetoableChange(event);

thread 1:  support.propertyChange(event);
thread 2:  support.remove(source);
```

Fig. 2. Client code that can cause deadlock in methods from Figure 1. In thread 1, `children` is locked, then `BeanContext.globalHierarchyLock` is locked (via a call to `remove`) while in thread 2, the ordering is reversed. Deadlock occurs under some thread interleavings. The initialization code shown above is designed to elicit the relevant path of control flow within the library

T•• [StringBuffer] • •••o•• ••• •yn••oni••• w•••• n••••••y •o •••• •ll ••• o•••••ion• on •ny ••••i••l•• in•••n•• ••••v• •• i• •••y o•••• in •o• • •••i•l o•••• •••• i• •on•i•••n• wi•• ••• o•••• o•••• • •••o• ••ll• • •••• •y •••• o•••• in•ivi••l ••••••• involv••.

I•••• o•••••ion• ••• •o •••• v• •• i• •••y o••••••• in •o• • •••i•l o••••, •••• lo•• •••w••n StringBuffer • •••o•• ••o•l• no•• • •o••i•l•. No •••i•l o•••in• ov•• ••• StringBuffer • •••o•• •o•l• l••• •o ••••lo•• •••••••• lo••• •••••i••• •y J•v•'• synchronized •on••••••• (w•i•• StringBuffer ••••) ••nno•••••l• ••w••n • •••o• ••ll•. Non•••••l•••, o•••ool ••• o•••• ••llin• •••••••n •••••••••••••• lo•• in StringBuffer.

Li•••i•• ••• o•••n v•ln•••••l• •o •••• lo••. W• ••v• in••••• 1• •i••in•• in-•••n••• o• •••• lo•• in 3 li•••i•• (•o• ••••il•• ••••l••, ••• S••ion 6). Si• • li••• •o•• •o• on• o• ••• ••••lo••• •o•n in S•n'• JDK i• ••own in Fi•••• 1. In ••• BeanContextSupport •l••• o• ••• java.beans.beancontext •••••••, ••• remove() •n• propertyChange() • •••o•• o•••in lo••• in • •iff•••n• o••••. T•• •li•n• •o••

•• own in Fi•••• • ••n in•••• ••••lo•• ••in• •••••• • •••o••. S•v•••l o•••• • •••-
o•• in ••• ••• • •••••••••••• ••• ••• •••• • lo••in• o•••••• remove() •n• •••• •x• i• i•
••• ••• • ••••lo•• v• ln••••ili•y.

T• i• ••••lo•• ••• • •i• •l• •ol••ion: ••• propertyChange() • •••o• ••n •yn-
•••oni•• on BeanContext.globalHierarchyLock •••o•• children, o• i• •o•l• lo••
only globalHierarchyLock. S•••ion 6.1 ••••i••• •ol••ion• •o• o•••• •••• lo•••.

An ov••vi•w o• o•• ••n•ly•i• i• •iv•n in S•••ion 3. W• ••v• i• •l•• •n••• o••
••••ni••• •n• •n•ly••• 1• li•••i•• •on•i••in• o• 1••5• lin•• o• •o••, o•••in••
••o• So•••Fo•••, S•v•nn••, •n• o•••• o••n •o•••• •••o•••••. U•in• o•• •ool,
w• v••i••• 13 o•••••• li•••i•• •o •• •••• o• •••• lo••, •n• •on••• •• 1• • i••in••
in•••n••• o• •••• lo•• in 3 li•••i••.

D•••••in• ••••lo•• •••o•• •ll •o••i•l• ••ll• •o • li•••y i• •iff•••n ••• n ••-
•••in• ••••lo•• in • w•ol• ••o•••• . • on••••• •li••in• ••l••ion•• i• •xi•• •n•
••n • • •••••• in•• •o• w•ol• ••o•••• , w••••••• ••• •n•ly•i• o• li•••y •••
•on•i••• •ll • o••i•l• ••ll• in•o ••• li•••y, w• i•• in•l•••• l•••• n•• ••• o• •li••-
in• •o••i•ili•i••. In ••o••••, ••• n•• ••• o• •••••••• ••n o•••n •• •••••• in••,
••• • •li•n• • •y ••ll in•o • li•••y ••o• •ny n•• ••• o• •••••••, •o o•• •n•l-
y•i• • ••• • o••l •n •n•o•n••• n•• ••• o• ••••••••. T•••• •iff•••n••• •o• •in•
•o yi•l• • • •••• l••••• n•• ••• o• ••• o••• ••n wo•l• •• • •••••n• in • ••o•••• ,
w• i•• • •••• i• i• •o•••n• •o •••••••••• ••l•• ••• o•••.

T•• ••• •in••• o• ••i• •••••• i• o•••ni••• •• •ollow•. S•••ion • •x•l•in• •••
••• •n•i•• o• lo••• in ••• J•v• ••o•••• • in• l•n•••••. S•••ion 3 •i•••••• o••
•n•ly•i• ••• • •i•• l•v•l, •n• S•••ion • ••ovi•• • • o•• ••••il•• •••••i••ion o•
••• •n•ly•i•. S•••ion 5 ••••i••• •••• ni•••• •o• ••••in• ••• n•• ••• o• ••••i-
o•• •••o•••. S•••ion 6 •iv•• o•• •x••i• •n••l •••• l••. • •l•••• wo•• i• •iv•n in
S•••ion •, •n• S•••ion • •on•l•••.

2   Locks in Java

In J•v•, •••• o• j••• •on•••••• lly ••• •n •••o•i•••• lo••; •o• •••vi•y, w• will
•o• ••i• •• •••••• o••n o•j••• •• •in• • lo••. T•• J•v• "synchronized (*expr*) {
statements }" •••••• •n• •v•l•••••• ••• •x•••••ion •o •n o•j••• ••••••n••, ••••i•••
••• lo••, •v•l•••• ••• •••••• •n• in ••• •lo••, •n• ••l•••• ••• lo•• w••n •••
•lo•• i• •xi•••, w•••••• no•• •lly o• ••••••• o••n •x•••ion. T• i• ••i•n ••••••
lo••• •o •• •••• i••• in •o• • o•••• •n• ••n ••l•••• in ••v•••• (•••• i•, in
LIF• o••••), • •••• •••• o•• •n•ly•i• ••••• ••v•n•••• o•. A J•v• • •••o• ••n
•• •••l•••• synchronized, w•i•• i• •yn•••i• ••••• •o• w••••in• ••• •o•y in
synchronized (this) { ... } •o• in•••n•• • •••o••, o• synchronized (*C*.class)
{ ... }, w• ••• *C* i• •••• •l••• •on••inin• ••• • •••o•, •o• ••••i• • •••o••.

A lo•• •••• i• ••l• •y on• •••••• ••nno• •• ••••i••• •y •no•••• ••••• • •n•il
••• •••• on• ••l•••• i•. A •••••• •lo••• i• i• ••••• ••• •o ••••i•• • lo•• •••• i•
••l• •y •no•••• ••••••, •n• •o•• no• •on•in•• ••o•••in• •n•il i• ••••••••• lly
••••i••• ••• lo••.

A lo•• i• ••l• •••-••••••; i• • •iv•n •••••• •••••• ••• •o ••-••••i•• • lo••, •••n ••• ••••i•i•ion •lw•y• •••••••• wi••o•• • lo••in•.[1] T•• lo•• i• ••l••••• w••n •xi•in• ••• synchronized •••••• •n• •••• •••• i••• i•.

T•• wait(), notify(), •n• notifyAll() • •••o•• o•••••• on ••••iv••• w•o•• lo••• ••• ••l•. An •x•••ion i• •••own i• ••• ••••iv••'• lo•• i• no• ••l•. T•• wait() • •••o• ••l••••• ••• lo•• on ••• ••••iv•• o•j••• •n• •l•••• ••• ••llin• •••••• in •••• o•j•••'• w•i• •••. W•il• • •••••• i• in •n o•j•••'• w•i• •••, i• i• no• ••••••l•• •o• ••o•••in•. T•••••• ••• •••n••l•• •o• ••o•••in• vi• ••• notify() •n• notifyAll() • •••o••, w•i••, •••••••iv•ly, ••• ov• on• o• •ll ••• •••••• ••o• ••• ••••iv•• o•j•••'• w•i• •••. • n•• • •••••• i• ••• ov•• ••o• •n o•j•••'• w•i• •••, ••• wait() • •••o• ••••• ••• •o •••••• i•• ••• lo•• •o• ••• o•j••• i• w•• invo••• on. T•• wait() • •••o• •••••n• only ••••• ••• lo•• i• ••••••i•••. T•••, • ••••••• • •y •lo•• in•i•• wait() •• i• ••••• ••• •o •••••• i•• ••• lo•• •o• ••• ••••iv•• o•j•••.

J•v• 1.5 in••o••••• n•w •yn•••oni•••ion • ••••ni•• • in ••• java.util.concurrent •••••••• ••••• •llow • ••o•••• • •• •o ••••i•• •n• ••l•••• lo••• wi••o•• ••in• ••• synchronized ••ywo••. T•••• • ••••ni•• • • • ••• i• •o••i•l• •o ••••i•• •n• ••l•••• lo••• in •ny o•••• (in ••••i••l••, •••• i••• •n• ••l•••• n••• no• •• in LIF• o•••••). • •• •ool •o•• no• ••n•l• ••••• n•w •••••ili•i•• in ••• J•v• l•n•••••. How•v••, • o•• •yn••oni••ion ••n •• •x••••••• ••in• ••• ••i• i•iv•• ••o• J•v• 1.•, •n• w• •••••o•• •x•••• •••• o•• •••• ni••• will •• ••• li•••l• • n•••• ••••••n• •n• •••••• ••l•••• o• J•v•.

3 Analysis Synopsis

W• •on•i••• • *deadlock* •o •• ••• •on• i•ion in w•i•• • ••• o• ••••••• ••nno• • ••• ••o••••• •••••• ••••• i• ••••• ••in• •o ••••i•• • lo•• •••• i• ••l• •y •n-o••••• • •• ••• o•••• •••. • •••••• lo•• •••••o• •••• •n in••••o••••l •n•ly•i• •o ••••• • o••i•l• ••••n••• o• lo•• ••••i•i•ion wi••in • J•v• li•••y. I• •••••- ••n•• •o••i•l• lo••in• •••••••n• ••in• • ••••• ••••••••—••• *lock-order graph*, ••••••i••• ••low. • y•l•• in ••i• ••••• in•i••• • •o••i•ili•i•• o• •••• lo••.

Fo• ••••• •y•l•, o••• •ool ••• o•••• ••• v••i••l• n•• •• o•• lo••• involv•• in ••• •••• lo•• •• w•ll •• ••• • •••o• •••• •••• •••• i•• ••o•• lo••• (••• S••ion •.•). • •• •ool i• •on•••v••iv• •n• ••• o•••• •ll •••• lo•• • o••i• ili•i•i•. How•v••, ••• •on•••-v••iv• •••oxi• ••ion•••• ••• •ool •o •on•i•• in••••i•l• ••••••n• i• •o••i•l• •li•• ••l••ion••i•, ••••l•in• in ••l•• •o•i•iv•• (•••••io••• •••• o•••).

3.1 Lock-Order Graph

T•• •n•ly•i• ••il•• • •in•l• lo••-o•••• •••••• •••• ••••••••• lo••in• in•o•• ••ion •o• •n •n•i•• li•••••y. T•i• ••••• •••••••n•• ••• o••••• in w•i•• lo••• ••• •••• i•••

---

[1] For our purposes, it is sufficient to consider multiple synchronized statements over the same object in one thread as a no-op. A Java virtual machine tracks the number of *lock/unlock* actions (entrance and exit of a synchronized block) for each object. A counter is updated for each synchronized statement, but if the current thread already holds the target lock, no change is made to the thread's lock set.

(BeanContextSupport.propertyChange() *locks* BeanContextSupport.children,
BeanContextSupport.remove() *locks* BeanContext.globalHierarchyLock)

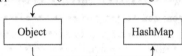

(BeanContextSupport.remove() *locks* BeanContext.globalHierarchyLock,
BeanContextSupport.remove() *locks* BeanContextSupport.children)

Fig. 3. Relevant portion of the lock-order graph for the code in Figure 1. The nodes represent the set of all `Objects` and `HashMaps`, respectively. Each edge is annotated by the sequence of methods (and corresponding variable names) that acquire first a lock from the source set, then a lock from the destination set

vi• ••ll• •o ••• li•••y' ••• li• • ••• o••. • o• •inin• in•o•• ••ion •• o•• ••• lo••-in• •••• vio• o• •••• ••• li• • ••• o• in•o on• ••••• •llow• •• •o •••••••n• •ny ••llin• •••••••n o• •••••• • •••o•• •••o•• •ny n•• • ••• o• •••••••.

• •••• no•• o• ••• lo••-o•••• ••••• •••••••••n•• • ••• o• o• j•••• ••••• • •y •• •li••••. (Ty•• •••• •n •••• oxi• ••ion •o • •y-•li•• in•o•• ••ion; S•••ion 5.1 •iv•• • • •n•• ••• ••ill li••w•i••• ••••oxi• ••ion ••• li•••l• •o ••l••.) An •••• in ••• ••••• in•i••••• n•••• lo••in• o• o• j•••• •lon• •o• • •o•• •••. T••• i•, i• in-•i••••• ••• • o••i•ili•y o• lo••in• •••• •n o• j••• ••o• ••• •o•••• no••, •••n •n o• j••• ••o• ••• ••••in••ion no••.

A •y•l• •on•i••in• o• no••• N_1 •n• N_2 ••n• ••••• •lon• •o• • •o•• •••••, •n o• j••• $o_1 \in N_1$ • •y •• lo•••• •••o•• •o• • o• j••• $o_2 \in N_2$, •n• •lon• •no•••• (o• ••• •••• •) ••••, o_2 • •y •• lo•••• •••o•• o_1. In ••n•••l, • •y•l• •x• o••• •o•• ••••• l•••in• •o •y•li• lo•• o••••, •n•, w••n ••• •o••••• on• in• ••••• ••• ••n in •••••••• •••••••, •••• lo•• • •y o••••. Fi•••• 3 •• ow• ••• lo••-o•••• ••••• •o• ••• •o•• in Fi•••• 1.

To ••il• ••• •••••, ••• •n•ly•i• i•••••• ov•• ••• • •••o•• in ••• li•••y, ••il•in• • lo••-o•••• ••••• •o• •••• o• ••••• . All •o••i• l• lo••in• •on••••••ion• o•• • ••• o• ••• • o••l••, in•l••in• lo••• ••••i••• •••n•i•iv•ly vi• ••ll• •o o•••• • •••o••. A• ••ll •i••, ••• ••ll••'• ••••• i• in••••• in•o ••• ••ll••. A••••• ••••• • •••o•'• lo••-o•••• ••••• ••• •••••••• • •x•• •oin•, ••• ••• li• • •••o••' lo••-o•••• ••••••• ••• • ••••• in•o • •in•l• ••••• •o• ••• li•••y. • y•l•• ••• •••n •••••••••, •n• ••• o••• ••• ••n••••••.

3.2   Deadlocks Detected by Our Technique

• ••• •o•l i• •o ••••• ••••• in w•i•• • ••••• n•• o• •li•n• ••ll• ••n ••••• •••• lo•• in • li•••y, o• •o v••i•y •••• no •••• •••• n•• •xi•••. • ••• •ool ••• o••• •••• lo•• • o••i•ili•i• in w•i•• •ll •••• lo•••• ••••••• ••• •lo•••• wi••in • •in•l• li•••y, ••••• ••in• •o ••••i•• lo••• vi• J•v• `synchronized` •••••• •n•• o• `wait()` ••ll•. Un•• •••••• in ••••• ••ion• ••o•• ••• •li•n• •n• ••• li•••y, o• •ool ••• o••• •ll •• •• • o••i•ili•i••.

• ••• •n•ly•i• •o••••• on •••• lo••• ••• •o lo•• ••••• i•i•ion• vi• J•v• `synchronized` •••••• •n•• •n• `wait()` ••ll•: ••o•••• o•• • ••o•••• i• ••l••• •••••• ••••••

in • ••• ••••• ••• •o ••••i•• • lo•• •l••••y ••l• •y •no•••• •••••• in ••• •••.
W• ••• no• •on••n•• wi•• o•••• w•y• in w•i•• • ••o•••• • •y ••il •o • •••
••o••••••. A ••••••• • i••• ••n• •o••v•• w•il• w•i•in• •o• in•••, •n••• •n in•ni••
loo•, •• ff•• liv•lo••, o• ••il •o ••ll notify() o• •o ••l••••• • ••••- o• li•••y-•••n••
lo•• (•••• i•, ••in• • lo••in• • ••••ni•• no• ••il• in•o J•v•). T•••• ••o•l•• •
in on• •••••• ••n •••v•n• •no•••• •••••• o• ••• w•ol• ••o•••• ••o• • ••in•
••o••••••: •on•i••• • ••ll •o Thread.join() (w•i•• w•i•• •o• • •iv•n •••••• •o
•••• in•••) on • •••••• •••• •o•• no• •••• in•••. D•••••in• •ll o• •••••• ••o•l•• •
i• o••i•• ••• ••o•• o•• •• i• •••••.

Assumptions About Client Code. W• • ••• •••••• ••••• • •ion• •• o•• •li•n•
•o••. I• • •li•n• ••vi•••• ••o• ••••• ••••• ••ion•, o•• •ool i• ••ill ••••l •o•
••••••in• •••• lo••, ••• i• ••nno• •••••• •••• lo••• in••o••••• •y ••• ••vi•n•
••• •vio•. Fi•••, w• ••••• • ••••• ••• •li•n• •o•• no• in•l••• • •l••• ••••• •x••n••
• li•••y •l•• o• ••lon•• •o • li•••y ••••••••. I••••• • •l•• •xi•••, i• n•••• •o ••
in•••••••• •y o•• •n•ly•i• •n• •••••••• ••••••• o• ••• li•••y. S••on•, w• ••••• •
•••• ••••• ••• •li•n• •o•• no• invo•• li•••y • •••o• wi•• in ••ll••••• ••o• •••
li•••y; •••• i•, •ll •li•n• • •••o•• M ••• •i•••• •n••••••l• ••o• ••• li•••y,
o• ••• li•••y i• •n•••••••l• ••o• M. Fo• •x•• •l•, i• • •li•n• •l•• ov••i•••
Object.hashCode() •••• •••• i• ••ll• • •yn••oni••• • •••o• in ••• li•••y, ••n
•ny li•••y • •••o• ••llin• hashCode() ••o•l• • o••l •••• •yn••oni••ion. T••
•l••• •••••••o•• n•••• •o •• •n•ly••• ••• ••o••• i• i• •••• o• ••• li•••y. T•i••, w•
••••• • ••••• ••• •li•n• •o•• i• *well-behaved*: •i•••• i• •o•• no• lo•• •ny o•j••••
lo•••• •y ••• li•••y, o• i• •o•• •o in •i••i•lin• w•y• (•• •x•l•in•• ••low).

Wi••o• ••• ••••• ••ion o• w•ll-•••v••n•••, i• i• •i• •i• •l• o• i• •o••i•l• •o
•••••n••• •••• lo•• •••••o• •o• • li•••y wi••o• •x•• inin• •li•n• •o••. An
••v•••••i•l •li•n• ••n in•••• •••• lo•• i• i• •••• •••••• •o •wo o•j••• lo•••• •y •
li•••y. Fo• •x•• •l•, •••• o•• •••••• • li•••y ••• • •yn••oni••• • •••o•:

```
class A {
  synchronized void foo() { ... }
}
```

T••n • •li•n• •o• l• ••••• •••• lo•• in ••• •ollowin• w•y:

```
A a1 = new A(), a2 = new A();
thread 1:  synchronized(a1) { a2.foo(); }
thread 2:  synchronized(a2) { a1.foo(); }
```

A •li•n• •••• lo••• • •iff••n• ••• o• o•j•••• ••n ••o•• lo•••• •y ••• li•••y
i• •lw•y• w•ll-•••v••. T•i• i• ••• •••• •o• •••i••••y •li•n•• i• ••• lo••• ••••
•y ••• li•••y •o no• •••••• i•; •••• i•, i• ••y ••• in•••••i•l• •o ••• •li•n•.
S••ion 5.1 ••••i•• • • •••o• •o• •••••••in• •o• in••••••i•l• lo•••.

• v•n i• ••• •li•n• •n• ••• li•••y ••••• • ••• o• lo•••, ••• •li•n• ••n ••
w•ll-•••v•• i• i• •••• •i••• ••o•• lo••• in • •••••i•••• •••••••n. T•••• ••••i••ion•
•o•l• •• ••••• o• ••• li•••y'• ••••i••••ion—•n• •••• •o••• •n••ion •o•l• •v•n
•• ••••o• ••i••lly ••n•••••• •o• ••• li•••y •y • •ool li•• o•••. A• •• ov•, on•

••• •i•n• ••••i••ion i• •••• •li•n•• •o no• lo•• o•j•••• •••• ••• li•••y • •y
lo••; ••i• •••• i••• ••• li•••y •o •••i•y ••• ••• o• o•j•••• •••• i• will lo••. A
• o•• li•••l ••• ••• •i•n• ••••i••ion i• ••• ••• •li•n• •••• i••• lo••• in •n o••••
•o• •••i•l• wi•• ••• li•••y. In ••i• •••n••io, ••• li•••y •••i•• ••• o•••• o• lo••
•••• i•i•ion• (••y, ••• lo••-o••• •••••), •n• •li•n• ••• •o•i••n ••o• •••• i•in•
lo••• in •n o•••• •••• in••o•••• •y•l•• in•o ••• •••••. W• •li•v• •••• ••••
••••i••ion• ••• ••i•• •••on••l•, •n• •••• in•o•• ••ion ••o• ••• lo••• •••• i•••
•y • li•••y ••• • •••i•••l• •••• o•i•• •••i•••ion.

Assumptions About Library Code. In •••••i••, li•••i•• •o no• •xi•• in
i•ol••ion. ••••••, •••• li•••y •••• •••i•ion•l li•••i•• (•.•., ••• JDK) •o ••l•
i• •••o• •li•• i•• •••••. • n• •••••o••• •o •n•ly•in• •••• •••••••• li•••i•• i• •o
•on•i••• •ll o• ••• li•••i•• •o••••••, •• i• ••y w••• • •in•l• li•••y. How•v••,
••i• ••• •••• • o••l•i•y, •• ••• •••••n•••• off•••• •o• on• li•••y •••n• on
••• i• •l•• •n••ion o• o•••• li•••i••. I• •l•o ••• •••• •••l••ili•y, ••••• •ff••iv•
li•••y •i•• ••n ••ow •nwi•l•y •o• ••• •n•ly•i•. Fo• ••••• •••on•, o•• •n•ly•i•
•on•i•••• •••• li•••y in••••n••n•ly. • on•i•• •••• ••• "• •in" li•••y •n•••
•on•i••••ion ••li•• on ••v•••l "••xili••y" li•••i••. Un••• •••••in ••••• ••ion•
••o•• ••• • •in li•••y, o•• •n•ly•i• ••••••• •ll •••• lo•• • o••i•ili•i• in w•i••
•ll •••••••• ••• •lo•••• wi•• in ••• • •in li•••y. I• ••o• no• ••• o•• ••••• in w•i••
•o• • •••••••• ••• •lo•••• in ••• • •in li•••y •n• o•••• •••••••• ••• •lo•••• in
••xili••y li•••i••.

W• ••• ••• •ollowin• ••••• ••ion• ••o• li•••y •o••. Fi•••, •• ••• li•••y
•n••• •on•i•••ion (•••• •in li•••y) • •y••• •li•n• o••o• •••xili••y li•••i••,
i• • ••• •••i•y ••• •li•n• ••••• ••ion• (•••••i••• •••vio••ly) •o •••••n••• ••••-
lo•• •••••o• •o• i•• own •••••. S••on•, ••• • •in li•••y ••nno• •••••o•• •ny
•yn•••oni••ion in • •••o•• ••••• ••• •••••••l• vi• ••ll••••• ••o• ••xili••y li-
••••i•• (•.•., in `Object.hashCode()`). • •ll••••• •••o•••• ••• ••xili••y li•••i••
••• in••••••i•l• •o ••• •n•ly•i•. T•i••, ••• li•••y ••nno• ••• ••fl••••ion. • •fl••-
•ion ••n in••o•••• o•••••• ••llin• ••••n••• •••• i• •••• ••• lo•• o•••••in•. A•
wi•• ••• •li•n• •o••, o•• •n•ly•i• o•••••• ••• ••••l •v•n i• •••••• ••••• ••ion•
••• ••o••n, ••• i• ••n no lon••• •••••n••• •••• •ll •••• lo•• • o••i•ili•i• •••
••• o•••••.

4 Algorithm Details

T•• •••• lo•• •••••o• •• •loy• •n in••••o••••••l ••••flow •n•ly•i• •o• •on-
••••••in• lo••-o•••• ••••••. T•• •n•ly•i• i• flow-••n•i•iv• •n• •on••x-••n•i•iv•.
A• ••••• ••o•••• • oin•, ••• •n•ly•i• •o• ••••• • •y• oli• ••••• • o••lin• •••
li•••y'• •x•••ion •••••. T•• •y• oli• ••••• •• ••• •n• o•• • •••o• •••v•• •••
• •••o• ••• • •y. T•• •n•ly•i• i• ••n •••••••ly ov•• •ll • ••o•• •n•il • •x••
• oin• i• •••••••; •••• in••ion o• ••• •n•ly•i• i• ••••n••••.

T•• •y•• • •o• •in• •o• ••• •n•ly•i• ••• •iv•n in Fi•••• •. Fo• i• • li•i•y, w•
•••••n• ••• •l•o•i••• •o• l•n••••• ••••• • o••l• ••• •••••• o• J•v• ••l•v•n• •o
o••• •n•ly•i•. T•• l•n•••••• o• i•• •l• •••i•n• •n••; ••y ••• no• ••l•v•n• •••••••

$$T \in \text{Type}$$
$$v \in \text{LocalVar}$$
$$method \in \text{MethodDecl} = T_r\ m(T_1\ v_1, T_2\ v_2, \ldots, T_n\ v_n)\ \{\ stmt\ \}$$
$$\text{where } v_1 = \texttt{this} \text{ if } m \text{ is instance method}$$
$$library \in \text{Library} = \text{set-of MethodDecls}$$

$$stmt \in \text{Statement} = \quad T\ v \qquad\qquad\ |\ \texttt{branch}\ stmt_1\ stmt_2$$
$$|\ v := \texttt{new } T \quad |\ \texttt{synchronized}\ (v)\ \{\ stmt\ \}$$
$$|\ v_1 := v_2 \qquad |\ v := m(v_1, \ldots, v_n)$$
$$|\ v_1 := v_2.f \qquad |\ \texttt{wait}(v)$$
$$|\ stmt_1;\ stmt_2$$

$$pp \in \text{ProgramPoint}_\bot$$
$$o = \langle \text{pp}, \text{T} \rangle \in \text{HeapObject} = \text{ProgramPoint} \times \text{Type}$$
$$g \in \text{Graph} = \text{directed-graph-of HeapObjects}$$
$$roots \in \text{Roots} = \text{set-of HeapObjects}$$
$$env \in \text{Environment} = \text{LocalVar} \rightharpoonup \text{HeapObject}$$
$$s = \langle g, \text{roots}, \text{locks}, \in \text{State} = \text{Graph} \times \text{Roots} \times \text{list-of HeapObjects} \times$$
$$env, wait \rangle \qquad\qquad \text{Environment} \times \text{set-of HeapObjects}$$

Fig. 4. Type domains for the lock-order dataflow analysis. Parameters are considered to be created at unique points before the beginning of a method. The "branch $stmt_1$ $stmt_2$" statement is a non-deterministic branch to either $stmt_1$ or $stmt_2$

o•• •n•ly•i• • o•• no• ••••• ••• flow o• v• l••• ••o••• ••l••. Syn•••oni••• • •••‐
o•• •••• • o••l•• in •• i• l•n•••• ••in• •••i• •••••••in• (••• S•••ion •) • n• loo••
••• •••• o•••• vi• •••••ion. ••• i• •l•• •n••ion ••n• l•• ••• •• ll J•v• l•n•••••.
••• •n•ly•i• o• •••••• on •y• • oli• •••• o• j••••. ••••• •y• • oli• •••• o• j•••
•••••••n•• ••• ••• o• o• j•••• •••••••• ••• • iv•n ••o•••• • oin• [6]; i• •l•o •on••in•
••i• •y••. Fo• •onv•ni•n••, w• •y ••••• •y• • oli• •••• o• j••• o i• *locked* w•• n
• ••••i••l•• •on••••• o• j••• •••wn ••o• o i• lo••••.

T•• **state** i• • 5-•••l• •on•i••in• o•:

- T•• ••••••n• lo••-o•••• **graph**. • •••• no•• in ••• ••••• i• • •y• • oli• ••••
  o• j••••. T•• ••••• •••••••n•• •o••i•l• lo••in• •••vio• •o• •on••••• ••••
  o• j•••• •••wn ••o• ••• ••••• • o••l•• •y ••• •y• • oli• •••• o• j••••. A ••••
  o• no••• $o_1 \ldots o_k$ in ••• ••••• •o•••••on•• •o • • o••n•i•l ••o•••• •••• in
  w•i•• o_1 i• lo••••, •••n o_2 i• lo•••• (•••o•• o_1 i• ••l•••••), •n• •o on.
- T•• **roots** o• ••• •••••. T•• •oo•• •••••••n• o• j•••• ••• ••• lo•••• ••• •o• •
  • oin• •••in• •x•••••ion o• • •iv•n • •••o• w••n no o•••• lo•• i• ••l•.
- T•• li•• o• **locks** •••• ••• ••••••n•ly ••l•, in ••• o•••• in w•i•• •••y w•••
  o•••in••.
- An **environment** • •••in• lo••l v••i••l•• •o •y• • oli• •••• o• j••••. T••
  •nvi•on• •n• i• •n i• • o•••n• •o• •on•n• o•••• in•••••o•••••l n•ly•i•, •• i•
  •llow in•o•• ••ion •o ••o••• •• •••w••n ••ll••• •n• ••ll•••. I• •l•o i• ••ov••
  ••••i•ion •y ••••in• ••• flow o• v• l••• •••w••n lo••l v••i••l••.
- A ••• o• o• j•••• •••• ••v• ••• **wait** ••ll•• on •••• wi••o•• • n •n•lo•in•
  synchronized •••••• •n• in ••• •••••n• • ••• o•.

4.1   Dataflow Rules

T•• ••••flow ••l•• •o• ••• •n•ly•i• ••• ••••n••• in Fi•••• 5. H•l••• •• n••ion•
•••••• in Fi•••• 6, •n• • •••••• ••i••l o••••o•• (in•l••in• ••• join o••••o•)
••• •••n•• in Fi•••• •. T••o••o•• ••• •ollowin• •x•l•n••ion, w• •••n• •••
current lock •• •••• • o•• •••n•ly lo•••• o• j••• w•o•• lo•• ••• •in••l•; i• i• •••
l••• o• j••• in ••• li•• o• •••••n•ly ••l• lo•••, o• ••il(*s*.lo•••).

T•• •y• •oli• ••••• i• •••••••• in ••• **visit_stmt** ••o•••••• (in Fi•••• 5)
w•i•• vi•i•• •••• •••••• •n• in • • •••o•. A v••i••l• •••l•••ion o• ini•i•li•••ion
in••o••••• • ••••• •••• o• j•••. An •••i•n• •n• ••w••n lo••l• •o•i•• •n o•j•••
wi•• in ••• lo••l •nvi•on• •n•. A ••l• •••••••n•• in••o••••• • ••••• o• j••• (•••
•n•ly•i• •o•• no• •o••l ••• flow o• v•l••• •••o••• ••l••). A branch • o••l•
•iv•••n• ••••• •n• i• ••n•l•• •y ••• join o••••o• ••low. ••ll• •o wait() •••
•••••i••• in S••ion •.•.

T•• ••l• •o• synchronized •••••• •n•• ••n•l•• lo•• ••••i•••; ••••• ••• •wo
•••••. Fi•••, i• ••• •••••• o•j••• *o* i• no• •••••n•ly lo•••• (i.•., i• *o* ∉ *s*.lo•••),
•••n •n •••• i• •••••• •o ••• lo••-o••••••••• ••o• ••• •••••••n• lo•• •o *o*, •n• *o* i•
••••n••• •o *s*.lo•••. I• no o•j••• w••• lo•••• •••o••• ••• synchronized •••••• •n•,
o •••o• •• • •oo• in ••• •••••• (•oo•• ••• i• •o•••n• •• • ••ll •i••, •• i•••••••
••low). N•x•, ••• •n•ly•i• •••••n•• in•o ••• •o•y o• ••• synchronized •lo••.
U• on •o• •l••ion, ••• •n•ly•i• •on•in•• •o ••• n•x• •••••• •n•, •••••vin• •••
lo••-o•••• ••••• ••o• ••• synchronized •lo•• ••• ••••o•in• ••• li•• o• lo••••
o•j•••• v•li• •••o•• ••• synchronized •••••• •n•. T•i• i• •o•••••, •in•• J•v•'•
•yn••x •••••n•••• •••• •ny o•j•••• lo•••• wi•• in ••• synchronized •lo•• •••
•l•o ••l••••• wi•• in ••• •lo••.

In ••• •••on• •••• •o• synchronized •••••• •n••, ••• •••••• i• ••••n•ly lo••••.
T•o••• ••• •o•y i• •n•ly••• •• •••o••, ••• •yn••oni••ion i• • no-o• •n• •o••
no• w••••n• •n •••• in ••• lo••-o•••• ••••••. To •x•loi• ••i• ••••, ••• •n•ly•i•
n••••••o •••••• in• w••••• n••••• synchronized •••••• •n••• ••• lo••in• ••• ••• •
•on•••• o• j•••. T•o••• •y• •oli• •••• o• j•••• •••••••••n• *sets* o••on••••• o• j••••,
•••y non••••l•••• •n • ••••• •o• •• i• •••••• in••ion: i• n••••• synchronized ••••••-
• •n•• lo•• v••i••l• •••••• ••• • ••••• •o ••• ••• • ••••• o• j••• (•••in• •n•ly•i•),
•••n •••y •lw•y• lo•• ••• ••• • •on•••• o• j••• (•••in• •x•••ion). T•i• i• ••••
wi•• in • • •••o• •••••••• •••• •••• o• j••• i• •••o•i•••• wi•• • •in•l• ••o••••
•oin•; •• ••i• •i• •li••• l•n••••• •on••in• no loo•••, •ny •x•••ion will vi•i• ••••
•oin• ••• • o•• on•• •n• ••n•• •••••• ••• • o•• on• •on••••• in•••n•• o• ••• •••••
o•j•••. T•i• no•ion •l•o •x••n•• •••o•• • •••o••, •• •o•• •••• o• j•••• •n• •on-
••••• o• j•••• ••• •i•••ly • •••••• ••o• ••ll•• ••••• •n•• in•o ••ll•• ••••• •••••
•• •••••i••• ••low. T•••, ••••••••• •yn••oni••ion on • •iv•n •••• o• j••• i•
••••ly i•no•••, •i•ni••n•ly i• ••ovin• ••• ••••i•ion o• ••• •n•ly•i•.

M•••o• ••ll• ••• ••n•l•• •y in••••••in• ••• •••••• •o• ••• ••ll•• in•o ••• ••ll••
•• •ollow•. In ••• •••• o• ov••i••n • •••o••, •••• ••n•i•••• i• •l•• •n••ion'•
••••• i• in••••••••. T•• •n•ly•i• •••• ••• • o•• •••n• lo••-o•••• ••••• •••••
•••n ••l••l•••• •o• ••• ••ll••. • ••••iv• •••••n••• ••• i••••••• •n•il ••••• in• •
•x•• •oin•. T•• ••llin• •on••x• i• •••• in•o•••o•••• in•o • •o•y o• ••• ••ll••'•
••••• •i•••• •y ••• ovin• ••• •o•• •l ••••• ••••• (i•••• •o••••• on• in• ••••• •n•

visit_stmt($stmt, s$) returns State s'
  $s' \leftarrow s$
  switch($stmt$)
    case $T\ v\ |\ v := \textbf{new}\ T$
      s'.env $\leftarrow$ s.env$[v := \langle$ **program_point**($stmt$), $T\ \rangle]$
    case $v_1 := v_2$
      s'.env $\leftarrow$ s.env$[v_1 := s$.env$[v_2]]$
    case $v_1 := v_2.f$
      s'.env $\leftarrow$ s.env$[v_1 := \langle$ **program_point**($stmt$), declared_type($v_2.f$) $\rangle]$
    case $stmt_1;\ stmt_2$
      $s_1 \leftarrow$ **visit_stmt**($stmt_1, s$)
      $s' \leftarrow$ **visit_stmt**($stmt_2, s_1$)
    case **branch** $stmt_1\ stmt_2$
      $s' \leftarrow$ **visit_stmt**($stmt_1, s$) $\sqcup$ **visit_stmt**($stmt_2, s$)
    case **synchronized** (v) { $stmt$ }
      $o \leftarrow s$.env$[v]$
      if $o \in s$.locks then
        // already locked o, so synchronized statement is a no-op
        $s_1 \leftarrow s$
      else
        // add o to g under current lock, or as root if no locks held
        if s.locks is empty // below, $\bullet$ denotes list concatenation
          then $s_1 \leftarrow \langle s$.g $\cup\ o, s$.roots $\cup\ o, s$.locks $\bullet\ o, s$.env$, s$.wait$\rangle$
          else $s_1 \leftarrow \langle s$.g $\cup\ o\ \cup$ edge(tail(s.locks) $\rightarrow o$)$, s$.roots$, s$.locks $\bullet\ o$,
              s.env$, s$.wait$\rangle$
      $s_2 \leftarrow$ **visit_stmt**($stmt, s_1$)
      $s' \leftarrow \langle s_2$.g$, s_2$.roots$, s$.locks$, s_2$.env$, s_2$.wait$\rangle$
    case $v := m(v_1, \ldots, v_n)$
      s'.env $\leftarrow s$.env$[v := \langle$ **program_point**($stmt$), return_type(m) $\rangle]$
      $\forall$ versions of m in subclasses of env$[v_1]$.T:
        $s_m \leftarrow$ **visit_method**(method_decl(m))
        $s'_m \leftarrow$ **rename_from_callee_to_caller_context**(s_m, s, n)
        // connect the two graphs, including roots
        s'.g $\leftarrow s'$.g $\cup\ s'_m$.g
        if s.locks is empty then // connect current lock to roots of s'_m
          s'.roots $\leftarrow s'$.roots $\cup\ s'_m$.roots
          s'.wait $\leftarrow s'$.wait $\cup\ s'_m$.wait
        else
          $\forall\ root \in s'_m$.roots:
            s'.g $\leftarrow s'$.g $\cup$ edge(tail(s.locks) $\rightarrow root$)
          $\forall\ o \in s'_m$.wait: if tail(s.locks) $\neq o$ then
            s'.g $\leftarrow s$.g $\cup\ o\ \cup$ edge(tail(s.locks) $\rightarrow o$)
    case **wait**(v)
      $o \leftarrow s$.env$[v]$
      if s.locks is empty then
        s'.wait $\leftarrow s$.wait $\cup\ o$
      else if tail(s.locks) $\neq o$ then
        // **wait** releases then reacquires o: new lock ordering
        s'.g $\leftarrow s$.g $\cup\ o\ \cup$ edge(tail(s.locks) $\rightarrow o$)

Fig. 5. Dataflow rules for the lock-order data-flow analysis

program_point(*stmt*) returns the program point for statement *stmt*

visit_method(T_r $m(T_1$ $v_1, \ldots, T_n$ $v_n)$ { *stmt* }) returns State s'
    $s' \leftarrow$ empty State
    $\forall$ parameters T_i v_i (including **this**):
        $s' \leftarrow$ **visit_stmt**(T_i v_i, s') // process formals via "T v" rule
    $s' \leftarrow$ **visit_stmt**(*stmt*, s')

rename_from_callee_to_caller_context(s_m, s, n) returns State s'_m
    $s'_m \leftarrow s_m$
    $\forall j \in [1, n] : formal_j \leftarrow s_m.\text{env}[v_j]$ // formal parameter
    $\forall j \in [1, n] : actual_j \leftarrow s.\text{env}[v_j]$ // actual argument
    $\forall o \in s_m.\text{g} :$ // for all objects o locked by the callee
        if $\exists j$ s.t. $o = formal_j$
            // o is formal parameter j of callee method
            then if $actual_j \in s.\text{locks}$
                // caller locked o, remove o from callee graph
                then $s'_m.\text{g}, s'_m.\text{roots} \leftarrow$ **splice_out_node**($s_m.\text{g}, s_m.\text{roots}, o$)
                // caller did not lock o, rename o to actual arg
                else $s'_m.\text{g}, s'_m.\text{roots} \leftarrow$ **replace_node**($s_m.\text{g}, s_m.\text{roots}, o, actual_j$)
            // o is not from caller, rename o to bottom program point $pp_\perp$
            else $s'_m.\text{g}, s'_m.\text{roots} \leftarrow$ **replace_node**($s_m.\text{g}, s_m.\text{roots}, o, \langle pp_\perp, o.\text{T} \rangle$)
    $s'_m.\text{wait} \leftarrow \emptyset$
    $\forall o \in s_m.\text{wait}$ // for all objects in wait set
        if $\exists j$ s.t. $o = formal_j$
            then $s'_m.\text{wait} \leftarrow s'_m.\text{wait} \cup actual_j$
            else $s'_m.\text{wait} \leftarrow s'_m.\text{wait} \cup \langle pp_\perp, o.\text{T} \rangle$

splice_out_node($g, roots, o$) returns Graph g', Roots $roots'$
    $g' \leftarrow g \setminus o$
    $\forall$ edges($src \rightarrow o$) $\in g$ s.t. $o \neq src$:
        $\forall$ edges($o \rightarrow dst$) $\in g$ s.t. $o \neq dst$:
            $g' \leftarrow g' \cup$ edge($src \rightarrow dst$)
    $roots' \leftarrow roots \setminus o$
    if $o \in roots$ then
        $\forall$ edges($o \rightarrow dst$) $\in g$ s.t. $o \neq dst$:
            $roots' \leftarrow roots' \cup dst$

replace_node($g, roots, o_{old}, o_{new}$) returns Graph g', Roots $roots'$
    $g' \leftarrow (g \setminus o_{old}) \cup o_{new}$
    $\forall$ edges($src \rightarrow o_{old}$) $\in g : g' \leftarrow g' \cup$ edge($src \rightarrow o_{new}$)
    $\forall$ edges($o_{old} \rightarrow dst$) $\in g : g' \leftarrow g' \cup$ edge($o_{new} \rightarrow dst$)
    if $o_{old} \in roots$
        then $roots' \leftarrow (roots \setminus o_{old}) \cup o_{new}$
        else $roots' \leftarrow roots$

Fig. 6. Helper functions for the lock-order dataflow analysis

---

$actual_j$ i• lo•••• •• ••• ••ll •i••, in w• i•• •••• ••• lo•• ••••i•• i• • no-o• ••o•
••• ••ll••'• •••••••••iv•) o• •y ••• l••in• •••• wi•• ••• ••ll••'• •••••l ••••• •n••
(i• $actual_j$ i• no• lo•••• •• ••• ••ll •i••). T•• non-•o•• •l ••••• •••• no••• •••

$g_1 \cup g_2$ returns Graph g'
  // nodes are HeapObjects: equivalent values are collapsed
  $\text{nodes}(g') = \text{nodes}(g_1) \cup \text{nodes}(g_2)$
  // edges are pairs of HeapObjects: equivalent pairs are collapsed
  $\text{edges}(g') = \text{edges}(g_1) \cup \text{edges}(g_2)$

$g \setminus o$ returns Graph g'
  $\text{nodes}(g') = \text{nodes}(g) \setminus o$
  $\text{edges}(g') = \text{edges}(src \rightarrow dst) \in g \;\; s.t. \;\; o \neq src \;\wedge\; o \neq dst$

$s_1 \sqcup s_2$ returns State s'
  $s'.\text{g} \leftarrow s_1.\text{g} \cup s_2.\text{g}$
  $s'.\text{roots} \leftarrow s_1.\text{roots} \cup s_2.\text{roots}$
  $s'.\text{locks} \leftarrow s_1.\text{locks}$ // $s_1.\text{locks} = s_2.\text{locks}$
  $\forall v \in \{v' \mid v' \in s_1.\text{env} \;\vee\; v' \in s_2.\text{env}\}$:
    if $s_1.\text{env}[v] = s_2.\text{env}[v]$
      then $s'.\text{env} \leftarrow s'.\text{env}[v := s_1.\text{env}(v)]$
      else $s'.\text{env} \leftarrow s'.\text{env}[v := \langle$**program_point**(join_point(v)), $T_1 \sqcup T_2 \rangle]$
  $s'.\text{wait} \leftarrow s_1.\text{wait} \cup s_2.\text{wait}$
$T_1 \sqcup T_2$ returns lowest common superclass of T_1 and T_2

Fig. 7. Union and difference operators for graphs, and join operator for symbolic state

••n •••l•••• wi•• no••• o• ••• ••• • •y•• •n• wi•• • •• ••i•l ••o•••• •oin• o• $pp_\perp$, in•i•••in• •••• •••y o•i•in•••• •• •n •n•nown ••o•••• •oin• (•o••o•). T•• ••ll••'• w•i• ••• i• ••j•••• in • •i• il•• ••••ion. A• ••i• •oin•, •n •••• i• ••••• ••o• ••• •••••n• lo•• in ••• ••ll•• •o •••• o• ••• •oo•• o• ••• • o•i••• ••ll•• •••••. Fin•lly, ••• •wo •••••• ••• • •••••, •oll•••in• i••n•i••l no••• •n• •••••.

T•• **join** o•••••o• ($\sqcup$) in Fi•••• • i• •••• •o •o• •in• •••••• •lon• •onfl••n• ••••• o• ••• ••o•••• (•.•., `if` •••••• •n••). W• ••• in•••••••• in lo••in• ••••••n• •lon• •ny •o••i•l• ••••, w•i••, •o• ••• ••••••, •oo••, •n• w•i• ••••, i• •i• •ly ••• •nion o•••• •wo in•o• in• ••••••' v•l•••. T•• li•• o•• •••n• lo•••• o•• no• n••• •o •• •••on•il•• •••w••n •wo •••••, •• ••• •i•••••y o• `synchronized` •lo••• in J•v• •••••n•••• •••• •o•• in•o• in• •••••• will •• ••• ••• •. T•• n•w •nvi•on• •n• ••• •in• ••• ••• • •o• • •••in•• •o• • on •o • o•• •••••. I• ••• • •••in•• •iff•• •o• • •iv•n v••i••l• •••n • ••••• •••• o•j••• • ••• •• in••o•••• •o• •••• v••i••l•. T•• ••••• o•j••• i• •••i•n•• • ••o•••• •oin• •o••••• on•in• •o ••• join •oin• •o• ••• v••i••l• (•••• v••i••l• i• •on•i•••• •o join •• • •••••••• lo•••ion). T•• •••on•••• •y•• •on••••in• •o• ••• ••••• o•j••• i• ••• join o• ••• v••i••l••' •y••• •lon• •••• ••••—•• •i• low••• •o• • on ••••••l•••.

T•• •l•o•i••• •o• •on••••••in• ••• •n•i•• li••••y'• lo••-o•••• ••••• i• •iv•n in Fi•••• •. T•• **top_level** ••o•••••• •••• •o• ••••• • •x•• •oin• ••••• v•l•• •o• •••• • •••o• in ••• li••••y. T••• in••ion i• •••••n•••• •in•• •••••••n •• •• • o•• |PP| · |Ty••| •••• o•j•••• in • • •••o• •n• ••• •n•ly•i• only •••• o•j•••• •o ••• ••••• ••• •iv•n •••••. A•••• •o• •••in• ••• •x•• •oin••, ••• ••o•••••• ••••o•• • • •o••-• •o••••in• •••• •o •••o• n• •o• •••l••in•. B•••••• ••• •n•ly•i•

top_level(*library*) returns Graph g
$s_1, \ldots, s_n \leftarrow$ dataflow fixed points over public methods in *library*
$g \leftarrow$ **post_process**$(s_1, \ldots, s_n)$

post_process$(s_1, \ldots, s_n)$ returns Graph g
$g \leftarrow$ empty Graph
$\forall i \in [1, n]$:
   $\forall$ edges $(o_1 \rightarrow o_2) \in s_i.g$:
     // Add edges between all possible subclasses of locked objects.
     // All heap objects now have bottom program point $pp_\perp$.
     $\forall$ subclasses T_1 of $o_1.T$, $\forall$ subclasses T_2 of $o_2.T$:
       $o_{T_1} \leftarrow \langle pp_\perp, T_1 \rangle$
       $o_{T_2} \leftarrow \langle pp_\perp, T_2 \rangle$
       $g \leftarrow g \cup o_{T_1} \cup o_{T_2} \cup \mathrm{edge}(o_{T_1} \rightarrow o_{T_2})$

Fig. 8. Top-level routine for constructing a lock-order graph for a library of methods

•o• •••• • •••o• w•• ••••• on ••• •••l•••• •y•• o• lo•••, •x••• •••••• • ••• •• •••••• •o• •ll •o••i•l• •on••••• •y••• •••• • •iv•n •••• o• j••• •o•l• •••••• •. W• il• i• i• •l•o • o••i•l• •o • o• i•y ••• • •••flow •n•ly•i• •o ••• l wi•• ••• •l•••in• •• ••••• ••••, i• i• •i• •l•• •n• • o•• •• •i•n• •o ••• •o••-•o•••in•.

4.2 Calls to `wait()`

A ••ll •o wait() on o• j••• o •••••••• ••• lo•• on o •o •• ••l••••• •n• •••••••••n•ly •••••• i•••, w•i•• i• • o••l•• •y •••in• •n •••• in ••• lo••-o••• ••••• ••o• ••• • o•• ••••n•ly •••• i••• lo•• •o o. How•v••, ••i• ••••• ••n •• o• i•••• i• o i• •l•o ••• • o•• ••••n•ly •••• i••• lo••, •• ••l••in• •n• •••••• i•in• ••i• lo•• ••• no •ff••• on ••• lo•• o•••in•. In •on••••• •o synchronized ••••••• •n••, wait() ••n infl••n•• ••• lo••-o••• ••••• •v•n ••o••• i•• ••••iv•• i• lo•••• •• ••• •i• • o• ••• ••ll. Fo• •x•• •l•, ••o•• ••• wait() ••ll in Fi•••• 9, a i• lo•••• ••o•• b. How•v••, •••in• ••• ••ll •o wait(), a'• lo•• i• ••l••••• •n• l•••• ••••i••• w•il• b'• lo•• ••• •in• ••l•, •o a i• •l•o lo•••• ••••• b. D•••lo•• i• •••••••o•• •o••i•l•.

I• i• ill•••l •o ••ll wait() on •n o• j••• w•o•• lo•• i• no• ••l•; i• ••i• ••••••n• •••in• ••o••••• •x•••ion, J•v• •••ow• • ••n•i• • •x•••ion. •v•n •o, i• i• •o•-•i•l• •o• • • •••o• •o ••ll wait() o••i•• •ny synchronized ••••••• •n•,. •in• ••• ••••iv•• •o•l• •• lo•••• in ••• ••ll••. W••n • • •••o• ••ll• wait() o••i•• •ny synchronized ••••••• •n•, o•• •n•ly•i• n•••• •o •on•i••• ••• ••llin• •on••x• •o •••••• in• ••• •ff•••• o• ••• wait() ••ll on ••• lo••-o••• •••••. Fo• ••i• ••••on, w••n no lo•••• ••• ••l• •n• wait() i• ••ll••, ••• ••••iv•• o• j••• i• ••o••• in ••• w•i• ••• •n• l•••• •••o•n••• •o• in • ••ll•• • •••o•.

Non• o• ••• li•••i•• w• •n•ly••• •••o•••• •ny •o••n•i•l ••••lo••• ••• •o wait(). T•i• •••••••••• •••• ••o•••• • •••• • o•• o•••n ••ll wait() on ••• • o•• ••••n•ly •••• i••• lo••.

```
void m1(Object a, Object b) {      void m2(Object a, Object b) {      Object a = new Object();
  synchronized(a) {                  synchronized(a) {                Object b = new Object();
    synchronized (b) {                 a.notify();
      a.wait();                        synchronized (b) {             thread 1:  m1(a, b);
      ...                                ...                          thread 2:  m2(a, b);
}}}                                }}}
```

Fig. 9. Method m1() imposes both lock orderings a→b and b→a, due to the call to a.wait(). Method m2(), which imposes the lock ordering a→b, can cause deadlock when run in parallel with m1(), as illustrated in the third column

4.3 Dataflow Example

An •x•• • l• o••• ••••flow •n•ly•i• •••••••• in Fi•••• 10. T•• •x•• • l• •on••in• • •l••• A wi•• •wo • •••o••, foo() •n• bar(). T•• •y• •oli• ••••• s_{foo} ••••••••n•• ••• • •••o• ••• • ••y •o• foo(). P•o•••• •oin••• ••• ••••••••n••• ••• • v••i••l• n•• ••n• • lin• n•• ••• •o••••• on•in• •o••• v••i••l•'•••i•n• •n•. Fo• •x•• • l•, ⟨•• $_{b1:5}$, B⟩ i• • •y• •oli• •••• o•j•••, o• •y•• B, •o• ••••• •••• b1 on lin• 5 o• foo(); ⟨•• $_{lock:11}$, B⟩ i• • •y• •oli• •••• o•j•••, •l•o o• •y•• B, •o• ••• ••l• lock •• ••••••n••• on lin• 11 o• foo() (••o••• lock i• •••l•••• on lin• •, ••••• ••l• •••••••n•• •••••••• • ••••• •••• o•j•••). T•• lo••-o•••• •••••• •o• foo() ill•••••••• •••• • ••••• ••••• b1 •n• c1 ••n •••• •• lo•••• in ••••••n••, wi•• lock lo•••• ••••••••ly. No•• ••••• ••• ••••• •on••in• •wo ••••••••• no••• •o• b1 •n• lock— •o•• o• •y• B—in •••• on• o• •••• ••n •• •••n•• w••n in••••••in• in•o ••• ••••• o•• ••ll••.

T•• •y• •oli• ••••• in bar() i• • ••i••ly •••o••• ••• ••ll •o foo() i• ••••••- ••n••• •y s_{bar1}. Sin•• bar() i• • •yn••oni••• • •••o•, • ••••• o•j••• •o• this •••••••• ••• •oo• o• ••• •••••. T•• ••••• ill•••••••• •••• •••••• ••••• b2 •n• c2 ••n •• lo•••• w•il• ••• lo•• •o• this i• ••l•. T•• li•• o• lo•••••l• •• ••• • •oin• o• ••• ••ll i• •iv•n •y s_{bar1}.lo•••; i• •on••in• this •n• c2.

T•• • o•• in••••••in• •••••• o• ••• •x•• • l• i• ••• • •••o• ••ll •o• bar() •o foo(). T•i• •••••• ••• ••••• o• s_{foo} •o •• ••j••••• •o• ••• ••llin• •on••x• •n• •••n in••••••• in•o ••• •••• o• s_{bar1} wi•• •••••••••••• ••o• ••• no•• •o• ••• •••••n• lo••, c2. T•• ••llin• •on••x• •••in• wi•• ••• •••••l ••••• •••• b2. Sin•• b2 i• no• lo•••• in s_{bar1} •• ••• •oin• o• ••• ••ll, ••• •o•• •l ••••• •••• b1 i• ••l•••• •y b2 ••o••o•• ••• ••••• o• s_{foo}. How•v••, ••• ••••••l ••••• •••• c2 i• lo•••• in s_{bar1}, •o ••• •o••••on•in• •o•• •l ••••• •••• c1 i• ••• ov•• ••o• ••• ••••• o• s_{foo}. T•• l••• no•• in foo() •o••••••on•• •o lock, w•i•• i• • ••l• •••••••n•• •••••••••••n• •o•• •l ••••• ••••; •••, i•• ••o•••• •oin• i• •••l•••• wi•• $pp_\perp$ •••o•• in••••••in• in•o bar(). T•• ••••l•, s_{bar2}, ••• on• n•w no•• ($pp_\perp$) •n• •wo n•w ••••• (••o• c2 •o • o•• b2 •n• $pp_\perp$). T•• o••••• ••••• •o• •on•n•• in s_{bar2} ••• •n•••n••• ••o• s_{bar1}.

T•• l••• •o• •on•n• o• Fi•••• 10 •iv•• ••• ov••ll lo••-o•••• •••••, ••••••in• foo() •n• bar() ••• li•••y o• • •••o••. A• ••••• i• no ••••l••in• in ••i• •x•• • l•, ••• •n•l lo••-o•••• ••••• ••n •• o•••in•• •i• •ly •y •••in• ••• •nion o• ••••••• ••o• s_{foo} •n• s_{bar2}, ••••in• •ll ••o•••• •oin•• •o $pp_\perp$. T•• •y•l• in ••• lo••-o•••• ••••• •o•••••on•• •o • •••l ••••lo•• •o••i•ili•y in w•i•• foo() •n• bar() ••• ••ll• •on••••n•ly wi•• ••• •••• • ••••• •n••.

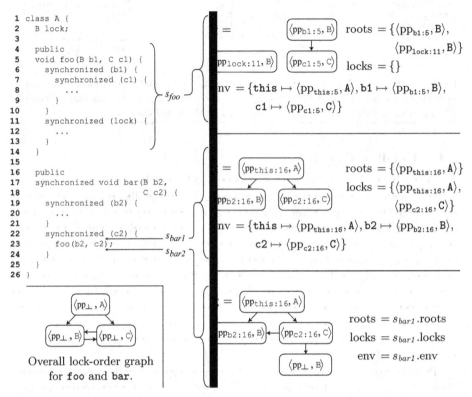

Fig. 10. Example operation of the dataflow analysis. The symbolic state is shown for the method summary of `foo`, as well as for two points in `bar` (before and after a call to `foo`). The `wait` sets (not shown) are empty in each case. The top-level lock-order graph for this library of methods is shown at bottom left

4.4   Reporting Possible Deadlock

To ••• o•• •••• lo•• • o••i• ili•i••, ••• •n•ly•i• •n•• •••• •y•l• in ••• lo••-o••••
•••••, ••in• • • o•i••• •••••-•••• ••••••• •l•o•i••• . • n•• • •y•l• i• •o•n•, •
••• o•• i• •on•••••••• ••in• i•• •••• •nno••ion•. •••• •••• in ••• lo••-o••••
••••• •••• • ••i• o• •nno••ion•, on• •o• ••• •o•••• lo•• •n• on• •o• ••• •••-
•in••ion lo••. •••• •nno••ion •on•i••• o• ••• v••i••l• n•• • o• ••• lo•• •n•
••• • •••o• •••• •••• i••• i•. A• •••••• ••• •o• •in••, •••••• • •y •o• ••o ••v•
• •l•i•l• •nno••ion•.

A ••• o•• i• •iv•n •o• •••• •i••in•• ••• o• lo•• v••i••l••. T•••• ••• o••• in•l•••
•••• o• ••• •••• o• • ••• o• •••• •••• j•• ••••• ••• o• lo•••. In •• i• w•y, • •••o••
wi•• ••• ••• • o• •i• il•• lo••in• •••vio• ••• •••••n••• •o ••• • •••• •o•••••. In
o•• •x••i•n•• wi•• ••• •ool, • o•• o• ••• ••o•••• • •••o• •••• •on••i••• •••
••• • lo••in• •••••••n, •o •• i• ••yl• ••n ••v• •i•ni••n• ••••• •ffo••.

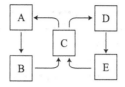

Fig. 11. The path {C, A, B, C, D, E} is a non-simple cycle: it visits node C twice

```
public void println(String s)    public void print(String s) {    private void write(String s) {
{                                  if (s == null) {                    try {
  synchronized (this) {              s = "null";                        synchronized (this) {
    print(s);                      }                                      ...
    newLine();                     write(s);                          }
  }                              }                                    }
}                                                                     ...
                                                                    }
```

Fig. 12. Code excerpt from Sun's `java.io.PrintStream` class. Due to the repeated synchronization on `this`, an intraprocedural analysis reports a spurious deadlock possibility while an interprocedural analysis does not

T•• •n•ly•i• ••• o••• •v••y *simple* •y•l• (•l•o •nown •• •n •l•• •n•••y •i•••i•) in • •iv•n •••••. A •y•l• i• •i• •l• i• i• •o•• no• vi•i• •ny no•• • o•• •••n on••. • iv•n • no•• •••• i• involv•• in • o•• •••n on• •i• •l• •y•l•, on• ••n •on•••••• non-•i• •l• •y•l• •y •••v••in• •••• •y•l• in •••••n•• (••• Fi•••• 11). I• i• • o••i•l• •o •on•••••• ••••• w•••• • non-•i• •l• •y•l• ••••••• ••••lo•• •v•n •• o•••• ••• •o• •on•n• •y•l•• •o no• [•6]. How•v••, •• w• ••v• n•v•• o•••v•• •••• • •••• in •••••i••, ••• •n•ly•i• ••• o••• only ••• •i• •l• •y•l•• ••• • w•y o• •o• •••••in• ••• •••• l••. Fo• •o• •l•••n•••, ••• •••• •• o•l• •on•i••• •••••• •y•l•• in •o• • in••ion.

4.5   Intraprocedural Weaknesses

• ••• n•ly•i• i• in•••• •o•••••l, ••••••• o•• •x• ••i•n•• i• ••••• •n in••••• o•••••l •n•ly•i• ••o••••• •oo • •ny ••l•• ••• o•••. Fo• •x•• •l•, Fi•••• 1• ill•••••••• •••• o• S• n'• java.io.PrintStream •l•••, in w•i•• • o•• println() •n• write() ••••• •• •o lo•• this. An in•••• •o••••••l •n•ly•i• ••nno• ••ov• •••• ••• ••• • o• j••• i• lo•••• in • o•• • •••o••. T•••, i• ••• o•••• • •••• lo•• • o••i• ili•y •o••••• on• in• •o ••• •••• w••n •wo •on•••••n• ••ll• •o println() •••• l• in • iff•••n• lo••in• o••••• on • ••i• o• PrintStream o• j••••. How•v••, •••••• ••• o• j•••• lo•••• ••• •lw•y• ••• iv• l•n•, ••• •••on• •yn•••oni••ion •o•• no• •ff••• ••• ••• o• lo••• ••l•. T• i• •••io•• ••• o•• i• o• i•••• •y o•• in••••• o•••••l •n•ly•i•.

5   Reducing False Positives

Li••• • ny ••••i• •n•ly•••, o•• •ool ••• o••• ••l•• • o•i•iv••. A ••l•• • o•i•iv• i• • ••- • o•• ••••• ••nno• • o••i• ly l••• •o •••• lo••, •••••••• (•o• •x•• •l•) i• •••• i•••• •n

in••••i• l• •li••in• ••l••ion••i• o• •n in••••i• l• ••• o• • •••• • ••o•• ••• ••• ••o•••• .
F•l•• •o•i•iv•• •••••• ••• ••••ili•y o• ••• •ool ••••••• v••i•yin• •••• ••• ••-
•o•• i• •••io•• ••n •• •••io••. W• ••v• i• •l•• •n•• •o•n• o••i• i••ion• ••••
•••••• ••• n•• ••• o• ••l•• •••o••• wi••o•• •li• in••in• •ny •••• ••• o•••. T•i•
••••ion •••••i••• •o• • o• ••• o••i• i••ion•; •wo •••i•ion•l i• •l•• •n••• o••i-
• i••ion• ••n•l• •yn••oni••ion ov•• •n o•j••• •n• on• o• i•• in••n•l ••l••,
•n• •yn••oni••ion ov•• • •••o• ••ll ••••n v•l••• [•6].

5.1 Unaliased Fields

An •n•li•••• ••l• i• on• •••• •lw•y• •oin•• •o •n o•j••• •••• i• no• •oin••• •o•y
•no••• v••i••l• in ••• ••o•••• . A• •n o••i• i••ion, o•• •n•ly•i• •••••• ••••••
••l••, •n• •••i•n•• •ni••• •y• •o•••• o••••• . T•i• •n •••••••• ••• n•• ••• o•
••••lo•• •••o••• •y •i••• •i•••in• •n•li•••• ••l• ••••••n••• ••o• o•••• no•••
in ••• lo••-o•••• •••••. (I• i• n•••••••y •o •••••• • no•• •o• ••••• ••l••, •••••
•••n •i•••••in• in•o•• ••ion ••o•• •yn••oni••ion ov•• ••••• . Al••o•• •••y
••v• no •li••••, •••y • •y ••ill •• involv•• in ••••lo••.)

T•• •ollowin• •n•ly•i• i• •••• •o •i••ov•• •n•li•••• ••l•• . Ini•i•lly, •ll non-
•••li• ••l•• ••• ••••• •• •o •• •n•li•••. A• ••• •n•ly•i• vi•i•• •••• •••••• •n•
in ••• li•••y, •••• •••••• ••ion i• n•lli••• •o• • ••l• f i• •ny o• ••• •ollowin•
•••••••n• ••• ly:

1. f i• •••i•n•• • non-n•ll, non-n•wly-•llo•••• •x•••ion.
•. f ••••••• on ••• •i••-••n• •i• o• •n •••i•n• •n• •x•••ion.
3. f ••••••• o••i•• •ny o• ••• •ollowin• •x•••ion•: • synchronized •••••• •n•
     ••••••, • •o• •••i•on •x•••ion (•.•., foo == bar), •n •••y •••••• o• •••y
     l•n••• •x•••ion, o•• •n ••••• •n• •o • • •••o• •••• •o•• no• •llow i• •o
     ••••••.

A •i• •l• i•••••iv• •••••• •n•ly•i• •••••• in•• w•i•• ••••• •n•• ••••••• •
• •••o•. ••ll• ••o• ••• li•••y •o i•• • •••o•• •• w•ll •• ••ll• •o ••• JDK •••
••••••••; ••••• •n•• ••• ••••• •• •o •••••• • •••o•• •• w•••• no •o•••• i• •v•il••l•.
T•• •n•ly•i• •••••n••• in S••ion •.1 in••o••••• • n•w •y• •oli• •••• o•j•••
•o• •v••y •••••n•• •o • ••l•. T•i• i• n••••••y •••••• ••• •n•ly•i• •o•• no•
• o••l ••• •o••i•l• v•l••• o••l••. Un•li•••• ••l•• ••• •••••i•••• in ••• •o••i•l•
v•l••• ••y• •y •ol•. In •••i••l••, •••y ••• •lw•y• •••i•n•• n•w o•j••••, •n•,
i• ••y ••• ••••i•n••, ••i• ol• o•j••• ••nno• •• •••••••. B•••••• o• ••i•
••o••••y, n••••• •yn••oni••ion ov•• ••• ••• • ••l• o• • •iv•n o•j••• ••n ••
•••••• •• • no-o• (••••••y •li• in••in• •••io•• ••• o•••), •in•• only on• o• •••
v•l••• lo•••• i• •••••i•l•. T••• i•, on• o• ••• •wo •yn••oni•• •••••• •n•• i•
on • lo•• •••• no lon••• •xi••• •n• ••o•l• •••••o•• •• i•no••. T•• •n•ly•i•
•••• •• •••• • •••• o•j••• •o• •ll •••••n••• •o ••• ••• • •n•li•••• ••l• wi••in
• •iv•n o•j•••, ••••••y ••••••in• n••••• •yn••oni••ion• •• no-o•• •• ••i•••.
T•i• •••• o•j••• ••o••••••• •••o•• ••ll •i•• •••••• •••n••in• • •••••• •o $pp_\perp$.

In •••i•ion •o ••••••in• •n•li•••• ••l••, o•• •n•ly•i• ••o••• ••• ••• o• o••i•l•
••n•i• • •y••• o• ••••• ••l••. T•i• in•o•• ••ion i• ••••ily •v•il••l• •o• •n•li••••
••l••, •• ••••y ••• only •••i•n•• ••••• o•j•••• (•••••• wi•• ••• new ••ywo••).

Wi•• •• i• in•o•• ••ion, ••• • n•ly•i• ••n •••••• in• • • o•• ••••i•• ••• o• o••i• l•
••ll•• • •••o•• w••n •n •n•li•••• ••l• i• •••• •• • ••••iv••.

D•••••in• •n• ••ili•in• •n•li•••• ••l•••n •• v••y ••n•••i•l. Fo• •x•• •l•,
•• i• o••i• i•••ion ••••••• ••• n•• ••• o•••o••• ••o• ov•• 909 •o only 1 •o• •••
j•••••• li•••y, •n• ••o• 66 •o 0 •o• ••• ••••• ni• li•••y.

5.2 Callee/Caller Type Resolution

A••••••• •nowl•••• •• o•• •yn•• i• •y••• •••v•n•• lo••• on on• o• j••• ••o•
••in• •on•••v•iv•ly ••••• •• •o ••• ly •o o•••• o• j••••. In ••n•••l, ••• •yn•• i•
•y••• o•••••• •n•• ••• • •••• l••• o• ••• ••• l•••• ••••• •••• •y••; li••wi••, •••
•yn•• i• •y•• o• ••• ••••iv•• i• • •••• l••• o• i•• ••• l•••• •y•• in ••• ••ll••.
• •ll••/••ll•• •y•• •••ol••ion •oll•••• •x••• •y•• in•o•• ••ion •y l•v•••in• •••
•••• •••• ••• ••• l•••• •y••• o• o• j•••• in ••ll••• •n• ••ll••• •o• ••i• ••• •iff••.

To • n••••••n• ••• ••n•••• o• •y•• •••ol••ion, •on•i•• ••• •ollowin•:

```
Object o;
o.hashCode();
```

W••n •n•ly•in• • ••••i••l•• i• •l•• •n•••ion o• `hashCode()`, ••y, in •l••• `Date`,
••• ••••iv•• i• •nown •o •• o• •y•• `Date`, no• `Object` •• i• w•• •••l•••• in •••
•• ov• •o••. T•• ••ll••/••ll•• •y•• •••ol••ion o••i• i•••ion ••••• ••v•n•••• o•
••i• in•o•• ••ion w••n in••••••in• ••• lo••-o•••• ••••• •o• • ••ll•• •••• ••
`Date.hashCode()` in•o •••• o• ••• ••ll••. In••••• o• ••in• ••• ••ll•• o• ••ll•• •y••
•x•l•iv•ly, ••• • o•• •••• i•• •y•• i• ••••. T•i• •••• l•• in • o•• ••••i•• •y•• in-
•o•• ••ion in ••• ov•••ll lo••-o•••• •••••, ••••••y ••••••in• ••• •i•• o• ••• •li••
••••. Ty•• •••ol••ion ••n ••v• • l•••• i• •••• on •••io•• ••• o•••: ••• o••• •o•
••• ••o•••o•• li•••y •••••••• ••o• 1•3• •o •, •n• ••• o••• •o• ••• j•••••••• o•••
li•••y •••••••• ••o• •• •o 0.

5.3 Final and Effectively-Final Fields

Fo• `final` ••l••, •ll ••••••n••• ••• •o ••• ••• • o• j•••. ••• •n•ly•i• •••••• ••-
v•n•••• o• ••i• •••• •y ••in• ••• ••• • •••• o• j••• •o• •••• o• ••• •••••••n••• •o
••• ••• • `final` ••l• wi••in • •iv•n o• j•••. T•• •n•ly•i• •l•o •••••••• ••l• ••••••
••• *effectively-final*: non-••• li• ••l•• •••• ••• no• ••• i•n•• • v•l•• (•x••• n•ll)
o• ••i• ••• i• •on•••• •o•. • x• loi•in• `final` ••l•• ••••••••• ••• n•• ••• o• ••• o•••
••o• •6 •o 3• •o• ••• • l•••••••• li•••y.

6 Results

W• i• •l•• •n••• o•• •••• lo•• •••••• o• in ••• Ko•i J•v• •o• •il•• [9], w• i••
in••••• J•v• •o•••• •o••. • ••• •n••• •••• •on•i•• o• 1• li•••i••, • o•• o• w• i••
w• o•••in•• ••o• So••••Fo••• •n• S•v•nn••[2]. T•• ••••l•• ••••••• in Fi•••• 13.

---

[2] ProActive [16], Jess [12], SDSU [20], and Sun's JDK [23] are not from SourceForge
or Savannah, but are freely available online.

Library	Code size			Graph size			
	sync	Classes	kLOC	Nodes	Edges	Reports	Deadlocks
JDK 1.4	1458	1180	419	65	278	70 *	≥7
Classpath 0.15	754	1074	295	15	22	32 *	≥5
ProActive 1.0.3	199	407	63	3	3	3 *	≥2
Jess 6.1p6	111	125	27	12	30	23 *	≥0
sdsu (1 Oct 2002)	69	139	26	2	2	3 *	≥0
jcurzez (12 Dec 2001)	24	27	4	1	1	1	0
httpunit 1.5.4	17	117	23	0	0	0	0
jasperreports 0.5.2	11	271	67	0	0	0	0
croftsoft (09 Nov 2003)	11	108	14	1	1	2	0
dom4j 1.4	6	155	41	1	1	1	0
cewolf 0.9.8	6	98	7	0	0	0	0
jfreechart 0.9.17	5	396	125	0	0	0	0
htmlparser 1.4	5	111	22	1	1	0	0
jpcap 0.01.15	4	58	8	0	0	0	0
treemap 2.5.1	4	47	7	0	0	0	0
PDFBox 0.6.5	2	127	28	0	0	0	0
UJAC 0.9.9	1	255	63	0	0	0	0
JOscarLib 0.3beta1	1	77	6	0	0	0	0

* Unsound filtering heuristics used (see Section 6.3)

Fig. 13. Number of deadlock reports for each library. The table indicates the size of each library in terms of number of synchronized statements (given in the column labeled sync), number of classes (source files), and number of lines of code (in thousands). The size of the lock-order graph is measured after pruning nodes and edges that are not part of a strongly connected component. "Deadlocks" shows the numbers of confirmed deadlock cases in each library. The JDK and Classpath results are for packages in java.*. We were unable to compile 6 source files in JDK due to bugs in our research compiler

T•• •n•ly•i• ••n in l••• •••n 3 • in•••• ••• li•••y on • 3.60• H• P•n•i•• • • ••• in•. Fo• ••• l••••• li•••i••, i• i• ••o• i• i•iv•ly •x••n•iv• •o •o• ••••• •ll •o••i• l• ••••lo•• •••o•••, •o w• i• •l•• •n••• • ••• o• •n•o• n• •••i••i•• •o •l••• •••• (••• S•••ion 6.3).

6.1   Deadlocks Found

W• invo••• 1• ••••lo••• in 3 li•••i••; 1• o• •••••• ••••lo••• w••• •••vio••ly •n• nown •o ••. W• v••i••• •••• in•••n•• •y w•i•in• •li•n• •o••• •••• •••••• ••••lo•• in ••• li•••y. T•••• ••• •• l•••• • ••••lo••• in ••• JDK, 5 in • NU • l•••••••, •n• • in P•oA••iv•.

A• ••••••i••• in S•••ion •.•, o••• n•ly•i• ••o••••• o••••••• on ••• lo•• v••i-•• l•• involv••. So• • o• ••• ••••lo••• •••••i••• ••low ••n •• in••••• •••o••• ••ll• •o •ny o•• n•• ••• o•• iff•••n• • •••o•• wi•• ••• ••• • lo•• in• ••••••n;

w• only •••••i• • •in•l• ••••, •n• •••o•• ••• n• • ••• o••••lo••• in ••i• •on-
•••v••iv• ••••ion.

Deadlocks Due to Cyclic Data Structures. • ••••• 1• ••••lo••• w• •o• n•, •
••• ••• •••• l• o••y•l•• in ••• •n••lyin• •••• •••••••••••. A• •n •x•• •l•, •on•i•••
java.util.Hashtable. T• i• •l••• ••n •• ••••lo•••• •y •••••in• •wo Hashtable
o•j•••• •n• •••in• •••• •• •n •l•• •n• o••• o••••, i.•., •y •o•• in• • •y•li ••-
l••ion••i• ••w••n ••• in•••n•••. In ••i• •i•••• •••n••, ••llin• ••• •yn••oni•••
equals() • •••o• on •o• o•j•••• in •iff•••n• ••••••• ••n yi•l• ••••lo••. T••
equals() • •••o• lo••• i•• ••••iv• •n• ••ll• equals() on i•• • •• ••••, •••• lo••-
in• •ny o•i•• in•••n•l Hashtable o•j••••. W••n ••n in •wo •••••••, •••• o• •••
••ll• •o equals() •••• •iff•••n• lo•• o•••in•, •o ••••lo•• ••n ••••l•.

Al••o••• ••i• •x•• •l• • •y •••• •••n•••••, ••• JDK Hashtable i• •l•• •n-
••ion ••••• ••• •o ••••o•• ••i• •y•li ••••••••: ••• hashCode() • •••o• •••v•n••
• •o••n•i•l in•ni•• loo• in •••• •••••• •y •••v•n•in• •••••iv• ••ll• ••o• •x••••-
in• ••• •••• v•l••• •o• ••••ion. A •o• • •n• wi•• in hashCode() ••y•, "T• i• •o••
•••••••• ••• ••••••ion •••••• •y •o• ••in• ••• •••• •o•• o• ••l•••••••n•i•l
•••• •••l• •n• •••v•n•• ••• ••••• ov••flow •••• wo•l• o•••wi•• ••••l•."

In •••i•ion •o Hashtable, •ll •yn••oni••• Collection• •n• •o• •in••ion• o•
•••• Collection• (•.•., • Vector in •y•li ••l••ion••i• wi•• • Hashtable) ••n ••
••••lo•••• in •i• il•• ••••ion. T• i• in•l••• Collection• ••o••••• vi• ••ll• •o
Collections.synchronizedCollection(), Collections.synchronizedList(), Col-
lections.synchronizedSortedMap(), •••. Fo• ••• •••• o••• o• ••• o••in•, •ll •••••
••••• ••• •o•n••• ••• •in•l• ••••lo•• in •o• ••• JDK •n• •l••••••.

D•••lo•• ••••l•in• ••o• •y•li •••• ••••••••• i• ••i•• •i• ••l• •o •o•••••.
Lo•••• • ••• • ••••i••• in • •on•i•••n• o••••, o• •••y • •••• •• ••••i••• •i• •l-
••n•o••ly. To •o •i•••• o• •••••• ••in• ••••i••• •nowin• w•i•• o•j•••• will ••
lo•••• •y ••llin• • •iv•n • •••o•. D••••• inin• ••i• in•o••ion wi••o•• ••••
lo••in• ••• •on••in•• o•j••• i• ••o•l•• ••i• •in• i•• in•••n•l• • •y ••n••• •••in•
in••••ion. I• ••••••• ••• ••• only •ol••ion i• •o ••• • •lo••l lo•• •o• •yn••o-
ni•in• in•••n••• o• •ll Collection •l••••. T• i• •ol••ion i• •n••i•••l•, •ow•v••,
•••••••• i• •••v•n•• • •l•i-•••••••• •••• o• •iff•••n• Collection o•j••••. Li•••y
w•i••• • •y in••••• ••oo•• •o l••v• ••••• •••• lo•• ••••• in •l•••, ••• •o••• •n•
••i• •xi•••n•• •n• •••••i•• • ow •o ••••o•i••ly ••• ••• •l•••.

No• only •o ••••• •y•li •••• ••••••••• l••• •o ••••lo••, ••• ••y • •y •l•o
••••l• in • •••••• ov••flow ••• •o in•ni•• ••••••ion. A n•• ••• o••• •l••••• ••vin•
••i• •in• o• ••••lo•• •l•o ••y• • •••o• ••••• ••o•••• •n•o•n•• ••••••ion •o•
••• •••• o• •y•li •••• ••••••••. I• •••• • •••• ••••• •••• lo•• ••••• ••v••l
in••n••• •••• •••• l invv•i•n•• (i.•., ••••• • •••n• o•j••• i• no• ••••••l• ••• •o•••
i•• ••il••n) ••o• ••• ••l•••• ••• •y involv•.

T•• ••• •inin• 5 •y•li •••• lo•••• ••• •i• il•• •o •••• •••••i••• •• ov•. D•••-
lo•• ••n •• in•••• in java.awt.EventQueue ••o• •o• JDK •n• •l•••••••, in
java.awt.Menu ••o• JDK, in java.util.logging.Logger ••o• •l••••••, •n• in
AbstractDataObject ••o• P•o••••iv•. •••• •l••••••• • •••o• •••• •llow• •y•li
••l••ion••i• •o •• •o•• ••, •n• •no•••• • •••o• (o• ••• o• • •••o••) •••• lo•••
••• •on••inin• o•j••• •n• ••• in•••n•l on•.

622 A. Williams, W. Thies, and M.D. Ernst

Other Deadlock Cases. In ••• i•ion •o ••• •y•li• •••• •••••i• •• •• ov•, P•oA•-
•iv• •x• i• i•• • ••••]• •••• lo•• in ••• ProxyForGroup •]•••. T••o••• • ••••••n•• o•
••ll•, ••• asynchronousCallOnGroup() • •••o• o• ProxyForGroup ••n • • • • ••• •o
lo•• • o•• this • n• • ny o•• •• ProxyForGroup. In••• n•i• •in• •wo o• • o•• ProxyFor-
Group o• j•••• •n• •o••in• •••• •o lo•• ••• o•••• in•• •••• ••••lo••. T•• •••••
n•••••••y •o ••o•••• •• i• •••n•io i• ••]••iv•ly •o• •]•x. T•• off•n• in• • •••o•
•on•• in•, wi•• in •o•• n••••••]•v•]• o• •on••ol flow, • • •••o• ••]] •••• ••••••n• •n
Object; • n•• •••••• in •i•••• •••n•••, ••• o• j••• ••••• •n•• i• • ProxyForGroup, ••
n••••••• •o ••o•••• •••• lo••. W• wo•]• no• •x• •••• • li•••• y w•i••• •o no•i•• •• i•
•••• lo•• • o••i• ili•y wi••o• • ••in• • •ool li•• o• ••.

W• invo••• • •••i•ion•l •••• lo••• in ••• JDK. • n• •••• lo•• i• in Bean-
ContextSupport •• •••• •i• •• in S•• ion 1. A •••on• •••• lo•• i• in StringBuffer.
append(StringBuffer), •• ill•••••••• in Fi•••• 1•. T• i• •••• lo•• o••••• • •••••••
append() i• • •yn•• •oni••• • •••o• (i.•., i• lo••• this), •n• i• lo••• i•• •••••• •n•.
T•••, ••in• ••• •li•n• •o•• in Fi•••• 1•, i• a i• lo•••• in •••••• 1, •n• b i• lo••••
in •••••• • •••o•• i• i• in •••••• 1, •••• lo•• ••••]••. No•• ••• •• •• i• i• •n •x•• •]•
o•• • •••• w•••• only • •in•]• • •••o• i• •••• •o ••• •• •••• lo••.

```
class StringBuffer {
  synchronized StringBuffer
    append(StringBuffer sb) {
    ...
    // length() is synchronized
    int len = sb.length();
    ...
  }
}
```

(StringBuffer.append(StringBuffer)
locks StringBuffer.this,
StringBuffer.length()
locks Parameter[sb])

StringBuffer

```
StringBuffer a =
  new StringBuffer();
StringBuffer b =
  new StringBuffer();

thread 1:  a.append(b);
thread 2:  b.append(a);
```

Fig. 14. Library code, lock-order graph, and client code that deadlocks JDK's
StringBuffer class. This deadlock is also present in Classpath

```
class PrintWriter {
  PrintWriter(OutputStream o) {
    lock = o;
    out = o;
  }

  void write(char buf[],
      int off, int len) {
    synchronized (lock) {
      out.write(buf, off, len);
    }
  }
}
```

```
class CharArrayWriter {
  CharArrayWriter() {
    lock = this;
  }

  void writeTo(Writer out) {
    synchronized (lock) {
      out.write(buf, 0,
              count);
    }
  }
}
```

```
// c.lock = c
c = new CharArrayWriter();
// p1.lock = c
p1 = new PrintWriter(c);
// p2.lock = p1
p2 = new PrintWriter(p1);

thread 1:  p2.write("x",0,1);
thread 2:  c.writeTo(p2);
```

Fig. 15. Simplified library code from PrintWriter and CharArrayWriter from Sun's
JDK, and, on the right, client code that causes deadlock in the methods. In thread
1, p1 is locked first, then c; in thread 2, c is locked, then p1. Because the locks are
acquired in different orders, deadlock occurs under some thread interleavings

```
DropTarget a = new DropTarget(), b = new DropTarget();
Component aComp = new Button(), bComp = new Button();

aComp.setDropTarget(a);
bComp.setDropTarget(b);

thread 1:  a.setComponent(bComp);
thread 2:  b.setComponent(aComp);
```

Fig. 16. Client code that induces deadlock in the JDK's `DropTarget` class

Ano••••• ••••lo•• ••o• ••• JDK o••••• in `java.io.PrintWriter` •n• `java.io.CharArrayWriter`. Si• •li••• •o•• •o• ••i• ••••lo•• i• ••own in Fi•••• 15. T•• `PrintWriter` •n• `CharArrayWriter` •l••••• •o•• •on••in • lock ••l• •o• •yn••• o-ni•in• I/• o•••••ion•. In `PrintWriter`, ••• lo•• i• ••• •o ••• o•••• •••••• out, w•il• in `CharArrayWriter`, ••• lo•• i• ••• •o this.

T•• l••• ••••lo•• in ••• JDK i• lo••••• in `java.awt.dnd.DropTarget`. T•i• •l••• ••n •• ••••lo•••• •y ••llin• `setComponent()` wi•• •n ••••• •n• (o• •y•• `Component`) ••vin• • v•li• `DropTarget` •••. W••n ••i• ••ll i• • •••, ••• •••••iv•• i• lo•••• •ollow•• •y ••• •••••• •n•'• `DropTarget`. T•••, ••• •o•• in Fi•••• 16 ••n l••• •o ••••lo••.

• NU • l•••••••• •x• i• i•• • •••• lo••• •••i••• ••o•• ••••i••• •o •••. T•• •••• i• in `StringBuffer`, •n• i• •n•lo•o•• •o ••• JDK ••• •••••i••• ••• ov•. T•• ••••on• i• in `java.util.SimpleTimeZone`. T•• `SimpleTimeZone.equals(Object)` • •••o• i• •yn••• oni•••• •n• lo••• i•• ••••• •n•; i• i• ••••••o•• •••••• i• l• •o ••• ••• • ••yl• o• •••• lo•• •• •••• o• `StringBuffer.append()`.

I• i• in••••••in• •o no•• •••• JDK •n• • l•••••••• i• •l•• •n••• ion• o• `Simple-TimeZone` •n• `Logger` •iff•• in •••i• lo••in• ••••vio•: i• i• no• •o••i•l• •o invo•• ••••lo•• in ••••• •l••••• ••in• ••• JDK. Si• il••ly, ••• • l•••••••• i• •l•• •n••-•ion• o• `PrintWriter` •n• `CharArrayWriter` •o no• •••• lo••; o•••• ••l•v• n• • o•-•ion• o•• l••••••• ••• no• ••lly i• •l•• •n•••.

Fixing Deadlocks. T•••• ••• • n•• ••• o• vi••l• •ol••ion• •o ••• ••••lo••• ••••• n••• •• ov•. T•• • ••• o•• •••o•• in •yn••• oni•••ion •o• l• •• w•i••n •o ••••i•• ••• n••••• lo••• in • ••• o••••. J•v• •o•l• •• •x••n••• wi•• • •yn-••• oni•••ion ••i• i•iv• •o ••o• i••lly ••••i•• • •l•i•l• lo•••. A ••ili•y •o••in• •o•l• •• w•i••n •o ••• o• •li•• ••• ••• • •ff••• ••• ••i• ••i• i•iv•, •••in• •• ••-••• •n•• • li•• o• lo••• •o ••••i•• •n• • •••n• •o •x•••••, •••n ••••i•in• ••• lo••• in • •x•• o••••. T•••• •ol••ion• ••••i•• •nowl•••• o• ••• ••• o• lo••• •o •• ••••• i•••. So• ••i• •• ••i• i• i• • ••i•••ly ••••••• n•• ••o• ••• •o••; o•••• wi••, • • •••o• •••• •••••• in•• ••• lo••• ••••i••• •o• •n o•••••ion •o• l• •• ••••• •o •n in••••••. In •ll ••••• •••••, ••• i• •l•• •n••• ion •o•l• o•••• ••• lo••• ••-in• `System.identityHashCode()`, •••••in• •i•• ••• i••••ily ••• •on•i••• n•ly. No•• •ow•v••, •••• ••••• •ol••ion• •••• • ••••••• n••••• lo••• will no• ••• n•• w•il• •••y ••• ••in• ••••• in••. I• •••y • i••• ••• n••, i• • •y •• n••••••••y •o ••• • •lo••l lo•• •o• ••• •l••••• involv•• in ••• •••• lo••.

6.2 Verifying Deadlock Freedom

U•in• o•• •ool, w• v••i••• 13 li•••i•• •o •• •••• ••o• ••• •l••• o• ••••lo•••
•••••i••• in S•••ion 3.•. No•• •••• ••••• li•••i•• • •y •••o•• ••ll••••• •o
•li•n• •o•, •o• • •x••n• ••• JDK, •n• • o•• •••o•• ••fl•••ion; o•• •••• ni••
•o•• no• • o••l •yn••oni••ion •••• l•in• ••o• ••••• •••• vio••. Fo• 10 o• ••••••
li•••i••, ••• v••i•••ion i• •• lly •••o• ••i•, wi•• 0 ••• o••• ••o• o•• •ool. A••o•
••• o•••• 3 li•••i••, o•• •ool ••• o•••• • •o••l o•• ••••lo••, w•i•• w• • •n••lly
v••i••• •o •• ••l•• • o•i•iv••.

T•• ••l•• •••o•• in j•••••• i• •o• • •••n••io in w•i•• •n in•••n•l ••l• f o•
••• ••• • •y•• • i•• •on••inin• •l••• i• ••• •o • ••••• •••• o• ••• •on••••••o•.
To •li• in••• ••i• ••• o••, ••• •n•ly•i• wo•l• ••v• •o •o• •in• ••v••l ••••• •n•
•••i•ion•l o••i• i•••ion•. • •o•••o•• iv•• •wo •••i o•• ••• o••• ••••••• •n o• j•••
involv•• in ••• •yn••oni••ion ••nno• ••v• ••• •• n•i• • •y•• ••••• o•• •ool •on-
•••v•iv•ly ••••• •• •o •• • o••i• l•. T•• •n•l •••o•• i• •o• •o• •j, •n• i• •••io••
••••••• o• in•••i•l• •on••ol flow.

6.3 Unsound Filtering Heuristics

Fo• •••• l•••••• li•••i••, ••• n•• ••• o••• o••• •iv•n •y o••• •l•o•i••• i• •oo •i••
(• o•• •••n 100,000 •o• ••• JDK) •o• •••• •o •• •on•i••••• •y •• n•. In ••• i•ion,
i• i• •o• •••••ion•lly ••• •n•in• •o ••• o•• •v••y •••• lo•• •o••i•ili•y. In o•••• •o
• ••• ••• •ool • o•• •••• l• •o• l•••• li•••i•• (• o•• in •••• • o• n•• ••• o• ••• o•••
•n• •i• • n•••••• •o •••••• ••••) o•• •ool •••• •n•o• n• •l•••in• •••i•i••. T•••
•••i••i•• •i• •o i• •n•i•y ••• o••• •••• ••v ••• ••••••• li•li•oo• o•••••••••n•in•
• •••• •••• lo••. How•v••, •• •n•o• n• •••i••i••, ••• y •l•o ••v• ••• • o••n•i•l •o
•li• in••• •••• •••• lo•• ••••• ••o• •on•i••••ion.

• ••• •ool ••• li•• •wo •l•••in• •••i••i•• on •••• in o••• li•••i•• in Fi•••• 13.
• n• •••i••i• i• •o ••••••i•• ••••n•ion •o •y•l•• in ••• lo••-o•••• ••••• ••••• •••
••o••• •••n • •iv•n l•n•••. Fo• ••• •l••••• li•••i••, only •y•l•• wi•• •wo o•
••w•• no••• w••• ••• o••••. S•o•••• •y•l•• •on•• in ••w• lo••, •n• ••• ••i•• •o
•x•• in• • •n• •lly. In ••• i•ion, •• o•••• •y•l•• i•••••• • o•• li••ly •o •o••••• on•
•o •••••l •••• lo••, •• •••• •••• in • •y•l• ••••••••n•• • ••i• o• lo•• •••• i•i•ion•
•••••••• •o• • •••n•• o• ••in• in•••i•l• (••• •o in•••i•l• •on••ol flow o• •li••in•
••l••ion•• i••).

T•• •••on• •l•••in• •••i••i• i• •o •••••• • •••••••• ••n•i• • •y•• o••••• o• j•••
i• ••• ••• • •• i•• •••l•••• •y••. T•i• •••• •••• ••• n•• ••• o•••• o••• in •wo w•y•.
Fi•••, ••• •n•ly•i• ••••• •o •••o•n• •o• •yn•• i• •i••••••, •• i• ••••• •• ••••
••••• i• •x••ly on• ••••• o• ••••• • •••o• ••ll. T•i• ••••••• ••• lo••-o•••• •••••
•o• • •iv•n • •••o• •o •• in••••••• •• ••w•• ••ll-•i••, ••••••y •••••••in• •••
n•• ••• o•••••• in ••• ov•••ll •••••. S••on•, ••i• ••••i••i• ••••••• ••• **top_level**
•o••in• (Fi•••••) •o •o••o •x••n•ion o••••• •••• in•o ••••••••••w••n •ll •o••i•l•
••••l•••••. T•i• ••••i••i• ••• •o• • in••i•iv• ••i• ••••••• i• •••••i••• ••••n•ion
•o •o•• •••• o• •••••• on • •••i•• •y••, •••••• •••n • • o•• ••n•••l •y••. Fo•
•x•• •l•, i• •on•i•••• ••• •ff•••• o• •ll •yn••oni••• • •••o•• o• • •iv•n •l•••,
••• i• •li• in•••• ••• ••••• ••ion •••• •ll o• j•••• •o•l• ••• •li•••• wi•• • ••l• o•
•y•• **Object** ••••• •y •• lo•••• •l••w••••.

7   Related Work

T•• lon•-•••n• in• •o•l o••n••in• •••• •on••••n• ••o•••• •••• •••• o••••• lo•• ••• •in• •n •••iv• •••••••• •o•••. M••••• ••vi•w• ••• v••io•• •••• •o••••• [••].

S•v•••l •••••••••••• ••v• ••v•lo••• •••i• •••• lo•• •••••••ion •ool• •o• J•v• ••in• lo••-o•• ••••••• [1•, 1, ••]. To ••• •••• o• o•• •nowl•••, ••• Jlin• •••• i• •••••••• [1•] i• ••• •••• •o ••• • lo••-o••• •••••. T•• o•i•in•l i• •l•• •n••ion o• Jlin• •on•i• ••• only synchronized • •••o••; i••o•• no• o••l synchronized •••••- • •n••. A•••o •n• Bi••• [1] •••• •n• Jlin• wi•• li• i••• •••• o•• •o• synchronized •••••• •n••. How•v••, •••i• •n•ly•i• •o•• no• ••• o•• •ll •••• lo•• •o••i• ili•i••. I• only •on•i•••••••••••y •••on ••• • o•• ••• i••• l •o• •n in• ••••: 1) •ll ••l•• •n• lo••l v••i••l•• ••• ••••• •• •o•••n•li••••, ••nin• •••• •wo •••••••• • ••• lo•• •x••ly ••• ••• • v••i••l• •o •li•i• • •••• lo•• •••o••, •) n••••• synchronized •lo••• ••• •••••••• only wi•• in • •in•l• •l•••, no• •••o•• • •••o•• in • iff•••n• •l••••, •n• 3) in••i••n•• i• no• ••lly •on•i•••••.

von P•••n •••••••• •••• lo•• •o••i• ili•i• in J•v• ••o••••••••in• • lo••-o•••• ••••• •n• •on••x-••n•i•iv• lo•• •••• [••–••.105–110]. ••• •n•ly•i• w•• ••v•l-o•• in••••n••n•ly [•5]. W•il• von P•••n'• •li•• •n•ly•i• i• • o•• •o••i••i•••• •••n o•••, i• i• •n•l•• •ow •o ••••• i••o • o••l •ll •o••i•l• ••ll• •o • li•••y. Al•o, in •n •ffo•• •o •••••• ••l•• •o•i•iv••, ••• •n•ly•i• ••••••••••• •••o••• in w•i•• •ll lo•••••lon• •o ••• ••• • •li•• •••; •• • •on•••••n••, i• •o•• no• •n• 1• o••••• 1• ••••lo•••x•o••• • y o•••ool. W•il• von P•••n'• •n•ly•i• •o•l• •• ••ivi•lly • o•i••• •o ••• o•• •••• •••••, i• wo•l• •••n •••o••, in ••• i•ion, •ll o• ••• •••ni•n ••••• ••• •••••••• ly lo•• • •in•l• o•j••• (•• in Fi•••• 1•). S•••••••-in• ••••• •••o••• i• ••• • o•iv••ion •o• ••• flow-••n•i•iv• •n• in•••••o•••••l ••••••• o• o•• •n•ly•i•: o•• •n•ly•i• ••n •••o•ni•• •••• •wo o•j••• ••••••n••• ••• i••n•i••l, ••••••y •••li•yin• •••••••• •yn••oni••ion• on • •iv•n o•j••• •• ••ni•n. von P•••n'• •n•ly•i• •o•• no• off•• ••i• ••n•••, in •••• •••••• i• i• flow-in••n•i•iv• •n• •ni•••ion-•••••. Al•o, i••o•• no• •on•i••• •••• wait() ••n in••o•••• • •y•li• lo••in• ••••••n (•• in Fi•••• 9). ••• •ool ••• o••• •ll •••• lo•• •o••i• ili•i••.

• ••••X [10] i• • flow-••n•i•iv•, •on••x•-••n•i•iv• •ool •o• •••••in• •••• lo•• •n• •••• •on•i•ion in • •y•••• ••o••. B•••••• o•• •ool •n•ly••• J•v• in••••• o•• , i• o•••••••• •n•••• • iff•••n• ••• o• •on•••in••. W• ••lly •••o• n• •o• o• j•••• •n• in••i••n••, ••• o••in• •ll •••• lo•• •o••i• ili•i••; ••••X o••••••• on • ••o-••••••l l•n••••••, •n• • i••• ••il •o ••• o•• ••v••y •••• lo•• •••• ••• •o ••n••ion •oin•••• •n• •i••-ov••••• •• n••ion•. ••• •ool •n•ly••• •n• o•i••• J•v• •o••, w•il• • ••••X •••• i••• •nno••ion• •o in•i•••• ••• lo••in• ••••vio• o• •y•••• -••••i•• • •• n••ion•. ••• •ool •x• loi•••••• i•••••• i••l •yn••oni••ion ••i• i•iv•• in J•v•; in • , ••••i•ion i• ••••i•••• ••• •o ••• •••o••lin• o• lo•• •n• •nlo•• o••••••ion• (•o• ••i• •• on • iff•••n• ••••• o••••• •• ••n••ion, •• no••• •y ••• •••• o••).

S•v•••l ••o•••••v• •••n • •• o••l-•••••in• •••••o••• •o •n•in• •••• lo•• in J•v• ••o•••• •. D•• •••ini, Io•i•, •n• Si••o [•] •••n•l••• J•v• in•o ••• P•o• •l• l•n•••••, •o• w•i•• ••• SPIN • o••l ••••••• v••i••• •••• lo•• •••••o• . T••i•

v••i•••ion •••o••• •ll •••• lo•• •o••i•ili•i•• •o lon• •• ••• ••o•••• •o•• no•
•x•••• ••• • •xi• •• n•• ••• o•• o••l•• o•j•••• o• •••••••.

J•v• P•••• n••• •l•o •••o•• •• o••l••••• in• •y •••n•l••in• J•v• •o P•o• •l•,
in•l••in• •••• o•• •o• •x•••• ion• •n• •oly• o•••i•• [13]. I• •••• •l•o •••n ••••
•o •n•ly•• •x•••• ion ••••••; • •••• lo•• v•ln•••• ili•y i• ••• o•••• i• •wo •••••••
o••• in lo••• in • •iff•••n• o•••• •• •• n•i• • [1•]. T•i• •••• o••• ••n •••••• "••••
lo•••": • ••••••• lo•• •••• •••••• •••• •••••• •• '• •n••y in•o • ••••••• o•• o••-o•-
o•••• lo••in• ••••• n••, •••••• y •••v•n•in• •••• lo••. T•• •••• ni••• ••• •volv••
in•o • ••n••• l onlin• • oni•o•in• •nvi•on• •n• ••ll•• J•v• P•••• x• lo••• [15].

B•••••• •n• V•ll• ••••• i• • ••• i• • •••••••ion o• •••• lo•• in ••• Lin•x •••n•l [3].
T••y ••••••• •••• lo•• ••••••• •y ••••••• ••••• ••ll sleep w•il• ••ill •ol•in• •
••• inlo••. • •••• i ••• •l. [•] ••• •o• n•••• x•• • l•-••j••• •••••••••• ion ••• n•• •n• •n•
••• MA• I• v••i•••ion •ool [5] •o ••••••• •••• lo•• in • •••••••-•••in• • • •o-
•••• •. T•• •••• ni••• i• •o• •o•i•ion•l •n• •• •i•n• (•o• •••• •o •••• i•ion•l
• o••l ••••• in•) •••••••• ••• •••••••••• ion •o• •••• •••••• ••n •• ••• n•• in••-
••n• •n•ly •n•il ••• ov•••ll •y•••• •x•i•i•• • ••• o• i• •ov•n •••• o• •••• lo••.
How•v••, ••• n•• ••• o•••••••• n• lo••• (•n• ••• i• in•••• •ion) • ••••• • nown
••••i••lly.

T•• A••••o•••• • in• l•n••••• •llow• •n••vo•• •o• • •ni•••ion •••w••n
• ••ll ••••••• •n• in on• •••• •n• •n ••••••• ••••••• •n• in •no••••. Mo•• •n•l-
y••• •o• A•• •i• •o v••i•y •••• ••n•••vo•• •o• • •ni•••ion ••••••••, •••••••
••• n •on•i••in• ••• o•••• o• yn•••oni•••ion on •••••• •••o••••• (lo•••). Fo•
•x•• •l•, M•••i•ol• •n• • y••• [19] •iv• • • olyno• i•l-•i• • •l•o•i••• •o• ••-
•o••in• •ll •o••i•l• •• n••vo•• •••• lo••• •o• • ••••••• o• A•• (•••y •l•o ••• o••
••l•• • o•i•iv••). • o••••• [•] •v•l•••• ••••• • ••• o•• •o• •n• in• •••• lo•• in A••
••o••••• •. M•ny •n•ly••• •ly on ••• •o• • on •••• w••••• A•• •••••• ••• •x••
•n• ini•i•••• •o••••••, in •on••••• •o J•v• ••••••• w•i•• ••• •lw•y• •••••••
•yn•• i••lly.

Boy••••i, L••, •n• • in••• [•] •••• •n• J•v• wi•• own•••• i• •y••• •o •n•••
•••• lo•• •••••• o• •• •o• •il• •i• •. W•il• •• i• i• •n •l••• n• •ol•ion, i• •••• i•••
•••n•l••in• •xi••in• ••o•••• • •o ••• n•w •y•• •nno•••ion•, •n• •o• • •o• ••••-
•ion• • i•••• • •••• •o •x••••• . Fl•n•••n •n• • •••••• •••• i•• • •y•• •n• •ff•••
•y•••• •o• ••o• i•i•y [11]. In ••i• •y•••• , • • •••o• i• ••o• i• i• i• ••••••• •o
•x••••• •••i•lly, wi••o•• in•••l••vin• o• o•••• •••••••. T••y i•n•i•y •n ••o• -
i•i•y viol••ion in StringBuffer.append, ••ovi•in• •••• o• ••• i• ••••• •o• o••
wo••.

••n• •n• M•••in •••• •n• • J•v• Vi••••l M•••in• wi•• • •••• lo•• •voi-
•n•• • •••• ni•• [••]. T•i• •••• ni•• ••on•••• ••• • lo••-o••• ••••• • yn•• i••lly,
•••••in• ••• •••• l o•j•••• ••• ••• lo•••• •••in• •x•••• ion. A• •y•l•• •o•• in
••• ••••••, "••o•• lo•••" ••• in••o••••• •o •••v•n• • •l•i•l• ••••••• ••o• •n•••-
in• ••• •y•li• •••ion•. W•il• ••i• •voi•••••• lo•• l•••• in ••• •x•••• ion, •••• lo••
•o•l• ••ill o•••• w•il• ••• •••••• i• ••in• ••il•.

••n• •••••i•• • •y•••• •••• •••• •x•••• ion• •o in•i•••• v••io•• •in• o•
•••• lo•• in • J•v• Vi••••l M•••in• [••]. S••• • • •••• ni•• •llow• •li•n• •o in-
••lli••n•ly •••• on• •o •••• lo•• in • li•••y •o• • on•n•. P•l•• [1•] i• •n o•••• •in•

•y•••• • •••• ni•• •••• •••••••• ••n•••1 •••• lo••• vi• •••••l••iv• •x•••ion o• •lo•••• ••o••••••. T•••• i• •l•o • l•••• • o• y o• wo•• on •yn•• i••lly •••••in• ••••lo•• in ••• •on••x• o• ••••••••••• •n• •i••i•••• •y•••• • [•1,••].

8 Conclusions

Li•••y w•i•••• wi•• •o •n••••• •••i• li•••i•• ••• •••• o• •••• lo••. B•••••• ••i• •••••n•• i• •i• •• l• •o o•••in •y •••in• o• •y • •n•, • •ool •o• i••n•i•yin• •o••i•l• •••• lo•• (o• v••i•yin• ••••o• ••o• ••••lo••) i• ••i••• l•. Mo••l •••••in• i• ••o••i•l• •••••o••• •o ••• ••o• l•• , •••••• w•ll-•nown ••••• •x•lo•ion ••o•l•• ••••• i• i• •••••i••l •o• • o•• li•••i••.

W• ••v• ••••••n•• • flow-••n•i•iv•, •on••x•-••n•i•iv• •n•ly•i• •o• •••••i• ••- •••••ion o• ••••lo•• in J•v• li•••i••. ••• o• 1• li•••i••, w• v••i•• 13 •o •• •••• o• ••••lo••, •n• •o•n• 1• •••••o•••i•l• ••••lo••• in 3 li•••i••. T•• •n•l- y•i• •••• lo••-o•••• ••••••• •o ••••••••n• lo••in• •on•••••••ion• •x••••• ••o• li•••i••. No••• in ••••• •••••• ••••••••n• •li•• ••••, ••••• •••••••n• •o••i•l• lo•• o•••••in••, •n• •y•l•• in•i•••• •o••i•l• ••••lo•••.

• ••• •n•ly•i• i• ••i•• •ff••••iv• •• v••i•yin• ••••lo•• •••••o• •n• •n•in• ••••- lo••, ••• i• ••ill ••o••••• • •i•••l• n•• ••• o• ••l•• ••• o•••. • •••••• ••n •••in• ••• ••••• •o inv••i•••• ••••• ••• o•••, ••• ••• o••• ••o•l• ••• •i•••••••• •o • • o••l ••••••• w•i•• •o•l• ••••o• ••i••lly ••••• •o• ••••lo••. In ••i• ••••• •wo••, o•• •ool wo•l• •••v• •o li• i• ••• •••••• ••••• o•••• • o••l •••••••, •o••i•ly •llow- in• •o•n• v••i•••ion o• l•••• li•••i••.

J••• •• ••••i• v••i•••ion o• •ll •o••i•l• ••o•••• •x••••ion• off••• •••on••• ••••••n•••• ••n •yn•• i• •n•ly•i• o• on• o• • ••w •x•••ion•, v••i•••ion •••• • li•••y ••nno• •••• lo•• i• ••••••• l• •o •••••in• ••• •••i••l•• •li•n• ••o•••• •o•• no• •••• lo•• w•il• ••in• ••• li•••y. To o•• •nowl•••, o•• •ool i• ••• •••• •o ••••••••• ••• ••o•l•• o• •••• lo•• •••••••ion in li•••i••. How•v••, ••• •••• ni••• i• •l•o ••• li••• l• •o w•ol• ••o•••• •, •n• • •y ••ov• •o •• •ff•••iv• in •••• •on••x•.

Acknowledgments

W• •••n• Vi••o• K•n•••, M•n• S•i•••••n, H•• H•i N••y•n, Wil•on H•i••, •n• S•••••n M•• •• •n• •o• ••i• ••••••• •n• ••••••••ion• on ••i• wo••, •n• M••- •in L•••n•• •o• ••••o•• wi•• Ko•i. T•• •••on• ••••o• •••n•• S•• •n A• •••- in••• •o• ••••o••in• •i• ••••i•i••ion in ••i• ••oj•••. W• •l•o •••n• ••• •nony- • o•• ••vi•w••• •o• ••i• •o• • •n••. T•i• wo•• i• ••••o•••• in •••• •y NSF •••n• • • • -01335•0, ••• MIT-• xy••n P•oj•••, •n• •n NSF ••••••••• • •••••••• F•llow••i• .

References

1. Artho, C., Biere, A.: Applying static analysis to large-scale, multi-threaded Java programs. In: ASWEC. (2001) 68–75
2. Boyapati, C., Lee, R., Rinard, M.: Ownership types for safe programming: preventing data races and deadlocks. In: OOPSLA. (2002) 211–230
3. Breuer, P.T., Garcia-Valls, M.: Static deadlock detection in the Linux kernel. In: Ada-Europe. (2004) 52–64
4. Chaki, S., Clarke, E., Ouaknine, J., Sharygina, N.: Automated, compositional and iterative deadlock detection. In: MEMOCODE. (2004)
5. Chaki, S., Clarke, E.M., Groce, A., Jha, S., Veith, H.: Modular verification of software components in C. IEEE TSE **30** (2004) 388–402
6. Chase, D.R., Wegman, M., Zadeck, F.K.: Analysis of pointers and structures. In: PLDI. (1990)
7. Corbett, J.C.: Evaluating deadlock detection methods for concurrent software. IEEE TSE **22** (1996) 161–180
8. Demartini, C., Iosif, R., Sisto, R.: A deadlock detection tool for concurrent Java programs. Software: Practice and Experience **29** (1999) 577–603
9. DMS Decision Management Systems GmbH: The Kopi Project (2004) http://www.dms.at/kopi/.
10. Engler, D., Ashcraft, K.: RacerX: Effective, static detection of race conditions and deadlocks. In: SOSP. (2003) 237–252
11. Flanagan, C., Qadeer, S.: A type and effect system for atomicity. In: POPL. (2003) 338–349
12. Friedman-Hill, E.: Jess, the Java expert system shell (2004) http://herzberg.ca.sandia.gov/jess/.
13. Havelund, K., Pressburger, T.: Model checking Java programs using Java PathFinder. STTT **2** (2000) 366–381
14. Havelund, K.: Using runtime analysis to guide model checking of Java programs. In: SPIN. (2000) 245–264
15. Havelund, K., Roşu, G.: Monitoring Java programs with Java PathExplorer. In: RV. (2001)
16. INRIA: Proactive (2004) http://www-sop.inria.fr/oasis/ProActive/.
17. Knizhnik, K., Artho, C.: Jlint (2005) http://jlint.sourceforge.net/.
18. Li, T., Ellis, C.S., Lebeck, A.R., Sorin, D.J.: Pulse: A dynamic deadlock detection mechanism using speculative execution. In: USENIX Technical Conference. (2005) 31–44
19. Masticola, S.P., Ryder, B.G.: A model of Ada programs for static deadlock detection in polynomial time. Workshop on Parallel and Distributed Debugging (1991)
20. San Diego State University: SDSU Java library (2004) http://www.eli.sdsu.edu/java-SDSU/.
21. Shih, C.S., Stankovic, J.A.: Survey of deadlock detection in distributed concurrent programming environments and its application to real-time systems. Technical report, UMass UM-CS-1990-069 (1990)
22. Singhal, M.: Deadlock detection in distributed systems. IEEE Computer **22** (1989) 37–48
23. Sun Microsystems, Inc.: Java Development Kit (2004) http://java.sun.com/.
24. von Praun, C.: Detecting Synchronization Defects in Multi-Threaded Object-Oriented Programs. PhD thesis, Swiss Federal Institute of Technology, Zurich (2004)

25. Williams, A., Thies, W., Ernst, M.D.: Static deadlock detection in Java libraries. Research Abstract #102, MIT Computer Science and Artificial Intelligence Laboratory (February, 2004)
26. Williams, A.L.: Static detection of deadlock for Java libraries. Master's thesis, MIT Dept. of EECS (2005)
27. Zeng, F.: Deadlock resolution via exceptions for dependable Java applications. In: DSN. (2003) 731–740
28. Zeng, F., Martin, R.P.: Ghost locks: Deadlock prevention for Java. In: MASPLAS. (2004)

Author Index

Lecture Notes in Computer Science

For information about Vols. 1–3501

please contact your bookseller or Springer